Studies in English Literature 1500-1900

VOLUME 28, 1988

CONTENTS

Ames, Clifford R., False Advertising: The Influence of Virgil and Isaiah on Pope's *Messiah* 401

Cheney, Donald, Recent Studies in the English Renaissance 149

Coiro, Ann Baynes, "To repair the ruins of our first parents": *Of Education* and Fallen Adam 133

Columbus, Claudette Kemper, The (Un)Lettered Ensemble: What Charley Does Not Lean About Writing in Bleak House 609

Crane, Mary Thomas, "Video et Taceo": Elizabeth I and the Rhetoric of Counsel 1

Crawford, Iain, Pip and the Monster: The Joys of Bondage 625

Davies, Stevie, and Hunter, William B., Milton's Urania: "The meaning, not the Name I call" 95

Ferry, Anne, Milton's Creation of Eve 113

Fisher, Leona W., Mark Lemon's Farces on the "Woman Question" 649

Griffin, Patsy, " 'Twas no *Religious House* till now": Marvell's "Upon Appleton House" 61

Horwich, Richard, "I Sing But After You": Shakespeare's Internal Parody 219

Hume, Robert D., Recent Studies in the Restoration and Eighteenth Century 513

Hunt, Maurice, Compelling Art in *Titus Andronicus* 197

Hunter, William B., and Davies, Stevie, Milton's Urania: "The meaning, not the Name I call" 95

Lamb, Jonathan, The Fragmentation of Originals and *Clarissa* 443

Levenson, Jill L., Recent Studies in Elizabethan and Jacobean Drama 331

Loewenstein, David A., *Areopagitica* and the Dynamics of History 77

Monahan, Melodie, Heading Out is not Going Home: *Jane Eyre* 589

Montuori, Deborah, The Confusion of Self and Role in Chapman's *Bussy D'Ambois* 287

Nelson, Nicolas H., Dramatic Texture and Philosophic Debate in Prior's *Dialogues of the Dead* 427

Novy, Marianne, *Daniel Deronda* and George Eliot's Female (Re)Vision of Shakespeare 671

Prager, Carolyn, The Problem of Slavery in *The Custom of The Country* 301

Priest, Dale G., *Oratio* and *Negotium:* Manipulative Modes in *As You Like It* 273

Reinert, Thomas, Johnson and Conjecture 483

Riede, David G., Recent Studies in the Nineteenth Century 713

Roark, Christopher, Lavatch and Service in *All's Well that Ends Well* 241

Shaw, Narelle L., Ancients and Moderns in Defoe's *Consolidator* 391

Simons, Louise, Rerouting *The Unfortunate Traveller:* Strategies for Coherence and Direction 17

Slights, William W. E., the Changeling in *A Dream* 259

Stewart, Mary Margaret, William Collins, Samuel Johnson, and the Use of Biographical Details 471

Stone, Donald D., Meredith and Bakhtin: Polyphony and Bildung 693

Thron, E. Michael, The Significance of Catherine Wordsworth's Death to Thomas De Quincey and William Wordsorth 559

van den Broek, A. G., Take the Number Seven in Cheapside 319

Van Tassel, Mary M., Johnson's Elephant: The Reader of *The Rambler* 461

Walker, Eric C., *Biographia Literaria* and Wordsworth's Revisions 569

Wehrs, Donald R., Rhetoric, History, Rebellion: *Caleb Williams* and the Subversion of Eighteenth-Century Fiction 497

Wilson, R. Rawdon, Shakespearean Narrative: *The Rape of Lucrece* Reconsidered 39

SEL

Studies in ENGLISH LITERATURE 1500-1900

The English Renaissance

VOLUME 28 WINTER 1988 NUMBER 1

Studies in English Literature
1500 - 1900

VOLUME 28 WINTER 1988 NUMBER 1

PUBLISHED BY RICE UNIVERSITY

CONTENTS

"Video et Taceo": Elizabeth I and the Rhetoric of Counsel — Mary Thomas Crane 1

Rerouting *The Unfortunate Traveller*: Strategies for Coherence and Direction — Louise Simons 17

Shakespearean Narrative: *The Rape of Lucrece* Reconsidered — R. Rawdon Wilson 39

"'Twas no *Religious House* till now": Marvell's "Upon Appleton House" — Patsy Griffin 61

Areopagitica and the Dynamics of History — David A. Loewenstein 77

Milton's Urania: "The meaning, not the Name I call" — Stevie Davies and William B. Hunter 95

Milton's Creation of Eve — Anne Ferry 113

"To repair the ruins of our first parents": *Of Education* and Fallen Adam — Ann Baynes Coiro 133

Recent Studies in the English Renaissance — Donald Cheney 149

U.S. Postal Service

STATEMENT OF OWNERSHIP, MANAGEMENT AND CIRCULATION

Required by 39 U.S.C. 3685)

1A. TITLE OF PUBLICATION	1B. PUBLICATION NO.	2. DATE OF FILING
Studies in English Literature, 1500-1900	0 0 3 9 3 6 5 7	9/23/87

3. FREQUENCY OF ISSUE	3A. NO. OF ISSUES PUBLISHED ANNUALLY	3B. ANNUAL SUBSCRIPTION PRICE
Quarterly	Four	U.S.: $20.00 Foreign: $25.00

4. COMPLETE MAILING ADDRESS OF KNOWN OFFICE OF PUBLICATION *(Street, City, County, State and ZIP+4 Code) (Not printers)*

SEL, Rice University, P.O. Box 1892, Houston TX 77251-1892

5. COMPLETE MAILING ADDRESS OF THE HEADQUARTERS OF GENERAL BUSINESS OFFICES OF THE PUBLISHER *(Not printer)*

Same

6. FULL NAMES AND COMPLETE MAILING ADDRESS OF PUBLISHER, EDITOR, AND MANAGING EDITOR *(This item MUST NOT be blank)*

PUBLISHER *(Name and Complete Mailing Address)*

William Marsh Rice University, P.O. Box 1892, Houston TX 77251-1892

EDITOR *(Name and Complete Mailing Address)*

Edward Doughtie, SEL, Rice University, P.O. Box 1892, Houston TX 77251-1892

MANAGING EDITOR *(Name and Complete Mailing Address)*

Lynne Wilson, SEL, Rice University, P.O. Box 1892, Houston TX 77251-1892

7. OWNER *(If owned by a corporation, its name and address must be stated and also immediately thereunder the names and addresses of stockholders owning or holding 1 percent or more of total amount of stock. If not owned by a corporation, the names and addresses of the individual owners must be given. If owned by a partnership or other unincorporated firm, its name and address, as well as that of each individual must be given. If the publication is published by a nonprofit organization, its name and address must be stated.) (Item must be completed.)*

FULL NAME	COMPLETE MAILING ADDRESS
William Marsh Rice University	P.O. Box 1892
	Houston TX 77251
	or
	6100 Main Street
	Houston TX 77005

8. KNOWN BONDHOLDERS, MORTGAGEES, AND OTHER SECURITY HOLDERS OWNING OR HOLDING 1 PERCENT OR MORE OF TOTAL AMOUNT OF BONDS, MORTGAGES OR OTHER SECURITIES *(If there are none, so state)*

FULL NAME	COMPLETE MAILING ADDRESS
There are none	

9. FOR COMPLETION BY NONPROFIT ORGANIZATIONS AUTHORIZED TO MAIL AT SPECIAL RATES *(Section 423.12 DMM only)*
The purpose, function, and nonprofit status of this organization and the exempt status for Federal income tax purposes *(Check one)*

(1) [X] HAS NOT CHANGED DURING PRECEDING 12 MONTHS

(2) [ ] HAS CHANGED DURING PRECEDING 12 MONTHS

(If changed, publisher must submit explanation of change with this statement.)

10. EXTENT AND NATURE OF CIRCULATION *(See instructions on reverse side)*	AVERAGE NO. COPIES EACH ISSUE DURING PRECEDING 12 MONTHS	ACTUAL NO. COPIES OF SINGLE ISSUE PUBLISHED NEAREST TO FILING DATE
A. TOTAL NO. COPIES *(Net Press Run)*	2011	2034
B. PAID AND/OR REQUESTED CIRCULATION 1. Sales through dealers and carriers, street vendors and counter sales	0	0
2. Mail Subscription *(Paid and/or requested)*	1759	1736
C. TOTAL PAID AND/OR REQUESTED CIRCULATION *(Sum of 10B1 and 10B2)*	1759	1736
D. FREE DISTRIBUTION BY MAIL, CARRIER OR OTHER MEANS SAMPLES, COMPLIMENTARY, AND OTHER FREE COPIES	76	76
E. TOTAL DISTRIBUTION *(Sum of C and D)*	1835	1812
F. COPIES NOT DISTRIBUTED 1. Office use, left over, unaccounted, spoiled after printing	176	222
2. Return from News Agents	0	0
G. TOTAL *(Sum of E, F1 and 2—should equal net press run shown in A)*	2011	2034

11. I certify that the statements made by me above are correct and complete

SIGNATURE AND TITLE OF EDITOR, PUBLISHER, BUSINESS MANAGER, OR OWNER

Lynne Wilson

Lynne Wilson, Business Manager

PS Form 3526, Dec. 1985 *(See instruction on reverse)*

Studies in English Literature 1500 - 1900

PUBLISHED BY RICE UNIVERSITY

Studies in English Literature is a quarterly journal of historical and critical studies. Each issue will be devoted to one of four fields:

WINTER: The English Renaissance
SPRING: Elizabethan and Jacobean Drama
SUMMER: Restoration and Eighteenth Century
AUTUMN: The Nineteenth Century

SEL: Studies in English Literature, 1500–1900 (ISSN: 0039-3657) is published quarterly (February, May, August, and November) at $15.00 per year for individuals, $20.00 per year for U.S. institutions, $25.00 per year for foreign institutions, and $6.00 per single issue, by Rice University, 6100 South Main Street, P.O. Box 1892, Houston, Texas 77251. Second-class postage paid at Houston, Texas. **Postmaster:** Send address changes to the Business Manager, *SEL,* Rice University, P.O. Box 1892, Houston, TX 77251.

Studies in English Literature invites historical and critical essays of moderate length (ten to twenty-five pages) that contribute significantly to the understanding of English literature, 1500-1900. Typescripts should be double-spaced throughout and prepared in conformity with the Chicago Manual of Style. Clean photocopy on uncoated paper is acceptable in place of the ribbon copy. We prefer not to have dot-matrix printed copy. We will not consider articles being simultaneously submitted elsewhere, nor will we print essays to appear in a book published within a year of scheduled publication of *SEL*. Those wishing to omit their identities from manuscripts may do so, but should include a covering letter.

Manuscripts submitted for publication should be addressed to the Editor, *Studies in English Literature*, Rice University, P.O. Box 1892, Houston, TX 77251. They must be accompanied by a sufficient number of unattached stamps for return. Receipt of manuscripts will be acknowledged by postcard. Editorial decisions usually take a minimum of three months.

Annual subscription rates: $15.00 for individuals, $20.00 for U. S. institutions, $25.00 for foreign institutions, $6.00 per issue for partial subscriptions and single copies. Regular subscriptions may be obtained for any or all quarterly issues. Remittance should accompany subscription requests. Notice of non-receipt of an issue must be made within ninety (90) days following the publication of that issue. No refunds for cancellations. Business communications should be addressed to Business Manager, *Studies in English Literature*, Rice University, P. O. Box 1892, Houston, TX 77251.

Microfilms of previous volumes (Vols. 1-27) may be obtained from University Microfilms, Inc., 300 N. Zeeb Road, Ann Arbor, Michigan 48106; xerox copies of individual articles may be ordered by calling (800) 521-0600 (toll free). Copies of articles are also available from ISI's The Genuine Article service, 3501 Market Street, Philadelphia, PA 19104; phone (800) 523-1850; telex 84-5305; electronic mail through CLASS; or facsimile transmission via FAXPAX.

Volumes 1 through 3 and 5 through 10 of *Studies in English Literature* are available from Johnson Reprint Corporation, 111 Fifth Avenue, New York, N. Y. 10003, or Berkeley Square House, London W. 1, England.

SEL 28 (1988)
ISSN 0039-3657

"Video et Taceo": Elizabeth I and the Rhetoric of Counsel

MARY THOMAS CRANE

Although one of her mottoes, "semper eadem," seems to claim a fundamental unity of character, Queen Elizabeth I nevertheless presents us with an array of poses and personae. A number of critics have shown how some of these stances represent strategies through which she upheld her status and power.[1] One group of critics, including Arthur Marotti, Louis Adrian Montrose, and Stephen Greenblatt, have explored how she manipulated and was manipulated by complex Petrarchan and pastoral paradigms, and how she and her courtiers used these traditions as sources for mediating symbols through which they both asserted power and mystified its origins.[2] Similarly, Daniel Javitch and Frank Whigham have stressed the rhetorical tools and tropes provided for power struggles at court by courtesy books such as Castiglione's *The Courtier*.[3]

Elizabeth's use of Petrarchan, pastoral, and courtly idioms, however, does not provide a full account of her strategies of power. In the first place, these symbols were most fully elaborated by male courtiers and writers and not by Elizabeth herself, and may tell us more about how men wanted to see her than about how she saw or presented herself. Such an approach stresses her most "feminized" roles, the marginal, seemingly powerless personae she assumed in order to mask her power and which her male subjects employed in order to manage the idea of a powerful woman. Historians of these strategies tend to present an Elizabeth who is, paradoxically, a passive symbol of power surrounded by active, scheming courtiers but who nevertheless embodies symbolically the absolute authority of a patriarchal state.[4]

I would like to explore Elizabeth's use of another symbolic system, that of political counsel, in order to show how she asserted and protected her authoritative involvement in the making of public

---

Mary Thomas Crane, Assistant Professor of English at Boston College, has also published articles on Shakespeare and on the epigram. This essay is from a work in progress on sententiousness and authority in sixteenth-century England.

policy. Unlike Petrarchan, pastoral, and courtly guises, the stance of educated advisor was one which she herself assumed in her speeches and writings, but in which her male contemporaries avoided depicting her. When her male subjects made use of this system of counsel, they attempted to assert their right, according to humanist paradigms of counsel, to give advice to her, and she responded with a variety of strategies which used their expectations about her role to subvert the system. As a result, unlike courtly paradigms which tended to freeze the queen in a static and symbolic posture removed from the actual operations of government, the system of advice-giving allowed her to assume an array of active roles—from patriarchal advisor to silent and obedient woman—within the political system, helping her to define her relation to her councillors, to Parliament, to her subjects, and to her fellow monarchs.

Recently, several critics have stressed the fact that Elizabeth denigrated her "female" weakness, asserting instead the masculine or androgynous authority of her divine "body politic."[5] For Allison Heisch, this strategy points to Elizabeth's status as "honorary male" who reaffirmed, rather than subverted, the patriarchal system.[6] I believe, however, that Elizabeth's use of the paradigm of advice-giving reveals a woman who was less completely bound by male structures than some critics have argued. Although she necessarily operated within the all-pervasive patriarchal system of her time, she used the tropes of counsel to exploit one aspect of that system against itself. The authoritative stance of advisor was, in the sixteenth century, almost always imagined as male, although its expressions and gestures were not explicitly gender-specific. Thus, Elizabeth could use its stratagems to assume in her own person an authority usually associated with men. Conversely, she could employ apparent complicity with patriarchy to mask stubborn resistance to it.

Another of Elizabeth's mottoes—"video et taceo"—expresses her ambiguous place in the advice-giving system with complex subtlety.[7] The first half of her motto, "video," implies silent judgment, the informed consideration of a person who must, and can, advise herself. The choice of "video" rather than "audio" indicates that she intends to make up her own mind on the basis of observation rather than to accept blindly her advisors' spoken counsel. "Taceo," however, implies that as queen, she will maintain the silence thought suitable for a woman in an age when women were relentlessly advised to remain "chaste, silent, and obedient."[8] As a whole, the motto displays the delicate balancing act between assertion and abnegation of authority upon which Elizabeth relied.

I

The purpose of humanist educational reform in England, according to its architects Desiderius Erasmus, Juan Luis Vives, Sir Thomas Elyot, and Roger Ascham, was to train young men in the serious moral purpose and copious Latin style that they needed to become authoritative advisors and public servants.[9] To these theorists of education, the two goals, moral probity and Latin fluency, were intimately related and to be achieved by the same means. Their educational programs were designed to turn the student into a wise advisor, a type of grave councillor exemplified in classical antiquity by Cato the Elder, in the sixteenth century most notably by Lord Burghley, and parodied by Shakespeare in the character of Polonius. Such a man would "bring forth good fruit" in the form of advice to his prince and to younger men, and in a prose style, in Latin and English, filled with authoritative sayings.[10]

Theories of how education in the classics could develop the wisdom, ethics, and prose style that such a figure would need were often accompanied by discussions, such as those found in More's *Utopia* and Starkey's *Dialogue*, of the obligations and problems involved in trying to give wise advice to the prince. Such an advisor asserted his authority through various rhetorical gestures; a copious style studded with learned and moral sayings and exempla taken from classical and religious works, and the assumption of a grave and serious demeanor. Princes were urged to accept the advice offered by such men, and to shun the more palatable advice offered by sycophantic flatterers. This system provided places for both providers and recipients of advice, and despite recent emphasis on the importance of Italianate models of courtly behavior, the humanist paradigm had a place in the semiotics of power at the Elizabethan court as long as men like Burghley were alive.[11]

Elementary education in England during this period was largely designed to teach boys to assert the proper kind of authority rhetorically, both in Latin and English. Women were excluded from power partly, as several scholars have shown, by being denied access to training in this code of authority.[12] In the rare cases when they received an education, women were taught to be familiar with Christian writings and to be chaste, silent, and obedient; many educated women found only religious outlets for their learning.[13] Without training in the rhetorical gestures of authority and without a sanctioned role as public advisors, women were effectively denied a place in the system of political counsel.

Nevertheless, historians agree that Elizabeth was, in fact, intimately involved in the making of political decisions.[14] To be sure, she did establish power and manipulate her courtiers by playing courtly games, but she also met with her council, corresponded with fellow monarchs, addressed parliament, and made decisions as part of her exercise of power. In these contexts, she often used gestures and strategies belonging to the system of counsel, defining herself with reference to the humanist ideal of authoritative statesman. She was able to use these strategies because she had been educated to do so, and her use of the system of council reveals the extent to which humanist education could empower a woman who was given the chance to exercise that power.

Unlike most women, Elizabeth received, at the hands of William Grindal, John Cheke, and especially Roger Ascham, the full humanist education.[15] She may have benefitted from the humanist concern that a prince, in particular, should be properly educated. Several letters written by Ascham reveal that Elizabeth was trained, as other women were not, in the use of rhetoric to assert authority.

She remained proud of her learning throughout her life, and realized the importance of displaying her education as a way of legitimizing her claim to power. She differs most sharply from other educated women of the period, and even from her fellow monarchs Mary Tudor and Mary Queen of Scots, by presuming to deliver public addresses. Her parliamentary speeches represent just the sort of authoritative, public discourse for which humanist education prepared men and in which women were not supposed to participate. She even, on several occasions, delivered public speeches in Latin, breaking womanly silence in the most exclusive language of male authority. And, as we shall see, she did not hesitate to use these speeches and her private letters to assume the role of advisor.

She also shows, in several letters, that she was familiar with the topoi of princely attitudes toward advice: as early as 1581, she urges the Duke of Anjou to be cautious in accepting advice and encourages one of his advisors to "give him good advice, and be bold, preferring his good to the desire of pleasing him."[16] She advises her cousin James VI of Scotland in a letter of 1592 that "if my counsels had as well been followed as they were truly meant, your subjects had now better known their King, and you no more need of further justice"; similarly, in 1593, she warns him against the "Siren's songs" of bad counsel: "May enough of God's reason befall you to resist so destroying advice."[17]

Nevertheless, her relation to the paradigm of educated statesman and advisor was necessarily oblique. In the first place, she was herself the prince, and the traditional system was designed to incorporate the giving of advice by trained men to their monarch. The topoi of counsel tend to stress the prince's need to avoid flattery and follow good advice, and not to generate such advice himself.[18] More importantly, there was no sanctioned way for female rulers, or, indeed, for women in general to assume this kind of paternal authority. Elizabeth's reliance on alternative images such as mistress or shepherdess reveals the extent to which conventional models of authoritative rule were closed to her. James I felt able, however ineptly, to assert this kind of learned authority through such works as his *Basilikon Doron* and his didactic speeches on the nature of kingship.[19] Elizabeth, however, was more circumspect in her assumption of this role, and was forced constantly to acknowledge her subjects' expectation that she would accept rather than give advice. She used her thorough grounding in the humanist system to formulate strategies for asserting her authority in different situations and before different audiences, often turning audience expectation that she would accept advice into a means of refusing it.

II

When Elizabeth passed through the streets of London on the way to her coronation, her subjects did not hesitate to give her an abundance of advice. At various points along her path, the citizens of London had placed "pageaunts," each concerned with a particular aspect of good government, offering sententious advice in the form of poems recited by children and in sayings inscribed on the structure itself. An unidentified witness tells us how in each pageant, in addition to the spoken advice, "there were placed in every voide rome of the Pageant, both in Englishe and Latin, such sentences as advaunced the seate of governaunce upholden by Vertue."[20]

Elizabeth seems to have accepted this torrent of sententious counsel quite graciously. Our witness tells how "ere the Quenes Majestie came wythin hearing of thys Pageaunt, she sent certaine, as also at all the other Pageauntes, to require the People to be silent. For her Majestie was disposed to heare all that shoulde be sayde unto her" (Nichols, 1:44). She is repeatedly described as listening attentively, asking for further explanation, and replying with thanks and promises to heed the proffered advice. She knew that as a young woman, undertaking to rule England when the right of women to succeed to the throne was questioned and criticized on all sides, she should expect to be told what to do.[21] Clearly, at the beginning of her reign even her lowliest subjects believed that she needed advice and that they had the right, even the duty, to offer it.

Significantly, later in her reign, the public entertainments presented to her avoided this vein of sententious moralizing and employed instead, extravagant praise based on chivalric, pastoral, and petrarchan modes.[22] Elizabeth may have discouraged the courtiers responsible for these entertainments from addressing her in this way, and they may have found courtly modes more easily manipulated in their quest for favor. Nevertheless, the queen tended to respond to flattery as if she had been given advice. Her famous reply to the recorder at Warwick (1572), whose speech consisted of praise of the queen and a history of Warwick, seems to acknowledge and accept non-existent counsel: "Come hither, little Recorder. It was told me that youe wold be afraid to look upon me, or to speak boldly; but you were not so fraid of me as I was of youe; and I now thank you for putting me in mynd of my duety, and that should be in me" (Nichols, 1:315-16).

Certainly at the beginning of her reign Elizabeth seemed to signal that she would preserve womanly silence and rely on the advice of her subjects, especially on that of father figures like Burghley and Sir Nicholas Bacon. Her statement appointing Burghley to serve on her council is instructive:

> I give you this charge that you shall be of my privy Council and content to take pains for me and my realm. This judgement I have of you that you will not be corrupted by any manner of gift . . . and that without respect of my private will you will give me that counsel which you think best and if you shall know anything necessary to be declared to me of secrecy you shall show it to myself only. And assure yourself I will not fail to keep taciturnity therein and therefore herewith I charge you.[23]

In appointing her chief advisor, Elizabeth was careful to stress his moral authority and her own willingness to keep silent and accept advice. Her choice of Burghley and her careful public maintenance of the appearance that she took his advice were vital strategies for the young queen.

This strategy was important because William Cecil, Lord Burghley, most clearly exemplified the style and stance of the humanist statesman-advisor. He was famous in his own time as the preeminent exemplar of this figure, the *pater patriae* who gave wise advice to the queen and to a number of young men whose education he supervised.[24] In the collections of precepts which he wrote for each of his sons, as well as in letters to Edward Manners, Earl of Rutland, John Harrington, and others, he exhibits the authority commensurate with his position.[25] He seems purposefully to have assumed this role of wise advisor, and to have manifested it through a sententious and didactic style.[26] His letters are full of proffered advice and quoted maxims: "Durus enim est sermo," "oculos habent et non vident," "Deus dabit meliora," "expecto Dominum, viriliter age, et confortetur cor tuum."[27]

Yet despite the pervasiveness of this style and stance in Burghley's correspondence, he seems never to have used it in addressing the queen. Although he often complains to others that she will not follow his advice, he does not approach her in an openly didactic manner.[28] His letters to her, even when she refuses his counsel, speak with the voice of a humble suppliant:

> It may please your most Excellent Majesty—With a sorrowful heart and watery eyes, I your poor servant and most lowly subject, an unworthy Secretary, beseech your Majesty to pardon this my lowly suit, that considering the proceeding in this matter for removing the French out of Scotland doth not content your Majesty, and that I cannot with conscience give any contrary advice, I may, with your Majesty's favour and clemency, be spared to entermeddle therein.[29]

She used Burghley to reassure her subjects that she was receiving suitable advice, but did not in practice allow him to approach her as an authoritative advisor. Nevertheless, she allowed Burghley to maintain such a public reputation for judicious advice that William Camden could write: "the Queen was most happy in so great a Councillor and to his wholesome counsels the state of England for ever shall be beholden."[30]

As Camden's remarks indicate, it was important for Elizabeth, especially as a young woman, to appear to receive good advice. On the other hand, as a prince, it was not to her advantage to appear to accept too much of it, especially from powerful male advisors. Through the delicate balancing act of her relationship with Burghley, she was able to assume absolute authority while seeming open to wise counsel.

III

In her own writings, Elizabeth continues to maintain a careful balance between authority and obedience and uses the full range of roles, from patriarchal advisor to silent and obedient woman, which the system of counsel made available to her. Her strategies differ according to her audience, and she is most willing to assert authority openly and without qualification in her letters to fellow monarchs, occasions when no subject was likely to be threatened by her unorthodox assertion of power.

Her letters to her brother, Edward VI, display an openly sententious authority as they attempt to manifest not only the humanistic education both she and Edward had received but also a sister's concern for her younger brother. In one instance, for example, she lets his request for a picture of her occasion a lesson:

> For the face I grant I might well blush to offer, but the mind I shall never be ashamed to present. But though from the grace of the picture the colours may fade by time, may give by weather, may be spited by chance; yet the other, nor Time with his swift wings shal overtake, nor the misty clouds with their lowering may darken, nor Chance with her slippery foot may overthrow.
>
> (Nichols, 1:28)

Later in the same letter, she gives herself advice: "I shall learn to follow this saying of Horace, *Feras non culpes quod vitari non potest*" (Nichols, 1:28).

When she herself becomes queen, her letters to brother and sister monarchs speak with the same authority. Her early letters to James VI of Scotland express their advice even more boldly: "Among your many studies, my dear Brother and Cousin, I would Isocrates' noble lesson were not forgotten, that wills the Emperor his Sovereign to make his words of more account than other men their oaths, as meetest ensigns to show the truest badge of prince's Arms."[31] She continues to advise him on matters of state, urging, for example, that "slacking of due correction engenders the bold minds for new crimes;" "weed out the weeds lest the best corne fester"; "I find an Old English proverb truly verified 'a feast long looked for is good when it cometh'."[32] She sounds much like Burghley in these letters as she combines homely proverbs, learned allusions, and original sententiae in a continual stream of political advice. Clearly, when she wanted to, she could make open use of the rhetorical gestures of authority.

Sometimes Elizabeth addresses advice to her subjects in a similarly bold fashion. She often felt the need to remind parliament of the limits of its authority to advise a prince. By casting such reminders in the form of advice, she is able to disguise the fact that they are commands. At the end of a speech to parliament in 1559, she warns them not to go any further in attempting to tell her what to do; they may urge her to marry, but must not attempt to give "limitation of place or person." She rises to an uncharacteristic lecture which ends in a saying: "a guerdon constrained and a gift freely given can never agree together" (Neale, 1:49). One of her favorite sayings alludes to the exemplum of the hierarchy of the human body: "A strange thing that the foot should direct the head in so weighty a cause; which cause hath been so diligently weighed by us, for that it toucheth us more than them."[33] With this saying, Elizabeth defines the limits of her subjects' advice-giving, at the same time claiming, as "head," to have "diligently weighed" the situation. By using a commonplace to express her thoughts, she asserts the learned authority of a trained advisor and claims the support of convention for her unconventional claim to male power. By casting a command in the form of sententious advice, she softens, and makes more acceptable, her claim to that power.

Sometimes, in reaction to unwanted counsel from parliament, Elizabeth directly asserts her own learned authority to give advice or in other ways affirms her ties to the humanist learning that was supposed to enable her to do so. Most directly, she occasionally makes full and serious claim to the authority of learning, assuming, if only briefly, the role of humanist statesman. At the end of the session of 1584-85, for example, she reminded parliament: "I am supposed to have many studies, but most philosophical. I must yield this to be true: that I suppose few, that be no professors, have read more. And I need not tell you that I am so simple that I understand not, nor so forgetful that I remember not" (Neale, 2:100). Through such claims of learning and wisdom the queen asserts personal authority and the ability to advise herself.

Upon occasion, Elizabeth demonstrates that she can provide her own counsel through the use of sententious advice addressed to herself. She often uses sayings to show that experience has taught her enough to advise herself on matters about which parliament has offered unwanted advice. In one instance, when parliament mentioned her attack of smallpox as reason to secure succession, she adduces a biblical *sententia* in her reply: "there needs no boding of my bane. I know as well as I did before that I am mortal. I know also that I must seek to discharge myself of that great burthen that God hath laid upon me. For of them to whom much is committed much is required."[34] Again, in 1586, she claims the fruits of experience: "I am not so void of judgment as not to see mine own peril; nor yet so ignorant as not to know it were in nature a foolish course to cherish a sword to cut mine own throat" (Neale, 2:127).

When it suits her strategy, however, usually as an excuse for delaying a decision or answer to some unpalatable suggestion, she will directly abdicate the learned authority which she has on other occasions taken such pains to establish. In a speech in 1563 on marriage, she runs through a repertoire of such tactics to justify her "answer-answerless":

> The weight and greatness of this matter might cause in me being a woman wanting both wit and memory, some fear to speak and bashfulness besides, a thing appropriate to my sex. But yet, the princely seat and kingly throne wherein God (though unworthy) hath constituted me, maketh these two causes to seem little in mine eyes, though grievous perhaps to your ears, and boldeneth me to say somewhat in this matter, which I mean only to touch but not presently to answer. For this so great a demand needeth both great and grave advice. (Neale, 1:107)

We might note, first of all, the claim that divine right overcomes womanly weakness, a strategy identified by both Heisch and Marcus.[35] Heisch says that in this passage, "Elizabeth hid behind her skirts and pointed to heaven" in order to claim divine sanction for her authority. I believe that her strategy here is considerably more complex, playing on the system of counsel in several ways. The opening sentence serves a double purpose—to indicate that she realizes the importance of the matter under consideration and accepts her role as recipient of advice, but also to excuse her avoidance of direct response to the particular advice that parliament has offered. Before denigrating her "wit and memory"—faculties which she stoutly defends in other speeches—she makes the point that she is well able to judge "the weight and greatness of this matter," and realizes that "so great a demand needeth both great and grave advice."[36] She does not identify the source of this advice, but rather uses her recognition of the need for it as an excuse to avoid responding directly to parliament's advice. She cannot give them a straight answer until she has had time to consider advice from other sources. In effect, she uses her acknowledged need for advice as an excuse for rejecting it, exploiting her ambiguous position within the system of counsel. In typical fashion, this passage moves purposefully between assertions and abnegations of authority: she claims to recognize the gravity of the situation, yet claims also that as a woman she lacks wit to deal with it; she asserts that her kingly power overrides womanly weakness, then admits that her kingly response may be unwelcome to parliament; she says that she will speak on the matter, then says that she will not answer it. The passage ends with an ambiguous acknowledgement of the need for advice from some unnamed source. In this passage, Elizabeth's claim that she lacks wisdom serves a specific purpose; to disarm male disapproval of her audacious speech, and to avoid direct refusal of unwanted advice. She uses male expectations about feminine behavior to protect her prerogative to circumvent those expectations.

The alternation of advice and diffidence found in several of Elizabeth's private letters may clarify the purpose of such tactics and help to place them in relation to some of her other strategies for asserting power. Although her missives to fellow monarchs often offer aphorisms and advice without qualification, those to her subjects rarely do so. She concludes a letter of consolation and advice to Lady Paget on the death of her daughter in this way: "Call to mind, good Kate, how hardly we princes can brook of crossing of our commands; how ireful will the Highest power be (may you be sure) when murmurings shall be made of his pleasingest will? Let Nature therefore not hurt herself, but give place to the giver. Though this lesson be from a silly vicar, yet it is sent from a loving sovereign."[37] Here the queen seems to offer sententious advice ("let nature therefore") with the full force of her authority behind it. But she immediately calls herself a "silly vicar" and returns the discourse from the system of counsel to that of love ("a loving sovereign"). She assumes the stance of authoritative advisor, and then undercuts it so that it cannot occasion anxiety. Similarly, she prefaces an extremely sententious letter to Henry Sidney with the disclaimer that had not necessity prevailed, the letter "shuld hardly have cumbered your yees."[38] The point here is that even when addressing her subjects, she does not avoid the assertion of her authority to advise, but rather follows the assertion with a softening qualification. In this way, she maintains her conveniently ambiguous place in the system of counsel, both manifesting her authority and taking pains that the manifestation of a powerful woman can occasion no anxiety. Thus, in a passage such as that addressed to Lady Paget, her recourse to the role of loving mistress can only be accurately read in the context of her initial stance as authoritative advisor.

Clearly, then, Elizabeth was extremely aware of humanist ideas about political counsel, and sought quite subtly to position herself with respect to a system of advice-giving. This system provided her with exceptionally flexible tools for the maintenance of power because, unlike courtly paradigms which froze her in a static pose, she could assume a wide array of stances within it. She could use Burghley's public reputation as wise councillor to reassure her subjects that she was receiving good advice, while refusing, in practice, to accept much of it. When writing poetry or addressing her equals, she could give advice as openly and imperiously as Burghley. She could assume the role of advisor to parliament in order to disguise blunt commands as wise counsel. She could almost simultaneously assert and deny her ability to advise herself in order to deflect outside advice. She was able to pose as a dutiful daughter in order to mask stubborn resistance to parliamentary advice. These assertions and abnegations of authority should not be taken as reflections of her true opinion of herself, but as strategic maneuvers within the complex system of counsel. This system, unlike its courtly fellows, furnished tropes which could represent and defend an active engagement in the formation of policy. And Elizabeth, as a female prince who had received a full humanist education and was influenced by humanist expectations about wise government, needed a way to express her relation to actual decision-making fully as much as she needed a way to express regal power.

Nevertheless, it frequently suited Elizabeth to remain a distant symbolic figure whose relation to policy was obscured. It was often in her best interest to let men see her as they would. As a woman who was, of necessity, chaste (but not too chaste), silent (but not too silent), and obedient (but not too obedient), it was important that she allow herself to be reflected in a number of mirrors chosen by her subjects. Her direct participation in the decisions of government, and her use of the authoritative rhetoric of counsel to defend that participation, however, shows that she did not always see herself in those mirrors. Although she necessarily worked within the patriarchal power structure, she was often able to use it against itself to protect her fragile position. Elizabeth saw quite clearly the dangers which accompanied her exercise of authority, but, despite her motto, did not always remain silent in the face of them. Her skillful use of the humanist rhetoric of authoritative counsel allowed her to break silence and speak the language of authority as a uniquely powerful woman in a man's world.[39]

NOTES

[1]Frances A. Yates, for example, has explored her use of traditions surrounding the classical goddess Astraea and the Virgin Mary to encourage a cult of secular monarchy, in *Astraea: The Imperial Theme in the Sixteenth Century* (London: Routledge & Kegan Paul, 1975), esp. pp. 29-112. See also Roy Strong, *The Cult of Elizabeth: Elizabethan Portraiture and Pageantry* (London: Thames and Hudson, 1977) for a study of similar iconographic strategies.

[2]See Louis Adrian Montrose, "'Eliza, Queene of Shepheardes,' and the Pastoral of Power," *ELR* 10 (1980):153-82; "Of Gentlemen and Shepherds: The Politics of Elizabethan Pastoral Form," *ELH* 50 (1983):415-59; and "'Shaping Fantasies': Figurations of Gender and Power in Elizabethan Culture," *Representations* 1 (1983):61-94; Stephen J. Greenblatt, *Sir Walter Ralegh: The Renaissance Man and His Roles* (New Haven: Yale Univ. Press, 1973), pp. 52-59; and *Renaissance Self-Fashioning: From More to Shakespeare* (Chicago: Univ. of Chicago Press, 1980), pp. 165-69; Arthur F. Marotti, "'Love is not Love': Elizabethan Sonnet Sequences and the Social Order," *ELH* 49 (1982):398-400.

[3]See Daniel Javitch, *Poetry and Courtliness in Renaissance England* (Princeton: Princeton Univ. Press, 1978), who argues that this Italianate courtly milieu fostered the development of imaginative poetry in sixteenth-century England; and Frank Whigham, *Ambition and Privilege: The Social Tropes of Elizabethan Courtesy Theory* (Berkeley: Univ. of California Press, 1984), who explores the "rhetorical semiotics" of courtesy through which the ambitious sought to rise and the already privileged sought to impede the ambitious.

[4]Leah Marcus, "Shakespeare's Comic Heroines, Elizabeth I, and the Political Uses of Androgyny," *Women in the Middle Ages and the Renaissance: Literary and Historical Perspectives*, ed. Mary Beth Rose (Syracuse: Syracuse Univ. Press, 1986), p. 148, notes that such recent studies have "frozen her into the ceremonial stasis of an object of worship."

[5]See Marcus, pp. 137-43; and Allison Heisch, "Queen Elizabeth I: Parliamentary Rhetoric and the Exercise of Power," *Signs* 1 (1975):31-55, 35; "Queen Elizabeth I and the Persistence of Patriarchy," *Feminist Review* 4 (1980):45-54; and Catherine Belsey, *The Subject of Tragedy: Identity and Difference in Renaissance Drama* (New York: Methuen, 1985), p. 180, who notes that "Elizabeth I, who spoke powerfully, did so most famously to deny her femininity."

[6]Allison Heisch, "Persistence of Patriarchy," p. 45; pp. 53-54.

[7]William Camden, *Remains Concerning Britain* (London, 1870), p. 373, notes that Elizabeth "most commonly" used two mottoes: "'video, taceo' and 'semper eadem,' which she as truly and constantly performed."

[8]See Suzanne W. Hull, *Chaste, Silent, and Obedient: English Books for Women, 1475-1640*, (San Marino: Huntington Library, 1982), pp. 142-43.

[9]See Desiderius Erasmus, *Literary and Educational Writings 2: De Copia/De Ratione Studii*, ed. Craig R. Thompson, in vol. 24 of *Collected Works of Erasmus*, 28 vols. (Toronto: Univ. of Toronto Press, 1978); and Juan Luis Vives, *De Tradendis Disciplinis*, vol. 6 of *Opera Omnia*, 8 vols. (Benedicti Montfort, 1745; London: Gregg, 1964); Thomas Elyot, *The Boke Named the Governour*, ed. Foster Watson (New York: Dutton, 1907); Roger Ascham, *The Scholemaster*, *English Works*, ed. W. A. Wright (1904; Cambridge: Cambridge Univ. Press, 1970). For the role of sayings and the commonplace book as a means of combining moral and rhetorical instruction, see my unpublished doctoral dissertation, "Proverbial and Aphoristic Sayings: Sources of Authority in the English Renaissance," Harvard, 1986.

[10]Richard Helgerson, *Self-Crowned Laureates: Spenser, Jonson, Milton and the Literary System* (Berkeley: Univ. of California Press, 1983), p. 27, associates Cato and Burghley with this stance. On the figure of paternal advisor in literature from ancient Egypt to the English Renaissance, see Rudolph Habenicht, ed., *John Heywood's "A Dialogue of Proverbs"* (Berkeley: Univ. of California Press, 1963), p. 9; on the expectation that young men so trained would enter public service, see G. K. Hunter, *John Lyly: The Humanist as Courtier* (Cambridge, Mass.: Harvard Univ. Press, 1962), pp. 26-35; on the centrality of the "problem of counsel" in Tudor government, see Arthur Ferguson, *The Articulate Citizen and the English Renaissance* (Durham: Duke Univ. Press, 1965), pp. 162-99.

[11]On Burghley as humanist advisor and statesman *par excellence*, see Helgerson, pp. 27, 57; and B. W. Beckingsale, *Burghley, Tudor Statesman* (New York: St. Martin's, 1967), pp. 196-97.

[12]On the importance of this educational system in perpetuating male authority, see Walter Ong, "Latin Language Study as Renaissance Puberty Rite," *Rhetoric, Romance, and Technology: Studies in the Interaction of Expression and Culture* (Ithaca: Cornell Univ. Press, 1971), pp. 113-41. On the limited nature of female education in the Renaissance, see Ruth Kelso, *Doctrine for the Lady of the Renaissance* (Urbana: Univ. of Illinois Press, 1956); and Joan Kelly-Gadol, "Did Women have a Renaissance?" in *Becoming Visible: Women in European History*, ed. Renate Bridenthal and Claudia Koonz (Boston: Houghton Mifflin, 1977), pp. 137-64, 150-52.

[13]See Hull, pp. 142-43. And on women who used their learning for pious ends, see the essays in Magaret Patterson Hannay, ed., *Silent But for the Word: Tudor Women as Patrons, Translators, and Writers of Religious Works* (Kent: Kent State Univ. Press, 1985).

[14]See Wallace T. MacCaffrey, *Queen Elizabeth and the Making of Policy*, 1572-1588 (Princeton: Princeton Univ. Press, 1981), p. 508, who says that Elizabeth "unfalteringly maintained her unquestioned command of English policy"; and Paul Johnson, *Elizabeth I, A Study in Power and Intellect* (London: Weidenfeld and Nicolson, 1974), p. 193, who argues that "there can be no doubt that the main lines of policy reflected her deepest convictions"; and J. E. Neale, *Elizabeth and her Parliaments*, 2 vols. (London: Cape, 1957), 2:418, 439, who concludes that she often opposed her council and parliament, and that her rule was personal.

[15]On her education, see J. E. Neale, *Queen Elizabeth* (New York: Harcourt, Brace, 1934), pp. 13-16.

[16]G. B. Harrison, ed., *The Letters of Queen Elizabeth I*, 2nd edn. (New York: Funk and Wagnalls, 1968), pp. 147-43.

[17]Harrison, p. 221; 228.

[18]Both More's *Utopia* and Starkey's *Dialogue* depict the prince as recipient of advice, for which, see Ferguson, pp. 180-82. On the difficulty of persuading a king to accept vertuous but unwelcome advice, see *Utopia*.

[19]See *The Basilikon Doron of King James VI*, ed. James Craigie, Scottish Text Society, 2 vols. (Edinburgh: Blackwood, 1944). This treatise addressed to his son resembles the tracts of advice to a son prepared by Burghley (for both sons), Henry Sidney, Sir Walter Raleigh, and other prominent sixteenth-century fathers. See Louis B. Wright, ed., *Advice to a Son, Precepts of Lord Burghley, Sir* Walter Raleigh, and Francis Osborne (Ithaca: Cornell Univ. Press, 1962); and see also Helgerson, p. 27, on the "paternal and governmental authority" of Burghley and Sidney.

[20]From a pamphlet entitled *The Passage of our most drad Soveraigne Lady Quene Elyzabeth through the Citie of London to Westminster, the daye before her Coronation, Anno 1558-9*, published by Richard Tottel and reprinted in John Nichols, *The Progresses and Public Processions of Queen Elizabeth*, 3 vols. (London 1823) 1:38-60.

[21]For a particular subject' s attempt to advise the queen, as well as an account of treatises questioning the right of women to rule, see Carole Levin, "John Foxe and the Responsibilities of Queenship," in Rose, ed., pp. 113-33.

[22]See Yates and Montrose on this. Even as early as the Woodstock entertainments of 1575, the queen was flattered rather than advised. At Wanstead in 1578, the entertainment, written by Sir Philip Sidney, includes a comic schoolmaster who makes a speech filled with inkhorn terms and sayings, and who is called "tedious fool" and banished by a "May-Lady" (Nichols, 2:97)—revealing how far entertainment of the queen had come from moralizing pageants. As we have seen, however, such courtly flattery served to manage the queen as surely as did the offer of counsel.

[23]As quoted in Conyers Read, *Mr. Secretary Cecil and Queen Elizabeth* (London: Cape, 1955), p. 119, from P. R. O., s. p. xii/1-7.

[24]See Beckingsale, pp. 196-97, 199, 245-50; and also Helgerson, pp. 25-27.

[25]See Wright, ed., *Advice to a Son.*

[26]See Beckingsale, p. 199, on Burghley's reliance on proverbs and adages.

[27]Quoted in Read, *Cecil*, p. 312, p. 395; and Conyers Read, *Lord Burghley and Queen Elizabeth* (New York: Knopf, 1960), p. 55; and Nichols, 1:346.

[28]See Read, *Cecil*, p. 171, for a letter to Throgmorton of 7 May 1560, in which Cecil complains: "I have had such a torment herein with the Queen' s Majesty" because she refused to take his advice.

[29]Quoted in Read, *Cecil*, p. 161, from a letter of December 1559.

[30]William Camden, *Annals*, as cited in Read, *Burghley*, p. 546.

[31]Harrison, p. 159.

[32]The first is from a letter of 11 September 1592, as quoted in Lacey Baldwin Smith, *Elizabeth I* (St. Louis: Forum Press, 1980), p. 45; the next on 26 November 1592; the next on 16 April 1590, both quoted in John Bruce, ed., *Letters of Queen Elizabeth and King James VI of Scotland* (London: Camden Society, 1849), pp. 45 and 165.

[33]I cite the parliamentary speeches from J. E. Neale, *Elizabeth I and her Parliaments*, 1:148; see also a letter to Catherine de Medici, 16 October 1567, quoted in Smith, p. 44: "I rejoice me very much to see that one prince takes to heart the wrongs done to another, having a hatred to that metamorphosis, where the head is removed to the foot, and the heels hold the highest place."

[34]Neale, 1: 108; again, in reply to a similar request in 1566: "As for my own part, I care not for death; for all men are mortal" (Neale, 1: 149).

[35]Heisch, "Persistence," p. 45; Marcus, p. 139.

[36]For her defense of wit and memory, recall her claim that she is not "so simple that I understand not, nor so forgetful that I remember not" (Neale, 2:104).

[37]Harrison, p. 200, undated letter.

[38]Nichols, 2:303-304. This letter is interesting for its large number of folk proverbs: "a fole to late bewares, when all the perrel is past"; "if we still advise we shall never do"; "thus are we ever knitting a knot, never tied," etc.

[39]I would like to thank Emily Bartels, Heather Dubrow, and Naomi Miller for their comments on an earlier version of this essay.

SEL 28 (1988)
ISSN 0039-3657

Rerouting *The Unfortunate Traveller*: Strategies for Coherence and Direction

LOUISE SIMONS

I

Thomas Nashe's prose fiction, *The Unfortunate Traveller*, written in 1593, is often viewed as a chain of enigmatic, picaresque-like adventures, unevenly strung together by the serial appearance of the main character. As we will see, however, two thematic strategies, one involved with plot and one with rhetoric, give the narrative a novelistic coherence. *The Unfortunate Traveller* predates the rise of the novel proper, of course, and, concerned with unstable motion as it is, it settles comfortably in no generic category. Nashe himself struggled to find the correct tag for it and was forced to make do primarily with "Tale," "Historie" "Treatise" or "Chronicle."[1] In modern terms, the work appears to be a proto-novel, even a kind of *Bildungsroman*. As such, it gains one aspect of its coherence and direction through a plot that unfolds the education of the protagonist, Jack Wilton, a page in Henry VIII's court. The hubristic Jack Wilton of the early jests is subdued on his Continental travels by a series of morally edifying misfortunes. The first aspect of Nashe's thematic coherence, then, is structural: it belongs to the work's surface structure and is portrayed in the overt story.

The second strategic coherence is formal: it is part of the work's deep structure and is uncovered from a rhetorical network of heavily invested words. In the underlying verbal network, Jack Wilton plays three roles: he is an *infant*, or noble spirited youth; a *maker*, or initiator and chronicler of his own tale; and a *monarch*, or centered subject and figure of rule (or misrule) of this chronicle. Invested words that are coordinated with each other tie seemingly discontinuous events into a unified subject, and in this way they provide thematic organization to a disjunctive text.

Louise Simons is an assistant professor of English at Upsala College. This article forms part of a longer study of Nashe. Her essay, " 'And Heaven Gates Ore My Head': Death as Threshold in Milton's Masque," was published in *Milton Studies* 24 (1987).

The complicated rhetoric of Nashe's text constitutes a challenge to interpretation. C. S. Lewis calls Nashe "the perfect literary showman" whose "sheer virtuosity" with words makes "the subject, in his sort of writing, unimportant."[2] In *The Unfortunate Traveller*, while the subject is not entirely unimportant, disjunctures in the narrative make it hard to decipher. As John Berryman and Walter Davis indicate, however, the organization of the narrative is triadic,[3] and indeed, the underlying motifs—infant, monarch, maker—inform the superficial action with their own special meaning. In that sense, at any given point, the momentary overt subject may indeed be less important than the continuous, or synchronic, underlying one. Because the conflicting codes of surface diachrony and underlying synchrony operate simultaneously, the text is perplexing and unrewarding when read merely as a type of picaresque or jestbook.[4] William Kerrigan describes Renaissance humanist schooling as reinforcing "the virtue of 'copiousness,' which . . . was the ability to say the same thing, clothe the same body, in a multitude of fashions. . . . Copiousness . . . was intended to guarantee a fulsome, ready plenitude of speech."[5] For an enhanced understanding of this peculiar work, we must attend to Nashe's special use of linguistic copiousness.

The reader is invited to understand *The Unfortunate Traveller* as a linguistic game, says Margaret Ferguson, "the 'newes of the maker' game," which Nashe, as the "self-reflective . . . maker," plays in earnest.[6] Taking our understanding of authorial word play a step further, we find that the verbal game provides a substructure for the surface events of the story. In particular, aging and *thanatos* are opposed to infancy and *aliveness* to form a narrative and psychological thread that holds together otherwise conflicting purposes. As the central figure, Jack Wilton is the "ingenious infant" (p. 209) of the story. In a second rhetorical maneuver, Nashe correlates the state of infancy, or childhood, with the occupation of writer; this conflates Jack, the narrator, with Nashe, the maker. As Nashe phrases his request to the reader at the end of the induction (p. 208):

> Heigh passe, come alofte: everie man of you take
> your places, and heare *Jacke Wil-*
> *ton* tell his owne Tale.

Simply by virtue of his role as central character, Jack Wilton becomes invested symbolically with the title of monarch. Earlier in the induction, the work is called the "Chronicle of the king of Pages" (p. 208). The status of ruler is Jack's because it is his tale being chronicled, for, in Nashe's formulation, a chronicle centers on a figure of rule. According to a conflicting mode of thought, however, only an actual monarch, and not an upstart one, is the fitting subject to be chronicled: the story opens with a tribute to "*Henrie* the eight (the onely true subject of Chronicles)" (p. 209). Jack Wilton is suspended between opposing systems: in one mode of thought, he is a monarch, centered in his own chronicle and hero of his own adventures; in the second, he is not authentic as either monarch or author but is a decentered false claimant in both categories, dangling between them, confused and unfortunate. In this reading of Jack as a generic usurper, his "unfortunate" travels become a kind of exile for misappropriating a monarch's status and powers, for Nashe was preoccupied with the propriety of his roguish hero for a role of eminence. The protagonist's irrepressible, high-spirited role playing and the author's own witty, audacious game playing thematically mask a serious intent.

II

The dialectical effect Nashe creates by setting up his character and undermining him at the same time begins in the dedication of the first edition to the Earl of Southampton. Extravagantly full of cringing praise, the dedication yet seems designed to give offense. It opens: "Ingenuous honorable Lord, I know not what blinde custome methodicall antiquity hath thrust upon us, to dedicate such books as we publish to one great man or other" (p. 201). "Ingenuous honorable Lord" rolls out rhythmically and oleaginously enough, but Nashe switches the tone of his adjectives from the ostensibly flattering "Ingenuous honorable" to the overtly pejorative "blinde" and "methodicall." The doubled set of positive adjectives, "Ingenuous honorable," is swiftly overweighed by the doubled set of negatives, "blinde . . . methodicall." Moreover, the verb "thrust," emphatic both in vividness and in accentual weight, is highly unflattering. Hence, if Nashe's true desire is to secure a patron, we may wonder at his method. Writers are aggrieved, or "thrust upon"; dedicatees are, derogatively, "one great man or another." In Nashe's handling, the fact that "methodicall antiquity hath thrust" the practice of dedication upon the author turns the dedication from a topos of courtesy into one of compulsion. By the time Nashe reaches his first full stop, he effectively reverses his elevated opening to imply that in reality Southampton is a disingenuous patron who knowingly accepts flattery in return for food, and who similarly is even dishonorable in that he cooperates in victimizing the "thrust upon" writers by demanding from them "custome." The dedication may have misfired in its stated purpose of wooing Southampton's patronage, for it is absent from the second edition, which contains instead, "The Induction to the dapper Mounsier Pages of the Court."

A key to understanding this perplexing text is found in the dedicatory sentence in the first edition, "My reverent duetifull thoughts (even from their infancie) have been retayners to your glorie." The words are forced, and they rebel on close reading. Here and elsewhere, Nashe's thoughts are demonstrably irreverent and undutiful to figures of authority. G. R. Hibbard makes a good case for our rejecting Nashe's assertion in *Have with you to Saffron-walden* of his prospects while at Cambridge: "My Father . . . brought me up at *S. Johns*, where (it is well knowen) I might have been Fellow if I had would." Hibbard shows that the "if I had would" clause is probably wishful, that Nashe was not "reverent" and "duetifull" enough.[7] The anonymous writer of *The Trimming of Thomas Nash*, 1597, mentions Nashe's "impudencie,"[8] and the scamp, Jack Wilton, appears to represent an extension of the independent, nonconformist aspect of Nashe's own self.

Nashe's thoughts about Southampton probably had not been "retayners to his glorie . . . even from their infancie," yet the first use of the word "infancie" is of interest to us, as the concept functions thematically. "Infancie" is exactly that primary, or self-generating and unreflective, state in which we are not "retayners" of "glorie" of any other person. In Nashe's usage, "infancie" resonates with associative meanings. It is a sheltered period in which the figurative child needs immunity from ordinary cares. Also, it is a time of freshness. Nashe's *infancy* has a later correspondence in the rhetoric of the English Romantics or in Henry David Thoreau's *morning*: "The morning, which is the most memorable season of the day, is the awakening hour. . . . Morning is when I am awake and there is a dawn in me. . . . To be awake is to be alive."[9] For Nashe, *infancy* has the freshness of Thoreau's dawn: the quickening period when the individual is most awake, most alive.

Accordingly, infancy represents a charmed state with a dual aspect; in it, one is exempted from ordinary vicissitudes and thus somehow freed into productivity. Specifically, what is produced during the infantile state is the output of the writer, the creative artist. For this reason, the period of infantilism is the equivalent of a period of being *in fancy* or *in fantasy* and thus of expressing one's own creative ego. Formally, then, the book is not an expression of the *realistic* world, but of a fantasized, or *fantastic* one, as Nashe indicates by naming Jack Wilton's tale a "phantasticall Treatise"

p. 201). Energized by the freshness of a novel kind of writing, with some hopefulness Nashe writes to Southampton, "A new brain, a new wit, a new stile, a new soule will I get mee, to canonize your name to posteritie," and he calls this a work in "a cleane different vaine from other my former courses of writing" (pp. 202, 201). In the joyfully ambitious project of becoming an "out-landish Chronicler" (p. 328), however, it is his own name that Nashe, as creator, wishes to "canonize . . . to posteritie."

Since dependency is implicit in the infantile state and nurture is required, it is consistent with Nashe's conception of author as infant that in *Lenten Stuff* he calls St. John's College (his *alma mater*, nourishing mother) "the sweetest nurse of knowledge" (p. 181). As the chiefest infant, the poet needs sustaining by a patron, or "braunch of Nobilitie." Nashe asks Southampton's aid as a well-known "lover and cherisher . . . of Poets,"[10] and compares the leaves of his book "to the leaves on trees . . . which as they cannot grow of themselves except they have some branches or boughes to cleave too, & with whose juice and sap they be evermore recreated & nourisht." Nashe continues, "Your Lordship is the large spreading branch of renown, from whence these my idle leaves seeke to derive their whole nourishing" (pp. 201-202). In Nashe's equation, the leaf of a tree equals the leaf of a book, a kind of leaf which is synonymous with the page of a book. Punningly, one type of page, the kind that is part of a volume, becomes another, the kind that is found in a royal court. In *The Unfortunate Traveller*, the paradigmatic page is Jack Wilton, who, as a page and also as the displaced self of the author, is the one who needs sustenance.

In this greatly pessimistic work, at the same time that Jack is the necessitous infant of the narrative as its narrator, he is also the false, or counterfeit, narrator because the actual writer, Nashe himself, tells Jack's tale. Jack is the leaf on a tree who "cannot grow of [him]self" unless he is *created & nourished* by the author, his maker. Jack Wilton, the page of Henry VIII's court, punningly, is a page of a book upon whom Nashe writes his story, just as Nashe claims in the induction Jack will be able to write his own story upon "the dapper Mounsier Pages of the Court." A page is unresisting by very definition. In the OED, Nashe is the first person credited with using *page* in its meaning of *printed sheet*.[11] Jack's attempts to reverse this fate of passivity through jests are punished in later adventures.

Jack is indeed a blank page before this story begins, with only the very barest previous history as "a Noble mans Page" (p. 224), former servant to the Earl of Surrey (p. 241). Since no details of his early life are provided, it is difficult to imagine Jack as the product of a family matrix. Considered in this way, Jack has an undifferentiated psychological self; Nashe explains that "the eye that sees round about it selfe, sees not into it selfe" (p. 201). Ego psychology applied to the fictional subject Jack Wilton considers him mainly in his role of surrogate, or vocalizing projection of the desiring ego, for his maker, Tom Nashe. This role is suggested by the initial description which Jack is given for self-reference: "I, *Jacke Wilton*, (a Gentleman at least,) was a certain kind of an appendix or page" (p. 209). He is a fictive, or subjective, appendix to the author's ego and a page upon which the author can express this created self.

Jack is, of course, the unfortunate traveler to whom the title refers, and Nashe uses the Bible as a source of negative exempla for Jack's travels. When Jack's misfortunes grow thick, he thinks, "Here beginneth my purgatorie" and "God plagud me" (pp. 295, 303). "A banisht English Earle" delivers a hectoring lecture to Jack in Rome: "God had no greater curse to lay upon the *Israelites*, than by leading them out of their owne countrey to live as slaves in a strange land." The earl points out, "The first traveller was *Cain*, and he was called a vagabond runnagate on the face of the earth" (pp. 296-97). Although the force of equating Jack with Cain is softened slightly by saying that Cain "*was called*" a renegade, still it would appear that the necessitous upstart will be scapegoated relentlessly by Nashe. Indeed, Nashe's religious revulsions arise from his underlying scruples over the suitability of his bumptious scapegrace, Jack Wilton, for the central role in a (parodic) morality.

In this "historie," Jack is activated as a character by the same events he relates as the narrator. He says of himself, "Let me be a historiographer of my owne misfortunes" (p. 281). As narrator, he addresses the audience directly at various stages: "list, lordlings, to my proceedings," "Gentle Readers (looke you be gentle now since I have cald you so)," "Oh my Auditors," "My masters," "gentle reader" (pp. 210, 217, 219, 226, 263). To indicate the passage of time, Nashe has Jack Wilton frame a request directly to the readers to allow peripheral events to pass by quickly: "I must not place a volume in the precincts of a pamphlet: sleepe an houre or two, and dream that Turney and Turwin is wonne, that the King is shipt againe into England, and that I am close at harde meate at Windsore or at Hampton Court" (p. 227). Nashe employs two devices for even greater intimacy between the audience and the author/narrator than can be gained by direct formal address. For one, he uses the humorous aside noted above: "(looke you be gentle now since I have cald you so)." Also, he tries to establish a *mutually* bantering tone between writer and audience; Jack Wilton first questions the readers on their conjecture about his own advancement in "signiorie over the [other] Pages" and then comments on the readers' "probable . . . suppose": "What, will you in your indifferent opinions allow me for my travell no more signiorie over the Pages than I had before? yes, whether you will part with so much probable friendly suppose or no, Ile have it in spite of your hearts. For your instruction and godly consolation, bee informed, that at that time I was no common squire. . . . I was the first that brought in the order of passing into the Court. . . . I was crowned King of the drunkardes with a Court cuppe" (pp. 227-28).

In Nashe's bantering tone, there is an eagerness for reader awareness of Jack's elevation to monarchy. Even as an ironic or playful or debased monarch, Jack is preeminent. As he says grandly, "I was the first." Jonathan Goldberg notes the correlation between politics, or monarchy, and literature: " 'Works' are opera, writing; discourse reigns supreme, its might is right, the sole truth: the acts of the king are crowned in words. There is an implicit politics in language: The root of author is *auctor*, originator, warrant of the truth, supporter of a law."[12]

III

The Unfortunate Traveller begins and ends on the notion of a chronicle. The story opens with Henry VIII, "true subject of Chronicles," at war "against the two hundred and fifty towers of *Turney* and *Turwin*" (p. 209). It closes: "And so as my storie began with the king at *Turnay* and *Turwin*, I thinke meete here to end it with the king at *Ardes* and *Guines*." In epilogue, Nashe/Wilton promises if the story does not please "never to bee out-landish Chronicler more while I live" (p. 328). With Henry VIII as the "onely" hero of chronicle, the text is set up as a false chronicle, an anti-chronicle or "out-landish Chronicle"; however, it is still a *kind* of chronicle, investing Jack with a kind of political standing (although "out-landish" also derogates both Jack's and Henry VIII's non-English ventures). The status of chronicler, then, authorizes the writer with the power of king-maker; as Nashe says in the induction, this tale is told to give "newes of the maker."

Interestingly, the sense of social duty in the three roles assigned to Jack Wilton corresponds to the underlying condition of central characters in the work of Sir Philip Sidney. Astrophel, especially, is a barely-disguised authorial surrogate: a poet, or maker, who relates, or chronicles, his own story. Moreover, he is an infant, or youth, of noble purpose.[13] As Nashe's preface, "Somewhat to reade for them *that list*," introduces one of the 1591 quartos of *Astrophel and Stella*, we know reliably of Nashe's familiarity with Sidney's work. Since the notion of a disguised prince who desires to regenerate society is not entirely a Renaissance commonplace, we may assume either the influence of Sidney on Nashe or their related thought. S. K. Heninger, Jr., states that Sidney's exalting of mimesis over metrification "leads in one direction to the development of prose narrative and eventually to the novel."[14] Although both Sidney and Nashe see the ability to cause ethical change as a possibility inhering in the heroic figure of fiction, Nashe's final vision is far bleaker than Sidney's, perhaps an index of the insecure status and remuneration of the new profession of practicing writer.

In *Astrophel and Stella,* Sidney elevates Astrophel to princedom as monarch of Stella's "high heart." As Arthur Marotti demonstrates, irony and ambition are displaced and disguised ingredients in the love imagery,[15] but Nashe overtly ironizes the rhetorical strategy. Jack bases his claim to royalty as a "prince of [the pages'] purses" or, by extension, a "peere of quart pottes" (p. 210). In the first "jest" which opens the book, Jack tricks an alehouse keeper into believing that the king thinks him a miser and a traitor and that to exculpate himself he must distribute free provisions in the army camp. The jest confirms Jack as monarch who assumes the care of his fellows. Despite the omnipresent satire, including self-denigrating references, Jack takes himself seriously as "king of the Pages." Even as Jack is enthroned, however, he is simultaneously toppled, with Nashe both asserting and undermining Jack's claim to be leader of his "company." Although Jack feels bound by honor to nourish his fellow pages, nevertheless, with deflating mockery, including self-mockery, Jack says he was the "sole king of the cans and blacke jackes, prince of the pigmies, countie palatine of cleane straw and provant . . . Lord high regent of rashers of the coles and red herring cobs. . . . Amongest [the pages] . . . I was prince of their purses, & exacted of my unthrifte subjects as much liquid alleageance as any keisar in the world could doe, yet where it is not to bee had the king must loose his right" (pp. 209-10).

With the pages unable to support him, for "men can doe no more than they can doe," Jack feels that leadership obliges him to remedy their need. Though their allegiance is but "liquid alleageance" which has been "exacted," Jack, as ruler, must come to their aid.

To gull the cider merchant, Jack tells a false tale, relying on his power of discourse. Since the "cunning" story is not for knavery's own sake, in one rhetorical move, the impudence of the plot against the merchant does not discredit Jack: "the lie" is a form of honor and youthful zest that activates the "device" (p. 212). By this tendentious reasoning, Jack's falsehood is transposed into the "stratagemicall act" of an "ingenious infant"; in addition, the crafty lie becomes even a "signe of good education . . . and argument of In grace and vertue to proceed" (p. 209). Nashe equates *infant* with a youth of high birth. The concept of *high birth* includes both a necessity of protecting inferiors who are dependents and an allowance for jests against oppressors whose class status is questionable. The alehouse keeper "dishonors" the aristocratic class in his undignified role as merchant; so also the mechanical captain and coistrel clerks of the next jests are appropriate victims because they are pretentious. When Jack Wilton says his lips "have but lately suckt milke" (p. 215), purity of infantile beverage is correlated to a purity of lively mischief in his spirit.

The first jest establishes the factitious nature of Jack's kingship. The victim, the tavern keeper whom Jack "chose out to damne with a lewd monilesse device," is a figure of some prestige in the army camp, "a Lord of misrule" (pp. 211, 210). Jack says that in fright at the intimidating tale of the king's disfavor, the victimized merchant "put his rustie ring on my finger, gave mee his greasie purse with that single mony that was in it, promised to make mee his heire, and a thousand more favours, if I would expire the miserie of his unspeakable tormenting uncertaintie. . . . Why (quoth I), my selfe that am but a poore childish well-willer of yours" (p. 213).

When the merchant puts the ring on Jack's finger and names Jack his heir, unification of their person and status will govern all Jack's future encounters. Increasingly, Jack becomes identified with the gull and the victim. True, at first Jack gulls the fools, but they insure his downfall, for as Jack observes, "*Adam* never fell till God made fooles" (p. 224). As the conflicting codes of the plot operate, Jack imagines himself on top of the events he puts in motion, but in the larger sense, he pulls the consequences down on himself. By accepting the ring Jack accepts transfiguration into a kind of lord, a status he desires; nonetheless, the change of rank is not an advancement. Jack becomes not a lord of high-minded rule, as he would wish, but a lord of misrule. The opening passage initiates Jack's slow descent, the debilitating and "unfortunate travel" that forms the progress of the book.

As the cider merchant episode reveals, no matter how central to power Jack may envision himself, in reality, he is made marginal by the wielders of authority. When Henry VIII discovers his trickery, the profit is turned to the king's advantage and Jack is whipped. Society and its monarch disregard him in every real sense. In his jest against the "ugly mechanicall Captain" (p. 217), Jack turns out to be of even less importance than in the one which opens the book. Just as Jack's "discourse" leads the "syder-merchant" into being tricked, his "solemne oration" (p. 218) gulls the captain, with Nashe, as usual, projecting the importance of tale-telling on to the impudent character, Jack Wilton.[16] In this case Jack's remorseless oration dazzles the foolish captain into believing himself to be a spy and propels him into disaster. Although eventually the captain "could not keepe his joynts from ransacking on the Wheele," and finally he pays for Jack's "good humors" with his life, society exacts no penalty from Jack. The captain even "said he was a poore Captaine in the English Campe, suborned by one Jacke Wilton (a Noble mans Page), and no other" (p. 224); but no sanctions follow.

IV

Jack declares that "if [the captain] had bin mine own brother, I could have done no more for him than I did" (p. 222). Kinship links Jack in brotherhood to the captain as well as in sonship to the merchant. After the jest against the captain, however, Jack subtly becomes lowered in his own self-esteem. A new style of judgmental, self-chastizing rhetoric comes into focus in which Jack does not clothe his tricks in the boastful and defensive euphemisms that characterize his irrepressible spirits at the start. In a transitional sentence, the "stratagemicall" jests are transposed into baseness: "Here let me triumph a while, and ruminate a line or two on the excellence of my wit: but I will not breath neither till I have disfraughted all my knaverie" (p. 225). "Knaverie" is no honorific: a *jest* is a verbal device of witty *high* spirit, which Jack Wilton boastfully and self-indulgently owns up to, but *knavery* implies a *base* strategem, which weighs *down* the perpetrator.

Jack's inevitable descent to the nether world which occupies most of the narrative is prefigured in a speeded-up episode in which he pretends to be a woman in order to gull a "Switzer Captaine that was farre gone for want of the wench" (p. 225). Disguised in the clothes of a "halfe crowne wench," Jack "had [his] curtsies in cue . . . for they dyvde into the verie entrailes of the dust" (p. 225). As a descent in miniature in which Jack objectifies himself, this precursor scene of Jack as a fallen woman prepares for his later important fall. The major moment of falling is at once a literal tumble into Zadoch's cellar and a figural descent into the torments of mental and physical purgatory. The immediate outcome of Jack's dive into the cellar is that he is victimized by Doctor Zachary, who plans to anatomize his "entrailes," and by Juliana, who keeps him enslaved in her chambers as a kind of pleasure object.

As the jests progress, Jack becomes more base. Nashe uses the rhetorical force of emblematic key words to rebuke Jack's knavery. Each of the three main precursor episodes is symbolized by a salient word that applies to the jest's partakers on both sides, instigator as well as victim, bonding them in a reciprocal relationship. The cider merchant adventure is identified at the end by a loss of exuberant spirit: the alcoholic spirits of "his *alie* honor" (p. 211) and the coltish high spirits of the "yong . . . prince of . . . purses." As the word *spirit* is emblematic of the first jest, so the mechanical captain adventure is identified by the tag "mechanicall," the adjective Nashe applies to the victim. *Mechanical* identifies the captain with manual labor and tradespeople, as well as with a lack of spontaneity and originality. Thus, it identifies Jack's *mechanical* repetition of disreputable—low and therefore *mechanical*—jests. The third such adventure, involving the "coystrell Clearkes," prefigures Jack's brushes with death. The baseness of the action on both sides is indicated by the word *coistrel* as applied to the clerks and the reciprocal word *scutchery* as applied to Jack's jest of pilferage from the clerks. Jack opens this section with, "Yet left I not here, but committed a little more scutcherie" (p. 225). The OED first exemplifies *scutchery* by both this sentence and by another of Nashe's, "Now that he [Senior Sathan] is thoroughly steeled in his scutcherie he plays above boord boldly," from *Terrors of the Night*, 1595. In fuller form, the passage from *The Unfortunate Traveller* runs: "Yet left I not here, but committed a little more scutcherie. A companie of coystrell Clearkes (who were in band with Sathan, and not of anie Souldiers collar nor hat-band) pincht a number of good mindes to God-ward of their provant. They would not let a dram of dead-pay ovre-slip them" (p. 225). Although "pinching" others' "provant" is Jack's aim also, he has not yet descended to stealing from the dead. His scutchery, however, connects him later with satanic characters.

In the above quotation, the word *dead* opens up the subterranean meaning of this episode. As *spirit* is the linguistic device of the first jest and *mechanical* of the second, so *dead* governs this trick and is increasingly central to the later unfortunate travels. In this fashion, Nashe establishes three opposed categories for Jack's three positive attributes: eventually, the infant becomes dispirited, the maker mechanical, the monarch dead. Before the story's end, Jack emulates the coistrel clerks, as well as those even more satanic villains, Esdras and Bartol, by stealing from the dead. In fact, his pillaging of Juliana's property even leads to her death. Although Juliana herself is established as an oppressor and wanton, Jack's act of robbery is not condoned by the didactic, or moralizing, rhetorical mode that forms one linguistic network under the surface activity of the plot.

The jest against the coistrel clerks illustrates Jack's double-binds, for as a leader he must provide for his followers. Jack confides to the reader: "I think confidently I was ordained Gods scourge from above for [the clerks'] daintie finicalitie. . . . One day [I] made a false alarum. . . . They betooke them to their heeles . . . and in fine, left me and my fellowes (their foole-catchers) Lordes of the field: How we dealt with them, their disburdened deskes canne best tell" (p. 226). Jack persuades himself that as prince of the impudent, thievish pages and instrument of God's justice, he has dispensation to wage a war of divine vengeance. The revenge motif is overturned, however, or exploited in order to be debunked; for every act of violence Jack perpetrates, Nashe insures he will be suitably victimized at a later time.

Jack's lively spirit, or aliveness, defeats the "finigraphicall" clerks. He and his followers pilfer the contents of their desks as he congratulates himself on the religious victory of the "Lordes of the field." In the variety of codes that govern the book, by one mode of reasoning Jack indeed acts on the side of morality. He avenges not only the clerks' thievery and overly refined finicality, but rather a special kind of "pusillanimitie." The clerks display a type of cowardice against which, even in a generalized scapegoating of Jack's impudent effrontery, Nashe privileges his actions. What especially counts against the clerks is their inability to "so much as throwe *a pen-full of inke* into the Enemies face" (p. 226; my italics).

This scornful jibe against the clerks opposes them to Jack in his most privileged role, of writer—or chronicler or historiographer—of the story he enacts. In their lack of language, the clerks become the enemies of that conflated figure, Tom Nashe/Jack Wilton, who so impudently and imprudently enjoys the copiousness of language. Literally, the clerks are associated with death because they steal the payment to the dead, and symbolically, because they cannot stay alive by words. Thus, the clerks are contrasted to the creative artist who lives by his wits and his ink pot. Agnes M. C. Latham comments: "One of the few things that we do know about Nashe is that he wrote for money, and that money was always short with him. This would not encourage a man to respect an artistic conscience. He was a satirist; a touchy, fleering, flyting pamphleteer; a professional wit; a stylist; and a hack dramatist. But always, through thick and thin, obstinately, sometimes unexpectedly and touchingly, Nashe was a literary man."[17] It appears that on one level Nashe aimed "to respect an artistic conscience," even though his observation of this type of honor might be "unexpected." As tale-teller even more than as infant/monarch, Jack is suspended between codes, compelled to battle the language-lacking clerks but not permitted debased weapons. For this reason, the theft *qua* theft from the "goose-quill Braggadoches" offends against an implicit moral imperative that the battle be an exalted one. The pettiness of the jest does not pass as mere "roguerie" but joins metaphorically with crimes committed by other low characters. By linguistic association, then, Jack's latest jest connects him to satanic actions, and he is punished accordingly.[18]

V

A returning kind of retribution punishes Jack on the three levels of his existence (infant, monarch, maker), bringing thematic coherence to the narrative. Each of the three main jests—against merchant, captain, clerks—will be revenged appropriately during the travels. In other words, "the houre of [Jack's own] punishment," the aspect of the work that Richard A. Lanham calls "this pleasure in punishment,"[19] unifies the book. First, Jack acts as a type of saviour, bringing cider and cheese to the needy. As the expected outcome, his harrowing follows. Retributive punishment comes in response to Jack's presumption as an upstart, which reveals him as a false hero, or knave; also, paradoxically, it comes in response to his effectiveness as a true leader, one whose acts are motivated morally and spiritually despite contrary appearances. Jack's high spirit is whipped out of him, and the merchant loses the alehouse, source of alcoholic "spirits." Just as the episode indicates the loss of spirit, or spirits, or even spirituality, so attainment of a rehabilitated life occupies the rest of the book.The unfortunate, or punishing, travels that ultimately regenerate Jack are associated with hellish underworld existence. Northrop Frye's explanation, "Ironic literature begins with realism and tends toward myth," describes the movement of the story. Punishment of villains who are surrogates for Jack, as well as Jack's own terror, accelerates bewilderingly. The journey leads to what Frye calls "the world of the nightmare and the scapegoat, of bondage and pain and confusion." This demonic world "is closely linked with an existential hell . . . or with the hell that man creates on earth. . . . Hence one of the central themes of demonic imagery is parody, the mocking of the exuberant play of art by suggesting its imitation in terms of 'real life.' "[20] The journey, then, a metaphoric descent for self-regeneration, occurs in three stages, each of which corresponds somewhat irregularly to one of the three main jests at the narrative's opening. Put differently, even before Jack leaves England, his jests, which may appear to be random, suggest by prefiguration his traits to be punished at various stages of the journey.

The opening jest forecasts the punishing events of the first level of the tripartite descent. Thus, the cider merchant episode presages two events which Jack witnesses early in his travels: the annihilation of the Anabaptists in Munster and the tournament with Surrey in Florence. In contrast to his active role in the jests, in both these scenes Jack is a spectator. Curiously, it appears that the author himself feels involved as a victim in the scene that depicts the massacre of John of Leyden and the Anabaptists although, superficially, an identification on Nashe's part with a radicalized Puritan sect seems unlikely. Still, these iconoclastic religious martyrs are Jack's analogues at least in that they also are impudent upstarts who briefly install themselves in the place of political and religious authority.

In telling the story of "*John Leiden*," Jack says, "Wherin let me dilate a litle more gravely than the nature of this historie requires, or wilbe expected of so yong a practitioner in divinity" (p. 234). Perhaps the fact that Nashe's father was a minister underlies Jack's parody of ecclesiastical language. We may infer a reference to Nashe's own father by associative contiguity of the parodic sermon and the simile, "like a father that weepes when he beates his childe, yet still weepes and stil beates" (p. 240). Ferguson notes the thematic father-son relationship that recurs throughout the story and is tied to the generalized sado-masochistic retributory punishment.[21] The ironic sermon which Jack delivers would constitute a type of discourse that Frye identifies with the demonic world. This satirized oratory is linked to the "ridiculous oration" at the University of Wittenberg by the "bursten belly inkhorne orator called *Vanderhulke*." Notably, Vanderhulke calls himself and his fellow students "Mechanicall men" with a "mechanike religion" (pp. 249, 247), using terms of cathected opprobrium.

The second travel event to depict an ending of spirit involves the reunion with the Earl of Surrey immediately upon Jack's quitting Munster. By rights, Surrey ought to incarnate the spirituality that Jack seeks because he is "a right noble Lord, liberalitie it selfe (if in this yron age there were any such creature as liberalitie left on the earth), a Prince in content because a Poet without peere" (p. 242). Surrey embodies the qualities that Jack would emulate, especially as poet, or truest form of maker, the privileged quality that assures peerage for the individual. Since Nashe uses essentially the same correspondences found in *Astrophel and Stella*, he may incorporate Sidney and his projected self, Astrophel, into the satiric depiction of the poet-aristocrat Surrey.[22]

Jack turns from the "catastrophe of this Munsterian conflict" to the meeting with Surrey by a transitional phrase in which he names himself a "knight arrant infant" (p. 241). This again is an emblematic moment that provides a hallmark for an entire section. Surrey's Petrarchanisms are systematically debunked; his tournament in defense of Geraldine's beauty burlesques true infantile chivalric honor. In fine, Surrey represents a leftover from a discredited romance-world, a figure of ridicule skewered by Nashe's quill. As Merritt Lawlis points out, "The romance element is inverted, becoming really anti-romance,"[23] with spirituality an attribute sought but not found. Through his involvement in the conventions of courtly love, the languishing Surrey represents what Lanham calls "the dying feudal social structure," here lampooned by "an emergent bourgeois attitude."[24]

Illustrating my thesis that by word play an ending of spirit takes place, Nashe/Wilton says both playfully and seriously of the Anabaptist segment, "This tale must at one time or other give up the ghost" (p. 241). Lacking spirituality, the world is counterfeit and mechanical in the sense conveyed by the episode of the captain. Jack devises a counterfeit persona for him, and the identity sticks to both "brothers," making Jack himself become part of the false, mechanical world. Nashe introduces counterfeit poetry into the story, and Jack is imprisoned as a counterfeiter in Venice and visits a counterfeit Eden in Rome. In Venice, he and Surrey are detained on a trumped-up, or "counterfeit," charge of counterfeiting coins. While in prison, Jack meets Diamante, also being held on a false charge. Mostly, their meeting contrasts Jack's societal impotence with his personal ability to pull off a jest against his master. Diamante, the correspondent in the jest, has the same adhesive quality as the other recipients of Jack's "lewd devices." Not only does she enter Jack's life permanently as "Curtizan" and wife, but for the remainder of the Italian travels, Jack becomes a surrogate Diamante, an imprisoned woman, as previously he was transfigured into merchant, captain, clerk.

In Rome, Jack describes an Edenic scene, a counterfeited paradise, as "a summer banketting house belonging to a merchaunt, that was the mervaile of the world, & could not be matcht except God should make another paradise. . . . For the earth, it was counterfeited in that liknes that Adam lorded out it before his fall" (pp. 282-83). At the merchant's summer house, Jack "sate and banketted" under a "conspiracie of pine trees" in which there were perched "many sortes of shrill breasted birdes" (p. 283). Unseen "organizing implements" cause the imitation birds to sing, to make a "spirting sound, such as chirping is" (p. 284). By metaphoric linkage, the mechanical, counterfeit birds become mechanical, counterfeit poets. The artificial birds, Jack says,

> were bodie without soules, and sweete resembled substances without sense, yet by the mathemeticall experimentes of long silver pipes secretlye inrinded in the intrailes of the boughs whereon they sate, and undiscerneablie convaid . . . into their small throats sloaping, they whistled and freely carold theyr naturall field note. . . . [The] tail of the silver pipe stretcht it selfe into the mouth of a great paire of belowes, where . . . it coulde not stirre or have anie vent betwixt.
>
> (p. 283)

In vivifying the inanimate boughs, birds, pipes, and bellows, Nashe builds the negative impression of strangulation: the pipes are "secretlye inrinded" and "undiscerneablie convaid under [the birds'] bellies *into their small throats.*" These substitute poets cleave to "the wel clothed boughs of this conspiracie of pine trees" much as the dedication states the "leaves" of poets must "have some branches or boughs to cleave too . . . some braunch of Nobilitie . . . with whose juice and sap they be evermore recreated & nourisht." Evidently, Nashe's assessment of what it means to "derive [one's] whole nourishing" from "a large spreading branch of renown" strangles his own dedicatory request in the act of asking. Imprisoning claustrophobia clings to the description of the juncture of pipe and bellows: "close soldered, and bailde about with yron, it coulde not stirre or have anie vent betwixt." As a tropic replacement for the nourished poets, the "inchained chirping birdes," mechanically singing in and of a perfect world, do not convey the underside, with invisible bellows which "dyd beate up and downe uncessently" although "all those organizing implements" are "obscured in the corpulent trunks of the trees" (p. 284). The captive birds that pipe conventional music exemplify the abhorrence of patronage that underlies and troubles the mock-"duetifull" dedication. Nashe, the quintessential needy infant, cannot allow himself to become a chained bird piping the official tune.

VI

After the two episodes that confirm the cider merchant jest—those at Munster and Florence—Jack, like the merchant, survives with his spirit in defeat. At the summer banqueting house, Jack sees another type of lesson in a perceived perfect world. In the book's most static scene, the "golden . . . good honest . . . age" (p. 285) turns out to be mechanical like the captain and dead like the clerks. As the antithetical figure to the mechanical birds, Jack's voice is non-synchronous with his society's because he is innovative and alive.

Indeed, Nashe's description of the controlling mechanism under the "conspiracie" of shady trees paranoically suggests a conspiracy against the creative artist: the subtext converts the "plummets" on a "wheele [which] dyd beate up and downe uncessantly" into a controlling father/society that beats conformity into its child/poet.

To some degree, Nashe's pessimism about the role of the creative artist in the Renaissance is confirmed by Kerrigan, who explains, " 'Imitation' was the key principle of humanist education," and specifically, the educational method of *imitatio* "denotes the imitation of model authors from the classical past."[25] In actuality, Renaissance childhood did not allow for the undutiful exuberance and creativity with which Nashe invests the concept of infancy. In Kerrigan's words, "Renaissance children peer at us from their portraits with the dour faces of adults, wearing the same clothes as adults: they seem invaded by their future maturity."[26] Significantly, Jack's panegyric on the "golden age" of the "banketting house" virtually ends his period of prankish and linguistic creativity. Although his education comes not so much from imitation as from a series of negative episodes, the result is the same. Kerrigan continues that "humanist imitation is a kind of grammar for the restraint of the creative act," and hence the "defenders" of "inspired creation . . . were mostly outside the academies."[27] One of Nashe's basic needs is to be assured that he could have had a career *inside the academy*, where he "might have been Fellow if [he] had would." Thus is Jack Wilton suspended between society's demand to pipe the right tune and the individual's desire to be historiographer of his own tale and to disfreight himself of his own knavery, not as Kerrigan describes the process, "in imitation of model authors from the classical past," nor as Nashe himself puts it, in the "blinde custome methodicall antiquity hath thrust upon" the writer, but rather in "a cleane different vaine."

After dining in the banqueting house, Jack exclaims, "O *Rome*, if thou hast in thee such soul-exalting objects, what a thing is heaven in comparison of thee" (p. 285). With this rhapsody, we come ironically to the first of Jack's three detentions in Roman homes, imprisonments which detail an inferno of physical and emotional torture. The final episodes comprise a *paronomastic* anatomy of thanatos, as Jack passively undergoes various brushes with death (counterfeit deaths): he faces the prospect of an *actual* anatomy—a medical dissection of his own body, and he is made to witness multiple deaths of other characters, all of whom suffer surrogatively for more wicked versions of his own early jests, or sins. For instance, Jack was the Jew who "exacted . . . liquid alleageance" from the pages, in anticipation of the way in which Doctor Zachary extracts even the "licour out of his shooes" (p. 306). The projected anatomy causes Jack's nightmares about his own bodily liquid allegiance: "phlebotomie, bloudie fluxes, incarnatives, running ulcers" (p. 305).

There are psychosexual overtones in Jack's bondage to Zachary, a "fore-skinne clipper" (p. 307): he is bought for his physical beauty ("of the age of eighteene, of stature tall, straight limd, of as cleare a complection as any Painters fancie can imagine" [p. 304]); he is stripped and kept "in a dark chamber" fantasizing about the blood gushing "out at [his] nose," the sweat trickling "down [his] breast and sides"; he has a "plumporredge of purgations ministred" to him (p. 305). Since the language and anxieties suggest fear of castration or loss of sexual potency, we may gather that Jack is punished for carnal misdoings. As a heedless womanizer who seduces Diamante, he is amply punished both emotionally and physically as Countess Juliana's prisoner. Of this period, he says, "Nere a sixe houres but the Countesse cloyd me with her companie . . . [with] harlot-like behavior" (pp. 316, 314). At the time of Jack's original seduction of Diamante, her husband is still alive, which may connect the jailhouse seduction to the prolonged episode in which Jack helplessly watches the tragicomic rape of Heraclide. In a brief early jest in the army camp, Jack imitates a woman of pleasure. In the passages involving Heraclide, Zachary, and Juliana, Jack becomes a type of counterfeit woman, defenseless and kept within quarters for his youth and comeliness. In Zachary's house, he is equated with a woman through the medium of his own imaginings about the forthcoming anatomy: "To die with a pricke, wherewith the faintest hearted woman under heaven would not be kild" (p. 308).

Jack's infancy is brought to a close by a mechanical and benumbing aggregation of cruel experiences. The incidents of robbery and death revise the knavish jest of theft from the coistrel and thanatotic clerks. As Jack launches into his first jest, he assesses the "povertie" of his fellow pages: "where it [liquid alleageance] is not to bee had the king must loose his right . . . what remained then, but the foxes case must help, when the lions skin is out at the elbowes" (p. 210). When Jack involves the reader in his foxy jest-as-logical-outcome, he initiates a relationship analogous to the one between the reader and Milton's Satan, as described by Stanley Fish.[28] Compromised by sin through implicit approval, the reader must perforce share in the punishment; Jack and the reader become immersed for cleansing purposes in the bloodbath of the later scenes. Jack has been an impudent upstart to whom the reader has not been immune; thereafter, the book's moralizing lesson sinks in on both protagonist and audience through gory depictions of lingering death.

VII

Jack's journey is marked by an increasing passivity. This quiescence symbolizes the loss of his infancy and the onset (or as Kerrigan puts it, the "invasion") of his "future maturity." The interpretation of Jack's travel as a descent accords with his statement upon leaving England, "Let mee *quietly descend* to the *waining* of my *youthfull* daies" (p. 228; my italics). In the word *quietly* we recognize the opposition established between liveliness-jest-voice on one side and death-punishment-silence on the other. To leave youth for maturity is to leave creativity for stillness. Although Jack Wilton may be imprinted on our imagination as eighteen years old, the travel adventures cover a period of time; in one instance, Cutwolfe pursues Esdras during "two yeeres" (p. 320) after Jack's Roman imprisonment. The passage of time makes Jack older than the legal and conventional definition of minority. Since by common law infancy extended through the twenty-first year of age, Jack is no longer a child. Symbolically, his aging is inscribed in the story as a concomitant of his misfortunes. Jack says, "Tracing uppe and downe the Cittie . . . till the Evening began to grow verie well in age . . . I fell into [Zadoch's cellar] as a man should tumble on a sodaine into hell" (p. 303). The waning, or aging, of the day signifies Jack's own aging; the descent is brought on by his youthful miscreance. In the dystopian underworld, his place is perpetually insecure in retribution for misuse of his formerly secure definition of page.

The outcome of Jack's misfortunes is akin to the outcome of the highly significant first jest, in which Jack accepts the ring and heritage of the Lord of Misrule and the alehouse keeper voluntarily retires. Just as Jack advises him "now in your old daies to be liberall" and the merchant retires to "a beadsmanrie," so in Jack's parallel expiation, he performs "many almes deedes" (pp. 215, 216, 327). Jack tells the merchant, "Credit my advice, you shall finde it propheticall" (p. 215), and such it is of Jack's own finale. He says, "The hunter pursuing the Beaver for his stones, hee bites them off, and leaves them behinde for him to gather up, whereby he lives quiet" (p. 215). Jack's metaphorical homily forecasts his own fate, as he himself becomes the quarry of unscrupulous hunters. At Doctor Zachery's, Jack fantasizes his emasculation by mutilation and at Juliana's undergoes another loss of masculinity. In self-preservation, paradoxically, he must emulate the merchant, the figural beaver of Jack's ironic sermon, and devise his own way to "live quiet."

The ending thus relates a kind of voluntary exile from infancy and chronicling and monarchy. Again, there is the sense of opposed modes of thought, both operant, both compelling. Jack is trapped, or "clogged" as he describes it, by Diamante and her wealth, yet he is simultaneously in need of them. Just as Cutwolfe shoots Esdras "full into the throat" (p. 326), so the narrative discourse seems simply to break off, leading to no future as it recounted no past, subdued finally by its own violence. In spirit, or as "a 'matter of style,' " as Jonathan V. Crewe says, "Nashe tempts us with the idea of a perennial modernism."[29] Self-consciously rhetorical and violently extreme, the text asks to be read not simply as a proto-novel, but rather as a proto-*postmodernist*-novel.[30] Nashe writes a story in which the honor of nobility is outmoded; the individual's spirit is broken, and he is silenced and bludgeoned into conformity. In this early depiction of mobility and bourgeois society, we may recognize the modern ethos of alienation: the stupefying carnage of senseless war and the brutalizing effects of false imprisonment, official bureaucracy, and other thanatoid aspects of city life.

At the finish, Nashe keeps his framework intact by again orienting the "out-landish" chronicle of Jack Wilton within the "English Chronicle" of Henry VIII, but he makes a wistful perorational reference to the possibility of sequels. Nashe's tentative uncertainty mirrors the conflicted and troubled finale. Having made amends, Jack returns to the king, who is still at bivouac in an English army campsite, now in a new location. The suggestion presents itself that if this king who is ever at battle is "the onely true subject of Chronicles," then society itself is the raptor and war is unending. After recounting the deaths of so many others, Jack is still alive, to be sure, but he is dazed by the enormity of mankind's capacity for evil. In essence, Jack is aged and dispirited and silenced. The end of the tale marks the end of the creative realm of infancy, which means the end of the page.[31]

NOTES

[1]All references to *The Unfortunate Traveller* (1594) cite *The Works of Thomas Nashe,* ed. Ronald B. McKerrow, 2nd edn., 5 vols. (Oxford: Clarendon Press, 1958), 2:201-328; also cited are *Have with you to Saffron-walden* (1596), 3:1-139, and *Nashes Lenten Stuffe* (1599), 3:141-226.

[2]C. S. Lewis, *English Literature in the Sixteenth Century Excluding Drama* (Oxford: Clarendon Press, 1954), pp. 410-11.

[3]John Berryman, "Thomas Nashe and *The Unfortunate Traveller,*" in *The Freedom of the Poet* (New York: Farrar, Straus, and Giroux, 1976), pp. 9-28; Walter R. Davis, *Idea and Act in Elizabethan Fiction* (Princeton: Princeton Univ. Press, 1969), pp. 218-19. The three-part structure is not easily pinned down, and most commentators disagree on salient points. For instance, Davis says, "The structural divisions . . . rest on the three main places visited: the English camp, northern Europe, and Italy" (p. 219; see pp. 190-237). On the other hand, Stanley Wells, who states the book "has no organizing principle," in *Thomas Nashe: Selected Works,* ed. Stanley Wells (Cambridge, Mass.: Harvard Univ. Press, 1964), p. 18, seems to overlook structural guideposts.

[4]To McKerrow, *The Unfortunate Traveller* is not a picaresque (5:23); however, Fredson T. Bowers, in "Thomas Nashe and the Picaresque Novel," *University of Virginia Studies* 1 (1941):12-27, and Madelon S. Gohlke, in "Wits Wantoness: *The Unfortunate Traveller* as Picaresque," *SP* 73 (1976):397-413, discuss the book as picaresque. Ann Rosalind Jones analyzes it as Menippean satire in "Inside the Outsider: Nashe's *Unfortunate Traveller* and Bakhtin's Polyphonic Novel," *ELH* 50 (1983):61-81; also see James Sutherland in *English Satire* (Cambridge: Cambridge Univ. Press, 1962), pp. 35-36. Richard A. Lanham provides the best summary of critical approaches in "Tom Nashe and Jack Wilton: Personality as Structure in *The Unfortunate Traveller,*" *SSF* 4 (1967):201-205.

[5]William Kerrigan, "The Articulation of the Ego in the English Renaissance," in *The Literary Freud: Mechanisms of Defense and the Poetic Will,* ed. Joseph H. Smith, M.D. (New Haven: Yale Univ. Press, 1980), pp. 261-308.

[6]Margaret Ferguson, "Nashe's *The Unfortunate Traveller*: "The 'Newes of the Maker' Game," *ELR* 11 (1981):165-82.

[7]G. R. Hibbard, *Thomas Nashe: A Critical Introduction* (Cambridge, Mass.: Harvard Univ. Press, 1962), pp. 3-7.

[8]*The Trimming of Thomas Nashe Gentleman* (1597), in *The Old Book Collector's Miscellany: or, a Collection of Readable Reprints of Literary Rarities,* ed. Charles Hindley, 3 vols. (London, 1871), 1:i-64.

[9]Henry David Thoreau, *Walden and Other Writings* (1854), ed. Brooks Atkinson (New York: Modern Library, 1937), pp. 80-81.

[10]In *A Cup of News: The Life of Thomas Nashe* (New York: Methuen, 1984), Charles Nicholl discusses this quotation as referring to Shakespeare. He states that in *Loves Labors Lost,* "Moth is Nashe in the guise of a 'knavish page', just as Jack Wilton is" (p. 161).

[11]See Jonathan V. Crewe, *Unredeemed Rhetoric: Thomas Nashe and the Scandal of Authorship* (Baltimore: Johns Hopkins Univ. Press, 1982), p. 69.

[12]Jonathan Goldberg, *James I and the Politics of Literature* (Baltimore: Johns Hopkins Univ. Press, 1983), p. 27.

[13]S. K. Heninger, Jr. (Folger Institute, 1984), and Daniel Traister, in " 'To Portrait That Which In This World Is Best': Stella in Perspective," *SP* 81 (1984):427, note the kingship of Astrophel. Any number of critics comment on

the ethical role of Sidney's characters; for different kinds of discussion, see D. H. Craig, in "A Hybrid Growth: Sidney's Theory of Poetry in *An Apology for Poetry*," *ELR* 10 (1980):187, and Louis Adrian Montrose in "Of Gentlemen and Shepherds: The Politics of Elizabethan Pastoral Form," *ELH* 50 (1983):448-49. Joseph F. Loewenstein emphasizes the infantilizing of Astrophel as a schoolboy in "Sidney's Truant Pen," Modern Language Association Convention, 1984.

[14]Heninger, "Sidney and the Drama," quoted in *Sidney Newsletter* 4 (1983): 31.

[15]See Arthur Marotti, " 'Love is not Love': Elizabethan Sonnet Sequences and the Social Order," *ELH* 49 (1982):400-406.

[16]In Jack Wilton's tale-telling are adumbrated two post-Renaissance definitions: the tale-teller as one who practices a deception and also as one who creates a novel.

[17]Agnes M. C. Latham, "Satire on Literary Themes and Modes in Nashe's 'Unfortunate Traveller,' " *ES*, n.s. 1 (1948):88.

[18]John Wenke discusses Jack Wilton's satanic fiction-making abilities and comments on Nashe's use of serpent imagery in "The Moral Aesthetic of Thomas Nashe's *The Unfortunate Traveller*," *Renascence* 34 (1981):26-27.

[19]Lanham, p. 212.

[20]Northrop Frye, *Anatomy of Criticism: Four Essays* (Princeton: Princeton Univ. Press, 1957), pp. 139, 140, 147.

[21]Ferguson, p. 177.

[22]Nicholl, however, sees no satire in the portrait of Surrey (see p. 158). He says, "Surrey was very much the Tudor prototype of Sir Philip Sidney" (p. 158).

[23]Merritt Lawlis, introduction to *The Unfortunate Traveller* by Thomas Nashe, in *Elizabethan Prose Fiction* (New York: Odyssey Press, 1967), p. 435.

[24]Lanham, p. 209.

[25]Kerrigan, p. 268.

[26]Ibid., p. 269.

[27]Ibid., pp. 272, 274.

[28]Stanley E. Fish, *Surprised by Sin: The Reader in "Paradise Lost"* (Berkeley: Univ. of California Press, 1967).

[29]Crewe, p. 68.

[30]According to Latham, "Nashe may fairly be judged as an embryo novelist" (p. 99). Barbara C. Millard says that *The Unfortunate Traveller* "anticipates the later work of the Schaur-Romantiks and consequently much modern fiction," in "Thomas Nashe and the Functional Grotesque in Elizabethan Prose Fiction," *SSF* 15 (1978):48. Lanham says of Nashe, "Perhaps it is because his neurosis is like ours that our novel is becoming so much like his" (p. 216).

[31]My grateful thanks to Bryn Mawr College and the Folger Institute for supporting my studies while I wrote this paper, and to Christopher Kendrick, S. K. Heninger, Jr., and John T. Shawcross for their attentive readings.

SEL 28 (1988)
ISSN 0039-3657

Shakespearean Narrative: *The Rape of Lucrece* Reconsidered

R. RAWDON WILSON

The Rape of Lucrece occupies an uncertain position in Shakespeare's canon. Generally neglected by students of the plays, and seemingly lacking the verbal magic of the sonnets, *Lucrece* most commonly has been relegated to the immeritorious categories of early, apprentice, experimental, passed-beyond, or failed. Perhaps few scholars would employ the last category explicitly, whatever their unspoken judgment, though the Arden editor of the narrative poems, F. T. Prince, chooses it without equivocation.[1] *Lucrece* normally has not been incorporated into analyses of Shakespearean drama and does not often figure in teaching Shakespeare to undergraduates. Nonetheless, there have been several positive efforts to recuperate *Lucrece* into a considered view of Shakespeare's canon as an admired (if overshadowed) preparatory work that either brilliantly encodes aspects of a complex rhetorical tradition or else manifests ghostly affinities with the plays, proleptically suggesting the shape of things to come.

These attempts at recuperation fall into four groups, overlapping and not exclusive, each one of which, canceling the temptations to harsh judgment and neglect, provides a reason for taking *Lucrece* seriously. First, it has been possible to argue that it demands critical judgment in terms of something that it is not (or is only by an aesthetic analogy), a work of visual art. According to this argument, the extended, vividly detailed ekphrasis (lines 1366-1570) of a "piece / Of skilful painting" depicting Troy's final moments provides the fulcrum upon which *Lucrece* turns. The motivation behind the ekphrastic tradition was, as S. Clark Hulse notes, "to surpass the limits of your material and achieve the perfection of the rival art."[2]

R. Rawdon Wilson, Professor of English at the University of Alberta and a member of the Editorial Board of *English Studies in Canada*, has written on Shakespeare, Spenser, Cervantes, and Milton, including several contributions to the forthcoming *Spenser Encyclopedia*. His current interests lie in the relations between Renaissance studies and recent narrative theory.

Although the ekphrasis extends through only slightly over two hundred lines, it can become a basis for valuing the poem as a whole. "Shakespeare's art," one critic observes, "represents the fullest and most complex triumph of the *ekphrasis* in its ambitious rhetorical function."[3] Second, F. T. Prince's austere judgment aside, it has been possible to approach *Lucrece* as, relative to its time and place, a kind of masterpiece: a work that shows its command of literary and rhetorical traditions, its absolute mastery of each convention available to the writing of an epyllion.[4] Third, it is relatively easy to find thematic anticipations of the plays in *Lucrece*. Lucrece's suicide alone links the narrative poem to several plays including *Othello* the hero of which, like Lucrece, elects to die upon a story. Its sombre atmosphere of gloomy nightstalking reminds one of *Macbeth*: a remembrance heightened by Macbeth's precise comparison of murder's personification ("withered murder") moving ghost-like towards his prey to Tarquin's "ravishing strides" (II.i.55). The subject matter of the famous ekphrasis anticipates the Player King's narrative in *Hamlet*. And, as Richard Lanham observes, "the dense cosmic imagery" of the poem may remind one of *Antony and Cleopatra*.[5] The thematic links are numerous and multiform. Fourth, the strongest argument available for the recuperation of *Lucrece* to a worthy canonical position would seem to be that, while *ostensibly* a narrative poem, it must be, in some powerful sense, a drama. It exhibits "close affiliations" with Shakespeare's plays, Harold R. Walley argues, and "its predominant concerns betray the hand of a poet whose preoccupations are basically those of a dramatist."[6] Viewed from that conflationary angle, *Lucrece* may easily be seen as "an examination of what constitutes tragedy and an explanation of how it operates. It is a rationale for tragedy . . . which underlies the whole of Shakespearean tragedy."[7]

Other kinds of argument are possible, including the biographical-psychological-cultural reduction that sees (or asserts) Shakespeare's mind-personality-*zeitgeist* playing through, and dominating, all of his work into a unitary object of investigation, but the four indicated above represent lines of argument that have been common during the past twenty years. The various efforts to recuperate *Lucrece* either isolate aspects of the narrative (rhetorical conventions, the formal ekphrasis) and claim Shakespeare's mastery of those aspects as a basis for revaluing the poem or they assimilate it to something else (a work of visual art, a drama) and make the plea that it be judged, henceforth, on these freshly revealed and supplementary terms. This essay does not dissociate itself from this common scholarly ambition. *Lucrece* deserves recuperation since, if for no other reason, it will be more interesting for all students of Shakespeare if this can be done. *Lucrece* is, one must feel certain, inadequately captured in such judgments as F. T. Prince's mordant dismissal. If recuperation is possible, then it will, evidently, follow generally either the procedure of singling out some aspect of the poem to constitute the basis for a fresh analysis or that of assimilating the poem to the plays themselves or to some sub-classification of them (the tragedies, say, or the Roman plays). This essay will differ from the ordinary directions of scholarly ambition only in its argument that the most sufficient method, and the most exciting, by which to recuperate *Lucrece* is narrative analysis. *Lucrece* is a compendium (an encyclopedia, or perhaps a seminary) of the conventions that constitute the embedded narratives, many and frequent, of the plays.

Repeatedly in the plays, characters tell stories. They become, in the midst of the dramatic action, narrators who, while the action is suspended or abandoned, narrate stories that project distinct, extra-dramatic at the very least, places and time-schemes. These narratives, embedded within the dramatic action, are told for many reasons and in many modes. The narrative voices are individual and highly differentiated. Hence an obvious, though not traditional, way of viewing the plays is to see them as conceptual spaces in which stories are told. Shakespeare's plays, to borrow a phrase from Tzvetan Todorov, create a realm of narrative-men.[8] These embedded narratives all possess dramatic functions, but these functions are not what make them narratives.[9] The many stories, told in such varying and distinct manners, that interweave Shakespeare's plays do more than serve the dramatic action and cannot be given a full account merely with respect to their dramatic functions. In order to understand their narrative status, one must examine their constitutive conventions. There must be something about them, as stories being told, that can be grasped as narrative *qua* narrative. No matter in what dramatic context they appear nor what dramatic functions they possess, these conventions will always be narrative: subject to narrative analysis and explicable in the terms of narrative traditions.[10]

The frequent recurrence of narrative within Shakespeare's plays should not be surprising if one considers the kind of education that writers in the Renaissance received: that education was essentially narrative, whether historical or fictional (and the distinction between the two kinds, as readers of *Don Quixote* will recognize, was not always as certain as it has seemed to subsequent periods), into the privileged literary mode.[11] Furthermore, it would be apparent even to a confirmed believer in the dramatic nature of Shakespeare's plays (pure drama, written by a man of the theater for the theater, a practical playwright whose plays are marvelously actable, and so forth) that the sources of these plays are mostly narrative. It has been argued that narrative pattern, as well as (the more obvious) themes, characters, and episodes, carry over from the sources to provide a "deep structure" for the action.[12] In any case, it would seem that whatever dramatic transformations Shakespeare worked upon his sources (dross into gold, mere flesh into things rich and strange), much of them remain including determinable aspects of their narrative nature. The argument of this paper, however, is specifically that Shakespeare wrote many narratives for his characters to tell, embedded them within the dramatic action, and in so doing created an important dimension for his plays. It would not seem to be the demands of plays, as plays, nor any idea of drama, theater, or production, that informs Shakespeare's embedded narratives, but only a comprehensive narrative understanding. Shakespeare's narratives in the plays are remarkable, but they are not so because of a non-narrative pressure from the direction of drama. Granted the Renaissance education in narrative, and assuming that someone as immensely literary as Shakespeare would have known the dominant achievements of his time, then it does not seem strange that Shakespeare should have written the embedded narratives out of a knowledge of how narratives are told, what they are good for, the purposes they serve (many and complex), and how they are heard. How well Shakespeare did understand narrative conventions may be seen in the construction of *Lucrece.* It is a superbly compelling work and its intricate narrativity foreshadows the manner in which the narratives of the plays are written.

In *Lucrece,* Shakespeare takes an old story and, in retelling it, greatly varies, intensifies, and expands it. The story of Lucrece was already, when Shakespeare took it up, a "well-handled piece of rhetorical baggage."[13] It had been told by Ovid in the *Fasti,* by Chaucer in *The Legende of Good Women,* and by Painter in the *Pallace of Pleasure,* to name only three.[14] The story requires 131 lines for Ovid to tell, 205 for Chaucer, and about three pages in Painter's prose version. Shakespeare elaborates the story in 1,855 lines. The pre-Shakespearean versions are essentially terse narratives of events (which are significant in themselves because they precipitated the overthrow of the Tarquins, ended the institution of kingship in Rome, and made possible the growth of consular government within the Republic) with some commentary, neither univocal nor always unmuddled, with regard to the paradoxical nature of Lucrece's suicide. Shakespeare extends the possibilities of the traditional story using most, if not precisely all, of the elaborative strategies made available by the sixteenth-century rhetorical topocosm. The diversity and range of his elaboration is impressive. *Lucrece* provides a lesson in the complex tactics by which rhetoric enables a writer both to intensify, and to defer, the teleo-graphic simplicities of old stories. Most importantly, two significant changes in Shakespeare's treatment of his inherited materials stand out.

First, Shakespeare transforms the inherited story by the means of a sustained elaboration, a virtuoso display of the rhetorical principle of *copia*. The primary vehicle of this transformation is the interior monologue, a familiar convention of the complaint, but the scope and variety of the reworking are manifest in the narrative's every part. The result of Shakespeare's transformation of the inherited story is (what it had never been before) a psychological narrative with a strong emphasis upon characterization. Second, he makes the narrative a comment upon the shortcomings, or the missed opportunities, of the previous versions and, as such, a comment upon narrative itself. There is, thus, in *Lucrece* a strong element of self-conscious reflexivity (which should not surprise any reader of Shakespeare who has thought about what happens in such plays as *Hamlet, A Midsummer Night's Dream*, or *The Tempest*). Though interior monologue occupies the rhetorical foreground, the transformation of the traditional story into a psychological narrative depends largely upon Shakespeare's command of the conventions of characterization available to sixteenth-century writers of narrative.

The conventions of characterization that dominate *Lucrece* are identical to those that function within the embedded narratives of the plays. Shakespeare's narratives typically build up a sense of place and time that is different from that of the dramatic action itself and then turn inwards towards a character's perception of events. In the plays, the inward movement often turns upon a character who does not exist outside of the embedded narrative; a focalizing character who has, that is, no role in the dramatic action itself and who appears nowhere else in the play. In *Lucrece,* the poem's narrative voice focalizes upon Lucrece's experience, but also upon that of Tarquin whose mind is split by dilemmatic conflict as he prepares to rape Lucrece. He is the kingly rapist who, it has been observed, rapes himself.[15] Moreover, the range of focalization in *Lucrece* also includes a number of characters embedded within Lucrece's own narrative which she tells herself about the fall of Troy and the responses to Lucrece's narrative version of her own story by her narratees, Collatine, Lucretius, and Brutus. The systematic emphasis upon the potential of characterization as a means to focalize a narrative (by investing it with an inside, an expressible experience) marks Shakespeare's narrative technique throughout his canon.

Two interactive constitutive narrative conventions underlie Shakespeare's creation of narrative. Shakespeare's narratives are normally both augmentative and culminative: they pile up details and they move towards a climactic moment.[16] First, all the embedded narratives develop an outward expansiveness (which goes beyond the simple need for exposition, either as background or as allusion) to establish a scene, often fairly complete, which is somewhere else, somewhere other than the scene of the dramatic action within which the narrative is being told. Second, the narratives culminate in an inward turn, a movement within the narrative to focalize upon a character that occurs somewhere else. Shakespeare's narratives are set elsewhere (though not always in the past) and are strongly focalized upon an absent character's experience. Hence the distinction which Genette has made clear in the analysis of modern narrative between voice and focalization applies to Shakespeare's command of narrative.[17] The narrator and the internal, or intradiegetic, characterization (which provides the narrative's focalization: the basis for its distinct grasp of incident, experience, and consciousness) are kept distinct. It is upon the focalized experience of a character, created by the character who narrates, that the embedded narratives turn. In *A Midsummer Night's Dream* (II.i.122-37), the tale of the changeling boy's mother is told in Titania's voice (for Oberon's ears), but it is focalized upon the experience of the boy's mother. The focalization is wholly upon the dead votaress. (It would be a much less precise account to say that in *MND* the tale of the changeling boy's mother is told from Titania's point-of-view.)

The outward expansiveness is augmentative, or dilatory, in nature: details build a scene different from the one in which the narrator speaks, and it is a scene often rich in complex visual imagery, but it is non-dramatic. Thus the embedded narratives seem to make the dramatic action more substantial. They vary it, deepen it (lending substance to the "four or five most vile and ragged foils"), and bring to bear the resources of the mind's-eye. Paradoxically, the embedded narratives also call attention to the nature of the drama itself. The action of the play becomes more real, being deepened, and less real, being framed. This is the point explicitly made by the Chorus in *Henry V*. As a narrator, the Chorus deepens the action of the play (calling to mind, for instance, the "vasty fields of France"), makes it more real through the potential of the imagination to visualize, yet makes it less real by framing it within narrative conventions. The other embedded narratives work similarly: for example, Horatio's second narrative (I.i.113-25) that takes his narratees (Marcellus and Bernardo) back to the "most high and palmy state of Rome," or Hotspur's second narrative *(1 Henry IV*, I.iii.95-111) that swings abruptly from the courtly confines of power to the Severn and the wild energies of battle.

The inward turn of Shakespearean narrative brings into the foreground a character (an essentially non-dramatic characterization) and focalizes upon its experience. The narrative creates an expanded scene and then interprets it through the perception of a character within that scene. Augmentation and culmination, outward expansiveness and inward turn, interact. The focalization of an embedded narrative can be quite minimal (a line or two, a single state of feeling, a trait or two at most), but it can be extremely forceful, vivid, and even empathetic as it catches the internal character in a moment of strong reaction. This culminative moment brings into the foreground the perceptions and feelings of a character within, and in response to, the expanded scene of action that the narrative has created. (There is a haunting, Borgesian quality of reflexivity in this narrative process: a character develops a characterization, a narrative-man makes a man.) Much as the expanded scene of the embedded narrative seems momentarily to frame (from within) the dramatic action, the internal characterization seems, however briefly, to frame the scene.

Hotspur's two narratives in the third scene of *1 Henry IV* are illustrative. The first narrative establishes the scene at Holmedon immediately after the battle and it turns upon the "popingay" courtier's experience of the battle which is a distant, verbalized experience. It is essentially a literary experience, unlike Hotspur's own, and unlike that which any of his narratees (Blunt, Worcester, Northumberland, and King Henry) might have had. The courtier talks, Hotspur sneers, so "like a waiting gentlewoman." In his second narrative, the scene expands outwards to the personal combat between Mortimer and Glendower, but it focalizes upon the terror felt by the observer who runs fearfully from the combat to hide his curly head in the "hollow bank" of the Severn. The affrighted observer, whose experience focalizes the scene, is actually the Severn personified. A forcefully characterized personification must seem, to anyone who has read the sonnets at least, a distinctively Shakespearean technique. (The threats that Beauty and Summer's Breath painfully confront in sonnet 65 come to mind.) In *Coriolanus*, when Menenius tells the story of the rebellion in the body, his narrative focalizes the Belly's experience of the body as a whole. Horatio's second narrative turns upon the experience of the "moist star" (the moon) who is "sick almost to doomsday with eclipse" in anticipation of Caesar's assassination. In *Antony and Cleopatra,* Cleopatra tells Dolabella the story of Antony's exercise of his heroic virtues and Antony becomes, within the expanded scene of her narrative, a personification, an island-striding Titan past "the size of dreaming" (V.ii.77-92) whose more-than-human bounty contrasts to, and shames, Caesar's own landlord's experience of the world.

The example of Titania's narrative suffices to clarify the point. Titania narrates the story of the changeling boy's mother in order to explain to Oberon why she sets upon the boy a value exceeding that of Oberon's fairy kingdom itself (I.i.122-37). Her narrative expands outwards to India ("The spiced Indian air") and the commerce of merchant ships upon the Indian Ocean, but then swiftly turns inwards to the characterization of the boy's mother, Titania's votaress. The boy's mother perceives the merchant ships in the spirit of comedy, though also with the eyes of metaphor. She is moved to laughter by the clumsy motions of the ships and the swollen sails ("big-bellied with the wanton wind") and, herself pregnant, responds to the ships with comic imitation. Her naturally awkward gait allows her to become a merchant ship made pregnant by the wind. It is the dead woman's metaphorical experience of the expanded Indian scene, not Titania's own, that focalizes the narrative.

In *Lucrece*, the narrative voice focalizes upon the experience of both Lucrece and Tarquin. It does this in dissimilar ways by employing distinct literary traditions for character development. Furthermore, in the two narratives that Lucrece tells there are multiple inward turns that involve correlative reactions in the immediate narratees. In Lucrece's first narrative, when she is her own narratee, her reaction to the events of Troy's destruction corresponds to Hecuba's own which has been chosen, in the first place, to symbolize, or externalize, her own grief at her loss of chastity. The inward turn towards a strong focalization upon a character internal to the narrative is many-leveled and intricate. As a procedure in characterization, it strongly anticipates the embedded narratives within the plays.

As Tarquin approaches Lucrece's bed, his mind is divided between two opposed values: the desire to satisfy his sexual appetite upon the lovely and virtuous woman (whose virtue is part of her sexual appeal) and the desire to keep his reputation as a soldier untarnished, to pass it on to his children as something that they will cherish. The narrative voice of the poem observes, "Here pale with fear he doth premeditate / The dangers of his loathsome enterprise" (lines 183-84). A few lines further on, Tarquin himself reflects, "O what excuse can my invention make / When thou shalt charge me with so black a deed?" (lines 225-26). And the narrative voice comments, "Thus graceless holds he disputation / 'Tween frozen conscience and hot burning will, / And with good thoughts makes dispensation, / Urging the worser sense for vantage still" (lines 246-49). This interior discourse, in which Tarquin feels himself split between the opposed values of sexual satisfaction and honor, is carried on in the form of a monologue for several hundred lines. The method of deepening characterization through a psychomachia, or dilemmatic meditation expressed in an interior monologue, is a powerful Ovidian technique for narrative development: probably the most useful, as well as the most widely used, convention of characterization available to a Renaissance writer.[18] This method splits a character's awareness between values and dramatizes the conflict in a rhetorically structured interior monologue during the course of which, typically, a rationalization on one side ("Urging the worser sense for vantage still") weighs down the claims of rationality on the other. Lanham argues that Tarquin's motive, essentially symbolic, is "at the same time narcissistic and self-dividing, suicidal" such that his "self" might be said to "split apart."[19] This shifts the problem to the level of interpretive exercise in which one may inquire what the split, or its two halves, *means,* but the mere presence of a split, some structure of self-division, seems evident. (If, as Brian Vickers argues, epideictic rhetoric provides the models, as well as the purposes, of Renaissance characterization, it is also the case that Ovidian split awareness makes available the distinctive formal strategy.)[20]

The narrative models for split awareness may be discerned in several characterizations in *The Metamorphoses,* such as that of Myrrha, in which a radical division between opposed values (love of her father, in Myrrha's case, against love of decorum) structures the consciousness of the character and prompts the distinctive monologue. In medieval and Renaissance literature, examples are commonplace. From Chrétien de Troyes (at least) split awareness constitutes the major narrative convention for characterization. It is important to observe that split awareness, frequently exemplified in the plays, is a narrative convention before it is a dramatic one. The comparison between Tarquin and Othello (two warriors, both men of honor and also criminals) has appealed to a number of scholars, but other examples are plentiful: Macbeth, split between ambition and honor, or Claudius, his consciousness split between what he would pray for and what he cannot relinquish, conspicuously stand out.

Shakespeare deepens Lucrece's characterization by the use of interior monologue and rhetorical device. After having been raped, Lucrece reflects upon the conditions of her downfall: Night, Opportunity, and Time. These are traditional *topoi* for rhetorical display, not only within the form of the complaint, and evident ways for a writer to satisfy the demands made by the principle of *copia* upon his virtuosity, but they are also genuine vehicles for the manifestation of subjectivity. This radical two-sidedness in the Ovidian interior monologue points towards what must be seen as a meta-rule of characterization: whether in a medieval romance or a modern novel, any manifestation of subjectivity in the form of a monologue, no matter how abstract the topic, deepens characterization. The dilemmatic force of split awareness is less apparent than in the case of Tarquin, but it is forceful, compellingly so, as Lucrece brings herself, through her meditations, to the conviction that suicide is the only recourse left to her if she is to preserve her honor.

In making an argument that draws a parallel between the interior monologues of the two characters, Jerome A. Kramaer and Judith Kaminsky observe that, in *Lucrece,* "Special emphasis is given to two ideas, fragmentation of the self and the perception and use of externals, both objects and persons."[21] The phrase "fragmentation of the self" may overstate what is essentially a double split only (incorporating into the model of characterization a number of Jungian notions, suggestive but anachronistic), but it vigorously makes the basic point that neither Tarquin nor Lucrece, nor indeed any complex Renaissance character, is psychologically unitary. The "perception of externals" must include concepts, such as night or time, as well as physical objects. It seems clearly to fall within the Ovidian convention of employing a speciously convincing rationalization on one side of the split awareness: an object (fact, activity, or concept) can support such a rationalization, as Ovid's Myrrha appeals to the behavior of animals to justify her lust for her father. In *Lucrece* the convention of split awareness, both as division of the character's mind and as rationalization calling upon an external object, is most clearly seen in Lucrece's empathetic scrutiny of the "piece / Of skilful painting" (1366-67) that depicts the sorrows of Troy. Not only does the ekphrasis extend Lucrece's characterization, as an external object which she perceives and correlates to her own state of mind, but it also extends the range of characterization itself since it introduces, as characters created within the ekphrasis, Hecuba and Sinon, who not only externalize the relationship between Lucrece and Tarquin but also, as characters, experience the events of *their* narrative. The ekphrasis actualizes a complex narrative juncture in *Lucrece* in which a number of discrete conventions are brought into play.

The second significant change that Shakespeare works upon the old story lies in the playfulness with which he treats it. *Lucrece* is, of course, an immensely serious tale written in rhyme royal, but, like any story, it is open to the possibilities of narrative play. To call Shakespeare's narrative procedures "playful," whether in *Lucrece* or in the plays themselves, is only to make a formal point concerning the evident level of authorial self-consciousness. Shakespeare's narratives reflect an understanding of narrative conventions; an understanding, that is, of their conditions, their scope and their inherent literariness. It has become commonplace, in contemporary literary theory, to call such an explicit emphasis upon the way in which a story is being told "metafictional," "self-representational," or "narcissistic": all designations of textual playfulness.[22] Shakespeare's narrative playfulness expresses itself through two conventions (or meta-conventions): recursiveness and reflexivity.

Recursiveness literally indicates a rerunning. A narrative rerunning exists when the *story* is picked up additional times and retold, in modified versions, in order to create both an incremental effect, as the story becomes more familiar through restatement, and an aesthetic effect, as the narrator's command of the story-materials becomes increasingly apparent. For example, the story that is told in *Romeo and Juliet* occurs in three versions with two untold versions indicated in the final scene. First, there is a prologue (a narrative sonnet), then there is the action of the play itself, then there is the summary of the action that Friar Lawrence narrates, there is also the letter which Lawrence has written and which Prince Escalus reads (V.iii.285), and finally there is the prediction that the story will never be forgotten. It will be retold again and again in the extra-textual future. The recursive treatment of the story in *Romeo and Juliet* corresponds to the four versions of the Ghost's story in *Hamlet*'s retellings and, quite strikingly, to the narrative strategies of *Lucrece* itself. It seems the case that recursiveness, normally more obliquely constituted, plays a significant role in Shakespeare's treatment of *story*.[23] The purposes of recursiveness in Shakespearean narrative are complex, but it must seem evident that they are not dramatic: calling attention to versions of the story creates incremental and aesthetic effects which have nothing, as such, to do with the development of the dramatic action and which, on the contrary, necessarily display Shakespeare's command of the story-materials and his narrative craftiness.

The second meta-convention, reflexivity, seems even more apparent in Shakespeare's writing. Reflexivity has both a dramatic and a narrative expression. In either case, the definition is the same: reflexivity is the semiotic means (gesture, diacritical mark, verbal formula, meta-commentary) by which attention is called to the nature of an act. The act itself becomes its own subject and purpose. To paint a picture of oneself painting a picture or even more forcefully, as Velázquez does in *Las Meninas,* to paint oneself painting the very picture in which one is painting, or to paint a pipe, as Magritte does, and then to label it with the phrase, "This is not a pipe," are self-consciously reflexive acts. To write a sonnet that calls attention to itself as a sonnet, as both Shakespeare and Sidney do, or to write a play that self-consciously asserts its existence as a play, as Shakespeare does in *Hamlet, A Midsummer Night's Dream,* and elsewhere, are powerfully reflexive acts. Narrative reflexivity is that dimension of narrative that acknowledges itself as narrative.[24] A reflexive narrative act, then, comments upon its own craft, the conventions of narrative, the techniques that are being employed, or even upon its own limitations. The Chorus in *Henry V* calls attention to the inadequacies of drama and, in so doing, to the greater capacity of narrative to fill in background, set scenes, supply detail, and to engage the imagination. Richard II's allusions to the *de casibus* tradition (the sad stories of the death of kings) which is also the form of his own story, and his final soliloquy in which he transforms his own existence into fiction, specifically into a *de casibus* narrative (V.v.1-66), are all essentially reflexive. Reflexivity occurs frequently and strikingly in Shakespeare's plays. Considered solely in its narrative dimension, Shakespeare's use of this meta-convention suggests his profound awareness of the many ways in which a story may be told (its potential for indefinite transcription) and the ways in which it may be deformed (compressed, modified, refocused, shared out between distinct narrators) for narrative effect.

Lucrece begins with a prose summary of the story, proceeds to a telling (which is, of course, a retelling), then gives the central character an occasion to tell the story over again to an attentive audience. Finally, the narrative concludes with the determination to "publish" Tarquin's offense in Rome: to tell the story, in an indefinite series of retellings, yet again. The down-razing consequences of the ultimate, but unnarrated, telling are suggested in the final two lines of *Lucrece*: "The Romans plausibly did give consent / To Tarquin's everlasting banishment" ("plausibly" clearly indicates "with applause, i. e., with a general acclamation").[25] Furthermore, *Lucrece* contains several suggestions that the story might have been told, and might still be told, in other ways by other narrators. *Lucrece,* as Heather Dubrow observes, is "packed" with allusions to language and to "various types of storytelling." Since Lucrece explicitly fears that she may become a character in ballads and nursery tales, the reader is invited, Dubrow argues, "to compare history-writing with other forms of story-telling."[26]

A number of points can be made concerning this recursiveness. First, the actual narrative tells a different version of the story than does the prose summary. The "Argument" is, as T. W. Baldwin demonstrates, close to the *Fasti* and to Livy.[27] Prince comments that the "result is a passage of English prose modelled on Latin, and completely different from any of Shakespeare's dramatic prose."[28] Second, the main narrative is expanded, as this paper has attempted to show, by inward turns towards characterization on multiple levels.

Third, there are actually two highly divergent versions of the story available in the narrative as Shakespeare tells it: the narrative voice contains, not merely its own version of the incidents, but also what Lucrece herself can tell *and* what Tarquin could tell. In part, Tarquin manages to overpower Lucrece's resistance by threatening her with a possible narrative. He could make it known, he tells her, that she had cooperated:

> So thy surviving husband shall remain
> The scornful mark of every open eye;
> Thy kinsmen hang their heads at this disdain,
> Thy issue blurr'd with nameless bastardy.
> And thou, the author of their obloquy,
>   Shalt have thy trespass cited up in rhymes
>   And sung by children in succeeding times.
>
> (519-25)

And Lucrece reflects, after having been raped, that "The nurse to still her child will tell my story" (813). Clearly, the potential to narrate, the fear of which occupies her mind, can be nearly as compelling as an actual narrative. In the plays, characters also dread the power of a hostile narrative: Cleopatra fears the stories that could be told, and how they might be told, for it is not merely the "quick comedians" in

Rome whom she dreads, but the "scald rhymers" as well (*AC,* V.ii.215-16); Hamlet fears the "wounded name" that he will leave behind him, "Things standing thus unknown" in the absence of a positive narrative (*Hamlet,* V.ii.355-56).

Fourth, there are narrative hints that the story could be told in still other ways and, it might be, in means other than words. Thus Lucrece, in the course of her apostrophe to Night, pleads that she should not become the

> object to the tell-tale day:
> The light will show character'd in my brow
> The story of sweet chastity's decay,
> The impious breach of holy wedlock vow;
> Yea, the illiterate that know not how
> To cipher what is writ in learned books,
> Will quote my loathsome trespass in my looks.
>
> (806-12)

A negative version of her story might be read in her face with such clarity that even unlettered people, for whom books are uninterpretable, would understand it. Similarly, in the account of the ekphrasis, Lucrece is said not merely to lend words to the characters within the painting but to "borrow" their looks (1498). In either case, the appearance of her face tells a version of a story (hers and that of Troy) and, however incomplete one must assume this to be, the point remains certain that other versions of any story are possible and words (even if they are the most forceful, always a "miracle" with the might to outlast all other monuments) are not the only medium of semiotic exchange. The face, too, is a compendium, a blazon, of signs that signify.[29] The ekphrasis itself underscores this point: the painting "tells" a story, one that Lucrece can renarrativize, and which might again be told in her merely physical "looks."

Fifth, Lucrece's own version of the story has an overwhelming effect upon her narratees, which implies how the story might be heard if only it could be heard with fresh ears: "stone-still, astonish'd" (1730) Collatine, Lucretius, and Brutus attend the closure of her narrative which ends with her shouting Tarquin's name and killing herself in the same instant. As does Othello, Lucrece dies upon a narrative: the end of life marks narrative closure.

The internal variations upon the inherited story indicate that Shakespeare was fully aware of how many ways it, like any other story, could be told. *Lucrece* makes evident that previous versions have underplayed the story's narrative potential. Shakespeare demonstrates his narrative mastery throughout *Lucrece*. Since it calls attention both to narrative potential and to variation, the story-recursiveness of the narrative contributes to this self-consciousness, but so do a large number of specific rhetorical devices. Indeed, the rhetorical elaboration, the very *copia* of the narrative, calls attention to its position as a self-conscious retelling of an inherited story: its implicit claim to be regarded as a masterpiece. Tarquin thinks within a divided consciousness, but he also thinks, as Lanham points out, in "heraldic pageants." A network of images that describe "treasons, leagues, and maps accompanies him to Lucrece's chamber and what he sees when he arrives is, again, not Lucrece but a miasma of feudal value-symbols, worlds unconquered, himself a foul usurper, Lucrece first a rich statue and then, and in overpowering detail, a castle which he, as diabolic hero, must storm, possess, sack."[30] The language makes sense, Lanham adds, only if rhetoric, and in particular feudal rhetoric, is the actual subject of the poem. It is certainly one subject: rhetoric constitutes the reflexive level of discourse that brings into focus the act of narration (with all, in terms of knowledge, consciousness, intention, command, and ambition, that such acts entail) and states, forcefully though obliquely, the narrative's claim to masterfulness.

The reflexive power of Shakespeare's rhetorical command seems evident throughout *Lucrece*. The immense distance, created by many specific rhetorical conventions, that opens between the narrative (in this retelling) and the story self-consciously acknowledges the master that has made it possible. Whatever the story seems to have been about, that which has traditionally filled the foreground in other narrative versions (malign intent, violence, rape, suicide, revolution), *Lucrece* concerns essentially itself: its own language, its rhetorical command, its comment upon historiography, its act of narration, and the distance between itself and the ground of its potential in the mere story. This narrative narcissism manifests itself everywhere.[31]

Consider the opening stanza. *Lucrece* begins in contrast to the "Argument" and to all previous versions by suppressing the background.[32] Sextus Tarquinius enters abruptly into the narrative unfolding without any account having been given of the inspiration he has taken from Collatinus's own unwise account of his wife's beauty and virtue. Tarquin hastens to Collatium from Ardea "all in post" with a precise intention. He is "lust-breathed" and bears the "lightless fire, / Which in pale embers hid, lurks to aspire" (4-5). Prince notes that the line is "good in itself" but shows "how the stanza encourages prolixity."[33] Prolixity (or *copia*) might rather seem to be the point. If the "lightless fire" ("smouldering, dark, hidden" as Prince glosses it) suggests Tarquin's lust, then the "pale embers" seem to imply his hidden genitalia. The likelihood of this equation draws support from commonsense: given the present tense, where else might lust smoldering hide as it awaits (it "lurks") the chance to "aspire"? The aspiration of lust must suggest, to the extent that the image carries any physical implication, the rising of tumescence. The galactic distance that Shakespeare's rhetorical mastery opens up, even in the initial stanza, between story and narrative retelling, between the incidents and the manner in which they are being narrativized, self-consciously calls attention to that mastery. Reflexivity pervades the narrative. The rape itself, the central violent incident of the story, occurs within ellipsis (860-66). That absence poses, with cool confidence, the narrative transaction both as game and as challenge.

The most striking instance of reflexivity enters into the narrative when Lucrece, concluding her long interior monologue (focused upon the three rhetorical *topoi*), looks around for something "external" that could be made to parallel her sense of anguish, loss, and downfall. In the painting in which the fall of Troy is depicted, Lucrece discovers a correlative to her own tragedy. Thus the ekphrasis, as was argued above, extends the convention of an inward turn towards internal characterization (by introducing Hecuba and Sinon) and intensifies Lucrece's own characterization. Furthermore, it accomplishes something peculiarly narrative in function. Like the embedded narratives of the plays, the ekphrasis invokes a story different from that which may be inferred from the narrative in which the ekphrasis itself occurs. An embedded narrative is always intrusive and normally heterodiegetic, or external to the main narrative or dramatic line. It shifts the narratees and (indirectly) the audience or readers to another place and time: a narrative elsewhere and elsewhen. An embedded narrative, always disruptive, creates a profoundly anachronic effect.

In the plays, this narrative anachronism interrupts the chronological on-goingness of the dramatic action (which, in Shakespeare, is uni-directional, end-pointed, and teleo-graphic) and supplies the only perturbation of temporal order that Shakespeare permits. In *Hamlet*, for example, the Player King's narration of Aeneas's tale to Dido (II.ii) plunges Hamlet, the Player King himself, and the audience into the dark, archaic world of classical legend, the deadly firestorms of Troy's final moments. The evident parallels on the level of theme and characterization (Pyrrhus, like Hamlet, Laertes, and Fortinbras, is a son avenging his father) provide yet another mirror to Hamlet's own dilemma and widen the sphere of the revenge motif, but the story is discontinuous with, even alien to, the world of *Hamlet.* It is exactly as if the narratees were thrust headlong into another world, following another time-scheme, and asked to make of it what they might. Indeed, as Martínez-Bonati observes, the story constitutes the world of a narrative.[34] It maps, at least, the minimal possibility for worldhood within a narrative. Thus the embedded narratives perturb the dramatic actions that contain them by the intrusion of a different story, an alien deictic field,[35] and, considered macrosemantically, a further fictional world.[36] Similarly, the ekphrasis in *Lucrece* intrudes upon the Roman world of the narrative, breaks open Lucrece's own story, and thrusts Lucrece (her own narratee) as well as the reader into a different time and space, elsewhen and elsewhere. Furthermore, since the creation of narrative anachrony is a profoundly reflexive act, one cannot experience anachrony without attempting to measure the gap that has opened between story and narrative.

All stories can be told in different ways, for a variety of diverse effects, and all stories can be made to reflect one another or even to contain one another. One narrative recalls another (whether in the play of allusiveness or along the implacable fields of intertextuality), bears upon another, can even become another, as the story of Troy becomes, in being contained by, the story of Lucrece or of Hamlet. Perhaps it is this narrative complexity, in part at least, that leads Ian Donaldson to remark that *Lucrece* "raises more questions than it manages to answer."[37] One of the questions that *Lucrece* raises concerns the function of narrative in Shakespeare's plays and the relation of those plays to the intricate narrative poem with which, in 1594, he made his public claim to literary mastery. The narrative infoldings of *Lucrece* publish the mark of all Shakespearean storytelling. Narratives catch, hold, illude, and frequently delude their narratees. These transactions, everywhere apparent in *Lucrece,* point forward to the important, if ordinarily overlooked, role of narrative in the plays: its distinctive conventions, its pervasiveness, its forcefulness, and its playfulness.

NOTES

[1]William Shakespeare, *The Poems*, ed. F. T. Prince (London: Methuen, 1960), pp. xxxiii-iv. For a recent overview of the critical positions that have been taken towards *Lucrece*, see Katharine Eisaman Maus, "Taking Tropes Seriously: Language and Violence in Shakespeare's *Rape of Lucrece*," *SQ* 37, 1 (Spring, 1986): 66-82. In this paper, all references to *The Rape of Lucrece* will be to F. T. Prince's edition; references to *Hamlet* will be to the Arden edition, edited by Harold Jenkins (London and New York: Methuen, 1982); references to other plays will be to *The Complete Works of Shakespeare*, ed. Hardin Craig (Chicago: Scott, Foresman, 1961). Line references will be given parenthetically.

[2]S. Clark Hulse, "A Piece of Skilful Painting' in Shakespeare's 'Lucrece'," *ShS* 31 (1978): 18.

[3]David Ronsand, " 'Troyes Painted Woes': Shakespeare and The Pictorial Imagination," *HUSL* 8 (1980): 81. Maus's discussion of the visual element in *Lucrece* is particularly interesting; see "Taking Tropes Seriously," pp. 79-82.

[4]Richard A. Lanham, *The Motives of Eloquence: Literary Rhetoric in The Renaissance* (New Haven: Yale Univ. Press, 1976), pp. 82-110. The intricate, self-conscious rhetoricity of *Lucrece* has become, since Lanham's study at least, commonly acknowledged. It would be difficult to overestimate Shakespeare's literary self-consciousness. In a brilliant essay on Renaissance historiography as this appears in *Lucrece,* Heather Dubrow argues for Shakespeare's self-conscious exploration of "the problem of reading and writing history." See "The Rape of Clio: Attitudes to History in Shakespeare's *Lucrece*," *ELR* 16, 3 (Autumn 1986): 425-41. This essay appears, in revised form, in Dubrow's *Captive Victors: Shakespeare's Narrative Poems and Sonnets* (Ithaca: Cornell Univ. Press, 1987).

[5]Richard A. Lanham, "The Politics of *Lucrece*," *HUSL* 8 (1980): 66.

[6]Harold R. Walley, "*The Rape of Lucrece* and Shakespearean Tragedy," *PMLA* 76, 1 (1961): 480.

[7]Walley, p. 487.

[8]Tzvetan Todorov, *The Poetics of Prose*, trans. Richard Howard (Ithaca: Cornell Univ. Press, 1977), p. 70.

[9]Most of the dramatic functions of narrative are self-evident. However, the constitutive conventions of the embedded narratives are distinct from their dramatic functions. Even if they function superbly in the plays (and with the most overwhelming effects), they are, nonetheless, narratives and open to narrative analysis. Considered only in terms of their dramatic functions, the embedded narratives serve to characterize (the Nurse's plain style, Hotspur's *altilogua*, Hamlet's biting paronomasia, and so forth), to provide needed exposition and to summarize action. No doubt, there are other dramatic functions but, however many, they may be clearly distinguished from the conventions that ground their narrativity.

[10]For a detailed examination of narrative in *Hamlet*, see R. Wilson, "Narratives, Narrators and Narratees in *Hamlet*," *HSt* 6, 1 and 2 (Summer / Winter 1984): 30-40.

[11]Studies of Renaissance education indicate the importance given to rhetoric. The emphasis upon narrative would seem to have been a consequence of the great models of the past having been themselves narratives. Sister Miriam Joseph observes that the "boys would memorize Ovid's *Metamorphoses* at the rate of twelve lines a week, five hundred lines a year, for two or more years" (*Shakespeare's Use of the Arts of Language* [New York: Columbia Univ. Press,

1947], p. 10). The theoretical disputes of the sixteenth-century centered around narrative, in particular the narrative poetry of Ariosto and Tasso. Sidney, in the *Defence*, clearly has narrative in mind, and Spenser, in the "Letter" to Raleigh, leaves no doubt that he perceives that his narrative task is to meet the standards of, and to make his claims within, a context (created by "all the antique poets historical") of previous narrative. Neither his stanza nor his metrics as such, judging from the "Letter," seem to have caused Spenser anxiety.

[12]See Joan Rees, "*Hamlet*: A Note on Structure," *HSt* 3, 2 (Winter 1981): 112-16. In her *Shakespeare and The Story*: *Aspects of Creation* (London: Athlone Press, 1978), Rees studies the narrative forms of the dramatic action; that is, how structural aspects of the narrative sources survive their dramatic transformations. In *Renaissance From More to Shakespeare* (Chicago: Univ. of Chicago Press, 1980), Stephen Greenblatt has a great deal to say concerning the Renaissance understanding of narrative purposes, the intellectual conditions that make narrative possible, and Shakespeare's grasp of narrative, particularly in *Othello,* as a powerful tool for psychological and conceptual construction (and reconstruction). However, the embedded narratives, *qua* narrative, have not been investigated. For a partial exception, see Chand Sunil, " 'A Tale Told': Shakespeare's Exploration of The Narrative Mode in *Venus and Adonis, Othello* and The Falstaff Plays," unpublished dissertation (Kent State Univ. 1982).

[13]Lanham, "Politics," p. 67.

[14]The multiple versions of the *story,* in both narrative and pictorial crystallizations, have been analyzed in Ian Donaldson's *The Rapes of Lucretia*: *A Myth and its Transformations* (Oxford: Clarendon Press, 1982). See also, D. C. Allen, "Some Observations on *The Rape of Lucrece,*" *ShS* 15 (1962): 89-98. Maus notes brilliantly that the "pell-mell momentum of the original Latin story becomes a marginal effect" in *Lucrece.* See "Taking Tropes Seriously," p. 67.

[15]Sam Hynes, "The Rape of Tarquin," *SQ* 10, 3 (Summer 1959):453. Donaldson comments (catching explicitly the Shakespearean mood) that, in *Lucrece,* rape is presented as both a destructive and as a self-destructive act.

[16]One could argue that "dilatory" would be a more acceptable term than "augmentative" since it bears within it the full weight of Renaissance rhetorical instruction. However, from the standpoint of contemporary narrative analysis, it also carries a baggage of largely anachronistic connotations. There is little doubt that Shakespeare and his contemporaries would have thought about "dilating" the narrative potential of a story matrix. In a series of interconnected essays, Patricia Parker has investigated the concept of dilation in Renaissance rhetoric and narrative. See "Shakespeare and Rhetoric: 'Dilation' and 'Delation' in *Othello,*" in Patricia Parker and Geoffrey Hartman, eds., *Shakespeare and The Question of Theory* (New York and London: Methuen, 1985), pp. 54-74. See also "Anagogic Metaphor: Breaking Down the Wall of Partition" in Eleanor Cook, et al, eds., *Centre and Labyrinth: Essays in Honour of Northrop Frye* (Toronto: Univ. of Toronto Press, 1983), pp. 38-50; "Dilation and Delay: Renaissance Matrices," *PoT* 5, 3(1984):519-35; "Deferral, Dilation, Differance: Shakespeare, Cervantes, Jonson," in *Literary Theory / Renaissance Texts,* Patricia Parker and David Quint, eds. (Baltimore: John Hopkins Univ. Press, 1986), pp. 182-209.

[17]The critical terminology of this discussion generally follows that developed for narrative analysis by Gérard Genette. See *Narrative Discourse: An Essay* in *Method,* trans. Jane E. Lewin (Ithaca: Cornell Univ. Press, 1980). For further

discussion of the narratological model, see Shlomith Rimmon-Kenan, *Narrative Fiction: Contemporary Poetics* (London: Methuen, 1983), and Mieke Bal, *Narratology: Introduction to The Theory of Narrative,* trans. Christine van Boheemen (Toronto: Univ. of Toronto Press, 1985). The vocabulary of narratology is, no doubt, "bristling," as Robert Alter comments [*The Art of Biblical Narrative* (New York: Basic Books, 1981), p. x], but it is extremely useful in that it accounts for certain conceptual distinctions far better than does the critical vocabulary of "normal" Anglo-American literary scholarship. For example, the term "focalization," originally deriving from film criticism, simply does more conceptual work, as I argue in the body of this essay, than does the more familiar expression "point-of-view." The term "focalization" (in the example cited) accounts for the distinction between Titania's voice and the dead votaress's experience.

[18]For discussions of Ovidian conventions, particularly that of split awareness, in Renaissance characterization, see Edward Milowicki and R. Wilson, "'Character' in *Paradise Lost*: Milton's Literary Formalism," *MiltonS* 14 (1980):75-94, and Wilson, "Drawing New Lessons from Old Masters: The Concept of 'Character' in The *Quijote*," *MP* 78, 2 (November 1980):117-38.

[19]Lanham, *Motives,* p. 99.

[20]Brian Vickers, "Epideictic and Epic in The Renaissance," *NLH* 14, 3 (Spring 1983):529-37.

[21]Jerome A Kramaer and Judith Kaminsky, "'These Contraries Such Unity Do Hold': Structure in *The Rape of Lucrece*," *Mosaic* 10, 4 (1977): 149.

[22]In *The Genesis of Secrecy*: *On the Interpretation of Narrative* (Cambridge, Mass.: Harvard Univ. Press, 1979), Frank Kermode speaks of the literary text itself as "playful" (p. 17). Playfulness, when it is perceived as a deliberate textual strategy, has been designated by a number of critical terms, of which "metafiction" is merely one of the more common. See especially Linda Hutcheon, *Narcissistic Narrative: The Metafictional Paradox* (Waterloo: Wilfred Laurier Univ. Press, 1980; rpt. London: Methuen, 1984), and Allen Thiher, *Words in Reflection*: *Modern Language Theory and Postmodern Fiction* (Chicago: Univ. of Chicago Press, 1984). For further citations of books and articles relevant to the concepts of play and game in the study of literature, see James A. G. Marino, "An Annotated Bibliography of Play and Literature," *CRCL* 12, 2 (June 1985): 306-58.

[23]"Story" has become one of the founding concepts of contemporary narrative analysis. The distinction between story and discourse, between a *what* and a *how*, seems basic to the formal analysis of literature and perhaps to common sense as well. Although it is implicit in Aristotle's *Poetics*, contemporary formulations derive from the work of the Russian Formalists. Their distinction between *fabula* (story-stuff) and *sjužet* (plot) made possible, among other things, the analysis of narrative according to models of textual codes and grammars. (Discourse, in this perspective, is invariably a matter of dilation: a regulated drawing out of story potential by means of codes, conventions, grammars, and rhetorics.) For a discussion of the concept of "story" as an analytic tool, see R. Wilson, "Narrative Allusiveness: The Interplay of Stories in two Renaissance Writers, Spenser and Cervantes," *ESC* 12, 2 (June 1986): 138-62.

[24]Reflexivity is that literary act by which a text refers to itself either explicitly (by self-reference) or implicitly (by genre or convention reference). It is one aspect of metafiction but not the only one. Some of the most interesting recent discussion of the concept of reflexivity may be found in Douglas R. Hofstadter,

Gödel, Escher, Bach: An Eternal Golden Braid (New York: Basic Books, 1979). However, one must bear in mind that Hofstadter conflates reflexivity and recursiveness: only the latter term appears in his index. In subsequent writing in *Scientific American,* Hofstadter makes the distinction and adds reflexivity to his vocabulary. See, *Metamagical Themas: Questing for the Essence of Mind and Pattern* (New York: Basic Books, 1985).

[25]F. T. Prince, ed., *The Poems,* p. 149, lines 1854-55 and n.

[26]Dubrow, "The Rape of Clio," p. 439.

[27]T. W. Baldwin, *On The Literary Genetics of Shakespeare's Poems and Sonnets* (Urbana: Univ. of Illinois Press, 1950), pp. 108-12.

[28]Prince, p. 65.

[29]On the signifying force of the blazon, see Nancy Vickers, " 'The blazon of sweet beauty's best': Shakespeare's *Lucrece,*" in Parker and Hartman, eds., *Shakespeare and The Question of Theory,* pp. 95-115.

[30]Lanham, *Motives,* pp. 97, 100.

[31]"Narcissistic" is Linda Hutcheon's term for metafictional self-consciousness. See her *Narcissistic Narrative.* I employ it here in a similar neutral, non-evaluative sense. The extension of her argument in this paper entails that terms such as "metafiction" or "narcissistic" are essentially transhistorical, and that they are not adequately exemplified by reference to modern literature alone.

[32]Dubrow discusses the opening of *Lucrece* in the context of Renaissance historiography; see "The Rape of Clio," pp. 428, 433-36.

[33]Prince, p. 67, fn. 5.

[34]Felix Martínez-Bonati, "The Act of Writing Fiction," *NLH* 11, 3 (Spring 1980): 425-34, esp. n. 4.

[35]Uri Margolin, "Narrative and Indexicality: A Tentative Framework," *JLS* 13, 3 (1984):181-204.

[36]The concept of a "fictional world" has been much discussed in recent literary theory. For a discussion that summarizes the different positions and provides a comprehensive bibliography, see Thomas G. Pavel, *Fictional Worlds* (Cambridge, Mass.: Harvard Univ. Press, 1986). Two valuable discussions, not cited in Pavel's bibliography, are Doreen Maitre's *Literature and Possible Worlds* (London: Middlesex Polytechnic Press, 1983) and Lubomir Doležel's "Towards a Typology of Fictional Worlds," *Tamking Review* 14 (1984 / 85): 261-76. The argument of this paper has been that the disruptive, anachronic effects of the embedded narratives stem from the perception of distinct worldhood (spatio-temporal difference), however incomplete, that these narratives create. For further discussion, see Wilson, "Narrative Allusiveness."

[37]*Rapes,* p. 49. Donaldson begins his discussion of *Lucrece* by noting that it "never quite adds up to a coherent whole, or to a totally compelling human drama" (p. 40). Profound disagreement characterizes the history of *Lucrece*'s reception. For a study of criticism of *Lucrece* since Hyder Rollins's *Variorum* edition (1983), see Robert Bernard DiGiovanni, "Shakespeare's *Lucrece*: A Topical Evaluation of and Supplement to The Scholarship and Criticism Since 1936," unpublished dissertation (Univ. of Michigan, 1971). See also, Maus, "Taking Tropes Seriously."

SEL 28 (1988)
ISSN 0039-3657

"'Twas no *Religious House* till now": Marvell's "Upon Appleton House"

PATSY GRIFFIN

Even some of the most sympathetic critics of Andrew Marvell's "Upon Appleton House" consider it flawed by the twenty-five stanza historical section—thrown off balance by the William Fairfax-Isabel Thwaites-nuns' story.[1] Yet as Marvell presents it, the history is essential to his purpose in the poem, which is to reconstitute the chronicle of Nunappleton House, representing the Fairfax possession as providential. As historiographer, Marvell guides us through a landscape, explicitly and covertly controlling the vista to cast the story of the Fairfaxes in its true mold. And rather than praise the modest General Fairfax, he eulogizes the traditions and ideals embodied in his family.

In 1650, Thomas Fairfax, Commander-in-Chief of all the Commonwealth of England forces, resigned in opposition to the Council of State's decision to invade Scotland. He would defend England, but the staunchly Presbyterian Fairfax would not act as the aggressor against Scotland with whom England was joined in the National League and Covenant. For Presbyterian to go against Presbyterian was a corruption of their united effort against episcopacy. His opposition extended to the commonwealth itself and the great estates ambitious Parliament men were gathering for themselves, which signaled to Fairfax the additional degeneration of the Civil War goals.[2] Marvell makes his poem an indirect witness and tribute to the integrity of Fairfax's conscience. He also reflects the religious dichotomy in opposing Nunappleton to Cawood Castle, the seat of the archbishop of York; thus Marvell suggests that Fairfax's Civil War participation was directed solely to the abolition of episcopacy and its abuses. Cawood Castle and the "Ambition of its Prelate great" (366) symbolize the ecclesiastical regime and its most secularized representative, Archbishop John Williams.[3] They represent an

---

Patsy Griffin recently completed her doctorate in English at the University of Rochester.

analogous situation to that presented in the estate's history of the cloister and the nuns' corrupt spirituality that Marvell shows as the reason for their dispossession by William Fairfax, whose "Religion taught him Right, / And dazled not but clear'd his sight" (227-28).

But Marvell's reshaping of the nuns' story answers another issue—the possession of Nunappleton House itself. To live in a former monastery or build on the site of one was widely regarded as sacrilege. Marvell's reconstruction of the Fairfax legend suggests an effort to relieve Fairfax's fears that Providence was acting against him or would do so because he assumed and retained the Nunappleton property. Nunappleton had been a Cistercian priory until 1542 when it was given to the sons of Isabel Thwaites and William Fairfax, and the first residence there was built from materials of the nunnery (whether actual sections of the nunnery were retained and expanded is not known). Nor is it certain that the General and his family were living in the new Appleton House. The consideration that John Newman has given the question[4] makes it easy to believe that they lived in the original house constructed out of the priory, which would encourage Fairfax's anxiety and Marvell's focus on the landscape.

Divine retaliation for such sacrilege might come suddenly or it might be worked out in time (usually three generations). In his excellent *Religion and the Decline of Magic*, Keith Thomas identifies Sir Henry Spelman as the popular disseminator of the belief that the impropriation of church lands was sacrilege. Spelman's work grew into a catalogue "of the punishments which God had bestowed for sacrilege from the time of the Old Testament onwards, but the most influential part related to the fate of the purchasers of the monastic lands in England."[5] According to Spelman, the former monasteries brought only misfortune to their new owners; families withered in them, producing a paucity of male heirs who seemed inordinately prone to "grievous accidents and misfortunes." The cloisters "flung out" their inhabitants. "It hath not happened that any of them, to my knowledge, or any other in all this country, hath been the permanent habitation of any family of note." Spelman also observed that "no man almost" dared "to build or dwell" on the former monastery sites, and lists the experiences of many who had and the dreadful "infelicity"[6] that pursued them.

General Fairfax held other properties that were formerly Church holdings, and unlike many others, he was punctilious in returning their tithes to the clergy. While this expresses some personal integrity, it may also be construed as an effort to ward off the curse.[7] *If* the Fairfaxes were indeed living in the house built with material from the nunnery, and constructing another house on the site, both sacrilegious acts, and *if* Fairfax had the strong seventeenth-century respect for divine retribution, then it is possible to see that Marvell's impulse in the historical reconstitution may rest in part on the desire to allay Fairfax's fears and convince his fastidious conscience that his ownership of Nunappleton fit a higher design in God's scheme than the nuns' possession did.[8] As a maneuver to disguise this propaganda, Marvell puts history into the whole of the landscape, thus expanding the traditional "walkabout" of the estate poem into a journey. Marvell introduces in stanza 5 the pilgrimage theme, and the trip itself begins at stanza 10, just before the account of the nuns, and ends only with his invitation at the end to reenter the house itself. The multiplicity of sights suggests also a pilgrimage—its goal the shrine of order and beauty that is Maria Fairfax in the garden of Nunappleton. Marvell, in a sense, makes destiny *his* choice by creating a poem that illustrates that Providence took a hand in placing the Fairfaxes at Nunappleton, and that General Fairfax's conscientious stewardship (in the best tradition) provides a pattern for England.

Thus in "Upon Appleton House," Marvell contends that the religious purposes of the house are "likely better thus fulfill'd" (276) by the seat's going to the Fairfaxes, for " 'Twas no *Religious House* till now" (280). Much of his description emphasizes Nunappleton House's religious character: the first line of the poem introduces it as a "sober frame," not extravagant or excessive, and *sober* is repeated in the fourth stanza to establish the relationship between the house and England's Golden Age:

> But all things are composed here
> Like Nature, orderly and near:
> In which we the Dimensions find
> Of that more sober Age and Mind,
> When larger-sized Men did stoop
> To enter at a narrow loop;
> As practising, in doors so strait,
> To strain themselves through *Heavens Gate.*
>
> (25-32)

This is a house "composed" to an earlier English tradition that was more God-fearing, when men practised humility and shunned ostentation in such things as houses and doorways for a moderate, pious expression of themselves. (It also seems possible that Marvell intends to erase the meaning of the tiny doorways still existing from the cloister and transform the narrow openings into the familiar image from Erasmus's *Paraphrases* of the "eye of the needle" through which a camel can more easily pass than the "covetous rich" can enter the gate of Heaven.)[9] The following stanza persuades the reader that the Fairfaxes belong to that "more sober Age"—those who could enter "*Heavens Gate*"—by projecting the "after Age" (33) pilgrims' wonder that the Fairfax magnitude could pass through such low and straight doors.

Moreover, Marvell presents Fairfax as illustrating his virtue through his employment of his wealth; he displays more than the customary *noblesse oblige.* The "Stately *Frontispice of Poor* . . . [that] Adorns without the open Door" (65-66) has the feel of a gracious almshouse, but when "*Furniture of Friends*" (68) is added to it, the house becomes something more than ordinary. In these two phrases, Marvell tranforms the inanimate into the animate and the house takes on a vital quality. The last four lines of the stanza reinforce this effect. Nunappleton had not been built to impress anyone, but "built upon the Place / Only as for a *Mark of Grace*" (69-70), that is, a mark of the family's grace (and favor) for the estate. It was to provide entertainment and occasional shelter for its lord, his friends, and the surrounding poor, and was never intended for continual occupancy.

But Marvell's parabolic language imparts a religious purpose to the Fairfaxes' building. As he begins the story of Nunappleton, he guides his audience out of the house into the landscape, effecting the transition by directing our eyes—"While with slow Eyes we these survey" (81)—to the landscape before us: "fragrant Gardens, shaddy Woods, / Deep Meadows, and transparent Floods" (79-80). He also directs our pace—"on each pleasant footstep stay" (82)—and thus constructs the ideal setting for telling us the "Progress of this Houses Fate" (84). In keeping with the vitality the house assumed earlier, we now find that it had a mother, a virgin mother who was violated, and thus "brought forth" the house: "all that Neighbour-Ruine shows / The Quarries whence this dwelling rose" (87-88). That is, the house was constructed of the ruins of the cloister.

The next stanza describes the nuns' seduction of Isabel Thwaites. Marvell creates the "suttle" speaking nun as a "distorted image" of his own role as "authority."[10] She, too, directs the eye of her audience: " 'Within this holy leisure we / Live innocently as you see' " (97-98). In reality, the nuns may have been innocent of all that Marvell accuses: the abbess was Isabel Thwaites's guardian, Lady Anna Langton, and she served as the head of the nunnery until the dissolution. Isabel Thwaites might often have been at the nunnery with her guardian, and Lady Langton possibly shut her up to keep her from William Fairfax, not to make a religious of her. Or perhaps William Fairfax seduced her from the nuns rather than the other way round. Whatever the actual circumstance, Marvell is charmingly slanderous, providing a justification for the Fairfax impropriation: he creates a dichotomy between false and true religious houses premised on the Protestant standard of personal faith and integrity of conscience. Marvell makes the nuns rivals to William Fairfax, perhaps to Christ, and also to his own role; the nun's inadvertent exposure of the order's hypocrisy—" 'And, if our Rule seem strictly pend, / The Rule it self to you shall bend' " (155-56)—makes Fairfax himself appear more righteous in a dubious action, just as the nun's suasion makes Marvell as poet and guide appear guileless in his manipulating of the reader.

"The *Nuns* smooth Tongue" (200) "sucks" Isabel into the convent,[11] and William Fairfax must go to the court to gain "the lawful Form; / Which licens'd either Peace or Force, / To hinder the unjust Divorce" (234-36). Marvell effects a neat inversion here, for Isabel cannot be Christ's bride when she is William Fairfax's: Marvell assumes as a postulate her previous betrothal to William Fairfax; thus, the seduction amounts to an "unjust Divorce." In Fairfax's remonstration with Isabel, Marvell allots him a diatribe against the building itself. Whereas Spelman documented cases of the monastic buildings avenging themselves by throwing their walls or stones on those who tried to put them to secular use,[12] Marvell upends this superstition and directs it at the nuns in the form of a humorous surmise:

> 'Were there but, when this House was made,
> 'One Stone that a just Hand had laid,
> 'It must have fall'n upon her Head
> 'Who first Thee from thy Faith misled.
>
> (209-12)

He makes it part of a larger strategy to subvert the belief that those given monastic property came to disorder and dispossession: so Marvell's first Fairfax asserts that the buildings themselves came to grief because they were "Founded by Folly, kept by Wrong" (218). Thus the orders, rather than Henry VIII, were responsible for their own misfortune, nullifying any possibility of sacrilege by the Fairfax family. Certainly William Fairfax has no desire to commit sacrilege:

> What should he do? He would respect
> Religion, but not Right neglect:

For first Religion taught him Right,
And dazled not but clear'd his sight.
Sometimes resolv'd his Sword he draws,
But reverenceth then the Laws:
For Justice still that Courage led;
First from a Judge, then Souldier bred.

(225-32)

Donald Friedman has observed that "The indecision is resolved, strangely enough, by the poet's reminder that William Fairfax is 'he whose Offspring fierce / Shall fight through all the *Universe*' (241-42)."[13] But it is not really strange that the reminder of the prophecy resolves William Fairfax to action ("Till one, as long since prophecy'd, / His Horse through conquer'd *Britain* ride" [245-46]): Marvell is putting forth the higher fate of the house as young Fairfax's spur to action.[14] Without the compunction that Fairfax has shown, "the *Nuns* his Right debar'd" (237) with their "holy Guard," which consists of "Their *Wooden Saints*," "their old *Holy-Water Brush*," and "The gingling Chain-shot of . . . [the Abbess's] Beads"; "their lowd'st Cannon were their Lungs; / And sharpest Weapons were their Tongues" (250-56). Fairfax, however, has the true holy guard of Providence, and "through the Wall does rise" (258). Whether the "Wall" through which Fairfax rises is that which the nuns claim can "restrain the World without" (99), or their "holy Guard" described above, it figuratively protects a false position. Its penetration by William Fairfax signals Marvell's intention to repudiate the "superstitions vainly fear'd" (260) which surround the current Lord Fairfax. That the cloister is immediately "dispossest" (272) is figuratively true and literally false, for it was only in the next generation that it came into the Fairfax family. Marvell's accomplishment in the lines—"The wasting Cloister with the rest / Was in one instant dispossest" (271-72)—is to equate the order's hypocrisy and evil with the cloister's physical decline. As a virgin building, Nunappleton is identified with Isabel: it has wasted as she would have if she had remained with the nuns. So the Fairfax line, Protestant warriors and English gentlemen, culminating in the Lord General of the Parliamentary Army, would not exist. The next stanza ameliorates the impropriation and conveys the triumphant rightness of Isabel Thwaites's new possession of the cloister:

At the demolishing, this Seat
To *Fairfax* fell as by Escheat.
And what both *Nuns* and *Founders* will'd

'Tis likely better thus fulfill'd.
For if the *Virgin* prov'd not theirs,
The *Cloyster* yet remained hers.
Though many a *Nun* there made her Vow,
'Twas no *Religious House* till now.

(273-80)

Marvell releases Nunappleton House to its destiny as the seat of a truly religious family, even as Isabel became that family genetrix.

The garden is the Fairfax amendment to the estate, laid out in the shape of a fort, a pentagon, by the first Sir Thomas, son of William and Isabel. The present Fairfaxes' Edenic life there emphasizes the appropriateness of the family's possession. The house and grounds flourish; the only prodigality is nature's, who has "laid so sweetly wast" (78) the gardens and woods:

From that blest Bed the *Heroe* came,
Whom *France* and *Poland* yet does fame:
Who, when retired here to Peace,
His warlike Studies could not cease;
But laid these Gardens out in sport
In the just Figure of a Fort;
And with five Bastions it did fence,
As aiming one for ev'ry Sense.

(281-88)

The bastions of the garden replace the cloister wall, and only the bees and flowers are the guardians of the Fairfax Eden:

When in the *East* the Morning Ray
Hangs out the Colours of the Day,
The Bee through these known Allies hums,
Beating the *Dian* with its *Drumms*.
Then Flow'rs their drowsie Eylids raise,
Their Silken Ensigns each displayes,
And dries its Pan yet dank with Dew,
And fills its Flask with Odours new.

(289-96)

Marvell opposes this new Paradise to the "holy Guard" of the nuns: he has the reality paradoxically parody the parody of the nuns. The "vigilant *Patroul* / Of Stars" becomes the counterpart to the fighting nuns, "the Tulip Pinke and Rose" to "their old *Holy-Water Brush*," the "fragrant Vollyes" of the flowers to the loud "Cannon" of the nuns' lungs, and the "Sentinel" bee who "if once stir'd, . . . runs you through, or askes *the Word*" to the sharp "Weapons" of "their Tongues" (298-320). Theirs is the only protection now needed, for Fairfax's integrity is its own holy guard, as was William Fairfax's. England, too, has had such protection:

> Oh Thou, that dear and happy Isle
> The Garden of the World ere while,
> Thou *Paradise* of four Seas,
> Which *Heaven* planted us to please,
> But, to exclude the World, did guard
> With watry if not flaming Sword;
> What luckless Apple did we tast,
> To make us Mortal, and The Wast?
>
> (321-28)

The protection of the sea, like the nuns' wall, is useless when the degeneration lies within; with the associations that Marvell has built up around *waste* in the poem, the false spirituality and greed that caused the cloister to waste would seem transferable to England's situation. The tour of the garden culminates in an unpleasant image of England as a nation where "We Ord'nance Plant and Powder sow" (344). It is Marvell's contention that Fairfax could have made England flourish like the garden at Nunappleton, but Marvell observes that it did not please Fairfax "and *God*" (346) that he do so. The very qualities that are the basis of his integrity, his conscience and his lack of personal ambition, prevent this; implicitly, they prevented his participation in the regicide and the invasion of Scotland, actions that he could not reconcile with God's will. For, paradoxically, conscience provides only immortal protection with its "prickling leaf . . . [that] Flowrs eternal, and divine": "Heaven" nurses this "Plant" (355-59), not earth.

But earthly profit from Fairfax's conscience is a reality for England. Fairfax's conscience would demand that he protect his country; he watches over it still from his Eden:

> The sight does from these *Bastions* ply,
> Th' invisible *Artilery*;,
> And at proud *Cawood Castle* seems
> To point the *Battery* of its Beams.
> As if it quarrell'd in the Seat
> Th' Ambition of its *Prelate* great.
>
> (361-66)

Marvell here presents the contemporary dichotomy between true and false religious houses, Nunappleton and Cawood Castle. The seat of the archbishop of York was something of a bastion itself, one of the last of the bishops' lands, many of which had been used by Parliament as collateral to raise monies for the war.[15] The archbishop of York is the counterpart of the abbess Lady Anna Langton, guardian of Isabel Thwaites. As William Fairfax despoiled the abbess, the present Lord Fairfax entered the war in 1642 to effect the deposing of the bishops.

In Marvell's allegorical landscape, Fairfax stands ready to defend England, that war-wasted "Abbyss" ("Garden of the World ere while") represented by the meadow the reader enters. His protective gaze—"Th' invisible *Artilery*"—watches Cawood Castle with a bellicose eye, but benignly guards the countryside: "ore the Meads below it plays, / Or innocently seems to gaze" (367-68).

Marvell's naming of the meadow "the Abbyss" invites its comparison to the cloister of the abbess, which wasted under her jurisdiction. The meadow wastes under the "massacre" (394) of the mower who "now commands the Field" (418). Unlike the undazzled sight of William Fairfax and the directed vision of the present Lord Fairfax, the perspective of no one in "the Abbyss" is reliable: "As, under Water, none does know / Whether he fall through it or go" (379-80). This untrustworthy perspective is characteristic of the land of grass and grasshoppers. Marvell has earlier created juxtapositions between the worthy and the unworthy; these frequently involve growth imagery which illuminates the poem's thesis that flowers and fruit prove the worth of what one does. The nuns' confine, where they artfully "dress the Altars" (179) in flowers, but where their "Gardens yield" perverse "Fruit" (219), has been juxtaposed to Fairfax's garden and to Maria, who "Seems with the Flow'rs a Flow'r to be" (302). The Fairfax garden guarded by the "Regiment . . . of the Tulip Pinke and Rose" (311-12) has been juxtaposed to the remembrance of England when "Tulips . . . Were then the *Switzers* of our *Guard*" (335-36). And, at the point of entry to the "Abbyss," Fairfax's good life, directed by an "*Ambition*"-free conscience of the sort that is nurtured by heaven and "Flowrs eternal, and divine" (354-58), is juxtaposed to the "Abbyss"-dwellers' existence, one so directed by ambition that they bring up "Flow'rs so to be seen, / And prove they've at the Bottom been" (383-84). This false position is equated with the unreliable vision; both result from a separation from the providential guidance that Fairfax relies upon. Yet Marvell does not specifically identify "The sight" that plies "Th' invisible *Artilery*," and thus leaves it free to be Fairfax's, ours, or his. If this indefinition constitutes a precursor of sorts of the shifting perspective that we are about to experience, it also persuades the audience that a union of effort can protect England. Thus Marvell manages to elaborate his new providential history of Nunappleton and England with a series of shifting allegorical foci.

When the reader enters the meadow, Marvell's allegorical fabric approaches the surreal:

> And now to the Abbyss I pass
> Of that unfathomable Grass,
> Where Men like Grashoppers appear,
> But Grashoppers are Gyants there:
> They, in there squeking Laugh, contemn
> Us as we walk more low then them:
> And, from the Precipices tall
> Of the green spir's, to us do call.
>
> (369-76)

He presents a panorama that is confusing and purposefully so. Rosalie Colie has likened it to a magic lantern show, dissolving one thing into another so we lose the sense of discrete objects and significances in the landscape.[16] The complex perspectives permit Marvell to traverse time and interject bits of circumstance that liken the meadow to England at civil war. Despite his first-person reference to himself, Marvell remains true to his persona—observer, not participant. Yet there is a sense of beleaguerment: the grasshoppers laugh and "contemn" him; the "bloody *Thestylis*" seems to shout, "he call'd us Israelites; / But now, to make his saying true, / Rails rain for Quails, for Manna Dew" (401-408). This scorn sufficiently identifies him as prophet; having undergone this initial experience, he will during the course of his journey complete his metamorphosis to become the authority, the providential historian.

He takes "Sanctuary in the Wood" (482), hesitating in awe before this "double Wood of ancient Stocks" (489), that is, of Fairfaxes and Veres:

> When first the Eye this Forrest sees
> It seems indeed as *Wood* not *Trees*:
> As if their Neighbourhood so old
> To one great Trunk them all did mold.
> There the huge Bulk takes place, as ment
> To thrust up a *Fifth Element*;

And stretches still so closely wedg'd
As if the Night within were hedg'd.

Dark all without it knits.

(497-505)

The last three lines are reminiscent of the nuns' enclosure, where the walls repel "the World without, / But hedge our Liberty about" (99-100). The cloister parodies retired life, whereas the wood provides a true retirement.[17] Its sanctity belongs to the union of English families represented by the Fairvax-Vere connection, unions that protect ancient natural order and oppose the chaos of the meadow world, that "naked equal Flat, / Which *Levellers* take Pattern at" (449-50). So the wood becomes a temple, the birds a choir.

Within the wood, Marvell creates an interior world as fantastic but not as threatening as the open meadow. The Thorn accommodates the nightingale by withdrawing its thorns. The Stock-doves "unto the Elms . . . moan" (526); the poet finds their music more pleasing than the nightingale's, yet wonders "why should such a Couple mourn, / That in so equal Flames do burn!" (527-28). The reader wonders, too, and wonders even more at "The hatching *Thrastles* shining Eye" (532). Rosalie Colie comments on Marvell's keen eye for detail: "the poet sees not the whole thrush upon her nest, but its 'shining Eye,' distinct from the surrounding leaves, a sharp eye which in its own right catches and holds the sharp eye of the poet. Montaigne and his cat; Marvell and the thrush—who plays with whom, who observes whom?"[18] Marvell evokes the self-conscious nature of introspection in the image of the "shining Eye," conveying another world, another eye watching him as he watches. More important, perhaps, this guarding eye of the natural world suggests an analogy with that of Fairfax: they watch to insure preservation of the good order.

But most the *Hewel's* wonders are,
Who here has the *Holt-felsters* care.
He walks still upright from the Root,
Meas'ring the Timber with his Foot;
And all the way, to keep it clean,
Doth from the Bark the Wood-moths glean.
He, with his Beak, examines well
Which fit to stand and which to fell.

(537-44)

The good order of the wood is maintained by the hewel who not only cleans the bark of parasites but also claims "the hollow Oak . . . for his building . . . /And through the tainted Side he mines" (548-50). The tree itself "fed / A *Traitor-worm,* within it bred" (553-54). That the tree hosted the treacherous worm yet hated its treason—"the Oake seems to fall content, / Viewing the Treason's Punishment" (559-60)—could be seen as an interesting accolade for Charles I, for the passage might suggest his fall. Since Marvell is justifying Fairfax's participation in the Civil War while also exalting the traditions of England, he does not condemn Charles, but one may consider that there were traitor-counselors who corrupted the essentially good king and reduced him from a healthy state to a sick one. As the hewel cannot rescue the oak, so Fairfax was unable to rescue Charles. Equally, however, the passage suggests that the decision—made like the hewel's with the practical economy of nature—was both just and fruitful: "yet that Worm triumphs not long, / But serves to feed the *Hewels young*" (557-58).

Marvell's self-mockery in calling himself "*easie Philosopher*" (561) in the next stanza implies that the previous passage has too summarily accounted for the trauma England has experienced. Yet he only appears to subvert his authority with the self-deprecating epithet: the role of philosopher is too limited. His theorizing on the trees and birds' presentation of the perfect model will now expand to communing with that world:

> Already I begin to call
> In their most learned Original:
> And where I Language want, my Signs
> The Bird upon the Bough divines.
>
> (569-72)

In this union, he finds his place and his true names of prophet and historian. Unlike the legendary Sibyl, he knows where all the leaves belong: "No Leaf does tremble in the Wind / Which I returning cannot find" (575-76); therefore, his prophecy, though "strange," will be true:

> Out of these scatter'd *Sibyls* Leaves
> Strange *Prophecies* my Phancy weaves:
> And in one History consumes,
> Like *Mexique Paintings,* all the *Plumes.*
>
> (577-80)

He can read all of history, philosophy, and theology: "What *Rome, Greece, Palestine,* ere said" (581), and with the understanding the light brings him through the leaves, the "light *Mosaick*" (582), he assumes the "*antick Cope*" (591) and becomes the "great *Prelate of the Grove*" (592), the antithesis of the "*Prelate* great" (366), the archbishop of York.

He commands his communicants to hold him in the wood:

> Bind me ye *Woodbines* in your 'twines,
> Curle me about ye gadding *Vines,*
> And Oh so close your Circles lace,
> That I may never leave this Place.
>
> (609-12)

The temptation to remain ("Oh what a Pleasure 'tis to hedge / My Temples here with heavy sedge" [641-42]) echoes the pleasure the nuns felt in their wall that "hedged" (100) them about. But retirement of this sort is not possible; rules may not be bent as the nun proposed to Isabel Thwaites. Placidly waiting for an answer (fishing) gets no tolerance. Conscience must respond to the right—Maria, here, as a part of the Fairfax continuity that represents the conscience-guided role: "But now away my Hooks, my Quills, / And Angles, idle Utensils" (649-50). In a transferral of the guiding vision, Maria's "judicious Eyes" return him to the world of natural order she creates. She has been reared in a "*Domestick Heaven*" (722):

> Under the *Discipline* severe
> Of *Fairfax,* and the starry *Vere;*
> Where not one object can come nigh
> But pure, and spotless as the Eye.
>
> (723-26)

Moreover, her purity has God's generative power to direct nature:

> 'Tis *She* that to these Gardens gave
> That wondrous Beauty which they have;
> *She* streightness on the Woods bestows;
> To *Her* the Meadow sweetness owes;
> Nothing could make the River be
> So Chrystal-pure but only *She;*
> *She* yet more Pure, Sweet, Streight, and Fair,
> Then Gardens, Woods, Meads, Rivers are.
>
> (689-96)

This purity is demonstrably different from the nun's suggestion to Isabel Thwaites that she should with the other nuns lie hidden away in a self-indulgent inactifity, "Like Chrystal pure with Cotton warm" (192). *That* was a false retirement; Maria is active virtue, springing from active virtue; her future marriage will be "for some universal good" (741).

In the creation of this Protestant saint and this Edenic world, Fairfax has made a shrine worthy of pilgrimage; together they constitute "*Heaven's Center, Nature's Lap, / And Paradice's only Map*" (767-68). And this "more decent Order" (766) could possibly tame those "wild Creatures, called Men" (102).

NOTES

[1]For example, while Rosalie L. Colie sees the section as thematically "important and integrated," she considers it "an incident interesting in itself but weighing heavily on the poem." *"My Ecchoing Song": Andrew Marvell's Poetry of Criticism* (Princeton: Princeton Univ. Press, 1970), p. 265. Donald M. Friedman expresses uncertainty that "there is a completely satisfactory answer" to "why so much effort has been spent on what should be an incidental allusion in the body of the poem." *Marvell's Pastoral Art* (London: Routledge & Kegan Paul, 1970), p. 220. My theory supplements and is essentially in harmony with a number of readings, including those of Annabel M. Patterson, *Marvell and the Civic Crown* (Princeton: Princeton Univ. Press, 1978), p. 103; Maren-Sofie Rostvig, " 'Upon Appleton House' and the Universal History of Man," *ES* 42 (1961):342; M. J. K. O'Loughlin, "This Sober Frame: A Reading of 'Upon Appleton House,' " in *Andrew Marvell: A Collection of Critical Essays*, ed. George deF. Lord (Englewood Cliffs: Prentice-Hall, 1968), p. 127; Kitty W. Scoular, *Natural Magic* (Oxford: Clarendon Press, 1965), p. 168; and Isabel G. Maccaffrey, "The Scope of Imagination in *Upon Appleton House*," in *Tercentenary Essays in Honor of Andrew Marvell*, ed. Kenneth Friedenreich (Hamden, Conn.: Archon Books, 1977), p. 229.

[2]Although Fairfax accepted a place in the newly formed Council of State in 1649, he refused to sign the declaration expressing agreement with the abolition of monarchy and of the House of Lords. When he resigned in 1650, he made a statement that suggests an explanation for his earlier refusal to participate in the regicide: "What my conscience yields unto as just and lawful, . . . I shall follow; and what seems to me to be otherwise I will not do. My conscience is not satisfied, and therefore I must desire to be excused." In Clements R. Markham, *A Life of the Great Lord Fairfax* (London: Macmillan, 1870), p. 360.

[3]Williams, the last archbishop of York until Accepted Frewen's appointment after the Restoration, died in Wales on 25 March 1650, and was buried there. Although the date of his death might be helpful in establishing a more exact date for the poem, probably Fairfax and Marvell were not aware that he was dead. At any rate, the reference allows also a general interpretation. For Williams, Cawood Castle had proved no sanctuary; within a few months of his arrival, he was set to rout by a Yorkshire troop (*DNB*). All quotations from Marvell are from the first volume of *The Poems and Letters of Andrew Marvell*, ed. H. M. Margoliouth, rev. Pierre Legouis with E. E. Duncan-Jones, 2 vols. (Oxford: Clarendon Press, 1971), cited by line numbers.

[4]John Newman, "Marvell's Appleton House," *TLS* (28 January 1972):99. See also A. A. Tait, "Marvell's Appleton House," *TLS* (11 February 1972):157, and James Turner, "Marvell," *TLS* (31 March 1972):367. When they were first married, General Fairfax and Ann Vere lived at Denton, the family's main residence, with Sir Thomas, the general's grandfather. Sir Thomas seems to have quickly grown uncomfortable with this arrangement and assigned his house at Nunappleton to them. It may have been intended as an interim dwelling, a place for the young couple to live for a few years; Fairfax, however, ever after preferred it (Markham, p. 22).

[5]Keith Thomas, *Religion and the Decline of Magic* (New York: Scribner's, 1971), pp. 96-102.

[6]Sir Henry Spelman, *The History and Fate of Sacrilege*, ed. Samuel J. Eales (London, 1888), pp. 136-58.

[7]As the third Lord Fairfax, he was also the possessor of Bilborough and Bolton Percy, both formerly belonging to the Church. He returned these properties' tithes to the clergy, assigning those of Bilborough to the clergyman, Mr. Topham, for his lifetime, and in his will, to the "preaching minister of Bilbrough for ever" (Markham, p. 397). When Parliament rewarded him with the seignory of the Isle of Man, he directed the entire proceeds from the sequestrated bishopric as supplement to the incomes of the lower clergy and for establishment of grammar schools in the surrounding area (Markham, p. 365).

[8]If assuagement were Marvell's aim, *Comus* may have been his precedent. See Barbara Breasted, "*Comus* and the Castlehaven Scandal," *MiltonS* 3 (1971): 201-24.

[9]Almost certainly Marvell would have known this paraphrase, as would many others, for since Queen Elizabeth's time, the law had required the placement of a volume of the *Paraphrases* in English so that it was accessible to all parishioners. William L. Edgerton, "Shakespeare and the 'Needle's Eye,' " *MLN* 66 (December 1951):549-50.

[10]Stephen Greenblatt's concept of "the alien constructed as a distorted image of the authority," in *Renaissance Self-Fashioning from More to Shakespeare* (Chicago: Univ. of Chicago Press, 1980), p. 9, prompted my awareness of the correspondences between the nun and the narrator, as well as of the nuns' gardens and behavior as a parody of Fairfax's garden and the bees and flowers' actions.

[11]An allegorical connection, albeit incomplete, might be seen between Isabel Thwaites's seduction by the nun's "smooth Tongue" (200) and Charles I's seduction by bad counselors.

[12]Spelman includes the story of Edward Paston in his accounting of the families who had suffered because of the possession of monastic lands. He makes particular note that Paston is the third generation. When Paston tried to clear the property for his "mansion-house upon or near the priory, . . . a piece of wall fell upon a workman and slew him: perplexed with this accident in the beginning of this business, he gave it wholly over, and . . . built his mansion-house, a very fair one, at Appleton" (p. 143). Though no connection seems to have been made between the Pastons and the Fairfaxes, Appleton property was part of the Fairfaxes' holdings, and tiny Appleton is only about two miles from Nunappleton. This section of Spelman's treatise was probably written in the late 1620s, so the incident is possibly within the time of General Fairfax. The story is the sort that might often be repeated, and perhaps Fairfax had heard it.

One cannot be sure that the Fairfaxes knew the Paston tale, but one can be fairly sure that they were superstitious. The general's grandfather, Sir Thomas, wrote to his brother Henry Fairfax in 1613 that he had heard the devil could "be seen upon the sea, and this morning I heard it credibly spoken that the devil was upon the Thames in a sculler." *The Fairfax Correspondence. Memoirs of the Reign of Charles the First,* ed. George W. Johnson, 2 vols. (London: Richard Bentley, 1848), 1: xxix. Edward Fairfax, the translator of Tasso's *Gerusalemme Liberata,* wrote an account of his two bewitched daughters entitled "A Discourse of Witchcraft. As it was acted in the Family of Mr. Edward Fairfax of Fuystone in the County of York, in the year 1621" (*DNB*).

[13]Donald M. Friedman, *Marvell's Pastoral Art,* pp. 224-25. Rupert Taylor observes that "Noblemen, if they belonged to the great political houses, collected prophecies relating to the fortunes of their families or kept books containing prophecies concerning the history of the realm." *The Political Prophecy in England* (New York: Columbia Univ. Press, 1911), p. 85. Horses were an interest grown into tradition with the Fairfaxes; the general wrote a treatise on horse breeding. His poem about the horse that Charles II rode in his coronation parade is a sad testimony to the hopeful prophecy that Marvell presents in the poem:

> Hence then Dispaire my hopes why should itt bury
> Sence this braue Steed Bredd first was in my Query
> Now thus aduanc't with highest honors loden
> Whilst his that bredd him on by most Mens troden
> But t'is noe matter Seing tho' has gott th' Aduance
> Then please the Royal Rider with thy Prance
> Soe may thy Fame much rayse thy Prayses higher
> Then Chessnut that begott the or Brid-la-dore his Sire.

The Poems of Thomas Third Lord Fairfax, ed. Edward Bliss Reed (New Haven: Yale Univ. Press, 1909), p. 284.

[14]Perhaps there were other prophecies particular to the Fairfaxes. The "Northern Star" of "Upon the Hill and Grove at Bilbrough" may be a reference to a prophecy.

[15]Commons decreed in 1646 that all cathedral lands were to be sold. Christopher Hill, *The Century of Revolution: 1603-1714* (New York: W.W. Norton, 1961), p. 163.

[16]Colie, pp. 211-13.

[17]Joseph Summers, introduction to *Marvell,* Laurel Poetry Series (New York: Dell, 1961), p. 19.

[18]"*My Ecchoing Song,*" pp. 206-207.

SEL 28 (1988)
ISSN 0039-3657

Areopagitica and the Dynamics of History

DAVID A. LOEWENSTEIN

The importance of the concept of struggle and confrontation in *Areopagitica*, of "triall . . . by what is contrary" (2:515),[1] has been understood well enough by critics, but the significant implications of this concept for Milton's perception of the historical process have not been sufficiently recognized.[2] Indeed David Aers and Gunther Kress have recently concluded that Milton's tract avoids any engagement with the historical process and reveals the "static, antihistorical, anti-empirical tendencies of [Milton's] outlook."[3] Similarly, a recent student of Milton's political thought has asserted that, in general, because Milton based "all the facets of his social philosophy upon the aesthetic appreciation of poetry and virtue, he displayed a severe lack of reality pertaining to human affairs," and consequently "his concepts of historical reality and politics became as elusive as Plato's spirit."[4] Contrary to these views, I believe that in *Areopagitica* Milton is highly conscious of history as a complex, dynamic process where vigorous ideological conflict and opposition generate radical reform. It is Milton's dynamic sense of history, in particular, which I wish to consider here: inseparable from his confrontational aesthetic and figurative imagination, it completely informs the politics of reformation in *Areopagitica*.

In his earlier revolutionary works, the radical pamphleteer had responded with the fierce rhetoric of "indignation and scorne" (1:664) to the crisis of social renewal in his age: the antiprelatical polemics—especially such heated tracts as *Of Reformation* and *Animadversions*—frequently project a troublesome, turbulent vision of history as an apocalyptic struggle of irreconcilable factions in the state and church. But no longer engaged in pamphlet warfare and having just completed two pro-divorce tracts, Milton composed a

---

An Assistant Professor of English at Loyola University of Chicago, David Loewenstein has recently completed a book on Milton's poetics of history and is presently editing a collection of essays on Milton's prose.

pamphlet which simultaneously lacks the intensely virulent rhetoric of his previous polemics and embraces conflict as a more positive feature of the historical process.[5] The vision of history in *Areopagitica* is therefore both like and unlike Milton's earlier polemics: like the antiprelatical tracts, *Areopagitica* concerns the interconnection between renovation and revolution in history; yet even more than the early polemics, it develops the notion that historical renewal occurs as a consequence of continual friction between opposing forces and ideologies—what Milton calls "brotherly dissimilitudes" (2:555) and "neighboring differences"—which paradoxically contribute to "*the unity of Spirit*" (2:565) in church and state alike. "The wars of Truth" (2:562) is the striking phrase Milton gives this historical process of conflict and confrontation which keeps the godly nation resilient and reformation ongoing. In particular, the tract's densely metaphorical passages—its descriptions of the militant and dismembered Truth, the great city of refuge, the temple of God, to cite only some of the most notable examples I will consider later—vividly demonstrate Milton's poetics of history embracing the conflicts and contradictions of a dynamic process unfolding "in these latter ages" (2:557).

I

Milton's frequent addresses to Parliament in *Areopagitica* and his other controversial prose works create in the minds of his contemporaries the impression that they stand at a crucial turning point in the drama of history—a time of "glorious changes and renovations both in Church and State" (2:585). Before *Areopagitica* Milton had addressed Parliament in *The Reason of Church-Government* (1642), *An Apology for Smectymnuus* (1642), *The Doctrine and Discipline of Divorce* (1643-44), and *The Judgement of Martin Bucer* (1644); and he would address its members soon again in *Tetrachordon* (1645). The ongoing presence of Parliament in Milton's prose works—often as immediate as his own presence—indicates Milton's unusual self-consciousness about the process of history. Parliament emerges as a revolutionary governing body powerful enough to shape and transform the uneven course of history itself. But *Areopagitica*, more than these other prose works, attempts to educate Milton's countrymen in the ideological contradictions and tensions which characterize the dynamic historical process.

At the very end of *The Reason of Church-Government*, Milton had envisioned Parliament as an apocalyptic "punishing force" (1:861) in history demolishing, with the furious and relentless judgment of divine vengeance, the prelatical oppressors of the godly people. His

Apology for Smectymnuus, published some two or three months later, presents Parliament's historical role in a spirit more closely resembling *Areopagitica*: there Milton's elaborate six-page eulogy makes a sharp break from the "harsh discord" and "jarring notes" of his fierce attack on prelatical power to "a smoother string" (1:922, 928). The men of the Long Parliament are depicted as wise, zealous, heroic figures capable of actively renovating the historical process. They possess the extraordinary power to reverse a regressive pattern in history—making it possible for them "to effect . . . the recovery of decay'd religion and the Commonwealth" (1:922) or, as Milton puts it in *Areopagitica*, to achieve "such a deliverance, as shall never be forgott'n by any revolution of time" (2:539). The remaking of the drama of history thus involves a dynamic collaboration between Parliament's members and God: if "the performance" is God's, then "the will and the endeavour" is "theirs" as they serve as "mediators" for God's actions (1:927-28). Their regenerative power leads Milton to believe intensely—if only for these six pages of impassioned prose—that he might someday see an end to "the long remedilesse afflictions of this kingdome" (1:927). In the self-conscious conclusion to this panegyric, Milton acknowledges to his readers that he has digressed into such "a path . . . much fairer and more delightfull then the rode way [he] was in." By modulating uneasily from eloquent panegyric back to seething invective, Milton draws attention to his own pressing desire to see history transformed radically from a thwarted process fraught with continual crisis into a process culminating in "full and perfet reformation" (1:928).

Milton's view of Parliament undertaking an active role in remaking the historical drama of the godly nation finds its fullest expression in *Areopagitica*. Indeed compared with Milton's other addresses to Parliament, this tract offers a considerably more sustained and probing exploration of how his elect countrymen should respond to the politics of history. The previous and contemporary addresses are all most impressive for their rhetorical force and for their attempt to include Milton's audience in the remaking of history.[6] Yet none represents the process of history quite as complexly or as subtly as *Areopagitica*. None attempts, like *Areopagitica*, to encourage Parliament to respond creatively to history as a dynamic process where an ideology of conflict may have regenerative rather than tragic consequences in the present and future ages of reformation.

Historical renovation, Milton's tract suggests, can be achieved creatively only through greater historical consciousness: that is the first step towards appreciating the regenerative implications of ideological combativeness in the process of history. Milton's argument from history concerning censorship is itself designed to encourage his countrymen to perceive their essential and innovative role in the historical process: they must "look back and revise what hath bin taught heretofore" in order "to gain furder and goe on." The task of remaking and revising history—of transforming the politics of thwarted reformation into a dynamic process which encourages "the discovery of truth" (2:566)—requires an acute consciousness of the past. In addition, Milton's brief survey of censorship reminds Parliament that writing itself has served and must continue to serve as a crucial means of renovating history and keeping it dynamic.

His historical overview manages skillfully to link the prelatical England of Laud, Charles I, and the Presbyterians with a tradition of tyranny that stretches back to Imperial Rome, and includes the increasing papal dominion of the Middle Ages and the Inquisition of the sixteenth century (2:499-504). The English bishops of Milton's age, as he punningly puts it, are "inquisiturient" (2:507)—a ridiculous but caustic word suggesting both their perverse inheritance from the Inquisition and their pruriency. Thus Milton's historical survey, however eclectic and cursory, recalls the earlier, elaborate account in *Of Reformation*, which traces history from the time of Wyclif to Milton's own troubled age: both pamphlets investigate those "Causes" (the very word Milton places in the title of his first revolutionary polemic) which have thwarted reformation and affected the historical process in the present.

Though not nearly as violently apocalyptic as Milton's anti-prelatical pamphlets, *Areopagitica* does project a millennial vision of history where national regeneracy might be perfected in the near future at the very time of the "second comming" (2:549). The emergence of Protestantism, first signaled by the appearance of such heretical reformers and visionaries as "*Wicklef* and *Husse* growing terrible" (2:502), augmented this historical drama in which England herself would continue to play a decisive millennial role: "the favour and the love of heav'n we have great argument to think in a peculiar manner propitious and propending towards us. Why else was this Nation chos'n before any other, that out of her as out of *Sion* should be proclam'd and sounded forth the first tidings and trumpet of Reformation to all *Europ*" (2:552). Indeed had the prelates not suppressed Wyclif as "a schismatic and *innovator*" (2:553), he might have eclipsed such Reformation lights as Huss, Jerome of Prague, even Luther and Calvin. *Areopagitica* is not completely free of that tension which makes *Of Reformation* such a powerful and disturbing work—the tension between Milton's sense of the extraordinary potential of millennial history and his sense of the tragic shortcomings of reformation.

Milton thus aims to make the members of Parliament conscious of both their revolutionary role and the failures of progressive history—"the slow-moving Reformation which we labour under" (2:565). The "apishly Romanizing" (2:504) prelates of Milton's age have used censorship as nothing less than a political weapon to thwart national regeneration. As a consequence, Milton interprets the history of censorship as another version of the history of hindered reformation: by focusing on the perfidious consequences of censorship, Milton adds a new dimension to the historical argument first presented at length in *Of Reformation*. Milton addresses the troubling issue of how the politics of reformation in England have failed in the past and how they could well fail again: "he who thinks we are to pitch our tent here, and have attain'd the utmost prospect of reformation, that the mortall glasse wherein we contemplate, can shew us, till we come to *beatific* vision, that man by this very opinion declares, that he is yet farre short of Truth" (2:549). The elect nation may have the potential to fulfill its national historic destiny, to achieve that "*beatifick Vision*" (1:616) of millennial history that Milton imagines so fervently at the very end of his first antiprelatical tract, but the process of reformation is far from complete. *Areopagitica*, for all its apparent idealism, directly confronts the difficulties of achieving reform in Milton's age before offering its compelling vision of a dynamic process of history.[7]

The men of Parliament, Milton suggests, should neither be constrained by the past nor the ideological narrowness of groups like the Westminster Assembly of Divines; rather they may choose to remake history—since "reason is but choosing" (2:527)—and to redefine the very social order they represent. In this spirit Milton reminds his countrymen that they may "repeal any Act of [their] own setting forth, as any set forth by [their] Predecessors" (2:490). Like other radicals of his period, Milton urges his countrymen to reject arbitrary precedent for a more flexible, imaginative response towards the present and future: "we are the men of the present age," remarked the historically self-conscious Leveller Richard Overton, "and ought to be absolutely free from all kindes of . . . *Arbitrary Power*."[8] To make Parliament aware of precedent, therefore, is simultaneously to make them aware of their ability to break away from it. *Areopagitica* thus boldly challenges the view of history as an inevitable, immutable process determined by the politics of the past. The failure of Parliament to act imaginatively—to diverge decisively from precedent and to recognize the need for the vigorous ideological conflict manifested in revolutionary writing—would eventually ensure a degenerative movement in history: "We can grow ignorant again, brutish, formall, and slavish, as ye found us" (2:559). The "fall of learning" (2:520) leads to regression in history, to the impoverishment of subsequent generations, and to "an undervaluing and vilifying of the whole Nation" (2:535). Such statements, moreover, remind us of Milton's self-consciousness about the worth of his own revolutionary works: he cries out against the Licensing Order because it poses an immediate threat to his own power—exercised through his radical polemics—to participate actively in the process of renovating and shaping the drama of history.

Indeed Milton realized, especially after his first, excited foray into pamphleteering, that the English Revolution was a revolution of words in two significant senses.[9] *Areopagitica*, with its sense of the vitalistic power of texts (which "contain a potencie of life" [2:492]), confirms and defends the power of words and the Word in history. Unlicensed writing has enabled a great visionary like Knox, "the Reformer of a Kingdom," to convey the revelation of the Word "utter'd in the height of zeal" and with "the dictat of a divine Spirit." Those radical reformers in Milton's age who dare to interpret the revolutionary meaning of the Word, as Milton himself had repeatedly done in his antiprelatical and pro-divorce polemics, might themselves be lost to posterity "for the fearfulnesse, or the presumptuous rashnesse of a perfunctory licencer" (2:534). Furthermore, those writers who saw in words themselves a revolutionary weapon for generating ideological controversy would now be at a loss for the means with which to remake the social order of their age: Milton recognizes that "all opinions, yea errors, known, read, and collated, are of main service & assistance toward the speedy attainment of what is truest" (2:513). The conflict between truth and falsehood, so important for the ethical and experiential vision of *Areopagitica*, is thus promoted to an essential force in the process of historical change: without such strenuous, intense conflict, much of it carried on in the sphere of revolutionary writing, the reformation of church and state, Milton warns his countrymen, must indeed remain as "slow-moving" as ever.

II

This sense of vigorous communal trial and ongoing ideological confrontation helps to explain why Milton is so critical in *Areopagitica* of utopian visions. For one thing, such social ideals are simply too static, never allowing for a dynamic process of historical renovation. A utopian vision, like "a fugitive and cloister'd vertue, unexercis'd & unbreath'd" (2:515) removes society from that world of confrontation and conflict through which it is able to regenerate itself: "To sequester out of the world into *Atlantick* and *Eutopian* polities, which never can be drawn into use, will not mend our condition; but to ordain wisely as in this world of evill, in the midd'st whereof God hath plac't us unavoidably" (2:526). Aers and Kress have stressed the limitations of Milton's viewpoint throughout *Areopagitica* which, they suggest, avoids "any statement concerning . . . specific temporal processes" and excludes "all engagement and dialogue with the empirical realities of human relationships, action and changing conflict."[10] Yet this critique misses the essential point of Milton's suspicion of utopias, as well as the complexity of *Areopagitica*'s richly metaphorical passages—with their significant implications for Milton's view of the historical process. If anything, Milton mistrusts utopias because they do not permit direct engagement and dialogue, the very activities upon which the godly nation thrives. His nation is a society which immediately confronts "this world of evill"—with all its conflicts, contradictions, and moral ambiguities—not a utopia which seeks to avoid it. Milton neither envisions nor desires a society wholly free from conflict and schism: to the contrary, such a nation, Milton believes, would remain unresponsive to dynamic historical change. Milton may not offer specific economic and social solutions for reform—that admittedly is not the primary purpose of his discourse—but he does envision a society which must directly engage and embody the complex and contradictory realities of this world rather than avoid or transcend them.

For this reason Milton mocks those who imagine a society where all activities are regulated:

> there be delights . . . that will fetch the day about from sun to sun, and rock the tedious year as in a delightfull dream. . . . These are the fruits which a dull ease and cessation of our knowledge will bring forth among the people. How goodly, and how to be wisht were such an obedient unanimity as this, what a fine conformity would it starch us all into? doubtles a stanch and solid peece of frame-work, as any January could freeze together.
>
> (2:545)

There is no room here for progress, conflict, vigor, all a consequence of a society which permits "brotherly dissimilitudes" in its political and religious constitution. The movement of history itself becomes a process of one "tedious year" succeeding another and yielding nothing more than "dull ease"—what Milton elsewhere in his prose calls "lukewarmenesse" (1:868) among the people. Conformity leads to political and spiritual staleness, as Milton observes later in *Areopagitica*, and ultimately to historical regression: "we may as soon fall again into a grosse conforming stupidity, a stark and dead congealment of *wood and hay and stubble* forc't and frozen together, which is more to the sudden degenerating of a Church then many *subdichotomies* of petty schisms" (2:564). Milton's imagery of icy congealment here—his personal addition to St. Paul's remarks on the Corinthians' unspiritual work as church builders (1 Cor. 3:10-13)—recalls the earlier reference to frozen congealment in January and contrasts directly with his dynamic image of the streaming fountain of Truth: "if her waters flow not in a perpetuall progression, they sick'n into a muddy pool of conformity and tradition" (2:543). Milton's Truth, then, not only represents the vitality of Scripture and the nourishing power of the Word,[11] but serves as a compelling image of history itself, a dynamic process characterized by vigorous progression rather than unhealthy stasis. The waters of Truth must flow in a "perpetuall progression," Milton suggests, just as the godly nation must continually renovate itself throughout history.

The description of Truth grappling with Falsehood dramatizes the ideology of confrontation at the very heart of Milton's historical imagination. Milton's England is itself a battleground where Truth and Falsehood continually engage in strenuous warfare, since Truth is rarely "put to the wors, in a free and open encounter" (2:561). This ideological combativeness not only refers to contentions among brethren, but presumably to ideological challenges from outside that arena as well. Truth in Milton's pamphlet thus emerges as a warrior much like some revolutionary Puritan saint: "who knows not that Truth is strong next to the Almighty; she needs no policies, nor stratagems, nor licencings to make her victorious" (2:562-63).[12] As Michael Walzer has shown in his important study of radical politics, the imagery of warfare is pervasive in Calvin's writings, and became a common theme in Puritan works, many of which envision the life of the saint as a permanent process of struggle and conflict. Moreover, the idea of the embattled saint, as Walzer's analysis suggests, also had profound social implications: the regenerate community as a whole would itself be strengthened and tested—for Truth, Milton suggests, is merely hindered "by *disexercising* . . . our abilities" (2:491; emphasis added)—as a consequence of militant struggle.[13]

Thus we find Milton's contemporary Puritan reformers, sympathetic to the millennial view of history, employing metaphors of warfare to suggest that social renewal is generated through energetic struggle. In his *Bloody Tenent of Persecution*, published in the same year as *Areopagitica* and censured by the Assembly of Divines, Roger Williams has the figure of Truth describe, in typical apocalyptic rhetoric, the wars of reformation taking place in the present age:

> The Israel of God now, men and women, fight under the great Lord-General, the Lord Jesus Christ: their weapons, armour, and artillery are like themselves spiritual, set forth from top to toe (Eph. 6), so mighty, and so potent that they break down the strongest holds and castles. . . . This glorious army of white troopers, horses and harness—Christ Jesus and his true Israel—gloriously conquer and overcome the Beast, the false prophet, and the kings of the earth, up in arms against them (Rev. 19).[14]

The vision of the wars of Truth in Milton's tract, while less aggressively apocalyptic than this, nevertheless emphasizes the vigor of political and spiritual struggle which tests and strengthens not only the Puritan individual or the "true warfaring Christian" (2:515) who, like Spenser's Guyon, must confront evil in order to "see and know" (2:516), but the godly nation as a whole. As Milton observes in *The Reason of Church-Government*, consciously echoing Paul's first epistle to Timothy (1.17), his countrymen might "warre a good warfare" in order to create a more "perfect state of the Church militant" and to bring about "a new and more perfect reformation under Christ" (1:757-58). Nor is it insignificant that in the same year he writes *Areopagitica*, Milton publishes an educational treatise which urges its young Englishmen to master the skills of "embattailing, marching, encamping, fortifying, beseiging and battering" since "they may as it were out of a long warre come forth renowned and perfect Commanders in the service of their country" (*Of Education*, 2:411-12). The wars of Truth in Milton's age, in other words, generate the conditions of ideological conflict necessary to realize his dynamic social vision of a people undergoing a continual transition into regeneracy, and of a Reformation continually reforming itself.

But while Milton's figure of the militant Truth may symbolize the dynamism of history and the regenerate power of the warfaring nation, his figure of *sparagmos*—Truth scattered—conveys a more troubling sense of the possibilities of historical renewal in Milton's age.[15] Hewn apart into a thousand pieces, Truth now becomes nothing less than a dramatic emblem for the fragmented body politic of the godly nation:

> Truth indeed came once into the world with her divine Master, and was a perfect shape most glorious to look on: but when he ascended, and his Apostles after him were laid asleep, then strait arose a wicked race of deceivers, who as that story goes of the *AEgyptian Typhon* with his conspirators, how they dealt with the good *Osiris*, took the virgin Truth, hewd her lovely form into a thousand peeces, and scatter'd them to the four winds. From that time ever since, the sad friends of Truth, such as durst appear, imitating the carefull search that *Isis* made for the mangl'd body of *Osiris*, went up and down gathering up limb by limb still as they could find them. We have not yet found them all, Lords and Commons, nor ever shall doe, till her Masters second comming.
>
> (2:549)

The horror of dismemberment, conveyed in the context of myth, haunts Milton elsewhere in his writing—one thinks of his description of the torn body of Orpheus in *Lycidas* (lines 57-63) and *Paradise Lost* (VII.32-38)—and expresses his anxiety about the violation and disfigurement of the sacred poet and his text. Here the violent image of dismemberment reverberates with political implications. It recalls Milton's references in the revolutionary prose to a fragmented, divided body politic—a nation so violated and abused by prelatical power that it is in danger of losing its original form. Milton laments in *The Reason of Church-Government* the "shatter'd and disjoynted frame of the Common-wealth" (1:860) which Parliament must now repair; and he laments, earlier in the same work, the prelates who "shatter the holy arke of the Church" (1:754-55). Milton's allegory of the dismemberment of Truth resonates with this sense of an afflicted, defiled Commonwealth. The treacherous "race of deceivers" who rose up after Christ's ascension—an allusion to the Roman Church with its hierarchy of popes, bishops, censors, and so on—has caused this violent defilement of the body politic. Milton's violated Truth, by far the most disturbing representation in *Areopagitica* of a thwarted, incomplete process of reformation, projects his worst fears of the English nation failing to fulfill her promise of historic regeneracy.

This poignant vision of dismemberment, however, is followed immediately by an equally powerful vision of unity in which Christ "shall bring together every joynt and member [of Truth], and shall mould them into an immortall feature of lovelines and perfection" (2:549). Here Christ as sculptor and refashioner creates perfection in the body politic where there was only shapelessness and fragmentation before. Later in *Areopagitica,* Milton's metaphor of bodily wholeness—his depiction of the body politic in "good plight and constitution" rather than "degenerated" and "drooping to a fatall decay" (2:557)—will serve as a contrast to the image of "the torn body of our martyr'd Saint," Truth (2:550): Milton's afflicted nation is reconstituted into a healthy body vigorously undergoing a dynamic process of reformation. But in comparison to these metaphorical passages, *Aeropagitica's* haunting fable about Truth's dismemberment conveys allegorically both the tragedy of failed reformation in Milton's age and the urgency of carrying on the incomplete process of historical renovation.

Milton's visions of the great city of refuge and the temple of God (2:553-57) are likewise both highly expressive of his historical consciousness, revealing its crucial interconnection with his figurative imagination.[16] These passages suggest that the historical process remains progressive and dynamic only when reformation permits, paradoxically, both union and conflict within the godly nation. The city of refuge passage—a vision of thriving London itself—is one of the most vivid representations of dynamic historical renovation in Milton's revolutionary prose works.

Milton's London is essentially a vision of the godly nation in microcosm, engaged in a kind of perpetual ideological warfare:

> The shop of warre hath not there more anvils and hammers waking, to fashion out the plates and instruments of armed Justice in defence of beleaguer'd Truth, then there be pens and heads there, sitting by their studious lamps, musing, searching, revolving new notions and idea's wherewith to present, as with their homage and their fealty the approaching Reformation: others as fast reading, trying all things, assenting to the force of reason and convincement.
>
> (2:554)

The "shop of warre" suggests that the godly people must not only challenge and refashion traditional religious and political authorities, but also keep the process of reformation in continual revolutionary activity. Rather than allowing themselves to degenerate into a state of "dull ease" (2:545), the people "should be disputing, reasoning, reading, inventing, discoursing, ev'n to a rarity, and admiration" (2:557). Such debates among Puritan reformers might well concern—as they in fact did in the Whitehall Debates of the late 1640s—the relevance of history to the politics of reformation.[17] Milton's portrayal of the teeming city preparing itself for war is therefore both literal—a reflection of the increasing evidence of civil war in and around London which had, in 1643, undergone a vast scheme of military fortification and defense[18]—and symbolic: an expression of Milton's dynamic vision of reformation and history. The passage suggests that ideological confrontation and combativeness within political and religious spheres generates more and more intellectual energy, activity, and progress: "Where there is much desire to learn, there of necessity will be much arguing, much writing, many opinions; for opinion in good men is but knowledge in the making" (2:554). Milton's emphasis here is clearly upon "knowledge in the making," upon energetic process rather than static completion.

The temple of God can itself be construed as a complex figure for the politics of historical renovation; it consequently serves as a vivid illustration of Milton's poetics of history in which aesthetics and ideology are inseparable. Milton understands the revolutionary saints of his age as architects engaged in the arduous process of rebuilding and reconstructing their society, as his address to Parliament in *Martin Bucer* suggests:[19] "it will be soon manifest to them who know what wise men should know, that the constitution and reformation of a commonwealth . . . is, like a building, to begin orderly from the foundation therof . . . to set right first what ever is amisse therein" (2:431). Nevertheless, Milton would have agreed with one Puritan contemporary who observed that "Temple-work is not easily, not suddenly accomplished."[20] "No Marble statue can be politely carv'd, no fair edifice built" without considerable "rubbish and sweeping" (1:796), Milton observes in *The Reason of Church-Government.* As he notes in *Areopagitica,* in the course of building the house of God there "must be many schisms and many dissections made in the quarry and in the timber" (2:555). It has been said that "to the zealous Puritan it was the finished temple that counted, not the process of building."[21] Yet Milton surely places as much emphasis on the rigorous, energetic *process* of reformation—the labor of "building . . . cutting . . . squaring . . . hewing" (2:555) the house of God—as he does on the completed work itself.

The Reason of Church-Government provides a valuable gloss on the importance of schism for Milton's vision of history. There, where Milton in effect argues for a kind of regenerative schism, he ridicules the idea of a "schismelesse estate" in which "all controversie may end in the finall pronounce or canon of one Arch-primat, or Protestant

Pope" (1:783). A certain degree of schism, Milton believes, is the very test of the godly nation's regenerative power, its capacity to contain and thrive upon ideological conflict and friction. But the prelates, terrified of any kind of schism at all, would enforce a deadly uniformity sapping the regenerate people's strength and vision—creating "an unactive blindnesse of minde upon the people by their leaden doctrine" (1:784). Milton's defense of schism develops from the concept of discipline at the very heart of this polemic: discipline requires "vigor" not "slacknesse" (1:751) and a paradoxical combination of order and conflict which permits the energetic "struggl[e] of contrarieties" (1:795). Indeed the dynamic movement of history itself depends upon the realization of this essential if paradoxical concept: "the flourishing and decaying of all civill societies, all the moments and turnings of humane occasions are mov'd to and fro as upon the axle of discipline" (1:751).[22]

With this discipline of contrarieties in mind, we may consider the figure of temple-building in *Areopagitica* for its historical and ideological implications:

> And when every stone is laid artfully together, it cannot be united into a continuity, it can but be contiguous in this world; neither can every peece of the building be of one form; nay rather the perfection consists in this, that out of many moderat varieties and brotherly dissimilitudes that are not vastly disproportionall arises the goodly and the gracefull symmetry that commends the whole pile and structure. Let us therefore be more considerat builders, more wise in spirituall architecture, when great reformation is expected. (2:555)

A paradoxical combination of unity (rather than uniformity) and dissimilitude constitutes the foundation and strength of this wondrous structure.[23] Its "gracefull symmetry" derives from the presence of contrary and disproportionate elements. Milton's double negative here—"brotherly dissimilitudes that are not vastly disproportionall"—the linguistic equivalent of his architectural image, conveys *Areopagitica*'s essential idea that "great reformation" in the body politic is generated by a paradoxical mixture of unity and schism. Opposites are not unopposed—either in Milton's text or his image. Indeed this image is itself an elaborate metaphor for Milton's text—that graceful structure artfully constructed out of the language of "brotherly dissimilitudes." The temple of God is thus both proportionate and disproportionate, in just the same way that it is "not impossible that [Truth] may have more shapes then one" or that she "may be on this side, or on the other, without being unlike her self" (2:563). Visually and linguistically, through double negatives, Milton is saying something about the process of historical renovation: if the body politic is to regenerate itself, then the dismembered pieces of Truth must finally be collected together in a spirit of unity paradoxically comprised not of "fine conformity" but of "brotherly dissimilitudes" and "neighboring differences."

III

Dynamic conflict, I have argued, is crucial to Milton' s historical imagination in *Areopagitica.* Milton's tract thus argues for a new kind of historical vision that involves the remaking of history itself: "not only to look back and revise what hath bin taught heretofore, but to gain furder and goe on." Gaining true historical vision—in this case, perceiving history as a complex process of continual but regenerative ideological conflict and schism—culminates in a simultaneous awakening of the godly nation and her revolutionary historian: "Methinks I see in my mind a noble and puissant Nation rousing herself like a strong man after sleep, and shaking her invincible locks" (2:557-58). Like Samson, and like Milton himself, the rejuvenated nation is a powerful, militant body vigorously fighting the wars of Truth in history. Milton's emphasis upon the nation's renewed powers of sight—identified with both the speaker's renewed vision and the phoenix-like eagle "kindling her undazl'd eyes at the full midday beam" (2:558)—underscores the essential connection between historical vision and radical regeneration. Milton had already stressed such a connection in his apocalyptic address to Christ in *Animadversions,* where his impassioned prayer for light—that "morning beam of *Reformation*"—is nothing less than an intense prayer for historical illumination, for God to remove "by degrees the inveterat scales from our nigh perisht sight" (1:704-705). In *Areopagitica,* Milton's godly nation renews her sight "at the fountain of . . . heav'nly radiance," a version of the streaming fountain of Truth that evokes simultaneously the notions of historical vision and renovation. Those incapable of understanding and interpreting these extraordinary signs of dynamic history—especially such "timorous and flocking birds" as the Assembly of Divines—misconstrue the historical process, envisioning in the future only terrible "sects and schisms" (2:558), a prophecy of historical conflict without the spirit of unity. But genuine historical vision in *Areopagitica*—"had we but eyes to lift up" says Milton to his countrymen (2:554)—should enable the godly nation to perceive the wars of Truth which exist at the heart of the regenerative historical process.

Milton's historical vision in *Areopagitica* thus remains as revolutionary as ever. Yet the apocalyptic rhetoric of this tract has been mollified to allow for a vision subtler and more generous than that of his earlier radical polemics. No other revolutionary prose work of Milton's, I think, shows a more resilient capacity to embrace conflict as the essential element of the historical process—a fact that seems especially striking when we consider that *Areopagitica* (despite its rhetoric of warfare) is so much less abusive and emotionally vehement than Milton's other polemical tracts. The drama of history for Milton is always dynamic, yet here he has highlighted its regenerative consequences: when some momentous historical change is about to occur, Milton writes towards the end of *Areopagitica,* "God shakes a Kingdome with strong and healthfull commotions to a generall reforming" (2:566). Although this sense of history as a dynamic process recurs in Milton's subsequent controversial pamphlets, these works depict an astonishingly turbulent and violent sense of the historical process that was emerging in the antiprelatical tracts. Rather than extending the complex vision of history in *Areopagitica,* with its remarkable capacity to transform conflicting ideologies into "brotherly dissimilitudes," Milton's regicide tracts would simultaneously look back to the fierce, unmediated vision of the antiprelatical tracts and ahead to the dramatic, iconoclastic vision of *Samson Agonistes.*

NOTES

[1]References to Milton' s prose, cited parenthetically within my text, are taken from the *Complete Prose Works of John Milton*, ed. Don M. Wolfe et al., 8 vols. (New Haven: Yale Univ. Press, 1953-82).

[2]Commentators who stress the importance of the concept of struggle in Milton's tract include its editor in the Yale edition, Ernest Sirluck, 2:515, n. 102; Alan F. Price, "Incidental Imagery in *Areopagitica,*" *MP* 49 (1952): 217-22; and John X. Evans, "Imagery as Argument in Milton's *Areopagitica,*" *TSLL* 8 (1966):200, 202.

[3]See "Historical Process, Individuals and Communities in Milton's *Areopagitica,*" in David Aers, Bob Hodge, Gunther Kress, *Literature, Language and Society in England, 1580-1680* (Totowa: Barnes & Noble, 1981), p. 182. Because it dissolves "the dialectical relations between individual and social circumstances" (p. 182), *Areopagitica,* Aers and Kress argue, is an example of "imaginative failure and intellectual closure" (p. 181); for their full discussion see pp. 152-83. The only other extensive treatment of history in Milton's tract

that I know of—one whose approach differs from both that of Aers and Kress and my own—is by Paul M. Dowling, "Milton's Use (or Abuse) of History in *Areopagitica*," *Cithara* 23 (1983):28-37, who examines Milton's work in terms of classical *historia*.

[4]Charles R. Geisst, *The Political Thought of John Milton* (London: Macmillan, 1984), p. 62.

[5]As some critics have noted, *Areopagitica* lacks the polemical bite of Milton's earlier pamphlets. See Evans, "Imagery as Argument," p. 188, and Edward S. Le Comte, "*Areopagitica* as a Scenario for *Paradise Lost*," in *Achievements of the Left Hand: Essays in the Prose of John Milton*, ed. Michael Lieb and John T. Shawcross (Amherst: Univ. of Mass. Press, 1974), p. 121, who also cites comments by William Haller, Don M. Wolfe, and Arthur Barker.

[6]See Nancy S. Struever's suggestive comments on the rhetor-historian who consciously includes his audience "in his effort to make history": *The Language of History in the Renaissance: Rhetoric and Historical Consciousness in Florentine Humanism* (Princeton: Princeton Univ. Press, 1970), pp. 89-90.

[7]As Joseph Wittreich has argued, Milton, far from being "an incurable idealist," envisions a regenerate nation in the future not in the present, and consequently assumes an ambivalent attitude towards Parliament's assertion of its power: see Joseph Anthony Wittreich, Jr., "Milton's *Areopagitica*: Its Isocratic and Ironic Contexts," *Milton Studies* 4 (1972):103-104. On Milton's sophisticated stance in relation to Parliament, see also Annabel Patterson, *Censorship and Interpretation: The Conditions of Writing and Reading in Early Modern England* (Madison: Univ. of Wisconsin Press, 1984), pp. 111-19.

[8]*A Remonstrance of Many Thousand Citizens* (1646), in *Tracts on Liberty in the Puritan Revolution, 1638-1647*, ed. William Haller, 3 vols. (New York: Columbia Univ. Press, 1934), 3:355.

[9]Lawrence Stone, *The Causes of the English Revolution, 1529-1642* (New York: Harper & Row, 1972), pp. 49, 97, notes that the wordiness of the English Revolution—with its vast amount of pamphlet literature—encouraged the rapid spread of radical ideas.

[10]Aers and Kress, "Historical Process, Individuals and Communities," pp. 165, 172.

[11]Cf. *Of Prelatical Episcopacy* where Milton refers to "the plentifull and wholsom fountaines of the Gospell" (1:626). For the relation of Milton's Truth to Scripture, see John R. Knott, Jr., *The Sword of the Spirit: Puritan Responses to the Bible* (Chicago: Univ. of Chicago Press, 1980), ch. 5.

[12]Evans, "Imagery as Argument," pp. 200-201, and Price, "Incidental Imagery," pp. 217-18, 221-22, note the tract's military images, though without connecting them to Milton's perception of the historical process.

[13]Michael Walzer, *The Revolution of the Saints: A Study in the Origins of Radical Politics* (Cambridge, Mass.: Harvard Univ. Press, 1965), pp. 57-65, 116, 278, 285, 288-90, 296.

[14]See the selection in *Puritanism and Liberty: Being the Army Debates (1647-9)*, ed. A. S. P. Woodhouse (London: J. M. Dent, 1938), p. 291.

[15]For a discussion of the metaphor of *sparagmos* and its tradition in relation to Milton, see James Nohrnberg, *The Analogy of "The Faerie Queene"* (Princeton: Princeton Univ. Press, 1976), pp. 268-70.

[16]For the correspondence between the representation of history and the figurative imagination, see Hayden White's important work, *The Tropics of Discourse: Essays in Cultural Criticism* (Baltimore: Johns Hopkins Univ. Press, 1978).

[17]See, for example, the exchange between John Goodwin and Henry Ireton in Woodhouse, *Puritanism and Liberty*, pp. 166-67, and F. Smith Fussner, *The Historical Revolution: English Historical Writing and Thought, 1580-1640* (London: Routledge & Kegan Paul, 1962), p. 24.

[18]In *London and the Outbreak of the Puritan Revolution: City Government and National Politics, 1625-43* (Oxford: Oxford Univ. Press, 1961), pp. 262-65, Valerie Pearl describes the enthusiastic support, from both the city government and citizens, to fortify London and its suburbs, thereby turning the city into a military magazine which the parliamentary forces could draw upon at their need.

[19]For a discussion of this theme in Puritan thought, see Walzer, *Revolution of the Saints*, pp. 3, 10.

[20]T. Hill, *The Season of Englands Selfe-Reflection* (London, 1644), p. 25, quoted in John F. Wilson, *Pulpit in Parliament: Puritanism during the English Civil Wars 1640-1648* (Princeton: Princeton Univ. Press, 1969), p. 191. The idea of repairing the house of the nation becomes a metaphor for reforming the Reformation itself in a sermon by the Smectymnuan Edmund Calamy, *Englands Looking-Glasse* (London, 1642), p. 46. For a good discussion of the Puritan idea of temple-building, see John S. Coolidge, *The Pauline Renaissance in England: Puritanism and the Bible* (Oxford: Clarendon Press, 1970), pp. 23-54.

[21]Arthur B. Ferguson, *Clio Unbound: Perception of the Social and Cultural Past in Renaissance England* (Durham: Duke Univ. Press, 1979), p. 205.

[22]Walzer discusses the context of the Puritan idea of discipline in *Revolution of the Saints*, pp. 12, 149, 211, 219, 303.

[23]The design of Milton's temple may express, metaphorically, something of the age's Antinomian critique of uniformity: thus the participants at the Putney Debates sought "not the outward compulsive uniformity of religious or political forms but the inward voluntary unity of God's truth, upon which, it was hoped, they would all be able to agree" (Leo Solt, *Saints in Arms: Puritanism and Democracy in Cromwell's Army* [Stanford: Stanford Univ. Press, 1959], p. 58; cf. pp. 43, 51).

SEL 28 (1988)
ISSN 0039-3657

Milton's Urania: "The meaning, not the name I call"

STEVIE DAVIES AND WILLIAM B. HUNTER

The identity of the Muse invoked in *Paradise Lost* has given trouble to many thoughtful readers of Milton's poem. In the addresses at the opening of Books I and III, the Muse appears as some mysteriously unnamed divine being or beings; then at the next exordium, which opens Book VII, the poet unexpectedly identifies her as the pagan Muse Urania, warning the reader, however, that he is invoking "The meaning, not the name" itself. A feminine Muse is to be expected: male poets' Muses are so generically; but that she is Greek and "plays" with her Hebrew sister Wisdom before the Father has proved to be cryptic.[1] One of us has,[2] however, argued that the images associated with the hymn to light which opens Book III—a luminary and its emitted radiance; a fountain of water and the stream which flows from it—derive from a well-established tradition dating back to the primitive church which employed them to explain the relationship pertaining between Father and Son.[3] In invoking light, Milton was metaphorically invoking the Son to mediate the necessary inward illumination for the creation of the poem (as well, of course, as invoking physical light after the dark underworld of the first two books). Hunter's conclusion was that the Son himself was to be ultimately identified with Milton's Muse, and indeed was Urania herself, though such an interpretation clearly had to turn a blind eye to the implications of the explicitly feminine personification addressed by Milton.

Not surprisingly a number of critics have been unwilling to accept so basic a disregard on Milton's part for so central a fact of life, a disagreement most recently registered by the other of us who, in *The*

Dr. Stevie Davies, of Manchester, England, has recently published a feminist reading of Spenser, Shakespeare, and Milton, *The Idea of Woman in Renaissance Literature: The Feminine Reclaimed.*

Dr. William B. Hunter, of Houston, Texas, is editing for publication a collection of his essays concerned with Milton's writings.

Idea of Woman in Renaissance Literature: The Feminine Reclaimed,[4] argued that Milton's evolving focus on the feminine nature of his Muse radically affects the meaning and emotional suggestion of the divine as it is experienced by the reader of the poetry of *Paradise Lost.* The quality of the emotion surrounding Urania is intense and personal: her communication of light and insight takes the form of a haunting and humane love-relationship, as of mother to son (by analogy with Calliope and Orpheus [VII.32-39]). We now agree that these opposite interpretations may be reconciled by redefining Milton's Muse not as a single but as a multiple figure, manifested in different combinations and with differing emphases in the three invocations of Books I, III, and VII. (We shall consider separately the reason for omitting from this series the statement which opens Book IX.) These three invocations suggest to us the Christian Trinity. Each appeals to the whole threefold unity of God whilst the second and third each emphasize a different person of the Trinity. We see the poem as embodying a structural representation, in the sequence of its invocations, of the wholeness of the Godhead to which the meditating poet must call for inspiration. The second invocation has already been definitively identified with the second member, the Son, through its imagery. The first we shall identify with the triune Godhead, and the third with the Holy Spirit, who may be equated with Urania. Although in Christian tradition the Spirit is ordinarily understood as or assumed to be masculine, a substantial tradition exists which associates this person of the Trinity with the feminine gender and more expressly with a mother-principle in the deity. Study of implied bisexuality within the deity will naturally widen to involve reflection on Urania's relation with her sister Wisdom, and exploration of the nature and meaning of Wisdom, in Book VII. The poem's unfolding structure of prayer searches toward a Godhead whose ultimate nature cannot be known save through the mediation of its second and third members. Full assurance of illumination is not complete until the third member of the Trinity has been addressed and contemplated in the third invocation.

Over three quarters of a century ago Verity, recognizing the problem of identifying Milton's Muse, proposed that the poet was really invoking two muses in Book I, the first in lines 1 to 17 and the second in lines 17 to 26, a duality which he found again in the Hymn to Light which opens Book III.[5] Rather than a double, we see a threefold development in this passage, marked by transitions of grammar, *or, and,* each stage having the internal coherence of an allusive topography. Milton distinguishes not two persons but the three of the Christian Godhead in lines 6 to 10a, 10b to 16, and 17 to 22a.

In the first Milton is addressing the Father

> that on the secret top
> Of Oreb, or of Sinai, didst inspire
> That Shepherd, who first taught the chosen seed,
> In the beginning how the heavens and earth
> Rose out of chaos.

The shepherd is Moses, to whom Jahweh delivered the Law, as Milton will later recount (XII.235ff.) on Mount Sinai (in Exodus) or Horeb (in Deuteronomy). The speaker on the mountain had to be, in Christian terms, the Father; for as Milton would argue in *Christian Doctrine*, Old Testament texts like these "refer to the virtue and power of God the Father. For the Holy Spirit had not yet been given, and was not believed in,"[6] and would not appear in the Christian tradition until Pentecost. The fact that the Father is the ultimate source of creation[7] gives these lines a special relevance to the transmission of sacred poetry, for Moses (as the author of the Pentateuch) is presented as obtaining first-hand knowledge of the story which *Paradise Lost* must also tell: "In the beginning God created the heavens and the earth." The Father, too, would be Milton's own ultimate source of creative inspiration.

But for the Christian poet there is available no direct theophany comparable with that of Moses: Milton moves across the significant conjunction *or* to contemplate the Son as Mediator of his poem. The manner is tentative, conditional, as if the poem were thoughtfully searching out the compass and sources of its inspiration in a world whose vestigial holy places memorialize the locations of God's long-past acts of communication with mankind. The distinctions between the persons of the Trinity are not experienced as discrete boundaries, but as subtle transitions mysteriously integrating the perception of the Godhead, as the narrator's vision pauses on each in turn. Here, we discern the shift in Milton's focus to the Son by allusion to a new landscape which, read in terms of the Gospels, reveals localities of Christ's significant actions for the writer of *Paradise Lost*:

> or if Sion hill
> Delight thee more, and Siloa's brook that flowed
> Fast by the oracle of God: I thence
> Invoke Thy aid to my adventurous song.

Now the identifying locality is Sion hill and Siloa's brook. "Sion," or "Zion," has a variety of associations in the Old Testament which center upon Jerusalem, "the city of David," with its location on a hill and the dwelling place of Jahweh in its temple there (see, e.g., Isaiah 18:7). For Christians it also refers to that city but now as the goal of Christ's ministry and the scene of his death. Even more significantly here, Jerusalem's hill became traditionally identified as the location of the scene of the Last Supper and it in turn, from Acts 2:1-4, with the scene of Pentecost when the Spirit was finally revealed directly to mankind.[8] Siloa's brook refers explicitly to Christ's ministry. John 9:1-7 recounts the miracle he performed to heal a man who was congenitally blind, by covering his eyes with moistened clay, telling him, "Go, wash in the pool of Siloam," where the man was indeed healed. This association with Siloam identifies the Son as healer of maimed and impaired human nature, veiling Milton's personal prayer for amelioration of his own blindness. It is a plea to which he hauntingly and explicitly recurs in the prayer to light in the invocation to Book III. Here, at the pool of Siloam, the pain of the blind Milton meets the human pain of the atoning Christ. Healer and healed are deeply one, for

> Thee Sion and the flowery brooks beneath
> That wash thy hallowed feet, and warbling flow,
> Nightly I visit.
>
> (III.30-32)

The plangent allusion to the woman who washed Jesus' feet in Luke 7:37-38 gives a power reminiscent of pastoral elegy to the sacramental, merciful countryside walked both by Christ the Muse and the Christian poet in his search for a gracious language.

The first invocation's movement from Christ to the Holy Spirit at line 17, on the connective *and*, again involves association with locality, but this time the location is twofold: the place within (the heart) and the place without (the abyss):

> And chiefly thou O Spirit, that dost prefer
> Before all temples the upright heart and pure,
> Instruct me, for thou know'st; thou from the first
> Wast present, and with mighty wings outspread
> Dove-like sat'st brooding on the vast abyss
> And madest it pregnant.

Critics who dispute that the Holy Spirit is specifically invoked here ignore the fact that Milton alludes to 1 Corinthians 3:16: the human body is "the temple of the Spirit," which is uncontroversially agreed to signify the third person of the Godhead.[9] The passage also suggests the Christian tradition which identifies this Spirit with the dove which descended at the baptism of Jesus to which all four gospels testify,[10] as well as with the Spirit which "moved upon the face of the waters" in Genesis 1:2. The power of this passage springs from its reenactment of the Creation: it is the first such visual declaration of the divine creativity in a poem which, taking us as if cyclically back to origins, will unfold as a series of such accounts of births and originations. As such it stands as a source-image for the whole future of the poem, and bears a special relation to the poet who now initially seeks to charge himself with the creative force to initiate such a process. We think it essential to note here that the image of release of latent energy from the cosmos ("Dove-like . . . brooding") and the simultaneous discharge of potency into it ("madest it pregnant") figures an integration of female and male acts of creation. Given that there are no gender-identifying pronouns in the entire invocation, the symbolism associated with the Holy Spirit assumes a totality and dynamic fusion of gender oppositions which directly prefigures the Urania of Book VII, and is based on the incorporation of the Hermetic conception (set forth in the *Pimander*) of the bisexual Creator and the bisexual universe.[11] We note that the invocation to Book I is throughout characterized by the ambiguity of "thou" which Milton can legitimately address to any one of the three divine persons or to the unity of the Godhead, nicely reflecting the ambiguity of the plural Hebrew word translated by the singular "God" in Genesis 1:1, and allowing for simultaneous analysis and synthesis of the Trinity throughout the invocation.

In the exordium to Book III, the Son becomes the focus of aspiration, though again all three persons of the Trinity are suggested. The Son is a "bright effluence" of light, the poet consciously hesitating between the Being of Christian orthodoxy who is coeternal with the Father, and the one begotten in time ("First-born of all creation") of his own more radical thinking argued at length in chapter 5 of *Christian Doctrine*:

> Hail, holy Light, offspring of heaven first-born,
> Or of the eternal co-eternal beam
> May I express thee unblamed? since God is light,
> And never but in unapproached light
> Dwelt from eternity, dwelt then in thee,
> Bright effluence of bright essence increate.
> Or hear'st thou rather pure ethereal stream,
> Whose fountain who shall tell?

The beautiful symmetry with which Milton composes the relationship between Father and Son as source and issue, their indivisibility implied by the reiteration of the single radiant epithet, their difference by minimal consonant variation within the verbal music that articulates them both (*bright effluence . . . bright essence),* reinforces the integrity of the Trinity whilst appealing primarily to its second member. Later at line 19 Milton refers briefly to the yet-unnamed Urania, his "heavenly Muse," acknowledging her guidance in the darkness of Books I and II, and completing the threefold pattern of invocation in Book III.

"Descend from heaven, Urania": finally, in the last true invocation, in Book VII, Milton names and reflects upon the nature and heritage of his most immediate source of poetic inspiration. The opening words expressly echo the coming of the dove at the baptism of Jesus, "and he saw the Spirit of God descending like a dove, and lighting upon him" (Matthew 3:16). The emphasis throughout this invocation is profoundly feminine, recalling the feminine element in the divine creativity so powerfully figured in the dove-image of Book I. Despite Urania's pagan name and associations with astronomy which is to be a major subject of the book he is making ready to compose (as it stands in the first edition) and equally those with Venus Urania, Milton's insistence on "the meaning, not the name" is a clear directive to the reader to avert the eyes from Urania's classical origins. The clues to this meaning we believe to lie in Urania's association with her sister "eternal Wisdom" and in the double-gendered traditions of the Holy Spirit, but before we explore these we think it essential to recognize the function that Milton believed to be played by the Spirit in religious experience. Commenting on Matthew 12:31-32, the famous statement about the "unpardonable sin" against the Holy Spirit, Milton in the *Christian Doctrine* argues that these verses "must refer to that supreme and indeed, final illumination by which the Father gives us light through the Spirit" (VI:295): exactly what the several invocations pray for. Thus although the Spirit "cannot be a God" in Milton's view and accordingly cannot be "an object of invocation" (VI:295)[12] it is the vehicle for appeals to the Father and for the Father's responses, just as is the Son, "in whose name" Christians pray. Thus the poet prays to the Spirit as Urania here as he had prayed to the Son as light in Book III, not as the finally divine and responsive God but as the medium of communication with the Father and specifically as the vehicle through which the ineffable Father bestows his Grace upon an individual. For Milton the Father is completely transcendent and may be approached only by way of an intermediary whose assistance he beseeches in these invocations. Before the advent of the Son on earth and the Spirit at Pentecost, that agent was Moses; for "to God [there] is no access / Without mediator" (XII.239-40). In the Christian era the mediator is either the Son or the Spirit, to whom Milton prays respectively in the proems to Books III and VII.

The sequence of prayers for divine assistance ends at Book VII, for the apparently analogous passage which opens Book IX is, properly speaking, of a different kind. Superficially, it makes a neat equation with the others in terms of structural rhythm—I:III::VII:IX. But the 1667 edition of *Paradise Lost* indicates that this pattern of symmetries was not intrinsic to the original design, for there, of course, it opens Book VIII and the formula disappears. Rather, it seems analogous to the similarly exceptional but much briefer beginning of Book IV (III::IV:VII:VIII in 1667) in which Milton wishes for

> that warning voice, which he who saw
> The Apocalypse, heard cry in heaven aloud,
> Then when the dragon, put to second rout,
> Came furious down to be revenged on men,
> *Woe to the inhabitants on earth*! that now,
> While time was, our first parents had been warned
> The coming of their secret foe, and scaped
> Haply so scaped his mortal snare.

In a comparable way Book VIII (1667) opens on a general statement about the coming development of its subject, whereas I, III, and VII had addressed themselves to the divine directly and at once. Indeed, only at about line 20 of Book VIII (1667) does Milton move to the question of whether "answerable style I can obtain / Of my celestial patroness." Here the *if* is conditional only in the most nominal sense: he refers to the Muse in the third person throughout, and in a mood of peaceful acknowledgment that Grace has been freely and fully extended for the composition of the poem. Hence, the parallel designed in the original scheme was to follow the invocation of the Son in III with the wish for a warning voice in IV, and the invocation of Urania / The Spirit in VII with the regretted necessity of describing the Fall of Man in VIII (1667). The vestige of this original patterning remains as a subtle underlying focus of emphasis in the 1674 revision. Furthermore, Milton wrote no true invocation to Book VIII (1667), for in this final exordium he offers no prayer for heavenly support but rather observes of Urania that he experiences "Her nightly visitation *unimplored*"(line 22, emphasis added). The state of mind he describes is tantamount to that of daemonic possession. The active feminine inspiration (operating below the level of consciousness to "dictate" or breathe into him an "Easy . . . unpremeditated verse"[23-24]) is fully integrated into his receptive and listening mind, implying a synthesis of creative power analogous to that of the double-gendered Dove-Spirit of Book I. The Muse now posesses him as his automatic companion.

This feminine element in the divine creativity, which we have interpreted as the action of the Holy Spirit, is most fully explored by Milton in the invocation to Book VII, in relation to Urania and her "sister" Wisdom. In attributing to his classically named Muse a biblically authorized sister in the person of Wisdom, Milton is uniting Hellenistic and Hebraic elements in what appears to be a novel and unprecedented synthesis. The hesitant and conditional naming of Urania "by that name / If rightly thou art called" (VII.1-2), together with the poet's concern to detach signifier from signified, "meaning" from "name," at the very moment of invocation, which we have already noted, indicates the extent to which Milton is at one with Renaissance sacred poetry in rejecting the profane fabrications of the classical epic tradition, whilst laying claim to a redeemed version of the genre itself.[13] The figure of Wisdom with whom Urania is twinned derives, of course, from the Old Testament, specifically Proverbs and Job:

> Before the hills appeared, or fountain flowed,
> Thou with eternal Wisdom didst converse,
> Wisdom thy sister, and with her didst play
> In presence of the almighty Father, pleased
> With thy celestial song.
>
> (VII. 8-12)

But the figure is also elaborated in that considerable body of Hebrew material referred to as the Wisdom Literature, including the apocryphal *Ecclesiasticus* and *The Book of Wisdom (The Wisdom of Solomon)*. *The Book of Wisdom*, itself a reconciliation of the Jewish and Greek philosophies for the Jewish diaspora in Hellenistic Alexandria by a Hellenistic Jew, interlaces the scriptural concept of wisdom with the Greek *logos*, as indeed does the whole tradition of Alexandrian Christian Platonism. It is to this source in Alexandrian wisdom literature and philosophy that we primarily turn for clarification and elucidation of the veiled meanings presented by Milton in his own Hebraic-classical synthesis of the figures of Urania and Wisdom. We believe that while the Muse addressed by Milton in Book VII and contemplated in the exordium to Book IX

(1674) is a poetic refraction of the Holy Spirit, the companion figure of Wisdom symbolizes the creating Logos.

The Hebrew word for God's spirit used in the Old Testament is *Ruah,* connoting God's breath, or the motion of breathing. It is associated with creativity, enlightenment, God's manifesting himself within the Creation, and the gift of prophetic inspiration. *Ruah* is a feminine noun which, like other feminine gender terms concerning the attributes of Jahweh, focuses on God's immanence, closeness to and interaction with mankind.[14] The gender of this noun became a source of traditions outside the main line of Christianity according to which the Holy Spirit was imagined, prayed to and described as feminine—traditions which were in origin Gnostic, Platonist, or otherwise apocryphal. Thus, for instance, in Gnosticism the Third Person of the Trinity becomes God the Mother, and is identified with the figure of Wisdom;[15] and in the first-to-second century hymnbook, *The Odes of Solomon,* the Holy Spirit is always "she": "I rested on the Spirit of the Lord, / and she raised me on high."[16] Such identifications are not solely located amongst heretical sects, but may also be found within mainstream Patristic traditions. So, for instance, Clement of Alexandria represents the divine Love as a feminine and maternal principle within the Godhead: "As nurses nourish new-born children on milk, so do I also by the Word, the milk of Christ."[17]

The feminine Hebrew *Ruah* was translated in Greek by the neuter noun *pneuma,* which allowed latitude in interpretation and for priority of the original Hebrew term in indicating that the Spirit could be apprehended as composing or containing a feminine aspect of God.[18] In turn, *Ruah* was from earliest times associated with the feminine personification of Wisdom (*Hokmah*): Irenaeus, Basil, and Victorinus all make this association.[19] The Alexandrian tradition especially brought about an interpenetration of ideas between Hebraic and Hellenic communities of thought, such that the Hebrew *Hokmah* equated with *sophia,* and *sophia* in turn was associated both with the Torah and with the Logos.[20] On the basis of I Corinthians 1:24 which names "Christ the power of God, and the wisdom of God," an identification could be made to the effect that, in Clement's words, "we assert that Christ Himself is Wisdom."[21] In this intricate interlacing of concepts and personifications, the gender of the Hebrew and Greek terminology is crucial in focusing meaning and enabling chains of association and allusion to be evolved.

Throughout the Wisdom Literature itself, pneuma and *sophia* (or *Ruah* and *Hokmah*) are linked or twinned. *The Book of Wisdom* raises Wisdom to the highest rank as God's associate in creation, "artificer of all things" (7:22), an emanation rather than a mere creation (7:25), mate and "throne partner" of God (6:14, 9:4).[22] This glorification of Wisdom is so extreme as to suggest hypostatization (a status which, when taken as a typological image for New Testament revelation, well qualifies the personification to be a "sister" to the Spirit). At the same time, however, Wisdom's lovable and humanitarian character is stressed—"For wisdom is a spirit that loves man" (1:6) *(philanthropon)*—together with her accessibility to human nature. Her association with *pneuma* is a constant feature of *The Book of Wisdom*, often to the point of blurring the distinction between God's spirit and the spirit of wisdom:

> For the spirit of the Lord has filled the world.
>
> (1:7)

> I called, and the spirit of wisdom came to me *(pneuma sophias).*
>
> (7.7)

> And whatsoever is secret and manifest I learned to know,
> For Wisdom the artificer of all taught me.
> For there is in her a spirit quick of understanding, holy.
> (7:21-22)

Eusebius links this last line with the Holy Spirit.[23] Such a link with the Spirit and identification with the creating Word is confirmed by the imagery traditionally associated with Wisdom. Thus in *Ecclesiasticus* Wisdom declares:

> I am the word which was spoken by the Most High;
> it was I who covered the earth like a mist.
> My dwelling-place was in high heaven;
> my throne was a pillar of cloud.
>
> (24:3-4)[24]

Figurative language here takes on threefold suggestiveness for the Christian exegete: "I am the word" identifies the speaker with Christ as creative logos; "like a mist" (correponding with "a vapour of the power of God" in *The Book of Wisdom* [7:25]) connotes the divine breath (*Ruah*) and remembers Genesis, the spirit of God brooding on the waters (1:2) and the breath of life by which God vitalized Adam (2:7); "a pillar of cloud alludes to the feminine manifestation of God's glory as the *Shekinah*, Indwelling Presence."[25]

To turn from the Wisdom and Wisdom-related texts to Milton's invocation of Urania in Book VII of *Paradise Lost*, bearing in mind the association of Wisdom with the Spirit, is to recognize several points of close association. The first word, which is also the verb of invocation, is "Descend"; and Book VII gestures us down to earth, in a world whose narrative (though it treats of creation) is on the verge of the Fall. This invocation represents a search for inner comfort and security of knowledge and articulation within a world which is personally experienced as profoundly unsafe, in external terms ("On evil days . . . fallen" [26]). For the first time in the poem the Muse is called upon to descend into a name, as Christ descended into his kingship in Book V ("he the head / One of our number thus reduced becomes"[842-43]),[26] and as the Spirit descended in the form of a dove at Christ's baptism, to name him God's Son. Hence the invocation to Book VII, the beginning of the end, returns to a source in the maternal-paternal dove-spirit of Book I, which becomes in terms of this radiant symmetry the focus of mediation between Heaven and earth in the fallen world. But between the dove-spirit of Book I and its refraction in the image of Urania in book VII, an alteration of emphasis has taken place. The Spirit in Book I incorporates the feminine as part of an elemental, cosmic energy, fused with her opposite in a dynamic dualism of gender, as in Orphic creation-myths: but in Book VII the aspect of the feminine archetype detached and presented is that of sanctuary, lucid guide, and mediatrix, a sared version of Calliope in her motherhood of Orpheus (37-38), evoking the role of the Holy Spirit as Paraclete, "the Comforter which is the Holy Ghost" (John 14:26). The linked figures of Urania and Wisdom stress the lovability and accessibility of the almighty, so dominant in the Wisdom tradition *(philanthropon)* where God's mighty emanation and beloved companion also stands to man as "bride" (*Book of Wisdom* 8:2):

> She will come out to meet him like a mother;
> She will receive him like a young bride.
>
> (Ecclesiasticus 15:2)

Wisdom in the Heavenly Mind extends as wisdom in the mortal mind: the "artificer" (*technites, Book of Wisdom*, 8:6) which helped to frame the Creation is also capable of immanence in God's creatures. Indeed, Wisdom is herself represented as a *Shekinah* in Ecclesiasticus (24:4-10).[27] It is Christ's indwelling presence as mediation to the Father toward which the poet searches through the channel of Urania in her association with Wisdom. The poem declares its need at this critical halfway point to be what Henry More called "that Divine Sagacity . . . that wisdome which is peculiarly styled the Gift of God,"[28] which assimilates the seeking soul to the divine. The association of Urania with the Platonic Venus Urania, previously noted by Hunter,[29] reinforces this pressure in the third invocation toward assimilation, for Venus Urania is traditionally Venus the reconciler, forgiving disparities, uniting opposites, restoring the mundane to the celestial. Hence Milton's "heavenly born" Muse presents a medium between earth and heaven (as divine messenger, God's agent, advocate and revealer of language and vision, the traditional functions of the Holy Spirit); her compass is at once the heights and depths of creation, Heaven and the home-world in which, as Comforter, she is a nightly and morning visitor (VII: 28-30).

The most profound association of Urania and Wisdom in the hexaemeral Book VII is, of course, with creativity. This is so in a double, or indeed treble form, in that the invocation presents a tableau of the Creator-Father listening (before the Creation itself) to the creation of "celestial song" by his two daughters:

> Before the hills appeared, or fountain flowed,
> Thou with eternal Wisdom didst converse,
> Wisdom thy sister, and with her didst play
> In presence of the almighty Father, pleased
> With thy celestial song.
>
> (8-12)

Just as the previous two invocations addressed a specific person of the Trinity within the context of the whole Trinity, so the idyllic threefold tableau presented here incorporates the relationship between Father, Son, and Holy Spirit, in an image of family harmony. The text is faithful to the immediate source in Proverbs 8:22-31, where Wisdom is seen as the Father's accompaniment throughout all stages of the Creation, an offspring who is at once a source of daily joy to the Creator and one who shares his joy in his creation, especially the creation of mankind (30-31), suggesting Christ's love of and identification with man. Milton's emphasis on "play" and "song" enacted by the persons of Wisdom and Urania indicates their active participation in the Creation (as set forth, for instance, in *The Book of Wisdom*) and reinforces the connection of Urania with *pneuma* and of Wisdom with *sophia / logos*:

> And if understanding works,
> Who of all beings is a greater artificer than she?
>
> (8.6)

For Philo, Wisdom supplied the mother-principle in the divine creativity: "We shall be justified in calling the Creator the Father of of the world, and his knowledge its Mother, with whom God dwelt and whom he made mother of the Creation, yet not after the manner of a man."[30] On another occasion he asserted that "the daughter of God, Wisdom, is both masculine and feminine, inseminating and engendering in souls a desire to learn."[31] Through Milton's feminine, almost Spenserian allegorization of the Trinity as heavenly family, he is able to suggest, without theological perversity, the fulness and wholeness (bisexuality) of the creative act.

The dogmatic and heretical insistence on the inferiority of the Holy Spirit which is everywhere found in *Christian Doctrine* is not specified in *Paradise Lost*, though it may be assumed in the poem. The allusion to Wisdom as "eternal Wisdom" in Book VII as against a "born" status for Urania (IX.7) may bring to mind the assertion in *Christian Doctrine* that "The Holy Spirit . . . was created . . . maybe before the foundations of the world were laid, but after the Son, to whom he is far inferior, was made" (VI, p. 298). This emphasis helps to consolidate the identification of Wisdom in *Paradise Lost* as the Word, which will issue out to create the world in the course of the same book (VII.216-42), accompanied by the Spirit who, performing his (secondary) role of incubating the Creation, leads the reader's mind inevitably back to the Spirit's "Dove-like . . . brooding" of the first invocation, and to Genesis 1:2:

> Thus God the heaven created, thus the earth,
> Matter unformed and void: darkness profound
> Covered the abyss: but on the watery calm
> His brooding wings the spirit of God outspread,
> And vital virtue infused, and vital warmth
> Throughout the fluid mass.
>
> (VII. 232-37)

This sacred duality of Word and Spirit divides between itself the processes of divine creativity: the transformation of chaos into cosmos through which the Word circumscribes and the Spirit incubates creation presents an elemental extension of the artistic energy described as orchestrated by Wisdom and Urania in "celestial song," in the invocation. The same pattern of creation is imitated by the sacred poet constructing the design and vitalizing the matter of his poem. The problem of turning the original "Matter unformed" into form, and casting light on the "darkness profound" of the "abyss" of fallen human experience, is mitigated for Milton by appeal through the channel of the Holy Spirit in her maternal aspect to the wisdom of Christ the Word in its intimate union with Omniscience, "Thou with eternal Wisdom didst converse, / Wisdom thy sister." It is this divine conversation to which Urania gives special and ready access. By the time of the fourth exordium, we think that Milton had attained such profound assurance of the continuity and audibility of his inspiration as to have reached a condition identifiable as the state of (poetic) Grace. The epic abdicates at this point its generic requirement of external support: the sacred source is fully internalized, the creating human author, confirmed in the power of his inner voice, to all intents and purposes independent. The "unimplored" Muse comes to offer herself as the free gift of God in the terms Milton's *Christian Doctrine* associates with the Holy Spirit in its descent on Christ at his baptism: "a sort of representation of the Father's supreme love and affection for the Son" (VI, p. 284). The Spirit affiliates the poet as a legitimate and justified son of the creating Father. If the exordia to *Paradise Lost* are, as we believe, real prayers incorporated by Milton in the body of his poem, the refusal of the final exordium to invoke at all represents a silent recognition that those prayers have already been answered, in full, through the mediation of the Comforter: "Howbeit when he, the Spirit of truth, is come, he will guide you into all truth: for he shall not speak of himself; but whatsoever he shall hear, that shall he speak; and he will show you things to come" (John 16:13).

NOTES

[1]See, e.g., the entries "Muse, Milton's" and "Urania" in *A Milton Encyclopedia*, ed. William B. Hunter, 9 vols. (Lewisburg: Bucknell Univ. Press, 1978-83), 5:157, and 8:106. Citations of Milton's poetic texts throughout are to the edition of Alastair Fowler and John Carey in *The Poems of John Milton* (London: Longmans Green, 1968).

[2]William B. Hunter, "Milton's Urania," *SEL* 4(1964):35-42, rpt. rev. in *Bright Essence: Studies in Milton's Theology*, ed. William B. Hunter et al. (Salt Lake City: Univ. of Utah Press, 1971), pp. 149-56.

[3]Jack Adamson independently reached the same conclusion. See *Bright Essence*, pp. 54-56.

[4]Stevie Davies, *The Idea of Woman in Renaissance Literature: The Feminine Reclaimed* (Sussex: Harvester Press, and Lexington: Univ. of Kentucky Press, 1986), pp. 119-21, 187.

[5]A. W. Verity, ed., *Paradise Lost* (Cambridge: Cambridge Univ. Press, 1910). Harris Francis Fletcher thought there is "ample support" for such an interpretation but doubted that any useful end could be "served by the plurality of muses involved." He concluded that "Milton conceived of his muse, not as now one, now another muse, but as one Muse, appearing and appealing under different aspects," though he did not clarify what these aspects were. *Milton's Semitic Studies and Some Manifestations of Them in his Poetry* (Chicago: Univ. of Chicago Press, 1926), pp. 118-121.

[6]*Christian Doctrine*, in *The Complete Prose Works of John Milton*, gen. ed. Don M. Wolfe, 8 vols. (New Haven: Yale Univ. Press, 1953-82), 6:283.

[7]See *Christian Doctrine*, p. 300.

[8]See also Milton's account in XII.485ff. The analogy of the hill where this gift of the Spirit from the Father took place, to the mountain where Jahweh had given the Law to Moses, is worthy of remark. As *The Interpreter's Dictionary of the Bible*, George Arthur Buttrick, gen. ed., 4 vols. (New York: Abingdon Press, 1962), observes s.v. "Zion," "the confusion between Davidic Zion and Christian Zion prevailed until the first decade of this century."

[9]See, e.g., Douglas Bush, ed., *Complete Poetical Works* (Boston: Houghton Mifflin, 1965), *Paradise Lost*, I.17n.; and, most recently, Mindele Anne Treip in *"Descend from Heaven Urania": Milton's "Paradise Lost" and Raphael's Cycle in the Stanza della Segnatura*, ELS Monograph no. 35 (1985), pp. 50ff., who thinks that the vagueness and shifting meanings of the term "Spirit" are exploited in *Paradise Lost* so as to blur into a "felt unity."

[10]E.g., Matthew 3:16. See *Christian Doctrine*, p. 284.

[11]See *Pimander*, 8-9, which ascribes the Creation to the action of "the breath-like Word which moved upon the face of the water. / And the first Mind,—that Mind which is Life and Light,—being bisexual, gave birth to another Mind, a Maker of things," and 14-15, in Hermes Trismegistus, *Hermetica*, ed. Walter Scott, 4 vols. (Oxford: Clarendon Press, 1924-36), 1:119, 121-23. Fowler also notes, in his edition of *Paradise Lost,* Milton's debt to "the Hermetic doctrine that God is both masculine and feminine," *PL* I/ 17-22n. For fuller treatment of this theme see *The Feminine Reclaimed,* pp. 198ff.

[12]See Maurice Kelley, *This Great Argument* (Princeton: Princeton Univ. Press, 1941), pp. 109-11.

[13]Du Bartas in *L'Uranie* refers to the strictly allegorical status of "la Muse, qu'on appelle / Du nom du ciel vouté," lines 249-50 in *The Works of Guillaume 10 vols. (London: William Heinemann, Loeb Classical Library, 1927-53), VIII,* Univ. of North Carolina Press, 1938), 2:184.

In *The Divine Weeks and Works,* he practises a twofold invocation which distinguishes between the Muse and the Father, using the Muse as an intermediate channel of Divinity, "Devinely-humane" (I. 135), who is not Sacred Light but something more dubious and low (II. 367, IV. 1), a near-equal whom he may hector and harrangue ("Soft, soft [my Darling]," II. 387). Tasso opens *Gerusalemme Liberata* with a statement of dissociation from the profane Muse "that . . . with fading baies / Deckest thy brow by th' Heliconian spring," I.2 (trans. E. Fairfax [Oxford: Oxford Univ. Press, 1981]).

[14]For the significance of the gender of *Ruah,* see Alasdair I. C. Heron, *The Holy Spirit: The Holy Spirit in the Bible, in the History of Christian Thought, and Recent Theology* (Philadelphia: Westminster Press, 1983), pp. 3-38; Virginia R. Mollenkott, *The Divine Feminine: The Biblical Imagery of God as Female* (New York: Crossroad Publishing, 1983), pp. 35, 36-39; Raphael Patai, *The Hebrew Goddess* (New York: Ktav Publishing House, 1967); D. L. Gelpi, *The Divine Mother: A Trinitarian Theology of the Holy Spirit* (Lanham, Md.: Univ. Press of America, 1984), pp. 11-12, 216.

[15]See Elaine Pagels, *The Gnostic Gospels* (London: Penguin), 1979), pp. 49-67.

[16]*The Odes of Solomon,* XXXVI, in *The Apocryphal Old Testament,* ed. H. F. D. Sparks (Oxford: Oxford Univ. Press, 1984).

[17]Clement of Alexandria, *Paedogogus.* He goes on, "Hence seeking is called sucking, for to those babes that seek the Word, the Father's breasts of love supply milk," in *The Ante-Nicene Fathers. Translations of the Writings of the Fathers down to A. D. 325,* ed. A. Roberts and J. Donaldson, 10 vols. (Grand Rapids: Eerdmans, 1971), 2:218, 221.

[18]See Pagels, p. 52.

[19]See Gelpi, p. 217.

[20]Succintly outlined by Samuel Sandmel in *Philo of Alexandria, An Introduction* (Oxford: Oxford Univ. Press, 1979), pp. 98-99.

[21]Clement of Alexandria, *The Stromata,* Bk. VI, ch. 7, in *The Ante-Nicene Fathers,* p. 494. Basil echoes these ideas in his *On the Spirit.*

[22]The edition cited throughout is *The Book of Wisdom,* trans. Joseph Reider (New York: Harper, 1957).

[23]Eusebius, *Praeparatio Evangelica,* VII. xii. 4 and XI. xiv. 4, in *La Préparation Evangélique,* ed. J. Sirinelli and E. des Places (Paris: Editions du Cerf, 1974). Eusebius's variant on *Estin gar en aute pneuma* is *Estin gar aute pneuma.*

[24]The edition cited is *Ecclesiasticus,* ed. John G. Snaith (Cambridge: Cambridge Univ. Press, 1974).

[25]On the significance of the *Shekinah,* see Mollenkott, pp. 36-43, and Michael Lieb, *The Poetics of the Holy: A Reading of "Paradise Lost"* (Chapel Hill: Univ. of North Carolina Press, 1981), ch. 10.

[26]For extended treatment of this theme see Stevie Davies, *Images of Kingship in "Paradise Lost": Milton's Politics and Christian Liberty* (Columbia: Univ. of Missouri Press, 1983), pp. 140-50, 175-79.

[27]See Harris Fletcher, *Milton's Semitic Studies,* pp. 115-25, for discussion of Milton's Muse as a version of the Semitic *Shekinah.* We think Fletcher's emphasis is misplaced, in view of the depth of Milton's New Testament commitment.

[28]Henry More, "Preface General," Section 7, in *Philosophical Writings,* in Aharon Lichtenstein, *Henry More: The Rational Theology of a Cambridge Platonist* (Cambridge, Mass.: Harvard Univ. Press, 1962), pp. 64-65.

[29]In "Milton's Muse," *Bright Essence,* pp. 151-53.

[30]Philo, *De Ebrietate,* 30, in *Philo,* trans. F. H. Coleman and G. H. Whitaker, 10 vols. (London: William Heinemann, Loeb Classical Library, 1927-53), VIII, 332.

[31]Philo, *De Fuga et Inventione,* 52, in *Philo,* V, 26.

SEL 28 (1988)
ISSN 0039-3657

Milton's Creation of Eve

ANNE FERRY

The critical debate referred to in the 1960s as "the Milton controversy" has disappeared so completely from current discussions of his poetry that it has to be recovered for students of Milton now as a piece of distant literary history.[1] His poetry has not ceased to provoke debate, however. A newer controversy has since come to occupy the attention and stir the various sympathies of writers about Milton. The issues of this debate have recently been explored in a helpfully inclusive essay by William Shullenberger called "Wrestling with the Angel: *Paradise Lost* and Feminist Criticism."[2] His discussion summarizes and responds to the attacks on Milton's treatment in *Paradise Lost* of Eve and her marriage to Adam which have been written by feminist critics in approximately the last fifteen years.[3] Central to the debate, as is pointed out in a recent article by Douglas Anderson, is whether the language of hierarchy in *Paradise Lost* can be assumed to prove that Milton "simply believed in the sexual subordination of women."[4]

The issue of what constitutes belief is of course far too complex to be explored here, but one tenet of faith we can be simply sure that Milton held with passionate conviction is that the Bible is a record of divinely inspired truth which it is the Christian's duty to interpret and follow, not to contradict or ignore. When we question Milton's ways of treating the material of *Paradise Lost,* we therefore have to take into account the givens, the fixed points of interpretation that he was unavoidably compelled to work with or to work around. In his presentation of Eve and her marriage to Adam, then, we have to think about what was dictated to Milton by their story in Genesis and its interpretations in the New Testament, how he shaped what he could not change, what decisions he made where some choices were allowed him.

Anne Ferry, Professor of English at Boston College, is the author of *Milton's Epic Voice, Milton and the Miltonic Dryden, All in War with Time, The "Inward" Language,* and a book about sixteenth-century poetic language, *The Art of Naming,* to be published in 1988.

Considering the account in Genesis, stripping away for present purposes many centuries of theological commentary and artistic representation known to Milton, the opening three chapters narrate several events to be taken into account in his presentation of Eve.[5] These episodes in the story of the first man and woman were considered to be factual history by all Englishmen when *Paradise Lost* was written (with the possible exception of Hobbes, who at least pretended to believe they were historically true). As sacred history the events in Genesis could not be changed in a telling of the story, nor could they be wholly ignored. An index of these fundamental, unalterable facts is given in the summaries placed before the chapters in the stoutly protestant Geneva Bible: God "createth man and giueth him rule ouer all creatures"; "He createth the woman"; "Mariage is ordeined"; "The woman seduced by the serpent"; "Enticeth her housband to sinne"; "They thre are punished"; "Man is cast out of paradise."[6] This is the unalterable outline elaborated in the actual chapters with some details which were also fixed points for Milton to work with or to work around.

Let us consider first how Milton used the details in the earlier parts of the story, according to which Eve was not only created after Adam, but was made for him, because God said: "It is not good that the man shulde be him selfe alone: I wil make an helpe mete for him" (Genesis 2:18). Eve was not only made for Adam, but from him: "Therefore the Lord God caused an heauie slepe to fall vpon the man; & whiles he slept, he toke one of his rybbe, and closed vp the flesh in steade thereof. And the rybbe which the Lord God had taken from the man, made he a woman, and broght her to the man" (Genesis 2:21-22). From this origin the bond of marriage was established: "Then the man said, This now is bone of my bones, and flesh of my flesh. She shalbe called woman, because she was taken out of man. Therefore shal man leaue his father and his mother, and shal cleaue to his wife, and they shalbe one flesh" (Genesis 2:23-24).

Milton of course assumes this order of events and incorporates all of them into his narrative. His presentation of them is also dictated by the fact that the history recounted in Genesis was interpreted in the epistles of St. Peter and St. Paul. As parts of the New Testament these passages were also held by all Christians to be divinely inspired truth which could not be ignored as, for instance, a Protestant with sympathies like Milton's could choose to avoid the misogynistic opinions of St. Jerome. To Puritans especially the Apostle to the Gentiles provided the crucial model of a Christian reading the letter of the Old Testament in the light of the spirit.[7] His pronouncements and those of St. Peter had inescapable authority in interpretations of the story of Adam and Eve, and therefore of the divinely ordained relationship between man and woman. For this reason their sayings were included in all kinds of writing about marriage, and were quoted in the English service solemnizing holy matrimony in the sixteenth and seventeenth centuries. Milton was married according to this rite in 1642.

The prayer book follows the order of creation in first addressing man: "Heare also what Saint Peter the Apostle of Christ, which was himself a married man, saith unto them that are married: Yee husbands, dwell with your wives according to knowledge, giving honour unto the wife, as unto the weaker vessell, and as heires together of the grace of life, so that your prayers be not hindred."[8] Next in the wedding service, St. Paul's words are called to the attention of women:

> Yee women, submit your selves unto your owne husbands, as unto the Lord: For the husband is the wives head, even as Christ is the head of the Church, and hee is also the Saviour of the whole body.
>
> Therefore as the Church or Congregation is subject unto Christ, so likewise let the wives also be in subjection unto their own husbands in all things. And againe hee saith, Let the wife reverence her husband. . . . And Saint Paul giveth you this short lesson: Ye wives, submit your selves unto your owne husbands, as it is convenient in the Lord.

Another authoritative passage which figures in discussions of the divinely appointed relation between man and woman is not quoted in the wedding ceremony because it is about conduct in church, not in marriage, but Milton follows common practice in applying it to Adam and Eve. The text is from the first epistle to the Corinthians:

> For a man oght not to couer his head: for asmuche as he is the image and glorie of God: but the woman is the glorie of the man.
>
> For the man is not of the woman, but the woman of the man.
>
> For the man was not created for the womans sake: but the woman for the mans sake.
>
> . . . .
>
> Doeth not nature it self teache you, that if a man haue long heere, it is a shame vnto him?
>
> But if a woman haue long heere, it is a praise vnto her: for her heere is giuen her for a couering.
>
> (1 Corinthians 11:7-15)

The events in Genesis are the necessary materials for Milton's story; these texts from the New Testament are their most authoritative interpretation. The ways they assume the facts of Eve's creation to define her nature and place as distinct from Adam's are echoed in a number of passages in *Paradise Lost,* beginning with the opening description of Adam and Eve in Book IV. They are first described together:

> Two of far nobler shape erect and tall,
> Godlike erect, with native Honour clad
> In naked Majestie seemd Lords of all,
> And worthie seemd, for in thir looks Divine
> The image of thir glorious Maker shon,
> Truth, wisdome, Sanctitude severe and pure,
> Severe but in true filial freedom plac't;
> Whence true autoritie in men.
>
> (IV.288-95)[9]

Then the narrator begins to differentiate between Adam and Eve:

> though both
> Not equal, as thir sex not equal seemd;
> For contemplation hee and valour formd,
> For softness shee and sweet attractive Grace,
> Hee for God only, shee for God in him:
> His fair large Front and Eye sublime declar'd
> Absolute rule; and Hyacinthin Locks
> Round from his parted forelock manly hung
> Clustring, but not beneath his shoulders broad:
> Shee as a vail down to the slender waste
> Her unadorned golden tresses wore
> Dissheveld, but in wanton ringlets wav'd
> As the Vine curles her tendrils, which impli'd
> Subjection, but requir'd with gentle sway,
> And by her yielded, by him best receivd,
> Yielded with coy submission, modest pride,
> And sweet reluctant amorous delay.
>
> (IV.295-311)

Many details here echo the New Testament readings of the events in Genesis. Once Adam and Eve are distinguished from each other by the wording "though both / Not equal," they are then presented in the order of their creation, with Adam first, expressing his superior dignity: "Hee for God only." The husband's position as head of the wife is represented by Adam's broad forehead and "Eye sublime" which "declar'd / Absolute rule." Eve's secondary creation, "shee for God in him," is reflected by her secondary place in the passage. Her nature as the weaker creature is expressed in the comparison of her ringlets to a vine which "impli'd / Subjection" to the husband who must support her with his strength, although the comparison had other suggestions, recalling Psalm 128 which was used as part of the marriage ceremony in the prayer book: "Thy wife shall be as the fruitfull Vine: upon the wals of thine house." Even the different hair-styles of Adam and Eve follow the prescriptions of St. Paul, signifying that the man should not hide the image of God by covering his head, whereas the woman should veil hers in token of submission to her Lord who is her husband.

Yet even in this passage there are slight modifications of the Pauline interpretation, which foreshadow much more radical treatment of biblical materials to be shown in later parts of the poem. Here, for instance, Milton begins by describing Adam and Eve in identical terms, both radiantly displaying "The image of thir glorious Maker," whereas St. Paul says that the man "is the image and glorie of God; but the woman is the glorie of the man." The Pauline distinction is traditionally imposed, for instance, in the headings summarizing the first and second chapters in the King James version of Genesis. They say of Adam's creation that God made "Man in the Image of God," but call Eve's merely "The making of woman."[10] Milton, however, dims this distinction in the beginning of the passage. He does so again in the line most often quoted to prove his interest in the subordination of women: "Hee for God only, shee for God in him."[11] Milton's rewording here brings Eve closer to her divine creator than St. Paul's formula that man "is the image and glorie of God: but the woman is the glorie of the man." At the end of the passage is another instance where Milton echoes but adjusts the effect of St. Paul's words, here the imperative that women "be in subjection unto their own husbands in all things." Milton says that Eve's vine-like ringlets "impli'd / Subjection, but requir'd with gentle sway, / And by her yielded, by him best receivd." Eve's subjection has its own authority to *require* gentleness. The balance of phrasing in "by her yielded, by him best receivd" also suggests a gracious reciprocity, granting Eve dignified choice in a courteous exchange. Yet even more striking than what is said here is what is not said, for in the whole of Milton's important introductory description of Adam and Eve there are two telling omissions. There is not the slightest echo here either of the passage in Genesis declaring that Eve was formed from Adam's rib, or of God's statement that Eve was created to make a "helpe mete for" Adam.

The pointedness of Milton's silence on those two episodes in this introductory description can be measured by contrast with a sermon preached by John Donne at an actual wedding ceremony about twenty years before Milton's first marriage. Donne weaves into his sermon the biblical passages quoted in the prayer book rite itself, echoing Genesis, St. Peter, and St. Paul when he addresses women with reminders presumably intended specifically for the bride on this happy occasion. Donne enjoins wives to remember

> that *they are the weaker vessell,* and *that Adam was not deceived* but *the woman was* . . . and it implies a weaknesse in the woman, and an occasion of soupling her to that just estimation of her self, *That she will be content to learn in silence with all subjection.* . . . that she is . . . but a Help: and no body values his staffe, as he does his legges. . . . Since she was taken out of his side, let her not depart from his side, but shew her self so much as she was made for, *Adjutorium,* a Helper.[12]

By contrast with Donne's archetypal wife—weaker vessel, temptress, dispensable staff or rib—Milton's Eve is first introduced as a regal figure sharing with Adam in "Majestie" signifying their joint position as "Lords of all."

Donne's sermon can be a measure of Milton's rendering of the same authoritative biblical passages in still other ways, for instance by contrast with the earliest lines where Milton does refer to Eve's formation from Adam's rib at the end of her first speech, where she tells the story of her creation. There she repeats Adam's earliest address to her, echoing the biblical words that consecrated their marriage. We know we are to approve Adam's unfallen speech, which teaches Eve the gracious yielding praised in the narrator's introduction of her. Eve remembers Adam's words:

> Return faire *Eve,*
> Whom fli'st thou? whom thou fli'st, of him thou art,
> His flesh, his bone; to give thee being I lent
> Out of my side to thee, neerest my heart
> Substantial Life, to have thee by my side
> Henceforth an individual solace dear;
> Part of my Soul I seek thee, and thee claim
> My other half: with that thy gentle hand
> Seisd mine, I yielded.
>
> (IV.481-89)

Here Eve's origin from the side nearest Adam's heart makes her part of his soul, not as Donne says, an expendable staff to which any man would prefer his own legs. She is by his side as "an individual solace dear," not as a subordinate forbidden to leave the place where she is meant to serve him.

Milton expands on the other biblical text avoided in his introductory description of Adam and Eve, the making of Eve as a "helpe mete for" Adam, in the story of Adam's creation which he tells to the Angel Raphael in Book VIII. Adam's account builds on the episode where God brings the creatures to man to receive their names, among whom "founde he not an helpe mete for him" (Genesis 2:20). Milton makes this an occasion for Adam to tell God what sort of mate he seeks, what ideal he has of marriage. As in Genesis, Adam finds no fit consort among the creatures presented to him, for reasons which Milton allows him to elaborate:

> Among unequals what societie
> Can sort, what harmonie or true delight?
> . . . .
> Of fellowship I speak
> Such as I seek, fit to participate
> All rational delight, wherein the brute
> Cannot be human consort.
>
> (VIII.383-92)

Adam desires "By conversation with his like to help, / Or solace his defects" (VIII.418-19). He wants what he calls "Social communication" (VIII.429), impossible with the creatures because

> I by conversing cannot these erect
> From prone, nor in thir wayes complacence find.
>
> (VIII.432-33)

We know that Adam has the right idea of marriage because God praises him for rejecting the creatures to seek a mate who, God says, bears

> My image, not imparted to the Brute,
> Whose fellowship therefore unmeet for thee.
>
> (VIII.441-42)

God then explains the test that Adam has just passed:

I, ere thou spak'st,
Knew it not good for Man to be alone,
And no such companie as then thou saw'st
Intended thee, for trial onely brought,
To see how thou could'st judge of fit and meet:
What next I bring shall please thee, be assur'd,
Thy likeness, thy fit help, thy other self,
Thy wish exactly to thy hearts desire.

(VIII.444-51)

What Adam wants in a mate is what God brings him in Eve—which both God and Adam in this dialogue define by terms like "societie," "fellowship," "conversation," "Social communication," "companie." This kind of union cannot take place, they say, between "unequals," but only between human beings both made in the image of God and therefore "fit to participate" in "All rational delight." The solace this union will offer to alleviate human loneliness is expressed in "conversation," which meant the whole conduct of life, but also specifically mutual speech.[13] The emphasis Milton gives to his ideal makes a pointed contrast between the mate God brings to Adam and the traditional ideal of wifely behavior preached by Donne to the bride, "*That she will be content to learn in silence with all subjection.*"

Adam's definition of marriage in this scene extends the pattern shown earlier in the narrator's introduction of Adam and Eve, and in Eve's retelling of Adam's first words to her. Yet here Milton more radically reshapes or works around the New Testament texts which constitute the most authoritative interpretation of Eve's nature and place as given in Genesis. Milton used these parts of the story—the naming of the creatures and the making of Eve—to put into the mouths of God and Adam a view of woman and marriage different from St. Peter's and St. Paul's, but very close to his own in his divorce tracts, written twenty years earlier to argue his radical view that divorce should be granted not solely for sexual misconduct.[14] Milton's opposing position was that marriage should be dissolved when there is between husband and wife none of what he calls in the tracts "cherfull conversation," "meet and happy conversation," "cheerfull society," "conjugall fellowship" with a "fit conversing soul," when there is no "fit union of their souls . . . where no correspondence is of the minde."[15] Passages in the divorce tracts show the same pattern that can be seen in the parts of *Paradise Lost* so far discussed: Milton's efforts to work with but also to work around the facts given in Genesis and their interpretations in the New Testament.

One passage from *Tetrachordon* can illustrate these efforts. Its movement parallels the first description of Adam and Eve in *Paradise Lost* by the way it accepts the authority of St. Paul's pronouncements but adjusts them to conform more comfortably to a different sense of man and woman in marriage. Milton's explicit subject is one commonly discussed in this period, whether Eve as well as Adam was made in the image of God:

> But *St. Paul* ends the controversie by explaining that the woman is not primarily and immediatly the image of God, but in reference to the man. *The head of the woman*, saith he, I *Cor.* 11. *is the man: he the image and glory of God, she the glory of the man:* he not for her, but she for him. Therefore his precept is, *Wives be subject to your husbands as is fit in the Lord, Coloss.* 3. 18. *In every thing, Eph.* 5. 24.[16]

Here Milton defers to Pauline authority, but then he immediately begins to work around it or away from it as the passage continues: "Neverthelesse man is not to hold her as a servant, but receives her into a part of that empire which God proclaims him to, though not equally, yet largely, as his own image and glory: for it is no small glory to him, that a creature so like him, should be made subject to him." In that sentence Milton sounds like the narrator of *Paradise Lost* who declares that Adam and Eve are "not equal" while at the same time he has made Eve a regal figure reigning in "Majestie" with Adam as "Lords of all," rather than declaring her a help or a missing rib. As the prose passage continues Milton's next sentence moves still farther from the Pauline definition of marriage as the subjection of wives to the absolute rule of their husbands according to the divinely established order of nature recorded in Genesis: "Not but that particular exceptions may have place, if she exceed her husband in prudence and dexterity, and he contentedly yeeld, for then a superior and more naturall law comes in, that the wiser should govern the lesse wise, whether male or female."

The distance between Milton's position here and traditional interpretations of Genesis can again be measured by Donne's marriage sermon in a passage where he also contemplates the exceptions when a wife may seem to be her husband's superior:

> I know there are some glasses stronger then some earthen vessels, and some earthen vessels stronger then some wooden dishes, some of the weaker sexe, stronger in fortune, and in counsell too, then they to whom God hath given them; but

> yet let them not impute that in the eye nor eare of the world, nor repeat it to their own hearts, with such a dignifying of themselves, as exceeds the quality of a Helper. S. *Hierome* shall be her Remembrancer, She was not taken out of the *foot*, to be troden upon, nor out of the *head*, to be an overseer of him; but out of *his side*, where she weakens him enough, and therefore should do all she can, to be a Helper.[17]

Donne's sentences illuminate Milton's efforts by contrast. For when Donne is confronted with actual experience which seems to contradict biblical views of woman's nature and place, he shapes the exception into a moral lesson supporting the authority, whereas what Milton does at the end of this passage, and in Adam's descriptions of the fit partner he seeks in marriage, is to reshape or work around the biblical texts inimical to his own deeply felt position about marriage.

The passages from *Paradise Lost* discussed up to this point, all treating events before the fall, show consistent efforts by Milton to acknowledge scriptural definitions of woman's nature and place, while elevating Eve above them to a stature that would make her a fit companion for Adam in marital conversation.[18] Yet there is hardly any disruptive conflict or confusion between his presentation of Adam and Eve and his use of biblical passages until the end of the scene where Adam tells the story of his creation and marriage at the close of Book VIII. Just before Milton begins to recount the temptation and fall of Eve and then Adam, he makes Adam describe to the Angel Raphael his feelings about his consummated marriage:

> here passion first I felt,
> Commotion strange, in all enjoyments else
> Superiour and unmov'd, here onely weake
> Against the charm of Beauties powerful glance.
> Or Nature faild in mee, and left some part
> Not proof enough such Object to sustain,
> Or from my side subducting, took perhaps
> More then enough; at least on her bestow'd
> Too much of Ornament, in outward shew
> Elaborate, of inward less exact.
> For well I understand in the prime end
> Of Nature her th' inferiour, in the mind
> And inward Faculties.
>
> (VIII.530-42)

Up to this point Adam defers to the facts of Genesis as St. Paul interprets them, but then he goes on to admit their discord with his feelings for Eve:

> yet when I approach
> Her loveliness, so absolute she seems
> And in her self compleat, so well to know
> Her own, that what she wills to do or say,
> Seems wisest, vertuousest, discreetest, best;
> All higher knowledge in her presence falls
> Degraded, Wisdom in discourse with her
> Looses discount'nanc't, and like folly shewes;
> Authority and Reason on her waite,
> As one intended first, not after made
> Occasionally; and to consummate all,
> Greatness of mind and nobleness thir seat
> Build in her loveliest, and create an awe
> About her, as a guard Angelic plac't.
>
> (VIII.546-59)

We are meant to understand that Adam is not valuing Eve rightly here. He should not admire her "As one intended first, not after made" because that view contradicts sacred history recounted in Genesis. He should not think that "Authority and Reason on her waite" because that image does not coincide with interpretations of her nature and place in the New Testament. Just as we expect, the listening Angel reproves Adam for allowing passion to distort his vision. Raphael preaches St. Paul's view of woman's relation to man:

> Accuse not Nature, she hath don her part;
> Do thou but thine, and be not diffident
> Of Wisdom, she deserts thee not, if thou
> Dismiss not her, when most thou needst her nigh,
> By attributing overmuch to things
> Less excellent, as thou thyself perceav'st.
> For what admir'st thou, what transports thee so,
> An outside? fair no doubt, and worthy well
> Thy cherishing, thy honouring, and thy love,
> Not thy subjection: weigh with her thy self;
> Then value: Oft times nothing profits more
> Then self esteem, grounded on just and right
> Well manag'd; of that skill the more thou know'st,
> The more she will aknowledge thee her Head,
> And to realities yield all her shows.
>
> (VIII.561-75)

If the dialogue between Adam and the Angel ended here, it would simply conform to the readings of this scene usually given in critical discussions of the poem.[19] Adam's speech could be said to foreshadow his fall, when his passion for Eve betrays him, while the Angel's reply would constitute a just and timely reminder of Eve's true nature and place by recalling events of Genesis in language echoing St. Paul. Yet Milton chose not to end the dialogue with this reproof by the Angel. He allows Adam to reply to it with what is not an apology or an excuse, but a correction of the Angel's view of human marriage. Adam, only "half abash't," restates his feelings for Eve:

> Neither her out-side formd so fair, nor aught
> In procreation common to all kindes
> (Though higher of the genial Bed by far,
> And with mysterious reverence I deem)
> So much delights me as those graceful acts,
> Those thousand decencies that daily flow
> From all her words and actions mixt with Love
> And sweet compliance, which declare unfeign'd
> Union of Mind, or in us both one Soule;
> Harmonie to behold in wedded pair
> More grateful then harmonious sound to the eare.
> Yet these subject not; I to thee disclose
> What inward thence I feel, not therefore foild,
> Who meet with various objects, from the sense
> Variously representing; yet still free
> Approve the best, and follow what I approve.
> (VIII.596-611)

Adam's reply is a lesson in human marriage, which closely resembles language used by Milton in the divorce tracts to praise the "sweet and mild familiarity of love," the "fit union of their souls" between man and wife.[20] Adam rephrases his feelings for Eve to make clear that they "subject not." What he wants the Angel to understand is that his marriage is a "Union of Mind, or in us both one Soule," a "harmonious" conversation between worthily matched rational beings. Adam's speech is therefore the culmination of Milton's efforts to lift Eve's unfallen nature out of the place assigned to it in the Old and New Testaments.

These adjustments allow Milton to present his own ideal of marriage, which is at the heart of his whole view of experience. The expression of this ideal in his presentation of unfallen Adam and Eve works in the poem to give tragic proportions to the temptation and fall of both Eve and Adam, for both are considerable figures.[21] Eve's stature before she eats the fruit makes her fall important in itself, not only as it occasions Adam's. Their marriage is the fulfillment of ideal human experience; its near destruction is an image of human damnation. Milton of course follows the dictates of Genesis in making Eve the temptress of Adam, but by contrast with centuries of fiercely misogynistic renderings of the story, Milton's in Book IX is balanced in the presentation of their falls. He expresses toward both Eve and Adam a mixture of sorrow and anger, sympathy and judgment.[22] They fare equally in his account of Eve's deception by the serpent, Adam's seduction by Eve, their mutually debasing sexual play, their later recriminations.

In Book X, however, Milton's balanced presentation of Adam and Eve is surprisingly disturbed, and in ways that invite questions because the disruption shows clearly in two important scenes in this later part of the poem. It is marked in the episode based on Genesis when God questions whether Adam and Eve have eaten the forbidden fruit, and also in the later scene of their reconciliation, which has no biblical prototype.

According to the episode in the third chapter of Genesis, when God questions the guiltily hiding pair he first asks Adam:

> Hast thou eaten of the tre, whereof I commanded thee that thou shuldest not eat in no case?
>
> Then the man said, The woman which thou gauest to be with me, she gaue me of the tre, and I did eat.
>
> And the Lord God said to the woman, Why hast thou done this? And the woman said, The serpent beguyled me, and I did eat.
>
> (Genesis 3:11-13)

The marginal commentary printed in this translation points to the sinfulness of both human replies. About Adam's it is said: "His wickednes & lacke of true repentance appeareth in this that he burdeneth God with his faute, because he had giuen him a wife." The gloss on Eve's reply makes a parallel accusation: "In stead of confessing her sinne, she increaseth it by accusing the serpent."

In Milton's version of the episode, God asks Adam whether he has eaten the forbidden fruit, "To whom thus *Adam* sore beset repli'd" with a long speech much more tortuously accusing of both God and Eve, more deviously self-exonerating than anything suggested in Genesis:

O Heav'n: in evil strait this day I stand
Before my Judge, either to undergoe
My self the total Crime, or to accuse
My other self, the partner of my life;
Whose failing, while her Faith to me remaines
I should conceal, and not expose to blame
By my complaint; but strict necessitie
Subdues me, and calamitous constraint
Least on my head both sin and punishment,
However insupportable, be all
Devolv'd; though should I hold my peace, yet thou
Wouldst easily detect what I conceale.
This Woman whom thou mad'st to be my help,
And gav'st me as thy perfet gift, so good,
So fit, so acceptable, so Divine,
That from her hand I could suspect no ill,
And what she did, whatever in it self,
Her doing seem'd to justifie the deed;
Shee gave me of the Tree, and I did eate.

(X.125-43)

After this burlesque of a confession, Milton's God rebukes Adam in the same Pauline terms that the Angel used to scold him earlier, reminding him that Eve was given to attract

Thy Love, not thy Subjection, and her Gifts
Were such as under Government well seem'd,
Unseemly to beare rule, which was thy part.

(X.153-56)

After God questions the woman, as in Genesis, Milton's narrator then describes Eve's response:

To whom sad *Eve* with shame nigh overwhelm'd,
Confessing soon, yet not before her Judge
Bold or loquacious, thus abasht repli'd.
The Serpent me beguil'd and I did eate.

(X.159-62)

Milton here has already forgiven Eve for her sin because he accepts her words as humbly penitent, not "Bold or loquacious," which would describe Adam's speech. By contrast with the commentator of the Geneva Bible, who finds hardness of heart equally in both replies, Milton's view is not so balanced.[23] For he exaggerates Adam's devious excuses to the point of ridiculing him, while he elevates Eve's accusation of the serpent to a form of truly penitent "Confessing," directly reversing the interpretation of the Geneva commentary.

The disruption of balanced judgment and sympathy in this scene might be explained partly by saying that Milton, like Milton's God, seems to take Adam's sin more seriously here, because man was created the guide and head of woman. Yet while this may illuminate the severe judgment of Adam here, it does not explain why Milton elevates Eve in spiritual dignity above any suggestion in the biblical episode, a question compounded in his treatment of the later scene of reconciliation between the fallen pair, where Eve is again made Adam's spiritual superior. This episode has no biblical model, and therefore no requirements for Milton to take into account.

In the later part of Book X Adam delivers an immensely long and bitter complaint for his lost innocence, which is overheard by Eve:

> Whom thus afflicted when sad *Eve* beheld,
> Desolate where she sate, approaching nigh,
> Soft words to his fierce passion she assay'd:
> But her with stern regard he thus repell'd.
> Out of my sight, thou Serpent, that name best
> Befits thee with him leagu'd, thy self as false
> And hateful.
>
> (X.863-69)

He goes on railing at length against Eve and against God for creating her, a "noveltie" in an otherwise masculine universe, and begins to generalize absurdly about the misery inevitably brought to man in marriage, of which there has so far been only one example:

> He never shall find out fit Mate, but such
> As some misfortune brings him, or mistake,
> Or whom he wishes most shall seldom gain
> Through her perversness, but shall see her gaind
> By a farr worse, or if she love, withheld
> By Parents, or his happiest choice too late
> Shall meet, alreadie linkt and Wedlock-bound
> To a fell Adversarie, his hate or shame:
> Which infinite calamitie shall cause
> To Humane life, and houshold peace confound.
>
> (X.899-908)

This tirade carries Adam's attention ludicrously far from recognizing his own sinful state, as Eve's conduct in response emphasizes:

> He added not, and from her turn'd, but *Eve*
> Not so repulst, with Tears that ceas'd not flowing,
> And tresses all disorderd, at his feet
> Fell humble, and imbracing them, besaught
> His peace, and thus proceeded in her plaint.
>
> (X.909-13)

The religious suggestions in Eve's "humble" posture, evoking Mary Magdalene, are intensified in her next speech of self-sacrifice.[24] As Joseph Summers was the first to point out, her moving words here resonate with echoes of Christ's speech in Book III where he offers himself for mankind's salvation:[25]

> Forsake me not thus, *Adam*, witness Heav'n
> What love sincere, and reverence in my heart
> I beare thee, and unweeting have offended,
> Unhappilie deceav'd; thy suppliant
> I beg, and clasp thy knees; bereave me not,
> Whereon I live, thy gentle looks, thy aid,
> Thy counsel in this uttermost distress,
> My onely strength and stay; forlorn of thee,
> Whither shall I betake me, where subsist?
> While yet we live, scarse one short hour perhaps,
> Between us two let there be peace, both joyning,
> As joyn'd in injuries, one enmitie
> Against a Foe by doom express assign'd us,
> That cruel Serpent.
>
> (X.914-27)

She then confesses herself to have sinned more gravely than Adam, which is a sterner judgment of herself than Milton has made of Eve: "both have sin'd, but thou / Against God onely, I against God and thee" (X.930-31). Finally she offers to sacrifice herself for Adam in words which directly reverse Adam's earlier excuse for blaming Eve to God

> Least on my head both sin and punishment,
> However insupportable, be all
> Devolv'd.
>
> (X.133-35)

Eve ends her speech in admirable contrast to this excuse of Adam's, with echoes in her words also of Christ's sacrificial offering:

> And to the place of judgment will return,
> There with my cries importune Heaven, that all
> The sentence from thy head remov'd may light
> On me, sole cause to thee of all this woe,
> Mee mee onely just object of his ire.
>
> (X.932-36)

Milton here invents Eve's declaration of repentance and self-sacrifice with no pressure for it from biblical authority, following it with lines in which he also chooses freely to make Eve the instrument of grace in man's restoration:

> She ended weeping, and her lowlie plight,
> Immoveable till peace obtain'd from fault
> Acknowledg'd and deplor'd, in *Adam* wraught
> Commiseration; soon his heart relented
> Towards her, his life so late and sole delight.
> . . . .
> As one disarm'd, his anger all he lost,
> And thus with peaceful words uprais'd her soon.
>
> (X.937-46)

One line of speculation about why Milton becomes so strongly of Eve's party in these two scenes is suggested by the pattern traced in earlier passages. In order to elevate unfallen Eve as a worthy partner in marital conversation, Milton has been in a sense her defender from her first introduction, making repeated efforts to rescue her from the place assigned to woman's nature on inescapable biblical authority. It may be that the pressure of Milton's sympathetic attitudes grew strongest at the point in the story most encouraging to severe judgment of Eve, after she has successfully seduced the husband from whom she was formed, for whom she was made.

Another, different kind of impetus behind Milton's special sympathy for Eve is also suggested by his ways of working with biblical definitions of woman in relation to man. As Milton's introduction of them acknowledges, man is the head of woman. This is declared in Adam's broad forehead and authoritative eye. He is said to be formed for "contemplation . . . and valour," and is therefore associated with the ruling rational powers of the soul. Yet Eve, Milton says often in the poem, is also part of that same soul. If not the rational part, with what powers is she especially associated? She is said to be formed for "softness . . . and sweet attractive Grace." This phrase, echoing praise of the poet Sidney's "sweet attractiue kinde of grace" in "An Elegie" appended to Spenser's "Astrophel," attributes to her the gifts of receptivity and a persuasiveness which is at once sensuous and divinely endowed.[26] Her beauty is said to imply rather than to declare its meaning. She is also described by the poet in less declarative terms, in more figurative, pictorial, musical language than Adam, qualities which also characterize her own mellifluous, descriptive speeches, by contrast with Adam's typically more abstract arguments. What these patterns suggest is that Eve is associated with those powers of the soul that belong especially to poetry, with imagination, sensation, and feeling. That association may suggest a reason why she is the poet's chosen instrument in man's redemption, and why Milton at that point in the story shows a special sympathy for her.[27] Eve's "Soft words" may represent what Milton in *Of Education* calls the distinctively "more simple, sensuous, and passionate" language of poetry.[28]

NOTES

[1]For discussions of the earlier Milton controversy see, for example: Bernard Bergonzi, "Criticism and the Milton Controversy," *The Living Milton*, ed. Frank Kermode (London: Routledge & Kegan Paul, 1960), pp. 162-80; Anne Ferry, *Milton's Epic Voice: The Narrator in "Paradise Lost"* (Cambridge, Mass.: Harvard Univ. Press, 1963), pp. xi-xv; Christopher B. Ricks, *Milton's Grand Style* (Oxford: Clarendon Press, 1963), pp. 1-21.

[2]William Shullenberger, "Wrestling with the Angel: *Paradise Lost* and Feminist Criticism," *MiltonQ* 23 (1986):69-84.

[3]Important articles in the more recent Milton controversy are: Barbara Lewalski, "Milton on Women—Yet Once More," *MiltonS* 14 (1980):3-24, responding to Marcia Landy, "Kinship and the Role of Women in *Paradise Lost*," *MiltonS* 4 (1972):3-18; Joan Webber, "The Politics of Poetry: Feminism and *Paradise Lost*," *MiltonS* 14 (1980):3-24, responding to Sandra Gilbert, "Patriarchal Poetry and Women Readers: Reflections on Milton's Bogey," *PMLA* 93 (1978):368-82. A later stage of this controversy about Milton's views on women is the exchange of Christine Froula, "When Eve Reads Milton: Undoing the Canonical Economy," *CritI* 10 (1983):321-47, followed by Edward Pechter, "When Pechter Reads Froula," and Christine Froula, "Pechter's Specter: Milton's Bogey Writ Small," *CritI* 10 (1984):163-70 and 171-78.

[4]Douglas Anderson, "Unfallen Marriage and the Fallen Imagination in Paradise Lost," *SEL* 26 (1986):141.

[5]For a recent discussion of examples of such commentary and representation see Diane K. McColley, *Milton's Eve* (Urbana: Univ. of Illinois Press, 1983), pp. 1-21.

[6]All citations to the Bible unless otherwise indicated are to the Geneva translation, *The Geneva Bible: A facsimile of the 1560 edition*, ed. Lloyd E. Berry (Madison: Univ. of Wisconsin Press, 1981). Quotations are from the headings for the first three chapters of Genesis. Contracted forms have been expanded throughout.

[7]For the importance of St. Paul to Puritan thought, especially the epistle to the Romans, see William Haller, *The Rise of Puritanism* (New York: Columbia Univ. Press, 1938), pp. 186-88. An example of such a Pauline reading is Romans 2.29: "But he is a Iewe which is one within, & the circumcision is of the heart, in the spirit, not in the letter, whose praise is not of men, but of God."

[8]"The forme of solemnization of Matrimony," *The Book of Common Prayer* (London, 1638). All citations to the rite of matrimony refer to this edition.

[9]John Milton, *The Works of John Milton*, ed. Frank Allen Patterson, 18 vols. (New York: Columbia Univ. Press, 1931), 2. All citations to *Paradise Lost* by book and line refer to this edition.

[10]*The Holy Bible. An Exact Reprint of the Authorized Version Published in the Year MDCXI* (Oxford: Oxford Univ. Press, 1833).

[11]The fact that Milton's wording of this line "assigns more dignity to Eve than was usual" is noted by McColley, *Milton's Eve*, p. 40.

[12]John Donne, Sermon 17: Preached at Sir Francis Nethersole's Marriage (shortly before February 12, 1619/20), on Genesis 2:18 (No. 2 in *Fifty Sermons), The Sermons of John Donne*, ed. George Potter and Evelyn Simpson (Berkeley: Univ. of California Press, 1955), 2:344-46.

[13]Milton's use of "conversation" is placed in the context of a discussion of Puritan tracts and courtesy books on marriage by John G. Halkett, *Milton and the Idea of Matrimony* (New Haven: Yale Univ. Press, 1970), p. 58.

[14]For discussion of Milton's position on divorce in relation to those of continental reformers and of the canon law adhered to by the English church see William and Malleville Haller, "The Puritan Art of Love," *HLQ* (1942):235-72.

[15]John Milton, *The Doctrine and Discipline of Divorce, Complete Prose Works of John Milton*, 8 vols., gen. ed. Don M. Wolfe (New Haven: Yale Univ. Press, 1959), 2:328, 246, 251, 326. All citations to Milton's prose are to this edition and volume.

[16]Milton, *Tetrachordon, Prose*, 2:589.

[17]Donne, Sermon 17, p. 346.

[18]That this view is representative of the attitudes toward the relation between women and men of Puritan writers on marriage is argued by William Haller, "Hail Wedded Love," *ELH* 13 (1946):79-97.

[19]For examples of this way of reading the episode see Halkett, *Milton and the Idea of Matrimony*, pp. 121-23; Joseph H. Summers, *The Muses's Method: An Introduction to "Paradise Lost"* (Cambridge, Mass.: Harvard Univ. Press, 1962), p. 148. The fact that Adam in his reply to Raphael "does not really admit" that he is guilty of uxoriousness is noticed by Webber, "The Politics of Poetry," p. 15.

[20]Milton, *Tetrachordon, Prose,* 2:603; *The Doctrine and Discipline of Divorce,* 2:326.

[21]That "few writers of any era—including our own—have taken women so seriously" as Milton is argued by Lewalski, "Milton on Women," p. 5.

[22]I discuss this mixture of judgment and sympathy in the presentation of the falls of Adam and Eve in *Milton's Epic Voice*, pp. 56-65.

[23]That Milton is more lenient than the Geneva commentators not only to Eve but also to Adam is the different interpretation of the scene of confession argued by Anderson, "Unfallen Marriage," p. 138.

[24]Eve's "feminine posture of supplication" as a "redefinition of heroism" substituted by Milton for "a masculine stance of heroic defiance" is argued by Maureen Quilligan, *Milton's Spenser: The Politics of Reading* (Ithaca: Cornell Univ. Press, 1983), pp. 174, 242.

[25]Summers, *The Muse's Method*, pp. 176-85.

[26]Edmund Spenser, *The Poetical Works of Edmund Spenser*, ed. J. C. Smith and E. De Selincourt (Oxford: Oxford Univ. Press, 1912), p. 557.

[27]I argue this association of Eve with poetry in a different context in *Milton and the Miltonic Dryden* (Cambridge, Mass. Harvard Univ. Press, 1968), pp. 106-109.

[28]Milton, *Of Education, Prose*, 2:403.

SEL 28 (1988)
ISSN 0039-3657

"To repair the ruins of our first parents": *Of Education* and Fallen Adam

ANN BAYNES COIRO

In *Of Education* Milton proposed a radical change in traditional educational strategies. Subjects normally taught to young children —rhetoric, logic, and original composition—were to be left until the very end of the process of education; instead, the concrete, pragmatic phases of education were to come first, preparing the student intellectually and emotionally for his leap into metaphysics and controversy.[1] Milton's educational tractate has been compared before to the education of Adam in *Paradise Lost*, but the similarities critics have noted have been general, drawn mainly from the first few paragraphs of the tractate where Milton enunciates the purposes of education. Furthermore, previous discussions of *Of Education* and *Paradise Lost* have found their parallels in Raphael's education of the unfallen Adam in Books V and VI.[2] It is, however, striking and significant that in Books XI and XII of *Paradise Lost* Michael leads Adam through an education that exactly parallels, down to the smallest detail, the "methodical course" that Milton had delineated with such precision in his educational tractate. Even the sharp and disturbing shift from vision to narration between Books XI and XII can be seen as a reflection of the bipartite structure of Milton's ideal education between the practical education of the senses and the more difficult education of the intellect and the conscience.

Books XI and XII demonstrate a clear shift in Milton's handling of his material, a shift which has been variously attributed to a loss of poetic power or of interest in the poem, on the one hand, or, on the other, to an intentional strategy to alter both Adam's perception of reality and our own.[3] The most striking difficulties which the conclusion of *Paradise Lost* presents are its shift from the evocative complexity of the body of the poem to a bare lean style; the

Ann Baynes Coiro is an Assistant Professor at Rutgers University, New Brunswick. Her book, *Robert Herrick's "Hesperides" and the Epigram Book Tradition,* will be published in spring 1988. This essay is the beginning of a study which will place together Milton's prose and poetry.

compression of all human history into so brief a space after the poem dwells expansively upon the initial creation and fall; and the further difficulty of the shift in Book XII from visions of history to a long narrative of events to come. The similarity of procedures between the education outlined in the tractate and the angelic education of Adam can, I believe, serve to illuminate some of these persistent difficulties and serve as well to illuminate Milton's stance as poet and teacher at the conclusion of *Paradise Lost.*

Indeed, the explicit statement of intent with which Milton begins the body of *Of Education* almost insists, in retrospect, upon a comparison with the epic:

> The end . . . of learning is to repair the ruins of our first parents by regaining to know God aright. . . . But because our understanding cannot in this body found itself but on sensible things, nor arrive so clearly to the knowledge of God and things invisible as by orderly conning over the visible and inferior creature, the same method is necessarily to be followed in all discreet teaching.[4]

In every detail, the clear, optimistic "method" of the tractate can be traced in Michael's education of Adam. But this recall of Milton's early work on education adds a dark resonance to the conclusion of *Paradise Lost*, especially because the procedures are so close as to seem at times almost an intentional self-parody of "that voluntary idea which hath long in silence presented itself to me, of a better education, in extent and comprehension far more large, and yet of time far shorter, and of attainment far more certain, than hath been yet in practice" (p. 630).

Of Education divides the process of teaching into two distinct halves: these two stages correspond to the division of Adam's education between Book XI and Book XII. Before placing tractate and poem together, let me give a summary list of the precisely arranged series of lessons Milton proposes for younger pupils before they reach the age capable of moral reasoning. They are to learn first the basic rules of grammar. Then they are to learn arithmetic and the practical sciences—agriculture, geography, geometry and trigonometry, fortification, architecture, engineering, navigation, geology, botany, biology, human anatomy, and medicine. The students are to consolidate this practical learning by observing demonstrations performed by visiting craftsmen. Finally, this phase of their education is to be capped by reading pastoral and georgic poetry. Even such a skeletal overview suggests the lessons of Book XI; retracing in more detail the early lessons of Milton's academy while at the same time moving through the lessons of Book XI demonstrates, I believe, close similarities of educational procedure—and profound differences of purpose.

The very youngest pupils at Milton's ideal academy were to learn the proper use of language by a simple grounding in the rules of grammar and of pronunciation. This very early stage of learning is, of course, unnecessary for the unfallen Adam who, untaught, can speak perfectly the names of all created things. But in *Of Education* Milton further recommends that in order to make young students adept at grammar "and withal to season them and win them early to the love of virtue and true labor, ere any flattering seducement or vain principle seize them wandering, some easy and delightful book of education would be read to them" for "here the main skill and groundwork will be to temper them such lectures and explanations upon every opportunity as may lead and draw them in willing obedience" (p. 633). This passage from early in *Of Education* may be read as a synopsis of Raphael's education of Adam before the Fall. But the passage is also charged with the tensions, even the very words that fill Books IX and X of *Paradise Lost* when, in spite of their "easy and delightful" education, Eve is by "flattering seducement" and Adam by "vain principle" seized wandering and drawn away from "willing obedience."

In the pamphlet on education Milton placed his faith in the power of a great teacher, "he who hath the art and proper eloquence to catch them with, what with mild and effectual persuasions and what with the intimation of some fear, if need be, but chiefly by his own example" who could thereby "in a short space gain them to an incredible diligence and courage, infusing into their young breasts such an ingenuous and noble ardor, as would not fail to make many of them renowned and matchless men" (pp. 633-34). The bitter lesson of *Paradise Lost*, however, is that not even mild Raphael, the perfect teacher of uncorrupted man, could prevent the fall into the knowledge of evil. Adam and Eve disobey; and all the rest of education must attempt to salvage something from that destruction.

Significantly, the early lessons outlined by Milton in *Of Education* were to be from "some easy and delightful book of education [which] would *be read to them*" (italics added). As the boys grew older, however, they were to become increasingly engaged in the process of their own education, first watching, then doing; first being read to, then reading, and finally writing themselves. It is the cornerstone of Milton's educational theory that a young student be *shown* first and experience directly what he is to learn, rather than be confined immediately to the dry theories of books. Clearly, Michael uses this "same method . . . to be followed in all discreet teaching" when he teaches Adam, first by showing him visions which gradually sharpen his responses, and then by withdrawing visions and lecturing the more sophisticated Adam on the history of Man after the Fall.

The close parallels between the tractate and Books XI and XII begin when the children in Milton's academy move beyond passive reception of knowledge and themselves begin to read.[5] The first books that the young students should attempt are practical works of agriculture, "for the matter is most easy" and will be "an occasion of inciting and enabling them hereafter to improve the tillage of their country, to recover the bad soil and to remedy the waste that is made of good" (p. 634).

The first lesson that Michael teaches Adam is the simple knowledge of his fate:

> to remove thee I am come,
> And send thee from the Garden forth to till
> The ground whence thou wast tak'n, fitter Soil.
> (XI, 260-62)

Michael here repeats exactly the message that God the Father charged him to deliver and every lesson Michael teaches Adam will be a version of this one. It is not an "easy" lesson: expulsion from paradise, limited knowledge, limited ambition, the inevitable linking of birth with death. Adam's lesson in "agriculture" is his first, but not his easiest; it is not a stepping stone to more difficult lessons, but the first strand in an interwoven web of self-knowledge.[6]

For Milton's hypothetical students it will next be "seasonable . . . to learn . . . the use of the globes and all the maps, first with the old names and then with the new" (p. 634). So also, at the very beginning of his lessons, Michael gives Adam a vantage point from which to "command wherever stood / City of old or modern Fame, the Seat / Of mightiest Empire," described in a catalogue of twenty-five lines (XI, 385-411). This gorgeous series of places beginning—

> Of *Cambalu*, seat of *Cathaian Can*,
> And *Samarchand* by *Oxus, Temir's* Throne,
> To *Paquin* of *Sinaean* Kings, and thence
> To *Agra* and *Lahor* of great *Mogul*
> Down to the golden *Chersonese*, or where
> The *Persian* in *Ecbatan* sat, or since

In *Hispahan*, or where the *Russian Ksar*
In *Mosco*, or the Sultan in *Bizance*,
Turchestan-born

—Michael spreads before Adam in a dazzling display of both temporal power and the power of magnificent words. Suddenly, however, Michael undercuts the hypnotic vision (and litany) with one concluding half-line—"but to nobler sights." Adam's vision must be cleared so that he can see again without the cloud cast over his eyes by the forbidden fruit. What he will see will not be the panoply of human magnificence, but the sordid details of death; what he will hear will not be sonorous, magical place names, but stark statements of reality. The maps and globes that in *Of Education* will be a means of opening children's eyes to the world around them, in Adam's more somber education is his first lesson "that God attributes to place / No sanctity" (XI, 836-37).

Since the primary thesis of *Of Education* is that before a student advances to abstract concepts he must have an education thoroughly grounded in sensible, physical knowledge, Milton recommends that the preliminary study of agriculture and geography be followed by practical sciences, culminating in anatomy and medicine so that the student "may at some time or other save an army by this frugal and expenseless means only, and not let the healthy and stout bodies of young men rot away under him for want of this discipline—which is a great pity, and no less a shame to the commander" (pp. 634-35). At the parallel moment in Adam's much more brutal and pessimistic education, Michael introduces him to the most grotesque aspects of anatomy—deliberate murder in the vision of Cain and Abel and disfiguring disease in the vision of the Lazar-house of Death. Adam is shown personified diseases, not to make him a more efficient military leader, but in order to demonstrate to him the need for temperance, a lesson vividly and ruthlessly impressed since it was through intemperance that Eve and he fell. He must learn to negotiate between his instinctive desire for pleasure and life and, after the fall, Eve's brave and horrifying suggestion: "Let us seek death" (X, 1001). Adam's lessons in the human body thus go far beyond the jaunty utility proposed in *Of Education*.

The younger boys at the academy Milton outlined in 1644 were at this stage to have mastered "the principles of arithmetic, geometry, astronomy, and geography, with a general compact of physics" and were now to "descend in mathematics to the instrumental science of trigonometry, and from thence to fortification, architecture, enginery, or navigation" (p. 634). As they learn the principles of these subjects they will be allowed to share "the helpful experiences of hunters, fowlers, fishermen, shepherds, gardeners, apothecaries; and in the other sciences, architects, engineers, mariners, anatomists" which should "give them such a real tincture of natural knowledge as they shall never forget, but daily augment with delight" (p. 635).

These practical arts Adam also sees and delights in as Michael allows him the analogous visions of the sons of God and the sons of Lamech. But Adam's delight is a sad deception and Michael must warn him:

> studious they appear
> Of Arts that polish Life, Inventors rare,
> Unmindful of thir Maker, though his Spirit
> Taught them, but they his gifts acknowledg'd none.
> (XI, 609-12)

The *purpose* of the practical lessons in *Of Education* is to inspire a lasting delight in the pupils; the delight that these same lessons give Adam is not the purpose of the lessons, but the means to a very different end. His delight is another fall into sin. He must learn to recognize the temptation of delight and temper it with moral judgment. Indeed, what Michael teaches him is that all of these worldly arts tend toward one end—and that is war. *Of Education* enunciates as one of its explicit goals the training of its students for military excellence. Milton concluded the introduction to his tractate by calling "a complete and generous education that which fits a man to perform justly, skilfully, and magnanimously all the offices, both private and public, of peace and war" (p. 632). But war and military heroism run like a sinister thread throughout Adam's education: Cain kills Abel, pastures are soaked with human blood (XI, 646-54), the spokesman for "Justice," "Religion," "Truth and Peace" (XI, 667) is threatened by violent hands. The students of 1644 were at this point to have enjoyed the pastoral and georgic poets; by the end of Book XI, Adam also sees pastoral and georgic visions, but, in every case, violence has intruded to destroy the idyll.

In *Of Education* the culmination of the practical phase of learning is the moment when Milton judged his pupils had by "years and good general precepts" been furnished with "that act of reason which in ethics is called Proairesis; that they may with some judgment contemplate upon moral good and evil. Then will be required a special reinforcement of constant and sound indoctrinating to set them right and firm, instructing them more amply in the knowledge of virtue and the hatred of vice; while their young and pliant affections are led through all the moral works of Plato, Xenophon, Cicero, Plutarch, Laertius, and those Locrian remnants" (p. 635). This process of reinforcement that Milton touches on briefly in the tractate is the cornerstone of Michael's pedagogy. He teaches Adam his lessons over and over again, allowing him to contemplate moral good and evil that he may judge correctly for himself. Over and over again, Adam judges incorrectly and learns from his mistake. The tractate, perhaps because it is so brief, never considers the possibility that students will *not* learn all the lessons spread so carefully before them. But Michael seems to expect that possibility and to use it in order to teach Adam.

Most delightful of all to Adam, for example, is the vision of the "Bevy of fair Women"—the vision which must be his most humiliating lesson. For Adam falls again and entirely into his original sin and cries:

> True opener of mine eyes, prime Angel blest,
> Much better seems this Vision, and more hope
> Of peaceful days portends, than those two past;
> Those were of hate and death, or pain much worse,
> Here Nature seems fulfill'd in all her ends.
>
> (XI, 598-602)

Tellingly, it is on this one crucial point that the students of the 1644 tractate were to receive a very tentative and insufficient lesson. When they reached the age of moral judgment, they were to be allowed "but with wariness and good antidote . . . [to] taste some choice comedies, Greek, Latin, or Italian; those tragedies also that treat of household matters, as *Trachiniae*, *Alcestis*, and the like" (p. 635). In this "complete and generous education which [should fit] a man to perform justly, skilfully, and magnanimously all the offices, both private and public, of peace and war" (p. 632), a few plays are to be his only introduction to women and marriage. The two plays Milton specifically recommends would demonstrate a wife whose jealousy inadvertently caused her husband's painful death and a wife so perfect that she gave her own life to save her husband's. What lesson is to be drawn from these instances of fallible and perfect woman is not clear except that it should be circled warily and with "good antidote."[7] Characteristic of the tractate, the hero of both plays is the warrior Hercules, the kind of hero who is cast in a very problematic light in *Paradise Lost*. At this parallel point in Book XI, Michael specifically warns Adam against the heroic ideal that Hercules embodies:

> styl'd great Conquerors,
> Patrons of Mankind, Gods, and Sons of Gods,
> Destroyers rightlier call'd and Plagues of men.
> (XI, 695-97)

The first lesson Milton's students were to learn once they had advanced to the second, contemplative stage of education was "the study of politics; to know the beginning, end, and reasons of political societies, that they may not in a dangerous fit of the commonwealth be such poor, shaken, uncertain reeds, of such a tottering conscience, as many of our great counsellors have lately shown themselves, but steadfast pillars of the state" (p. 636). Milton wrote these contemptuous words during the first steps of the commonwealth. Underneath his sarcasm seems to lie a belief that it will be possible to educate English youth truly to be "steadfast pillars of the state." In bitter contrast, the political lesson that Adam receives from Michael seems to reflect Milton's actual experience of the state he had endowed with so much hope. The lesson of politics becomes in *Paradise Lost* the central pivot of Adam's education—the same lesson taught over and over again—first by a vision of Enoch, "daring single to be just," speaking out in his nation's counsels, then in a vision of Noah reprimanding the assemblies of his decadent nation and a vision of the destruction of the Flood, then again, once Adam's visions are withdrawn, in Michael's reiteration and interpretation of the story of Noah, "One Man except, the only Son of light / In a dark Age" (XI, 808-809).

The lesson of Noah is of crucial significance both to the education of Adam and to the problematic structure of *Paradise Lost*'s conclusion. It is the cruelest vision that Michael shows to Adam and he subjects him to it twice—once in a vision and then again as a narration. This double lesson is a replication of the larger shift from vision to narration between Books XI and XII. It is Adam's lesson in proairesis, moral education, the moment when he must finally abandon his false optimism about man's happiness on earth and recognize the "only Son of light / In a dark Age." It is finally here, at the end of Book XI, that Adam must face the stunning humiliation of seeing men who do not give in to temptation as he has done, men whom he must recognize as morally superior to himself.

Finally, Adam's lesson in politics closes with the story of Nimrod, the rebel and tyrant who

> shall rise
> Of proud ambitious heart, who not content

With fair equality, fraternal state,
Will arrogate Dominion undeserv'd
Over his brethren, and quite dispossess
Concord and law of Nature from the Earth.

(XII, 24-29)[8]

Adam, indignant, once again misunderstands his lesson here at the beginning of the second phase of his education, but there is added poignance to his protestation against Nimrod since he could so easily be voicing Milton's own ideals before the realities of the commonwealth were borne in upon him:

but Man over men
He made not Lord; such title to himself
Reserving, human left from human free.

(XII, 69-71)

Michael must explain that "Since thy original lapse, true Liberty / Is lost, which always with right Reason dwells" (XII, 82-83). Instead,

Tyranny must be,
Though to the Tyrant thereby no excuse.
Yet sometimes Nations will decline so low
From virtue, which is reason, that no wrong,
But Justice, and some fatal curse annext
Deprives them of thir outward liberty,
Thir inward lost.

(XI, 95-101)

Adam receives a lesson in politics that goes far beyond what Milton had envisioned in 1644, a darker, sadder lesson than Milton would ever have intended for the students of his academy.

Following their readings in politics, the students in Milton's early academy were to cover "the grounds of law and legal justice; delivered first and with best warrant by Moses" (p. 636). At this point, Adam must go much further and come to understand the bitter underlying necessity of law. When Michael tells him the story of Moses, Adam, whose responses have become increasingly sophisticated as his education advances, asks why God should wish to live with men so sinful that they must be fenced in with innumerable laws. Michael replies:

Law appears imperfet, and but giv'n
With purpose to resign them in full time

> Up to a better Cov'nant, disciplin'd
> From shadowy Types to Truth, from Flesh to Spirit,
> From imposition of strict Laws, to free
> Acceptance of large Grace, from servile fear
> To filial, works of Law to works of Faith.
>
> (XII, 300-306)

Michael crowns his lesson with the story of Christ and the "Law of Faith" which his sacrifice to his Father shall institute.

The penultimate stage outlined in the pamphlet on education is the study of "the highest matters of theology and church history ancient and modern" (p. 636). The whole fabric of Michael's teaching, especially in the latter part of Book XI and in Book XII, has been theological and, at the end of Book XII, Adam listens to the history of the degeneration of the Church to the point where the Church would interfere in the laws that should spring from the heart of man. Readers of *Paradise Lost* have been disappointed and critics have been severe because Michael passes so quickly over the triumphant, climactic moment of Christ's act of salvation and then moves directly to the story of the Church's decay. It would indeed be comforting if Michael's lessons ended in a splendid burst of glory and optimism as Christ saved us all from ourselves. But it would not be the truth. Such a soft and happy ending would have been suitable for a young boy at the early stage of Milton's educational process when the teacher tells him "the easy grounds of religion and the story of scripture" (p. 634) as a relaxing bedtime story, carefully protecting his students from harsh truth, nurturing instead their curiosity and idealism. By the time Milton wrote *Paradise Lost*, however, his ideal teacher regarded it as unsuitable, even dangerous, to send a young man into the world without a forewarning that:

> Wolves shall succeed for teachers, grievous Wolves,
> Who all the sacred mysteries of Heav'n
> To thir own vile advantages shall turn
> Of lucre and ambition.
>
> (XII, 508-11)

The most striking difference between *Of Education* and Michael's education of Adam is that in *Paradise Lost* each lesson is weighted down by a darker, more complex vision of man's capability for corruption and failure and weighted by the admission that knowledge can lead not only to good, but to evil. It is understandable that Adam and the reader would want *Paradise Lost* to end on a great swelling note of triumph. The most important lesson of *Paradise Lost,* however, is that man has fallen, that dangers lurk around us and within us, and that we must both suffer because of our first parents' fall and learn from it.

The crowning movement of the education outlined in the tractate is the study of logic, rhetoric, and poetry so that the students may realize "what religious, what glorious and magnificent use might be made of poetry, both in divine and human things" (p. 637). Then, Milton concludes triumphantly, his students will be "fraught with an universal insight into things." Adam's final lesson, however, is very different; he acknowledges the rightful limitations of his knowledge and Michael approves: "thou hast attain'd the sum / Of wisdom; hope no higher" (XII, 575-76). In the disparity between these concluding lessons, the profound difference between Milton's early sketch of an ideal education and his later dramatization is most apparent.

Paradise Lost does not end with Michael's voice, however. There is one final lesson for us, if not for Adam. Michael's stern, rather unsympathetic voice ceases, and once again at the close of the poem the narrator's voice resumes and we do learn *Of Education*'s final lesson: "what religious, what glorious and magnificent use might be made of poetry, both in divine and human things."

In recent years impressive scholarly work has focused our attention upon the narrator of *Paradise Lost,* the central intelligence of the work whose mediating, meditative, and inspired presence adds rich dimensions to the first ten books. At the same time, some of Milton's most sympathetic critics have rejected Books XI and XII as a relative failure or have devised elaborate explanations for the aridity of the final books. Certainly a crucial factor in our response to Books XI and XII is the virtual disappearance of the narrator. The Cambridge Manuscript preserves four different stages of Milton's early plan for a drama, *Adam Unparadis'd.*[9] The drama was to have had a narrator, and for this role Milton considered, in turn, Michael, Moses, and Gabriel. Books XI and XII, then, are a curious return to Milton's earliest conception of a drama of the fall, in which the responsibility for shaping and narrating the story of man falls upon Michael.

Stella Revard has delineated a composite portrait of the archangel Michael as he was traditionally portrayed in the Renaissance.[10] The militant angel of judgment and expulsion, his strength lies in his sword and in his almost Roman figure of military charisma. In *Paradise Lost,* however, Milton subverts Michael's traditional stature as the supreme angel of undefeatable physical prowess, giving his traditional role of defeater of Satan to the Son and radically changing the means of that defeat from physical force to moral strength. Having limited Michael's traditional military power, Milton instead portrays him, still in his military garb, as teacher of fallen man.

There is no precedent for Michael as teacher; it is a curious and significant innovation on Milton's part. Yet Michael's soldierly demeanor perfectly embodies the military project of the early tractate on education:

> In which methodical course it is so supposed they must proceed by the steady pace of learning onward, as at convenient times for memory's sake to retire back into the middle ward, and sometimes into the rear of what they have been taught, until they have confirmed and solidly united the whole body of their perfected knowledge, like the last embattling of a Roman legion.
>
> (p. 637)

The final military metaphor is appropriate to a work that has advocated the training of civic and military leaders. It is also prophetic of Milton's soldier-teacher Michael who, having been superceded by the Son on the field of battle, his physical prowess superceded by spiritual strength, is sent by God to teach fallen man. He is to teach man reality and give him hope, but, finally, it will be Christ who will complete man's education. *Of Education* is shot through with confidence that the military skills Milton proposes for his students will be a powerful good for the state. That confidence is deeply shaken in the conclusion of *Paradise Lost,* spoken by Michael, who has been an actor in God's comedy of warfare. Adam's horror at the vision of Homeric heroes—

> Death's Ministers, not Men, who thus deal Death
> Inhumanly to men, and multiply
> Ten thousandfold the sin of him who slew
> His Brother
>
> (XI, 676-79)

—is a lesson learned by both pupil and teacher.

Milton framed *Of Education* with a telling image of his own stance as educational reformer: "I shall . . . straight conduct ye to a hillside, where I will point ye out the right path of a virtuous and noble education; laborious indeed at the first ascent, but else so smooth, so green, so full of goodly prospect and melodious sounds on every side, that the harp of Orpheus was not more charming" (p. 632). When Michael leads Adam to the top of the Hill of Paradise, he begins an education much more difficult than the lesson Milton had envisioned years before. A central theme of *Paradise Lost* and indeed, it may be argued, the central *action* of *Paradise Lost* is education, the pursuit of knowledge. Education was Milton's conscious concern throughout his life: from his own extended self-education, from his years as a teacher, from the publication of the tractate in 1644 for "the reforming of education . . . for want whereof this nation perishes," to Milton's republication of *Of Education* with the *Poems* of 1673 as part of his self-conscious presentation of his youthful work.[11] But the traces of the tractate's "discreet method" which structure the education of Adam serve to dramatize how Milton's thinking evolved. For Michael's lessons complicate the agenda and the imagery of *Of Education* and play its optimism against the tragic story of human history. Michael must lead Adam and the reader down from "this top of Speculation," out of the sympathetic clarity of the epic narrator's primeval world, out of the ideal academy, and into the dark, cold confusion of our contemporary world.

NOTES

[1]Milton was one of many voices in the Renaissance advocating educational reform. Donald C. Dorian, the editor of *Of Education* for the Yale edition of Milton's prose, argues convincingly, however, that Milton's stance was highly original. While at first glance there are certain obvious similarities between Milton's tractate and the Comenian educational reforms being championed by Samuel Hartlib, the philosophy and direction of Milton's argument are pointedly different from Hartlib's. For Milton, the Comenian insistence upon practical education should not be an end in itself, but only the groundwork for a broad and deep education in the humanities. See *Complete Prose Works*, gen. ed. Don M. Wolfe, 8 vols. (New Haven: Yale Univ. Press; London: Oxford Univ. Press, 1953-), 2:184-216.

[2]Murray W. Bundy, for example, has argued in "Milton's View of Education in *Paradise Lost*," *JEGP* 21 (1922):127-52, that *Of Education* contains two conflicting views of education, one based upon man's fallen nature, the other upon "the potential goodness of man's nature." He applies the general purport of *Of Education* to Raphael's education of Adam in Books V and VI, but only cursorily considers Michael's education of the fallen Adam. I believe that *Of Education* can be applied more exactly and more tellingly to Michael's lessons and I believe, too, that Milton recognized the conflict in *Of Education* and had it in mind as he constructed his final education experiment in *Paradise Lost*. Kathleen Swaim has recently argued in *Before and After the Fall: Contrasting*

Modes in "Paradise Lost" (Amherst: Univ. of Massachusetts Press, 1986), pp. 17-25, that *Of Education* is applicable to Raphael's education of Adam, *Areopagitica* to Michael's. See also George Williamson's article, "The Education of Adam," *MP* 61 (1963):96-109, and Lee A. Jacobus, *Sudden Apprehension: Aspects of Knowledge in "Paradise Lost"* (The Hague and Paris: Mouton, 1976), who discusses the role of logic in Renaissance education.

[3]A significant generative force for criticism of Books XI and XII was C. S. Lewis's dismissal of them as an "untransmuted lump of futurity" in *A Preface to "Paradise Lost"* (London: Oxford Univ. Press, 1942), p. 125. Other critics have also disparaged the final books. See, for example, John Barclay Broadbent, *Some Graver Subject: An Essay on "Paradise Lost"* (New York: Barnes and Noble, 1960), pp. 267-86, and Louis L. Martz, *The Paradise Within* (New Haven: Yale Univ. Press, 1964), pp. 141-67.

Among notable arguments for intentional structure and artistic purpose in Books XI and XII are: Ann Astell, "The Medieval *Consolatio* and the Conclusion of *Paradise Lost,*" *SP* 82 (1985):477-92; Stanley Fish, *Surprised by Sin: the Reader in "Paradise Lost"* (London: Macmillan; New York: St. Martin's Press, 1967), pp. 272-331; Northrop Frye, *The Return of Eden: Five Essays on Milton's Epics* (Toronto: Univ. of Toronto Press, 1965), pp. 19-20, 55; Barbara K. Lewalski, "Structure and the Symbolism of Vision in Michael's Prophecy, *Paradise Lost,* Books XI and XII," *PQ* 42 (1963):25-35; H. R. MacCullum, "Milton and Sacred History: Books XI and XII of *Paradise Lost,*" in *Essays in English Literature . . . Presented to A. S. P. Woodhouse,* ed. Millar MacLure and F. W. Watt (Toronto: Univ. of Toronto Press, 1964), pp. 149-68; F. T. Prince, "On the Last Two Books of *Paradise Lost,*" *Essays and Studies,* n.s. 11 (1958):38-52; Lawrence A. Sasek, "The Drama of *Paradise Lost,* Books XI and XII," rpt. in *Milton: Modern Essays in Criticism,* ed. Arthur E. Barker (London: Oxford Univ. Press, 1965), pp. 342-56; Joseph H. Summers, *The Muse's Method: An Introduction to "Paradise Lost"* (Cambridge, Mass.: Harvard Univ. Press, 1962), pp. 186-224; Raymond B. Waddington, "The Death of Adam: Vision and Voice in Books XI and XII of *Paradise Lost,*" *MP* 70 (1972):9-21; and Joseph Anthony Wittreich, Jr., *Visionary Poetics: Milton's Tradition and His Legacy* (San Marino, California: Huntington Library, 1979), pp. 184-91.

Stanley Fish also "narrates" the "story" of criticism of Books XI and XII in "Transmuting the Lump: 'Paradise Lost,' 1942-1982," in *Literature and History: Theoretical Problems and Russian Case Studies,* ed. Gary Saul Morson (Stanford: Stanford Univ. Press, 1986), pp. 33-56; 300-301.

[4]John Milton, *Complete Poems and Major Prose,* ed. Merritt Y. Hughes (New York: Odyssey, 1957), p. 631. I will use this edition throughout for quotations from both *Of Education* and *Paradise Lost,* citing both parenthetically in the text.

[5]Similarly, Kathleen Swaim argues that while Raphael attempts to teach the unfallen Adam how to read the book of God's works, Michael must teach him how to read God's word (*Before and After the Fall,* pp. 24-25, 36).

[6]See Christopher Fitter, " 'Native Soil': The Rhetoric of Exile Lament and Exile Consolation in *Paradise Lost,*" *MiltonS* 20 (1984):147-62.

[7]When Milton's students read the tragedies of Euripides and Sophocles, where women figure so powerfully, it will be to the political speeches only that their teacher should direct them (p. 636).

[8]At this point in Book XII Adam also learns the lesson of Babel. One of the aspects of *Of Education* that students and critics alike find amusing is the

offhand ease with which Milton expects his students to pick up languages by the way as they study other things. He clearly believes in the tractate that language is simply a vehicle, "but the instrument conveying to us things useful to be known" (p. 631). The study of languages should not, therefore, be an end in itself, but only a tool. In direct contrast, Adam must learn in Books XI and XII to understand that language can be much more complicated and dangerous than he at first assumes. Indeed, the reader's experience of all of *Paradise Lost* proves that language is much more than an "instrument."

[9]Allan H. Gilbert, *On the Composition of "Paradise Lost"* (1947; rpt. New York: Octagon Books, 1966), pp. 12-16.

[10]Stella P. Revard, *The War in Heaven: "Paradise Lost" and the Tradition of Satan's Rebellion* (Ithaca: Cornell Univ. Press, 1980), pp. 235-47.

[11]See Thomas Kranidas, "Milton on Teachers and Teaching," *MiltonQ* 20 (1986):26-28.

SEL 28 (1988)
ISSN 0039-3657

Recent Studies in the English Renaissance

DONALD CHENEY

I. LOGOCENTRIC ANXIETIES

> We know that ghosts cannot speak until they have drunk blood; and the spirits which we evoke demand the blood of our hearts. We give it to them gladly; but if they then abide our question, something from us has entered into them: something alien, that must be cast out, cast out in the name of truth!

Eighty years after Ulrich von Wilamowitz-Moellendorf wrote these words (in his *Greek Historical Writing*), they can serve as a cautionary epigraph to this review of the year's crop of Renaissance studies. Authors, editors, and publishers boast of the historical attentiveness of their work, of a care to place their subject in its proper cultural, political, or religious context as it has never been placed before. Not all worry openly about the risks of projecting their own cultural assumptions onto the past; those who do so are likely to be less confident than Wilamowitz about the possibility of identifying and casting out the alien. Although it is probably unrealistic to hope for much in the way of theoretical assistance in testing for historical accuracy—a more refined method of blood-matching—a warning of *caveat lector* should probably be attached to those works which seem casual in their provision of verifiable documentation of their claims about the past. It seems unlikely that all of this year's characterizations of the Renaissance can be valid.

I begin with a work in which the blood-drinking is at its most obvious and its most problematic. Jonathan Crewe's *Hidden Designs*

Donald Cheney is Professor of English at the University of Massachusetts, Amherst. He is the author of *Spenser's Image of Nature* and has translated Boccaccio's *Filocolo*. He is co-editor of *The Spenser Encyclopedia*.

is the most entertaining of the books under review, and the most difficult to evaluate. It contains (given its strategies of containment, I cannot say it "consists of") a collection of essays on various Renaissance authors: Spenser, Sidney, Puttenham, Shakespeare; and the designs which are briefly and fearfully revealed in its pages have an uncertain ontology. Perhaps they are patterns of meaning in the texts themselves; or they may be censored structures of authorial desire (the language of spycraft underlies the notion that Spenser is writing under the "deep cover" of pastoral fiction and disinformative glossing when he flirts with the "treason" of imagining Elizabeth's death in the "November" eclogue of *The Shepheardes Calender*); they are also, though not exclusively perhaps, reflections of similar patterns and desires in the critic and / or the critical profession.

Crewe creates a cover for himself no less deep or mischievously double-bluffing than what he finds in his Renaissance texts. The book is presented as an account of his encounters with criticism and the critical profession during 1980-85, at Johns Hopkins. In this it elaborates vastly on the model established by Stephen Greenblatt in his famous epilogue to *Renaissance Self-Fashioning*, where an account of his fear of lying, on a plane flight from Baltimore (where else?) to Boston, provides a final acknowledgement of the subjectivity that conditions his attempt to write the anthropology of an earlier period. For Crewe, this subjectivity is his subject, to the degree that I cannot be sure he is claiming legitimacy for his exemplary Renaissance essays any more than Joyce did for Stephen Dedalus's theory of *Hamlet*. It is not that their parent is unkent, but that they are shown to have been casually begotten in another critical country, in a cultural matrix that was never the same two days running.

Crewe does not limit himself to placing his essays in the context of his discussions with resident and visiting critics (the grey eminence of Stanley Fish is glimpsed obliquely from time to time); he casts them as well in the format of a detective story, modelled on the fiction of Leonardo Sciascia (two of whose novellae were reprinted in paperback during this period, with an introduction by Frank Kermode—who I suppose provides them with a bridge to our critical profession). The plot opens with a relatively accessible essay on Puttenham's rhetoric as "hegemonic theater" (reprinted from *ELR*), and proceeds to readings of Spenser which focus eventually on the more elusive theatricality of the *Theatre for Voluptuous Worldlings*. Gradually we learn that Crewe's "hermeneutic of suspicion" casts him in a role not unlike that of Sciascia's public investigator whose search for a crime brings him face to face with a criminal who is his mirror image. The "discovery" in chapter 5, to which this plot has been building, identifies Puttenham's *Arte of English Poesie* with Spenser's missing essay on the English Poet, and the shadowy George Puttenham himself with E. K. Although Crewe labels this a "Baconian fantasy," he stops well short of treating it as a cautionary example of misbegotten speculation. Indeed, he imbeds it in a hegemonic drama of vaster proportions, in which the 1588 *Arte* touts the supremacy of the forthcoming *Faerie Queene* in opposition to the case made for Sidney and against Spenser by Abraham Fraunce's *Arcadian Rhetorike* of the same year.

There are serious problems with this argument. Crewe claims that Fraunce's work treats Spenser "as virtually non-existent"; but one of the two Spenserian quotations there is from the unpublished *Faerie Queene*, which suggests rather the opposite. Furthermore, there is very extensive quotation of Spenser in Fraunce's *Sheapheardes Logike* manuscript of 1585, and this is largely retained in the *Lawiers Logike* published in 1588. It does not seem apparent that a confrontation between the Sidney and Spenser camps was forming at this time. I have trouble, too, in equating Puttenham and E. K. on stylistic grounds. Of course, it may be dull of me to take exception to the essay. Crewe emphasizes that it "was dictated to a very significant extent by the state of play in the Renaissance field, in which a scenario had been emerging whereby the sadomasochistic fantasies of the exiled [male] poet or laureate *manqué* could, under the particular conditions of Renaissance life, be translated into a political master plan." He avows and disavows it simultaneously, as an extreme instance of the profession's compulsion to "profess" a totalizing vision. Yet it seems clear that the fantasies of an exiled poet do belong to the Renaissance, even as they find a sympathetic and amplifying echo in the politics of poststructuralist poetics. I wish Crewe had given priority to recovering the former. Here and in his earlier book on Nashe, he shows a keen sense of the energies present in Elizabethan prose; and *Hidden Designs* may usefully serve as a basis for more strenuous readings of Puttenham and others.

Considered on its own terms, however, as a meditation on current critical debate, Crewe's book is at its most delightful in its self-destructive circularity. It is not quite a work of pseudo-critical fiction like *Pale Fire* or *Flaubert's Parrot*; its combination of autobiographical persona and exemplary texts links it more closely to the genre of the *Vita Nuova*. But at the same time Crewe celebrates the displacement of Sidney by Puttenham, he is claiming a Sidneian right to range in the zodiac of his own wit. Again, he disavows the role of amateur sleuth, in the manner of British detective fiction, as "reactionary fantasy," in favor of the European professional—he fancies himself as a public eye, not a private one. But a reader who puts Crewe's hermeneutic of suspicion itself under suspicion may come to a different conclusion: that this detection is more nearly akin to that of the British cadet aristocrat, like Lord Peter Wimsey or Mr. Campion, whose nervous diffidence betrays at once membership in the ruling class and personal estrangement from the sources of power. Detection, for them, is a fantasy of covert amendment and hence participation in their culture's power structure. Just so, one suspects, may be the fantasies in Baltimore of the crew of Jonathans —Jonahs, as it were, who testify to a "special and complicated form of indebtedness" to the great Fish. Revealingly, the only concrete evidence of Puttenham's attempt to demote Sidney in the *Arte* is his listing of him among "an other *crew* [my emphasis] of Courtly makers" (p.123). And elsewhere, in an admiring tribute to Joel Fineman's treatment of Shakespeare's sonnets, Crewe makes an observation that applies as well to himself: "although proceeding in terms of an essentially Lacanian schema, Fineman also places himself, Lacan, and everything else in poststructuralism inside Shakespeare, the new Leviathan" (p.172, n.1). Containment is finally the subject of Crewe's self-destroying artifact, as it is less directly or self-consciously of much of the more interesting criticism under review here.

In her own contribution to her edition of English Institute essays, Marjorie Garber reviews the Baconian and other fantasies of Shakespearean authorship, and after an entertaining account of the misadventures of Thomas Looney, George M. Battey, and other less ominously named anti-Stratfordians argues briefly that the plays themselves can be seen to dramatize the controversy in "an uncanny number of ways." Her examples of "ghost writers" presenting conflicting claims for authorship, and her discussion of Shakespeare's use of actual ghosts, "Senecan stalkers from the revenge tradition" asserting the rights of past authority transgressed, dovetail in their own uncanny fashion with the issues Crewe has raised about Puttenham and Spenser. Like Crewe, Garber recognizes that her Renaissance texts indisputably contain questions about the status of authorship that frequently end by rendering the texts themselves fundamentally problematic; like him, too, she recognizes the danger for the critic of exploring these questions too far. She ends by holding up Malvolio as the "strong precursor" of her nineteenth-century ninnies: an over-enthusiastic cryptographer trying to find his own name in Maria's forged letter, he cannot resist the temptation "to crush this a little" and make it "bow to me, for every one of these letters is [uncannily, he would probably say today] in my name."

The three essays on non-dramatic works in *Cannibals, Witches, and Divorce: Estranging the Renaissance* do not all suit the book's title as well as do the four on Shakespeare, but they do concern themselves with questions of authorship and authority. John Hollander's essay on the undersong of Spenser's *Prothalamion* is a characteristically subtle and learned tracing of the ways through which Spenser's linking of song and river or water's fall pass in becoming both a claim of origin and a virtual trademark, to be recognized and infringed by later poets. (When Spenser's sweet Thames flows under Wordsworth's Westminster Bridge, "The river murmurs at its own sweet will.") Patricia Parker similarly associates lyric with the anxious relation between poet and authorizing patroness in her study of the Bower of Bliss. And a long final essay by Mary Nyquist relates Milton's use of his biblical sources to problems of gendered subjectivity (in a study which complements Kendrick's Marxist interpretation of Milton discussed below).

Lecturing on the Greek historians in 1908, Wilamowitz was keenly aware of a gap between his historicism and theirs, and attributed it to the nineteenth-century development of a methodology that systematically questioned and evaluated received truths, as not even Gibbon had felt obliged to do. "Because we have over the Greeks the advantages of possessing a science of history," he argued, "the greatest of us can no longer claim the sort of authority which belonged for centuries even to a man like Livy." However brave this claim of possession may seem (and however condescending its attitude to Livy), he ends with a counsel of despair: today's historian must spend his life examining the tradition and showing it to be a collection of ruinous shards; but he must then also, somehow, breathe life into these ruins, give blood to the ghosts so they may speak to our age. That this advice, offered within the context of a university lecture, may easily be recognized as a conventional homily on combining teaching with scholarship should only emphasize the degree to which our profession is riven by a need to author the unauthorized and inauthentic, to profess what our learning has taught us we do not know. Small wonder, then, that we should be quick to respond to evidence of a comparable anxiety over authorship when we find it in our Renaissance texts; though we must also ask, like Hamlet, whether one can fully trust a ghost who expresses what can already be found in one's own prophetic soul.

In *Poetic License: Authority and Authorship in Medieval and Renaissance Contexts*, Jacqueline T. Miller has provided a very useful survey of the problem. Her most valuable contribution, I think, is the demonstration of the contradictions which are fundamental to every theoretical attempt to identify the issues, as well as to every attempt (in her reading of the texts in question) to resolve them in a specific act of authorship. She begins with the twelfth-century claim, by Bernard of Chartres, that "we are as dwarfs perched upon the shoulders of giants" and shows that this could be and was interpreted in opposing senses: that we are vastly inferior to our predecessors and yet that we *can* see further than they could, thanks to their stature and the availability of their shoulders. Burton not only expresses this desire to take the phrase both ways, but goes on to enact it in his wavering attribution of the *Anatomy* to a "Democritus Junior" who may or may not be an authority external to himself. Similarly, the concept of "poetic license," that (as Harington phrases it) "Astronomers, Painters, and Poets may lye by authoritie," carries at best a complex and backhanded authorization, though it may seem to echo Sidney's claim that poets do not lie since they do not affirm the truth of their fictions. At the very least, poetic license implies the existence of a licensing authority external to both poet and subject matter (comparable, Miller suggests, to other such abusive licenses and patents in Renaissance England); taken in the context of the Latin jingle Harington is paraphrasing, it disparages at once the professions that need such license and the motives of those who choose them. Elsewhere, it is used to excuse the need to twist sense or syntax for the sake of meter; in all cases it is far from affirming poetic autonomy.

As a means of unfolding these contradictions, Miller points to the multiple etymologies attributed to the term *auctor* by medieval grammarians. The word was related to *agere*, to act or perform: an author was an active maker—though he might be a mere "actor" by the same token, performing another's words. Or to *augere*, to grow; he caused the corpus of knowledge to increase—whether by adding something new, or by nurturing what was already there, is left uncertain. Or to an archaic *auieo*, to tie or bind, giving a more narrow sense of the author as a master of composition, ordering and binding verses. Dante favored a Greek source which he rendered as "autentim" and translated as "worthy of faith and obedience." In this last instance the question of authority is approached most directly, and with it the notion of a work's authenticity.

Miller does not go on to examine this etymology in detail, for she limits herself to medieval and Renaissance examples wherever possible. But it may be noted that the Greek *authentikos*, warranted (hence, Dante's "worthy of faith") or original, derives from *authenteo*, which means not only "to have full power or authority over" but also "to commit a murder"; an *authentēs* was a murderer (or on the evidence of Euripides, *Andromache* 172, a murderer's son). It would seem, then, that within this semantic field the power to create is radically bound up with the power to destroy, and indeed that authority is only fully realized when it has produced an *authentēs*. A sense of these primitive, tragic vectors in the complex of anxieties over authorship may help to explain its power and its ultimate resistance to resolution. Perhaps the clearest instance of the complex at its tragic pole may be the ultimate Shakespearean "ghost writer," Hamlet Senior, whom Shakespeare acted before he authored him, and whose authority mysteriously associates the killing of old Fortinbras with the birth of young Hamlet.

Miller's own examples of authorship in action are taken from medieval dream visions, from Spenser's allegory, and from Sidney's and Spenser's sonnets, and develop increasingly subtle versions of her thesis concerning the irreducible difficulties of establishing authorship in a literary text. The fact that Chaucer's *House of Fame* ends before the mysterious figure who "semed for to be / A man of gret auctorite" is either identified or allowed to speak becomes a paradigm of subsequent irresolutions. Repeatedly, for Miller, a moment or gesture of silence is taken as the most eloquent sign of an encounter between author and authorizing figure. A comparable moment, and the climax of her chapter on Spenser, is the silence of Nature at the end of the *Cantos of Mutabilitie*, which she sees as enabling the narrator to re-enter the poem. "In his final lines—his plea for the vision that Nature so easily articulated and that he so immediately dispels—the narrator of *The Faerie Queene* indicates his uneasiness with, and his desire to be released from, but his refusal to relinquish, his own authorial voice" (p.120). Earlier, she has argued for a similar impasse in the contrasting histories of Britain and Fairyland in Book II: she convincingly shows that they are mirror images of each other, each combining an act of "unjust possession" and visions of harmony lost or gained. By her reading, the poem recognizes from the start that its world is frail and contingent, destined to recede as it does in the 1596 instalment. Finally, in a concluding chapter on "Creative Imitation in the Sonnets," she explores the contradictions inherent in attempts to define the proper goal of imitation as an appropriation and transformation of the words of others. Whether the metaphor is one of digestion as opposed to regurgitation, or of making honey rather than florilegia, these definitions are uniformly vague as to where the poetic product achieves its legitimate identity. In lyrics where the desire for the beloved is identified with the desire for a poetic voice, the paradoxes may be playful but they are never finally harmonious.

Here too, as with the other works Miller has discussed, "the sense of ending is always sober and irresolute," dominated by the awareness that "a writer's authorship and the authority of his text are never final, never unassailable, never absolute" (p.175).

Although it is clear from the tone of such remarks that Miller does not feel she is describing a collection of poetic failures, she stops short of claiming explicitly that the anxiety of authorship is itself an authenticating force; that we are disposed today to recognize a sober irresolution as the only honest or realistic posture to strike in this life. Still, I think that the eloquence of her book—and the eloquence and pertinence of the texts she cites—must depend on some such implicit claim. It is instructive, therefore, to set *Poetic License* next to a work in which modern theory is much more clearly present, and the texts are made to speak much more explicitly about their predecessors. Ronald R. Macdonald's intertextual study of Vergil, Dante, and Milton draws its title from a remark by Macaulay on the magic of Milton's words: "No sooner are they pronounced, than the past is present and the distant near. New forms of beauty start at once into existence, and all the burial-places of memory give up their dead." Here, it is the belated poet who gives blood to his ancestors' ghosts, not the modern scholar, so we are distanced somewhat from the sources of logocentric anxiety. Further, Macaulay is writing with a comfortable "authority" that in the next century Wilamowitz will lack, thanks to his fortunate fall into *Wissenschaft,* and he evokes a transformative concept of memory that elides the question of just how these new forms are to be identified with the dead who are being given up.

Macdonald cites the song in *The Tempest* that "does remember my drown'd father," and takes the remembering there literally, as a general transformation of the father's members into pearls and coral. "Some such act of re-membrance," he suggests, "is what the epic poet aims at, to hear the nymphs ring the predecessor's knell, even as they turn him into something rich and strange." He invokes Freud as the basis for his central thesis: "true remembering," shown by the poet's meditations on the underworld, "as opposed to compulsive repetition, is the only way the past can be experienced as masterable" (p. 9). Coming on this argument with our sensitivity to contradiction heightened by Miller's analyses, we may pause to ask what constitutes true remembering here. Is it a total transformation of the past, as Ferdinand would have it? Hardly; this is only Act I and he has a lot to learn about fathers before he can be authorized as ready for marriage. Or is it a remembering in which the dead are given up, and given back to the living, in their original forms—as Aesculapius is said to have re-membered Hippolytus, all original parts? Macdonald grafts the traditional theory of memorial *loci* (as in the *Ad Herrenium)* to the idea of repression as active forgetting, to propose a psychoanalytic *ars memoriae* in which the burial-places yield repressed materials which are subjective in nature—already transformed, that is. Perhaps the paradigm should be Pelops or Osiris, who were recollected from largely original parts but with some artificial reconstruction as well: good as new, and perhaps better, but different in ways that may reward analysis.

At the heart of such difference is what Harold Bloom has mapped as the revisionary ratios of a poet's "misreading" of his predecessors. Macdonald has read his three poets very thoroughly indeed, and demonstrates brilliantly the points at which they reward such neo-Freudian interpretation. He starts from a discussion of antithetical language in Vergil which parallels Miller's oppositional readings, by noting that terms like *fama, sacer, altus* contain opposed meanings, and that terms relating to speech—*fatum, fama, infandum*—generate a problematic of authorship that he labels a "discourse of Fate" analogous to Lacan's "discourse of the Other." To summarize his argument is to risk implying that it is more rigorously theoretical (and trendy) than is in fact the case. Its most salient characteristic is its sensitivity to the texture of the poems under discussion; above all else it is a collection of readings, lovingly presented, in which echoes of an earlier author enhance our understanding. To choose one example among many, Macdonald suggests that the mysterious "dreadful Faces" that Adam and Eve see when they look back at Eden recall the *dirae facies* of gods hostile to Troy that Aeneas sees as he abandons his burning city (*Aeneid* 2.814). The allusion reminds us that Milton is ending his poem at the point where Vergil's began, having opened with a figure of heroic wrath, *indignata sub umbras*, that recalled Vergil's final picture of Turnus. At the same time, it evokes a sense of Adam and Eve as immature heroes, projecting their anxieties onto external objects as Aeneas had done at the beginning of his adventures; like him, they have a long way to go.

At times, I found myself wishing that Macdonald had himself gone further in the application of Bloom's theory of misreading, by making more of its agonistic aspects. To note that *sacer*, like *fama*, embraces opposing meanings is to be reminded that Vergil's *auri sacra fames* (*Aeneid* 3.57) is strikingly misread in just this way by Dante's Statius (*Purgatorio* 22.40-1), in an episode that probably outdoes anything in Milton for its wrestling with poetic forebears. Again, speaking of Milton's image of the "belated Peasant" at the end of Book I, Macdonald very helpfully notes that it recalls Aeneas's glimpse of Dido in the underworld; but he sees this as an indication of Milton's democratic feelings, in that it introduces an anonymous representative of humankind and rebukes the "aristocratic pretensions of the fallen angels" (p. 197). But since it is a scene of fairy revels that the peasant "sees, / Or dreams he sees," it would be more to the point of Milton's desire to "purge the heroic tradition" to say that the image questions both the Spenserian tradition and Shakespeare's "re-membering" of it in *Midsummer Night's Dream*. Our recognition of Vergil's linking of Dido and the moon, then, vastly increases the resonance of Elizabeth's association with both, as well as our sense of Milton's anxiety here which leads him to associate his great Elizabethan predecessors with the femininity and virginity of their queen. Here, surely, is an element of "something alien" in Milton's version of the past; and it needs to be identified, whether we propose to exorcise it "in the name of truth" or to see it as the truth we seek, the mark of a poet's authenticity. The psychoanalytic *ars memoriae* promises to be long indeed, but Macdonald's brief study affords us a precious introduction to it.

II. EDITIONS

This year's output of new scholarly editions is dominated by volumes from the Erasmus and More series. With the emergence of the third and final volume of the *Contemporaries of Erasmus*, edited by Peter G. Bietenholz and Thomas B. Deutscher, scholars have access to a marvelous collection of up-to-date biographies, with bibliographic information and portraits wherever available. Less purposeful denizens of reading rooms will have an equal opportunity to be distracted. Fredericus Nausea is represented by an appropriately queasy portrait; that Petrus Paludanus has no portrait at all is not surprising in that he is included because Erasmus three times protested that he never knew anybody by the name, despite the existence of a letter of his addressed to this apparent *ignis fatuus*. It is impossible to look up just one biography in this work.

Volume 7 of Erasmus's correspondence covers the period from 1519 to 1520, a painful period of controversy as the "Lutherana tragoedia" unfolded inexorably. Letters from and to More figure prominently here; and in letter 999, to Ulrich von Hutten, Erasmus provides his famous description of his English friend. The volume also includes the first translation of the *Dialogus bilinguium ac trilinguium*, attributed generally to Konrad Nesen but associated with Erasmus and at times attributed to him. Volumes 5 and 6 of the Literary and Educational Writings, edited by A.H.T. Levi, contain six of Erasmus's best-known works: the *Panegyric for Archduke Philip of Austria*, the *Julius Excluded from Heaven*, *The Education of a Christian Prince*, *A Complaint of Peace*, and above all the *Ciceronian* and the *Praise of Folly*. To cite these last two in their English forms is to call attention to the melancholy reality that an English Erasmus is a pale allusion to the real thing. As Betty Radice remarks of the Latin of the *Moria*, "It is almost impossible to reproduce its blend of erudite badinage, ironic ambiguity, delicate wit, trenchant satire, and simple eloquence on behalf of the Christian faith. Erasmus came to it in 1509 as soon as he had finished his commentary on over four thousand Greek and Latin quotations and proverbs in the *Adagia*, and nowhere else does he pile up so many allusions to classical authors ranging from Homer to Ausonius. For scholars like himself and More such verbal echoes would create what was virtually a private language, and one which must have been immensely enjoyable." Although we must remain intensely grateful to the Toronto project for its scrupulous treatment of translation and notes, and although I cannot pretend to have the Latin or the patience (or the money—the Amsterdam edition of the Latin text is currently coming out at a price of sixty-five cents a page, over four times the price of the Toronto edition, at a rough estimate) to read Erasmus in plain text, it is impossible not to feel a sense of loss, not only of enjoyment but of a fundamental understanding of what these humanists were doing with and to language. With the *Moria* we lose the personalized intimacy of shared readings; with the *Ciceronianus*, the very argument is virtually irretrievable, and we are left like Casca feeling that what may or may not be Ciceronian is Greek to us.

All the more reason, therefore, to be grateful to the editors of the Yale More for giving us the Latin original on facing pages; though we should probably give thanks to More for writing less, and to the Knights of Columbus for spending more. Volume 15, edited by Daniel Kinney, provides four major letters in defense of humanism (to Martin Dorp, to the University of Oxford, to Edward Lee, and to a Monk [John Batmanson]), along with the text and translation of the Paris manuscript of the *Historia Richardi Tertii* that was unfortunately not available to the late Richard S. Sylvester when he prepared his edition of the English and Latin versions of the work.

Kinney develops the text and context of these materials with scrupulous thoroughness; and (as with all the books surveyed here) it must be for others to give an adequate assessment of his achievement. Of the many controversies that More engages in his defense of Erasmus, of particular interest is the debate over Erasmus's Latin translation of the New Testament (which he entitled *Novum instrumentum* in the first 1516 edition; *Novum Testamentum*, perhaps less provocatively, thereafter). In general, More and his friend are championing the right and indeed the necessity to translate the Greek original in more than one way; not only is it possible that Jerome did not pick the best word, but it is positively desirable that a copious range of alternative translations replace a single, limiting one.

That such an argument should seem dangerously revolutionary to traditionalists, especially in view of the Lutheran threat, is not entirely surprising; but their anxiety seems the more understandable in view of the fact that Erasmus proposed to translate the opening of St. John as "In principio erat sermo," and went on: "et sermo erat apud deum, et deus erat ille sermo . . . Et sermo ille caro factus est, et habitavit in nobis." More seems slightly disingenuous in defending his friend here, for he admits that "logos" is perhaps one of those words like "Amen" or "Osanna" that should be left untranslated, "since it is wonderfully rich in holy meanings"; he only argues that since earlier translators have not done so, "the next-best procedure is for them to translate it variously so that none of the meanings . . . goes unknown or falls into disuse" (p. 239). Rather, what Erasmus seems to be doing, and what he seemed to traditionalists to be doing, involved a demystifying of the Word from internalized promise or potential, in the direction of knowable speech. He and More must have seemed as revolutionary then as do English critics and their Continental mentors today, when they speak of textual indeterminacy and *écriture*.

The advantage of a text in which the Latin original appears alongside the translation is that it allows a reader to seek an explanation of an apparently vacuous passage. Thus, for example, in the *Letter to a Monk*, More attacks an informant of the Monk's in terms that lose their pith in translation: "For though you call him a man of good faith, a man clearly both serious and (using your own pretty phrase) genial-mannered [*mor*igeratum], honorable by the standards of secular dignity, . . . he is drawn in a quite different light by the people who know him the best: not a man of good faith, far from genial in character [non valde *mor*atis *mor*ibus], and actually churlish [vere *mor*osum]" (pp. 206-207; emphases added). More seems to be establishing his territorial claim here, in the manner of a tomcat, by spraying the area with his own multivalent etymon, much as Erasmus and he had punned on the meanings of their names. Folly, moroseness, morality, delay, death—the humanist contains this cornucopia, and More.

H. A. Mason's selection of Wyatt's poems reflects a lifetime of study and response to the poet, but in a context that is not likely to be useful to many readers. At the center of the volume, he prints the poems in modern spelling, one to a page without distracting glosses or commentary. Extensive but apparently random collections of commentary, topical and textual, appear before and after. The announced purpose of the edition is to provide the reader with all the information necessary, without reference to other books. The result is a frustrating gathering of allusions to unspecified and untraceable materials. On page 327 we are given three stanzas of "a poem made up of proverbs" which "is not easy to come by." Elsewhere we hear of a similarly unidentified "Spanish chronicler" who is not to be trusted but is quoted. Wyatt's text remains in need of careful editing that is subject to collective scrutiny—as is clear from Mason's own 200-page "pamphlet" of 1972, *Editing Wyatt,* a review of the deficiencies of the Muir and Thomson edition—if we are ever to have an adequate sense of how original or idiosyncratic he really was. It is far too early, though, to have faith in any single scholar's sense of how he can be regularized for presentation to the modern reader.

The first volume of the Clarendon edition of Marlowe's works, edited by Roma Gill, contains what are loosely termed his "translations": the Ovid and Lucan, *Hero and Leander* (printed here without the Chapman continuation or the division into Sestiads that accompanied it), *Dido,* and "miscellaneous"—"The Passionate Shepherd" and a pair of Latin writings (the opposite of translations). One might suspect that the label was a half-hearted attempt to characterize the third of his *oeuvre* that did not contain the major plays; but in fact Gill takes it seriously and has some interesting remarks on Marlowe's evolution as a translator, which supplement what she has said elsewhere on the subject. If this first volume is any indication, I suspect that her edition will prove valuable as a supplement to the Revels volumes (which have fuller and more helpful notes, with a modernized text) and the Bowers edition (with more exhaustive if not wholly definitive justifications of the old-spelling text), rather than as a replacement to either or both.

In editing a translation, a commentator is faced with difficult decisions as to how much explanation the original text demands. The situation is aggravated when the translation is an early work full of errors or infelicities, as with Marlowe's versions of Ovid's *Amores.* In general, Gill assumes that the reader knows the modern text of Ovid, and will recognize the howlers without being nudged; she usually restrains herself to commenting when a sixteenth-century text has a reading that may help to explain the rendering. Marlowe tends to go astray when he needs to supply personal pronouns which are lacking in the original. An example is at II.xv.11, where Ovid apparently turns from addressing the ring to address his lady; Marlowe misses the turn, and asks the ring to "hide thy left hand underneath her lappe." The error is less gross than it seems, however, since Ovid is in the process of imagining himself transformed into the ring, and there is not the clear distinction between his hand and the lady's that an English version virtually necessitates.

Although Gill is committed to the creation of a sober, definitive edition, she shows a welcome readiness to call the reader's attention to her more delightful discoveries. One of these is a variant that Marlowe would surely have enjoyed: where the text at Elegy II.xiii.23 properly reads "In white, with incense Ile thine Altars greete," the Douce variant in the Bodleian reads "In wives, with incest." This information is available in Bowers, but not publicized there. And we must be grateful to Gill for the information that in the second century B.C. a Hero of Alexandria included in his *Pneumatica* (no. 44, "Notes produced from several Birds in succession, by a Stream of Water") the necessary hydraulic technology for the buskins worn by Marlowe's Hero.

Of this year's selection of anthologies and editions directed toward students, a work of particular distinction is Katharina M. Wilson's *Women Writers of the Renaissance and Reformation*, which contains an abundant range of texts from seven countries or language areas (including England), with each of the twenty-five authors introduced by a separate scholar who provides detailed biographical, historical, and bibliographic information. Anthologies of literature in translation tend to be rather perfunctory gatherings, but this is a carefully assembled work that deserves to have a profound impact on the curriculum.

Lawrence Manley's collection of writings illustrative of London in the age of Shakespeare will doubtless find its place in reserve book rooms, where it will provide a welcome alternative to "background studies" like the *Shakespeare's England* of 1916, relying on scholarly essays rather than on contemporary texts. Teachers will be glad for the freedom it offers to select materials of particular relevance to their syllabi. Another collection of original materials that will be similarly adaptable to selective assignment is the well-known *Elizabethan Lyrics* edited by Norman Ault (first published in 1925), now available in paperback. Changing times have given a certain irony, however, to the printer's dedication which still urges, "Doubt not to buy this pretty Book, / The price is not so dear."

Another reprint (though it comes with a sticker advertising it as "A

Penguin Original") is Gerald Hammond's selection of writings by Sir Walter Ralegh (first published by Carcanet in 1984); its selection of poetry is relatively slight and under-annotated, but it has the real merit of providing over two hundred pages of the prose. This should recommend it to courses which stress the historical and political contexts of Elizabethan literature.

The Penguin edition of Shakespeare's *Sonnets* by John Kerrigan is advertised as "the first full critical edition . . . to appear in almost a decade"—in moving to Shakespeare we encounter a new sense of the brutal shortness of an edition's life. Kerrigan does provide, however, an exceptionally thorough and thoughtful treatment of the sonnets in all their aspects; and his edition is a viable alternative to Stephen Booth's, if one is desired.

Methuen has begun a series of texts "designed to meet the needs of readers for whom the study of literature also involves the study of its historical and critical contexts," in the words of its general editor, John Drakakis. It seems from the two Renaissance volumes published this year that these needs can be addressed in quite different ways. Robert Wilcher's edition of Marvell's poetry and prose (in an 80-20 mix) opens with a brief introduction to the life and times, and prefaces its commentary on individual works with a longish essay on the history of Marvell criticism, stressing the poet's lyric and public voices. Though some will prefer to continue using the complete editions of the poems by Lord and Donno, Wilcher provides us with a sensible and balanced presentation of Marvell's works which seems generally close to the present critical consensus.

The edition of Donne's poetry and prose by T. W. and R. J. Craik is more idiosyncratic. The *Songs and Sonnets* appear in alphabetical order by title, and a determined effort has been made to cut back on what seem superfluous annotations, on the principle expressed by C.S. Lewis that Donne "knew what he was putting into his poem, and we cannot get out of it more than he knew he was putting in." This is probably not a principle that most of us would choose to enunciate today, or try to put into action. When the editors give us their reasons for not mentioning lachrymatories in their note on "Twickenham Garden," or state flatly of the *Epithalamion Made at Lincoln's Inn* that "It is unlikely that it was written for any special occasion, either for a real wedding or for a mock one," I am not convinced that I have a clearer sense of the poem's contexts.

Anthony Raspa's edition of Donne's *Devotions Upon Emergent Occasions* (1975) has been re-issued by Oxford University Press. In a new preface, the editor expresses his conviction that his claims for Donne's relationship to the Jesuit meditative tradition are no longer as controversial as they were formerly, and points for support to John Carey's book with its emphasis on Donne's Catholic upbringing.

III. GENERAL STUDIES

Two new journals of interest to students of the English Renaissance have made their appearance this year. The humble *Bulletin* of the Society for Renaissance Studies has been reborn as a handsomely designed *Renaissance Studies* published by Oxford University Press. It thus becomes a British counterpart to *Renaissance Quarterly*, which underwent a comparable transformation some decades ago. Articles in the first issue are devoted to the fields of history and the visual arts, but the entire range of Renaissance studies is its purview, as can be seen from the reviews. The burgeoning field of emblem studies has now produced *Emblematica*, the first issue of which (rather ominously dated Spring 1986) contains articles by John Manning on Continental emblem books in sixteenth-century England, by Michael Bath on the iconography of weeping stags in *As You Like It*, and by Mason Tung on Peacham's use of Camerarius's *Symbola et Emblemata*. Also worthy of note are the thirteenth volumes respectively of *The Renaissance Bulletin* and *Renaissance Monographs*, both products of the Renaissance Institute in Tokyo and testimony to the lively Japanese interest in the English Renaissance, under the guidance of Peter Milward.

A. *Translatio studii*

Two workmanlike and useful studies of English translations from the Latin have appeared this year. Deborah Rubin provides a detailed study of Sandys's Ovid, placing it in the contexts of seventeenth-century poetic practice as applied to translation and discussing the long tradition of commentary on which it drew. William Kupersmith casts his net more widely in his study of the Roman satirists as they were translated over the course of the seventeenth century, from Jonson to Dryden and his "Myrmidons." Too many authors appear in his brief survey to admit of much analysis in depth, but Kupersmith gives an attractive overview of this prelude to the golden age of imitation in the following century.

George deForest Lord gives us an engagingly frank indication of the origins of his *Classical Presences in Seventeenth-Century English Poetry*: he thanks one colleague for suggesting that a lifetime's collection of books, articles, and introductions could be "revised, cut, rethought" and made into a book, and he thanks another for putting all this material onto disks that he could edit. Even without

Lord's acknowledgment, however, the volume's lack of organic unity would be apparent. The notion of "classical presences" is itself a tenuous principle of organization, and the essays —at least those dealing with the pre-Restoration period—are too narrow in focus to point toward larger issues. Lord restates his claim for the "rightness" of Chapman's view of the evolutionary character of Odysseus, and thanks T.S. Eliot for a letter approving his claim, which was not widely accepted by reviewers of *Homeric Renaissance* where it first appeared. In the case of Milton, Lord's thesis is even more problematic: he continues to believe that the fair field of Enna recalls the Homeric Hymn to Demeter, even though the only known manuscript of that poem was first catalogued in Moscow in 1777; Milton must have seen an unrecorded manuscript in Italy, or perhaps his friend Marvell saw the Moscow manuscript on his visit to Russia. A chapter on "Andrew Marvell and the Virgilian Triad" strains to introduce the *rota* into what remains a general introduction to the poems.

Paulo maiora canamus. It is easier to praise than to summarize Leonard Barkan's *The Gods Made Flesh: Metamorphosis and the Pursuit of Paganism*, which is easily this year's most substantial study of the classical tradition in the Renaissance. Barkan has undertaken the extraordinarily complex subject of Ovidian metamorphosis and its effect on literature and painting; he has achieved a massive and monumental work of synthesis that keeps its balance and enthusiasm intact throughout. Chapters on Ovid, Dante, and Shakespeare provide the most sustained analysis of literary texts, while intervening chapters deal more generally with medieval and renaissance transitions. An introductory essay on "Tapestry Figures" gives an indication of Barkan's method: an analysis of Ovid's treatment of Arachne is followed by a discussion of Velázquez's *Las Hilanderas*, which is seen as a seventeenth-century reworking of the subject by a painter sensitive to the theme of artistic ambition (of authority and authorship, we could say) that was available in the original. Barkan describes the contrasting artistries of Arachne and Minerva, suggesting that Ovid's clear commitment to the Arachnid party may be not only human but a response to the monumental, Palladian influence of Vergil in late Augustan Rome. He indicates, too, the degree to which Arachne's figuring of the rape of Europa among her subjects was given increased prominence by later writers, so that it is not surprising that Velázquez too makes this quintessential instance of metamorphosis the subject of his background scene. Barkan's thesis is that metamorphosis stands at the heart of classical myth, and comes to stand for the classic tradition as well as for an "antiheroic upside-down world of flux" that challenges a masculine social order. "The history of metamorphosis," he proposes, "bound up with the great subject of the survival of antiquity, is the history of a two-thousand-year counterreligion of paganism."

Barkan is well suited to this project of reinterpreting the history of classical survival to our generation. As an art historian, he is able to write with insight on the appeal of Ovid to painters, as well as on the boundaries between description and illustration that are so important to Ovid's tracing of change. I suspect, too, that the experience of slide comparisons may lie behind his adroitness at mingling quotation and commentary. Although this is a long book, it is everywhere concise and even epigrammatic. The footnotes testify to an assimilation of the massive literature associated with each chapter's subject, and they provide a sympathetic guide to recent criticism. At the same time, they are filled with incidental insights and caveats. However inconvenient it may be to keep turning to them (a complaint that applies to most of the books under review, unfortunately; why hasn't electronic typesetting brought footnotes back to the foot of the page?), they are a valuable part of the book, and readers will ignore them at their peril. All in all, this is an essential source for future studies in Renaissance classicism and intertextuality.

B. Contexts

This year's most important attempt to expand our understanding of the social contexts of Renaissance literature, Leah S. Marcus's *Politics of Mirth*, has already been reviewed by Jean Howard last spring, but deserves mention here since non-dramatic texts are considered as well. Marcus argues for the political force behind the "defense of old holiday pastimes" sponsored by James and Charles and expressed by their poets and playwrights. What seems an innocently personal nostalgia in Herrick's pastoralism takes on a surprising resonance as one becomes aware of the Royalist overtones in a celebration of the countryside. I say "resonance" advisedly, choosing a neutral term that avoids any specification of the political goal or consequences of the poem itself: it is hard enough to say just how a play like *Bartholomew Fair* advanced royal policy at the scenes of its early performances, and harder still to say this of a poem, where the presence of earlier poems is likely to be felt more insistently and where the site of reading is left unspecified and uncontrollable. But we must be grateful to Marcus for the learning and tact with which she has made us realize that even mirth has its authorizing "license."

Several collections of essays approach contextual issues as well, and must be mentioned briefly for their similar consciousness-raising value for conjurors of Renaissance ghosts. Neil Fraistat's *Poems in Their Place* includes essays ranging from antiquity to the present, considering how the ordering or assembling of shorter works into a collective volume determines their meaning. S. K. Heninger, Jr., considers Sidney in this respect; John T. Shawcross, Donne; Annabel Patterson, the miscellanies; Joseph Wittreich, the linking of *Paradise Regained* and *Samson Agonistes*. The book enacts its thesis, to the degree that its value lies less in the substance of individual essays than in their collective impact. The final essay is the most powerful, and sums up the whole: Marjorie Perloff's demonstration of how the posthumous publication of Plath's *Ariel* contained additions, deletions, and juxtapositions that tilted the emphasis away from marital problems and toward parental ones. Just so contingent is the order we find in earlier texts, but it is unlikely that we shall ever have firm evidence of alteration of authorial intent such as appears here. As a whole, Fraistat's collection gives a clearer sense of the dimensions of the problems in this area.

Gerald P. Tyson and Sylvia S. Wagonheim have edited a collection of essays on print and culture in the Renaissance, largely devoted to European examples, although Fredson Bowers considers problems of authority in Shakespearean texts and John N. Wall discusses the effect of printing on the diffusion of the gospel. More directly pertinent to English studies is the collection on *Politics of Discourse* in the seventeenth century by Kevin Sharpe and Steven N. Zwicker. In essays that try variously to link literature and history, Barbara Lewalski writes on the Countess of Bedford; Blair Worden, on Marvell's "Horatian Ode"; Earl Miner, on Milton and the histories available to him; Mary Ann Radzinowicz, on the politics of *Paradise Lost*; Annabel Patterson, on the political contexts of fables. The volume opens with an especially clear and useful theoretical statement by J. G. A. Pocock, on "Texts as Events." Claude J. Summers and Ted-Larry Pebworth have published the proceedings of a 1984 conference on seventeenth-century religious lyric. Although by now the reader will have recognized a certain repetitiousness in these collections, which reflect the travels of a finite number of scholars (here is Wittreich on *Samson*, again), the collection does have its useful and distinctive elements. William A. Sessions's essay on abandonment in the religious lyric, for instance, only hints at the dimensions of that important theme, but suggestively treats the analogy of Ovid's *Heroides*.

Three volumes deal with seventeenth-century religious contexts.

James Holstun's *A Rational Millenium: Puritan Utopias of Seventeenth-Century England and America* looks at the ideological struggles which underlie utopian visions, whether in the Algonquian praying towns of John Eliot or in the republican political writings of James Harrington in Protectorate England. Though this is a work that is situated in intellectual history more than in literary studies, it is obviously pertinent to our field as well.

In *The Drama of Dissent: The Radical Poetics of Nonconformity, 1380-1590*, Ritchie D. Kendall argues that however anti-theatrical the Dissenters may have been in their attacks on the stage, they were in fact practicing a kind of theater of their own, so that we can talk of a "distinctly radical tradition of dissident poetics." He discusses the very different forms that this drama could take: Lollard writings with their displaced drama, the works of John Bale which included actual dramas, the "drama of disputation" in Thomas Cartwright, and the more overtly theatrical rhetoric of Martin Marprelate's publications. His argument, which obviously has points of contact with Crewe's notions of hegemonic theater or theatricality, seems a promising line of approach to the largely unconquered territory of Renaissance polemic. We have developed sophisticated vocabularies for applying a Protestant poetics to the more decorous texts, but we need a theory of oppositional rhetoric that will help us explain what is going on in those radically Protestant texts that refuse to conform to our linguistic expectations, or to meet us half way.

Jerome Friedman ventures into the wildest regions of Dissent in his survey of the Ranters, *Blasphemy, Immorality, and Anarchy*. He has read widely and tries to summarize what he has found; but lacking any theoretical basis for approaching his texts, he has not been able to make them accessible, or show that there is anything in them beyond the blasphemy, immorality, and anarchy that their contemporaries saw. The reader quickly wearies of the bizarre world he finds here; a better introduction to the subject, though more limited in scope, remains Christopher Hill's *The World Turned Upside Down*.

C. Generic horizons

Among the publications this year which investigate relations with the other arts is a collection of essays devoted to literature and the visual arts, edited by Richard S. Peterson for a special issue of the *John Donne Journal*. They include an essay on Bodley's bookcases and a fascinating analysis by John Dixon Hunt on elements of emblem and impresa in a portrait of William Style of Langley in the Tate Collection. Elizabeth Cook, in her *Seeing Through Words*, is concerned with a different aspect of the visual: the sense in which seventeenth-century poets as well as Shakespeare in his plays are attentive to the material world—"see" things and make us see them too—to a degree that is not true of earlier writers. An early chapter on shaped or figured poems sees their actual creation of pictures on the page as a specious but potentially initiatory form of what she has in mind. "The corporeal eye is bribed by the immediate gratification provided by the image on the page, to perform the more menial accessory task of scanning the words which stimulate a more subtle understanding, and suggest images less complete, but also less inert and more various than any dumb outline" (p. 47). She employs a concept of the mind that she finds in Hobbes, but as she goes on to explore specific images in the plays and poems, she is helped less by any evolving theory of metaphor than by an innate skill and tact in describing the relations between image and metaphor as she explicates her texts.

Winifred Maynard, in *Elizabethan Lyric Poetry and its Music*, has compiled a lucid and informative survey of her subject, with an emphasis on the present state of our knowledge about the music of the Elizabethan period, including evidence that may be derived from literary texts. I regret that I am in no position to evaluate this work, which appears to be a substantial synthesis of musicological learning although it makes no claim to sophisticated literary analysis.

In the area of specifically literary genres, Joseph M. Lenz has written a study of closure in romance. *The Promised End* contains essays on *Sir Gawain*, *Morte Darthur*, *The Faerie Queene*, and *The Winter's Tale*, comparing the different devices or closural gestures by which each achieves an ending that is characteristic of romance. Although little new ground is broken in this heavily cultivated field, the commentary is generally sensitive and trustworthy. I wish, though, that the publisher had chosen to modernize the thorns in all those *Gawain* quotations rather than employ the distractingly inappropriate phi or slashed o. And readers who despair at finding *peripeteia* misspelled four times on page 20 (there are a lot of endings still to be described) should be reassured that it is spelled correctly by page 40.

Peter Lindenbaum is similarly hampered by a lack of room for original commentary in his *Changing Landscapes: Anti-Pastoral Sentiment in the English Renaissance*. Although his treatment of Sidney, Shakespeare, Spenser, and Milton is convincing enough, it is all pretty familiar by now. As he admits, the "anti-pastoral" denial of escapism that he takes as his subject is widely considered to be inherent in the pastoral mode; so in the end this is simply another survey of pastoral.

Warren W. Wooden's collection of essays on Renaissance children's literature, posthumously edited by Jeanie Watson, suffers from a more serious problem: there was no children's literature in the English Renaissance, for there were no children then, in the sense of beings resident in a distinct, presexual garden state for which separate reading materials were felt appropriate. If Wooden had lived to complete his research into the origins of children's literature, he might have had something valuable to say about the representation in Renaissance art of those creatures that we today would identify as children; but there is no conceptual overview here that would enable an accurate naming of the subject. When Foxe describes the horrors of Bishop Bonner's mistreatment of children, he is certainly suggesting that Catholics are all the more clearly wicked for picking on little ones; but he is no more addressing himself to children than Chaucer's Prioress is when she tells her tale. Similarly, the attitude toward a less-than-adult figure in Skelton's "Philip Sparowe" is an interesting problem that can bear a good deal more discussion; but I can see little point in considering the poem as even potentially a part of children's literature.

Wyman H. Herendeen has written a book about rivers in literature which I hesitantly treat as a genre study, since it does talk about river poems (beginning with Ausonius's *Moselle*). But it is very hard to classify *From Landscape to Literature: The River and the Myth of Geography*. The author tells us that it has been a labor of love, and this is obvious: he has read everything he could find on rivers, and he gives us numerous illustrations of rivers and more or less related things. But he seems aware of his problems of organizing his material when he concedes in the preface: "An author can only ask the reader to allow himself or herself to be drawn into the current, to be led through varied landscapes by rivers which are not one's own." This is a fair description of the experience of reading the book, as well as a fair example of its style. The reader is very much adrift as he floats along unfamiliar but indistinguishible ways, longing for an overview of the geography, some sense of where he is going.

It is possible to say what the book is *not*. It is not a study of the river as trope. Herendeen does not mention recent books by David Quint and John Guillory which deal at length with the matter of origins (as does Hollander's essay in the Garber volume), nor does he cite their primary sources for the most part. For that matter, he does not cite much literary criticism. He is much more concerned (as we might have guessed from his title) with the representation of actual rivers in literature, and with the ways in which the river poem mythologizes landscape. These are valid and interesting subjects, and I only wish that Herendeen had been able to organize his material so that it could be presented more coherently.

D. Reputation studies

Sir Philip Sidney: 1586 and the Creation of a Legend commemorates the annversary of Sidney's death with a collection of essays that are about equally divided between descriptions of the circumstances of the death and funeral and more speculative considerations of the legend that was largely determined by that death. Essays in the former category contain much that is informative, especially as regards Dutch materials. In this the volume is a fitting memorial to the Anglo-Dutch scholarship of Jan van Dorsten, one of its editors, who died suddenly before it was published, and who contributes an essay on "The Final Year." The last essay in the volume, by Jackson Boswell and H.R. Woudhuysen, assembles some unfamiliar allusions to Sidney and urges the compilation of a full-scale "Sidney Allusion Book," a work that is clearly needed before we can see the true outlines of the legend. This service has now been performed for George Herbert: Robert H. Ray's *Herbert Allusion Book* has appeared as an issue of *Studies in Philology*. Writing in the *George Herbert Journal*, Ray summarizes his discoveries. Herbert's wide appeal is seen to rest on the fact that he could easily be adapted or read selectively to serve one or another sectarian interest, and at the same time he was seen as a universally admirable "divine poet." The same could probably be said of his twentieth-century reputation, to judge from recent studies.

Other reputation studies focus on periods outside the Renaissance. A special issue of the *John Donne Journal* treats the reputation of the Metaphysicals in the nineteenth century. In *Regaining Paradise: Milton and the Eighteenth Century*, Dustin Griffin takes issue with Harold Bloom's claim that Milton was an overwhelming predecessor and argues that he was an admired and supportive influence instead. And Jay A. Gertzman has surveyed nineteenth-century popular editions of Herrick. (His opening sentence does not inspire confidence: " 'Who now reads Herrick?' asked Walt Whitman, in a poem by Alan Tate." Who now reads Allen Tate?)

IV. STUDIES OF INDIVIDUAL AUTHORS

Arthur F. Kinney is concerned to show that John Skelton's "primary vocation was that of a priest, not a poet, and it is that which fundamentally informs much of his literary work." In *John Skelton, Priest as Poet,* he provides us with an abundance of information about the pre-Reformation English liturgy and festival that would have made up the stuff of Skelton's daily life, and he uses this information to provide systematic interpretations of the poems, challenging or qualifying the pictures of Skelton as Tudor humanist advanced by William Nelson, or as Stanley Fish' s reader-response manipulator. Kinney's enthusiasm for his subject is contagious; he is especially successful, I think, in locating the energies of Skelton's verse in the still-largely-unchallenged religious practices of his world. He argues persuasively against the comic priest of the merry tales who became a necessary stereotype of his Protestant admirers later in the century. To the extent that our own assumptions about Skelton are shaped by this jolly figure of misrule, Kinney's corrective is both timely and precious. Like the Goliardic tradition that seems generally pertinent here, Skelton's poetics assume an extensive familiarity with the liturgy and are in fact continuous with it.

I take it that it is this aspect of unbroken continuity between the sacred and the profane that constitutes the principal task of recuperation that Kinney is addressing. This is not always apparent, for much of the book is devoted to telling us about details of a largely unchanging Christian calendar. Though he bases his information on the Sarum ritual that Skelton would have known, he is not concerned to show where and how this differs from later Anglican or Roman practices; so it might seem that his repeated references to what we have since lost apply chiefly to a country that has no national church, or to readers who have chosen not to attend it. If that were the case, it would seem that Skelton's priestly poetics must be largely similar to George Herbert's, say. That those two poets have so little in common is rather a sign of the cultural changes brought by the century of Reformation and Counter-Reformation that separates them.

The Skelton described by Kinney is as ready to find traditional figures of Christian truth portrayed or parodied outside the church door as inside. Not for him the inward-turning meditative exercises that would shortly become characteristic of all religious verse. In fact, the very concept of "religious verse" as a distinct genre or subject matter is alien. Furthermore, Skelton is still composing in a tradition that is figural in the additional sense that the printed book has not fully determined the verbal status of the text. Philip Sparowe takes his place among the "sparowes soules / Set in our bede rolles" in that he is one with the sparrows of Scripture (Psalms 83 and 101; Matthew 10:29) and is also among those marginal figures of birds in manuscript illuminations. If Jane Scrope would give him a more privileged position "with the corner of a Crede" it is similarly in both these senses; figuring both the humblest of God's creatures and mankind's airborne aspirations, the bird fittingly decorates a creed which affirms the intersection of the human and the divine. A crucial part of the charm of Skelton's verse is that "multivalent density" (as Kinney terms it, p. 57) which accommodates simultaneously the naive perspective of Jane and the larger view of God's love that corrects and affirms it; here, the "corner" may be at once the humblest and most peripheral part, and the point on which the entire Creed turns.

I am not equally convinced by all of Kinney's interpretations, nor is it necessary that one should be in order to accept the general validity of his approach. As with any other interpretative apparatus, we are frequently given more information about the liturgies of specific feast days than seems likely to be operative in the poems at any given point. And to accept the aptness of the critical method being advocated is not the same as accepting specific applications. For instance, Kinney reads the opening lines of *Speke, Parrot* as describing a parrot who has been banished by "a flood as dreadful as Noah's" (p. 17) from Paradise into our fallen world, where he "must have an almon or a date" as anodynes to soothe the pain of remembering what he has lost. But I think we should take the present tense of Parrot's narrative as indicating that his "wonderous kynde," and his distinctive relationship to language, mark him as *not* belonging to our fallen human condition. The flood that brings him to India, and thence to Western "ladyes of estate," is not so much a catastrophic moment as a river, "Euphrates, that flode," which flows out of Eden and carries this "byrd of paradyse" into contact with humans. Boccaccio's Psittacus, a son of Deucalion who is changed into a parrot at his request, and so made eternally "green," seems to have given Skelton a model for a kind of speech that is both more and less immediate or authoritative than ours. Although C.S. Lewis may have been ill-advised in referring to *Speke, Parrot* as a "cryptogram of which we have lost the key"—for it is clear that we can make good sense of the poem as a whole—there may also be a sense in which his phrase accurately describes an essential aspect of the poem's meaning. Similarly, there are senses in which Kinney's valuable contribution to our understanding of Skelton may ultimately affirm the view of him as Tudor humanist. If nothing else, he suggests that Skelton would hardly have felt a need to distinguish between a priest's vocation and a poet's; given his lifelong "laureate" ambitions, it is well that he didn't.

Other books on sixteenth-century figures make substantial if more modest contributions. Uwe Baumann and Hans Peter Heinrich, editors of volumes in the German edition of More (Munich, 1983), have prepared a useful paperback introduction to the present state of scholarship on More's humanist writings: a thorough treatment of studies on the life of Pico, the translations of Lucian, the epigrams, and the *History of King Richard III,* and a more selective commentary on *Utopia* scholarship. O.R. Reuter has collected proverbial materials in Thomas Deloney's works, with rather predictable results: though the boundaries of proverb lore necessarily blur off into random instances of everyday speech, it is not surprising that Deloney's fiction should be at home in that neighborhood.

Breaking considerably more fresh ground than either of these studies, Peter E. Medine has surveyed the life and works of Thomas Wilson, best known probably for his *Rule of Reason* (1551) and *Arte of Rhetorique* (1553). Wilson was a loyal and assiduous Elizabethan whose most significant accomplishment—though he was too discreet and self-effacing for us to be sure if it was his at all—may have been the prosecution of the Duke of Norfolk and Mary, Queen of Scots. Medine produces a convincingly coherent portrait of a man of impressive intellect, his stiff-necked Protestantism the product of years of exile and trial at the hands of the Roman Inquisition, whose conservatism and patriotism were shown in an apparently disparate collection of publications, including a *Discourse upon Usury* (1572), in which, like Calvin himself, Wilson hewed to a line of traditional opposition to usury in an expression of his sense of the dangers he felt in the very changes to the social fabric that his Protestantism was bringing about; and a selection of translations from Demosthenes (1570) which obliquely argued for intervention in the Netherlands against Philip II of Spain.

This year has not seen major contributions to Sidney or Spenser scholarship, with the possible exception of Jonathan Crewe's book, discussed above. In addition to the Brill collection of Sidney essays, treated under reputation studies, the 1985 edition of *Spenser Studies* has appeared. Pride of place in it is given to John N. King's argument against the tradition of identifying Spenser with the Puritan cause in the ecclesiastical eclogues of *The Shepheardes Calender,* a tradition dating from the time of Milton, who found "some presage of these reforming times" in them. King finds that Spenser is consistently a spokesman instead for "the progressive Protestantism of his age." Anne Lake Prescott explores the sources of the thirsty deer of *Amoretti* 67, finding them in the liturgy of the latter part of Lent, especially in the Sarum rite; a parallel treatment of the image appears as well in Marguerite de Navarre. Harold L. Weatherby reopens the largely ignored question of Spenser's authorship of the 1592 *Axiochus* translation, and attempts to confirm Padelford's attribution by reference to a parallel in the Bower of Bliss. Here and elsewhere, the editors provide a forum for current scholarship, frequently in the form of extended notes rather than major revisionary or synthetic essays. Pamela J. Benson works out the role of Grace in Florimell's rescue; David O. Frantz, that of the sense of hearing in the union of Florimell and Marinell; Deborah Cartmell briefly suggests Psalm 137 as a model for the *Ruines of Time*; David J. Baker speculates that Spenser's *View* may have been suppressed because of an Irish counter-language that the authorities could sense as subversively operative beneath Spenser's official and conscious, authorized English; Louise Schleiner compares references in Sidney and Spenser to poetic inspiration; and Margaret P. Hannay edits four letters by Mary Sidney that flesh out our picture of that impressive woman's daily activities.

Elizabeth Heale's "reader's guide" to *The Faerie Queene* is explicitly directed to students who are approaching the poem for the first time, and must be evaluated on the grounds of its pedagogical usefulness rather than its advancing of any new readings of Spenser. Heale is quite aware that "In trying to explain the allegories as clearly as possible, I run the risk of over-simplifying and falsifying the poem's carefully achieved obliquity." Fair enough; we can probably agree that students need a preliminary guide of some sort if they are going to find their way into the poem. Heale provides a series of three- or four-page discussions of individual characters and episodes, for the most part advancing her interpretations with commendable restraint and caution. Inevitably, though, her format tends to encourage a dramatic view of Spenser's personages, implicitly attributing to them more in the way of "character" or consciousness than most Spenserians find in them. But whatever qualms we may have, we are probably going to find that our undergraduates will turn to this as the most accessible study guide now available.

Heather Dubrow's *Captive Victors* examines the ways in which rhetorical skill both describes and embodies a process of self-entrapment in Shakespeare's narrative poems and sonnets. Venus, Lucrece, and the poet-lover are seen as caught in linguistic webs of their own making. Dubrow's approach is to identify the specific rhetorical devices being employed and to show how they express judgments about self and world that define character and determine fate. In *Lucrece*, for instance, synecdoche is a sign of artistic triumph in the depiction of Troy's fall, where "A hand, a foot, a face, a leg, a head / Stood for the whole to be imagined"; at the same time, though, it is labelled "Conceit deceitful." Dubrow observes (p.167) that synecdoche is an apt metaphor for the experiences of a rape victim; in fact, both Lucrece and the men of Rome are variously generalizing from part to whole in "imaginary work" that seems to serve their separate interests but ultimately locks them into historical process. The poem's most characteristic rhetorical gesture, though, is that of oxymoron or syneciosis: Tarquin is "A captive victor that hath lost in gain"; and so, it emerges, is everyone and everything else here.

Dubrow is not the first to discuss the narrative poems as paired works that demand comparison (she exaggerates the degree to which they have suffered from critical indifference or condescension); and the first two-thirds of her book seems rather leisurely and unproductive, especially since she tends to focus on Venus and Lucrece and to understate the roles played by the other characters, the thematic and dramatic structures of the poems. This is true, I think, of her discussion of the Troy story mentioned above. She rightly comments that "Lucrece's responses to the depiction of Troy mirror—and invite us to compare—Aeneas' reactions when he views the story of Troy on Dido's temple doors" (p. 158). She limits her commentary, however, to a contrast of Aeneas and Brutus, when the comparison (especially to an Elizabethan reader with special interest in the figure of "widow Dido" and her alternative stories) seems rather to focus on Lucrece's inability to read the scene as Aeneas did, so that she is destined to become another Vergilian Dido, a footnote to Brutus's rising fortunes.

The novelty of *Captive Victors* consists in its treating the narrative poems alongside the *Sonnets*; and it is here that it seems most likely to prove of seminal importance. To see the speaker of the sonnets as characterized by his rhetoric (rather than by Shakespearean biography, however artfully fantasized), and to approach the sequence as sharing with the narrative poems a testing of the limits of the complaint genre, is truly liberating. Dubrow has some very useful things to say about closure in Shakespeare's nondramatic works; I would expect future critics to build on her insights as they find other respects in which the sonnet persona resembles those early, contrasting figures of Shakespeare's abiding sense of the tyrannizing powers of language, Adonis/Lucrece and Brutus.

The greater part of David Lindley's carefully argued study of Thomas Campion deals with the relation between words and music in the lyrics, a subject I am incompetent to judge. Lindley begins by quoting Campion's preface to *The Fourth Booke of Ayres*, "The

Apothecaries have Bookes of Gold, whose leaves being opened are so light as that they are subject to be shaken with the least breath, yet, rightly handled, they serve both for ornament and use; such are light *Ayres*." He appreciates that there is a "lightness" to the lyrics that is the essence of Campion's skill while being the antithesis of the kinds of density commonly admired and rendered subject to analysis by our critical vocabulary; that a critical "right handling" will demand a comparable lightness of touch; and finally, that a song book assumes a necessary blurring of the conventional boundary between writer and reader, for it is the performance by the latter that will produce the ornament and use of which Campion speaks. By careful attention to the rhythms of Campion's verse, and their interplay with what we know of his music, Lindley argues that Campion's significance as a poet lies in his witty play with convention, which "articulates itself in verse that also plays upon and with the rhythmic potential of the language" (p. 173). In a final chapter, Lindley makes a parallel claim for the masques, that Campion demonstrates a lightness and fluidity in adapting his theatricals to changing tastes, away from mythical elaboration and toward enchantment and self-congratulation. With the masques as with the lyrics, Lindley assumes the responsibility of defending Campion against charges of superficiality. He breathes as gently as possible on the fragile evidence of his texts; a graceful exfoliation is the result.

John Donne has been the object of contrasting book-length studies this year. Frank J. Warnke's survey of him for the Twayne series is a sympathetic, magisterial presentation of Donne as he seems to be understood today. Warnke is well equipped to place Donne in the Baroque tradition, and he is careful to note that twentieth-century scholarship has found too much evidence that Donne continued to write passionate love poetry throughout his life to support the tradition started by Walton that a mid-life conversion changed him from rake to preacher. Warnke's Donne is artist first and biographical subject secondarily; the cynical poems or "evaporations" are recognized as such and admired for their mischievous wit, though the Lincoln's Inn epithalamion is dismissed as atypical. Still, it is the dramatic persona of Donne that continues to validate his poetry; and it is probably fair to say that here he is more plausibly though no less symmetrically transformed, by his marriage, from passionate bachelor to passionate husband. The "Nocturnall Upon S. Lucies Day" is confidently associated with Ann's death in 1617, so that the solemnity of the occasion mirrors that of the art. Warnke is given to very extensive quotation from the poems and sermons, so much so that his volume is virtually an introductory anthology, in which

Donne's words are largely left to speak for themselves, after a minimal presentation of their contexts. Since this is the work of a mature and knowledgeable critic with an unerring sense for economical commentary, the result is entirely satisfying.

In a concluding survey of Donne's twentieth-century reputation, Warnke notes that Donne was given privileged status during a period, from 1920 to 1950, characterized by both formalism and eccentricity: the jazz age as well as the age of the New Criticism. His style—"dramatic, artificial, highly wrought, playful and serious at the same time"—seemed to embody perfectly what poetry should be; and explications of his text were the standard exercises by which newer and younger critics showed their mettle. Warnke notes with some relief that although Donne's poetry is no longer at the center of critical theory it continues to receive steady and respectful study, and has not been denigrated by postmodernist criticism "as modernist criticism had denigrated Shelley." But this is not surprising, nor I think particularly reassuring: denigration of individual texts or authors is not characteristic of postmodernism, and indifference to Donne's received reputation is hardly less damning. It seems odd that even after John Carey's attempt at presenting a newly problematized and anxious Donne, the profession should remain largely content to leave Donne in what amounts to an underprivileged position as sex object, passionate lover, and manly divine. A book entitled *John Donne, Undone*, with its promise of deconstructing the received image of Donne, seems long overdue.

Thomas Docherty takes his title, obviously, from Donne's wry comment on the disastrous consequences of his marriage to Ann More, a literally criminal act which easily epitomizes that act of transgression that poststructuralists labor to detect. (It seems no coincidence that this year's three most ambitiously theoretical studies, by Crewe, Docherty, and Kendrick, are all published by Methuen and share much terminology.) The etymological ties that bind crime, criticism, secrecy, and hypocrisy seem here to be evidence enough of a complex of undoing doings afoot. Donne's marriage becomes an attempt to embrace a Catholic past that is all that his wife's name can suggest—More, its anagram Rome, *moria*, Maria—so that his own poetry can be seen as a praise of folly, a quest for a female name and identity, and beyond that the ultimate transgressive self-naming, not merely as Mary but as God.

Docherty offers so many strange and wonderful claims for meanings in Donne that I am afraid many readers will quickly lose patience with him. He shows little interest in, or indeed familiarity with, previous studies of Donne. After an introductory essay in which he argues against the prevailing interest in dramatic characterization of Donne as individualized speaker—and cites a random list of critics who follow Crofts, Sanders, and Leavis in providing "more of the same"—there is virtually no mention of the critics, and frequently very little discussion of Donne's text itself. Perhaps the least exasperating essay in this respect, and so a good place to begin, is that on "The problem of women: authority, power, communication," in which he does quote from the poems at some length, while developing an interesting and generally convincing claim for a "failure of representation" in Donne's poetry: women are not independent or genuine presences in the poems, but ghostly figures of a space that the lover aspires to inhabit or colonize. There is evidence enough in Donne's language ("O my America! my new-found-land") to justify this claim, and Docherty cites much of the pertinent evidence. Even here, though, he does not hesitate to introduce readings that seem extraneous to the text. With reference to Elegy 19, he starts with Carey's remark that Donne "hardly seems to see the girl" in the poem, and then makes much of his claim to find the "girl" hidden anagrammatically in the "girdle" that she is being asked to remove. Highly speculative talk of hidden or perhaps censored names, in a somewhat Lacanian key, characterizes much of Docherty's approach. It might be noted that Warnke, speaking of "A Hymne to God the Father," remarked that critics have been reluctant to see a pun on Ann's name in the refrain, "thou hast not done, / For, I have more"; he suggests that the claim should not be rejected out of hand. The problem, I think, lies in a plausible explanation of how such a pun operates in context; and in this case Docherty does provide such an explanation (p. 218). But his more general claims for the centrality of "vocation" or self-naming in Donne's poetry rest on a discussion of the phenomenon in Du Bellay instead, with some questionable and indeed undemonstrable claims. For example, when the poet compares himself to "un aigneau que sa nourrice appelle," loyally calling out the name of France, we are told that he is covertly bleating (belêr) his adult identity as ram (bélier). Furthermore, he is most like the Donne we are being urged to recognize here, in seeing himself reflected in the "bel oeil divin" of Marguerite, the king's sister, who is reading his verse—and whose own name, in a later age, will be Latinized as the *Bellis perennis* or ox-eye daisy. "Bellay is 'forever' recognized in the pearly eye of Marguerite, gaining his name literally in perpetuity here" (p. 160).

Docherty's readiness to accept an obviously anachronistic reading like this is oddly contradictory of his claim to provide the first interpretation of Donne that is attentive to the "specific historical moment of the later European Renaissance" (p.1), but it seems in keeping with a tendency to see history as revealed and defined by a canon of modern texts. He can speak of Polonius as "a character who prefigures in many ways the dilemma of the contemporary [*sic*] Eliotic Prufrock" (p.149), without considering that this is an odd way of describing a situation in which Prufrock explicitly recalls Polonius. Karl Marx, himself a man widely read in earlier literatures and much given to the understated literary allusiveness of his times, seems to be invoked with some of the same sense of a new historical testament that uncannily affirms and completes the old, when at the beginning of chapter 6 his words are juxtaposed to similar words from Donne. Docherty's book seems to me an example of a frequently brilliant invocation of the past that would greatly benefit from the kind of corrective blood-filtering that Wilamowitz recommended, in the interest of letting the ghosts speak to us in something closer to their own words.

In time for the bicentennial of the French Revolution if not for that of the American, Eugene D. Hill has provided a most welcome reassessment of the life and works of Edward, Lord Herbert of Cherbury, widely recognized in his own time and in the following century as the father of English deism and forerunner of the Enlightenment, "one of the first," as Voltaire praised him in 1767, to have "the daring to stand up, not only against the Roman Church, but against the Christian Church." His death in 1648 was a model of the "philosophical" death to which eighteenth-century French would aspire, in which the clergy were evaded rather than defied openly, so that the faithful could be scandalized by the sight of a man dying calmly while deprived of the sacrament, yet without prejudice to the rights to civilized burial and normal inheritance. Aubrey describes how Herbert asked James Usher, Lord Primate of England (who Hill suggests was likely to have been in on the game to some degree) for the sacrament, with the offhand remark that "*if it did no good 'twould do no hurt.* The Primate refused it, for which many blamed him. He then turned his head to the other side and expired very serenely." It is probably a measure of the success of the Enlightenment, and of the vast gap that separates us from Lord Herbert's world, that we are more likely to be amused by this anecdote, as evidence of aristocratic bitchiness, than moved either to horror or to admiration. All the more reason, therefore, to be grateful to Hill for the care with which he has looked at the broad range of Herbert's works—philosophy, history, poetry, and autobiography—and composed a coherent portrait of a deist whose works have far greater consistency of substance and style than at first appears, so much so that with reason Donne could praise him: "you have dwelt upon / All worthy books, and now are such a one." Herbert's experiences as a diplomat, coupled with a need for discretion in expressing his personal philosophy, tended to foster an oblique and ironic style of understatement, and to give a special piquancy to his position among other metaphysicals. His lyrics in praise of black beauty combine a seventeenth-century paradoxical motif with more serious and esoteric elements; and in his principal poetic work, the "Ode upon a Question moved," the lover Melander responds to the argument of Donne's "Ecstasy" in terms that recall Herbert's major deist statement, the *De Veritate*. Hill's analyses help make more accessible and open the book that Herbert's contemporaries saw in his life and works.

Herbert's younger brother continues to receive serious attention this year, with two books devoted to his poetry. Stanley Stewart's Twayne volume reacts against recent interpretations of George Herbert that place him in an assertively Protestant or even Puritan context. He reviews the early lives of Herbert, evidence that runs parallel to that in Ray's collection of allusions mentioned earlier, and argues that the early tendency toward hagiography led the poet to be seen as a hero of Protestantism, championing all that that term came to mean in the later seventeenth century. In particular, the image of Herbert as heir to David's "mighty *Psaltery*," in Walton's phrase, led to his early adoption by hymnologists, notably in the *Select Hymns, Taken out of Mr. Herbert's Temple, and Turn'd into the Common Metre* of 1697. The alterations in Herbert's verse made by the Wesleys for their *Hymns and Sacred Poems* of 1739 provide amusing evidence of the process by which the Dissenter's Herbert emerged. Against this evolving tradition of an ever more Protestant poet, Stewart urges that Herbert be seen in the context of the religious practices of his day, and especially those of his friend and literary executor, Nicholas Ferrar, and the community at Little Gidding. He specifies that for Herbert, even the word "Protestant" may be anachronistic, as opposed to "reformed", noting that Herbert died before Laud's attempt to enforce conformity, and before Ferrar's practices came under attack from the establishment, Stewart suggests that Herbert's religion should be identified with the historical moment at Little Gidding when Herbert and Richard Crashaw alike could feel at home in forms of worship that enjoyed a broad base of tolerance and even approval.

Stewart's most substantial original contribution comes from the information he provides concerning the "Harmonies," volumes in which members of Little Gidding prepared concordances of related texts from Scripture for use in daily worship. He gives a general description of these volumes and points to some areas of similarity to Herbert's poetic practices. Although these are matters of analogy rather than of demonstrable indebtedness, an increased awareness of Little Gidding seems clearly to be central to further discussion of the vexed and elusive question of Herbert's priestly poetics. Stewart concludes his book with a claim for a School of Herbert comparable to that of Donne, and sees this as starting with Richard Crashaw's *Steps to the Temple* of 1646, and extending to Vaughan and Traherne as well as lesser figures like Christopher Harvey and Ralph Knevet.

In *The Opacity of Signs: Acts of Interpretation in George Herbert's "The Temple,"* Richard Todd traces an Augustinian tradition of sign theory which is developed by Hugh of St. Victor and Bonaventura into an emphasis on our damaged potential for reading the books of Nature and Scripture. "Man no longer possesses intuitive gifts for apprehending the Creator and his own place in the created order; instead, sense experience must be deployed in a semiological approach to what is perceived" (pp. 40-41). This theory, seen in sixteenth-century writers like Bernard Ochino, Peter Martyr, Jewel, and Hooker, is the basis for a view of Herbert's verse that is frankly indebted to Stanley Fish's reader-response theories: Herbert dramatizes the opacity of signs and our faltering efforts to read them. Todd attempts to locate a *via media* between conflicting critical viewpoints; the debate between Tuve and Empson over "The Sacrifice" is respectfully reviewed more than once here, for Todd would accept that an educated response to the poems by a present-day reader has to be the only practical basis for determining their meaning, while he is concerned to give that response a historical education. In effect, he finds the essence of the modern response in the culture that produced the poems; the ghosts turn out to have been given blood indistinguishable from their own. Todd's argument seems so clearly germane to the language and tone of Herbert's poetry, so little at odds with what I would like to think is the critical consensus, that I find his book an excellent place to start one's reading of Herbert criticism.

Jonathan Post gives us an introductory overview of an altogether more varied and complex figure in his study of Sir Thomas Browne. Like Todd, Post would take a conciliatory view toward contradictory critical viewpoints, but less from any personal sense of a point where they intersect than from his belief that his subject is all of the things others have found in him. Before such abundance, Post's solution is to offer a series of essays on aspects of the life and works, dealing separately with different elements in *Religio Medici* (in chapters on its "comic autobiography" and on its "playing down differences" of religion). In content as in style, Browne is seen as delighting the reader with his multifarious riches; Post seeks to convey that delight in this survey.

I confess that I am unable to speak with any confidence about Margarita Stocker's *Apocalyptic Marvell*, since I have trouble rereading the poems under her guidance and seeing the pertinence of many of the meanings she attributes to them. She starts from a claim (largely unsubstantiated here, though we are referred to unpublished materials in her dissertation) that seventeenth-century Protestantism was dominated by a "mainstream eschatological belief" in an imminent Second Coming. It seems axiomatic that to be a Protestant poet is to be a chiliastic poet as well, celebrating the thousand-year rule of the Church on earth which is to precede the Last Judgment. "We should recognize," she informs us at the outset, "that in this period, chiliasm was not limited to extremist groups or radical sects, and that such belief was not considered unusual (as it might be in the twentieth century). Equally, we must grasp an attitude of mind which—in distinction from our own age, with its apprehensions of nuclear holocaust—regarded the end of the world with hope and enthusiasm, as the triumph of God's saints and of His Justice, and as the prelude to bliss. To this degree seventeenth-century eschatology was optimistic" (p. xii). Although this statement disarms my initial reaction that Marvell's poetry does not strike me as "apocalyptic" in the normal sense of the term—as it might be applied to Blake's, for instance—I still have trouble in finding a steady prophetic strain in his lyrics, even an optimistic one.

Stocker further asserts that Spenser and Milton "represent the enterprise to construct an apocalyptic literature adequate to [the] historical crisis. For both . . . epic was to prove the vehicle best fitted for this enterprise, although it affects their shorter productions also. In Marvell's case the enterprise remained essentially lyrical; to that degree it is both less evident (epic is more readily seen as 'historical' in its pretensions) and perhaps more subtly difficult" (p. 46). Alas, since I cannot agree with the point about the epics, the subtler lyrics are all the more distant from my comprehension. I can grant the existence of an apocalyptic strain in Milton (as Joseph Wittreich defines it), but would hesitate to see him as totally committed to apocalypse as Stocker seems to see him, since this would seem to ignore all that is brooding and blinded in his poetry. And although Revelation is pertinent to specific passages in *The Faerie Queene* (the dragon in Book I, the longing for a sabbath's sight), I can see no evidence of a pervasive optimistic millenarianism there. Similarly with Marvell: there are passages where the language of Revelation and its glosses is clearly visible, but the Marvell I know seems an equally unlikely recruit for the enterprise. Stocker is determined to replace the current sense of Marvell as "a difficult, elusive, elegant, poised—one might even say etiolated—poet" with one who is consistently committed to a chiliastic program throughout his career. Since I am very happy with the former figure, etiolation and all, I may be constitutionally unsuited for a sympathetic reading of this extremely energetic reassessment of Marvell's works.

V. MILTON

As usual, this year has seen a substantial crop of Milton studies. The late C. A. Patrides has given us an annotated critical bibliography that should be of some help in coping with the overwhelming accumulation, though it is probably not the major new reference work its publishers claim. A selective checklist, with less annotation than an inexperienced reader might wish, and far more entries than an experienced one could look up, it is still an honorable footnote to a distinguished career whose untimely end is cause for regret. Galbraith M. Crump has edited a collection of essays on teaching *Paradise Lost* to those widely various student constituencies that pay our way. A pedagogical work like this fits uneasily into the confines of a scholarly review, awakening a vague sense—all the more powerful for being indefensible—that one ought not to boast about one's prowess in the classroom, and that it is letting the side down to separate mystery and *métier*. When one sees a colleague handing out tips on teaching, the tendency is to avert one's gaze, like two psychoanalysts meeting at a behaviorists' convention. Still, it is important to remember that virtually every author reviewed in this article is employed by an educational system that has placed Milton at the center of the humanities and frequently at the center of the "Judaeo-Christian tradition" as well; and much of the year's critical work is directly or indirectly trying to sort out the consequences thereof.

Gilles Mathis has published his Marseille dissertation, a mammoth stylistic analysis of *Paradise Lost*, "L'univers poétique: echos et correspondances." It is in two sections, on metaphoric structures and on "rythme et architectures sonores." Mathis is indebted to Riffaterre for a dynamic definition of style, and to Hollander for a sophisticated understanding of resonance; but the present shift away from formalism among English and American critics is likely to limit the impact of his work. (Readers who are worried about the present balance of trade in critical terminology will be pleased to learn that there is no precise equivalent in French for *pattern*; at last, we have something to make up for our lack of *jouissance*.)

The twenty-second volume of *Milton Studies*, like its younger sibling *Spenser Studies*, provides a sampling of current approaches and interests in its thirteen essays. Herbert J. Phelan tracks the entrances and exits of the persona in *L'Allegro* and *Il Penseroso*. Patricia Elizabeth Davis briefly explores the "figural tapestry" in *Paradise Lost*, of images that assimilate Christ's crown of thorns into a more positive "crown of Life." Kenneth J. Knoespel details Milton's expansion of Narcissus, noting that the words which Adam addresses to Eve ("Whom fli'st thou?" IV, 481-91) translate those of Ovid's Narcissus, and point to the applicability of the myth to all the major actors in the poem, Satan and Adam as well as Eve. In a similarly intertextual comparison, Carol Gilbertson convincingly treats Marvell's Mower poems as a subtle and intricate response to *Paradise Lost*. The unholy trio of Satan, Sin, and Death are treated by Samuel S. Stollman as an attack on Mosaic Law; his essay is followed, whether coincidentally or in application of a Fairness Doctrine, by Golda Werman's demonstration of the applicability of midrashic commentary to *Paradise Lost*, specifically to the theme of repentance. In the arena of intellectual history, James Obertino argues for the importance of Aquinas to the issues raised in *Comus*. Jun Harada speculates on Milton's changing attitudes toward the English Revolution and their reflection in his poetry, a subject treated far more elaborately and theoretically by Christopher Kendrick's book mentioned below. James Tatum argues with great skill and energy for a relation between Apollonius's *Argonautica* and *Paradise Regained*, as comparable reactions (in four books each) to the impossibility of writing epic in the shadow of a mighty predecessor (for Apollonius, Homer; for Milton, his own *Paradise Lost*). Finally, we have a collection of four essays on *Samson Agonistes*. Burton J. Weber explores the design of the middle part of the work, trying in the process to adjudicate debates between "regeneration theorists" and the "providential and revisionist critics." (*Samson* is evidently this year's trouble spot, perhaps because it is an important enough text to fight over and small enough to avoid risking major escalation.) Daniel T. Lochman sees Samson as prophet; Darryl Tippens applies the concept of kenosis to the work; William Kerrigan applies his thesis from *The Sacred Complex*—Samson, like Milton himself, must break free of a paralyzing chastity, and experience disastrous marriages, as a mysterious and paradoxical precondition for his triumph. Kerrigan prefaces this argument with an entertaining demolition of the critical tradition that has resisted such "irrational coherence."

In *Milton and the Paradoxes of Renaissance Heroism,* John M. Steadman returns to questions of Miltonic versions of the heroic that he has already addressed in several earlier books. If his judgments are frequently rather predictable, however, he delivers them with characteristic grace and with a richly resonant command of scholarship. His subject is the "temptation-ordeal" in *Paradise Lost, Paradise Regained,* and *Samson Agonistes,* and the transformations of the classical epic hero upon which Milton built in devising suitable protagonists for these ordeals. Particularly interesting is his tracing of the figure of Achilles as a type of the problematic hero. Statius's *Achilleid* had proposed to treat of his emergence from retirement on Scyros and his recruitment into the Greek forces at Troy. This aspect of his career seemed to Renaissance writers easier to treat as the rescue of a noble warrior from ignoble and effeminate idleness than the later episode of angry retirement treated by Homer. Steadman is especially skillful in describing the Achillean aspects of parallel figures in the Italian poems leading up to Tasso's Rinaldo: Ruggiero in the *Orlando furioso,* Corsamonte in Trissino's *Italia liberata,* and Lancilotto in Alamanni's *Avarchide.* The Italian poets "convert the *ferus* and *saevus* Pelides into a Renaissance nobleman" (p. 59).

Beside the figure of the Achillean hero, with its clear implications for Milton's Samson, Steadman sets a separate type which he attributes to Francis Bacon who borrowed the motto *Plus ultra* from Charles V, setting it with its accompanying illustration of the Pillars of Hercules on the illustrated title page of the *Magna Instauratio,* thereby expressing an intent to venture into the forbidden unknown, rejecting traditional limits to human knowledge. This celebration of the scientist as hero, with its Faustian overtones of transgressing divine restrictions in the pursuit of superhuman powers, sets the stage for an immediate discussion of Milton's major works as variously adapting these two traditions and capitalizing on their power to invoke some of the deepest ambitions of late Renaissance culture. Probably because he was reworking earlier essays rather than developing his argument from the start, Steadman moves rather indirectly and haphazardly into a series of discussions of Milton; and his book loses momentum after the third chapter, with instances of repetition and overlap.

In *Before and After the Fall,* Kathleen M. Swaim explores, in rich and rewarding detail, the contrasting styles of the two angelic messengers in *Paradise Lost,* Raphael and Michael, as expressive of lapsarian contrasts central both to the poem and to Milton's concept of our fallen condition. Since the angelic visits comprise nearly half of the poem's twelve books, and include the two least appreciated episodes—the battle in Heaven and Michael's review of biblical history—Swaim's enterprise includes a sympathetic reading of the poem at its most vulnerable points. In this, she rather charmingly embodies her thesis. She defines the pedagogical styles of the two angels as those of prelapsarian lecturer and postlapsarian discussion leader, and in her own education of her fallen audience she emulates Michael's employment of the latter role, giving us repeated instances of significant contrasts and letting us move at our own pace toward a justification of Milton's ways.

Swaim begins by demonstrating in great detail that Milton deliberately calls attention to the contrasting missions and methods of Raphael and Michael, through pervasive structural echoes in matters both great and small. For instance, Raphael offers Adam "the prime wisdom" that lies before both angel and unfallen man alike, in a world where earthly and heavenly realms are continuous and unified, and where the book of Nature is easily legible. The phrase is echoed when Michael speaks of Adam's attainment of "the sum / Of wisdom" when he has learned the lesson of his Redeemer, contrasting it to less profitable knowledge, in this fallen world where nature and grace are now dichotomous alternatives, as are also knowledge and wisdom, reason and faith. She proceeds, in the book's most substantial contributions to scholarship, to demonstrate that Milton's lapsarian dichotomies are reflected in, and informed by, his prose works, notably the *Art of Logic*, *Of Education*, and *Christian Doctrine*, and that comparable dichotomies are central to Ramist logic and faculty psychology. Successive chapters on lapsarian structures, imagery, logic, and poetics show just how much is meant by our sense that Adam and Eve are fallen humans akin to ourselves by the end of the poem: for they inhabit a world that is astonishingly close to that of Milton, in its fundamental methods and assumptions. In her epigraph to chapter 3, Swaim quotes Alfred North Whitehead to the effect that the philosophy of an epoch is not defined by "those intellectual positions which its exponents feel it necessary explicitly to defend," but by the range of philosophical systems enabled by those fundamental assumptions they do not bother to assert precisely because "no other way of putting things has ever occurred to them." By dint of much original scholarship, Swaim has enabled us to a firmer grasp of what was obvious to Milton, for these "lapsarian dichotomies" turn out to be central to the philosophy of the epoch as well as to Milton's plot.

Before and After the Fall makes a substantial contribution to our understanding of Milton, but it is also a profoundly conciliatory work so far as its relation to other critics is concerned. Swaim has an extraordinary command of what has been said about Milton in recent decades, and she documents extensively the points at which her commentary intersects with that of others. This is more than normal scholarly thoroughness: it seems that she is as concerned to show that other scholars have been saying much the same thing in slightly different words, as she is to assert the identical assumptions beneath the different systems in Milton's world. We are left at the end hand in hand with our discussion leader, with Adam and Eve, and with the critical tradition as well.

Christopher Kendrick, in *Milton: A Study in Ideology and Form*, is similarly concerned to locate Milton within the mentality of his epoch, but he is working with very different materials from Swaim's; readers will find few Miltonists cited in his densely packed and frequently polemical footnotes, and most of those few (like Waldock, who is unmentioned by Swaim and tolerantly rebuked by Steadman) belonging to the dissenters' chapel rather than the establishment. Kendrick's project is to define, from a Marxist perspective, the nature and consequences of the Puritan revolution of the 1640s, focusing not so much on the revolution itself—its self-awareness of collective struggle—as on "the dispersal of revolutionary energies, on the alienated effects of what had been collective action" (pp. 1-2). The distinction here is one which he notes is a central problem of classical Marxism, and is reflected in Marx's own divided career, between the Marx of the later 1840s, announcing and supporting a collective revolutionary agency in the *Communist Manifesto*, and "the Marx of the European Restoration, who devoted himself in *Capital* to the painstaking construction of the structural laws of capitalist development" (p. 3). It seems that a lapsarian dichotomy between revolution and historical determinism uncannily resembles those experienced two centuries earlier. Kendrick does not play with parallels between Marx and Milton, however, beyond his suggestive phrasing of this remark; there is very little critical playfulness in this volume (in this it differs from the similarly theoretical books of Crewe and Docherty). His argument is that Milton is "an ideologist and poet of emergent capitalism," of the period of primitive accumulation "in which capital had not yet learned to feel guilty about its origins, but which came to represent the repressed bad conscience of later capitalism" (p. 4).

Although Kendrick provides an introductory summary of Marxist theory for the benefit of Miltonists who are unfamiliar with its concepts and terminology, and rigorously argues every stage of his increasingly complex thesis, his book is heavy going, and readers are likely to cast about for a plausible reason to set it aside. If they decide that it is a misguided and historically naive Leavisite attack on their poet (the dust-jacket rather ill-advisedly claims it "takes issue with the canonical view of Milton as an isolated Great Man"), they will be seriously mistaken, however. Kendrick does not identify Milton as a capitalist ideologue in order to dismiss or displace him from the canon in favor of more enlightened figures, but rather as a basis for constructing a more effective theoretical framework for understanding the dynamics of his works.

If he must be faulted, let it be for his impatience with readers who need to catch their breath and make sure they have caught his drift, by means of a leisurely and explicit reading of texts. He repeatedly refuses to do this: "I do not intend here to attempt an extended psychoanalytic reading of *Areopagitica*, but only to indicate where such a reading might begin" (p. 36). "I do not want to read this passage, but rather to analyze the ethical logic that it presents and enacts" (p. 45). Here is the tone of the lecturer who expects his students to take notes and do the reading on their own, and who has at least one fallen mortal in his audience who longs for a discussion leader at this point. This objection is only not frivolous because the book has so much to say that enhances the mainstream view of Milton. Kendrick is strenuous and scrupulous (to a fault, I would suggest) in demonstrating the applicability of recent Marxist and psychoanalytic theory to an encompassing view of *Paradise Lost*. I hope that his next book will give us a reading of the poem, and perhaps attempt to bring in the critical tradition as well, in a gesture of amiable hegemony.

VI. IN CONCLUSION

Arnold Stein's *The House of Death: Messages from the English Renaissance* belongs to an uncommon and precious genre of critical study—Erwin Panofsky's *Tomb Sculpture* is another example—in which a distinguished scholar applies the tools of his profession to address the subject of death. It is not surpursing that so few attempt such an enterprise, for it is a little like posing for a Rowlandson caricature: death mocks the activities of iconologist or literary critic as cruelly as those of lawyer or physician. Furthermore, there may be ways of approaching the subject more obliquely or covertly, through themes of romance renewal, which are better suited to the conventional old age style. Stein resorts to no subterfuge: not only is death his explicit subject, but he approaches it in a way profoundly conscious of the problems of subjectivity, as a matter of messages from the past. "How past and present speak to each other is a question that a student of Renaissance literature lives with regularly," he observes, seeming to echo Wilamowitz; but he continues: "I have not tried to keep out of this book about the past everything learned from personal experience and from a normal interest in the present" (p. xi). His chapters on Renaissance poets are framed by references to the contemporary world, and it is finally the interplay between author and subject that gives the book its special excitement.

Donne, in the sermon from which Stein draws his title, speaks of the ambiguous status of death: "*As houses* that stand in *two Shires*, trouble the execution of Justice, the house of death that stands in two worlds, may trouble a good mans resolution." In his survey of sixteenth- and seventeenth-century poets who confront their own deaths or those of others, Stein is especially attentive to what is left unsaid for one reason or another. "Tichborne's Elegy" gains much of its power from its status as being written on the eve of his execution; Stein argues that its stiff conventionality is in fact suited to its context. He points out that Raleigh's verses written in his Bible before his execution are similarly stark and lack the boldness and wit of his other poems on death. Stein finds in such poems a sense of the pressure of time and an insistent adherence to a radically simplified view of the situation. The condemned Tichborne sees himself as poised between life and death, with the barest mark of punctuation separating the two: "And now I live, and now my life is done." The pendulum rhythm of the poem's antitheses conveys a determination to accept the finality of death; at the same time, if we consider (as Stein suggests we should) that dying will not be so simple or instantaneous but a protracted public agony, we can read the poem as an effort to deny that reality.

Ranging through his anthology of instances, Stein guides our appreciation of each poem's dynamics. Speaking of Marvell, he contrasts the tribute to Charles as "Royal Actor" on the scaffold with the radically different lines on the dead Cromwell, where the poet abruptly and uncharacteristically shifts to the past tense for a brief personal shudder at the physical fact of the body, and briefly interrupts the flow of his long elegy: "I saw him dead, a leaden slumber lyes, / And mortall sleep over those wakefull eyes." Here, Marvell enacts a personal emotion that is suppressed as he returns to a generalizing present tense where the survivor interprets the scene: "And in his alter'd face you something faigne / That threatens death, he yet will live again." In the "Horatian Ode," too, it is the selective presentation of details in the scene of death that enables a rich awareness of dramatic irony. People see what they look for; Charles was a graceful and finally willing actor in a play he did not write.

Stein's commentary is too varied, and too Marvellian in its capacity for multiple implication to be summarized here; his own style is characterized by the understatement he admires in others. At the end of the book, in a series of comments on modern attempts to describe the dying process, he quotes a scientific model that accounts for the serenity and out-of-body sensation testified to in near-death experiences: "the organism concedes that it is finished and the time for dying is at hand, and at this moment the events that lead to death are launched, as a coordinated mechanism. Functions are then shut off in sequence, irreversibly, and, while this is going on, a neural mechanism, held ready for this occasion, is switched on" (p. 280). Stein observes that beneath the modern vocabulary with its mechanistic orientation can be heard echoes of Ficino and Paracelsus as they describe the mind in Aristotelian terms. Here, too, the house of death stands in two worlds: the imagery of space flight suggests the launching of a new adventure, that of the computer a final logging-off at day's end. Even the latter image, however, balances finality against the silently awaited accessing of a new program. In a footnote, the former Sir William Osler Professor at Johns Hopkins tells us that Osler himself testified, after a lifetime of clinical experience, that he had never seen any "such state as an agony of death." With such genial demonstrations of continuities from past to present, the author adds his own voice to the message he is transmitting to his colleagues in Baltimore and elsewhere, offering the promise of a philosophical death and leaving open the possibility of an ecstatic encounter with the Logos, however one's personal program may have translated it: as *verbum* or as *sermo*, or (as did Flaubert's *coeur simple*) as a large, mute parrot.

BOOKS RECEIVED

Ault, Norman, ed. *Elizabethan Lyrics from the Original Texts.* London and Boston: Faber and Faber, 1986 (1949). Pp. xvii + 560. $17.95 paper. ISBN 0-571-13929-9.

Barkan, Leonard. *The Gods Made Flesh: Metamorphosis and the Pursuit of Paganism.* New Haven and London: Yale Univ. Press, 1986. Pp. xvi + 398. $30.00. ISBN 0-300-03561-6.

Bauman, Uwe, and Heinrich, Hans Peter. *Thomas Morus: Humanistische Schriften.* Mit einer Einführung von Hubertus Schulte Herbrüggen. (Erträge der Forschung, Band 243.) Darmstadt: Wissenschaftliche Buchgesellschaft, 1986. Pp. ix + 226. ISBN 3-534-02262-9. ISSN 0174-0695.

Campbell, Gordon, ed. *Renaissance Studies: Journal of the Society for Renaissance Studies* 1, 1 (March 1987). Oxford: Oxford Univ. Press, 1987. $60.00.

Cook, Elizabeth. *Seeing Through Words: The Scope of Late Renaissance Poetry.* New Haven and London: Yale Univ. Press, 1986. Pp. ix + 180. $20.00. ISBN 0-300-03675-2.

Crewe, Jonathan. *Hidden Designs: The Critical Profession and Renaissance Literature.* New York and London: Methuen, 1987. Pp. viii + 181. $33.00. ISBN 0-416-92350-X.

Crump, Galbraith M., ed. *Approaches to Teaching Milton's "Paradise Lost".* New York: MLA, 1986. Pp. x + 201. $27.50, cloth, ISBN 0-87352-4. $14.50, paper, ISBN 0-87352-494-2.

Cullen, Patrick, and Roche, Thomas P., Jr., eds. *Spenser Studies: A Renaissance Poetry Annual* 6 (1985). New York: AMS Press. Pp. xiv + 206. $45.00 institutions; $25.00 individuals. ISBN 0-404-19206-8; ISSN 0195-9468.

Daly, Peter M., and Russell, Daniel. *Emblematica: An Interdisciplinary Journal for Emblem Studies* 1, 1 (Spring 1986). New York: AMS Press, 1986. Pp. xii + 212. $55.00 institutions; $30.00 individuals. ISSN 0885-968X.

Deutscher, Thomas B. *Contemporaries of Erasmus: A Biographical Register of the Renaissance and Reformation,* vol. 3: N-Z. Toronto, Buffalo, and London: Univ. of Toronto Press, 1987. Pp. xii + 503. $80.00; $195.00 for three-volume set. ISBN 0-8020-2575-7 (vol. 3); -2507-2 (vol. 1); -2571-4 (vol. 2).

Docherty, Thomas. *John Donne, Undone.* London and New York: Methuen, 1987. Pp. xiii + 253. $35.00 cloth, ISBN 0-416-92040-3. $15.95 paper, ISBN 0-416-00592-6.

Donne, John. *Devotions Upon Emergent Occasions.* Ed. Anthony Raspa. New York and Oxford: Oxford Univ. Press, 1987. Pp. lvi + 192. $24.95 cloth, ISBN 0-19-504174-7. $9.95 paper, ISBN 0-19-504173-9.

Donne, John. *Selected Poetry and Prose.* Ed. T. W. and R. J. Craik. London and New York: Methuen, 1987. Pp. xi + 299. $7.95. ISBN 0-416-40220-8.

van Dorsten, Jan, Baker-Smith, Dominic, and Kinney, Arthur F., eds. *Sir Philip Sidney: 1586 and the Creation of a Legend.* Pp. xii + 246. Publ. of Sir Thomas Browne Institute, n.s. 9. Leiden: Brill, 1986. Gld. 86, ca. $38.25. ISBN 90-04-07923-8.

Dubrow, Heather. *Captive Victors: Shakespeare's Narrative Poems and Sonnets.* Ithaca and London: Cornell Univ. Press, 1987. Pp. 277. $29.95. ISBN 0-8014-1975-1.

Erasmus, Desiderius. *Collected Works of Erasmus,* vol. 7: The Correspondence, Letters 993 to 1121, 1519-1520. Trans. R.A.B. Mynors, annotated by Peter G. Bietenholz. Toronto, Buffalo, and London: Univ. of Toronto Press, 1987. Pp. xiv + 468. $75.00. ISBN 0-8020-5607-5.

Erasmus, Desiderius. *Collected Works of Erasmus,* vols. 27 and 28: Literary and Educational Writings. Ed. A. H. T. Levi. Toronto, Buffalo, and London: Univ. of Toronto Press, 1986. Pp. xxx + 322 (vol. 27), 323-638 (vol. 28). $95.00 the set. ISBN 0-8020-5602-4.

Fraistat, Neil, ed. *Poems in Their Place: The Intertextuality and Order of Poetic Collections.* Chapel Hill and London: The Univ. of North Carolina Press, 1987. Pp. vii + 344. $35.00. ISBN 0-8078-1695-7.

Friedman, Jerome, *Blasphemy, Immorality, and Anarchy: The Ranters and the English Revolution.* Athens and London: Ohio Univ. Press, 1987. Pp. xiv + 336. $32.95. ISBN 0-8214-0861-5.

Garber, Marjorie, ed. *Cannibals, Witches, and Divorce: Estranging the Renaissance.* Selected Papers from the English Institute, 1985, n.s. 11. Baltimore and London: Johns Hopkins Univ. Press, 1987. Pp. xii + 216. $19.50. ISBN 0-8018-3405-8.

Gertzman, Jay A. *Fantasy, Fashion and Affection: Editions of Robert Herrick's Poetry for the Common Reader, 1810-1968.* Bowling Green: Bowling Green State Univ. Popular Press, 1986. Pp. 240. Cloth, ISBN 0-87972-349-1. Paper, ISBN 0-87972-350-5.

George Herbert Journal 9, 2 (Spring 1986). Bridgeport, CT: Sacred Heart Univ., 1986. Pp. 58. $7.00. ISSN 0161-7435.

Griffin, Dustin. *Regaining Paradise: Milton and the Eighteenth Century.* Cambridge: Cambridge Univ. Press, 1986. Pp. xi + 299. $29.95. ISBN 0-521-30913-1.

Harrison, Antony H., ed. *The Metaphysical Poets in the Nineteenth Century. John Donne Journal* 4, 2 (1985). Raleigh: North Carolina State Univ., 1987. $8.00 individuals; $16.00 libraries.

Heale, Elizabeth. *The Faerie Queene: A Reader's Guide.* Cambridge and London: Cambridge Univ. Press, 1987. Pp. xi + 188. $39.50 cloth, ISBN 0-521-30386-9. $9.95 paper, ISBN 0-521-31679-0.

Herendeen, Wyman H. *From Landscape to Literature: The River and the Myth of Geography.* Pittsburgh: Duquesne Univ. Press, 1986. Pp. xii + 378. $32.00. ISBN 0-8207-0182-3.

Hill, Eugene D. *Edward, Lord Herbert of Cherbury,* Twayne's English Authors Series. Boston: G. K. Hall, 1987. Pp. 139. $22.95. ISBN 0-8057-6933-1.

Holstun, James. *A Rational Millenium: Puritan Utopias of Seventeenth-Century England and America.* New York and Oxford: Oxford Univ. Press, 1987. Pp. x + 371. $29.95. ISBN 0-19-504141-0.

Kendall, Ritchie D. *The Drama of Dissent: The Radical Poetics of Nonconformity, 1380-1590.* Chapel Hill and London: Univ. of North Carolina Press, 1986. Pp. ix + 286. $27.50. ISBN 0-8078-1700-7.

Kendrick, Christopher. *Milton: A Study in Ideology and Form.* New York and London: Methuen, 1986. Pp. x + 240. $29.95. ISBN 0-416-01251-5.

Kinney, Arthur F. *John Skelton, Priest as Poet: Seasons of Discovery.* Chapel Hill and London: Univ. of North Carolina Press, 1987. Pp. xiii + 236. $22.50. ISBN 0-8078-1730-9.

Kupersmith, William. *Roman Satirists in Seventeenth-Century England.* Lincoln and London: Univ. of Nebraska Press, 1985. Pp. xii + 193. $19.95. ISBN 0-8032-2710-8.

Lenz, Joseph M. *The Promised End: Romance Closure in the Gawain-poet, Malory, Spenser, and Shakespeare.* New York, Berne, and Frankfurt-am-Main: Peter Lang, 1986. Pp. xiii + 144. SFr 41.10. ISBN 0-8204-0301-6. ISSN 0741-0700.

Lindenbaum, Peter. *Changing Landscapes: Anti-Pastoral Sentiment in the English Renaissance.* Athens and London: Univ. of Georgia Press, 1987. Pp. xi + 234. $27.50. ISBN 0-8203-0835-8.

Lindley, David. *Thomas Campion.* Medieval and Renaissance Authors, vol. 7. Leiden: E. J. Brill, 1986. Pp. xii + 242. $38.75. ISBN 90-04-07601-8.

Lord, George deForest. *Classical Presences in Seventeenth Century English Poetry.* New Haven and London: Yale Univ. Press, 1987. Pp. viii + 224. $23.50. ISBN 0-300-03815-1.

Macdonald, Ronald R. *The Burial-Places of Memory: Epic Underworlds in Vergil, Dante, and Milton.* Amherst: Univ. of Massachusetts Press, 1987. Pp. x + 214. $20.00. ISBN 0-87023-558-3.

Manley, Lawrence, ed. *London in the Age of Shakespeare: An Anthology.* University Park and London: Pennsylvania Univ. Press, 1986. Pp. 372. $28.50. ISBN 0-271-00445-2.

Marcus, Leah S. *The Politics of Mirth: Jonson, Herrick, Milton, Marvell, and the Defense of Old Holiday Pastimes.* Chicago and London: Univ. of Chicago Press, 1987. Pp. ix + 319. $29.00. ISBN 0-226-50451-4.

Marlowe, Christopher. *The Complete Works of Christopher Marlowe,* ed. Roma Gill. Vol. 1: Translations. Oxford: Clarendon Press, 1987. Pp. xvi + 314. $79.00. ISBN 0-19-811878-3.

Marvell, Andrew. *Andrew Marvell: Selected Poetry and Prose.* Ed. Robert Wilcher. London and New York: Methuen, 1987. Pp. ix + 292. $7.95. ISBN 0-416-40230-5.

Mason, H. A. *Sir Thomas Wyatt: A Literary Portrait.* Bristol and Cranbury, NJ: Bristol Classical Press, 1987. Pp. 343. $32.50. ISBN 0-86292-086-8.

Mathis, Gilles. *Analyse stylistique du "Paradis perdu" de John Milton.* 4 vols. Aix-en-Provence: Université de Provence, 1987. Pp. 1490. Fr 550. ISBN 2-85399-149-0.

Maynard, Winifred. *Elizabethan Lyric Poetry and its Music.* Oxford: Clarendon Press, 1986. Pp. xiii + 246. $42.50. ISBN 0-19-812844-4.

Medine, Peter E. *Thomas Wilson.* Twayne's English Authors Series. Boston: G. K. Hall, 1986. Pp. 197. $24.95. ISBN 0-8057-6929-3.

Miller, Jacqueline T. *Poetic License: Authority and Authorship in Medieval and Renaissance Contexts.* New York and Oxford: Oxford Univ. Press, 1986. Pp. 223. $24.95. ISBN 0-19-504103-8.

Milward, Peter, ed. *Poetry and Faith in the English Renaissance*. Essays in Honour of Professor Toyohiko Tatsumi's Seventieth Birthday. Renaissance Monographs 13. Pp. 162. Tokyo: The Renaissance Institute, 1987.

More, St. Thomas. *The Yale Edition of the Complete Works of St. Thomas More*. Vol. 15, In Defense of Humanism, ed. Daniel Kinney. New Haven and London: Yale Univ. Press, 1986. Pp. cliv + 662. $55.00. ISBN 0-300-03161-0.

Patrides, C. A. *An Annotated Critical Bibliography of John Milton*. New York: St. Martin's Press, 1987. Pp. xii + 200. $35.00. ISBN 0-312-00480-X.

Peterson, Richard S., ed. *Essays in Literature and the Visual Arts*. Special double issue of *John Donne Journal* 5 (1986). Ed. M. Thomas Hester and R. V. Young, Jr. Raleigh: North Carolina State Univ., 1987. Pp. 310. $8.00 individuals, $16.00 libraries. ISSN 0738-9655.

Post, Jonathan F. S. *Sir Thomas Browne*. Twayne's English Authors Series. Boston: G. K. Hall, 1987. Pp. xvi + 189. $24.95. ISBN 0-8057-6948-X.

Ralegh, Sir Walter. *Selected Writings*, ed. Gerald Hammond. Harmondsworth: Penguin Books, 1986. Pp. 296. $6.95. ISBN 0-14-043257-4.

Ray, Robert H., ed. *The Herbert Allusion Book: Allusions to George Herbert in the Seventeenth Century*. *SP* 83, 4 (Fall 1986). Pp. ix + 182. $5.00. ISSN 0039-3738.

The Renaissance Bulletin 13. Tokyo: The Renaissance Institute, 1986.

Reuter, O. R. *Proverbs, Proverbial Sentences and Phrases in Thomas Deloney's Works*. Commentationes Humanarum Literarum 79, 1986. Helsinki: Finnish Society of Sciences and Letters, 1986. Pp. 146. ISBN 951-653-139-3. ISSN 0069-6587.

Rubin, Deborah D. *Ovid's Metamorphoses Englished: George Sandys as Translator and Mythographer*. New York and London: Garland Publishing, 1985. Pp. 190. $33.00. ISBN 0-8240-6716-9.

Shakespeare, William. *The Sonnets and A Lover's Complaint*, ed. John Kerrigan. Harmondsworth and New York: Viking Penguin, 1986. Pp. 458. $20.00 cloth, ISBN 0-670-81466-0. $5.95 paper, ISBN 0-14-070732-8.

Sharpe, Kevin, and Zwicker, Steven N., eds. *Politics of Discourse: The Literature and History of Seventeenth-Century England*. Berkeley and London: Univ. of California Press, 1987. Pp. viii + 361. $49.95 cloth, ISBN 0-520-05829-1. $14.95 paper, ISBN 0-520-06070-9.

Simmonds, James D., ed. *Milton Studies* 22. Pittsburgh: Univ. of Pittsburgh Press, 1987. Pp. 270. $32.95. ISBN 0-8229-3541-4.

Steadman, John M. *Milton and the Paradoxes of Renaissance Heroism*. Baton Rouge and London: Louisiana State Univ. Press, 1987. Pp. viii + 264. $32.50. ISBN 0-8071-332-8.

Stein, Arnold. *The House of Death: Messages from the English Renaissance*. Baltimore and London: Johns Hopkins Univ. Press, 1987. Pp. xv + 301. $28.50. ISBN 0-8018-3296-9.

Stewart, Stanley. *George Herbert*. Twayne's English Authors Series. Boston: G. K. Hall, 1986. Pp. 182. $21.95. ISBN 0-8057-6921-8.

Stocker, Margarita. *Apocalyptic Marvell: The Second Coming in Seventeenth Century Poetry*. Athens: Ohio Univ. Press, 1987. Pp. xv + 381. $37.95. ISBN 0-8214-0830-5.

Summers, Claude J. and Pebworth, Ted-Larry, eds. *"Bright Shootes of Everlastingnesse": The Seventeenth-Century Religious Lyric*. Columbia: Univ. of Missouri Press, 1987. Pp. xv + 222. $24.00. ISBN 0-8262-0618-2.

Swaim, Kathleen M. *Before and After the Fall: Contrasting Modes in "Paradise Lost."* Amherst: Univ. of Massachusetts Press, 1986. Pp. xiv + 291. $27.50. ISBN 0-87023-504-4.

Todd, Richard. *The Opacity of Signs: Acts of Interpretation in George Herbert's "The Temple."* Columbia: Univ. of Missouri Press, 1987. Pp. xiii + 223. $27.00. ISBN 0-8262-0609-3.

Tyson, Gerald P., and Wagonheim, Sylvia S., eds. *Print and Culture in the Renaissance: Essays on the Advent of Printing in Europe*. Newark, DE: Univ. of Delaware Press, and London and Toronto: Associated Univ. Presses, 1986. Pp. 266. $36.50. ISBN 0-87413-286-X.

Warnke, Frank J. *John Donne*.Twayne's English Authors Series. Boston: G. K. Hall, 1987. Pp. 143. $17.95. ISBN 0-8057-6941-2.

Wilson, Katharina M., ed. *Women Writers of the Renaissance and Reformation*. Athens and London: Univ. of Georgia Press, 1987. Pp. xl + 638. $40.00 cloth, ISBN 0-8203-0865-X. $19.95 paper, ISBN 0-8203-0866-8.

Wooden, Warren W. *Children's Literature of the English Renaissance*. Ed. with intro. by Jeanie Watson. Lexington: Univ. Press of Kentucky, 1986. Pp. xxii + 181. $19.00. ISBN 0-8131-1587-6.

SEL

Studies in ENGLISH LITERATURE 1500-1900

Elizabethan and Jacobean Drama

VOLUME 28 SPRING 1988 NUMBER 2

Studies in English Literature
1500 - 1900

VOLUME 28 SPRING 1988 NUMBER 2

PUBLISHED BY RICE UNIVERSITY

CONTENTS

Compelling Art in *Titus Andronicus* — Maurice Hunt 197

"I Sing But After You": Shakespeare's Internal Parody — Richard Horwich 219

Lavatch and Service in *All's Well that Ends Well* — Christopher Roark 241

The Changeling in *A Dream* — William W. E. Slights 259

Oratio and *Negotium*: Manipulative Modes in *As You Like It* — Dale G. Priest 273

The Confusion of Self and Role in Chapman's *Bussy D'Ambois* — Deborah Montuori 287

The Problem of Slavery in *The Custom of The Country* — Carolyn Prager 301

Take the Number Seven in Cheapside — A. G. van den Broek 319

Recent Studies in Elizabethan and Jacobean Drama — Jill L. Levenson 331

Studies in English Literature
1500 - 1900

PUBLISHED BY RICE UNIVERSITY

Studies in English Literature is a quarterly journal of historical and critical studies. Each issue will be devoted to one of four fields:

WINTER: The English Renaissance
SPRING: Elizabethan and Jacobean Drama
SUMMER: Restoration and Eighteenth Century
AUTUMN: The Nineteenth Century

SEL: Studies in English Literature, 1500–1900 (ISSN: 0039-3657) is published quarterly (February, May, August, and November) at $15.00 per year for individuals, $20.00 per year for U.S. institutions, $25.00 per year for foreign institutions, and $6.00 per single issue, by Rice University, 6100 South Main Street, P.O. Box 1892, Houston, Texas 77251. Second-class postage paid at Houston, Texas. **Postmaster:** Send address changes to the Business Manager, *SEL,* Rice University, P.O. Box 1892, Houston, TX 77251.

Studies in English Literature invites historical and critical essays of moderate length (ten to twenty-five pages) that contribute significantly to the understanding of English literature, 1500-1900. Typescripts should be double-spaced throughout and prepared in conformity with the Chicago Manual of Style. Clean photocopy on uncoated paper is acceptable in place of the ribbon copy. We prefer not to have dot-matrix printed copy. We will not consider articles being simultaneously submitted elsewhere, nor will we print essays to appear in a book published within a year of scheduled publication of *SEL*. Those wishing to omit their identities from manuscripts may do so, but should include a covering letter.

Manuscripts submitted for publication should be addressed to the Editor, *Studies in English Literature*, Rice University, P.O. Box 1892, Houston, TX 77251. They must be accompanied by a sufficient number of unattached stamps for return. Receipt of manuscripts will be acknowledged by postcard. Editorial decisions usually take a minimum of three months.

Annual subscription rates: $15.00 for individuals, $20.00 for U. S. institutions, $25.00 for foreign institutions, $6.00 per issue for partial subscriptions and single copies. Regular subscriptions may be obtained for any or all quarterly issues. Remittance should accompany subscription requests. Notice of non-receipt of an issue must be made within ninety (90) days following the publication of that issue. No refunds for cancellations. Business communications should be addressed to Business Manager, *Studies in English Literature*, Rice University, P. O. Box 1892, Houston, TX 77251.

Microfilms of previous volumes (Vols. 1-27) may be obtained from University Microfilms, Inc., 300 N. Zeeb Road, Ann Arbor, Michigan 48106; xerox copies of individual articles may be ordered by calling (800) 521-0600 (toll free). Copies of articles are also available from ISI's The Genuine Article service, 3501 Market Street, Philadelphia, PA 19104; phone (800) 523-1850; telex 84-5305; electronic mail through CLASS; or facsimile transmission via FAXPAX.

Volumes 1 through 3 and 5 through 10 of *Studies in English Literature* are available from Johnson Reprint Corporation, 111 Fifth Avenue, New York, N. Y. 10003, or Berkeley Square House, London W. 1, England.

SEL 28 (1988)
ISSN 0039-3657

Compelling Art in *Titus Andronicus*

MAURICE HUNT

In the judgment of many critics, the Ovid of the *Metamorphoses*—like the proverbial candle for the moth—possessed a fatal attraction for a Shakespeare groping at times for literary models capable of becoming drama.[1] "With Scene iii of Act II," Reuben Brower writes of *Titus Andronicus,* "heroic history gives way to literal enactment of myth. The first difficulty occurs when the rape of Philomel, the sufferings of Io, the vengeful feasts of Philomel and Procne and Thyestes, are spelled out on the stage. Though neither the rhetorical style nor the horrors can be entirely blamed on the Latin poets, some of the more outrageous passages are like Seneca in their cool use of gory language and even more like Ovid in combining physically painful images with startling metaphors."[2] In his concluding opinion, Brower may owe a debt to Eugene Waith, who—in an often-quoted essay—claimed that the boiling mixture of *Titus* contains raw bits of the *Metamorphoses,* mainly stylistic features (sweet verse), never reworked for the rough mode of revenge tragedy.[3] For Brower and Waith, Shakespeare's playgoers essentially stand in the same relationship to the unsavory play as Tamora does to the grisly "pastie" served up by Titus. For one camp of critics, authoritative art on occasion compelled a young Shakespeare to literalize source material, giving birth either to an unremarkable copy or—as in the charge against *Titus*—to a somewhat malformed offspring.[4]

Nonetheless, Shakespeare's characters' use of Ovidian myth to comprehend or order experience may comment more upon their world view than upon the relative quality of their creator's technical skills. In other words, the compulsive use of artistic prototypes may

---

Maurice Hunt, Associate Professor of English at Baylor University, has published twenty-six articles concerned with either Shakespeare or Renaissance drama. He is presently completing a study of medical metaphors in *The Duchess of Malfi.*

at times pertain to them rather than to Shakespeare; they—not the playwright—may deserve Brower's criticism. In the last two acts of *Titus* in particular, Shakespeare repeatedly dramatizes his characters' self-conscious reversion to literary models as patterns for their chaotic lives, at first with a certain ignorance on their part of the models' interpretive power and then later with an obsession bred of their belief that the present repeats the stories of the past.[5] A corollary of Shakespeare's staging of the relationship of art to life in *Titus* involves the divine use of art as a means of revelation. In fact, when Titus in Act IV cannot recognize a saving message of divine art, he becomes overtly destructive in his compulsive imitation of certain models of classical art. In this respect, the protagonist hurtles to his doom partly because he is unable to "read" the signs of heavenly art.

Chiron and Demetrius's brutal rape and mutilation of Lavinia involve the first self-conscious use of Ovidian story by characters in the play to determine their reality. Even though they are barbarians, Aaron and Tamora's sons, living in the world of the late Empire, have read Roman authors.[6] For example, Aaron alludes to Ovid's famous tale of the nightingale when, in Act II, he tells Tamora,

> This is the day of doom for Bassanius;
> His Philomel must lose her tongue to-day,
> Thy sons make pillage of her chastity.[7]
>
> (II.iii.42-44)

Struck in their reading of the *Metamorphoses* by muted Philomela's sewing of her rapist's name in a sampler, Chiron and Demetrius have profited devilishly from their exposure to Ovid; they not only cut out Lavinia's tongue but lop off her hands as well, thus barring Titus's daughter from the mythic character's means of discovery. In case his audience has missed the point, Shakespeare makes the association explicit. Seeing the ravaged girl, Marcus exclaims:

> But, sure, some Tereus hath deflow'red thee,
> And, lest thou should'st detect him, cut thy tongue.
>
> . . . .
>
> Fair Philomel, why, she but lost her tongue.
> And in a tedious sampler sew'd her mind:
> But, lovely niece, that mean is cut from thee;
> A craftier Tereus, cousin, hast thou met,
> And he hath cut those pretty fingers off,
> That could have better sew'd than Philomel.
>
> (II.iv.26-43)

At this stage of the dramatic action, Marcus's allusion to the Ovidian myth can only be conjectural on his part. Still, neither Chiron nor Demetrius is such a "craftier Tereus" that he can prevent Lavinia's eventual discovery of the crime and its actors. In fact, her means of revelation is the very book that originally suggested the nature of her mutilation to the criminals.

At the beginning of Act IV, grotesquely maimed Lavinia pursues her terrified nephew, who drops the books he has been carrying under his arm. Seeing his daughter feverishly turning pages with her stumps, Titus dimly apprehends that she seeks an artistic analogue to the outrage committed upon her, a pattern that might clarify it:

> Soft, so busily she turns the leaves!
> Help her: what would she find? Lavinia, shall I read?
> This is the tragic tale of Philomel,
> And treats of Tereus' treason and his rape;
> And rape, I fear, was root of thy annoy.
>
> (IV.i.45-49)

Lavinia's excitement confirms Titus's guess. "See, brother, see," Marcus states; "note how she quotes the leaves" (IV.i.50). Titus continues more confidently:

> Lavinia, wert thou thus surpris'd, sweet girl,
> Ravish'd and wrong'd, as Philomela was,
> Forc'd in the ruthless, vast, and gloomy woods?
> See, see!
> Ay, such a place there is, where we did hunt,—
> O, had we never, never hunted there,—
> Pattern'd by that the poet here describes,
> By nature made for murthers and for rapes.
>
> (IV.i.51-58)

Titus's ecstatic "See, see" indicates that ambiguous signs reveal clear truths when related to literary prototypes. In Titus's account, Ovid's tale of Philomela even includes a vivid portrayal of a woodland scene like that in which Lavinia was raped and disfigured. Ironically, the leaves of a book disclose a crime hidden by the leaves of a forest; Art is more powerful than Nature. In Shakespeare's staging, Ovid possesses prophetic powers greater than those of the Cumaean Sibyl herself, the writer of enigmatic messages on scattering leaves. And yet the *Metamorphoses* remains a *selva oscura* until experience—represented here by Lavinia's pregnant gestures—provides the code for reading the message latent in the dark leaves. While art can illuminate life,

life in turn on occasion renders intelligible prophetic art.

It is important to realize that Shakespeare, in this episode of *Titus*, is not simply dramatizing a case of art imitating (or mirroring) life. The "place . . . where we did hunt" is "pattern'd by that the poet here describes." Given Titus's "pattern'd," an uninformed auditor might think that Ovid wrote either contemporary with or after the fact of Lavinia's rape, copying, in the latter case, his account of Tereus's wood from the forest of Shakespeare's play. And yet of course it is the setting of the play and the details of the crime committed on Lavinia that providentially resemble those of Ovid's prior story.[8] Life imitates (or follows the pattern of) art. At least that appears to be Shakespeare's Wildean suggestion in Act IV of *Titus*. The question remains whether Ovid's art, which has been used in Shakespeare's tragedy both as a formula for evil and as a key to potential justice, finds a place in a larger design.

The providential aspect of compelling art appears almost immediately in the continuation of the episode from *Titus* under discussion. After Titus intuits that legend provides the means for clarifying Lavinia's personal tragedy, he pleads,

> Give signs, sweet girl, for here are none but friends,
> What Roman lord it was durst do the deed:
> Or slunk not Saturnine, as Tarquin erst,
> That left the camp to sin in Lucrece' bed?
>
> (IV.i.61-64)

Titus's instincts are right in seeking a literary model for the identity of Lavinia's ravisher, even though he is mistaken in his choice of story. Marcus, however, apparently benefits from divine inspiration:

> Sit down, sweet niece: brother, sit down by me.
> Apollo, Pallas, Jove, or Mercury,
> Inspire me, that I may this treason find!
> My lord, look here; look here, Lavinia:
> This sandy plot is plain; guide, if thou canst,
> This after me. *He writes his name with his staff and guides it with feet and mouth.*
> I have writ my name
> Without the help of any hand at all.
> Curs'd be that heart that forced us to this shift!
> Write thou, good niece, and here display at last
> What God will have discovered for revenge.
> Heaven guide thy pen to print thy sorrows plain,
> That we may know the traitors and the truth!
>
> (IV.i.65-76)

Marcus discovers God's stratagem for revealing hidden vice.[9] Despite his unorthodox method, Marcus's writing in sand duplicates the act of Ovidian Io.[10] Titus's brother realizes the artistic, especially the literary, medium by which the deity communicates with mankind. Lavinia in turn quickly emulates her uncle's method. After tracing *"Stuprum. Chiron. Demetrius"* (IV.i.78) upon the "plain" earth, she aptly, in light of our subject, concludes with some verses from Seneca's *Hippolytus,* which, in her mind, comment upon her disaster. Titus reads *"Magni dominator poli, / Tam lentus audis scelera? tam lentus vides?"* ("Ruler of the great heaven, art thou so slow to hear and see crimes?"). Lavinia believes that she finds in art's mirror a thought for exactly realizing her despair over the rape. Contrary to her sentiment, however, the God of *Titus* has not been slow to divulge secret crimes.

Interestingly, Marcus refers to the deity in the singular as "God"; certainly his prior allusions to Apollo and Mercury suggest that he addresses the supreme god Jove. Since we have no evidence for Shakespeare's seeing the quarto text of *Titus* through the press, and since Renaissance printers often capitalized important nouns, we have little reason to assume that Marcus ironically evokes the Christian God. Still, his use of the singular in naming divinity, coupled with the late-Empire setting of the play, permits a fleeting, ironic allusion to the non-pagan deity. In fact, Marcus's allusion creates the kind of dramatic ambiguity that Shakespeare shows a fondness for in other Roman plays when he places Christian references in the mouths of ancient speakers. Because *Titus* is the only Roman play historically set in the world after Christ, references to an elder tree growing by hell-pit (II.iii.277)—the tree associated with Judas—and to a "ruinous monastery" (V.i.21) where Aaron is captured do not represent clear instances of religious anachronism, as, for example, do Caesar's thirty-three wounds, which recall Christ's traditional age at the Crucifixion (*JC* V.i.53-54).[11]

Whatever the case, the first three acts of *Titus* present no evidence for resolving the ambiguity inherent in Marcus's allusion. However, by inspiring the Romans to discover Lavinia's rapists, the God of *Titus*—whether pagan or Christian—poses an ethical dilemma for the protagonist. For Marcus, the problem is easily solved—swift vengeance:

> My lord, kneel down with me; Lavinia, kneel;
> And kneel, sweet boy, the Roman Hector's hope;
> And swear with me, as with that woeful fere

And father of that chaste dishonoured dame,
Lord Junius Brutus sware for Lucrece rape,
That we will prosecute by good advice
Mortal revenge upon these traitorous Goths,
And see their blood, or die with this reproach.

(IV.i.87-94)

By invoking the Troy story and the legend of Lucrece, Marcus, appropriating the newly revealed divine *modus operandi,* finds cues for action in literary patterns. By recollecting Hector and Junius Brutus, Marcus gives the elder Lucius and Titus artistic models to imitate for heroic and bloody deeds. For Titus, however, the moral dilemma created by divine revelation appears stronger.

When Titus tells the boy Lucius that he has presents for Chiron and Demetrius, Lucius surmises that they will be daggers for their hearts (IV.i.118). "No, boy, not so," Titus exclaims; "I'll teach thee another course" (IV.i.119). Marcus, speaking to himself, in a sudden change of attitude can only admire Titus's apparent forswearing of blood revenge:

Marcus, attend him in his ecstasy,
That hath more scars of sorrow in his heart
Than foemen's marks upon his batt'red shield,
But yet so just that he will not revenge.
Revenge the heavens for old Andronicus!

(IV.i.125-29)

Marcus's final sentiment is orthodox Tudor myth—trusting God to rectify in His own time and inscrutable way injuries inflicted by tyrants.[12] Titus temporarily solves his dilemma by using art in an attempt to compel the villains to destroy one another, while he remains relatively blameless.

Once in court, the boy Lucius tells Aaron, Chiron, and Demetrius that

My grandsire, well-advis'd, hath sent by me
The goodliest weapons of his armoury
To gratify your honourable youth,
The hope of Rome, for so he bid me say;
And so I do, and with his gifts present
Your lordships, that, whenever you have need,
You may be armed and appointed well.

(IV.ii.10-16)

Titus's gifts consist of weapons strangely wrapped in Latin literary verses. His hand will not drive daggers into rapists' hearts; presumably the criminals themselves will do so under the compulsion attending an artistic insight on their part. Titus has chosen the Latin poetry so that it comments ironically upon Chiron and Demetrius's crime. For example, Demetrius, examining the paper wrapping a weapon, reads part of a Horatian ode: "*Integer vitae, scelerisque purus, / Non eget Mauri iaculis, nec arcu*" (IV.ii.20-21). "O, 'tis a verse in Horace; I know it well," Chiron naively claims; "I read it in the grammar long ago" (IV.ii.22-23)—so long ago in fact that he does not grasp the poetry's bearing upon his fragile safety.[13] A translation of the Latin—"The man who is pure of life and free from crime needs not the arrows or bow of the Moor"—reveals Titus's awareness of Tamora's sons' crime against Lavinia and Aaron's role in it. Reading the verse, whose message argues for a breaking of relationship between the man and the Moor, Chiron and Demetrius might, flattered by the hope of a pure life ensuing, turn upon Aaron and kill him. Conversely, Aaron, aware of Titus's knowledge and the poetry's relevance, might decide to kill the boys before they slay him, or before they act in a way divulging his role in the crime.[14] Whatever the bloody outcome, Titus assumes that art, once understood, will exert a savage but just retribution for his daughter's violation, fulfilling divine will in a way that keeps him free from guilt.

Titus's inclination to use art as an agent of vengeance may spring from his perception that the deity has employed artistic means to reveal truths seemingly demanding retaliation. However, Titus's artistry goes awry when Tamora's dull sons miss their bloody cues and when Aaron regards the scheme only as a bravura display of Renaissance wit.[15] "Now, what a thing it is to be an ass! / Here's no sound jest! the old man hath found their guilt" (IV.ii.25-26), the Moor exclaims. "But were our witty empress well afoot," he continues, "She would applaud Andronicus' conceit" (IV.ii.29-30). Apparently God intends to use Titus directly as an avenger of evil, perhaps judging that his pitiless sacrifice of Tamora's guiltless son at the play's beginning qualifies the old man to be divinity's self-destructive agent—a "scourge," in short, like Hamlet.[16] Still, Titus's art indirectly begins working good when it compels Aaron to break with his conspirators and seek personal safety in flight, a flight ending, significantly, in his capture in a monastery's ruins.

Our next view of Titus shows him continuing to use art in an attempt to compel behavior. Equipped with a bow and arrows with letters attached, Titus petitions the heavens for relief. "*Terras*

Astraea reliquit"—"Astraea, goddess of Justice, has left the earth"—reads one of the winged letters. Since in Titus's opinion justice dwells among the gods, retribution must proceed from above, perhaps in the form of a thunderbolt or a plague, rather than from man's hand. In other words, Titus's artistic conceit reflects his persisting desire to avoid personal revenge and trust divine providence. Because Titus's verse is taken from Book I of Ovid's *Metamorphoses,* the poetry testifies to his enduring belief that literary images can suggest meaningful patterns for behavior—in this case divine behavior. Publius believes that flattering Titus's humor will ease his madness. Consequently, when Titus asks if Publius has found Astraea, the latter Roman construes reality as a literary fable: Pluto "sends word" that Justice is employed, perhaps in heaven, but that Revenge is on call from hell (IV.iii.37-41). Unaware of Titus's belief that art molds life, Publius cannot understand the force of his personifications or the impact of his fiction on the old warrior. Convinced that "there's no justice in earth nor hell" (IV.iii.49), Titus again resolves to "solicit heaven and move the gods / To send down Justice for to wreak our wrongs" (IV.iii.50-51):

> *Ad Jovem,* that's for you: here, *Ad Apollinem*
> *Ad Martem,* that's for myself:
> Here, boy, to Pallas: here, to Mercury:
> To Saturn, Caius, not to Saturnine;
> You were as good to shoot against the wind.
>
> (IV.iii.53-57)

These pleas divinity apparently does not stoop to answer. "In this context," David Palmer remarks, "the last age of Rome under Saturninus in Shakespeare's play is something akin to a blasphemous parody, in which the 'Virgo' becomes neither Astraea nor Mary, but the violated chastity of Lavinia . . . while the son that is born into this world of woe is no redeemer, but Aaron's bastard."[17] Still, Shakespeare introduces the more tender virtues associated with Christianity into this late Roman world as values that Romans fail to appreciate or adopt.

This is made clear by the Clown-pigeon episode, which has usually been regarded by critics as dramatic filler. Titus's prayers are answered—not by a *deus ex machina* of Jupiter (like that staged in *Cymbeline*)—but by a heavenly response nonetheless (albeit a disguised one). Soon after the bizarre arrow-shooting, a country fellow carrying a basket containing two pigeons enters. Titus himself creates the context for valuing this interlude when he shouts,

> News, news from heaven! Marcus, the post is come.
> Sirrah, what tidings? have you any letters?
> Shall I have Justice? What says Jupiter?
> (IV.iii.76-78)

"Ho, the gibbet-maker?" the Clown whimsically exclaims, coining a kind of pun that captures ironically the vindictiveness of the classical gods. Distraught Titus repeats his question, "Why didst thou not come from heaven?" (IV.iii.87). Naturally the Clown protests: "From heaven? alas, sir, I never came there. God forbid I should be so bold to press to heaven in my young days" (IV.iii.88-90).

Nonetheless, Titus's madness has hit upon a veiled truth. The Clown, while obviously not a literal messenger from heaven, incarnates a heavenly ethos potentially redemptive for the wilderness of *Titus*. "Why, I am going with my pigeons to the tribunal plebs, to take up a matter of brawl betwixt my uncle and one of the emperal's men" (IV.iii.90-92), he continues. Clearly, the rustic intends the pigeons as a peace offering. In this respect, he represents the values of forgiveness and reconciliation, values which quickly would turn tragedy into divine comedy if adopted by Romans. The presence of the pigeons gives these values a Christian coloring; sixteenth-century iconography often employs pigeons—doves—as symbols for the Holy Ghost.[18] Titus's strange artistry has provoked a veiled response from a God unrevered by fourth-century Romans. That Titus—not to mention most viewers of the play—misreads God's dark conceit is not surprising. Only the audience that grasps the mimetic interplay between art and life understands that Shakespeare's God responds in kind; he challenges Titus and playgoers to interpret his symbols, his dark conceits, even as he has answered Titus's witty, artistic method of prayer. Titus's failure to fathom God's art, to imitate the model of the Clown's intended behavior, suggests a solipsistic blindness to anything that does not directly promote his revenge.

But does Titus really have a choice? Recently several critics have argued that the Rome of *Titus*, in its primitive customs of blood revenge, is no more enlightened than savage lands like that of Tamora's Goths.[19] In their view, Shakespeare weaves a mysterious Christian Providence through the play's events, pacifying both Goth and Roman, to bring forth a less tyrannous Rome represented in part by a crucial willingness to forgive seen in Lucius at the play's end. His pardoning of Aaron's son does break the cataclysmic series of filial sacrifices in the play.[20] In this argument, Titus becomes the necessary scourge making possible a Rome superior to Saturninus's wracked city. Titus's eye-for-an-eye sacrifice of Alarbus can qualify him as the corrupt agent who, in God's scheme, destroys greater evil—and yet himself in the process too (see note 16). Providence thus, in a certain economy of goodness, fully sweeps away corruption before forming a conciliatory society. In this respect, the special message of the Clown remains for the onstage and theatrical audiences—a message about a man hardened of heart, unable to embrace the reconciliation his role as scourge will help bring about in the character of Lucius.

In fact, the perversity of Titus's treatment of the well-meaning if bumbling Clown stamps him as the scourge worthy of ruin.[21] "By me thou shalt have justice at his [the emperor's] hands" (IV.iii.102), Titus predicts, secretly ordering Marcus to fold the Clown's knife in a bitter oration specially penned by Titus for Saturninus. "Then here is a supplication for you," Titus states, "and when you come to him, at the first approach you must kneel; then kiss his foot; then deliver up your pigeons; and then look for your reward" (IV.iii.107-10). "God be with you, sir; I will" (IV.iii.118), the innocent wishes as he departs to his brutal death, his final blessing on Titus clinching his piety. That the Clown is meant in his death to be thought of as a kind of martyr is signalled by his allusion to a Christian prototype in his greeting to Saturninus: "'Tis he. God and Saint Stephen give you godden. I have brought you a letter and a couple of pigeons here" (IV.iv.42-44).[22] "Go, take him away, and hang him presently" (IV.iv.45), Saturninus snarls, angered by Titus's claim in the delivered letter that the emperor has butchered Titus's sons. Thus the Clown-pigeon episode, while revealing God's symbolic artistry, casts Titus as unappreciative of its message—and so not worthy to be saved by grace. The larger art of Providence directs Titus one way, while, for a moment, God's local art fashions a spectacle for those uncorrupted enough to learn from Titus's example.[23]

At the beginning of Act V, the arch villainess Tamora, stung by the report that Titus's son, Lucius, leads an army of vengeful Goths against Rome, decides to use Titus in a scheme to thwart this new threat. Her plan involves concocting a little allegory based on the conventions of the recently established sub-genre of Elizabethan revenge tragedy. Approaching Titus's villa, she verbally creates a popular aesthetic context for the ensuing episode:

> Thus, in this strange and sad habiliment,
> I will encounter with Andronicus,

And say I am Revenge, sent from below
To join with him and right his heinous wrongs;
Knock at his study, where they say he keeps,
To ruminate strange plots of dire revenge;
Tell him Revenge is come to join with him
And work confusion on his enemies.

(V.ii.1-8)

With a cruel irony for Titus, Tamora's proposed drama fleshes out Publius's earlier, patronizing fable. Titus, however, first sees the empress Tamora, not the figure of Revenge (V.ii.25-26). "Is not thy coming for my other hand?" (V.ii.27), he awkwardly asks. Despite this question, Tamora, persuaded of Titus's blinding madness, insists on her delusion:

Know thou, sad man, I am not Tamora;
She is thy enemy, and I thy friend:
I am Revenge, sent from th' infernal kingdom
To ease the gnawing vulture of thy mind
By working wreakful vengeance on thy foes.

(V.ii.28-32)

This artistic conceit, Tamora's playlet, apparently takes in Titus. It is as though he and Tamora had noted well Revenge's dramatic assurance to the Ghost of Don Andrea at the beginning of *The Spanish Tragedy*. "Art thou Revenge? and art thou sent to me," Titus queries, "to be a torment to mine enemies?" (V.ii.41-42). Seemingly bewitched by Tamora's artistry, Titus allegorizes Chiron and Demetrius, who have accompanied their mother in her ruse:

Do me some service ere I come to thee.
Lo, by thy side where Rape and Murder stands;
Now give some surance that thou art Revenge:
Stab them, or tear them on thy chariot-wheels,
And then I'll come and be thy waggoner,
And whirl along with thee about the globe.

(V.ii.44-49)

"And day by day I'll do this heavy task," Titus repeats, "so thou destroy Rapine and Murder there" (V.ii.58-59). Has distracted Titus been completely fooled by Tamora's playlet so that he cannot tell fact from fancy? Has he become so persuaded that art models experience that he credits a destructive fiction, ready to act according to its aesthetic dictates? Or is Titus slyly engineering Chiron's and

Demetrius's deaths at their mother's hand (perhaps trying to absolve himself of the penalty for vengeance), by turning the logic of Tamora's allegory against itself?

Whatever the case, Titus and Tamora at this point engage in a struggle for art as an instrument of the will and a means for ordering experience for just or unjust ends. "These are my ministers," Tamora replies to Titus's suggestion, implying that Revenge cannot destroy its own agents for success. "Are these thy ministers?" Titus asks; "what are they call'd?" (V.ii.61). "Rape and Murder," Tamora answers; "therefore called so / 'Cause they take vengeance of such kind of men" (V.ii.62-63). J.C. Maxwell, in an appendix to his New Arden edition of the play, has argued that, in Tamora's mind, disguised Chiron and Demetrius lacked namable identities when they approached Titus's villa with her (pp. 131-32). Titus—not Tamora—first personified them in keeping with the iconography of Revenge. At length asking Revenge their names, he learns that he has correctly allegorized them. In doing so, Titus may have wrenched artistic direction of Tamora's playlet from the authoress herself. In other words, Titus may be reshaping an artistic pattern for experience rather than having his actions molded by it. "Good Lord, how like the empress' sons they are" (V.ii.64), Titus concludes:

> And you the empress, but we worldly men
> Have miserable, mad, mistaking eyes.
> O sweet Revenge, now do I come to thee;
> And, if one arm's embracement will content thee,
> I will embrace thee in it by and by.
>
> (V.ii.65-69)

Shakespeare carefully builds suspense by not quickly resolving the question of whether a deadly art deludes Titus or a clever protagonist knows it for an illusion, employing it secretly for the Goths' ruin. Tamora has cast herself as Revenge simply to gain Titus's confidence; she knows that he has been looking for Revenge everywhere. "See, here he comes," she concludes, "and I must ply my theme" (V.ii.80). "Show me a murtherer, I'll deal with him" (V.ii.93), Demetrius states in the spirit of his assigned identity. "Show me a villain that hath done a rape, / And I am sent to be reveng'd on him" (V.ii.94-95), Chiron iterates. Ironically, Tamora's sons are damning themselves as murderer and rapist; Chiron as Rape and Demetrius as Murder will destroy Chiron the rapist and Demetrius the murderer. Shadowed forth is a dynamism of just self-destruction, thrust upon the young men by means of a compelling artistry. Trusting ad-lib

Machiavellian policy becomes risky when art orders life; little room exists for improvisation. Suddenly caught up in an allegory escaping their control, Chiron and Demetrius find themselves subject to the righteous logic of the art. These points are not lost upon Titus:

> Look round about the wicked streets of Rome,
> And when thou find'st a man that's like thyself,
> Good Murther, stab him; he's a murtherer.
> Go thou with him; and when it is thy hap
> To find another that is like to thee,
> Good Rapine, stab him; he is a ravisher.
>
> (V.ii.98-103)

Moreover, Titus's direction of art's retributive working includes Tamora herself:

> Go thou with them; and in the emperor's court
> There is a queen attended by a Moor;
> Well shalt thou know her by thine own proportion,
> For up and down she doth resemble thee:
> I pray thee, do on them some violent death;
> They have been violent to me and mine.
>
> (V.ii.104-109)

Hoodwinked, Tamora agrees to let Rape and Murder remain with Titus while she promises to bring the queen and Saturninus to Titus's banquet. Martha Rozett has argued that "Tamora, by pretending to be a temptation figure, does in fact become one, by offering Titus the opportunity to seize her two sons. The very elements that make this scene seem so contrived to a modern audience might have served as evidence to a sixteenth-century one that Providence was indeed intervening, turning Tamora into the agent of her own destruction and Titus into the instrument of the revenging gods."[24] Finally, Titus, in a dramatic aside, ends the uncertainty over Tamora's disguise: "I knew them all, though they suppos'd me mad, / And will o'erreach them in their own devices" (V.ii.142-43). Art will undermine art. Once alone with Tamora's sons, Titus summons his friends Publius, Caius, and Valentine:

> *Tit.* Know you these two?
> *Pub.* The empress' sons, I take them, Chiron and Demetrius.
> *Tit.* Fie, Publius, fie, thou art too much deceiv'd;
> The one is Murder, and Rape is the other's name.
>
> (V.ii.153-56)

The artistry of the young men's disguise is so mediocre that they are easily recognizable. Tamora's understanding of the complex degree of artistry necessary for determining experience proves faulty. The question remains whether Titus's mastery is sufficient for his success.

Generally, Titus's Ovidian pattern for revenge exhibits decorum. He tells the bound criminals, "For worse than Philomel you us'd my daughter, / And worse than Progne I will be reveng'd" (V.ii.194-95). In revenge for Tereus's rape of her sister, Procne served him a meal made up of his son's flesh; similarly, Titus plans to cut Chiron's and Demetrius's throats:

> Hark, villains, I will grind your bones to dust,
> And with your blood and it I'll make a paste,
> And of the paste a coffin I will rear,
> And make two pasties of your shameful heads,
> And bid that strumpet, your unhallowed dam,
> Like to the earth swallow her own increase.
>
> (V.ii.186-91)

Titus's imitation of Ovid's story of Philomel and Procne reveals originality when Tamora ignorantly eats her slaughtered sons' remains, justly illustrating Appetite's self-consuming nature. Amorally greedy for absolute power, Tamora has cut down anyone standing in her ambition's way. A creature of earthy passions, she enacts a role in Titus's playlet in which she aptly swallows her own personified sins, grossly punishing herself in the process. This original enactment appears to be the "worse" (for the villains) in Titus's resolve to out-imitate his artistic model.

Shakespeare reserves the crowning blow of Titus's artistry for the play's final scene. Entering costumed "like a cook," Titus clearly plans to play a part in his final performance. Marcus expects that Titus's banquet will resemble a convivial feast, perhaps like that celebrated by Plato in the Symposium, or—at least from the audience's viewpoint—perhaps like that communion of brothers typified by the Last Supper: "The feast is ready which the careful Titus / Hath ordain'd to an honourable end, / For peace, for love, for league, and good to Rome" (V.iii.21-23). For a fleeting moment, the life-renewing values seen in the Clown are recalled. And yet before they can crystallize, intersecting the play's drive toward tragedy, Titus forces a grim pattern upon events:

> My lord the emperor, resolve me this:
> Was it well done of rash Virginius

To slay his daughter with his own right hand,
Because she was enforc'd, stain'd, and deflow'r'd?
(V.iii.35-38)

Editors wrestle gamely with the sense of these verses. According to G. Blakemore Evans, "this Roman centurion killed his daughter to *prevent* her rape. Either the dramatist has got the story wrong or he is failing to convey the idea that Titus has a better case for killing Lavinia than Virginius had for killing his daughter."[25] Surely the point lies otherwise. Titus has learned to adapt artistic patterns for his own advantage; in fact, he learned when the identities of Lavinia's rapists were discovered that God works in such a way.[26] For the moment, Saturninus replies to Titus's question about Virginius's homicide:

Sat. It was, Andronicus.
Tit. Your reason, mighty lord?
Sat. Because the girl should not survive her shame,
And by her presence still renew his sorrows.
Tit. A reason mighty, strong, and effectual;
A pattern, president, and lively warrant
For me, most wretched, to perform the like.
Die, die, Lavinia, and thy shame with thee;
And with thy shame thy father's sorrow die!
[*He kills her.*]
(V.iii.39-47)

Saturninus's horrified reaction represents that of most members of the audience: "What hast thou done, unnatural and unkind?" (V.iii.48). Art's logic is not life's logic. God employed artistic patterns to reveal truth, promote justice, and build a foundation for a better Rome; Titus adapts the Virginius story as a model for action in order to satisfy his perverted sense of honor. Clearly, Lavinia's death in Titus's staging is gratuitous. In this respect, Act IV, scene iv of *The Spanish Tragedy* most likely inspired Shakespeare's dramaturgy.[27]

There, Hieronimo, the master artist, adapts a play—*The Tragedy of Soliman and Perseda*—for the festivities following Balthazar's and Bel-imperia's wedding, which unites the Spanish and Portuguese kings. An aesthetic vehicle for Hieronimo's revenge, the drama requires Lorenzo to play a knight of Rhodes; Bel-imperia Perseda, the knight's beloved; and Balthazar Soliman, the heathen Sultan also in love with Perseda. Hieronimo himself will play a bashaw in the Sultan's service. Hieronimo's play demands that the bashaw (Hieronimo) stab the knight (Lorenzo) on command of the wildly jealous Soliman

(Balthazar). Enraged Perseda (Bel-imperia) then kills Soliman. During the court performance, the knives and blows are real, sending gullible Lorenzo and Balthazar to their dooms for their murder of Hieronimo's son, Horatio. Hieronimo's art conforms to the gory reality of the Spanish court; the protagonist kills the man most guilty of his son's murder while Bel-imperia slays the Portuguese prince who killed her first love, Don Andrea. In essence, Hieronimo's play-within-the-play provides a pattern for vengeance upon actual deeds.

When Hieronimo revises the ending of *The Tragedy of Soliman and Perseda* so that Bel-imperia might live, he reveals not only a vestige of humanity but also the fact that he works with an actual tragedy written in Toledo by himself many years earlier (IV.i.70-79).[28] Admittedly, Kyd's audience may hesitate to accept Hieronimo's account of the origin of his tragedy. One could argue that Hieronimo simply slapped together a play, fulfilling his and Bel-imperia's need for a vehicle for their notion of justice, and then misled his victims by persuading them that the drama represents a work completed in the days when Hieronimo, in his own words, "plied" himself to "fruitless poetry" (IV.i.71). After all, the coincidence of crimes in *The Spanish Tragedy* to the fictional events of an old student tragedy would be extremely remote. Nonetheless, Kyd indicates that such a coincidence has occurred. After stabbing Balthazar, Bel-imperia suddenly kills herself, directly contrary to the preservation that Hieronimo rewrote into his play's ending. "Poor Bel-imperia missed her part in this," Hieronimo confesses; "For though the story saith she should have died, / Yet I of kindness, and of care of her, / Did otherwise determine of her end" (IV.iv.140-43). Hieronimo's confession makes sense only if he in fact has resurrected an old play and revised its ending. And yet Bel-imperia chooses to ignore that revision and kill herself; experience in the Spanish court has in fact *fully* conformed to an artistic pattern created long ago in Hieronimo's youth.

However, with Bel-imperia's suicide, Hieronimo loses control of his art. In a mad act of violence, Hieronimo kills the duke of Castile, Lorenzo's and Bel-imperia's father, seemingly because the revenger regards him as his alter ego—a man left heirless by crime. Hieronimo does stab himself and the duke in virtually one motion with the same knife. The senseless killing of the duke of Castile suggests that the tragic protagonist who uses art as his model for experience can become so carried away by the spirit of his re-enactment that unjust outrages occur, bringing further damnation upon the artisan's head.

It is this dimension of Kyd's staging that Shakespeare may have noticed and developed in the catastrophe of *Titus*. In fact, Shakespeare's inspiration for Titus's shocking killing of Lavinia may have come from Hieronimo's pointless murder of the duke of Castile.[29] Both deaths warn against the danger of becoming compulsively caught up in acting out deadly artistic patterns.[30]

Nonetheless, in Shakespeare's play Titus provides a rationale for his wild deed. In reply to Saturninus's question—"What hast thou done?"—he attempts to justify Lavinia's death:

> Kill'd her for whom my tears have made me blind.
> I am as woeful as Virginius was,
> And have a thousand times more cause than he
> To do this outrage; and it now is done.
>
> (V.iii.49-52)

When Saturninus infers from Titus's repeated allusions to the Virginius story that Lavinia suffered rape, he asks Titus to name the criminals. The protagonist, however, after identifying the empress's sons, gruesomely points out that they may be sought in the pie which Tamora has eaten: "Why, there they are, both baked in this pie; / Whereof their mother daintily hath fed, / Eating the flesh that she herself hath bred" (V.iii.60-62). The final verse of Titus's speech stresses the previously mentioned moral about Appetite that prompted Titus's application of the Procne-Tereus story to the details of his revenge. In Titus's mind at least, this grisly moral marks the conclusion of an artistic pattern. His playlet over, he then stabs Tamora to death, receiving his death blow from Saturninus, who in turn is killed by the elder Lucius.

Amid the carnage, Marcus struggles to understand seemingly random acts of brutality. Not surprisingly, he does so by applying to them the pattern of art most tragic in the Renaissance mind. Addressing Lucius, Marcus states:

> But if my frosty signs and chaps of age,
> Grave witnesses of true experience,
> Cannot induce you to attend my words,
> Speak, Rome's dear friend, as erst our ancestor,
> When with his solemn tongue he did discourse
> To love-sick Dido's sad-attending ear
> The story of that baleful burning night
> When subtle Greeks surpris'd King Priam's Troy.
> Tell us what Sinon hath bewitch'd our ears,
> Or who hath brought the fatal engine in

> That gives our Troy, our Rome, the civil wound.
> . . . .
> Here's Rome's young captain, let him tell the tale,
> While I stand by and weep to hear him speak.
>
> (V.iii.77-95)

For Virgilian Rome, the tragic story of Troy became a tale of rebirth; Aeneas's founding of Rome was considered the rebuilding of Priam's great city. By comparing Lucius to Aeneas, Marcus unintentionally converts a tragic pattern of art into a redemptive legend. According to Reuben Brower, even the less-learned viewer of *Titus* "would have seen the point in the restoration of peace and order under Lucius," who was also "the 'first Christian king of England', as he 'was presented' in Foxe's *Book of Martyrs,* one of the more widely read works of Elizabeth's reign."[31] By identifying the Roman Lucius with the English Christian Lucius, Shakespeare suggests that the patterns of the past need not inexorably shape the future. By sparing Aaron's blackamoor child, Roman Lucius realizes, for an instant, the distinctively Christian virtue of mercy, breaking the deadly chain of eye-for-an-eye executions of sons—the catalyst to most of the disaster in *Titus.*[32] In his momentarily refined character, Roman Lucius, before lapsing into his terrible sentence upon Aaron, predicts his Christian namesake, who began a dynasty that would eventually bring Astraea back to earth in the form of Queen Elizabeth.[33] By recognizing the art of God's Providence in this design, Shakespeare's viewer gains insight into an aesthetic prototype more worthy of endorsement than Ovid's grim formulas. In fact, that awareness appears to be one of the more important dramatic effects intended by the creator of *Titus Andronicus.* Shakespeare's detached, often ironic perspective upon compelling art in this popular revenge tragedy makes charging him with naively imitating the works of Roman masters extremely difficult. Even at an early age (perhaps even in his late twenties), Shakespeare displays his remarkable ability for cooly exploring in his characterizations certain problems of art often committed by less thoughtful authors in their own persons.

NOTES

[1]The claim that Ovid's *Metamorphoses* provided the young playwright of *Titus Andronicus* with a pattern for tragedy scarcely needs demonstrating at this late date in Shakespeare studies. Still, the reader may wish to consult, among others, A. C. Hamilton, "*Titus Andronicus:* The Form of Shakespearian Tragedy," *SQ* 14 (1963):203-207; Nicholas Brooke, *Shakespeare's Early Tragedies* (London: Methuen, 1968), pp. 20-21; Andrew V. Ettin, "Shakespeare's First Roman Tragedy," *ELH* 37 (1970):235-36; and Grace Starry West, "Going by the Book: Classical Allusions in Shakespeare's *Titus Andronicus,*" *SP* 79 (1982):62-77.

[2]Reuben A. Brower, *Hero & Saint: Shakespeare and the Graeco-Roman Heroic Tradition* (Oxford: Oxford Univ. Press, 1971), p. 198.

[3]Eugene Waith, "The Metamorphosis of Violence in *Titus Andronicus,*" *ShS* 10 (1957):39-49.

[4]Some critics have argued that, in "literalizing" the *Metamorphoses,* the Upstart Crow was trying to "out-Ovid" Ovid, just as he had attempted to out-do Plautus by introducing a second set of twins in *The Comedy of Errors.* See Harold C. Goddard, *The Meaning of Shakespeare,* 2 vols. (Chicago: Univ. of Chicago Press, 1960), 1:34; David J. Palmer, "The Unspeakable in Pursuit of the Uneatable: Language and Action in *Titus Andronicus,*" *CritQ* 14 (1972):320-39; and Albert H. Tricomi, "The Aesthetics of Mutilation in *Titus Andronicus,*" *ShS* 27 (1974):16.

[5]My argument is anticipated by Mary Fawcett, who claims in "Arms/Words/Tears: Language and the Body in *Titus Andronicus,*" *ELH* 50 (1983):261-77, that in the play "words point to a pre-existing text which alone originates and sanctions action" (p. 269). Also see Grace Starry West, pp. 62-77. West argues that classical allusions often set precedents for characters' behavior in this early Roman tragedy. Yet, in her view (p. 65), art lacks compulsion; the difference between an artistic precedent and behavior based upon it reflects Shakespeare's characters' solipsistic, vicious willfulness. As West states, "Shakespeare's characters do learn from Ovid's book; but they learn how to be evil, not good" (p. 77).

[6]For the history of critical attempts to date the setting of *Titus,* see Clifford Huffman, "Titus Andronicus: Metamorphosis and Renewal," *MLR* 67 (1972):735, n. 3. Huffman notes that "the eighteenth-century prose tale, an earlier version of which is a probable source of the play, locates the events in the time of the Eastern Emperor Theodosius (A.D. 378-95)." Moreover, West remarks that "we should remember that the Rome of *Titus Andronicus* is Rome after Brutus, after Caesar, and after Ovid. We know it is a later Rome because the emperor is routinely called Caesar; because the characters are constantly alluding to Tarquin, Lucretia, and Brutus, suggesting that they learned about Brutus' new founding of Rome from the same literary sources we do, Livy and Plutarch" (p. 74). In this respect, Huffman describes the setting of Shakespeare's play as "late-Imperial Christian Rome" (p. 735). For an argument on the intended "unhistorical" nature of the Roman setting of *Titus,* see G.K. Hunter, "Sources and Meanings in *Titus Andronicus,*" *Mirror up to Shakespeare: Essays in Honour of G.R. Hibbard,* ed. J. C. Gray (Toronto: Univ. of Toronto Press, 1984), p. 181.

[7]All references to *Titus Andronicus* are taken from the New Arden edition, ed. J.C. Maxwell (London: Methuen, 1968). All other references to Shakespeare's plays are to *The Riverside Shakespeare,* ed. G. Blakemore Evans (Boston: Houghton Mifflin, 1974).

[8]Also see James L. Calderwood, *Shakespearean Metadrama: The Argument of the Play* (Minneapolis: Univ. of Minnesota Press, 1971), p. 34.

[9]In "Four Forms of Vengeance in *Titus Andronicus,*" *JEGP* 78 (1979):494-507, Ronald Broude also notes that the heavens inspire Marcus to fathom Lavinia's rape (p. 501).

[10]See Robert S. Miola, "*Titus Andronicus* and the Mythos of Shakespeare's Rome," *ShakS* 14 (1981):86.

[11]In "*Non sine causa:* The Use of Emblematic Method and Iconology in the Thematic Structure of *Titus Andronicus,*" *RORD* 13-14 (1970-71):158, Ann Haaker notes that "the elder tree from which the cross of Christ was made (a common belief in certain midland counties, for according to medieval tradition the elder tree was the tree on which Judas hanged himself), the taper in the monument, the slaughtered lamb of God—all form a bizarre mélange of the grotesque and the sacred in *Titus.*"

[12]The classic explication of this doctrine remains E.M.W. Tillyard, *Shakespeare's History Plays* (1944; rpt. New York: Collier, 1962).

[13]See Fawcett, p. 264.

[14]For an alternative account of Horace's bearing upon this episode, see West, pp. 70-71.

[15]That Aaron grasps the seriousness of the criminals' situation is evidenced by his aside "Pray to the devils; the gods have given us over" (IV.ii.48). Consequently, the Moor finds abandoning Tamora and Saturninus's court easy once the blackamoor child, his heir and first-born, is placed in his arms.

[16]At some point prior to the late sixteenth century, the idea of God's scourge as apocalyptic deluge (Isaiah 28:14-29) was translated into the notion of a bad man who punishes equal or greater evil. For specific references to the human scourge, see *Tamburlaine, Part One* III.iii.44-60, IV.ii.31-32, IV.iii.1-14; *Tamburlaine, Part Two* II.iv.78-80, IV.i.148-69, V.i.181-83; and of course *Hamlet* III.iv.173-77. Ronald Broude, in "Roman and Goth in *Titus Andronicus,*" *ShakS* 6 (1970):32-33, remarks that the Andronici "bring about the regeneration of Rome in much the same way that, in Shakespeare's later revenge play, Hamlet, acting as 'scourge and minister,' operates on Denmark's 'hidden impostume.' "

[17]"The Unspeakable in Pursuit of the Uneatable: Language and Action in *Titus Andronicus,*" p. 324.

[18]In *Dictionary of Subjects and Symbols in Art* (New York: Harper and Row, 1974), James Hall catalogues the many painterly versions of the dove as a symbol of the Holy Ghost (p. 109). "Pigeon" was a common sixteenth-century synonym for "dove," as the OED #1 and #2 definitions of the former term indicate.

[19]Roman barbarity equal to or greater than Goth savagery is described in *Titus* by Bertrand Evans, *Shakespeare's Tragic Practice* (Oxford: Clarendon Press, 1979), pp. 20-21; by Brooke, pp. 22-26, 39, 45-46; by Robert S. Miola, *Shakespeare's Rome* (Cambridge: Cambridge Univ. Press, 1983), pp. 47-57; and by Richard Marienstras, *New Perspectives on the Shakespearean World,* trans. Janet Lloyd (Cambridge: Cambridge Univ. Press, 1985), pp. 40-43.

[20]According to Ronald Broude, "notwithstanding the paganism of the characters . . . the guiding force in the play is something very much like the Christian Providence of Shakespeare's histories" (p. 496). For a reading of Providence at work in *Titus,* see Broude's "Four Forms of Vengeance in *Titus Andronicus,*" pp. 500-507, as well as his "Roman and Goth in *Titus Andronicus,*" pp. 27-34. Moreover, Irving Ribner, in *Patterns in Shakespearian Tragedy* (London: Methuen, 1960), argues that "Shakespeare tries also to place the fall of

Titus within a larger framework in which evil too is destroyed, so that the audience, while lamenting the damnation of one soul, may have a renewed awareness of the perfection of God's order and of the operation of justice in the world" (p. 18). For Shakespeare's "Christianizing" moments in Act V of *Titus,* moments replete with "Protestant phraseology," see Calderwood, pp. 42-43. On the other hand, see A. C. Hamilton's belief that, in *Titus,* "the gods delight in tragedies" (pp. 211-12). Hamilton implies that the gods have fiendishly crafted a plot for the characters to act out, a scenario with hell-pit the central stage property. This critic concludes that the action of *Titus* creates "a world without hope of redemption, where men are prey of their passions and the malignant gods" (p. 212). However, hell-pit, by entailing damnation, also implies possible salvation. In this respect, Hamilton's central stage property is hardly a pagan device.

[21]According to Alan Sommers, "what is lacking [in the Andronici] is not only the 'mercy' pleaded for [initially by Tamora] but also, more precisely, pity" (" 'Wilderness of Tigers': Structure and Symbolism in *Titus Andronicus,*" *EIC* 10 [1960]:277).

[22]Cf. Leslie A. Fiedler, *The Stranger in Shakespeare* (New York: Stein and Day, 1972), pp. 178-79. "Aaron's very name, of course, connects him with Jewish tradition; and like the tribe of Shylock, but unlike Othello and the Prince of Morocco, he is even described as 'misbelieving' and 'irreligious,' an enemy of the True God. Yet here, of course, Shakespeare gets into trouble, having no true believers to set against the pagan, only Titus and his sons, who are pagans, though Roman, as, indeed, he seems to forget, permitting, for instance, a clown entering the scene to swear by 'Saint Stephen,' first Christian martyr to the Jews." In my argument, however, the slip is scarcely accidental. In A. C. Hamilton's view, the Clown and his pigeons are a "cruel" answer to Titus's prayer for Justice—an answer on Pluto's part (p. 206).

[23]The Renaissance identification of Providence as God's art can be easily seen by comparing Robert Fludd's well-known engraving *Utriusque Cosmi Historia* (1617-19) with *The Winter's Tale* IV.iv.89-97. In Shakespeare's poetry, the Art "over that art / Which . . . adds to Nature"—the Art that "makes" Nature—clarifies the value of God's hand and chain in the Fludd engraving. God's attributes in the engraving symbolize the Art guiding that great Nature which rules her "ape," mankind, who in turn remains intent on rectifying fallen nature through his secular art (represented by the compasses).

[24]Martha Tuck Rozett, *The Doctrine of Election and the Emergence of Elizabethan Tragedy* (Princeton: Princeton Univ. Press, 1984), p. 198.

[25]*The Riverside Shakespeare,* p. 1049.

[26]Holger Nørgaard argues that, contrary to Livy's, Chaucer's, Gower's, and Lydgate's version of the Virginius story, Shakespeare based Titus/Virginius's killing of an already-raped Lavinia/Virginia upon the anomalous retelling of the classical legend by Lodowicke Lloid in *The Pilgrimage of Princes* (1573, 1586). See "Never Wrong But with Just Cause," *ES* 45 (1964):137-41. Arguing that Shakespeare grounded his understanding of source material in anomalies remains risky, however.

[27]In *Elizabethan Revenge Tragedy 1587-1642,* (Princeton: Princeton Univ. Press, 1966), Fredson T. Bowers argues that "*Titus Andronicus* is very similar in construction to *The Spanish Tragedy* and so deeply under its influence that, except for the omission of the supernatural, its outline conforms to that already given for Kyd's tragedy" (p. 111).

[28]References to *The Spanish Tragedy* are to the text in *Drama of the English Renaissance,* ed. Russell A. Fraser and Norman Rabkin, 2 vols. (New York: Macmillan, 1976), 1:167-203.

[29]For an extended analysis of the importance of *The Tragedy of Soliman and Perseda* for *The Spanish Tragedy* as a whole, see the chapter "Hieronimo's Play" in Peter B. Murray, *Thomas Kyd,* Twayne's English Authors Series 88 (Boston: Twayne, 1969), esp. pp. 135-52. Concerning Lorenzo's and Hieronimo's tragedies, Murray remarks that "in different ways each of them play-acts so well that he gets carried away in the fictions he has created and therefore loses sight of the relation between pretense and reality" (p. 138).

[30]The warning holds in Shakespeare's play even though the tragic character's role as scourge requires an indefensible killing as justification for his death. Compare Tamburlaine's killing of his son Calyphas in *Tamburlaine, Part Two* IV.i.81.

[31]Reuben Brower, *Hero & Saint,* p. 194.

[32]For example, when Lavinia begs pity of Tamora, the queen reminds her that Titus expressed none for Alarbus (II.iii.149-67).

[33]Frances A. Yates, *Astraea: The Imperial Theme in the Sixteenth Century* (London: Routledge & Kegan Paul, 1975), p. 75. While explaining the political relevance of classical Astraea and Lucius for their royal English namesakes, Yates notes that "Foxe's 'Book of Martyrs', it will be remembered, begins with Lucius and ends with Elizabeth."

SEL 28 (1988)
ISSN 0039-3657

"I Sing But After You": Shakespeare's Internal Parody

RICHARD HORWICH

"Parody-hunting has become as popular as (and sometimes synonymous with) parallel hunting" among students of Renaissance English drama, Richard Levin complained more than a decade ago.[1] Levin foresaw no waning of interest in either pursuit, and none has occurred; new expeditions have been mounted with increasing frequency during recent years, particularly by Shakespeareans. But the continued scrutiny of the parody-searchers and parallel-seekers has produced neither a definitive reformulation of parody and its function nor a consensus on the relationship between parodies and parallels. In 1965, Dean Frye took Allan Gilbert and others to task for assuming that the mere juxtaposition of "an idealised dramatic action" (such as the main plot of *Henry V)* with "an unheroic, romantic parallel" (the Pistol scenes) constituted a parody of the former by the latter.[2] But such strictures have had little effect, apparently; two decades later, the assumptions that dismayed Frye and Levin are still in evidence. Joan Hartwig (invoking Dr. Johnson's definition, by which almost any adaptation or imitation could be termed parodic) recently designated as parodies many analogical parallels between major and minor characters and between main- and sub-plots in Shakespeare's plays. For her, the final effect of these parodies is not reductively comic; though parody does "reduce the imitated scene, action, speech or gesture to simplistic terms," she tells us, "in the next instant . . . the original is recalled through the reduced terms of its imitation, and in the process of the original's being re-seen as it was meant to be seen, it regains authority and fresh meaning."[3]

Richard Horwich is Professor of English at Brooklyn College. He is the author of several articles on Shakespeare and other Elizabethan and Jacobean dramatists, and of a forthcoming book, *Shakespeare's Dilemmas*.

This tendency to view Shakespearean parody not as a vehicle of satire or ridicule but merely as a kind of two-way mirror represents a considerable departure from what Hartwig calls the "strict" definition of Frye and Levin.[4] Perhaps this neutralizing or even neutering of parody is rooted in the desire of earlier ages to safeguard Shakespeare's reputation from any possible taint of pettiness or vulgarity: let Jonson fire parodic salvos at his professional rivals in *The Poetaster* (even as Truewit bedevils Morose through parody in *Epicoene)*, but the Swan of Avon presumably flew at higher moral altitudes, both within the framework of his plays and without. In two other recent studies, however, by Margaret A. Rose and Linda Hutcheon, the comic and ironic elements of parody are to some extent recuperated. Rose argues convincingly that "the perception of any type of incongruity, be it dissimilarity or anachronistic similarity" between two texts is invariably comic, and that it is this comic element that distinguishes parody from "other types of literary criticism."[5] Hutcheon would appear at first to be a follower of Hartwig: warning her readers that parody (at least in the twentieth century) is "not just that ridiculing imitation mentioned in the standard dictionary definition,"[6] she chastises Rose and other modern commentators for confusing it with satire[7] and reminds us that what contemporary critics call parody is, formally at least, not substantially different from what in the Renaissance was called "imitation."[8] But, she continues, parody's "ironic 'trans-contextualization' and inversion" of the original text, though it "can be playful as well as belittling . . . critically constructive as well as destructive,"[9] distinguishes parody from mere parallel and other forms of imitation.

Thus the issues and conflicts besetting Shakespearean parody-hunters (whose company I shall shortly join) seem no closer to being resolved than they did twenty years ago. I propose to deal with this impasse partly by ignoring the difficult question of "external" parody—whether whole plays of Shakespeare's, or at least scenes and speeches in them, are (or were taken to be) parodies of other works known to his audience and to us in the "real" or "external" world outside the plays. Even to consider these possibilities is to court both the intentional and affective fallacies (though of course we do this whenever we recognize a work as parody, even when its author calls it one). How are we to determine, for example, that *Titus Andronicus* is a parody of Seneca, or of Kyd, or of the whole genre of gory hyperbolic tragedy, without vexing Shakespeare's ghost or reading the collective mind of his audience to discover whether he meant it, or they experienced it, as such? Admittedly, the ground becomes firmer when there is less of it to travel: Alvin B. Kernan, scrutinizing not whole plays but merely plays-within-plays, claims that these are invariably "old-fashioned in style and awkward" by the standards of Shakespeare's audience,[10] standards presumably shaped by the "modern" and graceful texts that contain them. But are they therefore to be considered parodies of an earlier generation's idea of drama, now thought crude and unfashionable? Kernan does not advance this contention, but others do, including Rose. In the case of everyone's favorite example of Shakespearean parody, Snug the Joiner's play of *Pyramus and Thisbe* in *A Midsummer Night's Dream*, some tendency to mock or ridicule does seem evident (notwithstanding Theseus's spirited defense of honest theatrical incompetence), though it is not easy to specify just what is being mocked or by whom. But Hamlet, who rejects all drama that departs from his standards of temperance and modesty, sees nothing ridiculous in *The Murder of Gonzago*, nor even in the blood-and-guts speeches on Pyrrhus that precede it; if either is a parody, then, it seems a gratuitous one, a case of Shakespeare whispering satiric commentary on his theatrical forbears to us over the heads of his characters. Occasionally, we find announcements of parodic intent within a play, when characters compare their own speech with that of "real" or external texts; one such example is Falstaff's statement that his impersonation of Henry in *1 Henry IV* will be carried out "in King Cambyses' vein,"[11] but in the speech that follows, he gives us a king who speaks in the accents not of Thomas Preston but of John Lyly.[12] Similarly, Bottom's claim that he will play Pyramus in "Ercles' vein, a tyrant's vein" *(A Midsummer Night's Dream* I.ii.40) may be an oblique reference to Seneca's *Hercules Furens*, but this fleeting allusion can hardly compel us to regard the whole of *Pyramus and Thisbe* as a burlesque of Roman tragedy.

Thus, the formidable difficulties of teasing external parodies out of Shakespeare's plays I will leave to others, along with what might be called "unconscious" parodies, like those studied by Gilbert and Hartwig: analogic structures, relationships and parallels between characters or plots of which the characters themselves are not aware and for which they have no responsibility, as when (Hartwig says) Polonius's relationship to Laertes "parodies" that of the Ghost to Hamlet.[13] Instead, I want to look at a group of parodies that are both purposeful and internal: conscious parodies of one character's speeches—or manner of speech—by another. If the root of all parody is imitation, Shakespeare's particular interest lay in imitation that occurs within the boundaries of the play; if all the men and women in his stage-worlds are "merely players," they are often embryonic playwrights as well: many of them possess a dramatist's ear for language, and in addition to playing their own parts, they may play each other's, often with parodic embellishment. I hope to show that even the most unlikely character may reveal an almost irresistible tendency toward this particular form of mimesis.

But if, as Wayne C. Booth tells us, parody is "the mocking by one author of another author's style,"[14] the question may legitimately be asked whether a *character* in a play who makes fun of another by imitating the peculiarities of his speech and behavior really deserves to be called a parodist. I would reply that any character who possesses a verbal style that is studied or self-conscious, whose speech seems designed more for dramatic effect than for the spontaneous expression of thoughts and feelings, should be considered an "author" in Booth's sense of the term. Every speech in a play exhibits, from one perspective or another, a style—either a rhetorical mode that dominates the play as a whole (prose, or blank verse, or rhymed couplets, for example) or a mode that distinctively identifies the speech as belonging to a particular character or class of characters—and in the latter case, we can and often do locate examples of parody.

In the former case, where the "style" of a given character's speech is merely the style in which most of the play is written, it is admittedly difficult to maintain that he or she is a potential target of stylistic parody. When a speech in a Shakespearean tragedy is not rhetorically distinctive save for being in blank verse, its style is not likely to register upon the audience as an identifying mannerism or peculiarity of the speaker. Laertes in *Hamlet* possesses a distinctive personal style, but in his first speech of mourning for Ophelia, he tells us that his grief prevents him from using it:

> *Laer.* Too much of water hast thou, poor Ophelia,
> And therefore I forbid my tears; but yet
> It is our trick, Nature her custom holds,
> Let shame say what it will; when these are gone,
> The woman will be out. Adieu, my lord,
> I have a speech a' fire that fain would blaze,
> But that this folly drowns it.
>
> (IV.vii.185-91)

The above speech does not particularly call attention to itself, does not seem characteristically "Laertian." In Act V, however, at Ophelia's funeral, Laertes's "speech a' fire" blazes in a style that is self-conscious and distinctive enough to invite parody:

Laer. O, treble woe
Fall ten times treble on that cursed head
Whose wicked deed thy most ingenious sense
Depriv'd thee of! Hold off the earth a while,
Till I have caught her once more in mine arms.
[*Leaps in the grave.*]
Now pile your dust upon the quick and dead,
Till of this flat a mountain you have made
T' o'ertop old Pelion, or the skyish head
Of blue Olympus.
(V.i.246-54)

Hamlet, who praises "temperance," "smoothness," "discretion," and "modesty" as the qualities without which players and playwrights cannot perform their proper function of holding the mirror up to nature, is so offended by grief that "Bears such an emphasis" (255)—the hyperbole of "ten times treble," the pedantry of the classical allusion, the flamboyant leap into the grave, the disingenuous call for self-immolation—that he cannot resist delivering a parodic rebuke:

Ham. Dost thou come here to whine?
To outface me with leaping in her grave?
Be buried quick with her, and so will I.
And if thou prate of mountains, *let them throw*
Millions of acres on us, till our ground,
Singeing his pate against the burning zone,
Make Ossa like a wart! Nay, an thou'lt mouth,
I'll rant as well as thou.
(277-84, emphasis added)

I have indicated through my italics what the actor must dramatize: that within these eight lines is a speech within a speech, a short parody that reduces the mountains of Laertes's conceit to mere foothills. In delivering it, Hamlet here as elsewhere employs parody as the means of adopting one of his many roles: in addition to the firebrand avenger, he has earlier put on the garrulous *senex* and the unctuous politician, and soon he will give us the flattering courtier. In almost every case, the target of Hamlet's parody is visible and audible to the spectators.[15] To adopt Rose's terminology, we have been given both "text-worlds" that every parody involves: TW_1 (the parody) and TW_2 (the target, or parodied text). Unless the reader is familiar with TW_2, he or she is likely to miss the parodic intention, and may even read it as part of TW_1, but this is not likely to occur in

Hamlet: Hamlet's parody of Laertes's alpine imagery follows immediately the speech that it targets, and "I'll rant as well as thou" makes his parodic intent explicit. The same is true of his subsequent parody of Osric—the two texts adjoin, TW_2 first displaying its absurd euphemism and TW_1 immediately hoisting the engineer with his own petar:

> *Osr.* Sir, here is newly come to court Laertes, believe me, an absolute gentleman, full of most excellent differences, of very soft society, and great showing; indeed, to speak sellingly of him, he is the card or calendar of gentry; for you shall find in him the continent of what part a gentleman would see.
>
> *Ham.* Sir, his definement suffers no perdition in you, though I know to divide him inventorially would dozy th' arithmetic of memory, and yet but yaw neither in respect of his quick sail; but in the verity of extolment, I take him to be a soul of great article, and his infusion of such dearth and rareness as, to make true diction of him, his semblable is his mirror, and who else would trace him, his umbrage, nothing more.
>
> (V.ii.106-20)

I quote the speech at length because it seems to me a clear and typical example of internal parody in Shakespeare. Referring to such a model will assist me in describing the limited and problematic subcategory of internal parodies on which my interest will focus: those in which the target of the parody is not as close, tempting or obvious as Osric is here, and in which the accuracy and ultimate success of the parody is thereby qualified or compromised.

The three plays in which I have located such parodies—*Romeo and Juliet, 1 Henry IV,* and *Antony and Cleopatra*—form rather a disparate group: neither do they constitute a discrete and coherent portion of the Shakespeare canon (like "the problem comedies," "the Henriad," or "the late romances"), nor can they be said to represent fairly Shakespeare's method or practice consistently throughout the body of his works. To the inevitable imputation that the scope of this paper is therefore too broad or too narrow, I can only reply that these seem to me the plays whose effect is most significantly determined by this kind of parody, and that the range of uses to which it is put is adequately reflected in them.

Early in *Romeo and Juliet,* Mercutio regales his friends with a parodic paraphrase of Romeo's amatory style:

> *Mer.* Romeo! humors! madman! passion! lover!
> Appear thou in the likeness of a sigh!
> Speak but one rhyme, and I am satisfied;
> Cry but "Ay me!", pronounce but "love" and "dove."
> (II.i.7-10)

The figure that Mercutio summons up is recognizable to the audience because we have met him before—not in the play, but in the lyrics of Wyatt, Spenser, Sidney, and Shakespeare himself, all practitioners of a native Italian tradition that Mercutio identifies for those of us who have failed to recognize it when he heralds a later entrance of Romeo's with "Now is he for the numbers that Petrarch flow' d in" (II.iv.38-39). In this instance, at least, Shakespeare has accomplished his internal parody by resorting to external parody, relying upon his audience's literary sophistication for at least part of the effect. But if the parody succeeds, it does so in a roundabout way, for the rhetorical signature of Romeo's early speeches is not the hackneyed rhymes that Mercutio attributes to him. Rather, Romeo's love for Rosaline is signaled by a fondness for long, almost syntaxless strings of oxymoron:

> *Rom.* Why then, O brawling love! O loving hate!
> O any thing, of nothing first create!
> O heavy lightness, serious vanity,
> Misshapen chaos of well-seeming forms,
> Feather of lead, bright smoke, cold fire, sick health,
> Still-waking sleep, that is not what it is!
> (I.i.176-81)

Still, these are as typical a feature of the Petrarchan convention as the groans and trite rhymes with which Mercutio taxes him, and the parody thus accomplishes its ends not by imitating any actual scene or speech of Romeo's in the play but by plausibly associating him with a tradition of love and of love poetry now partially discredited and thus susceptible of ridicule—by branding Romeo in his pre-Juliet phase as a boy passing through the age described (and parodied) by Jaques in *As You Like It* as that of "the lover, / Sighing like furnace, with a woeful ballad / Made to his mistress' eyebrow" (II.vii.147-49).

All this is as timely as Shakespeare's other external parodies of Petrarchism, like Sonnet 130, and equally effective. But we should notice that in terms of the play's internal chronology, it is slightly mistimed. We know that Mercutio's ridicule of Romeo's love for

Rosaline comes after Romeo has ceased to pine for Rosaline and begun to burn for Juliet in imagery that is significantly more vivid and more original: if Rosaline was to Romeo the mere collection of conventional features that Mercutio goes on to enumerate ("bright eyes," "high forehead," "scarlet lip" [II.i.17-18]), Juliet "hangs upon the cheek of night / As a rich jewel in an Ethiop's ear" (I.v.45-46)—much better poetry, with better yet to follow.

Romeo is not Mercutio's only target in the play. Tybalt also earns his share of parodic description intermixed with paraphrase—for fighting (as Romeo was wont to love) in a style that Mercutio identifies with a distinctive species of cant:

> *Mer.* O, he's the courageous captain of compliments. He fights as you sing prick-song, keeps time, distance, and proportion; he rests his minim rests, one, two, and the third in your bosom: the very butcher of a silk button, a duellist, a duellist; a gentleman of the very first house, of the first and second cause. Ah, the immortal *passado,* the *punto reverso,* the *hay*!
>
> (II.iv.19-26)

If Romeo's rhetorical style is ridiculous because it is antiquated, Tybalt's style, by contrast, is excessively modern and up-to-date:

> *Mer.* The pox of such antic, lisping, affecting phantasimes, these new tuners of accent! "By Jesu, a very good blade! a very tall man! a very good whore!" Why, is not this a lamentable thing, grandsire, that we should be thus afflicted with these strange flies, these fashion-mongers, these pardon-me's, who stand so much on the new form, that they cannot sit at ease on the old bench?
>
> (28-35)

What ties Romeo and Tybalt together, in Mercutio's view, is that they are slaves not to passion but to fashion, dandies who counterfeit emotion and conviction as a means to self-display. It is hard to tell whether Mercutio misjudges Tybalt to the degree that he has misjudged Romeo. Tybalt's indignation when Romeo appears at Capulet's feast may be genuine, or consciously feigned, or somewhere between the two—a sense of outrage perhaps duly summoned and given vent by the self-appointed defender of the Capulet family honor. But it is worth noting that, though Tybalt is certainly what the Elizabethans called a roaring boy, this is not the same thing as the "lisping, affecting phantasime" Mercutio thinks him. When Tybalt encounters Mercutio and Benvolio in Act III, his greeting is polite and restrained, in contrast to Mercutio's own pugnacity; Tybalt's insults to Romeo when the two meet soon after lack the studied quality of which a "new tuner of accent" might be presumed capable; and while Mercutio delivers his challenge in a torrent of whimsical invective, Tybalt accepts with a terse "I am for you" (III.i.83). Having been prepared by Mercutio's original description of Tybalt for the fanciest and most up-to-date swordsmanship imaginable, what we see instead is Tybalt delivering a single mortal thrust while Mercutio is distracted by Romeo—hardly what might be expected of "a gentleman of the very first house." It is possible to argue, then, that Mercutio has underestimated Tybalt as a fighter much as he has underestimated Romeo as a lover—that the habit of distortion and reduction that makes him a parodist blinds him alike to the profundity of Romeo's ardor and to the depth of Tybalt's menace, both of which he mistakes for empty posturing. No particular consequence attaches itself to his misjudgment of Romeo, but taking Tybalt for a mere "duellist" might be said to have cost Mercutio his life.

Thus Mercutio's parodies, striking their targets a glancing blow, recoil to his own disadvantage. The fact that they are internal parodies has deprived him of the security enjoyed by external parodists, who, separated from their targets by textual boundaries that do not exist where the parody-text and the target-text are contained in the same work, remain relatively immune to retaliation. And since the vehicle of Mercutio's parodies is dramatic dialogue, which is always to a marked degree emotionally and psychologically self-referential, he is again at risk of self-exposure in a way that external parodists usually are not. Hamlet, of course, is equally vulnerable to this tendency of internal parody to fall on the inventors' heads, but he is protected by the aptness and accuracy of his parodies themselves; he gets Osric's fulsome ineffectuality just right, where Mercutio, mocking the same qualities in Tybalt, pays a double price for his misjudgment: his wit misfires, and he loses his life.

In both cases, the success or failure of the parody is a factor to be considered in our interpretation of the play and our understanding of the characters' roles in it, but it is a more crucial factor in *Romeo and Juliet* than it is in *Hamlet* just because Hamlet's parodies succeed where Mercutio's fail. To conclude, after his demolition of Laertes and Osric, that Hamlet is good at parody is merely to gloss something we already knew: that he possesess a keen ironic wit. But to discover that Mercutio's parodies of Romeo and Tybalt are, though amusing, inaccurate, calls for a significant re-evaluation: the more we have earlier admired his extravagant inventiveness (in the Queen Mab speech, for instance), the more our admiration is tempered by the failure of his parodies to prove their case against Romeo and Tybalt, and the more dangerous seem the consequences of those failures.

Another play in which internal parodies create effects at variance with the apparent intentions of the parodists is *1 Henry IV*. These parodies are both more numerous and more varied than those of *Romeo and Juliet*; for one thing (as many critics have noted), not one but several of its characters display a tendency, even a compulsion, to mimic their friends and rivals. The most obvious are Hal and Falstaff, whose favorite pastime is ridiculing pretensions to heroism, honor, and dignity, often through such parodies as Hal's thrust at Hotspur in Act II:

> *Prince.* I am not yet of Percy's mind, the Hotspur of the north, he that kills me some six or seven dozen of Scots at a breakfast, washes his hands, and says to his wife, "Fie upon this quiet life! I want work." "O my sweet Harry," says she, "how many hast thou kill'd today?" "Give my roan horse a drench," says he, and answers, "Some fourteen," an hour after; "a trifle, a trifle."
>
> (II.iv.101-108)

Formally, this speech much resembles Mercutio's portrait of Romeo as a lovesick Petrarchist, but in this case the gap between the parodic target with whom we are acquainted and the conventional archetype against which he is superimposed is much wider, and the parody correspondingly less successful. Though the speech demonstrates Hal's considerable gifts for satire and dramatic invention, the Hotspur that Hal limns for us is all but unrecognizable. Hal couples him with Francis the drawer, who has "fewer words than a parrot" (98-99), but if he regards Hotspur as a taciturn man by nature, or one who has consciously adopted *litotes* as a favorite trope, he has misjudged him as thoroughly as he himself has been misjudged by Hotspur—not surprisingly in either case, for they have not yet met, and their opinions of each other rest upon rumor and unfounded assumption. Worcester is much closer to the mark when he observes that Hotspur is both loquacious and in love with the sound of his own voice, a man who "apprehends a world of figures . . . / But not the form of what he should attend" (I.iii.209-10). And since we have already had several opportunities to hear for ourselves Hotspur speaking volubly and in a variety of moods and styles—notably in his passionate argument with the king and in a conversation with his wife that is nothing like Hal's version of their dialogue—Hal's parody of him as a medieval version of the strong-but-silent hero of Western films, ignorant of the uses and delights of language, culture, and art, and devoid of all feelings save the lust for battle, falls short of producing the shock of recognition that parody typically engenders even as it distorts and ridicules the features that we recognize.

To be sure, Hotspur himself contributes substantially to the production of such a caricature, largely through what amounts to self-parody. In the actual conversation with Kate that precedes Hal's imagined one, he puts on the puritanical glory-seeker—"This is no world / To play with mammets and to tilt with lips. / We must have bloody noses and crack'd crowns" (II.iii.91-93)—before abandoning that role abruptly to show himself a more tender and more understanding husband than we would have suspected. Later in the play, he exploits the *persona* of the mulish, undiplomatic man of arms when he insists to Glendower that the Trent be turned to increase his share of the spoils, only to abandon that role too when his point is taken. Even his attacks on poetry and singing, though they may imply a genuinely Philistine component of his character, also reveal a man sensitive, rather than indifferent, to meter and melody, and are themselves expressed with a good deal of artfulness; in the first case, his own speech parodies the meter of bad poetry—"Tis like the forc'd gait of a shuffling nag" (III.i.133)—and in the second, he plays neatly on his wife's phrasing:

> *Lady.* Lie still, ye thief, and hear the lady sing in Welsh.
> *Hot.* I had rather hear Lady, my brach, howl in Irish.
> (III.i.233-36)

Hotspur's sensitivity to rhetoric—the fact that he can vary the modes and levels of his own speech as the situation and his whim dictate, together with his well-developed and strongly-felt critical perceptions of others' speech—thus makes him almost the antithesis of the non-verbal buffoon imaged by Hal's parody.

Hotspur's ear for language is nowhere more clearly revealed than in his own extended parody of the messenger, "perfumed like a milliner" (I.iii.36), who demands his Scottish prisoners in King Henry's name:

Hot. he made me mad
To see him shine so brisk and smell so sweet,
And talk so like a waiting-gentlewoman
Of guns, and drums, and wounds, God save the mark!
And telling me *the sovereignest thing on earth*
Was parmaciti for an inward bruise,
And that *it was great pity, so it was,*
This villainous saltpetre should be digg'd
Out of the bowels of the harmless earth,
Which many a good tall fellow had destroyed
So cowardly, and *but for these vile guns*
He would himself have been a soldier.
(53-64, emphasis added)

I have again indicated through italics where the actor speaking the speech might plausibly, by gesture, accent, and expression, leave off for the moment playing Hotspur and play instead Hotspur playing the fool. The lines of demarcation are not at all clear; narration grades into paraphrase, and paraphrase into what we assume to be quotation. Since the scene containing Hotspur's meeting with the lord is not in the play, we have no original text with which to compare the fidelity of the parody; all we have instead are Hotspur's accompanying descriptions of the speech-habits he is targeting: "With many holiday and lady terms," "like a waiting-gentlewoman," the messenger spoke "bald, unjointed chat" (46, 55, 65). This adds up to the stereotype of the pampered, effeminate courtier, with many affinities to Osric or the "lisping, affecting phantasime" Mercutio thinks Tybalt, but with the added imputation of cowardice. Such stage figures were familiar to Shakespeare's audience, so that though they could not have tested Hotspur's version against the character himself, they would at least have been able to refer to a recognizable type.

The dramatic point of the scene, though, is not whether Hotspur has hit his mark but that he has taken aim at it. The very fact of his resorting to parody establishes an affinity between Hotspur and Hal that neither is aware of: each is an actor, each is a critic, each is by turns a parodist and the target of parody, and each underestimates the other. When Hotspur offers his parody of the king's messenger to the king himself, he is performing an undiplomatic, even an insulting action, for which Worcester takes him to task, but he is also undertaking to entertain the audience in the characteristic mode of the madcaps, highwaymen, and sots who frequent the tavern in Eastcheap. Thus he establishes, by his employment of an essentially subversive rhetorical device in a politically and socially subversive context, his resemblances to the play's other critics of established authority, Falstaff and Hal.

As in *Romeo and Juliet*, parody in *1 Henry IV* cuts both ways: it tells us as much about the limitations of the parodist as it does about the excesses of its target, and in the process it partially restores the balance between them—a balance initially tipped in Hal's favor by an audience's conventional readiness, when watching ironic comedy, to identify more with those who ridicule than with those who are the targets of ridicule. Of course, the manipulation of our responses is more complicated than that. In this play, the reciprocal movement of parody sets up an infinite regress of opposed mirror-images whereby the parodist subsequently becomes the target of another parodist who is himself liable to the same fate, *ad infinitum*. Hotspur's unexpected penchant for parody shows us that Hal's parody of him as a witless clod is unfairly reductive, and thus tacitly raises doubts about Hal's and Falstaff's subsequent ridicule of the heroic myths attached to Owen Glendower, "he of Wales that gave Amamon the bastinado and made Lucifer cuckold" (II.iv.336-37), and to "that sprightly Scot of Scots, Douglas, that runs a' horseback up a hill perpendicular . . . and with his pistol kills a sparrow flying" (342-46). All of these heroes, including Hotspur, announce their presence to the world by creating their own self-serving mythology, which has the effect of flattening their characters as it proportionately increases their stature as heroes, and so assists the parodists in caricaturing and stereotyping them—but only to the extent that the parodies are apt. The play shows us independently that Hotspur and Glendower, at least, possess characters as various, as interesting, as human and as liable to internal contradiction as those of the parodists.

The limitations of the play's parodies of greatness are further seen in Falstaff's parodic impersonation of Henry, in which he makes the king into an early version of Polonius, intoning interminable Ciceronian *sententiae* and Euphuistic ornament:

> *Fal.* There is a thing, Harry, which thou hast often heard of, and it is known to many in our land by the name of pitch. This pitch (as ancient writers do report) doth defile, so doth the company thou keepest; for, Harry, now I do not speak to thee in drink, but in tears; not in pleasure, but in passion; not in words only, but in woes also.
>
> (II.iv.410-17)

By contrast, Henry's Act III summation of Hal's faults, of which Falstaff's speech is an anticipation, is (though lengthy) forceful and vivid, and shows us how far off the mark the parody is—as Hal implies when he derisively asks Falstaff, at its conclusion, "Dost thou speak like a king?" (433).

But Falstaff redeems his tarnished reputation as a parodist with his telling parody of Hal at the end of Act III, an example that functions (like no other in the play) as we expect a parody to function, being both an accurate imitation of an identifiable style and a ridiculing distortion of it. When Hal transforms himself into the simulacrum of Hotspur that he promised his father he would become, he transforms himself as well from a parodist of heroic pretension into a pretender to genuine heroism. Immediately, like Hotspur, the prince begins to speak in heroic couplets: "The land is burning, Percy stands on high, / And either we or they must lower lie," he exclaims to Falstaff, and exits, leaving Falstaff to remark, in parody, "Rare words! brave world! Hostess, my breakfast, come! / O, I could wish this tavern were my drum" (III.iii.203-206).[16] Where Hal and Falstaff once played together, parodying the mannerisms of self-styled heroes in concert, now Hal plays Percy alone, and later plays with Percy, leaving Falstaff to confront Douglas by himself. Like Hotspur, Hal is first a parodist and then the target of other parodists, and to the extent that these two roles determine our conception of the two characters—as hunters or prey, as wits or poetasters, as objects of sympathy or of derision—the effect of the play's parodic oscillations is to make the audience continually question and revise those conceptions, collapsing the categorical antitheses that separate Harry Monmouth from Harry Percy and obliterating the usual distinction between the parodist and his object. Hartwig's assertion that parody "heightens and expands, even as it qualifies, the meaning of that which it imitates"[17] may apply as usefully to the parodies of *1 Henry IV*, which she does not consider, as it does to any of those she discusses.

If the multiple perspectives of any Shakespearean play are the product of complex and overlapping ironies, the ironies of *1 Henry IV* characteristically take the form of parody. Rose tells us that the dual messages of all ironic utterances, the message from the ironist to the "initiated audience" and the "decoy" message that is its vehicle, are typically contained in a single code; parody, by contrast, gives us not one ambiguous code but two distinct ones, which, when juxtaposed, result in what Jakobson has called a *metalanguage*—"a commentary to another linguistic entity."[18] We have seen that in

1 Henry IV, the play's many "linguistic entities," each embodied in a characteristic style of discourse which is foregrounded through parody, comment upon each other as a means of continually adjusting the audience's conceptions of the characters associated with them, causing Hal and Hotspur to resemble each other ever more closely as the play goes on.

Parody serves an analogous (though not identical) function in *Antony and Cleopatra*: it mediates among the characters and their conflicts for us, disposing and adjusting our sympathies in a continuous process of redefinition. Shortly after the reconciliation between Mark Antony and Octavius Caesar, Enobarbus and Agrippa ridicule Lepidus's attempts at placating his two powerful colleagues:

> *Agr.* 'Tis a noble Lepidus.
> *Eno.* A very fine one. O, how he loves Caesar!
> *Agr.* Nay, but how dearly he adores Mark Antony!
> *Eno.* *Caesar? Why, he's the Jupiter of men.*
> *Agr.* *What's Antony? The god of Jupiter.*
> *Eno.* *Spake you of Caesar? How, the nonpareil!*
> *Agr.* *O Antony! O thou Arabian bird!*
> *Eno.* *Would you praise Caesar, say "Caesar," go no further.*
> *Agr.* Indeed he plied them both with excellent praises.
> (III.ii.6-14, emphasis added)

Thus Lepidus joins those other "new tuners of accent," including Romeo and Tybalt as Mercutio conceives them but better exemplified by the perfumed lord in *1 Henry IV* and Osric in *Hamlet*. So familiar is this conventionalized type that no one thinks to question whether these slanders accurately describe Lepidus; after all, the fact that Agrippa and Enobarbus can collaborate on a portrait of him suggests that they are working from the same model. But it is worth mentioning that we never see him cringe and fawn in quite this way; " 'Tis noble spoken" (II.ii.98) is the extent of his flattery of Antony in the earlier scene, and, with a few drinks in him, he finds the courage to bait Antony about Cleopatra at the feast on the barge (II.vii.24ff). As was the case in *Romeo and Juliet* and *1 Henry IV*, the character as we see him is not the character described through parody; Lepidus in his offstage moments may have earned his reputation as a sycophant, but he is also something more than that.

In any case, the most important effect of Agrippa's and Enobarbus's extended parody is to introduce into the play the equivocal and insincere accents of flattering speech, in a form designed to foreground that mode of speech; the parody of Lepidus, being a metalanguage, can do this more effectively than any flattery delivered by Lepidus himself might have done. Whether the parodists are quoting Lepidus accurately or exaggerating for satiric purposes, this exchange has the effect of underscoring, for later scenes and even retroactively for earlier ones, a suggestion made almost as soon as the play gets under way: that speeches of praise and ingratiation, including those of Antony and Cleopatra to each other, are as likely as not to be nothing more than courtly affectation or politic falsehood.

This is a crucial issue in *Antony and Cleopatra,* for the sole justification of Antony's conduct in particular, and Cleopatra's to a lesser extent, rests upon the possibility of their love being regarded, by posterity if not by their contemporaries, as noble, eternal, superior not only to other loves but to all other human pursuits. Accordingly, the play is full of potentially hyperbolic speeches in which extravagant praise is coupled with extravagant claims—speeches whose rhetorical sweep and power can support the extremes of their assertions when they are delivered, but that cannot stand up to the weight of repetition and paraphrase, let alone parody. And sometimes the speeches being cited, though they sound familiar to us, are not properly in the play:

Cleo. Nay, pray you seek no color for your going,
But bid farewell, and go. When you sued staying,
Then was the time for words; no going then;
Eternity was in our lips and eyes,
Bliss in our brows' bent; none our parts so poor
But was a race of heaven. They are so still,
Or thou, the greatest soldier of the world,
Art turn'd the greatest liar.
(I.iii.32-39, emphasis added)

Again the effect of quotation or paraphrase (it is impossible to say which) is of the ironic distortion and reduction of parody, whether or not any such distortion is intended by Cleopatra or deserved by Antony. If *Antony and Cleopatra* represents a development of Shakespeare's technique in handling internal parody, it is in the economy of means with which he achieves parodic effect here without explicit or recognizable exaggeration such as we find in Falstaff's parodies of King Henry and Mercutio's of Romeo. There is no way to determine whether Agrippa and Enobarbus are merely reciting, or editing, or embellishing Lepidus's flatteries, which become progressively more elaborate and stilted as their exchange progresses. But Antony's speeches cited here by Cleopatra, in terms of their emotional intensity and the way in which they employ conventional devices of rhetoric and romance, do not seem to me at variance with similar speeches that Antony delivers in the play. They sound like Antony. Thus, if they seem parodic, it is solely due to the present context of rancor and discord in which they are delivered, and the fact that it is Cleopatra, not Antony, who is delivering them.

The impression of insincerity is further exacerbated in that the introduction of these new speeches, so similar to those we have already heard from Antony himself, tells us that making such amorous protestations has become a habit of his. The effect of the original speeches, such as his famous lines beginning "Let Rome in Tiber melt," is diluted after the fact by Cleopatra's suggestion that Antony's restatements of the principle upon which their love is founded are merely pragmatic justifications of questionable conduct that have been dressed up like romantic vows. To Antony's claim that "the nobleness of life / Is to do thus *[embracing]*—when such a mutual pair / And such a twain can do't" (I.i.36-38), Cleopatra's reply is "Excellent falsehood" (40), which connects quite solidly with the point made by her paraphrase/quotation: that all such speeches will be proven false retroactively if Antony leaves her. Reproducing Antony's past declarations of love in the context of their present quarrel converts them not merely into parodies of Antony by Cleopatra but into Antony's parodies of himself, just as Lepidus was turned into a self-parodist if we assume that Enobarbus and Agrippa were not just vying with each other to invent new and more outlandish Lepidisms but quoting him *verbatim* from memory.

That is just what Charmian does to Cleopatra when, in speeches that closely resemble the Agrippa-Enobarbus exchange, she reproduces Cleopatra's former praises of Julius Caesar:

Cleo. Did I, Charmian,
Ever love Caesar so?
Char. *O that brave Caesar!*
Cleo. Be chok'd with such another emphasis!
Say "the brave Antony."
Char. *The valiant Caesar!*
Cleo. By Isis, I will give thee bloody teeth
If thou with Caesar paragon again
My man of men.
Char. By your most gracious pardon,
I sing but after you.
(I.v.66-73, emphasis added)

"I sing but after you"—that is, I merely quote your earlier speeches, and let them sing for themselves, as you did Antony's and Agrippa and Enobarbus did Lepidus's.

Cleopatra acknowledges the speeches and the sentiments to be hers, but defends herself by calling them the product of her "salad days" (73), of another, younger, less wise Cleopatra; Antony, though he did not formally acknowledge that the love-speeches attributed to him by Cleopatra were accurate, did not deny them. These citations, then, are a way of reminding us as well as the characters themselves that the lives of Antony and Cleopatra are not limited to what we see and hear on stage during the course of the play. The events of the play have a way of superimposing themselves upon what has occurred before the point of attack and what will occur after its conclusion, just as the characters tend to divide into a multiplicity of identities. Antony in particular appears to us, is referred to, or with relevance may be considered in many guises, including but not limited to the Antony who believes his own protestations of love to Cleopatra, and who believes in them as well; the Antony who, reluctantly and with difficulty, "must from this enchanting queen break off" (I.ii.128); the Antony who adopts Rome's view of Cleopatra as a "boggler" (III.xiii.110); the "real" or historical Antony who was the subject of Plutarch's *Life* and indirectly a source of Shakespeare's play; the Antony of earlier fictional and dramatic representations, such as the plays by Garnier and Daniel, with which Shakespeare was presumably familiar; the "hyperbolical vision" of a "gigantic and godlike" Antony[19] created by Cleopatra after his death; and Antony as both a character in the present play (who subsumes all these identities) and the actor who happens to be playing the role at any given performance.[20] And of course, many of these categories apply to Cleopatra as well. All this complicates our response to and our understanding of the play. We might, if we were discussing *Romeo and Juliet* or *Troilus and Cressida,* ask a straightforward question: whether the protagonists are true or false lovers. Here we must also ask whether they *believe* themselves to be true or false lovers, and to what extent their present status as lovers is determined by their respective pasts, or even by their ontological status as fictional characters modeled upon biographical reconstructions of real persons. In order to persuade us to ask these sorts of questions, some device was necessary which would discriminate not merely between utterances of different purport but between utterances of different kinds, so that certain speeches might be presented for the audience's inspection bracketed, as it were, by ironic quotation marks. Once again, that device proved to be parody.

Internal parody involves the audience in a simultaneous double movement, inclining its attention in two directions at once. Though the conventional thrust of parody is outward, away from the parodist and toward its target, it is nonetheless true, as Hartwig, Rose, and Hutcheon note, that all parody has a self-reflexive character, since we could not enjoy it, or even recognize it as parody, without being made aware of the tension between the two text-worlds involved. External parodies in plays are particularly self-reflexive, in that the playwright's parodic *persona*—the character whose speeches are the vehicle of parody—is visible, audible, and physically present on the stage, while the real target of the parody, though he may also have a fictive agent on the stage, is not.[21] The inequality between the two text-worlds, then, is more vividly dramatized to spectators in a theater than to readers of essays or novels. It might be supposed that internal parodies, if the target shares the stage on equal footing with the parodist, would thereby call less attention to themselves than external parodies, but in most of the cases we have examined, the converse is true. Mercutio's parody of Romeo as a literary archetype, Hotspur's of a character who is not in the play at all, Hal's of a Hotspur whom we do not recognize, Enobarbus's and Agrippa's of a Lepidus whose faults seem unfairly exaggerated, and Cleopatra's parodic citations of speeches made by Antony before the play began—all ostensibly encourage us to focus upon the objects of the parodies, but the inaccessibility or evanescence of those objects soon brings our attention back to the parodist. Only two parodies we have discussed illuminate their targets more than they do their authors, and thus are relatively free of this tendency toward self-reflection: Falstaff's parody of Hal's new "heroic" mode of address (which differs from Hal's earlier parodies of that mode only in its new context) and Charmian's recollections of a past Cleopatra energetically disavowed by the present one. In the main, by contrast, the peculiar tendency of Shakespearean internal parody is to recoil upon its inventor, as in the case of Mercutio and Hal, who only succeed in displaying their deficiencies as judges of character and as parodists in their attempts to ridicule Romeo, Tybalt, and Hotspur.

At the same time, all these parodies thrust outward, through the fabric of the play-worlds themselves, in a manner that is also typically Shakespearean. Though both external and internal parody are often employed by other Tudor and Stuart playwrights, none—not even Jonson[22]—has made such extensive use of parody that alludes to characters, speeches, and events that exist neither in the play-world nor in the world of the audience. This type of parody is part of Shakespeare's formidable arsenal of devices for breaching the dramatic frame, along with plays-within-plays, the world/stage metaphor in all its many versions, and on-stage discussions of the function of acting and of theater. I hope I have shown how such parodies can realign our sympathies among the characters and readjust the degree of credibility we are willing to grant them. Parody, by directing our attention to the undramatized offstage lives of such characters as Tybalt, Hotspur, and Lepidus, enhances our sense of their reality and prevents them from seeming merely peripheral figures who exist only to mirror or otherwise comment upon the protagonists. In a typical self-contained play, the relationships between characters are a function of the roles assigned them by the dramatist and of the point of view from which the audience perceives them; we are not encouraged to reflect upon the fact that each of the characters, no matter how minor, might be presumed to regard the action of the play, subjectively, as radiating out from a central point occupied by himself or herself, and similarly to regard the concerns of the protagonists as less important than his or her own. But in *Romeo and Juliet, 1 Henry IV*, and *Antony and Cleopatra* the parodies we have examined undercut these conventionally-determined ontological hierarchies, so that each play presents itself not so much as a fictive rendering of a world in which some characters possess more depth and weight than others but as a dramatization of a quasi-historical narrative in which, though we are more concerned with the lives of some characters than we are with others, every character's life, if we chose to examine it, would reveal equal complexity and wealth of detail.

Thus, the effect of parodies that break the dramatic frame is to make the play-world seem more "real"—or at least to make its reality seem more familiar—by connecting the world of the play with a larger plane or mode of existence outside itself. This is often perceived by the audience as an aspect of its own world, particularly when it puts before us some historical or literary person who is familiar to us as well as to the other characters—Petrarch or Julius Caesar, for example. But the mere act of referring to characters and events that have not been dramatized—to the flourishes of the king's messenger, to Lepidus fawning like a spaniel—similarly promotes the illusion that the play's world, like ours, stretches into shadowy, off-stage realms. And it is in these realms that the two worlds seem to meet. Through the complex signification of internal parody, Shakespeare creates the illusion that the play-world is not a fiction but, ontologically and even historically, a hitherto-unknown corner of the "real" world that has been made, for a moment, audible and visible to us.

NOTES

[1]Richard Levin, *The Multiple Plot in English Renaissance Drama* (Chicago and London: Chicago Univ. Press, 1974), p. 112.

[2]Dean Frye, "The Question of Shakespearean Parody," *EIC* 15 (1965):23. In fact, the parallel Allan Gilbert refers to is not between actions but between speeches, Henry's exhortations to his soldiers being imitated in comic terms "when Pistol talks of cutting throats or Bardolph exhorts his companies to enter the breach." ("Patriotism and Satire in *Henry V*" in *Studies in Shakespeare*, ed. Arthur D. Matthews and Clark M. Emery [Coral Gables: Univ. of Miami Press, 1953], pp. 61-62).

[3]Joan Hartwig, *Shakespeare's Analogical Scene: Parody as Structural Syntax* (Lincoln: Univ. of Nebraska Press, 1983), pp. 5-6.

[4]Hartwig, p. 4.

[5]Margaret A. Rose, *Parody//Meta-Fiction: An Analysis of Parody as a Critical Mirror to the Writing and Reception of Fiction* (London: Croom Helm, 1979), pp. 22-23.

[6]Linda Hutcheon, *A Theory of Parody: The Teachings of Twentieth-Century Art Forms* (New York and London: Methuen, 1985), p. 5.

[7]Notably Gerard Genette, whose *Palimpsestes* (Paris: Seuil, 1982) is regarded as an important contribution to modern theory of parody (Hutcheon, p. 20).

[8]Hutcheon, p. 10.

[9]Hutcheon, p. 32.

[10]Alvin B. Kernan, "Shakespeare's Stage Audiences" in *Shakespeare's Craft*, ed. Philip H. Highfill, Jr. (Carbondale: Southern Illinois Univ. Press, 1982), p. 154.

[11]II.iv.387. All quotations from Shakespeare's plays are taken from *The Riverside Shakespeare*, ed. G. Blakemore Evans (Boston: Houghton Mifflin, 1974).

[12]Dwight Macdonald has pointed out the close verbal parallel between Falstaff's "For the camomile, the more it is trodden on, the faster it grows, yet youth, the more it is wasted, the sooner it wears," and this passage from *Euphues his England*: "Though the camomile, the more it is trodden and pressed down, the more it spreadeth; yet the violet, the oftener it is handled and touched, the sooner it withereth and decayeth." (*Parodies: An Anthology from Chaucer to Beerbohm—and After*, ed. Dwight Macdonald [New York: Random House, 1960], pp. 14-16).

[13]Hartwig, p. 169.

[14]Wayne C. Booth *A Rhetoric of Irony* (Chicago and London: Univ. of Chicago Press, 1974), pp. 71-72.

[15]This is not true of Hamlet's early parodic enactment (as reported by Ophelia) of the complaining lover, a stock figure also parodied by Mercutio—see the following discussion of *Romeo and Juliet.*

[16]Compare Hotspur's

> My father and Glendower being both away,
> The powers of us may serve so great a day.
> Come, let us take a muster speedily.
> Doomsday is near, die all, die merrily.
>
> (IV.i.131-34)

[17]Hartwig, p. 6.

[18]Rose, p. 51.

[19]Janet Adelman, *The Common Liar: An Essay on "Antony and Cleopatra"* (New Haven and London: Yale Univ. Press, 1973), p. 102.

[20]See particularly Robert Martin Adams's discussion of the way in which the ontological relationships among the various *personae* break the dramatic frame of the play in his chapter on Shakespeare and Keats in *Strains of Discord: Studies in Literary Openness* (Ithaca: Cornell Univ. Press, 1958).

[21]A familiar example is Jonson's *The Poetaster*, in which Ovidius/Jonson purges Crispinus and Fannius in a scene whose point can be fully grasped only if the audience recognizes the phrases being regurgitated as direct quotations (functioning as parody) from the works of Marston and Dekker.

[22]Jonson, in fact, collaborated with Marston and Chapman on a play that extensively parodies Shakespeare. See my article "*Hamlet* and *Eastward Ho*," *SEL* 11 (1971):223-33.

SEL 28 (1988)
ISSN 0039-3657

Lavatch and Service in *All's Well that Ends Well*

CHRISTOPHER ROARK

> And let those that play your clowns speak no more than is set down for them; for there be of them that will themselves laugh, to set on some quantity of barren spectators to laugh too, though in the mean time some necessary question of the play be then to be consider'd. That's villainous, and shows a most pitiful ambition in the fool that uses it.
>
> (*Hamlet* III.ii.38-45)[1]

Of Shakespeare's wise fools, Lavatch in *All's Well that Ends Well* has been the most expendable in performance, and the most superfluous to critics. Tyrone Guthrie's 1953 production of *All's Well* at Stratford, Ontario, eliminated Lavatch's role.[2] Robert H. Goldsmith remarks, "he is unlike Shakespeare's other fools in that his role bears no significant relationship to the meaning of *All's Well*. He is in no way a measure of the play's meaning, as Touchstone, Feste, and Lear's fool are for their plays."[3] Hamlet's advice to the players tells us that fools like Lavatch are mere comic relief, provoking laughter which distracts the audience's attention from the play's necessary questions.

However, Jay Halio writes, "The clown's speeches pose some interesting problems of interpretation which scholarship has left almost entirely ignored; until they are worked out it seems wise to reserve comment on the true function of this character."[4] G. K. Hunter observes that "the action of the play is seldom allowed to make simple unimpeded effects, but is complicated throughout by a commentary, implicit as well as explicit, of which the principal agent is the clown." He notes that "we approach Helena's request to

---

Christopher Roark teaches and is completing his Ph.D. at SUNY Buffalo. This essay is part of a longer study of Shakespeare's wise fools.

the Countess that she may pursue Bertram by way of Lavatch's request that he may marry Isbel." Later, the fool speaks of his growing distaste for Isbel at the same time the Countess reads Bertram's letter of rejection for Helena. The fool points to "the distinction between physical nurture and moral discipline so important to the play," as when Lavatch describes himself as "highly fed and lowly taught." Hunter wisely remarks in a footnote that "it is dangerous to assume that Shakespeare's clowning is making only obvious points."[5]

I submit that Lavatch's part, especially when it appears to be most superfluous, can add a crucial dimension to our understanding of *All's Well that Ends Well*, and is useful for focusing the critical debate about the play's unsatisfying resolution and other problems. Lavatch's fooling with the Countess about an answer that "serves all," a scene that occurs during the King's healing, has been particularly singled out as obscure. It has been called "silly stuff" by John Dover Wilson, "almost pointless" by Glynne Wickham, and omitted in modern productions directed by Henson, Benthall, Guthrie, and Willman.[6] Yet in this scene I believe Shakespeare is doing something odd to startle us into paying close attention. The fool goes through an elaborate buildup (twenty-eight lines) to an answer that will serve all men and fit all questions, though this only leads to a disappointing answer—nothing more than an exclamatory remark, "O Lord, Sir!" (II.ii.40). The long prologue and the answer are ridiculous, seem to serve no one, and appear to do nothing more than mock the play's occasional affected courtly talk. It also seems to confirm that Lavatch's part is tenuous.

But, if we begin to consider the scene within the larger dramatic context, it is at this crucial moment that the King's miraculous cure takes place, an answer that does serve all in the sense of serving the entire kingdom. When the King appears in the following scene, after some elaborate introductory remarks by Lafew and Parolles about Helena's miracle cure, it is a moment of festive celebration. Like the ending of many comedies, something heavenly or magical, beyond human comprehension, has restored things to their proper place, after earthly reason has failed.[7] The folktale origins of the play's story have been noted by W. W.Lawrence, with Helena as a virgin whose magical powers show "a heavenly effect in an earthly actor" (II.iii.24).[8] Following closely Lavatch's mock invocation to heaven, "O Lord, sir!" as the answer that serves all things, we have Helena's answer that also invokes providence, now to cure the King and thus serving all men. We expect her actions to lead to a happy marriage, the usual comic conclusion.

But like Lavatch's answer, Helena's cure does not really serve all men, especially Bertram. Her remedy for the King is with the help of heaven, but the cure for her love sickness is in stark contrast to the healing because it lies within her own designs:

> Our remedies oft in ourselves do lie
> Which we ascribe to heaven. The fated sky
> Gives us free scope, only doth backward pull
> Our slow designs when we ourselve are dull.
>
> (I.ii.215-18)

Helena's thoughts are like the bastard Edmund's attitude in *King Lear.*[9] After Gloucester has attributed the kingdom's problems to heaven, Edmund also comments on false beliefs in providential control and such explanations for human behavior: "This is an excellent foppery of the world, that when we are sick in fortune—often the surfeits of our own behavior—we make guilty of our disasters the sun, the moon, and the stars, as if we were villians on necessity, fools by heavenly compulsion" (I.ii.121-25). Though it is an unflattering comparison, and though Helena does ally herself with heaven to cure the King, both she and Edmund forego dependence on providence and excel at the same kind of instrumental reasoning, employing various deceptions to rise in society. Both know providence cannot be depended upon and that "Our remedies oft in ourselves do lie." Whether it is for Bertram's own good or not, the ease with which Helena manipulates him to achieve her end is troubling, especially later in the play with the bed trick.[10] In spite of her professed admiration for Bertram, Helena's plot with the rings is based on an acute understanding of his weaknesses, on her knowledge that Bertram cannot control his lust, which she uses against him. I suggest that her manipulative reasoning, especially as it permits her to move up in society, was troubling for Shakespeare. In none of his other comedies do we find a marriage that attempts to cross such wide social boundaries, and those characters who dream of such things, such as Malvolio, are rudely put in their place. In the great tragedies to come, the skill with which Iago, Edmund, and Lady Macbeth are able to exploit the other characters' weaknesses helps to set the tragic wheels in motion. These characters also aspire to a higher social rank.[11]

Helena's manipulation of Bertram (even if it is out of love) so that he will recognize her new status (as the King and Countess do) is a basic problem in *All's Well that Ends Well* that reminds us more of

Shakespeare's tragedies than his comedies. However, Shakespeare was aware of this problem and indicates this to us through the fool's discussion with the Countess during the King's healing. At the same moment that Helena is at the height of her heavenly powers, inherited from her father, the fool is also put to the "height" of his "breeding" (II.ii.2), invoking providence, "O Lord, sir!" as the answer that serves all. Helena, following the comic form, has also called upon providence to heal the King so that society can be reconstituted and her marriage follow. But like the fool, and as the action of the play bears out, Helena (and Shakespeare) discover that comic solutions, as Lavatch remarks, "may serve long, but not serve ever" (II.ii.55). The fool's "O Lord, sir!" is a glance at a comic solution by Shakespeare that parodies Helena's solution, points out its limits, and takes place at the same moment she is invoking her solution. The providential solution perhaps serves well for the pastoral ("Tib's rush for Tom's forefinger") and holiday references ("Shrove Tuesday, a morris for May day") that the fool invokes, but then fails to serve when the Countess reminds Lavatch that he is a fool, not a courtier, and that his low station makes him subject to whipping. In an odd way, the fool's difficulty is Helena's: invoking heaven, a comic solution, fails to treat the problem of his low station, and similarly Helena's heavenly healing of the King, also a comic solution, is unable to change her station in Bertram's eyes and lead to marriage.[12]

Like these two scenes, the characters in *All's Well that Ends Well* again and again offer answers that only partially, temporarily, or simply cannot serve the problems they encounter. In Lavatch's "silly stuff" we find a clue to a dominant characteristic of the play: time and again Shakespeare gives us elaborate buildups that often try our patience but lead only to answers that do not serve the problem at hand. Shakespeare takes every opportunity to reiterate this pattern, pointing toward the final episodes, especially Parolles's exposure (his answers only serve to damn him during the elaborate inquisition) and the play's exasperating final scene, where Bertram's "answers" (or rather lies) continually fail, and Helena's plan to reveal the truth seems to bring as many problems as solutions.

In the opening scenes, the characters also dwell on problems that seem unsolvable: first the King's incurable fistula; then the defense of virginity, discussed by Bertram and Helena; and later the service of "our young Lords," which the King holds to be inadequate. In all three cases, the answer is in a dead or lost past: Gerard de Narbon could cure the King, remaining a virgin was "formerly better," and the King finds the dead Count Rossillion's service superior to the young lords. With the exception of Helena's cure, often when characters do offer solutions, their answers are contradictory. When the Countess, to assuage Helena's sorrow, calls herself Helena's mother, Helena can only see herself as Bertram's sister, contradicting her wishes for married love (I.iii.158-63); or later in the scene when Helena desires to "Wish chastely and love dearly, that your Dian / Was both herself and love," we again have an answer to her problematic love for Bertram that is contradictory. Lavatch's elaborate answer to Helena's inquiry about the Countess's health, expressing that she is both well and not well, underscores this tendency (II.iv.1-13). His answer simply doesn't serve, and it prepares us for the same mutually exclusive answers that Parolles and Diana give in the play's last scene. Parolles's drum is another example: his elaborate complaints trap him with a problem he cannot solve. This is particularly highlighted when the Lords spy on the parasitical soldier ticking off five answers to his dilemma, all of which the Dumains observe are inadequate (IV.i.46-61).

An earlier example of this dominant pattern is Bertram's response to the marriage. Again, the play presents a curiously prolonged, and seemingly unneeded, buildup to the "answer," Helena's choice of Bertram (II.iii.63-101). Yet thinking that Helena's solution will not serve, but rather corrupt his bloodline forever (II.iii.115-16), he responds to her choice by going to war and serving the Duke of Florence, an answer which serves himself but not the King, his mother, or Helena. For Bertram's difficulties, Shakespeare again offers an instructive parallel with the fool that focuses a necessary question of the play. When we are introduced to Lavatch, Shakespeare presents us with Bertram's problem in reverse. No one is forcing the fool to marry and corrupt his bloodline; rather, the fool petitions the Countess to allow him to marry so that he can "have issue o' my body; for they say barnes are blessings" (I.iii.24-25). The fool is knowingly driven on by the flesh to marry so he may "repent"; Bertram is also driven by the flesh to repent, though unknowingly. The Countess contends that Lavatch should be married before he is wicked, which again recalls Bertram, who is unfaithful after he is married. Lavatch's final reason for marrying strikes us as an absurd answer, and an example of perverted service:

> *Clown:* I am out o'friends, madam; and hope to
> have friends for my wife's sake.
> *Countess:* Such friends are thine enemies, knave.

> *Clown:* Y'are shallow, madam, in great friends; for the knaves come to do that for me which I am aweary of. He that ears my land spares my team and gives me leave to in the crop; if I be his cuckold, he's my drudge. He that comforts my wife is the cherisher of my flesh and blood; he that cherishes my flesh and blood loves my flesh and blood; he that loves my flesh and blood is my friend. Ergo, he that kisses my wife is my friend.
>
> (I.iii.39-50)

The fool tells us that a man who cuckolds him does him service by cherishing what he cherishes. Even here, the fool's twisted logic relates to Bertram: cuckoldry is not just a problem with an unfaithful wife, but also a problem of awareness: that is, a cuckold is someone whose wife has sex with a man without the husband's awareness, which is what Bertram does when he has intercourse with Helena in Italy. In essence, Bertram cuckolds himself, and if we follow the fool's "logic," in doing so he becomes his own best friend. Yet our usual logic tells us that the man who cuckolds another's wife is the husband's worst enemy. Shakespeare is careful to emphasize at the opening of the last scene that in losing Helena, along with his seeming ill behavior toward Diana which is revealed moments later, Bertram "Did to his Majesty, his mother, and his lady / Offense of mighty note; but to himself / The greatest wrong of all" (V.iii.13-15). The irony of this, as we sense with the fool's twisted logic, is that Bertram has been at once his own worst enemy and his own best friend, both without his awareness. Lavatch's fooling exposes an uncomfortable contradiction about Bertram, emphasizing that the Count's worst desires, by Helena's trick, do him service, just as the fool's worst embarrassment, cuckoldry, by a trick with logic, does Lavatch service.

Excessive lust, cuckoldry, and the need for greater social status (for whatever reason), are all potentially tragic problems that are linked to service in *All's Well.* Lavatch's remarks show that service in the play is somehow perverted, especially as that service is related to marriage. In the festive comedies, Shakespeare controls problems with lust or status by relegating them to minor characters, such as Touchstone or Malvolio. But in *All's Well* these are Helena's and Bertram's difficulties. Our sense of disjunction about the play is summed up by the fool's banter about cuckoldry: we see a tragic problem solved by a trick with logic in a comic or humorous context, after an elaborate buildup, but it is not an answer that we feel satisfied with: it provokes more questions, as most "answers" in the play do, and calls attention to its own inadequacy.

It is with the peculiar behavior of the fool that Shakespeare underscores these difficulties and guides critical assessment of the play. The Countess's response that Lavatch will "ever be a foul-mouth'd and calumnious knave" (I.iii.56) uncomfortably echoes how easy it is to relegate him to a role of mere bawdy mockery or simple parody, as the other characters do. Unlike Touchstone and Feste, whose intelligence is recognized by both Rosalind and Viola respectively, Lavatch's relevance is unnoticed, except for Lafew's brief recognition of his shrewdness (IV.v.63). When Lavatch responds to the Countess's accusation by saying "A prophet I, madam, and I speak the truth the next way" (I.iii.58), he seems to know that his remarks, especially when the fool mentions a man at a women's command, foreshadow Bertram's problems later. Here Lavatch's part hints at the prophetic qualities of fools that become significant in *King Lear*.

The remark which continues Lavatch's discourse on cuckoldry is also prophetic, "If men could be contented to be what they are, there were no fear in marriage" (I.iii.50-51). Even the wit and wisdom of a Rosalind or Portia does not serve entirely to unite the divisive forces in Shakespeare's festive comedies; rather, it is the characters' recognition of their wisdom's limits and their ability to understand their own weaknesses, or simply be what they are and trust in providence, that enables difficulties to be overcome. Helena's intelligence, especially when she interrupts her pilgrimage and devises the bedtrick, allows her to escape confronting what she is, a skillful doctor's daughter whose station is abhorrent to the one she loves. But both Parolles and Bertram must be rudely introduced to themselves. The difference between Parolles's contented capitulation, and Bertram's final skepticism about whether or not he has been foolish ("*If* she, my liege, can make me know this clearly, / I'll love her dearly," V.iii.313-14) will be discussed later.

Clearly, though, Bertram's inability to recognize his shortcomings is an important problem. At the end of the play, we can still ask, as the Lords ask of Parolles, can Bertram know what he is and be what he is? During the reconciliation he stands isolated from the others, united to society by the same trick that has exposed his foolishness. He has been a man unknowingly "at a woman's command." Whether or not any harm's been done, as Lavatch also remarks (I.iii.91), is a troubling question which will be explored properly in the tragedies that follow, where Shakespeare is able to confront questions of self-awareness, sexuality, and human folly that he can only suggest here with Lavatch and others. In any case, with *All's Well that Ends Well*, it is a lack of self-awareness that serves Bertram, and also the play's plot and purpose of reconciliation, just as the soldiers who capture Parolles know how they are to serve that plot though ignorant of what they say to each other: "Not to know what we speak to one another, so we seem to know, is to know straight our purpose" (IV.i.17-19).

Another indication that *All's Well that Ends Well* is an interesting midwife between the festive comedies and the birth of Shakespeare's later tragedies is the fact that virginity, rather than something inviolately preserved until the play's end as in the festive comedies, becomes a means to trap Bertram. Providential aid does not serve to unite the protagonists in marriage, and likewise virginity and virtue in a woman no longer serve to attract a husband. It is because women are no longer virgins in the plays that Shakespeare must confront problems with procreation, heredity, and incest that figure so largely in the tragedies. Just as the comic form no longer serves the questions about self-awareness and service that Shakespeare is now asking, so virginity is "a commodity will lose the gloss with lying; the longer kept, the less worth" (I.i.154-55). Yet where Parolles only sees "rational increase" coming from the loss of virginity, the fool knows better; "The danger is in standing to't; that's the loss of men, though it be the getting of children" (III.i.41-42). Lavatch's previous desire to get married is gone after visiting court; perhaps like Bertram, he begins to sense the problems with procreation and marriage. Isbel and a family, like the play's comic solutions, no longer serve, giving way to lust: "I have no mind to Isbel since I was at court. Our old ling and our Isbels o' th' country are nothing like your old ling and your Isbels o'th'court. The brains of my cupid's knock'd out, and I begin to love, as an old man loves money, with no stomach" (III.ii.12-16). The clown recites this as the Countess reads Bertram's letter announcing his intention never to bed Helena and to roam the world. Lavatch's remarks parody Bertram's inability to recognize any domestic values and remind us that the spoils of war for him include the lusty pursuit of women.

Bertram's letter closes with an ironic twist; he signs off with "My duty to you," though his behavior is in violation of his proper duty to his mother's wishes. The problem at the heart of *All's Well* is that Bertram cannot recognize that his duty or service is only to himself, nor can he recognize the true service of others. Shakespeare carefully illustrates the contradiction between Helena's constant offers of humble service to Bertram (II.iii.103; II.iv.47, 51, 54; II.v.55, 73, 75, 87) and Parolles's declaration that Bertram, a count by inheritance, is nothing more than his equal (II.iii.186-93, 243-45, 260-63). In choosing to follow Parolles to war, rather than accept Helena in marriage, Bertram is choosing the answer that literally does not serve. Parolles is mere language and clothes that pervert true service. Lavatch does not only attack Parolles's apparent (except to Bertram) opportunism and pompousness (as Lafew also does), but also his service to the count: "Marry, you are the wiser man; for many a man's tongue shakes out his master's undoing. To say nothing, to do nothing, to know nothing, and to have nothing, is to be a great part of your title, which is within a very little of nothing" (II.iv.23-27). Parolles's banter is a "nothing" that Bertram, his master, follows. His talk both shakes out Bertram's undoing as it goads him to Italy, and then also undoes his master at the play's end, when Parolles's attempt to say nothing conclusively ties Bertram to his seeming crime against Diana (V.iii.257-64). Here, Parolles has been reduced to a fool-like servant who desires to say, do, and know nothing. The fool's remarks about Parolles, like his remarks about Bertram, precisely describe what is to come. They are underscored when Lavatch says to Parolles "much fool may you find in you, even to the world's pleasure and increase of laughter" (II.iv.36-37).

The fool's, the play's, and the critic's search for answers that serve well leads us also to consider Helena's service. Yet even her behavior, though obviously a better choice than Parroles, is hard to swallow because she so thoroughly traps and exposes Bertram. Helena's love does not allow her to remain simply his servant, but rather to have the "best wishes that can be forg'd in . . . thoughts be servants" to her as she pursues him (I.i.75-76). The service that her calculating thoughts do for Bertram makes us uncomfortable, and even her initial service to the King is tainted; she thinks of helping him only because it may give her an advantage with Bertram (I.iii.229-33). Similarly, Shakespeare is careful to repeat three times that Helena must pay for Diana's services, thus suggesting that no service in the play is without some sort of blatant self-consideration.[13]

Lavatch proclaims himself "A fool, sir, at a woman's service, and a knave at a man's." First, for his own lusty sake, he would "cozen the man of his wife and do his service," and then "give his wife my bauble, sir, to do her service" (IV.v.23, 27-28). All service, the fool tells us, is somehow perverted into self-service. Even the fool's desire to satisfy the cuckolded man's wife results in nothing more than her own self-serving masturbation. Lavatch also suggests the cause of

All's Well's corrupt service when he responds to Lafew's admonition that he should continue to serve the devil:

> I am a woodland fellow, sir, that always lov'd a great fire, and the master I speak of ever keeps a good fire. But, sure, he is the prince of the world; let his nobility remain in's court. I am for the house with the narrow gate, which I take to be too little for pomp to enter. Some that humble themselves may, but the many will be too chill and tender, and they'll be for the flow'ry way that leads to the broad gate and the great fire.
> (IV.v.47-55)

In contrast to Lavatch's narrow gate suggesting domestic values and service, Bertram remarks to the Countess in his letter as he flees marriage: "If there be breadth enough in the world, I will hold a long distance" (III.ii.23-24). Service in the court world, the fool suggests, is tainted, and often merely self-service.

Parolles is more parasite than braggart soldier, and the play's most obvious example of self-service.[14] And yet his response to the exposure of his false service, linked to the fool's remarks here, is one of the strangest moments in the play. Just as Parolles is the play's most blatant example of self-service, so also is he the only character who is forced to acknowledge his limitations, then be truly humbled and so transformed by them. Parolles's search for any answer to serve the enemy elaborately builds towards his invocation "O Lord, sir" (recalling Lavatch) before he is unmasked. Following this, his answer to "live / Safest in shame: Being fool'd by fool'ry thrive!" (IV.iii.340-41), is borne out when he returns after his exposure, now unrecognizable in the rags of a fool, and ready to enter Lavatch's narrow gate for domestic service. When he encounters Lavatch, the fool's earlier observations about him become true, "'Before a knave th' art a knave'; that's, 'Before me th' art a knave.' This had been truth sir" (II.iv.29-31). Parolles, by becoming a fool, has found Lavatch in himself: "Did you find me in yourself, sir? Or were you taught to find me? The search, sir, was profitable; and much fool may you find in you, even to the world's pleasure and the increase of laughter" (II.iv.34-37). Appropriately, Lavatch's last words bequeath Parolles to Lafew, "I do pity his distress in my similes of comfort, and leave him to your lordship" (V.ii.25-26).

Lafew enlists Parolles into service that recalls Lavatch's woodland fellow:

> *Parolles:* It lies in you, my lord, to bring me in some grace, for you did bring me out.

Lafew: Out upon thee, knave! Dost thou put upon me at once both the office of God and the devil? One brings thee in grace and the other brings thee out . . . though you are a fool and a knave, you shall eat.

(V.ii.47-55)

Like Lavatch, Parolles also serves a devil. Like the fool with the Countess, Parolles has been introduced to his real status; however, when he looks to a "lord" for grace he is saved. Parolles will humble himself and serve Lafew ("I'll make sport with thee") as Lavatch used to serve his old master ("My lord that's gone made himself much sport out of him"). Both characters forego the wide gate of pomp and reputation and enter into honest domestic service. Instead of interrupting Lafew with worthless courtly verbage, Parolles now humbly begs one single word to identify himself. His answer, "Parolles" (V.ii.40), is of course a fool-like pun, a play on a word that means "words," and also a contradiction like so many answers in *All's Well.* But importantly, this is a contradiction that serves: it leads to Parolles's recognition, and his service to Lafew. In an odd way Parolles's former vice of excessive language, exactly that which denoted his perverted service, literally now leads to his honest service, again showing that a character's vices, by a trick with a pun here, aid him, and allow the plot to be worked out. Later, Parolles, like a wise fool, exposes Bertram's folly with Lavatchian contradictory answers and thus does the count service. It is appropriately a humble domestic's service that forces Bertram himself into marriage, a bond that requires humble and honest service to another.

But to assess Parolles's importance, his exposure should be compared with Bertram's, especially as it bears on the play's understanding of service. Unlike Parolles, we do not see Bertram enthusiastically accepting his exposure, and we thus cannot be sure whether he can serve others. Parolles can both know himself and be himself, and in doing so can commit himself to serve others. But for Bertram this is one of the play's most nagging problems, and one that Shakespeare knows he cannot serve well in a comic context.[15] Since Bertram qualifies his last remark, ("*If* she, my liege, can make me know this clearly"), we simply do not know whether he can be himself and know himself, and thus whether he can commit himself to serve Helena and their marriage, or merely fall back on more self-service. Here we are returned to Lavatch's earlier proposition, "If men could be contented to be what they are, there were no fear in marriage" (I.iii.50). Our fear is that Bertram cannot recognize his shortcomings, much less correct them and serve another. Parolles can understand his limitations through a kind of comic self-consciousness; thus for him "there's place and means for everyman alive."[16] For someone to find his place, the play emphasizes, admitting one's limitations is crucial, exactly what Bertram fails to do again and again in the play's last scene, as he continually lies and returns to answers that don't serve. Bertram's one short request for pardon ("Both, both, O, pardon"), as noted, is quickly qualified by the "if" of his last remark.

Bertram's shortcomings, especially his vain lack of self-knowledge, are too much like those found in Shakespearean tragedy to be resolved here by anything more than artificial tricks which do not serve to correct the problem, as Shakespeare evidently knows. By titling the play *All's Well that Ends Well* he ironically underscores exactly what we do not feel at the play's close, for this title is an answer that does not serve, a proverb pasted over our discomfort as the play's resolution is pasted over Bertram's unconfronted problems.[17] Along with Helena's all too calculating entrapment, the play fails to find a satisfying response to Bertram's self-service of his selfish needs. If we accept that Parolles's transformation, and offer of service, is a gesture that counters Bertram's selfishness, then Shakespeare makes this a weak gesture at best.[18] Parolles's transformation prefigures those of Kent and Edgar, both fool figures who serve, but his, too late and too little, lacks the powerful tragic context that makes their sacrifices so unforgettable.[19] In the same sense, Bertram's vain lack of self-knowledge is an extremely muted version of Lear's slender knowledge of himself, as the comic context of *All's Well* continually mediates against the development of these tragic issues.

Lavatch himself, compared with Shakespeare's other wise fools, fails to serve. Although he does focus the play's necessary questions, he is more detached than Touchstone, Feste, and Lear's fool, and it takes a more careful search to understand how he highlights the other characters', and the play's, failure to serve. No other characters in the play have any hint of his curious relation to the larger action, and we wonder just how conscious Lavatch himself is of how his parodies or perverse remarks parallel the behavior of others. Touchstone's parody is more direct and obvious than Lavatch's, and unlike Feste and Touchstone, Lavatch is not in the play's final scene, when Parolles appears to take over his role. Again, as Parolles's final behavior reminds us of Kent and Edgar, in an oddly reductionistic way Parolles's fool anticipates Lear; like him, Parolles is also stripped of his position along with his clothes, and so takes on the missing fool's part.[20] That part means speaking the "truth," as Lavatch himself asserts; he foreshadows events and consistently focuses our attention on the play's problems. And yet, if Lavatch does have a fool's traditionally prophetic powers, it seems out of place in the realistic world of *All's Well.* In addition, with the exception of Lafew, the others cannot pun or play with language like Lavatch; they are little more than straightmen when speaking to the fool, unlike those who banter with Touchstone or Feste. On the whole, the play is barren of engaging battles of wit. The fool fails to serve in the same way the play fails to serve, for the answer that there are no answers that serve, which Lavatch's fooling reveals and the play itself consistently returns to, is not an answer that serves.

Do we then conclude that Shakespeare has failed? In a strict sense, he has with this play. The answer that there is no answer which serves well lies at the heart of our dissatisfaction with *All's Well.* If Shakespeare is claiming "no adequate answer" to the problems he has raised as the law, in the sense of an enabling poetic, of this play, then he is failing at what he has set out to do as a dramatic poet creating comedy, just as if critics claimed the same "no adequate answer." To explain the play as an experiment for what will receive proper attention in the forthcoming tragedies, especially *King Lear*, as I have in part done, is not really to interpret the play, but rather to assuage the failure by pointing to examples or other sets of laws outside of the play itself.[21] This is Hunter's strategy when he looks to the romances at the close of his introduction.[22] As critics, perhaps we can make the play "explainable," but strictly speaking the play lacks if it can only be understood by laws outside of itself or by examples from other plays. As a poem which contains the rules of its own interpretation, as Shakespeare's better plays do, *All's Well that End's Well* fails, and Shakespeare in the process calls attention to that failure, especially with Lavatch.

Given this problem, we must ask why Shakespeare wrote *All's Well.* On the one hand, with the admission that to say so we are not really interpreting the play, we can say that Shakespeare is experimenting; he purposely tries to resolve what are tragic motifs in a comic context, and so works with the problems that he will render with brilliance in his later tragedies. But it is the way he experiments, I think, that we must also try to understand, specifically his service as an artist as he confronts problems that turn out to be unresolvable in a comic context. Sigurd Burckhardt, in a study of Shakespeare's Prince Hal trilogy, argues that Shakespeare discovers "a lethal mixture of two mutually inconsistent and severally inadequate models of succession." Burckhardt makes this helpful comment in an effort to understand Shakespeare's solution:

> Some three centuries before Niels Bohr, Shakespeare discovered the need of complementarity—i.e., of operating with two mutually inconsistent and severally inadequate models because, and as long as, a single, consistent, and adequate model has not been found. Complementarity differs from and is superior to mixing because it remains aware of its "illegitimacy" and *pays the price* for choosing one model over the other. It does not pretend to be a solution, hence it does not close the road of discovery but on the contrary compels us to take the risk of following it. Its passionate demand for order forces us to leave the safe prison of a static, once-for-all world picture, to suffer the grief of imperfection and disorder, and the joy of genuine action and creativity. Complementarity, in short, asserts the value of *human action in time*, which is to say, of history, of drama.[23]

A compelling way, I think, to reconcile the problems of *All's Well* with Shakespeare's awareness of those problems is to say that he understood the illegitimacy of what he was doing and also its consequences, that he knew he was paying a price for choosing the comic model over the tragic for the treatment of Bertram's selfishness and lack of self-awareness, or Helena's self-regarding manipulation of the count. Shakespeare is leaving the safe prison of the comic genre and posing problems that, he discovers, he cannot pretend to solve convincingly with comic solutions, especially providential help. But his passionate demand for a humane solution to human difficulties, to problems of self-awareness, uncontrolled lust, lying, one character's questionable manipulation of another, and social status, all problems that block significant relations between people, required him *first* to try to solve these difficulties in a manner that would not exact the awful human destruction of tragedy. Before he could confront these problems in the most destructive of tragic contexts such as *King Lear,* Shakespeare, I would like to suggest, had to try to solve them in a benevolent comedy.

Shakespeare, I believe, understands his failure in *All's Well*, and carefully expresses this to us with Lavatch. He also underscores this failure in the play's final lines. Like Bertram, Helena, "the shadow of a wife," also begins her final remark with an "if" (V.iii.315). In addition, the King hedges about whether or not the ending is complete, "*if* this suit be won": it is exactly the "oneness" of Helena's and Bertram's marriage that troubles us. The King, like

Parolles, is transformed to a humble "beggar" as he subtly thanks the audience for their patience, and asks them to put themselves in the actors' shoes, as the actors put themselves in the audience's place, "ours be your patience then, and yours our parts." While the King may have the audience "express content," one can't help but feel that the audience, like the King, senses the discontent, and has patiently endured the incomplete working out of the play's problems, and that Shakespeare is apologetically asking them to try to see it from the actor's point of view, whose service will "pay / With strife to please you, day exceeding day." The beggar-King's suggestion that the players will "pay" the audience uncomfortably echoes the fact that most of the service in the play is paid for rather than unselfishly given. The conclusion, then, is a tacit admission of *All's Well's* failure to serve the audience.

But service itself is an important idea for the ending of *All's Well.* Though there is no service that redeems the characters' severe problems or Shakespeare's failure to serve as a comic dramatist, Parolles hints that a character can free himself from false courtly artifice and deceit to serve honestly. But again, this does not tell us if Bertram can know himself and truly serve another or if Helena's manipulative intelligence, and the abuse that such control can lead to, will merely keep him "at a woman's command." Whether both can gain a comic understanding of their limits, and achieve an honest self-awareness, or whether their behavior will lead to tragic destruction, is an either-or proposition the play leaves us with, a problem of service and a question of complementarity insofar as the comic marriage and unresolved tragic problems clash. Burckhardt also writes:

> And the metaphor is one of *complementarity*, of either-or. It is neither a mixture nor a synthesis, but a metaphor: that strange entity which demands to be analytically dissolved because it *means* and creatively "made good" because it *is.* It is pregnant, hence promises birth; but the birth is never certain, while labor and pain *are* certain. Is even the father certain? Can we be sure of legitimacy? Will the offspring be the child of passion or of duty, of self-assertive lust or submissive routine? There are no guarantees, only the risk and the will—the need—to order.[24]

It is Bertram's inability to serve, and Helena's questionable methods of service, that lead to the pregnancy, an answer to the play that is literally and dramatically, and thus metaphorically, of questionable legitimacy. It is a clash of elements the play cannot resolve yoked together by pregnancy, by something with the potential to give birth both to good and bad. Shakespeare as dramatist has failed to serve because of this illegitimate answer, but the service itself that the play's creation also represents works metaphorically, a metaphor pregnant with possibilities that will be borne out in his great tragedies. As he wrote *All's Well that Ends Well* the birth of *King Lear* was not certain, but the labor and pain toward the highest achievements of drama, the "strife to please you," would be. The child in Helena now, of whom the father and the legitimacy is uncertain, is the child of both Bertram's lust and Helena's questionable service and duty, but what that child will turn out to be, and how the family and their love grows or is detroyed, is an either-or question the tragedies must answer as Shakespeare moves beyond complementarity to depict the clash of man's inhumanity with his humanity, of his selfish self-service with his service to others. It is a question that Shakespeare will serve with his greatest artistic skill, risking the road of discovery that leads to suffering, grief, and discord (especially as he questions the value of his own role as an artist), but also to the joy of genuine action and creativity.

The metaphor of pregnancy, it seems to me, is how we can understand this problem play: *All's Well that Ends Well* brings together clashing elements which lead to a product of questionable legitimacy. But the play itself is pregnant with questions which will be creatively made good in the great tragedies that follow, especially *King Lear*, where the necessary questions of duty and service, of both his characters and of the dramatist Shakespeare, will be presented along with the worst extremes of human destruction and self-service that poetic drama can portray, in a search for the questions and answers that will serve well. If Bertram's unresolved problem is his inability to recognize his limits, know himself, and serve others, and there is no adequate example in the play to counter his self-service (or something to counter Helena's self-regarding manipulation) then we must look ahead to Shakespeare's understanding of his role as an artist and his service to us in the later tragedies, as he leaves the seeming knowledge of comedy, of a static, once-for-all world picture, and submits himself and his characters to the unknown fear of tragedy. Miracles are past, and things unnatural and causeless must now be confronted head on.

NOTES

[1]All quotations from Shakespeare's plays are from *The Complete Works of Shakespeare*, ed. David Bevington (Glenview: Scott, Foresman, 1980).

[2]Oscar James Campbell, ed. *The Reader's Encyclopedia of Shakespeare* (New York: Crowell, 1966), p. 17.

[3]Robert H. Goldsmith, *Wise Fools in Shakespeare* (East Lansing: Michigan State Univ. Press, 1963), p. 60.

[4]Jay Halio, "All's Well That Ends Well," *SQ* 15 (Winter 1964):35.

[5]G. K. Hunter, introduction and notes to *The Arden Edition of All's Well That Ends Well* (London: Methuen, 1959), pp. xxxiv, xxxv, 47, 50.

[6]J. L. Styan, *All's Well that Ends Well: Shakespeare in Performance* (Manchester: Manchester Univ. Press, 1984), p. 55.

[7]Shakespeare takes pains to show that Helena's healing is an act of heaven. When she first argues with the King her language becomes religiously infused, "So holy writ in babes hath judgement shown / When judges have been babes; great floods have flown" (II.i.138-39). She goes on to speak of "miracles" (141); "Him," referring to God (149); "the help of heaven" (152); and "of heaven not me make experiment" (154) to the King. All this stands in stark contrast to how she must win Bertram, "Our remedies oft in ourselves do lie, which we ascribe to heaven" (I.ii.215-16).

[8]W. W. Lawrence, *Shakespeare's Problem Comedies* (New York: Ungar, 1960), pp. 35-63.

[9]W. L. Godshalk writes that "religious references are replaced by the appeal to nature, an appeal frequently made in the play" in Helena's speech at the end of II.i. He continues, "Nature allows man to bridge the gaps made by Fortune; and, like Edmund in *King Lear*, Helena accepts Nature as her guide." See *All's Well That Ends Well* and the Morality Play," *SQ* 25 (Winter 1974):64.

[10]David Scott Kastan writes, "In the problem comedies the contrivance is the character's own and is throughout too self-regarding, too unresponsive to the needs of others." See his fine essay *"All's Well that Ends Well* and the Limits of Comedy," *ELH* 52 (Fall 1985):579.

[11]Helena's remark cited in note 7 which links her to Edmund can be compared to Viola's "O time, thou must untangle this, not I; it is too hard a knot for me to untie" (II.ii.40-41). Rosalind and Portia do deceive their husbands, not to win a love they already possess, but rather to expose follies which do not mar the close of their comedies. Helena's social position, and her method for advancing, is part of the larger issue of social mobility that needs further treatment in Shakespeare. However, as Lawrence Stone persuasively argues, we can say that the Elizabethans would have been sensitive to the aristocracy's "crisis" regarding social mobility, its "unprecedented" expansion during Shakespeare's age and the conservative backlash that sought to control it. For a thorough study of this problem, see Lawrence Stone, *The Crisis of the Aristocracy, 1558-1641* (Oxford: Clarendon Press, 1965).

[12]Kastan's essay cited in note 10 is also concerned with the limits of comic solutions. However, he writes that the problem is "not Helena's social class or even Bertram's intractable snobbery but an inadequate conception of love—or, put differently, an inadequate conception of comedy, a conception that would exclusively formalize comic action, shaping comic characters and events to our desires" (p. 580).

[13]Godshalk notes that "the fact that Helena is conducting a dubiously moral

intrigue returns to haunt our excuses" each time Shakespeare reminds us that Helena is paying Diana (p. 65).

[14]Hunter, p. xlvii.

[15]See Phillip Edwards for an intelligent discussion of Bertram's behavior in *Shakespeare and the Confines of Art* (London: Methuen, 1968), pp. 113-15. Edwards points out that the count's "execrable" behavior is not a matter for critical debate: "The treatment of Parolles shows us a scoundrel changed by shame into a new recognition and a new way of life. Bertram is not so treated. Helena never saves Bertram. He is unredeemable: Shakespeare could not save him. It is not a matter of failing to write the lines that would have changed the soul of the play: it is a matter of not being able to force one's conscience to alter a character whose alteration would be, simply, incredible."

[16]Shakespeare's wiser comic characters have an acute sense of their own folly, a comic and unpretentious appraisal of their failings, exactly what Bertram shows no trace of in the last scene especially, but also when the blind-folded Parolles anatomizes the count's bad behavior (IV.iii.216-37). M. C. Bradbrook's analysis, like Edwards's, makes it clear that Shakespeare intends little sympathy for Bertram: "The Elizabethan code of honour supposed a gentleman to be absolutely incapable of a lie. . . . To give the lie was the deadliest of all insults and could not be wiped out except in blood. . . . Alone among Shakespeare's heroes Bertram is guilty of the lie" and by such conduct "forfeits his claims to gentility"; see "Virtue and Nobility in *All's Well that Ends Well*," *RES* 1.4 (October 1950): 289-301.

[17]Ann Barton makes this insightful comment on the proverbial nature of the play's title: "Like the proverbs continually employed in the perverse and contradictory fashion by the bitter fool Lavatch—traditional bits of lore existing uneasily in a world grown too complex for such simplifications—it serves as a gentle reminder that fairy tales, ultimately, are not true." See her introduction in *The Riverside Shakespeare*, ed. G. Blakemore Evans (Boston: Houghton, Mifflin, 1974), pp. 499-503.

[18]For an alternative view of Parolles's effect on the last scene, see Gerard J. Gross, "The Conclusion to *All's Well that Ends Well*," *SEL* 23 (Spring 1983):275-76.

[19]See Jonas A. Barish and Marshall Waingrow, "Service in *King Lear*," *SQ* 9 (1958):347-55.

[20]James Calderwood writes that Lear's fool's disappearence "makes foolish sense. When Lear has absorbed the fool's truths and begins to utter them himself, the fool becomes redundant." See "Creative Uncreation in *King Lear*," *SQ* 28 (1986):10.

[21]Sigurd Burckhardt, *Shakespearean Meanings* (Princeton: Princeton Univ. Press, 1968), pp. 296-98.

[22]Hunter, p. lv.

[23]Burckhardt, p. 183-84.

[24]Burckhardt, p. 185.

SEL 28 (1988)
ISSN 0039-3657

The Changeling in *A Dream*

WILLIAM W. E. SLIGHTS

Midway through the first scene of Act II in *A Midsummer Night's Dream,* Oberon, King of the Fairies, begs "a little changeling boy" of Titania. She responds, "The fairy land buys not the child of me" (II.i.120, 122), and from this exchange—or non-exchange—follows a highly determined though minimally textualized custody battle.[1] After a great deal has been done and said about the nature of love and marriage, and a quantity of flower juice has been squirted about, Oberon again "ask[s] of her her changeling child," and "straight" Titania gives it to him (IV.i.59-60), not because the snaky scales of feminine insubordination have fallen from her eyes, but because Oberon has caused her to become infatuated with a very funny-looking local weaver who is also not her husband. The quarrel over the changeling boy is powerful but also peripheral, erratically described, and never properly resolved. These and similar anomalies in Shakespeare's treatment of the changeling boy make it difficult to see how the other characters, followed by a group of usually reliable critics, can say with such fierce (over-)determination just what the boy and the fairy discords focused on him are all about. Although the text never calls for this "character" to appear on stage, theatrical directors, taking matters creatively into their own hands, tend to beg the question by assigning the changeling's "part" to some small member of the company. In the case of such a shadowy figure as the changeling in *A Dream*, however, we need to proceed with some care in order to be sure that what we are interpreting is, in some sense, *there*.

William W. E. Slights, Professor of English at the University of Saskatchewan, has recently completed a study of early printed marginalia in relation to contemporary socio-linguistic theories of *marginalité* (forthcoming in *Renaissance Quarterly*). He continues to work on Jonson and Shakespeare as reformers of literary genres.

There are just six direct references to the changeling boy in the text, three of which I have already quoted. In another, Puck, that perpetually amused vulgarizer of relationships, voices his view that the changeling is stolen goods that "jealous" Oberon wants to possess. He tells a unnamed fairy that Titania

> as her attendant hath
> A lovely boy stolen from an Indian king;
> She never had so sweet a changeling.
> And jealous Oberon would have the child
> Knight of his train, to trace the forest wild;
> But she, perforce, withholds the loved boy,
> Crowns him with flowers, and makes him all her joy.
> (II.i.21-27)

From these lines we learn that the boy, who started life as an Indian prince, is "lovely," "sweet," and "loved" by Titania.[2] Oberon's competing and exclusive claim suggests that perhaps, as Puck implies, no one in fairyland has a rightful claim to him. Anyone who wants the changeling, for whatever purpose, may have to withhold him "perforce," that is, forcibly. On the other hand, the line, "she, perforce, withholds the loved boy," also opens the possibility that Titania herself is acting under some form of compulsion.

While Puck's account of the changeling boy raises the problems of compulsive behavior and custodial rights among thieves, Oberon's way of seeing the matter is that he has suffered an intolerable injury (II.i.147) at the hands of a "wanton" wife (II.i.63).[3] To punish this act of sexual and social insubordination he employs the aphrodisiac juice of the flower called love-in-idleness, thereby creating a "hateful imperfection [in Titania's] eyes" (IV.i.63) that makes her lust after Bottom the ass. Eventually he chastens her and, we are to suppose, drives her back to his own conjugal bed with a second flower drug, "Dian's bud o'er Cupid's flower / [Having] such force and blessed power" (IV.i.73-74).

Titania's view of the changeling boy is altogether different from Puck's and Oberon's. To her, caring for the boy is an act of loyalty to a woman with whom she had shared the most intimate and delightful female companionship, until the fatal moment of the child's birth:

> His mother was a vot'ress of my order,
> And in the spiced Indian air, by night,
> Full often hath she gossip'd by my side,

And sat with me on Neptune's yellow sands,
Marking th' embarked traders on the flood;
When we have laugh'd to see the sails conceive
And grow big-bellied with the wanton wind;
Which she, with pretty and with swimming gait,
Following (her womb then rich with my young squire)
Would imitate, and sail upon the land
To fetch me trifles, and return again,
As from a voyage, rich with merchandise.
But she, being mortal, of that boy did die,
And for her sake do I rear up her boy;
And for her sake I will not part with him.

(II.i.123-37)

The passage captures the pleasure the two women take in gently mocking the world of marine commerce with the richer joys of sorority and pregnancy.[4] However perplexing we may find the phrase "a vot'ress of my order,"[5] the lines describe a relationship of deep understanding and trust based on their feelings as women. The experience of perfect empathy is expressed in the metaphoring, unmetaphoring, and remetaphoring of the big-bellied sails. What is conceived and imitated here is the very idea of conception. The sails, impregnated by the inspiring breath of the wind, transform the trading vessels into women great with child, one of whom (Titania's votaress and the mother of the changeling boy) in turn humorously imitates a merchandise-laden vessel by gliding gracefully across the land "with pretty and with swimming gait." One need only exchange the terms and, handy-dandy, which is the tenor, which the vehicle in this fully conceived metaphor? Ruth Nevo remarks wittily that "Oberon might mend his marriage more effectively by getting Titania with child than by trying to get Titania without child."[6] Though there is something vaguely absurd in the critic turning marriage counsellor to the Fairy King, Nevo has rightly seen that parenting emerges as central to Titania's consciousness. The Fairy Queen places herself in loco parentis when the Indian queen dies in childbirth. Now she must nurture and protect a child who, to her mind, is more adopted than kidnapped from the human realm. In Titania's eyes, the fact that he straddles the border between human and fairy in no way obviates his need for mothering.

Understanding what happens on the psychic boundary between human and fairy kind is a prime interpretive challenge in *A Dream*. The changeling boy, who in my view exists rather precariously in this bordering state, has seemed to some critics to provide a clear case of a lesson learned in fairyland and transferred back into the human realm. The lesson is largely concerned with the hypothesized superiority of reason (identified as a male strength) over will (identified as a female weakness) in Renaissance psychology, the dominant position of husbands over their wives in Renaissance society, and the advisability of graduating boy-children from women's care to men's hunting parties.[7] The difficulty with these claims is that they assume or assert a kind of particularity about the nature and function of the changeling boy that—as we have already seen from the conflicting views of Puck, Oberon, and Titania—Shakespeare's text does not provide. The changeling is an absent presence, existing only as a series of competing claims on his company. As such, he illustrates a principle of indeterminacy evident in many parts of the play.

The concept of indeterminacy has gained considerable currency over the past three decades, largely through the work of Ferdinand de Saussure, Jacques Derrida, and other semantic philosophers. One version of the concept grows out of Derrida's efforts to break down the simple model of one signifier and one thing signified by suggesting that signifiers may just go on indefinitely referring to other signifiers. Jonathan Culler is at pains to point out that this is not the same thing as arguing that any interpretation is as good as any other. He writes, "The combination of context-bound meaning and boundless context on the one hand makes possible proclamations of the indeterminacy of meaning—though the smug iconoclasm of such proclamations may be irritating—but on the other hand urges that we continue to interpret texts, classify speech acts, and attempt to elucidate the conditions of signification."[8] It is in this sense and spirit that I invoke the principle of indeterminacy. I do not propose to make common cause with those who, like Bottom, believe that "Man is but an ass, if he go about t'expound this dream" (IV.i.206-207). Expounding is a large part of the business of criticism as I practice it. What makes asses of us all, including the characters in *A Dream*, is announcing that we possess the sole, uncontestable truth, particularly about an area of experience as unstable as the one Shakespeare dramatizes in this play. As interpreters, we must always be prepared to deal with contending, contingent truths about matters as apparently simple as weather-reporting and as decidedly complex as love and marriage. While offering us a variety of insights into such topics as these, the play always slips free of formally restrictive readings. The changeling boy receives a wide range of responses from characters in the play and invites even more complex, unsettling responses from the audience.

Consider for a moment an apparently banal topic, the weather. Titania's account of the weather in a distinctly anglicized Athens and environs achieves mythic proportions but precious little fixity:

> never, since the middle summer's spring,
> Met we on hill, in dale, forest, or mead,
> By paved fountain or by rushy brook,
> Or in the beached margent of the sea,
> To dance our ringlets to the whistling wind,
> But with thy brawls thou hast disturb'd our sport.
> Therefore the winds, piping to us in vain,
> As in revenge, have suck'd up from the sea
> Contagious fogs; which, falling in the land,
> Hath every pelting river made so proud
> That they have overborne their continents.
> The ox hath therefore stretch'd his yoke in vain,
> The ploughman lost his sweat, and the green corn
> Hath rotted ere his youth attain'd a beard.
> The fold stands empty in the drowned field,
> And crows are fatted with the murrion flock;
> The nine men's morris is fill'd up with mud,
> And the quaint mazes in the wanton green,
> For lack of tread, are undistinguishable.
> The human mortals want their winter here;
> No night is now with hymn or carol blest.
> Therefore the moon (the governess of floods),
> Pale in her anger, washes all the air,
> That rheumatic diseases do abound.
> And thorough this distemperature, we see
> The seasons alter: hoary-headed frosts
> Fall in the fresh lap of the crimson rose,
> And on old Hiems' thin and icy crown
> An odorous chaplet of sweet summer buds
> Is, as in mockery, set; the spring, the summer,
> The childing autumn, angry winter, change
> Their wonted liveries; and the mazed world,
> By their increase, now knows not which is which.
> And this same progeny of evils comes
> From our debate, from our dissension;
> We are their parents and original.
>
> (II.i.82-117)

This perplexing set-piece of visionary verse moves from logic to chaos, from a precise time-frame to a seasonal jumble, from a complaint about infertility to a complaint about a "progeny of evils," from precise signs denoting natural objects, causes, and consequences to a "mazed world [that] knows not which is which." This sounds a good deal like a working definition of indeterminacy. Titania's catalogue of inclemency—fog, flooding, failed crops, decimated flocks, polluted air, and unseasonable temperatures—carries an implicit self-accusation of being either merciless (literally without clemency) or irresponsible towards the people whose weather she is making. But Titania is no bubble-headed woodland deity heedlessly upending the seasons. The thrice-repeated logical connective, "therefore," lends force to the carefully deployed argumentative structure aimed at forcing Oberon to accept joint responsibility for the weather, if not for the changeling child. For all that the fairies seem to be a source of disorder in the play, Titania here provides an orderly explanation of that very disorder. From the precisely defined "middle summer's spring" Titania plunges us into a *wintry* world incongruously crowned with "sweet summer buds," despite her assertion midway through the speech that "mortals want their winter here." Though phrases such as "wanton green" and "lap of the crimson rose" convey, as C.L. Barber points out, a strong "amorous suggestion" (p. 147), others such as "childing autumn," "progeny of evils," and "parents and original" create an equally strong maternal suggestion. As she arrives at her conclusion regarding the debate over the changeling child, she leaves us with an overwhelming sense that, for all her logical explanation, the progeny of evils remains a paradox, an indeterminate truth, and we a part of that "mazed world [that] knows not which is which."

Extending the indeterminacy of Titania's account of the grief caused by the struggle for custody of the changeling boy is the fact that no one else in the play seems to notice any bad weather. However much the Athenian lovers quarrel, not so much as a cloud emerges on their horizons. It is not an adequate response to this observation to say that Titania's lines apply only to the lofty idealities of fairyland and are not intended as a description of ordinary human reality when she has gone to such lengths to locate all that mud in the nine men's morris and to de-rhapsodize her speech with the sweat of redundantly "human mortals." René Girard amusingly demystifies the play's meteorology: "Scholars assume that the weather must have been particularly bad in the year Shakespeare wrote the play; this, in turn, gives some clues to the dating of the play. It must be true, indeed, that Shakespeare needed some really inclement weather to write what he did."[9] Girard goes on to argue that what lies behind all this literalized weather forecasting is the deeper problem of "conceptual undifferentiation" (p. 203), concluding with tongue in cheek that in the play's happy ending, "Good weather is back, everything is in order once more" (p. 208). The effect of omitting from the mimetic dimension of the play any corroborating text about the weather is to call into question the notion of a single, authorized version of reality, even though that version emanates from a royal source. Here is no privileging of the text but a willingness to launch the text on to the uncertain seas of human emotion.

If something as ordinary as the weather becomes a source of conflicting evidence in the play, we may expect a still higher degree of uncertainty to be generated around the presentation of love and marriage. It would be reasonable to conclude after reading the play or seeing it performed that love is the major source of indeterminacy, not quarreling, as Titania contends. It is hard to get a straight answer from a lover to even the simplest question: How do you like Athens, Hermia?

> Before the time I did Lysander see,
> Seem'd Athens as a paradise to me;
> O then, what graces in my love do dwell,
> That he hath turn'd a heaven unto a hell!
>
> (I.i.204-207)

Not only does the weather around Athens remain uncertain, the city itself evokes diametrically opposed responses in the same person, this time under the compulsion of love.

Some of this violent changeability can be credited to Shakespeare's Ovidian treatment of love. Love, especially youthful love, can never remain fixed for long in the *Metaphorphoses*. Similarly, Lysander's account of the course of true love broods with *Romeo and Juliet*-like awareness over the fate of a passion that is

> momentany as a sound,
> Swift as a shadow, short as any dream,
> Brief as the lightning in the collied night,
> That, in a spleen, unfolds both heaven and earth;
> And ere a man hath power to say "Behold!"
> The jaws of darkness do devour it up:
> So quick bright things come to confusion.
>
> (I.i.143-49)

That four of Shakespeare's bright young things quickly come to confusion in the night wood may be attributed to their youthful inexperience. Indeed, the skittishness of lovers becomes synonymous with childishness in the play. The two Athenian youths and their girlfriends are initially thought to be as much in need of parenting as the changeling boy. They are not fully formed persons but rather exude the still undetermined potential of childhood.

In the non-human world of *A Midsummer Night's Dream*, love's fickleness has not one but three childish faces. "Love [is] said to be a child" (I.i.238) in the iconographic tradition that transmitted the Cupid myth from classical times to the Renaissance, a tradition summarized in some detail by Helena (I.i.232-45). With delicate literalness, Shakespeare translates the erratic power of Cupid's arrows into the magic juice of Oberon's narrative of the fiery shaft that missed Diana's "imperial vot'ress," who figures the chaste Eliza, striking instead the flower called love-in-idleness (II.i.148-74). Oberon places Cupid's powerful drug in the hands of another "waggish boy," Puck, who, though himself no lover of mankind, is vastly amused by the emotional instability generated by his newly acquired ability to make people tumble in and out of love. The third is our old friend the changeling boy, who likewise represents no uniform or fixed approach to the meaning of love.[10] In each case, these spirits pose a threat to established hierarchy and its protective institution of marriage.

A widely accepted interpretation of the play's comic resolution is that the young people's unrealized potential for love is eventually given adult definition by traditional marriage celebrations in Act V.[11] The fullest and most persuasive account of this approach to determining the meaning of the play is Paul Olson's essay, "*A Midsummer Night's Dream* and the Meaning of Court Marriage."[12] After tracing a social and iconological tradition of marriage from the garden of Eden to the court of Elizabeth, Olson concludes that "In the total conceptual scheme of the play, the king and queen of the woods dramatize the two poles of the scale of values which gave meaning to marriage. They are types of the forces of Reason and Passion which in a more complex and human manner move through Theseus and Hippolita respectively" (p. 111).

One problem with this kind of reading is that it is clear both from literary and non-literary sources of the late sixteenth and early seventeenth centuries that marriage performed a great many functions besides subjecting women's passions to the control of men's intellects.[13] Some marriages were for gain, some for companionship, some for love, some for convenience. Some were equally shared, some enforced, some secret, and some nasty, mean, brutish, and short. Furthermore, given the favored male pastimes referred to in *A Midsummer Night's Dream* (war and the hunt), it is difficult to believe that Shakespeare was trying to depict Reason as an exclusive male preserve. Although Olson explains with admirable fullness and subtlety the significance of various literary representations of marriage, he overreads the text of Shakespeare's play. He refers, for example, to Titania's "erotic games with . . . the changeling" (p. 111), assignations we neither see nor hear about.

Far more prominent in the play than "the celestial love which preserves chaste marriages and keeps the cosmos in order" (Olson, p. 109), are the uncontrollable, carnivalesque impulses operating despite the best efforts of several patriarchs to rearrange or suppress the natural impulses of youth. As one recent critic points out, "the play represents several stories of resistance and discord, counter-models of the reconciliation and accommodation Theseus proposes."[14] Not only does the play confront us with the willful rebellion of a quartet of teenagers, but it sets in motion the maddest of low-life subplots, including Bottom's anarchic synesthesia (IV.i.204-19) and even in the fifth-act resolution the topsy-turvy indeterminacy of "very tragical mirth" (V.i.57) in the mechanicals' performance at court. The challenge for all the audiences, on-stage and off, is to hold in mind at once pairs of terms and concepts that point in opposite directions. It has become customary to discuss the reconciliation of opposites or *concordia discors* in *A Midsummer Night's Dream* in terms of a patriarchal triumph over female waywardness in the most obvious of institutional joining of opposites, holy matrimony.[15] This is the great Elizabethan humanist settlement for the problem of conflicting stories and emotional states in the play: Titania is forced to see the folly of her infatuation with the changeling boy by being made to fall in love with a second and more monstrous changeling, one that even she can eventually perceive as inferior to her proper husband. Like Helena, Hermia, and Hippolyta, she is taught that the only true concord for the sexes requires her to acknowledge the central fact of benign (and, by analogy, divine) male superiority in a patrilineal-patrological culture. Titania, in fact, acknowledges nothing of the kind when she gives up the changeling boy. All she says is that she now loathes the sight of the transfigured Bottom (IV.i.79). It can be argued, then, that in its pursuit of comic conflicts Shakespeare's play does more to unsettle than to inscribe traditional assumptions of courtly culture concerning marriage.

Traditional readings of *A Midsummer Night's Dream* do, of course, allow that conflicts exist within the hierarchical social structure depicted in the play, but they maintain that discord exists only to be chastized, corrected, and subsumed by a higher order. For a number of reasons I believe, on the contrary, that the indeterminacy of Shakespeare's text permits the characters to perpetuate their amorous and festive madness with all the illogic of a dream through and even beyond its formal end. Though the young lovers awake in Act IV as if from a dream, their present waking reality is as unfixed as their labyrinthine sleepwalking:

> *Her.* Methinks I see these things with parted eye,
> When every thing seems double.
> *Hel.* So methinks;
> And I have found Demetrius like a jewel,
> Mine own, and not mine own.
>
> (IV.i.189-92)

Shakespeare poses as a problem for his fictional persons as well as his would-be understanders outside the play, the proposition that any attempt to make something firmly one's own, whether it be a changeling boy, an eligible bachelor, or a unique interpretation of a text, is to expose the vaguely ridiculous limitations of the human condition. No tyrannical assertion of authority by a father, a duke, a lover, or a critic can manage to avoid the problem.

In writing a comedy that takes place almost wholly beyond the reach of ordinary domestic locales, exploring the haunts of Endymion rather than Gammer Gurton, Shakespeare ignores the centrality of traditional male power and respectability, instead mapping the terrain that Robert Frost in his poem "West-Running Brook" calls "lady-land." The male authority figures, Egeus and Theseus, cease to exert their powers of constraint after Act I. The genuine sources of human vitality and insight in Shakespeare are not to be found at the safe center of government or in the quiet domains of marriage but rather in the world of Falstaff and Hal at the Boars Head, Lear and his fool on the heath, Perdita in her garden, Prospero and Caliban on their uneasily shared island—places that harbor the mooncalves and changelings of the world. *A Midsummer Night's Dream* is not a celebration in the same genre as Jonson's court masques. It is not focused on the literal or even the symbolic seat of royal power but rather on the largely uncharted territory on the fringes or "margents" of society where the rules of power tend to break down, often with imaginatively liberating and extremely amusing results. Here,

Hippolyta's view that "the story of the night . . . grows to something of great constancy" (V.i.23-27) can brush aside Theseus's condescending and authoritarian pronouncements, leaving intact the claims of the imagination.

The point about discords in this marginal world is that they remain stimulatingly discordant. The changeling boy, so insubstantial in the text and so variously perceived as a source of conflict, is a prime example of the indeterminacy that the play postulates as the essential condition of people who love and people who dream. Try as they may to remain wrapped "In maiden meditation, fancy-free" (II.i.164), like the Imperial Virgin protected by chaste moonbeams from Cupid's fiery shaft, ordinary mortals are seldom free in their fancying. Even the perceptions of the Queen of Fairy can be constrained by the siren call of the strange mortal, Bottom:

> I pray thee, gentle mortal, sing again.
> Mine ear is much enamored of thy note;
> So is mine eye enthralled to thy shape;
> And thy fair virtue's force (perforce) doth move me
> On the first view to say, to swear, I love thee.
> (III.i.137-41)

Here are a woman and a piece of text about as determined as they can be. Bottom's perceived good looks, his "virtue," are closely shadowed by the root sense of *virtú*, power or force. A force perforce forces Titania triply to swear to a love that will evaporate from her eye and her tongue in the space of a single act. The real forces celebrated in the play would seem to be not marital restraint, chastity, or even, perhaps, constancy, but natural sexual impulses and radically unstable sense-perceptions. As Michael Andrews argues, the dewy tears that materialize in the "pretty flouriets' eyes" (IV.i.55) when Oberon upbraids Titania for bedecking first the changeling boy and then Bottom with flowers, are as likely to be shed for love repressed than, as usually glossed, for chaste women ravished.[16] Enforced chastity is no wellspring of joy in *A Midsummer Night's Dream*. Instead, the play gives full scope to desires that struck Puritan preachers and authors of courtly entertainments alike as anathema to Christian marriage and good government.

Still, matrimony has its hour when the moon is full, the rustics are fooling at the height of their bent, and the fairies are in gentle attendance. The troublesome changeling child, violator of the shifting but ever-present boundary between human and other worlds, has apparently been forgotten in the wake of the new amity between Titania and Oberon. This is not to say that the differences of perception regarding the changeling have been resolved, any more than the conflicting infatuations of the Athenian lovers or Hermia's dispute with her father have been "resolved." They have merely been swept to one side like the dust that Puck is sent to sweep behind the door on the wedding night. There the unpleasantnesses and competing truths will coexist with the joys of marriage and those of the comic stage. No single or higher truth emerges from the play but rather a slightly bewildering and highly amusing collection of apparently willful reinterpretations of the experience of being in and out of love. Like the changeling boy, *A Midsummer Night's Dream* itself is a masterwork of what I have called indeterminacy and what Keats called "*Negative Capability*, that is when man is capable of being in uncertainties, Mysteries, doubts, without any irritable reaching after fact & reason."[17]

NOTES

[1]Quotations from *A Midsummer Night's Dream* are from *The Riverside Shakespeare*, ed. G. Blakemore Evans, et al. (Boston: Houghton Mifflin, 1974).

[2]"The changeling," according to Minor White Latham, "seems to have been peculiar to the 16th-century fairies of England" (*The Elizabethan Fairies: The Fairies of Folklore and the Fairies of Shakespeare* [New York: Columbia Univ. Press, 1930], rpt. New York: Octagon Books, 1972, p. 150). The still more peculiar feature of this particular changeling is that he is not the usual deformed child left behind by the fairies to create consternation among distraught human parents, but instead the handsome young prince vied for on the far side, the fairy side.

[3]In his article, "Titania and the Changeling," *ES* 22 (1940):66-70, Donald C. Miller argues with single-minded determination that several epithets attached to Titania's name, including "proud," "rash," and "jealous," are synonymous with "wanton." Largely on this basis, he concludes that "Titania has made the boy her lover" (p. 66). As will become clear, I view the relationship very differently.

[4]I cannot agree with David Marshall's assertion that in this speech Titania "is perpetuating rather than rejecting terms that inscribe people in a system of economic relations." The tenderness of her language has little in common with characters such as Shylock whose purpose actually is so to "inscribe" people. See David Marshall, "Exchanging Visions: Reading *A Midsummer Night's Dream*," *ELH* 49 (1982):568. A more sensitive and persuasive reading of the lines is C. L. Barber's in *Shakespeare's Festive Comedy* (Princeton: Princeton Univ. Press, 1959), pp. 136-37. Louis Adrian Montrose reads the speech as an exclusively female version of carrying sons and argues that it "counterpoints" Theseus's account of how men, without the mediation of women, leave their imprint on their daughters (I.i.47-51). The upshot of this contest between male and female fantasies of parthenogenesis, according to Montrose, is repeated "male disruption of an intimate bond between women" (p. 71), a disruption that the play's

comic form eventually sanctions and, in doing so, "neutralizes the forms of royal power [in particular, the potent myth of the Virgin Queen] to which it ostensibly pays homage" (p. 85). See "'Shaping Fantasies': Figurations of Gender and Power in Elizabethan Culture," *Representations* 1 (1983): 61-94.

[5]Ernest Schanzer, with refreshing candor, admits his bafflement at the phrase: "The order of the fairy queen? With human votaresses? It does not make sense... the words 'vot'ress of my order' seem oddly chosen. Perhaps some topical allusion is the answer to the puzzle, with Titania at least in this episode standing for the Queen and the votaress perhaps for one of her ladies-in-waiting" ("The Moon and the Fairies in *A Midsummer Night's Dream*," *UTQ* 24 [1955]:241-42). More relevant to today's readers than surmised topicality is the sense of stability, as opposed to wantonness, conveyed by the word "order."

[6]Ruth Nevo, *Comic Transformations in Shakespeare* (London: Methuen, 1980), p. 104.

[7]In addition to Ruth Nevo's book, which I have already cited, and Paul Olson's essay, which I will discuss later, the following works read the play as endorsing certain sexist assumptions of Shakespeare's society: Paul N. Siegel, "*A Midsummer Night's Dream* and the Wedding Guests," *SQ* 4 (1953):139-44; James L. Calderwood, "*A Midsummer Night's Dream*: The Illusion of Drama," *MLQ* 26 (1965):506-22; David P. Young, *Something of Great Constancy: The Art of "A Midsummer Night's Dream"* (New Haven: Yale Univ. Press, 1966); Anca Vlasopolos, "The Ritual of Midsummer: A Pattern for *A Midsummer Night's Dream*," *RenQ* 31 (1978):21-29; and Alan W. Bellringer, "The Act of Change in *A Midsummer Night's Dream*," *ES* 64 (1983):201-17.

[8]Jonathan Culler, *On Deconstruction: Theory and Criticism after Structuralism* (Ithaca: Cornell Univ. Press, 1982), p. 133.

[9]René Girard, "Myth and Ritual in Shakespeare: *A Midsummer Night's Dream*," in *Textual Strategies: Perspectives in Post-Structuralist Criticism*, ed. Josué V. Harari (Ithaca: Cornell Univ. Press, 1979), p. 199.

[10]For an interpretation that finds a fixed, indeed a theoretically predetermined, pattern of behavior in the way adults and children relate to one another, see Vicky Shahly Hartman, "*A Midsummer Night's Dream*: A Gentle Concord to the Oedipal Problem," *AI* 40 (1983):356-69. Norman Holland's application of Freudian theory to the play ("Hermia's Dream," in *Representing Shakespeare: New Psychoanalytic Essays*, ed. Murry M. Schwartz and Coppelia Kahn [Baltimore: Johns Hopkins Univ. Press, 1980], pp. 1-20) avoids some of the problems of overdetermining the text that Hartman's essay exhibits. Paul Stevens argues from a rich matrix of allusion that the psychological origin of childishness in the play is the fancy uninformed by reason. See his *Imagination and the Presence of Shakespeare in "Paradise Lost"* (Madison: Univ. of Wisconsin Press, 1985), pp. 15, 85-87, et passim.

[11]The connection between this play about marriage and an actual aristocratic marriage of the mid-1590s has often been postulated, but the evidence for linking *A Midsummer Night's Dream* to one or another specific marriage is so far inconclusive.

[12]Paul A. Olson, "*A Midsummer Night's Dream* and the Meaning of Court Marriage," *ELH* 24 (1957):95-119.

[13]The fourth chapter of Keith Wrightson's *English Society, 1580-1680* (London: Hutchinson, 1982) presents evidence of some highly companionable marriages drawn from a variety of shires and social classes.

[14]Michael D. Bristol, *Carnival and Theater: Plebeian Culture and the Structure of Authority in Renaissance England* (New York: Methuen, 1985), p. 172. On the basis of Harold Brooks's source work with Plutarch and Seneca in the Arden edition, Louis Montrose argues that "sedimented within the verbal texture of *A Midsummer Night's Dream* are traces of those forms of familial violence which the play would suppress" (" 'Shaping Fantasies,' " p. 75).

[15]Hippolyta's lines concerning the hounds of Sparta suggest a possible analogue to this process:

Never did I hear
Such gallant chiding; for besides the groves,
The skies, the fountains, every region near
Seem all one mutual cry. I never heard
So musical a discord, such sweet thunder.

(IV.i.114-18)

[16]See Michael Cameron Andrews, "Titania on 'Enforced Chastity,' " *N&Q* 31 (1984):188.

[17]*John Keats: Selected Poems and Letters*, ed. Douglas Bush (Boston: Houghton Mifflin, 1959), p. 261.

SEL 28 (1988)
ISSN 0039-3657

Oratio and *Negotium*: Manipulative Modes in *As You Like It*

DALE G. PRIEST

Most of the *personae* in *As You Like It* address themselves in characteristic ways to the pastoral world Shakespeare has created in Arden. Each has his own distinct mode of response to that world. Still, a general bipartite pattern can be found in the various voices and strategies, a pattern that helps define two important polarities in the play. First we note the voices of accommodation—such characters as Corin, Orlando, and Duke Senior, who represent a spirit of inclusiveness in the play, and who function generally to promote integration and community. Other voices in the forest appear to be pitted against that spirit—chiefly those of Jaques, Touchstone, and Rosalind, among the persons who have significant dealings in Arden. These characters are manipulative by nature, and they project, or pretend to project, exclusive identities that seem to ridicule or reject the communal ideal. The polarities thereby established in the drama correspond roughly, and respectively, to the romantic and satiric modes of comic design.[1] This essay focuses on the decidedly different aims and methods of the manipulative *personae* in *As You Like It*—especially those of Touchstone and Rosalind—to show how and why Shakespeare gives us, in Rosalind, an *eiron* who uses the strategies of satire in the service of romance. In so doing, the playwright bestows upon her and her negotiative powers an implicit endorsement denied Touchstone and his rhetorical skills.

Of the three manipulators, Jaques receives the feeblest endorsement. That is, his vision is least compatible with the *telos* of the play—its direction, spirit, and outcome. It is Rosalind who is largely

Dale G. Priest is Assistant Professor in the Department of English and Foreign Languages at Lamar University. He is active in the South Central Renaissance Conference and has published essays on Marlowe, Shakespeare, and Milton.

responsible for that outcome, and Jaques will be left out. His scornful aloofness from the world is so practiced and extreme that it becomes an actual identity or fixity. His posturing is so iron-clad that it not only defines but confines him, separates him from the pastime. In the end he is invited to stay, and he does bestow his blessing—if with a touch of cynicism—on the magical pairings. But he cannot abide the community; he prefers the cave. In the effect of his withdrawal from the comic resolution, he shares with Malvolio a kinship of extremes. Malvolio, in *Twelfth Night*, proves petty and vindictive to the end and is almost totally without detachment. Jaques is irreversibly detached. Both will flee from the community as *pharmakos* figures, cast out so that the comic spirit may make conclusion. In leaving, they cast some doubt over that conclusion by suggesting its arbitrariness and artifice. Conversely, the festivity and play-making at the end undercut the seriousness of the threat represented by the outsiders.

Critics have often noted that Jaques and Duke Senior do not get along very well.[2] Only Jaques darkens the scene perceived through the Duke's rosy lenses. This is partly because Jaques's performance—his contrived, or manipulated version of the world—is a discomforting, inverted parody of the Duke's world-view. Jaques's persistent brooding on the "infected world" clashes with the Duke's optimism, to be sure; beyond that, the Duke is threatened by Jaques's posturing. The Duke wants people to be "sincere," as he believes himself to be. He is most pleased at the report of Jaques's "crying" over the wounded deer (II.i.25-70),[3] not realizing that Jaques's practiced melancholy is a far cry from sincerity. The Duke will then seek Jaques out and "cope" him when he is "full of matter." But when Jaques, admiring Touchstone, says he wants to become a satirist and heal the sick world with his detached, caustic commentary, the Duke is at odds with him again. Jaques has misjudged Touchstone's wry criticism of the passing world (II.vii.12-34), just as the Duke has misjudged Jaques's response to the wounded stag. We shall see that Touchstone, as fool and rhetorician, has the penetrating vision to see through pretense and the wit to express his critical perceptions. He is not, however, a satirist of the kind Jaques appears to admire—a misanthrope who delights in dragging man's dirtiest laundry out into full view.

Jaques, then, is clearly a manipulator of the exclusive and satiric kind. The temptation is great, in fact, to equate Jaques with Ben Jonson.[4] Jaques is original with Shakespeare, as is Touchstone; they have no parallel in Lodge's *Rosalynde*. Whether or not the playwright had Jonson in mind when he created Jaques, it is clear that

Jaques does not represent the vision recommended by the play. Certainly the Duke does not let Jaques's views go unchallenged:

> Most mischievous foul sin, in chiding sin:
> For thou thyself hast been a libertine,
> As sensual as the brutish sting itself,
> And all th' embossed sores, and headed evils,
> That thou with license of free foot hast caught,
> Wouldst thou disgorge into the general world.
> (II.vii.64-69)

The Duke is upset not only by Jaques's pessimism and his implicit threat to dump garbage, as it were, into the Duke's idyllic world, but also by his hypocrisy. The Duke alerts us to the vulnerability of the chronic unmasker, the cynic who views all conventions as social disguises which must be exposed. Wolfgang Iser notes that Jaques is himself forever alert to "double meaning," or hypocrisy, but that the double meaning Jaques purports to have seen through "might well rebound on him, for the code he keeps unmasking would also apply to himself. Excepting oneself from an otherwise universal law is indicative of . . . blindness."[5] Ultimately, Jaques's view leads to nothing, as Rosalind later reminds him (IV.i.1-38).

One important difference between Touchstone and Rosalind can be seen during the amusing and touching exchanges immediately after Orlando has been reported in the forest. When Celia tells her cousin that she found Orlando under a tree, "like a dropped acorn," Rosalind sighs, "It may well be called Jove's tree when it drops forth such fruit" (III.ii.236). Only a few lines earlier, when told that Orlando's poem had been found on a tree, Touchstone quips, "Truly, the tree yields bad fruit" (III.ii.116). The "fruit" in both cases is Orlando, or his poetry (in effect, the two are indistinguishable). The uses of the metaphor, however, are radically different. The contrast is not to be found in any great difference in wit or intelligence. Both Rosalind and Touchstone are very much alike in their powers of discrimination. But Touchstone's remark is pure wit; it is founded in thought only. Rosalind then takes the figure and infuses it with life. Her remark is spoken with thought and feeling reunited. She had earlier made it clear that Orlando's verse is truly "bad fruit" (III.ii.164-77), but she can use such a metaphor to express emotion as well—the fruit of genuine affection. Certainly Touchstone is not without feeling. There is clearly an authentic loyalty between him and the girls: "He'll go along o'er the wide world with me" Celia says just as they prepare to leave the court (I.iii.132). At the end of the play, he will press in among the "country copulatives" and marry Audrey, the country wench.[6] He has some reservations and an obvious measure of detachment about this (III.iii.90-94); still, he refers to his bride as "an ill-favored thing, sir, but mine own" (V.iv.58). Nevertheless, Touchstone's profession, and his primary function in the play, is that of the wise fool; his livelihood is essentially the detachment of his wit. He is the leveler, the designated critic who goes about puncturing pretense and testing this golden world for "fool's gold." He can parody Silvius's romantic agony with the story of his own passion for Jane Smile and how he would kiss the "cow's dugs that her pretty chopt hands had milked" (II.iv.46-56). He can also ridicule Orlando's stylized love poetry as "the very false gallop of verses" and compose his own priceless piece in response (III.ii.100-12).

Touchstone is a master of the ancient art of *oratio*—the purposeful use of mannered prose—and so illustrates a pervasive Renaissance interest in this use of a manipulative rhetoric employed to disarm or otherwise persuade an audience. The use of such discourse has its roots in Cicero,[7] and Socrates before him, and finds its Renaissance culmination in the *Encomium Moriae* (1509). Erasmus creates a persona who uses *oratio* masterfully to transvalue the meaning of the word "folly," who herself is folly transvalued as a source of wisdom, and who manipulates her audience with irony and word-play. Such is the folly and rhetorical skill Touchstone inherits in *As You Like It*[8]—even if, for the most part, he uses *oratio* for its own sake and without the sense of purpose which animates Rosalind. Still, Shakespeare has created in Touchstone a "master stylist and wit [whose] verbal adaptability gives him his astonishing range" (Young, p. 52). He confronts old Corin, for instance, with rhetorical proof that Corin and all his pastoral kind are damned for never having used good, courtly manners (III.ii.32-85). Later, he browbeats the poor bumpkin William with "figures in rhetoric" to show that William's wit is not as "pretty" as he thinks it is—showing him up, in effect, in front of Audrey (V.i.10-57). Then comes Touchstone's *pièce de resistance*, the extended discourse on the "degrees of the lie" (V.iv.43-103). Here he holds forth on the rules that govern quarreling about alleged lies and concludes that all malice can finally be avoided by a judicious use of the subjunctive: "Your If is the only peacemaker; much virtue in If" (V.iv.103). Shakespeare's comedies often recommend the use of manipulative, hypothetical modes as the best way to deal with real experience. But Touchstone's discourse as instructive model is weakened by the detachment of the *oratio* and by the removal of the performance from the world of actual human experience.[9] Rosalind will provide us a better model; her manipulative skills are generated by passion and directed by human needs. So the fool emerges as a somewhat distorted image of Rosalind.[10] He shares her powers of discrimination, but not her balanced personality. He is heavy on thought and light on feeling. Still I must think that Shakespeare took great delight in bringing Touchstone to life.

Rosalind is the negotiator in *As You Like It*, and that goes beyond the familiar definition denoting someone who deals with others in order to get things done or arrive at agreement. Rosalind does that, too. Like any effective negotiator, she has a goal, an awareness of conflicting claims on her attention, and a gift for tentativeness in policy and action. But the term is especially appropriate for Rosalind because of the etymology. The root of "negotiate" is *otium*, a classical term that variously denotes the pastoral ideal: leisure, contentment, the good life, and so on.[11] It also includes—especially for the Renaissance—the ideal of fulfilled, romantic love. *Otium* is advertised in the Duke's translation of Arden into a "golden world"; it is explicit in Amiens's music—especially the famous song about life under the greenwood tree (II.v.1-8, 38-45). *Negotium*, conversely, is "non-leisure" or business, a Ciceronian ideal antithetical to the Horatian *otium*.[12] In regard to Rosalind's aggressive business in Arden, the term is obviously appropriate to her. It also fits because her public business in Arden is to appear to be opposed to, or critical of, the very values she pursues—those associated with *otium* and the pastoral ideal. The true enemies of *otium* are ambition (shunned by the pastoral poet) and the aspiring mind. The enemies of the pastoral ideal in *As You Like It* are Oliver and Duke Frederick—overreachers of sorts, whose will to power and lordship over others provides the tension, the opposition that activates the drama. Their attitudes and activities are real and assertive; their imperative drive recalls the metaphysics of the tragic mode. If *otium* is the opposite of willful ambition, it is no less real in *As You Like It*. If not imperative, it is still engaging. As the goal that directs and impels dramatic activity, or as an actual state variously realized in the play, *otium* provides a core of reality, an ideal in relation to which the negotiator may act or proceed in various ways.

To illustrate we may recall Petruchio's "peace, love, and quiet life"—an ideal to lend meaning and direction to the supposings of that arch-negotiator of *The Taming of the Shrew* (V.ii.108). Such an ideal or goal clearly animates Rosalind as well, and it is more serious and perceivable than Petruchio's; we see it in her "fathoms-deep" love for Orlando. In *As You Like It*, the most specific representation of *otium*, in the literary sense, is Corin. Corin is a shepherd in a pastoral play, and to that extent he is a prop in a conventional mode. Still, he is older and wiser than the stylized Silvius, and there is an authenticity in his perception of himself and his place in the world: "Sir, I am a true laborer: I earn that I eat, get that I wear, owe no man hate, envy no man's happiness, glad of other men's good, content with my harm, and the greatest of my pride is to see my ewes graze and my lambs suck" (III.ii.73-77). This is an engaging statement—the simple profession of a man in whom the pastoral ideal is alive and well. Corin is not a character with much dimension, but he is honest and gracious. When Rosalind and her party arrive hungry and weary in Arden, Corin will do what he can to help them (II.iv.75-100). So, Touchstone has no actual quarrel with him; he acknowledges that the old shepherd is a "natural philosopher." Yet precisely because Touchstone recognizes in Corin an ideal—an unpretentious exemplar—he cannot resist exercising on the rustic his highly-developed skills as negotiator. I have suggested that the ensuing exercise is purely rhetorical; Touchstone's professionalism at this sort of thing is a key, again, to the difference between him and Rosalind. The fool's negotiations (certainly until he meets Audrey) are pure skill; they lack the motive and cue that move his mistress. Jaques also has potential as a negotiator, as he shows in his "ducdame" version of Amiens's song about pastoral idealism (II.v.50-57). The equivocal vision is wasted, however, because of Jaques's self-involvement and his excessive commitment to his own performance.

The balanced vision of Rosalind recommends her as the true negotiator of *As You Like It.* She acts "as if" to conceal purpose and feeling for tactical reasons; she also acts "as if" in order to infuse humanity into a world stifled by convention and to a great extent devoid of real life. The most obvious and most delightful instance of Rosalind's negotiations in Arden is her practice on Orlando (III.ii.315-456; IV.i.38-204). The scenario is familiar enough. Rosalind, as Ganymede, will help Orlando cure his lovesickness for Rosalind by pretending that she is Rosalind and by having him woo her. She will then portray the fickleness of woman so convincingly that he will see his folly and wish to have nothing more to do with the madness called love. Now this play-within-a-play business is mostly subterfuge. Almost everything about it is manipulated, contrary-to-fact. Rosalind is not really Ganymede, nor is Ganymede really Rosalind in the scenario. It is likewise clear that the real Rosalind does not wish to scoff at love or to purge Orlando's love for her, nor does Orlando really want his sanity restored: "I would not be cur'd, youth" (III.ii.425), he says when Rosalind promises guaranteed medicine. All is hypothetical.

At the same time, an audience is in touch with an underlying tissue of reality in Rosalind's genuine affection. The emotional component of the scenario is disguised, inaccessible to Orlando. But for us, the disguise actually serves to highlight the emotion through dramatic irony: our understanding of Rosalind runs deeper than Orlando's. We have already witnessed a private confession of Rosalind's feelings (III.ii.236), and we hear another one after Orlando departs following his second session with his "counselor": "My affection hath an unknown bottom, like the bay of Portugal" (IV.i.207). In the playlet itself we are alert to hidden confessions that draw us in. When Orlando wishes he could make Ganymede believe how much he loves his Rosalind, we have a telling response. Ganymede answers, but the real Rosalind speaks through the mask: "Me believe it? You may as soon make her that you love believe it, which I warrant she is apter to do than to confess she does" (III.ii.387-89). Poised in its response to this interplay of the real and the hypothetical, an audience is encouraged to infer meaning.

What is the meaning or value of Rosalind's negotiation here? I believe that Rosalind is using these manipulative tactics for three reasons. First, she simply finds it gratifying to do so. Framing her feelings in a theatrical mode gives her the double joy of both primary and vicarious experience. In another context, she calls this "feeding her love" (III.iv.58). In the company of Orlando, she can stand outside herself, as it were, and savor his professions of love with the satisfaction one can only get from overhearing someone say nice things about him to another person. The device prolongs and intensifies her pleasure in the same way that anticipation enhances a long-awaited, happy event. Second, the negotiation is designed to educate Orlando. He can be a sensible enough fellow, as he demonstrates in fending off Jaques's barbs when Monsieur Melancholy tries to belittle him and his love songs (III.ii.253-94). With regard to his feelings for Rosalind, however, Orlando's good sense is replaced by convention and stylized behavior. He lacks the element of detachment that gives Rosalind a happier and more clear-eyed understanding of her own emotions. Rosalind tries to teach him a bit of detachment by forcing him to dramatize himself in the playlet she construes. The attempt is similar to Petruchio's efforts to educate Kate in *The Taming of the Shrew*, in that both mentors use manipulative "supposes" to enlighten a subject who is mired in unreflecting behavior: Kate is excessively "real" and Orlando is too artificial. Rosalind's efforts are less "noisy" than Petruchio's, and the results are less dramatic. Four times Orlando forgets that he is supposed to be playing a part (III.ii.433; IV.i.110, 157, 197); and his response to Rosalind's lesson that "Men have died . . . but not for love" shows he has a bit more to learn: "I would not have my right Rosalind of this mind, for I protest her frown might kill me" (IV.i.109-10).[13] But the third and most important reason for Rosalind's use of a manipulative, hypothetical mode here is that it gives her power and control over her own feelings; it allows Rosalind to direct her experience as a playwright would his script. Rosalind's real goal is a happy integration of her real experience— marriage with Orlando. In her play world as well we see her directing the hypothetical activity in a way that culminates in the mock wedding between Orlando and his "Rosalind." There, at one of the most delightful moments in the play, we catch a glimpse of the happy girl behind the contrived role. Anticipating the formal question from the "priest" (Celia), Rosalind impulsively says, "I might ask you for your commission, but I do take thee, Orlando, for my husband. There's a girl goes before the priest, and certainly a woman's thought runs before her actions" (IV.i.138-41). Dramatizing herself as the impulsive girl allows her to be the impulsive girl and still remain in control of the scenario.

Probably the most interesting and most misunderstood of Rosalind's negotiations is her intervention in the Silvius-Phebe affair (III.v.1-80). Having overheard Phebe's icy rejection of Silvius's protestations of love, Rosalind jumps in to act her part (as Ganymede) in the scenario. Ralph Berry sees Rosalind's intrusion as an example of her will to master or to dominate certain others whom she finds disturbing in the play. Seeing herself in Phebe's antiromantic attitude, Rosalind is subtly threatened, the interpretation goes, and she is compelled to browbeat the shepherdess with one-upmanship.[14] Most of the evidence, however, seems to point to Rosalind's sense of purposeful play. When Corin, at the end of the preceding scene, invites her and Celia to come witness the encounter between the "lovers," Rosalind makes a telling remark:

> O, come, let us remove,
> The sight of lovers feedeth those in love.
> Bring us to this sight and you shall say
> I'll prove a busy actor in their play.
>
> (III.iv.57-60)

The lines are a fine instance of Shakespeare's simultaneous effects. Rosalind's confession of her own love is "real," while her allusion to theatrics reminds us that her action will be of a hypothetical nature. We are signaled that Rosalind will use a contrary-to-fact pose both to conceal and assert her own reality in a negotiation with another aspect of Arden.

Rosalind's lecture to Silvius and Phebe, then, is not real in the sense of the overbearing assertion of Rosalynde in Lodge's story. Shakespeare's Rosalind says,

> You foolish shepherd, wherefore do you follow her
> Like foggy south, puffing with wind and rain?
> You are a thousand times a properer man
> Than she a woman. 'Tis such fools as you
> That makes the world full of ill-favored children.
> 'Tis not her glass, but you, that flatters her,
> And out of you she sees herself more proper
> Than any of her lineaments can show her.
> But, mistress, know yourself, down on your knees,
> And thank heaven, fasting, for a good man's love;
> For I must tell you friendly in your ear,
> Sell when you can, you are not for all markets.
> Cry the man mercy, love him, take his offer.
>
> (III.v.49-61)

Rosalind's simultaneous detachment and involvement in this affair is another departure from his source made by Shakespeare, in keeping with his heroine's manipulative tactics. In Lodge, Rosalynde is "incensed," unable "to brook the cruelty of Phebe."[15] In Shakespeare's play, Rosalind is a player, incorporating both artifice and feeling in her negotiative art. Her objective is to infuse both sense and sensibility into the affair of Silvius and Phebe; in short, she will try to educate them while feeding her own love through theatrical participation in the love game. Rosalind seeks to impose a sense of balance upon the extremes of convention and hard reality represented in this scene, and she does this by reminding both parties of the relativity of time and beauty.

Silvius is a cardboard cut-out of the pastoral lover who fancies that the one "good life" lies somewhere behind Phebe's scornful eyes. Still he reminds Rosalind of her own affection for Orlando, as she had confessed in her earlier response to the slighted shepherd: "Alas, poor shepherd, searching of thy wound, / I have by hard adventure found mine own" (II.iv.44-45). She can "feed" her own love by helping Silvius see things more clearly, which is what she wants to do for Orlando as well. This educational process requires detachment, as well as empathy, in both cases. It requires the kind of manipulative power Feste uses on Orsino when the clown adapts his songs both to accommodate and to satirize the Duke in *Twelfth Night*. All three of the gentlemen—Orsino, Silvius, and Orlando—are essentially narrative. That is to say their identities are stories, stylized presentations fashioned from Ovid, Petrarch, pastoral complaint, and the manuals of courtly love. In *As You Like It* Rosalind not only knows this about Silvius and Orlando, but she understands them on an emotional level as well. This advantage gives her power, which she chooses to use apparently at their expense, but ultimately on their behalf. She will improvise upon their narratives with a narrative of her own.[16] Hers will take the form of stern counsel which, for Silvius, is designed to help him confront his own mindless behavior and to help him see the source and relative nature of female beauty.

Phebe represents a different extreme, but her single-minded antiromanticism is equally vain and without life. Rosalynde's rebuke of Phebe in Lodge's story is noteworthy in this regard: "Take heed, fair nymph, that in despising love you be not overreach'd with love, and in shaking off all, shape yourself to your own shadow, and so with Narcissus prove passionate yet unpitied" (p. 781). For Shakespeare, too, Phebe is a negative "overreacher," an enemy of *otium* in her willfulness. Her literalist response to Silvius's complaint that she kills him with her eyes would appear similar to Rosalind's own answer, as Ganymede, to Orlando's protest that he will die if Rosalind rejects him (IV.i.106-107). Phebe says sharply, "Lie not, to say mine eyes are murtherers! / Now show the wound mine eye hath made in thee / . . . I am sure there is no force in eyes / That can do hurt" (III.v.19-27). The harshness of Phebe's rebuff of Silvius sets her apart from the conventional coy mistress. She is not leading him on by pretending to be disinterested; she is trying to get rid of him. Rosalind's response to Orlando, that men do not die for love, is a tactic—part of her enterprise to cure him by counsel. The "truth" of her argument does not reflect her real concerns. The ostensibly cold fact about death for love belies her actual interest in keeping Orlando's love for her very much alive. Phebe, however, is serious in a straightforward way. She is engrossed in a rigid attitude that leaves room for no love but narcissism. Phebe also needs curing. The affliction is the opposite of Orlando's, but the medicine is fundamentally the same—a good dose of relativism. Single-mindedness is the enemy of contentment. Here, as elsewhere in Shakespearean comedy, the message is reinforced by the audience's awareness of the relative nature of role and identity. Phebe has a firmer identity than

Rosalind, but Phebe is the unhappy one. Rosalind uses her role as access to joy.

Rosalind's real feelings, then, are not the whole issue in the scene, since she is negotiating from behind the Ganymede mask. Her conclusion—"Down on your knees, / And thank heaven, fasting, for a good man's love"—is neither angry assertion nor sincere advice. For Rosalind to advise abject submission would not square with her own experience. The statement, rather, is an optative conclusion, the logical upshot of her argument. It is a tactic designed to jolt Phebe into alternate ways of seeing, to allow for the possibility of real affection. I am reminded, in Ganymede's advice, of Kate's lecture to the women at the end of *The Shrew*. I have compared Rosalind to Petruchio; Kate, after her conversion, likewise becomes an aggressive negotiator like them. Rosalind's motives are not Kate's; the former is "feeding her love," while the latter is winning a bet. But the manipulative postures are similar, and Rosalind can no more be held precisely accountable for her advice than can Katherina. Both speak "as if" they mean what they say. The result of the negotiations, in Rosalind's case, turns out to be an instance of comic irony. Phebe both misses the point and takes Ganymede's advice too literally. She surrenders to love surely enough, but she falls for Ganymede, not Silvius. Here is another of those reversals by which Shakespeare calls our attention to the fluidity of theatrical experience. Phebe, suddenly in love with Ganymede, has been cured of her intransigence; she is not really an enemy of love after all. Nor, an audience feels sure, will she "really" be in love with Ganymede for long, for it is clear that Rosalind is in firm control of this play world.

Rosalind's steadfast affection, together with her magical powers as playwright-negotiator, will result, finally, in all "earthly things made even." The magic word in this transformation—as in the play as a whole—is "if," the great peacemaker. Using the hypothetical to forge real happiness for all concerned, Rosalind asks Phebe, "You say you'll marry me, if I be willing? . . . But if you do refuse to marry me, / You'll give yourself to this most faithful shepherd?" Phebe agrees. And then to Silvius, "You say that you'll have Phebe, if she will?" Silvius agrees with enthusiasm (V.iv.11-17). The union of Phebe and Silvius, and the happiness of Orlando and Rosalind herself, await only the magic moment when Rosalind's "as if" identity becomes her real one. As she leaves to prepare herself for her bridegroom, Rosalind summarizes the conditional promises: "[To Phebe]: I will marry you, if ever I marry woman, and I'll be married tomorrow. [To Orlando]: I will satisfy you if ever I satisfied man, and you shall be married tomorrow. [To Silvius]: I will content you, if what please you contents you, and you shall be married tomorrow" (V.ii.113-18). Here is a set of assertions which the audience recognizes as true and not true at the same time. The promises both will and will not be fulfilled, depending upon the level of reality we choose as a reference point—whom we choose to identify with the first person voice of the promises. Ultimately, the voice is Shakespeare's, promising a magic we can believe in. The ending of *As You Like It* is both contrary-to-fact and alive with joy by virtue of Shakespeare's art. Rosalind, the playwright's "conjurer," uses her power to crystallize genuine emotion out of a highly contrived scenario. After she reveals herself to the company, there follows a remarkable exchange orchestrated around "if" (V.iv.118-24). Six times in seven lines, "if" becomes real happiness for Duke Senior and the lovers. Then Hymen enters to "make conclusion / of these most strange events," to join eight pairs of hands "if truth holds true contents." It does in *As You Like It,* because here, as elsewhere in Shakespeare's comedy, "if" and "truth" are one. And in the end, all are content, thanks largely to a heroine whose benign manipulations clearly have Shakespeare's blessing.

NOTES

[1]This useful generalization about comedy emerges out of Northrop Frye's comments on myth and archetype in *Anatomy of Criticism: Four Essays* (Princeton: Princeton Univ. Press, 1957), p. 177. For a discussion of the function of inclusive and exclusive personalities in romantic and satiric comedy, see Mark Bracher, "Contrary Notions of Identity in *As You Like It*," *SEL* 24 (1984):225-27.

[2]See, for instance, A. D. Nuttall, "Two Unassimilable Men," in M. Bradbury and D. Palmer, eds., *Shakespearean Comedy*, Stratford-upon-Avon Studies 14 (1972):210.

[3]All quotations of Shakespeare's plays are from *The Riverside Shakespeare*, ed. G. Blakemore Evans (Boston: Houghton, 1974).

[4]John Dover Wilson finds, for him, a more likely caricature of Jonson in Nym of *Henry V* and *The Merry Wives of Windsor*. See *Shakespeare's Happy Comedies* (Evanston: Northwestern Univ. Press, 1962), p. 153.

[5]Wolfgang Iser, "The Dramatization of Double Meaning in Shakespeare's *As You Like It*," *Theatre Journal* 35 (1983):314.

[6]Some critics choose to stress this aspect of Touchstone's personality and function. Harold Jenkins calls our attention to the fool's role as burlesque parodist by stressing the "material fool" in Touchstone—the realist, the "timekeeper," and even the "lusty, animal man." See "*As You Like It*," *ShS* 8 (1955):48-49.

[7]This is the definition I will use in my argument. There are numerous meanings and connotations associated with this versatile word. See P. G. W. Glare, ed., *Oxford Latin Dictionary* (Oxford: Clarendon Press, 1982), pp. 1262-63. On the power of oratio, Cicero says, "But so potent is that Eloquence (oratio) rightly styled by an excellent maker, . . . that she can not only support the sinking and bend the upstanding, but, like a good and brave commander, can even make prisoner a resisting antagonist." From *De Oratore* II.44.187 ff., in *Loeb Classical Library*, trans. E. W. Sutton (Cambridge, Mass.: Harvard Univ. Press, 1959), p. 333. This "making prisoner" is essentially what Touchstone does with his "antagonists" in Arden. David Young notes that in writing Touchstone into the play, "Shakespeare was inspired by his success with Falstaff and by his new clown, Robert Armin." See *The Heart's Forest: A Study of Shakespeare's Pastoral Plays* (New Haven: Yale Univ. Press, 1972), p. 52.

[8]On the "wise fool" motif as it appears in classical literature, in Erasmus, and in Shakespeare, see Robert H. Goldsmith, *Wise Fools in Shakespeare* (East Lansing: Michigan State Univ. Press, 1963), pp. 11-14. On Touchstone as wise fool, see pp. 47-51.

[9]According to C. L. Barber, Touchstone's verbal forays against Corin and William are not the work of a satirist mocking the real world, but a mocking of pastoral innocence. "Shakespeare's point of view," he says, "was not medieval. But his clown and fool comedy is a response, a counter-movement, to artistic idealization, as medieval burlesque was a response to the ingrained idealism of the culture." See *Shakespeare's Festive Comedy: A Study of Dramatic Form and its Relation to Social Custom* (Princeton: Princeton Univ. Press, 1959), p. 229.

[10]Critical views of Touchstone vary considerably. On the more positive side, Bracher argues that Touchstone's folly "leads to a greater relatedness among selves"; his irony produces humility, which opens the door to tolerance and love (pp. 233-34). Chris Hassel, arguing from an even more sharply defined theological perspective, has a different view. He admits that Touchstone

frequently alludes to Erasmian statements concerning the wisdom of folly, but he contends that Touchstone is naive, lacking in humility. Therefore he is not the wise fool that Feste is in *Twelfth Night*. See *Faith and Folly in Shakespeare's Romantic Comedies* (Athens : Univ. of Georgia Press, 1980), p. 110.

[11]Hallett Smith, *Elizabethan Poetry: A Study in Convention, Meaning, and Expression* (Cambridge, Mass.: Harvard Univ. Press, 1952), p. 2.

[12]The tension between these two classical standards is felt throughout the literature of the Renaissance and especially in humanistic thought. See Isabel Rivers, *Classical and Christian Ideas in English Renaissance Poetry: A Student's Guide* (London and Boston: G. Allen and Unwin, 1979), pp. 137-38.

[13]Rosalind does make some headway with Orlando, however. The contrived love game frustrates him and, if nothing else, tires him of artifice. "I can live no longer by thinking," he at last confesses. In Rosalind's reply, we sense that make-believe is about to become an image of real love: "I will weary you then no longer with idle talking" (V.ii.50-51). Kent van den Berg notes, "If Rosalind's deception of Orlando acts out his own self-deception, it also helps him to overcome it. The activity of pretending that Ganymede is Rosalind encourages in Orlando an awareness that the actual Rosalind is more real than the rarefied mistress of his Petrarchan fantasies." See "Theatrical Fiction and the Reality of Love in *As You Like It*," *PMLA* 90 (1975):891.

[14]Ralph Berry, *Shakespeare's Comedies: Explorations in Form* (Princeton: Princeton Univ. Press, 1972), pp. 183-85.

[15]Thomas Lodge, *Rosalynde. Euphues' golden legacie*, in H. E. Rollins and H. B. Baker, eds., *The Renaissance in England: Nondramatic Prose and Verse of the Sixteenth Century* (Boston: Heath, 1954), p. 781.

[16]I owe this observation to Stephen Greenblatt's analysis of Iago's improvisation of power in *Othello*. Iago sees Othello for what he is, a story which the story-teller takes seriously and believes is his own or his true self. "But Iago knows that an identity that has been fashioned as a story can be unfashioned, refashioned, inscribed anew in a different narrative." See *Renaissance Self-Fashioning: From More to Shakespeare* (Chicago: Univ. of Chicago Press, 1980), p. 238. This kind of awareness and just such a strategy might be said to describe Rosalind as well, but with some differences. Rosalind has motive, whereas Iago has only strategy perforce. Iago's strategy is entirely self-serving, whereas Rosalind's serves others as well.

SEL 28 (1988)
ISSN 0039-3657

The Confusion of Self and Role in Chapman's *Bussy D'Ambois*

DEBORAH MONTUORI

Criticism of George Chapman's *Bussy D'Ambois* is, on the whole, so diverse and dissatisfying that it does little more than validate the fact that this is indeed one of the most perplexing, disjunctive, and disturbing plays of the early Jacobean period. The reader of such criticism, pondering attempts to wedge the play into theories of Christian morality, Christian humanism, neo-Stoicism, Herculean epic, anti-Machiavellianism, rhetorical dialogue, supernatural knowledge, natural noblesse, and exploitative melodrama,[1] becomes aware of an uneasiness that is much akin to that experienced upon first reading the play itself. *Bussy D'Ambois* simply does not fit the given patterns. It is only too easy to deduce that Chapman's protagonist is, either directly or indirectly, a failure, that Bussy's failure ultimately makes the play a failure, and that therefore any critical theory applied to *Bussy D'Ambois* may be excused for its own failings. Selective study can partially fit the play into the shapes of all these theoretical conceptions, but the misfitted points and strained seams will eventually wear or glare. While clues helpful to understanding the play's social, philosophical, and moral milieu can be gleaned from these various theories, it seems to me that they stray too far from the character and dialogue of Bussy himself. The true tragedy, I believe, lies not in his maladaptation to the society defined by the French court nor in the gradual corruption of his character, but in Bussy's mistaken perception of himself.

I do not mean to discount scholarly work—most of it, however, written before 1965—which probes Chapman's interest in the classics and philosophy. Eugene Waith, for example, has done much to clarify the heroic role Bussy attempts to fill in accordance with the

Deborah Montuori is a Mellon Fellow in the University of Michigan's English Language and Literature doctoral program.

Renaissance concept of *virtú*;[2] Robert Ornstein, if one delves beneath the moralistic surface of his argument, enlightens the uninitiated about neo-Stoicism and the revival of Senecan tragedy;[3] and Ennis Rees traces the persistence of Chapman's philosophical bent and the pursuit of a higher truth, primarily through examples from the poetry.[4] But these citations only serve to illustrate the major problem with this line of criticism: it relies too heavily upon "proof" outside of the text itself, and while it enriches our approach to this densely written play, it does not provide the answers for which we yearn. *Bussy D'Ambois* is not pure poetry, it is not a philosophical or religious tract, it is not even a Senecan closet drama. It is, rather, a theatrical piece, designed for performance, not solitary contemplation.

Surprisingly, none of these critics have addressed the play's original performance sphere, which might elucidate Chapman's intentions. From 1600-1608, Chapman was employed to write plays for the Children of the Chapel at Blackfriars,[5] and it is likely that *Bussy D'Ambois,* entered in the Stationers' Register in 1607 but probably written and performed several years earlier,[6] was presented by this boy company.[7] While the youth of the actors would enhance Bussy's purity and naiveté, it would certainly also undermine his oft-mentioned *virtú*. One can safely assume that the boys of the company concentrated not upon abstract theory or political allegory, but upon action and characterization. It is Waith's contention, however, that Chapman, following the leads of Ficino and Pico della Mirandola, believed the poet should conceal a higher truth in his work which would be apparent only to the elite.[8] Indeed, Alfred Harbage concedes that because of its court connections, the Children of the Chapel probably played to a more "select" audience—aristocratic, educated, erudite.[9] But one must consider the effects of repeated attacks upon court morality and fashion, the arbitrariness of the law, a weak king, and, above all, the manipulation of "policy" upon such an audience. It is naive to assume that these sophisticated playgoers would identify these flaws as peculiar to the *French* court.[10] Again, in the mouths of boy actors, the seriousness of such attacks is lessened and they become instead a knowing, irreverent wink at the audience members' own experience. Policy, consistently labelled as Chapman's villain,[11] becomes no villain at all but merely the way of the world. Politic words are the human equivalent of the earth's natural exhalations, and they contain a similar power to conceal, to destroy, and to inspire action, rendering life itself nothing but "a courtier's breath." In this light, Bussy's posturings are absurd. Clues in the text reinforce this idea, for Bussy's only consistency seems to be in confusing what he is with what he would be.

Enough heat has been generated by Stephen Greenblatt's *Renaissance Self-Fashioning;* to add to it, at any rate, would go against my intention of keeping my finger on the text. Greenblatt's theory is a valid one for examining how an author creates an image, reflecting and reshaping a social stance through his work. Relevant to this discussion, however, Greenblatt's introduction touches upon the issue of two selves—the real, inward self and the outward role, self- or socially-imposed.[12] It is this confusion of "self" in *Bussy D'Ambois* that I propose to address.

It cannot be denied that Chapman relies heavily upon epic traditions in the depiction of Bussy D'Ambois. In *The Herculean Hero,* Eugene Waith presents a solid case for that model, noting parallels between the two heroes and citing Chapman's adoption of passages from Seneca's *Hercules Oetaeus.*[13] Still, the inconsistencies of time, place, action, and character suggest the epic mode itself as a flawed misconception in the context of *Bussy D'Ambois.* In the French court, the arrogance, pride, passion, impetuosity, and force of Bussy's classic *virtú* is applauded in the abstract, but in reality, it is far removed from behavior acceptable in this sphere and can only be perverted or destroyed. Furthermore, those who most praise his innate superiority are characters whose own motives, judgments, and natures are questionable. The ineffective King Henry, for example, describes his own court as a stable yet does not command the power or respect to set it back into order, and he rules, as the Guise points out (II.ii.24-29), according to circumstance and whim, not by law. Chapman makes it clear that the security of the throne is dependent upon the backing of the French nobles. In the king's service, Bussy's fearless *virtú* finds little application beyond expressing the ruler's hostilities towards his own chief supporters, who are ultimately beyond his direct control; in this regard, Bussy's role becomes allied to that of court jester. The king, then, can hardly be considered an exemplar of nobility whose conception of Bussy we can accept as infallible. Even less reliable is the friar, whose ghost delivers the final Herculean eulogy to the slain Bussy. He has perverted his holy office by acting as a pander to a married woman and conjuring up spirits from the depths of hell. While Waith relates the latter to Pico della Mirandola's interest in the supernatural as consistent with a neo-Platonic quest for knowledge,[14] we must consider once again the dramatic context: audiences caught up in the play's performance would be more likely to equate the Friar's role with that of Marlowe's Faustus and with contemporary anti-Catholic sentiment than with the work of Italian scholars, and his actions undermine his reliability as a judge of Bussy's superior nature. Monsieur is most aware of the very ordinary passions and desires beneath Bussy's surface and determines to appeal to his self-delusions in order to master him. The similarities and interdepend-dence between the two, discussed at length below, are primary factors in the exposure of the neo-mythic hero. Chapman's use of the epic mode and classical allusions, particularly in the poetic speeches of weak, perverse, or corrupted characters, therefore reinforces the reality of Bussy's self-delusion. It is not his fall but the inability to recognize himself, his true possibilities and his limitations, which give the play its tragic structure.

Bussy's discontented opening speech reveals at once his struggle to set himself above society and, simultaneously, to become an active part of it. He views successful courtiers as "unskilled statuaries" who have shaped themselves into outwardly heroic forms which "[w]ithin are nought but mortar, flint and lead."[15] The image is one of drossy matter, but a matter of enduring quality compared to the bleak metaphor that follows:

> Man is but a torch borne in the wind; a dream
> But of a shadow, summed up with all his substances.
> (I.i.18-19)

Here, the confusion between "I" and "they" becomes apparent. If Bussy truly believed this doctrine, he would not feel so strongly the neglect of the court, but clearly his dreams of shaping himself into a more viable, durable form drive him on. By line 28, his dissociation with his fellow men dissolves as the pronoun "they" is conspicu-ously replaced by a recurrent "we," which is thoroughly enmeshed in a struggle for fame and glory. Ironically, Bussy's assertion of ultimate reliance upon virtue is immediately followed by the stage direction, "He lies down." Heroic virtue indicates active manliness, the rational plan pursued to fulfillment; even moral virtue is active in its constant opposition to evil. Bussy's assumption of a passive, contemplative posture expresses a discrepancy between the inward and outward selves. Further, it is an open, undefended position which leaves him susceptible to Monsieur's temptations. The alteration of his original heroic ideal begins as the man beneath the mythic surface is detected.

Bussy and Monsieur are frequently dichotomized as the play's antagonists, the one embodying virtue, the other policy. The text itself, however, specifically in its parallel, repetitive language, reveals the two as startlingly similar beneath superficial appearances, almost to the point of needing one another to create a complete man. Under Bussy's protestations against court policy, Monsieur discerns his inward ambitions for material profit and personal fame: "None loathes the world so much, nor loves to scoff it, / But gold and grace with surfeit of it" (I.i.52-53). His appeal is craftily made, however, not to the denied avaricious nature, but to Bussy's projected self-righteous image:

> so our lives
> In acts exemplary not only to win
> Ourselves good names, but to others give
> Matter for virtuous deeds, by which we live.
>
> (I.i.77-81)

The successful baiting of Bussy's delusion is evidenced by his exaggerated belief that he is personally guided by fate. He speaks of a man's rise by merit as determined by Time's wheel, convincing himself that it is the moment, not Monsieur's persuasive rhetoric, which has moved him.

The two men are also alike in their basic lack of purpose. Neither has a well-defined plan of action (a failure of the heroic model, in Bussy's case), both tending to drift from one personal gratification to the next. As heir to the throne, it is Monsieur's intention to ally with powerful men like Bussy in order to secure his position in a country recently torn by rebellion; he voices no sinister plot to murder the king, although Bussy infers as much in Act III. Similarly, Bussy moves into the court sphere with no purpose other than to prove virtue as effective as policy in attaining one's desires, but the ends at which he aims are unspecified and seem to develop impulsively as his passions are aroused. This is far removed from the heroic ideal uniting *virtù* with a rational plan of action, moving toward a positive end which is not merely self-serving but also effects a general good. The court seems too small a sphere for true heroic ideals; but Bussy's ideals are equally small in relation to his grandiose behavior.

As closely as Monsieur hopes to rely upon Bussy's natural prowess, Bussy, in turn, relies upon Monsieur's mastery of court policy. His insulting approach to the ladies of the court and the slaughter wrought in the ensuing duel have brought the stables into the rooms of state, indeed, illustrating Henry's affirmation that "Pure innovation is more gross than error" (I.ii.35). Aware that his professed *virtù* does not bear the force of righteousness under the law, Bussy depends upon Monsieur to secure his pardon through the "policy" he himself lacks. The appeal is made upon the basis that reputation is more sacred than life itself and that "full men" in defense of their honor are instruments of justice that keep other men in check. Pardon granted, Bussy takes up Monsieur's strain, eloquently proclaiming himself beyond social law while diplomatically pacifying the king:

> since I am free,
> Offending no just law, let no law make
> By any wrong it does, my life her slave;
> Let me be king myself, as man was made,
> And do a justice that exceeds the law;
> If my wrong pass the power of single valor
> To right and expiate, then be you my king,
> And do a right, exceeding Law and Nature.
> Who to himself is law, no law doth need,
> Offends no king, and is a king indeed.
>
> (II.i.194-204)

Bussy's split with Monsieur is initiated by this speech as he firmly establishes his own anti-policy. It is not by virtue but by a novel posture of naturalness that Bussy rises in court, a means no less politic and artificial than that he condemns in others. His delusion of superior virtue is primarily expressed through verbal denunciations and reckless social behaviors, the outer role diminished by its own small sphere and petty ends. He has become little more than a new form of the statuary he belittled in his opening speech. By transferring his dependence from Monsieur to the king, he validates his sponsor's original opinion of the inward man: vain, disgruntled, and self-seeking, and his pose of self-sufficiency has significantly eroded. The bitter exchange between hero and former patron at the conclusion of Act III reveals a recognition of the self in one another; the speeches are, in effect, interchangeable:

> *Monsieur:* . . . in thy valor th'art like other naturals
> That have strange gifts in nature, but no soul
> Diffused quite through, to make them of a piece,
> But stop at humors, that are most absurd,
> Childish, villainous than that hackster, whore,
> Slave, cutthroat, tinker's botch compared before.
>
> (357-62)

Bussy: . . . your political head is the cursed font
Of all the violence, rapine, cruelty,
Tyranny, and atheism flowing through the realm
. . . .
you are utterly without a soul.
(401-11)

It is this complete destruction of their separate delusions of the self, the other, and of the degree of control each holds over their relationship which turns these mutual pawns into enemies. The physical strength and firmness of mind Monsieur had hoped to unite with his own political machinations have themselves become a diplomatic entity, and he is only too aware of the lost potential.

In his relations with Tamyra, Bussy is more successful in maintaining his delusions, perhaps because the role of the courtly lover relies heavily upon a structure of pretense. For Bussy, it is an outward, artificial role that transforms lust into a private game of service. His words, however, reveal that he is conscious of the delusion and comfortable in it. He never speaks directly of love, willingly accepts the pandering friar's proffered "art" and "cunning," belabors the importance of keeping a good reputation with the world, and downplays Tamyra's own guilt. His discourse on sin (III.i.18-42) rationalizes lust and ridicules remorse in a manner parallel to Monsieur's attack upon Tamyra's defense of her honor (II.ii.60-68), again emphasizing the importance of the gratification of passion that is the self-centered goal of each man. As the affair deepens, the harsh Bussy who verbally accosted the Duchess of Guise in Act I easily slips into an eloquent, artificial, public rhetoric. His elaborate conceit of women as the earthly moons under whose influence their lovers' emotions are controlled (IV.i.7-20) is nothing if not the mannered language of the court, another version of the "policy" he so frequently denounces. When the affair is discovered, both Behemoth and Tamyra urge Bussy to employ policy, not rage, to control Monsieur. Again, there is irony in the very language of Bussy's vow to outflank policy with policy, for his mode of speech echoes that of Monsieur and the technique he propounds is very like that Monsieur worked to bring him initially to court:

I'll bind his arm in silk, rub his flesh
To make the vein swell, that his soul may gush
Into some kennel where it longs to lie.
(IV.ii.157-59)

There will be no confrontation. Monsieur knows only too well that Bussy is incapable of resisting the lure of his own will, that he cannot admit caution or fear, and that he believes himself favored by fate and righteousness. The delusion of this outwardly asserted role brings about his ultimate pathetic fall (V.iii.).

Natural images abound in *Bussy D'Ambois,* many applied to the protagonist. Bussy himself sees his relationship with nature as positive, an affirmation of his superior role. But natural images in the play, like nature itself, are cyclical, both regenerative and destructive. In the beginning of Act II, for example, Henry spins an elaborate metaphor of Envy as a kite, feasting upon the corruption of men. The implication is clear: the king is confronting the hatred aroused by "D'Ambois' sudden bravery, and great spirit" (II.i.2). In Act III, scene ii, Henry likens Bussy's words to "brave falcons," states that "flatterers are kites," and gives Bussy the recurrent, affectionate sobriquet, "my eagle," clearly alluding to the relationship of Jove and his attendant eagle; Bussy, in turn, refers to himself as the king's hawk. The implications of and distinctions between these natural images are, in reality, less positive and absolute. Falcons, eagles, hawks, and kites are all predatory birds, closely related. At a distance, hovering in flight, falcon and kite are virtually indistinguishable; it is only when caught, tamed, and trained that the falcon earns its nobility. The bird's worth was measured not only in terms of its skill, but also by the degree of adaptation to role, dependence and obedience being the primary goals. While the Renaissance mind would surely value falcon above kite, the analogies behind the characters' biting badinage remind one that the court function of the former—sport—is dispensable. Similarly, Bussy's role at court is mere diversion, not vital to the administration of justice or policy. The distinctions between D'Ambois and his fellow courtiers, as those between falcon and kite, are exaggerated, and the exaggeration itself obscures the distinction between innate and learned behavior, character and role. The price of nobility is independence. The "natural" *virtú* prized by the king is thus molded and corrupted in Bussy's adaptation to a diminished role.

Similarly, recurrent images of clouds, vapors, smoke, and fumes[16] suggest not only hidden activity but obscured vision, reason, or reality, the presence of delusion and deceit. Tamyra refers to her passion for Bussy as a compressed fume raging for release (II.ii.34-43) and calls for nature's cover of darkness to conceal her guilt. Following their exchange upon the effects of sin, she employs like imagery to illustrate and rationalize the impotence of a virtuous soul overcome by the body's will:

Our bodies are but thick clouds to our souls,
Through which they cannot shine when they desire.
When all the stars, and even the sun himself,
Must stay the vapors' times that he exhales
Before he can make good his beams to us,
Oh, how can we, that are but motes to him,
Wandering at random in his ordered rays,
Disperse our passions' fumes with our weak labors,
That are more thick and black than all the earth's vapors?
(III.i.58-67)

These mists not only hide obvious evil, they also serve as temporary protection from damning truths. Exhalations, the result of the union of sun and earth, become an observable metaphor for policy as well. They are the verbal "breath" created by the self-contained confluence of reason and passion, the manipulative mind and the willful body cooperating to effect the individual will.

Bussy is frequently metaphorized as a lofty tree standing against the tempest (yet another form of exhalation), most notably in Monsieur's final exchange with the Guise. The image of the "full man" becomes a bending trunk more susceptible to destruction than his weaker fellows:

Yet as the winds sing through a hollow tree
And, since it lets them pass through, lets it stand;
But a tree solid, since it gives no way
To their wild rages, they rend up by th'root:
So this full creature now shall reel and fall
Before the frantic puffs of purblind chance.
(V.iii.42-47)

Tamyra, too, aware that Bussy's response to her summons will be his death, speaks of the state of man as a tree, recalling Bussy's first speech, which likens man to a torch in the wind: "Man is a tree that hath no top in cares, / No root in comforts: all his power to live / Is given no end, but t'have power to grieve" (V.iii.166-68). Both metaphors emphasize the role of chance in fickle nature, an alliance with blind Fortune's wheel—a force which Bussy can only identify as favorable to his will. The reader may recall that Barrisor, too, was depicted as a great oak falling to earth (II.i.94-101), an image prefiguring Bussy's ultimate defeat.

Finally, the unending sea recurs as a metaphor for Bussy's undaunted spirit.[17] Monsieur's initial wonder at his adamant posturing again points to the play's conclusion:

His great heart will not down, 'tis like the sea,
That partly by his own internal heat,
Partly the stars' daily and nightly motion,
Ardor and light, and partly of the place
The diverse frames, and chiefly by the moon,
Bristled with surges, never will be won—
No, not when th'hearts of all those powers are burst—
To make retreat into his settled home,
Till he be crowned with his own quiet foam.

(I.ii.145-53)

One recalls Bussy's conceit of a mistress as the moon who guides her lover's movements in his final entrance through the vault leading to Tamyra's chamber: the stage direction reads "D'Ambois [appears] *at the gulf*." His persistent outward role, conflicting with the inward self and its very ordinary desires, reiterates the Guise's image of the sea concealing the mud and dregs beneath it (II.ii.24-28).

The seeds of Bussy D'Ambois's inevitable fall are sown early on in the play because, I believe, the play is not about a superior man's fall but rather about a man's misreading of the world around him and his own role in it. His enormous pride and self-deception eventually lead to an assumption of knowledge beyond the supernatural, endowing him with a false sense of infallibility. Through supernatural knowledge, he is granted the means to manipulate fate, but Bussy persistently misreads or ignores the signs he is given. The double warnings against Tamyra's "hand" and summons (IV.ii.130-31; V.iii.54-56) are cast aside, the friar's ghost is denied, the hidden meaning of the letter written in blood is corrupted by a romantic ideal, and he follows the only dictate he has ever really known, that of his own will: "Should not my powers obey when she commands, / My motion must be rebel to her will, / My will to life" (V.iii.70-72). Meeting with his hired assassins, Bussy boasts of his personal alliance with fate, which is "more strong than arms, and sly than treason, / And I in all parts buckled in my fate" (V.iii.87-88). The long-held delusion of mastery over nature and fate is shattered by a bullet in the back—an ironic ending for the man of *virtù*.

Bussy's standing death is often viewed as a reaffirmation of his superiority, Chapman's melodramatic but rather unsuccessful attempt to redeem his failed protagonist.[18] Certainly he does become a visual image of self-control, and Chapman makes obvious allusions to the death of Hercules, including an almost word-for-word adaptation from Seneca's *Hercules Oetaeus*.[19] It is my contention, however, that the image is an emblem of the shattering of Bussy's initial delusion and that his final speeches delineate the conflict between the inward and outward selves.[20] Clearly Bussy is startled by his own mortal vulnerability:

> Is my body, then,
> But penetrable flesh? And must my mind
> Follow my blood? Can my divine part add
> No aid to th'earthly in extremity?
> Then these divines are but for form, not fact.
>
> (V.iii.125- 29)

Again, his ultimate identification with the courtiers he professes to despise emerges: "let my death / Define life nothing but a courtier's breath." His rise to a standing death is not glorious but simply "like a man," and the visual and verbal tableau he creates reverts to the ill-formed work of the "unskilled statuaries" reviled in his opening lines:

> Here like a Roman statue I will stand
> Till death hath made me marble.
>
> (V.iii.143-44)

The outward form of the Colossus filled with dross predominates as the illusion of *virtú* and mastery caves in, despite his imagined composition of solid marble. Clinging to his feeble desire for lasting fame, Bussy envisions his fall mourned by the deities of the Golden Age, carving for himself a niche in the classical universe, but the imposed reality of Tamyra's wounds reinforces the depths of his failure in the physical world. His delusion of a mythic self with powers superseding the political, social, natural, and supernatural spheres vanishes in death; he becomes the comet, barely glimpsed before it burns itself out; the lightning bolt that "Look'd to have struck, and shook the firmament" with superior force, but failed; an erroneous self-conception ending in ultimate insignificance.

NOTES

[1]Ennis Rees, in *The Tragedies of George Chapman* (Cambridge, Mass.: Harvard Univ Press, 1954), centers his comments around Christian morality and Christian humanism, using the latter term to encompass his conception of neo-Stoicism. He insists that the dying Bussy is a guilt-ridden, repentant man embittered by the waste of his own life. In *The Moral Vision of Jacobean Tragedy* (Madison: Univ. of Wisconsin Press, 1960), Robert Ornstein presents Bussy as a man of natural nobility and *virtú* on a "personal quest for values" in a Machiavellian world. Because Chapman has not been able to maintain a "moral" protagonist, Ornstein sees the playwright as falling back upon melodramatic conventions in order to elicit audience sympathy for his failed hero. Eugene Waith (*The Herculean Hero in Marlowe, Chapman, Shakespeare and Dryden*. London: Chatto & Windus, 1962) views Bussy as a tragic hero in the mold of Hercules and Achilles, following a drive for action which leads ultimately to his own destruction. Part of Waith's concept of the heroic is the pursuit of truth and knowledge, which he considers allegorized by the calling up of spirits in Act IV. Perhaps the most convincing is Joel B. Altman's theory in *The Tudor Play of Mind: Rhetorical Inquiry and the Development of Elizabethan Drama* (Berkeley: Univ. of California Press, 1978). Altman gives a concrete structure to the play which is non-reductive, non-moralistic, and non-judgmental. He poses the question, "What might happen if a naturally virtuous man came out of the garden and entered contemporary society?" debating the concerns of public justice, private morality, and cosmological speculation.

[2]Waith, pp. 39-59; 90-93.

[3]Ornstein, pp. 41-58.

[4]Rees, pp. 1-28.

[5]By revised license in 1603, the company's name was changed to the Children of the Queen's Revels; again, in 1607, to the Children of the Revels. See James E. Ruoff, *Crowell's Handbook of Elizabethan & Stuart Literature* (New York: Thomas Y. Crowell, 1975), pp. 64-65.

[6]Russell A. Fraser, "Introduction" to *Bussy D'Ambois* in Russell A. Fraser and Norman Rabkin, eds., *Drama of the English Renaissance*, 2 vols: (New York: Macmillan, 1976), 2:269-70.

[7]While the prologue to the 1607 quarto indicates that *Bussy D'Ambois* was first presented by the King's Men, performance by the Children of the Queen's Revels cannot be ruled out. The play was probably staged long before its 1607 publication date, and the prologue may have been written specifically for a later performance by an adult company. It was not infrequent for a play to shift back and forth between the boy and adult companies; Ann Jennalie Cook, in *The Privileged Playgoers of Shakespeare's London, 1576-1642* (Princeton: Princeton Univ. Press, 1981), cites *Bussy D'Ambois* as one such play (p. 213).

[8]Waith, pp. 99-100.

[9]Alfred Harbage, *Shakespeare's Audience* (New York: Columbia Univ. Press, 1941), pp. 35-36.

[10]Cook concurs that the boy companies probably played to a more aristocratic audience, partly because their enclosed playing areas allowed them to charge a higher admission fee. She also verifies that the Children of the Revels were "in and out of trouble for their indiscreet political satires and finally in disfavor with the court itself" (p. 131), a fact that lends credence to my view of *Bussy D'Ambois*

as social satire rather than tragedy and of Bussy himself as a misconceived and rather absurd hero.

[11]Roger Truscott Burbidge, "Chapman's *Bussy D'Ambois*"; *TSL* 17(1970):59-65. Also Ornstein, pp. 50-55; and Rees, p. 25.

[12]Stephen Greenblatt, *Renaissance Self-Fashioning* (Chicago: Univ. of Chicago Press, 1980), p. 11.

[13]Waith, pp. 98, 104.

[14]Ibid., p. 100.

[15]George Chapman, *Bussy D'Ambois*. All citations from the text of the play are taken from Fraser and Rabkin, *Drama of the English Renaissance*, vol. 2.

[16]II.i.110; III.i.21, 59-67, 112; IV.i.110-11; IV.ii.10, 53; V.i.13, 16, 46, 69; V.ii.45-48.

[17]I.ii.145-53; II.ii.3-4, 25-28; III.ii.295-99; V.iii.49-56.

[18]Ornstein, pp. 58-59; Rees, p. 47.

[19]Waith, pp. 104-106.

[20]Jane Melbourne comes to similar conclusions in her essay, "The Inverted World of *Bussy D'Ambois*," *SEL* 25(1985):381-95. She depicts the dying Bussy as "stripped of illusion after illusion—his heroic stance, his chivalry, his Platonic faith, his Stoic defiance" (p. 393). But while Melbourne stresses his realization that he is linked to the forces of nature which act upon him, it is my intention to expose his identification with the full range of the *human* world—passion, corruption, guilt, violence, materialism, physical frailty, competitiveness, and, above all, self-delusion. Bussy's death reveals him not as a superior demigod, but as a mere man, a truth supported by the striking inconsistencies of his words and actions throughout the play.

SEL 28 (1988)
ISSN 0039-3657

The Problem of Slavery in *The Custom of The Country*

CAROLYN PRAGER

Though Fletcher and Massinger's *The Custom of The Country* (1619/20) enjoyed enormous popularity throughout the seventeenth century, it is seldom read today, even by serious students of the drama. What, after all, can one hope to appreciate about a plot that involves intended rape, piracy, slavery, and fornication—on the marriage bed, on the high seas, and in the male stews, no less. Complicate the problem of critical evaluation still further with an extraordinary stage history. Before the closing of the theaters, the play was viewed twice at court. In its 1628 revival, it outgrossed *Othello*, *Richard II*, and *The Alchemist*.[1] With its frankly salacious material, it is easily dismissed as yet another example of degenerating Jacobean taste.

Last edited in 1905, it is apparent that the work has yet to find an editorial and critical response equal to its original popularity. Early commentators tend to denounce it as lewd. With some exceptions, modern commentators tend to restrict discussion to questions of theme or attribution. The latter commonly agree on Fletcher's responsibility for a good portion of the play, including the first act's provocative "custom" of the "droit de seigneur." Most recent critics find that the play illustrates Fletcher's love of the unusual and unique situation reflected in the use of this "custom" as part of a series of trials testing the chastity of the major characters.[2]

These critical viewpoints are shaped, in part, by the difficulty of dealing with the actual matter of the play, much of which involves chattel bondage. In a work that concerns itself with the manifesta-

Carolyn Prager is a former Associate Professor of English at the City University of New York and Vice-President of Academic Affairs at Hudson County Community College. She is working currently on a full-length study of the relationship between theories and practices of slavery and English Renaissance literature, especially the drama.

tions of institutional slavery in several forms—captivity, self-sale, transfer of the slave as property, and slavery to the oars—an informed perspective on the relationship of servitude to *The Custom of The Country* is conspicuous by its absence.

In *The Custom of The Country*, insistence upon proprietary sexual rights of feudal origin motivates the flight and pursuit of Zenocia, Arnoldo, and Rutilio—bride, bridegroom, and bridegroom's brother—from Italy to Portugal. Count Clodio seeks to exercise his right of *jus primae noctis*, precipitating the plot convolutions that make up the balance of the play. While the "custom" of the first night is underscored throughout the first act, it is paid scant attention beyond that, serving primarily as the provocative device triggering the complications of captivity and servitude, amatory and actual, that make up the balance of the play. Its primary function is structural, to stimulate and frame the subsequent activity. Its secondary function is thematic, to announce the dramatic exploration of slavery to the passions and service to love by polarizing a lustful count to faithful lovers. At the beginning, it precipitates the lovers' flight and ensuing trials that test their fortitude with experiences of real and figurative bondage. At the end, when the repentant count renounces further imposition of the "custom," it becomes one of a series of moral transformations that occur to the story's myriad licentious Italians and Portuguese.

Standard readings based narrowly upon the material of the first act tend to restrict the title's reference to the most obvious. To limit the title's application, however, to the first act's exploitation of the "droit de seigneur" ignores its relationship to the play's expansive treatment of customary servitude, to the detriment of the play as a whole. In building a topical base for the examination of amatory servitude, the treatment of customary servitude helps bind together seemingly disparate plot elements of seigneurial rights, flight, captivity, prostitution, piracy, lustful intrigue, service, and redemption.

To give dramatic form to the conflict between those who are slaves of passion and servants of love, *The Custom of The Country* exploits situations involving customary servitude in the form of the legitimate enslavement of Christians by other Christians, an increasingly troublesome reality of Mediterranean life, including the Iberian peninsula of the 1600s. The system of slavery that throve on Christian and Islamic Mediterranean shores resulted from the revival of the Mediterranean slave trade accompanying the commercial and maritime expansion of Renaissance Europe. According to Braudel, contemporary manifestations of slavery are a "structural" as opposed to a "conjunctural" feature of Mediterranean society, East and West. Largely an outgrowth of Christian-Moslem conflict and piracy, the Moslem slave-marts of Algiers have their historic parallel in the Christian ones of Malta and Leghorn. Although not as well documented, evidence also exists for the persistence of white bondage in Southern Europe in the period preceding and overlapping the English Renaissance.[3]

By linking one custom of the country, the right to the first night, to another, the right to take and dispose of men and women as property, Fletcher and Massinger seek to unify a multifaceted plot depicting amatory servitude, base and elevated, into a cohesive whole. The actual servile experiences of the fleeing Italians serve to underscore their roles and the roles of more minor characters as slaves of passion and servants of love. However imperfectly joined, the *droit de seigneur* protected by customary law in Italy (according to the given of the play, if not of history) is interwoven with the sanction of Christians to enslave other Christians protected by customary law in Lisbon (a given of the times, to be discussed below). In the end, each amatory character trapped in erotic or chattel bonds receives an appropriate manumission. Zenocia, the domestic slave of the courtesan Hippolyta, is freed from service. Rutilio, the male prostitute who sold himself to the stews to redeem himself from the galleys, is liberated by the coin and love of a generous benefactor. And Hippolyta and Clodio, slaves to their passions, are released by renouncing their lustful ways, the latter by abrogating the infamous custom of his country.

To explore the nature of amatory servitude, Fletcher and Massinger combine the familiar Platonic-Petrarchan images of the servant of love and the slave of passion with the topical correlative of the unfree servant entrapped in a world where bond slavery exists without moral censure, very much according to the custom of the country. The interplay of relative slaveries is accomplished poetically by exposure of the main characters to the slave-holding habits of fellow Christians. The first act culminates in the flight of Zenocia, Arnoldo, and Rutilio from Italy in a small boat. The duration of the play involves their seizure by pirates, the men's plunge into the ocean to escape captivity and servitude, the gift of Zenocia's person to Hippolyta, Arnoldo's search for his wife, his attempt to free her by exchange for himself, Rutilio's escapades and self-sale to a brothel, and their fortuitous redemption. Except for outrage repeatedly expressed against the tenured right of the count to the bridal bed, the play does not censure the right of some to hold others in chattel obligation.

The enslavement of the hapless travelers conforms to conventions of chattel bondage viable in Mediterranean Europe and its outreaches in the early seventeenth century familiar to Elizabethan and Jacobean audiences. The capture of thousands of English nationals in the Mediterranean inspires waves of sensational popular accounts of the experience of "Turkish" slaves, including those unfortunates enslaved by Christian renegades. The following excerpt from Nicholay, a French traveler whose eye-witness accounts are translated into English in 1585, typifies what Fletcher and Massinger's audience knew or thought it knew about such practices: "The most part of the Turkes of Alger, whether they be of the Kings household or the Gallies, are Christians renied, or Manhumetised, of all Nations, but most of them, Spaniards, Italians . . . living onely of rovings, spoiles, and pilling at the Seas . . . : and with their practick art bringing dayly too Alger a number of pore Christians, which they sell unto the Moores, and other merchauntes of Barbarie for slaves, who afterwards transport and sell them" (p. 8). Raising money for the redemption of captives and from publication of one's "true account" of suffering at the hands of Turks and renegade Christians becomes so prevalent that by the 1600s a certain cynicism had set in. Witness Cervantes's exposure in *Persiles y Sigismunda* of the two young men who try to beg money of a village audience by exploiting false tales of personal suffering as slaves in Barbary (pp. 275-76).[4] (Though the *Persiles* is the major source for *The Custom of The Country*, the incident is coincidental and without immediate relevance to the play.)

Fletcher and Massinger exploit conventional components of such accounts, including captivity as property, self-sale, and penal servitude. When their craft is set upon by Portuguese pirates, the two Italian men jump into the sea, rather than "taste the bread of servitude" (II.ii.15). Zenocia, however, is taken captive and given by the pirate Leopold to Hippolyta, as a "present" (III.i.13). Zenocia is unambiguously identified as a "bond-woman" (IV.ii.54), a "slave to this great lady" (IV.iii.46), and a living bond token of a lover's "service" (III.i.31). In the fortuitous advancement of plot, an insatiable Hippolyta becomes infatuated with Arnoldo after seeing him on the street. Introduced into her household, he rejects her lewd advances but pleads with her to trade his freedom for Zenocia's by becoming a slave in her stead "For ever to be fetter'd to your service" (IV.i.137). In the sub-plot, the vagrant Rutilio is sentenced to six hundred ducats or six years at the oars. Sulpitia, mistress of the "Male-Stewes," agrees to "redeem" him "from this slavery" (III.iii.65-66), if he will sell himself to her brothel servicing the ladies of Lisbon.

Fletcher and Massinger deliberately alter their source material in order to bring the story of portending sexual abuse more closely in line with both European contemporary practices of slavery and English constructions of servitude. The authors make use of a nuptial anecdote from the recently translated *The Travels of Persiles and Sigismunda* (registered with the Stationers 22 February 1619). In *Persiles*, the complaint against custom differs in degree and in kind from that of the English play. Transilla, Zenocia's counterpart in *Persiles*, flees her community to escape a custom whereby the bridegroom's brothers or nearest male kin "come to gather flowers in that garden where her husband onely should have entrance. A custome brutish and barbarous" (p. 58). Her father describes a marital practice within a primitive level of social organization:

> Now you must knowe, that in our country there is a custome, the worst of all those that are wickedly observed: which is, that the mariage agreed upon, and the wedding day comm, those that are espoused, and their brothers [i.e., the bridegroom's male kin], together with the nearest kindred of both parts, meet in a house; some to bee witnesses, others to be executioners: for I may well tearme them such.
>
> (p. 58)

The use of the bridal custom in the Spanish romance and English drama is similar only to the extent that it precipitates the resistance and flight of the respective heroines. In *Persiles*, however, it is retrospective, an incident from the past recounted in the flow of the romance, one of many phenomena that spur and test the pilgrim wanderers on the way to Rome. In *The Custom of The Country*, it is conjunctive, both framing the dramatic content and entering into it to illustrate the thematic rendering of bodily and amatory servitude.[5]

Other modifications of Cervantes point to Fletcher and Massinger's deliberate attempts to build their dramatic exposition of sensual bondage upon a firm topical base. Transilla's confrontation with the custom of bridal-rape takes place in or near Hibernia, one of Cervantes's vaguely defined northern locales. Zenocia's occurs in Italy. The choice of southern European locale is deliberate, most pointedly in the shift of the last four acts to Lisbon, a thriving contemporary center of the Renaissance slave trade to and from Mediterranean, African, and New World ports. Demographic records indicate that in 1551 there was one slave for every ten freemen in Lisbon; in 1620, the slave population has increased to 10,470, including white as well as African and Moorish slaves. To see *The*

Custom of the Country with more contemporary vision, it is important to remember that though overshadowed in degree by Moorish and black slavery, white servitude was an ongoing reality of Iberian peninsular life.[6]

By transferring stage action to Lisbon in the last four acts, the English authors depart further from the source to reflect contemporary history. The portrayal of the city by the Spanish and English writers differs markedly. In *Persiles,* the penitential "barbarian" wanderers who pass through Lisbon on their way to Rome discover a wealthy, civil, and spiritual metropolis. As they approach the city, one of them assures his wife, a Christian convert, that in Lisbon she shall "know the manner how to serve God": "Thou shalt now see the rich Temples in which hee is adored; the ceremonies of the Church, and the charity of Christians. . . . All the inhabitants are pleasing, courteous, liberall, amorous, and discreet. . . . Finally, this is the land which giveth to heven, a holy and rich tribute" (p. 217). By contrast, the fleeing Italians in *The Custom of The Country* discover a city of sensual, spiritual, and chattel entrapment and bondage.

Where both sets of characters experience spiritual redemption, the English play extrapolates the circumstances of their liberation from conditions of institutional servitude which they impose upon the Spanish material. Fletcher and Massinger enhance their source material with realistic references to the slave-holding practices of Europeans on European terrain. They do so to refurbish a threadbare worn-out poetry about spiritual bondage to the passions with the exotic apparatus of bond slavery in the contemporary world.

Because slavery is a structural part of southern European life, the Italian captives in *The Custom of The Country* anticipate a servile fate at Christian hands. The pirate Leopold testifies to this expectation:

> I see them [Arnoldo and Rutilio] yet when they were
>   brought aboard us,
> Disarm'd and ready to be put in fetters;
> How on the sudden, as if they had sworn
> Never to taste the bread of servitude,
> . . . .
> They leap'd into the sea.
>
> (II.ii.11-18)

Slavery is part of the situational normalcy of the play in a world where captives are routinely put to the oars or into domestic service. Leopold equates Zenocia with property in the time-honored tradition that allows the captor a legitimate claim to the captive's body in sparing his or her life: "Divide the spoil amongst you, this fair captive / I only challenge for myself" (II.ii.1-2).

Zenocia, Arnoldo, and Rutilio experience servitude with recourse only to redemptive policies established according to the custom of the country. As foreign prey, they are the legitimate booty of pirates, their physical emancipation dependent upon age-old customs of capital exchange between private parties, not upon theoretical or legal constructions of freedom. Rutilio's eventual release from the brothel's "fulling-mills" is owed to a generous benefactor willing to redeem him in coin. Zenocia's is initially negotiated by a husband willing to pay in flesh. When she ultimately gains her freedom, it is through a political accident that in no way challenges the legitimacy of institutional slavery *per se*. Upon Clodio's remorseful intervention and request to a peer, the governor of Lisbon orders her release on the narrowly construed legal ground that "she was no lawful prize, therefore no bondwoman: / She's of that country we hold friendship with" (IV.iii.208-209).

Although the period lacks a firm conceptual approbation of institutional slavery, its literature often struggles with the problem of slavery and the human dimension of bondage, especially in the drama. When she refuses to relate the story of her life to her captor, Zenocia articulates the extent to which the playwrights and presumably their audience intuit the pathos of the slave as an alien in exile. By virtue of her gender, foreign origins, and newly assumed "natal alienation," she is fitted into the paradigm that Patterson calls the "ultimate slave" whereby she accepts her "social death."[7] When her captor asks her to describe her history, she responds:

> A Captive, my fate and your power have made me,
> Such I am now, but what I was it skills not:
> For they being dead, in whom I only live,
> I dare not challenge Family, or Country,
> And therefore Sir enquire not, let it suffice,
> I am your servant, and a thankful servant
> (If you will call that so, which is but duty)
> I ever will be, and my honour safe,
> Which nobly hitherto ye have preserv'd,
> No slavery can appear in such a form,
> Which with a masculine constancy, I will not
> Boldly look on and suffer.
>
> (II.ii.41-52)

The slave woman accepts that the underlying authority for slavery rests in the power of the stronger over the weaker, a cultural legitimation that will not be fully challenged until the natural law debates of the Enlightenment. Without the intellectual referents of a later age that will find slavery reprehensible on its own terms, the Tudor-Stuart dramatist frequently resorts to the Stoics' notion of relative slaveries to palliate an unpleasant reality. Zenocia's only recourse then is in refusing to accept that she is truly enslaved, so long as she retains her virtue intact.[8]

In keeping with this Stoic resolution, she rejects release bought "basely, most basely / Stoop'd to the servile flames of that foul woman" (IV.iii.175-76), when Arnoldo offers to buy her freedom at the expense of his bondage. She reiterates the paradox of a chaste slavery which leaves her more free in bondage than freedom purchased with her husband's sacrificial adultery. Her defense reflects the Senecan argument that admits only to the bondage of the spirit. In Lodge's contemporaneous translation of Seneca's *De Beneficiis*,

> He is deceived, whosoever thinketh that servitude taketh possession over the whole man: the better part of him is exempted. The bodies are subject and obliged to their masters, but the mind is privileged in itselfe: . . . It is the bodie therefore Fortune hath submitted to the Master, This bought he, this selleth he: that interior part cannot be bought and sold, or suffer servitude.[9]

Without a moral vocabulary to condemn institutional slavery, the language of the play is one of stark moral antitheses where nobility in a slave mirrors degeneracy in the aristocrat. The play's diction exhausts the notional and actual slaveries of its characters by playing off the language of physical servitude against that of love and sexuality. The portrayal of chattel bondage helps to gradate dramatically the degrees of spiritual and bodily enslavement portrayed by the play's several amorous characters. Clodio betrays the nobility of his rank by enslavement to his passions so long as he insists upon his seigneurial right to Zenocia's body. Zenocia affirms the aristocracy of virtue by rising above the worldly condition of bondage. Arnoldo welcomes the relative freedom of physical bondage by accepting voluntary servitude to liberate his beloved—the servant of love literally enslaved as proof of service to his lady.

In *The Custom of The Country,* this literal enslavement accentuates the figurative bondage of those enthralled by appetite. Servile imagery of chattel slavery is nicely correlated to that of physical love. The ruttish Rutilio exchanges the shackles of the oars for those of the flesh. The lustful Hippolyta flaunts the "fetters" of her touch, and "soft chains" of her hair that "bind the arms of Princes, / And make them, in that wish'd for bondage, happy" (III.iv.24,25,26). The chaste Zenocia rejects freedom at the price of her husband's subjection to the "servile flames of that foul woman" (IV.i.176).

Despite poetic dependence upon the literal person of the slave in a topical setting, the play diverts attention from the real to the figurative slave. In distinguishing between the slavery to the body and that of the body, *The Custom of The Country* imparts a partial moral dignity to chattel bondage consonant with prevailing Stoic-Christian concepts of slavery. While slavery is associated with an unpleasant but tolerable worldly condition, lust is associated with an intolerable form of bondage. Typically for the period, the play thereby directs moral censure away from the enslaver and toward the enslaved, in keeping with the language of lecherous, amorous, and spiritual service of Western metaphor.

Aesthetically compelled to authenticate the jaded Petrarchan image of Love's servants and slaves with contemporary actuality, Fletcher and Massinger use situational reference to the surviving practice of white domestic and galley slavery on the continent. Though chattel slavery has virtually disappeared in England well before the writing of the play, its disappearance is not accomplished within a theoretical framework that easily condemns its practice. When William Perkins asks in 1604 whether or not "a Christian may with safe conscience have and use a man as a slave," he poses a question to which the period is unable to respond in terms which we call modern.

Perkins's response reflects the one worked out long before by Roman jurist and Church father arguing the authority of *jus gentium* in a fallen world. "The power and right of having bondmen, in the countries where it is established by positive lawes, may stand with good conscience." Like Sir Thomas More, who maintains that if not fortunate enough to be born Utopian, one is better off an alien slave in Utopia than a freeman elsewhere, English theorists often insist upon the potential of the Christian environment to improve upon the unfortunate lot of the slave. "Lastely," states Robert Pricke in *The Doctrine of Superioritie and of Subjection,* in pleading the necessity of bondage and service in a fallen world, "the worst estate of servants amongst such as are reputed Christians: is better and more tollerable, than the state of servants amongst many nations: . . . as appeareth in the Scripture, and in prophane Histories."[10]

In their desire to validate the literal condition of slavery on which they predicate the spiritual relationships of the play, Fletcher and Massinger echo the period's cultural assumptions about the potential therapeutic benefit of slavery to the slave. The pirate Leopold cloaks ancient understandings about the right to dispose of his spoils with such contemporary argument. When he gives Zenocia to Hippolyta, he elevates the act of enslavement by insisting upon the benefits that will accrue to her:

> To this incomparable lady I will give you,
> (Yet, being mine, you are already hers;)
> And to serve her is more than to be free,
> At least I think so: and when you live with her,
> If you will please to think on him than brought you
> To such happiness, (for so her bounty
> Will make you think her service,) you shall ever
> Make me at your devotion.
>
> (II.ii.63-70)

However incredible the passage may sound from the distance of the centuries, it accords well with the conceptual framework familiar to Fletcher and Massinger's audience that legitimates the institution of slavery within a world of actual servile activity.

In addition to reflecting concepts of slavery articulated by English statesmen and divines, *The Custom of The Country* mirrors those vestiges of customary law regulating villenage still embedded in English common law that control the disposition of a tenant's children in marriage on the manor. By so doing, Fletcher and Massinger overlay their exploration of relative slaveries with aspects of chattel slavery legitimated by the custom of the country and with aspects of seigneurial rights of ancient provenance also legitimated by the custom of the country. Historically, customary as distinguished from common and statutory law governs bonded service in the Renaissance. The rights and duties of those in tenure derive from medieval customary law in which the tenant in villenage is said to be "seised" of the land *de jure*, "according to the custom of the manor." In the period contemporaneous with *The Custom of The Country*, the authority of customary law still prevails in the treatment of servants selling service for passage who arrive in the colonies without written indenture. Lacking statutory protection, their varying terms of bondage are set according to the "custom of the country." In Fletcher and Massinger's play, the servile experiences of the young Italians in Portugal clearly reflect the tendency of the period to base the contractualism of master and servant or slave on regional practices unenacted in law.[11]

The playwrights also appeal to customary law in their efforts to connect organically seemingly disparate elements of defloration and slavery. In the Spanish source, the exercise of sexual custom on the first night is familial or tribal and designed to bond the female of one family with the male blood line of the other. Fletcher and Massinger transform the customary right of *jus primae noctis* from a tribal to a legal seigneurial right assuring the proprietary authority of the lord over his vassals. By changing the authority for the deplorable practice from tribal practice to legal custom, they try, however inconclusively, to bring their material into line with those aspects of English law derived from *constuetudo manierii,* the great bulk of unenacted law regulating those in tenure to the land.

Consonant with derivatives of feudal law still manifest in seventeenth century common law, the formal sanction given to customary law is underscored twice in the first scene. Arnoldo pointedly refers to "this custom, which this wretched country / Hath wrought into a law, and must be satisfied" (I.i.200-201). Zenocia's father urges her to remember the count's "power to possess" her, "by custom unresistible" to do "what law allows him" (lines 69, 71, 75). The proprietary basis of this custom is also underscored twice, by Arnoldo when he explains that the Governor of the country may claim the bride's "maidenhead, / Or ransom it for money at his pleasure" and then by Zenocia when she pleads with Clodio to take money for her "ransom" (lines 31-32, 54). Their exchange is conducted in the language of servile transaction tempered only by Stoic indifference to physical bondage. When Clodio insists that "No money, nor no prayers, shall redeem her," Zenocia declares that if her body must pay the price required by law, at least her "mind shall not pay this custom" (lines 362, 368).

Although neither English law nor recorded practice sanctions *jus primae noctis,* feudal law did forbid a tenant to marry his daughter outside of the manor in order to preserve property vested in the person of one's tenants, "according to the custom of the manor."[12] Remnants of such manorial custom appear to have survived into the seventeenth century, moving the jurist Sir Edward Coke in 1628 to remind his readers that although the lord of the manor may try to exact a fine if a tenant marries a son or daughter without license, "to claim such a fine by a generall custome within the Mannor, is against the freedome of a freeman that is not bound thereunto by particular Tenure." However, Coke goes on to state those conditions under which such a fine may be levied: "But a custome may be alledged within a Mannor, . . . That everie tenant (albeit his person bee free) that holdeth in bondage, or by native Tenure, the freehold being in the Lord, shall pay to the Lord for the marriage of his daughter without licence, a fine: and it is called Marchet, as it were a Chete or fine for marriage." Prompted by what must have been abuse of this distinction between freemen and copy-holders, only the latter having the obligation to pay a marriage fine, Coke reminds his readers that "if the Lord of a Mannor will prescribe that there hath beene a custome within his Mannour, time out of minde of man," that "every" tenant who marries his daughter without license must pay a fine, "such a prescription is against reason, such a prescription is voyd" ("Of Villenage," Lib. 2, Sec. 209).[13]

As late as 1679, Blount, in *Fragmenta antiquitas: Ancient Tenures of land, and Jocular Customs of some Manors,* points to the survival of the local custom of the marriage fine in Sussex: "This fine for the tenants marrying their daughters was without doubt in lieu of the *mercheta mulierum,* or first night's lodging with the bride, which the lord anciently claimed in some manors." Jack Cade's speech in *2 Henry VI* suggests that the notion lives on in the popular imagination: "The proudest peer in the realm shall not wear a head on his shoulders unless he pay me a tribute. There shall not a maid be married, but she shall pay to me her maidenhead ere they have it" (IV.vii.127-30).[14]

The study of Anglo-Renaissance poetic correlations of gender, sexuality, tenure, and slavery is beyond the scope of this paper to explore in full. Although white and black slaves figure thematically in plays as popular and influential as *Tamburlaine, Titus Andronicus, Lust's Dominion, Othello, The Tempest, The Bondman, The Royal Slave,* and *The Custom of The Country,* correspondences between the evocation of the dramatic slave persona and the practice of slavery in the Renaissance world has generated little academic interest.[15] Manifestly, there are discernible parallels between contemporary concepts and practices of tenure and slavery and Fletcher and Massinger's play upon custom in *The Custom of The Country.* If the parallels between real and figurative bondage insisted upon in *The Custom of The Country* do not seem to us to make for good poetry, it may be because the authors are struggling to make poetry out of material based on a reality that outstrips the culture's capacity to conceive of it in ways that we call modern. Although the English Renaissance dramatist sometimes tries to make poetry out of physical bondage, he can not readily comprehend that without the moral perspective and vocabulary to condemn it, there is little that is poetic about real slavery. Slavery is poetic only at the level of allegory, as when a noble Othello gives way to the "cursèd slave" (V.ii.276) who has destroyed that which sustains his soul.

In 1628, however, London theater-goers evidently prefer *The Custom of The Country* to *Othello*. It is possible that they respond so to the former because growing awareness of the actual practice of slavery in Southern Europe and its Mediterranean outreaches requires an intense and colorful actualization of slavery on stage in order to conduct dramatic inquiry into the nature of the slavish persona.

Exoticism and sensationalism aside, no other work in English Renaissance drama so clearly projects a coeval world of institutionalized and legitimated servile activity. *The Custom of The Country* reveals the extent to which Renaissance English men and women understand chattel slavery, even that of men and women most like themselves, as tolerable and normative in their world. More frequent in those dealing with the prospect of captivity in Barbary where English and European renegades and pirates sell their human booty into the markets of the Levant, the danger of servile seizure and sale within a European geography figures in a small group of Stuart plays.

To cite some examples, Eunuchus, the Christian slave of a Turk, lives at the Florentine court in Mason's *The Turke* (1609). Two Englishwomen in Heywood's *The Captives* (1624), the "shee chattyles" (line 271) of a Marseilles pimp, are forced aboard ship with the prospect of being sold, whether in England, Spain, Italy, or Morocco; as the pimp says, "tush these are wares in all parts vendible" (line 279). In the same author's *A Challenge for Beauty* (1634-35?), two Englishmen in Spain are hurried off "to the Male-Market" with their price upon their shoulders to face either fate as "slave to a Turke, or feare the bloodie usage / Of an ambitious Spanyard" (II.1). Massinger and Fletcher's *A Very Woman* (?—rev.1634) contains a vivid full-length scene (II.iii) attributed to Fletcher of slave barter in the markets of Palermo where Englishmen and Moors alike are bought for the Christian viceroy's household. Severino in Massinger's *The Guardian* (1634) calms a party captured by bandits outside of Naples with assurances that they need not fear "For profit, to be sold for slaves, then shipp'd / Into another Country" (V.iv.71-72).[16]

In each of these plays, slavery reflects political, economic, and geographic realities that tend to diminish the metaphoric usefulness of the slave figure to convey spiritual indenture. Explicitly rendered in later Jacobean drama, the chattel retention and sale of Englishmen, Europeans, Africans, Indians, and Turks on stage is sanctioned by the right of property. The enslavement of unfortunates belongs to the category of dubious acts contemporary audiences gladly ascribe to heathen and papists. If reprehensible, it is mainly so because practiced by Catholics and Turks. In the plays immediately cited above as in English letters of the period, the social phenomenon of slavery is neither censured nor condemned; it is simply displayed as an unappealing dimension of Christian experience in Christian but non-English lands.

Seen from a synchronous perspective, *The Custom of The Country* is a far more dramatically cohesive play than is generally allowed. It is not unreasonable to suggest that its popularity may owe something to its topical treatment of customary servitude as well as to its erotic excesses. Lacking a vocabulary of moral censure for slavery, *The Custom of The Country* tries to equate actual servile practice with the Renaissance metaphor of the slavish persona, not always with satisfactory aesthetic results. To the extent that it signals the diminishing utility of one of Western poetry's heretofore most enduring metaphors, the slave of passion, it merits reading by students of Renaissance literature. Until there are further gains in scholarship, discussion of continuities between white and black slavery must obviously be made on a cautionary note. However, to the extent that dramatic evidence can provide a perspective on the past, the play also merits reading for its date alone, 1619 marking the sale of the first cargo of slaves to the newly established English colony in Jamestown.[17]

NOTES

[1]For the play's colorful stage history, see Gerald Eades Bentley, *The Jacobean and Caroline Stage*, 7 vols. (Clarendon: Oxford Univ. Press, 1941-1968), 3:324-38. In 1700, Dryden castigates its erotic content in defense of the Restoration stage: "There is more Baudry in one Play of *Fletcher's* call'd *The Custom of the Country*, than in all ours together" and the anonymous author of the 1699 *Stage Acquitted* states that "there has been nothing so lewd as the bringing in *Bawdy-Houses* and *Stallions* of *Fletcher*; no not in the Plays in the two Late Reigns" (cited in Bentley, p. 328). See Lawrence B. Wallis, *Fletcher, Beaumont & Company, Entertainers to the Jacobean Gentry* (New York: Kings Crown Press, 1947), pp. 21-22, 83, 118, 175, for examples of eighteenth- and nineteenth-century criticism, much of it favorable.

[2]There are two "modern" editions, one of 1904 and the other of 1905: *The Works of Francis Beaumont and John Fletcher: Variorum Edition*, gen. ed. A. H. Bullen, 4 vols. (London: George Bell, 1904), 1, and *The Works of Francis Beaumont and John Fletcher*, ed. A. R. Waller and Arnold Glover, 10 vols. (1905; rpt. New York: Octogon, 1969), 1, ed. Arnold Glover. All citations are from the former. Among the critics, Clifford Leech in *The John Fletcher Plays* (Cambridge, Mass.: Harvard Univ. Press, 1962) attributes to Fletcher the love of a "rare situation" and to Massinger "a lachrymose quality in some of the scenes of distress," p. 57. He dismisses the play for its "haphazardness of structures," p. 57, none of which is properly explored and each of which is an incident in a densely packed plot, p. 59. Studies concerned primarily with problems of attribution include Cyrus Hoy, "Massinger as Collaborator: The Plays With Fletcher and Others," in *Philip Massinger: A Critical Reassessment*, ed. Douglas Howard (Cambridge: Cambridge Univ. Press, 1985), pp. 61-62; E. H. C. Oliphant, *The Plays of Beaumont and Fletcher: An Attempt To Determine Their Respective Shares and The Shares of Others* (New Haven: Yale Univ. Press, 1927), pp. 224-26; and Bertha Hensman, *The Shares of Fletcher, Field and Massinger in Twelve Plays of the Beaumont and Fletcher Canon*, 2 vols. (Salzburg: Universität Salzburg, 1974), 1:109. Hoy, pp. 64-65, and Nancy Cotton Pearse, *John Fletcher's Chastity Plays: Mirrors of Modesty* (Lewisburg: Bucknell Univ. Press, 1973), pp. 210-17, examine the play's dramatic structure in terms of separate plot elements, slavery excepted, designed to test the virtue of the major characters. Studies that use the play to illustrate the evolution of Jacobean stagecraft include Wallis, pp. 237-38, and Kathleen McLuskie, "The plays and the playwrights: 1613-42," in *The Revels History of Drama in English* , vol. 4, 1613-1660, ed. Lois Potter (London: Methuen, 1981), pp. 176-77. McLuskie reiterates the critical commonplace that "the unabashed contrivances of the plot make it impossible to be concerned with either the moral or emotional issues." However, she finds more consistency in the play than do most, which she attributes to style rather than content. She also finds some thematic coherence in that each major character demonstrates "the potentially disastrous consequences of sexual exploitation and the misuse of certain kinds of power." None of the above deal with the relationship between customary and amatory servitude as a unifying poetic and thematic device with which this paper is primarily concerned.

[3]See David Brion Davis, *Slavery and Human Progress* (New York: Oxford Univ. Press, 1984), pp. 51-52, for the relationship of slavery and expansion. Charles Verlinden in *L'Esclavage dans l'Europe médiévale: Tome Premier: Péninsule-Ibérique-France* (Brugge: De Tempel, 1955) explores the persistence

of white servitude on the Continent in the period preceding and overlapping the English Renaissance; see especially the "annexe," "Coup d'oeil sur l'esclavage à l'époque moderne dans la péninsule ibérique et en France," pp. 835-54. See also Fernand Braudel, *The Mediterranean and the Mediterranean World in The Age of Philip II*, trans. Sian Reynolds, 2 vols., 2nd. rev. edn. (New York: Harper, 1975), 2:865-91, for a well-documented description of Mediterranean piracy and the pointed reminder that European participation was behind its increased activity, particularly in the seventeenth century: "For it was not merely in Algiers that men hunted each other, threw their enemies into prison, sold or tortured them . . . : it was all over the Mediterranean," p. 867.

[4]The best introduction to the topic of Levantine slavery for students of English Renaissance literature is still Samuel C. Chew, *The Crescent and the Rose: Islam and England During the Renaissance* (New York: Oxford Univ. Press, 1937), esp. pp. 367-72. Nicholas Nicholay, *The Navigations, peregrinations and voyages, made into Turkie*, trans. T. Washington the younger (London, 1585). [Cervantes], *The Travels of Persiles and Sigismunda. A Northern History*, trans. anon. (London, 1619).

[5]The ritual defloration story was an alleged feature of primitive marriage ceremonies in many parts of the globe depicted by continental chroniclers and commentators. It is found in Piero de Cieca's *Chronica del Peru*, John Leo's *Description de l'Afrique*, and Lopez de Gomara's *Historia general de las Indias*, among others. See further, W. D. Howarth, "Cervantes and Fletcher: A Theme With Variations," *MLN* 56 (1961):563-66. Howarth restricts application of the custom to the motivation of the protagonists' flight; he does suggest, however, though without further elaboration, that Fletcher is reflecting a current English belief in the exercise of *jus primae noctis* rather than contemporary anthropology, p. 565.

[6]Verlinden, pp. 835-54; Braudel, p. 754.

[7]Orlando Patterson, *Slavery and Social Death: A Comparative Study* (Cambridge, Mass.: Harvard Univ. Press, 1982), p. 5 and ch. 11, pp. 299-333.

[8]"For some two thousand years men thought of sin as a kind of slavery. One day they would come to think of slavery as sin": David Brion Davis, *The Problem of Slavery in Western Culture* (Ithaca: Cornell Univ. Press, 1966), p. 90. Davis provides the best introduction to the complex subject of the development of moral perceptions of slavery before and after the Enlightenment as well as a comprehensive discussion of the historical application of Hellenic, Roman, and Christian Stoicism to temper the realities of institutional slavery; for the latter, see esp. pp. 72-90.

[9]Thomas Lodge, *The Workes of Lucius Annaeus Seneca, Both Morall and Naturall* (London, 1614), Lib. 3, ch. xx, p. 52.

[10]William Perkins, *A Commentarie or Exposition, upon . . . Galatians*, (Cambridge, 1604), pp. 697, 698; *The Yale Edition of the Complete Works of St. Thomas Mode*, ed. Edward Surtz, S.J., and J. H. Hexter, 15 vols. (New Haven: Yale Univ. Press, 1965), 1:185; Robert Pricke, *The Doctrine of Superioritie, and of Subjection* (London, 1609), sig. [M6r]. The use of *u, v, i*, and *j* is modernized throughout this paper.

[11]Sir Frederick Pollack and Frederick William Maitland, *The History of English Law Before The Time of Edward I*, 2nd edn., 2 vols. (1898; rpt. Cambridge: Cambridge Univ. Press, 1968), 1:361. The evolution of the Tudor legal framework of a labor system organized around bound labor rather than life-long or hereditary servitude is described by Winthrop D. Jordan, *White Over*

Black: American Attitudes Towards The Negro, 1550-1812 (Chapel Hill: Univ. of North Carolina Press, 1968), pp. 50-52. According to Jordan, the lingering vestiges of feudal bonded service that survived on the English manor were already anachronisms in the sixteenth century. He makes the important point, however, that "while villenage was actually extinct, it lay unmistakably fossilized in common law. Its survival in that rigid form must have reminded Englishmen that there existed a sharply differing alternative to personal liberty," p. 50. The application of customary law to colonial indenture is treated at length by Abbot Emerson Smith, *Colonists in Bondage: White Servitude and Convict Labor in America 1607-1776* (1947; rpt. New York: Norton, 1971), esp. ch. 11, "The Custom of The Country," pp. 226-52. Differences in the evolution of "white proto-slavery" in the English West Indies from 1624-45 and the feudal pattern of bonded service characterized by a contractual agreement with mutual legal obligation are described by Hilary Beckles, "Plantation Production and White Proto-Slavery: White Indentured Servants and the Colonisation of the English West Indies, 1624-1645," *The Americas: A Quarterly Review of Inter-American Cultural History*, 41(1985):21-46, pp. 37-39. White servitude in the colonies more closely resembles chattel slavery whereby the indentured servant is bought, sold, gambled away, mortgaged, taxed as property, etc., transactions which are governed only by the " 'custom of the Country'," p. 38. The use of bound white laborers preceded the use of black slaves in every Anglo-American colony, according to David W. Galenson, *White Servitude in Colonial America: An Economic Analysis* (Cambridge: Cambridge Univ. Press, 1981).

[12]Pollack and Maitland, pp. 372, 377.

[13]Sir Edward Coke, *The first part of the institutes of the lawes* (London, 1628).

[14]Cited by Howarth, p. 566. All citations from Shakespeare are from *The Complete Works*, ed. G. B. Harrison, (1948; rpt. New York: Harcourt Brace, 1968). Paul S. Clarkson and Clyde T. Warren appear to have misjudged the strength of contemporary belief in the persistence of *marcheta mulierum* in *The Law of Property in Shakespeare and The Elizabethan Drama* (1942; rpt. New York: Gordian, 1968). They suggest that Tudor-Stuart playwrights, including Fletcher, are probably not aware of it as an ancient English custom but may have read of it as a Scottish practice described by Holinshed and other chroniclers, pp. 35-36.

[15]For a preliminary inquiry into the relationship of the period's literature to contemporary theory and practice of slavery, see my unpublished Ph.D. dissertation, "Conceptions of Slavery in the English Renaissance: With Illustrations From the Drama" (Fordham Univ., 1974).

[16]Thomas Heywood, *The Captives*, ed. Arthur Brown (London: Malone Society, 1953), without act or scene division. *A Challenge for Beauty* in *The Dramatic Works of Thomas Heywood Now First Collected with Illustrative Notes and a Memoir of the Author*, ed. [R. H. Shepherd] 6 vols. (1874; rpt. New York: Russell and Russell, 1964), 5, without lineation. *A Very Woman* and *The Guardian* in *The Plays and Poems of Philip Massinger*, ed. Philip Edwards and Colin Gibson, 5 vols. (Oxford: Clarendon Press, 1976), 4.

[17]Jordan, p. 44. Despite the advances of recent scholarship, Davis reminds us that any discussion of the transition between white and black slavery requires a cautionary note, pending further research into such factors as "changing labor markets in the Americas, Europe, and especially Africa," *Progress*, p. 52.

SEL 28 (1988)
ISSN 0039-3657

Take the Number Seven in Cheapside

A. G. VAN DEN BROEK

The title of this paper is not altogether facetious, because by drawing attention to the number seven in Thomas Middleton's *A Chaste Maid in Cheapside* I hope to identify a clear moral point of view which the play is supposed to lack.[1] Recurring references to the number seven, I think, prove that there is nothing ambivalent about the play's characters; that their presentation does not "dip momentarily into horror," as R. B. Parker would have it,[2] suggesting a lack of artistic control; and, that Middleton does not stoop to a clumsy *deus ex machina,* implied by Susan Wells when she says, "Middleton only restores the play to the context of the popular festival by an audacious redirection of its tone in the final scene, as a bogus funeral leads to weddings, reunions of estranged spouses, and a feast."[3] Instead, I wish to consider the four components of the plot, so thoroughly discussed by Richard Levin and Parker, in terms of a social contract which expires during the seventh, climacteric year.

As a city comedy, *A Chaste Maid* has an urban setting with detailed and accurate references to London (cf. IV.i.313-15, where Tim refers to Trig stairs, Common stairs, Puddle wharf, and the "dock below," meaning Dung wharf).[4] It is also concerned with the "Jacobean moral and social world," and analyzes that world "in moral terms first and last,"[5] and it is otherwise typical, as Wells says, inasmuch as "the city comedy is an attempt to recover, by stating in new terms, [the] harmony between the commercial and the communal organization of the city which chroniclers like Stowe imaginatively portrayed as part of its recent past, but which was being compromised by the rapid growth, commercial development, and royal domination of the city during the Jacobean period."[6] However, more can be said than that Middleton's technique involves a "Formal

A. G. van den Broek is a graduate student at Dalhousie University, Halifax, Nova Scotia, Canada, and is currently writing a doctoral thesis on George Eliot, which he expects to complete later this year.

displacement, [in which] the presentation of a dramatic world [is] protected from the operations of conventional morality."[7] The "formal displacement," I think, takes the form of a society behaving in accordance with a perverse code of morality which is about to end.

After leaving his wife because they cannot afford any more children, and explaining about his "fatal finger" which has caused "no less than seven" pregnancies over the last several months (II.i.59-62), a sardonic Touchwood Senior is heard to say:

> I have known
> This city now above this seven year,
> But I protest in better state of government
> I never knew it yet, nor ever heard of;
> There has been more religious, wholesome laws
> In the half circle of a year erected
> For common good, than memory ever knew of,
> Setting apart corruption of promoters,
> And other poisonous officers that infect,
> And with a venomous breath taint every goodness.
> (II.i.108-17)

During this soliloquy, Sir Oliver and his wife have come on stage, and Lady Kix cries, "To be seven years a wife and not a child" (II.i.137). Allwit tells the audience that Sir Walter "h'as maintain'd my house this ten years" (I.ii.16), and tells Davy that Sir Walter and he "ever jump'd in one, this ten years" (II.iii.9), but, significantly, Allwit's wife has been "contracted" to Sir Walter for seven years. In an aside Allwit says that he "heard a citizen complain once that his wife's belly only broke his back: mine had been all in fitters seven years since, but for this worthy knight" (III.ii.71-74). Later he gives this description of Sir Walter to Yellowhammer: "He's an arrant whoremaster, consumes his time and state, [*Whispers*]—whom in my knowledge he hath kept this seven years" (IV.i.249-51). Lastly, Allwit tells Yellowhammer that Sir Walter has had seven bastards by the woman he keeps (IV.i.263-75).

This is how *The Oxford English Dictionary* (*O. E. D.*) defines "seven": "used (*a*) symbolically, often denoting completion of perfection (esp. in echoes of biblical phraseology), or (b) typically in expressions of time, etc. for a large number or quantity, esp. *(this) seven year (s,* etc. (= a long period)." C. T. Onions's *A Shakespeare Glossary* cites a number of instances where Shakespeare uses "seven years" to mean "a long time." Thus, possibly, Middleton means to suggest that Sir Walter and Touchwood Senior have known each other and the city for a long time, that they have many children, and so on.

But I think there is more to it than that. The Porter tells the Yellowhammers that he was a scholar forty years ago (I.i.76-77); Davy explains that he is forty years old (I.i.124); Maudline says that Tim "was eight years in his grammer" (IV.i.65); and the first Puritan says, "Children are blessings, if they be got with zeal, / By the brethren, as I have five at home" (III.ii.36-37). When he wants to, Middleton gives specific dates, ages, and numbers. So I think he is assigning a special significance to the number seven. Parker notes about Touchwood Senior and Sir Walter: "They are old acquaintances . . . and each has been in town seven years: Sir Walter's Welsh mistress is paralleled by Touchwood Senior's Country Wench; and Sir Walter's seven children by Mrs. Allwit (contrasting with Lady Kix's seven years of fruitless marriage) are matched by the seven country girls whom Touchwood Senior made lie in 'last progress.' "[8] Here Parker goes on to talk about the irony of Touchwood Senior replacing Sir Walter as a seducer, and that this creates further problems when it comes to interpreting the play's moral. But an interpretation is possible once the significance of the number seven is taken into account.

Seven is the first of a group of climacteric numbers, which, I think, is the key to its meaning in *A Chaste Maid.* My point will become clearer with a further definition from the O. E. D.:

> *Climacteric*: . . . Pertaining to or constituting a climacter or critical period in human life; as in *climacteric year*. . . . Constituting an important epoch or crisis; critical; fatal. . . . Applied to that period of life (usually between the ages of 45-60) at which the vital forces begin to decline (in women coinciding with the period of 'change of life'); pertaining to this period. *Climacteric disease*: a disease of unknown cause which often occurs at an advanced stage of life, characterized by loss of flesh and strength, sleeplessness, etc. . . . A critical stage in human life; a point at which the person was supposed to be specially liable to change in health or fortune. According to some, all the years denoted by multiples of 7 (7, 14, 21, etc.) were climacterics: others admitted only the odd multiples of 7 (7, 21, 35, etc.).

Thus Touchwood Senior's seven children, and comment, "I have known / This city now above this seven year," Lady Kix's barrenness (until "this seven year"), Sir Walter's seven children, and his seven year "contract" with the Allwits, all lend themselves to a particular motif. The play, I think, depicts Cheapside's society at a critical point, following a climacteric period of decadence and depravity. A change is inevitable. Middleton is not resorting to superstitious ideas associated with climacteric years to indicate that a supernatural agency is shaping events;[9] instead I think he refers to them to give his play a thematic unity. But at a time when astrology was still taken seriously, he could rely on people's awareness of the so-called mysteries surrounding the number seven, and, writing partly for members of the Inns of Court, he could expect his audience to think of a "Seven Years' Lease," which *The Dictionary of Phrase and Fable* defines as: "Leases run by seven years and its multiples, from the ancient notion of what was termed 'climacteric years,' in which life was supposed to be in special peril, (*Levinus Lemnius*)."[10]

Levin has shown how the four plots rely on "temporal cause-effect sequences," as well as "analogical or 'spatial' " connections.

> These symmetrical 'spatial' interrelationships, together with the causal or 'temporal' connections . . . can explain, I believe, how the four plots are combined into a single whole, but they cannot in themselves explain the significance of this combination, since that depends not only upon how the unity is achieved, but also upon what is being unified. Each of these four plots has its own distinctive tone or character which, weighed, and brought into proper focus through this cohesive structure, contributes to the total effect of the play.[11]

He thinks that the plot of Moll and Touchwood Junior is the most "serious" because the emphasis is on the "cruelty and venality of Moll's parents."[12] But I suggest that all the plots are "serious"—because of the "cruelty and venality" of Cheapside. Levin refers to Cheapside as "the real enemy,"[13] but he does not explain why its society falls apart. I think that the latter happens because the symbolic seven year period of social decadence and depravity has reached a crisis and is in a stage of moral revaluation.

Cheapside's corruption is all-pervasive. The denseness of its moral turpitude virtually props up society—just as the Allwits are financially propped up by Sir Walter. The Yellowhammers belong to the merchant class, but not content with their lot they display tacky and, in the case of Moll's well-being, dangerous social ambitions. Upon asking Yellowhammer whether news has come from their son at Cambridge, Maudline is told: "Had word just the day after when you sent him the silver spoon to eat his broth in the hall amongst the gentleman commoners" (I.i.56-58). Tim was not born with a silver spoon in his mouth, and so they send him one. Their laughable presumption is reflected in Tim's officious Latin note which no one will admit to not understanding. The Parson will not read it because he equates Latin with "Papistry" (I.i.102-103), but he probably "disclaims it" because he cannot read it. Regarding Sir Walter, however, the Yellowhammers' attitude is more disturbing. They fawn over a potential son-in-law, despite the fact that he oozes corruption. When Moll runs away at the sight of him, Maudline says, "you have a presence, sweet Sir Walter, / Able to daunt a maid brought up i'the city" (I.i.134-35). The observation is wonderfully ironic, because it flatters him while telling us that if city maids, who are normally promiscuous, are "daunted" by him, then Moll must be tottering on the brink of death, since she is the one chaste exception. Later it is made clear that Moll is in real danger of losing her life because of Sir Walter's presence.

Allwit's lifestyle is what the Yellowhammers unwittingly aspire to. Bragging about his enviable position since selling his soul for money and appearances, he scorns jealous "merchants [who] would in soul kiss Hell / To buy a paradise for their wives, and dye / Their conscience" (II.ii.42-44). "These torments stand I freed of" (I.ii.49), he says, and that is true: he stands free from everything good and decent. His name tells us that he is all wit, as in rationalization, and therefore he has no heart. Lovewit and Truewit, in Jonson's *The Alchemist* and *Epicoene*, respectively, are witty, well-balanced characters, but Allwit is weak and only perversely ironic. Nor is he free of torments, as he puts it: he is disgusted by the behavior of the Gossips and Puritans at the christening. His inability to enjoy the company of people who are essentially like him points to his insularity, and hints at a fragmented society.

Struggling in Cheapside's social sewer, Moll and Touchwood Junior show something that the Allwits and the Yellowhammers are impervious to: true love and affection. The "posy," *Love that's wise, blinds parents' eyes,* which Touchwood Junior gives Yellowhammer is at once funny, given the circumstances, and an indictment of the times. Love's wisdom, it turns out, is not sufficient to overcome the problems facing the young lovers. They need the help of Touchwood Senior to overcome the obstacles of society's hypocrisy and selfishness.

The Touchwoods contrast with the Allwits and the Yellowhammers inasmuch as they offer an unusual solution to the common problem of penury:

Mistress Touchwood. 'twill be so tedious, sir, to live from you,
But that necessity would be obeyed.
Touchwood Senior. I would it might not, wife, the tediousness
Will be the most part mine, that understand
The blessing I have in thee.
(II.i.1-5)

Circumstances beyond his control have made Touchwood Senior pull out his "fatal finger." He may not be virtuous, but at least he is honest with himself and others. The Wench he encounters is given an open account of his inability to do more than give money, and his analysis of the "religious, wholesome laws" of the land is frank and to the point. He has reached the end of his personal climacteric period, during which he only "please[d]" his "blood" (II.i.51), and he is ready to mend his ways. Unselfishly he helps his brother and the Kixes.

In helping the Kixes Touchwood Senior may be seen to please his blood, and to some extent that is true. Artificial insemination would have been better as far as his dealings with Lady Kix go, but, given the state of the art, he did the best he could. The old Sir Oliver is suffering from a climacteric disease, sterility, and needs a child for legal reasons. Lady Kix says, "Tis our dry barrenness puffs up Sir Walter; / None gets by your not-getting, but that knight; / He's made by th' means" (II.i.161-63). Touchwood Senior has not heard this remark, having left the stage after learning that they want, but cannot have, children. It is true that he charges Sir Oliver four hundred pounds for his troubles (IV.i.152-54), but this should be seen as a comic and strangely acceptable business transaction. He tells the Kixes when they squabble:

Pray cease;
When there are friendlier courses took for you
To get and multiply within your house,
At your own proper costs in spite of censure,
Methinks an honest peace might be establish'd.
(III.iii.66-70)

The last thing the Yellowhammers have in mind for Moll is "an honest peace," and Allwit is ever ready to maintain a dishonest peace by "poisoning / [Sir Walter's] hopes in marriage" (I.ii.117-18). In contrast to them, Touchwood Senior's behavior is well-inclined—"inspite of censure," as he admits. The Kixes need a child in order to inherit the legacy, but they also want one. Lady Kix and Sir Oliver have had sexual adventures in their days (cf. III.iii.54-57, 76-80), but during the last seven years they have attempted to make their marriage work. For them a child is not synonymous with meat or money, as it is for the two Promoters and the Wench, the Allwits, and the Yellowhammers. Like Moll and Touchwood Junior, the Kixes need help—and Touchwood Senior provides it.

The play is laced with varying levels of irony to underscore the social decadence and depravity of Cheapside. The lecherous knight plans to be a godparent to his own child (II.ii.34-35), which surprises even Allwit. Later, in an aside, Sir Walter says about Allwit:

> The more slave!
> When man turns base, out goes his soul's pure flame;
> The fat of ease o'erthrows the eyes of shame.
> (II.ii.39-41)

It is ridiculous that Sir Walter should accuse anyone of baseness, but he probably means that Allwit has become complacent about keeping up appearances. Sir Walter wants to become a "gossip" because "it prevents suspicion" (II.ii.36), and love of respectability also induces him to ask for Moll as the second godparent. Ironically, Allwit wants his rival, Touchwood Junior, to be the third. Thus Middleton creates the dramatic and moral impetus behind the young lovers' attempts to escape.

Meanwhile, the preparations for the christening are interrupted by the two Promoters, as well as the Puritans and the Gossips. The former mistake a child for meat, while the latter attend the christening feast and help themselves to the prohibited meat. We are left with the impression that christenings are good for catering to appetites, but without spiritual meaning, for we hear nothing about the ceremony. Even the decency of the Parson who almost marries Moll and Touchwood Junior is questionable:

> *Touchwood Junior.* O sir, if ever you felt the force of love,
> pity it in me!
> *Parson.* Yes, though I ner'er was married sir,
> I have felt the force of love from good
> men's daughters,
> And some that will be maids yet three
> years hence.
> (III.i.1-5)

The self-conscious Latin disputation between Tim and his Tutor (IV.i.1-21), concerning a point of logic, and Tim's misplaced admiration for the Welsh Gentlewoman's knowledge of Hebrew, when she really speaks Welsh (cf. IV.i.111-212), indicate that well educated people are also concerned with appearances and reputations. Of the Welsh Gentlewoman, Tim says:

> By my faith, she's a good scholar, I see that already:
> She has the tongues plain; I hold my life she has travell'd.
> What will folks say? 'There goes the learned couple!'
> Faith, if the truth were known, she hath proceeded.
> (IV.i.143-46)

The moral turning point comes with the bogus deaths, which are unusually handled by Middleton. In Marston's *The Dutch Courtesan*, for instance, Freevil feigns death with Malheureux's and the audience's knowledge. Hence, when Malheureux is on his way to be executed for Freevil's murder, we know that he will be saved. But in *A Chaste Maid* there is less certainty. The young lovers' attempts to escape end in failure and with increasingly severe consequences. After the first attempt, Moll is locked up by her parents, but the next time she is literally and symbolically dipped in the filthy Thames and almost drowns. Touchwood Junior is wounded by Sir Walter in Act IV, scene iii, and is not seen again until the final scene of Act V. Meanwhile, a servant tells Sir Walter, "O sir, the gentleman you wounded is newly departed" (V.i.117), and another servant says that legal proceedings are underway against Sir Walter for murder (V.i.139-40). Touchwood Senior tells Yellowhammer,

> He's dead: 'twas a dear love to him,
> It cost him but his life, that was all, sir:
> He paid enough, poor gentleman, for his love.
> (V.ii.58-60)

Moll sings her "swan song" before Touchwood Senior arrives with the letter that presumably informs her that Touchwood Junior is safe. But although a reader notes the stage direction, [*She faints*], an audience might well wonder what is going on, especially when Yellowhammer cries, "Oh, she's gone for ever! That letter broke her heart" (V.ii.97-98). Perhaps on stage Moll could make a gesture to Touchwood Senior, Susan, or the audience to indicate that she has only fainted. But even Touchwood Senior's speech, following the dumb funeral procession, suggests that the lovers died off stage.

This is what Parker means when he says that the presentation of the characters "dips momentarily into horror." However Middleton is making minor, although important, adjustments to comic conventions in order to remind the audience that the play is also about a corrupt society in which people are really threatened. Just as the endless vulgar word-play modulates between "exuberant vitality and a sense of degeneracy," as Parker notes,[14] so the dramatic conventions modulate between comedy and a sense of the pathetic. But this is not a flaw in Middleton's art. In the climacteric year, the corruption of Cheapside's society is at an all-time high; the young lovers are in danger, while also about to experience a new moral order—hence the "modulation."

Levin considers that Sir Walter is the principal link between the four parts of the plot,[15] and I agree. The knight is corruption personified (cf. V.i.74): he props up the Allwits and almost succeeds in propping up the Yellowhammers as well as Tim and the Welsh Gentlewoman. Virtuous people like Touchwood Junior and Moll offer him little resistance. In the duel, Touchwood Junior only assaults "part / Of [Sir Walter's] former life" (V.i.137-38). But the knight is also adversely affected by Touchwood Senior's acts of kindness to the lovers and the Kixes, and it is this combination of events which leads to Sir Walter's demise; and, since his presence helped to prop up the corrupt society, his removal helps to bring about its collapse.

Consequently, Allwit's "conversion" makes thematic sense. Suddenly the "wittol" purges his house of the murderous, not to mention penniless, Sir Walter. With some of the funniest lines in the play, he says:

> I must tell you, sir,
> You have been somewhat bolder in my house
> Than I could well like of; I suff'red you
> Till it struck here at my heart; I tell you truly
> I thought you had been familiar with my wife once.
> (V.i.151-55)

Immediately after Sir Walter's departure to "th' knight's ward," Allwit is busy formulating contingency plans: " 'Life, for furniture, we may lodge a countess!" (V.i.174). But when his wife upbraids him, he says:

> I have done wench;
> And let this stand in every gallant's chamber:
> 'There's no gamester like a politic sinner,
> For who e'er games, the box is sure a winner.'
> (V.i.177-80)

It is more than strange to hear Allwit trotting out aphorisms about gaming, but with Sir Walter's demise he has also reached a climacteric crisis, which makes his "conversion" possible.

Likewise, Sir Walter's sense of inviolability has been shaken by the encounter with Touchwood Junior, and he too begins to see that things are changing (cf. V.i.26-34). His bitter scorn for the Allwits is either an opportunistic response to knowledge that the rules are about to change, or an attempt to placate his awakening conscience. Davy is told to fetch the children to his bedside, and they appear before their father like seven Erinys:

> Oh my vengeance!
> Let me for ever hide my cursed face
> From sight of those, that darkens all my hopes,
> And stands between me and the sight of Heaven.
> (V.i.69-72)

Allwit encourages Nick and Wat to calm Sir Walter, but the latter's reaction is: "Wretched, death of seven" (V.i.87). The knight's Seven Years' Lease has expired; he is no longer the man who "wakes the slave, and keeps his flesh in awe" (I.ii.114-15). The idea of his seven Erinys is paralleled and echoed in Moll's song: "Cruel fates true love do soonest sever; / Oh, I shall see thee never, never, never!" (V.ii.44-45). But whereas Moll's fate is found in the Seven Years' Lease about to begin, Sir Walter's is found in the one about to end.

The idea of society substituting one "lease" for another, I think, helps to explain the play's ending. The funeral scene is not a clumsy *deus ex machina*, but an appropriate shorthand for a moral re-birth. When the new "lease" begins, everyone joins Touchwood Senior in wishing that the two lovers had married, and when they rise from their coffins, even Yellowhammer gives his approval. Earlier he was content to ignore Sir Walter's sins (cf. IV.i.288-98), but he too has been "converted."

It may seem that history is repeating itself when Sir Oliver bids the Touchwood Seniors to live in his house. In keeping with the suggestive innuendos which have characterized the play, Sir Oliver says, "Be not afraid to go to your business roundly; / Get children, and I'll keep them," to which Touchwood Senior replies, "Take heed how you dare a man, while you live, sir, / That has good skill at his weapon" (V.iv.86-88). Sir Oliver refers to their legitimate children, while Touchwood Senior pretends to interpret Sir Oliver's words to mean that he should do some more "business" by way of Lady Kix. But, given the playfulness of the exchange, and the fact that Mistress Touchwood is to join her husband, I do not think that a new seducer is about to take up residence in another man's household.

Only Tim and his new bride appear to have a strained relationship. Learning of his wife's past with Sir Walter, Tim makes snide remarks about "let[ting] her out to execution," and that he and his Tutor "will about her" (V.iv.96, 114). Maudline urges him to "prove" that a whore can be a honest woman, and his wife tells him: "Sir, if your logic cannot prove me honest / There's a thing call'd marriage, and that makes me honest" (V.iv.117-18). Her comment is not only right but logically valid. Her "conversion" makes her honest. Moreover, their marriage, given the new Seven Years' Lease, has the same moral worth as that of Moll and Touchwood Junior, and if Moll is honest, then she must be as well. Perhaps Tim recognizes both points when he decides to "love her for her wit" (V.iv.122-23).

Cheapside's new Seven Years' Lease will probably see some moral lapses, because characters are not made absolutely pure by their "conversions." Sir Oliver thinks about the way Moll was treated by her parents and declares, "I would not have my cruelty so talk'd on, / To any child of mine, for a monopoly," but he also says, "The child is coming, and the land comes after" (V.iii.17, 33-34); Touchwood Senior never loses his bawdy sense of humor, and neither does Tim who is quickly cut off by his father when he says, "and for my mountains, I'll mount upon—" (V.iv.123-24); and Yellowhammer is delighted that "One feast will serve [both marriages]" (V.iv.125-27), proving that his love of money remains undimmed. Nevertheless, the play ends on an optimistic note because the seven year cycle of corruption is finally over, while it remains to be seen what the future will bring.

NOTES

I am grateful to Dr. Ronald Huebert for helpful suggestions at various stages of this article.

[1]Cf. R. B. Parker, who says: "With the exception of Moll (and even her chastity is seen slightly askance), the characters are all morally ambivalent to a greater or lesser degree" (Introd. *A Chaste Maid in Cheapside*, by Thomas Middleton [London: Methuen, 1969], p. lix); also Richard Levin, who writes that the plot "cannot fit any simple formula," because the four levels of comic development have varying degrees of "seriousness" ("The Four Plots in *A Chaste Maid in Cheapside*," *RES* 16 [1965]:22-23); and Gail Kern Paster who argues that "the cruel atmosphere of London" only indirectly points to moral issues; that Middleton makes "farce the level of human interaction as a way of suggesting an ethical position—albeit an oblique one" ("The City in Plautus and Middleton," *RenD* 6 [1973]:42-44).

[2]Parker, p. lix,

[3]Susan Wells, "Jacobean City Comedy and the Ideology of the City," *ELH* 48 (1981):54.

[4]All quotations from *A Chaste Maid in Cheapside* are taken from the edition in David L. Frost, ed. *The Selected Plays of Thomas Middleton* (Cambridge and New York: Cambridge Univ. Press, 1978).

[5]Brian Gibbons, *Jacobean City Comedy* (Cambridge, Mass.: Harvard Univ. Press, 1968), pp. 29-30.

[6]Wells, p. 37.

[7]Wells, pp. 48-49.

[8]Parker, pp, xliv-xlv.

[9]Saturn, the malevolent planet, is usually associated with these periods. Cf. "Climacteric years," *The Dictionary of Phrase and Fable*, Classic ed. (New York: Avenel Books, 1978).

[10]"Seven Years' Lease," *The Dictionary of Phrase and Fable.*

[11]Levin, p. 17.

[12]Levin, pp. 20-21.

[13]Levin, p. 24.

[14]Parker, p. xlviii.

[15]Levin, p. 16.

SEL 28 (1988)
ISSN 0039-3657

Recent Studies in Elizabethan and Jacobean Drama

JILL L. LEVENSON

Last spring I trained for this *SEL* marathon by reviewing (a mere) nine books on Shakespeare, published in 1984 and 1985, for the *University of Toronto Quarterly*. Of course nine volumes, however various, cannot represent an enormous field that grows annually. Moreover this little collection—the haphazard offerings of five publishers—had barely felt the influence of current theory. It did not include Dollimore and Sinfield or Greenblatt, Adelman, Erickson or Neely; it missed these and other critics who had gravitated during the 1980s in theoretical directions which Coppélia Kahn describes as "psychological, social and historical, feminist, deconstructive" ("Introduction," *Shakespeare's "Rough Magic": Renaissance Essays in Honor of C. L. Barber* [Newark: Univ. of Delaware Press; London and Toronto: Associated Univ. Presses, 1985], p. 15). Organizing that brief survey of essentially orthodox scholarship, I depended on Robert M. Adams's metaphoric explanation of critical trends in Shakespeare studies: "the general shape of the twentieth-century critical changes . . . is that of successive, increasingly rapid waves of opinion" (*The New York Review of Books*, 6 November 1986, p. 50). The nine volumes of recent but not current opinion appeared more or less in the order of their waves' succession.

As I wrote the shorter review, cartons of books had begun to arrive from *SEL* headquarters in Houston. Meanwhile, I had started to compile a list of 1987 publications on English Renaissance drama from the *TLS* and other periodicals, as well as publishers' advertisements and academic gossip. By the end of the year, when I could check books received against the list, the discrepancy indicated that I

Jill L. Levenson, Professor of English at Trinity College, the University of Toronto, edited the quarterly journal *Modern Drama* for more than ten years. She has written *"Romeo and Juliet" in Performance* (Manchester Univ. Press, 1987) and is currently preparing an Oxford edition of this early tragedy.

should recycle one or two comments from the *UTQ* essay in setting the limits of this one.

First, it should be emphasized that the following review does not make an exhaustive survey even of book-length studies on Renaissance drama. (It does not treat journal articles at all.) Obviously coverage relies most on the availability of new volumes, and therefore on their publishers' arrangements for circulating them. Whatever policies obtain, it seems that all publishers of books on Elizabethan and Jacobean drama do not inevitably send all of their relevant book-length publications to *SEL*. If a few conscientiously post each volume as it appears, many offer a sampling—small, medium, or large—of the year's work. I confess that I have not asked *SEL* to acquire the missing volumes, because it would take a sabbatical leave to examine them all.

Second, the books which did arrive generally avoided the "turmoil and controversy" in literary studies which determined Jean Howard's position in writing last year's *SEL* review (see pp. 321-22). Yet the uproar has not subsided, especially on the Shakespearean front. Early in 1987 Terence Hawkes described it in terms anticipating Howard's: "The news that the current output of writings about the Bard may stand as high as 8.8 articles or books *a day* confirms him and all his works as one of the crucial battlegrounds in the struggle for cultural meaning" (*TLS*, 10 April 1987, p. 390). Academic conferences like recent meetings of the Shakespeare Association of America and the Modern Language Association also testify that the battle continues. Nevertheless, many of the full-length studies and collections of essays published last year remain outside the fray in well-established shelters. In my study I rarely encountered the partisans of psychological, social and historical, feminist, or deconstructive approaches; Tennenhouse (soft-spoken) arrived at the beginning of the year, Howard and O'Connor along with Womack (outspoken) toward the end. By Walter Cohen's account (in Howard and O' Connor's *Shakespeare Reproduced*), I missed only two books of political criticism: Stephen Greenblatt's *Shakespearean Negotiations* (Berkeley: Univ. of California Press) and Steven Mullaney's *The Place of the Stage: License, Play, and Power in Renaissance England* (Chicago and London: Univ. of Chicago Press).

In light of books received, this review will survey shelters for the most part and an occasional area of conflict according to the numbers of writers they attracted and the quantities of theoretical content they hold. Among theoretical books—those which argue a particular interpretive approach to a body of plays—the largest group take genre as their point of departure. The essay deals initially with these, and then with volumes which concentrate on politics, skepticism, linguistics, and an assortment of single themes. From this category it proceeds to discussions of staging, pre-Restoration theater, and texts in performance, all subjects which drew considerable attention last year. Next it treats books on individual playwrights and their associates, as well as books on individual plays. Having covered volumes on related topics, the survey will range over miscellaneous collections of essays, editions, other reference works, and reprinted books. For most citations of earlier scholarship in my text, full bibliographical information can be found in James G. McManaway and Jeanne Addison Roberts, *A Selective Bibliography of Shakespeare: Editions, Textual Studies, Commentary* (Washington: Folger Shakespeare Library, 1975). If McManaway and Roberts do not include the item, the review contains a full reference.

I should probably add that I write from a position of infinite tolerance, not only because I shrink from retaliation, but also because I still value the old humanism, New Criticism, and primary research which inform many of these volumes. Facing eighty-four books and an unyielding deadline, I felt grateful when I could understand an argument without having to master a foreign vocabulary. More important, a number of books vigorously exercised critical faculties not always active in teaching or specialized research projects. Like John Wilders, anxious as he undertook a comprehensive review of Shakespeare books mid 1987, I experienced relief as I calculated the results of reading: "on the whole, informative, challenging, illuminating and diverse in manner and approach" (*TLS*, 30 October-5 November 1987, p. 1199). Sheer giddiness may account for Wilders's figures of speech: "On this evidence the Shakespearean circus is in good health and . . . is performing new feats with which to enthrall and astonish its audiences." Yet in the end they suit the tone of last year's published proceedings more accurately than Hawkes's metaphor, rejoicing in books that made canons, not war.

I

Last year's most comprehensive treatment of genre also turned out to be its most sustained application of the "new" historicism: Leonard Tennenhouse's *Power on Display: The Politics of Shakespeare's Genres.* Tennenhouse has taken this theoretical approach to his subject in order to address crucial questions frequently unasked by conventional genre studies: why did certain dramatic forms prosper at specific times? why did particular genres undergo radical transformations or abandonment? On his way to these questions, Tennenhouse began his study with others intended to disclose "the historical principle which divides literary genres internally or makes them overlap in certain respects" (p. 5). The principle he discovered—the political conflicts of Renaissance England—governs his argument. In addition, this book's dialectic rests on two related assumptions: the English Renaissance had not yet differentiated literary from political discourse; and "Shakespeare exists for us as several different rhetorical strategies" (p. 2). Having isolated this principle and made these assumptions, Tennenhouse states his purpose: "My goal, then, is to argue for a Shakespeare whose dramatic forms participated in the political life of Renaissance England" (p. 6).

Disarmingly, Tennenhouse explains in the introduction how he built safeguards against the kinds of obstacles that impede a new historical approach. He developed "antiprocedures" to prevent himself from translating Renaissance culture into modern terms, forcing it to express "our notion of sexuality, the family, and the individual" (p. 10). In his argument he uses "strategies of defamiliarization," introducing a range of non-Shakespearean Renaissance texts—from official documents to plays and poems—as background for Shakespeare's drama (p. 15). As he went through these processes, Tennenhouse found himself "wriggling out of my cultural skin, much as someone might wriggle out of a particularly close-fitting turtleneck shirt" (p. 11). So he pursues his goal with caution, integrity, and some inconvenience.

Adapting his strategy from the beginning of Foucault's *Discipline and Punish*, Tennenhouse analyzes theatrical displays as forms of power: "I see [such displays] as providing a site where the iconography of state power was formulated in tension with various forms of representation that contested the ideology of the Renaissance court. The stage was in this sense a place where political events occurred and where history was being produced" (p. 14). Tennenhouse concentrates on certain figures of power which represent or derive meaning from the "aristocratic body," or Queen Elizabeth's body as he identifies it with the state (p. 16). In the variations of power's behavior on the stage, literary genres become distinguishable. Moreover, vicissitudes in the representations reflect vicissitudes in the aristocratic body and the new strategies opposed to it.

Tennenhouse's first and longest chapter treats romantic comedy through a discontinuous narrative in nine segments. For defamiliarization, the argument relies primarily on Sir Philip Sidney: the texts of his *Arcadia* and love poetry; his involvement in political life at court; and the interrelation of his art and career which made him a model of "the desiring courtier" (p. 36). Reinforcing this material, citations from William Camden and John Stubbs among others illustrate the general concern of writers with Elizabeth's potential marriage and the complexities of succession through the female line. As court literature attempted to resolve these dilemmas, and simultaneously mirrored the system of Elizabethan patronage, a social fantasy took shape in art. Theater and literature "displayed the same paradoxical figure organizing their political life: that of a perfect world to which an unavailable aristocratic woman alone could provide access" (p. 36).

In Tennenhouse's view, Shakespeare's romantic comedies add an element of parody to this figure and consequently represent the aristocracy from an outsider's perspective. The resulting genre, more tractable and inclusive than the object of parody, traces a specific pattern of action:

> [E]ven though Shakespeare endows each of his heroines with certain patriarchal prerogatives, this move always constitutes one step in a double move which relocates power in the male by way of marriage. Shakespeare thus restores the natural hierarchy of social relations as the wife subordinates herself to her husband. Having been so transferred from male to female and back again, however, the very nature of power changes.
>
> (p. 62)

Tennenhouse reads *The Taming of the Shrew, The Merchant of Venice, Twelfth Night,* and part of *A Midsummer Night's Dream* within this context.

The second and shortest chapter deals with plays which the author regards as undefined by traditional literary genres: in particular, *Henry VIII* (which does not belong with the chronicle histories) and *Hamlet* (which belongs with the chronicle histories rather than the Jacobean tragedies). At this point Tennenhouse emphasizes political changes at the turn of the century, challenges not only to royal prerogatives but to their artistic formulations. He considers the effects of Jacobean political history on Jacobean genres, introducing two major subjects in chapters 3 and 4: his definitions of Shakespearean tragedy and romance.

Whereas the aristocratic female body stands for the body politic in Elizabethan tragedy as well as other genres, Tennenhouse contends, the abused female body represents political difficulties and their resolution in Jacobean tragedy. With *Othello, King Lear, Macbeth,* and *Antony and Cleopatra,* he demonstrates how Shakespeare reworks earlier genres to make them portray "a more conservative form of patriarchy" (p. 123). "If Jacobean drama proves one single thing, . . . it is that sexual relations are always political. Jacobean tragedies maintain the patriarchal principles despite extravagant assaults on the monarch's natural body, despite illicit seizure of the instruments of state, and despite misuse of the rituals and symbols of power" (p. 124).

Like the rest of the iconography surrounding King James, the other Jacobean theatrical genres—"disguised ruler plays," city comedy, and romances—all display "a world without patriarchy as a world in grave danger" (p. 149). Together, they compose a picture of authority in Jacobean drama: "City comedy authorizes the positive representation of power displayed in dramatic romance. . . . The forces of disorder on the tragic stage or in the city comedies coexist with the idealized representation of order as a bounteous feast table in a mutually constituting relationship of figure to ground" (p. 153). In his fourth and concluding chapter, Tennenhouse scans nine absent monarch plays, the group of Jacobean city comedies, and Shakespeare's romances.

As my brief review suggests, Tennenhouse's strategies vary somewhat from chapter to chapter, although his antiprocedures stay in place throughout. For example, defamiliarization occupies a large space in the chapter on romantic comedy, but never again enjoys such expansiveness. Interpretations of dramatic texts—sometimes circumstantial, sometimes not—become prominent in other chapters. Divided into sections, the format of each chapter is fragmented, unique, hence unpredictable. The original mode of Tennenhouse's argument demands that a willing reader escape not only cultural biases but also most familiar habits of thought. His own display of intellectual energy makes for brisk wriggling.

Despite his alertness, Tennenhouse stumbles a few times at the edge of pitfalls. His readings of individual texts, while they focus on political implications, ignore or dismiss other possibilities (see, for instance, pp. 32-33 on the language of courtship and love). Occasionally they wrench Shakespearean plays into alignment with narrow concepts of the politics they reflect (see, for example, the discussions on pp. 77-81 of *Richard II* and on pp. 157-59 of *Measure for Measure*). Finally, Tennenhouse makes relatively little use of historical records, depending on conclusions from the old historicism especially for his understanding of King James's relationship to contemporary drama. As Leeds Barroll will show in his forthcoming study "A New History for Shakespeare and His Time," these documents allow for alternative readings of the era and therefore of the literature which contributed to its political debates. (Walter

Cohen's essay in Howard and O'Connor's *Shakespeare Reproduced* makes a similar point.) Terence Hawkes, admiring Tennenhouse's important book, summarizes its lapses in his single reservation (*TLS*, 10 April 1987):

> Rather too frequently the text seems smoothly conducive to what the creature "Shakespeare" thinks and believes, with small allowance made for its cross-grained recalcitrance, its equivocation, . . . The political state it engages with can seem correspondingly static, drained of a potential for radical resistance and sleekly recuperative of the dissent which we know lay in wait.
>
> (p. 393)

Except for Tennenhouse's *Power on Display*, the books on genre deal with one or (at most) two forms. Four studies concern Elizabethan and Jacobean tragedy: Dieter Mehl, *Shakespeare's Tragedies: An Introduction*; Thomas McAlindon, *English Renaissance Tragedy*; Peter Mercer, *"Hamlet" and the Acting of Revenge*; and C. L. Barber, *Creating Elizabethan Tragedy: The Theater of Marlowe and Kyd* (edited by Richard P. Wheeler).

Mehl's volume, a revised and freely translated version of his 1983 introduction for German students, surveys nine tragedies as well as *Timon of Athens* and *Troilus and Cressida*. Addressing English readers, Mehl has not changed his purpose: he offers background for each play—provenance, stage history, representative criticism—and his own exposition of the text in light of its genre. As Mehl follows each "late" and Roman/Greek tragedy from beginning to end (in chapters of about twenty-five pages), considering both text and context, he provides little new interpretation. This volume, an old-fashioned reader's guide, indicates which subjects have kept the critics busy (until c. 1980), celebrates the vitality of the texts, and "puts rather more emphasis on the dramatic characters than has been usual or fashionable for some time" (p. vii).

Mehl devotes a short first chapter to genre, avoiding schematization of the tragedies and citing Kenneth Muir's caution: "There is no such thing as Shakespearian Tragedy: there are only Shakespearian tragedies" (p. 2). In the end, however, Mehl prefers A. C. Bradley's definition; he believes the genre centers on the protagonist's experience of loss and on a moral vision: "The real substance of the tragic conflict . . . can only be understood in moral categories, by the experience that there is a fundamental opposition of good and evil determining all human intercourse but resisting any simple explanation" (p. 7). Although he does not cite Maynard Mack's seminal essay on "The Jacobean Shakespeare," Mehl shares some of its concepts about the dynamic between hero and community in Shakespeare's tragedies (pp. 6-7).

Arranging the plays by chronology and subject matter, Mehl begins with *Titus Andronicus* and *Romeo and Juliet* and ends with the two "problem" plays. He includes not only the standard Jacobean tragedies, but the three Roman dramas. As he journeys through the texts, Mehl varies his routes slightly. For instance, the chapter on *Hamlet* interprets the play chronologically, giving a thorough account of deviations from the traditional revenge-tragedy model; key themes and passages; and ambiguities in the text: a capsule version of John Dover Wilson's *What Happens in "Hamlet."* By comparison, the next chapter on *Othello* seems barely charted; the exposition here spends time describing interpretive controversies and catches up with itself by taking giant leaps through the play. Later, the discussion of *Antony and Cleopatra* stresses characterization rather than this tragedy's poetic and dramaturgical complexities.

Mehl's book succeeds as an introduction to the life and times of Shakespeare's tragic plays. Nevertheless, it misses some of the best criticism and most provocative approaches: the connection of *Titus Andronicus* with emblem poetry; the work of Rosalie L. Colie; the papers in *Some Facets of "King Lear": Essays in Prismatic Criticism*, edited by Rosalie L. Colie and F. T. Flahiff (Toronto and Buffalo: Univ. of Toronto Press, 1974); and cinematic renderings of these plays. Students and general readers should know that the bibliographical apparatus, while useful as a guide, does not thoroughly represent the best or most current studies.

More specialized, McAlindon's *English Renaissance Tragedy* covers the period from Kyd's *The Spanish Tragedy* (c. 1585-1590) and Marlowe's *Tamburlaine the Great* (1587-1588) to Ford's *The Broken Heart* and *'Tis Pity She's a Whore* (c. 1626-1633). It emphasizes the variety and interrelatedness of the tragedies, "the connections—conceptual, thematic, and formal" (p. 3). Like Tennenhouse, McAlindon has looked for overlapping in these texts; he has sought out "their shared ideas, preoccupations, and methods." But McAlindon focuses on non-Shakespearean tragedy, draws a large referential framework—not a principle—from his analysis, and establishes the structure's five component parts before examining the dramatic texts within its purview. Part I, his long opening chapter, defines these components: Violent Change; The Noble Death; The Violation of Justice and Love; Treacherous Entertainment: The Symbolism of Rite and Play; and Treacherous Words: The Language of Tragic Reality.

As he places each part in the frame, McAlindon identifies its source in the history of ideas. He traces fear of Violent Change back to Renaissance cosmology and forward to *The Spanish Tragedy*, *Tamburlaine*, and the Elizabethan Shakespeare, showing its influence on characterization and the shape of tragic action. In describing The Noble Death, he cites Christian and classical models—John Foxe's *Acts and Monuments*, Seneca's *Hercules Furens*—for the ritual of violent death which tests the hero's authenticity; then he points out variations on the model in a number of Renaissance plays. The general heading "The Violation of Justice and Love" introduces two more specific topics: justice and law, and law and marriage. The first allows McAlindon to investigate the connection between English Renaissance law and drama, especially with reference to the concept of revenge; the second brings him to the meaning of the bonds—"familial, matrimonial, and national" bonds among others (p. 39)—undone in English Renaissance tragedy. According to McAlindon, Kyd first linked these ideas of love, justice, marriage, and law not only to one another, but also to "the universal principle of harmonious contrariety." Kyd's achievement, seen in its cultural setting, leads the argument to a conclusion which bears comparison with Tennenhouse's view of the genre:

> [Kyd] showed his contemporaries and successors how to combine in a richly significant pattern the elements of romance and intrigue attractive to a popular audience with those matters of state traditionally thought proper to tragedy. As a result of his design, the interaction of socio-political and sexual disorder is a constant feature of Renaissance tragedy. What happens in courtship and marriage is reflected in or directly affects what happens in the state. Thus the changing configurations of sexual intrigue echo the great world's uncertainty as to who's in and who's out in the palaces of favour and fortune.
>
> (p. 39)

Kyd also created The Treacherous Entertainment, which McAlindon explains in terms of Renaissance concepts about ritual and play. When McAlindon comments on role as metaphor in characterizing the tragic hero, he provides a general gloss for Mercer's portrayal of the revenge protagonist. Both critics give close attention to The Language of Tragic Reality, McAlindon identifying recurrent metaphors, puns, rhetorical devices, and the most prevalent forms of semantic confusion.

Part II (chapters 2 to 6) offers McAlindon's readings of ten plays by Kyd, Marlowe, Tourneur, Webster, and Middleton. Rich in detail and insight, these employ the theoretical frame for reference, not constraint. McAlindon works inductively from texts he obviously knows very well; each explication assumes a different form and direction appropriate to its play.

McAlindon's most illuminating perceptions grow out of his close readings of individual passages: lines that weave myths through *The Spanish Tragedy, Tamburlaine, The Duchess of Malfi*; verbal and nonverbal patterns that make up for "figurative austerity" (p. 117) in *Edward II*; image clusters that refract the trajectory of Faustus; allusions to time, grace, and language that create aesthetic unity in *The Revenger's Tragedy*; manifestations of humor in the design of *The White Devil*; interrelated dualisms in *Women Beware Women*. Sometimes these passages add up to a whole scene, subplot, or play. In almost all cases, when McAlindon examines them against his frame—the shared ideas, preoccupations, and methods of English Renaissance tragedy—he discovers artfulness and meaning in the composition.

In *"Hamlet" and the Acting of Revenge*, Peter Mercer challenges two assumptions about Elizabethan revenge plays—that their structures are unproblematic, their central concerns ethical—and rethinks the genre before explaining how Shakespeare complicates it. The first half of this book defines a "structure of meaning" which includes some components from Maynard Mack's description of tragic form in "The Jacobean Shakespeare": "Essentially this structure registers a metamorphosis, a process whereby, through extremities of passion and extravagances of rhetoric, the hero is changed from his normal social self to a monster of revenging fury. This 'making of the revenger' invariably involves the assuming of a number of roles or disguises" (p. 2). More precisely, the revenge action takes place in three sequential phases introduced by an apparition, continuing in the hero's transformation, and ending with revenge through an artful stratagem. Mercer identifies this design in Seneca's *Thyestes* and two Renaissance plays: Kyd's *Spanish Tragedy* and Marston's *Antonio's Revenge*. He also examines *The Revenger's Tragedy*, because it shares with *Hamlet* mixed origin in both revenge and satire.

As Mercer considers the ghosts in revenge tragedy and then studies four examples of the genre, he interprets the meaning of structural or stylistic features. In his view, otherworldly presences insist that nonhuman forces shape the present action, however determined the gestures of individual men and women. The rhetorical flatness of choric voices betrays the distance of these witnesses from the tragic hero's experiences, the resulting lack of comprehension. Within the Elizabethan plays an "opposing" action—a plot controlled by an active villain—helps to rationalize the hero's transformation into a revenger while maintaining the audience's sympathy for him (p. 41). Moreover, the histrionic element conspicuous in these tragedies fills a void left by ritual. Since the Elizabethan world provided no system of rites adequate to the performance of revenge, the plays had to draw on ancient dramatic models. Their protagonists therefore struggle to master roles of intense passion articulated through the extreme rhetoric of vengeance.

The second half of this book analyzes *Hamlet* as a version of the structural paradigm. After acknowledging well-known distinctions—the development of potential ambiguities, the coloring of events with Hamlet's dark emotions—Mercer offers a speculation which will generate his most original insights: "We might almost say that Shakespeare has created for his tragedy of revenge a world so inherently resistant to the fierce simplifications of such an action, . . . that it is hard to see how any revenger could impose upon it the murderous artifice of his ritual of death" (p. 122).

In four chapters Mercer interprets *Hamlet*, sometimes line by line, giving his closest attention to the opening scene and act. His analysis of diction, syntax, and narration demonstrates that a "plurality of voices" conveys "the movement, the fluidity of life itself" (p. 135); the syntax alone "forces on us an overwhelming sense of the contingency of all things" (p. 136). Like Stephen Booth's essay "On the Value of *Hamlet*," Mercer's book finds the dynamic of Shakespeare's text in its details. It traces the revenge paradigm as Shakespeare filters it through language in particular.

While challenging old assumptions, Mercer discovers regions of *Hamlet* which attracted other writers last year from other directions. He pauses over Hamlet's first confrontation with the Ghost: "Whatever the scene leads us to expect, what it actually gives us is a hero sworn not to bloody revenge but to the memory of his father's suffering spirit" (p. 169). Similarly Stanley Cavell pauses in *Disowning Knowledge in Six Plays of Shakespeare* at this point of his philosophical/psychological inquiry into *Hamlet*: "the father's dictation of the way he wishes to be remembered—by having his revenge taken for him—exactly deprives the son, with his powers of mourning, of the right to mourn *him*, to let him pass" (p. 188). When Mercer discusses the way Shakespeare has subverted the traditional conclusion of revenge tragedy, he emphasizes Hamlet's release from fate to engage with chance. That encounter has a central place in William Beatty Warner's *Chance and the Text of Experience: Freud, Nietzsche, and Shakespeare's "Hamlet"*. In effect, Mercer employs conventional methods to relax the hold of standard genre criticism on the form and meaning of *Hamlet*.

With C. L. Barber's *Creating Elizabethan Tragedy: The Theater of Marlowe and Kyd,* published on the first day of 1988, Richard P. Wheeler presents a New Year's gift to admirers of the late scholar. Having gathered Barber's writings on this genre, Wheeler offers three essays along with his own generous introduction drawn from unpublished work. Parts of the first Barber essay, "Theatrical Magic in *Tamburlaine*," were printed in *Literature and Psychology* 16 (Winter 1966); most of the second, " 'The forme of Faustus fortunes good or bad,' " comes from *Tulane Drama Review* 8 (Summer 1964). However the third paper, "Unbroken Passion: Social Piety and Outrage in *The Spanish Tragedy*," appears in this volume for the first time.

Like other tributes to Barber over the past eight years, Wheeler's introduction attempts to define the nature of his influence, "the kind of insight" (p. 3) that made the late scholar such an important critic and teacher. This discussion places Barber's theory among the critical discourses that surrounded it, from formalist traditions to the still unnamed new historicism to modern psychology, comparative religion, and anthropology. In the end Wheeler maintains: "The special density of Barber's criticism partly derives from his effort to keep each of these contexts in view and in dynamic relation with one another" (pp. 20-21).

Wheeler's introduction also summarizes Barber's concepts of early Elizabethan tragedy, and with the essays this outline provides "a speculative inquiry into some of the enabling theatrical conditions of Shakespeare's tragic artistry" (p. vii). The new study on *The Spanish Tragedy* emphasizes the special forces operating in the play, the effect of the "Senecan mood and logic of violence" (p. 142) on these processes, verse mirroring of the action, and the Freudian implications of Hieronimo's experience. (Now and then Barber's conclusions seem to anticipate Mercer's.)

Wendy Griswold's book, *Renaissance Revivals: City Comedy and Revenge Tragedy in the London Theatre, 1576-1980,* reviews the histories of both genres from a sociological and humanist perspective. First it investigates the conditions—"cultural, theatrical, and social" (p. 2)—which initially produced these genres and their meanings; then it follows the Restoration-to-current pattern of their revivals which indicates how the original meanings changed over time. Like C. L. Barber and the new historians, Griswold understands plays as cultural phenomena which interact with the institutions and customs that form their immediate setting. She builds a thorough, multifaceted, and convincing argument for her view.

Griswold's concept determines not only the method but also the working vocabulary of *Renaissance Revivals*. Its fullest expression, graphic and verbal, is a device that Griswold calls "the cultural diamond":

> I conceive of the linkages between a cultural object and the social world as forming a diamond. . . . At the apex there is a social context, such as Elizabethan England; at the base there is a cultural object, such as the genre city comedy. The left point of the diamond represents creators or artists, here a set of dramatists and theatrical personnel, while the right point stands for the recipients, the audience.
>
> (p. 7)

Checking herself with this "accounting heuristic" (p. 8), Griswold proceeds to observe all the major contributors to the social-cultural interaction affecting two Renaissance dramatic genres in England.

Griswold has chosen to focus on city comedy and revenge tragedy because scholars have clearly distinguished them as genres; neither one playwright's style nor the Shakespeare industry has ever controlled them; and London theaters have revived them both in substantial numbers. As she arranges her research, chapters 2 and 3 examine each genre in its native habitat. The next three chapters track the revivals, and the last one tries to account for "periods of greater and lesser fit between these genres and their societal and institutional contexts" (p. 13).

With the two chapters on English Renaissance drama, Griswold identifies the plays in both categories and, working from authoritative scholarship, describes the types' basic features as well as the theaters in which they prospered. Each description leads to a detailed assessment of "the topical, archetypal, and social appeal of the genre" (p. 14). Considering the success of revenge tragedy, for instance, Griswold analyzes its perversity (or inversion of contemporary values), horror, and representation of social tensions within the state.

As she turns to the revivals of city comedy and revenge tragedy, Griswold wants to know "when and how post-Renaissance theatres and theatregoers reconstructed the meanings of these genres." The cultural diamond at hand, these chapters address the issue with accounts of "the social composition and physical arrangement of theatre audiences; the economic and organizational context in which managers and producers made their repertory decisions; the prevalent dramatic conventions; the competing modes of entertainment attracting audiences and worrying managers; and the socially based concerns and commonplaces, expectations and attitudes, of those individuals in each era that made up the London theatre's 'art world' " (p. 101).

Having presented a wealth of empirical evidence (much of it concentrated in tables), as well as interpretation, Griswold begins her last chapter with a summary of six general findings about Renaissance revivals and four observations about the two genres. She surveys the data by means of another figure, comparing cultural objects and social experience to the vehicle and tenor of metaphor. When the object connects efficiently with the interests and concerns of its recipients—creating and releasing tension as it plays on their expectations—it enjoys popular success. According to Griswold, the rascal in one genre and revenge theme of the other have worked metaphorically at different historical times, interacting with the tenors of economic conflict and failures of state. As a result, "the cultural resources of revenge tragedy and city comedy have been used to structure the social experience of succeeding generations of London playgoers" (p. 211).

Like several other books received, Harry Levin's *Playboys and Killjoys: An Essay on the Theory and Practice of Comedy* combines new essays on a theme with old. The twelve-part study which makes up the larger portion of the volume originated as a series of lectures at Oxford and Berkeley. At the end, four essays already published appear in slightly revised forms.

Levin proceeds in his main argument to observe the whole range of dramatic comedy by a synchronic method. As he considers matters of theory and definition, structure, characterization, setting, and effect—"a few first principles and basic elements" (p. 71)—he illustrates general points with instances from Tudor and Stuart plays. Among the four reprinted papers, "Notes on City Comedy" (from *Renaissance Genres: Essays on Theory, History, and Interpretation*, Harvard English Studies 14, ed. Barbara Kiefer Lewalski [Cambridge, Mass., and London: Harvard Univ. Press, 1986]) discusses the Renaissance subgenre while giving an account of comedy's long association with cities. Levin distinguishes two schools within Renaissance city comedy, represented in the article by about twenty plays.

Tracing one character type in early seventeenth-century comedy, N. J. Rigaud has written *Femme Mythifiée, Femme de Raison: La Veuve dans la comédie anglaise au temps de Shakespeare 1600-1625*. Rigaud considers the origins of the dramatized widow figure in reality and fiction (first chapter) and then surveys thirty-eight comedies where this type of character appears. From the evidence gathered, this book argues that the dramatists combine two sorts of features—one old, one new—in their widows: mythical feminine qualities (*la richesse*, provision, stability) and reasonableness (control of passions, intellectual lucidity, a sense of proportion). Consequently, remarriage with a young and ruined man in the plays carries a number of significations which Rigaud examines.

In *Renaissance Drama in England & Spain: Topical Allusion and History Plays*, John Loftis compares two versions of the same dramatic genre. Since the *comedia* and English history plays almost never interacted with one another, both forms independently resisted the control of neoclassical theory. As a result both, "alone in the Renaissance" (p. 5), presented sequences of events connected with national history and interpreted current issues in the process. Of course the nations interacted if their history plays did not. Given this network of analogues and links, Loftis has organized his book as a chronological account of Anglo-Spanish relations and the dramas which mirrored each phase. In order to give events "their European setting," he includes the Revolt of the Netherlands and the civil wars of France (p. 25). He writes in full knowledge that the dramatic texts, like all forms of history, are "culture-bound, not objective, not immutable":

> Historical drama and narrative history alike are conditioned by the time at which they are written, by social and institutional constraints, by the nature of available sources, by literary theory and convention, and—in the Spain and England of the Renaissance—by myth: in Spain, by the myth of the nation's imperial destiny; in England, by the myth known in the twentieth century as the "Black Legend."
> (p. 6)

With an introduction that briefly reviews sixteenth-century Anglo-Spanish politics, Loftis reads Shakespeare's *Henry VIII* and Calderón's *La cisma de Inglaterra* as typical Protestant and Catholic statements on the English Reformation. The succeeding chapters focus on the war of King Philip II in the Netherlands, the war of Queen Elizabeth I against Spain, the peace of King James I and the Palatinate, the Spanish courtship of Prince Charles and the Palatinate, and the Spanish victories of 1625. As the book covers the whole Renaissance, each chapter sketches individual events chronologically and describes the relevant plays, English or Spanish, alongside the episodes they reflect. This format undergoes some adjustment with each new historical phase. In the discussion of King Philip II and the Netherlands, events alternate with three texts by Lope de Vega. The section on Queen Elizabeth I, however, concentrates on English dramas—Shakespeare's *King John*, Marlowe's *Massacre at Paris*, Chapman's *The Conspiracy and Tragedy of Charles, Duke of Byron*—which approach their subject matter indirectly with plots set in foreign countries during recent times. Because the accession and reign of King James I accelerated the pace of Anglo-Spanish affairs, the chapters on this period juxtapose history and both kinds of plays with greater frequency. The Palatinate material includes, among English works alone, texts by Jonson, Massinger, and Middleton, as well as *Sir John van Oldenbarnevelt.* Not surprisingly the Spanish victories of 1625 inspired a number of Spanish dramas, Calderón's *El sitio de Bredá* having no equivalent among English history plays.

Drawing on evidence from the first six chapters, Loftis's conclusion summarizes the forces—from religious premises and censorship to chronicles and patronage—which shaped dramatic representations of history during the Renaissance. In the course of this book, the reader witnesses those forces in action, biasing Spanish drama toward the imperial tradition of its country and making English plays "alternative versions of European history in the sixteenth and early seventeenth centuries" (p. 6). Never overstepping the bounds of his comparison, Loftis has given a significant topic comprehensive and judicious treatment.

II

Year's end brought an important book of essays committed to politicizing Shakespeare not only in criticism and performance but especially in the classroom: *Shakespeare Reproduced: The Text in History and Ideology*, edited by Jean E. Howard and Marion F. O'Connor. With their introduction Howard and O'Connor identify feminism, new historicism, and Marxist criticism as the forms of contemporary discourse which the essays share. While the volume appropriates these and other current strategies (such as Bakhtin's discourse of carnival, or the discourse of deconstruction), however, "it modifies and reconfigures them" (p. 3). Moreover it defines terms as clearly as it presents genealogy, stating what the writers mean by "political analysis," "ideology" (pp. 3-4), and in particular "reproduced":

> By the title, *Shakespeare Reproduced: The Text in History and Ideology*, the editors intend to signal the nature of the

> countercriticism undertaken in these pages. If Shakespeare is often used to reproduce (to repeat and so continuously to give new life to) certain ideas about art's transcendence of history and politics, many of the essays included here aim to produce Shakespeare *differently* (reproduction understood as refashioning or making new) by exploring the political functions of the text at specific historical junctures within specific social practices.
>
> (p. 5)

This book therefore advances a program which it announces straightforwardly, at once; the editors and authors hope to change "the dissemination of Shakespeare in culture" (p. 5), beginning with pedagogical methods and the curriculum. By various means each paper supports the enterprise.

The first two essays provide useful historical contexts for ideological criticism in Great Britain and (with more detail) the United States. In "Political Criticism of Shakespeare," Walter Cohen describes the origins, methods, and boundaries of the three contemporary discourses which inform this book. Purposefully he juxtaposes feminist critics, British Marxist Shakespeareans, and American new historicists, "criticizing each [group] for its failure adequately to incorporate the theories, methods, and findings of the others" (p. 22). He proposes to consolidate and expand the gains of political criticism, which he partially records in "Bibliography 2: Political Studies of Shakespeare in the 1980s" (pp. 44-46). A complementary analysis, Don E. Wayne's "Power, Politics, and the Shakespearean Text: Recent Criticism in England and the United States," examines the historical/cultural factors which produced distinctions between British Marxists and American new historicists. In a compelling account Wayne reconstructs developments in the American academy since World War II, concluding with an outline of the new historicism and emphasizing the practitioner's "special responsibility to articulate the relationship between our constructions of the past and our present situation" (p. 60).

Nine of the remaining essays engage in the three formative political discourses, modifying and reconfiguring them as the introduction promised. For instance, O'Connor produces a long, well-documented, and fascinating study of a Shakespearean exhibition which reflected British ruling-class culture in the early twentieth century: "Theatre of the Empire: 'Shakespeare's England' at Earl's Court, 1912." Other papers apply political strategies to a range of Shakespearean plays: *The Tempest*, *The Merry Wives of Windsor*,

Othello, Much Ado About Nothing, The Merchant of Venice, Coriolanus, and *Macbeth*. Written by Margaret Ferguson, the afterword considers in some detail "the pedagogical project of producing Shakespeare differently in the classroom" (p. 279).

With the last essay, "Towards a Literary Theory of Ideology: Mimesis, Representation, Authority," Robert Weimann reviews the whole enterprise and raises many questions which the new historical and material-cultural critics have yet to address. Weimann creates his demanding prose from the vocabularies of several discourses: "how and to what extent do these mimetic uses of power either conflict with or corroborate the uses, in language, of an ideological signified which is always already given?" (p. 266); "on what ideological in terms of which legitimation gestures was it possible for these unsanctioned social interests in the public playhouses to authorize their own theatrical discourse?" (p. 270). Expressing critical tolerance, Weimann's multilingual notes close an earnest, analytical, and highly focused sequence of essays on a refreshing note of openness and play: "Ultimately, it may perhaps be said that one of the ways by which the Elizabethan theatre appropriated power was to challenge the representation of authority by an alternative authority of theatrical representation which derived at least part of its strength from vitalizing and mobilizing a new space for *Spass*, with all its irreverent and equalizing implications in the social process" (p. 272).

Two challenging books on the same topic occasionally cross each other's paths: Graham Bradshaw's *Shakespeare's Scepticism* and Stanley Cavell's *Disowning Knowledge in Six Plays of Shakespeare*. Both authors believe in "Shakespeare as a writer of human consistency, developing a particular problematic in and of a world, and in and of a language" (Cavell, p. viii). A literary critic, Bradshaw investigates the problematic by tracing Shakespeare's ideas about "the nature of Nature" (p. ix) through their poetic/dramatic permutations in a dozen assorted plays. A philosopher, Cavell examines Shakespeare's anticipation of a problematic associated with Descartes in five tragedies and one romance: "the issue suggested is how to live at all in a groundless world" (p. 3). Both Bradshaw and Cavell produce densely textured arguments that resist abstraction, each writing in a distinctive style that suits his case. Discovering correspondences within and between plays—and between plays and other art forms—Bradshaw expresses himself with wit that easily links Shakespeare's drama with a *concetto*, Banquo's wry humor (at II.i.4) with Woody Allen's. Proceeding through questions and intuition (in Emerson's sense), Cavell exercises a dynamic syntax that captures the intense spirit of his inquiry. The following sample intuits audience response to the death of Cleopatra: "And here we are, bystanders outside just now, drawn into a theater and then faced with a theater, buying a book and then faced with a text, perhaps imagining ourselves in the presence of, or service of, a woman in the process of transcendence: If there is eternity it is here, now, before a stage, or a page, finite things and others" (p. 32).

Bradshaw organizes his volume in two parts: a pair of opening chapters identify his theme and demonstrate his method with a selection of plays; the remaining four chapters analyze individual works in the context established by the first two. Starting from Troilus's famous question, "What's aught, but as 'tis valued?" Bradshaw concentrates initially on "that difficult triad, *value*, *valuer* and *valued*" (p. 3). Through Shakespeare's formulations of this triad, Bradshaw finds that two different concepts of the nature of Nature generate two different concepts of values: "In the affirmative, humanistic view of Nature, Nature itself provides a sanction for human values, which then appear to be discovered or recognised: ... But the opposed view of Nature allows no such affirmation: on the contrary, man is 'unaccommodated,' ... values appear to be created or invented" (p. 5). The Jacobean dramas particularly show these views in conflict, but Bradshaw exposes signs of radical skepticism in *A Midsummer Night's Dream* and *The Merchant of Venice* as he gives evidence of the full-scale collisions in *Hamlet*, *Othello*, and *Antony and Cleopatra*.

The second chapter, meant to complement the first, emphasizes "those respects in which the processes of poetic-dramatic thinking are not like those of logical-discursive thought" (p. ix). Here Bradshaw explores two crucial aspects of Shakespeare's style: changing registers of verse and prose which help to constitute meaning; and "Shakespeare's dramatic perspectivism—his habitual 'framing' of dual or multiple perspectives on characters and issues" (p. 92). He directs attention to *1 Henry IV*, *Hamlet*, *A Midsummer Night's Dream*, *Troilus and Cressida*, *The Merchant of Venice*, *Love's Labor's Lost*, *King Lear*, and *The Winter's Tale*, and offers an especially illuminating account of stylistic contrasts in *1 Henry IV*.

Each of the chapters on single texts—*Hamlet*, *Troilus and Cressida*, *Measure for Measure*, and *Macbeth*—approaches its subject from another angle. For instance, Bradshaw understands *Hamlet* as the result of Shakespeare's grafting the Prince onto the ur-play; the skepticism thus attached to the ethics of revenge constantly threatens the framework of Shakespeare's tragedy. In *Troilus and Cressida* a number of characters reflect or embody conflicting valuations, and Bradshaw explicates the most revealing passages. He singles out a major opposition in *Measure for Measure* between secular ethic and Gospel ethic—the problems of civil government and the consequences of invoking divine justice—explaining how the order of events in time "establishes the thrustingly interrogative, dialectical character of the play's dramatic rhythm" (p. 180). In order to track the sources of horror in *Macbeth*, the last chapter takes as its point of departure the image "nothing is, / But what is not" which Macbeth releases into the world. Bradshaw gives an extended comparison between the two marriages portrayed in the tragedy, suggesting that the Macduff narrative functions as a subplot.

In contrast with Bradshaw's volume, which consistently designs variations on its theme, Cavell's gathers five essays written over almost two decades and gives them a substantial introduction. According to Cavell, the introductory remarks have not turned out as he originally intended, "simple words of welcome": "I am hoping they will provide help to those who themselves welcome, or are prepared to welcome, the company of philosophy in reading works of, let us say, literature; and vice versa" (p. 2). Three of the essays—on *King Lear, Othello, Coriolanus*—have already been published; the two on *Hamlet* and *The Winter's Tale* will also appear elsewhere.

Cavell's introduction sets out the terms of his project and the context for reading his essays on Shakespeare. At the same time it describes his unhurried but steady progress through the canon since the mid 1960s. Its conclusion, more than half of its text, outlines Cavell's present thoughts about *Antony and Cleopatra*, ideas characteristically provocative and brilliant. He has come to see the final moments of this tragedy as offering "a new ceremony (or new sacrament) of marriage" (p. 18), and his speculations follow from the question: "What has caused the radicalization of the threat of skepticism, such that a ceremony of single intimacy is what we have to oppose to the threatened withdrawal of the world—of the realms of the natural, the social, the political, the religious?" (p. 19).

The title of the brief paper "Hamlet's Burden of Proof" refers to both Hamlet's stated purpose in using the play-within-the-play and "the surprising place of skepticism" (p. 179) in his burden of knowledge. Acting on W. W. Greg's intuition about the "Mousetrap," " 'It is such a play as Hamlet might have dreamed' " (quoted from "Hamlet's Hallucination" in Cavell, p. 182), Cavell applies two Freudian concepts to the dumb show and the protagonist: "primal scene" and "primal fantasies." Thus Freud interprets Shakespeare and Shakespeare interprets Freud (p. 189). In comparison with the *Hamlet* piece, "Recounting Gains, Showing Losses: Reading *The Winter's Tale*" engages with a whole play in detailed analysis of its structure, language, psychological and philosophic implications. Cavell centers his interpretation on Leontes' experiences of skepticism and recovery from it, proposing that the last scene—like the end of *Antony and Cleopatra*—represents a marriage ceremony as well as a study of theatrical impact ("theater as in competition with religion, as if declaring itself religion's successor," p. 218): "The final scene of issuing in *The Winter's Tale* shows what it may be to find in oneself the life of the world" (p. 221).

In *Dream Works: Lovers and Families in Shakespeare's Plays*, Kay Stockholder takes a less sanguine view of Leontes in the last episode of *The Winter's Tale*: "Only fairy-tale and magical forms can represent his restoration because there is nothing in the imagery to suggest an inner transformation of his desires" (p. 195). She has arrived at this conclusion toward the end of a generally thorough, consistent, and persuasive application of psychoanalytic theory to Shakespeare's canon. Specifically, she adjusts Rolf Loehrich's approach for literary use and reads the dramatic texts closely as analogues of dreams.

Stockholder's introduction both explains and justifies her strategy, but first it states her two main concerns. Like Bradshaw and Cavell, Stockholder recognizes a consistency in Shakespeare's writings established by certain themes and motifs that transmit "political and metaphysical significance" through many genres (p. 5). She identifies this problematic with Shakespeare's conflicting attitudes toward the family, his sense of its need to integrate romantic love and his sense of its harboring dark sexual forces. Analyzing this problematic, she considers how it affected the dramatist's treatment of his materials. She conducts her study through "literary interpretation based on dream theory, which assumes the protagonist to be the dreamer of the work in which he or she appears. This device . . . brings into relationship with one another underlying psychological forms, the overt ideas of moral, political, or cosmological import that relate works to their historical contexts, and the formal characteristics of literature" (pp. 5-6).

As Stockholder defines and uses this methodology, it concentrates primarily on character. The relationship of the protagonist to his or her world becomes comparable with that of the figure we identify as ourselves in dream to our dream world. Implicitly the critic's position corresponds with that of an awakened dreamer contemplating a dream: "In looking at one's own dream in this way, one would comment on the stance taken towards the figures with whom the dreamer is in confrontation, whether active or passive, manipulative or combative, as well as the kinds of figures (from past or present, male or female, parental or contemporary) with which, since it is our dream, we have surrounded ourselves" (pp. 13-14). Since the work of literature, another's dream, also includes "the fruits of the author's consciousness," associations multiply and become more complex and meaningful, "giving much greater significance to roles the protagonist adopts in relation to the configurations he or she is also seen to generate" (p. 14). These associations enhance as well the other components of dream, allowing for comprehensive readings which incorporate most elements of the dramatic texts: narrative structure, language, genre, and tone.

The ten chapters following the introduction systematically employ dream theory to interpret Shakespeare's plays in chronological order. Undergoing such analysis, the plays emerge uneven in aesthetic quality. Stockholder points out that her approach infers "an evaluative principle," because the more intricate and rich the network of associations, the more fully the work of art serves as "a mimesis of the overdetermined complexity of the 'knot intrinsicate of life' " (p. 23). According to this principle, her book favors the seventeenth-century tragedies, exploring earlier or contemporary plays in some haste and later ones with disappointment and signs of impatience. Consequently the seventeenth-century tragedies—*Hamlet, Othello, Macbeth, King Lear, Antony and Cleopatra*—benefit most from Stockholder's interpretations, which frequently illuminate the twilight reaches of their subtexts. (Now and then her explications support ideas intuited by Bradshaw or Cavell.) In her opinion, though, the romances evade psychological issues which the tragedies confront; and they achieve their resolutions uneasily by straining dramatic conventions.

With the concluding chapter Stockholder surveys the topography that she has covered: "different stages of Shakespeare's psychological enterprise in the changing kinds of protagonists, the changing attitudes of the protagonists towards the figures and circumstances they meet, the differing levels of their consciousness of their experience, and the changing degrees of control given the protagonists over their world" (pp. 216-17). Focusing on the subjects of women and power, she indicates how levels of control bring the author into his work. Finally she maintains that the narrative reconstructed by her argument belongs not only to Shakespeare, but to "the culture that bred him" (p. 232). Thus Stockholder's journey through the subterranean passages of Shakespeare's plays ends in the light of new historicism.

Margaret Loftus Ranald offers a substantial collection of essays on a theme with *Shakespeare and His Social Context: Essays in Osmotic Knowledge and Literary Interpretation*. Adding a general introduction, a general conclusion, and four new papers to five articles already in print, Ranald places the whole in the context of "osmotic knowledge": "the information, the moral and behavioral assumptions that a 'reasonable man,' that delightful legal fiction, should somehow have learned, or at least understood. . . . basically it formed a shared cultural frame of reference, something that could be taken for granted in the shorthand of dramatic dialogue" (pp. xi, xiv).

Arranged in four parts, this book concerns various aspects of courtship, marriage, tropes of power and chivalry; each section begins with its own introduction which gives background for the "shared cultural experience" (p. xv) it treats. With the new essays Ranald discusses "Trouser Roles and the Teachers of Love's Truth" in four romantic comedies; codes of matrimonial behavior in *The Comedy of Errors;* woman without power in *The Rape of Lucrece*; and loss of power signified by loss of clothing in *King Lear, Timon of Athens, Macbeth,* and *Henry VIII*. This volume contains much of value, in particular Ranald's essay on *The Taming of the Shrew* in light of falconry and conduct books (from *Essays in Literature* 1 [1974]) and her new study of "military language and military law as metaphorical and structural device" in *The Rape of Lucrece* (p. 153).

Of the three books received on language and prosody, only Ann and John O. Thompson's *Shakespeare: Meaning and Metaphor* tackles its subject aggressively. The authors set out determined to educate their audience, students and critics of literature without linguistic or philosophical background, in "extra-literary" theories of metaphor. When they describe these new theoretical developments, their own metaphors convey their intensity and some impatience: "The recent explosion of interest in metaphor within the fields of linguistics, psychology, anthropology and philosophy has as yet made little impact on English literary studies" (p. 1).

To introduce the latest approaches the Thompsons try four of them on individual Shakespearean texts, three plays and a sonnet, matching a theoretical framework "with an appropriate body of Shakespearean metaphor" (p. 1). With a fifth approach they "range across the entire Shakespearean canon" (p. 10). The reader willing to take this course in "extra-literary" theories has to master five different technical vocabularies. Moreover speaking these languages produces unconventional discourse, since the Thompsons do not use their analyses to argue full-scale interpretations of the plays or poem: "Our emphasis in this book will be less on ultimate meanings and more on immediate ones: we shall be asking not so much 'What does this metaphor mean'? but 'How does it come to mean what it means'?" (pp. 6-7).

The first chapter, "Time Metaphors in *Troilus and Cressida*," examines the play's linguistic thematization of time as a concept through George Lakoff and Mark Johnson's theory of everyday metaphor. Although the Thompsons carefully avoid traditional "thematic" readings—ascribing to Shakespeare or his characters "a set of Ideas About Time" (p. 41)—they do engage in some first-rate explications of the text. By means of its language, they demonstrate the play's cohesiveness and difficulty. Then chapter 2 attempts a more complicated theory, testing Eva Kittay and Adrienne Lehrer's arguments about semantic fields against "Animal Metaphors in *King Lear*." In these terms the Thompsons show how Shakespeare's images change unpredictably, manifest ambivalence: "The picture that begins to emerge is much more varied than we might expect from reading Spurgeon" (p. 59). Even more demanding, chapter 3 surveys theory on metaphor's relationship to synecdoche and metonymy (for instance, Roman Jakobson, Group Mu) in preparation for studying "Metaphors of the Human Body and its Parts in *Hamlet*": in *Hamlet* "synecdoche becomes more conceptually interesting than usual. This is because the wholes in question are the human body and the human person, and the decomposition of these entities into parts raises a number of conceptual problems. What are a person's parts? Are they immaterial as well as material, and if so what is the relationship between the two?" (p. 91).

Chapter 4 takes up philosophical semantics, summarizing J. F. Ross's *Portraying Analogy* and reading Sonnet 63 in light of Ross's ideas about differentiation and dominance. In the last chapter, "Meaning, 'Seeing,' Printing," the Thompsons investigate metaphors of books and printing; they consider their findings side by side with Donald Davidson's arguments against metaphorical meaning. Like the first chapter, the other four offer subtle interpretations of Shakespeare's lines. Together they insist on the complexity of Shakespearean metaphor, as chapter 5 directs attention, for example, to the tension between a metaphor's "intrinsic bias" (p. 199) and its context.

This stimulating book concludes that Shakespearean metaphor, rooted in still common everyday patterns, finds expression in sophisticated rhetorical devices. According to the Thompsons this metaphor does not distinguish among characters, but it can articulate themes, reflect the author's views, or voice contemporary social/political assumptions. *Shakespeare: Meaning and Metaphor* thus closes on a familiar note that it has struck elsewhere: "In the end, this is a study in literary criticism—more so, perhaps than we might have wished" (p. 214).

Less assertive and more specialized, Marina Tarlinskaja's *Shakespeare's Verse: Iambic Pentameter and the Poet's Idiosyncrasies* introduces the Russian linguistic-statistical method for analyzing poetic rhythm to students of English metrics. This book's introductory apparatus—a preface by James Bailey and foreword by George T. Wright—explains the value of the Russian Formalist approach, the ends to which Tarlinskaya has used it, and the results: "she describes how poets adapt the English language to a meter, summarizes the results in statistics, and on that basis derives metrical norms established by the poets themselves. . . . Most important, Dr. Tarlinskaja describes in precise detail how the English iambic pentameter alternates between periods of comparatively regular observance of the metrical scheme and periods of free treatment" (p. xvi). In the body of the text, Tarlinskaja employs her precision tools to explore such topics as the stylization of plays-within-plays, "differentiation of characters through rhythm" (p. 152), and "evolution of characters" (p. 154). The evidence she collects seems to confirm a great deal of established scholarship not only about these matters, but also about the plays' chronology and the development of Shakespeare's verse.

Often technical, *A Reader in the Language of Shakespearean Drama* addresses specialists in Elizabethan English and the history of the English language as well as curious Shakespeareans. Vivian Salmon and Edwina Burness have collected thirty-three essays, most published between 1965 and spring 1984, for readers without access to the kinds of libraries which house the originals. These papers represent four approaches to the language of Shakespeare's plays, indicating differences between Elizabethan and modern English; examining Shakespeare's artistic treatment of Elizabethan English; assembling data from the plays for information about Elizabethan English in general; and studying Elizabethan attitudes toward language. In the introduction, Salmon draws attention to recent Japanese work in these areas which does not appear in the book.

Of the remaining theoretical studies, three books on Shakespeare required more time at the drawing board before they reached print. As their titles suggest, two belong to the Procrustean school of literary criticism which ties dramatic texts to a single kind of reading: William F. Martin's *The Indissoluble Knot: "King Lear" as Ironic*

Drama and Barbara L. Parker's *A Precious Seeing: Love and Reason in Shakespeare's Plays.* The third, Diana Akers Rhoads's *Shakespeare's Defense of Poetry: "A Midsummer Night's Dream" and "The Tempest"* addresses a potentially fruitful topic: the plays' reflection of poetry's function in civil society. Having started life as a dissertation, however, this volume still needs to cut its redundancies and surplus information.

Four recent books include Elizabethan and Jacobean plays in studies which also treat drama from other periods: Phoebe S. Spinrad's *The Summons of Death on the Medieval and Renaissance English Stage*; Anthony Gerard Barthelemy's *Black Face, Maligned Race: The Representation of Blacks in English Drama from Shakespeare to Southerne*; Joanne Altieri's *The Theatre of Praise: The Panegyric Tradition in Seventeenth-Century English Drama*; and Richard Hornby's *Drama, Metadrama, and Perception.*

Both Spinrad and Barthelemy follow the path of an idea through a range of early English plays. In her volume Spinrad devotes six chapters and an epilogue to Renaissance texts, analyzing the (actual and impending) moments of death in *1* and *2 Tamburlaine*, *Doctor Faustus*, *Measure for Measure*, and *The Duchess of Malfi* (chapters 6 to 9) within the purview of earlier artistic conventions. The tenth chapter, "Memento Mockery: The Old Iconography Begins to Slip," covers a group of early seventeenth-century plays where death becomes "a puppet in the hands of the living, and in many cases, a joke" (p. 214); and the eleventh, "A Choice of Deaths: The Last Decades of Renaissance Theater," describes a "New Wave" of Renaissance drama where death is welcomed. Finally the epilogue considers *The Tragedy of Nero*, "a remarkable compendium of ways of dying, both old and new" (p. 279).

Barthelemy actually begins his survey with Peele's *The Battle of Alcazar* (1589), and he ends it with Southerne's *Oroonoko* (1695). In his comprehensive study he examines not only popular theater but also court masques and lord mayors' pageants. As he interprets these dramatic forms, he keeps before the reader three major influences on their representation of blacks: "English political, social, and theatrical history" (p. x); and he provides additional background by tracing the etymology of the word "Moor." According to Barthelemy's meticulous research, the roles of blacks remain depressingly negative throughout the period: they stand for evil in general, lust in particular, and alienation, the Other. If black figures represent positive values in the lord mayors' pageants, these shows reduce them to "exotic paraphernalia" (p. 47) to serve the purpose: "The Moor, in this context, becomes an emblem of London's, and consequently England's, global renown, power, and superiority" (p. 49). The handful of virtuous blacks on stage, "Ethiops Washed White" (p. 147), are in fact versions of the stereotypical villainous Moor, making potentially dangerous incursions into white communities.

Initially focused on the late seventeenth century, Altieri's project began with her interest in the "strange route" (p. 6) taken by Shakespearean opera, a way cleared of emotions. She worked backward from Dryden's comments on opera (and Purcell's achievement) and forward from Shakespeare, "meeting myself at William Davenant" (p. 7). Through an investigation which uses some new historical strategies, she traces the epideictic tradition from Renaissance to Restoration theater.

Altieri therefore starts from the masque on her way to opera and from Shakespeare, "whose history plays are, among many other things, a dramatic reaction to the masque venture" (p. 14). Stressing the political intention of masque, "whatever the form" (p. 25), she identifies those features of the Stuart version that lasted through the century: artifice, allegory, and didacticism. Together those features produce a hero accompanied by negative opposition: "Through the defeat or control of the negative forces, the ideal model asserts the power of monarchical values in a transference of moral values to the political sphere" (p. 26). If this format usually allegorizes common life to make it part of the heroic environment, epideictic theater allows the communal its identity. Placed in historical context, Jonson's masques sustain a monarchist ideology. Similarly placed, Shakespeare's *Henry V* is "focused on the nation in its dramatic embodiment and primarily communal in its orientation and desired effects" (p. 30). According to Altieri, epideictic theater links masque to ceremonial play and then opera through its communal function.

After the introduction, two chapters observe the diffusion of epideictic techniques during the first four decades of the seventeenth century, the complex response to those techniques, and their relation to heroic modeling. The first concentrates on Shakespeare's *Henry V* and *Henry VIII* , demonstrating how "both Henry plays consciously subject the forms of a courtly ideology to a broader, but not universally negative perspective" (p. 73). The second examines some ephemeral forms of epideixis in light of Bacon's essay "Of Masques and Triumphs"; it centers on Carew's *Coelum Britannicum* and the Stuarts' formalization of civic pageants. In both of these chapters, Altieri points out differences between her conclusions and those of Stephen Orgel and D. J. Gordon. On the whole, her book offers new and enlightening perspectives from which to view Stuart masques or theater.

As his title suggests, Hornby looks at world drama through a wide-angle lens. He calls the two parts of his book "Varieties of the Metadramatic" and "Drama and Perception," and the opening chapter discusses "Drama and Reality." In the second part, which seems tenuously related to the first, Hornby analyzes six texts ranging from Sophocles' *Oedipus the King* to Pinter's *Betrayal*, including Shakespeare's *As You Like It*. The discussion of *As You Like It* compares various characters with regard to their perceptions of the world.

At the level of theory, this volume exercises self-discipline irregularly. Hornby fails to define nineteenth-century realism in culturally precise terms, for example, and makes a number of simplistic assertions: "We can now see the distinction between the serious work of art and the work of a hack: the hack play merely reinforces the drama/culture complex in effect at the time of its composition, while the serious play attempts to attack that system in some way" (p. 23). Consequently this book might prove misleading to undergraduates with little background in the history of drama or theater, although its section on metadramatic devices offers a handy brief catalog of techniques along with the relevant plays.

Finally, Charles Warren's *T. S. Eliot on Shakespeare* retrieves unfamiliar or little-known work toward the portrait of "a great Shakespearean critic" (p. 1). But as George K. Hunter points out in his review of this book, and of Eliot (*Shakespeare Quarterly* 38 [Winter 1987]), Warren faces a stubborn problem in completing his task: the impact of Eliot's criticism relies on its expression, and copyright restrictions prevent extensive quoting. As a result, this volume reads like a commonplace book with short quotations and paraphrases arranged chronologically under various headings. Warren offers minimum explication, and his own prose shows no sign of Eliot's influence.

III

Interpreting both texts and their performances, Marion Lomax's *Stage Images and Traditions: Shakespeare to Ford* casts a broad net: "This book explores some of the many traditions behind the staging of adult company drama in the early years of the seventeenth century" (p. 1). For a fleeting moment in her preface Lomax sounds like a revisionist historian intending to view these Jacobean plays in the context of one another and their age (p. xi), amid the pressures of other discourses or practices. But the volume immediately takes a more conventional approach, emphasizing the influences of established traditions—"mythological, classical, religious, literary, and theatrical" (p. 1)—on the composers of English Renaissance drama. In its course Lomax also notices seventeenth-century crosscurrents resulting from "a wide range of dramatic entertainment . . . produced (often simultaneously) at different venues" (p. 1); she remarks how contemporary performances sparked one another to experiment with inherited traditions.

Each chapter starts from a new point of departure and comes to rest on specific texts. For instance the first defines spectacle ("any form of display, ceremony, show or pageant . . . used in the course of the drama," p. 10), then describes its manifestations in the late sixteenth and early seventeenth centuries. Having given illustrations from Shakespeare's late romances, Lomax pauses over Thomas Heywood's *Ages* and finally compares the two dramatists' handling of old and new traditions. The second chapter focuses on "emblematic or symbolic staging" (p. 34); it traces a few metaphoric stage properties associated with bloodstained cloths and Pandora's box through nine Elizabethan/Jacobean plays. From emblems Lomax moves to topical themes: the interest of King James I in an Anglo-Scottish union (1606-1607); the reflection of that issue in both Campion's *Lord Hay's Masque* and Shakespeare's *Macbeth*. Consequently the third chapter shows how the two forms of entertainment not only share certain elements but also differ from each other, speculating briefly about the emphatic duality and theatrical self-consciousness of *Macbeth*.

Lomax devotes two chapters to Shakespearean romances: the fourth demonstrates that *Pericles*, more closely related to pageant than to masque, draws on a number of medieval and contemporary traditions; the fifth shows that *Cymbeline*, arranged in layers of concrete and verbal images, employs popular customs as well as theatrical practices of the early seventeenth century. In chapter 6, Lomax examines the strategies Webster used as "he adapted traditions to stage particular metaphors crucial to his plays' understanding" (p. 127). She ends with a discussion of "conventions and improvised rituals in *The Changeling*, *'Tis Pity She's a Whore*, and *The Broken Heart*" (p. 155).

A large and abstract concept, "tradition(s)" resists categorization or any other logical mode of containment. As a result *Stage Images and Traditions* takes a number of directions after its wide-ranging introduction, pursuing divers conventions and plays in each chapter. More like essays on a theme than a continuing argument, it offers various fine explications of Renaissance texts set in their cultural backgrounds.

The format of *Jacobean Private Theatre*—whether required by the series Theatre Production Studies (to which it belongs) or invented by its author, Keith Sturgess—must have made this book difficult to write. Of its three parts, the first deals with theater history; the second, with hypothetical productions of *The Tempest*, *The Duchess of Malfi*, and *The Broken Heart*; and the third, with both the history and two performances of court theater. According to the introduction, "the approach is necessarily historical: to rediscover the 'private' play-in-performance by treating it as an historical object" (p. 4). The volume therefore attempts to bridge the gap between speculations about the venues and speculations about mounting individual dramatic texts—an extremely taxing endeavor.

Chapters 1 to 4 anchor the project as much as possible in data about "Jacobean" (meaning "Jacobean and Caroline," p. 7) private theater; Sturgess assembles information about the audiences, the playhouses and their accouterments, the companies, their playwrights and their repertories. (Sometimes this information is less accurate or complete than one might wish: for example, on the revivals at the Second Blackfriars and St. Paul's "in the 1590s," p. 17.) With the discussions of the plays, however, the argument often threatens to drift from its moorings. Analysis of the private play-in-performance becomes analysis of the private play-as-dramatic-composition, and Sturgess frequently lapses into readings of the texts. Sometimes the historical frame of reference seems to disappear completely, so that the play-in-performance might occur at any time. Describing *The Tempest* at the Blackfriars, for instance, Sturgess writes, "it is clear that in *The Tempest* Shakespeare was experimenting with graphic kinds of stage imagery. . . . The audience is given a series of stage pictures which, like the visions in a dream, have a sharp-edged clarity and a sense of careful composition" (p. 79). He reaches this conclusion about *The Duchess of Malfi*:

> Much of its dramaturgy—the mobile viewpoint, commentary devices, a certain narrative naivety (in, for example, its use of time-lags), and the reductive humour centred on Bosola—is intended to demystify. There are dark forces at the centre of Webster's universe and in the heart of man; but the audience is constantly invited to view, with judicious detachment, attempts by characters to dress up, glamorise or misrepresent the meaning of their actions.
>
> (p. 112)

The study of court theater, 1603-1642, registers the same tension. After reviewing the management, performance spaces, audience, function and repertory of "The King's Theatre" (phrase on p. 145), Sturgess imagines first Jonson's *Bartholomew Fair* and then Carew's *Coelum Britannicum* at the Banqueting House. At one point he says of dialogue in the comedy (at V.ii.1-18): "A passage like this makes poor, staccato reading but is brilliant theatre. The playwright juggles the various plots and involves the audience in a deadly serious game of truth-detection" (p. 187). When Sturgess loses direction in this interpretive pair of chapters, as in the earlier set, he loses the reader too. The road to rediscovery makes for a bumpy ride which sometimes arrives at its destination and sometimes goes off the map.

With *Shakespeare's Playhouses*, Herbert Berry has collected six of his essays about four playhouses associated with Shakespeare (a shareholder in their enterprises): the Theatre in Shoreditch, the Blackfriars, and the first and second Globes. Representing the valuable scholarship Berry has contributed to Renaissance theater history over more than twenty years, these papers interpret documents contemporary with the buildings. Five essays have appeared before; two have been revised for this volume; and C. Walter Hodges has provided the whole book with original drawings for each of the structures. In addition a previously unpublished sixth essay, almost one hundred pages long, analyzes "A New Lawsuit about the Globe." Berry has traced to the Public Record Office documents reported but not identified by C. W. Wallace (*The Times*, 30 April and 1 May 1914). When he places them in the order of their legal occurrence, Berry produces from these materials a coherent and remarkable narrative. Through his skillful rendering the documents, transcribed at the back of the essay, supplement the history of the Globe and the theatrical venture it housed: they reveal construction and reconstruction costs, information in the lease, the composition and value of building materials. Moreover, "they hint at the arrangements for rebuilding the Globe. They even give us a glimpse of that rival playhouse, the Swan, as it was four years later than our latest glimpse heretofore" (p. 153).

Working from both primary and fictional evidence, Andrew Gurr undertakes a much larger, more speculative topic than Berry's—*Playgoing in Shakespeare's London*. This book ends with two appendixes which gather the data that Gurr has explored: one names and describes 162 people known to have attended theatrical performances between 1567 and 1642; the other arranges chronologically all extant contemporary references to Elizabethan and Jacobean audiences. As Gurr points out when he considers "Who Went Where" (p. 59), the 367 items in the appendixes constitute a small fraction of close to fifty million visits to the playhouses, yet he gleans from them numerous details which multiply their implications. Although a study like this can never claim to provide definitive answers (or even definitive questions), it fills in and refines the modern picture of English Renaissance audiences. It revises its two important predecessors, Alfred Harbage's *Shakespeare's Audience* and Ann Jennalie Cook's *The Privileged Playgoers of Shakespeare's London, 1576-1642* (Princeton: Princeton Univ. Press, 1981), texts which Gurr addresses especially in his preface and introduction.

The first four chapters and the appendixes contain this book's most original subject matter. Here Gurr categorizes the four types of evidence assembled, and he demonstrates his technique for sounding the contemporary references (his largest category) with an illustration from Henry Peacham (pp. 5-9). In his system the evidence—physical circumstances, demographic information, contemporary allusions, mental composition—shades into a "most elusive" variety ("collective mind," "mindset," pp. 5-6) which becomes the most complicating feature in his long fifth chapter's survey of the period.

To re-create the physical conditions of playgoing, Gurr begins by reviewing the history, structures, and admission policies of both amphitheater and hall playhouses. Then he situates audiences in these venues, making almost palpable the discomforts they suffered as well as the distractions they caused. As he attempts to establish the composition of these audiences, Gurr initially distinguishes among the social classes in England and in London. Then he puts his evidence to use (about women, artisan and apprentice classes, gentry), along with his lack of evidence (about citizens), to infer how populations changed at the two kinds of theaters over seventy-five years. He draws a variety of conclusions: citizens remained a "staple" of the playhouses (p. 64); all social ranks came to the amphitheaters during the 1590s; students from the Inns of Court regularly attended the theater. Finally he tries to sort out the division of playhouse clientele into popular and privileged, the theaters they visited, and the chronology of this intricate branching which started after 1599.

Dealing with "the mental range," Gurr states: "Education and taste in reading, the contrasting social and political allegiances of blue apron and flat cap culture against the court gallants and law students, all influenced the kind of play written for the different playhouses and must to some extent therefore reflect at least the poets' and players' expectations of their customers" (p. 81). Much of this discussion analyzes evidence about the two sorts of playgoers identified by poets, those favoring verse and those favoring spectacle. Apparently the "hearer" or "auditor" held on tenaciously at the amphitheaters, and during Shakespeare's time competed on almost equal terms with the spectator. Afterward, however, the distinction faded. On the matter of dramaturgical tastes, Gurr believes that audiences remained passive whereas "the poets by their nature had more active tastes, always on edge to provide novelty." But "a comprehensive survey of audience reactions to the plays of this period suggests a complex and wide-ranging responsiveness which makes the eyewitness accounts of plays seem almost simple minded" (p. 105).

Finally Gurr traces "the evolution of tastes"; his last chapter recomposes the history of English theater in eight-to-twenty-year intervals from the opening of the Red Lion to the closing of the playhouses. Based on the four different kinds of evidence and Gurr's tentative or firm conclusions, the narrative focuses sometimes on a key performer or playwright, sometimes on a new or changing genre or repertory, sometimes on specific political events, plays, or dramatic characters. This shifting focus makes the fifth chapter more difficult to follow than the preceding four, which serve as the reader's main guide through otherwise unpredictable terrain. In its leaps, gaps, and idiosyncrasies, however, Gurr's survey fairly represents the current state of English Renaissance theater history.

Among the five books received (and at least one not received) on the performance histories of individual plays, only one does not belong to a series: R. Chris Hassel, Jr.'s *Songs of Death: Performance, Interpretation, and the Text of "Richard III."* Hassel has therefore worked out his own method for dealing with performances as interpretations of *Richard III.* At either end of this volume he examines significant twentieth-century productions: the 1955 Laurence Olivier film and the 1982 BBC videotape (starring Ron Cook, directed by Jane Howell) in chapter 1, and the 1984/1985 Royal Shakespeare Company staging (starring Antony Sher, directed by Bill Alexander) in the epilogue. The five chapters between analyze the play's text to uncover its "centers of energy and turbulence" (p. 3).

By framing his book with performances, Hassel encourages a reading of the main argument in light of modern productions. The first chapter compares the two media versions in some detail, concentrating on four segments of action—I, III.v-vii, IV.iv, V—to show how the BBC has restored dimensions of the play which Olivier had distorted or cut. Then Hassel looks at the same passages in the dramatic text, attempting to realize their "moral and aesthetic richness" (p. 3) through interpretations which rely on contemporary literature, documents, and commonplaces: Shakespeare's narrative and dramatic sources, Renaissance military manuals, and theology.

With a chapter to account for key textual cruxes, Hassel explicates the crucial passages and finally describes the RSC performance as a brilliant execution of the whole play: "its theatricality establishes beyond doubt the viability of Shakespeare's own *Richard III* as a stunning theatrical occasion" (p. 160).

Two impressive volumes relaunched the Plays in Performance series during 1987: J. S. Bratton's *King Lear* and Julie Hankey's *Othello*. Like the series as a whole, these books concern "the complex questions and answers of performance, their history, the theatrical, social and cultural reasons for their having been framed in different ways at different times" (series editors' preface). In each case a substantial introduction gives an overview of the play's theater history. Hankey's more elaborate version unfolds in thirty-two parts, from the original productions of *Othello* to the 1985/1986 RSC version (directed by Terry Hands, with Ben Kingsley as Othello and David Suchet as Iago). Bratton takes the centuries in broader leaps but nevertheless covers all the major performances of *King Lear*. With these essays, both authors interpret the effects of social/cultural factors as well as theatrical customs and personalities on staging the texts. Then they display the effects by means of facing pages with script on one side and available performance notes from major productions on the other. As the editors claim, "The text itself is no more than a sketch, an unfinished picture" (series editors' preface); it is based on old Cambridge editions. Yet the notes—on everything from inflections and gestures to sets and costumes—turn it into a composite promptbook, recording verbal alterations and other details of performance basically line by line. All in all, these editions help to re-create the experiences of witnessing and performing Shakespearean plays in changing social/political conditions since the English Renaissance.

Less successful in its purposes, the Text and Performance series allows its authors too little space "to introduce sixth-form and undergraduate students to the themes, continuing vitality and performance of major dramatic works" (series editor's preface). Bill Overton's *The Merchant of Venice* comes to eighty pages; Malcolm Page's *Richard II* to eighty-seven. Within those limits both writers have to raise key issues in their texts and describe stage management of those themes or problems in modern productions. The books also include plot summaries, outlines of the plays' major sources, and reading lists. Restricted in these ways, Overton works as efficiently as possible: he focuses on structure, characterization, and tone in *The Merchant of Venice*, then explains how five stagings between 1970 and 1984 dealt with these features. Page, however, seems addled by the task: he roams through the text, criticism, and theater history of *Richard II* without a clear sense of direction.

Manchester University Press published the second volume in its series Shakespeare in Performance with my study of *Romeo and Juliet*. To avoid reviewing the book and offending everyone, I shall quote the series editor's description of the guidelines I followed: "each contributor has selected a small number of productions and studied them comparatively. The productions, often from different periods, countries and media, have been chosen because they are significant interpretations in their own right, but also because they represent something of the range and variety of possible interpretations of the play in hand" (series editor's preface). During 1986 and 1987, a significant number of other Shakespearean plays were assigned for this treatment.

Lastly, Charles H. Shattuck has produced another model of theater history with *Shakespeare on the American Stage: From Booth and Barrett to Sothern and Marlowe*. Continuing from a first volume that stopped with Booth in his prime, Shattuck begins in the 1880s and makes his way through the early twentieth century. He places Shakespearean production in the dynamic context of American theater—its performers and other personnel, critics, managers and agents, audiences—showing how it responded to the pressures of constantly changing tastes and conventions. When I used the first volume extensively (in particular for its information about Charlotte Cushman, a famous Romeo), I found Shattuck's accounts of plays and players detailed, comprehensive, and therefore very useful. Of the same caliber, the new book also works not only as a scholarly resource but as a readable narrative. In both capacities it supplements the introductions of Hankey and Bratton, especially in its discussion of Tommaso Salvini, the Italian actor who visited the United States five times in the late nineteenth century with his repertoire of Shakespearean tragic protagonists.

IV

Among English Renaissance playwrights other than Shakespeare, Ben Jonson received the most attention last year in three books: Rosalind Miles's *Ben Jonson: His Life and Work*; Robert N. Watson's *Ben Jonson's Parodic Strategy: Literary Imperialism in the Comedies*; and Peter Womack's *Ben Jonson* (in the series Rereading Literature).

Miles set out to write "a modern scholarly biography" for Jonson, "because he incorporated so much of his own life in his work" (p. ix).

After ten years of research and consolidating, she has fulfilled her objective "to produce a reliable and accessible account to serve both those who wish to know Jonson in full and those who need simply to dip into some phase of his career" (p. x). As this statement indicates, Miles investigates Jonson's career thoroughly rather than analyzing his artistic development; she briefly describes the plays, masques, and some poetry in order to complete this detailed profile. Fifteen chapters arrange facts and apocrypha in a biography remarkable for its contradictions: the bricklayer's stepson who became a scholar and poet laureate; the Protestant who turned Roman Catholic and then Protestant again; the classical humanist who risked scandal and engaged in feuds; the playwright who lived through successes and disasters, financial security and losses. In this narrative Jonson's life takes shape against the backdrop of contemporary lives—actors, dramatists and other writers, members of court circles and the royal family.

Watson and Womack offer interpretive books, Womack more attentive than Watson to the intersection of Jonson's art and life. In both cases the authors know the vocabularies of new critical discourses: Watson uses them occasionally; Womack speaks them fluently most of the time. Watson reads eight of the comedies, giving the impression of Jonson as an innovative artist. By contrast Womack examines four components of the canon—"Speaking," "Characters," "Languages," and "Theatre"—generating the concept of Jonson as a bleakly conflictive psyche. When the two critics discuss the same play, the differences in their voices sound most clearly:

> The play strongly suggests a correspondence between Lovewit's house and the theaters of Elizabethan London. . . . As Jonson converts that stage into Lovewit's house, Face converts Lovewit's house into an overpopulated Jacobean stage.
>
> (Watson, pp. 113-14)

> Jonson's house of illusions is a scandalous reflection on, and of, the theatre in which it's exhibited. . . . "Lovewit's house," then, as its name neatly hints, is a self-referring image of the theatre. The image is a disgraceful and cynical one, opposed at every level to the aesthetic ideology of classical comedy.
>
> (Womack, pp. 117-18)

The general thesis of Watson's book and his chapter on *The Alchemist* first appeared as one of the outstanding essays in

Renaissance Genres, edited by Barbara Kiefer Lewalski (cited above for Levin). In his full-length study Watson elaborates the idea that Jonson builds his satiric city-comedies from other dramatic genres: the playwright appropriates the works of his rivals (thus yielding one sense of "literary imperialism") to satirize not only London society but also the London stage. According to Watson, "It is primarily a question of framing" (p. 4). Jonson decenters conventional plots or motifs, demonstrating at the same time his control over them and his dominance over their creators. Originating in these materials, Jonson's self-dramatizing characters play out their melodramatic fantasies to humiliating effect in nonmelodramatic scenarios. As he routs these figures, Jonson attempts to embarrass and drive away self-dramatizing instincts in general as well as melodramatic conventions in particular. Ultimately without success he tries to make room for his own mode, the kind of art that reforms society: "The reformed society, cured of its unhealthy melodramatic fantasies, will then support authors such as Jonson" (p. 14).

Tracing the "arc" discerned by Anne Barton, Watson's eight chapters mark the evolution of Jonson's views and techniques: "Jonson progresses from an openly combative attitude toward popular theater, to a brilliant assimilation of that tradition, and finally to a nostalgic immersion in it" (p. 9). Watson treats *Every Man In His Humor, Every Man Out of His Humor, Volpone, Epicoene, The Alchemist, Bartholomew Fair, The Devil Is an Ass*, and *The New Inn*, taking *Every Man In His Humor* as a model for examination of the other comedies. (Womack calls *Every Man In His Humor* "a rather overburdened workhorse in the interpretation of the plays," p. 37, but uses it anyway in his study of characters.) With his clear and economical analyses Watson usually starts from characterization, allowing it to lead him into matters of plot, literary conventions, and language. He identifies in each text the figures who represent the playwright or audience.

In the editor's preface to *Ben Jonson*, Terry Eagleton claims that Womack "rescues Ben Jonson simultaneously from the classical humanists and the romantic populists" (p. viii). Then Womack says that he has produced this volume with attention to the plays as scripts and the needs of students (p. ix). Finally this demanding book considers performance at Womack's discretion, and it requires knowledge of both Jonson's works and current theory. Moreover it formulates its argument in unpredictable ways. At some times Womack dives into a text to emerge with linguistic peculiarities, evidence of Jonson's opinions, or a bit of dramaturgy in the process of fracturing. At other times he scans the history of theater, print, or

England to reveal the pressures which formed Jonson's art. Often he appeals to nonhumanist, nonromantic thinkers, especially Bakhtin, to explain the patterns—or disintegration—that he has found. Rarely giving notice of the subjects coming next, Womack's book (like Tennenhouse's) insists on the reader's total concentration to forge logical connectives. The reader who cooperates should be able to extend his or her effort toward rereading Jonson's work from new perspectives.

As befits his format, Womack announces his thesis in the next-to-last chapter:

> I've argued in earlier chapters that the complex of values which is at issue here is exceptionally prominent in Jonson's plays. The idealization of the orator, the prestige of classical allusion, the latently sadistic conception of satire as correction, the value-laden oppositions of restraint and incontinence, singleness and multiplicity, sense and chatter—all these themes evince a didactic classicism which no doubt reflects Jonson's own grammar school education, a decisively male initiation in that it detached him permanently from his family and formed his passage to the career of an independent literary producer.
>
> (p. 124)

Womack concludes his argument by identifying another major component of Jonson's dramatic writing which interferes with its ideological coherence along with images of alchemy, sexuality, plague, and carnival: the image of capitalism, or money, which impedes Jonson's moralism as well as his presentation of language and character. Throughout the book Womack's prose sporadically loses its point in abstraction, but more often it draws attention incisively to elements in Jonson's personality and art neglected by classical humanists and romantic populists. At all times Womack makes his case aggressively: his rescue of Jonson threatens now and then to become a kidnapping.

Two volumes in the Twayne's English Authors Series edited by Arthur F. Kinney deal with Renaissance playwrights: Charles L. Squier's *John Fletcher* and Doris Adler's *Philip Massinger*. As introductions to the dramatists in well under two hundred pages, these books require effective organization to make the most of their formats. Squier has the more difficult task; Adler stretches the guidelines to fit her project.

Devising his frame of reference from genre and theatricality, Squier emphasizes "Fletcher's personal dramatic genius . . . for comedy" (p. 48) as well as "the copiousness of his dramatic invention in character and scene and in that play of conceited wit, the sudden turns of thought and image that can transform the relations of appearance and reality" (p. 153). Within this context Squier has to account for a canon of more than fifty plays written both alone and in collaboration. His first chapter surveys Fletcher's life and work; the second covers early collaborative plays along with those written for children's companies; three chapters address the genres of tragicomedy, tragedy, and comedy; and a brief conclusion sums up Fletcher's achievement. Despite the author's selectiveness (for instance, he only mentions collaboration with Shakespeare), the book sometimes reads like a catalog of plot synopses. Squier has little space for interpretive commentary, but he manages to include quite a bit of information about the plays' construction, sources, influence, and critical history.

With new data about Massinger—generally stemming from her own research—Adler examines his plays as reflections of his theater and age: "as small patterns in the tapestry of the time of James I and Charles I" (preface, n.p.). The first chapter gives an excellent digest of Massinger's life and work, concentrated but perfectly lucid, citing important scholarship (past and future) as it describes Adler's approach. At this early stage the book introduces fresh evidence, the manuscript prologue for a performance, to adjust dating for *The Maid of Honor* and *A New Way to Pay Old Debts*. Spanning the nineteen plays of Massinger's apprenticeship, the second chapter reviews the major political scandals of the period and notices their repercussions in the plays. Adler focuses on historical background, dramatic themes and (to some extent) structure, permitting herself only a nod toward the finer points of genre, language, and other stylistic features. In the rest of the book nonpolitical elements receive somewhat more attention. Discussing collaborations during the last five years of King James's reign, the third chapter sets up opposing paradigms of *Pericles* (which suggests resolutions of threats and problems) and Massinger's plays (which allude pessimistically to sensitive issues); it outlines nine plays in view of these models. The fourth to sixth chapters treat Massinger's independent plays from 1621 until 1639. As they regularly point out topical allusions, they recount the struggle between state and theater (1625-1640) and assess its impact on Massinger's publication history. In a short concluding chapter, Adler sums up the implications of her findings.

Donald K. Anderson, Jr., has assembled a first-rate collection of thirteen essays in *"Concord in Discord": The Plays of John Ford, 1586-1986*. While R. J. Fehrenbach's paper concerns bibliographical matters, the other studies interpret the dramatic texts according to their genres (Thelma N. Greenfield, Larry S. Champion), strategies of characterization (Robert B. Heilman, David M. Bergeron), use of sources and dramatic models (Eugene M. Waith, Richard S. Ide, Mark Stavig), modern performances (Alan C. Dessen), language and rhetoric (Coburn Freer, Glenn Hopp, Sharon Hamilton), and structure and manipulation of reader/audience response (Anderson). None of the critical essays analyzes more than three or four plays at length, and most concentrate on one or two texts. As a consequence this volume offers a range of perspectives on the seven works Ford wrote alone. It also argues convincingly for the dramatist's skillful experiments with Elizabethan/Jacobean conventions and the resulting contributions to Jacobean/Caroline theater.

For the Revels Plays Companion Library, E. A. J. Honigmann has written *John Weever: A Biography of a Literary Associate of Shakespeare and Jonson, Together with a Photographic Facsimile of Weever's "Epigrammes" (1599).* The first four chapters propose a variety of connections between Weever and Shakespeare, Middleton, Marston, Jonson, and Dekker among other literary and dramatic figures, and between Weever's *Epigrammes* and the Parnassus plays. When Honigmann reaches the fifth chapter, "Satirical Portraits of Weever in English Plays, 1598-1601," he warns the reader that "we tread upon treacherous ground" (p. 42). Tentatively he links Weever with Asinius Bubo in Dekker's *Satiromastix,* Simplicius Faber in Marston's *What You Will,* Shift in Jonson's *Every Man Out of His Humor* (Jonson may also have had Weever in mind for *Every Man In His Humor*), and Ingenioso in the *Return from Parnassus.*

With *The Elizabethan Theatre and "The Book of Sir Thomas More,"* Scott McMillin produces a contradiction in terms: compelling scholarship. He combines the skills of a textual scholar and theater historian to re-create the manuscript's history, but he underplays his erudition as he presents it. Disguising tedium—gathering statistics, analysis of handwriting, other bibliographical exertions—McMillin's urbane prose gives him the persona of an energetic detective solving a neglected mystery. The author/sleuth follows clues, makes hypotheses, and finally turns up one possibility that "brings me joy" (p. 154): "Let Hand D possibly be Hand C, Anon and Shakespeare at once, the genius and the functionary. That is just one way of stating the assumption behind this book, that all the writing in the manuscript of *Sir Thomas More,* even the censor's, holds to the similarity of addressing the coherent work of the Elizabethan theatre" (pp. 158-59).

On this assumption McMillin examines *Sir Thomas More* not as an " 'authored' document" (p. 16) but as a theatrical manuscript: "what kind of theatrical manuscript is this? how would it have been used in the theatre? how large a company does it require? which parts can be doubled? what kind of staging does it imply? why did the play have to be revised?" (p. 7). He pursues these questions through six chapters which provide a new frame of reference for the script. In the first and second he describes the manuscript as a type of promptbook readied for copying of actors' parts. In the third and fourth he attempts to identify the two companies that performed each version (original, revised) of *Sir Thomas More.* The fifth and sixth chapters concentrate on staging: the play's requirements and the style of the theater which originally had to fulfill them. Having explored all of his theatrical leads, McMillin acknowledges "Hand D" in the last chapter and addresses questions of authorship which he has done his best "to hedge . . . with speculations inimical to Bardolatry" (p. 8).

In its research and organization McMillin's book serves at least three useful purposes: it offers a new context for *Sir Thomas More* which restores the play's theatrical dimension; it demonstrates an effective method for analyzing Elizabethan and Jacobean scripts; and it calls attention to expanses of English Renaissance theater history (that is, various companies' repertories and individual techniques for staging) still uncultivated as scholarly resources. At the same time, of course, McMillin deals sensibly with the standard questions—of Edmund Tilney's censorship, topical allusion, dating—attached to this play. Yet he adds zest to the old chestnuts and transforms them into means for recovering *Sir Thomas More.*

Roy T. Eriksen works from analogies rather than questions in *"The Forme of Faustus Fortunes": A Study of "The Tragedie of Doctor Faustus" (1616).* Although he cites Michael J. Warren's definitive essay in his notes ("*Doctor Faustus*: The Old Man and the Text," *English Literary Renaissance* 11 [Spring 1981]), he does not take its main point to heart: "The nature of the original *Doctor Faustus* will probably always be beyond our reach; even an approach to its establishment is beyond the power of current bibliographical theory and practice" (p. 146). Six years after Warren's article, Eriksen "returns to the problem of textual integrity, adducing new internal and external evidence that support [*sic*] the view that the B text represents *Doctor Faustus* essentially as Marlowe conceived it shortly before he was killed" (p. 19). Since nothing has changed substantively on the bibliographical front since 1981, the book's argument faces a credibility problem. Compounding that problem, Eriksen treats the B text not as a theatrical script but as a literary artifact. At the very time when most critics/scholars have recognized the significance of Elizabethan theater as background for Elizabethan plays, Eriksen writes, "I shall argue that it is both possible and desirable to place Marlowe's textual arrangements within a purely poetic or nondramatic context" (p. 106).

Eriksen's case for the B text of *Doctor Faustus* rests primarily on assorted comparisons: he relates ideas in the play to those of Cambridge controversialist Peter Baro (chapter 1) and "aspiring magus" Giordano Bruno (chapter 2); he links formal elements and themes with classical and Renaissance epic (chapter 3), and typology with myth (chapter 5). In the sixth chapter Eriksen tests the integrity of the B text through verbal expressions and rhetorical schemes which he investigates in the disputed portions of *Doctor Faustus*, other Marlowe plays, and non-Marlovian texts (mostly dramatic) which date from 1562 to 1605. Chapters 3, 4, and 5 depend on a method which Eriksen calls "a *topomorphical* approach to the text"; they study "the distribution of topoi and themes, or textual segments devoted to specific topoi, with particular reference to their structure (morphe) and the interrelationships they form" (p. 14, Eriksen's italics).

As a whole, Eriksen's book surrounds the B text with so much data that the play often disappears from view. The chapters on influence especially block out *Doctor Faustus* as they focus on Bruno and Torquato Tasso. When the argument does settle on the play, Eriksen's dialectical strategies sometimes weaken his conclusions. In the first chapter, for instance, he tries to show that Marlowe's tragedy reflects the structure of Augustine's argument in *De libero arbitrio* without delineating the structure. In the sixth, a digression on rhetoric and tragedy in Aristotle, Longinus, and George Puttenham interferes with Eriksen's collecting of rhetorical schemes. Now and then this book's intricate route through the history of ideas and theory leads to an unexpected discovery about the play—its sequence and imagery in particular—but ultimately it becomes lost in the thicket described by Warren: "We encounter with these texts the mystery of the confused publication of a work on a controversial subject long after the death of the author, who was equally controversial" (p. 146).

Michael Hattaway has contributed a volume on *Hamlet* to The Critics Debate, a series relying on its two-part format to broaden its readers' horizons. With the first part each book introduces major critical trends associated with its text, stressing that English Studies advance through a plurality of approaches; with the second the author gives his own evaluation of the work, displaying literary criticism in action.

Hattaway serves The Critics Debate well, reviewing the criticism and reading his play in less than one hundred pages. As he notes all the high points in a style that makes them clear and memorable, he distinguishes historical, formal, romantic, psychological, philosophic, and "language-based" approaches. Along the way he defines terms (such as "ideology") and contexts (such as Renaissance attitudes toward revenge and ghosts) when he sees fit. His own interpretation of *Hamlet,* which demonstrates "the amount of ethical awareness the play generates" (p. 81), emphasizes "patterns of analogy" in the tragedy's structure.

In *Chance and the Text of Experience: Freud, Nietzsche, and Shakespeare's "Hamlet"*, William Beatty Warner combines psychological, philosophic, and language-based approaches to advance an original explication of Shakespeare's play. As the title suggests, Warner's study of *Hamlet* constitutes "Movement Three" (or the last long chapter) in an examination of conceptual narratives whose authors "interpret chance into experience" (p. 22). By "chance" Warner means "something which, befalling the person, and being construed by him or her, becomes a sign of a necessity that is opaque and resists the control of a presiding consciousness" (p. 16). "In articulating a relationship of chance and the person, narrative figures an experience for the subject which is obscure yet decisive because, in its single violent movement, chance helps constitute the very person it disrupts as a fixed identity" (p. 22).

The analysis of *Hamlet* falls into three sections promised by Warner in his introduction: he gives a thematic reading of the tragedy "from the vantage point of Hamlet the character, so we can understand how chance obscures and complicates his efforts"; then he interprets critical responses to show how they suppress the operation of chance in *Hamlet*; finally he rereads the play "outside the frame of Hamlet's desire" and analyzes "the series of binding contingent reversals which compose Hamlet's last act" (p. 222). Closely argued, both readings of *Hamlet* illuminate the tragedy with great intensity. Warner proves a dependable guide through the abstract realms of theory because he fixes his attention on Shakespeare's text, moves through it chronologically, and bases his conclusions on what he finds there.

First Warner follows the trajectory of the play's action as Hamlet tries to impose his "guiding interpretation" (that is, his understanding of the world and his situation) on Denmark and then gives up that interpretation for passivity which anticipates "a compromise formation—play as sport—that allows Hamlet's relationship to his adversaries and the act of revenge to take on an entirely new tone and character" (p. 260). Next the writer works through some of Hattaway's "patterns of analogy": "The text not only implicates Hamlet in the positions of his rivals; we also witness a symmetrical reversal. Just as Hamlet is beginning to throw off the terms of the guiding interpretation, Hamlet's rivals, Claudius and Laertes, begin to use its terms to define their own situations" (p. 285). Reversals occur both at the level of character and at the level of language in tropes of antithesis, negation, and chiasmus: "The reversibility of human positions in this text makes any kind of affirmation hopelessly entangled with its opposite" (p. 291). As the last scene becomes caught up in reversals—especially the duel which reenacts an earlier confrontation between Hamlet's father and Fortinbras's—its repetitions produce "incompatible alternative realities and interpretations suspended *in potentia* in the 'same' matrix of events" (p. 297). Hamlet has misgivings before this episode, intimations of hidden chance and his inability to control it; and the audience in the tragedy's closing moments may "glimpse the play of repetitions within which the life of the person appears as singular" (p. 295).

According to Hattaway these mysteries no longer fascinate critics as much as they once did, because *King Lear* has recently become the most acclaimed Shakespearean play (p. 20). Appropriately, a volume on *King Lear* brings Shakespeare into the series Approaches to Teaching World Literature. The Modern Language Association of America publishes these books intended for new teachers and nonspecialists who must cope with World Literature texts in undergraduate courses. In this series the two-part format provides a descriptive catalog of "Materials" (editions, useful secondary readings, audio-visual aids) and a collection of "Approaches" (short essays by experienced teachers about their methods). Robert H. Ray has compiled this thorough volume on *King Lear*, which includes sixteen "Approaches" that range from theme and images (Lynda E. Boose on "Marriage and the Family," Frances Teague on "Sight and Perception") to "Teaching with a Proper Text" (Michael Warren) to "*King Lear* as Performance and Experience" (J. L. Styan) and "*King Lear* in a Course on Shakespeare and Film" (Hugh M. Richmond).

V

Among miscellaneous collections of essays, the third volume of *Medieval and Renaissance Drama in England* offers the largest and most diverse number. This set of thirteen papers rarely deals with the medieval stage, but it runs the whole gamut from Tudor to Caroline, from Robin Hood entertainments in the Somerset parish of Yeovil

(James D. Stokes) to Ford's allegorical romance in *The Broken Heart* (Marie L. Kessel). In between it favors Jonson with three articles, two of them (by David M. Bergeron and Helen Ostovich) especially illuminating in connection with the theories of Watson and Womack. Other notable papers include two about staging (by Stephen K. Wright on an English chronicle drama and Leslie Thomson on Middleton's *Hengist, King of Kent*); one about language and the tragicomic genre (on Beaumont and Fletcher's *Philaster* by Nicholas F. Radel); and one about a dramatic source (on Middleton and Rowley's *The Changeling* by Dale B. J. Randall). In addition to its scholarly/critical essays, this volume contains five review articles and nineteen book reviews.

Leonard Barkan's last number of *Renaissance Drama* also ranges widely over texts from Kyd's *Spanish Tragedy* to Milton's *Comus*, and three essays share themes with criticism reviewed above (comparative items appear in parentheses): Diana Benet's on Jonson's *Epicoene* (Watson, Womack, two papers in *Medieval and Renaissance Drama in England*); Verna Ann Foster's on Ford's *Perkin Warbeck* (Coburn Freer in Anderson's *"Concord in Discord"*); and Mary Laughlin Fawcett's on "Chastity and Speech in *Othello* and *Comus*" (Karen Newman in Howard and O'Connor's *Shakespeare Reproduced*, Ranald on "Women without Power"). In this volume titled "Renaissance Plays: New Readings and Rereadings," four articles treat the dramatic constructions of *The Spanish Tragedy* (James P. Hammersmith), Greene's *Friar Bacon and Friar Bungay* (Charles W. Hieatt), Marlowe's *Edward II* (Susan McCloskey) and *Doctor Faustus* (Roy T. Eriksen, with material appearing in his book on the tragedy). Jonathan Baldo engages in "Reflections on 'Cause' in *Hamlet*," and Peggy Muñoz Simonds analyzes "The Iconography of Primitivism in *Cymbeline*."

Mary Beth Rose gives her first number of *Renaissance Drama* a distinctive stamp with a topic of immediate critical interest. Called "Renaissance Drama and Cultural Change," this volume comprises "seven essays . . . concerned with the effect that conflict in the social, political, and religious environment had on the drama" (pp. v-vi). Rose's thoughtful arrangement of these first-rate papers allows them to reflect on one another in provocative ways. For instance, she begins with Anthony J. Cascardi's "The Old and the New: The Spanish *Comedia* and the Resistance to Historical Change" (one of three articles on Spanish drama which add dimensions to Loftis's book) and follows it with G. K. Hunter's "The Beginnings of Elizabethan Drama: Revolution and Continuity." After Hunter argues for the influence of Reformation thinking on the "University

Wits'' and popular theater—stressing interrelationships between the playwrights and the institution—Jonathan Dollimore tackles "Subjectivity, Sexuality, and Transgression: The Jacobean Connection": "poststructuralism is helping us to see again what the Renaissance already knew: identity is in-formed by what it is not. It also helps us to see that if (as was apparent in the early seventeenth century) identity is clearly constituted by the structures of power, of position, allegiance, and service, any disturbance within or of identity could be as dangerous to that order as to the individual subject" (p. 55). Dollimore names his particular subject "transgressive reinscription," "a mode of transgression which seeks not an escape from existing structures, but rather a subversive reinscription within them—and in the process a dis-location of them" (p. 57). In the other two papers on English drama, Phyllis Rackin discusses "Temporality, Anachronism, and Presence in Shakespeare's English Histories" and Martin Butler studies accounts for "A Provincial Masque of *Comus*, 1636."

Last spring two small Japanese publications reached North America. *The Renaissance Bulletin* deals with both dramatic and nondramatic literature, and a few of its brief essays survey scholarship in the field; it includes an informative note on Akira Kurosawa's film *Ran* by Hiroshi Yamamoto. More specialized, *Shakespeare Studies* consists of three interpretive papers about *Julius Caesar*, *Much Ado About Nothing*, and *A Midsummer Night's Dream*; the last, Michiru Sasaki's, assembles material on folklore about the moon.

Editing Early English Drama: Special Problems and New Directions focuses on pre-Elizabethan plays; A. F. Johnston has compiled this volume of papers given at the nineteenth annual Conference on Editorial Problems at the University of Toronto. Although the printed versions rarely get past the early Tudors, their editorial topics concern most scholars who teach or do research involving Renaissance dramatic texts. In a very enlightening piece, David Bevington explains how editing anthologies of pre-Shakespearean dramas can determine the canon. David Parry and Peter Meredith interpret marginalia and stage directions in medieval and Tudor plays; J. A. B. Somerset emphasizes the usefulness of records to editors of pre-Restoration dramatic texts; and Johnston shows how such records have changed the chronology and "received understanding" (p. 121) of the English mystery cycles.

Last year the multifaceted Oxford Shakespeare sent *SEL* a major product of its enterprise, the second version of its *Complete Works*: the *Original-Spelling Edition*. Most of the Oxford team's innovative (if not radical) decisions became apparent in the modernized *Complete Works* published earlier and in scholarship the editors issued as they worked. Sharing the format of the modernized volume, the *Original-Spelling Edition* also begins with Stanley Wells's general introduction to Shakespeare's life, professional career, theater, and publication; continues with "Contemporary Allusions to Shakespeare" and "Commendatory Poems and Prefaces"; arranges the plays by chronology rather than genre; briefly introduces individual works; prints both the Quarto and Folio *King Lear*; includes new attributions not only to Shakespeare (of a few short poems, among them the now famous "Shall I die?") but also to Middleton (of revisions to *Measure for Measure* and *Macbeth*, and collaboration on *Timon of Athens*); and places its glossary at the back. The *Original-Spelling Edition* shares definitive principles with the modernized volume: it prints the most theatrical version of each play if possible; and when this practice results in leaving out Shakespearean lines, the editors restore the omissions at the end of the published script in "Additional Passages." Obviously the *Original-Spelling Edition* corresponds with the modernized *Complete Works* in many crucial ways; it springs few surprises.

But the latest *Complete Works* makes up in retrieval what it lacks in novelty: "The present edition follows the spelling, punctuation, and other 'incidentals'—capitalization, italicization, etc.—of the earliest edition of each work, or, where more than one edition survives, of that which we regard as being closest to Shakespeare's manuscript." Interfering as little as they could with the texts' evidence about pronunciation, wordplay, syntax, resonance, and the state of the language in Shakespeare's time, the editors have tried to make additions and emendations authentic: "When we have emended the text, or added directions, we have attempted to adopt incidentals characteristic of the text used as copy, or, where possible, of the manuscript underlying it" (p. xxxv). To help readers make the most of such evidence, the *Original-Spelling Edition* adds an essay by Vivian Salmon on "The Spelling and Punctuation of Shakespeare's Time." It also contains in diplomatic reprint the 1608 Quarto of *Pericles* for comparison with the editors' "Reconstructed Text."

The *Original-Spelling Edition* has its unauthentic moments, the effects of normalization, editorial stage directions (in square brackets), and conflated readings. On the whole, though, it fulfills its editors' intentions admirably and supplies a need. (As the general introduction understates the case, "Original-spelling editions of Shakespeare have rarely been attempted," p. xxxvi.) Nevertheless, like its predecessor this *Complete Works* requires the *Textual*

Companion announced for publication in July 1987 but not available for consulting by year's end. Evidently British reviewers have received extracts from this reference work to guide them through the editors' textual decisions for each play. In her *SEL* review for 1986, Jean Howard quoted Oxford University Press's assurance that the *Textual Companion* would provide "a discussion of the text of each of Shakespeare's works accompanied by detailed notes on individual readings, lists of departures from the early editions, a reprint of the stage directions in the primary text of each play, an Appendix recording changes of lineation, and other relevant material" (pp. 369-70).

In a less serious vein, A. L. Rowse has brought out ten more volumes in the Contemporary Shakespeare Series. Nothing about these "Modern Texts" has changed since Howard reviewed them fairly—and in unequivocally negative terms—last spring. Opening each edition on a silly note, the essay "Why a Contemporary Shakespeare?" patronizes the reader at once: "Just remember, I do not need it myself: *I live in the Elizabethan age,* Shakespeare's time, and have done for years, and am familiar with its language, and his. But even for me there are still difficulties—still more for modern people, whom I am out to help" (p. 4, Rowse's italics). With equally deathless prose Rowse condescends to Shakespearean editors and critics.

The format of these editions seems to allow for no more than six pages of introduction, some of them occupied by quotations from the texts and Rowse's perky questions. "Why all this? Why the subject?" he asks after a short paragraph touching the sources and atmosphere of *Cymbeline* (p. 14). "What matter?" he concludes about the textual difficulties of *Timon of Athens,* "we can only do our best to help the reader, and with so corrupt a text we are of necessity all the more free" (p. 15). One hopes that Rowse's tone and ideology will stop readers in their tracks, before they see his modern translations:

> *Gloucester:* Ah, Humphrey, this dishonour in your age
> Will bring your head with sorrow to the ground!
> I beseech your majesty give me leave to go;
> Sorrow would solace, and my age would ease.
>
> (*2 King Henry VI*, II.iii,p.61)

Queen Katherine: Take your lute, wench. My soul grows sad with troubles;
Sing, and disperse them if you can. Leave working.
(*King Henry VIII,* III.i,p.75)

Methuen has made generally available two of the program/texts which accompanied the Royal Shakespeare Company productions of *The Two Noble Kinsmen* and *The Fair Maid of the West.* For the Shakespeare and Fletcher play, the script comes from N. W. Bawcutt's New Penguin Shakespeare; square brackets in the text indicate cuts, and two pages of endnotes list alterations and additions. For the Thomas Heywood, director Trevor Nunn has made an adaptation: "In the playing version I have taken the liberty of conflating Heywood's two parts into one. . . . This has involved some transposition of both text and incident and a wholesale cutting of lines" (p. 5). Neither the director nor Simon Trussler, who writes the commentary for both program/texts, cites the edition from which Nunn started, and this script does not employ square brackets or endnotes. Each of these publications has fifteen or sixteen pages of apparatus at the front with everything from a cast list and plot summary to excerpts from scholarship, suggestions "For Further Reading," and background material on the dramatists as well as the plays. All in all the Swan Theatre Plays—named for the venue where these productions originated—serve as helpful records of the RSC's scripts and directorial choices.

Last year brought out at least three small collections of non-Shakespearean plays. With a second volume Peter Happé finished his edition of *The Complete Plays of John Bale,* this book containing unmodernized texts with notes and glossary of *God's Promises, John Baptist's Preaching, The Temptation of Our Lord,* and *Three Laws.* MacDonald P. Jackson and Michael Neill edited *The Selected Plays of John Marston* in the series Plays by Renaissance and Restoration Dramatists, having chosen five works: *Antonio and Mellida, Antonio's Revenge, The Malcontent, The Dutch Courtesan,* and *Sophonisba.* Reasonably priced (these days) in paperback, this book has much to recommend it for teaching: carefully edited texts with textual notes (in modernizing spelling, punctuation, and presentation, Jackson and Neill "profited from a discussion of the attendant problems by Stanley Wells in *Modernizing Shakespeare's Spelling* [Oxford: Clarendon Press, 1979]," p. xvii); substantial introductory apparatus including a "Life and Works" and extensive if "Selective Bibliography"; an "Introductory

Note" for each play covering text, date, source, auspices, and stage history; and two types—short and long—of annotations. Edited by Peter Corbin and Douglas Sedge, *Three Jacobean Witchcraft Plays*—Marston's *Sophonisba*, Middleton's *The Witch*, and Dekker, Ford, and Rowley's *The Witch of Edmonton*—appears in the Revels Plays Companion Library to "reflect the variety of witch belief and practice in the Jacobean period" (p. 1). In critical introductions to each play, Corbin and Sedge emphasize the contemporary opinion and customs which inform these texts as well as the dramas' theatrical potential. This edition includes notes on the texts, textual collations, commentary (at the back), and an appendix with music for Middleton's play.

To the very enthusiastic student of Elizabethan drama Jay M. Freyman, William E. Mahaney, and Walter K. Sherwin offer the Latin text and English translation (with notes) of Henry Bellamy's *Iphis*. This university drama—out of Ovid by way of English popular theater—was probably written and staged at St. John's College, Oxford, in the 1620s.

Two Shakespeare "companions" have appeared on each other's heels: *The Shakespeare Handbook* edited by Levi Fox and *The Cambridge Companion to Shakespeare Studies* edited by Stanley Wells. In the introduction, Fox calls his book "a convenient companion reference source for students, librarians, and Shakespeare enthusiasts in general" (p. 7). This volume includes a chronology and chapters on Shakespeare's era, life, theater, and poetry. Of course most attention focuses on the plays (organized by genres, each one introduced by two pages or so of text with visual illustrations), their performances on the stage and in film, and their interpretations through music. Working in limited compass a number of contributors—Eric Ives, David Daniell, Andy Piasecki, Ronnie Mulryne, Philip Edwards, John Steane, Roger Manvell—have nevertheless presented a great deal of information in their chapters.

Stanley Wells has restructured Cambridge's *New Companion to Shakespeare Studies* (1971), edited by Kenneth Muir and S. Schoenbaum, to produce his excellent version. In all nineteen essays cover every significant aspect of the field, and each ends with an up-to-date reading list. Wells has co-opted highly respected scholars to write about topics which helped to establish their expertise: for instance, Schoenbaum chronicles Shakespeare's life from documents; Inga-Stina Ewbank examines " 'his language' in terms that are practical-historical-dramatical" (p. 49); Alan C. Dessen distinguishes between Elizabethan and modern theatrical conventions in staging of the plays; Russell Jackson, Roger Warren, and Robert Hapgood cover theater history and the media.

Doing its part to make *The Cambridge Companion* a pleasure to read, each essay takes a different and original course through its material. The genre articles, for example, avoid strictly chronological arrangements: David Daniell stresses Shakespeare's transforming of conventions throughout the comedies; G. K. Hunter groups four tragedies which use love "as a central interrelating emotion" (p. 129), the later Roman plays, and "chronicle tragedies" (p. 136), concluding with *Hamlet*; R. L. Smallwood considers the histories as "an exploration of human political behaviour, of the desire for power" (p. 147) and begins his paper with illustrations from *Henry V*, *Richard III*, *Richard II*, and *1 Henry VI*. According to their individual lights W. R. Elton discusses the history of ideas; Robert Ellrodt, the nondramatic poetry; Peter Thomson, playhouses and players; MacD. P. Jackson, the transmission of the text; and Harry Levin, critical approaches from 1660 to 1904. In addition Muir, Lawrence Danson, and Edward Berry review twentieth-century criticism of the three major genres, and Dieter Mehl compiles a useful listing of reference books. Toward the end Terence Hawkes accomplishes a tour de force with characteristic polish: he describes new critical approaches—structuralism, poststructuralism or deconstruction, semiotics, feminism, Marxism and discourse, reception theory—in sixteen pages of lucid prose. As a whole *The Cambridge Companion* works successfully as an introduction for students, a reference book for scholars, and a first-rate demonstration of research and criticism.

Among other reference books, two concern Shakespearean drama in particular: Naseeb Shaheen's *Biblical References in Shakespeare's Tragedies* and Robin Headlam Wells's *Shakespeare, Politics and the State*. Shaheen maintains that his "study of Shakespeare's biblical references differs from previous ones in that it considers Shakespeare's references in the light of his literary sources" (p. 7). Consequently Shaheen attempts to differentiate between allusions deriving from Scripture and those coming from narrative sources, and among the passages Shakespeare added, rejected, or adapted; he also listens for echoes from the *Book of Common Prayer* and the *Book of Homilies*. For the catalog of references at the heart of this volume, Shaheen employs a system to indicate whether he believes allusions certain, probable, or possible in eleven Shakespearean tragedies which include *Julius Caesar*, *Troilus and Cressida*, and *Timon of Athens*. Preceding the catalog, two introductory chapters give a historical survey of English Bibles to Shakespeare's time and an account of the Anglican liturgy in the second half of the sixteenth century. Together the listings and apparatus make a useful reference tool.

Robin Headlam Wells's volume belongs to the series Context and Commentary edited by Arthur Pollard: "It is the aim of this series to trace the interweavings of history and literature, to show by judicious quotation and commentary how those actually working within the various fields of human activity influenced and were influenced by those who were writing" (p. ix). After a short introduction, therefore, six chapters define major political themes from a twenty-year period of Shakespeare's dramatic career—concepts such as "The Just Ruler," "Rebellion," "Providence and History," "Natural Law"—and exemplify the treatment of these ideas with citations from a variety of Renaissance texts: Wells juxtaposes the extracts with related passages from Shakespeare's histories and tragedies primarily. Since this kind of procedure generates interpretation in fits and starts, the volume will probably serve undergraduates best as an introduction to primary sources concerning Renaissance thought. At the back Wells provides convenient (though short) bibliographies of both primary and secondary materials.

Mark W. Scott has edited two more volumes in the series *Shakespearean Criticism*, each book giving excerpts (in chronological order) from four centuries of commentary on the dramatic and nondramatic works. For each Shakespearean text a summary at the beginning reviews date, text, source, and critical history; an "Additional Bibliography" at the end supplements the studies quoted. The fourth volume just published includes *Othello, Titus Andronicus, The Merchant of Venice*, and *Cymbeline*; the fifth covers *Romeo and Juliet, Henry V, As You Like It*, and *The Merry Wives of Windsor*, and it introduces a "Cumulative Index to Topics." Although this series gives students an indication of Shakespearean commentary's scope (and bulk), I prefer *The Cambridge Companion* for its interpreting of critical trends—and its economy.

During 1987 the Dictionary of Literary Biography issued companion volumes edited by Fredson Bowers: *Elizabethan Dramatists* and *Jacobean and Caroline Dramatists*. In line with the series as a whole, "Each of these freestanding volumes provides a biographical-bibliographical guide and overview for a particular area of literature" (p. vii). Individual entries in the Bowers's dictionaries start with a list of the author's play productions and his books in their first and last authoritative editions (compiled as accurately as evidence permits); and each one ends with a catalog of bibliographies, secondary references, and manuscripts. Covering nineteen dramatists (Shakespeare among them) and five anonymous plays, *The Elizabethan Dramatists* contains an introduction by Bowers and three appendixes on theater, publication, and sources for study. *Jacobean and Caroline Dramatists* prints the same foreword and includes twenty-six dramatists as well as *A Yorkshire Tragedy*. Together these two books provide a useful resource for any student of English Renaissance drama.

Six books have been reissued, most as paperbacks for the first time: Terry Eagleton's *William Shakespeare*; Robert Marchant's *A Picture of Shakespeare's Tragedies*; Kenneth Muir's selection of British Academy Shakespeare Lectures, *Interpretations of Shakespeare*; Steven Urkowitz's *Shakespeare's Revision of "King Lear"*; Robert Weimann's *Shakespeare and the Popular Tradition in the Theater: Studies in the Social Dimension of Dramatic Form and Function*, edited by Robert Schwartz. First published in 1971, J. W. Lever's *The Tragedy of State: A Study of Jacobean Drama* reappears with a new introduction by Jonathan Dollimore which defines the book's context as "the larger critical, intellectual, aesthetic and political issues" contributing to literary criticism over the past two decades (p. vii).

BOOKS RECEIVED

Adler, Doris. *Philip Massinger.* Twayne's English Authors Series 435, ed. Arthur F. Kinney. Boston: Twayne, 1987. Pp. 152. $22.95. ISBN 0-8057-6934-X.

Altieri, Joanne. *The Theatre of Praise: The Panegyric Tradition in Seventeenth-Century English Drama.* Newark: Univ. of Delaware Press; London and Toronto: Associated Univ. Presses, 1986. Pp. 240. $32.50. ISBN 0-87413-275-4.

Anderson, Donald K., Jr., ed. *"Concord in Discord": The Plays of John Ford, 1586-1986.* New York: AMS Press, 1987. Pp. xiv + 298. $34.50. ISBN 0-404-62287-9.

Bale, John. *The Complete Plays of John Bale,* vol. 2, ed. Peter Happé. Wolfeboro, NH: Brewer, 1986. Pp. 193. $45.00. ISBN 0-85991-219-1.

Barber, C. L. *Creating Elizabethan Tragedy: The Theater of Marlowe and Kyd,* ed. Richard P. Wheeler. Chicago: Univ. of Chicago Press, 1988. Pp. xii + 169. $29.95 cloth, ISBN 0-226-03703-7. $11.95 paper, ISBN 0-226-03704-5.

Barroll, Leeds, ed. *Medieval and Renaissance Drama in England: An Annual Gathering of Research, Criticism, and Reviews,* vol. 3. New York: AMS Press, 1987. Pp. xiv + 368. $30.00. ISBN 0-404-62303-4.

Barthelemy, Anthony Gerard. *Black Face, Maligned Race: The Representation of Blacks in English Drama from Shakespeare to Southerne.* Baton Rouge and London: Louisiana State Univ. Press, 1987. Pp. xii + 215. $27.50. ISBN 0-8071-1331-X.

Bellamy, Ralph. *Iphis,* trans. and ed. Jay M. Freyman, William E. Mahaney, and Walter K. Sherwin. Salzburg: Univ. Salzburg, 1986. Pp. 116.

Berry, Herbert. *Shakespeare's Playhouses.* New York: AMS Press, 1987. Pp. x + 260. $34.50. ISBN 0-404-62289-5.

Bowers, Fredson, ed. *Elizabethan Dramatists.* Dictionary of Literary Biography, vol. 62. Detroit: Gale Research, 1987. Pp. xxi + 492. $92.00. ISBN 0-8103-1740-0.

Bowers, Fredson, ed. *Jacobean and Caroline Dramatists.* Dictionary of Literary Biography, vol. 58. Detroit: Gale Research, 1987. Pp. xxi + 370. $92.00. ISBN 0-8103-1736-2.

Bradshaw, Graham. *Shakespeare's Scepticism.* New York: St. Martin's Press, 1987. Pp. xiii + 269. $35.00. ISBN 0-312-00964-X.

Cavell, Stanley. *Disowning Knowledge in Six Plays of Shakespeare.* Cambridge and New York: Cambridge Univ. Press, 1987. Pp. x + 226. $34.50 cloth, ISBN 0-521-33032-7. $10.95 paper, ISBN 0-521-33890-5.

Corbin, Peter, and Sedge, Douglas, eds. *Three Jacobean Witchcraft Plays: "The Tragedy of Sophonisba," "The Witch," "The Witch of Edmonton."* The Revels Plays Companion Library. Manchester and Wolfeboro, NH: Manchester Univ. Press, 1986. Pp. xii + 260. £29.50. ISBN 0-7190-1949-4.

Eagleton, Terry. *William Shakespeare.* New York: Basil Blackwell, 1987. Pp. x + 114. $7.95. ISBN 0-631-14554-0.

Eriksen, Roy T. *"The Forme of Faustus Fortunes": A Study of "The Tragedie of Doctor Faustus" (1616).* Oslo: Solum Forlag A/S, and Atlantic Highlands, NJ: Humanities Press, 1987. Pp. 233. $35.00. ISBN 0-391-03440-5 (US); 82-560-0416-9 (Norway).

Fox, Levi, ed. *The Shakespeare Handbook.* Boston: G. K. Hall, 1987. Pp. 264. $29.95. ISBN 0-8161-8905-6.

Griswold, Wendy. *Renaissance Revivals: City Comedy and Revenge Tragedy in the London Theatre, 1576-1980.* Chicago and London: Univ. of Chicago Press, 1986. Pp. 288. $24.95. ISBN 0-226-30923-1.

Gurr, Andrew. *Playgoing in Shakespeare's London.* Cambridge and New York: Cambridge Univ. Press, 1987. Pp. xv + 284. $49.50. ISBN 0-521-25336-5.

Hassel, R. Chris, Jr. *Songs of Death: Performance, Interpretation, and the Text of "Richard III."* Lincoln and London: Univ. of Nebraska Press, 1987. Pp. x + 196. $21.95. ISBN 0-8023-2341-2.

Hattaway, Michael. *"Hamlet."* The Critics Debate. Atlantic Highlands, NJ: Humanities Press, 1987. Pp. 112. $22.50 cloth, ISBN 0-391-03459-6. $7.95 paper, ISBN 0-391-03476-6.

Heywood, Thomas. *The Fair Maid of the West.* A program/text with commentary by Simon Trussler. London and New York: Methuen, 1987. Pp. 75. $7.50. ISBN 0-413-4-580-X.

Honigmann, E. A. J. *John Weever.* The Revels Plays Companion Library. New York: St. Martin's Press, 1987. Pp. 134. $35.00. ISBN 0-312-00788-4.

Hornby, Richard. *Drama, Metadrama, and Perception.* Lewisburg: Bucknell Univ. Press; London and Toronto: Associated Univ. Presses, 1986. Pp. 189. $26.50. ISBN 0-8387-5101-6.

Howard, Jean E., and O'Connor, Marion F., eds. *Shakespeare Reproduced: The Text in History and Ideology.* New York and London: Methuen, 1987. Pp. vi + 292. ISBN 0-416-00922-0.

Johnston, A. F., ed. *Editing Early English Drama: Special Problems and New Directions.* New York: AMS Press, 1987. Pp. 143. $29.50. ISBN 0-404-63669-1.

Lever, J. W. *The Tragedy of State: A Study of Jacobean Drama.* London and New York: Methuen, 1987. Pp. xxi + 100. $9.95. ISBN 0-416-70000-4.

Levin, Harry. *Playboys and Killjoys: An Essay on the Theory and Practice of Comedy.* New York and Oxford: Oxford Univ. Press, 1987. Pp. viii + 214. $18.95. ISBN 0-19-504856-3.

Loftis, John. *Renaissance Drama in England & Spain; Topical Allusion and History Plays.* Princeton: Princeton Univ. Press, 1987. Pp. xvi + 281. $34.50. ISBN 0-691-06706-6.

Lomax, Marion. *Stage Images and Traditions: Shakespeare to Ford.* Cambridge and London: Cambridge Univ. Press, 1987. Pp. xiii + 202. $37.50. ISBN 0-521-32659-1.

Marchant, Robert. *A Picture of Shakespeare's Tragedies.* Doncaster: Brynmill Press, and Atlantic Highlands, NJ: Humanities Press, 1987. Pp. 180. $12.50. ISBN 0-907839-21-5.

Marston, John. *The Selected Plays of John Marston*, ed. MacDonald P. Jackson and Michael Neill. Plays by Renaissance and Restoration Dramatists. New York: Cambridge Univ. Press, 1986. Pp. 535. $54.50 cloth, ISBN 0-521-21746-6. $19.95 paper, ISBN 0-521-29247-6.

Martin, William F. *The Indissoluble Knot: "King Lear" as Ironic Drama.* Lanham, MD, and London: Univ. Press of America, 1987. Pp. vi + 87. $16.75. ISBN 0-8191-6604-9.

McAlindon, Thomas. *English Renaissance Tragedy.* Vancouver: Univ. of British Columbia Press, 1986. Pp. xiii + 269. $20.50. ISBN 0-7748-0253-7.

McMillin, Scott. *The Elizabethan Theatre and "The Book of Sir Thomas More."* Ithaca and London: Cornell Univ. Press, 1987. Pp. 170. $18.95. ISBN 0-8014-2008-3.

Mehl, Dieter. *Shakespeare's Tragedies: An Introduction.* Cambridge and New York: Cambridge Univ. Press, 1986. Pp. x + 272. $39.50 cloth, ISBN 0-521-30423-7. $12.95 paper, ISBN 0-521-31690-1.

Mercer, Peter. *"Hamlet" and the Acting of Revenge.* Iowa City: Univ. of Iowa Press, 1987. Pp. viii + 269. $27.50. ISBN 0-87745-171-0.

Miles, Rosalind. *Ben Jonson: His Life and Work.* New York: Routledge & Kegan Paul, 1987. Pp. xiv + 306. $55.00. ISBN 0-7102-0838-3.

Muir, Kenneth, ed. *Interpretations of Shakespeare.* Oxford: Clarendon Press, 1987. Pp. 215. $14.95. ISBN 0-19-812952-1.

Overton, Bill. *"The Merchant of Venice."* Text and Performance. Atlantic Highlands, NJ: Humanities Press, 1987. Pp. 80. $7.95. ISBN 0-391-03469-3.

Page, Malcolm. *"Richard II."* Text and Performance. Atlantic Highlands, NJ: Humanities Press, 1987. Pp. 87. $7.95. ISBN 0-391-03466-9.

Parker, Barbara L. *A Precious Seeing: Love and Reason in Shakespeare's Plays.* New York and London: New York Univ. Press, 1987. Pp. xi + 213. ISBN 0-8147-6603-X.

Ranald, Margaret Loftus. *Shakespeare and His Social Context: Essays in Osmotic Knowledge and Literary Interpretation*. New York: AMS Press, 1987. Pp. xvi + 288. $42.50. ISBN 0-404-62280-1.

Ray, Robert H., ed. *Approaches to Teaching Shakespeare's "King Lear."* New York: Modern Language Association, 1986. Pp. ix + 166. $30.00 cloth, ISBN 0-87352-497-7. $16.50 paper, ISBN 0-87352-498-5.

The Renaissance Bulletin 12. Tokyo: The Renaissance Institute, 1985. Pp. 48.

Renaissance Drama, n.s. 16, *Renaissance Plays: New Readings and Rereadings*, ed. Leonard Barkan. Evanston: Northwestern Univ. Press, 1985. Pp. vii + 182. $42.00. ISBN 0-8101-0677-9.

Renaissance Drama, n.s. 17, *Renaissance Drama and Cultural Change*, ed. Mary Beth Rose. Evanston: Northwestern Univ. Press, 1986. Pp. vii + 174. $42.00. ISBN 0-8101-0678-7.

Rhoads, Diana Akers. *Shakespeare's Defense of Poetry: "A Midsummer Night's Dream" and "The Tempest."* Lanham, MD, and London: Univ. Press of America, 1987. Pp. vii + 255. $14.50. ISBN 0-8191-4980-2.

Rigaud, N. J. *Femme Mythifiée, Femme de Raison: La Veuve dans la comédie anglaise au temps de Shakespeare 1600-1625*. Aix en Provence: Univ. de Provence, 1986. Pp. 280. 130,00 F.F. ISBN 2-85399-150-4.

Salmon, Vivian and Burness, Edwina, eds. *A Reader in the Language of Shakespearean Drama*. Amsterdam and Philadelphia: John Benjamins, 1987. Pp. xxii + 523. $21.95. ISBN 0-915027-99-2.

Scott, Mark W., ed. *Shakespearean Criticism*, vol. 4. Detroit: Gale Research Co., 1987. Pp. 714. $85.00. ISBN 0-8103-6128-0.

Scott, Mark W., ed. *Shakespearean Criticism*, vol. 5. Detroit: Gale Research Co., 1987. Pp. 625. $85.00. ISBN 0-8103-6129-9.

Shaheen, Naseeb. *Biblical References in Shakespeare's Tragedies*. Newark: Univ. of Delaware Press; London and Toronto: Associated Univ. Presses, 1987. Pp. 245. $29.50. ISBN 0-87413-293-2.

Shakespeare, William. *The Complete Works. Original-Spelling Edition*. Ed. Stanley Wells and Gary Taylor. Oxford: Oxford Univ. Press, 1986. Pp. lxiii + 1456. $98.00. ISBN 0-19-812919-X.

Shakespeare, William. *Cymbeline*. Ed. A. L. Rowse. Lanham, MD, and London: Univ. Press of America, 1987. Pp. 140. $3.45. ISBN 0-8191-3938-6.

Shakespeare, William. *King Henry the Eighth*. Ed. A. L. Rowse. Lanham, MD, and London: Univ. Press of America, 1987. Pp. 137. $3.45. ISBN 0-8191-3936-X.

Shakespeare, William. *King Henry the Sixth, Part One*. Ed. A. L. Rowse. Lanham, MD, and London: Univ. Press of America, 1987. Pp. 135. $3.45. ISBN 0-8191-3941-6.

Shakespeare, William. *King Henry the Sixth, Part Two.* Ed. A. L. Rowse. Lanham, MD, and London: Univ. Press of America, 1987. Pp. 145. $3.45. ISBN 0-8191-3942-4.

Shakespeare, William. *King Henry the Sixth, Part Three.* Ed. A. L. Rowse. Lanham, MD, and London: Univ. Press of America, 1987. Pp. 146. $3.45. ISBN 0-8191-3943-2.

Shakespeare, William. *King John.* Ed. A. L. Rowse. Lanham, MD, and London: Univ. Press of America, 1987. Pp. 120. $3.45. ISBN 0-8191-3946-7.

Shakespeare, William. *King Lear,* Plays in Performance. Ed. J. S. Bratton. Cranbury, NJ, and Bristol: Bristol Classical Press, 1987. Pp. xix + 247. $29.50. ISBN 0-86292-233-X.

Shakespeare, William. *Much Ado About Nothing.* Ed. A. L. Rowse. Lanham, MD, and London: Univ. Press of America, 1987. Pp. 114. $3.45. ISBN 0-8191-3937-8.

Shakespeare, William. *Othello,* Plays in Performance. Ed. Julie Hankey. Cranbury, NJ, and Bristol: Bristol Classical Press, 1987. Pp. xviii + 354. $35.00. ISBN 0-86292-231-3.

Shakespeare, William. *Pericles.* Ed. A. L. Rowse. Lanham, MD, and London: Univ. Press of America, 1987. Pp. 117. $3.45. ISBN 0-8191-3945-9.

Shakespeare, William. *Timon of Athens.* Ed. A. L. Rowse. Lanham, MD, and London: Univ. Press of America, 1987. Pp. 116. $3.45. ISBN 0-8191-3939-4.

Shakespeare, William. *Titus Andronicus.* Ed. A. L. Rowse. Lanham, MD, and London: Univ. Press of America, 1987. Pp. 107. $3.45. ISBN 0-8191-3944-0.

Shakespeare, William, and Fletcher, John. *The Two Noble Kinsmen.* A program/text with commentary by Simon Trussler. London and New York: Methuen, 1987. Pp. 64. $7.50. ISBN 0-413-40530-3.

Shakespeare Studies, vol. 23, ed. Jiro Ozu. Tokyo: The Shakespeare Society of Japan, 1986. Pp. 93. ISSN 0582-9402.

Shattuck, Charles H. *Shakespeare on the American Stage: From Booth and Barrett to Sothern and Marlowe,* vol. 2. Washington, DC: Folger Shakespeare Library; London and Toronto: Associated Univ. Presses, 1987. Pp. 339. $65.00. ISBN 0-918016-77-0.

Spinrad, Phoebe S. *The Summons of Death on the Medieval and Renaissance English Stage.* Columbus: Ohio State Univ. Press, 1987. Pp. xii + 334. $30.00. ISBN 0-8142-0443-0.

Squier, Charles L. *John Fletcher.* Twayne's English Authors Series 433, ed. Arthur F. Kinney. Boston: Twayne, 1986. Pp. 167. $19.95. ISBN 0-8057-6923-4.

Stockholder, Kay. *Dream Works: Lovers and Families in Shakespeare's Plays.* Toronto, Buffalo, and London: Univ. of Toronto Press, 1987. Pp. 281. $35.00. ISBN 0-8020-5743-8.

Sturgess, Keith. *Jacobean Private Theatre.* London and New York: Routledge & Kegan Paul, 1987. Pp. ix + 228. $55.00. ISBN 0-7102-1017-5.

Tarlinskaja, Marina. *Shakespeare's Verse: Iambic Pentameter and the Poet's Idiosyncrasies.* American Univ. Studies. New York and Bern: Peter Lang, 1987. Pp. xxi + 383. $49.90. ISBN 0-8204-0344-X.

Tennenhouse, Leonard. *Power on Display: The Politics of Shakespeare's Genres.* New York and London: Methuen, 1987. Pp. viii + 206. $33.00 cloth, ISBN 0-416-01271-X. $12.50 paper, ISBN 0-416-01281-7.

Thompson, Ann, and Thompson, John O. *Shakespeare: Meaning and Metaphor.* Iowa City: Univ. of Iowa Press, 1987. Pp. xi + 228. $25.00. ISBN 0-87745-166-4.

Urkowitz, Steven. *Shakespeare's Revision of "King Lear."* Princeton: Princeton Univ. Press, 1980. Pp. 170. $11.50. ISBN 0-691-10228-7.

Warner, William Beatty. *Chance and the Text of Experience: Freud, Nietzsche, and Shakespeare's "Hamlet."* Ithaca and London: Cornell Univ. Press, 1986. Pp. 308. $29.95. ISBN 0-8014-1754-6.

Warren, Charles. *T. S. Eliot on Shakespeare.* Studies in Modern Literature 66. Ann Arbor: UMI Research Press, 1987. Pp. x + 139. $39.95. ISBN 0-8357-1784-4.

Watson, Robert N. *Ben Jonson's Parodic Strategy: Literary Imperialism in the Comedies.* Cambridge, Mass., and London: Harvard Univ. Press, 1987. Pp. 269. $25.00. ISBN 0-674-06601-4.

Weimann, Robert. *Shakespeare and the Popular Tradition in the Theater: Studies in the Social Dimension of Dramatic Form and Function*, ed. Robert Schwartz. Baltimore and London: Johns Hopkins Univ. Press, 1987. Pp. xxii + 325. $10.95. ISBN 0-8018-3506-2.

Wells, Robin Headlam. *Shakespeare, Politics and the State.* Context and Commentary, ed. Arthur Pollard. Houndmills and London: Macmillan Education, 1986. Pp. x + 174. $29.95 cloth, ISBN 0-333-37590-4. $9.95 paper, ISBN 0-333-37591-2.

Wells, Stanley, ed. *The Cambridge Companion to Shakespeare Studies.* Cambridge and New York: Cambridge Univ. Press, 1987. Pp. xi + 329. $42.50 cloth, ISBN 0-521-26737-4. $12.95 paper, ISBN 0-521-31841-6.

Womack, Peter. *Ben Jonson.* Rereading Literature, ed. Terry Eagleton. Oxford: Basil Blackwell, 1986. Pp. x + 181. $19.95 cloth, ISBN 0-631-14375-0; paper, ISBN 0-631-14376-9.

SEL

Studies in ENGLISH LITERATURE 1500-1900

Restoration and Eighteenth Century

VOLUME 28 SUMMER 1988 NUMBER 3

Studies in English Literature
1500 - 1900

VOLUME 28 SUMMER 1988 NUMBER 3

PUBLISHED BY RICE UNIVERSITY

CONTENTS

Ancients and Moderns in Defoe's *Consolidator* — Narelle L. Shaw 391

False Advertising: The Influence of Virgil and Isaiah on Pope's *Messiah* — Clifford R. Ames 401

Dramatic Texture and Philosophic Debate in Prior's *Dialogues of the Dead* — Nicolas H. Nelson 427

The Fragmentation of Originals and *Clarissa* — Jonathan Lamb 443

Johnson's Elephant: The Reader of *The Rambler* — Mary M. Van Tassel 461

William Collins, Samuel Johnson, and the Use of Biographical Details — Mary Margaret Stewart 471

Johnson and Conjecture — Thomas Reinert 483

Rhetoric, History, Rebellion: *Caleb Williams* and the Subversion of Eighteenth-Century Fiction — Donald R. Wehrs 497

Recent Studies in the Restoration and Eighteenth Century — Robert D. Hume 513

Studies in English Literature
1500 - 1900

PUBLISHED BY RICE UNIVERSITY

Studies in English Literature is a quarterly journal of historical and critical studies. Each issue will be devoted to one of four fields:

WINTER: The English Renaissance
SPRING: Elizabethan and Jacobean Drama
SUMMER: Restoration and Eighteenth Century
AUTUMN: The Nineteenth Century

SEL: Studies in English Literature, 1500–1900 (ISSN: 0039-3657) is published quarterly (February, May, August, and November) at $15.00 per year for individuals, $20.00 per year for U.S. institutions, $25.00 per year for foreign institutions, and $6.00 per single issue, by Rice University, 6100 South Main Street, P.O. Box 1892, Houston, Texas 77251. Second-class postage paid at Houston, Texas. **Postmaster:** Send address changes to the Business Manager, *SEL*, Rice University, P.O. Box 1892, Houston, TX 77251.

Studies in English Literature invites historical and critical essays of moderate length (ten to twenty-five pages) that contribute significantly to the understanding of English literature, 1500-1900. Typescripts should be double-spaced throughout and prepared in conformity with the Chicago Manual of Style. Clean photocopy on uncoated paper is acceptable in place of the ribbon copy. We prefer not to have dot-matrix printed copy. We will not consider articles being simultaneously submitted elsewhere, nor will we print essays to appear in a book published within a year of scheduled publication of *SEL*. Those wishing to omit their identities from manuscripts may do so, but should include a covering letter.

Manuscripts submitted for publication should be addressed to the Editor, *Studies in English Literature*, Rice University, P.O. Box 1892, Houston, TX 77251. They must be accompanied by a sufficient number of unattached stamps for return. Receipt of manuscripts will be acknowledged by postcard. Editorial decisions usually take a minimum of three months.

Annual subscription rates: $15.00 for individuals, $20.00 for U. S. institutions, $25.00 for foreign institutions, $6.00 per issue for partial subscriptions and single copies. Regular subscriptions may be obtained for any or all quarterly issues. Remittance should accompany subscription requests. Notice of non-receipt of an issue must be made within ninety (90) days following the publication of that issue. No refunds for cancellations. Business communications should be addressed to Business Manager, *Studies in English Literature*, Rice University, P. O. Box 1892, Houston, TX 77251.

Microfilms of previous volumes (Vols. 1-27) may be obtained from University Microfilms, Inc., 300 N. Zeeb Road, Ann Arbor, Michigan 48106; xerox copies of individual articles may be ordered by calling (800) 521-0600 (toll free). Copies of articles are also available from ISI's The Genuine Article service, 3501 Market Street, Philadelphia, PA 19104; phone (800) 523-1850; telex 84-5305; electronic mail through CLASS; or facsimile transmission via FAXPAX.

Volumes 1 through 3 and 5 through 10 of *Studies in English Literature* are available from Johnson Reprint Corporation, 111 Fifth Avenue, New York, N. Y. 10003, or Berkeley Square House, London W. 1, England.

SEL 28 (1988)
ISSN 0039-3657

Ancients and Moderns in Defoe's *Consolidator*

NARELLE L. SHAW

The *Consolidator* has long been recognized as an allegory pertaining to political events during the period 1660-1705—in particular, to the problems posed by the Spanish succession, and the High Church's move to tack an important land bill onto a bill designed to prevent the occasional conformity of dissenters.[1] Less apparent is the fact that the *Consolidator* represents a substantial contribution on Defoe's part to the ancients-moderns controversy, the only indication of this dimension of the *Consolidator* being provided by Marjorie Nicolson's brief comments upon the relevance of this work to "the perennial controversy between 'ancient' and 'modern.' "[2] Both political and philosophical material is introduced by the narrator who, after rhapsodizing upon a recent visit to China, undertakes a voyage to the moon to review lunar politics. The apparent purpose of the China section is to promote the claim that ancient Chinese learning exceeded all modern efforts. Nicolson, accepting this material at face value, sees Defoe as turning the tables upon the moderns "by implying that all the inventions on which they prided themselves had been known to [the ancient Chinese]" (p. 184). Similarly, John F. Ross argues that Defoe "in his own person" is the narrator, documentation of superior Chinese inventiveness and learning allowing him "to glance satirically at many aspects of the English world."[3] This, however, is not the case. The narrator's "ancient" perspective upon issues ranging from the circulation of the blood to a plurality of worlds is debunked in an ironic manner which both recalls and at the same time inverts Swift's manipulation of his modern hack in *A Tale of a Tub*—a work which is disparagingly acknowledged in the *Consolidator* (p. 33).[4] As Swift's persona "thro' the Assistance of our Noble *Moderns*" investigates "the weak sides of the *Antients*" (p. 96) and unwittingly

Narelle L. Shaw is a graduate of the University of Toronto and now teaches at the Tasmanian State Institute of Technology in Australia. She is writing a book on Defoe's reflections on the battle of the ancients and moderns.

sabotages his allies' arguments, so Defoe's persona applauds ancient Chinese ingenuity in terms which inevitably vindicate his antagonists, the moderns.[5]

Defoe's allusion to China has obvious topicality.[6] The question of Chinese pretensions to ancient wisdom had been recently disputed in such works as Sir William Temple's *An Essay upon the Ancient and Modern Learning,* William Wotton's *Reflections upon Ancient and Modern Learning,* and Thomas Baker's *Reflections upon Learning,* and it is within the context of the ancients-moderns controversy that the narrator's full-blown praise must be viewed.[7] Defoe introduces Chinese learning casually, as a foregone conclusion: "as all Men know the *Chineses* are an Ancient, Wise, Polite, and most Ingenious People" (p. 4). The statement is a provocative one. The exceptions which Wotton takes to Temple's exaltation of the extent of Chinese knowledge illustrate the contentiousness of this issue. Wotton objects that if the Chinese applied themselves to learning "for near so long a Time, as their History pretends to, there is no Question but we should have heard much more of their Progress" (p. 146). Defoe's narrator follows Temple in making effusive claims concerning China's pre-eminence in the sphere of knowledge:

> as the *Chineses* have many sorts of Learning which these Parts of the World never heard of, so all those useful Inventions which we admire our selves so much for, are vulgar and common with them, and were in use long before our Parts of the World were Inhabited. Thus *Gun-powder, Printing,* and the use of the *Magnet* and *Compass,* which we call Modern Inventions, are not only far from being Inventions, but fall so far short of the Perfection of Art they have attained to, that it is hardly Credible.
>
> (p. 5)

While this seems to be clear praise of Chinese learning, Defoe himself did not actually believe the Chinese to be the inventors of gunpowder, printing, and the compass. In *An Essay upon Projects* (1697), the compass and gunpowder are presented as feathers in the moderns' cap, while in Defoe's writings of the 1720s Chinese claims to all these inventions are soundly refuted.[8] This external evidence of Defoe's attitude is substantiated by clues imbedded in the *Consolidator* itself.

The narrator plans an exhibition of Chinese arts "for publick View, by way of Detection of the monstrous Ignorance and Deficiencies of *European* Science; which may serve as a *Lexicon Technicum* for this present Age, with useful Diagrams for that purpose" (pp. 5-6). In this scientific compendium, he promises to enlighten the world on the art of artillery as practised in China before the war of the giants. His source will be a work written "*Anno mundi* 114" by the historiographer-royal to the Chinese emperor. There are manifest absurdities in such a project. Most importantly, European science had already produced its *Lexicon Technicum*—a fact which convincingly discredits the allegation of modern ignorance. John Harris's *Lexicon Technicum* appeared in 1704, complete with "useful Diagrams."[9] In later scholarly writings, Harris's *Lexicon* served Defoe as a convenient reference source; the *Consolidator* allusion evinces that Defoe's respect for this modern text was formed at an early stage of his literary career.[10] Furthermore, the narrator's proclamation that an ancient Chinese treatise on artillery exists in the library at Tonquin is palpably ridiculous. Certainly, his insistence that such is the case conflicts with what Temple, that staunch advocate of Chinese antiquity, knows of the subject. Temple relates that an ancient emperor ordered all books except those on medicine and agriculture to be burned (p. 46). Defoe's purpose in allowing the narrator's ancient tome, made of vitrified diamond, to survive the flames is clearly ironic.

The discrepancy between Defoe's position and that of the narrator also informs the reference to Chinese navigation and mathematics. Indefatigable in his praise of ancient ingenuity, the narrator decides that, on his next visit to China, he will compose "an Abstract of their most admirable Tracts in Navigation, and the Mysteries of *Chinese* Mathematicks; which out-do all Modern Invention at that Rate, that 'tis Inconceivable" (p. 7). The rhetoric rings false, the underlying contention being that such rivalry of modern invention is, literally, inconceivable. The narrator's project will entail his reading of the 365 volumes of one Augro-machi-languaro-zi, "the most ancient Mathematician in all *China*." The sheer extravagance of the claim and, indeed, of the alleged author's name point up the narrator's lack of credibility.

The information on Chinese navigation forms a useful preliminary to ensuing material dealing with China's weathering of the deluge. Noah, it seems, was not the only human being apprised of the upcoming disaster: the emperor Tangro was also privy to the secret and consequently equipped a fleet of 100,000 ships to carry China through the flood. Every town in his dominion had at its disposal a vessel large enough to accommodate its entire population as well as provisions for 120 days. The ships were equipped with 600 fathoms of chain "which being fastned by wonderful Arts to the Earth . . . rid out the Deluge just at the Town's end" (pp. 7-8). When the waters subsided, "the People had nothing to do, but to open the Doors . . . come out, repair their Houses . . . and so put themselves in

Statu Quo" (p. 8). Theirs was a situation vastly preferable to that of poor Noah who, when his ark rested upon Ararat, faced the immense task of rebuilding a world. Clearly, the narrator's apparent belief in such an absurd scenario does not correspond to Defoe's own opinion. The plan of the monstrous Tonquin vessel which the narrator diligently promises to obtain from the Chinese emperor is just another pin with which Defoe bursts the bubble of ancient Chinese learning.

A sharp invective against modern pretensions to learning complements the narrator's praise of China. He feels driven by benevolence to enlighten the ignorant scientists, artists, and philosophers of the west:

> as these things must be very useful in these Parts, to abate the Pride and Arrogance of our Modern Undertakers of great Enterprizes, Authors of strange Foreign Accounts, Philosophical Transactions, and the like; if Time and Opportunity permit, I may let them know, how Infinitely we are out-done by those refined Nations, in all manner of Mechanick Improvements and Arts.
>
> (p. 8)

One invention which strikes him as being most noble is an engine to prompt the memory, and the narrator plans to procure a draft of it "that it may be Erected in our Royal Societies Laboratory" (p. 9). Reference is made to the merchants, creditors, preachers, and lawyers who would find the memory engine particularly helpful. The insinuations of dishonesty and vice in these professions prevailing in Europe must be conceded; however, only the credulous narrator believes that such practices have been eradicated in the east. In "some Parts of *China*," knowledge has arrived at "such a Perfection" that "all sorts of Frauds, Cheats, Sharping, and many Thousand *European* Inventions of that Nature, *at which only we* [the west] *can be said to out-do those* [eastern] *Nations*" (p. 10) have been stamped out. Although he confesses he has not yet had the leisure to visit these parts, the narrator's faith in this instance of Chinese integrity is unswerving, his firm conviction of modern supremacy in fraudulent enterprise and of ancient Chinese supremacy in the field of learning being unequivocally expressed. While Defoe may be sympathetic to the complaint of human iniquity, it is most unlikely that he would confine it to one corner of the globe. On the issue of Chinese perfection, he is profoundly skeptical. Not so the narrator: a convert to the Chinese cause, he announces that his "search after the Prodigy of humane Knowledge the People abounds with" (p. 11) soon brought him among the circle of principal artists, engineers, and men of letters. The degree to which he is impressed proves impossible to conceal: "I was astonish'd at every Day's Discovery of new and unheard-of Worlds of Learning" (p. 11). Nowhere does he experience greater pleasure than in browsing among the vast collection of books in the library at Tonquin, to which he is given access by the library-keeper himself. Surrounded by "wonderful Volumes of Antient and Modern Learning," the narrator takes particular notice of "a few" (p. 11).

Along with questions concerning the inventions of gunpowder, printing, and the compass, that involving the discovery of the blood's circulation constituted a significant aspect of arguments regarding ancient and modern learning. In *An Essay upon the Ancient and Modern Learning,* Temple expressed reservations as to whether the circulation of the blood was in fact a modern discovery, attributable to Harvey rather than Hippocrates, and indeed whether the theory were viable at all: "for though reason may seem to favour [it] more than the contrary opinions, yet sense can very hardly allow [it]; and, to satisfy mankind, both these must concur" (pp. 56-57). On the other hand, Wotton's *Reflections upon Ancient and Modern Learning* claimed the discovery on behalf of the moderns. Wotton relates how, in Frankfurt in 1628, Harvey demonstrated "even to the most incredulous, not only that the Blood circulates through the Lungs and Heart, but the very Manner how, and the Time in which that great Work is performed" (p. 215). Wotton dismisses the possibility that Hippocrates made the original discovery and suggests that Temple was unwilling to believe in the blood's circulation because he could not see it (pp. 207-208, 217).

Not surprisingly then, the narrator's abbreviated catalogue of the Tonquin library includes works dealing with the circulation of the blood:

> two famous Volumes in Chyrurgery [contain] an exact Description of the Circulation of the Blood, discovered long before King *Solomon's* Allegory of the Bucket's going to the Well; with several curious Methods by which the Demonstration was to be made so plain, as would make even the worthy Doctor B——— himself become a Convert to his own Eye-sight, make him damn his own Elaborate Book, and think it worse Nonsense than ever the Town had the Freedom to imagine.
>
> (p. 15)

While the narrator contends that the ancient Chinese held the secret of the blood's circulation, Defoe's own attitude towards the debate becomes apparent in later writings. In *A General History of Discoveries and Improvements,* Defoe, basing his opinion on Ecclesiastes 12:6, states that Solomon understood how the blood circulated. He concedes the possibility that the blood's motion was perceived by the ancient Tyrians and Egyptians but assumes that the knowledge was subsequently lost when the Romans conquered the learned world (p. 94). It remained a mystery until rediscovered by Harvey in the early seventeenth century. Thus, Defoe aligns himself in a circuitous manner with the position of the moderns. Robinson Crusoe illustrates the arbitrary will of Lutheran princes by an image of the blood's circulation in *Serious Reflections,* and in *The Compleat English Gentleman* the discovery is one of many accomplishments which establish the superiority of the modern age.[11]

The allusion to the work of "the worthy Doctor B———" is more revealing of Defoe himself than of the narrator. "Doctor B———" is Dr. Joseph Browne, whose *Lecture of Anatomy against the Circulation of the Blood* abounds with references to the ancients-moderns controversy.[12] Despite Browne's profession in his preface that there is "no design in my head to oppose any received Notions, either of the Moderns or Ancients," his criticism of the moderns is undeniably severe. He rejects "all the Proofs urged by the Circulators" in favor of "a Motion in the Blood which is not always one and the same." The world, Browne complains, has not been made sensible of the "prodigious Difficulties" attending the doctrine of circulation. There can be no other explanation of the universal acclaim with which it has been heralded. He "will not rob [Harvey] of the Honour of bringing this ingenious Hypothesis into the World"—the ancients were not guilty of such folly (p. 2). Defoe's reference to the reception of the *Lecture* is surely calculated to make Browne wince. In the preface to his work, a self-righteous Browne complains that he did not meet with "candid Usage" from his audience, who opposed "every sentence" he delivered: "Some . . . denyed my Quotations, others denyed matter of Fact, and some offer'd to show the Experiments quite contrary." Defoe's thrust in the *Consolidator* may very well have precipitated their later literary war.[13]

A reference to the phenomenon of tides further reveals the distance separating Defoe and his narrator in the ancients-moderns debate. The narrator assesses the value of a favorite treatise on navigation:

> It was a certain Sign *Aristotle* had never been at *China*; for, had he seen the 216th Volume of the *Chinese* Navigation, in the Library I am speaking of, a large Book in Double Folio, wrote by the Famous *Mira-cho-cho-lasmo,* Vice Admiral of *China,* and said to be printed there about 2000 Years before

> the Deluge, in the Chapter of Tides he would have seen the Reason of all the certain and uncertain Fluxes and Refluxes of that Element, how the exact Pace is kept between the Moon and the Tides, with a most elaborate Discourse there, of the Power of Sympathy, and the manner how the heavenly Bodies Influence the Earthly: Had he seen this, the *Stagyrite* would never have Drowned himself because he could not comprehend this Mystery.
>
> (pp. 16-17)

The passage is rich in details which undercut the narrator's wonderment. Of most compelling interest is the role played by Aristotle. The narrator's claim that had Aristotle visited China he would have benefited from a long intellectual tradition and arrived at a complete understanding of the phenomenon of tides betrays a wanton ignorance of Aristotelian thought. In *De Mundo,* Aristotle recognized the lunar influence upon tides: "Many tides and tidal waves are said always to accompany the periods of the moon at fixed intervals."[14] As Henry Pemberton points out in his *View of Sir Isaac Newton's Philosophy,* the ancients had grasped the essential fact of the moon's governing of tides "[t]hough how the moon caused them, and by what principle it was enabled to produce so distinguish'd an appearance, was a secret left for [Newton's] philosophy to unfold."[15] In the *Principia* (1687), Newton demonstrated that the mutual gravitation between the earth and the moon, and that between the earth and the sun, was responsible for tidal action.[16] Judging by the evidence provided by the fabulous Vice Admiral, the assertion that the ancient Chinese understood tides is spurious and discloses the narrator's gullibility.

According to popular legend, Aristotle was unable to fathom tidal movements and committed suicide in a fit of frustration.[17] Even if Defoe accepted the legend, he did not believe that Aristotle was pre-empted by the ancient Chinese, as is implied in the reference to the Chinese publication's having been issued 2000 years before the deluge. According to contemporary chronologies, the volume in question pre-dates the creation of the world. Raleigh and Ussher, for instance, agreed that the flood occurred in the year of the world 1656—an opinion which Defoe later supported in *An Essay upon Literature.*[18] In this work too, Defoe explicitly denounces the Chinese claim to a chronology extending for 7000 years.[19] The Chinese, Defoe insinuates, would have offered Aristotle no enlightenment.

A later reference to China's survival of the flood constitutes a strong indictment of the narrator as a defender of ancient superiority.

Allegedly, Chinese knowledge far surpasses "our common Pitch" because it is derived from a "more Ancient Original":

> We are told, that in the early Age of the World, the Strength of Invention exceeded all that ever has been arrived to since: That we in these latter Ages, having lost all that pristine Strength of Reason and Invention, which died with the Ancients in the Flood, and receiving no helps from that Age, have by long Search arriv'd at several remote Parts of Knowledge, by the helps of reading Conversation and Experience; but that all amounts to no more than faint Imitations, Apings, and Resemblances of what was known in those masterly Ages.
>
> Now, if it be true as is hinted before, That the *Chinese* Empire was Peopled long before the Flood; and that they were not destroyed in the General Deluge in the Days of *Noah*; 'tis no such strange thing, that they should so much out-do us in this sort of *Eye-sight* we call *General Knowledge,* since the Perfections bestow'd on Nature, when in her Youth and Prime met with no General Suffocation by that Calamity.
>
> (pp. 60-61)

To identify narrator and author here as one and the same would be to disregard a violation of the biblical evidence in which Defoe placed his trust. As Chinese chronology is fictitious so too are the grandiose claims to knowledge. As is made clear in *A System of Magick,* Defoe believed that the patriarchs of the antediluvian world were divinely blessed with a consummate knowledge of nature and that this knowledge was lost at the flood.[20] Sympathetic to the Baconian notion that man had made substantial progress in recovering his ancient heritage, Defoe nevertheless insisted that the "brightest part of human wisdom" was the product of the last two centuries.[21]

A detail concerning the origins of the famous Chinese mathematician, Augro-machi-languaro-zi, makes plain Defoe's refusal to believe that China was an ancient source of knowledge. It turns out that the mathematician was "no Native of this World," but "Born in the Moon" (p. 17). In later life, Defoe was to evaluate seriously the evidence for a plurality of worlds, but in 1705 he peoples the lunar world simply for satiric purposes.[22] His man from the moon, having arrived in China, is prevailed upon by the Chinese emperor to remain and educate the Chinese in the accomplishments of the lunar regions: "it is not to be wonder'd at, why the *Chinese* excell so much in all these Parts of the World, since but for that knowledge which comes down to them from the World in the Moon, they would be like other People" (p. 33). The illusory nature of China's claims is deftly exposed by the imputation that Chinese enterprise originates in the moon.

Defoe's argument yields even greater complexities. The political section of the *Consolidator* is dominated by the notion popularized by John Wilkins in *The Discovery of a World in the Moone,* that the world is to the moon as the moon is to the world.[23] Defoe's narrator voyages to the moon and encounters a lunar philosopher with whom he discusses the nature of their respective worlds: "they were both Moons and both Worlds, this *a Moon* to that, and that *a Moon* to this" (p. 65). Wilkins's conceit serves Defoe's satiric purpose admirably. Moon and earth become interchangeable entities: by deriving its learning from the moon, China is indebted, necessarily, to the earth. Those inventions and advancements which the narrator heralds as belonging to the Chinese are actually the property of the moderns.

To assume that the voice constantly deriding the state of modern learning and lauding Chinese ingenuity is that of Defoe is to misconstrue his *"damn'd Satyrical way of Writing"* (p. 68). This heretofore unnoticed distinction between author and narrator in the China section of the *Consolidator* is of much importance, representing as it does Defoe's first extended contribution to the battle of the ancients and moderns.

NOTES

[1]Daniel Defoe, *The Consolidator: or, Memoirs of Sundry Transactions from the World in the Moon* (London, 1705).

[2]Marjorie Hope Nicolson, *Voyages to the Moon* (New York: Macmillan, 1948), p. 184.

[3]John Ross, *Swift and Defoe: A Study in Relationship* (Folcroft: Folcroft Press, 1940), pp. 37-38.

[4]Jonathan Swift, *A Tale of a Tub*, ed. A. C. Guthkelch and D. Nichol Smith, 2nd edn. (Oxford: Clarendon Press, 1958).

[5]John Ross attributes the allusiveness of the *Consolidator*, its materialistic vocabulary, and the citing of mock treatises to the influence of Swift's *Tale*. See *Swift and Defoe: A Study in Relationship*, pp. 37-55.

[6]William W. Appleton records the Chinese vogue in England and notes Defoe's unreceptive attitude towards China in *A Cycle of Cathay* (New York: Columbia Univ. Press, 1951), pp. 55-60.

[7]Sir William Temple, *An Essay upon the Ancient and Modern Learning*, in *Five Miscellaneous Essays by Sir William Temple*, ed. Samuel Holt Monk (Ann Arbor: Univ. of Michigan Press, 1963), pp. 37-71; William Wotton, *Reflections upon Ancient and Modern Learning (1694)* (Hildesheim: George Olms, 1968); Thomas Baker, *Reflections upon Learning* (London, 1699).

[8]Daniel Defoe, *An Essay upon Projects* (London, 1697), pp. 22-23; *A General History of Discoveries and Improvements* (London, 1725-26), pp. 25, 223, 226; *An Essay upon Literature* (London, 1726), pp. 15, 76-77.

[9]John Harris, *Lexicon Technicum: or, An Universal English Dictionary of Arts and Sciences* (London, 1704).

[10]Refer to Daniel Defoe, *The Political History of the Devil* (London, 1726), pp. 384-85, for Harris's definition of magic as a branch of mathematics, and *An Essay upon Literature*, pp. 120-26, for his history of the art of printing.

[11]Daniel Defoe, *Serious Reflections during the Life and Surprising Adventures of Robinson Crusoe with His Vision of the Angelic World*, vol. 3 of *The Works of Daniel Defoe*, 16 vols. (New York: George D. Sproul, 1908), p. 144; Daniel Defoe, *The Compleat English Gentleman*, ed. Karl D. Bulbring (London: David Nutt, 1890), p. 231.

[12]Joseph Browne, *A Lecture of Anatomy against the Circulation of the Blood* (London, 1701).

[13]In the *Review* of 21 April 1705, p. 84, Defoe advertises the publication of *The Moon Calf: or, Accurate Reflections on the Consolidator. Giving an Account of Some Remarkable Transactions in the Lunar World.* He identifies Browne as the author of this work in the *Little Review* of 8 June 1705 and proceeds to take apart Browne's sample translations of Horace (pp. 5-6). Browne responds with *A Vindication of the Specimen Design'd for a General Translation of Horace, from the pretended Criticisms of Mr. De Foe, in his "Little Review"* (London, 1705). While this pamphlet deals with Defoe's blunders in the field of classics, a sizeable portion of it treats the *Moon Calf* issue. Browne notes that Defoe is "very angry with the *Moon Calf*, which he Fathers upon me without any Grounds, I believe" (p. 5). While remaining non-committal on the question of authorship, Browne defends the work against Defoe's charges of inconsistency and falsehood. The conflict was acerbated by the political differences separating the two men.

[14]*De Mundo*, vol. 3 of *The Works of Aristotle*, ed. J. A. Smith and W. D. Ross, 12 vols. (Oxford: Clarendon Press, 1914), p. 396a.

[15]Henry Pemberton, *A View of Sir Isaac Newton's Philosophy* (London, 1728), p. 283.

[16]See *Sir Isaac Newton's Mathematical Principles of Natural Philosophy and His System of the World*, trans. Andrew Motte (Cambridge: Cambridge Univ. Press, 1934), bk. 3, pp. 435-40.

[17]For example, Galileo made use of the legend to emphasize the value of his own ideas on the causal principle of tides. See *Dialogue Concerning the Two Chief World Systems—Ptolemaic and Copernican*, trans. Stillman Drake, 2nd edn. (Berkeley: Univ. of California Press, 1967), p. 433.

[18]Sir Walter Raleigh, *The History of the World* (London, 1614), see bk. 1, ch. 7, p. 102 and chronological table; James Ussher, *The Annals of the World* (London, 1658); *An Essay upon Literature*, p. 31.

[19]*An Essay upon Literature*, p. 15.

[20]Daniel Defoe, *A System of Magick* (London, 1727), pp. 6-8, 10-11.

[21]*A General History of Discoveries and Improvements*, p. 238.

[22]*The Political History of the Devil*, pp. 51, 83, 90-91, 213; *An Essay on the History and Reality of Apparitions* (London, 1727), pp. 26-28, 52, 54.

[23]John Wilkins, *The Discovery of a World in the Moone* (London, 1638), p. 143.

SEL 28 (1988)
ISSN 0039-3657

False Advertising: The Influence of Virgil and Isaiah on Pope's *Messiah*

CLIFFORD R. AMES

I

Pope's "Advertisement" to the *Messiah* was intended literally "to direct" (*advertis*) the reader's "mind" (*mentem*) towards an appreciation of the poet's motives in adapting an established classical form to accommodate the essentially antithetical spirit and prosody of Hebraic verse. By examining this self-assessment and then determining the extent to which it accounts for the poet's use of his sources in the poem, we can gain some insight into what Pope intended and what he actually accomplished in undertaking the highly controversial task of reworking Isaiah to accept the contours of a pagan poem. The "Advertisement" begins: "In reading several passages of the Prophet *Isaiah,* which foretell the coming of Christ and the felicities attending it, I could not but observe a remarkable parity between many of the thoughts, and those in the *Pollio* of *Virgil.* This will not seem surprising when we reflect, that the Eclogue was taken from a Sybilline prophecy on the same subject."[1] Pope appears to dress himself in the critical robes of the commentator. His directness and economy of expression convey a sense of artlessness that invites the reader's confidence while it boldly maneuvers him into accepting questionable testimony for disinterested historical truth. Addressing the reader informally in the first person singular, Pope implies that the traditional association of passages in Virgil's fourth eclogue with the Messianic prophecy in Isaiah occurred to him as a spontaneous revelation while "reading several passages of the Prophet." The specifically Christian problem of having to explain the curious similarity of vision in what appear to be entirely isolated and incompatible prophetic traditions, the author dismisses with a simplified version of the conventional

Clifford R. Ames is currently teaching English literature at the University of Hawaii where he is completing his doctoral dissertation. Ames has also published on American literature and has collaborated on translations of articles and books on Japanese philosophy.

argument that the *Pollio*, when traced through the versified prophecy of the Sibyl of Cumae, reaches back to the sacred literature of the Jews.

By following the practice of "Christianizing" Virgil (popular in the seventh and eighth centuries, or the *aetas Vergiliana*), and admitting him as a latecomer to the distinguished company of Old Testament prophets, Pope need not justify his use of a pagan form as a vehicle for sacred materials, because the authority and precedent for this cross-breeding had been long established by a view of Virgil as *anima naturaliter Christiana*.[2] Also, Pope's suggestion that he arrived at the historical connection between the book of Isaiah and Virgil's so-called "Messianic Eclogue" as a "remarkable" personal discovery without, as it were, prior knowledge of their similarity, dissociates his view of Virgil from the centuries of learned argument over the source of the fourth eclogue, and the extravagant secular and religious legends that characterized him variously as a sorcerer and as the "prophet of the Gentiles." Similarly, by addressing himself directly to the poem and closing his eyes to the intervening centuries of monastic scholarship corrupted by religious bias, myth, and superstition, Pope escapes the inevitable identification of his eclogue with one or more of the imitative and largely discredited genres that appeared wherever there were Christian enthusiasts of Virgil.

The way in which Pope selects fragments from virtually the entire book of Isaiah and disposes them in a coherent poem that has an integrity and an order of its own, is immediately reminiscent of the architects of the Virgilian centos who, like Pomponius in his *Tityrus*, Proba in her life of Christ, and Lelio Capilupi in his eclogues, collected passages from the Latin texts into a new unity which preserved the idiosyncratic *lumina* while it retold a familiar Christian story. Furthermore, the tradition of the pastoral is not silent from 40 B.C. until 1712 A.D., and although it disappears after Nemesianus in the third century, its revival in the fourteenth century is followed closely by the emergence of the devotional eclogue treating the Nativity and using Virgil's genethliacon as one of its principal models.

While the eleventh pastoral of Giovanni Boccaccio in the early fourteenth century shows only a slight dependence upon Virgil, the influence gathers strength with Francesco Patrizi's *De natali Christi*, Andrea Fulvio's *De ortu Servatoris*, Chateillon's *Sirillus*, Mambrun's fourth eclogue, *Christus nascens*, and especially Antonio Geraldini's first eclogue in his *bucolica sacra*, Cornelius de Schryver's *Theander* and Gregor Bersman's *Natalicia Iesu Christi*.[3]

Pope's unqualified claim in his "Advertisement" is that Virgil's *Pollio* "was taken from a *Sybilline* prophecy on the same subject" as

Isaiah. This claim not only preserves the tradition of identifying the Roman poet with the Old Testament Hebrew prophets, and his fourth eclogue with Old Testament Messianic prophecy (popular since before the twelfth century and Vincent of Beauvais's *Speculum Marius*), but also carries with it the tradition of viewing the pastoral as a form of cryptic allegory which, as Petrarch insists in his letter to Cola Rienzo, "ut . . . omnino non possit intellegi."[4] A contemporary of Petrarch similarly associated with the repopularization of the pastoral form and equally an advocate of the medieval school of poets who saw the activity of the poet as architectural, and the labor of the reader as archaeological, is Dante Alighieri.[5] Writing to Can Grande della Scala on his *Commedia*, he describes four levels upon which the poem may be read: "one sense that we get through the letter, and another which we get through the thing the letter signifies; and the first is called literal, but the second allegorical or mystic . . . although these mystic senses have each their special denominations, they may all in general be called allegorical, since they differ from the literal and historical."[6] A "literal and historical" reading of Virgil's fourth eclogue might see the work as a celebration of the bright prospect of an end to the agonizing civil wars and the dawning of a *nova ordo* heralded by the treaty of Brundisium and personified by the poet in the miraculous birth of a *cara deum suboles*—variously identified as the child of Octavian and Scribonia, Mark Antony and Octavia, or C. Asinius Pollio. Pope ignores this "literal" sense, however, and by relying upon the historical identification of pastoral with allegory and his own tenuous connection of the *Pollio* with the prophetic tradition of the Jews, he elevates Virgil to the order of the inspired Prophet and imposes a symbolic interpretation upon the work comparable to Dante's second allegorical level. The *Messiah. A Sacred Eclogue, In Imitation of Virgil's Pollio*,[7] as the title implies, follows the Procrustean custom of equating Virgil's genethliacon eclogue with the Nativity, and imitates not only the classical form of its Latin model, but also its presumed Christian content. Avoiding explicit assertion, Pope avoids explicit criticism and possible refutation, and at the same time escapes the need to justify his use of a pagan literary form as a vehicle for sacred material.

Pope reported at the outset of the introduction that his reading in Isaiah had been confined to those passages "which foretell the coming of Christ and the felicities attending it." To the reader unprepared to dispute the author's claim that the *Pollio* is descended indirectly from inspired Hebrew parentage, there would be no question of the superiority of the original sacred text of Isaiah over a derivative, classical variation, even from the distinguished pen of

Virgil.[8] Indeed, "Virgil who copies Theocritus" was recognized first for "refin[ing] upon his original" (*A Discourse on Pastoral Poetry,* p. 30), and therefore the reader might suppose (even had it not been suggested by Pope) that his prime concern in selecting passages from the Sibylline books was not a pious determination to chronicle faithfully a presumably sketchy rendition of the Nativity, but rather a desire to improve upon his master by selecting "such Ideas as best agreed with" the character and the integrity of the verse form—a function of artistic "Judgment,"[9] not faith. Moreover, conceding Pope's argument that after the destruction of the Sibylline books in 83 B.C., their reconstruction incorporated elements from the sacred literature of the Jews, and assuming further that the Romans' enthusiastic association of Virgil with the oracles is valid and is applicable to the *Pollio,* then the reader must suppose that the prophecy of a Messiah would have been substantially modified by the Sibyl to conform with the established myth of successive ages, degenerating from the golden through the silver and the bronze to the iron. By way of allowing for this inexactness in transmitting the prophecies, and by interpreting the fourth eclogue as a partial or imperfect religious allegory predicting the birth of the Christian Messiah, Pope can exaggerate the importance of those "images and descriptions" which agree with Isaiah, and discount those which demonstrate no apparent correlation with the biblical text.

Pope claims the same freedom as Virgil in extracting passages from his source, and the same liberty to dispose them as his judgment directs. However, Pope's explanation that his "Sacred Eclogue" was written with the specific intention of providing an approximation of Virgil's form to contain the unalloyed "thoughts" of Isaiah so that a comparison between the prophet and the poet would be possible, takes for granted a concurrence of "thought" where only a concurrence of image exists. Indeed, to evaluate Virgil in terms of his ability to communicate effectively a Christian sense irrelevant and probably contrary to his historical purpose simply because the physical exterior of his poem suggests Old Testament prophecy, is as unjust as to judge Isaiah on his ability to capture the optimistic climate of Post-Republican Rome. Furthermore, if the reader accepts Pope's argument that in borrowing passages from Isaiah and organizing them into a verse mosaic he follows Virgil's example of selecting from a "Sybilline prophecy," then any comparison involving the author of the *Messiah*'s transcriptions from the prophet Isaiah would necessarily refer to the source from which the poet Virgil transcribed, or the Sibyl of Cumae. Yet, if Pope's emphasis is meant to fall upon Virgil's criteria in selecting passages which he felt were suitable to the pastoral, the comparison is entirely independent of

Isaiah. It involves only the artistic discretion of the two poets in determining what "best agree[s] with the nature of pastoral poetry" and how it should be disposed in order to maximize the beauty of the piece—a relative judgment of taste. In any case, regardless of the terms of the comparison, Isaiah is the indisputable winner and the *Pollio* must finish second to the *Messiah*[10] simply because, whatever Virgil's dependence upon pirated Old Testament revelation embodied in the Sibylline books, he relies upon an adulterated version of a Hebraic prophecy which Isaiah received from an unimpeachable source, and which Pope claimed to reproduce faithfully. Moreover, if Virgil's choice of "image and description" from the versified prophecies of the Sibyl is evaluated on artistic grounds, Pope, by insisting that he quotes Isaiah "without admitting any thing of [his] own," can summon the full weight of seventeen centuries of Christian faith in the sublimity of the prophet's words to load the scales in his favor.

Were we to give full credence to Pope's assertion that his *Messiah* is nothing more than an orchestration of Isaiah executed according to the rhythms of the Virgilian pastoral, and that it was composed intentionally as an imitation of the fourth eclogue in order to illustrate the superiority of a Christian prophet over a pagan poet, he could not be accused of attempting to improve upon biblical verse by draping it in classical robes. However, the question of the extent to which the reader can safely accept Pope's modest self-assessment that his role in writing the *Messiah* was primarily editorial rather than creative, and the extent to which this self-assessment serves merely as an ingenious justification for violating a set of conventions which he had earlier publicly upheld, can be responsibly addressed only by a detailed examination of the author's management of his materials in the poem itself. Before proceeding to this examination, it is perhaps worthwhile to note that the most interesting and most valuable insights we shall gain will have less to do with Pope's poetic aspirations and intentions and more to do with the complex and nuanced manner in which the poet constructs his *Messiah* by celebrating intertextual resonances with the *Pollio* and Isaiah.

II

Virgil opens his fourth eclogue with an address to the Muses of Sicily, the sources of inspiration for his Theocritean models which had celebrated the simple life of the Sicilian shepherd against an idealized rural landscape. This is not, however, an ordinary invocation.[11] Rather, the author elevates himself to the imaginative level of his hosts and invites them to accompany him as an equal in transcending the conventions of the pastoral by paradoxically admitting a consul, symbol of military power and temporal change, into the static, timeless world of the poem.[12] Virgil employs the hortative subjunctive *canamus* in order to encourage the Muses to aspire beyond the artificial to the real, for it is only by uniting the ideal with the actual that man can liberate himself from conventions—both literary and social. He writes:

> Sicelides Musae, paulo maiora canamus!
> non omnis arbusta iuvant humilesque myricae;
> si canimus silvas, silvae sint consule dignae.

> Muses of Sicily, let us sing a little more grandly! not all are delighted by arbors and lowly shrubs; if we sing of the forests, let the forests be worthy of a consul.

Pope's imitation of Virgil's address to the Muses is remarkable in that although the heroic couplet replaces the dactylic hexameter the verse is able to capture the external metrical features and the stately musical tone of the original. The *Messiah* begins (lines 1-5):

> Ye Nymphs of *Solyma!* begin the Song:
> To heav'nly Themes sublimer Strains belong.
> The Mossie Fountains and the Sylvan Shades,
> The Dreams of *Pindus* and th' *Aonian* Maids,
> Delight no more.

The opening three lines of Pope's imitation display not only an approximate syntactic and qualitative equivalence, but also an attempt to reproduce the phonetic resonances of his model. The powerful rhythms and the distinctive orchestration of sound that characterize Virgil's invocation and that account for its stately tone are captured by Pope through his careful attention to the rhetorical surface of the work.[13] In the opening lines of the *Messiah*, Pope is not attempting anything as specific as reproducing onomatopoeia. Rather, he is attempting to imitate the overall texture of the Latin verse by copying Virgil's patterns of sound.

Pope sets an ancient composition to modern music—and his execution is virtuoso. However, the variations which he does make in translating and adapting the language of the *Pollio* for his own idyl, while they may appear slight and technically necessary for the phonological effect, alter the meaning of the piece entirely. Virgil's low-key invocation to the pagan Muses of Sicily to sing "paulo maiora" because there are those who do not delight in the rustic trappings of the pastoral is replaced in the *Messiah* by a demand for the "Nymphs of *Solyma*"—the lesser divinities (perhaps angels) of

Jerusalem—to "begin the Song," for the pastoral is not equal to the sublime task at hand. Pope's address to the "Nymphs," reminiscent of the Douai Bible's "ye inhabitants of Jerusalem"[14] is not, as in the *Pollio*, an appeal for inspiration. Rather, it is an emphatic rejection of the bucolic vision which "Delights no more," followed by a prayer spoken in the manner of Isaiah and calling upon the Divine Spirit to cleanse the pagan images from the poetic voice. Pope's "O Thou my Voice inspire / Who touch'd *Isaiah's* hallow'd Lips with Fire!" (*Messiah* lines 5-6) has its source in Isaiah 6:6-7: "And one of the Seraphims flewe to me, and in his hand an hote cole, which he had taken with tonges from the altar. And he touched my mouth, and said: Behold this hath touched thy lippes, and thine iniquitie shal be taken away and thy sinne shal be cleansed."

Virgil's innovative break with Theocritean pastoral convention implicit in his introduction of a figure representative of time and political authority into the garden of Arcadia, has its counterpart in Isaiah 32:8: "But the prince wil thinke these thinges, that are worthie of a prince." Even so, this connection is avoided by Pope, first because such a figure recalls the infamous Herod, and second because he is not attempting to reconcile an ideal with an actual world, but confidently predicting a historical event in retrospect. Moreover, this disruption of the self-contained and essentially myopic world of the idyl brought about by intruding history, with its conception of linear time extending forward into the future, into a timeless present, is reversed by Pope in the *Messiah* and carried into the meter of the poem itself. The measured progress of the Roman *aetas* captured in the rhythms of the classical *carmina* is suddenly brought to a full stop as the mounting force of Christian prophecy gathers momentum towards apocalypse and leaves time, history, and convention in its wake. Pope exaggerates the dignified canter of the *Pollio* in the third and fourth lines of the *Messiah* by stressing the medial caesura and using it to separate balanced half-line clauses opening anaphorically and joined only by the connective "and." As the repetition of this simple metrical pattern takes control of the reader's expectation, hurrying to close the larger syntactic unit by sliding over the weak end-stop of the fourth line, it falls dramatically to an abrupt rhythmic and semantic conclusion at the fourth-place caesura of the fifth line.

> The Mossie Fountains and the Sylvan Shades,
> The Dreams of *Pindus* and th' *Aonian* Maids,
> Delight no more.
>
> (*Messiah* lines 3-5)

At this point the elevated tone and the emotional urgency of the second invocation are released in an explosion of sudden feeling. The classical regularity of the verse carrying the pastoral vision is gone, and in its place an exalted appeal for Divine inspiration responds almost antiphonally to the silence following "more." The vocative "O Thou" introduces a rhythm suggestive of the fluidity of biblical verse which is accomplished by allowing the fifth line to run on without hesitation into the sixth, quickened by the feminine ending "inspire" and by the absence of internal pause. Pope, then, has broken his own rules of metrical composition in order to make the "*Sound* . . . an *Eccho* to the *Sense*." Indeed, the poet's enthusiastic rejection of the pagan Muses in favor of Christian inspiration is represented in the verse itself by the sudden departure from the features of classical verse at the precise moment when the Spirit of Christian prophecy enters and takes control of the author's powers of expression. The abrupt transformation in the character of the verse from the stern regularity of the first four lines to the intoxicating momentum of the following two registers the changing emotional intensity of the poet as he raises his voice to the sublime task which he has undertaken.

Following Virgil's example, Pope indents the line after this impassioned invocation, suggesting perhaps that he must pause breathlessly to receive the Spirit of Isaiah's loving Angel, and to allow the reader a moment to reflect upon the sublimity of the author's petition. Entering the mind of Virgil as he himself has been entered, Pope views the Nativity through prophetic eyes. The ability of the "cleansed" poetic spirit to transcend the present moment (albeit on borrowed wings) is emphasized by the initial and final verbs in the seventh line that bind the notion of prophetic vision motivating the poetic voice into a closely knit open voiced consonant of the active verb describing the ecstatic condition of the speaker.

  Rapt into future Times, the Bard begun;
A *Virgin* shall conceive, a *Virgin* bear a Son!
From *Jesse*'s Root behold a Branch arise,
Whose sacred Flow'r with Fragrance fills the Skies.
Th' Aethereal Spirit o'er its Leaves shall move,
And on its Top descends the Mystic Dove.
(*Messiah* lines 7-12)

Although Virgil stresses the imminence of his vision through the repetition of *iam* and the semantically equivalent *redit* and *redeunt*, Pope alternates lines recording the past as if it were the present (lines 7, 9, 10, 12) with lines predicting past events as if they were in the future (lines 8, 11) in order to emphasize his new historical perspective. Moreover, knowing that there are exactly forty years separating the composition of the *Pollio* from the birth of Christ, Pope can fix one eye on the prophecies of Isaiah while he searches beneath the literal sense of Virgil's words to discover allegorical meanings that will support not only Old Testament scripture, but also his own knowledge of the historical event.

Pope continues to imitate the external features of his model by, as it were, continuing to adapt the distinctive Virgilian *lumina* to the conditions of the heroic couplet. For example, he compresses the anaphora of the sixth and seventh lines of the *Pollio* ("iam redit . . . iam nova") and the balanced epexegesis of line six incorporating semantic, phonic, and positionally equivalent verb forms into the eighth, Alexandrine line of the *Messiah*. At this point, however, Pope's leading concern has shifted from the rhetorical ornaments of style to the images which they are designed to elevate. Approaching the fourth eclogue as a religious allegory, he focuses upon those "images and descriptions" which resemble—however tenuously—the prophetic vision of Isaiah. Assuming a common tradition, Pope then selects those passages from the Old Testament which correspond figuratively with the *Pollio* and disposes them in an equivalent syntagmatic order.

Virgil disrupts the quiet of the idealized pastoral landscape by insisting, paradoxically, that it must be elevated to receive the military and political influences of a representative of an empire torn by civil unrest. Without explaining how a fictional world characterized by rustic simplicity and permanence can accommodate its opposite, Virgil brings the timeless present into collision with chronological time by insisting that this minister of change will preside over a world reborn into time. The eternal present *iam* becomes the intersecting point for past, present, and future in an inversion of the Hesiodic pattern of the ages recorded in the Sibylline verses.[15] The artificial perfection of the bucolic vision is violated by the entrance of those destructive elements which had been the cause of its preservation as an image of a utopian past, and while both the real world without and the imaginative world within collapse, the ancient golden age returns. At this point Virgil is not a prophet advocating that the real may be made one with the ideal through renovating existing social, intellectual, and political conditions, nor is he proposing that it may be accomplished by fashioning an entirely new system using the debris of the old. Rather, he claims to witness the timely exit ("desinet") of the debased iron race together with a rebirth of the great order of the ages—the original golden race ("gens aurea")—conceived by the gods independent of man's now ignoble nature. This glorious new universe is animated to receive an infant boy ("nascenti puero") who acts as a mediator between man's temporal existence and the eternal home of the gods, and whose symbolic birth initiates the return of Justice (the goddess Astrea) and the dethronement of Apollo by Saturn, his grandfather and the chief of the immortals during the first golden age. The poet appeals to chaste Lucina (the patroness of childbirth, also named Juno as the daughter of Saturn) to look with favor upon the auspicious child whose birth will restore the magnificent past.

Examining the fourth eclogue as Christian allegory, Pope interprets the last age of Cumaean song as the end of pagan prophecy (Isaiah 26:13-14; 31:7) brought about by the rebirth of the great line of the ages. Searching for an appropriate Old Testament image, Pope associates the *magnus saeclorum ordo* with the geneological tree linking Christ and the root of Jesse by way of David (Isaiah 11:1, 2, 11; I Sam. 16:12 and Rom. 15:12). In lines nine through twelve of the *Messiah* this symbolic tree becomes the central image: "From *Jesse*'s Root behold a Branch arise, / Whose sacred Flow'r with Fragrance fills the Skies." (*Messiah* lines 9-10). Pope's source in Isaiah is strengthened by Virgil's use of the verb *surgo*, meaning to arise or spring up (Isaiah 45:8): "be the earth opened, and bud forth a saviour: and let justice spring up withal: I the Lord have created him." Translating line seven of the *Pollio* into Christian terms, Pope has the Dove of Matthew 3:16, symbol of the Holy Spirit, sent down from heaven above ("caelo demittitur alto") to identify the "sacred Flow'r" as the "progenies" of God. Furthermore, by interpreting "virgo": as virgin and associating it with "casta Lucina," the chaste goddess of childbirth who is to look kindly upon the "nascenti puero," Pope has an image of the virgin mother that is reinforced in Isaiah 45:8 by its connection in the *Pollio* with Astrea or Justice. Virgil's "iam redit et virgo, redeunt Saturnia regna" suggests Isaiah 7:14: "Behold a virgin shal conceive, and beare a sonne," and, in the hands of Pope, it becomes "A *Virgin* shall conceive, a *Virgin* bear a Son!" (*Messiah* line 8). Although Pope continues to imitate Isaiah's invocatory style, he relies upon Virgil's poem to supply the controlling images that determine his selection of passages from the prophet.

A single word may now provide the only connection between the *Pollio* and an entire verse from Isaiah. Moreover, the order in which these images are borrowed and transferred to the *Messiah* is determined essentially by the coherence of Pope's own work rather than by their disposition in either of his sources. Perhaps recalling Virgil's allusion to "caelo alto" (*Pollio* line 7), Pope imitates Isaiah's recurrent apostrophe "ye heavens" (Isaiah 1:2; 44:23; 45:8) to introduce Isaiah 40:8, no doubt inspired by the repetition of *fundo* (*Pollio* lines 20,23) and the application of the verb *surgo* in a similar metaphorical context. Isaiah writes (45:8): "Droppe dew ye heavens from above, and let the cloudes rayne the just: be the earth opened, and bud forth a saviour: and let justice spring up withal: I the Lord have created him." Isaiah's constant allusion to the restoration of justice and world peace (for example Isaiah 26:2, 3, 7, 8, 9, 10, 12) provides an easy link with the return of Astrea in Virgil ("iam redit . . . virgo": *Pollio* line 6), to which Pope adds the Divine scales (Isaiah 40:12). The prophet writes (Isaiah 32:15-18): "until the spirit be powred out upon us from on high . . . And the worke of justice shal be peace, and the service of justice silence, and securitie for ever. And my people shal sitte in the beautie of peace." Pope's extension of Virgil's "progenies" who "demittitur caelo alto" (*Pollio* line 7) is "white-roab'd Innocence from Heav'n descend" (*Messiah* line 20), and the function of both these figures is to rule a world made peaceful by their father's virtues (*Pollio* line 17): "pacatumque reget patriis virtutibus orbem." This peace is achieved by erasing our *sceleris vestigia*, thereby releasing the land from terror. Pope transforms Virgil's "te duce, si qua manent sceleris vestigia nostri, / irrita perpetua solvent formidine terras" (*Pollio* lines 13-14), into "All Crimes shall cease, and ancient Fraud shall fail" (*Messiah* line 17), using Isaiah 26:3 as his Old Testament reference: "The old errour is gone: thou wilt keepe peace: peace because, we have hoped in thee."

Finally, Pope draws upon the ancient reputation of *baccar* (*Pollio* line 19) as a charmed plant capable of protecting against evil in order to personify the auxiliary service of his "kindly Show'r" (*Messiah* lines 15-16): "The Sick and Weak the healing Plant shall aid; / From Storms a Shelter, and from Heat a Shade." His acknowledged debt is to Isaiah 25:4: "thou art become a strength to the poore, a strength to the needie in his tribulation: an hope against the whirlwinde, a shadow against the heate." Responding perhaps to Isaiah's injunction to "Seeke ye our Lord whiles he may be found, invocate him, whiles he is neere" (Isaiah 55:6), Pope replaces Virgil's account of the increasing benevolence arising out of Pollio's administration (*Pollio* lines 11-12), "teque adeo decus hoc aevi, te consule, inibit, / Pollio, et incipient magni precedere menses," with an image that combines his earlier modification of the pastoral silvan landscape (lines 9-16) and Isaiah's continuous association of the Lord with the light of the rising sun (Isaiah 51:4; 58:8-10; 59:9; 62:1), but especially (Isaiah 60: 1-20):

> Arise, be illuminated Jerusalem: because thy light is come, & the glorie of our Lord is risen upon thee . . . upon thee shal

> our Lord arise, and his glorie shal be seene upon thee. And the Gentiles shal walke in thy light, and kinges in the brightnes of thy rising . . . the Lord shal be unto thee for an everlasting light, and the daies of thy mourning shal be ended.

Pope's abrupt apostrophe to the propitious child (Messiah line 22), "Oh spring to Light, Auspicious Babe, be born!" retains traces of Virgil's use of *surget* and "magnum Iovis incrementum" (*Pollio* lines 9, 49). Moreover, he develops Virgil's image of a child—a *cara deum suboles*—who is seen as a miraculous plant flowering under the auspices of the gods and acclaimed by a pastoral garden animated through its influence (*Pollio* lines 18-25, 28-30). In the *Messiah,* however, this personified landscape is translated into a symbolic figure representing Nature, in the guise of Spring, entering a barren world and restoring the profusion of life. Appropriating three lines from Menalcas's speech celebrating the apotheosis of Daphnis in Virgil's fifth eclogue, Pope exaggerates his image of Nature rejoicing. The shepherd sings (*Daphnis* lines 62-64):

> ipsi laetitia voces ad sidera iactant
> intonsi montes; ipsae iam carmina rupes,
> ipsa sonant arbusta: 'deus, deus ille, Menalca!'

Menalcas's description of the natural sounds of the wooded mountains, echoing cliffs, and cultivated fields, harmoniously reassuring him of the deification of beautiful Daphnis, is transformed by Pope into an antiphonal chorus in which the "vocal Hills" respond with "A God, a God!" echoing the "lonely Desert['s]" command "Prepare the Way! a God, a God appears." The subtle, private melody of Nature, inaudible to all but the devotee who desires to hear, becomes in the *Messiah* a miraculous personalization of the elements of Nature—lofty mountains and common rocks—who announce publicly the "approaching Deity." The relevant passage in Isaiah is 44:23: "Prayse ye o heavens, because the Lord hath done mercie: make jubilation ye endes of the earth: ye mountaynes sound prayse, thou forest and everie tree therof."

As the *Messiah* continues, and presumably as the moment of the Savior's birth draws near, the celebration assumes universal proportions (*Messiah* lines 33-37):

> Lo Earth receives him from the bending Skies!
> Sink down ye Mountains and ye Vallies rise:
> With Heads declin'd, ye Cedars, Homage pay;

Be smooth ye Rocks, ye rapid Floods give way!
The SAVIOR comes!

Responding to Virgil's image of the domed universe trembling in anticipation at the approach of the child of the gods (*Pollio* lines 50-51), "aspice convexo nutantem pondere mundum, / terrasque tractusque maris caelumque profundum," Pope combines Isaiah's description of the "day of our Lord" (Isaiah 13:9) as a day of judgment and devastation (Isaiah 13:13), "For this I shal truble heaven: & the earth shal be moved out of her place," and as a day of forgiveness and reward (Isaiah 40:4; 42:11; 54:10; 55:12):

> Everie valley shal be exalted, and everie mountaine and litle hil shal be humbled. . . . Let the desert be exalted and the cities therof. . . . For the mountaines shal be moved and the little hilles shal tremble: but my mercie shal not depart from thee, and the covenant of my peace shal not be moved. . . . the mountaines and the litle hilles shal sing prayse before you, and al the wood of the countrie shal clap the hand.

Pope's "The SAVIOR comes!" (*Messiah* line 37) echoes both Isaiah's "Behold thy saviour cometh!" (Isaiah 62:11) and Virgil's "Behold how all things rejoice with the age that shall come!" ("aspice venturo laetentur ut omnia saeclo!"—*Pollio* line 52).

Although there is little textual support in the fourth eclogue for Pope's consolatory address to the "Blind," the "Dumb," and the "Lame" in his *Messiah* (lines 38-44) other than Virgil's repetition of *video* in his account of the child's familiarity with the gods (*Pollio* lines 15-16), the image of the cripple restored to health and the powerful reduced to impotence is of central importance in the book of Isaiah, usually taking the form of the loss or recovery of sight and hearing as an indication of an equivalent spiritual condition (Isaiah 6:10; 11:3; 29:18; 42:7, 16; 43:8; 50:5; 52:15). The passage which most nearly approximates Pope's fervent appeal to the lame,

Hear him ye Deaf, and ye Blind behold!
He from thick Films shall purge the visual Ray,
And on the sightless Eye-ball pour the Day.
'Tis he th' obstructed Paths of Sound shall clear,
And bid new Musick charm th' unfolding Ear.
The Dumb shall sing, the Lame his Crutch forego,
And leap exulting like the bounding Roe,
(*Messiah* lines 38-44)

and is likely his primary source, is Isaiah 35:5-6: "Then shal the eies of the blind be opened, and the eares of the deafe shal be open. Then shal the lame leape as an hart, and the tongue of the dumme shal be opened." Entirely without counterpart in the fourth eclogue, Isaiah's 25:8, "and our Lord God shal take away teare from al face," provides the original for Pope's line 46: "From ev'ry Face he wipes off ev'ry Tear." And the context for this Divine mercy in the *Messiah* (line 45), "No Sigh, no Murmur the wide World shall hear," may be derived from the prophet (65:19): "and there shal no more be heard in it [Jerusalem] the voice of weeping, and the voice of crying."

Gradually, then, Pope's reliance on a "remarkable parity between many of the thoughts [of Isaiah] and those in the *Pollio* of *Virgil*" that had allowed him to remain largely faithful to the design for his poem outlined in his "Advertisement" tapers off as he shifts his primary focus to the images in Isaiah. Indeed, thus far he has encountered little difficulty in matching Virgil's predictions of a new golden age ushered in by the birth of a "magnum Iovis incrementum" with biblical imagery depicting the coming of a new era of peace and justice initiated by the birth of a Messiah. In the fourth eclogue the achievement of Virgil's *nova ordo* is qualified, however, by a period of gradual improvement during which time the child will learn to praise the heroic man and be taught to understand his own *virtus*, and humanity will purge itself of the "priscae vestigia fraudis" (*Pollio* line 31) in a reversal of the Hesiodic pattern of the ages. Under the military administration of C. Asinius Pollio, Virgil's world must pay for the ultimate suspension of arms and the blessing of complete prosperity by restoring its honor and its nobility on the field of combat. Warfare, then, is a glorious trial in which men must

> cingere muris
> oppida, . . .
> alter erit tum Tiphys, et altera quae vehat Argo
> delectos heroas; erunt etiam altera bella
> atque iterum ad Troiam magnus mittetur Achilles.
> (*Pollio* lines 32-36)

This intervening "heroic age" delineated in the fourth eclogue is inconsistent with Isaiah's apocalyptic vision in which the day of the Lord is a day of reward and punishment—of universal destruction in concert with universal salvation—and the "later days" (Isaiah 2:2) preceding judgment are characterized by man's realization that heroic virtue lies not in the continuation of *bellum*, but in the recovery of *otium*. Isaiah predicts that eventually the Lord will "Judge the Gentiles, and rebuke manie peoples: and they shal turne their swordes into culters, and their speares into siethes: nation shal not lift up sword against nation, neither shal they be exercised any more to battel" (Isaiah 2:4). This state of harmony will arrive, however, only after a period in which the Lord will turn back hostility upon itself in a bloody inversion of friendship and brotherhood. The prophet's description of battle is the antithesis of heroic: "And I [the Lord] will make the Aegyptians to runne together against the Aegyptians: and a man shal fight against his brother, and everie man against his friend, citie against citie, hingdom [sic] against kingdom" (Isaiah 19:2).

In order to escape this radical disagreement in his source material, Pope ignores Virgil's account of the maturing novitiate and man's attempts to redeem his honors by re-enacting ancient heroic exploits (*Pollio* lines 31-36), and concentrates exclusively on Isaiah's concession of a merciful side to Christ as the instrument of Divine justice. Using as his original Virgil's claim that the insidious forms of nature that threaten the infant by concealing death behind an exterior of alluring beauty (represented by the "serpens" and the "fallax herba veneni") will be eliminated in the new age, Pope centers upon the repetition of the verb *occidet* (*Pollio* lines 24-25) to recall Isaiah 25:8, "He shal cast death downe headlong for ever," and 51:9, "Hast not thou striken the proude, wounded the dragon?" Pope's version is "In adamantine Chains shall Death be bound, / And Hell's grim Tyrant feel th' eternal Wound" (*Messiah* lines 47-48).

Similarly, Virgil's fourth eclogue offers nothing even remotely approximating Pope's anti-pastoral vision of the future age as an advanced period of architectural reconstruction, "Then Palaces shall rise" (*Messiah* line 63), and, while Pope identifies his source as Isaiah 65:21-22, the prophet's reference to the year of the Lord as a time in which the ruined civilizations will be restored certainly provides additional support: "And they shal build the desertes from the begynning of the world, and shal erect the old ruines, and shal repayre the desolate cities, that were dissipated in generation and generation" (Isaiah 61:4). Moreover, Pope finishes his couplet by alluding to "the joyful Son" who "Shall finish what his short-liv'd Sire begun" (*Messiah* lines 63-64), a rendition of Virgil's *cara deum suboles* who inherits a world made peaceful through Pollio's military achievements ("pacatumque reget patriis virtutibus orbem": *Pollio* line 17), and who is transformed in Pope's eclogue to a figure possessing immortality and representing the great order of generations born anew ("magnas ab integro saeclorum nascitur ordo": *Pollio* line 5). Pope's debt to Isaiah is unclear, but it is possibly Isaiah 61:10: "I wil rejoyce in our Lord, and my soule shal be joyful in my God."

Another image that is crucial to the *Pollio* but incompatible with Isaiah is the view of Nature in the new golden age as an inexhaustible cornucopia furnishing, without human effort or assistance, all the requirements and conveniences for a vigorous, independent life (*Pollio* lines 18-25, 28-30, 37-44). Virgil insists that once man has regained his honor the whole world will minister to his needs ("omnis feret omnia tellus": *Pollio* line 39). In Isaiah, however, the "new heavens" and the "new earth" (65:17) are not handmaidens to an idle race, but rather a strict mistress whose favors a man must court with his love and hard labor. The improvement in man's physical condition, then, is that henceforth he will be rewarded in proportion to his efforts—a matter of social reform, not magic. The prophet writes,

> And they shal build cities, and inhabite: and they shal plant vineyardes, and eate the fruites therof. They shal not build, and an other shal dwel: they shal not plant, and an other shal eate: for according to the daies of the tree, shal be the dayes of my people, and they shal make old the workes of their handes. Myne elect shal not labor in vayne nor ingender in conturbation.
>
> (Isaiah 65: 21-23)

Again Pope follows his biblical source emphasizing the idea of labor of long continuance with a line that strains itself across ten monosyllables: "Their Vines a Shadow to their Race shall yield; / And the same Hand that sow'd shall reap the Field" (*Messiah* lines 65-66). The revelation of the future granted to the prophet Isaiah entails a vision of the universe spiritually and naturally revitalized. Although this miraculous rebirth of creation will concern the unfolding of Divine Justice, its opulence will take the form of spontaneous growth which, without cultivation, will be deficient in the essentials necessary to support human life. Virgil's heroic race will reenter the Garden of Eden replete with bending harvest, ripening grapes, and oak trees that drip with honey:

> molli paulatim flavescet campus arista
> incultisque rubens pendebit sentibus uva,
> et durae quercus sudabunt roscida mella.
>
> (*Pollio* lines 28-30)

Pope, however, follows the biblical text, and the absence of available means of support is intentional. Pope cites Isaiah 55:13 and 35:7: "For the shrubbe, shal come up the firre tree, and for the nettle, shal grow the myrtle tree." "And that which was drieland, shal be as a poole, and the thirstie ground as fountaines of waters. In the dennes wherein dragons dwelt before, shal spring up the greennes of reede and bulrush." But Isaiah 41:18, 19 certainly provided additional material:

> I wil open rivers in the high hilles, and fountaynes in the middes of plaine fildes: I wil make the desert into pooles of waters, and the land not passable into rivers of waters. I wil geve into the wildernes the cedar, and the thorne, and the myrtle and the olive tree: I wil set in the desert the firretree, the elme, and the box tree together.

Pope introduces the conventional rustic lover into the pastoral landscape as an extension of the reader's own senses. Using what has been called "a kind of 'prophetic perfect' tense, a device by which a future event is vividly depicted as already present,"[16] Pope narrows the distance between his reader and the prophet's vision, allowing him, as it were, to move with the "Swain" and "See Lillies spring, and sudden Verdure rise" (*Messiah* line 68). Moreover, Pope follows the early Christian practice of superimposing Greco-Roman landscape onto the Hebraic setting. An examination of a hymn by Prudentius reveals how closely Pope's technique approximates that of the earlier composer. Upheld by traditional pastoral imagery, Prudentius's spring landscape finds a counterpart in Pope's eclogue, though in following Virgil he projects the golden age into the future, and following the Christian interpretation of Virgil's *Pollio* replaces Roman values with Hebraic. Pope's Christian perspective creates a bond between his poem and the hymn of Prudentius that, in terms of isolated surface expression, is stronger than his dependence on Virgil and Isaiah. For example, his treatment of the shepherd and his care bears more resemblance to the traditional Christian interpretation of the pastoral convention exemplified in Prudentius than to Virgil's fourth eclogue. Compare Prudentius's

> The busy shepherd calls back
> [the lost sheep] and, driving off wolves,
> carries it on his shoulders
> back to the open sheep pen,

with Pope's

> As the good Shepherd tends his fleecy Care,
> Seeks freshest Pasture and the purest Air,
> Explores the lost, the wand'ring Sheep directs,
> By Day o'ersees them, and by Night protects;

The tender Lambs he raises in his Arms,
Feeds from his Hand, and in his Bosom warms.
(*Messiah* lines 49-54)

In addition to Prudentius, many poets within this Christian pastoral tradition could supply equally remarkable echoes of the *Messiah*.

As Virgil's child moves from infancy, through adolescence, towards manhood, and the silver age descends into the golden, the tranquility that is achieved by military superiority and the elimination of accumulated dishonor spreads to encompass the world and its creatures. The coveted patronage of the gods is restored to humanity in the form of the maturing child who brings back the remote knowledge of heroic deeds and moral purity by studying the lessons of his father and reliving the victorious ancient campaigns. Once the human spirit has ascended the scale from insignificance to greatness, and from there to near divinity, the entire universe pays homage to the new race of heroes by offering itself as a tribute. And once man is in possession of his "Destiny," weakness and fear—in fact any form of imperfection—is abolished from the newly transformed world. Virgil writes "ipsae lacte donum referent distenta capellae / ubera, nec magnos metuent armenta leones" (*Pollio* lines 21-22). In Isaiah's apocalyptic vision man is not himself the source of harmonious co-existence. Rather, universal peace is a gift to the faithful on the day of judgment and proceeds from God alone. One is a process that begins in self-improvement and the other is a reward for service rendered, but the finished product is much the same. Using Virgil again as his point of reference, Pope reproduces the language and the spirit of the prophet with little modification. Isaiah 11:6-9 reads:

> The woolfe shal dwell with the lambe: and the leopard shal lie with the kid: the calfe, and lion, and sheepe shal abide together, a litle child shal leade them. The calfe, and the beare shal feede: their yong ones shal rest together: and the lion shal eate strawe as it were an oxe. And the infant from the brest shal be delighted upon the hole of the aspe: & he that is weyned, shal thrust his hand into the hole of the cockatrice. They shal not hurt, and they shal not kil in al my holie mountayne, because the earth is replenished with the knowledge of our Lord.

The prophet abbreviates this prediction in Isaiah 65:25 with a minor variation that Pope develops in his own poem. "The wulfe and the lambe shal feede together, the lion and the oxe shal eate straw: *& to the serpent dust shal be his bread*: they shal not hurt, nor kil in al my holie mountaine, sayth our Lord" (emphasis added). Pope's contribution to this Garden of Eden is to introduce the Adamic traveller whose successful journey through the ages has brought him full circle so that he returns to his original state where the now debased serpent impotently licks the dust from his feet.

> The Lambs with Wolves shall graze the verdant Mead,
> And Boys in flow'ry Bands the Tyger lead;
> The Steer and Lion at one Crib shall meet;
> And harmless Serpents lick the Pilgrim's Feet.
> The smiling Infant in his Hand shall take
> The crested Basilisk and speckled Snake;
> Pleas'd, the green Lustre of the Scales survey,
> And with their forky Tongue shall innocently play.
> (*Messiah* lines 77-84)

As Pope's "Sacred Eclogue" rises towards a passionate evangelic finale, the author casts off the restraining lines that had held Virgil's fourth eclogue in tow, and harnesses a succession of Isaiah's more conspicuous images to lift his verse pasticcio to a sublimer elevation. Pope ignores obvious similarities between the prophet and the poet, such as the parallel between Virgil's petition for an extended life (*Pollio* lines 53-54) and the prayer of Ezechias for deliverance from the grave (Isaiah 38: 3-5), and again the *Pollio's* "incipe, parve puer, risu cognoscere matrem" (line 60) and Isaiah's "For before the childe know to cal his father and his mother" (8:4). He does, however, exploit the multiple connotations of the word "Salem" as at once the city of David and the birthplace of Christ, the core of the Jewish community and the focus of its worship, consequently the Jewish faith itself, Israel, the house of God, the Christian church, and finally Heaven. Without an assignable prototype in the fourth eclogue, Pope personifies the city of Jerusalem (called *Salem* in the book of Genesis) as a sleeping form invested with a regal crown in which the ornamental turrets are the turrets of the walled city. "Rise, crown'd with Light, Imperial *Salem* rise! / Exalt thy Tow'ry Head, and lift thy Eyes!" (*Messiah* lines 85-86). This figure, representing in particular the spirit of Christ, the "King of Kings," whose crown is at once a symbol of spiritual sovereignty as the sun and an emblem of suffering as the crown of thorns, is entreated to rise and occasion the dawning of the new era.

In Isaiah, Jerusalem is the kingdom of Judah and the object of enlightenment, not its source. "Arise, be illuminated Jerusalem: because thy light is come, & the glorie of our Lord is risen upon thee" (Isaiah 60:1). Echoing Virgil's repetition of "aspice" (*Pollio* lines 50-52) and Isaiah's habitual use of the jussive "Behold" (Isaiah 24:1; 41:24,29; 42:1,19; 47:14, and so on), Pope reiterates the verb "See," thereby dramatizing his account of the supremacy of Christianity over the world, past, present and future.

> *See*, a long Race thy spatious Courts adorn;
> *See* future Sons, and Daughters yet unborn
> In crowding Ranks on ev'ry Side arise,
> Demanding Life, impatient for the Skies!
> *See* barb'rous Nations at thy Gates attend,
> Walk in thy Light, and in thy Temple bend.
> *See* thy bright Altars throng'd with prostrate Kings,
> And heap'd with Products of *Sabaean* Springs!
> For thee, *Idume's* spicy Forests blow;
> And Seeds of Gold in *Ophyr's* Mountains glow.
> (*Messiah* lines 87-96; emphases added)

Although the notion of Christian superiority originates in Isaiah, its significance is considerably altered with its incorporation into the *Messiah*. The prophet's words do not suggest that Christianity will be the prevailing religion of future generations, but rather advise that Judaism will take its place as the spiritual center of the world, radiating the brilliant light of true belief into the dark souls of the Gentiles. Isaiah writes:

> Because loe darkenes shal cover the earth, & a mist the peoples: but upon thee shal our Lord arise, and his glorie shal be seene upon thee. And the Gentiles shal walke in thy light, and kinges in the brightnes of thy rising. Lift up thine eies round about, and see al these are gathered together, they are come to thee: thy sonnes shal come from a farre, & thy daughters shal rise from the [sic] side.
> (Isaiah 60:2-4)

The conversion of the "barb'rous Nations" (*Messiah* line 91) or "incredulous people" (Isaiah 65:2) is an essential ingredient of the prophet's vision, occurring at Isaiah 27:13; 54:3; 55:5; 64:1, and 66:19. Pope transforms the image of the Sabaean nation paying homage to the chosen people into a description of the kings of the material world offering the wealth of Sheba in tribute to the Savior. The poet's initial debt is to Isaiah 60:6, 10 and 11:

> al of Saba shal come, bringing gold and frankincense: and shewing forth prayse to our Lord . . . and their kinges shal minister to thee. . . . And thy gates shal be open continually: day and night they shal not be shut, that the strength of the Gentiles may be brought to thee, and their kinges may be brought.

However, Pope reinforces this image by drawing upon Isaiah 49:6-7, "Behold, I have geven thee to be the light of the Gentiles, that thou mayst be salvation even to the fardest part of the earth. . . . kinges shal see, & princes shal rise, & adore for our Lords sake, because he is faythful," as well as Isaiah 45:24, "because everie knee shal be bowed to me, and everie tongue shal sweare." Following his pattern of introducing a symbolic meaning associated with *Salem* after the initial verb "See" in lines 87, 88, 91, and 93, Pope introduces the ultimate definition in lines 97 and 98, "See Heav'n its sparkling Portals wide display, / And break upon thee in a Flood of Day!" and then revives his earlier depiction of Christ's birth as the spiritual dawning of a new day, "rise th' expected Morn! / Oh spring to Light, Auspicious Babe, be born!" (*Messiah* lines 21-22). Pope's image of the rising sun in lines 97 and 98 recalls Isaiah 60:19 and 20:

> Thou shalt haue the sunne no more to shine by day, neither shal the brightnes of the moone lighten thee: but the Lord shal be unto thee for an everlasting light, and thy God for thy glorie. Thy sunne shal goe downe no more, and thy moone shal not be diminished: because the Lord shal be unto thee for an everlasting light, and the daies of thy mourning shal be ended.

Pope personifies Isaiah's moon (*Messiah* line 100) as the chaste goddess Cynthia. Although this mythological figure can be traced to the fourth eclogue through the suggestion of Diana in the epithet *casta* and the implication of "tuus iam regnat Apollo" (*Pollio* line 10), Pope rejects it as a representative of the spiritual imperfection of the natural world, while Virgil employs it conversely as an image of Divine indulgence.

Continuing his imitation of the *Pollio*, then, with only this conjectural evidence of a sustained Virgilian influence, Pope collects Isaiah's images associating light and heat with the simultaneous destructive and restorative powers of Divine justice into an apocalyptic vision which owes little to any single passage from the prophet, and almost nothing to Virgil. Again relaxing the metrical and semantic integrity of his couplets, Pope connects successive epexegetical statements into an overlapping series that reflects the distinctive biblical pattern of impulsive flights of intoxicating passion. Combining images from Isaiah 10:17, 18; 29:6; 30:26, 27; 51:4; 60:1-3, 19, 20; 62:1, and 66:15, Pope hurries his verse towards an ecstatic celebration welcoming God's redemption of the world:

> No more the rising Sun shall gild the Morn,
> Nor Evening Cynthia fill her silver Horn,

But lost, dissolv'd in thy superior Rays;
One Tyde of Glory, one unclouded Blaze,
O'erflow thy Courts: the LIGHT HIMSELF shall shine
Reveal'd; and *God's* eternal Day be thine!
(*Messiah* lines 99-104)

Returning to a pasticcio of Isaiah, Pope describes the general dissolution of the natural world as "The Seas shall waste; the Skies in Smoke decay; / Rocks fall to Dust, and Mountains melt away" (*Messiah* lines 105-106) recalling Isaiah 19:5, "And the water of the sea shal be dried up, and the river shal be made desolate, and drie," and Isaiah 50:2: "Behold, in my rebuke I wil make the sea desert, I wil turne the floodes into drie land." By alternating balanced half-lines that direct the reader's vision from the nadir to the zenith—from the wasting "Seas" to the smoking "Skies" and from the disintegrating "Rocks" to the melting "Mountains"—Pope sets up an agitated see-saw movement that heightens the tension of his description of universal destruction. While Isaiah 51:6 and 34:3 provide support for this vision, his primary source is Isaiah 64:1-3: "Would God thou wouldest breake the heavens in sunder, and wouldst descend: at thy presence the mountaines should melt away. As the burning of fyre would they melt, the waters would burne with fyre . . . thou art descended, and at thy presence the mountaines are melted." Pope relieves the reader's anxiety by qualifying his account of the catastrophic end of the world with an assurance that God's "Word" remains unbroken, and his mercy supreme. This distinction between impermanent Nature and Divine will provides the counterpart for Pope's final celebration of the eternal kingdom. Using terms which imply that provisional human government is a shallow imitation of an omnipotent, everlasting spiritual monarchy, Pope turns his thanksgiving address from the dissolving creation to its Creator, from Jerusalem to Jehovah, and from the Son to the Father, "But fix'd His Word, His saving Pow'r remains: / Thy *Realm* for ever lasts! thy own *Messiah* reigns!" (*Messiah* lines 107-108). As if inflamed by the grandeur of the vision that has opened before him, and impatient to return thanks, Pope divides the hexameter line into an anaphoric, epexegetical construction with strong medial caesura, suggesting that his passion carries him beyond the formal restrictions of the verse in a two-fold effort to voice his admiration.

III

Pope explicitly claims in his "Advertisement" to the *Messiah* that he is not writing a poem in competition with Isaiah, but composing a pasticcio in the likeness of the *Pollio* to demonstrate the superiority of the prophet over the poet. Presumably, to forestall the objection that his *Messiah* represents a sacrilegious attempt to improve upon the inspired testament of Isaiah by rewriting it along classical lines, Pope argues that his poem is merely a receptacle sanctioned by the Church into which he delivers fragments from the prophet with the understanding that the new contents will better an old container. Pope's claim, then, is that his function is not one of enhancing already sublime "images and descriptions," but of selecting and disposing them in a predetermined order—not a creative, but an editorial activity. If we accept this claim, we cannot fault Pope for the content of his poem, nor for its structure, since both were received, and the question of the propriety of grafting sacred prophecy onto a pagan root is answered by his contention that he found it growing there already. Furthermore, the enormous task of selecting passages from the entire book of Isaiah and adapting them to suit a heroic-couplet rendition of Virgil's fourth eclogue, like the tedious editorial parquetry of the authors of the Virgilian centos, is ample testimony to the poet's religious dedication independent of the literary merit of the finished product.

Nonetheless, it is possible to evaluate Pope's artistic honesty while respecting his spiritual sincerity by determining the extent to which his poem is faithful to the "Advertisement" he made available to his reader after the poem had been completed. Using the comparative discussions of the second section of this essay as our point of departure, we can now make some observations on the reliability of the poet's self-assessment.

The "remarkable parity" between the *Pollio* and the book of Isaiah allows, for the most part, a relatively smooth transfusion of "thought." However, Pope's reading of the fourth eclogue as religious allegory is occasionally interrupted by, for example, Virgil's attempt to mesh the stationary pastoral world with the advancing wheels of history, or by his notion of a transitional period involving the restoration of heroic virtue before the ideal can become one with the real. Consequently, in order to preserve the sense of Isaiah Pope insists upon the same editorial license in excerpting passages from his Old Testament source as he assumes Virgil permitted himself in borrowing from the Sibyl. Yet there is an essential difference. Granting that Virgil appropriated elements from the Sibylline verses and adapted them to suit his purpose, his labor is assimilative and his motive is, as Pope indicates, based upon artistic impression, or "what best agreed with the nature of pastoral poetry . . . [and] serv'd most to beautify his piece." In order to write coherent verse Pope must assume a similar artistic authority, but because the final decision on what is appropriate to his subject rests with the prophet, the author of the *Messiah* is forced to extend his editorial powers to include making substantial modifications in the work which he claims to be imitating. Indeed, in every situation in which Virgil's meaning is irreconcilable with the prediction of the Nativity as it is recorded in Isaiah, Pope either ignores the inconsistent material in his model, or transforms it to agree with Christian prophecy.

In the closing lines of the *Messiah* (lines 85-108) Pope's dependence on Virgil's fourth eclogue has diminished to the point where it is almost non-existent, and the images that he lifts from the text of Isaiah have blurred from the particular and the specific to the general and the indefinite. Consequently, while it may be possible to argue that Pope's industry early in the work is collative and his contribution limited primarily to supplying transitions between fragments extracted from the prophet on the basis of their correspondence with the *Pollio*, this description becomes less accurate as the poem continues. In fact, towards the end of the *Messiah* the author's technical function has been overridden by his creative concerns, and Old Testament motifs provide the transitions and the biblical texture for an essentially Popean vision. The discrepancy between what Pope claims in his "Advertisement" that he has done, and what the poem itself reveals that he has done, might well lead critics to challenge Pope's sincerity. Yet an equally defensible, and certainly a more charitable interpretation would find in the "Advertisement" nothing more sinister than an innocent misinterpretation of the poet's personal investment in his work. Far more interesting, however, than any such attempts to uncover Pope's motivations with respect to the construction of his *Messiah*, is to chart the fascinating manner in which that poem is made to resonate with Isaiah and the *Pollio* while nonetheless maintaining its own considerable integrity.

NOTES

[1]*Messiah: A Sacred Eclogue, In imitation of Virgil's Pollio, The Twickenham Edition of the Poems of Alexander Pope*, 11 vols., vol. 1: *Pastoral Poetry and An Essay on Criticism*, ed. E. Audra and Aubrey Williams (London: Methuen, 1969), p. 111. All subsequent references are to this edition.

[2]Paul F. Distler, *Vergil and Vergiliana* (Chicago: Loyola Univ. Press, 1966), p. 156.

[3]For a more comprehensive discussion of the growth of Neo-Latin literature and the popularity of Latin models for religious subjects in the sixteenth and seventeenth centuries in Europe, see Jozef Ijsewijn's *Companion to Neo-Latin Studies* (Amsterdam, New York, Oxford: North-Holland, 1977). And for an examination of the influence of Virgil's fourth eclogue on the pastoral tradition,

see W. Leonard Grant, *Neo-Latin Literature and the Pastoral* (Chapel Hill: Univ. of North Carolina Press, 1965), pp. 258-59. Pope's familiarity with the tradition of employing the pastoral as a vehicle for Christian subjects, and his disapproval of this practice, is apparent in his allusion to the eclogues of Mantuan, or Baptista Spagnuoli, in "A Discourse on Pastoral Poetry," *Poems*, 1:122, and in his remarks on Spenser in *Guardian* 40.

[4]Grant, *Neo-Latin Literature*, p. 87.

[5]Dante alludes to this view of the relationship between the poet and his readers in the *Commedia*, Canto IX, lines 61-63. He says:

> voi ch'avete li 'ntelletti sani,
> Mirate la dottrina che s'asconde
> sotto'l velame de li versi strani.

[6]Charles S. Singleton, "Two Kinds of Allegory" in *Modern Critical Views: Dante*, ed. Harold Bloom (New Haven: Chelsea House, 1986), p. 13.

[7]Pope's poem first appeared in the *Spectator* under the longer title, *Messiah: A Sacred Eclogue, compos'd of several Passages of Isaiah the Prophet. Written in Imitation of Virgil's Pollio*. At this time, 14 May 1712, it was not accompanied by the "Advertisement" which first followed the poem in the *Works* of 1717.

[8]Murray Roston discusses the prevalent seventeenth-and eighteenth-century attitude towards the Bible as literature of the highest order in his book *Prophet and Poet, The Bible and the Growth of Romanticism* (London: Faber and Faber, 1965), pp. 15-59.

[9]Pope claims in "A Discourse on Pastoral Poetry," *Poems*, 1:30, that Virgil surpasses Theocritus "in all points where Judgment is principally concerned." Although he does not identify those areas where judgment might be concerned, he condemns Dryden a few lines later for an error that, in writing the *Messiah*, he was guilty of himself, and before him Spenser and Virgil. He claims that Dryden "treats of matters of religion in a pastoral style as *Mantuan* had done before him." As contemporary readers of the *Messiah*, however, we need not use these criteria to evaluate the poem even though they were the author's own, but the obvious discrepancy between the censures of the young critic and the practice of the mature poet must lead us to seek some explanation in the prose introduction to the poem.

[10]This is certainly the order of literary merit which many of Pope's contemporaries would have ascribed to the book of Isaiah, the *Messiah* and the *Pollio*. See especially Steele's letter to Pope dated 1 June 1712 in *The Correspondence of Alexander Pope*, 5 vols., ed. George Sherburn (Oxford: Clarendon Press, 1956), 1:145-46, and Warton's *An Essay on the Genius and Writings of Pope*, 2 vols., 1st edn. (London, 1756), 1:11-15.

[11]Paul Alpers, in *The Singer of the Eclogues: A Study of Virgilian Pastoral* (Berkeley: Univ. of California Press, 1969), pp. 158-59, argues that the invocation that begins the fourth eclogue is not a bold departure from pastoral convention as so many critics have insisted, but that it has acquired this reputation because of its fame and influence. Whatever the case, our only concern here is with Pope's reading of the poem as an inspired prediction of Christ's nativity.

[12]Michael C.J. Putnam makes a similar observation in *Virgil's Pastoral Art: Studies in the Eclogues* (Princeton: Princeton Univ. Press, 1970), p. 143.

[13]For example, Pope converts Virgil's medial pauses to respectively sixth, fourth, and fifth place caesuras. Furthermore, the profusion of sibilants that dominate the opening of the *Pollio* (initially in "Sicelides," alliteratively in "si . . . silvas, silvae stint," medially in "Musae, arbusta, humilesque," and

"consule," and terminally in "canamus, omnis, canimus," and "silvas") are repeated within an equivalent phrase structure with the final and initial "s" sounds in "Nymphs" and "Solyma" balancing the initial and medial "Sicelides Musae," the initial "s" in "Song" balancing the final "s" in *canamus*, the alliterative "sublimer Strains" and "Sylvan Shades" corresponding to the "s... silvas, silvae sint," and the remaining terminal sibilants in "Themes," "Strains," "Fountains," "Shades," "Dreams," "Pindus," and "Maids" echoing their counterparts in the original.

[14]Isaiah 5:3, from "The Prophecie of Isaie," in the Douai Version of the Old Testament. All further references to Isaiah will be cited from this edition first published at the English Jesuit College at Douai in 1609.

[15]Putnam, *Virgil*, p. 145.

[16]The quotation is from the introduction to Pope's *Messiah* in the *Poems* 1:106.

SEL 28 (1988)
ISSN 0039-3657

Dramatic Texture and Philosophical Debate in Prior's *Dialogues of the Dead*

NICOLAS H. NELSON

Since ancient times, the dialogue has proven itself one of the most versatile of all the forms of literature. One offshoot of this form, the dialogue of the dead, has had, however, a much less fertile literary history.[1] The three most eminent writers of this more restricted form are probably Lucian, Fontenelle, and Fénelon, but there is another who merits, and is beginning to receive, a wider recognition. In the final years of his life, Matthew Prior composed several dialogues of the dead that have received high praise from their few commentators. K. N. Colvile declares that they are "among the very best of their kind ever written in any tongue,"[2] and Frederick Keener, in the most comprehensive and illuminating discussion of this genre, says that "they do not pale when set beside acknowledged masterpieces of eighteenth-century literature."[3] Since they were first published only in 1907 and since only four of them were written (of which one is unfinished), these dialogues have received relatively little scholarly attention. Two aspects of these works in particular, I believe, could use further exploration: the nature of Prior's thought, his central philosophical values, and the various techniques he uses to dramatize these ideas. In this paper I propose to show how Prior blends the different uses of such dialogues, from satire to a discussion of ethics, into dramatic confrontations between two personalities with radically conflicting ways of looking at the world. To understand Prior's distinctive contribution to this form, we need to look briefly at the three writers mentioned above before turning to the Englishman's writings.

Writing in the second century of the Christian era, Lucian is generally credited with originating the dialogue of the dead, and he placed it firmly in the satiric tradition. Lucian depicts mythological or historical figures who discover, to their chagrin, that death obliterates all worldly distinctions and that their earthly obsessions

Nicolas H. Nelson is Associate Professor of English at Indiana University at Kokomo. He has written on Samuel Butler, Charles Cotton, and Jonathan Swift, and is currently working on Prior's poetry.

no longer matter. He ridicules those who cling to their possessions or to their physical beings after death, though he makes little effort to render human personality in his conversations. A typical example occurs in the debate between Nireus and Thersites about which one is better looking. They appeal the decision to Menippus the Cynic, Lucian's satiric mouthpiece, whose decision underscores their absurdity: "Bones are all alike. The only way of distinguishing your skull from Thersites'," he tells Nireus, "is that yours wouldn't take much cracking; it's fragile—not very masculine." And at the end of this brief dialogue Menippus sums up: "There aren't any distinctions in Hades; everybody's equal."[4] Thus Lucian initiates one of the central themes of the dialogue of the dead, the leveling power of death. Lucian's attack on man's pretensions is harsh and cynical, since, as Bryan Reardon has observed, his "merciless rationality never reaches any but negative conclusions. Lucian knows all the answers; and they are all 'No'."[5]

Closer to Prior in time if not in spirit are the French dialogists of the late seventeenth and early eighteenth centuries, Fontenelle and Fénelon. Fontenelle first established himself as a writer with his dialogues published in 1683, in which he mixes ancient and modern characters in urbane, witty, and often ironic explorations of the vagaries of human nature or the paradoxical quality of life. Like Lucian's, they are brief discussions of general ideas, but they lack his strongly marked satiric impulse. One of the characters commonly acts as the instructor of the other as they probe the subtleties of their topic. Socrates, for example, explains to Montaigne that the nature of man is essentially constant throughout history: "La politesse ou la grossièreté, la science ou l'ignorance, le plus ou le moins d'une certaine naïveté, le génie sérieux ou badin, ce ne sont là que les dehors de l'homme, et tout cela change; mais le coeur ne change point, et tout l'homme est dans le coeur."[6] But there are few moments of high tension or sharp intellectual debate in these conversations, which, for the most part, remain smooth, polite, and clever, and without much passion or personality.

At the end of the seventeenth century, Fénelon adopted the dialogue of the dead for the instruction of his prince-pupil, the Duke of Burgundy. His conversations naturally have a strong didactic element, with their goal of showing the future king of France the proper values and attitudes of a wise and benevolent monarch. In one of these, Achilles confesses to the centaur Chiron in the afterlife that he was an impetuous young man whose passion got the better of him, as youth is prone to allow: "la jeunesse," he remarks, "serait charmante si on pouvait la rendre modérée et capable de réfexions." Chiron replies, however, that this will only be possible if one learns "de se craindre soi-même, de croire les gens sages, de les appeler à son secours, de profiter de ses fautes passées pour prévoir celles qu'il faut éviter à l'avenir, et d'invoquer souvent Minerve dont la sagesse est au-dessus de la valeur emportée de Mars."[7] Moral judgments permeate these dialogues as Fénelon lays bare for his young student the shocking ignorance or misguided intentions of past leaders and civilizations. In commenting on recent French history, for example, Fénelon has Richelieu condemn Mazarin for being weak, timid, secretive, and lacking in principle. The Italian, Richelieu declares, is responsible for undermining the morality of the French: "vous avez corrompu le fond de leurs moeurs, vous avez rendu la probité gauloise et ridicule."[8]

Such are the major dialogists of the dead before Prior. The Englishman, despite the few dialogues he wrote, manages to strike a new and distinctive note in this tradition, by combining the satire, irony, and didacticism of his predecessors with a greater sense of the dramatic, together with a fuller exploration of the philosophical issues in question.

In his dialogues Prior depicts historical characters who engage in serious discussions of issues and ideas, defending their lives according to their conception of man and the world. Philosophy comes alive through personality; the human clash is elevated by the debate about general principles. Though not all of the dialogues are equally successful, they point to a more theatrical approach to the form than found in the past. Before detailing some of the dramatic aspects of these dialogues, we must look carefully at Prior's central ideas.

Critics have generally identified Prior as a philosophical skeptic. Forty years ago, in a series of seminal articles on Prior, Monroe Spears, though acknowledging Prior's fideism, made Pyrrhonism the key to his religious thought. Prior, Spears declared, "is, throughout his work, a consistent exponent of Pyrrhonism and a disciple of Montaigne," and he cites the Locke-Montaigne dialogue for an important piece of evidence. Montaigne's "chief argument" in Prior's dialogue, Spears says, is "the basic Pyrrhonist one against the possibility of any knowledge of absolute truth beyond the uncertain realm of sense-impressions."[9] Recently, John Higby and Frederick Keener have concurred with this judgment, though Keener speaks more generally of "Prior's distinctive blend of skepticism and energy, disillusionment and generosity."[10] Prior's skepticism has, in effect, become a critical commonplace.

But I believe we have accepted this designation too easily. True Pyrrhonist or skeptical doctrines are less evident in Prior's dialogues, or his work as a whole, than we are given to believe. Many years ago, C. K. Eves, Prior's biographer, pointed out that Prior wrote a number of religious poems throughout his career, some of which were among his favorites, and that he "was as loyal a Church of England man as he was a patriotic Englishman. For the natural religion of many of his contemporaries or for irreligion, he had neither patience nor understanding."[11] It is difficult to believe that a man who can casually refer to Christ as "our Savior" in his own commonplace book at this time (1720-21) could be a true skeptic.[12]

Nor do his dialogues support a skeptical or libertine interpretation. Montaigne himself, in Prior's dialogue, refers disparagingly to the founder of Greek skepticism in discussing a contemporary philosopher: "Descartes in the middle of the Joy he felt when he was certain he doubted of every thing and only knew his own Ignorance, was just in the same piteous estate where Pyrrho found himself two thousand years before" (1:633). In the passage from the Locke-Montaigne dialogue that Spears cites to support his claim for Prior's Pyrrhonism, Montaigne's purpose is to demonstrate the fallibility of man's sensory knowledge, thus undermining Locke's philosophy. Arguments against the validity of sense impressions are not unique to skepticism, nor does Montaigne assert that certain knowledge does not exist. From his other comments it is clear that he believes there is plenty of knowledge and wisdom about life available to man if he will only open his eyes a little more. Moreover, some other characteristics of skepticism are missing from Montaigne's arguments. The goal of the skeptic was, according to Long, "freedom from disturbance,"[13] since it was impossible to determine any absolute truth. Montaigne neither argues for such tranquility of mind nor does he exhibit it. And, finally, a proper skeptic would suspend judgment on any question and refuse to discriminate between good and evil for the same reason that he values imperturbability: ultimate reality can never be known for certain. On the contrary, Prior's Montaigne, like the real one, is positive, cheerful, dogmatic, and fully engaged with life. He is a vigorous Gascon with a Gallic wit and a rapid-fire mind. There is very little of the true skeptical philosopher about him or his arguments.

If Prior is not a skeptic, what is he? His own philosophy is difficult to characterize because it is unsystematic and eclectic. Like Montaigne, he draws on a variety of sources, both classical and Christian, for his themes. He is a traditional moralist who harks back to Horatian moderation as an antidote for the excessive zeal or enthusiasm with which human beings generally pursue their selfish goals. He sees clearly the limits of our reason and knowledge, and he roundly condemns our inclination to presumption and pretense. He wants us to know ourselves and our limitations better and not to impose ourselves on others as we strive to realize our ambitions or our happiness. Prior's dialogues affirm the values of simplicity, honesty, and moderation, in part by satirizing the human tendency to self-righteousness and an inflated sense of self-worth. Humility, restraint, and tolerance are key words in Prior's lexicon, or implicit assumptions in his satiric mode. Like Swift, he chooses not to depict humanity's spiritual condition, focusing instead on the ethical dimension of our behavior. Prior's ideas are scarcely original, but they are threaded throughout his dialogues, providing a continuous basis for judging what is being said.

As many have pointed out, one of Prior's characters appears to speak for the author in each of his dialogues, though he may not embody absolute truth or represent the perfection of humanity. This character, in the course of the dialogue, instructs the other one not only in ideas but also in feelings and sensitivity, though he himself may show some failings or weaknesses of character along the way. Aristotle's Golden Mean furnishes one of the truths that Prior's characters keep returning to in their discussions. Montaigne is perhaps Prior's chief exponent of this idea, especially when he summarizes some of his own axioms on life in opposition to Locke. "There is no pleasure," Montaigne asserts, "so just and Lawfull but is blamable if used in Intemperance or Excess" (1:627). "Valor," too, according to Montaigne, "has its Limits as well as the other Virtues, and foolhardiness is as great a Vice as Cowardise" (1:627). Even the concept of courtesy includes the possibility of excess: "I have seen," Montaigne remarks, "People impertinent by too much good Manners, and troublesome with the greatest Decorum" (1:627).

Prior's other dialogues contain a similar concern with virtue as a mean. The Vicar of Bray suggests to Thomas More that virtue itself requires restraint, and quotes some verses from a "Freind" (actually Prior himself) that were originally composed for *Alma*:

> Your Conscience like a Firy Horse
> Shou'd never know His native force
> Ride him but with a Moderate Rein
> And stroke him down with Worldly gain;
> Bring him by Management and Art
> To every thing that made him Start;
> And strive by just degrees to Settle
> His native warmth and height of mettle.
>
> (1:653)

Occasionally, this theme is adapted directly from Horace, whose poetry Prior admired and imitated. Nicolas Clenard, a learned and lively professor of languages, in his conversation with Charles V, former Emperor of the Holy Roman Empire, cites Horace's first satire from Book I to support his contention that moderation should guide our attitudes and actions in life, in contrast to the hauteur that Charles displayed. As Clenard translates Horace's famous lines on this theme:

> One equal bound there is, one Stated line,
> Which shou'd the Justice of our Act confine:
> There Right resides, what goes beyond is Wrong:
> Grows idly vast, and trails absurdly long.
>
> (1:603)

Clenard further advises Charles that "Reason should Direct your view, but Ambition dazles it, So you never attain your Desires, because you never sufficiently consider what will satisfy them" (1:603). The grammarian proceeds to condemn heroic virtue, which, according to him, once it transcends "the measure of Nature from Sublime turns to Ridiculous" (1:603). All of this sounds very much like Aristotle's discussion of virtue in his *Ethics*, where he says that virtue "is a mean between two kinds of vice, one of excess and the other of deficiency; and also for this reason, that whereas these vices fall short of or exceed the right measure in both feelings and actions, virtue discovers the mean and chooses it."[14] Like Horace, then, who based his satires on the idea of the "happy medium,"[15] Prior centers his dialogues on the same commonplace, though he gives it his own dress and style.

Because of its wide-ranging nature, the Locke-Montaigne dialogue, especially in Montaigne's axioms for life, summarizes most of Prior's central themes. Throughout Montaigne's long monologue, he emphasizes simplicity in life, integrity, and tolerance. "To be honest is the end and Design of our Life" he declares (1:627), though the difficulty of this modest goal is clearly implied. Another statement about the purpose of life suggests an even more limited end: "Our chief Business in life is to learn to bear the ills of it" (1:627). Life, Montaigne implies, will furnish enough suffering for us without our creating more problems for ourselves through imaginary anxieties or a crusading zeal. We should learn to accept ourselves and our conditions, and not seek out greener pastures elsewhere. But human beings are eternally restless: "we are always beyond our selves, fear, Desire, hope, throw us forward into futurity, and take away our sense of what is to amuse us, with what shal be, and that too possibly when we cannot perceive it" (1:627). Because of our restlessness we find it difficult to live peaceably in a community: "Have you composed your own Manners, and lived as you ought to do with Your Neighbors? You have done more than he who has written Volumes or taken Cities" (1:627). Even in education restraint is the key: "As to Science," Montaigne asserts, "Plants may be Killed with too plentifull Nourishment, and Lamps Extinguisht by too great a supply of Oyle; We may have so much Science that it may confound our Judgment" (1:628). To find stability in life we must recognize that many apparently desirable goals are illusions, such as the lives of the "great," who suffer from many serious "Inconveniences and hindrances" (1:628) by being constantly in the public eye. Finally, Prior paraphrases Montaigne's thoughts on death, where he tries to moderate our natural fear of it and to lessen the importance we attach to life: "Comfort Your self, You have good Company in the way. A thousand Men and ten thousand Animals Dye in the very same moment with You" (1:628). In such maxims carefully selected from Montaigne's essays, Prior inculcates the virtues of temperance and modesty, of limited goals and realistic visions, and, in doing so, sounds a good deal more like a traditional moralist than a philosophical skeptic.

Similar sentiments occur in Prior's other dialogues. One common theme is that happiness may be found in any station of life. Clenard makes this point to Charles after the Emperor has wondered how people of inferior rank can possibly be considered as happy as their superiors: "Every Wise Man has [an equal share of happiness] . . . for . . . he must form it himself, and this is soon done, when the necessarys of Life very few and easy to come at, almost within every Mans reach are once acquired" (1:606). Cromwell's porter, too, defends his life in a prison cell after the Lord Protector expresses his astonishment that anyone could be happy there, especially one who was judged to be mad. Simplicity of desire, the porter remarks, mocks all of Cromwell's "Splendor and Magnificence, Gardens Parks and Palaces." After all, the porter notes: "I had every thing which I desired or wanted, My Potage well dressed, my Straw fresh and my Coverlet Clean, Whilst in the midst of the Plunder of Three Nations You were always in Necessity, and every Week laying New Taxes upon an opprest People For the Support of an awkward ill founded Greatness" (1:657). The simple life of a madman in his cell was certainly not Prior's literal ideal, but it favorably contrasts with Cromwell's extravagant and immoral attempts at self-glorification. Simplicity also appears in the Vicar of Bray's disarmingly plain answer to Thomas More's question about his goal in life: "Why," the Vicar replies, "to teach my Parish and Receive my Tythes" (1:644). To the extent that he retains his integrity, the Vicar is right. His modesty acts as a satiric counterpoint to More's self-righteousness.

As these examples show, the defense of the simple life leads naturally to some of Prior's most telling blows against social pretense and snobbery. Clenard's description of Charles V's exploits as a conqueror reduces them to an immoral spectacle: "Now of the Hundred thousand Men, with whom You went Dub a Dub, and Tantara rara thrô the World Nineteen parts in Twenty were only Machines, meer Instruments of War, made use of to fill Trenches, or stop Breaches, played off by whole Battallions, Food for Powder, as Sir John Falstaff calls it, in the English Play" (1:601). A number of such passages appear in this dialogue as Clenard's satiric imagination catches fire when he denounces Charles's abuse of his power and his contemptuous attitude toward the common people. In a statement that does much to discredit his own judgment, Thomas More exhibits a similar attitude toward the people when he exclaims: "the Mass of Mankind is a Multitude of Such Animals as this Vicar, the Burden of the Earth, who only feed upon it without endeavoring to deserve the Bread it affords them, Wretches, who in having done nothing have done ill" (1:654-55). Sympathy for the common man is one of Prior's most constant and most endearing themes.

Another snobbery that Prior ridicules is the intellectual, with Locke being the chief target. Locke opens the dialogue musing upon his very important role in the history of philosophy: "Is it not wonderfull," he remarks, "that after what Plato and Aristotle, Descartes and Malbranch have written of Human understanding, it should be reserved to Me to give the most clear, and Distinct Account of it?" (1:615). Montaigne, of course, cannot allow such vanity to go by without laughing at it, but he also levels some serious as well as satiric criticisms at the Englishman's philosophy. In particular, he attacks Locke's use of language, especially his penchant for giving circular or meaningless definitions. In a parody of Locke's method, Montaigne imagines the following interchange:

> I hold a Stone in my hand, and ask you what it is, You tell me 'tis a body, I ask you what is a Body, You reply it is a Substance; I am troublesome enough once more to ask You what is a Substance, you look graver imediately, and inform me that it is something whose Essence consists in Extension in such a manner as to be capable of receiving it, in Longitude, Latitude, and Profundity.
>
> (1:618)

Intellectual pretense joins with social snobbery when Locke scorns the effort to write "to the Vulgar" as he defends the difficulty of his philosophy. Montaigne counters that common readers are "the only People that should be writ to," pointing out that many of the greatest writers either came from the "Vulgar" themselves or wrote for them:

"Esop and Epictetus had more Sense than their Masters. Sophocles shewed his Tragedies to his Maid. Since our time Racine, said, he doubted of the Success of his Phaedra till his Coachman told him he liked the Character of Hypolitus, and Boileau, addresses one of his Epistles to Antoine his Fav'rite Gardiner" (1:624). Montaigne concludes his debate with Locke by showing how impractical the Englishman's philosophy is when applied to everyday life. He imagines Locke's servant trying to carry out the simplest command from his master ("You may go down and Sup, Shut the Door" [1:635]) by analyzing it in Lockean terms. Such a process effectively reduces the command to nonsense, confusing the servant and embroiling him with his fellow servants. Wisdom is clearly not served by such a method of reasoning.

In ridiculing Locke's search for truth, Prior does not adopt the premise that it is impossible ever to know anything for sure, as a good Pyrrhonist would. Rather, through Montaigne and his other spokesmen, he shows how selfishness, pride, and presumption cloud our vision and obstruct the search for wisdom, and how simplicity, integrity, and moderation could provide a positive set of norms and attitudes for guiding our lives toward a reasonable measure of happiness and fulfillment. The dialogue form enables Prior to present such values indirectly without preaching, but they emerge nonetheless clearly and distinctly. The personalities Prior sets in conflict, especially his favored speakers, defend their lives and their ideas vigorously and often eloquently, with the result that these dialogues are unusually lively and dramatic. It is to this human side of the dialogues, with its theatrical aspect, that I now wish to turn.

Each dialogue opens with a sudden and apparently accidental meeting of the two characters in the afterlife. No exposition of situation or setting introduces the discussion, but the issues in the debate emerge clearly in the opening statements. In a kind of reverie, Charles V reviews his conquests on earth: "Burgundy with Brabant and Flanders, Castile, Arragon, Germany Possessed: Italy, France, Africa, Greece Attempted" (1:599). Hearing this, Clenard, without an introduction, recites his own achievements as if in mockery: "Noun Substantive and Adjective, Pronoun, Verb, Participle Declined: Adverb, Conjonction, preposition Interjection undeclined" (1:599). Thus Prior pits the warrior against the intellectual, the active life against the contemplative, to the detriment of the proud conqueror. We have already noted Locke's complacent dream of his place in the history of philosophy being shattered by Montaigne's pointed challenges, but there is also the Vicar of Bray's fond farewell to his parish that is upset by Thomas More's rebuke for his reluctance to go to his eternal home. From the start, then, Prior's characters square off in abrupt confrontations over their lives and values, with one of them challenging the other to philosophical debate.

Other dramatic techniques heighten the characterization in the dialogues and increase the tension between the debaters. Monologues not only enable one of the speakers to develop his ideas at length, but they also more fully reveal him as an individual. Clenard's speeches tend to turn into monologues because he is a "Word-Man" as Charles notes (1:605) and because he is defending a difficult position. The power of language is rarely accorded much recognition in contrast to the power of the sword, yet Clenard maintains that "Swords Conquer some, but words Subdue all Men" (1:611). These arguments, which Charles is unable to counter effectively, reinforce Clenard's central theme, though we see that he too goes overboard in his assertions. Like Clenard, Montaigne loves to amplify and embroider his ideas, not only to win the debate but also to show his wit and to indulge his love of invention and expression. We sense the joy in his verbal powers as his recital of various axioms for life extends to over two pages. When he finally stops to look up for a moment, he discovers that Locke has fallen asleep. On waking up, Locke naturally ridicules Montaigne's garrulous, rambling treatment of his ideas, a criticism sometimes made of the *Essays*, yet despite this comic incident, Montaigne's arguments are not seriously undermined but only given a human context. In the other two dialogues monologues are less in evidence since no personality dominates them as do Clenard and Montaigne in theirs.

Another dramatic device Prior uses effectively, though sparingly, in the dialogues is the aside. The speaker of the aside is generally in the process of losing the argument, and it enables us to see into his feelings about the course of the discussion. After Clenard concludes his long diatribe on the power of language, Charles comments to himself with a typical image: "I'l e'en draw down my main Argument, my great Battering Piece upon him, and Strike him Dead at once" (1:612). Charles's confidence is, however, seriously misplaced, since he cannot repel Clenard's verbal assault so easily. A variation of the aside occurs when Thomas More, true to his character, moralizes on the foolish Vicar's worries about his curate outliving him: "Strange Illusion! of which even Death has not cured this Wretch, We join Ideas which in Nature have no Coherence: Our fear of Death gives us not sufficient leizure to consider what Death it self is" (1:648). More goes on to speak of the Vicar in the third person as if he were not there in front of him: "What was it to this Vicar who should enjoy that Benefice from which Death has given him an Eternal Quietus. Yet with Regret he considers who shall possess the

Tythes when he shal neither have Mouth to Receive or Stomach to Digest the produce" (1:648). No doubt More is right about the Vicar's silly concerns, yet the interesting element is More's contempt for people of lesser intellectual capacity than his own. The aside, then, momentarily interrupts the flow of the discussion to allow a sudden perspective on it that often suffuses it with dramatic irony.

Prior uses language effectively to heighten our sense of two personalities in conflict over basic issues. It is considerably more varied than the language of Fontenelle and Fénelon, ranging from the highly formal to the colloquial or idiomatic. The colloquial expressions of some of his most educated speakers stand out, with such words as "Od zooks," "Pough, hang it," and "Egad" cropping up rather frequently. Even the Emperor Charles flavors his comments with a "prythee Man" (1:609) and "hark You" (1:615) that imitate an actual conversation taking place. Montaigne's language is naturally spiced with French exclamations like "Mort de ma Vie" (1:629) and "foy de Gentilhomme" (1:617), as well as a number of idiomatic English phrases such as "Who the Devil" (1:618), "come in for a Snack with my Landlord" (1:633), and "knock Your heart out" (1:638). He also uses contractions like " 'tis," " 'em," and "t'other," and coins some words like "Ergoismes" (1:631) and "Sectators" (1:619). Characters occasionally employ nicknames for their opponents that contribute to the satirical tone of the dialogue. Cromwell's porter calls the great man "Noll" to his face, Clenard refers to the Emperor as "Neighbor Charles," and More speaks of the Vicar as a "Drole." The Vicar is consistently respectful toward Sir Thomas, but he does call two of Henry VIII's queens "Old Kate" and "Nanny Bullen" (1:645). This informal language clearly gives us the impression of a vivid, almost realistic conversation taking place before us.

Language is also wittily employed in these dialogues, especially by Prior's favored speakers. Clenard, for instance, often introduces satiric analogies to deflate Charles's self-importance, as when he asks if Charles has never noticed "a large Ship going out of Port . . . with her Sails all spread, and her Streamers flying? . . . yet how soon her Bulk diminishes to the Eye of those that stand upon the Shoar 'till as the distance increases She becomes quite lost" (1:608). Applying this directly to Charles's career on earth, Clenard mocks his dependence upon the writer for his future reputation:

> You are launched into the Ocean of Eternity with all your Scutchons and Bandirolls about your Hearse, and probably you may have Four Marble Virtues to Support the Monument you were Speaking of just now. But alas, the Funeral Pomp is soon diminishd worn out and forgotten: Age and

> Accident deface the Tomb, And, it is only one of Us Scholars that must take an Account of Your true Worth, and transmit it safe to succeeding Generations.
>
> (1:608)

In his defense Charles asserts that men of words are the parasites of men of action, but his language lacks the expressiveness of Clenard's and thus fails in persuasive power.

The wittiest of Prior's characters is undoubtedly Montaigne. His speeches are filled with analogies, metaphors, similes, and imagery, much as his actual essays were, giving them an energy and an appeal that Locke cannot hope to match. When he ridicules Locke's penchant for defining terms without discussing his topic in a substantive fashion, Montaigne declares: "You seem, in my poor apprehension, to go to and fro upon a Philosophical Swing like a Child upon a wooden Horse always in motion but without any Progress, and to Act as if a Man instead of Practising his Trade should spend all his Life in Naming his Tools" (1:620-21). And when he defends his apparently confused method of treating his own subjects, Montaigne asserts that he is simply following the mode of Nature herself: "Is it not the variety it self that pleases while it instructs?" he asks. After all, "If all your Lillies were Collected together in one bed next your House, then all your Roses in an other, and all your Sun flowers in a Third, Who would admire the Beauty of your Garden?" (1:630). In answering Montaigne's critique of his lack of substance, Locke briefly introduces his own figure ("if a Man does not leap Hedge and Ditch, in your Opinion, he stands stock stil" [1:621]), but he is soon overwhelmed by a profusion of images and arguments from the Frenchman.

The other dialogues offer fewer imaginative passages than these because of the characters involved, yet the ones that do exist help reveal character or convey Prior's point of view. The Vicar of Bray, though a rather simple and uncomplicated man, exposes More's rigid moral approach to life after he hears some of the saint's hard-hitting maxims: "you mix't too much Gall with your Ink," the Vicar declares, "Egad with these Maximes of Your's you would raise both Court and Country against You, and if You had as many heads as there are Loops upon Your Gown You might run a fair risk to have 'em all cut off" (1:655). The Vicar speaks the truth here and more effectively because of his figurative language. More himself, as Prior depicts him, is not a very imaginative character, but when he does employ some figures, they are more bitter than most, as in the passage quoted above where he calls the common people "Animals" who are the "Burden of the Earth." Cromwell's porter is inherently not very imaginative, yet even he can introduce his own metaphors, as when he describes his master's own madness in despoiling his enemies of their property: "You find others," he tells Cromwell, "bitt with the same Tarantula who Second your fury pertake of the Plunder and justify your error. Yee all herd together, and it is a very hard thing to catch one of You" (1:661-62). Without this witty, imaginative language, Prior's characters, and hence his dialogues, would lack much of their interest and persuasiveness.

A final ingredient in these dialogues as miniature human dramas remains to be considered, that is, the range of emotion expressed. Prior's characters defend their convictions and attack their opponents with vigor and sometimes passion. Abrupt changes of tone occur, as characters react to one another in the flow of the exchange. All of the emotions we would expect are here, from the consternation of an emperor at being challenged by a lowly scholar to the haughty dogmatism of Cromwell. Montaigne himself plays most of the notes on the scale of feeling except perhaps those of deep anger or bitterness. There are, however, other feelings present that we would not anticipate and that lend a human richness to these conversations. Thus the Emperor Charles, by the end of his discussion with Clenard, is so frustrated with the professor that he breaks off any further debate, yet he solicits Clenard's help in concealing their talk because of its potential embarrassment for him. "Pray," he begs Clenard, "dont take the least Notice to any of my Fellow Princes of the Discourse we have had" (1:615). Fear of shame humanizes this haughty prince. The Vicar of Bray is remarkably mild and gentle throughout his dialogue until the last sentence when he allows himself a pointed thrust at Sir Thomas: "Thou Great Chancellor of England, without a head, Adieu" (1:655). Sarcasm humanizes the saintly Vicar. When Cromwell's porter describes the effect the execution of Charles I had upon him, we cannot help being struck by the depth of his disillusionment: "I imitated You, I looked upon You as my Idol till running from your Door with my Staff in my hand one thirtieth of January, I Shal never forget the Day, I saw You order your Master to be brought out of the Window, and Murthered at his own Palace Gate. I confess when You cut off the Kings head you turned mine into the bargain" (1:657). Though this dialogue may have the appearance of being Prior's most Lucianic work,[16] the porter's unusual sensitivity gives it a pathos not found in the Greek author. Prior thus enriches the human side of his dialogues with these diverse and unexpected emotions.

Each of the dialogues ends with the two characters going their separate ways without having found any common ground of agreement. The reader, I believe, knows which one has had the better of the argument, though he also knows that neither has an exclusive option on the truth. Even Montaigne has to admit the justice of Locke's comment that many of his best ideas are taken from other writers. Prior, in other words, achieves a richer characterization in his dialogues, a greater "negative capability," than most other dialogists of the dead. Without sacrificing his central theme of Horatian moderation, Prior depicts a scene of conflicting personalities whose views and characters are unchanged since their earthly careers. The fusion of mimetic, satiric, and philosophical elements into a coherent dramatic scene is a remarkable achievement. It is a pity Prior had so little time to pursue his work in this genre.

NOTES

[1]The land of the dead was used as the setting for a large number of literary works from the Renaissance down to modern times, as Benjamin Boyce has shown in "News from Hell," *PMLA* 58 (1943):402-37. As a distinct form, however, the dialogue of the dead appears only sporadically since Prior's time, from Lord Lyttleton's *Dialogues* (1760) to W. S. Landor's *Imaginary Conversations* (1824-29; 1853), George Santayana's *Dialogues in Limbo* (1925), and Steve Allen's television series "Meeting of Minds" (published in book form in 1978).

[2]K. N. Colvile, "Dialogues of the Dead," *Quarterly Review* 267 (1936):312.

[3]Frederick M. Keener, *English Dialogues of the Dead: A Critical History, An Anthology, and a Check List* (New York: Columbia Univ. Press, 1973), p. 55.

[4]Lucian, *Selected Works*, trans. Bryan Reardon. The Library of Liberal Arts (Indianapolis: Bobbs-Merrill, 1965), p. 45.

[5]Bryan Reardon, Introduction to Lucian, *Selected Works* (Indianapolis: Bobbs-Merrill, 1965), p. xxix.

[6]Bernard le Bovier de Fontenelle, *Nouveaux Dialogues des Morts*, ed. Donald Schier (Chapel Hill: Univ. of North Carolina Press, 1965), pp. 65-66.

[7]François de Salignac Fénelon, *Oeuvres*, ed. Jacques Le Brun. Bibliothèque de la Pléiade (Paris: Gallimard, 1983, p. 285.

[8]Fénelon, p. 493.

[9]Monroe K. Spears, "The Meaning of Matthew Prior's *Alma*," *ELH* 12 (1946):285.

[10]Frederick Keener, *English Dialogues of the Dead: A Critical History, An Anthology and a Check List* (New York: Columbia Univ. Press, 1973), p. 69. John Higby, "Idea and Art in Prior's *Dialogues of the Dead*," *Enlightenment Essays* 5(1974):62-69.

[11]Charles Kenneth Eves, *Matthew Prior: Poet and Diplomatist* (New York: Columbia Univ. Press, 1939), p. 207; see also p. 404.

[12]See Matthew Prior, *The Literary Works*, ed. H. Bunker Wright and Monroe K. Spears, 2nd edn., 2 vols. (Oxford: Clarendon Press, 1971),1:1011. All references to Prior's dialogues and other writings are to this edition.

[13]A. A. Long, *Hellenistic Philosophy: Stoics, Epicureans, Sceptics* (New York: Scribner, 1970), p. 79.

[14]Aristotle, *The Ethics: The Nichomachean Ethics*, trans. J. A. K. Thomson, rev. Hugh Tredennick (Harmondsworth and New York: Penguin, 1976), p. 102.

[15]Niall Rudd, *The Satires of Horace* (Cambridge: Cambridge Univ. Press, 1966), p. 23.

[16]Richard Morton, "Matthew Prior's *Dialogues of the Dead*," *Ball State University Forum* 8 (1967):74.

SEL 28 (1988)
ISSN 0039-3657

The Fragmentation of Originals and *Clarissa*

JONATHAN LAMB

In eighteenth-century Britain the idea of originality is tied to a number of related principles, such as the importance of primitive simplicity, the irregularity of the national temperament, the creative power of genius, and the priority of sublimity over all other categories of art and experience. These principles help to emphasize the value of things and people that are detached from over-elaborate and usually foreign influences, and to isolate that peculiar quality of self-subsistence—of being like yourself or of being like the thing itself—which it is the province of the sublime to represent. The debate about originality allows an easy passage therefore between these related principles. Tillotson's celebrated sermon on sincerity, where he reprobates the imitation of French manners and phrases and mourns the loss of old English plainness,[1] sits quite comfortably beside Edward Young's recipe for an original national literature: "Something new may be expected from *Britons* particularly; who seem not to be more sever'd from the rest of mankind by the surrounding sea, than by the current in their veins; and of whom little more appears to be required, in order to give us *Originals,* than a consistency of character and making their compositions of a piece with their lives."[2] The terms of Young's argument comprehend *Spectator* No. 160, where Addison applauds the splendor of art derived from nothing but "the mere Strength of natural Parts," and No. 350, where Steele has Captain Sentry draw a neat parallel between sublime writing and the modest bearing of the best sort of Englishman.

Close to the center of this discourse of originality, and well aware of its ramifications, is Samuel Richardson. He is an accurate, if rather niggardly critic of the practice ("Pray, sir, may it not be hinted

Jonathan Lamb, senior lecturer at the University of Auckland, is currently a visiting fellow at the University of Sussex and visiting fellow elect at the William Andrews Clark Memorial Library. He is preparing a study of Job-like scenes of consolation in eighteenth century literature, of which this essay is a specimen, exploring the differences between pleonastic solace and tautological damage.

. . . that Addison was sometimes *original* . . . in his Sir Roger?"[3]); he also prompts and exemplifies Young's discussion of the theory. Although the *Conjectures* is addressed to the "Author of *Sir Charles Grandison*," there is good reason for suggesting that *Clarissa* is at once the most impressive and flawed monument to Richardson's speculations and achievements in the sphere of originality. It is a novel that assimilates every conflict between Lovelace and Clarissa—sexual, political, aesthetic, linguistic—to a struggle between a man whose instincts are imitative and a woman who believes it is possible to deliver herself as she is. The skill—the genius—of Richardson's dramatization of this struggle is evident in the consonance of recent interpretations of *Clarissa* with his own. When Terry Castle maintains that all interpretations of the novel are repetitions of the hermeneutic violence committed by Lovelace upon Clarissa's papers; or when Terry Eagleton assaults William Beatty Warner's *Reading Clarissa* with devastating sarcasms ("It seems logical, then, that a contemporary deconstructionist should find Lovelace the hero and Clarissa the villain, without allowing a little matter like rape to modify his judgement"), it is as if in the twentieth, even more than in the eighteenth century, critics are ready to sacrifice their ingenuity in a good cause.[4] Like so many Peter Walshes, they account for their terror and ecstasy with the bare assertion, "It is Clarissa."

In an era when readers have been instructed in the importance of their role, when books are understood to be in endless dialogue with other books, when doubt has fallen on the status of origins and originality, Richardson is lucky to have won such a consensus. It has been made possible by the association of readerly disobedience with the palliation of a rapist's stratagems, as Eagleton shows. The violence always falls to the side of exegesis—that is, to the production of multiple meanings from constellated texts—never to the side of the original text, consubstantial with the self-evidence of its message. In this paper I am going to set up a colloquy between *Clarissa* and six other books in order to estimate the damage caused by the pursuit of this sort of originality, as distinct from the damage caused by a rapist with a talent for reading, writing, and quotation. Two of these are prior to *Clarissa* and are quoted in it: Montaigne's essay "Upon Some Verses of Virgil" and the book of Job. The remaining four appear in the half century after the publication of *Clarissa*; but all are part of the same constellation and glance at, or talk to, one another. These are Wollstonecraft's *Vindication* and *The Wrongs of Woman*; Rousseau's *Émile*; and Sterne's *Journal to Eliza*.

Because his gaze is widest and he talks to everyone, it seems right to start with Montaigne. He appears several times in *Clarissa* as an authority for libertine behavior and skeptical judgment, along with

Mandeville, Swift, and Rochester. On the charms of difficulty, the allurements of modesty, the importance of lies in courtship, the advantages of bashfulness, and the resemblance between rape and necrophilia Montaigne and Lovelace have opinions in common. They are especially fascinated by the excitements of obscurity and obliquity, what Wordsworth calls "a low hankering after the double entendre in vice."[5] Therefore "Ladies cover their Necks with Network, as . . . Painters shadow their pictures to give them greater Lustre"; so whoever "has no Fruition but in Fruition, who wins nothing unless he sweeps the stakes; and who takes no pleasure in the Chase, but in the Quarry, ought not to introduce himself into our School."[6] Shortly after the elopement Lovelace shows himself a connoisseur of this sort of *chiaroscuro*: "A white handkerchief, wrought by the same inimitable fingers, concealed—O Belford! what still more inimitable beauties did it not conceal! And I saw . . . the bounding heart . . . dancing beneath the charming umbrage."[7] He announces himself a collegian of Montaigne's school of erotic indirection when he tells Belford, "Always of Montaigne's taste thou knowest—thought it a glory to subdue a girl of family. More truly delightful to me the seduction progress than the crowning act" (2:371).[8]

After pondering his friend's addiction to fantastic obliquity, Belford comes up with a solution borrowed (presumably unconsciously) from the very essay which has sponsored it. It is his *soul*, expressing itself as nicety of appetite and awe of virtue, which has turned him to stratagems that are always "preparative."

> The very appetite is *body*; and when we ourselves are most fools, and crazed, then are we most eager in these pursuits. See what fools this passion makes the wisest men! . . . Do not even chaste lovers choose to be alone in their courtship preparations, ashamed to have even a child to witness their foolish actions, and more foolish expressions? Is this deified passion, in its greatest altitudes, fitted to stand the day: Do not the lovers, when mutual consent awaits their wills, retire to coverts and to darkness, to complete their wishes. And shall such a sneaking passion as this, which can be so easily gratified by viler objects, be permitted to debase the noblest? (2:487-88)

Belford is paraphrasing that portion of Montaigne's essay where he impersonates sexual self-disgust, and complains as follows:

> It is in Mockery, that Nature has order'd the most troublesome of Actions to be the most common, by that to make us

> equal, and to parallel Fools and wise Men, Beasts and us.... In every thing else a Man may keep some Decorum, all other Operations submit to the Rules of Decency; this cannot so much as in Imagination appear other than vicious or ridiculous.... 'Tis a Man's Duty to withdraw himself from the light to do it.
>
> (*Essays*, 3:126)

Twenty years later, in the last chapter of *Tristram Shandy*, Walter Shandy will paraphrase the same portion of the essay for the same mistaken purpose as Belford; they both try, as Montaigne puts it, "to honour their Nature by denaturing themselves [and to] value themselves upon their Contempt of themselves" (*Essays*, 3:129). One imagines that Richardson was rather pleased to think he had caught Montaigne out in the admission that a revolted palate keeps him from his fruit; and not simply because it confirmed him in his opinion that all intelligent libertines *know* at heart their delights are grievous, but also because it helped explain the worthy outset of that particular essay.

For someone as committed to the idealization of the familiar letter as Richardson, Montaigne's opening gestures must have been instantly recognizable. Alone in his study he tries to wean his mind from his body by taking pen in hand to recollect past pleasures: "Let Infancy look forward, and Age backward.... Seeing it is the privilege of the Mind to rescue it self from old Age, I advise mine to it with all the power I have, let it . . . flourish if it can like Misseltoe on a dead Tree" (*Essays*, 3:73, 77). The success of the exercise depends upon absolute candor: "I dare to say all that I dare to do." He even imagines that his readers will be women, who will read his confessions in the privacy of their closets. Writing to a woman whose closet he called a paradise, Richardson explains how the pen ought to "engross the writer's whole self"—*engross* in the compound sense of *absorb* and *retail*, so that every impulse of the heart is "*embody'd*" in letters. He asks the same correspondent if she can resist the converse of a pen that so exquisitely and innocently transforms desire into satisfaction: "The pen that makes distance, presence; and brings back to sweet remembrance all the delights of presence; which makes even presence but body, while absence becomes the soul" (*Letters*, pp. 64-68).

The strategic arrangements of privacy, writing, the self and pleasure are remarkably similar; and Edward Young helps show why. The British are isolated by the ocean, individualized by the blood in their veins, and provided they write like themselves they will prove original. Richardson simply scales down island to closet, and substitutes a female correspondent for the true-born Briton; otherwise his recipe for originality is the same. Montaigne's contribution to this cult of British originality is far larger than Tillotson would have liked. When Pope strikes attitudes of Anglo-Saxon sincerity, confiding how much he loves "to pour out all myself, as plain / As downright Shippen, or as old Montagne," when Addison laughs at the egotism of "this lively old Gascon [who] has woven all his bodily Infirmities into his Works," and when Tristram Shandy begins to decant himself into print with a quotation from Montaigne's essay on Virgil, they confront the exotic element in the peculiarities of the British.[9] To Richardson, Montaigne and his pupil Lovelace represent a perversion of originality, an engrossment of the self by the pen for purposes alien to the cultivation of a moral genius; but he recognizes in their oddly forthright accounts of their indirections an ambivalence, even a comicality, that belongs to the originality he favors.

Before her story properly begins, Clarissa has intervened in a quarrel between Mrs. Drayton and her daughter by writing a letter in the character of an elderly woman. Her theme is Montaigne's: that youth looks forward, and age backward. Although old folk have no other consolation than the memory of past ardors, they know how imperfectly the "fruits" of life answer expectation; young folk, on the other hand, have no notion that the only "fruit" awaiting them is the wisdom of understanding this (1:295). In one sense Clarissa's advice chimes with Richardson's eulogy of the pen as an instrument delightfully situated between the extremes of privation and possession; in another she seems to be echoing Lovelace's earliest recitation of Montaigne's libertine creed: "*Preparation* and *expectation* are in a manner everything; *reflection* may be something . . . but the *fruition*, what is there in that?" (1:172). If absence and distance are necessary to the keenest intuitions of presence, and if the mind ministers to the body's desires by denying them, who is to say whether asceticism or hedonism has the upper hand? This indeterminacy prompts the mock piety of Lovelace's praise of writing ("Not the heart only, the *soul* was in it. Nothing of body . . . the mind impelling sovereignly the vassal fingers" [2:431]), and Belford's misreading of Montaigne. Once Clarissa's "conditional liking" for Lovelace puts her at the mercy of her family and her lover, she is forced into an endless series of conjectures. Her writing can never engross her because it is devoted to establishing hypotheses about the past and the future. So rarely is she out of the subjunctive mood that Mrs. Howe is more acute than she knows when she says of Clarissa, "That *if* is everything" (1:298). These hypotheses are just like Lovelace's lies:

fictions inserted between an absent ideal and a present imperfection, preparations and reflections that defer the fruit.

Even if Clarissa were to pour herself out plain, and to make her writing of a piece with her life, her originality would not be free of troublesome ambiguities. Richardson himself was aware that singular moral grandeur can be made visible to the world's eye sometimes only through the medium of the ludicrous. "We are condemned," he wrote to Aaron Hill, "to live in such a trifling Age, that to make Wisdom looked upon as worth regarding, we must shew her with a Monkey's Grin" (*Letters,* p. 129). Willy-nilly he has to develop Clarissa as an *original* in the sense already being used by Smollett: that is, as an example of singularity so extreme that it must strike others as eccentric. Richardson aims to give a tragic luster to oddities of behavior which verge upon the humorous. Towards the end of her story Clarissa is being referred to frequently as a "dear extravagant" and a "sweet oddity" (4:41). The coffin in her bedroom is called a "whimsical choice," a "shocking whimsy" (4:442, 271); and it causes Belford to reflect that "great minds cannot avoid doing extraordinary things" (4:256). In short, her coffin becomes a macabre hobbyhorse on which she means, in Sterne's phrase, "to canter it away from the cares and solicitudes of life." On the road to this dismal originality Richardson has posted the signs of unborrowed excellence. With her inimitable fingers Clarissa gives, but never copies fashions (1:512); she refuses to be lent what she does not own, and she despises compositions which are no more than "*notes* and *comments* upon other people's *texts*" (4:495). Inimitable and nonimitative, "*Nature* was her *art*... her *art* was *nature*" (4:500). That is why so skilled a forger as Lovelace cannot reproduce the cut of her letters, and why on one occasion he is unable even to transcribe a piece of her writing because "the original is too much an original" (3:204).

All comic originals in the eighteenth-century novel fulfill a double function related to the double meaning of the word. As *original* implies a source and derivation as well as a self-generative uniqueness, so they represent mythic national virtues while behaving in unaccountable ways. The straddling of representative and nonrepresentative roles is symptomatic of a tension between public duty and private whim that is never resolved in the career of an original. As far as they are concerned there is a perfect coincidence of public utility and private virtue. Sir Roger de Coverley lays it down for a rule, "That the whole Man is to move together, that every Action of any Importance is to have a prospect of publick Good" (*Spectator* No. 6). But precisely because his extravagances are "particularly *his*" (*Spectator* No. 106) their representative or public value is missed. It takes an observer with a foot in both camps to appreciate the centrality of marginalized virtue and to hear in the language of a private memorandum sentiments fit for a public bulletin. Tristram Shandy tests his audience for this sort of receptivity when he *confides* his intention of *publishing* to the world at large a map of his miniature "world" (*Tristram Shandy*, p. 36). Lovelace has begun to understand something of this paradox when he defines Clarissa's originality as a unique copy: "Miss Clarissa Harlowe, indeed, is the only woman in the world, I believe, that can say in the words of her favourite Job (for I can quote a text as well as she): *But it is not so with me*" (4:135).[10]

Whether inventing, subsisting in, observing, or trying to express originality, difficulties are generated for those who expect it to be unequivocally present to itself. Richardson's belief in the coincidence of literary and moral genius puts beyond any doubt the exemplary quality of Clarissa's tragedy, as far as he is concerned. But when Clarissa, anticipating originals like Matthew Bramble and Walter Shandy, cries out, "I am quite sick of life; and of the earth in which innocent and benevolent spirits are sure to be considered as *aliens*" (3:383), it seems as if the world she confronts is beyond the reach of example and therefore cannot be the same as the one Richardson writes for. Or are we to assume that Richardson no sooner sets the world the example of Clarissa, than he removes her on account of her inimitability and its insensibility to virtue? Even if an adequate idiom is sustained between the world and the virtuous original, it is probable that the one will understand the other (as Lovelace does Clarissa) in terms of the imitation of models. He sees her as Job in her dying, Belford compares her with Socrates, and it seems likely that Richardson privately compared her death with Addison's. Publicly he justified it by quoting from *Spectators* Nos. 40 and 548. The familiar letter compounds these difficulties by its substitutive play of absence and presence. On all fronts originality seems to define itself, or be defined, in terms of the loss or displacement of what ought to belong to it: presence is distributed over distances in time and place; virtue is either invisible or eccentric; integrity is known by the fragments it is left lying in; and inimitability is calculated in terms of its imitative potential. While Richardson is content to interpret a comic original like Sir Roger as one who moves "in his intire and proper Motion" (*Spectator* No. 6), and whose appearance of oddity is owing to the world's exorbitance, the comic novelists are fascinated by quixotic disintegrations which arise from a radical instability in the identity of the original. A scene typifying these rival views takes place between Yorick and the Count de B**** in *A Sentimental Journey*, when Yorick identifies himself by pointing to a page in *Hamlet.* The count is sure that there is only one Yorick; and to Yorick's urgent demonstrations that there are in fact two, he imperturbably responds, "'Tis all one."[11]

We left Montaigne as he was about to exploit these paradoxes. He does so first of all by revising his aim of a mind-oriented candor and cultivating instead that sentimental pliancy Anna Howe calls "*consentaneousness* of corporal and animal faculties" (1:202). By studying their resemblances he starts to relish what is missing from his body and from the best love poetry: that is, the means and the representation of fruition. "One poor inch of pitiful Vigour," and kidney stones whose voiding he compares to pissing out his life piecemeal, comprehend the facts of his genital condition. His impotence is figured in the erotic poetry of Ovid and Virgil, which hides its fire under modest, uncertain, and incomplete gestures that rehearse his loss. After quoting a line of Ovid he exclaims "Methinks I am *eunuch'd* by the Expression" (*Essays*, 3:130). The metaphor keeps in play the substitutive relation of privation, tact, and delight: the fragment of his cock and the fragments it yields are consolingly mocked by verses which are fragments because they are quoted and because they say less than everything. No longer does Montaigne admire those who dare to say all they dare to do.

Richardson does everything he can to avoid such an obscene compromise. He erects a vast dualist structure designed to sink Lovelace and his consentaneous equivocality to the lower level of "sensual dream," and to buoy Clarissa up towards her native skies by ridding her of all carnal ballast. It is clear from his next novel, where Sir Charles is variously characterized as a man who lives to himself, who is present to himself, like himself and "the man of men,"[12] that Richardson had abated none of his belief in the self-identity of the original hero. Clarissa's rape and death should be construed as two plenary literalizations of his remarks about the familiar letter. The first is intended to clear away all real ambiguity from Lovelace's behavior and our judgment of it, as it shows him reducing presence to mere body in an act of shattering brutality. The second shows the soul liberated from the clinging body in an absence that is final and eternal.

Helping Richardson towards these successive literalizations is an Addisonian notion of the upper limit of originality allied with an aesthetics of the sublime supplied by Anthony Blackwall. The three levels of singularity, in Addison's opinion, comprise pointless eccentricity at the bottom; the lovable oddities of Sir Roger in the middle; and at the top the Catonic stoicism he imitated on his deathbed: "Singularity in Concerns of this Kind is to be looked upon as heroick Bravery, in which a Man leaves the Species only as he soars above it" (*Spectator*, No. 576). As Thomas Tickell was witness to Addison's singular piety in the moment of his death, so Belford is improved by the Christian composure with which Clarissa prepares for hers. Helping him to appreciate what he sees and hears is Blackwall's *The Sacred Classics Defended* (1727). It is a book, he tells Lovelace, that has taught him to prize the natural art of the Bible above all ancient pagan writers (4:8). Belford has just transcribed one of Clarissa's meditations, verses culled from Job and psalms which Richardson subsequently collected, printed, and privately circulated, and which he thought of entitling *Simplicity the True Sublime* (*Letters*, p. 222). To read Blackwall with this title in mind is to get an inkling of how Richardson associated soaring singularity with the illocutionary force of the sublime. Originality speaks in a tongue of primordial simplicity—"an original and essential language, that borrows of none, but lends to all"—operating in rare proximity both to the feelings of the speaker ("their noble and animated sentiments fill'd out their expressions") and to the object of the speech, "the infinite greatness and dignity of the thing."[13] When original language knits a sensibility that is like itself to a thing that is itself, the result is speech so powerful it fuses the nature of word and deed, description and action: "What a man endeavours to do, or commands to be done by this strong and comprehensive way of expression, he is said to do . . . what he offers, to give; and what he promises, to perform" (Blackwall, p. 120). Addison's and Clarissa's deaths authenticate everything they have ever written because their last words are just such original coalitions of tongue, sentiment, and act. Like the very best familiar letter, they exhibit nothing but "*Soul* and *Meaning*" (*Letters*, p. 68). Such sublime simplicity satisfies Richardson's high hankering after the univocal in virtue.

Wollstonecraft and Rousseau embody between them the qualities of Clarissa and Lovelace and help shed further light on the fragility of originals. Wollstonecraft is a fine example of how the British original evolves into the British radical. In her work the pursuit of sincerity and a contempt for social and sexual arts are allied to a distinctly republican idea of how private and public virtue ought to intersect. In *A Vindication of the Rights of Woman* she argues for the political as well as the moral utility of shedding double meanings from female discourse and consentaneousness from the female sensibility. However, the ultimate point of this simplicity is Clarissa-like: the acquirement of those spiritual garments that are "to clothe the soul when it leaves the body."[14] This is why she is particularly hostile to Rousseau's misreading of Sophy's clothes in *Émile*, when he interprets their "charming umbrage" in a sense not at all spiritual: "Her dress is extremely modest in appearance, and yet very coquettish in fact: she does not make a display of her charms, she conceals them; but in concealing them, she knows how to affect your imagination" (*Vindication*, p. 97). Rousseau justifies this sexualization of a young woman's appearance in terms drawn directly from Montaigne's academy: "The imagination, which decks the object of our desires, is lost in fruition."

On the wings of this imagination Rousseau skilfully places all sorts of fruition at a distance. His "original pleasure" is at its most intense when he entertains the *prospect* of reading his *reflection* upon it shortly before he dies.[15] As Derrida has exhaustively demonstrated, it is not the thing itself but its iterations and copies that please Rousseau; and these in a context of present distress (exile, persecution) whose bitterness dying will intensify. His strategy is very similar to Montaigne's: it is to confront present ruin with fragments of himself in written form.

After her separation from Gilbert Imlay ("a sort of separation of the soul . . . something torn from [myself]"[16]) Wollstonecraft deploys her imagination in the same way. The novel written in the aftermath of that unhappy love affair is about "Maria who, locked in a madhouse, uses writing (like Rousseau) as the focus of forward and backward glances. Backward, "Maria lived again in the revived emotions of youth"; forward she consoles herself with the thought that her daughter will learn to avoid such ruin by reading about it.[17] The correspondence between Maria and her felllow prisoner Darnford—initiated by means of a note passed in a copy of Rousseau's *La Nouvelle Heloise*—blossoms into an avowal of love after he reads this memoir. Despite the literary fragments she gets from him and this written record of ruin he gets from her, the novel never escapes the horrid limitation of the subtitle: *Maria, a Fragment.* Her final disintegration is delivered in broken form: "Her lover unfaithful-Pregnancy—Miscarriage—Suicide" (p. 202). Clearly the story covers the same emotional terrain traversed by Wollstonecraft between Imlay's infidelity and her attempted suicide, and it performs the same consoling function as Maria's autobiographical fragment. Darnford's literary love even mimics Godwin's, who fell in love with the author of the *Letters from Sweden* before he met her. What utterly disrupts the comforting accumulation of these "fragments" upon fragments is Wollstonecraft's death, *post partum*: a dreadful literalization of the metaphor of fragmentation with which Wollstonecraft commenced her travels two years earlier. That literalization is not ameliorated by Godwin's preface, where he writes, "There are few, to whom her writings could in any case have given pleasure, that would have wished this fragment should have been suppressed, because it is a fragment. There is . . . a melancholy delight in contemplating these unfinished productions of genius" (p. 71). Pleonasm (fragment on fragment) is replaced by tautology (fragment as fragment) in order to emphasize the originality—the creative self-identity—of the missing author. It is no wonder that Mary Shelley, the human fragment left in the wake of this absence, should write a story about a creature composed of fragments which are literally bits of dead bodies.

The difference between the pleonasm and the tautology is critical to this discussion. As long as one can quote a fragment at one's own disintegration, the substitutive play of writing is kept up and the missing element of originality makes room for imitation. But as soon as that originality is interpreted as the essence or agent of an uncompounded self-sufficiency, damage will occur; or (much the same thing) the consoling mockery of ruin—pieces on pieces—will be reduced to ruin itself—pieces as pieces. That is why Montaigne avoids those who tautologize fruition ("who have no Fruition but in Fruition"), and why Lovelace is irritated by Belford's pious circularities ("So awkwardness is a perfection in the awkward!" [4:34]). It is also why Wollstonecraft was horrified by the embalmed corpses in the church at Tonsberg: the antithesis of "noble ruins" they were "something worse than natural decay," a macabre artifice transforming the death of death into death itself, not unlike the fragments in which Godwin commemorated her departed genius (*Letters from Sweden,* p. 71).

Armed with this distinction, the reader ought to be able to make some independent sense of the two great literalizations of *Clarissa*:. the sinking into body and the rising into soul. Both involve the ruin of a body and the disturbance of a mind, and both are followed by scenarios of fragmentation. Ten disjointed meditations are written by Clarissa on torn and crumpled scraps of paper after she has been raped; and after her death Lovelace forms the ghastly plan of opening and embalming her corpse. Are these scenarios literalizing tautologies or figuring pleonasms? Nine of Clarissa's written fragments are continuous with destruction, fragments as fragments; but the tenth, consisting of ten fragments of poetry, makes fragments of fragments by matching each bit of wreckage with a quotation. In this way she saves herself from the measureless and inimitable agony suffered when "the original is too much an original" (3:204). Lovelace seems too sunk in the project of dividing Clarissa's body to make this restorative turn: "Her *heart*. . . I *will* have. I will keep it in spirits" (4:376). He even seems unconscious of the pun. But when he gets further in his anatomy, he shows how ingeniously he is managing his words: "Her bowels, if her friends are very solicitous about them, and very humble and sorrowful (and they have none of their own), shall be sent down to them." Punning, John Hollander explains, is a form of quotation;[18] and here each pun, like each of Clarissa's fragments, is quoted against a disastrous originality, that "original dust" which embalmers and certain literary executors only thicken.

Sterne's *Journal to Eliza*, a series of rapid alternations between reckless nostalgia and fantastic expectation, ought to belong with Montaigne's, Rousseau's, and Wollstonecraft's literary self-consolations. In fact Yorick takes the same route as Richardson towards the originalization of a woman, simplifying and spiritualizing as he goes. When Eliza Draper sailed out of his life, "Yorick" experienced the "Separation of Soul & Body"—the same self-tearing heartache suffered by Wollstonecraft when she set off for Scandinavia—with the addition of a severe lung hemorrhage. Figure gruesomely coincided with fact as his broken heart bled copiously into his handkerchief.[19] His written response to this joint fragmentation is an elaborate strategy of spiritualization, designed at first to expel the literal and physical elements of heartbreak from what he wishes to interpret as a figurative death, in whose aftermath he lingers a "gawsy" spirit, a shadow, a pale ghost. Death is redeemed from the letter, however, only to serve the purpose of a sublime literalization, in which Yorick and Eliza, two spirit beings, will be reunited forever in a sort of pastoral-theatrical heaven. To get there Yorick arranges himself as shadow in front of Eliza's "sweet Shadow," the miniature she had painted shortly before she left. The trick is to transform the copy into the original; so he talks to the picture, takes it out to dinner, kisses it, declares it has a soul, until the tautology is complete: "Yr picture is Yrself" (*Journal*, p. 357). The labored pretence that the *Journal* is translated from the original French manuscript (p. 322)—that is, that the original is a copy—develops a reverse symmetry with the further pretence that the copy of an absent body is the original of spiritual presence.

Yorick suffers a series of comic disasters as a consequence of turning the representation of Eliza into an original. Unless it was dying while trying to correct Lady Bradshaigh's opinion of Clarissa, Richardson suffered none for doing the same thing to his heroine. He published her meditations; he added a volume of letters to the third edition under the heading, "Restored from the Original MSS"; he had Joseph Highmore paint two portraits of her; and all the time he was thinking about originality. It is Clarissa who complains of the "author of her ruin" in words borrowed from Job, "How long will he vex my soul, and break me in pieces with words!" (4:120). But the author himself is immune to such equivokes: he has been so perfectly original about her originality that her story, especially at its consummation, bears itself out, explains itself, resists all interpretations not conformable to the frame he has placed her in and to the self-evident doctrines it proclaims. Richardson would have endorsed a suitable translation of Eagleton's account of Clarissa's death: "She achieves that pure transparency of signifier to signified which she seeks in the integrity of her script. Such transparency—the baffling enigma of that which is merely itself—is bound to appear socially opaque, a worthless tautology or resounding silence" (The *Rape of Clarissa*, p. 75). It is, however, linguistically and dramatically necessary that Clarissa be divided ("Self, then, be banished from *self*" [3:321]) if she is to be tautologized; for as Wittgenstein points out, the tautology of identity requires that the self be split so that the two halves may be compared and asserted of one another.[20] That is why Roland Barthes takes such a dim view of it, calling tautology a murderous magic governing a world that is dead and motionless.[21]

Richardson could invoke authorities for what he had done. Longinus was sublime about the sublime, Tillotson was sincere about sincerity (*Spectator*, No. 103). It was a point of honor among theorists of genius to be novel on the topic, because "in an ESSAY on ORIGINAL GENIUS, Originality of Sentiment will naturally be expected."[22] Practitioners of the simple sublime assume that this collapsing of a representation into what it represents is always the last proof of the intense unity of the sublime phenomenon. But what happens when an imperfection is doubled up—when, for example, Longinus is pusillanimous about pusillanimity?[23] Neil Hertz suggests that the Longinian sublime more often than not turns upon the representation of what is imperfect or violent, and that the force of destruction is appropriated by the creative impulse which, in figuring it, removes the threat. This "movement of disintegration and figurative reconstitution" is complicated by the way Longinus quotes, or cuts, sublime texts into his own: by means of this further mimicry of the disintegration represented in them, an extra reconstitutive flourish is given to "the sublime turn."[24] It isn't difficult to see the resemblance between these pleonasms of reconstitution and Montaigne's transformation of impotence into the castrating pleasure of reading bits of Ovid. In both texts damage is controlled by setting up an oscillation between its literal and figurative manifestations. That control is lost when figurative difference is pared away to leave the "tautegorical" expression of identity.[25]

The status of this oscillation in the books I have been talking about may be measured by the role played by books within them, especially when the books act as mediators between lovers. Montaigne makes an emblem of his reconstitutive turns out of Socrates, who remembers falling in love (like Dante's Paolo) over a book (*Essays*, 3:147). Rousseau's Émile and Sophy exchange books before they exchange vows: she gives him Fénelon's *Telemachus* and he gives her the *Spectator*. His *Heloise* brings Darnford and Maria at least temporarily together in *The Wrongs of Woman*. But in the *Vindication*, where Wollstonecraft is aiming for the fullness of original sentiments, books—"the reveries of the stupid novelists" (*Vindication*, p. 203)—are put aside. In Yorick's *Journal* the transformation of Eliza's shadow into Eliza's self will be thoroughly accomplished when she comes ashore with her half of the book he has been writing; then the *Journal* will be like itself. This is like Pamela's surrender of her journal-girdle to Mr. B, like Harriet's reading of Sir Charles's letters to Dr Bartlett, and like Sir Charles's perusal of Clementina's celebrated paper. The only book of any importance to these characters is the book they are in: they write and read only themselves because their compositions are entirely of a piece with their lives. Ann Radcliffe, as ardent an exponent of the simple sublime as Richardson, deserves to be mentioned as a writer partly aware of the consequences of pursuing it. She knows that descriptions of uncompounded sublimity demand repetitions which "must appear tautologous"; and when Emily St. Aubert crosses the frontier dividing sublime spectacle from implication in the violence and terror of the thing itself, the transition is clearly marked: she laments "the irresistable force of circumstances over the taste and powers of the mind" which prevents her from being able to concentrate on a book.[26]

Clarissa has a choice. When Belford hands over extracts of the letters he has had from Lovelace, her story is complete; and if it were as full of soul and meaning as Richardson supposes, she would have no more trouble in reading it than Pamela or Yorick have reading their journals. As it happens, she finds it a dismal story, one she is unable to read with patience because it is a chronicle of sufferings she doesn't understand (4:74). In this state of unexemplary perplexity she turns to the book of Job, where her feelings of self-division, doubt, and impatience are most aptly represented. Job describes the agony of being turned into a public symbol, ripe with meaning for everyone but himself: "He hath broken me asunder . . . and set me up for his mark. . . . He hath made me also a byword of the people" (Job 16: 12; 17:6). When Clarissa quotes this complaint at her own ruin (4:101), it is hard not to think that she has her creator in mind, between whom and Job's intriguing parallels may be run. They both risk their favorite creatures in a bet with their antitypes (Satan and Lovelace), and when questions are asked they quote their creation at itself. God quotes leviathan and the war-horse as the self-evidence of the creative will's coincidence with power and meaning; rather milder but of the same order are Richardson's directions, "In page 95 of this volume the reader will see. . . ." Neither loses faith in his creature's capacity to survive the upward collapse into pure symbolization, and neither understands that a tested mark, a tried byword, can no longer plentifully declare the thing as it is.

With this book Clarissa is able to reproduce the sublime turn of her tenth paper. Finding in Job a complaint that matches her fragmented condition, she quotes (cuts) it into "fragments" on fragments. The pleonasm offers the same figurative refuge from tautology that Montaigne finds in quoting Ovid, or that Longinus gets from cutting up Demosthenes. Lovelace understands what she is doing because he has always understood the difference between fruit and pursuit, and between deadening tautegoricality and figurative oscillation. That is why, in the joke he plays on Hickman, he tries desperately to allegorize Death out of his exclusively deathly function (3:495). Richardson's failure to understand this difference, or his desire to obscure it, suggests that he is not quite guiltless of the violence Lovelace and the hermeneuts are generally blamed for.

NOTES

[1]"Of sincerity toward God and Man," in *The Works of the Most Reverend Dr. John Tillotson, Late Lord Archbishop of Canterbury*, 2 vols. (London: Ralph Barker, 1712), 1:7. Excerpted in *Spectator* Nos. 103, 352, 557.

[2]Edward Young, *Conjectures on Original Composition* (London, 1759; rpt. Leeds: The Scolar Press, 1966), p. 76.

[3]Samuel Richardson, *Selected Letters*, ed. John Carroll (Oxford: Oxford Univ. Press, 1964), p. 335.

[4]See Terry Castle, *Clarissa's Ciphers* (Ithaca: Cornell Univ. Press, 1979); Terry Eagleton, *The Rape of Clarissa* (Oxford: Basil Blackwell, 1982), p. 66. Warner seems to have taken a much bigger risk in floating this hypothesis in the twentieth century than Joseph Priestley in the eighteenth. Nobody called him heartless for suggesting that "Even the prudent and virtuous Mr. Richarson hath interested his reader so much in the character of *Lovelace* . . . that, I believe, there are few of his readers who would be displeased with the success of his base designs upon any other woman than Clarissa herself": *A Course of Lectures on Oratory and Criticism* (London, 1777; rpt. Menston: Scolar Press, 1968), p. 129. To the objection that Priestley's and Warner's readings are typical of males, it needs to be said that the authorized reading insisted upon by Richardson (who was notorious for rejecting all readerly advice and for sharply correcting heretical readings), and then endorsed by Eagleton, are male interpretations too. It is significant that Priestley concedes the impossibility of free interpretation faced with "Clarissa herself."

[5]Preface to *The Borderers, Wordsworth's Poetry and Prose,* ed. W.M. Merchant (London: Rupert Hart-Davis, 1955), p. 105.

[6]"Upon Some Verses of Virgil," *Essays of Michael Seigneur of Montaigne*, trans. Charles Cotton, 3 vols. (London, 1711), 3:130-31. I have used Cotton's translation because it was popular in the eighteenth century. There are no clear

echoes to indicate that it was this translation Richardson used; perhaps, like Sterne, he caught the flavor of Montaigne's essay secondhand from Charron's compilation *Charron on Wisdom,* "englished by Dr. Stanhope" (1729).

[7]Samuel Richardson, *Clarissa: or, the History of a Young Lady,* 4 vols. (London: Dent's Everyman's Library, 1932; rpt. 1976), 1:512.

[8]He seems to associate two ideas with Montaigne here—upper class women and postponement. In the latest edition of the novel Angus Ross identifies the source of the first as the essay "Of Three Commerces"—*Clarissa* (Harmondsworth: Penguin, 1985), p. 1517. But Lovelace's preference for deferred delights and a winding game—one he never tires of declaring—belongs to "Upon Some Verses of Virgil."

[9]Alexander Pope, "The First Satire in the Second Book of Horace," in *Imitations of Horace,* ed. John Butt (London: Methuen, 1939), lines 51-52; Joseph Addison, *Spectator* No. 562; Laurence Sterne, *The Life and Opinions of Tristram Shandy, Gentleman,* ed. James A. Work (New York: Odyssey Press, 1940), p. 7.

[10]For more extensive discussions of what Thomas McFarland has named "the originality paradox" see Thomas McFarland, *Originality and Imagination* (Baltimore: Johns Hopkins Univ. Press, 1985); David Quint, *Origin and Originality in Renaissance Literature* (New Haven: Yale Univ. Press, 1983); Robert L. Chibka, "The Stranger within Young's Conjectures," *ELH* 53, 3 (1986): 541-65.

[11]Laurence Sterne, *A Sentimental Journey through France and Italy by Mr. Yorick,* ed. Gardner D. Stout (Berkeley: Univ. of California Press, 1967), p. 223.

[12]*Sir Charles Grandison,* ed. Jocelyn Harris, 3 vols. (Oxford: Oxford Univ. Press, 1972), 2:78, 189; 3:75.

[13]Anthony Blackwall, *The Sacred Classics Defended* (London, 1727; rpt. New York: Garland, 1970), pp. 10, 334, 332. Blackwall writes conscious of Addison on the force and translatability of primitive languages, particularly Hebrew and English. See p. 324 and *Spectator,* No. 405.

[14]Mary Wollstonecraft, *A Vindication of the Rights of Woman* (London: J. M. Dent, 1929), p. 60.

[15]Jean-Jacques Rousseau, *Reveries of the Solitary Walker,* trans. Peter France (Harmondsworth: Penguin, 1979), p. 32.

[16]Mary Wollstonecraft, *Letters Written during a Short Residence in Sweden, Norway and Denmark,* ed. Carol H. Poston (Lincoln: Univ. of Nebraska Press, 1976), p. 176.

[17]Mary Wollstonecraft, *The Wrongs of Woman,* ed. Gary Kelly (Oxford: Oxford Univ. Press, 1976), p. 82.

[18]John Hollander, *The Figure of the Echo* (Berkeley: Univ. of California Press, 1981), p. 63.

[19]Laurence Sterne, *The Journal to Eliza* in *Letters of Laurence Sterne,* ed. Lewis Perry Curtis (Oxford: Clarendon Press, 1935), pp. 374, 366.

[20]Ludwig Wittgenstein, *Philosophical Investigations,* trans. G.E.M. Anscombe (Oxford: Basil Blackwell, 1968), paragraphs 84e, 216.

[21]Roland Barthes, *Mythologies,* trans. Annette Lavers (London: Granada Publishing, 1973), p. 152. Studying the self-reflexive imagery in the poetry of Andrew Marvell and Seamus Heaney, Christopher Ricks comes to the interesting conclusion that tautological conceits are especially prevalent in times of civil war: *The Force of Poetry* (Oxford: Clarendon Press, 1984), pp. 34-59.

[22]William Duff, *An Essay on Original Genius* (London, 1767; rpt. Gainesville: Scholars' Facsimiles and Reprints, 1964), p. x.

[23]Of Longinus's remarks about the loss of political liberty and the decay of the sublime, Gibbon observes, "Here, too, we may say of Longinus, 'His own example strengthens all his laws.' Instead of proposing his sentiments with a manly boldness, he insinuates them with the most guarded caution, puts them into the mouth of a friend, and . . . makes a show of refuting them." Edward Gibbon, *The Decline and Fall of the Roman Empire,* ed. Dero A. Saunders (Harmondsworth: Penguin, 1981), p. 84, n. 10.

[24]Neil Hertz, "A Reading of Longinus," *CritI* 9 (March 1983): 585, 591.

[25]The neologism is invented by Coleridge in *Aids to Reflection* to name the shift from "expressing a different subject but with a resemblance" to "expressing the same subject but with a difference"—that is, from allegory to tautology. The passage is cited by Stephen Knapp in a remarkable chapter, "Coleridge on Allegory and Violence," in *Personification and the Sublime* (Cambridge, Mass.: Harvard Univ. Press, 1985), pp. 7-50.

[26]Ann Radcliffe, *A Journey made in the Summer of 1794* (London, 1795), p. 419; *The Mysteries of Udolpho* in *The Novels of Ann Radcliffe* (London: Hurst, Robinson, 1824), p. 396.

SEL 28 (1988)
ISSN 0039-3657

Johnson's Elephant: The Reader of *The Rambler*

MARY M. VAN TASSEL

> It is well known by experience to the nations which employed elephants in war, that, though by the terror of their bulk, and the violence of their impression, they often threw the enemy into disorder, yet there was always danger in the use of them . . . for, if their first charge could be supported, they were easily driven back upon their confederates. . . .
>
> I know not whether those, who have so vehemently urged the inconveniences and dangers of an active life, have not made use of arguments that may be retorted with equal force upon themselves; and whether the happiness of a candidate for literary fame be not subject to the same uncertainty with that of him who governs provinces, commands armies, presides in the senate, or dictates in the cabinet.[1]

It is a critical commonplace that Johnson's audience for the Rambler is the "common reader," that ordinary man who is "the perfect representative of all mankind,"[2] a reasonable person whose learning and experience take in the whole circle of polished life, an allegorical or archetypal figure emblematic of those "select minds" fitted for judgment "by learning and by virtue" (3, 3:18). The common reader stands for public opinion in the author's lifetime, and for the eventual reckoning of posterity. He is the "higher judicature, and the publick, which is never corrupted, nor often deceived, is to pass the last sentence upon literary claims" (23, 3:128). The reading process is a trial at which the author cannot hide or dissemble, but "necessarily discovers the degree of his merit to his judges" (1, 3:5), readers sophisticated enough to rule upon the text according to the "extent of his [the author's] knowledge, or the sprightliness of his imagination" (1, 3:7), who judge the author's work without "prepossessions" and see clearly those faults to which the author is "blinded . . . by innumerable prejudices" (21, 3:120).

Mary M. Van Tassel is a PhD. candidate at the University of Maryland, College Park.

The traits and attainments that qualify a man for the bench of common readership in Johnson's court are not always directly stated, but can be inferred from the Rambler's topics, references, and allusions. The reader is a highly social being who, though he follows no particular profession, is familiar with the vocabulary and customs of all. He has sufficient learning to be conversant with classic literature, but is "uncorrupted with literary prejudices."[3] He is a well-informed Lockean in a universe whose workings are revealed by contemporary natural philosophy. A city-dweller, he has the sophisticate's familiarity with the pastimes and habits of the world. To judge from the sense of otherness which accompanies his references to women, he is a man. He is not a youth, but has lived long enough to distill his experience into habitual attitudes and thoughts. He is willing and able to subject his own motives and behavior to introspection, and he is a moral person, a Christian who is motivated by "the two great movers of the human mind, the desire of good, and the fear of evil" (1, 3:6). In short, he is the counterpart and mirror of the Rambler himself.

When we look for his direct presence in the *Rambler* essays, however, we find not this generalized, steady, moral, and just reader, but a crowd of more alarming individual beings. Just as Samuel Johnson works through and behind the Rambler, so combining to compose the common reader is a hydra-headed real reader whose peculiar attitudes and attributes make him intimidating to the author. *Rambler* 1, the Rambler's curtain-opener on the stage of the periodical essay, dwells humorously on the writer's anxieties. With every new publication, the author appears before the public as a defendant in a trial in which the judges may not even hear his case unless they are already inclined to favor him (1, 3:5). From the outset he is aware of "dangers" and anticipates censure (1, 3:4). Tropes of trial lead by latent association to similes of wooing. In his desire to win over his audience, the writer must go courting like a suitor, and can expect that if his suit fails, his presumption will be rewarded with "an unbounded contempt, indulged by most minds without scruple, as an honest triumph over unjust claims, and exorbitant expectations" (1, 3:6).

Smooth it over how he may (*Rambler* 1 smooths it over with self-deprecatory laughter), the engagement of writer and reader is a hazardous one whose recurrent metaphor is that of warfare. For many reasons, writers and their works are "in danger from every common reader" (4, 3:20). The text in the hands of the reader is the ground for a battle to the finish; before the reader has read very far, "The question concerning the merit of the day is soon decided" (1, 3:7). In this battle, the writer's heavy weapon—the elephant he sends out to trample his opponent (21, 3:116)—is his ability to arouse the imagination. Whether by his manner, where his "spirit and intrepidity" can force surrender "as to a resistless power" (1, 3:5), or by his matter, in which examples "take possession of the memory by a kind of violence, and produce effects almost without the intervention of the will" (4, 3:22), the writer must conquer by force of words. Like the elephant to which it is compared, this weapon carries with it its own dangers.

The author needs all the power he can muster because his opponent is not disposed, by inclination or by attribute, to surrender easily. The reader's attitudes and behavior ever threaten the security of the writer's fond delusion that his work will ensure lasting fame, that he has been "furnished by the muses with the arms which never can be blunted, and which no art or strength of their adversaries can elude or resist" (21, 3:116). Indeed, the writer's strategic victory with any particular work can set in motion a long-range defeat, can become the cause of a greater subjugation; for he who has enforced the regard of the public must keep it by paying continual "tribute" to a master who is by nature capricious, fickle, captious, and demanding. The author's popularity can be lost as easily by overconfidence as it can be destroyed by anxious overwork (22, 3:118). His vassalage of "past service" counts for nothing today (22, 3:118). Like a jaded tyrant, the hydra-headed real reader constantly demands novelty, and is apt without warning to transfer his favors to a new subject (22, 3:118). The writer is at the mercy of a public which frequently changes its object and grants favor according to the winds of taste (1, 3:8). All the innate qualities, individual and social, of the human species fight against the author's victory over such an opponent:

> He that endeavours after fame by writing, solicits the regard of a multitude fluctuating in pleasures, or immersed in business, without time for intellectual amusements; he appeals to judges prepossessed by passions, or corrupted by prejudices, which preclude their approbation of any new performance. Some are too indolent to read any thing, till its reputation is established; others too envious to promote that fame, which gives them pain by its increase. What is new is opposed, because most are unwilling to be taught; and what is known is rejected. . . . The learned are afraid to declare their opinion early, lest they should put their reputation in hazard; the ignorant always imagine themselves giving some proof of delicacy, when they refuse to be pleased: and he that finds his way to reputation, through all these obstructions,

> must acknowledge that he is indebted to other causes besides his industry, his learning, or his wit.
>
> (2, 3:14)

This troublesome reader is not disposed to be dispassionate about his contest with the author. He has a stubbornly good opinion of himself, is reluctant to think himself in error or ignorance (3, 3:15), and constantly asserts his right to be entertained and pleased on his own ground. Wanting to see in the text only a flattering mirror, he nags the author to write about transient current affrays or trivial social affairs (10, 3:52). He prefers reading what he knows to venturing where he is unsure, so complains when the Rambler does not echo the Spectator (23, 3:129). He often believes that he can write as well as, if not better than the professional, and complains if his letters are not published. If he is given the chance to comment upon a work in progress, he harasses the author with "heterogeneous ideas" (23, 3:126) and offers proposals for "specious alteration" (23, 3:127). He pesters for details about the author's personal life, but hides his own epistolary lights under assumed names, in which anonymity he proffers advice for the regulation of Rambler's conduct and contributions for the assistance of his understanding (20, 3:111). The common reader in his everyday person is often affected, pretentious, inconstant, and malicious; the writer who would climb to fame upon the "unsteady" "pinacles" of popular praise cannot promise himself the blessing of fame, but trusts his happiness to the winds (20, 3:114).

There are several things to say about this reader of Johnson's. One is that to some extent he must have been the exaggerated projection of his author's anxieties, fears which every writer shares. Another is that he is perhaps projected as a challenge to the reader's sense of fair play. Nevertheless, whether their antagonism was real, imagined, or rhetorical, the constant presence of two audiences—the "common reader" and the real, not surely friendly daily reader—determined many of Johnson's strategies in *The Rambler.* For reasons that had to do not only with his desire for popular acceptance, but that lay deep in Johnson's conception of the human condition; for important and central reasons, in the workshop of the text, the daily reader, with all his prejudices and animosities, had to be converted to the common reader. And if he was not to be antagonized or driven away, this process had to be accomplished with subtle skill. The most important technique Johnson uses to achieve his end is to enlist the reader on the side of the Rambler. It is for this reason that most of Johnson's criticism of everyday foolishness, weakness, or evil is accomplished in letters from created personae. Here the letter-writers either betray their own shortcomings or point the finger at others'.

Either way, the reader is elevated to a superior moral vantage point and stands with the Rambler, condemning or laughing at others. Furthermore, if he is brought by analogy to laugh at himself, he is supported by the brotherly presence of the Rambler, who constantly uses the pronoun "we," includes his own failings in his great catalogue of human weakness, and tempers his condemnations with assertions of compassionate acknowledgment and forgiveness.

In the engagement between reader and writer, another of Johnson's devices for disarming his readers is satire directed against authors. The Rambler constantly pokes fun at writers by exaggeration. We smile at the writer whose "alacrity" is heightened "to think in how many places he shall hear what he is now writing, read with *ecstasies* tomorrow" (1, 3:8, emphasis added), and while we smile, we forgive him. Who can resist an author who sets out for our laughter his own temptation to "the pleasure of wantoning in common topicks" (2, 3:9)? The surprise of the verb as well as the playfulness of the assonance compel our pleased surrender. In the *Dictionary,* Johnson gives many meanings to *wanton,* and all of them play in the phrase here: the writer is "frolicsome; gay; sportive; airy"; he is also a "trifler" and an "insignificant flutterer." If he is "lustful," he is also "luxuriant"; if his work is "irregular," or "turned fortuitously," it is also worthy of "a word of slight endearment." Johnson never grants the writer a privileged position; he is not the representative of a kind of intellectual priesthood, but merely "a man of lively fancy" with a propensity to suffer from an incurable malady, the "infatuation" of appealing to "the tribunal of succeeding times" (2, 3:12).

When Johnson joins with his reader, either to criticize others or to step back and laugh at himself, his aim is not to defeat his reader, or even to jolly him into complaisant approbation. His ultimate intention is to demonstrate that the reader and the writer are one. If Cowley is criticized for deluding himself about his desire for solitude (6, 3:33), he held a delusion common to most men. By analogy, if the public is a mass of fickle readers, capricious and changeable, their desire for variety is but part of the natural condition of man. Like Cowley, his readers (and Johnson's) must find the causes of their unhappiness within themselves; like his readers, Cowley should have remembered that changes "keep the mind in action" (6, 3:35). If the reader is unreasonable, it is in part because no one is able to be reasonable all of the time. He is dependent upon his "animal faculties" and finds it difficult to withstand their impulses. As Wimsatt reminds us, in Johnson's Lockean epistemology a man's soul was "a kind of anomalous prisoner in an invisible world of matter, receiving through the operation upon it of corpuscular agents many and vivid reports of its milieu, but all indirect, and the most vivid having a low degree of reliability."[4] To demonstrate our relationship to natural law, the Rambler uses the metaphor of civil law: the "motions of sense are instantaneous, its objects strike unsought; we are accustomed to follow its directions, and therefore often submit to the sentence without examining the authority of the judge" (7, 3:39). The "trepidations of the balance" which are unendurable to the author (1, 3:7) are also "the equipoise of an empty mind, which, having no tendency to one motion more than another but as it is *impelled by some external power,* must always have recourse to foreign objects (5, 3:27, emphasis added). Here the metaphors commingle: the uneasy, frightening, and incomplete balance of ambivalent desires and influences is a phase in the life process which is itself a battle.

It is in the realm of metaphor that Johnson unites the daily reader to the writer, creating that "common reader" who is in some sense both reader and writer. As Fussell points out, in "the precariousness of genuine civilization,"[5] that civilization which must be the joint creation of author and reader, military metaphors are figures for the moral battles of life. In the *Rambler* essays, tropes of warfare and battle are not limited to the struggles of writer against reader, but symbolize a man's moral strife in all areas of life: "Such is the state of all moral virtue, that it is always uncertain and variable, sometimes extending to the whole compass of duty, and sometimes shrinking into a narrow space, and fortifying only a few avenues of the heart, while all the rest is left open to the incursions of appetite, or given up to the dominion of wickedness" (70, cited by Fussell). Warfare was an appropriate trope for a dualistic view of life. Fussell suggests that this Augustan, "humanistic myth of dualism" is twofold: "(1) man's inner convictions are in conflict—or should be—with the practices of a 'corrupt' world outside; and (2) within man himself the inimical element of his psychic hierarchy, the will and the flesh, conduct with each other an analogous battle."[6] What seems at first a simple metaphor—the author apparently pitted in battle against his reader—thus assumes a more complex and quite different meaning in the context of all the *Rambler* essays. From the viewpoint of the writer pitted against his public (Fussell's first dualism), the Rambler speaks for inner convictions. The metaphors of struggle embody his sense of being alone against an antagonistic world. By various stratagems, he lifts the reader out of the hostile crowd to enlist him on the author's side in the struggle against corruption. In a deeper sense, however, the writer becomes a metaphor for the soul, that part of any man where his reason and conscience join to fight, not so much against others as against his own sense-bombarded, wind-blown, and fallible impulses. When the Rambler writes "I know not

. . . whether the happiness of a candidate for literary fame be not subject to the same uncertainty with that of him who governs provinces, commands armies, presides in the senate, or dictates in the cabinet" (21, 3:117), he is identifying the writer with the will itself, that ruler or general who endeavors to command the uneasy outlying dominions of his own being.

This moral battle which creates the common reader is exemplified at all levels of *The Rambler.* Not only does it color episode and character, lexicon and figure; it can be seen as determining the structure of many essays. *Rambler* 107 presents a particularly vivid example. Here a hilarious monologue from Properantia, a teenaged scatterbrain burbling in paragraph-length, breathless sentences about the forthcoming change in the calendar, is paired with a sombre letter from Amicus, appealing to our compassion for the plight of prostitutes, victims more of society's cruelty than of their own weakness.[7] The Rambler provides no transition between the letters, and offers as explanation of their juxtaposition only the pretext of pleasing the reader by "uniting gay and solemn subjects in the same paper" (107, 4:205). Thematic links between the first, funny essay and the second, tragic one, are left to the reader's reason to discover. Properantia writes about time, but her attitude to it is that of the pampered young girl who, without a care to darken her sheltered world, regards only her own pleasure and thinks of the time "as little as I can" (107, 4:206). She longs for "a year of confusion" and would like to "leap over . . . months of restraint" (108, 4:207). The "new style," which she delightedly conceives will be her liberation, will free her to "run from ball to ball, and from drum to drum; and spend all my time without tasks, and without account, and go out without telling whither, and come home without regard to prescribed hours, or family-rules" (107, 4:207). Immediately follows the account of the piteous prostitutes, with its reminder that "the opportunities which every day affords of relieving the most wretched of human beings are overlooked and neglected, with equal disregard of policy and goodness" (107, 4:209). No visible stones are thrown, either at Properantia or at the prostitutes, but a complex relation of cause and effect is implied. The time that is Properantia's opportunity for license should be her opportunity to behave herself and to do good. No change in "style" should disburden us of the moral obligations requisite to civilized life, and no change in nomenclature will relieve us of the necessity to use for good the all-too-short time of mortal existence. The Properantias of the world not only endanger their own lives—if, naive and pleasure-loving, she is allowed to run riot, she may end up like the tragic prostitutes—they also by their shallow vanity perpetuate a society to whose tragedies they are blind. In juxtaposing these letter-parables, the Rambler reminds his colleague reader that moral warfare, though uncomfortable, is unavoidable. To turn one's back on the battle is to condemn oneself and others to tragedy. This moral is unstated, and must be drawn by the reader. The writer's rhetorical power, which has led the reader from laughter to reflection, forces him to think about his own reaction to the two letters. Both the intensity of his emotions (the Properantia piece is very funny; the prostitute piece very sad) and the indeterminacy of the juxtaposition insist that the reader place himself in the essay, if only to put its two warring parts together. As the *real* reader, he has demanded variety from the Rambler—and the Rambler has given him variety. As the *real* reader, he has been forced by the writer's power to laugh and to sigh. When he goes a further step, when he reflects upon the meaning of the halves of the essay, upon their bearing on each other, and upon their application to his own life, then he is changed. He must look past the "secondary qualities" of life—its glittering color, its amusing variety—and infer its "primary" qualities—its grim realities, its sober obligations, and its opportunities for moral choice.

Johnson does battle with his reader just as he believed a man should do battle with his own weaknesses, and for the same reason. It is only in this struggle that we become completely human. Since we are mortal, divided and imperfect, we can no more win the battle than can the individual, real reader become a generalized abstraction. Both transformations must await the processes of time. The soul will find its triumph and its identity with others only in heaven; the real reader will become the common reader only as he merges into posterity. Nevertheless, we achieve in diurnal battle occasional moments of revelation. In a microcosm of the entire *Rambler* series, *Rambler* 107 transforms the real reader of Johnson's essays into the common reader of the Rambler's moral domain.

NOTES

[1]Samuel Johnson, *The Rambler* 21, 3:116. I have used the following edition, from which all quotations are taken: *The Yale Edition of the Works of Samuel Johnson,* 15 vols. New Haven: Yale Univ. Press, 1958-, cited by *Rambler* number followed by volume and page numbers.

[2]Robert DeMaria, Jr., "The Ideal Reader: A Critical Fiction," *PMLA* 93 (May 1978):463-74.

[3]Samuel Johnson, *Lives of the English Poets,* ed. G. B. Hill, 3 vols. (Oxford: Clarendon Press, 1905), cited in DeMaria, "The Ideal Reader," p. 463.

[4]William K. Wimsatt, Jr., *Philosophic Words: A Study of Style and Meaning in the Rambler and Dictionary of Samuel Johnson* (New Haven: Yale Univ. Press, 1948), p. 94.

[5]Paul Fussell, *The Rhetorical World of Augustan Humanism: Ethics and Imagery from Swift to Burke* (Oxford: Clarendon Press, 1965), p. 142.

[6]Fussell, p. 41.

[7]The letter from Amicus, written in a very different, softer style from Johnson's, was attributed by Bishop Percy to "Mr Joseph Simpson, a young Lawyer of Lincoln's Inn." (D. Nichol Smith, *Bodleian Quarterly Record* 7 (1934):508-509. See the note to *Rambler* 107 in 4:207.) As the pairing of the letter with the Properantia essay is Johnson's, who was willing to have the essay attributed to himself, my point about the rhetorical relation between the two is unaffected by the dual authorship.

SEL 28 (1988)
ISSN 0039-3657

William Collins, Samuel Johnson, and the Use of Biographical Details

MARY MARGARET STEWART

In April 1756 Samuel Johnson wrote Joseph Warton and asked: "What becomes of poor dear Collins?" His epithet "poor Collins," a phrase he used five times in letters to the Warton brothers between 1754 and 1756, has remained associated with the poet William Collins. Johnson, using the term *poor* to mean "deserving pity or sympathy, unfortunate," refers to Collins's physical and mental or emotional condition.[1] Today, as indeed in the latter part of the eighteenth century, scholars and biographers have been intrigued by Collins's life in the 1750s, the decade in which Collins became ill, weak, and reportedly "mad."[2] An examination of his activities during the previous decade, however, may yield information useful to our understanding of Collins.

Because the adjective *poor* also means "having little money or means," Johnson's epithet has also characterized Collins during the decade of the forties, a decade in which he was struggling to achieve fame as a poet, a struggle made more severe, his contemporary biographers tell us, because of his lack of money.[3] His "poorness," or poverty, according to the traditional account, kept him distracted and contributed significantly to his inability to complete his various projects. Samuel Johnson, John Langhorne, and Gilbert White all use the term *poverty* when discussing Collins. In supporting his maxim that "man is not born for happiness," Johnson observes that "Collins, who, while he 'studied to live,' felt no evil but poverty, no sooner 'lived to study' than his life was assailed by more dreadful calamities, disease and insanity."[4]

Indeed, Alexander Hay, a historian of Chichester and a resident of that city during years that Collins's sister Ann lived there, relates Collins's poverty of the 1740s to his "nervous disorder" of the 1750s: "His mind had been so long harrassed with anxiety, his distress had made so deep an impression on him, that he fell into a nervous

Mary Margaret Stewart, Graeff Professor of English, Gettysburg College, is working on a biography of William Collins. Her other current interests include eighteenth-century marriages and parent-child relations.

disorder, followed by a great depression of spirits, which reduced him to the most deplorable weakness."[5]

When Oliver Sigworth published his study of Collins in 1965, he speculated that Collins's "hardships" during the years 1744-1749 "have no doubt generally been sentimentally overstated." P. L. Carver, in his biography of Collins published in 1967, raised doubts not only about the poverty of Collins during the forties but also about the reported size of Collins's inheritance in 1749 after the death of his uncle, Lt. Colonel Edmund Martin, concluding both reports had been exaggerated.[6] Yet no evidence has been produced to confirm these suspicions, and the traditional image of Collins persists—a struggling, poverty-stricken poet, who in 1749 inherited a sizable estate only to become sick, weak, even "mad" and thus could neither develop his talents uninhibited by anxiety produced over financial concerns nor enjoy the freedom a large cash balance provides.

Vital evidence is now provided by property leases executed during the 1740s. These leases, never fully explored by Collins's previous biographers, not only reveal facts about Collins but also help us to verify contemporary accounts of Collins, or at the least to make more reliable judgments about these accounts. Among these, none is more ambiguous or tantalizing than Samuel Johnson's short *Life of Collins* nor is any more central to the creation of what has become the prevailing image of Collins. The leases of the 1740s, used with other information we have, enable us to analyze Samuel Johnson's role as biographer of Collins, to reexamine his relationship with Collins, and to question the image of Collins which has emerged from Johnson's biography.

While Collins was a student at Magdalen College, Oxford, supported by his allowance as a demy, his uncle, Charles Collins, a resident of Charterhouse, began writing his will on 2 September 1741 and completed it almost one year later on 19 June 1742. In this will he left his nephew William Collins freehold property just outside the west gate of Chichester in St. Bartholomew parish. He also instructed that "all Rents Arrearges and Profits" from this property "from one Year" after his death should go to his nephew William. If Charles Collins died in December 1742, as records seem to indicate he did, then William Collins would have begun to collect rent on this freehold property in December 1743. This small sum and source of income may have been one of several factors which prompted Collins to leave Oxford for London sometime between December 1743 and May 1744.[7]

Once in London, he received a small allowance from his uncle, Lt. Colonel Edmund Martin, who was then stationed in Scotland and whose agent in London was William Collins's cousin George Payne, an apothecary who lived just off Berkeley Square on Bruton Street.[8] He must have received at least a small sum for the sale of his *Epistle to Thomas Hanmer,* which was published by Dodsley and Cooper on 11 May 1744. He also raised money from the sale of his proposals for *A History of the Revival of Learning,* which were circulating in Oxford and London at least by July 1744.[9]

On 3 July 1744 Collins's mother died in Chichester, and thus Collins and his two sisters inherited property their father had accumulated through the years and which their mother had endeavored to retain for them.[10] Although Elizabeth Collins's will indicates that her three children are to divide equally all the revenues from her estate, Collins, in fact, inherited property at her death that went directly to him and to him alone—six small holdings containing approximately twenty-three acres in Cackham Manor, property secured in 1704 by his grandfather Edmund Martin and then settled upon his mother. On 6 November 1744, at the Court Baron of Cackham Manor, Collins was admitted to these copyholds, a copyhold being a "customary estate in England, the only visible title to which consists of the copies of the court rolls, which are made out by the steward of the manor, on a tenant's being admitted to any parcel of land, or tenement belonging to the manor."[11] Just one month later, on 18 December 1744, he raised £100 by signing a conditional surrender of the land to Anne Challen; that is, he used his Cackham Manor land as collateral for a loan. When the interest and principal on this loan came due on 18 June 1745 the interest but not the principal was paid to Anne Challen. Shortly thereafter, on 29 June 1745, Collins signed an absolute surrender of these Cackham Manor lands to his cousin George Payne, who eventually paid all the principal and interest on Collins's loan. The manor records indicate that Collins remained in London rather than returning to Chichester for the negotiations and transactions in November and December but that both Collins and his cousin Payne were in Chichester at the end of June when Collins signed over his copyholds to Payne.[12]

On 12 August 1745 Elizabeth Collins (the poet's sister) proved her mother's will.[13] On October fourth and fifth Collins was in Chichester, where he and his two sisters negotiated the sale of four leasehold properties their family held in St. Bartholomew parish. Francis Soan paid £400 for these four leases. Since, however, their father's cousin, Mrs. Elizabeth Staker, had redeemed one of these leases for their mother in 1743, the three Collins heirs received only £274.[14] Because their mother's will directs that the moneys raised from sales of her real and personal estate were "equally to be divided between them [Elizabeth, Ann, William] share and share alike," Collins's share would have been about £91.

On 5 March 1746 George Payne proved Charles Collins's will in London.[15] By early April Collins was in Chichester negotiating to raise money on the freehold property his uncle left him in St. Bartholomew parish, the property from which he had been receiving rent since December 1743. On 10 April he signed a mortgage loan for £50 from Thomas Sefton. On 30 May 1746 Collins was again in Chichester, this time negotiating the sale of his freehold property. William Milton, Junior, who bought the property, paid Collins £12 and assumed the principal and interest of his loan from Sefton (51/05/00). As in April, Collins described himself as "of the City of Chichester."[16]

On 1 May 1747 Collins was in Chichester, for on that day he and his sisters sold the East Street house, lease, and easement to Williams Crowcher of Chichester, an apothecary. Crowcher paid the Collinses £230, of which sum Collins's share would have been somewhat over £76. When Collins signed the documents he described himself for the first time as "of London Gentleman." Thus, with the sale of the large flintstone house in which he had grown up, Collins changed his legal residence from Chichester to London.[17]

By the middle of April 1749 Lt. Colonel Edmund Martin, now sixty-seven years old, lay gravely ill in Chichester. On 19 April he wrote his will. After making small bequests to a daughter and son of his late younger brother and to his servant, he bequeathed all the rest of his real and personal estate "wheresoever and whatsoever" to his nephew William Collins and his nieces Elizabeth Collins and Ann Collins. Finally, he appointed his niece Elizabeth Collins sole executrix of his will. Later that day he died.[18]

On 26 April 1749 Edmund Martin's name was removed from the Army List; the next day Major John Lafausille, who had served under Martin for several years, was promoted to the rank of Lt. Colonel in Martin's old regiment, the prestigious Eighth Regiment of Foot, the King's Own Regiment.[19] On 30 May 1749 Elizabeth Collins proved her uncle's will in London. At the end of May, then, Collins and his sisters would have received considerable sums of money, for whatever else was included in Martin's unspecified estate, we can assume there was some back pay and can be sure there was the sale of his commission. The price of Martin's commission of Lieutenant Colonel and Captain would have been worth at least £2,000, and if, as his obituary indicates, he was also Colonel Commandant, his commission would have been worth at least £5,000.[20]

These legal documents, primarily leases, tell us a number of things:

First, they help us locate Collins on particular dates, and they indicate what he considered his legal residences during the 1740s.

Second, they reveal that Collins did not strike a good bargain; that is, they suggest he was not a very good business person. When he raised money on property which was his rather than that which he shared with his sisters, he always got less than market value for the property, perhaps only because he wanted cash at a particular moment. In 1744 he took £100 on the same copyholds for which his grandfather had been willing to loan £200 in 1704.[21] In 1746, for £63, Collins sold the freehold which his uncle had purchased for £83 in 1720, even though the property had been improved and even though property values were higher in 1746 than in 1720. Twenty years later in 1765, William Milton sold this same copyhold for £120. Milton, that is, almost doubled his investment in twenty years, while Collins took a £20 loss on a twenty-five year investment.[22]

Third, and most important, they indicate that Collins, while certainly not wealthy or even well-off, had visible means of support, investments and funds that, if managed prudently, should have provided adequate support. In less than three years, or more precisely, within twenty-nine months, he grossed £329 on the property transactions we know about. It is true that by the time he paid court costs, attorney fees, and other related expenses he would have netted something less than that amount. Meanwhile, however, he had other funds coming to him: rents from the freehold, copyhold, and leasehold property held by the Collins family; at least £10 for his promise to translate and comment upon Aristotle's *Poetics;* and £10 from Andrew Millar for the copyright on his odes.

More light is shed upon Collins and upon Samuel Johnson as a biographer if we examine Collins's property transactions in the spring of 1746 along with other information we have from letters, newspapers, and Johnson's *Life of Collins.*

On 5 March 1746, as we have noted, Charles Collins's will was proved. On 10 April Collins was in Chichester and raised £50 on the property left to him by his uncle Charles. On 23 April John Gilbert Cooper wrote Robert Dodsley: "If you should See that wandering Knight Collins, pray tell him, that I have not wrote to him because I did not know where to direct my letters, but should think myself honour'd in receiving that Knowledge from his own pen."[23] By the end of April and the beginning of May, the pleasure gardens in London had opened for the season. On May twentieth through May twenty-second Collins attended the races at Merrows Downs near Guildford, for Joseph Warton wrote his brother Thomas that he had met Collins there. Collins then accompanied Warton to Milford, a few miles south of Guildford in Surrey, where Warton's mother and sister were. Collins probably returned to London on Saturday 24 May.[24]

On Wednesday, 28 May, John Mulso reported to Gilbert White: "I can't help telling You, tho' 'tis a little uncharitable, that Collins appears in good cloathes & a wretched carcass, at all the gay Places, tho' it was with the utmost Difficulty that He scrap'd together 5 pound for Miss Bundy at whose Suit He was arrested & whom by his own confession He never intended to pay. I don't believe He will tell the Story in Verse, tho' some circumstances of his taking would be burlesque enough. The Bailiff introduc'd himself with 4 Gentlemen who came to drink Tea, & who all together could raise but one Guinea. The ἀναγνώρισις (a word he is fond of) was quite striking & the catastrophe quite poetical & interesting."[25]

In his *Life of Collins* Samuel Johnson recalls: "By degrees I gained his confidence; and one day was admitted to him when he was immured by a bailiff that was prowling in the street. On this occasion recourse was had to the booksellers, who, on the credit of a translation of Aristotle's *Poeticks,* which he engaged to write with a large commentary, advanced as much money as enabled him to escape into the country. He shewed me the guineas safe in his hand."[26] That Mulso and Johnson are discussing the same incident seems almost certain, particularly when we remember that Johnson was negotiating between the end of April and 18 June 1746 with Robert Dodsley on behalf of the booksellers of London to do the dictionary.[27]

By reading these passages together and by referring to the two property transactions in Chichester, we can reconstruct the probable scene. By the beginning of April, Collins, greatly in need of cash, raised £50 on his property in Chichester. He then may have traveled a bit; certainly he bought new clothes, entertained, and went to the gardens, concerts, and theaters. He traveled to the races in Surrey and more than likely dropped a few pounds on the horses. When it came time to pay Miss Bundy what he owed in rent, he had no money. Miss Bundy had no success in getting Collins to pay his debts; she therefore brought charges against him for non-payment of debt, and a bailiff was sent by the court to secure the funds or to arrest Collins. When the bailiff appeared, Samuel Johnson must have been one of the four gentlemen Mulso refers to in his note to White. He slipped out to a bookseller, more than likely Robert Dodsley, and made arrangements for Collins to borrow money on a promised translation of and commentary upon Aristotle's *Poetics.* With this money he was able to pay his debt and thus avoid imprisonment and trial. He obviously received more than £5; he got that plus enough to travel out of town "into the country," in all probability, directly to

Chichester. The diction of Mulso's letter, the wit of which no doubt pleased him exceedingly, supports Johnson's story of the Aristotle translation and commentary and suggests that Collins was currently working with Aristotle's concepts.

With the guineas Collins received from the bookseller, he left London and traveled back to Chichester, where he arrived by at least Friday, May thirtieth. On that date, he sold the property he had used for collateral the month before and received £12.

When we read Johnson's account of Collins, it is important to remember these transactions of April and May 1746. Fifty pounds was a sizable amount of money in the mid-eighteenth century. Wisely managed, it would have supported Collins for five to six months if he had been willing or able to live frugally, or perhaps just sensibly. Remarking in his *Life of Savage* that Richard Savage received regularly £50 a year, Samuel Johnson points out that £50 a year is "a Salary which though by no Means equal to the Demands of Vanity and Luxury, is yet found sufficient to support Families above Want, and was undoubtedly more than the Necessities of Life require."[28] Yet in less than two months, specifically within forty-eight days, Collins had spent more than £50.[29]

Did Collins go through the money he had raised from other property transactions as quickly? Probably.[30] James Hampton says "he soon dissipated his small fortune"; Gilbert White observes he spent "his time in all the dissipation of Ranelagh, Vauxhall, and the playhouses . . . In this pleasurable way of life he soon wasted his little property." Evidence now bears out these reports. After commenting that Collins "suffered the greatest inconveniences," John Langhorne reports: "Day succeeded day, for the support of which he had made no provision, and in which he was to submit either by the long-repeated contributions of a friend, or the generosity of a casual acquaintance. —Yet indolence triumphed at once over want and shame; and neither the anxieties of poverty, nor the heart-burning of dependence had power to animate resolution to perseverance." John Ragsdale observes that he "lived with and upon his friends."[31]

All those who were Collins's friends and all those who had ready access to Collins's acquaintances mention that Collins was a man of great ability, even of genius, who showed great promise; that he was a delightful companion and a warm friend; but that he lacked resolution; and that he had financial difficulties and embarrassments. Of all the accounts, Samuel Johnson's is the most sympathetic. We should keep in mind the statements made by Langhorne and Ragsdale when we turn to Johnson's account in his *Life of Collins:* "He designed many works, but his great fault was irresolution, or the frequent calls of immediate necessity broke his schemes, and suffered him to pursue no settled purpose. A man, doubtful of his dinner, or trembling at a creditor, is not much disposed to abstracted meditation or remote enquires."[32]

Johnson's version does not contradict either Langhorne's or Ragsdale's account but certainly presents Collins in a different light. Perhaps Johnson did not know Collins had a small inheritance that could have supported him if used prudently; more likely, he chose not to mention that detail.[33] By deciding *not* to select that biographical detail and by also avoiding mention of debts or loans and yet without straying from "the truth," Johnson lets his reader believe that Collins was a poor, struggling poet.[34] He presents a rather romantic image. The *Life of Collins* by Johnson, besides giving us valuable information about Collins and our best analysis of his character, reveals almost as much about Johnson himself as it does about Collins.[35]

Collins became close to Johnson during 1745 and 1746, a period of Johnson's life of which little is known. He was still a hack writer of small means and little fame, dissatisfied with himself and his career, increasingly concerned and anxious about the condition of Tetty.[36] His growing friendship with Collins must have been one bright spot in an otherwise rather low and bleak period of his life. Here was a young man who was learned, well read in classic and modern poetry and criticism, who was vivacious and cheerful, and who was an excellent conversationalist. Johnson tells us that Collins was full of projects; and at this time, we should remember, Johnson was also making a list of projects he could carry out to earn subsistence and fame. Collins was, according to James Clifford, the only one of Johnson's early London friends who "came close to being a genius."[37]

Johnson's obvious fondness for Collins influenced his selection and presentation of details. Furthermore, Johnson saw in Collins the thing about himself which distressed him most—his indolence and resulting procrastination. He also saw in Collins the thing he feared most—madness or at least the inability to direct his actions rationally. We know, however, that Johnson was far more generous and tolerant about excusing weaknesses in others, particularly in those for whom he had special affection, than he ever was with himself.[38] Thus he mentions Collins's irresolution but then rationalizes it and provides Collins an honorable excuse, one he would not have accepted for himself. In his character of Collins, first written in 1763, Johnson speaks of "that depression of mind which enchains the faculties without destroying them, and leaves reason the knowledge of right without the power of pursuing it."[39] Johnson was, as Walter Jackson Bate has pointed out, "speaking partly for himself."[40] And, important for our consideration, he was softening the disturbing elements of Collins's character, both his indolence and his "madness."[41]

Because of the biographical details we now have, we know that Collins disposed of property rashly, accepted considerably less than market value for his copyholds and leaseholds, and then failed to manage in a prudent manner the funds he had raised. We have always known that Collins did not live in some garret on Grub Street when he went to London. He took rooms in a fashionable section of Westminster just off Soho Square. He traveled to the continent in the summers of 1745 and 1746. We must, therefore, be willing to reexamine the term *dissipation,* a term used by Hampton, White, and also Johnson. While Johnson defines the term as "scattered attention," as G. B. Hill has pointed out, he also defines it as "the act of dispersion."[42] In the eighteenth century the term also clearly meant "wasteful expenditure or consumption of money, means, powers, faculties, etc.; squandering, waste."[43] We may still admire Collins as a poet and visionary and yet admit he wasted and squandered his money as well as his time and talents.

NOTES

[1]*Letters of Samuel Johnson,* ed. R. W. Chapman, 3 vols. (Oxford: Clarendon Press, 1952), 1:90. In his *Dictionary of the English Language* (London, 1755), Johnson defines *poor* as "depressed; low; dejected" and also as "[A word of tenderness.] Dear." Although he may have been indicating Collins's depression or dejection by using the term *poor,* he clearly is also expressing pity and sympathy. See also *Letters,* 1:53, 58, 59, 60.

[2]"Introduction," *The Works of William Collins,* ed. Richard Wendorf and Charles Ryskamp (Oxford: Clarendon Press; New York: Oxford Univ. Press, 1979), p. xxiii.

[3]Johnson first defines *poor* as "Not rich; indigent; necessitous; oppressed with want."

[4]Samuel Johnson, *Lives of the English Poets,* ed. G. B. Hill, 3 vols. (Oxford: Clarendon Press, 1905), 3:337.

[5]Alexander Hay, *The History of Chichester* (Chichester and London, 1804), p. 528. Alexander Hay served as a clergyman, schoolmaster, and chaplain of St. Mary's Chapel in Chichester from 1760 to his death in 1807. Since Ann Collins did not die until 1789, Hay could well have known her. Certainly he would have known her contemporaries and those of her brother, the poet.

[6]Oliver Sigworth, *William Collins* (New York: Twayne Publishers, 1965), p. 32; P. L. Carver, *The Life of a Poet: A Biographical Sketch of William Collins* (London: Sedgwick and Jackson; New York: Horizon, 1967), p. 68.

[7]P.R.O. Prob 11/745. The parish records of St. Peter the Great in Chichester indicate a Charles Collins was buried 3 December 1742. In the parish records abbreviations *P* for Parish or *Ext* for Extra (persons outside the parish) appear beside the name of each person buried in the parish. The abbreviation *Ext*

appears before the name of Charles Collins (West Sussex Record Office [hereafter referred to as W.S.R.O.] Par 44/1/1/3, f. 47v). On 17 July 1728 Charles Collins had been nominated by the Duke of Newcastle for admission to Charterhouse as vacancies occured, and he probably took up residency sometime the following year. It was at Charterhouse that he began to write his will on 2 September 1741 and then completed it on 19 June 1742. When N. Long-Brown, Registrar and Clerk to the Governors of Charterhouse, searched the records of Charterhouse for me, he could find no actual note of Charles Collins's arrival and could find nothing about Collins's death. Since Charles Collins had such strong feelings of family, it is likely that he went back to Chichester to die or at least instructed that his body be returned to Chichester for burial in the parish in which he had been baptised (Par 44/1/1, f. 40v) and in which he had been married (Par 44/1/1/2).

[8]John Ragsdale provides this information in his letter to William Hymers, dated July 1783 ("Particulars of Mr. William Collins, the Poet," *The Monthly Magazine* 21 [1806]:494). A successful jeweller and goldsmith, Ragsdale operated a shop under the sign of the Golden Vause on New Bond Street near the corner of New Bond Street and Bruton Street and thus lived within a block of Collins's cousin George Payne, an apothecary on Bruton Street just off Berkeley Square. For further information on Ragsdale, his access to information, and his reliability, see M. M. Stewart, "Further Notes on William Collins," *SEL* 10 (1970):572-78.

[9]*The Letters to Gilbert White of Selborne from His Intimate Friend and Contemporary the Rev. John Mulso,* ed. Rashleigh Holt-White (London, 1906), p. 3.

[10]Date of death is given on a memorial plaque on a wall of St. Andrew's parish church where she was buried on 6 July 1744 (W.S.R.O. Par 37/1/1/2, f. 173). Elizabeth Collins's will is general and thus does not specify her real and personal estate (W.S.R.O. STD I/7).

[11]Henry Campbell Black, *Black's Law Dictionary. Definitions of the Terms and Phrases of American and English Jurispurdence, Ancient and Modern,* rev. 4th edn. (St. Paul: West, 1968), pp. 405-406.

[12]W.S.R.O. Ep VI/30/1, pp. 449-52; Ep VI/34; Ep VI/30/1, pp. 455-58. For a discussion of this marriage settlement which benefited William Collins, see M. M. Stewart, "William Collins and Cackham Manor," *RES* 20 (1969):310-14. I suspect that George Payne acted for Colonel Martin on behalf of the Collins sisters, for at Payne's death in 1762, these same copyholds went to Ann Collins, the only surviving Collins sibling. See Cackham Manor records, W.S.R.O., Ep VI/30/2, p. 1.

[13]W.S.R.O. STD 1/7.

[14]W.S.R.O. Harris MSS. 688, 689, 690, 686.

[15]P.R.O. Prob 11/745.

[16]W.S.R.O. Add. MSS. 925, 926, 927; W.S.R.O. Add. MSS. 926, 928, 929, 933, 934.

[17]W.S.R.O. Add. MSS. 5999, 6000.

[18]P.R.O. Prob 11/770; obituary in the *Daily Advertiser,* 27 April 1749.

[19]General Cunningham Robertson, *Historical Record of the King's Liverpool Regiment of Foot,* 2nd edn. (London, 1833), p. 276, and App. I, p. 210; P.R.O. S.P. 44/187, f. 109.

[20]P.R.O. W.O. 26/16, pp. 40 and 46.

[21]In 1700 Richard Zouch raised money, as Collins did in 1744, by using these Cackham Manor copyholds as collateral. When he was unable to pay Collins's

grandfather, Edmund Martin, £216 at the end of two years, Martin negotiated with Zouch a two year extension, but, still unable to repay his loan to Martin in 1704, Zouch forfeited his mortgage to the copyhold lands, and Martin was admitted to these lands on 24 October 1704 (W.S.R.O. Ep VI/34 and Ep VI/30/1, pp. 177-78).

[22]Collins's sister Elizabeth handled the family's affairs after her mother's death. When she negotiated the property transactions in 1745 and 1747 the Collinses received at least fair market price for their leaseholds.

[23]Bodleian MS Eng. misc. d. 174, f. 11.

[24]*The London Evening-Post,* 26-29 April 1746; John Wooll, *Biographical Memoirs of the late Revd. Joseph Warton, D.D.* (London, 1806), pp. 14-15, note m.

[25]*The Letters to Gilbert White . . . from . . . John Mulso,* p. 14.

[26]*Lives of the English Poets,* 3:336.

[27]Walter Jackson Bate, *Samuel Johnson* (New York: Harcourt Brace Jovanovich, 1977), pp. 241-42; James L. Clifford, *Young Sam Johnson* (New York: McGraw-Hill, 1955), pp. 292-93.

[28]Samuel Johnson, *Life of Savage,* ed. Clarence Tracy (Oxford: Clarendon Press, 1971), p. 96. Walter Jackson Bate estimates that Johnson had an annual income of about £100 or £125 in the middle 1740s. According to Bate, Johnson "may very well have devoted two-thirds of it to Tetty while keeping his own personal expenses to a minium." He also points out that an ordinary hack writer would earn approximately £27 a year (*Samuel Johnson,* pp. 237-38).

[29]After James Boswell arrived in London on 20 November 1762, he calculated a scheme that would permit him to live comfortably for a year within the £200 allowance he received from his father. If he adhered to his scheme, he figured he would have a surplus of £36 (James Boswell, *London Journal,* ed. Frederick A. Pottle [New York: McGraw-Hill, 1950], Appendix 1, pp. 335-37). Samuel J. Rogal ("Boswell's 'Scheme of Living': London on Six Shillings a Day," *Research Studies* 44, 2 (June 1976):126-36) demonstrates that Boswell stayed within this scheme. In his eight and one half months in London, Boswell spent something over £79 or approximately £9 per month. "For the most part," Rogal tells us, "he spent his money on necessary articles and services—necessary, at least, to a man who would be a gentleman, a seeker of prestigious employment and of the best company" (p. 136).

[30]Mulso wrote White on 28 May that Collins appeared "in good cloathes." The Mulso letters to White are now housed in the John Rylands Library, and an examination of the manuscript of the 28 May letter reveals that Mulso first wrote "gay Cloathes," but then crossed out *gay* and wrote above it the word *good,* perhaps because he immediately used the word *gay* to describe the places Collins had frequented (Rylands English Ms 911, vol. 1, letter 9). John Ragsdale also comments upon Collins's clothes: "When Mr. Wm. Collins came from the University, he called on his cousin Payne gaily dressed, and with a feather in his hat." When Collins left Oxford, according to Ragsdale, he was "in arrears" to his tailor as well as to his bookseller and other tradesmen (*The Monthly Magazine,* p. 494). If Collins liked good or gay clothes, as these comments indicate he did, this indulgence may explain in part at least his expenditure of funds, for clothing was particularly expensive in the eighteenth century. Based upon John Burnett's study, *A History of the Cost of Living* (London: Penguin, 1969), Bate concludes: "If rent or food were proportionally much cheaper in the eighteenth century than now, dress was far more expensive. With just a little indulgence or even relaxation there, one's annual expenses—if one's income were in the £100-a-year range—could leap 50 percent" (*Samuel Johnson,* p. 238).

[31]James Hampton, "Some Account of the Life and Writings of Mr. William Collins," *Gentleman's Magazine* 34 (January 1764):23; Gilbert White, "Memoirs of the Life of William Collins, the Poet," *Gentleman's Magazine* 51 (January 1781):11; John Langhorne, *The Poetical Works of Mr. William Collins. With Memoirs of the Author; and Observations on His Genius and Writings* (London, 1765), p. x; John Ragsdale, *The Monthly Magazine* 21 (1 July 1806):495.

[32]*Lives of the English Poets,* 3:335.

[33]If Johnson did not have this information in the 1740s, he surely realized Collins's circumstances by the mid-fifties, for he knew James Hampton, Joseph and Thomas Warton, and Hester Mulso, the sister of John Mulso, who had known Collins at Winchester College and Oxford University. Since Collins took rooms in the Bundy house which was next door to the Mulso residence on King's Square Court, Hester, who lived with her parents during the years Collins lodged in Miss Bundy's house, would have known Collins personally and would, no doubt, have heard her brother and Gilbert White talk of Collins. The letters of John Mulso to Gilbert White indicate White stayed at the Mulso home in London.

[34]In his study *Samuel Johnson, Biographer* (Ithaca: Cornell Univ. Press, 1978), Robert Folkenflik observes that Johnson "resolves to tell the truth about his contemporaries, but not the whole truth" (p. 84).

[35]Richard Wendorf in his study of "The Making of Johnson's 'Life of Collins'" (*PBSA* 74 [1980]:96-103) notes that "Johnson's commentary is essentially protective in nature" (p. 99) and that Johnson's account is more sympathetic than James Hampton's account in *Gentleman's Magazine.* Wendorf compares Johnson's biography of Collins with Hampton's earlier biography of Collins and analyzes particularly the difference in tone. I would argue that selection of detail as well as tone produces the sympathetic version.

[36]See Bate's discussion of this shadowy period of Johnson's life in *Samuel Johnson,* pp. 231-39.

[37]*Young Sam Johnson*, p. 243.

[38]Another example is Johnson's treatment of Savage.

[39]*Lives of the English Poets*, 3:338.

[40]*Samuel Johnson,* p. 383.

[41]Johnson may also have sympathized with Collins's inability to manage money carefully. In a study of "Samuel Johnson's Literary Earnings," J. D. Fleeman indicates that Johnson "did not exercise careful management of his affairs" (*Studies in the Book Trade in Honour of Graham Pollard,* Oxford Bibliographical Society Publications, n.s., vol. 18 [Oxford: The Society, 1975], p. 220).

[42]*Lives of the Poets,* 3:338, n. 2; *Dictionary of the English Language.*

[43]*OED.*

SEL 28 (1988)
ISSN 0039-3657

Johnson and Conjecture

THOMAS REINERT

Hester Piozzi reports that, whenever Johnson felt his imagination "disordered, his constant recurrence was to the study of arithmetic."[1] Once during the period of near-breakdown he went through in the 1760s, she found him in his room "in the midst of a series of elaborate calculations. He was taking the national debt, computing it at 180 millions sterling, and then calculating whether it 'would, if converted into silver, serve to make a meridian of that metal, I forget how broad, for the globe of the whole earth'" (p. 415). In other bad times, he applied similar calculations to his own projects. A couple of weeks before he left Oxford, in despair, debt-ridden, unable to finish his degree, he made a sort of chart "in which he outlines for himself what reading a certain number of lines per day (10, 30, and so on up to 600) would amount to in a week, then a month, then a year" (p. 106). Bate notes that Johnson kept making charts like this throughout his life, even when he was old and famous.

This habit was a form, Bate suggests, of Johnson's "anticipative imagination," his strategy of allaying a fear of the unexpected by considering beforehand all of the turns of fortune that might befall him. His calculations and charts warded off the unexpected specifically by breaking experience—even the "globe of the whole earth"—into comparable units, a move which would put the future into a predictable and knowable relation to the present and past. At more sober and circumspective moments—and this would include most of his published writing—he argues that such schemes for regulating the flow of events are generally doomed, if not to fail, then at least to struggle against a mass of unpredictable contingencies. Instead of warding off the unexpected, such schemes give it occasions in which to unfold itself—in the form, for example, of the laziness that keeps one from sticking to a schedule, or of unavoidable external distractions, or of unforeseen confusions. But since Johnson is less interested in preventing the unexpected from happening than in warding off its shock effects, he concentrates most of his attention not on concocting schemes, but, according to Bate, on figuring out

Thomas Reinert teaches English at Wellesley College. He is currently working on a book about Johnson and the crowd.

in advance all the ways things can turn out. Johnson's mobility as a writer—the multiple perspectives he adopts in arguments, his constant movement from propositions to qualifications, his enumerative turn of mind—can be seen as a defensive effort, in Bate's words, "to overlook nothing, to take it all into account beforehand" (p. 107). By covering all the possibilities in his mind, he does not get around the impossibility of predicting the future, an impossibility he often gloomily calls attention to in his writing, but things that come unpredicted at least do not come to him completely unexpected, or at any rate do not come as a shock he is unprepared for.

A century after Johnson, such structures of consciousness had become the norm, according to Walter Benjamin, for people taking shelter psychologically against the shocks of big city life. Consciousness itself, Benjamin argues (citing Freud), is essentially defensive. It is opposed to memory: instead of retaining experiential impressions, it protects one against stimuli. It dissipates "the effects of the excessive energies at work in the external world" by registering them in the place of "other systems," in which, Freud writes, stimuli leave "permanent traces as the basis of memory."[2] Paradoxically, consciousness wards off shocks by registering them, as if registration were simultaneously an erasure. Benjamin suggests one interpretation: consciousness protects by isolating. The more efficiently it is "alert as a screen against stimuli . . . , the less do these impressions enter experience (*Erfahrung*), tending to remain in the sphere of a certain hour of one's life (*Erlebnis*)" (p. 117). But Benjamin also observes that anticipation, that is, some structure of repetition and contextualization, is necessary for parrying shocks. "According to [psychoanalytic] theory, fright has 'significance' in the 'absence of any preparedness for anxiety.'" The unconscious comes into play here: the nightmares of accident patients "endeavour to master the stimulus retroactively, by developing the anxiety whose omission was the cause of the traumatic neurosis" (p. 115). The dilemma of consciousness is thus how to isolate shocks but at the same time stay prepared for them; circumscribe them without suppressing the premonitory halo of anxiety whose absence transforms them from excitement into trauma. Consciousness does it through the construction of what Benjamin calls "empty" time, a time in which all moments are equivalent, abstract, and interchangeable. Benjamin cites the newspaper and the mechanization of labor under industrial capitalism as products of experience organized around "empty" time; he might have cited Johnson's "anticipative imagination" as well. In this conceptualization, anticipation and isolation go together, for present, past, and future are equivalent to the same extent that every moment is discontinuous with every other. Assigning an experience a place in this chronology isolates it by contextualizing it. "Perhaps the special achievement of shock defense may be seen in its function of assigning to an incident a precise point in time in consciousness at the cost of the integrity of its contents" (p. 117).

Benjamin describes the difficulties faced by a nineteenth-century poet like Baudelaire, for whom the shock defense has become so prevalent a psychic mode that it is a matter of luck to have an experience which would still retain the "integrity of its contents." For Baudelaire, poetry reacts less to the "excessive energies" of the external world—the big city crowd in particular—than to the psychic defense against these energies. On the one hand it seeks out unrationalized experiences, and on the other it demystifies attempts to enrich the poverty of modern experience. But for Johnson, whose hold on the shock defense seems more tenuous and desperate than Baudelaire's, embracing the desolating effects of conscious structures such as anticipation and routinization can still appear as a grave moral obligation. Far from trying to disrupt their constant and oppressive operation, he struggles to maintain the spell of these structures against a persistent barrage of tempting arguments for letting them go. For him their dismalness does not tell against them; it is only an occasion for moral effort, one effort among others to endure something awful that can't be made any better. Nor does he try to legitimate these structures by fabricating some continuity between them and the sort of experience whose contents Benjamin would consider still to be intact. Johnson's account of consciousness is consistently grim: he hates routine, and he writes hopelessly and incessantly about the despair of a fully comprehended and anticipated world, a world bereft of novelty. But still he remains faithful to the demands of routine and anticipation; with an apparently senseless tenacity, he bestows on them enormous reserves of anxiety and self-recrimination.

Benjamin outlines some literary corollaries to the shock experience, particularly "the replacement of the older narration by information" (p. 113). Information, which Benjamin associates with newspapers, is not assimilated by readers as part of their own experience: rather it "isolate[s] what happens from the realm in which it could affect [their] experience" (p. 112). Items of information are unconnected to one another and do not imply a personal relation between those who receive and those who purvey the information, nor a relation to its content. Such items do not "enter 'tradition'." They seek to "convey a happening *per se*." Storytelling, on the other hand, "one of the oldest forms of communication," embeds an event "in the life of the storyteller in order to pass it on as experience to those listening" (p. 112).

Benjamin does not try to show that information replaced storytelling at a particular period, but he links this movement to the experience of big cities and to the technology of mechanical reproduction. Following Benjamin, Benedict Anderson argues that the conception of the nation, a community of so many members that it cannot be apprehended in any direct experiential way, arose along with the experience of what Benjamin calls "homogeneous, empty time," the only mode of experience open enough to contain the dispersion of vast anonymous crowds without having recourse to the idea of the sacred. In the Middle Ages, Anderson points out, it was common to represent biblical stories as if they happened in the present, not by way of imagining them in "modern dress," but rather because the link between past, present, and future was conceived to be essentially a timeless relation of prefiguration and always already consummated fulfillment. Anderson argues that this conception of simultaneity gave way to homogeneous, empty time, the conception of simultaneity as "temporal coincidence . . . measured by clock and calendar," first with the development of the printing press and then with the rise of "two forms of imagining which first flowered in Europe in the eighteenth century: the novel and the newspaper."[3] The printing press contributed to the rise in power of vernacular languages, a movement which destabilized the status of Latin as a sacred language, and at the same time it established a common language between speakers whose dialects were otherwise typically unintelligible to one another. In so doing, it crystallized a mode of figuring or imagining community that was unavailable before (p. 47). But the newspaper not only constructed a writing-oriented figure for community, it assembled experiences on the basis of their association in calendrical time: in newspapers events appear together because they share the same date (p. 37).

In Johnson's writing, then, we can detect his preoccupation with information not only in his massive efforts of accumulating facts—the dictionary and the edition of Shakespeare—but also, following Anderson, in the disconnectedness of his periodical essay writing. He contrasts essay writing with the compilation of a "system of science," an extended work elaborated according to "long trains of consequence," by pointing out that periodical writing follows only the law of the calendar: every "day calls afresh upon [the writer] for a new topick, and he is again obliged to choose, without any principle to regulate his choice."[4]

Johnson's tasks of information-gathering, like his charts and calculations, evidently helped him pull himself together; at least we know that he never brought himself to start working except under the pressure of a deadline. But on the other hand, he is conscious of a disorienting tendency in such constraints. Though Benjamin argues that structures of consciousness protect one against the "excessive energies" of city crowds, they seem to dazzle Johnson with a sense of these crowds by putting him into an obsessively enumerative relation to the world. Writing for a daily deadline makes the world disintegrate into a chaotic mass before his eyes: "It is indeed true, that there is seldom any necessity of looking far, or enquiring long for a proper subject [for a periodical essay]. Every diversity of art or nature, every public blessing or calamity, every domestick pain or gratification, every sally or caprice, blunder or absurdity, or stratagem of affectation may supply matter to [a writer] whose only rule is to avoid uniformity" (*Rambler* 184, p. 141). Not only does this mass churn before him with incomprehensible variety, but it scatters his thinking across the expanse of its apparent boundlessness: as one contemplates it, "it often happens, that the judgment is distracted with boundless multiplicity, the imagination ranges from one design to another, and the hours pass imperceptibly away till the composition can no longer be delayed" (*Rambler* 184, p. 141). Thus, while periodical writing isolates and disjoins events to keep them from entering experience, it also intimates the possibility of their endless proliferation, and the mechanism that is supposed to protect one from the crowd also turns it into a determining figure of one's thought. Understanding an event (or in Johnson's case, choosing a topic) requires that it be placed in the right context—which is also understood to mean a complete context—but who can tell what that would be with a newspaper, where decontextualization is the governing principle of organization? This is a problem with any reading, but newspapers thematize the problem in their layout. It would be a particularly disconcerting problem for someone like Johnson, to the extent that he defends himself against shock, as Bate says, by "taking it all into account beforehand." What happens when trying to take it all into account beforehand draws one instead into the midst of "boundless multiplicity"?

The only way to stop this proliferation is by some arbitrary intervention; and this is what Johnson describes. However boundless routine and information-gathering may be potentially, in practice they invariably run up against contingent disruptions. In the case of periodical writing, deadlines make it necessary finally to choose topics at random; by a kind of violence, one reduces the multiplication of possibilities, but only at the cost of giving way to chance determinations (*Rambler* 184).

But in discussing failures of long routines elsewhere, Johnson pushes this argument further and gets to the point of coming to terms, in a certain way, with such chance influences. The disruptions of routine he discusses in these passages are only random contingencies, not the arbitrary decisions that resolve a long search; but the main thing is that they're disruptive. His further move is to generalize about how accidents of this sort occur. Any long, complicated undertaking, he argues, just because of its length and complexity, is bound to be plagued with problems. In the preface to the dictionary he apologizes for the "wild blunders . . . from which no work of such multiplicity was ever free."[5] In the "Life of Pope" he says of Pope's representation of himself as translating fifty verses of *The Iliad* a day: "According to this calculation, the progress of Pope may seem to have been slow; but the distance is commonly very great between actual performances and speculative possibility. . . . Perhaps no extensive and multifarious performance was ever effected within the term originally fixed in the undertaker's mind."[6] Such an argument is familiar anid sensible enough but also conceptually complicated inasmuch as it involves a major discursive shift from the logic of experience to a logic of probabilistic calculation. It explains problems by linking them to the multifariousness of an undertaking, but the linkage is not directly causal and not even determinate. Even if the complexity of a long task necessarily brings problems in its train, it is on the other hand also the case that any specific problem is contingent: inevitably there are lapses in a routine, but saying this doesn't explain why there are these lapses in particular. Instead of a causal relation which would establish a continuous relation between a general principle and particular experiences, this argument allows the specific to lapse into mere contingency, and it searches for structures of necessity on the level of the aggregate. This disjunction is what is probabilistic. The argument is statistical: mistakes are understood as a percentage of a large work, lapses in routine as a margin of error.

Through this blurring of a specific event's contours, a conceptual shift takes place from which one can only return to specific events in the empiricist mode of taking a random sample. The literary effects of this mode can be attractive: it becomes possible to spin out long, desultory lists of random experiences and still give the impression that the writing is driving at a coherent point. For instance, in the preface to the dictionary Johnson gives the following account of the kind of unexpected contingencies that can beset a writer: one must remember, he says,

> that a writer will sometimes be hurried by eagerness to the end, and sometimes faint with weariness under a task, which

> *Scaliger* compares to the labours of the anvil and the mine; that what is obvious is not always known, and what is known is not always present; that sudden fits of inadvertency will sometimes surprize vigilance, slight avocations will seduce attention, and casual eclipses of the mind will darken learning; and that the writer shall often in vain trace his memory at the moment of need, for that which yesterday he knew with intuitive readiness, and which will come uncalled into his thoughts tomorrow.
>
> (p. 259)

Similarly, in the "Life of Pope" he treats particular obstructions to routine as random and virtually imperceptible: "Indolence, interruption, business and pleasure all take their turns of retardation, and every long work is lengthened by a thousand causes that can, and ten thousand that cannot, be recounted" (p. 229). The pleasure of such lists lies in the feeling that they can include anything and yet not have to organize their contents in any overarching, systematic way. At best, they are organized strictly according to rhetorical force: the randomness of their elements allows Johnson to think entirely in terms of surface effects. But this kind of writing is available to him because of the frame of probability around them; and if this stylistic mannerism is prevalent in his work, that is an indication of how deep-seated probabilistic thinking is with him. It even affects his moralizing style. What readers call his "generosity," his willingness to put himself in the place even of someone whose faults he is criticizing, manages to accompany a severe code of rights and wrongs because he never moves to specific cases without crossing a probabilistic space that attenuates any experience's particularity. Even when any given fault might have been avoided, it is hard to hand down a harsh judgment on it if one imagines at the same time that *some* quantity of faults is inevitable.

In the preface to the dictionary Johnson excuses the errors he has committed as "human" errors: the preface gets its effect by drifting between a remark at the beginning about "the imperfection of human things" (p. 235) and the pathos-laden image of the frail lexicographer, laboring under the shadow of death, incapable of sustaining his efforts with the machine-like regularity asked of him (p. 259). It is of course a traditional Christian idea to define the "human" as a liability to error. But Johnson's preface reconceives that idea in terms of factory-like labor, as though Christian faith and humility would take the form of a rigorous adherence to a dehumanized, mechanical routine. One can gauge the bizarreness of this confluence of rhetorical modes by considering the pathos Johnson brings to bear on the topic of Pope's failure to follow his translation schedule: "Perhaps no extensive and multifarious performance was ever effected within the term originally fixed in the undertaker's mind. He that runs against Time has an antagonist not subject to casualties" (p. 229). It takes a minute, given the solemn and funereal overtones of this last sentence, to realize that Johnson is only trying to come to terms with Pope's laziness. But for Johnson, the failure to follow a routine is not only a contingent matter of laziness: it is also, on the contrary, an inevitable failing which marks the vanity of human undertakings. The discourse organized around the disjunction between these two notions of failure—as contingent and as inevitable—is that of probability and statistics. Human vanity is the margin of error, statistically defined, in any large work. Consequently, the "human" becomes a conceptual wild card: it personifies the array of elusive contingencies which upset the unfolding of routine—likewise any effort to gather information—and which the language of statistics derives its power from presupposing the inexplicability of. It personifies the random, the non-conceptual, and ultimately the unrepresentable.

Presumably one attraction of this statistical conception of the "human" would be that it is more coherent—less "perplexing and suspenseful"—than the "boundless multiplicity" Johnson has to contend with when he is aimlessly gathering information and has not yet taken the risk of making a decision. Furthermore, to the extent that it motivates his catalogues of random examples, catalogues in which he indulges the pleasure of multiplying surfaces and discontinuities, it is responsible for one of his most seductive literary practices. But at the same time it radically marginalizes a personal conception of the "human"—much more radically than the gestures of self-sacrifice he diffidently analyzes in his writing about marginal characters like Richard Savage and Dr. Levet. Martyrdom is a gesture in which the self asserts its power: in it, self-sacrifice becomes self-aggrandizing. But when the human becomes a statistical representation of a routine's inexplicable disruption, its marginality undermines the concept of specific experience *in general* and, as Benjamin says, destroys the "integrity of its contents." This discourse derives its power precisely from regarding the moment and the personal axiomatically as random and contingent and examining the patterning of large masses. It assumes from the outset that the task of describing the general is disconnected from the task of describing the particular. The results of this thinking are apparent in a poem like "The Vanity of Human Wishes," where personal agency is a statistical construct. The figures in this poem are not "typical" in Georg Lukács's sense;[7] there's no dialectical interplay between the particular and the general, no attempt to make the universal concrete. They are "average" figures: Johnson imposes identity on them by means of a synecdochic use of the definite article ("the hireling judge" replaces the literal phrase "hireling judges"). Their identity is merely figurative, and the construction of the figure is authorized only statistically. Since no construction of identity in this discursive register refers to personal experience, empirically inconceivable figures are possible: this is the kind of language that allows a family to have 2.5 children. In a discursive mode such as this, it is apparent that the marginalization of the self can have nothing to do with the gratifying transfers of power and structures of consolation available in the martyr's experience of self-sacrifice. The self is not marginal here because one has given up its power: it is marginal in that it is the figurative construction of some bureaucratic imagination.

Johnson never writes explicitly about probability and statistics, but he does write frequently about conjecture. Usually he attacks it on the grounds of its vanity and idleness. But in the preface to his edition of Shakespeare, he sifts out a discreet use of conjecture from among some examples of its misuse. The results elaborate the notion of marginality I have been talking about.

Like many of his writings about attempts to regulate the confusions of language, this essay revolves around a version of Benjamin's distinction between storytelling and information. In this case the distinction is between original composition and editing, and ultimately between Shakespeare and Johnson. Editing, as Johnson sees it, is essentially and radically marginal. It is marginal with respect to original composition, which comes first in order of literary priorities and which moreover controls most of the power available in literature. Literary power for Johnson means the power not only to please but to produce emotional involvement in general, a power without which literature becomes empty drudgery. It's what we read for—so much so that even a badly garbled edition of a great work impresses readers, according to Johnson, almost as strongly as a good edition. Johnson imagines the movement from original composition to editing in temporal terms: the period of critical commentary follows that of composition as a stage of decline, a stage of decayed power, as if the literary scene were organized entropically, like a machine perpetually winding down. Commentary provides virtually nothing of value to anyone reading for the sake of the text's power—Johnson even urges readers who are coming to Shakespeare for the first time to ignore the notes. Commentary is intended instead for readers concerned with "exactness" of understanding.[8] But since Johnson imagines such readers as cold and jaded scholars who have lost their susceptibility to the text's power, the propagation of critical commentary appears as a circulation of waste: worthless services provided to those who would be incapable of receiving a service of value. What makes its basic economy skewed and eccentric is that, even despite its virtual worthlessness, editing is nevertheless exorbitantly difficult. Critics need extensive knowledge of texts, and their judgment in cases of emendation must be exceptionally fine; meanwhile they also engage in vicious battles with one another, and the accumulation of their learning ceaselessly proliferates; but at bottom virtually nothing is at stake. Johnson speculates that there is some logic of compensation in this: "Perhaps the lightness of the matter may conduce to the vehemence of the agency; when the truth to be investigated is so near to inexistence, as to escape attention, its bulk is to be enlarged by rage and exclamation" (p. 298).

This wretched and virtually meaningless activity is to be understood, though, as an approach to the way things really are; as some kind of advance on original composition, which is the source of energy and meaning, the center of literary activity, but also a fraud. For Johnson entropy has two incompatible meanings which allow him to conceive of marginality as the worst of both worlds: it means loss and decay, the fall from meaning, but it also implies that what has been lost never really existed. Thus, Shakespeare could be "read, admired, studied, and imitated, while he was yet deformed with all the improprieties which ignorance and neglect could accumulate upon him"(p. 306), but still: "It is to be lamented, that such a writer should want a commentary; that his language should become obsolete, or his sentiments obscure. But it is vain to carry wishes beyond the condition of human things; that which must happen to all, has happened to *Shakespeare*, by accident and time" (p. 307). In other words, Shakespeare lives despite all the deformities heaped upon him by time, but nevertheless they have also managed to kill him (as "must happen to all"). Editing presides over this scene where no one is singled out, not even the greatest geniuses. Because Shakespeare lives, editing is a worthless falling away from his immortal vitality, but because he is dead, editing remains necessary and becomes representative of the powerlessness that disables everything human, even the works of Shakespeare. This contradiction constitutes its radical marginality: even though it is worthless, it must nevertheless be pursued in all its poverty. Original composition is doubly displaced in this line of thought. Not only is its power doomed to decay: from the outset it lacks authority, for, as Johnson represents it, it is blind to the inevitability of the decay of power in general. But editing is not blind to this necessity; and this is the sense in which it is the more lucid of the two pursuits.

Conjecture comes into this argument like the moment in *Rambler* 184 where Johnson has to choose a topic after scattering his thoughts over a boundless multiplicity of possibilities. He has to fill in a gap that the pursuit of information has left him with (in this case, he has to repair a corruption in Shakespeare's text; in the other case, he has to say something coherent) but he can only do it by making a random move—an arbitrary decision or guess—which exposes him to error (p. 304). To contain the problem of error (which he can't fully resolve), he relies on the probabilistic nature of conjecture: he dispels the threat of making a mistake by pointing out that he is only guessing. When a proposition is marked as a conjecture, it is immediately freed from the risk of error. As Johnson says, "There is no danger in conjecture, if it be proposed as conjecture" (p. 303).

But having taken these precautions, he is absorbed with the question of what they have cost him. The unguarded mode of conjecture he has renounced leads one to make mistakes, but it is also the only task available to an editor that appears to bring one back into contact with the pleasure of original composition and literary power. According to Johnson, the "allurements of emendation are scarcely resistible"; and its primary allure is the promise of originality, a promise so gratifying that it seduces editors away from their responsibility to the dessicated obligations of correctness: "Conjecture has all the joy and all the pride of invention, and he that has once started a happy change, is too much delighted to consider what objections may rise against it" (p. 304).

The risk of making a guess at random presumably adds to the flutter of excitement here, a flutter one can also hear in that *Rambler* essay where Johnson speaks of choosing an essay topic at random: "necessity enforces the use of those thoughts which then happen to be at hand [and the] mind rejoicing at deliverance on any terms from perplexity and suspense, applies herself vigorously to the work before her." Another remark about conjecture suggests what would link originality to risk-taking. When Johnson is attacking critics for covering up the flimsiness of their conjectures under a mass of irrelevant verbiage, he makes a surprising claim for the possibility of a certain kind of easy, unmistakeable critical mastery: "I have always suspected that the reading is right, which requires many words to prove it wrong; and the emendation wrong, that cannot without so much labour appear to be right. The justness of a happy restoration strikes at once, and the moral precept may be well applied to criticism, *quod dubitas ne feceris* (when in doubt, refrain)" (p. 303). Apparently for a certain masterful criticism, conjecture manages not to be doubtful: its justness "strikes at once." But at the same time, all conjectures are doubtful, even those of a critic of "wonderful sagacity and erudition": "when [a critic] succeeds best, he produces perhaps but one reading of many probable, and he that suggests another will always be able to dispute his claims" (p. 304). The allure of mastering conjecture would lie in the fantasy of reconciling these two imaginings of chance. It's the allure of the professional gambler: constantly exposed to chance, but skilled at dealing with it. It would likewise be the allure of the writer of original compositions, especially one who can write powerfully about a topic chosen at random.[9]

Most of Johnson's account of editing is an attempt to cut his losses by weakening this link between unguarded conjectures and original composition. The link between them is merely apparent, he argues. Conjecture is structured not like original composition but like editing and information-gathering. It has "no system, no principal and axiomatical truth that regulates subordinate propositions"; it is repetitive inasmuch as the critic's "chance of errour is renewed at every attempt"; it subjects the critic to the domination of random influences: "an oblique view of the passage, a slight misapprehension of a phrase, a casual inattention to the parts connected, is sufficient to make him not only fail, but fail ridiculously" (p. 304). Johnson writes generally in a harsh, satirical tone about the critics who have engaged in conjecture; but his distaste for them has less to do with moral disapproval than with a cold recognition that their efforts at mastery have only gotten them lost in a crowd of bunglers.

> To dread the shore which he sees spread with wrecks, is natural to the sailor. I had before my eye, so many critical adventures ended in miscarriage, that caution was forced upon me. I encountered in every page Wit struggling with its own sophistry, and Learning confused by the multiplicity of its views. I was forced to censure those whom I admired, and could not but reflect, while I was dispossessing their emendations, how soon the same fate might happen to my own, and how many of the readings which I have corrected may be by some other editor defended and established.
>
> Criticks, I saw, that other's names efface,
> And fix their own, with labour, in the place;
> Their own, like others, soon their place resign'd,
> Or disappear'd, and left the first behind.
>
> Pope.

What is striking here is the conjunction of futility and anonymity: the wrecks are particularly terrible because there are "so many" of them, and the "struggling" recalls the turmoil of a blind, seething crowd. The awfulness of undergoing the "same fate" as everyone else is not so much that it involves making mistakes, but that it is the *same* fate. It is equivalent to the wretchedness of repetition that goes with editing, only here these critics lack even the dignity of having known what they were getting into. This is the advantage, such as it is, that Johnson has over them.

He marks his conjectural emendations as such by putting them in the footnotes, outside the body of the text, where they won't be mistaken for solid information. This is a strange kind of composition: one can neither take it nor leave it. It is no sooner offered than withdrawn. If one begins to incorporate it, one has to reject it at the same time; but since it is in the text, neither can one dismiss it altogether. Johnson seems to want his writing to take a reader through a detour like the wishes granted by demons in fairy tales: after it's over, they leave you where you were before. As long as the magic cancels itself out, like imaginary numbers in physics, one can make room for any extravagance: "Since I have confined my imagination to the margin, it must not be considered as very reprehensible, if I have suffered it to play some freaks in its own dominion" (p. 303).

But Johnson is clear about the cost of writing in this mode. If he has cut his losses by dispelling the temptation of unguarded conjectures, he is still acutely conscious that he is engaged only in a choice of evils. Since his conjectures are marginal, they have no power. At most, they have the power of sapping the text's power. They mark its absence; and they fragment it by pointing to a corruption without guaranteeing that it is a corruption. In a dull, unproductive way, they invite suspicion, but they neither let the corrupt passage go nor supplant it with a substitute. Instead of staying confined to the margins, they minimally *multiply* the text. But Johnson gets no power over the text or the reader in this process. The most he can say for himself is that he did the *correct* thing, and this assessment is purely negative, like the remark in the preface to the dictionary: "It is the fate of those who toil at the lower employments of life, to be rather driven by the fear of evil, than attracted by the prospect of good; to be exposed to censure, without hope of praise; to be disgraced by miscarriage, or punished for neglect, where success would have been without applause, and diligence without reward" (p. 234). He would have betrayed the obligation to give correct information if he had put his conjectures in the body of the text; but putting them in the margins earns him no praise, the less so given that they exist strictly in order to cancel themselves; and since correctness is a value one embraces only after one no longer has contact with literary power, even the negative virtue of not betraying it seems to be no virtue at all. Johnson himself appears to be left halting within the doubleness of these constraints. He insists that the need to be correct is an imperative obligation: "The greater part of readers, instead of blaming us for passing trifles, will wonder that on mere trifles so much labour is expended, with such importance of debate, and such solemnity of diction. To these I answer with confidence, that they are judging of an art which they do not understand" (pp. 302-303). But to be in the right on this issue does him no good; the obligation he is faithful to is pointless and wasteful: "[I] cannot much reproach [those readers] with their ignorance, nor promise that they would become in general, by learning criticism, more useful, happier, or wiser" (p. 303).

NOTES

[1]Walter Jackson Bate, *Samuel Johnson* (New York: Harcourt, Brace, Jovanovich, 1975), p. 106.

[2]Walter Benjamin, "Some Motifs in Baudelaire," in *Illuminations*, trans. Harry Zohn, ed. Hannah Arendt (New York: Schocken Books, 1968), p. 115.

[3]Benedict Anderson, *Imagined Communities: Reflections on the Origin and Spread of Nationalism* (London: Verso Editions, 1983), p. 30.

[4]Samuel Johnson, *Rambler* No. 184, in *Samuel Johnson: Rasselas; Poems and Selected Prose*, ed. Bertrand H. Bronson (3rd edn.; New York: Rinehart Editions, 1971), p. 141.

[5]Samuel Johnson, "Preface to a Dictionary of the English Language," in Bronson, p. 259.

[6]Samuel Johnson, "The Life of Pope," in *Johnson's Lives of the Poets: A Selection*, ed. J.P. Hardy (Oxford: Clarendon Press, 1971), p. 229.

[7]Georg Lukács, *Studies in European Realism*, (New York: Grosset and Dunlap, 1964), pp. 91, 147ff.

[8]Samuel Johnson, "Preface to Shakespeare," in Bronson, p. 306.

[9]I picked up the drift of these remarks about the fascination of conjecture from a conversation with Mark Seltzer.

SEL 28 (1988)
ISSN 0039-3657

Rhetoric, History, Rebellion: *Caleb Williams* and the Subversion of Eighteenth-Century Fiction

DONALD R. WEHRS

Much recent literary theory argues that critics, faced with the complicity of Western literature in false values and baneful social practices, must choose between the alternatives of, as Frank Lentricchia puts it, working "on behalf of a dominant hegemony by reinforcing habits of thought and feeling that help to sustain ruling power" or working "counter-hegemonically as a violator, in an effort to dominate and to re-educate" by revealing "naturalized conventions" to be "all bourgeois encrustations of consciousness."[1] The value of counter-hegemonic criticism may be questioned by examining Godwin's *Caleb Williams*. Written by a committed radical, *Caleb Williams* represents the consequences of rebellion while being itself a sustained act of rebellion against the norms and "lessons" of eighteenth-century fiction. By probing the inconsistencies of Falkland's "official" story—a story that follows the conventional patterns of eighteenth-century "realistic" novels—Caleb resists Falkland's domination by means of a form of "counterhegemonic" criticism, but the freedom he gains remains strangely illusory. Instead of achieving spiritual independence, Caleb grows to identify with his persecutor/victim and ends by doubting the propriety of resistance. Both internally, as a vehicle for persuading readers of certain positions, and externally, as an event in literary history, *Caleb Williams* challenges central premises underlying current "political criticism."[2]

Like many contemporary Western Marxists, Lentricchia insists that any critical stance is always already a political stance while

---

Donald R. Wehrs received a Ph.D. from the University of Virginia in 1986, has held assistant professorships at Emory University and Illinois State University, and is currently an assistant professor at Auburn University, teaching English, comparative literature, and cultural studies. This discussion of *Caleb Williams* forms part of a larger study of the generic evolution of prose fiction from the eighteenth century through the Romantic era, other portions of which have appeared in *ELH* and *Comparative Literature Studies*.

rejecting the base/superstructure model underlying traditional Marxism.[3] His position does not depend upon "Marxism or any other philosophy rest[ing] on the foundations of reality or history" (p. 12). Instead, Marxist theory "is itself a kind of rhetoric whose value may be measured by its persuasive means and by its ultimate goal: the formation of genuine community" (pp. 12-13). Justifying Marxism through its abstract goal, Lentricchia makes the experience of Marxist government irrelevant to the theory's truth as rhetoric.

One might reply to Lentricchia by recalling Edmund Burke: "Abstractly speaking, government, as well as liberty, is good; yet could I, in common sense, ten years ago have felicitated France on her enjoyment of a government . . . without enquiry what the nature of that government was . . . ? Can I now congratulate the same nation upon its freedom?"[4] Burke's observations bear upon the "persuasive means" of a goal of "genuine community" because the power of such rhetoric cannot be evaluated apart from the history of such rhetoric. Both Lentricchia and Eagleton distinguish rhetorical from formalist criticism, but to the extent that the effectiveness of rhetorical modes is viewed separately from the history of their effects, rhetorical analysis becomes formalism. Lentricchia's determination to keep Marxism as "rhetoric" isolated from "reflectionist" theories leads him to neglect historically-created imperatives to get beyond pleasant abstractions (who wants an un-genuine community?) if, after the French Revolution, a rhetoric of radical social change is to be persuasive. In its portrayal of rebellion, *Caleb Williams* challenges Lentricchia's rhetorical justification for counter-hegemonic activity at the same time that it undercuts his theory of rebellion.

Lentricchia argues that "[o]ur identities are very nearly hopelessly complicated . . . by a hegemonic process that would enroll us in a range of corporate identities, some concentric, others in conflict," but nonetheless, the "shifting forces of hegemonic authority" are pregnant with "structural instability" because every age is "transitional" and because language is intrinsically "undecidable" (pp. 78-80). If freedom lies in resistance to cultural formation, then literature, by promoting a sense of cultural continuity, abets hegemony. But a pedagogy designed to neutralize influence by historicizing text and critic risks producing de-historicized students, students who find cynicism and indifference preferable to what Foucault calls "the endlessly repeated play of dominations."[5] Sensing the danger of a quietism he associates with Paul de Man, Lentricchia insists that counter-hegemonic criticism should call attention to "the historically stubborn story of resistance, whose marks continue to be made within those very mechanisms that reproduce existing, stratified power relations" (p. 143). However,

Godwin's novel suggests that the division of literature into two opposed traditions is no more tenable than the segregation of rhetoric from history. Revealing the *literary* origins of Caleb's rebellion, Godwin delineates an interplay between literature's twin roles as "story of resistance" and enforcer of "sociocultural conservation and continuity" (p. 140); similarly, the rebellion of Godwin's novel against the generic tradition it inherits is inseparable from fidelity to the forms and values inscribed within that tradition.

Before turning to *Caleb Williams,* we must consider the objection that to use a novel to evaluate the assertions of a literary theory is to compare apples and oranges. Such an objection assumes that while a novel and theory may consider a common subject—in this case, the origin and consequences of rebellion—their claims belong to different spheres, to literature in the first case and life in the second. But the isolation of literature from life, the relegation of the former to "pseudo-statements," is precisely what rhetorical criticism rejects. Godwin's novel, no less than Lentricchia's theory, seeks to persuade readers through distinct rhetorical modes. It is my argument that those modes are shaped by and gain efficacy through their historicity.

When Caleb, fascinated by Falkland's brooding, inconsistent conduct, asks the steward Collins for an explanation, he receives a story that follows the conventions, echoes the themes, and re-stages scenes familiar to any reader of Richardson, Fielding, Goldsmith, and Burney. Falkland's story, taking up the first third of Godwin's novel, is "official" in several senses: put forth for public consumption, it has been sanctioned by universal assent; woven from patterns typical to eighteenth-century fiction, it draws upon previously established traditions of interpretation; the story is thrice attenuated from a speaker (Caleb recounts in the third person Collins's account of Falkland's account). However, once Caleb begins, in the manner of a counter-hegemonic critic, to question the "official" version, he places in doubt the "naturalized conventions" that underlie Falkland's representation of himself.

But deconstruction alone does not foster successful rebellion. Though Caleb discovers the fraudulence of eighteenth-century fictional norms as they operate in Falkland's "cover story," he cannot conceive of his own "story" in their absence. Godwin pursues, through Caleb's "memoirs,"[6] a deconstruction similar to his hero's, exposing the unwillingness of eighteenth-century "realistic" fiction to trace the "practical effects" of "the existing constitution of society"[7] by writing a novel that shows the "true" consequences of social circumstances reversing and rendering ironically implausible the standard patterns of fiction from Richardson to Burney. Just as Falkland's descent from nobility to murder inverts *Sir Charles Grandison,* so Caleb's story, orginally conceived as a tale of persecution and pursuit ending in the hero's madness, reverses the "virtue rewarded" scheme of *Pamela.*[8] However, the novel's irony toward novels emerges from its generic consistency, from its insistence that novels should really present the true, unadulterated consequences of actual conditions. Godwin's revolt, like Caleb's, never moves beyond dependence upon what it reveals to be duplicious: *Caleb Williams* remains an anti-eighteenth-century novel that is not yet a nineteenth-century novel.

Falkland's "official" story corresponds to distinct fictional conventions. However opportune, the apparently "chance" murder of Falkland's adversary, Squire Tyrrel, stands within a tradition of "providential" resolutions for the heroes of eighteenth-century novels, extending from Mr. B.'s proposal of marriage to Mr. Burchell's transformation into Sir William Thornhill. After seemingly intractable problems, grounded in social circumstances, are placed before a protagonist, and after the protagonist bears up under their weight, the problems simply disappear through sudden conversions (Mr. Square's repentence), the discovery of mistaken identity (Joseph Andrews, young Wilson in *Humphry Clinker*), or strokes of fortune (Lord Orville proposes to Evelina; Amelia recovers her stolen inheritance). Falkland intends, as a young gentleman of means early imbued by his "favorite authors" with "the love of chivalry and romance" (p. 10), to use his privileged social position to cultivate politeness, inspire rectitude, and render moral service. In effect, he expects to imitate Sir Charles Grandison. As with Grandison, his generosity and nobility bring him the respectful affection of all his country neighbors—except Squire Tyrrel. Ignorant and boorish, Tyrrel enjoys local pre-eminence through his mastery of "horseflesh . . . , shooting, fishing and hunting" (p. 17) before he is challenged by someone who, through a "transvaluation of values," shifts the basis of merit from the manly arts to the practice of civility and magnanimity.

When Tyrrel's dependent niece conceives an infatuation for Falkland, he seeks to punish her for admiring "modern" virtues by forcing her to marry "the uncouth and half-civilised animal" Grimes (p. 47). Tyrrel re-creates the situation of *Clarissa,* but with a difference. Instead of pursuing wealth through coerced wedlock, he seeks, much in the manner of Lovelace, ideological vindication: by proving the superiority of force and pride upon the body of his niece, Tyrrel can enforce a "story" that will expose the inefficacy of Falkland's values and hence undermine the basis of his character. As with the conflict between Mr. B. and Pamela, Lovelace and Clarissa, the fate of the body is important not for its own sake, but because it provides an index for evaluating the claims of competing worldviews; its destiny discloses the judgment of "real experience" or Providence upon the assertions of contradictory sets of words. After Falkland's opportune appearance foils Grimes's attempted rape of Emily, Tyrrel imprisons the girl on a trumped-up charge of owing him back rent. Up to this point, Falkland has been able to translate his moral notions into effective action. Just as the approbation he receives recalls similar praise lavished upon Sir Charles Grandison, so his chance rescue of Emily very nearly repeats the circumstances of Sir Charles's rescue of Harriet Byron: in both cases, the young lady struggles against a seducer in a carriage on a lonely road when the hero happens to ride within earshot. Even Tyrrel's imprisonment of Emily repeats a pattern already encoded in eighteenth-century fiction: Lady Booby finds legal means to persecute Joseph in Book IV of *Joseph Andrews;* Squire Thornhill imprisons the Primroses in *The Vicar of Wakefield.*

Whereas Lentricchia makes rebellion contingent upon finding an "oppositional" story embedded within the "official" one, Godwin makes the principles implicit in eighteenth-century fiction the source of his critique. By tracing the "realistic" consequences of legal corruption, Fielding and Goldsmith reveal the "practical effects" of the "existing constitution of society" to be unsavory indeed; but instead of pursuing those "effects" to their logical conclusion, they arrest the implications of their own stories: the accidental discovery of Joseph's true birth frees him from Lady Booby's persecutions; when Mr. Burchell resumes his identity as Squire Thornhill's powerful, benevolent uncle, he rights the wrongs done the Vicar's family. More than faint-heartedness is involved in the eighteenth-century novel's oscillation between realistic circumstances and romance resolutions. The novel would, on the one hand, derive its "truth" from mimetic accuracy and probable causation, limiting itself to "natural Means" of sparing the hero lest "the Truth and Dignity of History" be violated;[9] on the other hand, it would have "happy endings" reveal a providential guidance or moral logic at odds with immoral probabilites. By freeing the Primroses, Sir William Thornhill institutes essential justice despite social realities; Amelia's rescue from the degradations of London through an unexpected inheritance suggests an *ultimate* rewarding of virtue, even though the dark public world Fielding presents provides little reason to expect one. Godwin exposes the inconsistency of conflating the facts of this world and the principles of a better one by pointedly refusing to dilute the tragic potential of real conditions. Emily contracts a fever and dies in jail before Falkland can save her. Since Falkland "places" himself within the norms of eighteenth-century fiction, the violation of those norms by Emily's death cannot but threaten his very being: "He burst away from the spot with a vehemence, as if he sought to leave behind him his recollection and his existence . . . . [H]e could not prevent himself from reproaching the system of nature, for having given birth to such a monster as Tyrrel" (pp. 89-80). Tyrrel's success in frustrating Falkland's good intentions suggests that the "truth" of ordinary experience and the "truth" of a providential order do not converge in fact, however they may in fiction; if eighteenth-century novels are broken, inconsistent narratives, then the exemplary character Falkland has sought by "assiduously conform[ing] to [a] model of heroism" (p. 10) might prove illusory and ineffectual.

His fears seem confirmed when, shortly after Emily's death, Tyrrel brazenly enters an assembly. Falkland delivers an eloquent rebuke that forces the villain to retreat in confusion. Tyrrel's embarrassment recalls Mr. B.'s similar embarrassment when challenged by Pamela's articulation of inner nobility. The retreat of vice before virtue, "full of wildness and horror" (p. 95), suggests that experience really does confirm moral values. But, in an act equivalent to Mr. B. raping Pamela despite her moral superiority, Tyrrel returns, surprises Falkland with a blow, and thrashes him publicly. The assault fuses generic and political implications. By refusing to play under Falkland's rules, Tyrrel reveals the vulnerability of civility to barbarism, underlining, with his fists, the gap between rhetorical power and practical effect.

Once the "story" Falkland encounters suggests that an eighteenth-century hero may be an imaginary social-linguistic construct, he first longs "for annihilation, to lie down in eternal oblivion" (p. 98) and then murders Tyrrel in a moment of blind rage. Yet, by constructing an eighteenth-century "official" version of the event, shifting responsibility for the plot resolution to a convenient third party (Hawkins and son), he would ask others to acknowledge a self he knows to be illusory. Falling back on Tyrrel's methods, Falkland reveals the presence of Tyrrel's instincts within himself as well as the dependence of civilized values upon force in order to prevail. Falkland loses the ability to seek confirmation of his character in the implications of events once he falsifies events to fit a character. In a manner typical of much eighteenth-century fiction, Falkland's story arrests the consequences of the action artificially: he is "baffled of the vengeance" he would have sought because Tyrrel happens, by chance, to turn up dead immediately after the beating (p. 88).

Whereas the incongruence between realism and romance in Fielding and Richardson reflects genuine opposing conceptions of truth (one based on observation, the other on faith), by the time of

Goldsmith and Burney, generic tension dissipates as the inconsistencies of form become conventional. Falkland's "official" story resembles the subplot of Burney's *Camilla.* Eugenia, a wealthy maiden deformed by smallpox, is kidnapped and forced into marriage by the fortune-hunter Bellamy. While she refuses to "lower" herself by annulling the marriage, Bellamy plans to extort her family's fortune. Burney resolves the tension between ideal conduct and its practical effects by having Bellamy accidently shoot himself. The tale Falkland constructs fits the Goldsmith-Burney mold; it is a type of story whose inner inconsistencies and blurred implications reveal less the conflict between two notions of truth than a strained effort to convince others, through worn conventions, of what one can no longer believe oneself.

As Caleb broods upon the story, probing its points of divergence from eighteenth-century norms, its seeming self-evidence grows "mysterious" (p. 107). The apparent murderers, tenants mistreated by Tyrrel, hardly fit their roles: "So firm, so sturdily honest and just, as [Hawkins and son] appeared at first; all at once to become . . . murderer[s]!" (p. 107). Tyrrel's convenient death, instead of resolving matters in the hero's favor, leaves Falkland tormented by "agonies and terrors" (p. 107). Just as Falkland's efforts to oppose Tyrrel's disruption of his "story" lead him, ironically, to supersede the norms that he would have circumscribe his character, so Caleb's effort to assimilate Falkland's story to a familiar discursive field leads, ironically, to his own estrangement from that field. Instead of rebellion being explicable, as in Lentricchia, only in terms of unstable cultural formation or the "undecidability" of language, it arises in *Caleb Williams* from the struggle to maintain a form of life and belief. Falkland seeks to erase any ironic gap between experience and the conceptions of self and world he derives from literature. But Tyrrel's murder reinforces the very irony it would abrogate by increasing the distance between self-projection and actuality, between rules of formation and the realities they would order. Caleb's rebellion assumes, ironically, a similar pattern.

Just as Godwin subjects eighteenth-century fiction to irony by adhering to one of its principles (truth derived from observation) at the expense of another (truth as providential order), so Caleb deconstructs Falkland's story by demanding that it achieve the "realistic consistency" it pretends to. Caleb's rebellion, no less than Falkland's, rests upon a "self" constituted by eighteenth-century norms. As Falkland expects reality to translate virtue into effective action, Caleb expects reality to reward intellectual inquiry with certain knowledge: "I could not rest till I had acquainted myself with the solutions that had been invented for the phenomena of the universe" (p. 4). His love of "natural philosophy" is allied with "an invincible attachment to books of narrative and romance"; in both he seeks principles that make meaningful sense of experience. Godwin traces the conservative impulse in rebellion, the desire to maintain a form of belief and self-projection through rendering its implications consistent with itself and with external experience.

But Caleb's pursuit of truth and consistency is complicated by a compulsive, pervasive delight that, as with Falkland's susceptibility to instinctual violence, places the character's actions outside his ability to explain them: "I remembered . . . [Falkland's] terrible looks; and the recollection gave a kind of tingling sensation, not altogether unallied to enjoyment. The farther I advanced, the more the sensation was irresistible" (pp. 107-108). From sadistic games of reminding his master of the murder, Caleb proceeds to reading Falkland's correspondence and breaking into his private trunk. He accuses himself of acting "contrary to every received principle of civilized society . . . [by] trampling on the established boundaries of obligation" (pp. 137-38). Paradoxically, even as the abstract good of "truth" leads him into guilt and self-estrangement, Caleb's rebellion remains grounded in admiration and solicitude: "I feel that my soul yearns for [Falkland's] welfare. . . . I had known [him] from the first as a beneficent divinity" (pp. 137-38).

Jauss's reception theory, not Lentricchia's oppositional criticism, clarifies the connection between admiration and rebellion. Arguing that ideological critics ignore art's "communicative function,"[10] Jauss maintains that aesthetic communication balances identification and distance: total distance engenders mere curiosity about the "other"; uncritical identification permits ideological (de)formation. Caleb's freedom of judgment emerges from, and is retained by, viewing Falkland aesthetically, as a hero. Only to the extent that Caleb identifies with Falkland's desire to "conform . . . to [a particular] model of heroism" (p. 10), only to the extent that he shares Falkland's hope of experiencing life as a consistent story, does his critical sense gain focus. Its historical specificity invests his rebellion with a shape of its "own": by attempting to replace a defective story with the "true" one, Caleb would shore up the eighteenth-century norms that Falkland's inconsistencies threaten.

As Caleb's rebellion grows out of admiration, so his actions repeat, inadvertently, Falkland's and his story becomes, like his master's, an ironic subversion of the historical norms his identity demands. Falkland could describe Tyrrel's murder in the terms Caleb employs for describing his forcing open Falkland's trunk: "In the high tide of boiling passion I had overlooked all consequences. . . . I have always been at a loss to account for my having plunged thus headlong into an act so monstrous. There is something in it of unexplained and involuntary sympathy" (p. 133). Since, at critical moments of transgression, Caleb and Falkland share with Tyrrel a blind, "involuntary" impulsiveness, their degree of guilt is blurred in a way that makes problematic the relation between an event and its interpretation. Godwin moves, in Caleb's story, from exposing the incongruence between the eighteenth-century novel's dual sources of truth (observation and faith) to challenging the notion that truth may be drawn from observation; in doing so, he undermines the "character" that Caleb hopes his discourse will "justify."

Godwin displays, in *Political Justice*, faith in the irresistible force of truth strangely juxtaposed with skepticism about the ability to determine truth in particular cases.[11] On the one hand, the natural self-validation of truth renders violent revolution unnecessary: "Who ever saw an instance in which error unaided by power was victorious over truth? . . . Has the mind of man the capacity to choose falsehood and reject truth, when her evidence is fairly presented?"[12] On the other hand, Godwin argues that "[n]o two crimes were ever alike; and therefore the reducing them . . . to general classes . . . is [as] absurd" as making punishment proportionate to a "degree of delinquency" that "can never be discovered."[13] But how can a character prove his merit if the evaluation of individual acts becomes uncertain? Moreover, if an individual's conduct is shaped by outer circumstances and "involuntary" compulsions, how can one distinguish between deeds that display character and deeds that disclose its (de)formation? While Caleb would justify himself through the self-validation of a realistic story, Godwin's novel portrays truth as neither irresistible nor certain—nor is its diffusion necessarily moral.

Like Falkland, Caleb expects his story to adhere to rules of formation derived from eighteenth-century fiction. His "memoirs" should vindicate the writer by having "that consistency, which is seldom attendant but upon truth" (p. 3). Caleb would reduce his life to the morally unequivocal pattern of pursuit by an enemy "inaccessible to intreaties and untired in persecution," a persecution his intrinsic character has "not deserved" (p. 3). From Pamela and Clarissa on, the distresses of eighteenth-century novelistic heroes and heroines arise from misrecognition. Were Pamela and Clarissa known for what they are, they would have no stories; the evidence of their letters justifies them by showing the ironic gap between how they are perceived and how they are "really." For this reason, reading Pamela's journal converts Mr. B. to virtue and Clarissa's letters enforce her posthumous vindication. In *Northanger Abbey* Catherine Morland is possessed by feelings "rather natural than heroic"[14] when, instead of allowing the Tilneys to misconstrue her character, she immediately explains how the Thorpes tricked her into missing their intended walk. Placing himself inside inherited generic norms, Caleb assumes that his "meaning no ill" will eventually be transparent to others, keeping any one from being "seriously angry" with him (p. 108). After he has goaded Falkland into confessing the "truth" and his attempt to flee his master's oppressive surveillance ends with arrest on a false charge, Caleb expects to be vindicated by a simple relation of the truth: "Innocence and guilt were, in my apprehension, the things . . . most opposite to each other. I would not suffer to believe, that the former could be confounded with the latter. . . . Virtue rising superior to every calumny, defeating by a plain, unvarnished tale all the strategems of vice . . . was one of the favourite subjects of my youthful reveries" (p. 180).

Having driven Falkland from the refuge of an inconsistent, self-contradictory Goldsmith-Burney story, Caleb hopes to "locate" himself within a typical eighteenth-century "plain, unvarnished tale" of persecution and victimization. Godwin suggests that the dissemination of particular values (in this case, the values encoded in the norms of eighteenth-century fiction) fosters criticism and revolt by constituting specific patterns of identification, specific modes of emulation: Caleb suspects Falkland's "official" story because it inadequately answers the requirements of the novelistic tradition; he seeks first to construct a "better" version of Falkland's story and then to construct his own story as an exemplary—and hence convincing—realization of eighteenth-century fiction's assumptions. Caleb's independence of judgment emerges not from instabilities in cultural formation, but from his insistence that inherited norms and principles be realized consistently and universally.

Up to a point, his experience, like Falkland's, seems to confirm the pattern it would realize: he *is* persecuted and misrecognized. After hearing Falkland's charge of robbery, Caleb's old friend Thomas will not listen to his explanation: "For your sake, lad, I will never take any body's word, nor trust to appearances, thof it should be an angel" (p. 176). When Caleb applies to an "amiable old man" for protection, he receives a favorable hearing until he divulges his name, at which the old man retreats in horror (p. 249). In Godwin's orginal ending, Caleb was to continue the victim of everybody's faith in Falkland's lies until, imprisoned once again, he was to go mad from despair of ever being believed. The "existing constitution of society" would produce an ironic anti-*Pamela*, leaving intrinsic merit and innocence forever misrecognized and slandered.

Though Godwin retains his indictment of society, Caleb's simple persecution-victim scheme grows increasingly suspect as real persecution and paranoia blend together, bringing Caleb to declare, "I could almost have imagined that I was the sole subject of general attention, and that the whole world was in arms to exterminate me" (p. 238). Both Caleb's ability to discern truth and the capacity of events to yield univocal interpretation become questionable. His rebellion and insistent distinction between himself and "the other" notwithstanding, Caleb's fugitive's life resembles Falkland's experience after murdering Tyrrel: either might observe, "My life was all a lie. I had a counterfeit character to support. . . . I was not free to indulge, no not one, honest sally of the soul" (pp. 255-58). Even the reality of Falkland's persecution grows murky. Released from prison because Falkland fails to appear against him, Caleb later hears his master declare, "Were you so stupid and undistinguishing as not to know that the presevation of your life was the uniform object of my exertions?" (p. 281). Rendering uncertain the extent to which Falkland's persecution is magnified by Caleb's paranoia, showing Caleb repeat Falkland's "story" unawares, Godwin creates a narrative that transgresses the rules of formation upon which Caleb's "character" depends. Indeed, the complexities that subject Caleb's conception of his story and himself to irony also render his pursuit of "truth" morally ambiguous.

Falkland challenges the "merit" of allowing any abstract good to determine conduct: "Is truth . . . entitled to adoration for its own sake . . . ? Will a reasonable man sacrifice to barren truth, where benevolence [and] humanity . . . require that it should be superseded?" (p. 282). While Falkland is, of course, implicated by his own guilty secret, the honest, simple people Caleb meets reinforce his Burkean point. After Laura, an exemplary, charitable country woman, learns of Caleb's reputation, she refuses to hear his "true" story: "The good man and the bad, are characters precisely opposite, not characters distinguished . . . by imperceptible shades. The Providence that rules us all, has not permitted us to be left without a clue in the most important of all questions" (pp. 299-300). Collins elaborates on the harm Caleb's "truth" might do: "If you could change all my ideas, and show me that there was no criterion by which vice might be prevented from being mistaken for virtue, what benefit would arise from that?" (p. 310). Though Falkland is a murderer, and bringing murder to light is good in the abstract, the practical effects of revealing this particular truth make its disclosure potentially criminal. Collins notes, "If you even succeed in perplexing my understanding, you will not succeed in enlightening it. . . . Meanwhile for the purchase of this uncertainty I must sacrifice all the remaining comfort of my life" (p. 310).

While Lentricchia may be confident of the rhetorical efficacy of the abstract goal of "genuine community," Godwin's novel suggests that by 1794 such modes of persuasion were already suspect. Subjecting their expectations to irony, the events Falkland and Caleb encounter make dubious the prospect of reducing polyvalent experience to univocal patterns; by emphasizing the difficulty of inferring an interpretation from events, Godwin implies that the inherence of ambiguity and unexpectedness in actual experience renders equivocal and potentially reprehensible conduct that abstract idealism would seem to vindicate. Their efforts to realize self-projections bring Falkland and Caleb to confront "surprises" (Tyrrel's attack, Falkland's ambiguous persecution-solicitude) which in turn disclose "surprise" inner depths (Falkland's murderous instincts, Caleb's abiding devotion to his compromised master) that place each character outside the "self" he would vindicate. Making surprise part of "a more profound principle of order" that "frustrate[s] . . . expectations modeled on older conventions,"[15] the very form of Godwin's novel encodes suspicion of a rhetoric that would make an abstract goal the justification of radical action. Not only do Falkland and Caleb harm others, imposing death, injustice, and incertitude in futile efforts to retain selves their stories have already repudiated, they remain locked into the same Lacanian "imaginary" however much events subject it to irony.[16]

Caleb Williams begins with the intent of exposing the frauds of eighteenth-century fiction but ends by questioning the moral consequences of unmasking them for the sake of abstract "truth." The rewritten conclusion, in which Caleb, moved by Falkland's sad decrepitude, changes his intended accusation into a self-accusation only to have Falkland so "penetrated" by "grief and compunction" (p. 323) that he announces his own guilt, has often been seen as an example of the selfless morality Godwin urges in *Political Justice*.[17] It might also be viewed as the vindication of "a plain, unvarnished tale" after all. But Falkland's confession, no less than Caleb's self-accusation, exchanges one feverishly unreliable reading of events for another. When Caleb declares, "I proclaim to all the world that Mr. Falkland is a man worthy of affection and kindness, and that I am myself the basest and most odious of mankind!" (p. 323), his "sincerity" provokes an equally extreme assertion by Falkland: "My name will be consecrated to infamy, while your heroism, your patience and your virtues will be for ever admired" (p. 324).

Caleb and Falkland would see themselves as villains rather than allow ambiguity of conduct and responsibility to set them outside eighteenth-century fiction's range of "the true."[18] No more willing than Laura and Collins to recognize as "truth" the problematic implications of Godwin's story, both expect moral clarity from experience and believe—as good eighteenth-century readers—that stories are about the "vindication of character," describing either triumphant virtue (Grandison, Amelia) or the gradual recognition of misjudged merit (Pamela, Tom Jones, Primrose, Evelina). To the extent that Godwin portrays outer circumstances and inner compulsions shaping individuality, he anticipates the nineteenth-century novel's concern with character formation.[19] But since Caleb and Falkland place themselves within eighteenth-century norms, they experience vulnerability to "involuntary" forces as a terrifying lack of autonomy; once their stories fail to affirm the presence of "intrinsic merit," being unable to imagine any other basis for character, they are left with none. Caleb concludes his self-justifying "memoir" by confessing, "I began . . . with the idea of vindicating my character. I have now no character that I wish to vindicate" (p. 328).

Linked by a common incapacity to imagine any transformation of self that is not a subjugation or annihilation of self, Caleb and Falkland struggle to enclose daily experience within specific rules of formation, to prevent events from casting doubt on certain interpretative models, in part to secure themselves against the threat of change. There is something ultimately reactionary in their resistance to the challenge posed by other people and unanticipated events to the "stories" they would realize, as though experience could be kept from "surprising" an established perspective with new circumstances or contrary viewpoints. In the readiness of Falkland and Caleb to condemn themselves in terms of the eighteeenth-century novel's rules of formation rather than acknowledge the inadequacy to experience of those terms, there is a foretaste of the dread of change and uncertainty that Nadezhda Mandelstam found lurking within abstract revolutionary idealism: "People had been promised that all change was at an end, and further changes were inadmissible. . . . Let time stand still. The stopping of time means peace and stability. They need it so much, the leaders of our age."[20]

The rhetorical force of Godwin's novel is inseparable from its historicity. Just as Caleb's resistance to Falkland is shaped by his identification with distinct cultural-linguistic norms, so the persuasiveness *for us* of Godwin's portrait of moral revolt degenerating into "involuntary" tyranny does not simply rest upon its obvious affinities with the Orc cycle and Byronic Prometheanism. Rather, the ambivalence towards rebellion encoded in the form of *Caleb Williams* enters, at a historical moment that Blake, Byron, and Godwin demarcate, the realm of literary expression in response to specific interactions between rhetoric and history in the "real world" (namely, the French Revolution). Falkland and Caleb attempt to evade their historicity by seeking to render an inherited worldview free from the revision and challenge of particular experience. Similarly, a criticism that would isolate rhetorical analysis from the interplay between history and rhetoric would not historicize literature, but shield itself from the "subversive" potential implicit in historicity.

NOTES

[1]Frank Lentricchia, *Criticism and Social Change* (Chicago and London: Univ. of Chicago Press, 1983), pp. 147-48. Further references are to this edition and will be cited parenthetically in the text.

[2]In general, Adorno and Marcuse emphasize the liberating function of aesthetic form, its resistance to the rationalizing, normalizing hegemony of consumer culture, while Jameson, Lentricchia, and Eagleton, drawing on the French tradition, emphasize its mystifying function, its promotion of false consciousness. See T. W. Adorno, *Aesthetic Theory,* trans. C. Lenhardt (London: Routledge & Kegan Paul, 1984); Herbert Marcuse, *The Aesthetic Dimension: Toward a Critique of Marxist Aesthetics,* trans. Herbert Marcuse and Erica Sherover (Boston: Beacon, 1978); Frederic Jameson, *The Political Unconscious: Narrative as a Socially Symbolic Act* (Ithaca: Cornell Univ. Press, 1981); Terry Eagleton, *Literary Theory: An Introduction* (Minneapolis: Univ. of Minnesota Press, 1983). Traditional readings of *Caleb Williams* divide between political and psychological approaches. See David McCracken's introduction in *Caleb Williams* (New York: Norton, 1977), pp. vii-xxii; Gerald A. Barker, "Justice to Caleb Williams," *Studies in the Novel* 6 (1974): 377-88; John Pesta, "*Caleb Williams:* A Tragedy of Wasted Love," *TSL* 16 (1971): 67-76. In "*Caleb Williams* and the Attack on Romance," *SNNTS* 8 (1976): 81-86, C. R. Kropf remarks the novel's critique of eighteenth-century fiction, arguing that Godwin follows Fielding's portrayal of things "as they are" against Richardson's portrayal of things as they ought to be. Mitzi Myers notes Falkland's resemblance to a "tragic Quixote" (p. 604) in "Godwin's Changing Conception of *Caleb Williams,*" *SEL* 12 (1972):591-628.

[3]Just as reflectionist aesthetics (Lukács and Goldmann) are rejected by Marcuse (*The Aesthetic Dimension,* pp. 1-21), Adorno (*Aesthetic Theory,* pp. 326-29, 358-59), and Jameson (*The Political Unconscious,* pp. 43-44), so Jameson and Lentricchia use the doctrine of semi-autonomy to undermine the base's determination of superstructure. See *The Political Unconscious,* pp. 23-43; *Criticism and Social Change,* pp. 122-23. Lentricchia even minimizes Althusser's preservation of economic "determination in the last instance":"The stress . . . is not on the metaphysical temptation of the 'last instance' but on semi-autonomous levels, each possessing its own structural and internal necessity" (p. 122). Citing Althusser's "antiteleological formula for history" (p. 34), Jameson flirts with a "paradigm" enfolding all literature into a master narrative of Freedom struggling against Necessity (pp. 101-102). Less coy, Lentricchia flatly rejects the "teleological ideal" underlying "all traditional Marxist acts of interpretation" (p. 12).

[4]Edmund Burke, *Reflections on the Revolution in France* (Harmondsworth: Penguin, 1969), p. 90.

[5]Michel Foucault, *Language, Counter-Memory, Practice: Selected Essays and Interviews,* trans. Donald F. Bouchard and Sherry Simon (Ithaca: Cornell Univ. Press, 1977), p. 153.

[6]William Godwin, *Caleb Williams* (New York: Norton, 1977), p. 3. Further references are to this edition and will be cited parenthetically in the text.

[7]William Godwin, 1794 Preface, *Caleb Williams* (New York: Norton, 1977), p. 1.

[8]See D. Gilbert Dumas, "Things as They Were: The Original Ending of *Caleb Williams*," *SEL* 6 (1966):575-97. In his 1832 account, reprinted in *Caleb Williams* (New York: Norton, 1977), pp. 335-41, Godwin notes that he began with a story of persecution, conceiving first Caleb's flight, then Falkland's story.

[9]Henry Fielding, *The History of Tom Jones, A Foundling,* ed. Martin C. Battestin (Middletown, Conn.: Wesleyan Univ. Press, 1975), p. 876.

[10]Hans Robert Jauss, *Aesthetic Experience and Literary Hermeneutics,* trans. Michael Shaw (Minneapolis: Univ. of Minnesota Press, 1982), p. 20; also see pp. 152-88.

[11]Just as Godwin advocates anarchism by conjoining confidence in man's ability to see his individual interest in the general good with a hard-headed analysis of how every form of government opens avenues for moral corruption, so he maintains that the progressive diffusion of reason will allow truth to be apprehended clearly while denying the justice of criminal penalities because the same act may be evaluated variously. See Peter H. Marshall, *William Godwin* (New Haven and London: Yale Univ. Press, 1984), pp. 93-117.

[12]William Godwin, *An Enquiry Concerning Political Justice,* ed. Raymond A. Preston, 2 vols. (New York: Alfred A. Knopf, 1926), 2:82-83.

[13]*Political Justice,* 2:169.

[14]Jane Austen, *Northanger Abbey and Persuasion* (London: Oxford Univ. Press, 1975), p. 83.

[15]Paul Ricoeur, *Time and Narrative,* trans. Kathleen McLaughlin and David Pellauer, 3 vols. (Chicago and London: Univ. of Chicago Press, 1985), 2:22.

[16]See Wilfried Ver Eecke's discussion of Lacan's account of aggressivity as a means of conserving the imaginary in "Hegel as Lacan's Source for Necessity in Psychoanalytic Theory," in *Interpreting Lacan,* ed. Joseph H. Smith and Walter Kerrigan (New Haven and London: Yale Univ. Press, 1983), pp. 113-37, esp. pp. 126-35.

[17]See Barker, pp. 377-88; *Political Justice,* 2:116-27.

[18]See Foucault's discussion of speaking "within the true," "The Discourse on Language," p. 224, in Michel Foucault, *The Archeology of Knowledge,* trans. A. M. Sheridan Smith (New York: Pantheon, 1972).

[19]See Anthony Winner's discussion of Balzac's portrayal of character in *Characters in the Twilight: Hardy, Zola and Chekhov* (Charlottesville: Univ. Press of Virginia, 1981), pp. 9-27.

[20]Nadezhda Mandelstam, *Hope Against Hope: A Memoir,* trans. Max Hayward (New York: Antheneum, 1970), p. 50.

SEL 28 (1988)
ISSN 0039-3657

Recent Studies in the Restoration and Eighteenth Century

ROBERT D. HUME

We live in a golden age of eighteenth-century studies. This may seem a surprising way to open a survey that will not consist of unmitigated rapture. Omnium gatherum surveys tend more to gloom than rhapsody; we have plenty of mediocre or pedestrian books to consider. But this has always been so, and, waiving plaints about the rising tide of academic Grub Street, we will make a very different judgment if we look at the best of what is appearing, and at the overall level of quality. A number of books have come out this year that should make a major difference in their realms for some decades. Most notably I would point to James Winn's biography of Dryden; Dene Barnett's revolutionary account of eighteenth-century acting; Thomas Kaminski's study of the early career of Samuel Johnson; the Jordan-Love edition of Southerne; volumes 5 and 6 of the "California" Dryden, giving us his *Virgil*; the Bond *Tatler*; and volumes 11 and 12 of the ongoing *Biographical Dictionary* of theatrical personnel in London. In the realm of criticism—always harder to judge for the long term—we have interesting and important books by W. B. Carnochan on Gibbon and Kristina Straub on Fanny Burney.

No organization of an essay of this sort can be wholly satisfactory. I propose to work by rough categories. I shall begin with editions, and go on to major authors (omitting dramatists and novelists); and then to drama; fiction (general and particular); prose and satire; cultural and intellectual history; and finally collections. Dealing with more than 100 volumes in fifty typescript pages makes serious "review" of any of them impossible, but I will describe some books only very briefly in order to leave more space for the most important ones.

Robert D. Hume is Professor of English at The Pennsylvania State University. His numerous books range from *Dryden's Criticism* (Cornell Univ. Press, 1970) to *Henry Fielding and the London Theatre, 1728-1737* (Oxford Univ. Press, 1988).

I. Editions

Editions have not seemed glamorous in recent years, but they remain the underpinning on which many of our critical enterprises depend, and much of this year's most important work falls in this category. An edition is not, of course, an end in itself. Enormous effort can be expended to no useful end, and all of us are familiar with examples of mindless or inaccurate editions, not to mention pointlessly reduplicative ones. How many "student" editions of *The Country-Wife* and *Moll Flanders* do we need? But when an edition makes scattered or inaccessible material available, or makes difficult material easy to use, it changes the field in a truly important and welcome way. Two sorts of editions seem especially desirable—"standard" full-dress *Works* and inexpensive "make-it-available" editions of neglected texts. We have admirable examples of both genres to consider.

The Works of Thomas Southerne, edited in two volumes by Robert Jordan and Harold Love, is the most important and exciting edition of a playwright from this period to have appeared in the last half-century. This statement will surprise readers who are wondering "Who he?"—but let me explain. Decent editions of virtually all major Restoration and eighteenth-century playwrights were published by the 1930s, often more than one per author. Since then new editions have hardly ever forced us to reconsider basic canon judgments—but this one does. Both as a writer of serious satiric comedy (*The Wives' Excuse, The Maid's Last Prayer*) and pathetic tragicomedy (*The Fatal Marriage, Oroonoko*) Southerne produced work that will stand comparison with the handful of plays that have long constituted "the canon." In 1948 John Harrington Smith boldly called *The Wives' Excuse* "one of the five most considerable comedies written between 1660 and 1700," a judgment endorsed by a number of later scholars—but lack of a widely available modern edition and general ignorance of Southerne have kept criticism to a minimum for fully forty years. In my view Southerne is a better playwright than Etherege or Wycherley, and though more uneven, arguably as good as Congreve. The Oxford edition is a truly major event, giving us an accessible and well-presented text of a writer unfairly marginalized by the vagaries of literary history. And happily, it is a superlatively good edition. The text has been edited with intelligence and good judgment; the annotation is knowledgable; the introduction and apparatus helpful, unobtrusive, and accurate. Southerne deserves the serious critical attention that this edition now makes possible.

The appearance of volumes 5 and 6 of the "California" Dryden is another major event. Strange as it seems, this is the first scholarly edition of Dryden's Virgil ever published. Only in recent years has the excellence and importance of this translation been understood, a development to which Steven Zwicker's recent book contributed substantially. Even more than Pope's Homer, Dryden's Virgil has been wrongly treated as a digression or distraction from his central poetic endeavors. Both poetically and ideologically, the Virgil translation has much to tell us about Dryden and the 1690s—and this edition should spark a great deal of work in the next twenty years. These particular volumes attempt to recreate a sense of the original physical book in a way this edition has never previously done. Thus the entire contents of the 1697 folio are included—which gives us Knightly Chetwood's Life of Virgil, Addison's essay on the *Georgics,* commendatory poems, etc., along with all the original illustrations (some 100 in all). We are also, of course, given the elaborate textual bibliography and historical annotation we expect from this source. The bibliographic and textual complexities are considerable (neither the 1697 nor the 1698 edition can be straightforwardly accepted as copytext). Dryden drew extensively on a long tradition of Virgil translation—here helpfully expounded. And his growing habit of covert allusion to recent and contemporary events poses considerable headaches for any editor, who must avoid overingenuity while trying to expound important indirect references. The nearly 300 pages of notes and commentary (helpfully indexed) are an enormous step forward in letting us understand Dryden's magnum opus. These volumes are the fourteenth and fifteenth to appear in a series that began publication in 1956 and has remained at state-of-the-art standards ever since. The 1980s volumes tend to be decidedly better than those published twenty years earlier, something that cannot be said for all long-term editions. When the edition is complete, Dryden will have been served about as well as any major English author has been by twentieth-century editors. And because of the unreasonable neglect of the Virgil, this installment of the edition has serious claim to being the most vital of all.

Donald F. Bond's three-volume edition of *The Tatler* is not quite so ground-breaking a venture. Aitken's edition of 1898-99 was excellent for its day, and the periodical has hardly been neglected. Nonetheless, this edition deserves high praise. Editorial policy and format parallel Bond's admirable five-volume *Spectator* of 1965 (out of print for some years, but now made available again by Oxford). That edition has stood the test of time, and I suspect this one will too. People who have read only particular *Tatlers* in collections may not realize how compulsively readable it is. The *Spectator* is the more literary and intellectual journal, but *The Tatler* is grounded in the daily cultural life of its times, and is the better source for context and detail ca. 1710. It needs a lot of annotation—generously but tactfully provided here. There is an index in each volume; that in volume 3 is cumulative and 136 pages long. This is destined to be one of those standard editions that is used by generations of scholars, and I have spent many hours reading it for the sheer fun of doing so.

Three single-volume installments in ongoing standard editions deserve an enthusiastic welcome. *The True Patriot and Related Writings,* edited by W. B. Coley, is the latest addition to the Wesleyan/Oxford Fielding. It comprises Fielding's contributions to the title periodical and three pamphlets likewise related to the "Forty-Five": *A Serious Address to the People of Great Britain, The History of the Present Rebellion in Scotland,* and *A Dialogue Between the Devil, the Pope, and the Pretender.* Massive annotation is necessary, and is provided. The general introduction runs eighty-five pages, with another six on the text. "Uncertain" parts of *The True Patriot* are placed in a lengthy appendix, and there is a substantial index. The volume represents historical and textual scholarship of a high order and allows us confident access to a part of Fielding's canon that clearly needs more study. I regret that this volume was already in press when Thomas R. Cleary's important *Henry Fielding: Political Writer* (1984) appeared; Cleary would have been of some use to Coley. And I must lament what I take to be a decision made for economy: to exclude those parts of the thirty-three numbers of *The True Patriot* definitely not by Fielding. This throws the reader back on Miriam Austin Locke's facsimile edition of 1964 for the remainder of the periodical. Even granted that this is an edition of Fielding, the exclusion seems regrettable.

The earlier volumes of Karina Williamson's edition of *The Poetical Works of Christopher Smart* have been widely praised, and rightly so. Volume 4, "Miscellaneous Poems English and Latin," is well up to the standard of the series, and very welcome indeed. Thirty of the poems have not been printed in any earlier collection, and several are reprinted here for the first time since the eighteenth century. The thirty-page introduction is brisk, helpful, and sound—a model of its kind. The most important of the contents is *The Hilliad* (great fun), but there are many surprises and pleasures to be found here. Williamson's edition is helping Smart claim his place as a major poet, and the succinct but meaty notes are a great help even to the specialist reader. I might quibble with the decision to use *1752* as a typographical model, but this edition is so good that complaint seems ungenerous.

The last contribution to a standard edition is, fittingly, the fifth and final volume of *The Letters and Prose Writings of William Cowper*, edited by James King and Charles Ryskamp. The contents are heterogeneous—some occasional essays and book reviews, the commentary on *Paradise Lost*, and three addenda to the 1303 letters already printed. Editing and presentation are elegant, and the fifty-page "Cumulative Index" is a pleasure to use. The existence of this edition will do much to change and deepen our view of Cowper.

An enthusiastic welcome is also due to the "Mothers of the Novel" series, published by Pandora and distributed by Routledge/ Methuen. For review I have received a representative sample: Sarah Fielding's *The Governess* (1749), Eliza Haywood's *The History of Miss Betsy Thoughtless* (1751), Frances Sheridan's *Memoirs of Miss Sidney Bidulph* (1761), Mary Hamilton's *Munster Village* (1778), Elizabeth Inchbald's *A Simple Story* (1791), Charlotte Smith's *The Old Manor House* (1794), and Mary Hays's *Memoirs of Emma Courtney* (1796). The prices range from £3.95 to £5.95 (with American prices around $10.00). None of them is a great novel, but having them available is wonderful and should do much to facilitate critical attention to more than a few big names. Texts are set in attractive modern type; there is no textual apparatus. Introductions are brief and for the most part superficial and unscholarly. But infinitely better that we should have many neglected novels in this form than an occasional novel fancily edited at a high price. This series deserves our investigation and support.

We have four editions that fall somewhere between the extremes of "standard" and popular reprint. The most ambitious is *John Dryden*, edited by Keith Walker in the "Oxford Authors" series. The book gives us (in 967 pages of readable type) modernized texts of the *Essay of Dramatic Poesy*, all the usual poems and many minor ones, and lots of the *Fables*. Virgil is represented by the *Georgics*; beyond prologues and epilogues and some scraps of criticism, Dryden the playwright does not appear. Eighty-five pages of helpful endnotes are signalled by degree signs in the text. For $14.95 in paperback this is a generous representation of Dryden. The audience, however, is definitely the lower-level student or the general reader. The book is a convenience to teachers, and perhaps a source of profit for its publisher, but hardly an advance on Oxford's own Kinsley edition, let alone the "California" Dryden. California would be well advised to try a couple of competing paperbacks of its own, preferably unmodernized and more fully representative of Dryden.

Selected Prose of Alexander Pope, edited by Paul Hammond (Cambridge), strikes me as an odd enterprise. Hammond is good scholar, and he provides a sensible short introduction and helpful notes. The texts include the prefaces to the 1717 *Works* and Pope's *Iliad* and Shakespeare edition, essays for the *Spectator* and *Guardian, The Art of Sinking in Poetry*, and some fifty-five pages of letters.

The blurb suggests that "This anthology is intended to make Pope's major prose works more widely available," but why and for whom? At $39.50 one hopes for a bit more. An inexpensive paperback might be a useful teaching aid, but at this degree of scholarship and price, why not simply redo and supplant the "Ault" edition? A similar venture from Cambridge is *English Science, Bacon to Newton*, edited by Brian Vickers, which comprises familiar extracts from Bacon, Boyle, Hooke, Sprat, Newton, and others. Title notwithstanding, the focus is on the 1660s—a sensible decision. The editor provides a competent brief introduction, a helpful glossary, minimal notes, a useful "Select Bibliography," but no index. Textual policy is left rather cloudy, but less is modernized than in the Pope. Once again, however, I have to wonder how much real need there is for this edition. By comparison with Oxford, Cambridge's ventures into edition publishing have not been altogether happy of late.

The last edition to be considered here is George Campbell's *The Philosophy of Rhetoric* (1776), which has been reissued by Southern Illinois. Originally published in 1963, with a brief introduction by Lloyd F. Bitzer, this reprint has a substantially enlarged introduction by the same editor. Having the text readily available again is welcome: it was an exceedingly important influence for more than fifty years. Campbell's attempts to build a rhetorical theory on empirical principles, and his ultimate reliance on theological assumptions, make fascinating reading. The introduction is now substantial and helpful. I wish, however, that the text were not simply a facsimile reproduction of the 1850 edition, especially as the choice of copytext is both peculiar and not properly justified. In this age of Kurzweil optical scanners and laser printers, Southern Illinois might have presented a reset text, as they did in their recent *The Rhetorics of Thomas Hobbes and Bernard Lamy* in the same series.

Reflecting on these editions, I must salute Oxford University Press for the service it is rendering our field. Of the six "standard" editions considered here this year, five are from Oxford. Nor is this a statistical fluke. Already advertised—though I have not yet seen them—are major editions of Farquhar, Halifax, and Crabbe, all from Oxford. Scholars and libraries groan at the prices, and £50 a volume is steep. The market has shrunk, however, and even at these horrid prices such editions tend to be losing propositions. But we badly need them, and we should be grateful to Oxford (and to California for its Dryden) for continuing commitment to a vital if unfashionable kind of scholarship.

II. Major Authors (excluding dramatists and novelists)

In the realm of Dryden-Pope-Swift-Johnson (and this year Gibbon) we have eleven books to consider. The most important is unquestionably James Anderson Winn's *John Dryden and His World.* When Charles E. Ward published *The Life of John Dryden* in 1961 it was widely praised, and most scholars have assumed that only scraps could be added to it. Indeed, most sorts of biographical information remain woefully lacking, and the biographer is forced to go to works and context. No vast amount of new information has turned up in the last thirty years, but reading this massive and densely-packed volume and then going back to Ward, one immediately realizes how comparatively narrow and shallow the earlier biography is. Ward provides less than half of Winn's documentation, and is much less scrupulous about giving his basis for everything from dates to character analysis. Winn has taken infinite trouble—to read his predecessors, dig in context, and return to many original records. Ward could have done many of the same things in the 1950s, but did not. The new biography benefits enormously from Winn's grasp of detail and his judicious handling of scanty or biased evidence. He is by no means afraid to guess and to say so. As he remarks, "in the case of Dryden, inference and speculation are particularly necessary, since the kinds of primary material usually available for later writers are almost entirely absent in his case" (p. xiii).

Biographers too often write either without apparent reason for doing so or because they have an axe to grind. Mary Edmond's *Davenant* is a recent example of the former; Helene Koon's *Cibber* of the latter. Winn has written very simply in the belief that Dryden is a great writer and that he can help us understand Dryden's aims, point of view, and contexts. This book is mercifully free of apology for what Dryden was or did: Winn accepts and explains his subject. Lacking the personalia available to most biographers, Winn concentrates heavily on what Dryden wrote. He is more partial to the poems than to the plays, but he has done a thorough and conscientious job with theatrical context, dates, and casts. He is perfectly willing to point out Dryden's failures and unevenness. One of the most welcome differences from Ward is that Winn has read a great deal more of Dryden's rivals and friends and sees his work in a much more balanced way. Dryden's numerous literary quarrels are presented with a no-nonsense fairness that is unusual and refreshing. Unlike Ward, Winn has been able to escape the slurs and broils of past generations. For the first time we have here a Dryden stripped of tired smears and partisan defense.

One of the great successes of *John Dryden and His World* is Winn's emphasis on his youth and upbringing. The chapters on Westminster School, Trinity College, and the puritan world of the 1650s take us far beyond Ward and the ordinary limits of biography, and help us understand why Dryden grew up viewing the world as he did. The perspective narrows considerably after the 1660s as Winn is forced to deal with Dryden's busy career. And I must confess to finding the last two chapters (1687-1700) overcompressed and very closely focused. This book comprises 650 large pages, but another hundred would have been welcome.

This biography has plainly been written for two audiences, as the publisher implies in offering so massive a book (with some forty-five illustrations) for just $29.95 hardbound. Winn reserves the text for discussion of Dryden and the seventeenth century; scholarly controversy has been "suppressed to the notes" (p.xvi). The documentation and discussion of scholarship is formidable—ninety pages of smallish print—and not only helpful but very good reading in its own right. In sum, this is a major book. It gives us an immensely fuller, clearer, and fairer picture of its subject than we have ever had before, and it does as much for its subject as any biography has done for an important eighteenth-century author. Given the difficulties of the evidence, this is a remarkable achievement. One of the functions of major books is to be quarrelled with, and no doubt this one will be. But it gives us a new foundation for Dryden studies, and it will assuredly be a key point of reference for all Dryden scholars of our time.

After so massive and learned a book, others tend to seem skimpy, however unfair the comparison. Our one Pope book of the year is in fact a good one. In *The Imaginative World of Alexander Pope* Leopold Damrosch, Jr., gives us a short, readable reconstruction of how Pope viewed and understood the world around him. The perspective is unusual and salutary. For once Pope is not a "late Renaissance poet" stoutly upholding cultural truisms. Instead, Damrosch finds a Pope who, living in a chaotic "modern" world, very much wanted to affirm traditional order but had great difficulty in doing so. Damrosch is particularly effective in explaining Pope's lack of the "cultural authority" (p. 303) that he craved and sought, and his painful discovery that "great literary forms had ceased to be effective" (p. 245). Organization is thematic, giving us chapters on such subjects as self-image, "Society, Money, Class," Pope's ultimate choice of satire as a vocation, and "Religion and Metaphysics." I particularly liked the account of money and class, which is scrupulously nonideological, but helpful in seeing Pope in his setting. The footnotes are modest and strictly documentary, but this book is written with a thorough knowledge of recent scholarship, and in an undogmatic way the author proffers a useful counterview to Popean orthodoxy. At times I wished for a broader perspective and some comparisons to other figures of the time—this is very much a book about Pope—but what the book sets out to do it accomplishes gracefully and well.

The two Swift books of the year are pretty small beer. The more useful is Dirk Friedrich Passmann's *"Full of Improbable Lies": "Gulliver's Travels" und die Reiseliteratur vor 1726.* This 505-page monograph, offset from typescript, investigates the relation of Swift's book to earlier travel literature and searches for "elements" relevant to Swift. Little is done with *Gulliver's Travels* itself—eleven pages on *GT* "als Werk der Reiseliteratur." But the study is heavily documented (120 pages of notes) and will be of use as a sourcebook. Charles H. Hinnant's *Purity and Defilement in "Gulliver's Travels"* is a monograph of 114 pages (at $29.95) set up to suggest "that impurity is best understood . . . not in a contemporary psychological or hygenic sense, but rather in relation to rational norms and categories" (p. ix). We are given an introduction, a chapter on each book, and a brief conclusion. Such thematic study can be carried out on virtually any text, and many texts permit application of a wide variety of themes. This book is very lightly footnoted indeed and does not make much contribution to ongoing debates. It is not necessarily "wrong," but I do not see for whom it is useful.

On Samuel Johnson we have five books, three of them of considerable merit. Let me start, briefly, with *A Bibliography of Johnsonian Studies, 1970-1985*, compiled by Donald Greene and John A. Vance. I need hardly say more than that this volume continues "Clifford" (1951) and "Clifford and Greene" (1970). Organization and numbering systems tie directly into the latter, and there is a good index. Like its predecessors, this tool will be much used by all Johnsonians.

The major Johnson book of the year—and one of the highlights of this review—is Thomas Kaminski's *The Early Career of Samuel Johnson.* To the reader who is muttering "Boswell . . . Clifford . . . Bate . . . who needs it?" I say "dip into it." You will soon find yourself gripped. Kaminski's title is precise: he is talking about the career, not the life. The subject is what Johnson was doing in the world of Grub Street, not biography per se. Kaminski starts in 1737 and ends in 1746 with the contract for the *Dictionary.* In an uncontentious but convincing way he gives us substantially new views of the book trade in the 1740s, the *Gentleman's Magazine*, the issue of Johnson's "poverty," the abortive 1745 plan to edit Shakespeare, Johnson's early political principles, and his relations with Savage. Kaminski writes clearly; asks straightforward questions; and stays away from Boswell. The fifty pages of endnotes are solidly helpful. I particularly liked the calculation of Johnson's income—the results of which are surprising. This book is scholarly, readable, and strikingly original.

Another unusual and worthwhile book is Mark J. Temmer's *Samuel Johnson and Three Infidels*. It comprises three autonymous studies—on Johnson and Rousseau, *Candide* and *Rasselas*, and *The Life of Savage* and *Le Neveu de Rameau*. The perspective may be disconcerting to some Johnsonians. Temmer is practicing a speculative kind of comparative intellectual history, fully aware of the risks and methodological problems. He is content to show suggestive and unnoticed parallels and to admit substantial differences. ("What, one may ask, does Johnson's melancholic biography have in common with Diderot's crisp satire? What values might they share and how might they differ in terms of style and dramatic structure?"—p. 124.) No "thesis" is argued here, but out of this book comes a sharpened sense of later eighteenth-century intellectual history.

Our last two Johnson books are less important. *Dr Johnson: Interviews and Recollections*, edited by Norman Page, is simply a collection of snippets (mostly one to three pages). Only one Boswell passage is used, but Mrs. Piozzi, Hawkins, Murphy, and Fanny Burney are familiar sources. This collection is tidily done but has little to offer specialists. *Domestick Privacies: Samuel Johnson and the Art of Biography*, edited by David Wheeler, is a decided disappointment. The contributors—Lawrence Lipking, James L. Battersby, John A. Dussinger, James Gray, Catherine N. Parke, Stephen Fix, William R. Siebenschuh, and Michael Stuprich—include some noted Johnsonians, but most of these essays seem short and lightweight. The most interesting, to me, was Fix's "The Contexts and Motives of Johnson's *Life of Milton*," arguing for a substantial revision in our assumptions about Johnson's view of Milton. But overall, this collection does not cohere well enough to be a book.

The last work to be considered in this section is both unusual and very fine indeed. W. B. Carnochan's *Gibbon's Solitude: The Inward World of the Historian* is really a study of *outlook*, a notoriously difficult thing to bring off both gracefully and convincingly. Carnochan uses the six overlapping drafts of Gibbon's autobiography as a route into this complex and contradictory person, looking to see how Gibbon moved from Catholic convert to skeptic and how the diverse impulses of his character are embodied in the *Decline and Fall*. This is not a tidy thesis book, and it does not summarize conveniently. But anyone who reads it will come away with a clearer understanding of why Gibbon's masterpiece is the way it is. This book is good because Carnochan is smart and also unpretentious. Would that all subtle readers could write so simply and engagingly. Abstract and wide-ranging though the book is, it makes very pleasant reading. And it reminds us that Gibbon is too often neglected by those determined to concentrate on fiction, poetry, and drama. He was a major figure, and we need to reckon with him as we try to make sense of the age.

III. Drama and Theater

Since the completion of *The London Stage* twenty years ago we have benefitted from the publication of a great deal of excellent work in this realm. "New Criticism" failed to do much for "Restoration drama," but the push toward theater- and performance-oriented criticism in the last decade has opened up new methods and new views. Editions of something other than chestnuts have been a major desideratum and continue to be so. The Jordan-Love *Southerne* is discussed above. The "California" Dryden is moving along toward completion; Shirley Kenny's *Farquhar* is advertised (though not yet out as I write). We have sound versions of Wycherley, Gay, and Sheridan; and Oxford promises Etherege, Congreve, Buckingham, and Lillo. But what about Aphra Behn? Vanbrugh? Foote?—not to mention a host of others.

The second major drama-related edition of the year is volumes 5 and 6 of Pierre Danchin's *The Prologues and Epilogues of the Restoration 1660-1700*, completing the text with the years 1691-1700. (A seventh volume, due out shortly, will contain three indexes and some corrigenda.) The first two volumes appeared in 1981; the second set in 1984; and their enthusiastic reviews should have generated more notice and use than this important edition has yet received. Collecting 1229 prologues and epilogues is by no means a simple matter. A substantial number are buried in collections or survive only in manuscript, and not all copies of play quartos have the prologue and epilogue. Multiple versions and variants are not uncommon; dating problems are numerous. Professor Danchin has done an exemplary job of assembling texts, collating and dating them, and presenting explanatory introductions. He has labored mightily over *POAS* items and other collection pieces, leaving us all in his debt. I have spotted few significant errors or problems. I might point out that the author of the prologue for the opening of Drury Lane in 1695 is Colley Cibber (*Apology*, ed. Lowe, 1:195-96), and that *The Fairy-Queen* (1692) is no longer attributed to Settle; hence its prologue should be regarded as anonymous. No serious student of the drama should ignore this edition as a source of valuable context, criticism, and topical perspective. It stands as an important source of difficult-to-assemble material, but so far one that has found its way into too few libraries.

Another welcome edition of a totally different sort is Bruce Redford's *The Origins of "The School for Scandal,"* comprising "The Slanderers" and "Sir Peter Teazle" from the Taylor MSS at Princeton. These have never before been completely and accurately printed, and Redford is able definitively to show that they were conceived as sketches toward a single play. This handsome book presents facsimile of manuscript against facing transcription. From it we can learn a great deal about Sheridan's habits of composition and revision and his concept of play design.

Turning from editions to reference books, we arrive at one of the joys of the year, volumes 11 and 12 of the Highfill-Burnim-Langhans *Biographical Dictionary of Actors, Actresses, Musicians, Dancers, Managers & Other Stage Personnel in London, 1660-1800.* The first two volumes appeared in 1973; the present set comprise "Naso to Pinkey" and "Pinner to Rizzo." No titans are covered in this installment—no Betterton nor Garrick—but the Norris, Palmer, and Rich families, Anne Oldfield, Hannah Pritchard, and James Quin are of considerable interest. The *Biographical Dictionary* gets unfairly taken for granted: we grumble about lack of detail or documentation, and somehow the name one wants is always in the next volume awaiting publication. Inevitably, a specialist can find minor errors or gaps. Thomas Odell did not, for example, obtain "Letters Patent" in 1729 (though he claimed to), and the "fixed overhead" of £16 at Goodman's Fields is not credible (11:93). What the authors take to be an "unrecorded burlesque" of Lee's *Rival Queens* ca. 1706 is in fact Colley Cibber's *The Rival Queans* (11:322). British Library "Add MS 2201" should be 12,201 (11:329—an error repeated from earlier volumes). The account of John Potter (builder and owner of the Little Haymarket) should have mentioned his participation in censorship in 1732 and his letter to Grafton about shutting Fielding down at Walpole's behest in 1737 (12:97). The discussion of the building costs of Covent Garden is off by several thousand pounds, as the *Survey of London* account makes clear (12:344). But a few such blemishes do not detract from an achievement of staggering proportions. With some twenty-five years of labor, the three authors have put together a reference work that permanently changes the nature of its field. As literary critics come to understand that they really *must* take into account the actors for whom parts were written, and to see that cast history allows us to recreate the concept and impact of eighteenth-century productions, they will understand that the *Biographical Dictionary* makes not only possible but easy a kind of scholarship that has heretofore been feasible only for a few specialists. A critic must be very stupid or old-fashioned to refuse to see the power of what the *Biographical Dictionary* opens up for us.

The second reference book—hardly by coincidence—is Edward A. Langhans's *Eighteenth Century British and Irish Promptbooks: A Descriptive Bibliography*. This is a tool of considerable value. No previous reference work has ever pulled together a list of eighteenth-century promptbooks, and given current interest in staging and theater, they represent an important and hitherto almost unutilized source of information. Langhans lists some 380 prompt copies located all over the world and describes succinctly the production at issue and the types of notes the particular copy contains. This will be an invaluable source for anyone trying to identify and analyze a new find. Introduction, bibliography, and index are all extremely helpful.

The third drama/theater reference book of the year is Ronald W. Vince's *Neoclassical Theatre: A Historiographical Handbook*. I must confess to wincing at the title: Vince covers England, France, and Italy from roughly 1650 to 1800, and "neoclassical" applies better on the continent. The ninety pages devoted to England, however, are quite splendid. Vince provides a brisk, expert, and authoritative survey of available primary sources—both printed and MS. He covers playtexts, criticism, early biography, P.R.O. MSS, the Larpent collection, promptbooks, account books, prompters' histories and diaries, inventories, actors' handbooks, theater plans, scene design, and music. Modern scholarship is judiciously utilized.

The greatest impediment to "historical" interpretation of eighteenth-century plays has always been the vexed issue of acting style. How did *they* perform these plays, and how are we to interpret such commentary as has come down to us? Like baroque musicologists of two generations ago who realized that performers added ornamentation to printed texts, but had no idea exactly what the ornaments consisted of, we find ourselves at a loss in facing a gap we can hardly begin to measure. Most of what has been written in textbooks and surveys is rubbish, based on little but prejudice and conjecture. Happily, we are now entering a new phase. Dene Barnett's *The Art of Gesture: The Practices and Principles of 18th Century Acting* is a truly seminal piece of research. Working painstakingly through a great mass of printed and manuscript evidence in several European languages, Barnett has constructed at 500 pages' length and with elaborate illustration such explanation of the theory and practice of acting as the eighteenth century has to offer us. Of course this is only a beginning: we have now to learn to interpret and apply what Barnett has discovered. Many a literary critic will gape at this book in dismay and incomprehension, and hasten to close it. But what it tells us is going to serve as the underpinning of a basic reassessment of how we analyze this drama. Mark these words: a century hence this book will be viewed as one of the principal twentieth-century contributions to the history of acting.

Making useful generalizations about this drama has seemed harder and harder in recent years. Edward Burns's *Restoration Comedy: Crises of Desire and Identity* is an intelligent, readable, old-fashioned survey of some fifteen major writers from Etherege to Steele (with a coda on *The Beggar's Opera*), written loosely around the notion that "Restoration comedy" is prose comedy of London life shaped by conventions of pastoral intrigue. Discussion proceeds virtually without reference to prior criticism, making the book pleasantly unargumentative but leaving it in something of a vacuum. I must confess myself skeptical about the genre theory and the emphasis on Etherege as a model, but the author does not insist overmuch on these matters. Readers should be warned that the book is riddled with erroneous and inconsistent dates, and liberally sprinkled with typos and errors in names—e.g., "Montagne" Summers, "Maidmont and Cogan," and "Stone" for "Fone."

One of the seriously understudied realms in drama remains literary and theatrical relations with France, especially in the late seventeenth century. John Wilcox's *The Relation of Molière to Restoration Comedy* (1938) was an exemplary account of the degree to which Molière served as a "source," but a great many important and difficult questions remain, even in the realm of comic drama. Unfortunately, few of them are raised in Harold C. Knutson's *The Triumph of Wit: Molière and Restoration Comedy*. I admire Knutson's earlier *Molière: An Archetypal Approach* (1976), but I find the present book a severe disappointment. Knutson makes a passing gesture toward "sociocritical method," but what he really seems interested in doing is applying Fujimura's tired old Truewit-Witwoud-Witless distinction to Molière—without much useful result, in my opinion. Knutson appears to be ignorant of virtually all scholarship and criticism relevant to English drama and theater—at least he cites precious little of it. A book that relies on Montague Summers (and ignores Langhans and Richard Leacroft) for information on physical theater cannot be taken seriously by specialists. The few English plays that get discussed are dealt with in such vague and general terms as to make the treatment entirely superficial.

Brief mention of two broader studies is in order. Anthony Gerard Barthelemy's *Black Face, Maligned Race* is largely concerned with Renaissance drama, but contains a useful account of the Black in Southerne's *Oroonoko*, stressing the use of "otherness." Alice Rayner's *Comic Persuasion: Moral Structure in British Comedy from Shakespeare to Stoppard* contains chapters on Wycherley's *Country-Wife* and Cumberland's *West Indian* (with a glance at Steele's *Conscious Lovers*). The book is an intelligent and nonscholarly series of reflections on *dulce et utile* in comedy, and of very limited interest to specialists.

Coming to books about single dramatists—always a tricky form to make work—we find three of them. Perhaps not coincidentally, all are essentially biographical. Mary Edmond's *Rare Sir William Davenant* has some virtues. It is written with an attractive enthusiasm for its subject; it is handsomely illustrated; and it is elaborately documented as to marriage licences, wills, etc. Unfortunately, the author seems to have no interest in the plays, and no understanding of theater management. The text post-1660 is a pastiche of Pepys and anecdotes about actors, hardly a biography at all. Edmond ignores almost all modern literary and theatrical scholarship, including Mongi Raddadi's important *Davenant's Adaptations of Shakespeare* (1979); her idea of context is often supplied by the "Companion" volume in the Latham-Matthews edition of Pepys. This book contains some useful documentary citations, but is a dismal failure as a piece of literary/theatrical biography.

Arthur R. Huseboe's *Sir George Etherege* is altogether more satisfactory, Twayne though it is. Perhaps because Etherege wrote so little, Huseboe has enough space for biographical detail and historical context. His accounts of plays are critically limited, but perfectly sensible; scholarship and criticism are liberally cited and judiciously assessed; and the standard of accuracy is high. If all Twaynes were like this, the series would enjoy a higher reputation.

The importance of Sir John Vanbrugh has become increasingly obvious in the past twenty years or so. His plays were excellent and long influential; his Haymarket Theatre was an important part of the London theater world for many decades; and his part in the introduction of Italian opera in London was a major one. The last serious biography was Laurence Whistler's in 1938, and a large amount of new documentary information has come to light since then. Kerry Downes's *Sir John Vanbrugh: A Biography* makes a genuine advance in its subject. Downes is an architectural historian (and author of an excellent book on Vanbrugh as architect [1977]), but this book is centered on life, not works, and demonstrates excellent scholarship. In 560 pages (plus 40 illustrations) Downes gives a sober, sensible, well-documented, and unfanciful picture of his subject. Vanbrugh emerges as a decent and likeable man, as a good and innovative playwright, and as a conscientious public servant. The plays are described with enthusiasm and genuine appreciation, albeit without reference to criticism. There are no footnotes, but each chapter is supplied with a list of specific references and citations that allow specialists to follow up on particular points. All in all, this is a very competent and helpful book.

IV. Fiction: General Studies and Reference Books

Eighteenth-century fiction proved decidedly more fruitful for New Critics than the drama. But there was only so much paydirt in those particular fields, and a generation later we find ourselves confronted with basic problems and questions. Twenty-five years ago, Ian Watt's *The Rise of the Novel* was taught as gospel. That it offers a grossly misleading historical model is now widely understood, but—fortunately or unfortunately—no genuine alternative has replaced it. The first serious attempt to do so was not published until 1987—Michael McKeon's *The Origins of the English Novel 1600-1740* (Johns Hopkins), which was greeted with enthusiasm by my predecessor in *SEL* last year. While we try to come to terms with McKeon's undeniably impressive and important book, and await J. Paul Hunter's forthcoming study, we stand at a crossroads.

As critics, what are we to *do* with eighteenth-century fiction? Most of it is eminently comprehensible, and the future for explicative criticism seems dim indeed. Historicist approaches have proved illuminating (particularly with regard to Defoe), and Terry Castle's account of *Clarissa* proves that modcrit approaches have something important to tell us, at least about selected texts. Part of our problem is the extremely limited canon. Another difficulty has to do with our predisposition to work within texts, or at least to stay safely within the realm of the literary. A healthy sign among this year's books is a number of authors' willingness to work in the broader regions of psychology and sociology. There are risks and problems to such extra-textual approaches, but they undeniably get us out of the rut dug by a generation of in-text critics.

A few words about McKeon's book are in order. Let me say at once that I admire it and disbelieve it. It is a massive, learned, heroic enterprise. McKeon endeavors via dialectical method to define a "genre" (i.e., "novel") able "to comprehend" both Richardson and Fielding (p. 21). The book is comprehensive, schematic, and quite astonishingly committed to a virtually unequivocal belief in genre. "The argument of this study has been that the origins of the English novel, whose climax is signaled by the Richardson-Fielding rivalry of the 1740s, consist in the establishment of a form sufficient for the joint inquiry into analogous epistemological and social problems which themselves had a long prehistory of intense and diversified public debate. . . . The function of literary genres is to mediate and explain intractable problems. . . . The problem the novel was formulated to mediate is, on the most general level of all, not questions of truth and questions of virtue in themselves so much as their division, their separation from each other" (pp. 410, 419). But what if there really was no such genre? McKeon labors to find order and system, and constructs an elaborate machine to comprehend untidy particulars. I sympathize with the desire to find order, and genuinely admire the attempt. McKeon's range of reading is impressive, and I have plundered his learned footnotes with gratitude and pleasure. But I look at a book like Geoffrey Day's *From Fiction to the Novel* (Routledge)—an unscholarly little survey of eighteenth-century fiction seen from the perspective of eighteenth-century commentary on it—and I wonder if such cheerful acceptance of chaos is not only the easiest but the wisest course. Poking dubiously at McKeon's dialectical machine I wonder why the "destabilization" he defines was not at least equally present a hundred years earlier in England? And why stop short in 1740? If the machine works, the best proof lies in what it tells us about the major works of Richardson, Fielding, and their successors. Watt's much tidier and simpler construct seemed—once upon a time, anyway—to work beautifully for Defoe and Richardson; only when we came to Fielding did qualms arise. I wish McKeon had taken a crack at the next decade. Pondering this book, I feel like a nineteenth-century atheist regarding a major theological treatise with bemused wonder. Perhaps, of course, I am merely a savage looking uncomprehendingly upon a rocket ship.

Let me start consideration of this year's books with an unequivocally warm welcome for James Raven's *British Fiction 1750-1770: A Chronological Check-List of Prose Fiction Printed in Britain and Ireland.* A great deal of labor went into this compilation, and anyone interested in getting beyond the Big Five will certainly want to use it. The 1750s remain scandalously underexplored—and here is a tidy map of the territory. Each entry gives author (if known), title, publication information, references to reviews in the *Critical* and *Monthly*, library locations, and so forth. Subsequent editions are included (clearly marked). The *ESTC* will no doubt add some items, but for the present this compilation represents a most welcome addition to our research tools, and it is certainly a major advance on Leonard Orr's unsatisfactory *A Catalogue Checklist of English Prose Fiction, 1750-1800* (1979). Orr presents just 282 items in 24 pages for the years of Raven's book. Special praise is due for the 50 pages of helpful front matter, chock full of useful tables. For example: the number of new novels vs. reprints in London and Dublin, year by year; total number of titles each year (1700-1769), treating new books and all editions separately; number of novels by women; number of titles translated from French and Spanish; percentage of novels published by various London and Dublin booksellers. If we are to expand the canon, and if we want to do sound historicist work, this is precisely the kind of basis we need to build on. Unglamorous this kind of work undeniably is, and certainly not an end in itself—but done this well it is truly useful.

Three books this year focus on matters pertaining to criminals, and I have chosen—perhaps misleadingly—to treat them together here under the heading of fiction. Lincoln B. Faller's *Turned to Account: The Forms and Functions of Criminal Biography in Late Seventeenth- and Early Eighteenth-Century England* might more fairly be dealt with in Section VII below, but it relates to the next two books and I suspect it will mostly be used by students of fiction looking for sources and context. Faller gives us (as far as I am aware) the first serious study of a major popular genre. We all know that Defoe used it, and that it was popular—but the full range and depth of the form was revealed to me here for the first time. Faller aims both to describe and to analyze the form. Like the original documents, this account is highly readable. And the analysis—mercifully sensible and unpretentious—is easy to accept. Faller asks what crime meant to the seventeenth- and eighteenth-century reader, making particularly good points about the combination of fear and fascination that attached (for example) to highwaymen. His many references to both primary and secondary sources are welcome, as is his bibliography of criminal biographies. The appendix on "Who read the popular literature of crime?" makes a beginning on an important and largely undocumented problem. In sum, a good piece of work.

Georges Lamoine's *Littérature et Justice Pénale en Angleterre au Dix-Huitième Siècle* is an odd but readable enterprise—basically an attempt to construct a picture of the English system of justice out of a combination of novels and historical documents. There are chapters on the basis of the judicial system, the "King's officers," courts, punishments, prisons, and eighteenth-century views and the spirit of reform. Lamoine relies too much on fiction to make this a solid piece of history, but he certainly provides a readable account of this part of the eighteenth-century world.

The third crime-related book is far and away the most ambitious, difficult, and problematical. Summarizing John Bender's *Imagining the Penitentiary: Fiction and the Architecture of Mind in Eighteenth-Century England* without radical reduction or travesty is virtually impossible. I presume the author approved the jacket copy, and so I shall quote it. "Bender investigates the role of the novel in the development of institutions. Drawing on history, sociology, anthropology, law, and aesthetics, as well as contemporary literary theory, Bender considers literature and the visual arts as advanced forms of knowledge, cognitive instruments that anticipate and contribute to institutional formation—vehicles rather than reflections of social change. Bender argues that attitudes toward prison which were formulated in narrative literature and art—especially prose fiction—between 1719 and 1779 enabled the conception and construction of actual penitentiary prisons later in the eighteenth century. He shows how these penitentiaries assumed novelistic ideas of character and represented the sensible world—both to their inmates and to the public—in order to alter motivation and, ultimately, the very notion of selfhood." The author is unquestionably brilliant, and the book is impressively erudite. I have read it with interest and profit, and many of the specific points and arguments are convincing (or at least usefully provocative). Helpful light is shed on such works as *Moll Flanders* and *Amelia*, and the whole book is stimulating about views of self and man. The chapter on Bentham and Adam Smith ("The Aesthetic of Isolation as Social System") is particularly good. The seventy-two illustrations help us picture both actuality and the concepts at issue. In sum, there is a great deal of worth here, but the book's subtext—which seems to be that novelists are the unacknowledged legislators of the world—strikes me as exaggerated and offputting.

In passing, let me mention two excellent books that touch our field only briefly. Paul K. Alkon's *Origins of Futuristic Fiction* is a wide-ranging and genuinely original book. By "futuristic fiction" Alkon means "prose narratives explicitly set in future time" (p. 3). As he demonstrates, this device developed surprisingly late: until the mid-seventeenth century it was not used, and until the nineteenth it was a rarity. Utopias and fantasies get distanced in space, but almost never forward in time. This "taboo against tales of the future" tells us something important about pre-Romantic *Weltanschauung*. Many of the texts Alkon considers are French (e.g., Mercier's *L'An 2440*, Souvestre's *Le Monde tel qu'il sera*), but detailed discussion of Samuel Madden's *Memoirs of the Twentieth Century* (1733) introduced me to an astonishing English text with which I was totally unfamiliar. Alkon's book is elegantly written, handsomely printed, and an absolute pleasure to read. It manages the rare feat of being well-documented and critically sophisticated without ponderousness or pretension. The second study, Edward H. Friedman's *The Antiheroine's Voice: Narrative Discourse and Transformations of the Picaresque*, is almost entirely concerned with Spanish literature over a wide span, but contains a well-informed chapter on *Moll*

Flanders (with excursions elsewhere in Defoe) that is well worth the reader's attention. The avowed method is "deconstructive," but I would call this a successful generic study: Friedman aims to "define a model that will illuminate particular narrative strategies in a group of texts" (p. xvii). He uses the notion of intertextuality effectively; does a good job of defining alternative viewpoints in texts; and has something useful to say about the differences between real and professed messages in Defoe.

The last four books to fall under the "general fiction" heading all have substantial feminist concerns. So very different are these books that they constitute a reminder of the unfairness of making categorical judgments. I will start with the simplest case—Christine van Boheemen's *The Novel as Family Romance: Language, Gender, and Authority from Fielding to Joyce.* The title implies a broader book than this is: it is really a politely hostile feminist account of *Tom Jones, Bleak House,* and *Ulysses.* This is too narrow and selective a basis on which to found generalities about the novel and its history. The intellectual texts with which van Boheemen associates each novel are likewise carefully picked—Descartes, Darwin, and Derrida, respectively. The three chapters on *Tom Jones* usefully sensitize us to Fielding's biases and ideology. I would not criticize van Boheemen's hostility to the "patriarchal" assumptions embedded in these and many other texts. But the book does not seem convincing to me in its claim "to sketch the story of the functional relation of the [novel] genre to the Western individual's self-constitution as transcendent subject" (p. 195). Novels are appropriate evidence in such an enterprise—but I would want many novels as well as other kinds of evidence.

Nancy Armstrong's *Desire and Domestic Fiction: A Political History of the Novel* is another book that bases sweeping statements on rather few texts—in this case *Pamela, Emma,* some books by the Brontës, and the case history of Freud's Dora. Misleading subtitle notwithstanding, this book is basically an argument to the effect that what was written by and for women in the eighteenth and nineteenth centuries both reflects and affects the process by which "the modern English middle class" evolved. I find the book intelligent, scrappy, and awkwardly split between its slender literary basis and the broader historical/sociological argument its author wants to make.

For me, the most successful of these four books is unquestionably the most radical. Jon Stratton's *The Virgin Text: Fiction, Sexuality, and Ideology* will certainly raise some hackles (and I deduce that it had problems finding a publisher). Stratton's topic—handled more abstractly than I would like—is how novels mirror sex in bourgeois society. Stratton writes with verve and has no hesitation in making

Clarissa and *Dracula* his most prominent examples. The author's ideological commitment is never concealed in any way. He starts chapter 1 with the statement "In bourgeois capitalist society everyday life is experienced as being pervaded by the sexual, and simultaneously, as being asexual since sex is repressed." I very much like his refusal to accept the usual distinctions between fantasy and realistic fiction (p. 117) and his vigorous denial of the ontological status of the novel (p. 199). How far one accepts the argument that texts become fetishized female objects is really beside the point. This book is genuinely provocative and highly entertaining—arguably outrageous, but worth taking seriously.

I do not know quite what to say about Dale Spender's *Mothers of the Novel: 100 Good Women Writers Before Jane Austen*—published in conjunction with the reprint series I welcomed so enthusiastically in Section I. It is not an academic book, and perhaps it should not be assessed in academic terms. It has both genuine virtues and alarming shortcomings. Spender writes to recuperate a host of forgotten (she would say "suppressed") women novelists. The text wobbles between straightforward appreciations of the life and works of women writers (Katherine Philips, Behn, Manley, Haywood, Sarah Fielding, Inchbald, et al.) and polemic against the international male plot to deprive women of their credit as great novelists and inventors of the novel form. I rather enjoy the frequent diatribes against Ian Watt—I had never even guessed that he had cloven hooves and a tail—but the stridency grows tiresome and the more paranoid bits of feminist extremism are sad. Cranky and uneven as it is, however, this remains a worthwhile book. We do need to rethink the canon; women wrote several hundred novels during the eighteenth century; and if Spender's enthusiasm for these writers helps win them some attention, we have to be grateful for the book (and certainly for the reprint series). Unfortunately, the lists of works are shaky; the bibliography is weird, limited, and full of omissions; and parenthetical citations are few (there are virtually no notes). When Spender says "I must confess that my researches have turned up more than one hundred women novelists before Jane Austen and no more than thirty men" (pp. 5-6) I am not sure whether she is joking, flaunting her own biases, or simply crazy. Can she have looked at *NCBEL*? But there is no point in belaboring a book not written for scholars. As a puff for some neglected writers it has some value.

V. Fiction: Single Authors

Of the dozen titles devoted to single novelists none is truly exciting, though Kristina Straub's book on Burney is a solid piece of work and Clarence Tracy's biography of Richard Graves is a welcome account of a neglected writer. The lack of "readings" of the Big Five is testimony to the sterility of that genre. Such readings as we have of Defoe and Richardson this year are explicitly addressed to students. The cul-de-sac in which New Critics of the old school find themselves has not often been breached by vigorous attention to Bage, Holcroft, Brooke, Lennox, Mackenzie, or others—which given the probable results may be just as well.

On Defoe we have four books: two reference books, a monograph, and a Twayne. Defoe has, of course, benefitted immensely from twenty-five years of serious criticism and close reading. Looking back to the debates of the 1960s one wants to laugh. A major biography of Defoe is clearly needed, and an account of him as political writer is a major desideratum; what we do with him beyond that is not so easy to say. Current views of Defoe are well summarized in John J. Richetti's *Daniel Defoe*. Only rarely has a leading scholar undertaken a Twayne. The contrast between Richetti's *Defoe* and the recent, lamentable *Otway* boggles the imagination. Richetti's book is expert, authoritative, and well-balanced. Defoe is presented as the varied professional writer and journalist he was, not just as a novelist. This is purely and simply an introduction for students, but a good one. Concerning Thomas Keith Meier's *Defoe and the Defense of Commerce*, let me say merely that it makes a useful footnote to Novak's *Economics and the Fiction of Daniel Defoe* (1962). Meier is not concerned with analyzing Defoe's economic theories or putting them in context, but rather with elucidating "Defoe's opinions toward business—its function, its potential, and its place in the scheme of things—as revealed in his major nonfictional writings" (p. 8).

I have radically different responses to the two fat reference books on Defoe that have appeared from Garland. Spiro Peterson's *Daniel Defoe: a Reference Guide 1731-1924* strikes me as a solid and useful piece of work. Method and format are familiar from other Garland bibliographies in the series—year by year listings with descriptive annotation. Peterson is a respected veteran Defoe scholar, and he seems to have carried out his task with care and devotion. Some of the annotation is quite substantial. I should stress that this volume is particularly useful because it does *not* duplicate MLA/MHRA coverage, and it overlaps John Stoler's 1900-1980 Garland Defoe bibliography (1984) only slightly. Peterson gives us access to a lot of out of the way eighteenth- and nineteenth-century sources, and he had the good sense to include prefaces and introductions to reprints of Defoe's works—which can be extremely valuable. If we compare, for example, Novak's excellent *NCBEL* list with this one, we find that it jumps from 1762 to 1785—a gap in which Peterson lists 56 items. I cannot, I fear, summon much enthusiasm for *A KWIC Concordance to Daniel Defoe's Robinson Crusoe*, edited by I. J. Spackman, W. R. Owens, and P. N. Furbank. "KWIC" means "key word in context": the word at issue is centered on the page, surrounded by as much context as will fit on one line. In 1141 pages we get a very clear idea how Defoe used each word. Some common words are omitted—5933 instances of "the" and 876 of "them," though 230 occurrences of "then" are duly displayed. The word-counts are interesting, as are the alphabetical appendix of word endings and the appendix of frequency order. This is, in fact, quite a good concordance—keyed, by the way, to the rather makeshift Crowley edition of 1972. I have doubts, however, about its utility. How much criticism of Defoe will require such a tool? Milton and Yeats, yes, but Defoe? At $150 for 1141 pages of computer printout, this does not seem like a good investment even for a library. Microfiche or CD-ROM seems an appropriate way to distribute such a work, supposing we need it at all.

We have two books on Richardson. Jocelyn Harris's *Samuel Richardson* is published by Cambridge in its "Introductory Critical Series." In the words of its blurb, "This book provides a concise introduction to Richardson, by combining a close reading of *Pamela, Clarissa,* and *Sir Charles Grandison* with a discussion of their central themes." The book is, in sum, a descriptive appreciation aimed at students, not peers. Harris is a deservedly respected Richardson scholar, and she provides a clear, vigorous, and well-informed account of the subject. Like Richetti's Twayne *Defoe,* this is a good place to send a student in need of basics. But is the business of Cambridge University Press to outTwayne Twayne? Dimiter Daphinoff's *Samuel Richardsons "Clarissa": Text, Rezeption und Interpretation,* as best my rusty German can decipher it for me, provides a detailed, rather mechanical analysis of Clarissa and Lovelace, followed by a lengthy survey of responses by contemporaries. Few of these will be new to specialists, and interpretively the book seems limited after Warner and Castle.

Fielding is likewise the subject of two items. *Henry Fielding in His Time and Ours* comprises Clark Library lectures by J. Paul Hunter and Martin C. Battestin. Hunter's *Occasional Form* (1975) remains the best general study of Fielding yet written, and Battestin is unquestionably the foremost Fielding scholar of our time. Hunter addresses the problems Fielding's "didacticism" poses for the twentieth-century reader. Battestin points out the presence of neglected and unnoticed "autobiographical dimensions" in Fielding's writings. As one would expect, both talks represent scholarship of a high order.

I am sorry to say that I do not find James J. Lynch's *Henry Fielding and the Heliodoran Novel* very convincing. Looking back to such works as Heliodorus's *Aethiopica*, Cervantes's *Persiles y Sigismunda*, and Scudéry's *Ibrahim*, Lynch defines a romance genre inclined to the heroic, and tries to relate it to Fielding. Lynch is honest about the fuzziness of the connection: "I do not claim the Heliodoran novel as a hitherto unacknowledged source of Fielding's novels. There is no evidence that Fielding was familiar with the *Aethiopica*, or with Cervantes' *Persiles*. . . . I do contend, however, that the synthesis between epic and romance in the Heliodoran novel parallels the synthesis between romance and history in Fielding's novels" (p. 15). I agree that this is true, but do not find the parallels terribly illuminating. Lynch does not significantly change the way we read Fielding's fiction.

Tobias Smollett: The Critical Heritage, edited by Lionel Kelly, is the usual collection of snippets—going up as far as 1821, with codas from Scott and Dickens. The introduction is sensible; the selection offers few revelations. The book has the virtues and vices of its series, but whether it is worth $69.95 I am inclined to doubt. If the series is uneconomic at more reasonable prices, perhaps it should quietly be brought to a halt.

Clarence Tracy's *A Portrait of Richard Graves* is a pleasant surprise. Like many others, I suspect, I found *The Spiritual Quixote* (1773) delightful when Tracy's OEN edition appeared in 1967—but I never dug further on Graves, or looked up *Columella* (1779), *Eugenius* (1785), or *Plexippus* (1790). Friend of Shenstone and parson-of-letters, Graves (1715-1804) was indubitably a minor writer, but one good enough to deserve some readers and some scholarly attention. Tracy's affectionate and readable biography makes no extravagant claims for him, but gives us a solid and satisfying picture of an eighteenth-century life. Thanks are owed to Toronto for numerous illustrations and a handsome printing job, not to mention a $30 price that seems moderation itself when you see what St. Martin's will give you for the same money.

Two books on Fanny Burney conclude this rather scrappy section on individual authors. D. D. Devlin's *The Novels and Journals of Fanny Burney* is merely a lightweight student introduction ($27.50 for 118 pages from St. Martin's). Devlin does a sensible job with context and political background; his accounts of the novels are very scanty. Kristina Straub's *Divided Fictions: Fanny Burney and Feminine Strategy* is another matter altogether. Critical neglect of Burney up to the present makes writing a significant book easier, and rumor says that heavyweight competition will be along shortly. But by getting away from the dead end of literary explication, Straub has made a genuinely significant contribution to our understanding of Burney's fiction. Her emphasis is on *Evelina* and *Cecilia*. The book benefits greatly from its feminist perspective: judiciously considering biographical issues, Straub is able to show—very convincingly—that these novels are expressions of Burney's female outlook and her problems in a world of male authority with which she had serious difficulties. The novels really come to life this way: thinking back to dreary accounts of them as aesthetic entities unrelated to life, one wonders why someone did not take a biographical/ideological approach long ago. Straub is particularly good on the ambivalence with which marriage is presented, and the degree to which these novels express the contradictions and insecurities of the woman's position in eighteenth-century society. All in all, an excellent and welcome book.

VI. Satire, Biography, and Language

Books on "intellectual prose"—the soggy title I am avoiding here—are in short supply this year, and what we have is extremely uneven. Perhaps the small number is a healthy sign: scholars seem more inclined to pull intellectual prose into ambitious cultural history books than to write earnest monographs about particular texts, some of them already overworked. The day of graduate courses in "Augustan Prose" has passed, and coming to these texts in the 1980s the critic has to wonder what to *do* with them. Foucault is often brandished, if seldom seriously applied. "Prose style" seems to have become a dirty phrase in most quarters. Trendy doubts about the adequacy of language make this an awkward time to turn to linguistics, historical or otherwise, for answers—though I have a sneaking suspicion that this might be a fruitful line to pursue. We know alarmingly little about the education of eighteenth-century readers, the application of aesthetic theory to literature, or how language relates to class structure in this period. (Carey McIntosh has made a start on the third problem in a book published just two years ago.) Close attention to Campbell, Lowth, Kames, Gibbon, Alison, et al. would be extremely healthy. And we could usefully start by simply attempting to recover their sense of problems, answers, and world view.

The particular books we must consider here comprise two on satire, three on biography, and three that I am categorizing together under "language." Both of the "satire" books, despite footnotes to recent work, give me a sense of having fallen backwards twenty-five years in time. David Nokes's *Raillery and Rage: A Study of Eighteenth Century Satire* is another St. Martin's special for the wealthy general reader—though for St. Martin's, a comparative bargain at 211 pages for $35.00. Nokes is an intelligent critic, well-grounded in this material. But though the jacket copy of the American edition trumpets the book as the "first major study of the dominant literary genre of the Augustan Age" (a claim for which I am prepared to hold Mr. Nokes entirely blameless) the book is no more than a lightweight survey aimed at "students" and "general readers," as Nokes plainly says in his preface. The "problem" posed is how to read eighteenth-century texts without worrying about classical and topical allusions. Chapters on "Satire and Society" and "Themes and Forms of Augustan Satire" are followed by sketchy appreciations of Pope, Gay, Fielding, and Swift (20 pages for Pope, 18 for Swift). The text is dotted with contemporary allusions (*Dallas*, *O What a Lovely War*) and the notes with errors (Eleanor "Hitchens," Rawson's *Order from Confusion Sprung* dated "1935"). I deduce that Nokes's heart was not in this venture.

Leon Guilhamet's *Satire and the Transformation of Genre* is more scholarly but hardly more satisfactory. Despite the invocation of "structuralism, hermeneutics, and modern mimetic theory," this book takes an extremely old-fashioned view of its subject. Guilhamet's announced purpose is to define the unity and integrity of satire as a literary genre. The "major argument of this study is that satire is known essentially by its form" (p. x)—a contention that I continue to find unconvincing. Guilhamet devotes general chapters to sketching "Demonstrative" satire (i.e., direct attack), "Deliberative" satire (recommending a course of action), and "Judicial" satire. He then goes on to particulars in chapters devoted to Dryden, Pope, and Swift. But nine pages on *Mac Flecknoe* do not much change the way we see the work, especially when Guilhamet does not directly engage his predecessors. This is an honest, sober, careful book—but ultimately I must confess to finding it short on original substance.

The three books on biography are so different that they sit uncomfortably on the shelf together. Reed Whittemore's *Pure Lives: The Early Biographers* is aggressively nonacademic (though published by Johns Hopkins) and an unalloyed pleasure to read. Whittemore writes with enthusiasm of Plutarch, Aelfric, Vasari, Holinshed, Johnson, and Boswell, adding excursions into the likes of Machiavelli and Cellini. The final chapter is an exuberant appreciation of Sterne—not, to be sure, a biographer, but a writer doing things relevant to the development of biography. Whittemore takes a sardonic view of hagiography (he does not like *purifiers*) but his accounts of his subjects are affectionate if unsanctimonious. The publisher's letter to *SEL* requesting coverage for the book says that "*Pure Lives* is not a survey of biography. It is a discursive, essayistic, and personal approach to the subject." This is quite accurate. The book is clearly aimed at general readers, and I hope it finds some, for it is very good fun.

Reading William H. Epstein's *Recognizing Biography* is rather like falling into porridge. One can swim in it, but doing so is hard work. Sodden prose aside, the book has its virtues. Epstein has read many biographies and a lot of work about biography, and he has useful things to say about both theory and practice. (Epstein himself is the author of a biography of Cleland.) This book comprises a chronological overview of particular texts—Walton's *Life of Donne*, Johnson's *Savage*, Boswell's *Johnson*, Strachey's *Eminent Victorians* —but it is really a kind of sustained and entangled meditation about biography. Epstein moves from "Life-Text" to "Subject" to "Biographer" to "Life-course"—the last discussion seeming to me the most persuasive. He is given to lists and ritual genuflections toward Foucault, but the notes are up to date and will be useful to readers. Granting the book erudition and earnest concern for its subject, I shudder to think what Reed Whittemore would say about it. In fairness, I must admit that I hate to think what Reed Whittemore would say about the likes of me.

The third biographical book—or so I am classifying it—is William B. Ober's *Bottoms Up! A Pathologist's Essays on Medicine and the Humanities*. Ober will be familiar to most readers as the author of *Boswell's Clap* (1979). Like that collection, this one is wide-ranging—murder by Gesualdo, Margery Kempe's hysteria, Rimbaud's sex life. The title essay concerns flagellation (though to my innocence the implication was unclear). Three essays directly concern us here. In "The Iconography of *Fanny Hill*" Ober reprints (with analysis) a variety of highly pornographic illustrations. A chapter on Johnson and Boswell offers sober and unsensationalized commentary on their struggles against depression. And a brief account of the trial of Spencer Cowper (1699) sheds interesting light on trial procedures and expert witnesses in a murder case. Those curious about Peter Anthony Motteux's death of "autoerotic asphyxia" will find considerable illumination in a chapter on the demise of the Czech composer František Kocžwara. Judgment of the technicalities I leave to those more qualified than I, but like its predecessor this is a delightfully readable book by a distinguished practicing physician.

The one previously-unpublished "language" book of the year is Ann Cline Kelly's *Swift and the English Language*. This is a sober, careful, and somewhat understated piece of work, well-written and efficiently organized. Kelly comes right to the point in her first paragraph: "This book focuses on an important and somewhat neglected aspect of Jonathan Swift's thought: his fascination with language in general and his commitment to the English language in particular. Swift's linguistic concerns structured his vision of the world and determined his strategies for altering it." In a series of pleasantly brief chapters she then proceeds to describe Swift's interest in language, his belief in language "as a social fabric," the social function of conversation (personal and national), Swift's views of proposals for linguistic improvement, his own proposal for an English "Academy," and so forth. The proposition that Swift's concept of "proper words" parallels his belief in the established church and the monarchy is argued in a very low key, but seems to me convincing. The book concludes with a discussion of Swift's belief in the permanent value of writing. I could have wished for more extensive consideration of Swift's linguistic playfulness ("private language" *is* discussed) and especially for more account of the problem of irony (which Kelly does not seem anxious to grapple with). But this book makes a useful addition to our knowledge of an important part of Swift's outlook.

Two excellent recent books related to "language" have been issued in paperback and sent along for review, so I will take the opportunity to commend them to the reader's attention. Robert DeMaria, Jr.'s *Johnson's Dictionary and the Language of Learning* starts from Eco's dictum that dictionaries are disguised encyclopedias and proceeds to analyze Johnson's 1755 *Dictionary* to see what "concept of knowledge" is revealed therein. DeMaria shows very convincingly that there are definite patterns and purposes in Johnson's selection of quotations, and that by analyzing them we can reconstruct his sense of evidence and his way of looking at the world around him. The other book, likewise well received in hardback, is Olivia Smith's *The Politics of Language, 1791-1819*. Despite the stiff sobriety of its style, this set of six related studies is quite accessible and has a great deal to tell us about elitism and class distinctions in the theory and use of language at the end of the eighteenth century. The chapter on "*Rights of Man* and its Aftermath" should certainly be read by every student of the 1790s. Given the subject matter Smith is either undoctrinaire or remarkably well able to affect impartiality. Much of the methodology seems to me eminently transplantable—for example, to the period of the Exclusion Crisis or the age of Walpole. Both North Carolina and Oxford deserve thanks for making relatively inexpensive paperbacks available—for other than via review copies, how else are starving scholars to acquire them?

VII. Cultural and Intellectual History

Under this sweeping heading I shall compass some rather heterogeneous studies dealing variously with religion, law, history, feminism, the press, and so forth. I must confess that in parts of this territory I have less confidence than I do when dealing with accounts of poetry, fiction, and drama. I do not, for example, have an exhaustive acquaintance with recent scholarship on nonconformity, and my grip on the intellectual history of Scotland gets shaky after the obvious names and titles. I shall try not to retreat into pure description and abstinence from evaluation, but the reader will have to excuse some diffidence and perhaps some lapses in judgment. That said, let me hasten to say once again how very welcome I find books that are not exclusively grounded in the reading of literary texts. Intellectual history is a great deal harder to bring off than explication du texte, but in the last decade the need to look beyond particular texts has become painfully obvious.

For me, the most exciting of the books under this heading is undoubtedly N. H. Keeble's *The Literary Culture of Nonconformity in Later Seventeenth-Century England.* Keeble jumps off from the perception that scholars have seen Milton and Bunyan "in the light of their Puritan predecessors rather than in the context of their nonconformist contemporaries" or alternatively have seen them as "idiosyncratic genius[es]" who transcend the minds and world of their brethren (pp. 21-22). Both views remain commonplace in criticism, and both are untenable. (How many major writers are not deeply rooted in their own times?) Keeble sets out to recreate the intellectual contexts from which Milton and Bunyan worked. I should stress that this is *not* a book about those writers, but rather about the world from which they sprang. We are given chapters on such subjects as literary responses to persecution, nonconformity and the press, nonconformist writers and their readers, education, individualism, and "'Answerable style': the linguistic dissent of nonconformity." This is a book of genuine erudition and wide range, though the focus settles in the 1660s. The method of the book is resolutely simple: Keeble describes what is there, leaving "application" almost entirely to others. This can be frustrating: at times one wants analytic explanations and demonstrations of significance. Keeble becomes superficial when on rare occasions he launches into comparisons with establishment writers (for example, Wycherley and Congreve, whose plays he tends to misdate). I would have enjoyed more development of the longterm connection of nonconformists to Blake and the Romantics. But what this book sets out to do it accomplishes in a careful, well-documented, and readable way.

A second book I shall treat as "religious" is *Deism, Masonry, and the Enlightenment: Essays Honoring Alfred Owen Aldridge,* edited by J. A. Leo Lemay. Some of the contents concern American subjects, but four essays are of immediate relevance to us here. In "Latitudinarianism and the English Deists" Roger L. Emerson argues vigorously against the usual connections asserted between the two groups, finding "liberal Anglicans and deists . . . farther apart than most recent commentators have appreciated" (p. 45). In a short essay on "Spinoza, Stillingfleet, Prophecy, and 'Enlightenment'" Gerard Reedy, S.J., reconsiders John Lough's strictures on the term "Enlightenment," granting some of the objections but finding some utility to the concept as well. David Berman's "Deism, Immortality, and the Art of Theological Lying" insists on the degree to which deist writers had to utilize both irony and outright deception in order to cover "covert atheism." And finally, Maximillian E. Novak, in a piece on "Defoe, the Occult, and the Deist Offensive during the Reign of George I," offers the first satisfying explanation for several works of 1726 and 1727 on magic and occultism.

Sir Robert Chambers's *A Course of Lectures on the English Law 1767-1773*, edited by Thomas M. Curley in two fat volumes (over 900 pages), could have been put under "Editions" or tossed in with Samuel Johnson, but seems best dealt with under the heading of context. This is a major publication, and the more welcome in that only a part of this massive survey of English law has ever before been published. Chambers was Blackstone's successor as Vinerian Professor of English Law at Oxford. He published virtually nothing in his lifetime, and the full course was preserved only because George III had a copy made for his library—now British Library King's Manuscripts 80-97. This edition makes available what is virtually a whole new primary source. Chambers was a friend of Samuel Johnson, and Johnsonians will remember that E. L. McAdam long ago argued that Johnson gave Chambers substantial aid in the writing of these lectures. This is clearly true (from extrinsic evidence), but how much assistance and in what form we have no way to acertain. Curley is commendably cautious in his claims for the degree of Johnson's involvement in the actual writing, and about whether he wrote particular passages. (McAdam was far less restrained.) At any rate, what we have here is 75 pages of learned and helpful introduction; a very readable modernized text of the 56 lectures; a bibliography of sources cited; excellent indexes of cases, laws, and statutes cited (as well as a substantial general index); and a straightforward set of textual notes. The University of Wisconsin Press deserves credit for making this important edition available.

Moving from law to history, we come to Ian Haywood's *The Making of History: A Study of the Literary Forgeries of James Macpherson and Thomas Chatterton in Relation to Eighteenth-Century Ideas of History and Fiction*. Haywood argues that the forgeries should be viewed in light of eighteenth-century debates about the relation of fiction to history. The context is interesting, but the degree of direct "influence" is cloudy, particularly in the case of Chatterton. There is an intriguing hypothesis here, but the book is lacking in cohesion, and the final chapter wanders off toward Scott. Attention to these writers is welcome, but a major book on eighteenth-century forgery and its relation to the simulation of history in fiction remains to be written.

The one press-related book this year is Jeremy Black's *The English Press in the Eighteenth Century*. The subject is dishearteningly difficult. Information about writers, readers, sources, distribution, and finances is scattered and unsatisfactory. The number of newspapers was large; the number of complete or even substantial runs of issues preserved is now maddeningly small. Generalizations are risky to make and hell to document. What the papers say cannot safely be taken at face value: editors steal, invent, distort, and occasionally subvert their ostensible positions—never mind the issue of irony. Seventeenth-century newspapers have been much more studied (the mass of evidence is less intimidating). Given the difficulties, Jeremy Black has made a good job of his attempt "to provide a general introduction to the eighteenth-century English press," both metropolitan and provincial (p. xiii). He deals helpfully with such matters as contents/coverage, sources and distribution, censorship, and moral content. The large number of citations to particular issues of specific papers is exceedingly welcome and highly commendable. For my own purposes, the coverage is too broad: each chapter ranges all over the country and up and down the length of the century. I would have welcomed cohesive accounts of particular major papers (which Black avoids because they can be misleading), and more attempt to divide consideration of London and provincial papers. I am disappointed that "For reasons of space only a select list of sources consulted has been given" (p. 309) and especially that Black does not cite locations for particular newspaper issues—space-consuming, but a godsend to anyone trying to find them. Black admits the need for research on particular papers (p. 289), and we must be grateful for as good an overview as he has been able to give us. Analysis of newspapers and their contents is going to occupy scholars for a long time to come.

Two feminist books offer little that is new. Alice Browne's *The Eighteenth Century Feminist Mind* is a straightforward survey of "eighteenth-century notions of women" and "feminist responses." It covers legal status, advice to women (exercise, eating, clothes, etc.), the presence of women in novels (emphasizing *Clarissa* and Rousseau's *Julie*), the beginning of feminism (Astell), education, place in society, the double standard, and the 1790s (Wollstonecraft). Documentation is adequate. But there is really no argument here, and little of what is said will be new to any specialist in the period. Though not so billed, this is essentially an introduction for students. The other book is a mish-mash collection with a grand title—*The Ideology of Conduct: Essays on Literature and the History of Sexuality*, edited by Nancy Armstrong and Leonard Tennenhouse. The contents range from an essay on medieval courtesy literature to a pair of rather pop essays on "Modes of Modern Shopping" and "The Beauty System." There are two eighteenth-century essays. Nancy Armstrong's "The Rise of the Domestic Woman" is an adaptation of material in her *Desire and Domestic Fiction* (discussed in Section IV, above). Carol Houlihan Flynn's "Defoe's Idea of Conduct: Ideological Fictions and Fictional Reality" seems to me the best piece in the collection—a vigorous discussion of the interior tensions and ideological contradictions in Defoe's *The Family Instructor* (both versions). As a whole, however, this volume is a scrappy beginning to what is announced as a series of "Essays in Literature and Society."

I am treating together three books that might pompously be described as recuperations of marginalized territories—the Caribbean, Scotland, and rural England, respectively. By far the most stimulating is Peter Hulme's unusual study of *Colonial Encounters: Europe and the Native Caribbean 1492-1797*. The author describes this as "a case study rather than a theoretical work on the subject of colonial discourse" (p. 5). The cases are Columbus's view of cannibals in his *Journal*, Prospero and Caliban, John Smith and Pocahontas, Robinson Crusoe and Friday, and the popular Inkle and Yarico story. Hulme acknowledges a "generally Marxist" bent, with a wave at Foucault, but his method is psychological/explicative. He tries "to make a text speak more than it knows," "to identify key locations in a text—*cruces* . . . where the text stutters in its articulation, and which can therefore be used as levers to open out the ideology of colonial discourse" (p. 12). This is a smart, stimulating, and unusual book. Hulme has interesting things to say when he asks a question like "What was the fundamental difference between Algonquian and English cultures?" (p. 147). The account of *Robinson Crusoe* seems to me excessively fettered to Watt. But overall, the focus on the collision between European and Colonial helps define interior tensions and contradictions in a culture we tend, as insiders in it, to take for granted.

John Dwyer's *Virtuous Discourse: Sensibility and Community in Late Eighteenth-Century Scotland* is basically an account of "the moral preoccupations of eighteenth-century Scotsmen" (p. 1). Dwyer is concerned to describe and document prevalent views of such subjects as civic humanism, adolescents, women, the novel, and "community cohesion." He argues that counter to common emphasis on "an age of improvement" in Scotland, "running through all of these rich cultural tapestries was one darkly, coloured thread—the conviction that increased wealth, individualism and specialization threatened the integrity of the moral community." The picture drawn is clear and adequately documented, and attention to Adam Smith's neglected *The Theory of Moral Sentiments* is particularly welcome. The last of the "margins" books is *Life and Labour in Rural England, 1760-1850*, edited by Pamela Horn. This turns out to be a collection of snippets illustrating "Change in the Countryside," "Village Life and Labour," and so forth. On the latter we get bits of *Wuthering Heights, Adam Bede, Emma, The Vicar of Wakefield*, Wordsworth's *Michael* (etc.), along with less familiar extracts from Saint-Fond's *Travels*, the *Gentleman's Magazine*, the *Torrington Diaries* (etc.). The editor does a tidy job of tacking this agglomeration together, but there is nothing here for the specialist, and I suspect that libraries could find a better use for $29.95.

I can think of no polite rubric under which to place the last item in this section, a reprint of T. H. White's *The Age of Scandal: An Excursion Through a Minor Period* (1950). The author calls the volume a "little scrap-book of a nostalgic Tory" (p. 5). It consists of undocumented anecdotes strung together in a careless way. This is the sort of book in which Horace Walpole is called "Horry" (p. 4), and Samuel Johnson referred to as "the old rhinoceros" (p. 3). If there are readers for such bilge, perhaps we can hope that they will graduate to something better. I do not understand why this book, originally published by Cape, should be reissued by OUP. The reappearance of this book under such an imprint is simply contemptible.

VIII. General and Reference Books and Collections

The books lumped together under this final heading range from excellent to regrettable. I start with a pair of books placed here strictly *faute de mieux*. *A Dictionary of British and American Women Writers, 1660-1800*, edited by Janet Todd (1985), has been reissued in a revised paperback edition. It covers "almost 500 women writers" in some 344 double-column pages. No such reference book can be perfect, especially when so many of the relevant sources are scanty and inadequate, but this dictionary fully deserved the praise it won when it first appeared, and its emergence in paperback is extremely welcome. Accounts of the best-known women writers are, inevitably, the least satisfactory—but on a large number of the writers included this is literally the only modern source to which we can turn. Coverage is selective—the editor notes, for example, the omission of many Quaker pamphleteers—but one will seldom look for a writer of fiction, poetry, or drama without success. Specialists can find flaws: Aphra Behn's *The History of the Nun* is not a play, and her *Love Letters Between a Nobleman and His Sister* is not a "200,000-word" novel. The account of Susanna Cibber's affair with Sloper and the resultant crim. con. trial is curiously prudish and misleading. I particularly regret the total lack of bibliographic aids. One does not expect footnotes in a dictionary, but *DNB*-style hints would not have occupied much space and would have been immensely useful. Let us hope such addenda can be incorporated when there is another edition. But all grumbles aside, this is a splendid addition to reference books in our field.

The one book I feel compelled to classify as "general" is Peter Conrad's *The History of English Literature: One Indivisible, Unending Book*. In 740 pages it offers us a footnoteless survey of English literature from Beowulf to Seamus Heaney. For our period there are chapters on "Comedy from Wycherley to Sheridan"; Swift and Pope; Defoe; Richardson and Fielding; Sterne; Johnson and Boswell; and "Gothic Follies." In essence the book is an elementary introduction written in a lively style. Its great virtue is the author's insistence on getting away from "period" blinkers and simply responding to particular texts taken seriatim. The lack of clichéd generalities is refreshing; this would not be a bad place for an undergraduate to get some help with specific authors.

We have four "original" collections and three reprint collections to consider. *Studies in the Eighteenth Century 6*, edited by Colin Duckworth and Homer Le Grand, comprises papers presented at the sixth David Nichol Smith Memorial Seminar in Melbourne in 1983—published as a special issue of *Eighteenth-Century Life* in 1987. Some useful structure is supplied by division into three parts: "The Uses and Abuses of History," "Performing Arts," and "Literature and Fine Arts." The essays vary in substance, but all are respectable or better. Those of particular relevance for us here are Peter Sabor on "Horace Walpole as a Historian," Paul Turnbull on "Neglected Aspects of Gibbon's Roman Conversion," Harold Love on "Continuities in English-language Theatre, 1660-1860," Keryl Kavanagh on "Goldsmith's Fictive Histories," Bryan Coleborne on "James Arbuckle and Jonathan Swift," and T. G. A. Nelson on "Women of Pleasure."

The second collection is *Anticipations of the Enlightenment in England, France, and Germany*, edited by Alan Charles Kors and Paul J. Korshin. Perhaps because it is the product of a carefully-structured "year-long conference," the contents are of unusually high quality. All four of the "English" essays are excellent. In an elegant and sensible essay on "Shaftesbury's Optimism and Eighteenth-Century Social Thought" John Andrew Bernstein asks "where cosmic optimism, the belief in a Providential world order, stood in relation to progressivism on the one hand and traditionalism on the other" (p. 86). In a resolutely anti-doctrinaire conclusion he suggests "that all attempts to divide eighteenth-century English writers into separate camps must proceed entirely issue by issue, belief by belief. The bewildering ambiguities of optimism and its implications demonstrate the pitfalls awaiting unwary definers of mutually exclusive schools" (pp. 98-99). Margaret C. Jacob's "Scientific Culture in the Early English Enlightenment" asks "Was there an aggressive, self-conscious movement for Enlightenment in England (as distinct from Scotland)?" And if so, how did science, often believed to have "grown moribund" in England, contribute to this movement? Jocelyn Harris's "Sappho, Souls, and the Salic Law of Wit" considers womens' claims to be serious writers, and objections to such claims, jumping off from John Duncombe's *The Feminead* (pub. 1754). Finally, J. Paul Hunter's " 'The Young, the Ignorant, and the Idle': Some Notes on Readers and the Beginnings of the English Novel" asks "Who were the first readers of novels?"; "What did they want novels to do for them?"; and "How were cultural needs translated into the emergence of a new literary species?" (p. 260). This ambitious but unpretentious essay offers an exciting preview of Hunter's forthcoming book on the beginnings of the novel—one that promises to escape the trap of genre and deal more flexibly with the multitude of forces that make eighteenth-century "novels" what they are.

The third original collection is *Man, God, and Nature in the Enlightenment*, edited by Donald C. Mell, Jr., Theodore E. D. Braun, and Lucia M. Palmer. It comprises twenty studies, most of them so short as to seem insubstantial. The British portions are Sophia B. Blaydes on "The Duchess of Newcastle and Seventeenth-Century Philosophy"; Melissa Butler on "Wollstonecraft versus Rousseau" concerning natural religion; Hilda Smith on education in the seventeenth century; Brian McCrea on *Joseph Andrews*; Spencer Davis on "Scottish Philosophy and Political Economy"; Leslie Friedman Goldstein on constitutional theory; James E. May on "Early Eighteenth-Century Paraphrases of the Book of Job"; Sylvia Kasey Marks on *Grandison*; David Wheeler on *Douglas*; and Robert W. Uphaus on "The Fear of Fiction" (a highlight of the volume). There are some good pieces here, but fewer and more substantial would have been better.

The last original collection is another special issue of *Eighteenth-Century Life* (October 1986), edited by Robert P. Maccubbin and

Oliver F. Sigworth and entitled *British Literature and Culture: Essays by Students, Colleagues, Friends, and Other Admirers of Bertrand H. Bronson.* Bronson was a twentieth-century giant well deserving a *festschrift,* but this one strikes me as unfocused and uneven, especially in the contributions from senior scholars. The contents range from "Wren and the Restrained Baroque" to "Johnson on the Metaphysicals," with stops along the way at Gay, Pope, Eva Maria Garrick, "sentimental comedy," the gothic novel, and Smollett. John Samson's "Politics Gothicized: The Conway Incident and *The Castle of Otranto*" is the prize in a very mixed bag—a radical challenge to Walpole's account of the genesis of his novel and an attempt to fix it squarely in contemporary events.

The three "reprint" collections vary even more drastically in quality. The best by an immense margin is *Modern Essays on Eighteenth-Century Literature,* edited by Leopold Damrosch, Jr. This volume is explicitly announced as successor to James Clifford's collection of 1959, long a classroom standard. Damrosch gives us predictable coverage: three essays on Swift, two on Pope; something on each major novelist; a sprinkling of broader pieces; and one on Fanny Burney (a token concession to feminism?). Predictable names are selected—Rawson, Wimsatt, Ehrenpreis, Paulson, Spacks, et al., and the choices are unexceptionable. If the collection seems unsatisfying as a total picture this is hardly the editor's fault, for in 1988 so does Clifford's. As Damrosch rightly says, "no collection can now hope to represent the field as fully as Clifford's did" (p. vii)—a great deal has happened in the last thirty years, and never again will we enjoy the relative clarities and simplicities of those days. Nor, to be sure, should we want to.

Volumes 5 and 6 of *Literature Criticism from 1400 to 1800,* edited by James E. Person, Jr., have been published by Gale Research. I regard these, frankly, as expensive exercises in pointlessness. Each installment of what is planned as a massive series is a kind of miniature "Critical Heritage" for eleven or twelve authors apparently selected at random from a four-hundred year span and several countries. Thus volume 5 covers Congreve, François de Malherbe, Rabelais, Spenser, Tasso, and Mary Wollstonecraft (among others). Each entry (ten to eighty double-column pages) presents a potted biography, a list of major works, a series of critical snippets from the author's lifetime to the present, and an "Additional Bibliography." The snippets are at least properly identified, though longer selections are ruthlessly hacked up and the bits rejoined in sometimes nonsensical ways. Footnotes are treated as irrelevancies and omitted. The selections are seemingly random, and the representation of current criticism so scanty as to be badly misleading. The bibliographies would disgrace a first-year graduate student—weird mélanges that include the trivial or discredited while omitting major work. At roughly $90 per volume this series seems to exist more for the sake of endless library sales than for the service of any clientele I can imagine.

We come, finally, to what is for me unequivocally the low point of the year—a volume in Harold Bloom's "Modern Critical Interpretations" series called *Thomas Gray's "Elegy Written in a Country Churchyard,"* "Edited and with introduction by Harold Bloom." This is announced as one of more than a hundred such volumes, and seems at first glance merely to be a wildly overpriced 1987 hardbound version of "Twentieth Century Views." The choice of nine essays is perfectly reasonable—Brady, Lonsdale, Weinbrot, et al.—and the apparatus is pretty standard for student texts: half a page of "Chronology," notes on contributors, two pages of further bibliography, and a brief index. The "introduction" is five and a half superficial pages, well larded with quotation, and can hardly have cost the editor half an afternoon's labor. What appalls me about this volume—and others in the series—is that without saying he is doing so Bloom *omits all footnotes* from the essays he reprints. To my way of thinking this renders the book worthless not only to scholars but to all serious students. What is deplorable in a snippet-collection from a commercial publisher seems unspeakable in a series sold on the basis of Harold Bloom's name. I wonder how many libraries that are buying these books realize the fraudulent nature of these reprints? I am afraid I can see no object to this series other than gouging money out of libraries. Harold Bloom is unquestionably a brilliant man and an important twentieth-century critic. Why such a person—and a MacArthur fellow at that—should need or wish to spend his time on such academic prostitution I do not pretend to understand.

Looking back over the mass of work covered in this essay, I am struck once again by how good the best of it is, and how high the overall average is. Granting the potboilers and library rip-offs, one finds a lot of sound and useful criticism and scholarship. Finishing up, I would like to echo and amplify comments by two of my recent *SEL* predecessors, one negative, one positive. Writing in 1986 Paul Korshin lamented that "many scholars who write about eighteenth-century literature . . . are doing less primary research than once was usual." Too true: even among the useful pieces of work quite a few do not go beyond modern editions and recently published scholarship. A lot of scholars are not using genuinely rare books, pamphlets, and newspapers, let alone manuscripts. I presume that this is the effect of a generation of New Critical training in universities, followed by a rush to embrace critical theory. There is much of value to be done in this field via New Historicism, reader-response criticism, feminism, and semiotics, but we need to train our students to get beyond obvious primary sources. On a more positive note, let me add to Howard Weinbrot's 1985 salute to publishers who have demonstrated special commitment to our field. Taking them in alphabetical order, we owe particular thanks to the presses of Delaware, Georgia, Kentucky, Oxford, the University of Pennsylvania, and Southern Illinois. This is not a profitable field for publishers, and presses that regularly print work in it need and deserve our support.

Any lively field should be in the throes of a certain amount of doubt and turmoil, and this one certainly is. Finding appropriate methodologies for dealing with fiction and poetry is a glaring problem at the moment. Learning to cross disciplinary boundaries competently and profitably is another—theater, music, art, history, economics, political science, and comparative literature all beckon, sometimes treacherously. The kinds of work we do have changed markedly in the last ten or fifteen years, and the process of change has only begun. But however confusing and disconcerting the changes sometimes are, the field is plainly flourishing.

BOOKS RECEIVED

Armstrong, Nancy. *Desire and Domestic Fiction: A Political History of the Novel.* New York: Oxford Univ. Press, 1987. Pp. x + 300. $22.50. ISBN 0-19-504179-8.

Armstrong, Nancy, and Tennenhouse, Leonard, eds. *The Ideology of Conduct: Essays on Literature and the History of Sexuality.* New York and London: Methuen, 1987. Pp. 243. $12.95. ISBN 0-416-38600-8.

Alkon, Paul K. *Origins of Futuristic Fiction.* Athens and London: Univ. of Georgia Press, 1988. Pp. xii + 341. $30.00. ISBN 0-8203-0932-X.

Barnett, Dene, with the assistance of Jeanette Massy-Westropp. *The Art of Gesture: The Practices and Principles of 18th Century Acting.* Reihe Siegen, Band 64: Anglistische Abteilung. Heidelberg: Carl Winter Universitätsverlag, 1987. Pp. 503. ISBN 3-533-03716-9 (cloth); 3-533-03715-0 (paper).

Barthelemy, Anthony Gerard. *Black Face, Maligned Race: The Representation of Blacks in English Drama from Shakespeare to Southerne.* Baton Rouge: Louisiana State Univ. Press, 1987. Pp. xi + 215. $37.50. ISBN 0-8071-1331-X.

Bender, John. *Imagining the Penitentiary: Fiction and the Architecture of Mind in Eighteenth-Century England.* Chicago and London: Univ. of Chicago Press, 1987. Pp. xvii + 337. $29.95. ISBN 0-266-04228-6.

Black, Jeremy. *The English Press in the Eighteenth Century.* Philadelphia: Univ. of Pennsylvania Press, 1987. Pp. xv + 321. $44.95. ISBN 0-8122-8062-8.

Bloom, Harold, ed. *Thomas Gray's "Elegy Written in a Country Churchyard."* New York: Chelsea House, 1987. Pp. vii + 151. $19.95. ISBN 0-87754-420-4.

Browne, Alice. *The Eighteenth Century Feminist Mind.* Detroit: Wayne State Univ. Press, 1987. Pp. viii + 237. $25.00. ISBN 0-8143-1941-6.

Burns, Edward. *Restoration Comedy: Crises of Desire and Identity.* New York: St. Martin's Press, 1987. Pp. viii + 183. $27.50. ISBN 0-312-67789-8.

Campbell, George. *The Philosophy of Rhetoric.* Ed. Lloyd F. Bitzer. Carbondale: Southern Illinois Univ. Press, 1988. Pp. lxxvi + 423. $29.95. ISBN 0-8093-1417-7.

Carnochan, W.B. *Gibbon's Solitude: The Inward World of the Historian.* Stanford: Stanford Univ. Press, 1987. Pp. xiv + 225. $29.50. ISBN 0-8047-1363-4.

Chambers, Sir Robert, and Johnson, Samuel. *A Course of Lectures on the English Law, 1767-1773.* Ed. Thomas M. Curley, 2 vols. Madison: Univ. of Wisconsin Press, 1987. Pp. 483 and 445. $60.00. ISBN vol. 1: 0-299-10011-1, vol. 2: 0-299-10012-X.

Conrad, Peter. *The History of English Literature: One Indivisible, Unending Book.* Philadelphia: Univ. of Pennsylvania Press, 1987. Pp. x + 740. $39.95. ISBN 0-8122-8067-9.

Cowper, William. *The Letters and Prose Writings*, vol. 5. Ed. James King and Charles Ryskamp. Oxford and New York: Oxford Univ. Press, 1987. Pp. xxvi + 245. $57.00. ISBN 0-19-812690-5.

Damrosch, Leopold D., Jr. *The Imaginative World of Alexander Pope.* Berkeley: Univ. of California Press, 1987. Pp. ix + 310. $32.00. ISBN 0-520-05975-1.

Damrosch, Leopold D., Jr., ed. *Modern Essays on Eighteenth-Century Literature*. New York and Oxford: Oxford Univ. Press, 1988. Pp. 288. $32.50. ISBN 0-19-504923-3.

Danchin, Pierre. *The Prologues and Epilogues of the Restoration 1660-1700.* Part 3: 1691-1700. Nancy: Presses Universitaires de Nancy, 1985. Vol. 5. Pp. li + 322. Vol. 6. Pp. 323-697. The two-vol. part: 650 FF.

Daphinoff, Dimiter. *Samuel Richardsons "Clarissa": Text, Rezeption und Interpretation.* Bern: Francke Verlag, 1986. Pp. 324. DM 92,—. ISBN 3-317-01550-0.

Day, Geoffrey. *From Fiction to the Novel.* London: Routledge, 1987. Pp. vii + 223. $45.00. ISBN 0-7102-0911-8.

DeMaria, Robert, Jr. *Johnson's Dictionary and the Language of Learning.* Chapel Hill and London: Univ. of North Carolina Press, 1987. Pp. xiv + 303. $25.00 cloth, ISBN 0-8078-1713-9. $9.95 paper, ISBN 0-8078-4201-X.

Devlin, D.D. *The Novels and Journals of Fanny Burney.* New York: St. Martin's Press, 1987. Pp. viii + 118. $27.50. ISBN 0-312-00034-0.

Douglas, William. *The Cornutor of Seventy-Five* (1748) and Smollett, Tobias (?). *Don Ricardo Honeywater Vindicated* (1748). Augustan Reprint Society. Los Angeles: Univ. of California, William Andrews Clark Memorial Library, 1987. Pp. xiv + 52.

Downes, Kerry. *Sir John Vanbrugh: A Biography.* London: Sidgwick and Jackson, 1987. Pp. xxxi + 560. ISBN 0-283-99497-5.

Downie, J.A., introd. *Swift, Temple, and the Du Cros Affair, Part II: A Letter from Monsieur de Cros (1693) and Reflections upon Two Pamphlets (1693).* The Augustan Reprint Society. Los Angeles: William Andrews Clark Memorial Library, 1987. Pp. xi + 40.

Dryden, John. *The Works of John Dryden*; vols. 5 and 6 "*The Works of Virgil in English.*" Ed. William Frost and Vinton A. Dearing. Berkeley and Los Angeles: Univ. of California Press, 1987. Vol. 5: pp. 568; 72 illust.; $55.00; ISBN 0-520-02121-5. Vol. 6: pp. 641; 33 illust.; $55.00; ISBN 0-520-02122-3.

Duckworth, Colin, and Le Grand, Homer, eds. *Studies in the Eighteenth Century* 6. *Eighteenth-Century Life* 11,1 (February 1987). Williamsburg: College of William and Mary. Pp. 198. $9.00 single issue. ISSN 0098-2601.

Dwyer, John. *Virtuous Discourse: Sensibility and Community in Late Eighteenth-Century Scotland.* Edinburgh: John Donald, 1987. Atlantic Highlands, NJ: Humanities Press, 1987. Pp. viii + 204. $45.00. ISBN 0-85976-174-6.

Edmond, Mary. *Rare Sir William Davenant.* The Revels Plays Companion Library. New York: St. Martin's Press, 1987. Pp. ix + 264. $29.95. ISBN 0-312-00783-3.

Eighteenth-Century Life 10, n.s. 2 (May 1986). Ed. George R. Healy. Williamsburg: College of William and Mary. $15.00. ISSN 0098-2601.

Epstein, William H. *Recognizing Biography.* Philadelphia: Univ. of Pennsylvania Press, 1987. Pp. x + 231. $28.45. ISBN 0-8122-8081-4.

Faller, Lincoln B. *Turned to Account: The Forms and Functions of Criminal Biography in Late Seventeenth- and Early Eighteenth-Century England.*

Cambridge and New York: Cambridge Univ. Press, 1987. Pp. xiii + 347. $39.50. ISBN 0-521-32672-9.

Fielding, Henry. *The True Patriot and Related Writings*. Ed. W.B. Coley. Middletown: Wesleyan Univ. Press; Oxford: Oxford Univ. Press, 1987. Pp. cxii + 446. $50.00. ISBN 0-8195-5127-9.

Fielding, Sarah. *The Governess or, Little Female Academy*. London and New York: Pandora, 1987. Pp. xv + 126. $8.95. ISBN 0-86358-182-X.

Friedman, Edward H. *The Antiheroine's Voice: Narrative Discourse and Transformations of the Picaresque*. Columbia: Univ. of Missouri Press, 1987. Pp. xvii + 261. $30.00. ISBN 0-8262-0641-7.

Greene, Donald, and Vance, John A. *A Bibliography of Johnsonian Studies, 1970-1985*. Victoria: Univ. of Victoria, 1987. Pp. vi + 116. ISBN 0-920604-31-5.

Guilhamet, Leon. *Satire and the Transformation of Genre*. Philadelphia: Univ. of Pennsylvania Press, 1987. Pp. xii + 200. $49.95. ISBN 0-8122-8053-9.

Hamilton, Mary. *Munster Village*. London: Pandora Press of Routledge & Kegan Paul, and New York: Methuen, 1987. Pp. x + 150. $8.95. ISBN 0-86358-133-1.

Harris, Jocelyn. *Samuel Richardson*. Cambridge and New York: Cambridge Univ. Press, 1987. Pp. xii + 179. $39.50 cloth, ISBN 0-521-30501-2. $11.95 paper, ISBN 0-521-31542-5.

Hays, Mary. *Memoirs of Emma Courtney*. London: Pandora Press of Routledge & Kegan Paul, and New York: Methuen, 1987. Pp. xix + 100. $8.95. ISBN 0-86358-132-3.

Haywood, Eliza. *The History of Miss Betsy Thoughtless*. London: Pandora Press of Routledge & Kegan Paul, and New York: Methuen, 1987. Pp. xii + 594. $8.95. ISBN 0-86358-090-4.

Haywood, Ian. *The Making of History: A Study of the Literary Forgeries of James Macpherson and Thomas Chatterton in Relation to Eighteenth-Century Ideas of History and Fiction*. Rutherford, NJ: Fairleigh Dickinson Univ. Press, 1987. Pp. 228. $28.50. ISBN 0-8386-3261-0.

Highfill, Philip H. Jr., Burnim, Kalman A., and Langhans, Edward A. *A Biographical Dictionary of Actors, Actresses, Musicians, Dancers, Managers & Other Stage Personnel in London, 1660-1800*, Vol. 11: Naso to Pinkey. Carbondale: Southern Illinois Univ. Press, 1987. Pp. 331. $45.00. ISBN 0-8093-1280-8. Vol. 12: Pinner to Rizzo. Pp. 387. $45.00. ISBN 0-8093-1281-6.

Hinnant, Charles H. *Purity and Defilement in "Gulliver's Travels."* New York: St. Martin's Press, 1987. Pp. xi + 114. $29.95. ISBN 0-312-008290-5.

Horn, Pamela. *Life and Labour in Rural England, 1760-1850*. London: Macmillan Education, and Atlantic Highlands, NJ: Humanities Press, 1987. Pp. x + 184. $9.95 paper, ISBN 0-333-37585-8. $29.95 cloth, ISBN 0-333-37584-X.

Hulme, Peter. *Colonial Encounters: Europe and the Native Caribbean, 1492-1797*. London and New York: Methuen, 1987. Pp. xv + 348. $39.95. ISBN 0-416-41860-0.

Hunter, J. Paul, and Battestin, Martin C. *Henry Fielding in His Time and Ours.* Los Angeles: William Andrews Clark Library, Univ. of California, 1987. Pp. x + 64. $8.00.

Huseboe, Arthur R. *Sir George Etherege.* Boston: Twayne, 1987. Pp. 143. $24.95. ISBN 0-8057-6946-3.

Inchbald, Elizabeth. *A Simple Story.* London: Pandora Press of Routledge & Kegan Paul, and New York: Methuen, 1987. Pp. xi + 294. $8.95. ISBN 0-86358-136-6.

Kahler, Erich. *The Inward Turn of Narrative.* Trans. Richard and Clara Winston. Evanston: Northwestern Univ. Press, 1987. Pp. xvi + 238. $12.95. ISBN 0-8101-0736-8.

Kaminski, Thomas. *The Early Career of Samuel Johnson.* New York and Oxford: Oxford Univ. Press, 1987. Pp. xi + 268. ISBN 0-19-504114-3.

Keeble, N.H. *The Literary Culture of Nonconformity in Later Seventeenth-Century England.* Athens: Univ. of Georgia Press, 1987. Pp. xi + 356. $37.50. ISBN 0-8203-0951-6.

Kelly, Ann Cline. *Swift and the English Language.* Philadelphia: Univ. of Pennsylvania Press, 1988. Pp. xiii + 169. $24.95. ISBN 0-8122-8084-9.

Kelly, Lionel, ed. *Tobias Smollett: The Critical Heritage.* London and New York: Routledge & Kegan Paul, 1987. Pp. xvii + 380. $69.95. ISBN 0-7102-0905-3.

Kenrick, William. *Love in the Suds; A Town Eclogue.* Augustan Reprint Society. Los Angeles: Univ. of California, William Andrews Clark Memorial Library, 1987. Pp. xiii + 33.

Knapp, J. Merrill, and Mann, Alfred. *George Frideric Handel's Chamber Duets.* Los Angeles: Univ. of California, William Andrews Clark Memorial Library, 1987. Pp. x + 45.

Knutson, Harold C. *The Triumph of Wit: Molière and Restoration Comedy.* Columbus: Ohio State Univ. Press, 1988. Pp. xi + 192. $22.50. ISBN 0-8142-0438-4.

Kors, Alan Charles, and Korshin, Paul J., eds. *Anticipations of the Enlightenment in England, France, and Germany.* Philadelphia: Univ. of Pennsylvania Press, 1987. Pp. viii + 290. $29.95. ISBN 0-8122-8057-1.

Lamoine, Georges. *Littérature et Justice Pénale en Angleterre au Dix-Huitième Siècle.* Etudes Anglaises Cahiers et Documents, 8. Paris: Didier Erudition, 1987. Pp. 269. ISBN 2-86460-108-7.

Langhans, Edward A. *Eighteenth Century British and Irish Promptbooks: A Descriptive Bibliography.* Westport, CT: Greenwood Press, 1987. Pp. 304. $49.95. ISBN 0-313-24029-9.

Lemay, J.A. Leo, ed. *Deism, Masonry, and the Enlightenment: Essays Honoring Alfred Owen Aldridge.* Newark: Univ. of Delaware Press, and London: Associated Univ. Presses, 1987. Pp. 209. $28.50. ISBN 0-87513-317-3.

Lynch, James J. *Henry Fielding and the Heliodoran Novel.* Rutherford, NJ: Fairleigh Dickinson Univ. Press, 1986. Pp. 128. $19.50. ISBN 0-8386-3268-8.

Maccubbin, Robert P., and Sigworth, Oliver F., eds. *British Literature and Culture: Essays by Students, Colleagues, Friends and Other Admirers of*

Bertrand H. Bronson. Eighteenth-Century Life. 10, 3. (October 1986). Williamsburg: College of William and Mary, 1986. Pp. 203. $15.00 annual subscription. ISSN 0098-2601.

McKeon, Michael. *The Origins of the English Novel 1600-1740.* Baltimore and London: Johns Hopkins Univ. Press, 1987. Pp. xi + 529. $29.95. ISBN 0-8018-3291-8.

Meier, Thomas Keith. *Defoe and the Defense of Commerce.* Victoria: Univ. of Victoria, 1987. Pp. 117. ISBN 0-920604-29-3.

Mell, Donald C., Jr., Braun, Theodore E. D., and Palmer, Lucia M., eds. *Man, God, and Nature in the Enlightenment.* East Lansing, MI: Colleagues Press, 1988. Pp. xv + 247. $28.00. ISBN 0-937191-03-5.

Nokes, David. *Raillery and Rage: A Study of Eighteenth Century Satire.* New York: St. Martin's Press, 1987. Pp. xii + 211. $35.00. ISBN 0-312-00958-5.

Ober, William B. *Bottoms Up! A Pathologist's Essays on Medicine and the Humanities.* Carbondale: Southern Illinois Univ. Press, 1987. Pp. xix + 335. $19.95. ISBN 0-8093-1419-3.

Page, Norman, ed. *Dr. Johnson: Interviews and Recollections.* Totowa: Barnes and Noble, 1987. Pp. xxii + 176. $28.50. ISBN 0-389-20628-8.

Passmann, Dirk Friedrich. *"Full of Improbable Lies": "Gulliver's Travels" und die Reiseliteratur vor 1726.* Frankfurt am Main, Bern, and New York: Peter Lang, 1987. Pp. 505, sFr. 77.—.

Person, James E. Jr., ed. *Literature Criticism from 1400 to 1800.* Vol. 5. Detroit: Gale Research, 1987. Pp. 549. $88.00. ISBN 0-8103-6104-3.

Person, James E. Jr., ed. *Literature Criticism from 1400 to 1800.* Vol. 6. Detroit: Gale Research, 1987. Pp. 539. $92.00. ISBN 0-9103-6105-1.

Peterson, Spiro. *Daniel Defoe, A Reference Guide, 1731-1924.* Boston: G.K. Hall, 1987. Pp. xxxiii + 455. $45.00. ISBN 0-8161-8157-8.

Pope, Alexander. *Selected Prose.* Edited by Paul Hammond. Cambridge and London: Cambridge Univ. Press, 1987. Pp. xi + 322. $39.50. ISBN 0-521-25011-0.

Raven, James. *British Fiction 1750-1770: A Chronological Check-List of Prose Fiction Printed in Britain and Ireland.* Newark: Univ. of Delaware Press, 1987. Pp. 349. $39.50. ISBN 0-87413-324-6.

Rayner, Alice. *Comic Persuasion: Moral Structure in British Comedy from Shakespeare to Stoppard.* Berkeley and London: Univ. of California Press, 1987. Pp. ix + 169. $29.00. ISBN 0-520-05917-4.

Redford, Bruce, ed. *The Origins of "The School for Scandal": "The Slanderers" and "Sir Peter Teazle."* Princeton: Princeton Univ. Library, 1986. Pp. 165. $30.00. ISBN 0-87811-027-5.

Richetti, John J. *Daniel Defoe.* Boston: Twayne, 1987. Pp. x + 154. $17.95. ISBN 0-8057-6955-2.

Sheridan, Frances. *Memoirs of Miss Sidney Bidulph.* London: Pandora Press of Routledge & Kegan Paul, and New York: Methuen, 1987. Pp. xi + 431. $9.95. ISBN 0-86358-134-X.

Smart, Christopher. *The Poetical Works of Christopher Smart*, vol 4. *Miscellaneous Poems English and Latin.* Ed. Karina Williamson. Oxford and New York: Clarendon Press, 1987. Pp. 1 + 498. $92.00. ISBN 0-19-812768-5.

Smith, Charlotte. *The Old Manor House.* London: Pandora Press of Routledge & Kegan Paul, and New York: Methuen, 1987. Pp. xi + 516. $9.95. ISBN 0-86358-135-8.

Smith, Olivia. *The Politics of Language, 1791-1819.* Oxford: Clarendon Press, 1986. Pp. xvi + 269. $15.95. ISBN 0-19-812878-9.

Southerne, Thomas. *The Works of Thomas Southerne*, 2 vols. Ed. Robert Jordan and Harold Love. Oxford: Clarendon Press, 1988. Vol. 1: Pp. l + 508. £50.00. ISBN 0-19-811859-7. Vol. 2: Pp. viii + 503. £48.00. ISBN 0-19-812798-7.

Spackman, I.J., Owens, W.R., and Furbank, P.N., eds. *A KWIC Concordance to Daniel Defoe's "Robinson Crusoe."* New York and London: Garland, 1987. Pp. viii + 1141. $150.00. ISBN 0-8240-6388-4.

Spender, Dale. *Mothers of the Novel: 100 Good Women Writers Before Jane Austen.* London: Pandora Press of Routledge & Kegan Paul, and New York: Methuen, 1986. Pp. x + 357. $13.95. ISBN 0-86358-251-6.

[Steele, Richard.] *The Tatler*, 3 vols. ed. Donald F. Bond. Oxford: Clarendon Press, 1987. Vol. 1: Pp. xxxvii + 590. £60.00. ISBN 0-19-812484-8. Vol. 2: Pp. xiv + 539. £55.00. ISBN 0-19-818533-2. Vol. 3: Pp. xiv + 563. £55.00. ISBN 0-19-818534-0.

Stratton, Jon. *The Virgin Text: Fiction, Sexuality, and Ideology.* Norman and London: Univ. of Oklahoma Press, 1987. Pp. xxii + 237. $22.50. ISBN 0-8061-2054-1.

Straub, Kristina. *Divided Fictions: Fanny Burney and Feminine Strategy.* Lexington: Univ. Press of Kentucky, 1988. Pp. viii + 237. $22.00. ISBN 0-8131-1633-3.

Temmer, Mark J. *Samuel Johnson and Three Infidels: Rousseau, Voltaire, Diderot.* Athens and London: Univ. of Georgia Press, 1988. Pp. xiii + 212. $25.00. ISBN 0-8203-0962-1.

Todd, Janet, ed. *A Dictionary of British and American Women Writers, 1660-1800.* Totowa: Rowman & Littlefield, 1987. Pp. xxiv + 344. $19.50. ISBN 0-8476-7125-9 (paper).

Tracy, Clarence. *A Portrait of Richard Graves.* Toronto and Buffalo: Univ. of Toronto Press, 1987. Pp. xiv + 199. $30.00. ISBN 0-8020-5697-0.

van Boheemen, Christine. *The Novel as Family Romance: Language, Gender, and Authority from Fielding to Joyce.* Ithaca: Cornell Univ. Press, 1987. Pp. xi + 221. $24.95. ISBN 0-8014-1928-X.

Vickers, Brian, ed. *English Science, Bacon to Newton.* Cambridge and New York: Cambridge Univ. Press, 1987. Pp. xii + 244. $44.50. ISBN 0-521-30408-3.

Vince, Ronald W. *Neoclassical Theatre: A Historiographical Handbook.* Westport, CT: Greenwood, 1988. Pp. x + 229. $45.00. ISBN 0-313-24445-6.

Walker, Keith, ed. *John Dryden.* Oxford and New York: Oxford Univ. Press, 1987. Pp. xviii + 967. $39.95. ISBN 0-19-254192-7.

Wheeler, David, ed. *Domestick Privacies: Samuel Johnson and the Art of Biography*. Lexington: Univ. Press of Kentucky, 1987. Pp. vii + 192. $18.00. ISBN 0-8131-1612-0.

White, T.H. *The Age of Scandal: An Excursion Through a Minor Period*. Oxford and New York: Oxford Univ. Press, 1986. Pp. v + 250. $10.95. ISBN 0-19-281948-8.

Whittemore, Reed. *Pure Lives: The Early Biographers*. Baltimore and London: Johns Hopkins Univ. Press, 1988. Pp. ix + 159. ISBN 0-8018-3548-8.

Winn, James Anderson. *John Dryden and His World*. New Haven and London: Yale Univ. Press, 1987. Pp. xviii + 651. $29.95. ISBN 0-300-02994-2.

Woodhead, Abraham. *The Protestants Plea for a Socinian*. The Augustan Reprint Society. Los Angeles: William Andrews Clark Memorial Library, 1987. Pp. xii + 45.

SEL

Studies in ENGLISH LITERATURE 1500-1900

The Nineteenth Century

VOLUME 28 AUTUMN 1988 NUMBER 4

Studies in English Literature
1500 - 1900

VOLUME 28 AUTUMN 1988 NUMBER 4

PUBLISHED BY RICE UNIVERSITY

CONTENTS

The Significance of Catherine Wordsworth's Death to Thomas De Quincey and William Wordsworth — E. Michael Thron 559

Biographia Literaria and Wordsworth's Revisions — Eric C. Walker 569

Heading Out is not Going Home: *Jane Eyre* — Melodie Monahan 589

The (Un)Lettered Ensemble: What Charley Does Not Learn About Writing in Bleak House — Claudette Kemper Columbus 609

Pip and the Monster: The Joys of Bondage — Iain Crawford 625

Mark Lemon's Farces on the "Woman Question" — Leona W. Fisher 647

Daniel Deronda and George Eliot's Female (Re)Vision of Shakespeare — Marianne Novy 671

Meredith and Bakhtin: Polyphony and Bildung — Donald D. Stone 693

Recent Studies in the Nineteenth Century — David G. Riede 713

Studies in English Literature 1500 - 1900

PUBLISHED BY RICE UNIVERSITY

Studies in English Literature is a quarterly journal of historical and critical studies. Each issue will be devoted to one of four fields:

WINTER: The English Renaissance
SPRING: Elizabethan and Jacobean Drama
SUMMER: Restoration and Eighteenth Century
AUTUMN: The Nineteenth Century

SEL: Studies in English Literature, 1500–1900 (ISSN: 0039-3657) is published quarterly (February, May, August, and November) at $15.00 per year for individuals, $20.00 per year for U.S. institutions, $25.00 per year for foreign institutions, and $6.00 per single issue, by Rice University, 6100 South Main Street, P.O. Box 1892, Houston, Texas 77251. Second-class postage paid at Houston, Texas. **Postmaster:** Send address changes to the Business Manager, *SEL,* Rice University, P.O. Box 1892, Houston, TX 77251.

Studies in English Literature invites historical and critical essays of moderate length (ten to twenty-five pages) that contribute significantly to the understanding of English literature, 1500-1900. Typescripts should be double-spaced throughout and prepared in conformity with the Chicago Manual of Style. Clean photocopy on uncoated paper is acceptable in place of the ribbon copy. We prefer not to have dot-matrix printed copy. We will not consider articles being simultaneously submitted elsewhere, nor will we print essays to appear in a book published within a year of scheduled publication by *SEL*. Those wishing to omit their identities from manuscripts may do so, but should include a covering letter.

Manuscripts submitted for publication should be addressed to the Editor, *Studies in English Literature,* Rice University, P.O. Box 1892, Houston, TX 77251. They must be accompanied by a sufficient number of unattached stamps for return. Receipt of manuscripts will be acknowledged by postcard. Editorial decisions usually take a minimum of three months.

Annual subscription rates: $15.00 for individuals, $20.00 for U. S. institutions, $25.00 for foreign institutions, $6.00 per issue for partial subscriptions and single copies. Regular subscriptions may be obtained for any or all quarterly issues. Remittance should accompany subscription requests. Notice of non-receipt of an issue must be made within ninety (90) days following the publication of that issue. No refunds for cancellations. Business communications should be addressed to Business Manager, *Studies in English Literature,* Rice University, P. O. Box 1892, Houston, TX 77251.

Microfilms of previous volumes (Vols. 1-27) may be obtained from University Microfilms, Inc., 300 N. Zeeb Road, Ann Arbor, Michigan 48106; xerox copies of individual articles may be ordered by calling (800) 521-0600 (toll free). Copies of articles are also available from ISI's The Genuine Article service, 3501 Market Street, Philadelphia, PA 19104; phone (800) 523-1850; telex 84-5305; electronic mail through CLASS; or facsimile transmission via FAXPAX.

Volumes 1 through 3 and 5 through 10 of *Studies in English Literature* are available from Johnson Reprint Corporation, 111 Fifth Avenue, New York, N. Y. 10003, or Berkeley Square House, London W. 1, England.

SEL 28 (1988)
ISSN 0039-3657

The Significance of Catherine Wordsworth's Death to Thomas De Quincey and William Wordsworth

E. MICHAEL THRON

Catherine Wordsworth, aged three, died on the morning of 5 June 1812; Thomas De Quincey, an intimate of the family, was twenty-seven years old. The grief and affliction brought by Catherine's death, coupled with the death of De Quincey's nine-year-old sister Elizabeth on 2 June 1792 when Thomas was seven, formed the inexhaustible fuel of his imaginative and autobiographical writings. His excessive grief went beyond that expected from a friend of the family. Henry Crabb Robinson was present when De Quincey, having received a letter announcing the death from Dorothy, met William in London; Robinson noted in his diary that "Mr. De Quincey burst into tears on seeing Wordsworth and seemed to be more affected than the father" with Wordsworth far more in control expressing himself in language "that became a man both of feeling and of strength of mind."[1]

Catherine was a special child to both men before her death. Her lameness stemming from "convulsions" or, more likely, polio marked her early in her life.[2] At nine months, Dorothy Wordsworth writes of her as "a sweet creature—very fair, very bonny, but not *beautiful* in spite of her blue eyes" and her gentle manners led to a promise by Mary Wordsworth, here echoed by Dorothy, that De Quincey "is to be her sole tutor. . . . His gentle sweet manners must lead her to sweetness and gentle thoughts."[3] Her gentleness did not reflect docility but a way of living. Dorothy sees her at a year and two months with a face that is "perfectly comic" and with an "uncommonly quick and lively" way of moving about in the world.[4] And at a year and a half "Catherine makes you laugh. . . .

E. Michael Thron, Professor of Literature at the University of Wisconsin-Green Bay, has written several articles on De Quincey and is currently investigating the theoretical relationships between literature and cultural geography.

She is a plain child, has something peculiar in the cast of her face which probably adds to the comic effect of her looks and gestures."[5]

Dorothy Wordsworth's precise observations of Catherine's face and gestures are abstracted by the imagination of William in his tribute to Catherine written a year or more before her death, "Loving she is." The complete first line, "Loving she is, and tractable, though wild," captures that quickness of movement and gentleness of manner noted by Dorothy. This poetic Catherine is set apart from the adults who watch and admire her so that "this happy Creature of herself / Is all-sufficient; solitude to her / Is blithe society." She is another of Wordsworth's solitaries, not one cast off by the world, but a solitary by her very nature who "fills the air / With gladness and involuntary songs." Catherine's wild innocence is matched by the fawn who, startled, comes "unthought of, unexpected" from the woods; and, echoing the earlier tone of the *Lyrical Ballads,* Catherine is a new William and Dorothy in "Tintern Abbey." The imagery associated with Dorothy has that same untamed gentleness of Catherine which is seen "in the shooting lights / Of [her] wild eyes." The repetition of "wild" as a word characterizing both Catherine and Dorothy is a tenuous link to be sure, but the character of Dorothy in "Tintern Abbey" and of Catherine in "Loving she is" are too similar to be dismissed as coincidence. De Quincey, too, sees this wildness in Dorothy when he depicts "Her eyes [as] wild and startling, and hurried in their motion."[6] Dorothy, Catherine, and William as youths were all participants in the energetic forms of Nature that are repeated so often in Wordsworth's poetry but seldom so directly as in "Tintern Abbey":

> Their colours and their forms, were then to me
> An appetite; a feeling and a love,
> That had no need of a remoter charm
> By thought supplied, nor any interest
> Unborrowed from the eye.
>
> (lines 79-83)

William and Dorothy gained the "abundant recompense" of the philosophic mind through maturity and reflection, but Catherine was deprived of the self-awareness, and pain, necessary for maturity. She was forever trapped in "all-sufficient" innocence.

The self-sufficiency of innocence became an obsession for De Quincey in his precise, and what we might call neurotic, description of Catherine's life and death many years later in 1840.[7] In his *Literary Reminiscences,* Catherine is "Kate" and she "walked with me, slept with me, and was my sole companion" while he was living solitarily at Dove Cottage in Grasmere. She was his secret love, as he passionately tells Dorothy in his letter to her upon learning of Catherine's death: "Nobody can judge from her manner to me before others what love she shewed to me when we were playing or talking together alone. On the night when she slept with me in the winter, we lay awake all the middle of the night—and talked oh how tenderly together: When we fell asleep, she was lying in my arms. . . . Many times on that night—when she was murmuring out tender sounds of endearment, she would lock her arms with such passionateness round my neck—as if she had known that it was to be the last night we were ever to pass together."[8]

Though obviously comfortable to De Quincey's pen, the letter is embarrassing to read aloud in the late twentieth century. An odd twist. De Quincey senses the deep anxieties within this love, however, when he attributes it to witchery twenty-eight years later, and cites Wordsworth's "Loving she is" as evidence that one other saw her in the same light.[9] De Quincey saw himself as "blindly, dotingly, in a servile degree, devoted to this one affection." But there was another, his companion for much of his life, opium. He was using opium regularly at this time and in the year following Catherine's death he took 320 grains (8,000 drops of laudanum) a day, his highest dosage before the writing of the *Confessions* in 1821.[10] His only higher dosage came during the terrible times during and following the deaths of his two sons and his wife Margaret (1833-37) and while he was struggling to write the *Literary Reminiscences* of 1840 that I have been quoting.

After Catherine's death he reports that he haunts her grave, often spending all night beside it, and sees her ghost "in broad noonday" by "weaving, out of a few simple elements, a perfect picture of little Kate." His stomach pains increased, his opium use reached a new high, but the obsession suddenly stopped in November of 1813. It was as if a tiger had dropped him from its mouth: "I had been shaken and wrenched; and, in short, a case more entirely realizing the old Pagan superstition of a nympholepsy [falling impossibly in love and against one's will with an immortal nymph] in the first place, and secondly, of a Lethe or river of oblivion, and the possibility, by one draught from this potent stream, of applying an everlasting ablution to all the soils and stains of human anguish, I do not suppose the psychological history of man affords."[11] But she was not forgotten. Rather, Catherine Wordsworth was transformed by De Quincey's dreams and pen and joined his sister Elizabeth in the pantheon of dead and worshiped children, an untouched, pure, self-sufficient but passionately desired Innocent.

We have now entered De Quincey's unsolvable labyrinth of secrets, guilt, and dreams. The more he confesses, the stranger the world revealed becomes as each confession hides yet another secret. It is a far more dangerous world than Wordsworth's and, for that, a far more interesting one. His odd combination of analysis and emotional devotion, all in the form of literary and public confessions or gossip, lends itself to our modern interest in secrets, darkness, and the unconscious. Wordsworth's Catherine remains the poet's child, and sister/companion, captured in his images of wild and gentle innocence. But for De Quincey, she becomes a part of his "magnificent apparatus" of the Innocent left behind and the Innocent hidden from him by the forces of darkness. Her death on a sunny morning in June matches the death on another bright day in June of De Quincey's sister Elizabeth. Both deaths are dark ironies of Nature. The Innocent lost at sunrise can be our deepest tragedy and an experience that calls into question the justice of life itself. The dream world that Catherine enters is the primary opium dream of De Quincey's "Pains of Opium," the death chamber of his sister Elizabeth: "Again I am in the chamber with my sister's corpse, again the pomps of life rise up in silence, the glory of summer, the Syrian sunlights, the frost of death. Dream forms itself mysteriously within the dream." This powerful nightmare brought on by the opium becomes the basis for De Quincey's horrors and the vision of the dead Elizabeth will repeat itself many times over the years. Catherine's image joins Elizabeth's, and he re-mourns the death of his natural sister through the death of his adopted sister.[12]

At this point, the two men divide in their relationship to Catherine. Henry Crabb Robinson's observation, noted earlier, that De Quincey took her loss harder than Wordsworth is the outward reflection of the division. For Wordsworth Catherine remains a daughter and a companion symbolically participating in the forms of Nature as do he and Dorothy; she is someone who might have been welcomed into the maturity of the philosophical mind. Her loss is deeply felt, certainly, but it is held within the context of domestic and natural tragedy. Catherine was a sister in the sense that she was a fellow traveler on earth outside the push and pull of lust and commerce, two forces that defined corruption for Wordsworth.

In contrast, De Quincey's loss of "Kate" fuels his excesses of emotion and reason. By thinking obsessively upon the loss, he loses control in the labyrinth of his mind; and this convulsion of grief and thought, complicated and enhanced by physical pain and opium, wrenches apart the conventional combinations of child/father, brother/sister, wife/husband, lover/beloved and produces new and dangerous configurations. But they are acceptable for public disclosure because De Quincey views them as transformed by his visions and his mind. De Quincey sees opium as transforming the experiences of his life into mythical proportions fueled by his experiences as a child and his life as a scholar. Common experiences are combined with his life as a scholar so that his sublime visions and sublime sufferings are informed by both the everyday world and the grandness of the scholarly past. The metaphor of music incarnates and captures this transformation as "the detail of its [an experience's] incidents [are] removed, or blended in some hazy abstraction; and its passions exalted, spiritualized, and sublimed."[13] The capturing of the incident by the exalted and spiritualized takes it from the pain of particular guilt and permits it to be placed side by side with another incident which is equally sublime. Hence, sister/beloved can be realized. But not for long. The forbidden combination hovers between the pleasures and pains of opium, between the dream and the nightmare. The tension, almost insupportable, between desire and guilt enhanced by (maybe even caused by) opium produces the excesses and peculiar relationships between intimates and family reported by De Quincey.

A few examples of these dangerous combinations are instructive. Agnes, the young woman in *The Household Wreck* and probably modeled after the young Margaret Simpson, his future wife, "retained a most childlike expression of countenance so even then in absolute childhood she put forward the blossoms and the dignity of a woman. . . . she was also a mother. Whilst, therefore, to her child she supported the matronly part of guide and the aire of an experienced person, to me she wore, ingenuously and without disguise, the part of a child herself, with all the giddy hopes and unchastised imaginings of that bouyant age. This double character sits most gracefully upon many a young wife whose heart is pure and innocent."[14] Of course, in what can be described as a domestic gothic novella, De Quincey has her threatened from early in the story with crime, false imprisonment and disaster—the Innocent, that he holds dear and desires, brings, as he says of the tale, "whisperings from paradise and fierce mockeries from the anarchy of chaos."[15] De Quincey writes *The Household Wreck* while Margaret is dying of typhus and with few prospects for a better financial future. Agnes seems a tribute to the loss of his wife's hope for life and the story itself a lashing out at the isolation of his family from his past acceptance by the Wordsworths.

If the imagined Margaret is the child/wife/mother, she is also Electra to De Quincy's Orestes in the *Confessions.* The first section of the 1822 *Confessions* describes his vagabond existence in London and his camping out in an abandoned house that an orphaned little girl shares with him in the cold and where he meets and befriends the teenage prostitute Ann of Oxford Street. After losing track of both the orphaned girl and Ann, he places them in his bank of memories where they will later join his sister Elizabeth's and Catherine's deaths as prelude to the symphony of pleasure and pain in opium; all are women, all spiritual Innocents, all under fifteen years of age, all lost and abandoned. Margaret Simpson is eighteen when he marries her, she was seventeen when she became pregnant with their first child, and she was living in Dove Cottage while De Quincey was in London desperately writing the *Confessions.* De Quincey, in typical fashion, sees himself as the guilt-ridden and tormented Orestes on his couch: "There it was, that for years, I was persecuted by visions as ugly, and as ghastly phantoms as ever haunted the couch of an Orestes . . . but, watching by my pillow, or defrauding herself of sleep to bear me company through the heavy watches of the night, sat my Electra, for thou beloved M., dear companion of my later years, thou wast my Electra."[16] The metamorphosis of two people into two mythological murderers of parents (De Quincey is using the myth as presented by Euripedes, certainly one of the more perverse renderings) and seeing in that transformation a brother and sister comforting each other before their Fate and more murders is certainly an unsettling reference. It is one quite typical of De Quincey but quite perverse for the previous tenants of Dove Cottage; we just cannot imagine Dorothy or Mary and William as Electra and Orestes. Can we imagine Thomas and Margaret? No, but we can see by asking that question that the imaginations of the two writers diverge considerably even though they share a deep respect for and an understanding of childhood as a wellspring for the imaginations of artists.

The child/sister/wife Margaret shares in the life of pain and guilt because she has reached maturity, but the imagined Elizabeth and Catherine were cut off before they could understand or really be guilty. This lack of guilt in the child is an idea and emotion shared by Wordsworth's vision and De Quincey's, and a fact seemingly as entrenched in the interpretation of the Romantic Movement as the theory of evolution is in scientific circles. The great energy driving De Quincey's version of the child Innocent is his opium dreams that abstract the Innocent and place her within his own guilt, his own desires and maturity, without corrupting her. But it is dangerous, and if I read De Quincey correctly, he could not control her once the visions began: the real danger is losing her forever in the darkness of the labyrinth.

Yet De Quincey never seems to have lost this vision of the child nor the appearance himself of a child. His daughter Emily records his last words as "They are all leaving me but my dear little children," "My mother," and "Sister, Sister."[17] From this distance we can never settle on the facts and say that the sister mentioned is Elizabeth nor that it is his sister at all, but I think we can say that his last words as recorded by a daughter are certainly deeply informed by his first and second families and his imagined children. His autobiography, his reminiscences, his dream visions revolve around the innocent children that he experienced and lost. Children were to him, and to many of his contemporaries, like Catherine Wordsworth as described in the 1840s *Literary Reminiscences*: "[she was] an impersonation of the dawn and the spirit of infancy; and this abstraction seated in her person, together with the visionary sort of connexion which, even in her parting hours, she assumed with the summer sun, by timing her immersion into the cloud of death with the rising and setting of that fountain of life."[18]

A familiar passage from "Tintern Abbey" is a play upon De Quincey's last words:

> My dear, dear Sister! And this prayer I make,
> Knowing that Nature never did betray
> The heart that loved her; 'tis her privilege,
> Through all the years of this our life, to lead
> From joy to joy.
>
> (lines 121-125)

The progression from joy to joy is the great hope of our lives, particularly when sanctioned by Nature and shared with those closest to our hearts. As we all know, the poem is a prayer to sanction and continue a bond of spirit between two people. That bond is strengthened by the presence of his sister Dorothy. Later, Wordsworth records one of those moments of joy but the companion, this time his daughter Catherine, is gone:

> Surprised by joy—impatient as the Wind
> I turned to share the transport—oh! with whom
> But thee, deep buried in the silent tomb,
> That spot which no vicissitude can find?
>
> (lines 1-4)

Wordsworth *is* stronger and wiser than De Quincey; Robinson was right to see that he was "a man of feeling and of strength of mind"—the very qualities that attracted De Quincey. He lays Catherine to rest even as he remembers her death. He forgets her death, turns to her and expects her there. When she is not, the reexperienced death forces the reexperiencing of the acceptance of that death. In contrast, De Quincey's everlasting Innocent forms and re-forms within his imagination so that even the control, and catharsis, that comes from writing the journeys of these dead children can not stop the pain, the loss, and the guilt. They will not die for De Quincey until he dies because they have not settled *in* the earth. Wordsworth is wiser, but De Quincey has his attractions for those who cannot settle their quarrel *with* the earth.

NOTES

[1]*The Diary, Reminiscences and Correspondence of Henry Crabb Robinson*, ed. Thomas Sadler, 2 vols. (London and New York: Macmillan, 1872) 1:204.

[2]The cause of the lameness or the death can never be settled but Cecilia Hennel Hendricks's argument in "Thomas De Quincey, Symptomatologist" *PMLA* 80, 2 (1945): 828-40 would suggest polio.

[3]Dorothy Wordsworth to Catherine Clarkson (Catherine Wordsworth's godmother), 15 June 1809, from *The Letters of William and Dorothy Wordsworth*. ed. Ernest De Selincourt 2nd edn., rev. Mary Moorman, 6 vols. (Oxford: Oxford Univ. Press, 1969), 1:357.

[4]Dorothy Wordsworth to Jane Marshall, 19 November 1809. *Letters*, 1:377.

[5]Wordsworth to Lady Beaumont, 28 February 1810. *Letters*, 1:389.

[6]*The Collected Writings of Thomas DeQuincey*, ed. David Masson, 14 vols. Edinburgh: A. and C. Black, 1889-90) 2:238.

[7]*Literary Reminiscences* from *The Autobiography of An English Opium Eater*, 2 vols. (Boston: Ticknor, Reed and Fields, 1851) 2:214-19.

[8]Thomas De Quincey to Dorothy Wordsworth 13-15 June 1812 in John E. Jordon's *De Quincey to Wordsworth: A Biography of a Relationship* (Berkeley: Univ. of California Press, 1982), p. 265.

[9]*Literary Reminiscences*, 2:214-215.

[10]Alethea Hayter, *Opium and the Romantic Imagination* (Berkeley: Univ. of California Press, 1988), p. 228, footnote 13.

[11]*Literary Reminiscences*, 1:219.

[12]See Grevel Lindop's argument in his *The Opium-Eater: A Life of Thomas De Quincey* (London: J. M. Dent, 1981), pp. 207-208, for a more detailed link between the two deaths. In addition, Thomas McFarland in his *Romantic Cruxes: The English Essayists and the Spirit of the Age* (Oxford: Clarendon Press, 1987), sees Catherine's death as a reinforcement of the mental wanderings begun with the rememberance of Elizabeth's death, and Robert Lance Snyder in his essay, "De Quincey's Literature of Power: A Mythic Paradigm," *SEL* 26 (1986):691-711, sees such "overpowering losses" as essential to the evolution of De Quincey's concept of the dark sublime and the literature of power.

[13]Grevel Lindop, *The Opium Eater*, pp. 45-46.

[14]*The Household Wreck*, in *Writings*, 12:158, 173.

[15]*Writings*, 12:158.

[16]*The Confessions of an English Opium-Eater and other Writings* (Oxford and New York: Oxford Univ. Press, 1985), p. 35-38.

[17]William Hallam Bonner, *De Quincey at Work: As Seen in One Hundred and Thirty New and Newly Edited Letters* (Buffalo: Airport, 1936), Emily De Quincey to James Fields, 12 December 1859, p. 42. Miss De Quincey also records that "I heard him one night say, 'My dear little girl, you may be called in some measure the child of my old age.' I wondered for a minute if he was going back to my childhood but I heard soon after the name of Maggie's Eva [his oldest daughter Margaret's child]."

[18]*Literary Reminiscences* 2:216.

SEL 28 (1988)
ISSN 0039-3657

Biographia Literaria and Wordsworth's Revisions

ERIC C. WALKER

William Wordsworth once claimed only to have skimmed *Biographia Literaria,* but students have long noticed that he later revised many of his verses discussed by Samuel Taylor Coleridge.[1] These revisions, however, often have been misrepresented in criticism of both Wordsworth and Coleridge.[2] My purpose here is to take a fresh look at Wordsworth's revisions after the publication of *Biographia Literaria* in 1817. Although such a list would be useful, an annotated catalogue of the revisions is not the present objective; my examples are chosen instead chiefly to illustrate problems that occur in any study of Wordsworth's revisions but that are especially prominent in this famous chapter in their history.[3] A more careful account of these specific materials should help to illuminate at least two larger subjects, Wordsworth's lifelong habit of revision and his relationship with Coleridge.[4]

To review the characteristic manner of citing Wordsworth's post-*Biographia* revisions and the usual conclusions that are stated, three well-known examples, changes to "The Thorn," "The Blind Highland Boy," and the "Ode: Intimations of Immortality," will serve as an introduction.[5] Among other alterations to "The Thorn," Wordsworth revised for the 1820 edition of his poetry the description of the pond, "I've measured it from side to side: / 'Tis three feet long, and two feet wide" (Brett and Jones, p. 71), to "Though but of compass small, and bare / To thirsty suns, and parching air," after the original couplet was quoted by Coleridge as a "sudden and unpleasant sinking" (2:50-52). The blind highland boy's loch-going vessel, originally a "Household tub," was amplified from "The Shell of a green Turtle, thin / And hollow;—you might sit therein, / It was so

Eric C. Walker, Director of Graduate Studies in the English Department at Florida State University, has published essays on Wordsworth in *PQ* and the *Papers of the Bibliographical Society of America,* and others are forthcoming in *JEGP, Studies in Romanticism,* and *The Wordsworth Circle.*

wide and deep" (1815) to, in 1820, "A Shell of ample size and light / As the pearly Car of Amphitrite, / That sportive Dolphins drew" (Curtis, pp. 225, 337) after Coleridge cited the 1815 passage in context as an example of "disharmony in style" (2:123). Finally, four verses about the child's conception of death in the "Intimations Ode," originally

To whom the grave
Is but a lonely bed without the sense or sight
Of day or the warm light,
A place of thought where we in waiting lie,

became in 1820 one verse, "In darkness lost, the darkness of the grave" (Curtis, p. 274), after Coleridge's comment that the reader "must at once understand the words *contrary* to their common import, in order to arrive at any *sense*" (2:140-41). In the recent Bollingen edition of *Biographia Literaria*, these and other of Wordsworth's revisions are recorded in footnotes, introduced by phrases such as "in response to Coleridge," "in reaction to Coleridge," or "in deference to Coleridge." Such evidence has led to the long-standing judgment of Wordsworth's reaction to the *Biographia*, which was phrased most influentially by Stephen Parrish in a 1958 *PMLA* essay: "But there is no need to guess at the impression left by the *Biographia Literaria*. For the 1820 edition of his collected poems Wordsworth revised the passages that Coleridge had singled out for criticism. The revisions had a consistent aim—to elevate the language, making it accord more closely with Coleridge's notion of poetic diction."[6] It almost goes without saying that this "consistent aim" is often assumed to be a lapse or a retreat on Wordsworth's part, evidence of his poetic decline. Phrased extremely, as in the following example from a 1984 essay in *The Wordsworth Circle*, the conclusion is that Wordsworth "took the *Biographia* itself sufficiently to heart to mutilate a number of his poems in subordination to Coleridge's judgement."[7]

Careful attention to all the poetry in Wordsworth's four-volume 1820 collected edition, *The Miscellaneous Poems of William Wordsworth*, suggests different conclusions about the revisions: Wordsworth revised only selectively in what appears to be response to Coleridge, and the changes to material singled out by Coleridge are only a portion of Wordsworth's revisions at the time, including work on numerous texts about which Coleridge is silent. Furthermore, these "alterations," as Wordsworth liked to call them, often can be read as coherent stylistic experiments, chiefly with poetic diction, and these experiments are consistent with regularly encountered features of Wordsworth's poetry. When it is recalled that Wordsworth was revising his poetry long before and long after the *Biographia* was published, the following limitations appear in the usual manner in which the post-*Biographia* revisions are presented and studied: normally, little attention is directed to pre-*Biographia* revisions; little notice is taken of revised passages in poems outside the passages specified by Coleridge; little or no attention is drawn to the instances when Wordsworth did *not* revise passages Coleridge criticized; little notice is taken of changes to passages Coleridge *praised;* little awareness is expressed of Wordsworth's other revisions at this time of poems unmentioned by Coleridge; little account is taken of the bulk of unrevised poetry; and little attempt is made to connect the revisions with Wordsworth's new poetry of the same years.[8] Throughout these remarks, I assume that, to be discussed usefully, Wordsworth's post-*Biographia* revisions must be reported accurately and fully (which includes awareness of unrevised material) and that these revisions then need to be located in several overlapping contexts: the complete texts of poems in which they occur, the entire range of revising activity (which includes work on much poetry not mentioned in the *Biographia*), and, finally, new poetry of the same period.

The following comments are divided into two main sections, the first devoted to Wordsworth's poetry noticed in the *Biographia* and the second devoted primarily to Wordsworth's other poetry, including revisions of earlier texts and new composition. Three goals govern selection and discussion of examples. First and most regularly, I want simply to illustrate problems of method in the study of Wordsworth's revisions, particularly those revisions associated with Coleridge's commentary in the *Biographia.* Second, because prevailing opinion tends to assume the opposite case, I use many of the same examples to test the hypothesis of Wordsworth's independence in his post-*Biographia* revisions. Finally, especially in the last section of the essay I select examples to argue that Wordsworth's various kinds of revision during this period participate in an ongoing stylistic experiment with poetic diction—specifically, an experiment in the contrasts within single poems between apparently more elaborate and apparently simpler language, an experiment, moreover, that Coleridge (among others) considered infelicitous. These latter remarks can only indicate the project toward which they are a preliminary step, a better sense of Wordsworth's style as he neared his fiftieth year.

II

Coleridge keyed his examples in the *Biographia* to Wordsworth's first collected edition, the two-volume *Poems of William Wordsworth,* published in 1815, which presented about two hundred and fifty poems. In *Biographia Literaria,* Coleridge mentioned about sixty of these poems in about seventy-five references, about a third of which references are by title alone.[9] Of these approximately six dozen total references, roughly half are complimentary and half are critical. Of the three dozen critical references, about two-thirds specify a passage, by either quotation or page reference. Of these two dozen specifically criticized passages, some as brief as a couplet, Wordsworth revised about two-thirds. Thus, in unquestionable "response," "reaction," or "deference" to Coleridge, Wordsworth revised about sixteen passages among hundreds of poems.

This section of examples from poems that Coleridge remarked in the *Biographia* has been organized to illustrate the necessity of accounting for 1) earlier, pre-*Biographia* revisions, 2) the revisions in poems mentioned by Coleridge that lie outside passages specified by Coleridge, 3) passages Coleridge criticized that Wordsworth left untouched, and 4) changes to passages Coleridge praised.

The first category in which to consider the possibility of Wordsworth's independence is earlier, pre-*Biographia* revisions. In their notes to "The Thorn," the editors of a standard edition of the *Lyrical Ballads* state that "no significant changes were made in the text of this poem until 1820, that is, until *after* Coleridge had singled the poem out for criticism."[10] Similarly, an important essay on "The Thorn" suggests that "the event that led to its alteration was the appearance of *Biographia Literaria.* . . . Wordsworth . . . was now ready to abandon the struggle: he revised the poem extensively for the edition of 1820. The revisions had a single end, to elevate the language . . . their importance is that they marked a retreat on Wordsworth's part from a daring and skilful experiment."[11] In light of such assessments, two facts about the revisions should be recorded: not all the 1820 revisions can be seen unequivocally "to elevate the language," and some revisions to the passages specified by Coleridge in 1817 had already appeared in the 1815 edition. In addition to the couplet reproduced at the beginning of this essay, Coleridge quoted fifty-eight verses from the middle of the poem as additional "sudden and unpleasant sinkings" (2:50-52); for the 1820 edition, Wordsworth omitted eleven and revised twelve of these verses. Several of these revisions, however, seem to elevate language only a little if at all: " 'Tis now some two-and-twenty years" became " 'Tis known, that twenty years are passed," for example, and "Last Christmas when we talked of this" became "Last Christmas-eve we talked of this" (Brett and Jones, pp. 73-75). Moreover, a notable instance among these fifty-eight verses of revisions that do indeed elevate language had already appeared in 1815 (a fact unremarked by Coleridge in the *Biographia*), where the earlier version of four verses—

A cruel, cruel fire, they say,
Into her bones was sent:
It dried her body like a cinder,
And almost turn'd her brain to tinder
(Brett and Jones, p. 74)

had become in 1815—

A pang of pitiless dismay
Into her soul was sent;
A Fire was kindled in her breast,
Which might not burn itself to rest.

The evidence suggests that Wordsworth undeniably devoted additional attention to "The Thorn" in the wake of Coleridge's commentary, but also that some—not all—of these 1820 revisions continued a kind of change that was initiated before the *Biographia* appeared.

A few additional examples of earlier revisions will serve as reminders of Wordsworth's complex revising procedures. "Anecdote for Fathers," which Coleridge offered as an example of "occasional prolixity, repetition, and an eddying instead of progression of thought" (2:136), was, as the most recent editors of the *Biographia* note, "later altered," apparently to modify these features, but this process had begun in revisions that appeared as early as 1800, where the twelfth stanza in the original had been revised in part to eliminate the phrase "so fair and slim," which was a close echo—a repetition—of "so slim / And graceful" in the fifth stanza (Brett and Jones, pp. 64-65). This feature of Wordsworth's revisions—the continuation, in revisions of passages specified by Coleridge, of a kind of change that is in evidence before the *Biographia* was published—may also be noticed in the fourth stanza of "The Sailor's Mother," which Coleridge had quoted (with the two following stanzas) as language "exclusively colloquial" (2:69-70). Four of the six verses in the stanza were revised for 1820, apparently to temper the colloquialisms, but a fifth verse in the same stanza had been revised to similar effect for the 1815 edition (a regular way Wordsworth modifies the colloquial is to substitute polysyllabic for monosyllabic diction): "And I have been as far as Hull, to see" had become "And I have travelled far as Hull, to see" (Curtis, p. 78).

A number of other poems Coleridge criticized had already accumulated extensive histories of revision, a feature of Wordsworth's habit of composition that again is often forgotten in the study of the post-*Biographia* revisions. Notable examples include "Ruth," which Coleridge both praised and blamed (2:43, 101-102), and which was revised for 1820, but which also had been extensively revised for 1802 and 1805 (Brett and Jones, pp. 179-88), and, to a lesser extent, for 1815. "Simon Lee" (Brett and Jones, pp. 60-63), which Coleridge included among a quartet of poems "more delightful to me in prose" (2:68), was reworked for 1820, but it also had been heavily revised for 1815 and was altered again for 1827. The point seems almost too obvious to state, but a reminder seems in order: Wordsworth did not require the *Biographia* to take up revising.

The examples to this point of course beg an obvious question: what are the influences upon and purposes of Wordsworth's revisions at *all* these stages, both long before and long after the *Biographia*? Specifically, the appearance of a critical comment in the *Biographia* of course does not necessarily mean that Wordsworth had not heard it—or something like it—much earlier, so that the extensive revision history of a poem perhaps represents a response to Coleridge all along. It is important to keep in mind that some of Wordsworth's revisions may represent his response to unrecorded discussions within the Wordsworth circle, so that we cannot be absolutely certain that he was not responding to Coleridge—or to someone else, such as Dorothy Wordsworth, Sara Hutchinson, Mary Hutchinson, Charles Lamb, or the reviewers—when he revised material not singled out in the *Biographia* or in other records. It is not my purpose here, however, to address extensively the full phenomenon of Wordsworth's revisions; my point instead is simply this: when we study Coleridge's comments in the *Biographia* and Wordsworth's subsequent revisions, we should remember that Wordsworth's revisions form an extraordinarily complex and extensive record, and that those revisions which appear after the *Biographia* was published have been misinterpreted in part because they have been tied too closely to Coleridge's commentary in the *Biographia*.

A second category of revisions points less equivocally toward Wordsworth's independence: in numerous instances, Wordsworth revised for the 1820 edition passages in poems outside the passages in the same poems that Coleridge singled out for criticism. For example, Coleridge quoted one stanza of "The Emigrant Mother" as an example of "disharmony in style" (2:124) and Wordsworth reworked part of this stanza for 1820, but at the same time he also revised verses much earlier in the poem: "Once did I see her clasp the Child about, / And take it to herself; and I, next day, / Wish'd in my native tongue to fashion out" became, in 1820, "Once did I see her take with fond embrace / This Infant to herself; and I, next day, / Endeavoured in my native tongue to trace" (Curtis, p. 248). Another example of this feature occurs in "The Brothers," from which Coleridge paraphrased ten verses to demonstrate "prosaisms" in Wordsworth's verse (2:79-80); Wordsworth then extensively reworked the paraphrased passage for the 1820 edition, arguably making it less "prosaic." But he also at this time reworked verses not specified by Coleridge; for instance, four verses in the original,

> With two or three Companions whom it chanced
> Some further business summoned to a house
> Which stands at the Dale-head. James, tired perhaps,
> Or from some other cause, remained behind
> (Brett and Jones, p. 148)

became five in 1820:

> With two or three Companions, whom their course
> Of occupation led from height to height
> Under a cloudless sun, till he, at length,
> Through weariness, or, haply, to indulge
> The humour of the moment, lagged behind.

Of course these examples in isolation can be used to argue that Wordsworth took Coleridge's criticism so much to heart that he fitfully applied its spirit elsewhere, but I want to counter such a conclusion by maintaining that no one feature of Wordsworth's revisions should be studied in such isolation; an alternative and to my mind more useful conclusion is that, when studied in the context of the larger process of revision, these passages supply additional reminders that Wordsworth exercised his own judgment. At times his changes evidently produced some effects that appear to be not inconsistent with Coleridge's criticism, but revisions were by no means restricted to passages specified by Coleridge.

Wordsworth's independence comes into unmistakable focus in a revision of "The Idiot Boy." Coleridge noted that this "fine poem" is nevertheless "pitched at a lower note," and lodged one particular objection: "the author has not, in the poem itself, taken sufficient care to preclude from the reader's fancy the disgusting images of *ordinary, morbid idiocy,* which yet it was by no means his intention to represent. He has even by the 'burr, burr, burr,' uncounteracted by any preceding description of the boy's beauty, assisted in recalling them''(2:48). Through the 1820 edition, Wordsworth made very few changes to this poem, but he did revise for 1820 one of the two stanzas in which Johnny's "burr, burr, burr" occurs; the original,

> Away she hies to Susan Gale:
> And Johnny's in a merry tune;
> The Owlets hoot, the Owlets curr,
> And Johnny's lips they burr, burr, burr,—
> And on he goes beneath the Moon.
>
> (Brett and Jones, p. 90)

became in 1820

> Away she hies to Susan Gale:
> Her Messenger's in merry tune;
> The Owlets hoot, the Owlets curr,
> And Johnny's lips they burr, burr, burr,—
> And on he goes beneath the Moon.

Wordsworth let stand the one quoted feature of the poem that Coleridge singled out for blame, and made one of his few revisions in the very same stanza, substituting a mock-heroic epithet—"Messenger" for "Johnny"—that heightens the effect Coleridge objected to, the bathos of Johnny's burr. Here we can begin to glimpse the nature of Wordsworth's experiment, which I discuss at greater length in the last section: the deliberate juxtaposition (enforced here by the bathetic rhyme "messeng*er* / burr") of different levels of diction.

The most pointed evidence of Wordsworth's independence is offered by two last categories of revision, passages Coleridge criticized that Wordsworth left untouched, and revisions of passages that Coleridge praised. Numerous examples of both groups again often go unremarked in comments on the post-*Biographia* revisions. In the first group, in addition to the unrevised "burr, burr, burr" in "The Idiot Boy" noted above, Coleridge objected to the concluding couplet of "I wandered lonely as a Cloud" (2:137), but Wordsworth left the couplet untouched (Curtis, p. 208). More extensive examples include the unrevised opening stanza (ten verses) of "The Last of the Flock" (Brett and Jones, p. 78), which Coleridge singled out prominently at the beginning of chapter 18 as an example of how even

Wordsworth's seemingly simple language did not reproduce "the language of ordinary men . . . in *real* life" (2:58-59). Coleridge criticized three long passages in *The Excursion* (2:127, 135-36), but Wordsworth made extensive revisions to only one of these, the passage in Book I (Book I, lines 112-38; III, lines 23-73; VI, lines 1-80). Before he complained about the verses concerning the child's sense of death in the "Intimations Ode," Coleridge also protested the preceding ten verses about the "best Philosopher" (2:138), but Wordsworth let these verses stand (Curtis, p. 274). Finally, in the face of the notoriety surrounding the evolution of the blind highland boy's vessel from a "Household tub" to a "Turtle Shell . . . light as the pearly Car of Amphitrite," it should be pointed out that Coleridge quoted two separated stanzas of "The Blind Highland Boy" as equal examples of "disharmony in style" in the poem (2:123); the second read in 1815

> Our Highland Boy oft visited
> The house which held this prize, and led
> By choice or chance did thither come
> One day, when no one was at home,
> And found the door unbarred.
>
> (Curtis, pp. 225, 339)

Wordsworth revised the vessel stanza again but left this stanza, which appears later in the poem, untouched.[12]

The last group of revisions related to Coleridge's commentary in the *Biographia*, revisions to passages that Coleridge praised, includes verses in "To the Cuckoo," "The Green Linnet," and "Elegiac Stanzas, Suggested by a Picture of Peele Castle, in a Storm." As an example of Wordsworth's fourth "excellence," "the perfect truth of nature in his images and descriptions," Coleridge cited "To the Cuckoo" (2:149), which Wordsworth not only had revised for the 1815 edition but continued to revise for the 1827 and 1845 editions (Curtis, pp. 213-15). In this same category of "excellence," Coleridge quoted the last two stanzas of "The Green Linnet," commenting "what can be more accurate yet more lovely?" (2:149). Of the eight verses in the final stanza, Wordsworth revised one for 1820 ("And mock the Form which he did feign" became "The voiceless Form he chose to feign"), recast the whole stanza for 1827, and then continued to rework the opening couplet through 1845 (Curtis, p. 230). Finally, when Coleridge came to declare Wordsworth's "pre-eminent" excellence, "the gift of IMAGINATION in the highest and strictest sense of the word," and then bestowed his greatest compliment, "in imaginative power, he stands nearest of all modern writers to Shakespear and

Milton; and yet in a kind perfectly unborrowed and his own," he immediately quoted three verses of "Elegiac Stanzas, Suggested by a Picture of Peele Castle" as "at once an instance and an illustration": "add the gleam / The light that never was on sea or land, / The consecration, and the poet's dream" (2:151). Among few revisions ever to this poem, these verses became in the 1820 edition "add a gleam, / The lustre, known to neither sea nor land / But borrowed from the youthful Poet's dream" (Curtis, p. 267). The very choice of the passage and the denial of Coleridge's "perfectly unborrowed" phrase render the independence of this revision rather prickly, and the passage thus illustrates an essential problem in the study of Wordsworth's revisions: although to argue that Wordsworth "mutilated" poems only in response to Coleridge's criticism at best states only a very partial truth, few who would at least consider the essential integrity of Wordsworth's procedures would hold that they yield uniformly successful results. Wordsworth himself did not, and restored the original reading of these "Peele Castle" verses for the 1832 edition.[13]

The last body of evidence pointing to Wordsworth's independence is material from the same period as the post-*Biographia* revisions that lies outside the immediate scope of Coleridge's commentary. Before turning in the last section to examples from this body of work, it is useful briefly to notice all the preceding kinds of revisions in a single poem, "Resolution and Independence" (Curtis, pp. 123-29), as a summary of the argument to this point. In the last section, I will inspect in greater detail one revision to "Resolution and Independence" as a transition to the larger issues addressed there.

Coleridge commented on "Resolution and Independence" in several places in the *Biographia* (2:125-26, 152), and Wordsworth's attention to the poem after first publication demonstrates not only his response to Coleridge's remarks but also earlier revisions, changes to passages not specified by Coleridge, passages criticized by Coleridge that are left standing, and alterations to passages Coleridge praised.[14] The only one of these groups usually remarked is the first, Wordsworth's omission of a stanza that, as Coleridge pointed out, presented repetitious imagery (lines 57-63 in the original) and the alteration of one verse, "Beside the little pond or moorish flood," to "Upon the margin of that moorish flood" in the other stanza Coleridge quoted. In addition to these related changes for 1820, however, Wordsworth had already reworked another verse for the 1815 edition: "And now, not knowing what the Old Man had said" had become "But now, perplex'd by what the Old Man had said." Moreover, this verse occurs in a stanza that Coleridge quoted with approval in 1817 (in contrast to the following stanza), but Wordsworth revised the verse again for 1820: "Perplexed, and longing to be comforted." Furthermore, Wordsworth left unchanged the following stanza that Coleridge disliked (I return to this example of Wordsworth's independence in the last section). Elsewhere in the poem, Wordsworth revised for the 1820 edition a number of verses outside sections that had attracted Coleridge's notice; for example, "And now such freedom as I could I took" became "And now a stranger's privilege I took," and "What kind of work is that which you pursue?" became "What occupation do you there pursue?" This pattern of revision to "Resolution and Independence" offers a model that should be kept in mind when Wordsworth's revisions after the *Biographia* are studied: Wordsworth often revised poems before the *Biographia* appeared; while it is clear that a number of subsequent revisions occurred in response to Coleridge's critical comments, it is also clear that Wordsworth did not necessarily revise a passage Coleridge disliked, nor did he restrict revisions to passages singled out by Coleridge, nor did he hesitate to change passages Coleridge praised.

III

A central question remains: if Wordsworth did not revise simply in response to Coleridge, what purposes do govern Wordsworth's revisions during this period of his career? A full discussion lies well beyond the scope of this essay because the question poses the larger problem of Wordsworth's later style. Nevertheless, a useful beginning is to restate this problem in terms of Wordsworth's revisions for the 1820 collected edition of his poetry, and then to notice by way of conclusion some features common to three groups of Wordsworth's verse: 1) his revisions connected to the *Biographia* commentary (I include one last example from this material) 2) his revisions at the same time of other, earlier poetry, and 3) his new poetry of the period. Awareness of these shared features may begin to point the way toward a better sense of Wordsworth's stylistic habit in the years after Waterloo.

In a recent discussion of Wordsworth's style—significantly, in the context of his relationship with Coleridge—Thomas McFarland seeks to discriminate the "poetically meretricious" from Wordsworth's "first-rate work" and offers three examples of "poetic pabulum," two couplets from *An Evening Walk* (published 1793), "In thoughtless gaiety I coursed the plain, / And hope itself was all I knew of pain" and "There, bending o'er the stream, the listless swain / Lingers behind his disappearing wain," and one couplet from "Resolution and Independence" (published 1807), "Ere he replied, a flash of mild surprise / Broke from the sable orbs of his yet-vivid eyes.''[15] The argument is the familiar one, that Wordsworth the novice began writing in a derivative, artificial style (the *Evening Walk* examples) and that this style occasionally reappeared in even his best work from the "great decade" (the "Resolution and Independence" example). These three specific examples are what is interesting about this restatement of an old argument: none of the three appeared in the quoted form in the first published version (1793 and 1807) of either poem, and in fact two of the couplets—one of the *Evening Walk* examples and the "Resolution and Independence" example—first took the quoted form in the 1820 edition. In other words, the general problem of Wordsworth's style as McFarland presents it is, in these examples, more accurately a problem of Wordsworth's revisions, and even more precisely, a problem of Wordsworth's revisions in the wake of *Biographia Literaria*.

Before turning to material unconnected to the *Biographia* commentary, consider one last example from poems mentioned by Coleridge, the revised couplet in "Resolution and Independence" quoted by McFarland. Originally, the couplet read "He answer'd me with pleasure and surprize; / And there was, while he spake, a fire about his eyes" (Curtis, p. 127); it appears in stanzas that were not singled out by Coleridge, and the couplet had not been revised before 1820. The change centers in the move from the suggestive, simple language of "was . . . a fire about his eyes" to the far more elaborate and explicit language of "a flash . . . / Broke from the sable orbs of his yet-vivid eyes." Out of context, the manifestly artificial diction of "sable orbs" might strike some readers as a poor exchange, and might be used as additional evidence that the later Wordsworth yielded not only to Coleridge but to the other critics of his "simplicity." Yet when other facts about the changes to the whole poem are recalled, and when the revised couplet is placed in context, a more complex picture emerges of Wordsworth's purposes.

Wordsworth left entirely unrevised in 1820 one of Coleridge's two examples of disharmonious "sinkings" in the poem (2:125), the third stanza from the end, which conveys the poem's most memorable simplicity, the leech-gatherer's method: "stirring thus about his feet / The waters of the Ponds where they abide." Other similarly "simple" descriptions, unremarked by Coleridge, are also unchanged, such as "did look / Upon the muddy water, which he conn'd / As if he had been reading in a book." Moreover, some rather elaborate language that is present in the original also remains: "And I bethought me of the playful Hare," for example, or "with demeanour kind / But stately in the main" (Curtis, pp. 123-29). The point is that the poem presents, at every stage, contrasts between seemingly simple and comparatively elaborate poetic language. In the revisions, while adjusting in places the proportions of the contrasting elements, Wordsworth preserves the essential feature of contrast itself.

Indeed, some of the revisions introduce or heighten contrasts. Even though "sable orbs" will probably please few modern readers, consider the unrevised verses that immediately follow the revised couplet:

> His words came feebly, from a feeble chest,
> But each in solemn order follow'd each,
> With something of a lofty utterance drest;
> Choice word, and measured phrase; above the reach
> Of ordinary men; a stately speech!
>
> (Curtis, p. 127)

The newly ornate description of the leech-gatherer's eyes stands in pointed contrast to the following simply-phrased image of the "feeble chest," a contrast that is not as prominent in the original. Wordsworth also emphasized in revision a link between the leech-gatherer's vivid eyes and his "stately speech" (the new "sable orbs" is echoed two verses later by the unrevised "solemn order," and echoes continue in "word" and "ordinary") and both elements are in marked contrast to his physical decay. These effects of the revised couplet are not evident apart from its context; as with all revisions, this example presents losses and gains, but the important conclusion is that this revision—and others—can be understood, not as Wordsworth's unthinking lapse into the "poetic diction" he had once decried, but as a regularly encountered feature of his style.[16]

To move at last to poems outside the scope of Coleridge's commentary, consider one of the two couplets from *An Evening Walk* offered as an example of the early style that the mature Wordsworth outgrew: "In thoughtless gaiety I coursed the plain, / And hope itself was all I knew of pain." In its originally published form in 1793, the couplet read "When link'd with thoughtless Mirth I cours'd the plain, / And hope itself was all I knew of pain"; the revision first appeared in 1820 (and was probably drafted near that time), when *An Evening Walk* was first reprinted complete in a collected edition.[17] The remarkable feature of this revision is that it *reduces* the conspicuous artifice of the language, exchanging the original conceit of a journey with personified Mirth for a more psychologically realistic—if still relatively elaborate—statement. This unexpected feature of Wordsworth's 1820 revisions, that he at times simplified language, should change the way we read the more generally encountered feature, what has been called "elevated" expression. Examples of both procedures are evident in revisions for the 1820 collected edition of a number of other poems unmentioned by Coleridge, such as *Peter Bell, Benjamin the Waggoner,* and other shorter lyrics.[18]

Because it is readily accepted that Wordsworth's later revisions often heighten the artifice of the poetic idiom, examples of this procedure can be presented quickly as additional reminders that Wordsworth revised much verse that Coleridge did not publicly inspect in the *Biographia. Peter Bell* and *Benjamin the Waggoner,* earlier poems first published in 1819, were both revised again for inclusion in the 1820 collected edition, and revisions to both poems show Wordsworth in places exchanging simpler, more unconventional poetic language for more conventionally poetic expressions.[19] For example, the opening stanza of "Part First" of *Peter Bell,* in 1819

> All by the moonlight river side
> It gave three miserable groans;
> "'Tis come then to a pretty pass,"
> Said Peter to the groaning Ass,
> "But I will *bang* your bones!"

became in 1820

> All by the moonlight river side
> Groaned the poor Beast—alas! in vain;
> The staff was raised to loftier height,
> And the blows fell with heavier weight
> As Peter struck—and struck again.
>
> (Jordan, p. 59)

Revisions to the opening lines of *Benjamin the Waggoner* demonstrate a similar movement; an earlier manuscript version in 1812,

> 'Tis spent—this burning day of June,
> Its latest gleams are going out
> The Night-hawk is singing his frog-like tune
> While restlessly he wheels about

became in 1820 (after intermediate changes in 1819)

> 'Tis spent—this burning day of June,
> Soft darkness o'er its latest gleams is stealing;
> The dor-hawk, solitary bird,

Round the dim crags on heavy pinions wheeling,
Buzzes incessantly, a tiresome tune.

(Betz, pp. 43, 284)

Similar changes are evident in revisions to shorter lyrics not mentioned by Coleridge. In "Beggars," for example, the couplet "Two Brothers seem'd they, eight and ten years old / And like that Woman's face as gold is like to gold" became in 1820 "In their fraternal features I could trace / Unquestionable lines of that wild Suppliant's face" (Curtis, p. 115). In all of these cases, the revisions should be studied in the context of the newly created poem to determine Wordsworth's purposes; often the revisions—which in isolation may seem simply to introduce "elevated" language—may be seen in context to heighten contrasts existing in the original between apparently simpler and apparently more elaborate forms of expression, similar to the heightened bathos noted earlier in the "Idiot Boy" revision.

The opposite, generally unexpected feature of some 1820 revisions—that Wordsworth sometimes revised to simplify expression—argues with additional force that the poet sought to develop contrasts within poems between different levels of poetic language. Even in *Peter Bell,* which presented some of Wordsworth's most daring experiments in "simplicity"—and which would thus seem open to revisions only of the elevating kind—Wordsworth occasionally worked in 1820 to emphasize original simplicity; for example, in addition to quiet shifts such as from "Meanwhile the Ass to gain his end" (1819) to "Meanwhile the Ass, to reach his home" (1820), Wordsworth in 1820 added the italicized emphasis to one of the poem's least fancy moments: "making here a sudden pause, / The Ass turn'd round his head—and *grinn'd*" (Jordan, pp. 111, 125). Other examples are found in *Benjamin the Waggoner,* where earlier manuscript descriptions of morning mists as "bright empurpled steam" and "a rainbow-coloured shroud / Such as doth round Angels blaze" disappeared in the 1819 version of the passage and did not reappear in 1820 (Betz, pp. 307-308), and in shorter lyrics such as "To the Daisy," where an earlier manuscript revision, "beguil'd by sportive similes," became in 1820 "sit and play with similes" (Curtis, p. 238). Similarly, in a revision of *The White Doe of Rylstone* between 1815 and 1820, the earlier phrase "the verdant sod" became "the grassy sod" (Dugas, p. 104). The bulk of Wordsworth's 1820 revisions do present elevated poetic language, but it should be remembered that the bulk of the earlier poetry, dominated by a generally plainer idiom, is unrevised. These several characteristics of the process of revision—that the revisions are selective and not pervasive, that some of the revisions simplify existing stylistic complexity and artifice, and that many of the revisions do indeed render the expression much more elaborate—together suggest that Wordsworth was at times experimenting with the effects of contrasts within poems between different kinds of poetic language.

Finally, although Wordsworth's new poetry of the same period is often dominated by a conspicuously artificial idiom that has long vexed commentators, contrasts between simpler and more elaborate modes of speech can be found even there, just as an apparently decorative idiom sometimes appears in the earlier, often deliberately "simple" verse. For example, a blank verse poem of 1819, "The Haunted Tree," presents a juxtaposition of the rough sound made by an old dead tree with very fancy mythological machinery:

> for when the wind
> Blows keenly, it sends forth a creaking sound
> Above the general roar of woods and crags
> Distinctly heard from far—a doleful note
> As if (so Grecian shepherds would have deem'd)
> The Hamadryad, pent within, bewailed
> Some bitter wrong.[20]

The stylistic problem here is essentially the same as that encountered in an earlier poem such as "Gipsies" (1806-1807), where we find the verse "Then issued Vesper from the fulgent West" (Curtis, p. 211). In the *Biographia*, Coleridge quoted this "Gipsies" verse and others in the poem as examples of "thoughts and images too great for the subject" (2:137-38); Wordsworth let the verse stand.[21]

Because Coleridge lamented that Wordsworth did not use a more formal poetic language more regularly, and because many of Wordsworth's revisions in 1820 seem to change language in just that direction, it has often been assumed that Wordsworth revised almost exclusively in deference to Coleridge. The evidence—a complex process of revision of poems Coleridge mentioned and of numerous other poems, and even new verse at the time—suggests instead that Coleridge's idea of a uniformly elevated style remained at odds with an essential feature of Wordsworth's habit, the juxtaposition of different kinds of language, even within single poems. The first "defect" of Wordsworth's poetry that Coleridge diagnosed in *Biographia Literaria,* what he also called "disharmony in style," is, as we might expect, right on the mark:

> The first *characteristic, though only occasional* defect, which I appear to myself to find in these poems is the INCONSTANCY of the *style*. Under this name I refer to the sudden and unprepared transitions from lines or sentences of peculiar felicity (at all events striking and original) to a style, not only unimpassioned but undistinguished. He sinks too often and too abruptly to that style, which I should place in the second division of language, dividing it into the three species; *first,* that which is peculiar to poetry; *second,* that which is only proper in prose; and *third,* the neutral or common to both.
>
> (2:121)

Wordsworth's apparently deferential responses to *Biographia Literaria* instead often persisted in this disharmonious, inconstant, and unrepentant path.

NOTES

[1]*The Letters of William and Dorothy Wordsworth,* 7 vols. Vol. 3: *The Middle Years, Part II, 1812-1820,* ed. Ernest de Selincourt, 2nd edn., rev. Mary Moorman and Alan G. Hill (Oxford: Clarendon Press, 1970), p. 399. Henry Crabb Robinson recorded late in 1817 that "Coleridge's book has given him no pleasure. . . . With the criticism on the poetry too he is not satisfied. The praise is extravagant and the censure inconsiderate"; *Henry Crabb Robinson on Books and Their Writers,* ed. Edith J. Morley, 3 vols. (London: Dent, 1938), 1:213.

[2]For example, the presentation of Wordsworth's revisions in the new edition of the *Biographia* in the Coleridge *Collected Works* is in several instances misleading (details follow in the course of these remarks; see especially note 8 below); *Biographia Literaria,* ed. James Engell and W. Jackson Bate, 2 vols. (Princeton: Princeton Univ. Press, 1983). My comments are keyed parenthetically (by volume and page number in the text) to this edition, which I hasten to add is an invaluable scholarly tool; for more strongly stated reservations about this edition, see Norman Fruman, "Aids to Reflection on the New *Biographia,*" *SIR* 24 (1985): 141-73. See note 6 for previous accounts of Wordsworth, Coleridge, and the *Biographia.*

[3]As the evidence accumulates in the Cornell Wordsworth edition, more systematic and theoretical attention to Wordsworth's lifelong process of revision would be helpful, especially comparisons with other habitual revisers such as Pope, Tennyson, and Yeats; for example, David Morris's recent comments on Pope's techniques in "Seeing Anew: The Nature of Popean Revision," *Alexander Pope: The Genius of Sense* (Cambridge, Mass.: Harvard Univ. Press, 1984), pp. 76-81, are resonant for Wordsworth studies. Wordsworth's revisions of published material can be added as an important category of "self-reference" to the other kinds Stephen Gill has begun to explore in "'Affinities Preserved': Poetic Self-Reference in Wordsworth," *SIR* 24 (1985): 531-49.

[4]Since these remarks were completed, three books on the Coleridge-Wordsworth relationship have been published, a fact sufficient to reaffirm its

hold on our imaginations; all three books, however, are essentially limited to the earlier stages of the relationship, and none inspects the materials of this essay: Lucy Newlyn, *Coleridge, Wordsworth, and the Language of Allusion* (Oxford: Clarendon Press, 1986); Nicholas Roe, *Wordsworth and Coleridge: The Radical Years* (Oxford: Clarendon Press, 1988); Paul Magnuson, *Coleridge and Wordsworth: A Lyrical Dialogue* (Princeton: Princeton Univ. Press, 1988). In "Desynonymizing the Self in Wordsworth and Coleridge," *SIR* 26 (1987): 513-26, William Galperin considers anew Coleridge's representation of Wordsworth in the *Biographia*, but he does not take up the issue of Wordsworth's response.

[5]My texts of Wordsworth's poetry and system of references are as follows: For readings of poems in the *Lyrical Ballads* volumes through the 1805 edition: *Lyrical Ballads,* ed. R. L. Brett and A. R. Jones (London: Methuen, 1965), cited parenthetically in the text as Brett and Jones (in a few quoted instances, I have silently introduced non-verbal variants from the 1815 *Poems* text). For subsequent (post-1805) readings of these poems through 1827, I use the following first editions: *Poems by William Wordsworth,* 2 vols. (London, 1815); *The Miscellaneous Poems of William Wordsworth,* 4 vols. (London, 1820); *The Poetical Works of William Wordsworth,* 5 vols. (London, 1827); which of these three editions I am citing for a later revision of a *Lyrical Ballads* poem is indicated by the date (1815, 1820, 1827) of the revision in the text. (Wordsworth's responses to Coleridge usually appeared in the 1820 edition, but sometimes in the 1827 edition and even later; I do not, however, regularly cite readings of the *Lyrical Ballads* poems after 1827.) For original texts and revisions of other poems, I rely on the following volumes in the Cornell Wordsworth series: chiefly, *"Poems, in Two Volumes," and Other Poems, 1800-1807,* ed. Jared Curtis (Ithaca: Cornell Univ. Press, 1983), cited parenthetically in the text as Curtis; and also *Peter Bell*, ed. John E. Jordan (Ithaca: Cornell Univ. Press, 1985) (Jordan); *Benjamin the Waggoner,* ed. Paul F. Betz (Ithaca: Cornell Univ. Press, 1981) (Betz); *The White Doe of Rylstone; or The Fate of the Nortons,* ed. Kristine Dugas (Ithaca: Cornell Univ. Press, 1988) (Dugas); *An Evening Walk,* ed. James Averill (Ithaca: Cornell Univ. Press, 1984); *Descriptive Sketches,* ed. Eric Birdsall (Ithaca: Cornell Univ. Press, 1984). Until the Cornell series is complete, the 5-volume *Poetical Works* edited by Ernest de Selincourt and Helen Darbishire (Oxford: Clarendon Press, 1940-49) remains the standard edition for citation, but I have not keyed my examples to that text because the history of revisions is not an unfailingly reliable feature of the edition. I am indebted to the staffs of the rare book collections at Cornell University, the University of North Carolina at Chapel Hill, and Duke University for much kind assistance.

[6]Stephen M. Parrish, "The Wordsworth-Coleridge Controversy," *PMLA* 73 (1958): 373. I call these sentences "most influential" chiefly because they have been quoted twice by Thomas McFarland, first in "The Symbiosis of Coleridge and Wordsworth," *SIR* 11 (1972): 297, and then in the chapter of the same title in *Romanticism and the Forms of Ruin* (Princeton: Princeton Univ. Press, 1981), p. 95. Other notable treatments of Wordsworth, Coleridge, and the *Biographia* (excluding those numerous studies that focus almost exclusively on the early relationship) include Don H. Bialostosky, "Coleridge's Interpretation of Wordsworth's Preface to *Lyrical Ballads*," *PMLA* 93 (1978): 912-24; Stephen M. Parrish, *The Art of the Lyrical Ballads* (Cambridge, Mass.: Harvard Univ. Press, 1973); Kenneth R. Johnston, *Wordsworth and "The Recluse"* (New Haven: Yale Univ. Press, 1984); Roy Park, "Coleridge's Two Voices as a Critic of Wordsworth," *ELH* 36 (1969): 361-81; Thomas M. Raysor, "Coleridge's Criticism of Wordsworth," *PMLA* 54 (1939): 496-510.

[7]Richard Gravil, "Coleridge's Wordsworth," *The Wordsworth Circle* 15 (1984): 38; see also his "Imagining Wordsworth: 1797-1807-1817," in *Coleridge's Imagination: Essays in Memory of Pete Laver,* ed. Gravil, Lucy Newlyn, and Nicholas Roe (Cambridge: Cambridge Univ. Press, 1985), pp. 129-42.

[8]Compounding these problems of method is misleading information in the new Princeton edition of the *Biographia.* A troublesome feature of the annotation, for example, is the dating of the revisions: two revisions dated 1827 actually appeared in the 1820 edition, to "The Brothers" (2:80) and to "The Blind Highland Boy" (2:123), and elsewhere, a number of undated revisions are reported (2:118; 2:125), which renders the dating of other revisions less useful. Furthermore, because editorial silence cannot be assumed to mean that Wordsworth did not respond to Coleridge's criticism (the editors do not note, for example, that Wordsworth removed "Alice Fell" from the collected state in 1820 [2:68]), the evidence in the annotations does not allow accurate conclusions about which passages Wordsworth revised and which he did not. Also, when the editors report a post-*Biographia* revision, they do not regularly note any earlier revision history (e.g., 2:136), which presents a distorted picture of Wordsworth's procedures. Finally, a curious feature of the annotation, indicative of the tendency in some criticism to load the case, is the use of the adverb "completely," as in "Wordsworth completely dropped the final four lines" (2:124; see also 2:80); the emphasis would appear to be unnecessary.

[9]The figures in this paragraph are presented approximately because no two readers would arrive at exactly the same totals in these various calculations: Coleridge's references are sometimes unclear, sometimes he quotes Wordsworth not to praise or blame the poetry but just to illustrate a point, and sometimes it is arguable whether he intends praise or blame. Most readers, however, would probably find these approximate values not far from their marks.

[10]Brett and Jones, eds., *Lyrical Ballads,* p. 287.

[11]Stephen M. Parrish, "'The Thorn': Wordsworth's Dramatic Monologue," *ELH* 24 (1957): 161-63.

[12]The revision of the vessel stanza in "The Blind Highland Boy" offers a memorable example of the complicated process of Wordsworth's revisions. In this case, to summarize briefly, Wordsworth had revised the stanza between 1807 and 1815 at Coleridge's suggestion; Charles Lamb then argued for the original reading, and Coleridge further criticized in the *Biographia* the revised passage that he himself had inspired (should we then wonder that Wordsworth's subsequent revisions occasionally seem exasperated?), after which Wordsworth revised the stanza again for 1820. Barron Field then took up Lamb's case in 1828, at which time Wordsworth washed his hands of the matter. See Curtis, pp. 420-21; *The Letters of Charles and Mary Anne Lamb,* 3 vols., Vol. III, 1809-1817, ed. Edwin W. Marrs, Jr. (Ithaca: Cornell Univ. Press, 1978), p. 139; Barron Field, *Memoirs of Wordsworth,* ed. Geoffrey Little (Sydney: Sydney Univ. Press, 1975), p. 132; *The Letters of William and Dorothy Wordsworth,* Vol. 4, *The Later Years, Part I, 1821-1828,* ed. Ernest de Selincourt, 2nd edn., rev. Alan G. Hill (Oxford: Clarendon, 1978), p. 641. The editors of the Princeton *Biographia* note some of this famous history (2:123).

[13]Wordsworth took up the original reading again in response to Barron Field, commenting that "I need not trouble you with the reasons that put me upon the alteration"; *Letters: Later Years,* 1:645. See also Curtis, p. 428.

[14]For the earlier, complex revision history of this poem, see Jared R. Curtis, *Wordsworth's Experiments with Tradition: The Lyric Poems of 1802* (Ithaca: Cornell Univ. Press, 1971), pp. 97-113; 186-95.

[15]Thomas McFarland, "Problems of Style in the Poetry of Wordsworth and Coleridge," *Romanticism and the Forms of Ruin* (see note 6), pp. 217, 231, 251-52.

[16]Wordsworth's attack on "what is usually called poetic diction" is presented of course in the prefatory material to the *Lyrical Ballads* volumes; see *The Prose Works of William Wordsworth,* ed. W. J. B. Owen and Jane W. Smyser, 3 vols. (Oxford: Clarendon Press, 1974) 1:145.

[17]*An Evening Walk,* ed. Averill, p. 32. This early poem and *Descriptive Sketches* (also published 1793) had been represented by "extracts" in the 1815 edition; Coleridge commented on *Descriptive Sketches* in the *Biographia* (1:77-79), and Wordsworth revised portions of both poems for the 1820 edition; for details of these revisions, see the volumes in the Cornell Wordsworth series. In particular, for a description of the revising process to *An Evening Walk* between 1815 and 1820, see Averill's introduction, pp. 16-17.

[18]Increasingly detailed study of Wordsworth's revisions is made possible as new volumes in the Cornell Wordsworth series appear; better accounts of Wordsworth's revisions in the wake of the *Biographia* will be facilitated in particular by volumes devoted to *Lyrical Ballads* poems and to the most familiar example of Wordsworth's revising habit, *The Prelude.* One reason to clarify now Wordsworth's response to the *Biographia* is that subsequent criticism can address issues such as different purposes that possibly govern Wordsworth's revisions at different stages in their long history. Other than poems mentioned by Coleridge in the *Biographia,* I limit my examples in this section to volumes currently available in the Cornell series.

[19]Jordan summarizes the 1820 revisions to *Peter Bell* in his introduction to the poem (p. 18), and Betz summarizes the 1820 revisions to *Benjamin the Waggoner* in his introduction (pp. 27-28).

[20]My text is that of the first edition, *The River Duddon* (London, 1820). I explore some other features of style in this poem in "Wordsworth's 'Haunted Tree' and 'Yew-Trees' Criticism," *PQ* 67 (1988): 63-82.

[21]Wordsworth did revise some of the other verses; see also David Ferry's comments on style in this poem in *The Limits of Mortality* (Middletown, CT: Wesleyan Univ. Press, 1959), pp. 5-9 (Ferry's discussion, however, omits the "Vesper" verse from the portion of the poem quoted by Coleridge).

SEL 28 (1988)
ISSN 0039-3657

Heading Out is Not Going Home: *Jane Eyre*

MELODIE MONAHAN

To comfort Jane Eyre after her trauma in the red room, Bessie brings Jane's favorite book, *Gulliver's Travels.* Considering her former responses to modes of fantasy, Jane explains how she now reads the text differently:

> This book I had again and again perused with delight; I considered it a *narrative of facts,* and discovered in it a vein of interest deeper than what I found in fairy tales: for as to the elves . . . I had at length made up my mind to the *sad truth* that they were all gone out of England . . . whereas, Lilliput and Brobdingnag being, in my creed, solid parts of the earth's surface, *I doubted not that I might one day, by taking a long voyage, see with my own eyes* the little fields, houses, and trees, the diminutive people, the tiny cows, sheep, and birds of the one realm; and the corn-fields forest-high, the mighty mastiffs, the monster cats, the tower-like men and women, of the other. Yet, when this cherished volume was now placed in my hand—when I turned over its leaves, and sought in its marvelous pictures the charm I had, till now, never failed to find—all was eerie and dreary; the giants were gaunt goblins, the pygmies malevolent and fearful imps, Gulliver a most desolate wanderer in most dread and dangerous regions. I closed the book, which I dared no longer peruse.[1]

Jane's earlier response asserted the authority of *Gulliver* and its relevance to her own experience: if not in England, then at least somewhere and someday she believed she could replicate its quest model. But now, subjugated by the Reeds, Jane finds both the world of the text and her own reality darkened. In the same scene she notes how the painted plate is strangely faded: and how Bessie's once lively tune now resounds like a "funeral hymn"

Melodie Monahan is an editor of Charlotte Brontë's early writings and is currently working on quest-romance and the female hero as author.

(p. 21). In closing the book, Jane displaces received narratives for her own facts. What was once taken as "true" is now set aside as belief. Sudden self-awareness of her female status (heightened by the red room crisis as the literalized stage of the onset of menses) dispels for Jane the promise of escape offered by androcentric scripts and makes problematic her once easy identification with male questers.

All of a sudden, for Jane as female reader and hero, quest-romance breaks apart: instead of a hyphenated whole, a linear progression, the pattern confounds with a mixed message. From the female hero's point of view, quest-romance is self-contradictory, a conjunction of contrary imperatives which press the female hero into antithetical terms and push her in opposite directions. On the one hand, quest beckons her, like her male counterparts, to head out in search of stimulus and adventure, to find another perhaps better world. But on the other hand, romance invites her into the patriarchal home where female autonomy is sacrificed for safety and connection. Clearly, the contradiction is gender-specific. Heading out *is* going home for the male hero in at least the one sense that he exists in an androcentric culture, and he has access to male privilege whether he is in the world or at home. The female's relationship to both heading out and going home are problematic, particularly so when the two are conjoined. The woman who undertakes the journey and feels the struggle and empowerment in her revolt against marginality will resist subordination in a household. In the act of discounting what appear to be either-or narrative trajectories, Jane asserts her emerging role as author; in putting down *Gulliver's Travels*, she effectively takes up her own autobiography.[2] Yet by undertaking to write the text she would *rather* read, she enters a hostile zone where as female hero and author she is always at odds with literary and linguistic tradition.

The androcentric paradigm of quest-romance, as Frye defines it, automatically shrinks the female to the role of the feminine and relegates her to a place at the end of the narrative where the hero reaps his reward. Frye makes this point perfectly clear by citing the Crusades as the quintessential quest-romance in which the prized Chalice is an abstraction of female genitalia: Frye asserts that "The Holy Grail . . . like other cups and hollow vessels . . . has female sexual affinities."[3] Shifting these implications to the level of language itself, Margaret Homans generalizes that "the dominant myth of Western languages has [its] operation structured as a quest-romance, based on the boy's postoedipal renunciation of the mother and his quest for substitute objects of desire."[4] In quest-romance, then, the female hero-as-author simultaneously asserts herself as subject and writes herself as object into the ending. Language, it would seem, gives the promise; Homans calls it the hyphen, offering the hope of crossing the gap. Yet, as Lacan tells us, "a sign presupposes the absence of the object it signifies."[5] Thus Jane Eyre can dismiss *Gulliver's Travels* as irrelevant to her narrative of facts, but she can no more escape the patriarchal structure which subjugates her as female hero than she can escape the linguistic system which silences her as author.

Heading out is the quest form seen in *Jane Eyre* in Jane's repeated departures from households, from Gateshead, Lowood, and Thornfield. Going home is enacted each time Jane establishes community, at Lowood with Miss Temple and Helen, at Thornfield with Rochester and Adele, and at Marsh-End with Diana and Mary Rivers.[6] Heading out breaks down in the nadir of Whitcross and the night on the moors. Going home accrues with the establishment of the Morton Cottage school and the recognition of the Rivers as relatives; it culminates in the family found at last with Rochester and a son. The recurrent ambivalence, however, undermines any final claim of perfect happiness. Each cycle in this female enactment of quest-romance turns in against itself; what the female hero is as a questing protester against patriarchal tyranny, she cannot be as an assimilated member who connects and stabilizes with others. To end the search is to settle for the known; to become a member of the group is to forget the feel of alienation. For male and female heroes alike, to quest is to test the power within and have the chance of self-determinism. But for the female hero, to be absorbed, then, into the patriarchal economy of romance is to be relegated to the homebound periphery of action and into the margins of importance. Charlotte Brontë's narrative strategy, then, is to enact the fundamental contradiction of quest-romance on at least two levels: the female hero-as-author writes self into subject in a script which traditionally objectifies the female; the female author defines her own authority *vis-a-vis* literary tradition within the system of symbols which requires her absence. In order to maintain this counterstance, subversion must permeate *Jane Eyre,* and it does so in the narration of events themselves and in the medium of language that transforms the script into art.[7]

Let us first consider how Brontë derails traditional romance and its heroine. The romantic legacy she displaces in *Jane Eyre* consists of programmatic scenarios which trap beautiful, middle- and upper-class heroines in passive, mimetic roles as, to use Nancy K. Miller's terms, ornamental "objects of circulation" in "plausible plots" of sexual exchange.[8] Automatically an insider, the beautiful heroine symbolizes the prevailing ethic that physical appearance is the first measure of female worth. Moreover, the script she inhabits maximizes the erotic and leaves no psychic dimension or literal space for non-erotic female ambition, the quest.[9] Such narrative pattern and heroine type are peripheralized and overturned in *Jane Eyre* by the "demolition" of Georgiana Reed and Blanche Ingram and by the subtext about the young Bertha Mason.[10] Of central importance is Jane Eyre's "physical inferiority" (p. 7) which disrupts convention and generates the reflexive social exclusion that creates the literal space for quest.[11] Jane can undertake the journey because she is an outcast. Thus, paradoxically, Jane Eyre is both an agent in her own quest-romance and the anomaly which subverts for Brontë the received values of the traditional romance paradigm.[12]

As these predictable romantic scenarios are sidelined, the center of Brontë's narrative evolves a bifurcated pattern which enhances the erotic fantasy of romance with the ambitious wish to restructure power. Jane's journey is both a literal leave-taking from oppressive hierarchical groups and a process of negotiating for lateral connection. The quest for a better world expresses itself in her repeated efforts to challenge binary and vertical constructs: the haves and the have-nots, the saved and the damned, the insiders and the outcasts, the masculine and the feminine. A noteworthy early example of this insurgence is her tart reply to Brocklehurst's idea that hell consumes the wicked. To avoid hell fire, Jane asserts, "I must keep in good health, and not die" (p. 32). In response to Helen Burns's excessive compliance with Christ's Doctrine of Love, Jane powerfully contends that equality is worth fighting for: "If people were always kind and obedient to those who are cruel and unjust, the wicked people would have it all their own way: they would never feel afraid, and so they would never alter, but would grow worse and worse. When we are struck at without a reason, we should strike back again very hard; I am sure we should—so hard as to teach the person who struck us never to do it again" (p. 58). Jane repeatedly speaks and acts in an attempt to topple the sanctioned superstructures of social and literary design. Self-ordained as author and subject, Jane and her narrative attempt an insurrection against the normative, and in this sense, Jane's asserting her own values in her *narrative of facts* can be seen as "literalized" in Bertha's burning Thornfield to the ground.[13] The edifice is both patriarchal house and literary convention. Thus, through the medium of dissent and disruption, the romantic inscription is revised.

The female quest-romance is a narrative of empowerment which attempts to act on the world in the same way other narratives do, by imaging forth and evaluating particular patterns of behavior and belief. However, because this pattern is cast from the margin across the grain of dominant constructs, it is as much a revolutionary model as it is a commentary on the constraints that come to bear on the woman writer's fictive representation of female life. If we analyze Brontë's quest-romance in terms of the dialectic between members of vertical groups and the ousted Jane Eyre, then we can better understand how the female quester takes her uneasy stand against the received power design and how she negotiates for parity within the resistant network of heterosexual romance. We can also come to understand the author's own equivocation in a linguistic process which replicates a model in order for the female hero as author to transform it.

Repeatedly we see in *Jane Eyre* how the narrative exposes the prevailing group's cruelty in imposing arbitrary prerogatives on inferiors. In the Reeds' bullying at Gateshead, in the hypocrisy of Brocklehurst and his family at Lowood, in the sanctioned ostracism of the governess by the drawing-room guests at Thornfield, even in Hannah's attempt to reject the destitute Jane on the doorstep at Marsh-End, we see the group's mechanism of exclusion and self-aggrandizement. These communities share the hierarchical and superficial values of monied society; they endorse the arbitrary power of privileged birth and the middle- and upper-class objectification of women. When ten-year-old Jane wonders, "Why could I never please?" she cites her physical plainness as cause, for Georgiana's beauty seems "to purchase indemnity for every fault" (p. 15). The novel opens on the day when "the mad cat" (p. 12) chooses no longer to "endure the blow" (p. 10): on the day when, Jane Eyre admits, "I resisted all the way: a new thing for me" (p. 12). Conjuring tumult and insurrection, Jane becomes an "infantine Guy Fawkes" (p. 25). Midway through the novel, Aunt Reed remembers dealing with Jane Eyre on that first day: "I felt fear, as if an animal that I had struck or pushed had looked up at me with human eyes and cursed me in a man's voice" (p. 241). As Jane speaks the truth, she acquires rank: the "animal" in her seems human; its voice sounds male. By asserting her own facts Jane wins space as well as status: "my soul began to expand, to exult, with the strangest sense of freedom, of triumph" (p. 37). Empowered by protest, Jane subverts the system which attempts to devalue her, claiming her superiority through aggressive counter-statement.

The place the child Jane Eyre is to occupy and the manner in which she is to behave are outlined for her by the female keepers of patriarchy. The Gateshead servant, Abbot, declares, "you ought not to think yourself on an equality with the Misses Reed and

Master Reed . . . your place [is] to be humble, and to try to make yourself agreeable to them," and Bessie adds, "try to be useful and pleasant, then perhaps you [will] always have a home here" (p. 13). Miss Temple and Helen would put down Jane's rebellion with the dictates of the Sermon on the Mount and the delayed gratification of wrongs righted in Heaven. Mrs. Fairfax and Hannah preserve the canonized codes in their directives about the station and conduct of Jane at eighteen. By assuming Blanche is an unequal match for Rochester, Mrs. Fairfax renders invisible the even more unequal Jane who harbors the same private hopes. Hannah, whose impulse is to turn out Jane "on a night when you should not have shut out a dog" (p. 346), suspects anyone bereft of house and brass. To be "useful" in patriarchy is to accept objectivity in place of selfhood. But against these pronouncements, Jane declares her own superior nature, her integrity and independent moral sense. For example, at Gateshead, Jane claims that the Reed children "are not fit to associate with [her]" (p. 27). Despite Blanche Ingram's preeminence, in both Jane's masochistically disparate paintings and Rochester's feigned preference, Jane is confident about her own superiority: "Miss Ingram was a mark beneath jealousy: she was too inferior to excite the feeling. . . . I mean what I say. She was very showy, but she was not genuine: she had a fine person, many brilliant attainments; but her mind was poor, her heart barren. . . . She was not good; she was not original" (pp. 187-88). At Marsh-End, Jane pushes Hannah to apologize for her failure as a Christian to recognize that "Some of the best people that ever lived have been as destitute as I am" (p. 347). In this reiterative fashion, then, Jane pronounces against the established order a new moral design which affirms humane values and charitable acts. In these pronouncements, moreover, Jane is reinforced by marginalized individuals with whom she identifies, for example the kindly apothecary Mr. Lloyd, nurturant Bessie and Miss Temple, and of course the in many ways victimized Rochester.

With Jane's sexual maturation and the advent of Rochester, the contradictory imperatives of quest-romance become more explicit. Jane's need for a sexual partner, for kinship and a sense of home are at variance with her need to achieve autonomy through self-sufficiency and through the process both as teacher and author of defining reality from her own perspective. Coupled with these difficulties are the special problems of Rochester's past, his conditioning with regard to sex roles, and his perverse experience with marriage. In negotiating for her divergent needs with this particular partner, Jane speaks within the erotic grammar of romance, while at the same time her narrative redistributes power.

Though loving Rochester subjects Jane to the very system which devalues her, she continues to resist the assigned passivity of marginal status and becomes here the active negotiator, one who can set some conditions, one who can comply or refuse. In this give-and-take process, the quest impulse reroutes romance, creating a fantasy about equitable partnership that requires both female empowerment and male reduction. This emergent fantasy is constantly undermined, however, by both the momentum of the conventional romance dyad, with its heterosexual economy of power, and by the requisite autonomy of quest. Staging the contest in this way, Brontë authorizes the "extravagant wish . . . for a *story* that would turn out differently" (Miller, p. 352).

While one aspect of Jane's quest is to react against arbitrary privilege, another important part of it requires the appropriation of terms. Bessie thinks of usefulness, for example, as the ability to prop the preordained order. But Jane translates the concept into the reflexive use of one's talent to confirm the self and create community by helping others. Asserting that beneficence enriches the self, that profit increases as it is shared, this reciprocal sense of usefulness counteracts the materialism and selfishness of the Reeds and Ingrams and betrays the supposed martyrdom of St. John as calculated self-interest parading as altruism. It substitutes connection for hierarchy. So, for example, when Jane is newly engaged to Rochester, she impetuously gives her whole purse of three or four shillings to a beggar-woman and her son, so that they can "partake of [her] jubilee" (p. 260), and, similarly, with the "compassion" of Mary and Diana Rivers, not the "charity" of St. John (p. 353), Jane divides her legacy among her kin. To do otherwise is to "feast alone" (p. 387); whereas to experience the interconnection of family is "wealth indeed" (p. 390). Moreover, Jane tries to give a better education than the one she has received. With Adele and later with the village students at Morton, she tries to revise the received value system by confirming the worth of poor country students. In these ways, Jane speaks and acts in the role of leveler, working to eliminate advantage and to create connection. Yet, ironically, communities tend to acquire hierarchical designs which in turn can threaten the democratic purposes which cause marginal individuals to make alliances in the first place. Similarly, in literary terms, revision of the paradigm requires recapitulation: in order for Brontë to rewrite quest-romance she must repeat it.

At Thornfield, Jane understands her desire for usefulness as both the need for stimulus in the world and for "more of intercourse with [her] own kind" (p. 110). In Hay Lane, these combined desires are met in the appearance of Rochester, to whom she can be immediately useful. She helps because he is *like her*, an unattractive outsider; downed by his horse he is literally and metaphorically dispossessed of his power. Significantly, bonding and usefulness are in this case made possible through inferior physical appearance. "Had he been . . . handsome," Jane explains, "I should not have dared to stand thus questioning him against his will" (p. 114). Rochester's hostility, in fact, sets free her assertive nature: "I retained my station when he waved to me to go, and announced:—'I cannot think of leaving you, sir, at so late an hour, in this solitary lane'" (p. 115). Set on the estate's periphery, this night scene simultaneously provides adventure (quest) and initiates the formation of a new community (romance). The Hay Lane scene is emblematic, then, of the novel's bifurcated pattern, wherein the female hero's quest for usefulness converts into her romance about connection which is itself realized on the periphery of the old order.

Community requires recognizable sameness. In addition to looking alike, members of a group sound alike. The "natural sympathies" (p. 152) Rochester denotes to explain his kinship to Jane are signaled by the fact that he and Jane speak the same language. In choosing not to make polite exchanges, Jane and Rochester exclude anyone who, like Mrs. Fairfax, only knows how to make small talk. Setting aside for the moment Rochester's duplicitous courtship of Blanche and his artifice in the gypsy scene, we can say that Jane and Rochester frequently communicate with abruptness, reticence, and candor, and that their verbal rudeness often signals what is for them an immediacy of meanings and complementarity of perspectives. Perhaps, the sadomasochism in some of their exchanges is the grammatical sign of the process by which they align themselves to one another through a shared struggle to adjust the received power imbalance; it may also encode how that power structure resists adjustment. Certainly, their communication style is exactly opposite the so-called polite conversation used by the Ingrams as they exult themselves at others' expense. In the drawing-room scene Jane and Rochester's covert *true* union opposes the overt yet *false* association of Rochester with his wealthy guests. While Jane insists on her connection to Rochester and her ability to help him, the Ingrams trivialize the "anathematized race" (p. 179) of governesses and tutors. When Rochester appears, Jane immediately fantasizes about that moment in the "baptism scene" when she "rendered him . . . an essential service—and he, holding [her] hand . . . revealed a heart full and eager to overflow" (p. 176). Watching Rochester speak to Louisa and Amy Eshton, Jane believes "[the women] were in no sense moved," which she takes as proof that "he is not of their kind . . . he is of mine . . . I feel akin to him—I understand the language of his countenance and movements" (p. 177). For Jane, Rochester is an essential member in the marginal group she defines, one that is to admit Adele, the "emblem" of Jane's own childhood, and Mary and Diana, her longed-for sisters.

Poised against Jane's interior monologue in the drawing room is Blanche's supercilious harangue about "the whole tribe" of governesses and tutors (p. 179). Of course, Blanche demonstrates Jane's earlier reading of the Ingrams' haughtiness. As Jane says of Blanche, "Her face was like her mother's . . . the same low brow, the same high features, the same pride. . . . Her laugh was satirical, and so was the habitual expression of her arched and haughty lip" (p. 174). Contrary to Blanche's own claim to superiority in these matters, Jane is the *true* "judge of physiognomy," and it is in Blanche that Jane sees "all the faults of her class" (p. 179), faults which betray an almost genetic link to Bertha.[14] By discounting lateral bonds between governesses and tutors, the Ingrams are predictably blind to any potential relationship between Jane and Rochester. Blanche outlines the dangers arising from bonds between employees: "mutual alliance and reliance; confidence thence resulting—insolence accompanying—mutiny and general blow-up" (p. 180). And if community on this level threatens the establishment, then an implausible bond between members of different classes, between employer and employee, is truly subversive. Despite the gap in status between her and Rochester, Jane claims Rochester is her kind; after all, he said himself he owed her an "immense debt" (p. 152). Blanche aspires to marry Rochester *because* his status and money identify him as aristocratic, while Jane envisions him as kindred *despite* those economic assets which put him in a class above her. In terms of narrative structure, then, the trajectory of Blanche's conventional romance plot crisscrosses with the trajectory of Jane's partially realized quest for usefulness. Tension arises from these counternarratives because they make opposite assumptions about power and social structure. In this double pattern of dialogue and interior counterstatement, the drawing-room scene depicts the exclusionary dynamics of the established community. Placed side by side, the Hay Lane scene and the drawing-room scene illustrate the emergence of a new model and the resistance of the old. As Jane creates community on the outside, so to speak, and rearranges courtship narrative to suit her particular terms, we see how Brontë transforms romance to accommodate female ambition.

This dramatic intersection is reinforced verbally by the use of bird metaphors to measure the power of women at Thornfield.

When likened to larks, wrens, and doves (pp. 178, 209), the female guests are both trivial and transitory. Bertha is dominant and eternal when dichotomized as beast and supernatural evil, "a carrion-seeking bird of prey" and "the Fury" (pp. 211, 212). In Jane's case, however, equivocation in bird metaphors reveals the power dynamics in her relationship to Rochester. In one way Jane is the metaphoric equivalent of the winter robin she fed on the window sill at Gateshead (pp. 30, 353). She confesses that "to taste but of the crumbs [Rochester] scattered to stray and stranger birds like me, was to feast genially" (p. 247). But when Rochester retells the Hay Lane scene, he compares Jane to a powerful linnet, one that "proposed to bear [him] on its tiny wing," one that "stood by [him] with strange perseverance, and looked and spoke with a sort of authority" (p. 317). In the memorable scene when Jane angrily attacks Rochester's sadism (beginning with the question, "Do you think because I am poor, obscure, plain, and little, I am soulless and heartless?"), Rochester typifies Jane as an ensnared bird, "rending its plumage in desperation" (p. 256). His confession of love comes side by side with terms of entrapment. Community offers comfort, but connection extracts its price in terms of lost liberty. When the connection is marriage, the price is prescribed by the sanctions of the institution and the history of its reenactment. But against this traditional economy of male dominance in marriage, Jane's narrative envisions another structure for heterosexual love.

In this new structure, power is distributed so that the female role can be defined as essential not extraneous, useful not decorative. So that while romantic attachment seems to disempower Jane by drawing her like a "magnet" (p. 244) to Rochester, it also enhances her with vitality and gives her "keener hopes" (p. 159). In her evening conversations with Rochester, Jane recognizes her "power to amuse him" (p. 147), not as an entertainer like Blanche singing and playing the piano, but rather as one who can help him realize a sense of communion, a oneness that supersedes the hierarchy of class and the polarization of gender. Validated as an individual through her connection to Rochester, Jane can visit her dying aunt and discover that a sneer is "no longer powerful" (p. 231). She can see that for Aunt Reed the lament "we are getting poor" (p. 234) veils the terrifying realization of common mortality. Jane can *now forgive* the unforgiving. I would assert, moreover, that her attachment to Rochester, entailing as it does the enhancement of female power, prevents Jane's victimization in the narrative Rochester would himself authorize, one which evolves through sadistic teasing about Blanche to his hope for a bigamous marriage and his final desperate plea for an extramarital alliance, all painful distortions of the romance script.

Against Rochester's seemingly endless machinations and lies, Jane remains resistant and powerful. Though she claims she would give her life to serve him, Jane still negotiates the terms of her connectedness: "I am no bird; and no net ensnares me: I am a free human being with an independent will" (p. 256). Later she calls his proffered engagement gifts "a degradation." In courtship she shows Rochester "the rugged points" (p. 276) of her character, noting and resisting his desire to "attach [her] to a chain" (p. 273). In his description of former illicit relationships, she hears his belief that mistresses are slaves, his assumption that "to live familiarly with inferiors is degrading" (p. 316). Thus Rochester exposes for Jane the false economies of sexual systems which objectify women, either as wife or mistress: If Jane were "to become the successor of these poor girls, he would one day regard [her] with the same feeling" (p. 316). Sanctioned or illicit, heterosexual coupling is immoral in so far as it operates as a vertical construct requiring female inferiority and marginality. The old language of romance which inevitably tracks the genders in self-limiting, rigid, and eventually debilitating sexual roles constitutes a discourse of lies; the old romance about traditional marriage, about male dominance and female dependence, cannot be confused with the true story Jane tells.

As practiced by the Masons and Ingrams, the process of courtship and marriage is duplicitous and therefore must be read as disruptive in a narrative of facts. DuPlessis characterizes the Thornfield section as "a landmine of cunningly intertextual false marriages": "the hidden wed*lock* with Bertha . . . a charade 'wife,' Blanche Ingram . . . a dramatically arrested false marriage ceremony, with Jane as . . . bride."[15] DuPlessis argues that Brontë creates here "a critical context in which the normal activities of courtship (and the normal narratives as well) take on a lurid and foreboding quality" (p. 9). In an attempt to disrupt the normative, Brontë makes Thornfield a house of mirrors where identity superimposes identity and parodies of identity multiply, where identity becomes what is refracted. For example, Blanche replicates the young Bertha, and the Ingrams' hope to ensnare Rochester replays the Mason family's manipulation of him. Adele is both a younger version of Blanche and a recreation of her actress-mother, Celine Varens, especially when the child parrots an operatic song about illicit love, disguise, and betrayal (p. 103), or dresses with such mimetic care for a drawing-room evening with the Thornfield guests (p. 172). Moreover, despite her prettiness and access to money, Adele is like Jane, a parentless dependent (p. 146). Jane is a young Grace Poole, unattractive warden, silent outsider, "the living enigma" (pp. 205, 267). Yet antithetically, Jane is also a young Bertha, maddened by confinement, enraged by a system which provides no options, where she is more pawn than agent. Imprisoned in the red room, sequestered behind a bolted bedroom door, locked-in caring for Mason on the third floor, Jane knows captivity. Like Bertha, she is the "dread instrument of evil" (p. 326). Bertha, conjoined with Blanche, is "the bride that stands between" Rochester and Jane (p. 357). Even Rochester is drawn into this mirroring overlay of female identities, for when he is disguised as a gypsy, Jane mistakes him for Grace. Rochester *is* like Grace—the cell keeper, the keeper of locks, the one who would secure Jane with a chain.

The literal game of charades is emblematic of role-playing at Thornfield. Masquerade reverberates in Rochester's false courtship of Blanche and in her feigned infatuation with him, in his impulse to objectify Jane by decking her out in jewels and in her systematic coldness, her "needle of repartee" which holds him at a distance (p. 276), even in Rochester's wedding day fight with Bertha that resembles a "conjugal embrace" (p. 296). In this disturbing array of mimicry and artifice, the fixed binary opposition of husband and wife is shattered *because it is false*. In all, the "landmine" of marriage and marital distortions clearly puts Jane at risk (as it does all participants whether they know it or not), and the ambivalence in her struggle to realize the self *within* a community expresses itself through metaphors of abortion, stillbirth, crying dream children, and dying babies. For example, Jane characterizes the threat of separation from Rochester as a "newborn agony—a deformed thing which I could not persuade myself to own and rear" (p. 246). And later she wonders if her persona as Mrs. Rochester "will come into the world alive" (p. 277). Finally, after the wedding ceremony is broken off, Jane likens her dashed hopes to the Slaughter of Innocents: "my cherished wishes . . . lay stark, chill, livid—corpses that could never revive," and her love for Rochester "shivered in [her] heart, like a suffering child in a cold cradle" (p. 298). Homans points out that "The transitory experience of being a mother is the central and recurring metaphor for the abundant sense of danger in *Jane Eyre*" (p. 88), aptly so because childbirth objectifies, literalizes, the self in the same way that traditional marriage objectifies and *therefore infantilizes* woman when it defines her only in reference to her husband. This process of objectification constitutes erasure; it denies the integrity and autonomy, the *selfhood*, essential for quest. In giving birth to Mrs. Rochester, Jane faces the death of self, "augmented by a feeling of powerlessness in relation to the process that has been set in motion" (Homans, p. 89). At the same time, she courts the reinscription of insanity and imprisonment which Bertha enacts. At Thornfield, then, the superimposing of characters and plot sequences fractures the romance narrative, effectively confounding Jane's normative progression toward marriage.

The ambitious wish for a story that would turn out differently shows itself in Jane's refusal to be either Rochester's mistress or St. John's unloved wife. Jane again *imposes her terms* on the received pattern and *affirms her power* in the face of a process already set in motion. But these denials of male prerogative are heightened immeasurably by the three nighttime descents of Bertha and by Rochester and Jane's wedding day confrontation with her, "the beast or human being . . . on all fours" (p. 295). Distorted by parody, marriage is now wholly debased by the image of Bertha who connotes the dead-end of conventional marriage as the structure which reduces, rigidifies, and imprisons. When Jane points out that Bertha "cannot help being mad" (p. 305), she emphasizes Bertha's victimization. Bertha does not author the system, the exploitation of Rochester, or her own objectification; rather, these are parts of a larger cultural design in which Bertha is only an object of sexual exchange. The fracturing of narrative which culminates with Bertha's disclosure is meant to demonstrate how resistant marriage is to quest. In order for Jane to synthesize her needs for autonomy and usefulness she has to re-create marriage, but this re-creation cannot occur at Thornfield.

The disclosure of Bertha impels Jane to Whitcross, whitewashed arms marking the intersection of two moorland roads. At this nadir, Jane is forced from the group identification which membership in a community affords into the anonymity of absolute solitude. Whitcross is the literal intersection where she confronts and eventually rejects the inescapably solitary nature of quest. She has refused Rochester's plea, maintaining instead "the law given by God," insisting that "the more friendless, the more unsustained I am, the more I will respect myself" (p. 321), but at Whitcross that absolute must undergo transformation. Respect quickly gives way to the "moral degradation" of begging, fraught with "the consciousness of having no claim to ask—no right to expect interest in [her] isolated lot" (p. 332). When Providence leads her to Marsh-End, she is once more poised on the edge of community, looking through a narrow aperture at the cozy kitchen. Out of life-threatening isolation and exposure, Jane again approaches the group. The crisis at Whitcross is pivotal: it reenacts the helplessness and ostracism Jane experienced at Gateshead and Lowood; it juxtaposes absolute separation with the duplicitous *net*works at Thornfield; and, more important still, it provides the necessary space Jane requires in order to imagine her future. In this last sense, the *future facts*, the uncle's legacy, the burning of Thornfield, the death of Bertha, the reduction in Rochester's power, all necessary steps in re-creating marriage with Rochester, are realized at Whitcross.

If the Thornfield section condemns traditional narratives of courtship and marriage because they preclude quest, then the Marsh-End section faults spiritual quest because it denies romance. In this final section, Brontë subverts St. John's quest, along with his version of the Pauline Doctrine, as she attempts to literalize a fantasy about equitable marriage in the union of Jane and Rochester. In protest against St. John's asceticism, which is so akin to Eliza Reed's brand of Catholicism, and in machinations to equalize heterosexual connection, Brontë asserts the importance of human bonding. Centered in the hyphenation of quest-romance, attempting to locate a balance between these contradictory parts, Brontë connects quest and romance by making Jane's search for usefulness converge with her erotic attraction to Rochester. Jane's return to Rochester is motivated by these two desires. As Jane's quest for usefulness merges with the fantasy of lateral connection, romance claims to incorporate quest. Thus in the final section of the novel, Jane's chosen path toward community is poised against St. John's denial of what Barry Qualls identifies as "fellow-feeling" (*The Secular Pilgrims of Victorian Fiction*, pp. 63 ff.). And in the juxtaposition of these quests, spiritual and mortal, Brontë "retailor[s] the scripture" of Revelation, writing the New Jerusalem into this world as well as leaving it in the next (Qualls, p. 68).

In the figure of St. John, Brontë suggests that the spiritual quester who denies humanity in seeking to transcend it is destined to fail. "Cold, hard, ambitious" (p. 379), St. John "lived only to aspire" (p. 397). Incapable of rest, pleasure, love, he relentlessly pursues the most spiritual of missions, glorification in heaven, yet with a self-righteousness, a "self-idolatry," which defeats his objective (DuPlessis, p. 10). Unlike Rochester who tries to overleap "an obstacle of custom" (p. 220), St. John speaks within patriarchy and for it; he presumes to rule, own, curb. Jane notes: "he acquired a certain influence over me that took away my liberty of mind . . . I daily wished more to please him: but to do so, I felt daily more and more that I must disown half my nature, stifle half my faculties, wrest my tastes from their original bent, force myself to the adoption of pursuits for which I had no natural vocation" (pp. 402, 403). Controlling with "marble kisses," he elicits either submission or revolt, and when he presses Jane to marry him, he unwittingly ignites her rebellion. While denying his erotic attachment to Rosamond Oliver, St. John is categorical about the complete dominion he wants over Jane: "I want a wife: the sole helpmeet I can influence efficiently in life, and retain absolutely till death" (p. 411). In effect, St. John welcomes the benefits of wifely service, but at the same time he is repelled both by overt sexuality and non-erotic human connection. If his repugnance for intimacy implies his spirituality, it also betrays his failure to live by Christ's Doctrine of Love. St. John's ministry contains a "strange bitterness; an absence of consolatory gentleness," and at Marsh-End Jane surmises that St. John "had not yet found that peace of God which passeth all understanding" (pp. 356, 357). In his letters to Jane, St. John mouths the words of Revelation; he declares heaven is his home. What St. John never comprehends, however, is "that redeeming work involves first of all a generous concern for one's brother'" (Qualls, p. 64). Despite all his spiritual longing, St. John denies the Christ in "the least of these" (Matthew 25: 40-45); thus his quest denies the value Brontë places on human relationship and work in the world. Indeed, his failure is anticipated in the telepathic exchange between Rochester and Jane which not only literalizes their psychic connection but locates Providence in the natural world and envisions the New Heaven and Earth in this life. Like *Gulliver's Travels*, Revelation remains a favored text, but it too is displaced in this narrative.

Autobiography is self-assertion: in order to speak her own narrative Jane must deny as temptation the self-abnegation which St. John recommends. But at the same time that his vision is tarnished by his arrogance, her "vision of apocalyptic marriage" (Qualls, p. 68) diminishes the role of usefulness which Jane assumes as her worldly calling. At first, Jane's needs for equity and purpose seem mechanically fulfilled by her financial independence and by Rochester's physical dependence. Yet these arbitrary stabs at equalization leave a tottering imbalance in Jane and Rochester's loving relationship. In one sense, Jane appropriates Rochester's narrative as she concludes her own: "He saw nature—he saw books through me; and never did I weary of gazing for his behalf, and of putting into words the effect of field, tree, town, river, cloud, sunbeam—of the landscape before us" (p. 456). Moreover, without qualification, Jane states that the intervening ten years of married life have brought "perfect concord" (p. 456). Yet below this apparent fulfillment resides the ambivalence and hesitancy palpable in their living at Ferndean, the estate Rochester earlier confesses is too unhealthy to house Bertha, and in their being withdrawn from society, without the stimulus of urban life Jane has long since desired.

To understand the ending of Jane Eyre's narrative, we have to see its revision of received scripts and we have to remember the novel's beginning. Some readers see the ending as reinstating Providential design. Thomas Vargish asserts, for example, that "[Jane] will do what she can to raise [Rochester] from despondence and return him to power" and that the ending "contains no subversive negations" but rather enacts the "providential intention . . . in its most apprehensible and humanly gratifying form."[16] Seen this way, the ending reenacts the well-known moment when Cinderella's foot slides into the glass slipper, when Prince Charming's kiss wakes Sleeping Beauty. In this sense, the ending gives us what we expect and want, the plausible plot. But, I suggest, it also gives us a number of cues that Jane's expectations are confounded by some insidious authorial impulse to unhinge the plausibilities. Let us examine how this textual crosscurrent alters the prescribed resolution.

Returning to Thornfield in ruins, Jane rounds the building to see it from the front and then, before describing the scene, she interrupts with an "illustration":

> A lover finds his mistress asleep on a mossy bank; he wishes to catch a glimpse of her fair face without waking her. He steals softly over the grass, careful to make no sound; he pauses—fancying she has stirred: he withdraws; not for worlds would he be seen. All is still: he again advances: he bends above her; a light veil rests on her features: he lifts it, bends lower; now his eyes anticipate the vision of beauty—warm and blooming and lovely in rest. How hurried was their first glance! But how they fix! How he starts! How he suddenly and vehemently clasps in both arms the form he dared not, a moment since, touch with his finger! How he calls aloud a name, and drops his burden, and gazes on it wildly! He thus grasps and cries, and gazes, because he no longer fears to waken by any sound he can utter—by any movement he can make. He thought his love slept sweetly: he finds she is stone-dead.
>
> I looked with timorous joy towards a stately house: I saw a blackened ruin.
>
> (p. 429)

If the illustration is a parable, then it jars intriguingly with Jane's description of her happy future. As the returning lover, Jane approaches the house, the dead mistress, in an explicitly sexual and yet unmistakably ambivalent way. If the ruined house conjoins with its burned and dead mistress, then Jane's illustration seems to be her way of authorizing Bertha's revenge. Certainly, Brontë's strategy involves rewriting the script, and the ending she distorts here both in the illustration and Jane's own reunion with Rochester cannot be confused with the predictable formula. Identifying herself with the male lover who approaches uneasily, Jane seems to align the dead mistress with the past, with the whole patriarchal house and all its plausible plots. Yet at the same time, she is the female quester-turned-lover, killed by distortion.

The unrentable Ferndean is hidden in the thick, dark timber of a "gloomy wood," "the house—scarce . . . distinguishable from the trees; so dank and green were its decaying walls" (p. 435). When Jane sees Rochester's face, she describes it in terms of entrapment: "I saw a change: that looked desperate and brooding—that reminded me of some wronged and fettered wild-beast or bird, dangerous to approach in his sullen woe. The caged eagle, whose gold-ringed eyes cruelty has extinguished, might look as looked that sightless Samson" (p. 436). The power factor implied here is reinforced in her first touch: "I arrested his wandering hand, and prisoned it" (p. 438). These images of his enslavement are adjacent to her celebration of atonement in marriage: "There was no harassing restraint, no repressing of glee and vivacity with him; for with him I was at perfect ease, because I knew I suited him: all I said or did seemed either to console or revive him" (p. 442). His dependency makes her important: she reassures him, "I love you better now, when I can really be useful to you, than I did in your state of proud independence, when you disdained every part but that of the giver and protector" (p. 451). Clearly, the terms of her importance are set by his neediness, and by implication, then, as he recovers she must become less essential. Ten years after, Jane reports they are "precisely suited in character," and yet literally in the same breath she inserts, "*He loved me so truly, that he knew no reluctance* in profiting by my attendance: *he felt I loved him so fondly*, that to yield that attendance was to indulge my sweetest wishes" (p. 456, emphasis added). The relationship rigidifies with assumption and obligation.

Why must it end this way, we ask. The answer is that the ending is inextricably tied up with the beginning, with the gendered sense of self. Quest-romance affords no exit for the female hero. Enmeshed in her internalized split concept of gender, the female hero remains a trapped animal, powerfully resisting the limits of social enclosure, longing for connection and space, articulating these contradictory imperatives as a traumatic collision. Moreover, if the separate paths of romance and quest are dead-ends, then the female hero lives in the conjunction of forked roads, in the hyphenation of quest-romance. In writing her autobiography, Jane speaks her life into art, and in this sense, she *has taken the long voyage and seen with her own eyes* a reality in keeping with her creed. At the same time, however, the act of liberation has required that she set herself like an object within the frame. What the female-as-hero enacts as conflict, the female hero-as-author inscribes as paradox. Revelation stands and at the same time is unhinged. In the conventions of her time, Brontë writes *to the ending and not beyond it*, but to the degree that twentieth-century readers recognize this narrative of facts as a distortion of the familiar story, they can appreciate Brontë's nervy appropriation of an age-old paradigm. Female authorized quest-romance locates the hostile zone as that place where the new story writes itself against the old. *Jane Eyre* is about this revolutionary commitment to patterns which resist sanctions and embrace contradictions.

NOTES

[1]*Jane Eyre*, ed. Margaret Smith (London: Oxford Univ. Press, 1973), p. 21 (emphasis added). All quotations are from this edition and pagination is given in the text. Karen E. Rowe connects Jane's response to *Gulliver's Travels* to the duality in her own psychology, her acquiescence to servitude and her defiance of authority. See " 'Fairy-born and human-bred': Jane Eyre's Education in Romance," *The Voyage In: Fictions of Female Development*, ed. Elizabeth Abel, Marianne Hirsch, and Elizabeth Langland (Hanover, NH: Univ. of New England Press, 1983), p. 75. See also Rowe's discussion, "Feminism and Fairy Tales," *Women's Studies* 6 (1979):237-57, for an analysis of gender-related implications in fairy tales and how these tales constitute "one of culture's primary mechanisms for inculcating roles and behaviors" (p. 238). Rowe asserts that tales, such as "Cinderella," "Sleeping Beauty," "Beauty and the Beast," "prescribe approved cultural paradigms which ease the female's assimilation into the adult community" (p. 240).

[2]See Janet H. Freeman's fine analysis of the challenges Jane faces in achieving her own narrative authority, in "Speech and Silence in *Jane Eyre*," *SEL* 24 (1984):683-700.

[3]Northrop Frye, *Anatomy of Criticism: Four Essays* (Princeton: Princeton Univ. Press, 1957), p. 194.

[4]Margaret Homans, *Bearing the Word: Language and Female Experience in Nineteenth-Century Women's Writing* (Chicago: Univ. of Chicago Press, 1986), p. 41.

[5]Lacan's idea as discussed in Terry Eagleton, *Literary Theory: An Introduction* (Minneapolis: Univ. of Minnesota Press, 1983), p. 166.

[6]My focus here on the self-contradictory literary paradigm is distinct from Sandra Gilbert and Susan Gubar's thoughtful examination of enclosure and escape; see *The Madwoman in the Attic: The Woman Writer and the Nineteenth-Century Literary Imagination* (New Haven: Yale Univ. Press, 1984), pp. 338-39.

[7]For discussions centered on the implications of romance and quest in *Jane Eyre*, see the following: Shirley Foster, "Female Januses: Ambiguity and Ambivalence towards Marriage in Mid-Victorian Women's Fiction," *IJWS* 6, 3(1983):219-29; John Hutcheson, "Subdued Feminism: Jane Austen, Charlotte Brontë, and George Eliot," *IJWS* 6, 3(1983):230-57; Margaret Miller, "Happily-Ever-After: Marriage in Charlotte Brontë's Novels," *MSE* 8, 2(1982:21-38; and Jean Wyatt, "A Patriarch of One's Own: *Jane Eyre* and

Romantic Love," *TSWL* 4,2 (1982):199-216. Of these, Wyatt's essay alone sees the structural contradiction as a strength since, she claims, it permits simultaneous contradictory fantasies in readers. Wyatt argues, however, that among these fantasies, the one which envisions rebellion and equality is defeated by the myth of romantic love and its requirements of male power and female-male fusion. The structural contradiction, I suggest, is the effect of the quest-romance model on the female hero which in this text generates a dialectic through which moral assessment can occur and needs for change can be defined.

[8]Nancy K. Miller, "Emphasis Added: Plots and Plausibilities in Women's Fiction," *The New Feminist Criticism: Essays in Women, Literature, and Theory*, ed. Elaine Showalter (New York: Pantheon Books, 1985), p. 351. Miller's analysis of plot structures used by French women novelists applies directly to Brontë's fiction. I suggest that the romantic formulas derailed in the novel include "Cinderella," so frequently seen as the archetype for Jane Eyre's own narrative.

[9]Brontë's juvenilia, especially between 1829 and 1836, replicates the most conventional formats for gender roles and romantic plot lines. Heroines are repeatedly poised in a domestic setting; their fine dress and personal grace greatly exceeding in interest anything they say or manage to do. In *Arthuriana: Or Odds and Ends* (1833), a collection of stories about the Duke of Wellington's first son, Arthur Wellesley, the hero repeatedly comes to the rescue, single-handedly securing a happy ending, after his beautiful but inept and meddling wife, Marian, oversteps her bounds by getting involved with suspect characters or by going out at night to aid friends without her husband's permission. Resolutions frequently include renewed promises of wifely submission. For a summary of these early plot patterns see Christine Alexander, *The Early Writings of Charlotte Brontë* (New York: Prometheus Books, 1983).

[10]The apt word is Elaine Showalter's, regarding Eliot's treatment of Rosamond Vincy; see *A Literature of Their Own: British Women Novelists from Brontë to Lessing* (Princeton: Princeton Univ. Press, 1977), p. 24.

[11]In *The Life of Charlotte Brontë*, Elizabeth Gaskell reports on Brontë's remarkable decision to make "her heroine plain, small, and unattractive, in defiance of the accepted canon" (p. 308). Gaskell quotes a relevant anecdote from Harriet Martineau's *Daily News* obituary article on "the death of Currer Bell": "[Charlotte] once told her sisters that they were wrong—even morally wrong—in making their heroines beautiful as a matter of course. They replied that it was impossible to make a heroine interesting on any other terms. Her answer was, 'I will prove to you that you are wrong; I will show you a heroine as plain and as small as myself, who shall be as interesting as any of yours.' Hence *Jane Eyre*, said she in telling the anecdote" (Gaskell, p. 308; the obituary is reprinted in the *The Brontës: Their Lives, Friendships and Correspondence*, ed. Thomas J. Wise and John A. Symington, 4 vols. (Oxford: Basil Blackwell, 1932), 4:180 ff. For a worthwhile overview of physiognomy and female characterization in nineteenth-century English fiction, see Jeanne Fahnestock's excellent essay, "The Heroine of Irregular Features: Physiognomy and Conventions of Heroine Description," *VS* 24 (1981):325-50. The fascinating connection to Charlotte Brontë is that the century-long pattern Fahnestock traces in which heroines are described in increasing detail and with increasing frequency of physical irregularity matches Brontë's own development in her fictional portraiture of female characters. In the juvenile writings the heroines are invariably beautiful; with the novelettes (1836-1839) and *Ashworth*, several plain heroines appear

who are antecedents of Jane Eyre and Lucy Snowe. Fahnestock points out that "the heroine of irregular features is capable of irregular conduct" (p. 331).

See my discussion of the evolution of Brontë's plain heroines in "*Ashworth*: An Unfinished Novel by Charlotte Brontë," *SP* texts and studies 80, 4 (Winter 1983):12-24.

[12]For an early study of *Jane Eyre* as Cinderella myth, see Helene Moglen, *Charlotte Brontë: The Self Conceived* (New York: Norton, 1976), p. 108 ff. Gilbert and Gubar also draw these parallels; see *Madwoman*, p. 342.

[13]See Margaret Homans's discussion of literalization in *Jane Eyre*, in *Bearing the Word*, pp. 68-99.

[14]Significantly, Brontë subverts birthright by using physiognomy to undermine class distinction, and in this way a genetic scheme tries to replace an economic one. Gilbert and Gubar discuss the parallels between Jane, Grace, and Bertha in *Madwoman*, p. 351. Miller's conception of texts about female destiny as either euphoric or dysphoric helps explain why romance narrative concludes with either marriage or death. See *The Heroine's Text: Readings in the French and English Novel, 1722-1782* (New York: Columbia Univ. Press, 1980), pp. 218-19.

See Gayatri Chakravoty Spivak's reading of Bertha's character and role in the text and its relationship to the imperialism taken for granted in nineteenth-century English narrative in "Three Women's Texts and a Critique of Imperialism," *CritI* 12 (Autumn 1985):243-61.

[15]Rachel Blau DuPlessis, *Writing beyond the Ending: Narrative Strategies of Twentieth-Century Women Writers* (Bloomington: Indiana Univ. Press, 1985), p. 9. DuPlessis argues that as the chosen resolution of marriage becomes clear, the quest impulse is displaced on the figure of St. John, because quest and marriage are irreconcilable for nineteenth-century narratives by women (pp. 10-11). I suggest that St. John's quest, aimed as it clearly is at personal salvation and enthronement, is subverted just as certainly in this text as is the proposed enthronement of Blanche Ingram through marriage to a wealthy man.

[16]Brontë's use of Providence is variously understood. Thomas Vargish explains that the reliance on Providence as a *deus ex machina* in Victorian plot resolution reflects the common Victorian mind set about Divine order and intention. Vargish argues that "the power play that infests . . . the earlier chapters of *Jane Eyre* is resolved in a temporal equality of nature and grace." See *The Providential Aesthetic in Victorian Fiction* (Charlottesville: Univ. Press of Virginia, 1985), p. 67. In effect, he traces the romance but denies the contending quest. More persuasive is Barry Qualls's discussion of Brontë's this-worldly humanism and secularization of the Word in *The Secular Pilgrims of Victorian Fiction: The Novel as Book of Life* (Cambridge: Cambridge Univ. Press, 1982). From as early on as the Roe Head Journal (1836) and in her teen letters to Ellen Nussey, Brontë repeatedly expresses an unsettling yet persistent suspicion of religious teachings. In one letter, she confesses, "If Calvin is right, I am already an outcast." See Clement K. Shorter, ed., *The Brontës: Life and Letters*, 2 vols. (London: Hodder and Stoughton, 1908). Qualls points out correctly: "All her novels assert a this-worldly ethic. Self-knowledge is nowhere possible unless the individual can find some work, some activity that will define the self in relation to other human beings" (p. 45). Influenced certainly by Bunyan, Brontë writes a secular narrative which may be compared constructively to Carlyle's *Sartor*, but in Brontë's articulation of the quest-romance, the pilgrim's progress is accounted for by the power within and the female hero's affinity with Nature. Gender makes Brontë's a different story from Carlyle's.

SEL 28 (1988)
ISSN 0039-3657

The (Un)Lettered Ensemble: What Charley Does Not Learn about Writing in Bleak House

CLAUDETTE KEMPER COLUMBUS

Charles Dickens's use of parallel plots, leitmotifs, and visual symmetries create covert as well as overt connections among the characters in *Bleak House* (1853).[1] Speaking of Dickens's novels in general, Harry Stone observes the "intricate subtlety" with which Dickens reveals the "divergent yet related identities of the persons named and their divergent yet related roles."[2] Each character "enacts his name," but, although the practice is widely recognized, the reach of the interconnections continues to surprise, as when Stone notes murder and hardheartedness embedded in Murdstone, Merdle, Stony Durdles, Headstone.[3]

Units as small as vowels and consonants suggest interconnections among Dickens's characters. Julia Kristeva argues that "grams" or "paragrams," verbal bits, transmit meanings. These resonate with metarational networks, linguistically and psychologically "open."[4] Communicating liminally on the microlevel of consonants and vowels, paragrams also reveal connections among divergent emotions and contexts. On the microlevel of paragrams, the meanings expressed extend beyond an author's deliberate and conscious intent.

However deliberately crafted Dickens's parallel or concentric fictional structures, at the level of the paragrams, even he could not have known how the linguistic network opens into his own emotional life. Paragrams help communicate the fictional world that the author projects. Paragrams also unintentionally help reveal the psychological world the author inhabits.

To picture a fictive social world that spells fragmentation, corruption, selfishness, darkness exacts a terrible toll. But to

Claudette Kemper Columbus, Professor of English and Comparative Literature at Hobart and William Smith Colleges, is a devoted fan of Charles Dickens. Her publications range from Comparative Romanticism and Victorian Studies to Contemporary Latin American Literature.

recognize one's own entrapment and arrested development, one's own mutilation by one's actual social world is worse. And yet the paragrams in *Bleak House* reveal the degree to which such representations of society as projected shed light on the depth to which Dickens himself was stricken. Although Dickens willed himself to believe it was possible to win some separation from the society he describes in *Bleak House*, he inscribes in its networks the impossibility of escape. *Our Mutual Friend* (1865) shows transformative, resurrectional possibilities. Good people learn collectively to read history and society and themselves. They thereby transfigure the death imprinted on their social world. But *Bleak House* shows nobody truly transformed.

In most of his novels, Dickens separates a few characters from the bleak house, the prison of society, by introducing a representation in miniature of a sunshiny "alternative," a happy household tucked into the novel, usually at the end.[5] But the Bleak House in litigation that emblemizes England in the novel of that name becomes a second Bleak House where the inhabitants appear to be "reading and writing" in a happy corner of the great darkness, but are shown to be reenacting the self-promoting world they believe themselves to have escaped. Ostensibly *Bleak House* achieves a "bridal" conclusion. Ostensibly its young inhabitants escape the corruption and alienation pervasive in the greater world. Yet the concentric ripples of the social world they believe they have escaped prove inexorable. The new Bleak House is a prison in the cradle, although, in other novels with similar endings, Dickens clearly does not even liminally nor inadvertently intend the absence of real alternatives to the greater social world.

Dickens himself desired comfortable, middle class resolutions to major social problems. At the very least, characters could win sweet marriages and, if not a fortune, a livable income; and enough education of heart to share one's good fortune. But in *Bleak House,* Dickens inscribed how delusory these privatized resolutions that he himself desired must be in such a social world as he represented. Only, he could not let himself read what he had written, the extent to which his own life was inextricably implicated in the open network enlettered by the paragrams. Dickens could not consciously accept that his imagination, contaminated by the failure of his social world, failed to go beyond the parallels and paragrams that Dickens himself set up and that leave *Bleak House*'s second narrator, Esther Summerson, an immature mother. Esther Summerson and her companion, Charley, depict Dickens's failure to draw more daring and more drastic resolutions than theirs.

Dickens declares in the "Author's Preface" (p. xxxi) that the novel's injurious ensemble has dragged down the spirit of the author and "subdued" his nature "To what it works in, like the dyer's hand: / Pity me then, and wish I were renew'd!" But he has succumbed more deeply than he knows to the disease that captures his characters and keeps the perceptions of sympathetic Esther and Charley unlettered.

The character of society that emerges in *Bleak House* is to a considerable extent the character of all its inhabitants. Gradually their numerous plots and plans converge in a monstrous plot, driven by the systematic concealment of connections among individuals and among the social classes. Absorption in the pursuit of private interests delimits their cognition and their social interaction. Their predatory social relations preserve the illiteracy that demonizes the character of the society they inhabit and blasts them all. Innocence, incapacity, isolation, poverty prevent even the best among them from seeing themselves as parts of a whole, from seeing themselves collectively, from seeing the similarities among them despite the gradations among them that seem like differences. That the characters are joined is evident to the reader on the level of nomenclature and the level of paragram. But, since no reader in the text sees the interconnections, and since even Dickens could not admit how far they extended, society remains disjointed and so too does the discourse of disconnected, metonymic characters reduced to jagged, minimal, verbal units.

Initially, the liveliness of the characters distracts the reader from the social similarities that reduce them to ambulatory alphabetical letters. Even "nice" characters focus all but exclusively on the pursuit of their own interests, perhaps particularly those characters who are self-deceived in believing they have no personal interests. Not a character expresses nor represents a coherent, legible, larger social goal. Few characters see, far less read, the death plot, that is, their general failure to attend to the collective good. The eleven death scenes that punctuate the novel not only conjoin burial plots and the novel's plot, but delete the difference between burial ground and bridal bed.

Eventually, what makes a reader take note of the centrality of the deathly character of society and the deadly plot is the absence of depth despite the liveliness of Dickens's characters. The sharing of letters of the alphabet shows how the lives of the characters partake in the life of the malevolent figure of the collective whole. The interconnections of the lives of each of these characters impinging on the lives of all the rest are rung by modulations in their sharing of vowels and consonants, until the reader becomes aware of the degree to which the characters' names follow the trajectory of paragrams such as the alphabetical character of "J."

"J" chalks in the lineaments of all the characters. The hook of "J" and the hook of its homophonous other, "G," ensnare other paragrams that gradually reveal blind individual bondage to the monstrous body politic. Characters of the alphabet draw the character and the body of society.

Shortly after Esther Summerson first encounters the illiterate Mr. Krook, rapacious owner of a rag and bone shop, fascinated by the transactions of the courts of chancery, Krook chalks a crooked J on the wall. Esther describes it as done "in a very curious manner, beginning with the end of the letter, and shaping it backward. It was a capital letter, not a printed one, but just such a letter as any clerk in Messrs. Kenge and Carboy's [law] office would have made" (p. 44).

Esther makes superficial note of the handwriting on the wall; yet the "J," ominous as it is, does not rupture Esther's pacificatory attitudes. She cannot see how much it ensnares.

Soft "J" and "G" form visual echoes in hard "G." So too does the hard "c" of *court* connect to the soft "ch" of *chancery*. Through the *C*ourt of *C*hancery, deeply embroiled in the interminable case of Jarndyce vs. Jarndyce, *K*rook's *J* connects to General *G*eorge and *G*ridley and *G*uppy and *G*uster and Mrs. *J*obling and the various *J*arndyces and *J*o the "Unfortnet" (p. 478) and *J*oseph *B*agnet. "Grid," "bag," "net": not only do initials indicate the paragrams of entrapment; so too do parts of names. Bagnet bags, nets *B*. "B" draws in *B*adger and *B*oythorn, joined to *C*arboy and *K*enge and *C*arstone, the young bridegroom worn away by the law until he ends as raw Mr. *C*. As for the females, Mrs. *J*ellyby, *J*enny, the cat Lady *J*ane, *J*udy, and *C*addy *J*ellyby Turveydrop circulate until, at last, the "unfortnet" baby Esther at the beginning of the book is replaced by another, an echo baby, Esther, at the end of the book. The first Esther's deaf and dumb goddaughter, Esther, who has absorbed ink into her veins, who has absorbed not only the ink that stained her mother and grandmother, has also absorbed the Inquest Jo hears as Inkwhich. "I had almost forgotten Caddy's poor little girl" (p. 664) notes Esther, our "sympathetic" heroine, whose grown body veils the infant buried in her.[6]

Like her missing mother, Lady Honoria Dedlock, like Caddy and Ada Clare, et cetera, Esther will never mature. Instead, like Richard Carstone on the occasion of his death declaring he is ready to begin a new world, Esther of Inkwhich will repopulate a second Bleak House. Both Bleak Houses are metonyms for England, repeating or echoing itself.

The assembly of personages in *Bleak House* subject to phonetic shrinkage is also subject to the reductiveness of society's academic exercises, such as taxonomic authority. Naming indicates to which "kingdom" a character has been consigned: animal (Vholes), vegetable (Chick Weed), and mineral (soft rock Mr. Carstone).[7] Categories ornithological, entomological, ichthyological portray / betray, entrap and bag Miss Flite, Weevle, Guppy. The hard woods, Lignum Vitae (Mr. Bagnet) and Mr. Skimpole, a pole(cat) of, say, Lignum Mortis, show Dickens using letters to dismantle differences among his characters.

Dickens's taxonomies differ from those Roland Barthes sees writers formulating by means of raids on cultural artifacts. Dickens is showing words, letters, characters, as husks, the native rhythms threshed out of them by the unfeeling mechanics of religious, legal, academic, and fiduciary systems.

The short first chapter opens with "mud" and ends with "Mlud." The legal system of nineteenth century England (Mlud) eclipses the passage of time as progressive. Meaningful history is deleted, because justice and the legal system have remained "m[l]ud," the term Lawyer Tangle uses to refer to My Lord Chancellor of the Court of Chancery where he sits "in the midst and the heart of the fog" (p. 4). "Mlud" introduces at the paragram level the deformation of language, the illiteracy of supposedly civilized people who cannot read what they do and who they are.

These unalienated individuals wish to belong to the system. They wish to believe in the system. But most of the characters in *Bleak House*, such as lawyer Vholes, have holes in them instead of hearts and pockets instead of heads. Metonymic consonants and vowels of the social alphabet, all are, willy-nilly, malevolently averaged into a malevolent society with a hole instead of a heart. Unaware of the fragmentation they share, shown by the consonants and vowels they share, these characters with a lizard-like and unreflecting consciousness mirror a world that causes the first of the novel's two narrators to remark, "and it would not be wonderful to meet a Megalosaurus, forty feet long or so, waddling like an elephantine lizard up Holborn Hill" (p. 1).

Neither the novel's older, "omniscient" nor the novel's young, "innocent" narrator escapes the eclipse of the middle years. Neither reveals the middle. The older narrator buries his private emotional life by omitting it. The ingenue who is a character does not know her personal history and moves from abused childhood to life in the doll house. The absence of an accounting for either one of the middle years, that is, the years of sexual maturity, parallels the deletion of erotic competence that could exist between the infancy of society and its old age.[8] These absent middles parallel the deletion of the personal histories of most of the characters' lives.

If a mature understanding of history evolves from a mature

social world, populated by people capable of loving with maturity, it follows that, if society damages the maturational processes of its young, if it forces children to be old before their time, no mature and libidinal history, personal or national, is possible. Rather than engaging in discourse, rather than exchanging stories and histories, most of the characters must resort or choose to resort to a secrecy and a silence that sabotage history on the one hand and that, on the other hand, expose history as absent to itself. Whenever the missing middle emerges, it emerges in the form of scandal and reveals that one character or another has either been "shirking" or "sharking" (p. 4). It is because the characters have endured processes of socialization with the middle missing that they are telescoped into the letters of their own names, showing them, old and young, enslaved by the system that has grown old without growing up. These are the sentimental and elemental facts *Bleak House* encodes.

The absence of space between "mud" and "mlud" parallels the absence in history of the recorded maturation of society, and parallels the lack of distance between youth and old age. Indeed, the alternating voices of the narrators reveal halves of one personality, each harmed by a terrifyingly rapacious and numbingly indifferent society. The third person narrator denouncing the viciousness of the social system is the alter ego of the orphan secretly aspiring to be accepted by it. The omniscient narrator's voice, male, sardonic, witheringly witty, enraged, old, is, in an earlier time frame, also the first person narrator's voice, young, naive, female, hopeful, the voice of illegitimate Esther Summerson who intends to be a decent member of society.

The tragedy of alphabetical letters and human characters telescoped into letters, crushed into one another, is the eclipse of space and the absence of innovation. Despite superficial distinctions, society exacts a paralytic and parasitic uniformity from its members. The missing roundness of characters, the missing fullness of letters, is indicated not only by the absence of history, but by the missing documents and the missing letters (epistles). The most important of these critically absent texts could have told a tale of lost love (Honoria Dedlock's for Captain Hawdon). The search for the missing love letters drives the obsessed Tulkinghorn to make lethal rather than vital connections among people. He not only threatens to expose the missing "middle" of Lady Honoria Dedlock's life and story; he extorts a letter from Captain Hawdon to General George. Tulkinghorn also threatens Honoria Dedlock's feline servant, Hortense, whom she has dismissed. As is only to be expected, Tulkinghorn's private history is missing. Lovelessness is so voracious of his life that it consumes his history and makes him a predator on the missing histories of others.

Like Nemo or No One (Captain Hawdon's alias), like General George, like Miss Barbary, Tulkinghorn acknowledges no family relations, no background, no history. His surname indicates the pathology of his sexuality. But in his name, the growl of society is heard. *R, ar, haw* betray society's otherwise inarticulate, barbaric, primordial voice. The scenes of violence that distinguish Tulkinghorn's life make clear the cost of repression of history, the negation of sexuality. Captain Hawdon (alias Nemo or No One), Honoria Dedlock, General George are all likewise refugees from maturity and from history. Honoria's servant's name, Hortense, signals Honoria's suppressed horror at the price Honoria Dedlock pays for a compressed life of formality in a "labyrinth of grandeur" (p. 662).

Honoria has borne an illegitimate child whom she cannot acknowledge, even if she believed the child alive. Lady Honoria cannot flesh out either her sterile life as a lady or her name (honor). She can only act alive behind the veil of respectability she uses to delete her history. Letters and characters that can expand into history through stories shared and that allow for mobility and invention in the social system remain crooked and cramped. Lady Honoria must keep her background and her passion secret, hidden from her life, private and public, at the cost to her of an authentic marital relationship.

The horrid and hard "Hor" of *Hor*tense and Tulking*hor*n and *H*on*or*ia and the unrelenting (doubled and hence infinitized) "ar" of B*ar*b*ar*y and J*ar*ndyce, though softened in Ada Cl*ar*e, have to be, could be transformed into roundness, wholeness, by the open, mature heart of those who can love and speak and read. Rosa, Rouncewell, Esther herself hint at emotional and consequently social transformation, at a living language bespeaking acknowledged relationships rather than the shattering language of categorization and privatization. But these softer consonantal characterizations remain peripheral, "obedient" to the social conventions; servile, and therefore almost powerless to alter the Megalosaurine society. Although each of these three is able to change a personal situation to some degree, each ultimately welcomes social normalization. Not one learns to speak with the resonance of maturity. Only Rouncewell acts in the larger world through his ironworks, but, by Carlyle's definition of a captain of industry, he does not gain the stature of an organic figure nor does he become an organic filament or relational paradigm.

Honoria plots to visit her former lover Nemo's grave. Nemo's corpse, described as a "deserted infant" (p. 110), indicates how not only his childhood, not only his history, but his entire life has been eclipsed. Honoria disguises herself as Hortense, her name echoing "whore." Later, Hortense dons the same clothes to play the part of Honoria. The purity-prurience that resonates in the words "Honoria," "Hortense," "honor," "whore" suggests the figure of the overall social Character, its hair standing on end with horror of the genital, whether the genitals be missing or flashed. Society has willed the absence of its middle. Yet, without an adult, erotic life, history, society cannot differentiate between the honorable and the dishonorable. The legal system that should support honor has gone whoring and inkhorning. That representative of putative respectability, lawyer Tulking*horn,* sounds in his name the sickness of the deleted middle with its echoes of underlying ugliness that such society, such "history," such a legal system sounds.

These veiled characters all lurk alike. Honoria veils herself in Hortense's veil. Hortense wears the same veil to duplicate Honoria.[9] The shared veil show them aspects of one being, particles echoing the same sound, figures mirroring the greater veil of the system.

The unconscious connections suggested by similar sounds among what might otherwise seem distinct human beings playing distinct social roles in distinct classes ring in their names and also resound in their missing stories. With history(ies) missing, the cohesive element of a clear, a speaking plot line disappears. So, also without the middle ground of mature experience, extremes collapse into a muddle: pride into prurience, honor into whore, predator into prey, the living into the indicated and veiled grave. Esther's bridegroom, Doctor Woodcourt, he who would, with love, court, suffers a phonetic eclipse into Wood Cot. His long-distance courtship of Esther is scarcely ardent. His priggish mother and John Jarndyce arrange the marriage behind Esther's back.

Honoria's incriminating letters, the love letters, are missing; honor's letters are missing. All the plots of Bleak House revolve around the absence of missing love letters.

Although he is learning to write, Krook cannot read the love letters that Lady Dedlock wrote Captain Hawdon and that Krook has hidden. Avarice drives Krook to learn to read. He may achieve a moment of reading. It may be that the discovery that what he is reading is a letter of love consumes him in apt manner, by spontaneous combustion.

Lady Dedlock cries "Who copied that?" when she sees a legal document copied by her former lover (p. 10). Her agitation reveals to Tulkinghorn a missing meaning in the copied document that will bring about Lady Dedlock's downfall.

Esther remembers reading aloud to Miss Barbary about "our Saviour's" goodness to the sinful woman. Our "Saviour stooped down, writing with his fingers in the dust, when they brought the sinful woman to him" (p. 14). This text strikes Miss Barbary with her unforgiving and immature heart as dreadful. This reaction on the part of Esther's undeclared, secret aunt (her history is also missing) to open-heartedness is so violent that Miss Barbary collapses and dies, presumably after suffering a heart attack and only after she has done Esther permanent injury by branding her her mother's "disgrace."

The legalese in which the letter informing Esther that she will be the companion of a ward of court is a small masterpiece of the eclipse of heart in a mangle of letters. Esther, however, is so eager to become a part of the system that she cries, "O, never, never, never shall I forget the emotion this letter caused in the house!" (p. 20). Shortly after, a carriage bears her to the lawyers' office, indistinguishable from a cemetery, "for I saw the gravestones from the staircase window. This was Kenge and Carboy's" (p. 22). Even John Jarndyce, Esther's kind guardian, uses writing to distance himself from emotional life. He welcomes the young wards of chancery who are coming to live with him by sending them identical notes advising them not to be demonstrative (pp. 46-47).

The permutations on the theme of letter-writing are extensive, but perhaps Mrs. Jellyby's should be mentioned as the most tragicomic. She is distracted to mindlessness by the volume of "unaccountable" correspondence, meaningless to her family, and takes no care whatever of her family. The most pitiable writing is probably Lady Dedlock's letter to her newly acknowledged daughter to advise her that her mother will be No More: "I have done all I could to be lost" (p. 612). Lady Dedlock's letter to her husband "is discovered on her table, —but it is doubtful yet whether he has not received another missive from another world, requiring to be personally answered; and all the living languages, and all the dead, are as one to him" (p. 576).

The desolation of letters written touches the desolation of letters un-written. Gallant General George wonders "Why should I ever write?" (to his family [p. 567]). The sinless innocent, the pauper Jo, having passed directly from infancy to old age without passing through puberty, much less maturity, considers the reading and writing in the world of Tom-All-Alone's "unaccountable" (p. 169), which it surely is. But, before he expires, he absorbs the lesson of a society with a legal system legible as mud: guilt falls to the victim. Jo is to blame. To be poor is to be "illegitimate," sinful. In his abjection, Jo finally confesses a need for writing. He wants his guilt inscribed on his grave.

> "Wot I wos a-thinkin on, Mr. Sangsby, . . . wos, as you wos able to write wery large, p'raps?" [I'M WERY SORRY THAT I DONE IT.]
> The stationer . . . asks him, what it is that he is sorry for having done?
> "I went and giv a illness to the lady as wos and yit as warn't the t'other lady. . . . might [you] be so good p'raps, as to write out, wery large so that anyone could see it anywheres, as that I wos wery truly hearty sorry that I done it and that I never went fur to do it. . . . What I wos a-thinkin on, Mr. Sangsby," proceeds Jo, "wos, as you wos able to write wery large, p'raps?"
> "Yes, Jo, please God," returns the stationer.
> "Uncommon precious large, p'raps?"
>
> (p. 490)

No author accidentally inscribes his own name in a novel, particularly not in a novel that calls attention to grams, paragrams, patronyms, diagrams, grids, nets, hooks, and bags. Dickens had felt himself abandoned as a child when he was about Jo's age. In the years preceding *Bleak House,* Dickens entered his forties, successful in letters but, like John Jarndyce, cheated of emotional fulfillment. His marital and family problems were exacerbated by his sense of social outrage from which neither national polity nor liturgy offered refuge.[10] Appalled by the very people who applauded him, yet wishing to be numbered among them, as an artist, Dickens was contradictorily committed to transcend and to preserve class barriers that Bleak House breaches and preserves. He attacked the social milieu, but he did not perceive an alternative to it.

The kind of mythology that genuine communal interaction generates could have inspired Dickens to posit genuine social maturity. A communal mythology can generate a sense of shared destiny and intent that can sustain the individual and humanize society. But if language has no relation to a revitalizing mythology, language becomes categorical, reductive, castrating, mechanical, and disjunctive, providing no place to store either personal or cultural experience. But, judging by all but one of his novels, Dickens's social world went no further in that direction than fairy tale.

D. W. Winnicott describes "culture" as

> something that is in the common pool of humanity, into which individuals and groups of people may contribute, and from which we may all draw *if we have somewhere to put what we find.*
>
> There is a dependence here on some kind of recording method. No doubt a very great deal was lost of the early civilizations, but in the myths that were a product of oral tradition there could be said to be a cultural pool giving the history of human culture spanning six thousand years. This history through myth persists.[11]

Struggling to humanize his nation, Dickens found no "*potential space* between the individual and the environment,"[12] where children can store and share experience, a place necessary because its security gives children enough security to separate themselves from their parents; that is, it gives them enough security to become mature. Into that space, at that time, Dickens could only project a Ruined house, the Solitary House where the Wind howled; the Solitary House that was always Shut up and never Lighted, Bleak House and the East Wind: How they both got into Chancery and never got out (all possible titles).[13] It cannot be other than deliberately that Dickens gives his given name to the orphaned "slavey" already too damaged by society to separate herself from it, the thirteen-year-old, pre-pubescent, female character *C*harley *C*oavinses (Neckett).[14] But Dickens seems not to have consciously accepted what the paragrams reveal he was feeling: that the middle of his own life had been eclipsed.

Like Esther, Dickens felt himself socially mutilated by the failure of his guardians to guard. This sense, transposed to the social scene, includes everyone, in and out of the novel. The third person voice of the fulminating narrator changes in a pronomial shift to "we" in "The Appointed Time" of Krook's very special death. At the scene of the crime, "we" the witnesses run away. "Horror, he [the corpse] is here; and this from which we run away, striking out the light and overturning one another into the street" (p. 346) is a statement that our missing love letters have entombed our maturity.

"'Coavinses has been arrested by the great Bailiff,' said Mr. Skimpole. 'He will never do violence to the sunshine anymore'" (p. 157). Skimpole does not give the abandoned children a second thought. Less heartless than Skimpole, Esther Summerson and John Jarndyce track down Charley, daughter of the deceased Coavinses, collector of bad debts who had "lived" in Cursitor St., Cook's Court, Chancery Lane, in what Skimpole calls Coavinses' Castle. Taken from Mrs. Blinder's penurious lodgings, Charley is given to Esther Summerson as a Christmas gift.

Like their circumstances, like Honoria and Hortense and Tulkinghorn, Esther and Charley and Charles are intricately intertwined. Becoming the companion to the companion to a ward of the Court of Chancery, Charley "Coavinses" becomes as "convincing" a social housekeeper as Esther in the "benign" coven of domestic slavery in which Esther and Charley and Charles leap from childhood into premature old age, doing other people's laundry and sweeping away cobwebs.

Esther undertakes to teach young Charley to write, in a scene of instruction, "Nurse and Patient," that repays contemplation. For it may be that the scene strikes the note that reveals the devastation of the multiplicity of unconscious systems blindly operant and ruining language and the national character. It may be that, like Mr. Swills, who is "like an empty post-office, for he hadn't a single note in him" (p. 347), Charley will nonetheless strike the note that rings the noisy and deadly chorus of the "inkwhich" of the social system.

If the identification between two Charleys is granted, Dickens has been more than "feminized," the role David Simpson sees Dickens giving redeemer figures such as Riah of *Our Mutual Friend*.[15] She has been defeated by a social system grounded on categorization and devoted to a writing not of space but of possession. The character of Charley hints at a *dies irae* rising from the illiteracy and immaturity of a society that sustains avarice and prizes pennies and shillings and half-crowns instead of sunshine; a society that uses writing Tulk-ink-horn-ishly to control exchange, gregariousness, and relation; a society that makes writing deadly.

In "Nurse and Patient," Charley is first patient, and Esther, nurse. Distinction between nurse and patient proves very temporary, for soon Esther is the patient. She ends the chapter by requesting her nurse to "sit beside me for a little while, and touch me with your hand. For I cannot see you, Charley; I am blind" (p. 336). In addition to being metaphorically blind, she consents to remain an object. As John Jarndyce has given Charley to Esther as a gift, so, without speaking to her about it beforehand, he gives Esther to her future husband. Moreover, no word of love is heard spoken between Esther and Allan Woodcourt at their betrothal. Rather, the pair is shown through another Jarndyce gift, a furnished, second Bleak House, "quite a rustic cottage of doll's rooms" (p. 648).

When one Bleak House breeds another of the same ilk, nothing has changed. Although ostensibly a comfortable and kind way of life is lived in both Bleak Houses, the unsilenceable "eek"s and "ow"s of the Bleak Houses leave even critics who interpret the ending as optimistic uneasy. As for Esther, whom her guardian had made old before her time, and who has enjoined her to utter not a word as she accepts her doll-house existence, she writes, "Because he was so dear, so good, so admirable, I tried to tell him what I thought of him, but I could not articulate a word" (p. 647).

So what does Esther teach Charley about writing in "Nurse and Patient" in which the teacher-nurse becomes ill and blind?

> Writing was a trying business to Charley, who seemed to have no natural power over a pen, but in whose hand every pen appeared to become perversely animated, and to go wrong and crooked, and to stop, and splash, and sidle into corners, like a saddle-donkey. It was very odd, to see what old letters Charley's young hand had made; they, so wrinkled, and shrivelled, and tottering; it, so plump and round. . . .
>
> "Well, Charley," said I, looking over a copy of the letter O in which it was represented as square, triangular, pear-shaped, and collapsed in all kinds of ways, "we are improving. If we only get to make it round, we shall be perfect, Charley."
>
> (pp. 324-25)

As they chat, Charley makes it clear she has been or will be exposed to the smallpox that Jo has brought to Jenny's and that Charley and then Esther will contract. The future writes itself on Charley's face. "If Charley could only have made the letters in her copy as round as the eyes with which she looked into my face, they would have been excellent" (p. 325). Her round, her perfect "O" eyes fill with tears, for the sick boy reminds her of her father's death. To visit Jenny, young Charley, with her bonnet and shawl, "made herself look like a little old woman" (p. 326).

Neither Charley nor Charles writes down with perfect clarity the zeroes their eyes go round in seeing. Instead, both jump from youngsters seeing the zeroes the social system figures and encodes to old age, Charley shawling herself to protect herself from the "lurid glare that overhung the whole dark waste." As Lady Dedlock veiled herself in a futile effort to protect herself, so too will Esther veil her mirror to avoid seeing. She is ruined, not, however, because her face is pocked, but because she relies on her mirror. That reliance on the image in herself of the way others see her keeps her from writing the deformation she sees as surely as it does Charles Dickens. Who can openly admit having missed the middle, the heart of life, through no fault of one's own, but because the connections among people make evident the large, ghostly figure of a deadly society?

Relations with marginal people can give a creature many eyes, can make a body a social being and can humanize the character of society. But the thrust in *Bleak House,* despite itself, despite its author, is either to kill off or to normalize marginal people. Doing so is to sacrifice the eyes. The image of reliance on the mirror exposes one defense of the threatened, the need to be reflected in society. The desire to be legitimate, to be legitimized, to belong devastates Esther in her ruthlessly immature social world. If society is infected, the natural desire to have a place in the world ends in illiteracy (blindness, the lack of an historical perspective, the absence of emotional courage). The letters of that society spell its death as they stray / prey through halls of mirrors and echoes, where evil conventions dictate even to good people and keep them disguised to themselves, until, consciously or not, they become as veiled and violent as the world around them.

Bleak House ends with Esther, who seems to have everything she ever wished for, asking her husband to reassure her about her looks. Even if her looks are gone, she consoles herself with "I know that my dearest little pets are very pretty, and that my darling is beautiful, and that my husband is very handsome, and that my guardian has the brightest and most benevolent face that ever was seen; and that they can very well do without much beauty in me—even supposing——THE END." This conclusion counts another victory, another victim. Supposing she is conventionally beautiful, Esther shows herself still enslaved to ingrained normative standards. So society remains unaltered. As for Charley, who has gone to work at the mill, she too loses her middle. She becomes a member of society.

NOTES

[1]The edition used for purposes of quotation in this article is Charles Dickens, *Bleak House,* ed. Morton Dauwen Zabel (New York: Basic Books, 1956).

[2]See Harry Stone, ed., "Introduction," *Dickens' Working Notes for His Novels* (Chicago and London: Univ. of Chicago Press, 1987), p. xxv; hereafter cited as Stone.

[3]Stone, p. xxv.

[4]Julia Kristeva, *Desire in Language,* ed. Leon S. Roudiez (New York: Columbia Univ. Press, 1980).

[5]Some instances are *David Copperfield, Great Expectations, Our Mutual Friend, Little Dorrit.*

[6]In "Esther Summerson Rehabilitated," *PMLA* 88 (May, 1973):429-39, Alex Zwerdling investigates several of the themes that also appear in this essay, notably the trapped infant in the old body and the "grammatical cripple" (Zwerdling on Esther).

Of the larger canvas, Joseph I. Fradin uses the phrase "numbing stupidities of our institutions," but casts the social struggle as being between the forces of good and evil, a struggle so unequal the best can attain only passive goodness. See Joseph I. Fradin, "Will and Society in 'Bleak House,' " *PMLA* 81 (March 1966): 95-109.

[7]David Simpson, *Fetishism and Imagination: Dickens, Melville, Conrad* (Baltimore and London: Johns Hopkins Univ. Press, 1982), identifies carstone as a soft, Norfolk stone, "pretty and decorative but of little use for building foundations" (p. 53); hereafter cited as Simpson.

[8]Fredric Jameson explores "libidinal transfiguration" and social change in, for instance, "On Interpretation," *The Political Unconscious: Narrative as a Socially Symbolic Act* (Ithaca: Cornell Univ. Press, 1981), pp. 73-74.

[9]As well as having the qualities of a good, realistic detective story, *Bleak House* ranks as a first rate Gothic romance, its scenes surrealistic and its acoustics Wagnerian. Possibly Gothic tales initiated narrative representation of human beings reduced to characters of the alphabet. Possibly the device of substituting an alphabetical character for a human one emblemizes enletterment as enslavement. Such Gothic scenes as the paragramic Lockwood shut inside Catherine's bed and book in *Wuthering Heights* are possessed by letters and haunted by inscriptions.

The idea seems in the air anywhere that market considerations outweigh human considerations. In the United States, Edgar Allan Poe devised spectacular effects to show the dehumanization in writing that regulates the lives of others, the totalitarian writing of ownership, of possession. "Autography" and *The Narrative of Arthur Gordon Pym*, both preceding *Bleak House* (1852-1853), anatomize human character terrorized by an incomprehensible, usurpative alphabet that in *The Narrative* dries people out until, like Dirk Peters, they are what their names letter. In France, Charles Baudelaire's "Les Septs Vieillards" in *Fleurs du Mal* (1857) and Victor Hugo's calling cards of the 1850's and 1860's fuse human-and-alphabet-and-land- or city-scape, so that Victor Hugo's initials become nightmare territory for a life "grounded" in letters.

Mark Spilka has shown how Kafka learned from Dickens what both Poe and Hugo knew. Perhaps Dickens derived the idea that we do not write so much as we are written from his years as a reporter.

[10]A glance at, say, page 659 in vol. 2 of Edgar Johnson's splendid *Charles Dickens* (Boston and Toronto: Little, Brown, 1952), 2 vols., gives a sense of Dickens's misery as it was in 1848. Hereafter cited as Johnson.

[11]D. W. Winnicott, *Playing and Reality* (New York: Basic Books, 1971), p. 99. Hereafter cited as Winnicott.

[12]Winnicott, p. 100.

[13]Stone, pp. 183-205. See also Johnson, p. 746.

[14]My sense of the Charley [Hexam] in *Our Mutual Friend* is that the use of Charley as a name bears no relationship to Dickens, although some sly game may be being played in naming one of the pickpockets in *Oliver Twist* Charley Bates. Nevertheless, that Dickens uses names that link fictional to life characters is incontrovertible. In *Dickens and the Social Order* (Philadelphia: Univ. of Pennsylvania Press, 1985), Myron Magnet notes three fathers named John in Dickens's work, on all of whom, Magnet shows Charles taking out his aggressions against his own father, John Dickens (p. 66).

[15]Simpson, p. 56.

SEL 28 (1988)
ISSN 0039-3657

Pip and the Monster: The Joys of Bondage

IAIN CRAWFORD

"Poetic history," according to Harold Bloom, "is . . . indistinguishable from poetic influence, since strong poets make that history by misreading one another, so as to clear imaginative space for themselves."[1] My concern here is not with poetry but fiction and with the "misreading" Dickens imposes upon Mary Shelley's *Frankenstein* in his own *Great Expectations*. I hope to argue that Dickens's novel is, quite deliberately and to an extent that has not been fully explored, an elaborate reworking of its predecessor. In Bloom's terms, *Great Expectations* is both a completion of and antithesis to Shelley's work, since it retains its predecessor's terms but transforms their significance.[2] In particular, where Shelley's work posits an ideology of assertive individual self-reliance in a godless world, Dickens's text emphasizes the values of human community and, especially, of submission to divine grace. While this emphasis may not completely resolve all the issues raised in the novel, *Great Expectations* nevertheless ultimately embraces the influence of Shelley's text with more resilience than anxiety, and the two novels thus confront one another as almost paradigmatic expressions of Romantic and Victorian culture.

Frankenstein was and is surely the most popular and widely diffused of all Romantic writings. Appearing towards the end of that great wave of literature which marks the first two decades of the nineteenth century and enjoying, as it were, a rebirth in the form of its much revised 1831 edition, the novel became perhaps the Victorians' most familiar contact with the impulse of Romanticism. Contemporary reviews, such as the 1818 *Edinburgh Magazine*'s, immediately caught that peculiar force of the novel which has been responsible for so much of its massive and lasting

---

Iain Crawford is Assistant Professor at Berry College, Georgia. He is now working on the *Barnaby Rudge* volume in the Dickens Companions series.

appeal. To the *Edinburgh* reviewer, it was the delicious combination of "dark and gloomy views of nature and of man, bordering too closely on impiety," together with a "power of fascination . . . in harsh and savage delineations of passion," and finally the soothing balm of the "gentler features of domestic and simple feelings" which engendered the novel's special attraction of repulsion.[3] By 1823, *Frankenstein* had begun to spawn progeny of its own and, with the presentation of five separate dramatizations on the London stage, was well on its way to that transmutation into the broad cultural myth which is still very much alive. A year later, the novel was sufficiently established in the national consciousness and highly enough regarded by the political elite for Secretary Canning to allude to it in a complimentary fashion as he likened emancipating the West Indian slaves to raising up "a creature resembling the splendid fiction of a recent romance; the hero of which . . . being unable to impart to the work of his hands a perception of right and wrong . . . finds too late that he has only created a more than mortal power of doing mischief, and himself recoils from the monster he has made."[4] Throughout the century, such dramatizations and appropriations of the story would continue, as Lee Sterrenburg and others have shown,[5] and it is readily apparent that Mary Shelley's novel thus quickly achieved that firm position in western culture which it still maintains.

One would expect a writer so attuned to popular culture as Dickens to be well aware of a novel with the appeal *Frankenstein* clearly possessed, and we know that he owned a copy of *Bentley's Standard Novels,* the series which included the second edition of Mary Shelley's work. Allusions to her writing have also been detected both in a letter Dickens wrote Forster during his Alpine sojourn of 1846 and in *The Haunted Man* of 1848;[6] twelve years later, when he came to write *Great Expectations,* it is apparent that he had not forgotten *Frankenstein*:

> I had got on so fast of late, that I had even started a boy in boots—top boots—in bondage and slavery to whom I might have been said to pass my days. For, after I had made the monster (out of the refuse of my washerwoman's family) and had clothed him with a blue coat, canary waistcoat, white cravat, creamy breeches, and the boots already mentioned, I had to find him a little to do and a great deal to eat; and with both of those horrible requirements he haunted my existence.[7]
>
> The imaginary student pursued by the misshapen creature he had impiously made, was not more wretched than I,

> pursued by the creature who had made me, and recoiling from him with a stronger repulsion, the more he admired me and the fonder he was of me.
>
> (p. 354)

A number of critics have noted the second of these allusions Pip makes to *Frankenstein;* the earlier, and quite different echo of Shelley's work has also been remarked, though it has received far less attention.[8] No one, however, has explored the full implications of the narrator's decision to refer so pointedly to the earlier work or discussed the extraordinary variety of ways in which Shelley's novel operates within the narrative of *Great Expectations.* My intention here is to argue that the links between the texts go far beyond the two overt allusions and to suggest that Dickens's novel radically explores the value of the cultural metaphor *Frankenstein* offers to western civilization. Above all, I would maintain that Dickens's Victorian version of the *Frankenstein* myth denies the original's emphasis upon the sufficiency of the individual will, stresses instead the values of human community and, finally, embraces the supremacy of divine authority. If *Frankenstein* establishes a bleak universe, stripped of a deity and thus of underlying meaning, *Great Expectations,* despite and perhaps indeed because of the suffering through which most of its major figures pass, ultimately accepts and endorses the will of God. To demonstrate the nature of Dickens's repetition of Mary Shelley's work, I shall first consider how the two novels depict the relations between creators and their progeny, then examine their treatment of the Romantic themes of nature and childhood, and, finally, explore their ranges of intertextual response and the manner in which Dickens in particular reinscribes his inherited texts.

That concern with the nature of creation and the process of forging one's identity which lies at the heart of both novels is, *pace* Secretary Canning, altogether more complex than the simple imparting of notions of right and wrong, especially for Pip. Just as Victor and the Monster are clearly alter-egos, so too Pip and Magwitch exist in a curious form of bondage to one another, each tied into the union by a series of events of which neither is fully aware. Where their relationship differs from the earlier one, however, is in that widely noted blurring of the roles of creator and created, man and monster.

A "parcel of bones" (p. 105), assembled almost out of the grave beside which his maker discovers him and from, as it were, his mother's tomb untimely ripped, young Pip is indeed to be compared with Frankenstein's Monster in the moment of his creation. Moreover, as he grows up he will become an adolescent of singular egoism and unreflecting social prejudice who is monstrous in his behavior to those with whom he spends his childhood. Yet we should also note that he himself is his most urgent accuser and that the ingratitude for which he so unsparingly berates himself neither prevents the majority of the characters in the novel from responding to him with delicacy and affection nor is perceived by them as anything other than the somewhat unconventional form of an otherwise entirely normal, indeed laudable social mobility. Further, though Pip himself may forget it, neither Magwitch nor the reader fails to grasp that his behavior out on the marshes that miserable Christmas Eve revealed a capacity for charity and sympathy which the convict had seldom encountered and which was indeed anything but monstrous. In the light of this dichotomy between his general behavior and the occasional better promptings of his moral nature, the sense of bewilderment which Pip expresses for much of the novel should come as no surprise to the reader.

If Pip is thus perceived by his society as normal and by himself as a hideous aberration, with Magwitch the case is precisely reversed. Like the Monster, Magwitch's first recollection is of the primal need for warmth; both then move on from craving the basic necessity of fire and shelter to seeking an entree into human society. But just as the Monster is repulsed and thus permanently scarred by the educated and ostensibly civilized De Laceys,[9] so too Magwitch is twisted by his early induction into the world of crime and, above all, by the influence of Compeyson, the fake lover and phoney gentleman. At his trial he is thus represented as a violent monster whose evil corrupts the social ideal ostensibly embodied in Compeyson. However, and by contrast with *Frankenstein,* in Dickens's world the human spirit retains its capacity for good and its potential to survive such traumas as these; thus it is that Magwitch, nurtured by memories of Pip's charity while sitting by his fire in the Australian outback, is able to keep his own spark of natural feeling alive and be encouraged in his plan to give the boy those opportunities he himself never had. Yet the trauma has been controlled, not removed, and, for all the charitable impulse of Magwitch's plan, it is also clear that he sees Pip as a vehicle for his fantasies of revenge over Compeyson in particular and the structure of the English class system in general. Where the Monster had sought consolation in the creation of a fearsome bride, Magwitch, more subtly, would create a son, a gentleman, and an authentic version of the social type Compeyson, his creator, had counterfeited. His dog-like affection for Pip and repeated addressing him as "Master" are thus qualified and undermined by his all too apparent delight in the joy of owning a "brought-up London gentleman" (p. 339) who will enact his revenge. Such is the refusal of the novel to escape to simplifications, however, that even here there may be latent potential for good. For, while Magwitch is indeed guilty of reifying Pip into an instrument of his revenge, unlike Victor Frankenstein he neither denies his responsibility for his creation nor ceases to care for him. And it is precisely this insistence upon the father-and-son link between them that will eventually allow each to transcend the social stereotypes through which he perceives the other and thus finally to attain that bond of love in which their relationship ends.

To anticipate such a conclusion at this point, however, would be premature since both characters have a considerable distance to go before they can escape the bondage of class-determined perceptions. It is for Pip that this struggle will be the most difficult and the most rewarding. Although it is in his tie with Magwitch that *Frankenstein* is specifically evoked and given an especially Victorian bent through the combination of tension between father and son with the antagonisms of social class, several of Pip's other childhood relationships also deal with the manner in which he is created and misshaped by class envy. Mrs. Joe, eternally lamenting her marriage to a village blacksmith; Pumblechook, abetting her in the attempt to cut Pip away from that same Joe; and, most crucially, Estella with her comments on his coarse hands and thick boots—all spur Pip into an effort at upward social mobility which compromises what tenuous sense he possesses of his own identity. Even when he does escape to find in Herbert Pocket and his father new, attractive, and generally beneficent role models, his sense of alienation from the village and the forge, and thus from himself, remains. For Pip's dilemma is that, while he may apparently come to fit into the social niche his part as a gentleman provides, in reality his inner life ties him to the village and, as Bentley Drummle, Orlick, and Trabb's boy unfailingly remind him, to the marshes.

And yet if the story of Pip's creation is thus one of the undermining of identity through the attempts of others to shape it in terms of class ambition, envy, and revenge, his actual narrative and, above all, his evocation of the tale of Frankenstein and the Monster is an act of defiance, an assertion of identity on his own terms. The guilt-tormented child whose extraordinary agonies over helping Magwitch and robbing Joe are intensified by his torture at Estella's hands is all too readily disposed to see himself as a monster; throughout his youth, he thus lives in a state of restless anxiety and self-doubt, a doubt which may well be honest but which also undermines what little faith he has in himself.

That he should then respond to the truth of his great expectations and the identity of his creator in terms of Frankenstein's story makes perfect psychological sense, since, by casting himself thus, he is relieved from all responsibility for that identity with which he has been so chronically dissatisfied. If his allusion to himself as the "imaginary student" and to Magwitch as the "misshapen creature" suggests that role confusion to which I have referred, it also marks the beginning of his fight back through a redefinition of the myth that has been imposed upon him. Though he is at first as crushed by Magwitch's news as his allusion to the Arabian Nights suggests (p. 330), even in this moment of defeat he begins to employ the education his patron has made possible as a means of self-defence: the child at the forge had no means of resisting anything that was forced on him and lacked even the literacy to decode his parents' tombstone; the young gentleman who devotes hours to his books each day (p. 330) is immediately able to delve into his reading and emerge with a narrative that will enable him to encode and thus control his trauma.

Indeed, in re-telling his life he constantly reshapes its raw material so as to diminish the pain caused by his ambivalent relations with his quasi-parental figures; in particular, he twice uses comic inversions of *Frankenstein* to this effect. Both of these occasions resemble the night of Magwitch's return in that each involves a confrontation of Pip's new world with his true origins: the first, previously cited, account of the Avenger appears immediately after Pip learns of Joe's imminent arrival in London and, through the contrast between his agonized feelings on the occasion itself and the comic self-deprecation of his retrospective narratorial parallel with *Frankenstein,* suggests that the older Pip has succeeded in controlling and assimilating the experiences his younger self had found overwhelming. The second allusion occurs when, in the aftermath of Joe's disastrous visit, Pip penitentially rushes down to Kent to be at once confronted with the dirty and stained form of the local newspaper asserting that it is Pumblechook to whom he owes his gratitude. The narrating Pip, however, is able to laugh off this particular form of textual authority and respond with another comic reversal of the converging travellers in *Frankenstein*: "I entertain a conviction, based upon large experience, that if in the days of my prosperity I had gone to the North Pole, I should have met somebody there, wandering Esquimaux or civilized man, who would have told me that Pumblechook was my earliest patron and the founder of my fortunes" (p. 253). But before he attains such awareness and this competence to narrate his life the young Pip must evolve and mature considerably. To do so, he must first understand the nature of the fictive models by which those around him live and then comprehend both their significance and their indispensability. If his early adulthood is thus a form of semi-intentional forensic probing as he endeavors to piece together all the lives which have bearing upon his own, his maturity will consist in realizing that to know these narratives is not in itself sufficient to fulfil his own humanity.

It is, of course, Estella who most intrigues him and bears most responsibility for shaping his social ambition. Yet his narrative can be seen as a progress from total subjection to her towards an eventual comprehension of both the true quality of her social origins and of her emotional nature. Like Pip, Estella is the victim of a creation myth, a myth which does her immense harm and from which, for her, there is to be no real recovery. Both children are snatched out of the worlds into which they are born, educated according to the standards and tastes of the social elite, and bred for a single purpose—to act as proxies in the taking of revenge upon a world whose deficiencies of humanity are encapsulated in Compeyson. Although Estella's case is never explicitly drawn into parallel with the Frankenstein story, it is evidently as much an instance of monster-making as Pip's fashioning at the hands of Magwitch. Like Pip, Estella is subjected to a process of moulding —by Miss Havisham, Mrs. Brandley, and finally at the hands of Bentley Drummle—and left with no coherent identity to call her own. Like Pip again, she is all too aware of her limitations but, having none of that residual sense of love and care Pip derives from Joe and which is so essential to his own continuing humanity, can see herself only as the hapless product of her creator (pp. 323-24). Even though she has no reason to feel that sense of ingratitude and moral inadequacy which so racks Pip's conscience, there is nevertheless something truly monstrous about her actual dehumanization itself and her lack of the imagination even to begin to comprehend this until the end of the novel. Pip at least possesses both the conscience and the imaginative vitality to have some sense of the wider context of his feelings. Thus it is a measure of both this distance between them and the overall dream-like logic of his narrative that he should so hauntingly anticipate what Estella will mean for him in the very moments before he learns of his first summons to Satis:

> Joe made the fire and swept the hearth, and then we went to the door to listen for the chaise-cart. It was a dry cold night, and the wind blew keenly, and the frost was white and hard. A man would die tonight of lying out on the

> marshes, I thought. And then I looked at the stars and considered how awful it would be for a man, to turn his face up to them as he froze to death, and see no help or pity in all the glittering multitude.
>
> (p. 80)

For it is Miss Havisham who is shaping Estella and her cold love drills all responsiveness out of her creation; the result is a woman entirely devoid of amatory feeling, a creature whose polished and brilliant external form only masks an inner monstrosity. Well indeed might Estella, even more than Pip, have echoed that poignant cry of Adam which also stands as the epigraph to *Frankenstein:* "Did I request thee, Maker, from my clay / To mould me man? Did I solicit thee / From darkness to promote me?"[10]

Pip, who early begins to revolt from the monstrous aspects of his behavior, is in no danger of imitating the worst of Estella's fate. For, by contrast with Estella's acceptance of the manner in which she has been shaped, he portrays himself as the flawed product of Magwitch's imagination. He thereby frees himself to begin a quest for the true quality of his nature, the truth that lies beyond the fiction which has been imposed upon him. To some degree, his progress here is simply a result of the opportunities his new life gives him, but, ironically, it is mostly through his deliberate attempt to put together the pieces of Estella's story that he comes to discover the character of the lives of all the people in his world, recognize the other versions of *Frankenstein* co-existing with his own, and thus establish a coherent narrative that can both account for his own creation and enable him to accept it. His exploration of Estella's past reveals to him the variety of compromises people make in order to retain their humanity and sense of identity in an overwhelmingly hostile world and, crucially, allows him to come to terms with his own self and realize that he is far more than Magwitch's monstrous creation. This process will not be complete, however, until he comes to a larger understanding of the relationship between the mundane world and the divine. Where Victor Frankenstein had aspired to divinity through discovering the secret of creativity, Pip carries his exploration back into the source of his own and Estella's origins. It is thus in their responses to the shaping worlds of childhood and nature that *Frankenstein* and *Great Expectations* find the next aspect of their curiously symbiotic relationship.

Both novels quite clearly display a conscious reaction to the Romantic, specifically the Wordsworthian, concern with the relationship between the child and the adult selves: Shelley's novel is founded upon the conflict between the Monster's innate moral beauty and his corruption through the experience of rejection; Dickens's, as U. C. Knoepflmacher has shown, shares in that debt all his later work owes to *The Prelude* and its depiction of childhood.[11] Similarly, both novels treat of the relationship between the animal and the human, nature and civilization, the demonic and the divine. However, if each text is skeptical about the chances of innate goodness naively surviving the endemic hostility of the human world, where *Great Expectations* essentially dissents from its predecessor is in its presentation of the consequences of a destruction of innocence. While in *Frankenstein* a blood-dimmed tide is indeed loosed by the rejected and desperate Monster, *Great Expectations* suggests that there are less extreme responses to the loss of one's innocence and that even a Pip may find viable and benign sources of consolation.

At the outset of Dickens's novel, we are presented with a highly Wordsworthian image of Pip contemplating the graves of his entire family. In a manner reminiscent of the little maid in "We Are Seven," he is quite unable to comprehend either the tombstones which he is incapable of deciphering or the distinction between life and death that is both represented by the place itself and which Magwitch is about to thrust upon him. Never again in his narrative will Pip be far from either the fact or sense of death. As the convict springs up out of the grave, Pip's freshly awakened "first impression of the identity of things" (p. 35) is abruptly twisted into anguished fear, an emotion which is intensified when Magwitch conjures up a lurking alter-ego in the form of that dismembering young man. Pip's entire life is given its shape by this one brief scene and, as Knoepflmacher has pointed out, the fear engendered in him not only recalls *The Prelude* but also becomes the underlying motive for much of his later behavior.[12] This trauma is, moreover, one with which Pip is helpless to come to terms, largely because it so completely accords with the conditions of his bringing up by the rough and ready hands of his sister. Unlike the eight-foot-tall Monster, whose response to rejection by his creator and then the De Laceys is to wreak destruction and death, Pip, small for his age, morally timid, and very sensitive (p. 92), can only suffer in silence and remain scarred for years to come. And yet it may also be precisely this helplessness which saves him. For, unable to follow the Monster in fulfilling his childlike fantasies of house-burning and murder, Pip is restricted to the minor, even comic peccadillos of purloining the file, brandy, and pork pie. Even when he is later humiliated by

Estella on his first visit to Satis, his wrathful response comes out as nothing more than pulling his hair and kicking the brewery wall (p. 93), neither of which actions, one may feel, leads to any great destruction. Thus the conditions of his childhood effectively prevent Pip from acting out any desire for revenge and, even though the stolen file will later implicate him in Mrs. Joe's death, his direct response to trauma remains dissipated into ostensibly trivial forms. Indeed, not only is Pip restrained from the violence to which the Monster gives free play, but he is also propelled by his suffering towards Joe who, with "the influence of [an] amiable honest-hearted duty-doing man" (p. 135), supplies him with those "little, nameless, unremembered acts / Of kindness and of love" which constitute the other half of the Wordsworthian legacy, a half which Pip, crucially, will never quite forget and which distinguishes him from both the Monster and Estella.

If the two novels thus differ in their treatment of Wordsworthian notions of childhood, so too they diverge in their responses to the world of nature itself. In *Frankenstein,* despite the initial beauty of the Swiss setting and the later tour of the English Lakes undertaken by Victor and Henry Clerval, the overall thrust of the narrative is to alienate the central characters from that "never-failing source of joy." The two figures who do respond to nature in conventionally Romantic terms and specifically in those of *Tintern Abbey,* are both destroyed by the Monster: Henry Clerval, "a being formed in the 'very poetry of nature' " and who loves the natural as much as the human world (p. 156), is strangled and cast up on the Irish shore; while Elizabeth, who delights in the "majestic and wondrous scenes" of her Swiss homeland (p. 36), is murdered on her wedding night. Victor and his Monster, by contrast, do indeed learn that they can receive but what they give; however, they offer one another only vengeful hate, an emotion to which they subsume all other sensibilities until their final trek across the northern wastes towards the extinction of all their early fire in the barren reaches of the Arctic.

If Dickens's endeavors at painting Romantic nature all too often seem like babbling of green fields, in *Great Expectations* his most significant treatment of the natural world is of a quite different order. While there is an element of decorative writing in such passages as the description of Joe and Biddy's wedding day (p. 486), a far more significant force of nature is to be found in the role more usually allotted to the marshes, a setting which may be seen to parallel and yet revise the part of the Arctic in *Frankenstein.*

Both the Arctic and the Kent marshes with the Thames beyond them form a natural geography that is also psychic and social. Existing beyond the fringes of civilization, these regions objectify and externalize the inner depths and darknesses of human consciousness. It is on the frozen ocean alone that Victor and the Monster can come together and, such is their mutual hatred, even this reunion can only occur after the former's death. Similarly, it is on the marshes and the river—which together constitute the one setting in the novel that is not a product of the human social world—that Pip, at moments of high crisis, confronts both his creator and, in Orlick, that alternative self who seems to leach out of him so many of his own blackest emotions. Magwitch, too, will twice struggle here with his own creating alter-ego Compeyson: first, at the beginning of the novel, they will fight like "two wild beasts" (p. 67) in the marsh ooze; then, much later, they will finally resolve their differences in a fight to the death beneath the waters of the Thames. On this second occasion, the scapegoat convict and the counterfeit gentleman will become as one in their struggle in a murky world where nothing can divide them, and Magwitch will, albeit at the cost of his life, at last succeed in triumphing over the man who has been both his maker and his torturer. Pip's part in all of these miry conflicts with which he is involved is almost intensely passive: he can do nothing but watch on helplessly during that first fight on the marshes; for all his brave resolve, he could not have prevented Orlick taking his revenge; and he can only watch and wait as Magwitch and Compeyson wrestle beneath the river.

It is, however, characteristic of the difference between the two novels' senses of the relation between the individual and social worlds that Pip should be rescued in the very nick of time. Where Walton's letters to his sister only bear passive witness to events far beyond his comprehension, let alone his control, Pip's chance dropping of Orlick's rough note will find a response in Herbert, Startop, and the irrepressible Trabb's boy. As was the case with the novel's modification of *Frankenstein*'s image of childhood, here too Pip's passivity itself affords an opportunity for the power of human sympathy and community to find expression and, unlike the isolated figures of Victor and the Monster, he is always secured within the bonds of human society. Even his personal version of that physical violence which frames his relationship with Magwitch and Magwitch's with Compeyson seems to emphasize this. Where his counterparts battle out on the marshes in the manner of beasts, he ventures into the highly structured and exquisitely comic fray of his bout with Herbert in the garden at Satis (pp. 119-20). However guilty Pip may feel at affronting the laws of social convention, this is an altogether different order of struggle from the others in the novel and one which is securely defined within the codes of that social world to which he aspires and into which he will eventually be assimilated.

Moreover, it is Herbert Pocket—an ideal representative of such codes—who plays an essential part in Pip's transformation from apprentice blacksmith into young London gentleman. Unlike Henry Clerval, who for all his love of Victor is never able to relieve him of his self-imposed burden, Herbert provides Pip with a confidant vital to his emotional health. If Pip's entire narrative is a form of *ex post facto* confession, then his friendship with Herbert allows him the interim opportunity to express and thus, to a degree, come to terms with his feelings. Moreover, Herbert himself has a range of qualities that perfectly match Pip's needs in his struggle to align his nature and behavior with the requirements of the social world for which he is being shaped. Herbert's charm, ready sympathy and savoir-faire are all of considerable appeal to the raw, yet warm and ardent country boy who is eager to learn. But of all the things Herbert can teach Pip it is perhaps his lessons in social refinement that are the most significant. From their first meeting at Barnard's Inn, Herbert manages things with style and grace and eventually transforms Pip into a young man of some polish and elegance. These are qualities that Pip himself values intensely. Not only does he never forget Estella's brutal comments on his boorishness but he is also extraordinarily sensitive to the feelings of others, even when he manages to ignore them, and throughout the novel he displays a fine sensibility to the value of courtesy and social consideration. In this respect, he may also be seen in the wider context of that importantly intermediary social category upon which the Victorians placed such emphasis and which both Robin Gilmour and Shirley Robin Letwin have so usefully discussed in their considerations of the gentleman in the Victorian novel.[13]

The concept of the gentleman, which provided an invaluable staging point in the rapidly shifting class structure of nineteenth-century Britain, is clearly essential to Pip's entire progress; it is also, however, important to the novel's treatment of nature and its reworking of *Frankenstein*. For Pip, as for the Victorians at large, it is the code of gentlemanliness which tames the beast and acts as a civilizing force that enables a blacksmith's boy to climb up out of the marshes into a world that is both more sophisticated and, albeit rather problematically, more cultivated. At the same time, however, this very stress upon the civilizing impulse also implies an admission of the proximity of the bestial, a conjunction of which few Victorians could fail to be aware in their daily existence and which was widely perceived as a diachronically thin line separating their progressive age from the far more brutal period in which *Great Expectations* is set.[14] Pip is indeed the seed that comes to bear a fruit very different from his convict progenitor; yet both he and Estella are also hybrids and are divided from Wemmick's Newgate plants by little more than the jail's bars. If the prison thus symbolizes the segregation of mankind's darker elements from society at large, both Pip and Estella are walking embodiments of the fact that the distinction between the criminal and conventional worlds is little more than a fictive convenience and one which all too frequently permits the orthodox to regard and treat the criminal exiles as nothing other than beasts.

The case of Pip and Estella, however, both undermines this entire assumption and, in the topical context of the debate over Darwinian theory, also raises a variety of questions about the vitality of the ostensibly superior classes. On the one hand, there is a real sense of evolutionary progress in the social elevation Estella and, especially, Pip enjoy: not only does the novel repeatedly immerse the principal criminals in the primeval world of the marshes and their liquid mud, but even the convicts being transported to the Hulks seem little more than "lower animals" (p. 249). Pip's desperation to escape such a fate is almost palpable and his external success in so doing would appear both to endorse conventional Victorian social ambition and catch nicely that fashionable concern with theories of evolution that had been stimulated by the publication of *The Origin of Species* in November 1859. Dickens was, of course, aware of Darwin's work; not only did he allow it to be favorably discussed in *All the Year Round* a few months before he began serializing *Great Expectations,* but also, as Gillian Beer has shown, intellectually he and Darwin had a great deal in common.[15] In particular, as Dr. Beer points out, Darwin shared Dickens's fascination with Romantic ideas of growth and development, ideas especially found in *Frankenstein,* which depicts the effects of not allowing "full recourse to those secret, pre-conscious and beyond consciousness experiences of growth which are the full conditions of creativity."[16] In *Great Expectations,* however, we should note that it is Pip who portrays the convicts as beasts and articulates the theory of social evolution as a form of theoretical legitimization of his own progress. The text at large more fully endorses Darwin's conception of the common ancestry of species and portrays the ancestry of the gentleman, and thus by implication of the bourgeoisie as a whole, in, if not the monkey, then at least the criminal classes. While this assertion might in itself be sufficiently troubling to the Victorian mind, what is perhaps even more disturbing is the novel's intimation of the price that is demanded for this evolution into a state of refinement, grace, and sophistication. For not only does

Pip achieve his social mobility at the price of losing both his roots in the marshes and his closest ties of affection, but also, like Herbert, he lacks the raw power of Magwitch, Orlick, and, indeed, Mary Shelley's Monster. In this sense, if *Great Expectations* revises *Frankenstein,* it does so with the implied acknowledgement that Victorian social progress may also comprise the descent of man himself, that the beast may have been worked out but that with him has also vanished the primal energy of both the ape and the tiger.

Finally, however, Pip's relationship with his particular Monster is seen in larger terms than those of vitiated social evolution. For his text makes its ultimate appeal not to the categories by which society classifies human existence but, instead, to the overriding power of divine authority. This is not to claim that *Great Expectations* is by any means an overtly religious novel; nor is it to suggest that Dickens's Christianity here is anything other than that rather diffused sentiment Dennis Walder has shown to be characteristic of his belief in general.[17] What can be argued, however, is that *Great Expectations* and *Frankenstein* are linked and then finally divided through their diverse ideological responses to a series of parallel intertexts and that where the later work most significantly dissents from its predecessor is in its ultimate subsuming of human will to the operations of divine Providence.

Both novels are, as numerous critics have noted,[18] extraordinarily conscious of their literariness and allude to a plethora of other texts. As we have seen, the Wordsworthian image of childhood and nature derived from *Tintern Abbey* plays an important though differing part in both novels; other common intertexts include *Hamlet, Paradise Lost,* Gray's *Elegy,* and the Bible. Given that in writing *Great Expectations* Dickens was at the height of his powers, it seems unlikely that these analogies are merely coincidental, and at least two of the novels' major intertexts appear to have been invoked precisely to be challenged both in their own right and in terms of the readings given them in *Frankenstein.* Where Shelley's novel employs *Paradise Lost* and related images from the Gothic tradition to reinforce its own depiction of a restless, deracinated, and finally godless world, *Great Expectations* implicitly attacks and finally overthrows this model through an inverted treatment of the selfsame text and tradition. Beyond Milton's Christian epic, however, stands the larger intertext of the Bible. It is in the role that this book plays in *Great Expectations,* together with its conspicuous absence from *Frankenstein,* that we most fully see the distance between the two novels and the extent to which Shelley's Monster is remade as his tale is used to generate its own counter-text.

Mary Shelley's deploying of *Paradise Lost* as a subtext to her novel has been amply documented and Milton's epic is an undeniably appropriate analogue for a narrative that begins with Victor's defiance of parental authority and then develops into his own conflict with an unruly scion. What is finally so chilling about *Frankenstein* is the manner in which it demonstrates that the mind is indeed its own place and that Victor has most assuredly made himself a hell of heaven. For in Shelley's world there is no evidence whatsoever of a deity and, thus deprived of any larger context for its meaning, the human mind is left to determine its own signification.

What Victor does is simply take this to a logical conclusion and literally attempt to define the nature of existence; his struggle is thus not the conventional hubristic revolt against his Maker but, ultimately, merely an act of supremely egotistic solipsism. His failure derives from a refusal to accept his own creation and takes the form of a collapse inwards; by contrast with Satan who derives so much vitality from the sheer fact of his rebellion, Victor is left gnawing at himself and is finally consumed by his own desire for revenge and destruction. The Monster himself is little better, since, dealing only in absolutes of love and hate and responding in totalitarian terms to the experience of rejection, he devotes himself to the wholesale slaughter of all his creator holds dear—friends, family, and, finally, bride. The ultimate responsibility for even these acts of evil, however, must remain with Victor, since not only does he fashion the Monster but he also shares in the latter's fantasies of destruction. Its murders remove from Victor's path such rivals as his father, brother, and Henry Clerval, as well as Elizabeth, the bride for whom he has never been able to feel anything other than a primly asexual love. Indeed, it is Victor's neglect on the wedding night that allows the Monster to carry out the murder he should have predicted yet seems almost to have anticipated, as his ambiguous words, "But death was no evil to me, if the loss of Elizabeth were balanced with it" (p. 191), suggest. In *Frankenstein*'s version of *Paradise Lost,* then, we find not only a deliberate modelling of the Monster upon Satan but also, and far more disturbingly, Victor's own corruption by the overweening desire for knowledge to extend his power. In a world evidently lacking any divine authentication, the darkest elements of the human psyche operate freely; Victor's overreaching desire for uniqueness is left with neither inner nor outer restraint and brings about not only his own death but also those of his alter-ego and all whom he himself holds dear.

Great Expectations is certainly not without its darker side and Pip's doubling with a character such as Orlick in the attack upon Mrs. Joe would suggest that Dickens is no less responsive to the capacity for human evil than Mary Shelley. Yet his novel's tone is predominantly elegaic and comic and is largely free from the bitter rage that is so prevalent in *Frankenstein*. Perhaps not surprisingly, then, when *Paradise Lost* appears in *Great Expectations* it does so in tones that are appropriately softened and which carry a value quite different from the allusions in *Frankenstein*.

Again, two explicit references suggest the larger borrowing: first, Pip concludes the initial stage of his expectations with words that recall the closing lines of the poem, "And the mists had all solemnly risen now, and the world lay spread before me" (p. 186); and secondly he ends the novel with a similar image of himself and Estella quitting Satis for the last time rather as Adam and Eve, "with wandering steps and slow," depart from Eden. In broad terms, what Pip does here is align himself with that tradition of English fiction which derives from *Paradise Lost* its underlying pattern of allegorized picaresque wandering through the wilderness of the world. However, his particular departure from the pristine rural sanctuary is rendered problematic both by the questions raised throughout the text as to the idyllic character of the life of retreat and by the complex nature of his relationship with the father-figure who imposes a new knowledge of life upon him. For, although his feelings towards Magwitch do include the same kind of resentment that exists between Victor and the Monster, they later grow into a love which, blending the human and the divine, will finally enable Pip to avoid Victor's inner vacuum by finding signification in both the world and himself. His allusions to *Paradise Lost*, then, make an appropriate contrast with the poem's appearance in Shelley's novel, since he is able to rewrite the text, transforming it from an image of suffering into a poignant emblem of his own blend of emotional and moral loss and growth.

A broader version of a related reworking may also be seen in *Great Expectations*'s treatment of the Gothic, a genre which is clearly so basic to *Frankenstein* as not to require further discussion here. The settings, action, and, above all, the doubling of Victor and his Monster do much to place Mary Shelley's novel within that popular Gothic tradition which, in its challenging of established forms of authority, is also related to the broader Romantic revival and reinterpretation of *Paradise Lost*. In *Great Expectations*, however, and as is characteristic of Dickens, Gothic forms are less dominant and are to be found mostly as a subtext to the main narrative. While the pairs of mirroring characters in which the novel abounds owe much to Gothic tradition, the most significant appearance of the form lies in the contrasting images presented by Miss Havisham's Satis and Wemmick's Gothic castle in Walworth, images which continue the novel's redefinition of *Frankenstein*'s anguished image of the parent-child relationship.

By contrast with his other exercises in intertextual gauging of his spiritual and psychic progress, Pip is unable to control his Gothic allusions as readily as he had those to *Paradise Lost* or to *Frankenstein* itself. Much of the reason for this failure must surely lie in the fact that the novel's Gothic forms are at their strongest precisely in the center of his own emotional life, Satis and the younger of its imprisoned maidens:

> The nooks of ruin where the old monks had once had their refectories and gardens, and where the strong walls were now pressed into the service of humble sheds and stables, were almost as silent as the old monks in their graves. The cathedral chimes had at once a sadder and a more remote sound to me, as I hurried on avoiding observation, than they had ever had before; so, the swell of the old organ was borne to my ears like funeral music; and the rooks, as they hovered about the grey tower and swung in the bare trees of the priory garden, seemed to call to me that the place was changed, and that Estella was gone out of it for ever.
> (p. 407)

Although Pip's description is actually based firmly in Dickens's recollections of Rochester, such is the power of Satis in the novel that the Gothic details of its barred windows, darkened rooms, and entrapped maidens diffuse themselves into and take over the real-life topography. Pip's poignant confession to Estella that she has been in every prospect he has ever seen (p. 378) is amply borne out by this coloring of the land to which she and Miss Havisham have laid waste, a devastation confirmed by the final destruction of the house and the text's refusal to support unequivocally any hope that its hero may indeed rescue the maiden from the ruins. And yet, despite the bleakness of these Gothic forms offered by Satis, Miss Havisham, and Estella, in Wemmick's Walworth home we are allowed to feel a world in which a harmonious resolution of the parent-child relationship empowers a rewriting, a taming of the Gothic.

Wemmick's enchanting castle, with its moat, abundant estate, and inimitable pig, may well be a gentle parody of that Victorian craze for the medieval in domestic architecture, but it is also quite precisely an inversion of the Gothic image of Satis. It is at Walworth that Pip finds sanctuary when his world appears to be collapsing upon him and the visits he pays to the Wemmicks and Miss Skiffins are by far the most endearing episodes in the novel. And yet, although Satis and Walworth appear to be two quite opposed versions of Gothic, they are, in fact, closely linked; if, for example, it is in Walworth that Pip begins his plans to assist Herbert to a career, it is from Satis that the means to complete them will eventually come. Though the tone of the narrative is very different when dealing with these two Gothic citadels, the assumption upon which each regime is founded is identical—that the parental authority must remain imprisoned for the child to be released. Dickens's mid-Victorian Gothic is a far gentler thing than Mary Shelley's, though also a less urgent, quieter version of the impulses which so relentlessly drive Victor and the Monster to both their dooms and their unique power and stature. Nevertheless, it too centers upon that conflict between tyrannical parent and supplanting child which is central to *Frankenstein*. What finally distinguishes *Great Expectations* from both Shelley's text and much of Dickens's own earlier work is the very presence of Walworth, a sanctum in which the perennial conflict between parent and offspring is subsumed by the greater power of the love that exists between Wemmick and his father. And it is this taming of the Gothic impulse which is in keeping with the two novels' very different treatments of *Paradise Lost*, with the manner in which they respond, or fail to respond, to the ur-text of Christian tradition, the Bible, and, finally, with the relationship Pip and Magwitch will at last come to achieve.

Pip's initial response to the notion that Magwitch is his creator, however, is certainly hostile and, even in the plan to help the convict flee, we may detect something of Victor's covert desire to rid himself of those closest to him. For the escape is surely a fiasco: Pip's involvement in the actual mechanics of the operation, his failure to throw pursuit off the track by any diversion, and, above all, his refusal to be warned by the figures who lurk around the boat, are all appalling blunders that, despite Wemmick's later assertion of the impossibility of getting Magwitch away (p. 461), surely hint at Pip's underlying complicity in his patron's capture and death. For it is precisely this recapture which removes Magwitch from Pip's life, frees him of the burden of his creator, and, most importantly of all, allows Pip to express the love he certainly does feel for the man who gave him being. Like Victor, Pip acquiesces in an outcome his conscious self would reject; like the Monster, he can be reconciled to his maker only at the end of the latter's life; and, like the Gothic Wemmick, he achieves control over his "parent" by consigning him to imprisonment. But, unlike Victor or the Monster and yet like Wemmick once again, he can also admit that his feelings for his alter-ego are positive as well as negative and we surely question neither the truth nor the sincerity of his final love for Magwitch. This is an older, wiser, more compassionate Pip, who has learned profoundly from his life, grown, and both understands and loves the man who has, in the fullest sense, made him what he is. How does this come about? How can Pip reconcile the apparently contradictory impulses within him? The answer is to be found in the novel's final intertext, the Bible, an authority to which Pip's entire narrative gives precedence and which it most certainly does not attempt to rewrite.

While the opening of the novel is indeed redolent of the language of Wordsworthian Romanticism, it is even more significantly, if less overtly, colored by the tones of the Bible. For, if both Magwitch's starting up from and subsequent near return to the grave and Pip's explosion into self-consciousness remind us of the Monster's creation, they also find strong scriptural parallels. The day, as we soon learn, is Christmas Eve and, even on these marshes, is one marked by forms of birth, the bearing of gifts, and the presence of a guardian Angel. An even more exact biblical parallel is to be noted in the links between both Pip and Magwitch and the story of Lazarus: not only do Pip's brothers number five, as did those of the rich man who spurned Lazarus at his door, but they also include an Abraham—in whose bosom Lazarus at last finds rest. And Lazarus, moreover, is an entirely appropriate analogue for Magwitch, the beggarly outcast from society who will achieve grace at the last. Finally, the religious subtext is further strengthened both when Pip sees Magwitch as "torn by briars" (p. 36) and when the convict defines himself as an Angel in comparison with the lurking young man. If the novel's version of the biblical text seems far removed from the original, such is precisely the point, for these characters have much to undergo before they can come into divine grace. At this point in their lives, neither Pip nor Magwitch seems aware of the implications latent within their allusive language; the narrator's encoding of the scene in such religious terms would seem to imply both his own subsequent spiritual growth and his belief that an overseeing Providence was operating even upon such an unlikely occasion as this.

When Magwitch next appears in the action, moreover, both he and Pip are evidently still in a state of emotional and spiritual lack of grace. Though he may have returned from that new world the Victorians so readily fantasized into a healing Arcadia,[19] Magwitch's true condition is superbly epitomized in the "greasy little clasped black Testament" (p. 349) that he always carries with him but which, as Pip notes, he appears to regard merely as "a sort of legal spell or charm" to guarantee the swearing of any oath. Pip himself, absorbed in the whole notion of his expectations and obsessed with Estella, may be refined and elegant but is otherwise little better than his maker. Nevertheless, in the few months they spend together, these two men, whose entire lives have been governed by fantasies now under such assault from reality, will not only find peace with one another but also come to see the insignificance of their desires when set against the larger truth of divine Providence.

It is Pip who must lead the way here, since he has at least been educated and trained to be more receptive to conventional religion than the outcast convict and may thus return Magwitch's gifts in a manner their donor little anticipates. His spiritual development is crucially assisted by a growing understanding of and sympathy for Miss Havisham, and in this we see again that characteristic emphasis in Dickens upon charity as the central tenet of Christianity. Freed from the burden of perceiving her as his creator, Pip can see Miss Havisham with newly-opened eyes as a woman whose entire life has been an appalling waste:

> I knew not how to answer, or how to comfort her. That she had done a grievous thing in taking an impressionable child to mould into the form that her wild resentment, spurned affection, and wounded pride, found vengeance in, I knew full well. But that, in shutting out the light of day, she had shut out infinitely more; that, in seclusion, she had secluded herself from a thousand natural and healing influences; that, her mind, brooding solitary, had grown diseased, as all minds do and must and will that reverse the appointed order of their Maker; I knew equally well. And could I look upon her without compassion, seeing her punishment in the ruin she was, in her profound unfitness for this earth on which she was placed. (p. 411)

It is this new understanding that is so instrumental both in Pip's transformation into the character who can create such a profoundly sympathetic narrative and which frees him from that cycle of revenge in which Victor and his Monster remain trapped. Before he can finally blend this capacity into his relationship with Magwitch, however, he must reconcile it with that forensic process of questioning which has been such an important motive for him.

Of all people, it is Jaggers who teaches him the greater wisdom of allowing appropriate fictions to stand in place of the unduly naked truth.[20] For, after Pip has at last succeeded in outwitting his guardian by obtaining information that even he had not known, Jaggers admonishes him to think of the effect upon Estella of revealing Miss Havisham's, and her, secret. Taking as his text Matthew 5:30, Jaggers advises Pip rather to cut off his own hands than let her know the secret of her parentage (p. 426), and it is thus the Sermon on the Mount, Dickens's own favorite piece of scripture, that is evoked as Pip draws towards the end of his relationship with his earthly maker and which sets the tone for this last phase of the novel.

Magwitch's reform is heralded at his trial where the bond between himself and Pip is clearly one both rejoice in and which they deliberately set apart from the ritual of the courtroom and the social world it represents. When all is said and done and the thirty-two prisoners at the bar have been sentenced to die, Magwitch rises and, standing in that beam of light so much a part of popular religious iconography, entrusts himself into the hands of God with the only words he makes in his defense: "My Lord, I have received my sentence of Death from the Almighty, but I bow to yours" (p. 467). From here, it is but a short step to one of the more successful death-beds of Victorian fiction, a scene that is not only effective in its own right but also, crucially, inverts its counterpart in *Frankenstein*. There, unrepentant pride and despair leave the creator tormented to the end, and his Monster racked with penitential remorse and impelled towards suicide. Here, we find both the loving reconciliation of creator and created and also, of especial value in a novel where fact and fantasy have existed in such a precarious relationship, the supreme generosity of Pip's bestowing upon Magwitch the lovingly selfless illusion that Estella, found and a lady, will marry the son, gentleman, and heir. None, surely, would deny Magwitch this final consolation and yet we should also recognize both that Pip's action marks his own emancipation from the illusion and, even more significantly, that the scene does not end on this note of fine sentiment. For the chapter in fact concludes with Pip's apostrophe over Magwitch: "Mindful, then, of what we had read together, I thought of the two men who went up into the Temple to pray, and I knew there were no better words that I could say beside his bed, than 'O Lord, be merciful to him, a sinner!' " (p. 470).[21] The reader, continuing the allusion to Luke 18, can also complete the text by reading on—"this man went down to his house justified . . . he that humbleth himself shall be exalted"—and thus shape the perfect cycle of the novel as a whole with the knowledge that Magwitch indeed now rests in Abraham's bosom.

With this final reconciliation of creator and created we find that

Dickens's text has comprehensively rewritten Shelley's *Frankenstein*. The monster and his maker have been, first, confused in one another and then, each coming to recognize the other's true identity, fused in a love which embraces the human and the divine. If Pip might well have begun by lamenting his creator's having raised him out of preconscious obscurity, he concludes by acknowledging, with a full heart, that the thing of darkness is most truly his. Unlike Prospero, he has not burned his book, but rather taken the subtler course of reshaping Mary Shelley's novel as a parable for nineteenth-century England in which the virtues of the New Testament speak out powerfully against the dehumanizing tendencies of a class-ridden society. Pip's success is indeed to be qualified. Cairo notwithstanding, he remains a gentleman with little true interest in that work ethic upon which Victorian prosperity rested, and he is thus wed only to a social code that would become ever more out-dated. Nor, of course, will he have children, and natural selection thereby passes its verdict on both him and his species. Nevertheless, he has grown wise and found grace not hereafter but in human life, and it is this growth which enables him to create a narrative that so finely blends trauma and healing, loss and recovery, comedy and elegy. His expectations of fortune and Estella as his bride may be well lost, but those of a larger salvation are, indeed, well-founded, and it is surely this fact which accounts for the manner in which a novel whose content might appear bleak becomes richly moving in its tones, able both to leave Paradise with equanimity and to accept the Monster who waits beyond.[22]

NOTES

[1]Harold Bloom, *The Anxiety of Influence: A Theory of Poetry* (New York: Oxford Univ. Press, 1973), p. 5.

[2]*The Anxiety of Influence,* ch. 2, "Tessera or Completion and Antithesis."

[3]*Edinburgh Magazine,* 11 (March 1818); cited in R. Glynn Grylls, *Mary Shelley: A Biography* (London: Oxford Univ. Press, 1938), p. 317.

[4]*Hansard's Parliamentary Debates,* n.s. 10 (1824): 1103.

[5]See George Levine and U.C. Knoepflmacher's invaluable collection of essays, *The Endurance of Frankenstein: Essays on Mary Shelley's Novel* (Berkeley: Univ. of California Press, 1979). Sterrenburg's "Mary Shelley's Monster: Politics and Psyche in *Frankenstein*" is on pp. 143-71.

[6]Dickens's ownership of the Bentley series is evidenced in the 1844 inventory of his library which is reproduced in *The Letters of Charles Dickens,* ed. Madeline House, Graham Storey, Kathleen Tillotson, et al., 6 vols. (Oxford: Clarendon Press, 1965-), 4:711-25. His epistolary echo of Mary Shelley is noted by Lawrence Frank in *Charles Dickens and the Romantic Self* (Lincoln and London: Univ. of Nebraska Press, 1984), p. 35, and is to be found in *Letters,* 4: 618-19. The allusion in *The Haunted Man* is noted in *The Endurance of Frankenstein*, pp. 22-23.

[7]Charles Dickens, *Great Expectations,* ed. Angus Calder (Harmondsworth: Penguin Books, 1965), p. 240. Subsequent references will be included parenthetically.

[8]The principal discussions of the novel's debt to *Frankenstein* are J. Hillis Miller, *Charles Dickens: The World of His Novels* (Cambridge, Mass.: Harvard Univ. Press, 1958), pp. 272-73; Levine's introductory essay to his and Knoepflmacher's collection, especially pp. 21-22; and Chris Baldick's *In Frankenstein's Shadow: Myth, Monstrosity, and Nineteenth-century Writing* (Oxford: Clarendon Press, 1987), especially pp. 117-20.

[9]*Frankenstein or The Modern Prometheus,* ed. M.K. Joseph (Oxford and New York: Oxford Univ. Press, 1969; paperback edn. 1980), pp.135-38. Subsequent references will be inserted parenthetically.

[10]John Milton, *Paradise Lost and Selected Poetry and Prose,* ed. Northrop Frye (New York: Rinehart, 1951), X, 743-45.

[11]U.C. Knoepflmacher, "Mutations of the Wordsworthian Child of Nature," in U.C. Knoepflmacher and G.B. Tennyson, eds., *Nature and the Victorian Imagination* (Berkeley: Univ. of California Press, 1977), pp. 391-425.

[12]*Nature and the Victorian Imagination,* p. 424.

[13]Robin Gilmour, *The Idea of the Gentleman in the Victorian Novel* (London: George Allen and Unwin, 1981); Shirley Robin Letwin, *The Gentleman in Trollope: Individuality and Moral Conduct* (London: Macmillan, 1982).

[14]Dickens's own sense of the remarkable yet precarious achievements of Victorian civilization is evident in many of the remarks of his later years, from the opening sentences of *Hard Times* to such speeches as that he made to the Newsvendors' Benevolent Institution on 9 May 1865; see *The Speeches of Charles Dickens,* ed. K.J. Fielding (Oxford: Clarendon Press, 1960), p. 340.

[15]Gillian Beer, *Darwin's Plots: Evolutionary Narrative in Darwin, George Eliot and Nineteenth-Century Fiction* (London: Routledge & Kegan Paul, 1983), passim. The *AYR* article, "Natural Selection," appeared on 7 July 1860; 3: 293-99.

[16]*Darwin's Plots,* p. 111.

[17]Dennis Walder, *Dickens and Religion* (London: George Allen and Unwin, 1981), passim.

[18]Discussions of intertextuality in the two novels include Harold Bloom, "Frankenstein, or the New Prometheus," *Partisan Review* 32 (1965): 611-18; Burton R. Pollin, "Philosophical and Literary Sources of *Frankenstein,*" *CL* 17 (1965): 97-108; Elliot L. Gilbert, "'In Primal Sympathy': *Great Expectations* and the Secret Life," *DSA* 11 (1983): 89-113; and Harry Stone, *Dickens and the Invisible World: Fairy Tales Fantasy, and Novel-Making* (London: Macmillan, 1980), pp. 298-339.

[19]The best discussion of this Victorian myth is to be found in Coral Lansbury's *Arcady in Australia* (Melbourne: Univ. of Melbourne Press, 1970). Dickens himself ran a number of articles in *All the Year Round* on the rich opportunities of the Antipodes; see, for example, "A Piece of Blood-Money," *AYR* 1 (20 August 1859): 394-96, or "A Two-Year Old Colony," *AYR* 5 (22 June 1861): 294-97.

[20]See Anthony Winner's essay, "Character and Knowledge in Dickens: The Enigma of Jaggers," *DSA* 3 (1974): 100-21, for a full discussion of Jaggers on lines similar to those I suggest here.

[21]See Walder's discussion of this scene in *Dickens and Religion,* p. 203. I follow Walder in my interpretation of the text here, rather than Julian

Moynahan's suggestion of a distancing irony at Pip's expense; see "The Hero's Guilt: the Case of *Great Expectations*," *EIC* 10 (1960): 60-79.

[22]Several of my friends and colleagues greatly helped me in developing this essay and I should like to thank here: the members of the Faculty Colloquium of the English Department at the University of Alabama; Henry E. Jacobs; Donald R. Noble Jr.; Robert L. Patten; John Tibbetts; Mack L. Smith; and Mirjana Zec.

SEL 28 (1988)
ISSN 0039-3657

Mark Lemon's Farces on the "Woman Question"

LEONA W. FISHER

Victorian critics were generally in agreement that the stage was a low, debased form of entertainment, its producers not to be called artists. Indeed, twentieth-century readers and playgoers notice that there are no great, producing playwrights to be found between Oliver Goldsmith and George Bernard Shaw. While we may view Victorian farces and melodramas as insipid and noncontroversial, contemporary critics frequently saw them as immoral and even dangerous, as an 1851 article in *The Theatrical Journal* demonstrates. Entitled "The Stage—Its Impurity," the piece proceeds in a tone of high moral dudgeon:

> The stage certainly wants purifying. There is much that is offensive to refined taste, and discordant with a pure morality. It panders to the lowest passions of man, and responds to promptings that ought to be repressed. It exhibits the path of wrong in an alluring light, and sneers at immortal virtue. This wickedness we will never wink at but it shall at all times receive our most earnest condemnation.
>
> We would like to know why we cannot have a pure stage? Is there a positive necessity for moral filth? Have playgoers an irrepressible penchant for sensuality, disgusting impudence, and the vernacular of Billingsgate?[1]

The reason for the defection of serious writers from the stage during the early Victorian period is, perhaps, partly to be found in the impossible canons of taste and propriety imposed upon the literary artist. This gap was, of course, not unknown in other eras, the Restoration among them, but the Victorians seem to have had a particularly tight control over stage manners and mores regard-

Leona Fisher is Associate Professor of English and Co-ordinator of Women's Studies at Georgetown University. She is the author of *Lemon, Dickens, and "Mr. Nightingale's Diary": A Victorian Farce* (1988).

ing sexuality; after all, even revivals of Shakespeare included the deletion of bawdy language and the substitution of "happy" endings.[2] Those who might have produced successful plays converted their energies into other genres, especially the novel—where the rules of propriety of course followed them, but with a difference.

Charles Dickens, himself an actor and playwright, helped to shape and preserve Victorian verbal delicacy in regard to sexual or gender-related topics. While in *Our Mutual Friend* (1865) he could ironically comment on the "cheek of the young person" and the need to protect it from a blush, each of his novels illustrates the premise that sexual crime does not pay—and dare not go unpunished in the world of Dickens's novels, as in Victorian society. Despite this sentimental approach to sexual complexity, however, Dickens's novels do offer us courageous and incisive social criticism, even of marriage and the family, while in the eight or nine plays Dickens wrote or collaborated on, propriety reigns—even at the sacrifice of plot and substance. As Edgar and Eleanor Johnson have described them, "Whatever vitality these [plays] may have had in the nineteenth century has trickled out of them, leaving flabby and lifeless dummies."[3] Whether or not we agree with the Johnsons' extreme judgment, we do not expect to find representative dramatic virtues and defects in the narrow range of Dickens's plays.

In the plays of his friend and colleague Mark Lemon, whose works Dickens approved and encouraged, we do have a chance to see the scope, the best as well as the worst, of mid-nineteenth-century English drama, including its relationship to family and sexuality. A middle-class Victorian gentleman, Lemon wrote plays in order to support a large family (eventually spirited away to the suburbs to save them from the temptations of London); he wrote, translated, adapted, or collaborated on more than eighty dramatic works between 1836 and 1867: operas, burlettas, extravaganzas, melodramas, burlesques, and farces.

But before I turn to three of these plays on the "woman question," I would like to look at Mark Lemon as the editor of *Punch* magazine during the first twenty-nine years of its existence, since he was chosen by his colleagues for that position because he combined consistent integrity with genial humility—a middle-class standard of morality with a keen sense of humor (even when that wit was turned in self-parody on his own Philistine class). The "code" of the *Punch* school of journalism was, according to a *Times Literary Supplement* reviewer in 1929, a narrow and "male" one: "Among the jokes that 'are not done' are the 39 of the 40 possible jokes that cannot . . . be told to ladies. On the other hand, the one possible joke is exquisitely turned out. . . . Invective, sarcasm and the fiercer forms of satire"[4] were inappropriate to the maintenance of Victorian decorum. "It may sacrifice what the codeless world would be capable of calling 'punch'; but how much that is essentially unpleasant is eliminated therewith!" Lemon would have been proud to reaffirm the periodical's absence of malice and spirit of noncontroversial optimism, although he would also have defended *Punch*'s appeal to the critical intellect and the social conscience.

Gentle, essentially positive commentary and caricature, rather than nasty satire, defined *Punch*'s early days. But its 1851 issue on the Crystal Palace Exhibition, for example, also reveals the philosophical firmness of Mark Lemon's editorial policy. Difficult topics are not eschewed: war, class-consciousness, nationalism and patriotism, racism, marital relations, the habits of women, and Prince Albert are all touched lightly with satirical pen and brush. The Crystal Palace itself merits some raillery: there are comments on the desirability of allowing beer to flow in its fountains, and the suggestion that the erection of a "glass bowl" over all of London would insure peace and preservation. Included is Mr. Punch's (and Lemon's own) moral: "That the different nations of the world, and the different classes of society, might meet oftener, with much advantage to each other." This kindly philosophy could be condescendingly paternalistic, but this issue even half-seriously gives the following advice:

> The wives and daughters of England are unfortunately very averse to using their legs, except for the purpose of executing Schottisches, Polkas, and so forth; hence doctor's bills of stupendous amount. But as natural curiosity will take ladies all round the Exhibition, . . . they will be forced to walk the whole distance. The reward of this exertion will be bloom in the cheek, brilliancy in the glance, warmth in the extremities, appetite for dinner, and domestic happiness, by reason of a saving of many fees, effected by an economical investment in a few tickets.[5]

It is the joke that could be told, of course, but it recommends quite sensibly that increased exercise would benefit both the "legs" (not the more innocuous "limbs") and the dispositions of the sedentary sex. As Professor Arthur Adrian points out in his biography of Lemon, most of the *Punch* "club" held the "Victorian attitude" toward women and took "the conservative Victorian stand" on women's suffrage.[6] But they were also capable of submerged wisdom, if only in the interest of laughter or the unconscious exposure of a problem.[7]

Although subject both to self-censorship and the licensing of the Lord Chamberlain, Lemon's plays likewise reveal a far-ranging awareness of significant political and social controversies. For example, *The M.P. for the Rotten Borough* (1838) satirizes methods of choosing members of Parliament, while *Domestic Economy* (1841) examines husband-wife relations and the management of the household. *Knight and the Sprite; or, The Cold Water Cure* (1844) puns on a new method of popular medical treatment (a ship sinks: hence the "cold water cure"), while *The Camp at Chobham* (1853) makes farce of the conduct of the Crimean War. Gamblers are chastised in the drama *Hearts are Trumps* (1849) and gossips are exposed in *Mind Your Own Business; or, The Man of Tact* (1852).

Particularly interesting for the examination of both sexual propriety and male-female relations are Lemon's three plays dealing explicitly with women's rights: first, *The Ladies' Club* (1840); then, *The House of Ladies* (also 1840) and its revised version, *The Petticoat Parliament* (1867).[8] Although almost thirty years apart, the first and last plays predictably make the same point: clubs and Parliament properly "belong" to men—even though men have not fulfilled the responsibilities of that privilege. The pieces are slight, designed as after-pieces to full-length plays, but their messages are surprisingly subtle, at least in their subtexts, which reveal a complexity and ambivalence, even naughtiness, that Lemon may not have intended. They raise and expose the very possibilities for impropriety (on the part of "ladies") that they are consciously designed to ridicule and refute.[9]

Of all dramatic forms, farce (and its musical relatives: burletta, burlesque, and extravaganza)[10] may be best suited for breaking down sexual codes and manners. Because of their reliance on fantasy and the incredible incident, these forms can mask their serious issues with frivolity, self-parody, and musical spectacle, trivializing their serious concerns, and rendering morbid or sentimental their lighter themes. They thereby protect their point of view from both the censors and the audience, who miss the danger and let the vulgarity pass.

Mark Lemon's two-act burletta *The Ladies' Club,* presented at the Olympic Theatre on 25 February 1840, is typical of early Victorian farce. Witty language, especially word play; cross-dressing, disguises and secret plots; ethnic and racial stage business and accents; and ludicrous male-female role reversals—all take attention away from the serious domestic problem that the play addresses: women are being deserted by husbands who claim to be "going to the club" while engaging in undisclosed, vaguely immoral activities.

After the servants' introduction of the issue, Major and Mrs. Mortar argue about his persistent absences, and three more of the ladies burst in, complaining passionately about their husbands' desertion of home and hearth. Finally, the central character Mrs. Fitzsmyth arrives, dismisses her husband with delight, and has a pre-arranged tete-a-tete with the dandy, Sir Charles Lavender. She wittily blackmails Lavender into helping the women plot against the wayward men, then declares: "Come ladies, I'll be your leader,—for tho' to arms unknown, women can conquer by their wits alone!" (*Ladies*, p. 6). Vowing "Death rather than unsatisfied curiosity" (*Ladies*, p. 15), two of the women disguise themselves and infiltrate the men's club, overhearing an incriminating conversation. After a confrontation over the men's sins, the husbands repent and plan a conciliatory dinner. Meanwhile, the women have begun to lose cohesiveness as each attacks the others' husbands. But they nonetheless proceed to form a "Ladies' Club," with Mrs. Fitzsmyth as "Chairwoman," in order to teach the men a lesson. Reversing the plot, the men enter surreptitiously and overhear the proceedings, including the women's bickering. But all is finally reconciled in this tit-for-tat structure, as the men promise "more home" and "less club."

Insignificant as the piece may seem, on one level the "ladies" do seem to win their battle without fundamentally relinquishing their dignity or their moral ascendancy. Even their two brief skirmishes among themselves are resolved, as in Aristophanes' *Lysistrata*, by a sense of their common purpose—and by Mrs. Fitzsmyth's leadership.[11]

But the play's language, both conscious wit and unconscious buffoonery, seeks to undermine our sympathy for them from the beginning. For example, the ladies' case and presence are repeatedly devalued by syllepsis or zeugma—used by Lemon, as well as Dickens, as a form of comic implied metaphor. The rhetorical figure syllepsis is a grammatical construction in which a single word, usually a verb or adjective, is used to modify or govern syntactically two or more words in the same sentence, though the word literally agrees with only one of them. The figure is related to zeugma, used by Alexander Pope and other satirists to set up compact juxtapositions with a comic effect. Thus Pope's Belinda in *The Rape of the Lock* may "stain her *honor* or her new *brocade*" (Canto II, line 107) or "lose her *heart* or *necklace*, at a ball" (line 109) [emphasis mine].

Similarly, Lemon's wits (usually servants) use zeugma to analyze and render ludicrous a character or situation. Thus, before we learn the justice of Mrs. Mortar's cause, the servant Flammer introduces her as "descending the chromatic scale, and the stairs, at the same time" (*Ladies*, p. 8). Mrs. Derby arrives "in tears, and a hackney coach"; and Mrs. Twankay, "in a rage, and— . . . a bonnet!" (*Ladies*, p. 11). One automatically suspects that Mrs. Mortar is conscious of both her singing and her descent, that Mrs. Derby considers her hackney coach indispensable to her desired effect, and that Mrs. Twankay's bonnet is integral to her rage. Or at least, we sense that the perceptive and witty Flammer sees through the ladies' agony to their superficiality and lack of self-consciousness. Sir Charles Lavender confirms this satiric use of syllepsis when he later tells Mrs. Fitzsmyth that he will deny her nothing "from my heart to my tiger!" (i.e., his valet—*Ladies*, p. 15).

In contrast, the women's language at first seeks to establish their injured innocence, however histrionically, with such words as "brute," "destroyed," "wretches." But once Mrs. Mortar and Mrs. Derby have eavesdropped on the men, the women turn viciously against one another and defend those same brutes and wretches. Each tries to outdo the others—criticizing their husbands while defending her own spouse.

Mrs. M. Well . . . my dear Mrs. Twankay, your horrid Mr.T.—

. . . .

Mrs. M. Spoke in the most affectionate terms of two little ebony cherubs. . . .

Mrs. T. Cherubs! the black monster! . . .

. . . .

Mrs. F. For my part, I always suspected Twankay; for he creeps about the house, like a cat stealing cream. . . .

Mrs. T. Mr. Twankay, ladies, may have his failings, but he is still a gentleman.

Mrs. F. My dear, I hope I've said nothing to annoy you; but I always find it extremely agreeable to abuse my husband, when I am out of temper. Well, my dear Mortar?

Mrs. M. As for Mrs. Derby—but I won't wound the feelings of Mrs. D. by a repetition of her husband's failings.

Mrs. F. Oh, my dear, don't deny us our only consolation.

Mrs. D. (*aside.*) Savages! I shall go into hysterics.

Mrs. M. Well then, Mr. Derby, is very partial to Brompton. . . . There can be but one opinion as to its attraction.

Omnes. Oh, dear no! . . .

Mrs. F. Well, ladies, as Mrs. Derby, *does not* believe it——it would be cruel to try and persuade her, though I *do* think if it was Fitz, I should draw a very different conclusion. . . .

Mrs. D. Mrs. Mortar, ladies, has forgotten to inform you that the major, once had the honor of being beloved by a washerwoman.

Mrs. M. No, Mrs. Derby, the person was not a washerwoman.

. . . .

Mrs. F. Delightful automaton! Really ladies, you seem to have made some very fortunate selections.

Mrs. D. . . . We have not married men whom we are ashamed to own.

Mrs. F. O, bless you, I'm not ashamed of Fitz!—not I, a dear little goose.

Mrs. M. The butt of the clubs!

Mrs. F. Is he? Well, I'm delighted to hear he is so useful.

(*Ladies,* pp. 22-23)

The scene grimly demonstrates a clichéd notion of women's rivalry and inability to support one another. The reason that propelled them toward Mrs. Mortar's house in the opening scene has abandoned them—and their need to defend the men on whom they depend, financially and socially, asserts itself. Only Mrs. Fitzsmyth is free of this compulsion, and presumably because she does not uphold the fiction of romantic love. She doesn't depend on Mr. Fitzsmyth for either her livelihood or her self-worth.

This failure of female power and bonding is strongest in the Ladies' Club scene, in which they argue over amendments; their disagreement allows Mr. Twankay to comment, "I thought they couldn't agree long," and Major Mortar to respond, "They never do at home" (*Ladies*, p. 29). Silly, irrational, argumentative, and competitive, these women (who began with a legitimate complaint) have been set up by Lemon to undermine their own just cause.

This farce/burletta conforms perfectly to the criteria common to farce and comedy in the Victorian period, as defined by Michael Booth in *English Plays of the Nineteenth Century, Volume Four: Farces*, especially the "glorification of the domestic ideal, and the assertion of the husband's rightful authority over his wife."[12] Perhaps even more important for our discernment of Mark Lemon's point of view in the play is Booth's claim that "All farce is fantasy; all farce must involve its audience in this fantasy as well as indicate clearly that it *is* fantasy."[13] In this case the play makes clear the absurdity of the situation: women would never join together in clubs because they could never agree long enough to form such a bond. As Maurice Charney has phrased his definition of farce in *Comedy High and Low*: "Farce may be the purest, quintessential comedy, since it so rigorously excludes any sentiment at all, especially feelings of sympathy, compassion, or empathy for the characters. It is also unintellectual, unpsychological, and uncomplex. . . . The prevailing mood is one of a world gone mad, or at least a world where wish-fulfillment fantasies are acted out by the characters."[14] Applied to Mark Lemon's choice of genre for his exploration of marriage, these definitions confirm that the formation of a "ladies club" is a short-term, fantastic strategy designed merely to challenge the men and to reestablish domestic equilibrium. It will not (and should not) effect a revolution of values and structures. An audience would feel no complex challenge from such an outlandish plot, because they could not imagine the action to be plausible, much less significant or threatening. They would see no impropriety in behavior, because the ladies merely confirm the stereotype of female hysteria and capitulation. Thus one seasoned theater-goer, Henry Crabb Robinson, saw the farce as merely "an amusing squib against the clubs. Nothing offensive in it."[15] Likewise, the *Times* reviewer claimed that the play contained "no low vulgarism or obscenity, . . . and it is refreshing to find a modern burletta at which ladies can laugh without blushing, and gentlemen enjoy merriment without being disgusted."[16] Neither Crabb Robinson nor the anonymous reviewer saw the potential offensiveness in the play's themes and language.

But Mark Lemon should both be given credit for something more than mere inoffensiveness—since the play also reexamines the clichés and imagined impropriety—and criticized for perpetuating a mood of decorous hypocrisy. Like all farce at its best, *The Ladies' Club* is not so innocuous as the reviewers believed. As the few theorists of farce have noticed, farce lives on the edges of other genres, and establishes a dialectic between surface and substance, conflict and resolution, revolt and convention.[17] As a genre in tension simultaneously with the pathos of tragedy and the grotesqueness of comedy, for example, farce in the last century began to assert its immunity from censorship. It could flirt with the ugly underside of human behavior, as well as with iconoclasm and radical social schemes—so long as its conclusions reaffirmed a centrist, bourgeois *status quo*.

Here, for instance, Lemon had to expose the gentlemen's ethical weaknesses in order to construct the plot; and the themes of illegitimacy, racism, adultery, and prostitution are therefore included in the men's conversation at the men's club in Act I. Twankay declares, "I expect the two little ebony cherubs over by the next ship. Of course as a father I shall provide for them"

(*Ladies*, p. 19). The Major, excusing Twankay and himself on the grounds that "imprudence" characterizes the young, adds that he is periodically visited by a previous paramour disguised as a washerwoman, who had been the "wife of a tailor" when Mortar "ran away" with her. Derby seems to be engaged in an extramarital affair at Brompton, and all the men ask Sir Charles Lavender to introduce them to Mademoiselle Entrechat, surely a courtesan for whom Lavender acts as procurer.

Add to all this that the milksop Captain Fitzsmyth brags of "pulveriz[ing]" his wife, that the men are gambling as they speak, and that they mean to indulge themselves at the ballet (certainly a euphemism, since it included "dancers") without their wives—and the picture of upper-middle-class male morality is thoroughly damning. The scene is closer to brutal exaggeration than to innocuous fantasy, and the men are revealed as liars, cheats, hypocrites, braggarts, voluptuaries. The two disguised women are allowed to overhear this conversation—responding with some shock, but few blushes, since they return with obvious relish to tell the other women. Only a thin veneer of gentility separates this club scene from a locker room conversation, and yet the women have difficulty sustaining their outrage and each fiercely defends her husband. A touch of almost French "bedroom" cynicism intrudes on the humor in Act I, but contemporary critics may have missed the offensiveness because the stock sex roles prevail: "boys will be boys" and "must sow their wild oats"; "girls'" primary loyalties are to men, not to other women.

Less palatable to Victorian taste, one would have thought, is the characterization of the rebellious and controversial Mrs. Fitzsmyth. Her "Somewhat suspicious!" (*Ladies*, p. 14) meeting with Charles Lavender suggests adultery; and even as she betrays her husband, she also confirms her role reversal with the effete Lavender: "My dear fellow, don't look alarmed; ha, ha! you'll positively spoil your dimples!" (*Ladies*, p. 15), making implicit fun of her own sex—which practiced smirking before mirrors—but also humiliating the elegant fop. Mrs. Fitzsmyth has certainly been encouraging Sir Charles's attentions, to further her plot against the husbands, and she also declares very disloyally that her home situation is "unfortunate" and that "Fitzsmyth is neither useful nor ornamental" (*Ladies*, p. 14).

Beyond her sexual indiscretion, Mrs. Fitzsymth could offend because she is in charge throughout the play, and through a gender reversal serves as Lemon's chief vehicle of male wit and irony. Like Aristophanes' Lysistrata, she knows her own sex and refuses to succumb to the stereotype. She has chosen to marry Captain Smyth, adding the "Fitz" for glamour, because he is "very docile, obedient, and wealthy." She calls him her "lord and master" with conscious irony, declaring in the next breath: "I want a slave, and not a master" (*Ladies*, p. 13). Her methods are not typically "feminine"—that is, naive or cunning; she is direct, verbally adept, and courageous. Her realism declares that "faithless husbands have been known to exist" (*Ladies*, p. 13) and that their clubs provide cover for the men's vices. In Act II, when the others tell her that Fitz has been bragging about his power over her, she remains distanced: "Well, I never gave him credit for so much courage as that even. It's of no use my dears, you can't make me angry, and I forgive you, for your desire to do so, knowing the cause you have to be vexed yourselves" (*Ladies*, p. 23). Depending on how the actress delivers this last line, it can be either straightforwardly magnanimous and disinterested, or devastatingly cool and sarcastic; in either interpretation, she wins this round as well.

But most importantly (again, like Lysistrata), she also believes fundamentally in the women's potential power and cleverness. First she devises the scheme, manipulating a man to achieve it; then she states the women's purpose and goals to the men; finally, she prevents her husband from speaking during the closing rhymed couplets, and has the last word in the play—thereby reasserting her central place in the plot and leaving us the final image of a tough-minded, influential woman. With right (and the playwright, apparently) on her side, Mrs. Fitzsmyth can afford to set her terms: "this is *our* club-room, and we shall appeal to a court of honor, to justify our proceedings, and to judge of yours" (*Ladies*, p. 31). Echoing Aristophanes' classic depiction of the war-between-the-sexes-to-end-all-wars, Major Mortar surrenders: "Gentlemen! my experience tells me that a treaty is better than a war—for one, I accept the condition. More home, and less club" (*Ladies*, p. 31).

"Less club" tells us that the women have won—but what have they achieved? Mrs. Fitzsmyth can be tolerated (in small doses) because the women have gained only the increased attendance of their husbands at the home fires (a dubious accomplishment, given the men's apparent characters). The men promise moral amendment, too, but certainly do not intend to relinquish their ascendancy or withdraw from their clubs. Just as adultery and illegitimacy have merely signified minor domestic disruption, so the reinstitution of marital tranquility symbolizes no fundamental subversion of conventional domestic rule.

But in fact, to shift the irony once again, Lemon *has* presented the weakened moral condition of the bourgeois gentleman—and the possibility of female solidarity and control. While the farce ultimately reaffirms the conservative ideal of domestic reconciliation, the imagination has been allowed to free itself momentarily from the conventions and to envision a radical state of affairs. As we read or view, the irony turns over at least three times: (1) what seems to be a spoof on the "ladies" turns out to be a serious criticism of the men; yet, (2) what appears to be a "squib against the clubs," does not seriously threaten their perpetuation; but nonetheless, (3) what constitutes a reinstitution of the *status quo* contains within it the fantastic possibility that women can take power, assert their "rights," and win the "war." Because of its successive rereadings of itself, *The Ladies' Club* is one of Mark Lemon's more problematic and interesting farces, comically undermining its own staid conclusion. Linguistically, thematically, and structurally, the play allows its own ambivalence in point of view, and therefore questions its own complacency.

Lemon's second play about the Woman Question, *The House of Ladies*, starts more firmly in the realm of fantasy: women have gained control of the world. Produced only two months after *The Ladies' Club*, this one-act burletta opens on Time and Fancy as they discuss the future—1845, as Fancy describes it:

> *F.* Well, let the vile monopoly of men
> That long with discord hath made earth a den
> Of noisy troubles, for a while give way,
> And leave the earth to women's gentle sway.
>
> *T.* To Women give dominion? Well, that's strange!
> Egad, I'll do it Fancy, for a change!
> For man so long hath murmured at my rule:
> Woman, shall teach the world that man's a fool!
>
> (*House*, Prologue)

The point of view seems firmly opposed to the "vile" mess that men have made of government, but the issue of power itself is suggested by Fancy (who is, of course, a female, stereotypically granted her whim by an indulgent grandfather). Time grants that men have botched the business, but offers the usual Victorian saw about women's true power over males: "Man—tho' the boasted lord, hath been her slave—/From childhood's cradle, even to the grave!" (*House*, Prologue). Since woman has been in control anyway, Time can justify indulging Fancy by granting her wish. Yet the possibility that women could actually run Parliament is so fantastic that the premise for safe farce is built in to the plot.

Furthermore, the play confirms Albert Bermel's generalization about "women in farces," whose "roles . . . make them less prisoners of tradition or convention than the men are."[18] For the length of one act, even the Victorian patriarch could condescend to the ladies, give them their unconventional spell in Parliament.

Joe, Sir Charles Lavender's servant, declares in the play's opening speech: "Well, things be come to a pratty pass—the world seems turned topsy turvy loike! The women ha' got the whip-hand o' the men wi' a vengeance, and I s'pose by and bye they'll do wi'out us altogether!" (*House*, p. 7). Released from their everyday sphere, women have taken over the reins of power: "no lords of the creation now!" says Susan, Mrs. Fitzsmyth's tigress. Joe responds, "men are now nothing more—" and Susan interrupts, "Than women used to be; we are now in the ascendant as missus says—you have to *obey*, whilst *we* have to *cherish*!" (*House*, p. 8).

The women appropriate the clichéd language of male sexual dominance and this turnabout prepares us for a continuation of the conflict from the earlier play, setting up what Jessica Milner Davis calls a "quarrel-farce," in which the ladies' "reversal" at the conclusion of *The Ladies Club* is reversed yet again.[19] Unsatisfied to remain at home, even with their husbands present, the ladies have overturned the structure of power and entered the public sphere. If the two Lemon burlettas are seen as companion or consecutive pieces—and their repeated characters, situation, and intertextual references suggest that they are—then this oscillation can be interpreted as the playwright's rethinking of the earlier conflict: women may give up their clubs, but they will next aspire to political power.

In *The House of Ladies*, Mrs. Fitzsmyth (now conveniently a widow) is a member of Parliament, and "what with the late hours and long speeches, she's been a little ailing" (*House*, p. 9). As Sir Charles Lavender moralizes, "Poor creature! she'll soon discover that place and power are not the beds of roses they appear to be" (*House*, p. 9). But the women have not yet lost their vitality, for Mrs. Fitzsmyth (accompanied by Mrs. Derby, Mrs. Twankay, and Mrs. Bookly) comes to Tattersall's to place her bets on the horses, while the husbands complain of being neglected and patronized. Derby's complaints occasion Mrs. Fitzsmyth's characteristic response: "My dear fellow, don't blame us! For some thousands of years you have had the management of all worldly matters, you were never satisfied with each other, and I really think you ought to be grateful to us for relieving you from your position! Sir Charles, can't you find Derby some employment—clerk of the stud—surveyor of the straw—or inspector of oats?" (*House*, p. 12). Repeating her masculine parody from *The Ladies' Club*, she teases: "Come, Derby, don't be sulky! you know you're an especial favourite of mine! Bless those charming whiskers! (*Tickles him*)" (*House*, p. 12). The men are shocked at the betting and at the ladies' new "privileges," and the scene ends as the women go off to their respective jobs.

Mrs. D.	Derby, you may walk down with me to the House.
Derby.	Of correction—if I had my way!
Mrs. T.	Twankay, you can leave me in Downing Street.
Twan.	I wish I could leave her there till I called for her!
Mrs. B.	Bookly, I'll honor you as far as the Record Office.
Book.	Would that our acquaintance terminated there!
Mrs. F.	Sir Charles, you can drop me at the treasury!
Sir Chas.	The treasury! the paradise of office!

(*House*, p. 13)

The remainder of the play consists of lying to creditors, political backbiting, and a climactic scene in the House of Ladies, in which, after several ludicrous petitions (one on behalf of "the dogs in these realms," *House*, p. 19), the clerk reminds them that the matter before the House is the Rouge Tax. Mrs. Fitzsmyth speaks eloquently in favor of the tax:

> Madam, *Rouge* is the article proposed to be taxed—Rouge—the treacherous ally of the dissipated—Rouge that hides the last lingering light of modesty on the sallow cheek of the midnight scandal-monger—Rouge that ever deceives those who trust to its blandishments! What then can influence the opponents of this tax? Can it be that they officiate as priestess's [sic] at the midnight orgies of Terpsichore and Epicurus? Can it be that divested of all love of country they patronize Souchong and China—the one so destructive to the nerves, the other so inimical to the potteries? No, no, they have the experience of age to guide them, and they should support this tax.
>
> (*House*, p. 20)

Mrs. Derby speaks sarcastically against it, and the debate soon degenerates into a match of witty insults, as both women emphasize beauty and youth, the presumed preoccupations of their sex:

Mrs. D. If by that cheer, the honourable Member for Chatterton means to insinuate the use of Rouge in this House, I distinctly assert that there is no colour for the charge.

Mrs. F. I rise to explain—I have more confidence in the honourable Ladies' age.

Mrs. D. If that observation is intended to apply to me, I at once tell the honorable member for Chatterton, I am *by some months* her *junior.*

Omnes. Question! order.

Speaker. Order!

Mrs. F. I rise to order! The honorable member for Melton has with a singular aptitude for self-annoyance appropriated my remarks to herself. I am at once ready to admit her juvenility, I had almost said *childishness.* As to the use of rouge, that is a secret known only to herself; her looking-glass and her pocket-handkerchief.

(*House*, p. 21)

Soon the whole House is quarrelling, as Derby, Twankay, and Bookly rush gleefully down from the gallery, citing the Ladies' Charter and reasserting men's rights: "Should general dissension occur, their [the women's] present privileges are forfeited for ever!" (*House*, p. 18). The play concludes with Mrs. Fitzsmyth's applying "archly" to the audience to let the "House of Ladies" "sit again" (*House,* p. 22)—referring, of course, to a repeat performance of the farce, but with the secondary implication that the women are not finished suing for their rights.

This play's tensions (and ambivalence) are much less complex than those of *The Ladies' Club*. Since the women hold power from the start, the men are never shown abusing their own privileges. Hence, when the women quarrel, they are merely humiliated, and the cause of women's suffrage and autonomy, simply dismissed. Mrs. Mortar's despair at her creditors' pressure reveals her willingness to regain dependency; the chief issue itself—the Rouge Tax—demeans women and impugns their political seriousness. Only Mrs. Fitzsmyth retains her strength, appears conscious of her verbal parody of women's behavior, and maintains the sex role reversal that she began in the earlier burletta. Even though Sir Charles Lavender is reduced to the role of an elegant bookie with little function in the plot, he reasserts his male superiority by verbally assaulting the women and expressing the author's ultimately unambiguous view: women belong at home; if they entered the political and financial sphere, they would soon realize that they are truly privileged in being spared those worldly agonies. Since the audience's sympathy here is never with the quarrelsome, vain, hypocritical females, the play lacks the multiple ironies of *The Ladies Club*. *The House of Ladies* never rises above its conservative reaffirmation that ladies belong in the house. Public governance is clearly a much more controversial issue than domestic power and must be presented unequivocally.

The title *The House of Ladies* may produce a smirk because of its possible duplicity: what kind of "house" is referred to? a family home? a brothel? certainly not a Parliament! But its very ambiguity also preserves a measure of the ladies' self-respect, as "The Ladies' House" would not do. In his revival of the play twenty-seven years later, however, Lemon borrows a phrase uttered by the servant Susan in scene one and retitles the piece unambiguously, *The Petticoat Parliament; or, Woman's Suffrage*.[20] The multiple meanings are precluded and the smirk becomes a guffaw, if only because of the metonymy—"petticoat" for "ladies." Reduced to an article of apparel designed to confine their movements, the ladies are defeated before they appear. The use of "suffrage" in the subtitle therefore implies ironical "suffering" as well as the right to vote: women don't really suffer, so why would they want to relinquish their protected status and enter Parliament?

Given the battle for women's rights waged in Parliament during 1866 and 1867,[21] it is no wonder that Mark Lemon saw the opportunity to revive his burletta (as an "extravaganza") for the Christmas Amusements at the Olympic Theatre on 26 December 1867. The play received considerable critical attention because of its timely subject. The *Sunday Times* showed sympathy for Lemon's sexist point of view, using its typically arch tone to praise the play, poke fun at John Stuart Mill (who had headed the Parliamentary fight), and refute the notion that women are oppressed:

> The seasonable novelty consisted of a piece by Mr. Mark Lemon which, under a different name and with some slight variation, has already been performed, but which recent debates in the houses of legislature have rendered specially appropriate at the present time. *Petticoat Government* [sic]: *or, Woman's Suffrage* shows what is the state of affairs to be expected when acceptance has been found for the views of woman's rights propounded by our parliamentary philosophers. Chronos has carried time forward for a few years, and fancy shows with what result. Woman has got the upper hand, and is making the best use of her supremacy. She has ejected man from all the offices he has

> hitherto monopolised, and has reduced him to a state of subordination such as that women are sometimes supposed now to occupy. Men are mere objects to be flirted with. They dress themselves in extravagant attire to secure the notice of their superiors, are thankful for a smile, and receive a chuck under the chin with a "curtsey."[22]

Taking a very different perspective, another reviewer gave a comprehensive summary of the play, then criticized its lack of intellectual seriousness:

> This description sufficiently indicates the character of the piece, which will be differently appreciated by those familiar with and those ignorant of Parliamentary procedure. It leaves the impression that opportunities for witty and suggestive dialogue have been sacrificed to mere wildness and boisterousness, and that the extravagance is overdone. It might have been expected that there would have been one strong minded woman who could have been earnest without losing her temper, and a little more intellectuality would certainly have made the piece a greater success.[23]

In one respect, the reviewer errs: Mrs. Fitzsmyth (now Mrs. Clareton) does exhibit strength and disinterestedness, and she does manage to persevere without losing her composure. But, of course, her cause is futile—and she (as "Clare") so "clearly" serves as the female exception, that she can ultimately be dismissed. Indeed, except for name changes (all directed toward greater realism), there are only a few significant omissions or additions, each of which extends and accentuates the women's lack of seriousness and solidity.

For example, at the end of scene one of *The House of Ladies*, as we have seen, the women all head to their businesses, allowing their husbands to accompany them (and then to proceed to their own idleness). But in *The Petticoat Parliament*, all allusions to "the House," "Downing Street," the "Record Office," and the "treasury" are omitted; instead, only Mrs. Clareton speaks, and the frivolous women are only off to a boat race.

A second change introduces Mrs. Dr. Caulker, who is ridiculed by a male servant for adopting the behavior and occupation of a man. She has come to counsel the overweight Jenkins (formerly Flammer): "You must take more exercise— . . . Have you left off drinking brandy and water? . . . And porter? . . . No sugar? . . . No potatoes. . . . Hum! (*play with cane solemnly*) Well, I think we shall get you round in time" (*Petticoat,* p. 11). Jenkins puns awkwardly on her comment, then reaffirms the sexual stereotype: "Get me *round*! Egad, I think I have done that myself. Ladies may play the Psyché well enough, but physics is a little above 'em, to my thinking" (*Petticoat*, p. 11). Both of these scenes emphasize the common Victorian belief that, given the vote, women would become unacceptably "masculine."

Lemon has also added an entire scene—on women's new, inappropriately masculine recreations—which furthers his rejection of expanded roles for women. The men are playing croquet and the women, billiards. In the interest of balance, each group is seen arguing among themselves. First, the men quibble affably over a score:

Clipper.	If we can't make up our minds on the point, let's throw dice for it!
Cantel.	Ride for it!
Tumbrel.	Shoot for it!
Damper.	Let's refer it to the authorities—
All.	The authorities?
Damper.	(*lugubriously*). Our wives! [All *groan and run* Damper *off.*]

(*Petticoat*, p. 14)

By contrast, in their dispute over billiards, the women want justice, not chance, to decide. Two of the women appeal to Sir Charles, whom they (wrongly) see as disinterested—and, I think, safe and androgynous. His self-interest lies in calming their anger, so he tells them, "In a word you are both wrong" (*Petticoat*, p. 15). "I'll never defer to a man again," snaps Mrs. Clipper as she exits, while Mrs. Clareton declares, "I'll write to Bell's Life" (a magazine for the sporting gentleman), presumably to appeal to its unbiased expertise on the fine points of the game. But Sir Charles has the last word at the women's expense: "I've no exact idea of the man's feelings who enters the tiger's den, but if they equal mine, he earns his money" (*Petticoat*, p. 15). The scene is somewhat mean-spirited, forced, and not very funny. Good will can only be artificially renewed by the scene's conclusion, which shows the women and men in boats and barges on the Thames, cheering and waving. In the spirit of "extravaganza," the burletta with increased spectacle, the scene ends irrelevantly with a hornpipe by the Ballet.

The final scene is largely unchanged, except for Sir Charles's more significant role, since he reappears at this climactic point and is given Derby's powerful lines about the Woman's Charter (*Petticoat*, p. 17) and the "weaker sex" (*Petticoat*, p. 19). Thus he finally has his revenge for being "seduced" in *The Ladies' Club*: the elegant, widowed Mrs. Clareton may ask the audience's indulgence, but this time she and her women have definitively lost their power and their cause. In order to reinforce their defeat visually, Lemon adds this stage direction—"(*her armful of papers falling*)" (*Petticoat*, p. 19)—to Mrs. Clareton's last speech before Sir Charles interposes.

At best, Lemon's perspective suggests that all lawmakers, male or female, are immoral and trivial. At worst, however, women are shown to be particularly susceptible to self-interest and verbal viciousness. Given the reins of power, the "whip-hand," they lose their "moral ascendancy" and end by beating the horse and one another. If they were granted the vote and seats in Parliament, they would reveal their true pettiness and corruptibility: "Your sex from being *weak* is now much *weaker*" (*Petticoat*, p. 19).

Taken together, the three plays make a strong case for gender distinctions, for women's inferior intellect and judgment, and for the need to keep "ladies" protected from the taint of public affairs. Once they are allowed into the realms of power, their purity will be spoiled and they will no longer preserve domestic morality. Unable to overcome their vanity or their jealousy, they will merely transfer these traits to the public sphere, worsening both their own condition and the country's.

But Mark Lemon's three plays on the Woman Question also raise the very issues that they are designed to deflect or dismiss, and thus can serve as a useful index of the preoccupation with sex roles and power that concerned, perhaps even terrified, the Victorian patriarchy. Lemon does present a pathetic picture of men reduced to powerlessness: they plead with the women, argue among themselves over a croquet game, whine about their financial dependency, and plot to regain control over lives that have become a "sinecure"—that is, useless. Though the farces argue the inappropriateness of this state, the men's temporary condition accurately mirrors the permanent sphere of Victorian women. In reading these plays from a feminist perspective, therefore, we can infer both the disrespect that men felt for their wives' minds and daily occupations, and the depths of fear that lurked in the idea of sharing their political and economic power with women.

It would of course offend against dramatic, as well as social, propriety, if the women in each farce were actually to demonstrate consistent initiative, conscious wit, intellectuality, and solidarity. Indeed, the very definition and etymology of the word "propriety" means both the "fitness, appropriateness, aptitude, suitability" of something (in this case, a heroine to a given role); and "something owned, a possession." (The Latin noun *proprietas* is translated as "a property," a "peculiarity," or "ownership.") The two senses of the word (and concept) meet in a notion of "decorum": appropriate behavior is also owned—by society and the playwright. Sexual decorum, therefore, demanded that absolute control remain in the hands of the stronger sex and that the rules of sexual conduct make a sharp distinction between the owner and his weaker possession. Dramatic propriety allowed for the fanciful overturning of that decorum, but could not permit more than temporary lapse from the structure of male dominance; it certainly could not admit a compromise. A Parliament in which women and men sat together would have been even more threatening than the female one—simply because it would have seemed more realistic, less absurd. In exaggerating the fiction of female power, Lemon could preserve society's belief in the inviolability of men's superiority. As the "workers" of the domestic "factory" structure, women could dream of subversion, but had to be regarded as an absolute, revolutionary threat to their "masters" in order to be kept in line. As with workers in real factories, women were easier to control if one defined their abilities and needs as limited—and their demands as unnatural, inordinate: the more exaggerated their claims, the more easily mocked and refuted.

In his essay on "Farce" in *The Life of the Drama,* Eric Bentley makes a distinction between melodrama and farce which may be applied to our discussion of fear and social control: "the principal motor of farce is not the impulse to flee (or Fear), but the impulse to attack (or Hostility). In music, says Nietzsche, the passions enjoy themselves. If in melodrama fear enjoys itself, in farce hostility enjoys itself."[24] If, however, Freud is right that jokes are indeed to be associated with the displacement characteristic of dreams (as similar expressions of the Unconscious), it is possible to see hostility as itself the expression of a fear that does *not* "enjoy itself," or indeed, even fully know itself. It is further possible to see the musical burletta as the least threatening form of farce—a sublimating structure which chooses to treat its passions lightheartedly and with apparent propriety—softening both the terror and the aggression. Paradoxically, though, as we have seen, Victorian burletta about sexual politics has the capacity to deconstruct its own "proper" designs.[25]

NOTES

[1]"The Stage—Its Impurity," *The Theatrical Journal* 12 (June 1851):190-91.

[2]Perhaps the best known objection to licentiousness in the theater belongs to the Restoration period and the so-called "Collier controversy." In 1698 the clergyman Jeremy Collier wrote *A Short View of the Immorality and Profaneness of the English Stage*, producing renewed debate on immorality in the theater and even leading to the prosecution of actors for uttering licentious speeches. Critics in the early eighteenth century also foreshadowed Victorian complaints that the current theater showed a decline in taste and compared unfavorably with its artistic heyday in the past. For a discussion of these conflicts see, for example, William Van Lennep, ed., *The London Stage: Part I: 1660-1700* (Carbondale: Southern Illinois Univ. Press, 1965), pp. xxx, lxiv, and Emmett L. Avery, ed., *The London Stage: Part II: 1700-1729* (Carbondale: Southern Illinois Univ. Press, 1960), pp. cxxi, clxxi-clxxiii.

[3]Edgar and Eleanor Johnson, eds., *The Dickens Theatrical Reader* (London: Victor Gollancz, 1964), p. ix.

[4]"Punch Writers," *Times Literary Supplement*, 21 November 1929, p. 963.

[5]*Records of the Great Exhibition, extracted from "Punch"* (1851), p. 8.

[6]Arthur A. Adrian, *Mark Lemon: First Editor of "Punch"* (London: Oxford Univ. Press, 1966), pp. 27, 75, 77, 93, 158-59, 173.

[7]My comments on the 1851 Crystal Palace edition of *Punch* and on Lemon's attitude towards the "Woman Question" are substantially repeated from my monograph, *Lemon, Dickens, and "Mr. Nightingale's Diary": A Victorian Farce*" (Victoria, B.C.: English Literary Studies Monograph Series, 1988).

[8]Mark Lemon, *The Ladies' Club*, in vol. 1, no. 9 of *The Universal Stage* (London: J. Pattie, 1840), Olympic Theatre, 25 February 1840; *The House of Ladies*, in vol. 2, no. 4 of *The Universal Stage* (London: J. Pattie, 1840), Olympic Theatre, 25 April 1840; *The Petticoat Parliament*, in vol. 23 of *DeWitt's Acting Plays* (New York: Robert M. DeWitt, 1867), Olympic Theatre, 26 December 1867; hereafter referred to in parentheses within the text, followed by the page numbers on which the quoted passage appears, as *Ladies*, *House*, and *Petticoat*, respectively.

[9]These plays differ markedly from Lemon's melodramas and farces about sentimental heroines, dramas whose very titles—such as *The Semptress* (1844), *The Loving Woman* (1849), *The Railway Belle* (1854)—signal their conventionality.

[10]The early Victorian theatrical prescription specified that farces were all to take the musical or "burletta" form, introduced around 1740 and borrowed from the Italian diminutive of *burla*, joke or mockery. These musical farces were designed to circumvent the terms of the 1737 Stage Licensing Act, which stipulated that all plays must be registered with the Lord Chamberlain two weeks before production and that serious or "legitimate" (non-musical) theater would be confined to the two patent theaters, Drury Lane and Covent Garden. By 1833, however, the strict rules for burletta had been somewhat softened, and a *Morning Chronicle* reviewer suggested: "it means a drama, with amusing plot, sprightly dialogue, and light sketchy characters, without any music." Still, the "minors," as the unlicensed theaters were called, usually retained the lightness of touch and the spontaneous introduction of song into their productions.

[11]I have cited the example of *Lysistrata* because Mrs. Fitzsmyth is similarly contemptuous of her sex, the farce uses war imagery, and *Lysistrata* is well-known. But I am grateful to classics professor Joseph F. O'Connor for pointing out to me Aristophanes' less well-known play, *The Congresswomen*

(Ecclesiazusae), whose plot may apply more directly to Lemon's farces, though its extreme obscenity does not. As its translator, Douglass Parker, has summarized it, "Bearded and cloaked, the ladies of Aristophanes' transvestite Chorus pack the assembly, or Congress" (William Arrowsmith, ed., and Douglass Parker, trans., *The Congresswomen*, in *Four Comedies by Aristophanes* [Ann Arbor: Univ. of Michigan Press, 1969], p. 2).

[12]Michael R. Booth, ed. *Farces*, vol. 4 of *English Plays of the Nineteenth Century*, 5 vols. (Oxford: Clarendon Press, 1973), p. 5.

[13]Booth, p. 15.

[14]Maurice Charney, *Comedy High and Low: An Introduction to the Experience of Comedy* (New York: Oxford Univ. Press, 1978), p. 97.

[15]*The London Theatre 1811-1866; Selections from the Diary of Henry Crabb Robinson*, ed. Eluned Brown (LondonSociety for Theatre Research, 1966), p. 163.

[16]Review of *The Ladies' Club*, by Mark Lemon, *London Times*, (6 March 1840); p. 6, col. 3.

[17]See, for example, Eric Bentley's "The Dialectic of Farce," in *The Life of the Drama* (New York: Atheneum, 1965), pp. 241-44; and Albert Bermel's "The Shadowy Edges of Farce," ch. 4 in *Farce: A History from Aristophanes to Woody Allen* (New York: Simon and Schuster, 1982), pp. 49-64: "Farce may be said to exist on the lunatic fringe of comedy and on the ludicrous fringes of tragedy and melodrama."

[18]Bermel, p. 39.

[19]"A rebellious or mischievous practical joke will often produce a counter-attack by those whose dignity has been offended, so that the rebels are either checkmated or suffer humiliation in their turn. . . . When reversal-farce focuses narrowly upon the repeated oscillation of the counterpoise, . . . it takes a shape which I shall call 'quarrel-farce.' This choreographs the progress of multiple exchanges between the quarrelling partners." Jessica Milner Davis, *Farce: The Critical Idiom*, 39 (London: Methuen, 1978), pp. 43, 50.

[20]From the first, apparently, there has been some confusion about this play's title. Adrian lists the play as *Petticoat Parliament: or, A Woman's Suffrage*, omitting the definite article in the title and adding the indefinite article in the subtitle. The *Sunday Times* reviewer calls it *Petticoat Government; or, Woman's Suffrage,* and the *Times* reviewer, *Petticoat Parliament; or, A Women's Suffrage.* My copy of the play, owned by the Duke University Special Collections, is the New York printing, entitled *The Petticoat Parliament, An Extravaganza* (in obvious reference to its genre as a musical farce with extravagant scenes of singing and dancing).

[21]John Stuart Mill defended Gladstone's Reform Bill in the House of Commons on 17 July 1866, moving that "return" be made to those "excluded from the Franchise by reason of their sex." The amendment passed, but Gladstone's bill was defeated. As author of the *The Subjection of Women* (1869), Mill was prepared to continue the women's rights battle when Disraeli introduced his own Reform Bill during the 1867 session. Mill introduced a womanhood suffrage petition with 1500 signatures, and on 20 May 1867 proposed that the word "man" be replaced with "person" throughout the bill. The amendment lost, but received seventy-three votes. On 1 June 1867 Mark Lemon's *Punch* ran a cartoon entitled "The Ladies' Advocate," in which Mrs. Bull speaks to a diminutive Mill (who is dressed in Parliamentary robes and wig and is carrying a scroll entitled "Womanhood Suffrage"): "Lor, Mr. Mill! What a lovely speech you did make. I do declare I

hadn't the slightest notion we were such miserable creatures. No one can say it was your fault that the case broke down." See John B. Ellery, *John Stuart Mill* (New York: Twayne, 1964), p. 94; the cartoon and caption are printed in Eugene August, *John Stuart Mill: A Mind at Large* (London: Vision Press, 1976), pp. 207-209.

[22]Review of *The Petticoat Parliament*, by Mark Lemon, *Sunday Times*, 29 December 1867, p. 3, cols. 2-3.

[23]Review of *The Petticoat Parliament*, by Mark Lemon, *London Times*, 27 December 1867, p. 8, col. 4.

[24]Bentley, p. 255.

[25]I would like to thank my colleagues Susan S. Lanser and Joseph Sitterson, Jr., for their painstaking and multiple readings of this piece in its various forms. An earlier version of this essay was read as a paper at the Southeastern Nineteenth Century Studies Association Conference at Virginia Military Institute, Lexington, Virginia, in April 1984.

SEL 28 (1988)
ISSN 0039-3657

Daniel Deronda and George Eliot's Female (Re)Vision of Sheakespeare

MARIANNE NOVY

U. C. Knoepflmacher noted in 1961 that "*Daniel Deronda,* George Eliot's last work of fiction, is the most consciously Shakespearean of all her novels."[1] Knoepflmacher points to "a deliberate process of imitation on the part of the novelist" and suggests that she incorporates "the playwright and his works into the novel itself as an original means of characterization and differentiation."[2] Much feminist criticism written in the twenty-five years since has suggested that such use of a male model is problematic for the woman writer. As a reader of male texts, argues Judith Fetterley, she undergoes a process of "immasculation" unless she sympathizes with their female characters and thereby becomes a "resisting reader."[3] Such resistance, and the related attitudes found in women writers by Sandra Gilbert and Susan Gubar, would seem to preclude conscious imitation of the male writer, except to mock or subvert him.[4] In this view, if George Eliot did identify with Shakespeare, it seems a sign of alienation from her sex.

However, in this paper I will argue that these alternatives are too simple. As Mary Poovey has suggested, "confrontation is not the only profitable way of formulating women's relationship to their literary fathers."[5] More specifically, the claim in *The Madwoman in the Attic* that the male precursor's images of women "by reducing her to extreme stereotypes (angel, monster), drastically conflict with the woman writer's own sense of her self"[6] does not fit Eliot's view of Shakespeare's women. George Eliot read Shakespeare with distinct though not exclusive interest

Marianne Novy teaches English and women's studies at the University of Pittsburgh. She is the author of *Love's Argument: Gender Relations in Shakespeare* (Chapel Hill: University of North Carolina Press, 1984), and editor of an anthology of essays on women writers' responses to Shakespeare, forthcoming from the University of Illinois Press.

in his female characters, as did many Victorians, but unlike many Victorians, she emphasized his female characters' autonomy. I suggest that she enjoyed Shakespeare partly because she saw him as a creator of powerful women, and that she saw herself as writing both in his tradition and from a female viewpoint.

The contrast between Eliot's attitude to Shakespeare and the Fetterley-Gilbert-Gubar model is partly a result of the difference between Shakespeare on the one hand and Milton and male American novelists on the other. It also results from two aspects of Victorian culture that Gilbert and Gubar do not mention—its praise of Shakespeare for the wide range of his sympathy, a trait considered particularly accessible to women, and its celebration of his female characters, discussed recently by Nina Auerbach in *Woman and the Demon.*[7] These factors may have made the Shakespearean tradition more accessible to women writers than the Miltonic one at issue in *The Madwoman in the Attic.*

George Eliot's writings give an especially extensive record of interest in Shakespeare, and the Shakespearean allusions in *Daniel Deronda* gain resonance when we can situate them in a context that is both personal and cultural. Gwendolen's identification with Rosalind looks back to Eliot's own past; however, Eliot stresses the contrast between Rosalind's plot in *As You Like It* and Gwendolen's in *Daniel Deronda,* and points up the aspects of women's experience that do not fit into Shakespeare's comedy. In her characterization of Deronda himself, she emphasizes his wide-ranging sympathy—important both in her culture's image of Shakespeare and in her own aesthetic—and relates it to irresolution, important in her culture's image of Hamlet. One way of describing the contrast between the plots of *Daniel Deronda* is as a contrast between a realistic rewriting of *As You Like It* and a romantic rewriting of *Hamlet.* In these rewritings, Shakespeare provides materials for her interest in Victorian ideals of womanhood and womanly qualities, ideals that she partly shared and partly criticized, as well as for her attempt, as an author, to transcend the limitations her culture associated with her gender.

Long before she wrote *Deronda,* long before she became a novelist, George Eliot read Shakespeare with a special interest in his female characters.[8] Her letters, especially the first volume (written between the ages of sixteen and twenty-two), abound in Shakespearean references. Ten of the more than twenty in that volume are from *As You Like It,* and throughout her life it is the play she most often alludes to in her correspondence.[9] The friendship between Rosalind and Celia is often a model for her own friendship with other women. To Maria Lewis, she writes, "I heartily echo your kind wish that we should be 'like Juno's swans' coupled together" (1:51; *AYLI* I.iii.75). To Martha Jackson, "I have as many queries rising to my lips as, if you were here to have them orally delivered, would make you wish, like Rosalind, that the answers were corked up in you like wine in a bottle" (1:92; based on *AYLI* III.ii.197-200). To Sara Sophia Hennell, "Not a word more to throw at a dog. So said Rosalind to Celia and so says one to thee, who loves thee as well as Rosalind did her Coz" (1:203; based on *AYLI* I.iii.3). In some of her other letters from this time she playfully puts on a male identity to express this affection, suggesting another dimension of her interest in the cross-dressed Rosalind and anticipating her later use of a male pseudonym. "I have not been beyond seas long enough to make it lawful for you to take a new husband—therefore I come back to you with all a husband's privileges and command you to love me whether I shew you any love or not" (1:279). These letters place her relationships within the tradition of romantic friendship discussed by Lillian Faderman.[10] Yet the *As You Like It* allusions make the note of playfulness more explicit.

Eliot's longest discussion of Shakespeare focuses on his representation of women. In 1855, writing criticism for the *Leader,* she uses Shakespeare's women as models to attack what she calls "the doctrines of modern propriety."[11] Discussing Girardin's *Cours de Litterature Dramatique,* she energetically refutes the claim that Shakespeare's women, unlike those of ancient dramatists, declare their love only after a lover has declared himself to them. On the contrary, "Shakspeare's women have no more decided characteristic than the frankness with which they avow their love, not only to themselves, but to the men they love." By contrast to Hazlitt's view that these characters show "weakness leaning on the strength of its affections for support," note the active power that George Eliot finds.[12]

> If Romeo opens the duct [duet?] of love with a few notes *solo,* Juliet soon strikes in and keeps it up in as impassioned a strain as he. Sweet Desdemona, "a maiden never bold," encourages Othello, not only by a "world of sighs," but by the broadest possible hint that he has won her heart. Rosalind, in her first interview with Orlando, tells him that he has "overthrown more than his enemies"; Portia is eloquent in assurances of her love before the casket is opened. . . . Curious it is to contrast these Shakspearean heroines with some of Walter Scott's painfully discreet young ladies.

She sees the "respectability" of Scott's ladies as a violation of nature: "they are like trees trained in right lines by dint of wall and hammer." At the end of the paragraph she explicitly uses the concurrence of Shakespeare and Greek dramatists in portraying "feminine frankness" as evidence that "it must be simply a natural manifestation which has only been gradually and partially repressed by the complex influences of modern civilization." Here George Eliot begins to sound like Freud!

Her enthusiastic emphasis on the initiative of Shakespeare's women was unusual. Hazlitt's picture of Shakespeare had influenced her greatly, as we shall see, yet her view here differs markedly from his. For many Victorian critics, as Russell Jackson has shown, "Rosalind, Beatrice, and Viola, for all the affection they attracted, could not be accepted without some special pleading. They enjoyed a freedom of speech and mind beyond what was proper in a well-brought-up Victorian girl."[13] In her notebook, Eliot herself commented on this peculiarity of Victorian criticism: "It is remarkable that Shakespear's women almost always *make love,* in opposition to the conventional notion of what is fitting for woman. Yet his pictures of women are belauded."[14]

However, she can also criticize women's roles in Shakespeare's plots. In her journal the same year (16 March 1855), she writes, "After dinner read 'Two Gentlemen of Verona.' . . . That play disgusted me more than ever in the final scene, where Valentine, on Proteus's mere begging pardon, when he has no longer any hope of gaining his ends, says 'All that was mine in Silvia, I give thee!' Silvia standing by."[15]

Each of these Shakespearean allusions has a strong personal resonance for Eliot. She borrows phrases from the dialogues between Rosalind and Celia when female friendships are the most important ones in her life; when her defining relationship becomes her love of G. H. Lewes, she writes on Shakespeare's portrayal of unconventional, frankly passionate women. She objects to a Shakespearean woman's passive role while Lewes is away, apparently to determine whether his marriage with Agnes is irretrievably broken.[16]

In her first published fiction, *Scenes of Clerical Life,* after drawing on memory to a large extent for "The Sad Fortunes of the Reverend Amos Barton," she wrote "Mr. Gilfil's Love Story," which borrows from a number of Shakespeare's plays.[17] Like Helena in *All's Well that Ends Well,* mentioned in the Girardin review, the main female character is a ward in love with a man of higher position. Eliot's narrator modulates a comment on Caterina's educational limitations into a claim that puts her explicitly in the tradition of Shakespeare's tragic heroines. "It is very likely that to her dying day Caterina thought the earth stood still, and that the sun and stars moved round it; but so, for the matter of that, did Helen, and Dido, and Desdemona, and Juliet; whence I hope you will not think my Caterina less worthy to be a heroine on that account. The truth is, that, with one exception, her only talent lay in loving; and there, it is probable, the most astronomical of women could not have surpassed her."[18]

Caterina is Eliot's most explicit experiment in portraying the frank passion in women that she so enjoyed seeing in Shakespeare, and her publisher was rather taken aback (*Letters* 2:297). As Blackwood and Eliot discuss the story, they reenact the conflict between civilized respectability and passion that Eliot sees exemplified in the contrast between Scott's women and Shakespeare's. Like Madame de Staël, who wrote in *Corinne* that "*Romeo and Juliet,* translated into Italian, seems but resuming its own mother-tongue," she depicts an Italian heroine who shocks English decorum even though that decorum has managed to accommodate itself to the passionate stage Italy of Shakespeare's comedies and love tragedies.[19] Although most of Eliot's other female characters in later works show more of "the complex influences of modern civilization," a critique of those influences is one of her continuing concerns.

The passion Eliot noted and valued in Shakespeare's female characters, I argue, is closely linked with the strong emotions she experienced while watching his plays. A letter she wrote in 1859 indicates how central to Eliot's image of Shakespeare is this experience. "In opposition to most people who love to *read* Shakspeare I like to see his plays acted better than any others: his great tragedies thrill me, let them be acted how they may. I think it is something like what I used to experience in the old days in listening to uncultured preachers—the emotions lay hold of one too strongly for one to care about the medium. Before all other plays I find myself cold and critical, seeing nothing but actors and 'properties'" (*Letters* 3:228).

But, somewhat as in the woman's poetics theorized by Lawrence Lipking (who draws especially on de Staël), Eliot valued Shakespeare's plays not only for the emotions they created in her, but also for the sympathy they aroused.[20] As Knoepflmacher has noted, wide-ranging sympathy was one similarity many Victorians saw between Eliot and Shakespeare, and I believe that this aspect of his cultural image, combined with an emotional response that included a personal concern with his female characters, contributed to her choice of Shakespeare as an important model in her writing.[21] To her, Shakespeare's plays meant both emotion and sympathy—passion becoming compassion—and such conversion she gave central importance in her life and work.

Lewes, who as a man of the theater helped sustain Eliot's interest in Shakespearean performance—unusual among Victorian Shakespeare critics—also phrased one of the earliest comparisons between Eliot and Shakespeare. He wrote to Blackwood describing the anonymous manuscript of "Amos Barton" as "exhibiting in a high degree that faculty which I find to be the rarest of all, viz. the dramatic ventriloquism" (*Letters* 2:274). His image is one Hazlitt used for Shakespeare: "By an art like that of the ventriloquist, he throws his imagination out of himself, and makes every word appear to proceed from the mouth of the person in whose name it is given."[22] Later Lewes explicitly likened Eliot and Shakespeare in terms of "that wonderful intuition with which genius throws itself into all forms of life" (*Letters* 3:420). This aspect of her culture's image of Shakespeare, developed especially by Keats and Hazlitt, is crucial for Eliot's imaginative use of him. He was the perfect example that it was possible to be great without egotism through sympathy and identification, to write while seeming to put the self aside, projecting it into a variety of other characters.

Keats opposed Shakespeare as the "camelion poet" with "no self" to the "wordsworthian or egotistical sublime."[23] Hazlitt wrote that Shakespeare "seemed scarcely to have an individual existence of his own, but to borrow that of others at will, and to pass successively through 'every variety of untried being.' . . . His talent consisted in sympathy with human nature, in all its shapes, degrees, depressions, and elevations. . . . He was the least of an egotist that it was possible to be."[24]

This view of the great writer as sympathetic rather than egotistical was particularly important because Eliot, influenced by Victorian constructions of womanhood, was extremely anxious about egotism.[25] She calls herself too egotistical at least sixteen different times in the first volume of her letters—usually with regard to writing too much about herself. As Ruby Redinger shows, she frequently felt uneasy about an interest in herself that she could not suppress; indeed that very uneasiness added to her self-consciousness.[26]

Writing to her friends from Geneva in 1848, she begs for letters on the grounds that she has both too much identity and too little, with one allusion to a Shakespearean text (*Macbeth* III.iv.24) and one to the animal that was one of Keats's images of Shakespeare.[27] "My nature is so chameleon I shall lose all my identity unless you keep nourishing the old self with letters" (*Letters* 1:302); "When one is cabin'd, cribbed, confined in oneself, it is good to be enlarged in one's friends" (1:324). The cumulative effect of her letters suggest that these comments are not simply jokes but also reflections of an uncertainty about identity rather similar to that discussed by Erik Erikson in *Young Man Luther.*[28]

In Erikson's interpretation, Luther resolved his crisis by writing lectures on the Psalms and by reformulating his theology; Eliot helped herself resolve this crisis by her work as an essayist and translator and by formulating views about both life and fiction in which the growth out of egotism into sympathy is seen not simply as a need of her own, but as a process of maturing more generally important, and one in which the role of the artist is especially important. "When we are young we think our troubles a mighty business—that the world is spread out expressly as a stage for the particular drama of our lives and that we have a right to rant and foam at the mouth if we are crossed. I have done enough of that in my time. But we begin at last to understand that these things are important only to one's own consciousness" (*Letters* 2:156). In "The Natural History of German Life," July 1856, she declares, "The greatest benefit we owe to the artist, whether painter, poet, or novelist, is the extension of our sympathies."[29] Yet she found no English novelist really adequate in presentation of the life of the people. Dickens is her best example, but, when dealing with "the emotional and tragic," he is "transcendent in his unreality."[30] Praising him, however, she grants him "the same startling inspiration in his description of the gestures and phrases of 'Boots,' as in the speeches of Shakspeare's mobs or numbskulls." Implicit in this essay is the image of the sympathetic Shakespeare as the quintessential artist.

By the end of her career, descriptions of the impression she created in person as well as in her novels often resemble the Victorian image of Shakespeare. When Lewes contrasts Shakespeare to Goethe, for example, he writes, "He uttered no moral verdict; he was no Chorus preaching on the text of what he pictured. Hence we cannot gather from his works what were his opinions."[31] Cross's summary at the end of his *Life and Letters* makes a similar point: "And it was this wide sympathy, this understanding of so many points of view, that gained for her the passionate devotion not only of personal friends, but also of literary admirers from the most widely sundered sections of society. . . . This many-sidedness, however, makes it exceedingly difficult to ascertain, either from her books or from the closest personal intimacy, what her exact relation was to any existing religious creed or to any political party."[32]

To the reader of *Daniel Deronda*, this description may recall not only the Victorian image of Shakespeare but also the initial presentation of Daniel himself, where many-sided sympathy has its drawbacks. In his characterization, Eliot treats her ideal of compassion in a self-conscious way. Partly because of the link between aesthetic manysidedness and inactivity, nineteenth-century critics often identified Shakespeare and Hamlet; I will show that Daniel has something of what they saw in both.[33]

Like Rosalind, Hamlet interested George Eliot throughout her career, but while the greatest concentration of *As You Like It* allusions in Eliot's correspondence is early, her *Hamlet* allusions, the second most numerous overall, increase as time proceeds. Any cultured Victorian probably knew this play well, but Eliot's interest in it can be related to her particular situation within her culture. I suggest that she often sees Hamlet from a woman's viewpoint, in several different ways.

In *The Mill on the Floss*, her narrator turns a cold demythologizing eye on its hero and takes critical note of his attitude toward Ophelia. "Hamlet, Prince of Denmark, was speculative and irresolute, and we have a great tragedy in consequence. But if his father had lived to a good old age, and his uncle had died an early death, we can conceive Hamlet's having married Ophelia and got through life with a reputation of sanity notwithstanding many soliloquies, and some moody sarcasms towards the fair daughter of Polonius, to say nothing of the frankest incivility to his father-in-law."[34] The narrator of *Middlemarch* refers to Hamlet in a rather different context: when Dorothea returns with a "triumphant power of indignation" from the visit in which she sees Rosamond with Ladislaw, and moans, "Oh, all the troubles of all people upon the face of the earth," Celia is "uneasy at this Hamlet-like raving" and asks, "Dear me, Dodo, are you going to have a scheme for them?"[35] This association in Celia's mind suggests that Eliot finds in Hamlet the universal sympathy she sees in his creator, a quality congenial to the self-image of an idealistic Victorian woman, if not to the pragmatic Celia.

In Hamlet, Eliot chose a hero whose manhood is often questioned by himself and others. David Leverenz, who writes that Hamlet is "as Goethe was the first to say, part woman,"[36] has shown how often Hamlet and other characters use female imagery of him: Claudius calls his grief "unmanly" (I.ii.94) and Hamlet associates his powerlessness with that of a whore or a drab. According to Bernard Grebanier, starting with Sarah Siddons in 1775, more than fifty women have played Hamlet, many in the nineteenth century. Like Eliot, they were interested in transcending the limits usually set on women, but their particular focus on Hamlet, like hers, I would argue, resulted from seeing him as a figure who also transcended the bounds of gender.[37]

Many male critics of the nineteenth century used words such as "sensitivity," with feminine associations, to apply to Hamlet. What is unusual in the Middlemarch passage is the implied association of Hamlet with sympathy—a word much harder to find in nineteenth-century descriptions of Hamlet.[38]

Hamlet is the one Shakespearean character for whom Eliot tells us directly a character of hers is named: "A College Breakfast-Party" begins with "Young Hamlet, not the hesitating Dane, / But one named after him."[39] This character is "held inert / 'Twixt fascination of all opposites. . . . / Having no choice but choice of everything." Speculative and irresolute indeed! He asks a priest:

> I crave direction, Father, how to know
> The sign of that imperative whose right
> To sway my act in face of thronging doubts
> Were an oracular gem in price beyond
> Urim and Thummim lost to Israel.
> That bias of the soul, that conquering die
> Loaded with golden emphasis of Will—
> How find it where resolve, once made, becomes
> The rash exclusion of an opposite
> Which draws the stronger as I turn aloof.[40]

Ruby Redinger comments on the poem: "She herself had known well the Hamlet-road of quest and questioning."[41] It was published in 1874, an incidental project while she was writing, in her last novel, about another character whose "sensibility and reflectiveness had developed into a many-sided sympathy, which threatened to hinder any persistent course of action."[42] This blending of Hamlet-characteristics with the Shakespeare-characteristic most associated with female values is one of the main ways that *Daniel Deronda* shows Eliot reading and revising Shakespeare from a woman's point of view.

The two main characters in *Daniel Deronda* are, in different ways, rewritings of these two Shakespearean figures Eliot found so interesting—Rosalind and Hamlet. The identification of Gwendolen with Rosalind is the most explicit, although, as Knoepflmacher observes, the effect is ironical.[43] It is partly because George Eliot loves the frank passion that she sees in Shakespeare's women that she recalls them so emphatically in the creation of a character as far removed from frank passion as Gwendolen. On a festive day in the forest, "It was agreed that they were playing an extemporized 'As you like it'; and when a pretty compliment had been turned to Gwendolen about her having the part of Rosalind, she felt the more compelled to be surpassing in liveliness" (p. 135). Gwendolen has Rosalind's charm, commanding personality (except with Grandcourt), and love of role-playing, but she lacks the affection towards others that is one of the most salient characteristics of Rosalind in Eliot's allusions to her. When Gwendolen says to Anna, "You are a dear little coz," (p. 50) she echoes Rosalind's words to Celia, and recalls the relationship that Eliot enjoyed evoking in her early letters. But Gwendolen lacks Rosalind's easy sisterly communication, and thus seems more isolated.

Comparison to a scene in *As You Like It* points up the emphasis in two early incidents on how much stronger Gwendolen's feeling for herself is than her feeling for others. During Rosalind's time disguised as a boy, she is accosted by Orlando's brother Oliver, who explains that Orlando has saved him from a starved lioness, and flourishes a cloth stained with his brother's blood. At this sight Rosalind faints, revealing the depth of the feeling under her disguise. However, she tries to cover this up by claiming that she was acting: "I pray you," she says to Oliver, "tell your brother how well I counterfeited" (IV.iii.165-66).

Early in *Daniel Deronda*, Gwendolen acts in a Shakespearean tableau: she plays Hermione in the statue scene from *The Winter's Tale*. When Paulina calls for music and Herr Klesmer, the musician, plays a chord on the piano, a panel flies open to reveal a dead face, and Gwendolen is terrified. Obviously her terror is not an intended part of the performance, but Herr Klesmer pretends it is: he twice praises it as a "bit of *plastik*" (pp. 54-55). In both scenes, self-possessed characters are momentarily shocked out of their poise. Rosalind's shock comes out of her feeling for Orlando, and she has enough aplomb to invent a quick excuse for herself; Gwendolen's shock comes out of a more primitive fear of death; she is not resourceful enough to invent an excuse, and is so self-deceived that she thinks Herr Klesmer really means the praise of her acting that he offers.

But if Gwendolen's fear is heartfelt, Eliot shows her acting soon after. Her uncle Gascoyne tells her about her cousin Rex's fall on a riding expedition from which Gwendolen has returned with great success. Gwendolen's response is "'Oh, poor fellow! he is not hurt, I hope?' with a correct look of anxiety, such as elated mortals try to superinduce when their pulses are all the while quick with triumph" (p. 68). Gascoyne is carefully watching Gwendolen to determine what she feels about his son; when he explains that Rex has put his shoulder out and is bruised, "Gwendolen, instead of any such symptoms as pallor and silence, had only deepened the compassionateness of her brow and eyes, and said again, 'Oh, poor fellow! it is nothing serious, then?'" As he deliberately emphasizes the incongruity of his description, Gwendolen gives up attempts at a sympathetic face and bursts into laughter. Comparison with Rosalind, who can't help fainting when she hears about Orlando's injury, emphasizes Gwendolen's lack of feeling for Rex, and by extension for other people in general. As Bonnie Zimmerman has shown, many details place Gwendolen as a type of the "new woman" of the 1860s and 1870s, the "Girl of the Period," whose highest priority, in the critical view of Eliza Lynn Linton, was fun.[44] By contrast, the sympathetic qualities of Rosalind were emphasized by the Victorians, including Eliot's friend, the actress Helen Faucit, who helped moved the character "from an eighteenth century hoyden, a comic breeches part, into the sentimental 'womanly woman.' "[45]

Gwendolen's most disastrous act is a further contrast to Rosalind. Rather than choose a husband she loves, as Rosalind does with the frankness Eliot praises in her essay on Girardin, Gwendolen marries Grandcourt. To others, this appears the climax of a romantic courtship: on the day of the forest party, for example, the earl interprets Grandcourt's lateness as if it belonged to a character like Orlando—"a lover so absorbed in thinking of the beloved object as to forget an appointment which would bring him into her actual presence" (pp. 134-35). When Gwendolen is asked if she has met him on a walk, she replies, "No. . . . And we didn't see any carvings on the trees either" (p. 138).

What she has seen shows how much darker the world of Deronda is than the world of Shakespeare's comedy, even when both are dealing with marriage. In the play, infidelity is something to be laughed at ("Wilt thou have me?" "Ay, and twenty such" IV.i.11-12) and the emphasis is on cuckoldry—the husband's perspective on a wife's behavior. In the novel, infidelity results in children and has more serious consequences for women: Gwendolen meets Lydia Glasher, who has left her husband for Grandcourt and has then been rejected by him. In *As You Like It,* realism is making fun of Petrarchan convention; here the inadequacy of literature goes deeper: "Gwendolen's uncontrolled reading, though consisting chiefly in what are called pictures of life, had somehow not prepared her for this encounter with reality" (p. 140).

Gwendolen has read Shakespeare, but, as Knoepflmacher has observed, without understanding.[46] Her strongest passion is for self-assertion, and she uses the plays for this purpose. In the *Winter's Tale* tableau, she changes the staging from Shakespeare's text so that she will be paid the tribute of a kneeling Leontes. "This awakened Hermione is to maintain the remoteness and detachment of the carved figure."[47] The scene interests her because of the opportunity of appearing in a statuesque pose in her Greek dress. Elsewhere she quotes—slightly misquotes—Othello's lines about Desdemona (III.iii.92-93) only to make fun of her suitor's lack of expression: "If he had to say, 'Perdition catch my soul, but I do love her,' he would say it in just the same tone as, 'Here endeth the second lesson' " (p. 49). (It is ironic that after this dismissal of Mr. Middleton she marries a man whose emotionless manner is much more ominous.) She often sees life in terms of theater, but without understanding the demands of either. "She had never acted—only made a figure in *tableaux vivans* at school; but she felt assured that she could act well," and she wondered "whether she should become an actress like Rachel, since she was more beautiful than that thin Jewess" (p. 48). In calculating her chances for success, she uses arguments which recall Sarah Siddons's writings about Lady Macbeth's femininity: "I think a higher voice is more tragic: it is more feminine; and the more feminine a woman is, the more tragic it seems when she does desperate actions" (p. 48).[48] Though these lines hint something of Gwendolen's future in this book, at this point she knows nothing of tragedy or desperation. For her the plays exist mainly as opportunities for actresses to be seen. She knows them as part of what George Eliot calls "the sort of culture which combines Shakespeare and the musical glasses" (*Letters* 5:174; corrected 8:352).

The *As You Like It* allusions suggest a doubleness in the way Eliot now takes a woman's viewpoint on Shakespeare: she enjoys his representation of women who could combine power and love, and recalls it to criticize Gwendolen; but she associates Gwendolen's illusions about her power as a wife with Gwendolen's interest in the power of Shakespeare's women, and thus she criticizes a reading of the comedies to foster romanticism about marriage.

Gwendolen has less feeling for others and more ambition than her culture's ideal of woman. Eliot juxtaposes her with Daniel, who has more feeling and apparently less ambition than his culture's idea of man. The narrator makes it explicit that Daniel transcends traditional gender expectations—he is "moved by an affectionateness such as we are apt to call feminine, disposing him to yield in ordinary details, while he had a certain inflexibility of judgment, an independence of opinion, held to be rightfully masculine" (p. 295).

In a different way from the associations of Gwendolen and Rosalind, the *Hamlet* allusions in this novel also show Eliot reading Shakespeare as a woman. Like Hamlet, Gwendolen and Daniel in turn each receive a "ghastly vision (p. 137) and "a new guest who seemed to come with an enigmatic veiled face, and to carry dimly-conjectured, dreaded revelations" (p. 152). Both Gwendolen's literal visitor, Mrs. Glasher, and Daniel's metaphorical one, the idea of his illegitimacy, carry secret messages connected with another's sexual behavior. For both characters, Eliot is rewriting Hamlet's ghostly visitation, except that the message in *Deronda* is presented more as the wrong done to women and children than, as in *Hamlet,* wrong that inspires disgust with women.

Daniel is like the Victorian Hamlet and the Hamlet of "A College Breakfast-Party" because of his "reflective hesitation" (p. 164). He returns to England after studying on the continent "questioning whether it were worth while to take part in the battle of the world" (p. 169). Like Hamlet he has a Polonius-like foil in Sir Hugo. When he asks permission for his continental studies, Sir Hugo says, with both the superficiality and the interest in selfhood in Polonius's famous speech to Laertes: "For God's sake, keep an English cut, and don't become indifferent to bad tobacco! And—my dear boy—it is good to be unselfish and generous; but don't carry that too far. It will not do to give yourself to be melted down for the benefit of the tallow trade; you must know where to find yourself" (p. 168). But unlike Hamlet's "incivility" to Polonius, Deronda maintains a tolerant affection for his uncle.

Deronda is given an Ophelia as well as a Polonius. He meets his future wife for the first time as she is on the point of drowning herself. The willows in the background recall the setting of Ophelia's drowning as described by Gertrude—a frequent subject for painting and other allusions in the nineteenth century. It is as if Eliot's rewritten Hamlet must reverse the course of the original in dealing with women, and so become even more idealized. Shakespeare's Hamlet moves from disgust with his mother—"Frailty, thy name is woman" (I.ii.146)—to rejection of Ophelia—"If thou wilt needs marry, marry a fool, for wise men know what monsters you make of them" (III.i.138). Deronda, seeing Mirah's misery, thinks, "Perhaps my mother was like this one" (p. 175) and saves her from drowning.

Deronda is more like Hamlet and like the Shakespeare of the sonnets in his intense involvement with male friendship. At the university he gives up much of his own study time to help his friend Hans Meyrick (whose Holbein associations and classical interests link him to the humanist cult of friendship exemplified also by Erasmus and Thomas More) but he longs for a friend to whom he can confide more about himself, toward whom he feels more of an equality. His friendship with Mordecai, who communicates mystical visions of Zionism, is presented in language echoing that of the idealizing sonnets, without their tensions or disillusionment. When they are about to have their first conversation, the two have "as intense a consciousness as if they had been two undeclared lovers" (p. 462).[49]

In general, Daniel's Shakespearean associations idealize him. While with Gwendolen we repeatedly find less sympathy than with her Shakespearean prototype, with Daniel we find more.[50] By contrast with Gwendolen, he reads with empathy: "He was a boy of active perceptions and easily forgot his own existence in that of Robert Bruce" (p. 154). He learns most of what he knows about illegitimacy from reading "Shakespeare as well as a great deal of history" (p. 152); he gives "ardour" to the "imaginary world in his books" before his realization that his title of nephew may be a euphemism turns that ardour to his own history. The narrator repeatedly suggests that "many-sided sympathy" is the cause of his inaction (pp. 335-36). Like the revision of Hamlet's disgust with women into Deronda's "interest in the fates of women" (p. 174), this interpretation shows Eliot writing from a female perspective. Pre-eminence in sympathy links Deronda not only to Hamlet but to Shakespeare himself. Eliot calls it "An activity of imagination on behalf of others" (p. 162) and gives an explicitly Shakespearean reference point for this sympathy when "Grandcourt held that the Jamaican negro was a beastly sort of baptist Caliban; Deronda said he had always felt a little with Caliban, who naturally had his own point of view and could sing a good song" (pp. 303-304). Although he is not a poet, the imagery presenting him often compares him to one; the narrator calls his "meditative interest in learning how human miseries are wrought . . . as precocious in him as another sort of genius in the poet who writes a Queen Mab at nineteen" (p. 163).

Reading Shakespeare with Eliot's passion, imagining others' sorrows as she saw her own art as doing, Daniel becomes identified not only with Hamlet and Shakespeare but also with Eliot's own public image. Consider, for example, the account of a meeting with Eliot late in life that her childhood friend Mary Sibree Cash wrote to Cross: "It touched me deeply to find how much she had retained of her kind interest in all that concerned me and mine, and I remarked on this to Mr. Lewes. . . . When I added, inquiringly, 'The power lies there?' 'Unquestionably it does,' was his answer; 'she forgets nothing that has ever come within the curl of her eyelash.' "[51] Compare these descriptions of Daniel:

> What he felt was a profound sensibility to a cry from the depths of another soul; and accompanying that, the summons to be receptive instead of superciliously prejudging. Receptiveness is a rare and massive power, like

> fortitude; and this state of mind now gave Deronda's face its utmost expression of calm benignant force.
>
> (p. 463)

> His eyes . . . were of a dark yet mild intensity, which seemed to express a special interest in every one on whom he fixed them, and might easily help to bring on him those claims which ardently sympathetic people are often creating in the minds of those who need help.
>
> (p. 304)

Critics have found a number of autobiographical elements in Gwendolen's early life. Many of the passages I cite here suggest ways in which Daniel is also a projection of Eliot's own experience. Eliot links them both with Shakespearean figures important to her: the novel's Shakespearean dimension is closely related to its personal dimension because Shakespeare was so much a part of Eliot's personal mythology. Eliot's letters and her narrators' voices speak of maturity as a conversion from self-concern to sympathy. But both self-concern and sympathy, as Eliot imagined them in Gwendolen and Daniel, possess the intense feeling that Eliot associated with Shakespeare. Daniel gently urges to Gwendolen the conversion that Eliot enacted in her own life: "I suppose our keen feeling for ourselves might end in giving us a keen feeling for others, if, when we are suffering acutely, we were to consider that others go through the same sharp experience" (p. 420).

The conclusions of both plots in *Daniel Deronda* rewrite literary tradition. Gwendolen's expectations that Daniel will stay in her life as, at least, a mentor, coalesce with novelistic and comic conventions that, like a Mr. Knightly or a Felix Holt, having educated her, he will marry her. But there is no comic ending for Gwendolen. She is left in an openness and uncertainty that recalls something of Deronda's situation near the beginning.

The epigraph of chapter 32 implies that writing about Daniel's love in relation to his intellectual worldview is rewriting the great love stories of literature in another way. The reversal in emphasis from the passage in *Clerical Life* which declares Caterina's astronomical ignorance irrelevant to her talent for loving suggests how much more ambitious Eliot had become about the scope of her fiction:

> In all ages it hath been a favourite text that a potent love hath the nature of an isolated fatality, whereto the mind's opinion and wonted resolves are altogether alien: as, for example, . . . Romeo in his sudden taking for Juliet,

> wherein any objections he might have held against Ptolemy had made little difference to his discourse under the balcony. Yet all love is not such, even though potent; nay, this passion hath as large scope as any for allying itself with every operation of the soul: so that it shall acknowledge an effect from the imagined light of unproven firmaments, and have its scale set to the grander orbits of what hath been and shall be.
>
> (p. 332)

Daniel chooses to commit himself to making a Jewish nation in terms that, as Bonnie Zimmerman has pointed out, idealize Judaism as the "heart of mankind, . . . the core of affection" (p. 492).[52] From one point of view, this suggests the breakdown of the public/domestic dichotomy in his final vocation; from another, it suggests how visionary is his and Eliot's final image of public life. His valuation of Judaism for its transmission of emotion is rather like the valuation that Eliot places on "that exquisite type of gentleness, tenderness, possible maternity suffusing a woman's being with affectionateness, which makes what we mean by the feminine character" (*Letters* 4:468). Thus, in his membership in an oppressed group as well as in his temperament, Daniel's viewpoint is close to what Eliot sees as a woman's.

Eliot's "Notes on the Spanish Gypsy and on Tragedy in General" emphasizes the role of hereditary conditions in tragedy, using as main examples Othello and the Virgin Mary, designated because of her heredity for a fate different from "the ordinary lot of womanhood."[53] But that "ordinary lot," or what remains of it even for an atypical woman, is itself a hereditary condition in a different sense.

Eliot herself had dealt with the conflict between the ideal of female domesticity and her interest in accomplishing something in the larger world. Her discovery of herself as a fiction-writer coincided with her discovery that her own life had given her subject matter in the lives of women as well as the lives of her former neighbors whose provinciality had seemed a burden to her. Her attitude toward being a woman eventually came to be rather like that of Deronda's attitude toward being a Jew: ultimately she gloried in defining herself as "wife" and "mother" and wrote to other women in ways that assumed much more community with them in these roles than contrast.[54] If she saw her writing as an act of sympathy, it was consistent with the ideals she saw in womanhood, and thus very different from the art of Alcharisi, who could not combine her role as an artist with her role as a mother.

But Eliot was no longer simply the interested correspondent and good listener, or even the translator and anonymous journalist. She was the internationally known novelist-sage whose novels dealt with events in world history. Shakespeare's female characters, though she early found them models of autonomy, did not exhaust the plots of women's lives, as her portrayal of Gwendolen emphasizes, and could not be models for her in making that transition. Instead she behaved somewhat as Carolyn Heilbrun urges contemporary women to do, and reinterpreted male literary figures for her own purposes.[55] The romantic and Victorian Hamlet, with his concern for the world's wrongs and his contemplative nature, was a suggestive model, though imperfect, and the romantic and Victorian Shakespeare, whose writing was motivated by his universal sympathy, was an even better one. And both because she felt that "Woman has something specific to contribute"[56] to art and literature, and because he had written so many years previously, he was the kind of model that left her much of her own to say, somewhat as Daniel leaves Gwendolen to find her own work.

Thus in *Daniel Deronda* Eliot was rewriting Shakespeare in several ways. Gwendolen's story ends more sadly than Rosalind's because of Gwendolen's own limitations as well as because of the greater harshness of the world where Eliot places her. Daniel, on the other hand, is a Hamlet idealized enough to represent Eliot's own ego-ideal. In Gwendolen's plot we can see Eliot's interest in Shakespeare's women turning into a concern to represent the experiences of women more realistically; in Daniel's plot we see Eliot claiming both Shakespeare and Hamlet as figures that she could identify with partly because of their possession of qualities that she associated with women. Her interest in women as a distinct and diverse group, sharing many social restrictions, predominates in the realistic mode of Gwendolen's plot; her interest in traditionally female values predominates in the idealizing mode of Daniel's plot. Comedy revised toward realism, tragedy revised toward romanticism—this description of the two plots may help to account for the disjunction many readers have felt between them.[57]

Among Victorian women novelists, Eliot was unusual in the importance she gave to Shakespeare. The letters and novels of Charlotte Brontë and Elizabeth Gaskell show an occasional allusion, but nothing like the affinity that Eliot's references suggest. Let me sketch, however, a necessarily brief contrast with the effect on Charlotte and Emily Brontë of their fascination with a very different male literary figure. Helene Moglen and Donald Stone have shown Charlotte Brontë's interest in the literary mythology of Byron and its relation to Rochester, and an analogous argument may be made about Emily Brontë and Heathcliff.[58] Byronic influence mediates the role of these figures as female rewritings of Milton's Satan, an interpretation suggested for Heathcliff by Sandra Gilbert and Susan Gubar.[59]

Like women, Deronda, Heathcliff, and Rochester are all outsiders, disadvantaged by their birth. All of them have been criticized as characters in whose creation a female author's fantasy predominates over realism. But Heathcliff and Rochester eminently lack that wide-ranging sympathy that Deronda shares with Eliot's image of Shakespeare and, apparently, of Hamlet. Rather than a special concern for the fates of women, the Brontë hero has an identification with one special woman, which can coexist with a generally egoistic treatment of her and condescension toward the rest of the world. Their authors' identification with them is combined with repulsion.

In Eliot's novel, by contrast, it is with Gwendolen that we may see ambivalent authorial identification. Daniel is idealized, partly by giving him solidarity with women and the sympathy Eliot associated with women; Gwendolen begins with all the egotism that Eliot attributes to her own past self, but unlike Rochester or Heathcliff receives a detailed and effective psychological education. On the other hand, neither Gwendolen nor Daniel, fascinating as they may be, has the demonic power that many readers have found in Rochester and Heathcliff. Though they all write from a perspective influenced by gender, and they all respond to literary tradition, Eliot and the Brontës are writing two different kinds of novels, and the greater importance of Shakespearean allusions in the one case and of Byronic/Satanic allusions in the other helps to mark that difference.

Eliot's reading was vast, and the number of writers who stirred her imagination was not small. Ellen Moers has shown her interest in such women writers as Jane Austen, Charlotte Brontë, George Sand, and Harriet Beecher Stowe; Gillian Beer has added Geraldine Jewsbury and Fredrika Bremer.[60] But Shakespeare played a special role for her, as he would for such twentieth century writers as Virginia Woolf and H. D.[61] Paradoxically, taking him as a model permitted her to affirm her aspirations and deny self-centeredness at the same time. Reading Shakespeare from a woman's viewpoint, emphasizing qualities in him and in his characters that crossed gender boundaries, Eliot reimagined a literary tradition that she could claim as her own.[62]

NOTES

[1]U. C. Knoepflmacher, "*Daniel Deronda* and William Shakespeare," *VN* 19(1961):27.

[2]Knoepflmacher, p. 28.

[3]Judith Fetterley, *The Resisting Reader: A Feminist Approach to American Fiction* (Bloomington: Indiana Univ. Press, 1978), pp. xx-xxii; see also Adrienne Rich, "When We Dead Awaken: Writing as Re-Vision," *CE* 34 (October 1972): 18-25.

[4]Sandra M. Gilbert and Susan Gubar, *The Madwoman in the Attic* (New Haven: Yale Univ. Press, 1979).

[5]Mary Poovey, *The Proper Lady and the Woman Writer* (Chicago: Univ. of Chicago Press, 1984), p. 44.

[6]Gilbert and Gubar, p. 48.

[7]Nina Auerbach, *Woman and the Demon* (Cambridge, Mass.: Harvard Univ. Press, 1982), pp. 207-17. Auerbach writes that "for Victorian audiences Shakespearean characters represented the apotheosis of selfhood and a glorification of womanhood in particular" (p. 207).

[8]Throughout I will use the name George Eliot, although my discussion includes works written before her adoption of this pseudonym, and letters signed, for example, Marian Lewes, as well as the novels. The persistence of her pseudonym, as distinguished, for example, from Charlotte Brontë's, seems in part a sign of the "created" nature of her identity; see Ruby V. Redinger, *George Eliot: The Emergent Self* (New York: Alfred A. Knopf, 1975).

[9]See *The George Eliot Letters*, ed. Gordon S. Haight, 9 vols. (New Haven: Yale Univ. Press, 1954-78). Further references to these volumes (*Letters*) will be parenthetically included in the text. The letters include eighteen references to *AYLI*, and she frequently includes it in short informal lists of Shakespeare's works, for example in 6:113. *AYLI* I.iii.12 is the source of what she calls "my favorite little epithet 'this working day world'" (1:44), a phrase which appears frequently in her essays and novels; see her *Essays*, ed. Thomas Pinney (New York: Columbia Univ. Press, 1955), p. 302n. Shakespeare citations are from *The Complete Works*, ed. David Bevington, 3rd edn. (Glenview, IL: Scott, Foresman, 1980).

[10]Lillian Faderman, *Surpassing the Love of Men* (New York: Morrow, 1981).

[11]George Eliot, *A Writer's Notebook 1854-1879, and Uncollected Writings*, ed. Joseph Wiesenfarth (Charlottesville: Univ. Press of Virginia, 1981), p. 255. The *Leader* was Lewes's journal and it was just the previous year that she had chosen to violate "propriety" by living with him. Of course the review, like most journalism then, was published anonymously. For an earlier violation of propriety, see her passionate letter to Herbert Spencer (8:56-57).

[12]William Hazlitt, *Round Table and Characters of Shakespeare's Plays* (New York: E. P. Dutton, 1936), p. 180.

[13]Russell Jackson, "'Perfect Types of Womanhood': Rosalind, Beatrice and Viola in Victorian Criticism and Performance," *ShS*, ed. Kenneth Muir (Cambridge: Cambridge Univ. Press, 1979), p. 16. Jackson shows such unease even in Mary Cowden Clarke and Anna Jameson, two of Auerbach's major examples of the Victorian celebration of the individuality of Shakespeare's women. The mythic female power Auerbach finds in such Victorian Shakespeare criticism, as elsewhere in Victorian culture, must be distinguished from Eliot's interest, social assertiveness.

[14]Eliot, *Notebook,* p. 11.

[15]J. W. Cross, ed., *George Eliot's Life as Related in her Letters and Journals,* 3 vols. (Boston: Dana Estes; rpt. Grosse Pointe, Mich.: Scholarly Press, 1968) 1:287-88.

[16]Elizabeth Deeds Ermarth, *George Eliot* (Boston: Twayne, 1985), p. 14.

[17]Characters love at cross-purposes somewhat as in *AYLI*: Captain Wybrow uses a phrase from this play when he says, "I've a fellow-feeling for a poor devil so many fathoms deep in love as Maynard"; see *Scenes of Clerical Life,* ed. Thomas A. Noble (Oxford: Clarendon Press, 1985), p. 146; *AYLI* IV.i.198. But he is arguing in favor of moving up an arranged marriage, which precipitates a disaster somewhat as in *Romeo and Juliet.* Maynard fears Caterina has drowned, and "seems to see part of her dress caught on a branch, and her dear dead face upturned" (p. 165), like Ophelia. On the obsession with Ophelia's drowning in nineteenth-century art and literature, see Auerbach, *Woman and the Demon,* pp. 94-96, and Elaine Showalter, "Representing Ophelia: Women, Madness, and the Responsibilities of Feminist Criticism," in *Shakespeare and the Question of Theory,* ed. Patricia Parker and Geoffrey Hartman (New York: Methuen, 1985), pp. 83-85.

[18]*Scenes,* p. 110.

[19]Madame de Staël, *Corinne; or, Italy,* trans. Isabel Hill (New York: W. I. Pooley, 1870), p. 124.

[20]Lawrence Lipking, "Aristotle's Sister: A Poetics of Abandonment," in *Canons,* ed. Robert von Hallberg (Chicago: Univ. of Chicago Press, 1984), pp. 85-105.

[21] Knoepflmacher, p. 27.

[22]William Hazlitt, "On Shakespeare and Milton," in *The Complete Works of William Hazlitt,* ed. P. P. Howe, 21 vols. (1930; rpt. New York: AMS Press, 1967), 5:50.

[23]John Keats, *Selected Letters,* ed. Lionel Trilling (New York: Farrar, Straus, and Young, 1951), p. 152.

[24]Hazlitt, *Round Table,* pp. 23, 346-47; *Complete Works* 5:47.

[25]Anxiety about whether the vocation of writer was too selfish was, as Elaine Showalter shows, generated by the nineteenth-century construction of women's role; see *A Literature of Their Own* (Princeton: Princeton Univ. Press, 1977). However, Eliot's letters mention anxiety about egotism much more than those of such other authors as Charlotte Brontë or Elizabeth Gaskell.

[26]Redinger, p. 42.

[27]On her "chameleon" nature and her ambivalence about it, see Nina Auerbach, *Romantic Imprisonment* (New York: Columbia Univ. Press, 1985), p. 257.

[28]Erik Erikson, *Young Man Luther* (New York: W. W. Norton, 1958).

[29]*Essays,* p. 270.

[30]*Essays,* p. 271.

[31]G. H. Lewes, *Life of Goethe,* 2nd edn. (London: Smith, Elder, 1864), p. 54.

[32]Cross 3: 344-45.

[33]Jonathan Bate, *Shakespeare and the English Romantic Imagination* (Oxford: Clarendon Press, 1986), p. 19. The similarity between Hamlet and Deronda has also been noted by Linda Bamber in *Comic Women, Tragic Men* (Stanford: Stanford Univ. Press, 1982), p. 89.

[34]George Eliot, *The Mill on the Floss,* ed. A. S. Byatt (Baltimore: Penguin Books, 1979), p. 514.

[35]George Eliot, *Middlemarch,* ed. W. J. Harvey (Baltimore: Penguin Books, 1965), p. 833.

[36]David Leverenz, "The Woman in Hamlet: An Interpersonal View," in *Representing Shakespeare: New Psychoanalytical Essays,* ed. Murray Schwartz and Coppelia Kahn (Baltimore: Johns Hopkins Univ. Press, 1980), pp. 110-28; quote is from p. 111.

[37]Bernard Grebanier, *Then Came Each Actor* (New York: David McKay, 1975), pp. 253-54. Grebanier suggests that the common belief in Hamlet's sensitivity encouraged actresses to think of him "as a sister under the skin" (p. 253).

[38]See for example *Readings on the Character of Hamlet 1661-1947,* ed. Claude C. H. Williamson (London: Allen and Unwin, 1950).

[39]George Eliot, *Poems,* in *Works,* 10 vols. (New York: Bigelow, Brown and Coe, 1908), 8:416.

[40]*Poems,* p. 420.

[41]Redinger, p. 366.

[42]George Eliot, *Daniel Deronda,* ed. Graham Handley (Oxford: Clarendon Press, 1984), p. 335. Further page references to this novel will be parenthetically noted in the text.

[43]Knoepflmacher, p. 28.

[44]Bonnie Zimmerman, "Gwendolen Harleth and 'The Girl of the Period,'" in *George Eliot: Centenary Essays and an Unpublished Fragment,* ed. Anne Smith (Totowa, N.J.: Barnes and Noble, 1980), pp. 196-217.

[45]Charles Shattuck, *Mr. Macready Produces As You Like It* (Urbana: Beta Phi Mu, 1962), p. 55n.

[46]Knoepflmacher, p. 28.

[47]Ian Adam, "*The Winter's Tale* and its Displacements: The Hermione Episode in *Daniel Deronda,*" *Newsletter of the Victorian Studies Association of Western Canada* 9 (Spring 1983):10.

[48]Thomas Campbell, *Life of Mrs. Siddons* (New York: Harper and Brothers, 1834), p. 124, quotes Siddons's description of Lady Macbeth as "fair, feminine, nay, perhaps even fragile"; but she also described her as someone who "had probably from childhood commanded all around her with a high hand" (p. 129), like Gwendolen. Gwendolen's pose as Hermione, "her arm resting on a pillar," is borrowed from the stance used by Siddons and other eighteenth century actresses in this part, in which she was famous, according to Hugh Witemeyer, *George Eliot and the Visual Arts* (New Haven: Yale Univ. Press, 1979), pp. 93-94.

[49]With cross-gender imagery like that in the sonnets, Mordecai has "something of the slowly dying mother's look when her one loved son visits her bedside" (p. 462) and says to Daniel, "It has begun already—the marriage of our souls" (p. 698).

[50]And emphatically more than the Shakespearean characters who contributed to his image of the experience of illegitimacy—he is "the reverse of that type painted for us in Faulconbridge and Edmund of Gloster" with their "coarse ambition for personal success" (p. 437).

[51]Cross 1:385.

[52]Bonnie Zimmerman, "The Mother's History in George Eliot's Life, Literature, and Political Ideology," in *The Lost Tradition: Mothers and Daughters in Literature,* ed. Cathy N. Davidson and E. M. Broner (New York: Frederick Ungar, 1980), p. 92. It should be noted that these are Mordecai's images. Donald D. Stone makes the related point that "in Judaism Eliot observed the triumph of the Romantic principle: in the survival of a nation through the power of shared memories and feelings"; see *The Romantic*

Impulse in Victorian Fiction (Cambridge, Mass.: Harvard Univ. Press, 1980), p. 243. In *The Figure of Theater* (New York: Columbia Univ. Press, 1986), p. 219, David Marshall construes Daniel's "decision to identify himself with his Jewish heritage . . . as a far-reaching act of sympathy."

[53]Cross 3:32.

[54]Though not as activist as Deronda's, this solidarity involved an interest in social change; Gillian Beer has recently shown her familiarity with the "writing and actions of the women's movement." See her *George Eliot* (Bloomington: Indiana Univ. Press, 1986), p. 180. Beer also notes the active feminism of many of Eliot's close friends: Clementia Doughty, Bessie Rayner Parkes, Barbara Bodichon, and Edith Simcox (p. 181), and recalls that Eliot signed Bodichon's petition in support of the Married Women's Property Bill and distributed sheets for it (p. 169).

[55]Carolyn Heilbrun, *Reinventing Womanhood* (New York: Norton, 1979).

[56]*Essays,* p. 53.

[57]However, Daniel's plot becomes more "realistic" in such moments as his confrontation with his mother, where, as Marshall shows on p. 215, Eliot explores the limits of sympathy.

[58]Helene Moglen, *Charlotte Brontë: The Self Conceived* (New York: W. W. Norton, 1978), pp. 25-33, 118, and Stone, pp. 101, 106-107, 117.

[59]Gilbert and Gubar, p. 253.

[60]Ellen Moers, *Literary Women* (Garden City: Doubleday, 1977); Beer, pp. 41-51, adds to the intertextuality with the writers Moers discusses as well.

[61]Susan Stanford Friedman, "'Remembering Shakespeare Always, But Remembering Him Differently': H.D.'s *By Avon River,*" *Sagetrieb* 2 (1983):45-70.

[62]Time for the research and writing of this paper was provided by a fellowship from the Educational Foundation of the AAUW. I am also grateful for helpful comments on earlier versions from Jonathan Arac, Shirley Nelson Garner, Harriet Gilliam, Helene Moglen, Liane Ellison Norman, Josephine O'Brien Schaefer, Elizabeth Segel, William J. Sullivan, and Richard Tobias.

SEL 28 (1988)
ISSN 0039-3655

Meredith and Bakhtin: Polyphony and Bildung

DONALD D. STONE

Although much distinguished criticism of the novel appeared in the two decades following the publication of *The Rhetoric of Fiction* (1961), very few books since Wayne Booth's have proven at once so stimulating and usable as *The Dialogic Imagination,* the assortment of essays written by Mikhail Bakhtin between 1934 and 1941 but not published in the Soviet Union until the 1960s and 70s, nor translated into English until 1981. The fine new translation by Caryl Emerson of Bakhtin's *Problems of Dostoevsky's Poetics,* together with the reprinting of *Rabelais and His World* (both in 1984), has confirmed Bakhtin's eminence; and Booth himself has written generously of Bakhtin's "astonishingly broad enterprise—his passionately reasoned celebration of what the novel can do."[1] Despite recent detractions and retractions of support—from nervous Deconstructionists, from latter-day New Critics, from Marxists mistaking Bakhtin's dialogism for dialectics—Bakhtin's vocabulary of terms such as dialogism, heteroglossia, carnivalization, chronotopes, and character zones has enriched the way we read, teach, and talk about novels.[2] For example, the old argument over Joyce's attitude to Stephen Dedalus becomes resolved once we apply Bakhtin's description of novelistic polyphony to *A Portrait of the Artist as a Young Man.* Instead of brooding over whether Joyce is treating his hero sympathetically or ironically, or whether narrative control is lacking in that book, we might instead appreciate Joyce's presenta-

---

Donald D. Stone, Professor of English at Queens College, CUNY, has published widely in nineteenth and twentieth-century literature. The author of *Novelists in a Changing World: Meredith, James, and the Transformation of English Fiction in the 1880s* (1972) and *The Romantic Impulse in Victorian Fiction* (1980), he is currently co-editing *Nineteenth-Century Lives: Essays Presented to Jerome H. Buckley,* as well as working on a book on Matthew Arnold, a portion of which appears in the December issue of *NCL* ("Arnold, Nietzsche, and the 'Revaluation of Values'").

tion of a world of contending voices—Stephen's, his friends', his would-be mentors'—and his juggling of the internal voices and styles that speak through Stephen (including that which composes the "precious villanelle" and another which mocks his "vague words for a vague emotion"). The inability of critics to hear Joyce's polyphony in *Portrait* underscores the truth of Bakhtin's remark, "The utter inadequacy of literary theory is exposed when it is forced to deal with the novel."[3] Other genres respond to the rules laid down for stabilized forms, but the novel flaunts its instability; it thrives on the rejection of rules.

The modern novelist most often cited (although not by Bakhtin) to illustrate Bakhtin's views in practice is Joyce. Among nineteenth-century English novelists, however, George Meredith best validates Bakhtin's principles. In their background and education, Meredith and Bakhtin received a similar training in heteroglossia, "the mingling of different language groups, cultures, and classes."[4] Both acquired the habit of looking at their respective cultures from an outsider's point of view: as Bakhtin observes, "it is possible to objectivize one's own particular language, its internal form, the peculiarities of its world view, its specific linguistic habits, only in the light of another language belonging to someone else" (*DI*, p. 61). Each had a German training—Meredith initially from the Moravian Brethren and subsequently from German Romanticism, Bakhtin from tutors and colleagues who introduced him to Kant, Kierkegaard, Buber, even Nietzsche (whose suggestion that the novel form emerged out of the Platonic dialogue proved invaluable).[5] Although Bakhtin became a scholar of enormous erudition, while Meredith became a novelist of considerable range, both writers, in their commitment to multiple perspectives and styles, paid homage to the ideal of German cultivation as embodied in the master of all-inclusiveness, Goethe. Idealist and Realist, as Meredith describes him, Goethe brings us to "Earth; but it is Earth with an atmosphere." In Goethe, two key ingredients of Bakhtin's critical and Meredith's creative philosophy are united: Polyphony (the recognition and celebration of multiple voices and perspectives) and Bildung (the need for development, both of the individual and his society).[6]

Born seven years after Bakhtin's own exemplary novelist, Dostoevsky, Meredith has from the beginning of his career baffled his readers, who have wondered what to make of his hybrid fictions, comic one moment and tragic the next, alternately romantic and realistic, with their startling shifts in tone and point of view. Oscar Wilde, lamenting his inability to "define him," memorably describes Meredith's style as "chaos illumined by flashes of lightning." And Virginia Woolf, while praising his lyricism and intellectual power, seems almost surprised as to why Meredith should have "been at great pains to destroy the conventional form of the novel." Meredith, along with George Eliot and Hardy, was an "imperfect" novelist "largely because [he] insisted upon introducing qualities, of thought and of poetry, that are perhaps incompatible with fiction at its most perfect." Yet, Woolf concedes, if Meredith had not "destroyed all the usual staircases by which we have learned to climb," the novel might have died.[7] The first edition of Bakhtin's book on Dostoevsky appeared in Russia the year following Woolf's 1928 centenary tribute to Meredith, and a good deal of what Bakhtin has to say there applies to the most seemingly chaotic of English novelists: "Dostoevsky's world may seem a chaos, and the construction of his novels some sort of conglomerate of disparate materials and incompatible materials for shaping them," yet there is, in Dostoevsky's poetics, a "profound organic cohesion, consistency and wholeness" (*Dost.*, p. 85). What Woolf regards as "incompatible" elements in fiction, Bakhtin sees as indispensibles: for the novelist to develop, he (like his protagonist) must be open to the multitudinousness of life's and fiction's possibilities.

"The novel is the only developing genre," Bakhtin writes in his comparison of novel to epic, "and therefore it reflects more essentially, more sensitively and rapidly, reality itself in the process of unfolding. Only that which is itself developing can comprehend development as a process" (*DI*, p. 7). The novel is *about* change; its characters exist in order *to* change in a world of competing values, voices, and styles. History, poetry, philosophy, tragedy, comedy—all belong properly to the novel just as they coexist in reality. Dostoevsky is Bakhtin's model novelist because his is an aesthetic of fluidity, of plenitude, of polyphony. The *"chief characteristic"* of his fiction, Bakhtin maintains, is *"a plurality of independent and unmerged voices and consciousnesses, a genuine polyphony of fully valid voices"* (*Dost.*, p. 6). Dostoevsky aims at reproducing the plurality of points of view that exist in life, even as he draws upon the multiplicity of literary styles that make up the novel. He combines the Bible with the daily tabloid, Menippean satire with the adventure story; and the result is the wildly heterodox Dostoevsky novel in which farce coexists with tragedy, religious idealism with parody and burlesque. Everything is in motion and nothing is fixed—neither ideas nor characters. "A character in Dostoevsky," Tzvetan Todorov explains, "is an unaccomplished, incomplete, heterogeneous being, but that is the reason of its superiority." Dostoevsky's task (here Bakhtin is quoting Leonid Grossman) is "to create out of the heterogeneous and profoundly disparate materials of varying worth a unified and integral artistic creation" (*Dost.*, p. 15). Bakhtin's theory of the novel (if such an anti-theory can properly be called a theory) corresponds to a philosophy of life—a kind of "polyphonic idealism" which embraces life's fullness and possibilities and which celebrates the individual's capacity for development.[8]

If it were discovered that *The Ordeal of Richard Feverel* had in fact been translated from Russian, perhaps the reputation of Meredith's first great novel would be higher. Its commingling of comedy and tragedy, Byronic romance and Restoration-style wit, Shakespearean lyricism and analytical psychology seems perverse to readers expecting consistency in narrative tone and design. Like Pushkin's *Eugene Onegin* (which Bakhtin much admired), *Richard Feverel* might be called "an encyclopedia of the styles and languages of the epoch" (*DI*, p. 329).[9] Meredith, in 1859, wanted to include everything in the texture of his novel because, like his Russian counterpart, he wanted his fictive characters to participate in the plenitude of reality. Nothing should be left out, no options withheld. Hence, we find, for example, Sir Austin Feverel's systematic outlook, Adrian Harley's cynical epicureanism, Austin Wentworth's rugged idealism, Mrs. Berry's Dickensian earthiness, Clare Foley's pathological introversion, all sharing the same novelistic universe—and, in the midst of it all, a Bildungsroman hero trying to find his bearing among voices variously labelled "Nature," "Science," "Poetry," and so on. Meredith's novels are "dialogic"in form and substance: their theme is the fact of otherness, which makes life tragic (as in Richard's case) or redemptive (as in the case of Clara Middleton in *The Egoist)*. Later works like *Harry Richmond* and *Beauchamp's Career* are made up of characters who embody opposing political and philosophical views. Sometimes, as in *The Amazing Marriage,* we even have competing narrators: Dame Gossip, who sees characters in fixed, conventional terms, and the Novelist, who tries to allow for the complexity and changeability of character.[10]

Merely to accumulate opposing voices into the framework of a novel is scarcely new; Peacock, Meredith's father-in-law, had already done so in his fictions. Meredith's gift, as J. Hillis Miller asserts, is for creating "living" figures who respond from within to the pressure of outside presences, in the manner of "realistic" Victorian novel characters, but who also exist as fluid, changeable identities. Or, as V. S. Pritchett says, "His originality lies in rejecting realism [conventional realism] and parcelling events out among many people's minds."[11] For all the overbearing nature of the Meredithian narrator, his own viewpoint is not to be confused with that of any individual speaker. An astute contemporary, in a review of *Beauchamp's Career*, noted that Meredith, by liberating his characters, was doing something new: "His outlook is too wide and his understanding of character too deep to permit him to use men and women as puppets summoned merely to enforce and expound a particular creed, nor is the author in his own behalf disposed to suggest any sure and ready solution of the many problems he loves to present. What he attempts is merely to bring individual character into sharp and close relation with the dominant influences of a chosen period. He forces the actors of his drama not only to wear the appropriate costumes of the time, but to bear its intellectual burdens, and he does not permit them even for a moment to indulge the placid indifference which in actual life is enjoyed by so vast a proportion of the human race." It was thus that Meredith arrived at the process which Todorov, drawing upon an early Bakhtin essay ("Author and Character in Aesthetic Activity"), calls "exotopy": the means by which a novelist first empathizes with his created character and then returns to his own "outside" position. Thus freed from authorial control, but poised among the historical tensions that lie outside the novel but are expressed in it (and through him), the Meredith character must actively shape his or her own outlook and career. Meredith's hero resembles, in this respect, a Dostoevsky character who lives in active dialogue with history and who embodies a historical *idea* which contends with the ideas of his fictive compatriots.[12]

Bakhtin's description of life-as-polyphony corresponds to Meredith's image, effectively used in *Beauchamp's Career* and *One of Our Conquerors*, of society as an orchestra. In the latter novel, Radical and Conservative, optimist and pessimist, ironist and deep thinker (one, that is, with "German views"), among others, are "harmonized" as parts of an amateur orchestra, while nevertheless remaining "pointedly opposed" to each other's individual positions.[13] "The essence of polyphony," Bakhtin declares, "lies precisely in the fact that the voices remain independent and, as such, are combined in a unity of a higher order than in homophony" (*Dost.*, p. 21). For Meredith, as for Bakhtin, the individual is part of a communal structure; but as soon as one realizes one's communal position and interdependence, one attains, paradoxically, the freedom to develop. Learning to engage in dialogue with the other is a demonstration of one's freedom. For Bakhtin, "Dostoevsky always privileges the other [in Caryl Emerson's phrase], because it alone can protect individual personality from the awful trap of the final word." Finality, for Bakhtin, implies unresponsiveness, silence: dialogue is the means of saving oneself. (It is here that the religious side of Bakhtin's thought becomes apparent: "Whoever wants to preserve himself, loses himself"—

thus Todorov glosses a passage from the Dostoevsky book.)[14] Clara Middleton is emancipated from her engagement to Sir Willoughby Patterne once she learns to express her feelings honestly to herself and others and to join in harmony with them. "Her cry for freedom," she senses early on, is "a cry to be free to love"—to love "unselfishness and helpfulness, and planted strength in something." Armed with such freedom, she conjectures, she might then find "the words needed" to speak out. Meredith's egoists, on the other hand, find themselves increasingly fixed in place, trapped within their inflexible rhetoric of self. Willoughby's inability to join the dialogue puts him among the company of Dostoevsky's disengaged and unalterable egoists, Stavrogin and Ivan Karamazov, for all of whom hell is (in Father Zossima's words) "the suffering of being unable to love."[15]

For the remainder of this essay, I will touch on four important areas in which Bakhtin's and Meredith's dialogical imaginations intersect: their views regarding, first, the role of the hero in fiction; second, the Idea in fiction; third, the relations between the fictive self and the other; and finally, the novel's link with what Bakhtin calls the "culture of laughter." With these connections established, I can then, very briefly, consider Meredith's fiction, particularly *Diana of the Crossways*, from a Bakhtinian perspective. In a polyphonic world the hero must always struggle, says Bakhtin, "to destroy that framework of *other people's* words about him that might finalize and deaden him" (*Dost.*, p. 59). The Dostoevsky or Meredith protagonist is granted an independence within the structure of the novel; he is free to be the subject of his own discourse (if he chooses) rather than the object of the novelist's or another character's discourse. Both novelists' characters find themselves in a "profoundly *pluralistic*" world, filled with people expressing opposing viewpoints which correspond to the contradictoriness of their historical "social reality" (*Dost.*, pp. 26-27). Each writer chooses settings which maximize the chance of verbal pyrotechnics: Meredith preferring a dining or drawing room (just as Balzac or Stendhal would have chosen a parlor or salon [*DI*, p. 246]), Dostoevsky indulging in melodramatic "mass scenes," concentrating, "often at the expense of credibility, as many persons and themes as possible in one place at one time." In such scenes, Dostoevsky characteristically splits characters in two, often "forcing a character to converse with his own double" (*Dost.*, p. 28). The Meredith hero, too, is located in a world of opposing selves—Harry Richmond, for example, is torn between a Romantic, posturing father and a down-to-earth grandfather; Nevil Beauchamp between a Radical mentor and a feudal uncle—

with each polarity reflecting the division within the hero.

The aim of all this contending dialogue is the testing of the hero and his beliefs. According to Bakhtin, Dostoevsky typically utilizes an adventure plot which "places a person in extraordinary positions that expose and provoke him," and which "connects him and makes him collide with other people under unusual and unexpected conditions precisely for the purpose of testing the idea and the man of the idea, that is, for testing [what Dostoevsky calls] the 'man in man'" (*Dost.*, p. 105). This tallies with Meredith's description of "the novel, exposing and illustrating the natural history of man," and Meredith's own method of subjecting his heroes to an ordeal, "a scene [that exposes] the fullest of their blood and brain under stress of a fiery situation."[16] The best European novels, Bakhtin contends, combine the theme of the hero's development (Bildung) with the "theme of testing" (*DI*, p. 393); and the classic Bildungsroman of this type, for both Bakhtin and Meredith, is Goethe's *Wilhelm Meister's Apprenticeship*. The idea of Bildung is crucial to German thinkers of both the Enlightenment and Romantic periods. (For Herder and Lessing, it is identified with the ideal of self-cultivation, with "reaching up to humanity," in Herder's famous phrase; while for Hegel, Bildung becomes a means by which the self can transcend its limitations and be objectified in Culture.) For Goethe, who straddled the two epochs, the Bildungsroman hero is on the "border" of two time zones; hence, Wilhelm Meister personifies a new kind of individual, one who develops in real time and real space: one who *becomes*. Since Bakhtin's conception of the hero and Meredith's actual heroes are heavily indebted to Goethe's prototype, one deeply regrets the loss of Bakhtin's book on Goethe and the Bildungsroman. (The surviving portion of the manuscript is in the Bakhtin collection, *Speech Genres and Other Late Essays*.) Clearly, Goethe's portrayal of a developing hero in a developing world greatly influenced Bakhtin's description of the novel as "the only developing genre."[17]

Oscar Wilde's description of Meredith in "The Soul of Man Under Socialism" strikingly anticipates Bakhtin's description of Dostoevsky. "To him," Wilde states, "belongs philosophy in fiction. His people not merely live, but they live in thought. One can see them from myriad points of view. They are suggestive. There is soul in them and around them. They are interpretative and symbolic."[18] Wilde's claim for Meredith resembles Bakhtin's view that Dostoevsky's novels, rather than containing ideas, are "*about the idea*": for Dostoevsky, "the idea is a *live event*, played out at the point of dialogic meeting between two or several consciousnesses" (*Dost.*, pp. 23, 88). Hence, a Nevil Beauchamp or a Raskolnikov can be said "to live in thought" (in Wilde's phrase), to live out their ideas in that epoch which Dostoevsky conceived "as a great dialogue," when "the reigning dominant ideas" of the present and "ideas . . . just beginning to ripen" clashed head on (*Dost.*, p. 90). Such characters, Bakhtin says in another context, "both illuminate the world and are themselves illuminated" (*DI*, p. 45)—they are, to repeat Wilde on Meredith, "interpretative and symbolic." It is imprecise to say of such figures that they use ideas; rather, ideas use them.

The task for the Dostoevsky ideologue (notes Bakhtin) is "to find one's own voice and to orient it among other voices, to combine it with some and to oppose it to others, to separate one's voice from another voice with which it has inseparably merged" (*Dost.*, p. 239). Meredith's characters, too, as a contemporary reviewer observed, "feel the intellectual pressure of their time. They are compelled to live and breathe in an atmosphere that is heavily charged with the strong and conflicting currents of modern thought, and by the skill of the artist they are made to absorb into themselves some of the elements of this conflict, and to express its progress and development in their own persons."[19] Because they are impelled by their own ideas, characters in Meredith or Dostoevsky have the freedom to make their own fates, to intersect freely with the times they live in and thus, in a manner of speaking (as it is said of Beauchamp), to "bother the world," to alter the times they live in. The optimistic and radical thrust behind Meredith's and Bakhtin's aesthetic is obvious. For Bakhtin, since the hero in fiction contains an "unrealized potential and unrealized demands," he is always on the threshold: for him, "the future exists, and this future ineluctably touches upon the individual, has its roots in him" (*DI*, p. 37). The major idea for Meredith and Bakhtin, thus, is human potentiality, becoming—in short, human freedom. They are both (to borrow the phrase Bakhtin's biographers apply to him) "philosophers of freedom."[20]

For Meredith and Bakhtin, to be is to be part of a dialogue, part of nature, part of history. "*To be*," Bakhtin contends, "means *to communicate*. Absolute death (non-being) is the state of being unheard, unrecognized, unremembered. . . . To be means to be for another, and through the other, for oneself. A person has no internal sovereign territory, he is wholly and always on the boundary; looking inside himself, he looks *into the eyes of another* or *with the eyes of another*" (*Dost.*, p. 287). There is no such thing as an isolated ego; and egoism itself is a contradiction in terms. In the critique of Freud, Bakhtin (writing with V. N. Vološinov) charges that psychoanalysis postulates an imaginary concept called the unconscious, which is, in fact, a fictive "scenario" created by the patient to sustain his dialogue with his analyst.[21] The self always assumes a listener; it has no linguistic identity separate from the language of its society, its class. Bakhtin's description of the self has considerable relevance when applied to Meredith's most famous egoist, Sir Willoughby Patterne—seemingly detached from the world and yet at its mercy, terrified of what the world thinks of him. ("Doubtless some ancient Greek," writes George Eliot, "has observed that behind the big mask and the speaking-trumpet, there must always be our poor little eyes peeping as usual and our timorous lips more or less under anxious control.") Incapable of a human relationship, cut off from dialogue and from nature, Willoughby can only deal with others in the form of imaginary scenarios. "The most important acts constituting self-consciousness," Bakhtin says, "are determined by a relation toward another consciousness (toward a *thou*)." Hence, "separation, dissociation, and enclosure within the self" are "the main reason for the loss of the self" (*Dost.*, p. 287). Or, as Meredith remarks of Willoughby's eventual fate: "Through very love of self himself he slew" (*Egoist*, Prelude). Bakhtin's biographers observe that whereas for Freud, "the more [there is] of the other, the less [there is] of the self; in Bakhtin, the more of the other, the more of the self."[22] Where Willoughby loses by withdrawing into the self, Clara Middleton, in contrast, gains freedom and fullness by acknowledging her place in the "great dialogue."

The force that unites people is laughter; and on the role of comedy and its relation to reality Bakhtin and Meredith are in substantial agreement. The novel, says Bakhtin, derives in part from the "culture of laughter" (*DI*, p. 20), from the public demand to see reality at close range:

> As a distanced image a subject cannot be comical. . . . Laughter has the remarkable power of making an object come up close, of drawing it into a zone of crude contact where one can finger it familiarly on all sides, turn it upside down, inside out, peer at it from above and below, break open its external shell, look into its center, doubt it, take it apart, dismember it, lay it bare and expose it. . . . Laughter demolishes fear and piety before an object, before a world, making of it an object of familiar contact and thus clearing the ground for an absolutely free investigation of it. Laughter is a vital factor in laying down that prerequisite for fearlessness without which it would be impossible to approach the world realistically. (*DI*, p. 23).

This sounds like Meredith's comic method: exposing an authoritarian figure through laughter. The pompous Shagpat is shaved (which removes the source of his power); the princely Willoughby is brought down from his pedestal and exposed to the scrutiny of his fiancée Clara and to the "world" surrounding Patterne Hall; Victor Radnor, the financial and would-be political leader, is laid low. Such figures resemble the monarch of carnival celebration; first puffed up, then dethroned, stripped, humiliated. "A carnival sense of the world" lurks behind many literary forms, Bakhtin argues (*Dost.*, p. 157); and *The Egoist*, for all its refined setting, draws in part upon the carnival tradition which Bakhtin so brilliantly evokes in *Rabelais and His World*. "The love-season," Meredith writes, "is the carnival of egoism, and it brings the touchstone to our natures" (*Egoist*, ch. 11). Carnivalization brings us down to earth (literally so, in the case of Victor Radnor, who is first seen in *One of Our Conquerors* falling to the ground). It helps answer the question of what is fundamental: "What is under our feet?" Comedy, for Bakhtin and Meredith, rejects all forms of authoritarianism. It is a communal activity which valorizes physical space and actual time; it rejects stasis and celebrates a world of "becoming, change, and renewal."[23] For Bakhtin, Rabelais's culture of laughter is a forerunner of Goethe's culture of Bildung.

Nietzsche's Zarathustra urges that we "learn to laugh at [ourselves] as one must laugh." If Meredith's comedy is less robust than Rabelais's, it is partly because he is more sensitive a writer, one who shares many of the weaknesses he exposes.[24] When the comic imps gather around Willoughby Patterne ("our fountainhead, primeval man"), "restlessly plucking at the garments which cover our nakedness," the novelist, while admitting the need for such humiliation, nevertheless is reluctant to abet "the imps whose revelry is in the frailties of our poor human constitution." (He allows them their fun, however, since they are now participants "in these festival hours" in which lack of restraint is unavoidable [*Egoist*, chs. 39, 49].) The culture of laughter partakes of seriousness, Bakhtin notes—and he points to plays by Euripides and Shakespeare in which comedy and tragedy coexist—although, more optimistically than Meredith, he sees laughter as purifying the world of the atrophied seriousness which takes the form of dogma, didacticism, illusion, sentimentality (*Rab.*, pp. 122-23). For Meredith, who attacks these same forces, a new illusion invariably replaces the old—thus he ends his first novel, *The Shaving of Shagpat*. And in *The Tragic Comedians*, the novel which followed *The Egoist*, Meredith selects as his hero "a grand pretender, a self-deceiver, one of the lively ludicrous," but one, for all that, "whom we cannot laugh at, but must contemplate, to distinguish where their character strikes the note of discord with life."[25]

Bakhtin's model comic writer is Rabelais, whereas Meredith's (in his "Essay on Comedy") is Molière. Bakhtin's comic spirit looks up from "below," from the arena of the public carnival, while Meredith's, "humanely malign," looks down "from above." Also, in Meredith the country-house typically replaces the market-place as the scene of comic activity. Even so, both writers see comedy as a "corrective of reality" (in Bakhtin's phrase, *DI,* p. 55), a force that (in Meredith's words) "appeals to the individual mind to perceive and participate in the social." Both writers reject the "reduced" forms of laughter prevalent in much modern literature—a humor stressing irony or sarcasm, the comic forms of writers distanced from the world and their own creations (*Rab.*, p. 38). True laughter, rather than detaching us from others, draws us toward others into a community where all are equal. Just as, for Bakhtin, comedy necessarily dissolves social hierarchies, so, for Meredith, true comedy can only flourish in a society where women are "on the road to an equal footing with men, in attainments and in liberty."[26]

Despite their common radicalism, their belief in human development and freedom, Meredith differs from Bakhtin on the subject of the efficacy of discourse. Whereas for Bakhtin language is a social act, with every word determined both by its speaker and its auditor, for Meredith language threatens to become a personal possession. The tragedy of egoism is being cut off verbally from others; the difficulty in writing novels is, increasingly for Meredith, making oneself understood. In a notable passage of *Rhoda Fleming* (ch. 43), Meredith gives us both the words of his characters and the characters' real meaning, which the words belie. True dialogue, in Meredith, is often of a nonverbal nature. After weighing the opposing verbal positions presented to him, Harry Richmond comes to realize, "There is more in men and women than the stuff they utter."[27] In preferring Vernon Whitford to Willoughby Patterne, Clara Middleton admits, "I wanted his voice; but silence . . . did tell me more" (*Egoist*, ch. 48). In the late Meredith novels, language seems increasingly problematic. Discourse obfuscates rather than reveals, and the Meredith hero and heroine look for refuge in a world beyond language. In this respect, the novelist anticipates the Wittgenstein of the *Philosophical Investigations*: "My own relation to my words is wholly different from other people's." And yet the mention of the Austrian philosopher reminds us that Bakhtin's brother Nikolai was an influential member of Wittgenstein's circle—and one recalls Todorov's sober thought that perhaps Bakhtin's "whole theory of dialogue may have originated from the desire to understand this unbearable state [his own inability to be heard in Russia]—the absence of response."[28] Dialogism, for Bakhtin and Meredith, was an ideal condition from which they were, very often, excluded.

In the prehistory of the novel which Bakhtin sketches in his book on Dostoevsky, we find something resembling Meredith's own development as a novelist. A genre, Bakhtin insists, "always *remembers* its past, its beginning" (*Dost.*, p. 106); hence, Meredith's and Dostoevsky's novels reveal their origins in Socratic dialogue and Menippean satire. Meredith's first novel, *The Shaving of Shagpat*, is an exuberant version of Menippean satire, a hybrid genre (as Bakhtin defines it) in which comedy, fantasy, and lowly realism coexist in the form of an improbable narrative whose aim is "the provoking and testing of a philosophical idea" (*Dost.*, p. 114). From *The Ordeal of Richard Feverel* on, Meredith draws upon the Goethean Bildungsroman, which combines the Baroque novel tradition of the testing of a potential hero with a new emphasis on a developing protagonist in a historically changing world (*DI*, p. 393). Meredith builds upon the novel's dialogic structure: his heroes (Richard Feverel, Evan Harrington, Harry Richmond, Nevil Beauchamp, for example) must find their way in a world of competing voices, competing philosophies. Any one finalized position, any "system," is always to be regarded with suspicion. As Meredith observes in *Richard Feverel,* "There is nothing like a theory for blinding the wise." The main danger is singularity of point of view: reading others "from our own book."[29] Meredith's villains are his monologists, egoists deaf to the polyphony of life, who (like Willoughby Patterne) try to impose their sentimental scenarios upon others.

Yet if Willoughby is himself frozen in place at the end of *The Egoist,* Clara is last seen, together with Vernon, high up in the Alps, with all the world before her. She is literally on the "border" (in Bakhtin's term for the Bildungsroman hero)—located, as J. Hillis Miller notes, in an indeterminate geographical position (somewhere between Austria and Switzerland, suspended between mountains and lake) and in an indeterminate state of identity.[30] Meredith's heroines do considerably better than his heroes, especially in the late novels, responding to polyphony, holding up under their ordeals, developing. Besides Clara and Sandra Belloni (of the earlier *Sandra Belloni* and *Vittoria*), he offers a series of liberated heroines that is unmatched among Victorian novelists: Nesta in *One of Our Conquerors*, Aminta in *Lord*

Ormont and His Aminta, Carinthia Jane in *The Amazing Marriage*. Among this company, none is tested more than Diana Warwick in *Diana of the Crossways*.

The idea for *Diana* came from a historical event: Caroline Norton's leaking to the press of the impending repeal of the Corn Laws. Fifteen years ago, in *Novelists in a Changing World*, I considered the book and its heroine a failure, a depiction of (what I called) "schizophrenia posing as sanity."[31] My reassessment is based, to some extent, on my having read Bakhtin in the interim. Diana now strikes me as the most free and perhaps most complex of Meredith's characters, the most striking example of his ability to stand outside a character with whom he has identified (exotopy). That she should betray her lover's secret and yet remain a heroine no longer seems to me a sign of confusion on Meredith's part. For Diana is, by Bakhtin's standards, an unfinished character, one who rebels against being frozen in place by others. With all her wit, her intelligence, her creative abilities, she is capable of mistakes, is capable, in short, of continued development. Diana is herself a novelist; and here one recalls Bakhtin's remark that "every one of Dostoevsky's heroes is a potential author" (*Dost.*, p. 45). She is in the process of fashioning her own identity, even as she fashions her characters. The title of one of her works, "The Man of Two Minds," reflects her growing awareness of human dualism. Diana is "at war with" herself, and she is at odds with all those in the novel who dare to fix her in place, confine her, turn her into an object: "the woman Warwick."[32]

Despite his growing skepticism concerning the intelligibility of language—despite the attempts of his characters to arrive at a state beyond language—Meredith remains committed in *Diana* to the ideal of verbal dialogue. However obscure reality may seem to his characters (and to his readers), who judge by fixed standards and are baffled accordingly, Meredith remains convinced that the novel can embrace "Philosophy" and be true, like no other form, to the complexity of life. Philosophy, he contends, is the enemy of fixed positions, whether, for example, of a sentimental or cynical cast. It "bids us to see that we are not so pretty as rose-pink, not so repulsive as dirty drab; and that instead of everlastingly shifting those barren aspects, the sight of ourselves is wholesome, bearable, fructifying, finally a delight" (*Diana*, ch. 1). For Diana to be a liberated woman, she must be liberated from verbal persiflage, proceeding from others or from herself. "Metaphors were her refuge," Meredith warns. "The banished of Eden had to put on metaphors, and the common use of them has helped largely to civilize us" (ch. 24). To regain Eden, hence, it is necessary to return by means of language to the truths concealed by language. And Meredith's Eden is, like Bakhtin's, the dialogical universe.

The novel opens with a dialogue of voices trying in vain to pin down the elusive Diana. She resists even Meredith's attempt to lead her to a conclusion. "She has no puppet pliancy," he noted in a letter to Mrs. Leslie Stephen; "it is she who leads me."[33] Unlike the women in earlier fiction who accepted their "dolly-dolly" status, Diana demands the right to make her own fate, to "muse on actual life," to speak "a language distinct from the mercantile, trafficking in ideas" (*Diana*, ch. 39), to write her own novels! Like Clara Middleton, like a Dostoevsky protagonist, Diana is a woman on the "threshold" (*Dost.*, pp. 169-70). Although she is tempted on several occasions to regress, to escape from the world and lock herself away in her ancestral home, the Crossways, Diana is obliged to move on, to test herself, to make blunders, even (and especially) to fall in and out of love. She inhabits a historical world in which events and other voices impinge upon her, but she also thrives as an individual who looks, thinks, questions, acts, interacts. "What is realized in the novel," Bakhtin avers (in words applicable to *Diana*), "is the process of coming to know one's own language as it is perceived in someone else's language, coming to know one's own belief system in someone else's system" (*DI*, p. 365).

Resisting the idea of ending up a conventional heroine, Diana yearns to be "an unclaimed self" (ch. 15); she rails against the accepted definitions of good versus bad women. Under trial, she groans at her dependency as a woman in a male-dominated society. "Give us," she demands, "the means of independence, and we will gain it, and have a turn at judging you, my lords!" (ch. 14). Reluctantly accepting the hand of Tom Redworth—the only male in the book depicted as "a friend of women" (ch. 8)—Diana murmurs, "Is marriage to be the end of me?" (ch. 42). Yet there is much to be said for Redworth as Diana's fit partner. "An open-minded clear-faced English gentleman" (ch. 8), he respects both her sovereignty as an individual and her capacity for growth. He is represented as forward-looking, while she is sometimes tempted to look back; he is (in Meredith's phrase) "of the finest Saxon type" (ch. 5), practical, generous, not always verbally fluent, while she is a representative Celt, imaginative, humorous, articulate. He builds railways, while she writes novels. Theirs is a working dialogue that extends beyond the novel, linking invaluable linguistic and cultural traditions with the needs of a developing world. Together, they are Meredith's most persuasive demonstration of the polyphonic principle in operation. "A single voice ends nothing and resolves nothing," as Bakhtin observes. "Two voices is the minimum for life, the minimum for existence" (*Dost.*, p. 252).

By demonstrating how Meredith can be read in the light of Bakhtin, I have been doing what Paul de Man has cautioned against: "To imitate or to apply Bakhtin, to read him by engaging him in a dialogue, betrays what is most valid in his work." But de Man's Bakhtin is a monological Deconstructionist, yet another creator of "a reflective system of *mise en abýme*."[34] Perhaps the current interest in Bakhtin indicates that some humanists have grown weary of dogmatic skepticism and blindered insights, tired of Marxist, New Critical, or Deconstructive pieties. Many critics, to be sure, have no room for Bakhtin in their systems. Geoffrey Hartman has wondered whether we can "tolerate [in Bakhtin] such ambiguity, such unresolved diversity, without structures of domination or dialectic"; and Denis Donoghue has contemptuously dismissed Bakhtin for defying the sacred principle of "authority." (Donoghue charges that "he has been turned into a hero for our time for reasons mostly sentimental.") Yet Bakhtin's defiance of authoritarianism is not to be confused (as Donoghue implies) with an endorsement of "hippie culture." Few modern critics—very few contemporary critics—approach texts with even a portion of Bakhtin's exuberant and expansive humanism. Todorov has called him "the greatest theoretician of literature in the twentieth century," all the while showing how Bakhtin draws upon some of the most vital of literary sources and philosophical traditions.[35]

While the ideas of polyphony and Bildung are not new, they have been celebrated and combined by Bakhtin with a particular urgency in our time. Harking back to Socrates and Rabelais, Goethe and Dostoevsky, Bakhtin speaks, as a literary critic, in behalf of human variety and human potentiality; and he celebrates the novel precisely because, in its all-inclusiveness, it is (as D. H. Lawrence also perceived) "the one bright book of life." Meredith and Joyce wonderfully demonstrate the polyphonic principle in their novels, while, among philosophers, Bakhtin's companions include not only the German Romantics, with their "diversitarian" impulse and their reverence for Greek culture, but also American ethical pluralists ranging from William James to Wayne Booth. Like all of them, Bakhtin extols otherness. Among contemporary humanists, Hans-Georg Gadamer has demonstrated affinities with Bakhtin, both in his appeal to the Socratic dialogue as the surest basis for moving toward (though never arriving at) truth, and in his willingness to face the future with undimmed faith in humankind. According to Bakhtin and Gadamer—and to

Meredith too—we live through language, tradition, history; they speak through us; they transmit their legacy even as we are developing as individuals. "It is completely mistaken," Gadamer declares, in response to those who want absolutes or nothing, perhaps nothing *as* an absolute, "to infer that reason is fragmented because there are various languages. Just the opposite is the case. Precisely through our finitude, the particularity of our being, which is evident even in the variety of languages, the infinite dialogue is opened in the direction of the truth that we are."[36]

NOTES

[1]Wayne C. Booth, introduction to Mikhail Bakhtin, *Problems of Dostoevsky's Poetics*, ed. and trans. Caryl Emerson (Minneapolis: Univ. of Minnesota Press, 1984), p. xxvii, hereafter cited in text as *Dost.*

[2]It was inevitable, given the enthusiastic reception accorded to Bakhtin (MLA sessions, a special issue of *CritI* [December 1983], a *Bakhtin Newsletter*, etc.), that there would be a critical backlash. See, for example, Paul de Man, "Dialogue and Dialogism," *Poetics Today* 4 (1983): 99-107, on the "unlikely bedfellows" invoking Bakhtin (p. 104); Rene Wellek, "Dostoevsky's Carnival," *New Criterion* 2 (June 1984): 89-93, on the exaggerated and borrowed aspects of Bakhtin's thinking; Robert Young, "Back to Bakhtin," *Cultural Critique* 2 (Winter 1985-86): 71-92, on the Marxists' appropriation of, and then discontent with, Bakhtin. Besides Booth's, three good recent tributes to Bakhtin are Don H. Bialostosky, "Booth's Rhetoric, Bakhtin's Dialogics and the Future of Novel Criticism," *Novel* 18 (Spring 1985): 209-16; David Patterson, "Mikhail Bakhtin and the Dialogical Dimensions of the Novel," *Journal of Aesthetics and Art Criticism* 44 (Winter 1985): 131-38; and Joseph Frank, "The Voices of Mikhail Bakhtin," *NYRB* 33 (23 October 1986): 56-60. I am grateful to Bialostosky and to Caryl Emerson for their useful comments and suggestions.

[3]Bakhtin, *The Dialogic Imagination*, ed. Michael Holquist, trans. Emerson and Holquist (Austin: Univ. of Texas Press, 1981), p. 8, hereafter cited in text as *DI*. See Booth on Joyce in *The Rhetoric of Fiction* (Chicago: Univ. of Chicago Press, 1961), pp. 323-36 (for the "precious villanelle," see pp. 328-29). James Joyce, *A Portrait of the Artist as a Young Man: Text, Criticism, and Notes*, ed. Chester G. Anderson (Harmondsworth: Penguin Books, 1977), p. 251. (Anderson devotes pp. 446-80 to the critical debate over Joyce's "aesthetic distance" from Stephen.)

[4]Katerina Clark and Michael Holquist, *Mikhail Bakhtin* (Cambridge, Mass.: Belknap Press of Harvard Univ. Press, 1984), p. 22. Among those who link Joyce with Bakhtin are Clark and Holquist, p. 317; Allon White, "Bakhtin, Sociolinguistics and Deconstruction," in *The Theory of Reading*, ed. Frank Gloversmith (Brighton: Harvester, and Totowa: Barnes & Noble, 1984), pp. 132-33; Julia Kristeva, *Desire in Language*, ed. Leon Roudiez (New York: Columbia Univ. Press, 1980), p. 71 (she lists Joyce, Proust, and Kafka among modern polyphonic novelists). Meredith's influence on Joyce has long been recognized. (See, for example, Donald Fanger, "Joyce and Meredith: A Question of Influence and Tradition," *MFS* 6 [Summer 1960]: 125-30; Richard Ellmann, *James Joyce* [New York: Oxford Univ. Press,

1959], e.g. pp. 54, 116; and my *Novelists in a Changing World* [Cambridge, Mass.: Harvard Univ. Press, 1972], p. 336.)

[5]"What sets Meredith apart is the effect of his education in Germany" (V. S. Pritchett, *George Meredith and English Comedy* [London: Chatto & Windus, 1970], p. 37). And see Lionel Stevenson, *The Ordeal of George Meredith* (New York: Scribner, 1953), pp. 12-15; and my *The Romantic Impulse in Victorian Fiction* (Cambridge, Mass.: Harvard Univ. Press, 1980), pp. 292-94. For the connections between Bakhtin and German literature and philosophy, see Clark and Holquist, pp. 54, 60, 27, 26; and Tzvetan Todorov, *Mikhail Bakhtin: The Dialogical Principle*, trans. Wlad Godzich (Minneapolis: Univ. of Minnesota Press, 1984), pp. 86, 87. Fredrich Nietzsche, *The Birth of Tragedy* (with *The Case of Wagner*), trans. Walter Kaufmann (New York: Vintage Books, 1967), pp. 90-91. There may also be a connection between Bakhtin's carnival and Nietzsche's Dionysian revelry (see *Tragedy*, pp. 36-37). James M. Curtis, in "Michael Bakhtin, Nietzsche, and Russian Pre-Revolutionary Thought" (*Nietzsche in Russia*, ed. Bernice Glatzer Rosenthal [Princeton: Princeton Univ. Press, 1986], pp. 331-54), speculates that Bakhtin may have been inspired by Nietzsche's arguments in behalf of pluralism and dialogism (see pp. 335, 336).

[6]George Meredith, *Letters*, ed. C. L. Cline, 3 vols. (Oxford: Clarendon Press, 1970), 1:161. For Meredith as for Goethe, Bildung involves both the widening of one's perspective (*An*bildung) and the developing of one's abilities (*Aus*bildung). See W. H. Bruford, *Culture and Society in Classical Weimar: 1775-1806* (Cambridge: Cambridge Univ. Press, 1962), p. 37.

[7]Oscar Wilde, "The Decay of Lying," in *Works*, ed. G. F. Maine (London: Collins, 1948), p. 915; Virginia Woolf, "The Novels of George Meredith," *The Second Common Reader* (New York: Harcourt, Brace, 1932), pp. 206, 211-12. The vogue for Meredith, beginning in the 1880s, coincided with the discovery of Dostoevsky. Woolf wrote appreciatively on both writers.

[8]"Polyphonic Idealism" was the charge levelled against Bakhtin in Russia in 1930 (Todorov, p. 9; and see p. 103 for the comment on Dostoevsky's characterization).

[9]Here Bakhtin is echoing Belinsky on *Onegin* ("an encyclopedia of Russian life"). See Holquist, introduction to *DI*, p. xxviii. "The point [of *Richard Feverel*]," as Juliet Mitchell observes, "is . . . that the novel is not inconsistent, but heterogeneous; not chaotic, but strangely inclusive." "*The Ordeal of Richard Feverel*: A Sentimental Education," in *Meredith Now. Some Critical Essays*, ed. Ian Fletcher (London: Routledge & Kegan Paul, 1971), p. 73.

[10]Allon White, invoking Bakhtin, calls Meredith's novels "dialogical"; but he doesn't elaborate. *The Uses of Obscurity: The Fiction of Early Modernism* (London: Routledge & Kegan Paul, 1981), p. 27. For Meredith's use of dual narrators in *The Amazing Marriage*, see Gillian Beer, *Meredith: A Change of Masks: A Study of the Novels* (London: Athlone Press, 1970), p. 173.

[11]Miller's suggestive comments are directed toward Clara in *The Egoist*, but they apply to other Meredith protagonists. J. Hillis Miller, "'Herself Against Herself': The Clarification of Clara Middleton," *The Representation of Women in Fiction*: Selected Papers from the English Institute, 1981, ed. Carolyn G. Heilbrun and Margaret R. Higonnet (Baltimore: John Hopkins Univ. Press, 1983), pp. 98-123. Pritchett, p. 107.

[12]J. C. Carr, *Saturday Review* 41 (May 1876); rpt. in *Meredith: The Critical Heritage*, ed. Ioan Williams (London: Routledge & Kegan Paul, 1971), p. 182; Todorov, p. 99; see *Dost.*, ch. 3 ("The Idea in Dostoevsky"); Arnold

Kettle, "Beauchamp's Career," in Meredith Now ("The characters of the novel are all . . . seen as characters in history"), p. 188.

[13]Meredith, *Beauchamp's Career*, ch. 12; *One of Our Conquerors*, ch. 8. And see Walter F. Wright, *Art and Substance in George Meredith, A Study in Narrative* (Lincoln: Univ. of Nebraska Press, 1953), p. 31. According to W. H. Bruford, in *The German Tradition of Self-Cultivation: "Bildung" from Humboldt to Thomas Mann* (London: Cambridge Univ. Press, 1975), Goethe cites, in *Wilhelm Meister*, the "obvious analogy of the orchestra to suggest how the individual can fulfill himself while performing a useful social role"(p. 98).

[14]Caryl Emerson, "The Tolstoy Connection in Bakhtin," *PMLA* 100 (January 1985): 71; Todorov, p. 97. And see Patterson and Clark and Holquist on Bakhtin's religious views.

[15]Meredith, *The Egoist*, ch. 21 (further citations in text); Fyodor Dostoevsky, *The Brothers Karamazov*, trans. Constance Garnett, Bk. 6, ch. 2.

[16]Meredith, *Letters*, 2:876.

[17]I am very grateful to Caryl Emerson for allowing me to read Bakhtin's commentary on Goethe ("The *Bildungsroman* and its Significance in the History of Realism") in advance of its publication in *Speech Genres and Other Late Essays*, ed. Caryl Emerson and Michael Holquist, trans. Vern W. McGee (Austin: Univ. of Texas Press, 1986). (Todorov, pp. 91-92, writes of the "maturity of thought" evidenced in this fragment.) Meredith's importance as a writer of *Bildungsromane* has been demonstrated by Jerome H. Buckley in *Season of Youth: The Bildungsroman from Dickens to Golding* (Cambridge, Mass.: Harvard Univ. Press, 1974), pp. 63-91; Susanne Howe, *Wilhelm Meister and His English Kinsmen, Apprentices to Life* (New York: Columbia Univ. Press, 1930), ch. 9; Margaret Tarratt, "*The Adventures of Harry Richmond—Bildungsroman* and Historical Novel," in *Meredith Now*, pp. 165-87; G. B. Tennyson, "*The Bildungsroman* in Nineeenth-Century English Literature," in *Medieval Epic to the "Epic Theater" of Brecht, Essays in Comparative Literature*, ed. Rosario P. Armato and John M. Spalek (Los Angeles: Univ. of Southern California Press, 1968), pp. 135-46. For Hegel on Bildung see G. W. F. Hegel, *The Phenomenology of Mind*, trans. J. B. Baillie (New York: Harper & Row, 1967), pp. 514-48. Bruford, in *The German Tradition of Self-Cultivation*, treats the idea of Bildung with caution, noting that some German Romantics were prone to develop themselves but to ignore the corresponding need for social development. For more favorable views of the idea of Bildung see Ruth apRoberts, *Arnold and God* (Berkeley: Univ. of California Press, 1983), ch. 4; and Hans-Georg Gadamer, *Truth and Method*, trans. and ed. Garrett Barden and John Cumming (New York: Seabury Press, 1975), pp. 10-19. Like Bakhtin, Georg Lukács, in *The Theory of the Novel*, trans. Anna Bostock (Cambridge, Mass.: MIT Press, 1971), treats the novel as dealing with man's "becoming" (pp. 72-73); but unlike Bakhtin, Lukács looks wistfully back to the epic sense of order and stability. (Todorov, p. 87, cites Friedrich Schlegel's view that the novel as a genre is still in a state of "becoming.")

[18]Wilde, "The Soul of Man Under Socialism," in *Works*, p. 1037. Meredith's protagonists, Pritchett contends, "are always extremists because they have to carry this thing he called Idea" (p. 50). See Emerson, "The Tolstoy Connection," p. 76.

[19]Carr, in *Meredith: The Critical Heritage*, p. 182.

[20]Meredith, *Beauchamp's Career*, ch. 50; Clark and Holquist, p. 11. As in the case of Hegel, Bakhtin's celebration of freedom is based on his belief in Bildung.

[21]V. N. Vološinov, *Freudianism: A Marxist Critique*, trans. I. R. Titunik and ed. in collaboration with N. H. Bruss (New York: Academic Press, 1976), p. 79. Whether the words in this and the other "Bakhtin Circle" writings are or are not (in part or wholly) Bakhtin's, the impulse behind them seems to have been Bakhtin's.

[22]George Eliot, *Middlemarch*, ch. 28; Clark and Holquist, p. 206.

[23]Bakhtin, *Rabelais and His World*, trans. Helene Iswolsky (Bloomington: Indiana Univ. Press, 1984), pp. 272, 403, 10, hereafter cited in text as *Rab.* Here, as in other respects, Bakhtin allies himself with William James, whose Pluralism privileges real space and historical time: "Pluralism, in exorcising the absolute, exorcises the great de-realizer of the only life we are at home in, and thus redeems the nature of reality from essential foreignness" (*A Pluralistic Universe* [London: Longmans, Green, 1920], pp. 49-50).

[24]*Thus Spoke Zarathustra*, in *The Portable Nietzsche*, trans. and ed. Walter Kaufmann (New York: Viking Press, 1954), p. 404. See White on Meredith's sensitivity (*The Uses of Obscurity*, ch. 4).

[25]Meredith, *The Tragic Comedians*, ch. 19.

[26]Meredith, "An Essay on Comedy" (originally "Essay on the Idea of Comedy and the Uses of the Comic Spirit"), in *Comedy*, ed. Wylie Sypher (Garden City: Doubleday, 1956), pp. 48, 10, 13-14, 46 ("Those who detect irony in comedy do so because they choose to see it in life"), p. 32. Despite Wayne Booth's musings over the anti-feminist implications in Rabelais, *Bakhtin's* Rabelais is an apostle of egalitarianism (see, for example, *Rab.*, p. 264). A belief in dialogism, as we see in Meredith, is necessarily feminist. Booth, "Freedom of Interpretation: Bakhtin and the Challenge of Feminist Criticism," *CritI* 9 (September 1982): 45-76.

[27]Meredith, *Harry Richmond*, ch. 56. For Bakhtin, language is not the only medium of communication: he also discusses intonation, "contextual overtones" (*DI*, p. 293), and other ways in which meaning is conveyed. The fullest account of the social nature of language is that of Bakhtin's associate Vološinov in *Marxism and the Philosophy of Language*, trans. L. Matejka and I. R. Titunik (New York: Seminar Press, 1973).

[28]For Meredith and the limits of language, see Beer, p. 185, and her essay on *One of Our Conquerors* ("Language and Music") in *Meredith Now*, pp. 265-80 ("Music, in this novel, is the liberating alternative to language," p. 275); and see my chapter on this novel ("The Limits of Articulation") in *Novelists in a Changing World*, pp. 154-72. Ludwig Wittgenstein, *Philosophical Investigations*, trans. G. E. M. Anscombe (New York: Macmillan, 1968), p. 192. See Clark and Holquist, pp. 20-21; and Terry Eagleton, "Wittgenstein's Friends," *Against the Grain, Essays 1975-1985* (London: Verso, 1986), pp. 111-19. Todorov, p. 111. As early as *Modern Love* (1860) and *Richard Feverel*, Meredith had doubts about the chances of verbal comprehension and communication. In the latter work he writes, "There are ideas language is too gross for, and shape too arbitrary, which come to us and have a definite influence upon us, and yet we cannot fasten on the filmy things and make them visible and distinct to ourselves, much more to others" (ch. 23).

[29]Meredith, *The Ordeal of Richard Feverel*, chs. 12, 30. Michael Mendelson has discussed the Menippean elements in *The Shaving of Shagpat* in a paper ("The Comic Spirit in the Land of Fantasy") read in 1985 at the Fantasy in the Arts conference.

[30]Miller, "'Herself Against Herself,'" pp. 121-22. What Miller sees as a new, Deconstructive "theory of character" in Meredith may be explained in terms of Bakhtin's and Goethe's view of the changeability of character.

[31]Stone, *Novelists in a Changing World*, p. 148.

[32]Meredith, *Diana of the Crossways*, chs. 4, 13 (further citations from *Diana* are in the text). Dostoevsky's characters, says Bakhtin, "do furious battle with such definitions of their personality in the mouths of the other people" (*Dost.*, p. 59). In *One of Our Conquerors*, another author concocts a dialogical fiction, "The Rival Tongues."

[33]Meredith, *Letters*, 2:743.

[34]De Man, "Dialogue and Dialogism," pp. 107, 105.

[35]Geoffrey H. Hartman, "The Culture of Criticism," *PMLA* 99 (May 1984): 389; Dennis Donoghue, "Reading Bakhtin," *Raritan* 2 (Fall 1985):115-16, 118; Todorov, p. ix. Don H. Bialostosky has recently called for a "dialogical critical practice" in "Dialogics as an Art of Discourse in Literary Criticism," *PMLA* 101 (October 1986): 788-97.

[36]D. H. Lawrence, "Why the Novel Matters," *Phoenix* (New York: Viking Press, 1978), p. 535. See Arthur O. Lovejoy, "Romanticism and the Principle of Plenitude," *The Great Chain of Being, A Study of the History of an Idea* (Cambridge, Mass.: Harvard Univ. Press, 1950), pp. 288-314; James, *A Pluralistic Universe*; Wayne C. Booth, *Critical Understanding: The Powers and Limits of Pluralism* (Chicago: Univ. of Chicago Press, 1979; Hans-Georg Gadamer, *Philosophical Hermeneutics*, trans. David E. Linge (Berkeley: Univ. of California Press, p. 16.

SEL 28 (1988)
ISSN 0039-3657

Recent Studies in the Nineteenth Century

DAVID G. RIEDE

The experience of reading through vast amounts of the year's work teaches many things, but nothing more emphatically than that life is short, art is long, and criticism is interminable. To prevent my own from becoming interminable I have had to say far less about the books reviewed than I would have liked, and of course I have had to be selective about what books to review. Despite my agreement that the canon needs to be opened up, I have chosen to review primarily those works concerned with canonical texts and authors on the assumption that they would still be of the widest general interest, and I have avoided collections of essays by diverse hands (mainly because it seemed impossible to review them adequately in limited space), collections of previously printed essays by single authors, and most volumes of letters. My only other caveat is to note that with the current triumph of the New Historicism there has been much discussion of the sources of authority in discourse, and in particular of the spurious authority bestowed upon an author by the prestige of the organ he writes for—so despite my desire to take the reactionary position that I do indeed speak with authority, and not as other critical scribes do, I must confess that the whole idea of an omnibus review conducted by a single all too limited critic is obviously highly problematic. The several books reviewed that discuss the policing functions of literature have made me, I confess, acutely self-conscious.

The attempt to review such a book as Jerome J. McGann's *Social Values and Poetic Acts: The Historical Judgment of Literary Work* quickly exposes both the practical and theoretical limitations of a period-bound omnibus review. Its immense

David G. Riede is Professor of English at Ohio State University. He is the author of *Swinburne: A Study of Romantic Mythmaking*, *Dante Gabriel Rossetti and the Limits of Victorian Vision*, and *Matthew Arnold and the Betrayal of Language*.

range, from Homer's Greece to contemporary America removes it both from the limited field of nineteenth-century British literature and from the far more limited field of the reviewer's expertise, and its theoretical argument and methodology call into question the whole idea of studying literary works isolated and sealed off within the artificial bounds of periodization. But for just these reasons, among others, McGann's work is of great importance to students of nineteenth-century British literature. Like other New Historicist critics, McGann calls into question the fundamental premises of literary study that our own age has inherited from the Romantic domestication of Kantian aesthetics. In particular, he examines the consequences of separating an aesthetic realm from the social world, establishing an autonomous realm of art, examining artistic works as timeless artifacts rather than time-bound acts, and acquiescing in the totalizing, imperialist gestures of a Romantic aesthetic that claims to transcend the ideological constraints of partial or partisan views. The complex, multi-faceted argument incorporates the insights of deconstructionists, New Historicists, formalists, and Marxists, drawing them into a dialectic that aborts the absolutist or totalizing drive of each approach by thwarting it with the contrary views of the others. In fascinating discussions of Blake, Arnold, Pound, Aeschylus, and others, McGann demonstrates how an awareness of an artist's work as an active intervention in the life of his time increases our sense both of the practical function of art, and of its necessary limitations within given historical horizons.

Another important contribution to both the emergent New Historicism and to nineteenth-century studies is Jonathan Arac's *Critical Genealogies: Historical Situations for Postmodern Literary Studies*. The special relevance of this study of postmodernist critical theory to students of the nineteenth century is evident in Arac's "claim that to read contemporary criticism requires recognizing the interrelations of at least three layers, like geological strata. Coleridge's Romantic metaphysics of symbol and imagination; Arnold's Victorian stance of disinterested, yet worldly, discrimination; and modernist, technical specifications of professional critical tasks together form the ground that current literary study has begun to shift" (p. 3). Arac does not attempt the impossible task of fitting all literary critical theory from Coleridge to yesterday into a totalizing narrative, but instead adapts "Benjamin's thoughts on 'constellating' moments of the past into a shape with present meaning" into a methodological principle (p. 6). With excellent results, he "constellates," for example, Coleridge, the New Critics, M.H. Abrams, and Paul de Man; and elsewhere, Matthew Arnold, the New Critics, and Geoffrey Hartman. These and other "constellations" provide the grounds for analyses that reveal both the strengths and weaknesses of current critical methodologies, and lead to revisionary assessments of writers whose achievements have been misrepresented and often underestimated because of the ideological biases in various post-modernist theoretical stances. Arac's methodology thus enables him to offer significant revisionary studies of Wordsworth, Arnold, and others by supplementing the language- and text-centered analyses of modernist/post-modernist methodologies with a New Historical awareness of literary works as ideologically conditioned and conditioning. Arac's most important contribution to the new literary history he hopes to influence is his emphasis on the historical, cultural, and political conditions that help shape not only literature, but critical theory as well.

Another ambitious New Historicist study is Clifford Siskin's *The Historicity of Romantic Discourse.* Siskin argues that criticism of Romantic discourse has remained within the parameters of that discourse, and so has failed to gain sufficient critical-historical detachment to see such fundamentally Romantic concepts as the deeply interiorized self, the development of mind and imagination, and the authoritatively charged lyric burst as constructs *invented* at a specific historic moment, not as timeless realities *discovered* by the Romantics. Consequently, according to Siskin, the texts of Blake, Wordsworth, Austen, Malthus, the Wedgewoods, Darwin, and hosts of others share in "a common enterprise: the naturalizing of a new complex of human behaviors" (p. 163) and the texts of critics as diverse as de Man, Hartman, McFarland, and McGann share a common error: the acceptance of these naturalized constructs as reality. I emphasize the texts rather than the writers because, according to Siskin's Foucauldian argument, there are only texts—authors are "written," "pre-scribed" or "inscribed" by the discourse they perpetuate in writing. Siskin would presumably agree that his own discourse is "pre-scribed" by Foucauldian discourse, particularly by the arguments that "reality . . . is a matter of representation—a construct of changing discursive practices that define the 'nature' of experience in culture-specific terms" (p. 72), and that the human subject came into existence—with remarkable abruptness—in the late eighteenth century, and that "development" (the "growth" of the individual mind, the "growth" of culture) is a Romantic construct imposed on change. Siskin's contribution to this discourse (actually his discourse's contribution—personal agency is written out of this discourse, since the New Historicist dominance in the profession has "pre-scribed" that the author be proscribed) is to urge a new literary history that would emphasize differences in genre rather than in quality among works, and thus, Siskin hopes, avoid the psychologizing and thematizing across generic lines that has enabled critical discussion to "naturalize" differences in "kind" as differences in "degree." The point is a political one, since the proposed change would replace hierarchical judgments with analysis, and would force reassessments of our still Romantic conceptions of topics as diverse as the nature of "genius," of gender differences, of economics, and even of drug addiction. Siskin's Foucauldian assumptions are, of course, not above question, and his criminalization of Romantic modes of thought is perhaps overdone, but his range is vast and impressive, his arguments important and provocative.

Studies of intellectual movements over a two hundred year span helpfully isolate certain trends and tendencies of thought, but they also formally suggest a linear view of historical change, and a sparsely populated historical line at that, with the chain or thread of history strung across a few monumental works. Richard L. Stein's decision to look at a specific "moment" in *Victoria's Year: English Literature and Culture, 1837-1838,* leads to a very different perspective, one that enables us to see a densely figured culture in a historical vision that aspires to reflect the Carlylean axiom that history is not linear but solid. Our methodologies, as Stein is well aware, always determine the nature of our results, so it is perhaps not surprising that Stein's methodological concern with the issue of how best to focus on a given historical moment is reflected in his discovery of a culture that is obsessed precisely with the question of how to focus on itself. Stein's approach, in other words, makes him especially sensitive to the ways in which the earliest Victorians were anxious to define and fix a world view in an increasingly changing, uncertain, relativist world, and leads him to excellent analyses of such works as Harriet Martineau's *How to Observe* and of her actual observations of American life, of Ruskin's concerns with how to see architecture and nature in *The Poetry of Architecture,* and of the young Darwin's concerns with how to see nature and man in his first scientific notes. Further, Stein's subtle analyses show that even seemingly untroubled representations of the world in the late 1830s are deeply problematic, and show how a society constructs its own versions of reality. His excellent discussions of representations range from the young Victoria's sketches of gypsies, Boz's sketches of London life, Cruickshank's sketches for Boz's sketches, to a judge's representation of a would-be suicide's self-representation, to a newspaper version of the judge's version, and so on through all levels of early Victorian culture. Stein's method cannot, of course, present the moment in its full "solidity," but it does enrich our understanding of the dense web of interrelations, and of the pervasive common ground shared among all classes and among all philosophic, scientific, and aesthetic pursuits at the beginning of Victoria's reign. It goes a long way towards defining the common "order of things" that all discourse spoke within or against.

Pamela Horn's *Life and Labour in Rural England, 1760-1850* is designed to provide "context and commentary" for the literature of the period, and does provide a host of often fascinating quotations from poems, novels, memoirs, and historical records, but though Horn is aware that her various quotations are not always to be taken at face value, that they are distorted by the biases of particular speakers, she does not do enough to assess and analyze them. For the most part, lengthy quotations from Austen, Cobbett, and (slightly anachronistically) Eliot and Trollope are left to speak for themselves about the conditions they describe—polemical rhetoric and literature are too little sifted. Nevertheless, the book will be very useful to beginning students of the period who are seeking general background information about how the age saw itself. More grimly fascinating historical context for the Victorian novel is provided by A. Susan Williams's accounts of the "socio-political discourse" (p. ix) generated by the actual horrors of pestilence in early Victorian England. *The Rich Man and the Diseased Poor in Early Victorian Literature* describes the miasma, the disease mists, the loathsome sanitary conditions, and the ways in which the actuality and imagery of disease contributed to upper and middle class perceptions of the poor, who bore the brunt of the cholera, typhus, and typhoid epidemics.

In *Doubt and Identity in Romantic Poetry,* Andrew M. Cooper argues that Romantic narrative poetry responded to eighteenth-century skepticism—and especially to David Hume's deconstruction of essentialist ideas of personal identity—by constructing a self that "emerges as the provisional outcome of a continuous welter of perceptivity" (p. 15). Cooper offers versions of Romantic irony and Romantic indeterminism to argue that the self-reflections and repetitions of various narratives are the means to the poet's self-formation as an identity, a shaping consciousness, and that this identity is recognized (indeed, realized) in the shaping consciousness of the projected reader. His suggestive readings of *Milton, Christabel,* the second canto of *Don Juan,* and *Alastor* argue that the poems enact a process of self-realization in which the poetic subject evolves simultaneously in poet, poem, and reader. In effect, Cooper's method of reading echoes his version of Romantic creation as he works through Humean skepticism to a reader-response criticism that reconstitutes the identity of the poet in that of the reader. The end result is a somewhat qualified phenomenological affirmation that the "poems offer what Blake terms a merciful 'female space' of time wherein poet and reader, by recognizing their mutual dependence, are each enabled to objectify a provisional identity for the other" (p. 186). Arguably, at any rate, Cooper is a little too ready to accept the Romantic project on its own terms; the strongest part of this intriguing, important study, I think, is its recognition of the profoundly disquieting importance of Hume's skepticism on the Romantics, and I would be inclined to argue that the Romantic efforts to reestablish personal identity, like Cooper's still Romantic phenomenology, never fully succeed. But Cooper, like the authors he discusses, is well aware of the shakiness of a personal identity that can only be "provisional," that is always prey to skeptical deconstruction—consequently his careful, sympathetic readings of the poems offer important (though certainly disputable) insights into their complex workings.

In *Language, Music and the Sign: A Study in Aesthetics, Poetics and Poetic Practice from Collins to Coleridge,* Kevin Barry argues that critical emphasis on the analogy of poetry and painting in the eighteenth and early nineteenth centuries has resulted in neglect of the analogy of poetry and music. He demonstrates that music, when understood as an expressive rather than a representational art, offered a semiotic system of "empty signs" that eighteenth-century and Romantic writers could use to lessen the perceived tyranny of the word in order to shift from a representational to an expressive theory of language. In separate chapters on Collins, Blake and Cowper, Wordsworth, and Coleridge, Barry places the poets in relation to various major and minor theorists to highlight their uses of musical theory in relation to their own developing thoughts about language and the arts. Barry's erudition is impressive, and his thoroughness in reviewing aesthetic traditions and debates is compelling, but in the cases of Blake and Wordsworth, at least, his findings do not convincingly challenge generally accepted views. The discussion of Coleridge also does not radically alter received ideas about his aesthetics, but it does offer a new perspective on his thought by showing clearly how his preference of music to painting correlates with his ideas about imagination and poetry.

Alan Richardson's *A Mental Theater: Poetic Drama and Consciousness in the Romantic Age* urges a reassessment of Romantic experiments in dramatic form that would see them not as a retreat from the stage, but as a new subgenre, the "mental theater." Such works as Wordsworth's *The Borderers*, Byron's *Cain* and *Manfred,* and Shelley's *The Cenci* and *Prometheus Unbound* have too often been seen as drama collapsing into monodrama as they explore the developing Romantic individualism of a too dominant central character, but Richardson's shift in generic perspective enables him to argue that the differentiation of characters in "mental theater" characteristically portrays a pattern of seduction into a state of self-consciousness that is not a Romantic good in itself, but a limited condition of alienation and guilt. "Mental Theater," according to Richardson, is a better term than "closet drama" for such forms because it insists upon the creative responses of the reader, who is to become a participant in the mental strife of the drama. Richardson's perspective is not especially new for such works as *Prometheus Unbound* and *Manfred*, and his collapsing of plays as different as the very stageable *The Cenci* and the utterly unstageable *Cain* leads to some neglect of traditional theatrical elements in these works, but it also leads to the recognition of surprising and intriguing patterns among the various plays. And despite a somewhat single-minded effort to refer the intertextuality of all of these works back almost exclusively to *Othello, Macbeth,* and *Paradise Lost,* Richardson's readings are always fresh, insightful, and illuminating.

In the year's only monograph on Blake, Harold Pagliaro passes over the historical, biographical, theological, and literary contexts to argue that the "psychology of redemption" (p. ix) in Blake's prophecies is also, and more immediately and urgently, present in the *Songs of Innocence and Experience.* The approach in *Selfhood and Redemption in Blake's "Songs"* is, I think, not only unnecessarily limiting, but actually distorting, since the only context offered for reading the *Songs* is, anachronistically, the late prophecies. Pagliaro, like many other Blakeans, assumes that Blake's works form a canon of unified, consistent doctrine, but freighting the songs with the language of the prophecies produces such unjustifiable and unhelpful readings as the comment on the relatively late "To Tirzah" that "in moments Satan cannot find, Selfhood is 'visited' and 'displaced' by eternal Identity" (p. 103). Discussions of the earlier poems in these terms are, of course, still less justifiable. Further, Pagliaro's emphasis on the "psychological process as process" (p. 2) leads to surprising questions about Blake's "characters"—what they thought before the experience of the poem, what they will be like after it, and so on. Pagliaro's accounts of the dynamics of character are sometimes helpful in discussing dramatic speakers, but they seem startlingly inappropriate when he speaks of the Sick Rose, or the Youth and pale Virgin of "Ah! Sun-Flower" as "highly individual persons with histories of their own" (p. 125). One effect—and perhaps cause—of these readings is that distinctions of genre are blurred as the *Songs* are not read as songs but as studies in redemptive psychology.

In *Wordsworth's Historical Imagination: The Poetry of Displacement,* David Simpson challenges the traditional view of Wordsworth as "the poet of nature and of solitude," arguing that Wordsworth's thought is historically and socially influenced to a far greater extent than is generally realized, that his imagination does not transcend but reflects material circumstance. Further, Simpson argues that even the Wordsworthian "self," that coherent inward core of being that justifies the "egotistical sublime," is a historically, socially, materially conditioned intersubjective construct. But Simpson resists what he sees as the totalizing impulses of all theory, preferring a moderate, pragmatic approach to such issues as the nature of subjectivity: "Subjectivity is neither a 'historically' created automaton, nor an exclusively individual entity governing itself by choice and free will. It is, awkwardly, something between the two" (pp. 5-6). The subject described in Wordsworth's writing is "a subject in conflict, a subject defined by a condition of acute alienation, both vocational and social" (p. 2). Denying himself the luxury of a totalizing theory, or even of a fully coherent Wordsworthian self for analysis, Simpson must also deny himself the luxury of a vast overview and convenient summarizing generalizations. Consequently he concentrates on just a few poems, among them "Simon Lee," "Michael," "The Old Cumberland Beggar," and *The Excursion,* and attempts to demonstrate his contention about Wordsworth's alienation by reading them within a detailed historical and biographical context. Simpson does not provide a coherent Wordsworth, nor does he try to—instead he provides a strong demonstration of the inadequacy of a Romantic view of Romanticism, a challenge to the fiction of "an intelligence continually evolving in ways that typify the life of a Coleridgean organic whole" (p. 212).

Recent writers on Wordsworth, including Simpson, have regretted that emphasis on the so-called "great decade" has limited our understanding and appreciation of Wordsworth's late career. That imbalance is partially redressed in Theresa M. Kelley's *Wordsworth's Revisionary Aesthetics.* Kelley gains a somewhat unusual perspective on Wordsworth's writings by taking as her starting point two relatively little discussed prose works written after the "great decade": *A Guide Through the District of the Lakes* and the unfinished study of aesthetics, "The Sublime and the Beautiful." Study of these works leads Kelley to careful differentiation of the Wordsworthian from the Burkean and Kantian versions of the sublime, to a subtle analysis of the importance of topography in Wordsworth's aesthetics, and to the conclusion that, contrary to critical tradition, Wordsworth valued the beautiful above the sublime, that he in fact valued the beautiful precisely because it could control and domesticate the sublime. Recognizing Wordsworth's emphasis on the beautiful may well provide a key to appreciating his late works on their own terms as opposed to viewing them as a falling off from the sublime, though some may initially question Kelley's decision to use late Wordsworth to interpret early poems. But her analyses of various earlier works, and especially of various versions of *The Prelude,* demonstrate that fears of the revolutionary sublime engendered in response to mayhem in France in the early to mid 1700s had led Wordsworth, even then, to begin confining the energies of the sublime within the controlling structures of the beautiful.

The complex relation of Wordsworth and Coleridge is the subject of two books, Nicholas Roe's *Wordsworth and Coleridge: The Radical Years,* and Paul Magnuson's *Coleridge and Wordsworth: A Lyrical Dialogue.* Roe's scrupulous and detailed archival research illuminates the nature and extent of Wordsworth's involvement with various factions and individuals in Orléans, Blois, and London, and of Coleridge's rather different—but overlapping—involvement with radicals and dissenters in Cambridge, Bristol, and London. He provides a full and rich account of the contexts of Wordsworth's and Coleridge's early thought through detailed accounts of government policies, radical associations, and the thought of, among others, Michel Beaupuy, Henri Grégoire, Priestley, Frend, Thelwall, and Godwin. By following the paths of the poets separately to their eventual collaboration, Roe clearly demonstrates not only the common ground that brought them together (a common interest in politics as much as in poetics) but also the different directions in which they were moving, and as a result he is able to offer a new perspective on the collaboration. Roe is certainly not the first to note the extreme importance of Wordsworth's and Coleridge's early radicalism, but his excellent study admirably substantiates the exact nature of their political involvement. Nevertheless, he does not find in mutual radicalism a sufficient context to explain the "surprising" fact that Coleridge seems to have expressed what Jonathan Wordsworth calls the "central Wordsworthian mystical experience" before Wordsworth himself did (p. 233). Magnuson is helpful in this respect, arguing that the two poets constructed their poetic identities in a common body of texts that are so dialogically interwoven as to constitute, in Coleridge's phrase, "*one work . . . as an Ode is one work*" (p. 16). Magnuson effaces the boundaries of individual works, seeing poems as stanzas in a vast, jointly composed ode. He begins with works written before the close collaboration began, arguing that Coleridge's reading of the Salisbury plain poems and *The Borderers*, and Wordsworth's reading of "Religious Musings" and *Osorio* drew them towards one another's viewpoints, and even towards the perceived dangers of "amalgamation." He then proceeds to readings of numerous works in which the poets respond to one another's poems—the "Ancient Mariner," for example, is a response to the sailor of Salisbury plain, and the "Discharged Soldier" is a response to the "Ancient Mariner"; similarly, "Christabel" responds to "The Ruined Cottage," "Tintern Abbey" to "Frost at Midnight," *The Prelude* (1799) to the conversation poems in general, *Home at Grasmere* to "Reflections on Having Left a Place of Retirement" and so on. The limitations of this approach are implicit in the notion that the poems are to be read as stanzas in a single ode; despite Magnuson's desire to eliminate the boundaries of individual poems and so to read them in a larger context, he ends up, in effect, positing a mega-poem to be read as an autonomous entity, cut off from the larger socio-historical context. He is also, I think, too eager to find that each poem is "a commentary on a succeeding one" (p. 139), with the result that he sometimes distorts poems by reading them too single-mindedly in response to a single precursor. Nevertheless, his study helpfully complements Roe's, and illuminates how intimately and intricately the two poets' works are interwoven. Magnuson depends heavily on the magisterial editions of Wordsworth and Coleridge being issued by Cornell and Princeton respectively, and his final chapter, on the relations of the "Intimations Ode," "Dejection: An Ode," and "Resolution and Independence" would have been facilitated by—as it happens—a new Coleridge edition from the general editor of the Cornell Wordsworth. Stephen Maxfield Parrish's *Coleridge's "Dejection": The Earliest Manuscripts and the Earliest Printings* provides reading copies, variants, photographic duplications, and transcripts of the newly discovered earliest version of "A Letter to ———," of early and late versions of "Dejection: An Ode," and of the related "The Day-Dream" (first published in the *Morning Post* in 1802 and never republished by Coleridge). The edition is valuable not only for making new MS material available, and for its lucid and thorough presentation of the various texts, but also for Parrish's helpful introduction, which provides the background for the writing and transformation of a 339-line love letter addressed to Sara Hutchinson to a 139-line ode addressed first to a fictitious "Edmund," then to Wordsworth and finally to an unnamed "Lady."

The major event this year in Coleridge studies is the publication of two large volumes in *The Collected Works of Samuel Taylor Coleridge. Lectures 1808-1819: On Literature,* edited by R.A. Foakes, maintains the extraordinarily high standards of the edition as a whole. Coleridge, always a difficult author to edit because of the chaotic state of his literary remains, presents an even greater challenge to the editor of his lectures, since they were never prepared for publication, never even fully written out. But Foakes has assembled, arranged, introduced, and annotated whatever information is available for each lecture, from Coleridge's own notes, notes taken by auditors, newspaper reports, and letters and comments about the lectures. Foakes not only arranges the familiar materials chronologically for the first time, but he also publishes a large amount of new, previously unpublished material, outlines the conditions under which the lectures were written and delivered, and discusses the contemporary responses. As a result, an enormously important part of Coleridge's career is now conveniently available for study for the first time. But *The Collected Works,* alas, is not for everyone's budget, either of money or, for the nonspecialist, of time, so selections from Coleridge's writings are still necessary. H.J. Jackson's cullings from Coleridge's correspondence, *Samuel Taylor Coleridge: Selected Letters,* offers about one-tenth of Coleridge's published correspondence, and the one-tenth is carefully and well chosen to "display his achievement as a writer in the minor genre of the familiar letter; to reveal his complex personality in evolution; and to record his astute judgement, especially in literary matters" (p. xii). The selection shows Coleridge at his mercurial best as his mind and pen fly from topic to topic, from profundity to whimsy, and shows him also at his pitiful worst, wheedlingly apologetic and self-deprecatingly self-serving. But the volume is woefully lacking in apparatus—the introduction offers far too little to the nonspecialist audience that such a selection should serve, and the somewhat haphazard annotations far too often fail to gloss names, quotations, references, and circumstances that the reader must have for a full understanding of the text.

H.W. Piper's *The Singing of Mount Abora: Coleridge's Use of Biblical Imagery and Natural Symbolism in Poetry and Philosophy* argues that Coleridge has been too often misread by critics who have not appreciated the consistently religious context of his thought and therefore of his symbolism. Piper traces the shifts in Coleridge's religious thought from his Unitarianism in the 1790s through his readings of German philosophers in the first decade of the nineteenth century to the Trinitarian position of his later writings, and demonstrates that both the symbols actually used in his poetry, and the philosophical discussions of symbolism in his prose must be understood in relation to his concurrently held religious position. Stated this baldly, Piper's argument seems merely obvious, and indeed it is not strikingly novel in its broad outlines; but it does, nevertheless, serve as a useful corrective to common readings of Coleridge that see his work as all of a piece, all interpretable through the metaphysical lenses of the *Biographia*.

Coleridge is also prominently discussed in the year's only study of the Romantic essayists, Thomas McFarland's *Romantic Cruxes: The English Essayists and the Spirit of the Age*. McFarland's announced purpose is, in part, to explore the difficult relations of Lamb, Hazlitt, and De Quincey with Coleridge, and more importantly, to show that the three essayists are not foothills but bona fide "mountains in the Romantic range" (p. 15). He succeeds best in this endeavor when he lets the essayists speak for themselves in numerous extended blocks of quotation, but when he speaks for them he actually makes them look small in relation to "the snow-capped peak of Coleridge" (p. 25). Arguing, for example, that Hazlitt is a great stylist, McFarland actually demonstrates that Hazlitt's style gains its force at the considerable expense of flexibility and subtlety. Despite a proclivity for tired metaphors, McFarland himself writes forcefully, but unfortunately he has no real thesis to advance, and no new information to offer.

Byron, whose life and works are so complexly interwoven with the ideological clashes of his times, would seem to be a likely beneficiary of the current rage for New Historicist criticism, but he is the subject of only one major study this year, Frederick Garber's *Self, Text, and Romantic Irony: The Example of Byron*. Garber seems at first likely to take something like a New Historicist perspective, eschewing what he calls "naive biographism" and arguing that "Romantic selves, texts, and worlds flow into each other in ways that still dazzle" (p. x). It soon becomes clear, however, that he avoids all "biographism," that in his analysis of the perpetual weaving and unweaving of selves, texts, and worlds, the selves and worlds he examines are exclusively the fictional ones—Harold, Manfred and their worlds, but rarely or never Byron and his world. Consequently Garber, who sees himself working somewhere between the poles of Abrams and de Man, finds himself closest to the de Manian disregard of history, and pays little attention to the historical Byron and the interplay of *his* self with the actualities of experience and with the transformations of self and world in the generation of texts. Indeed, Garber speaks of the Byronic "canon" as though it were somehow self-generating, so that he can speak, for example, of "acts the canon performs as it goes along" (p. 126). But on their own somewhat formalist grounds, Garber's readings are often brilliant. His discussion of the early books of *Childe Harold,* of *The Giaour,* and of *Manfred* superbly explicate the inter-involvement of selves and settings in a constant dialectic of making and unmaking a coherent self in a coherent text. Further, Garber extends his discussion beyond formal analysis by lengthy and fruitful comparisons of Byron's practices with those of other artists—Byron's orientalism is usefully compared with that of Beckford and Delacroix, his firm insistence on outline with that of Blake, his Romantic irony with that of Hoffman and Heine. Similarly, his ironic mode, with its constant emphasis on gaps, discontinuities, and open-endedness is very usefully contrasted with the traditionally "normative" Romanticism of Wordsworthian organicism and closure—a contrast that leads Garber to one of his characteristically pithy formulations, a paraphrase of Wordsworth that sees the mind of the ironist "acting as if its whole vocation were endless dislocation" (p. 181).

In *Wordsworth's Influence on Shelley: A Study of Poetic Authority*, G. Kim Blank exhaustively argues "what many critics have intuited: that Wordsworth is the single most important influence in Shelley's poetic development" (p. x). Blank usefully points out Shelley's frequent comments on and allusions to his older contemporary, and offers interesting discussions of a number of poems, from *Alastor* to *The Triumph of Life*, that show Shelley contending with the figure of the poet he inherited from Wordsworth. But Blank's speculations, based on Bloom's model of poetic anxiety, often seem far-fetched and reductive—Wordsworth comes to seem Shelley's all but exclusive concern, as Blank identifies not only the *Alastor* poet and narrator, but the maniac of *Julian and Maddalo*, and Jupiter of *Prometheus Unbound* as types of the Wordsworthian poet, and at times it seems that every cloud is the one that Wordsworth wandered lonely as, every flower the celandine that Wordsworth celebrated. Wordsworth's influence on Shelley was undoubtedly profound and pervasive, and Blank's study can be a useful guide to it—but his speculations should be read with a healthy skepticism.

The Monster in the Mirror: Gender and the Sentimental/Gothic Myth in "Frankenstein" by Mary K. Patterson Thornburg ambitiously attempts not just a reading of Mary Shelley's novel, but a history and explication of what she calls the "sentimental/

Gothic myth, our culture's dominant world-view" (p. 11). Unfortunately her survey of western culture since the Renaissance suffers from relentless generalizing, and naive conceptions of myth, of the sentimental, and of the gothic. Her analysis of *Frankenstein* adds little new to our understanding of the novel, and in fact badly distorts the work by imposing upon it her general thematic categories as well as a somewhat less pertinent and somewhat more distorting Freudian analysis. It is symptomatic of the lack of precision in Thornburg's thematic analysis that her last chapter sweepingly associates with *Frankenstein* such films as *Shane, The Thing, Alien,* and *Cujo*. A much better book on the same topic is Chris Baldick's *In Frankenstein's Shadow: Myth, Monstrosity, and Nineteenth-Century Writing*. Baldick offers a wide ranging examination of Mary Shelley's novel as well as of the subsequent "series of adaptations, allusions, accretions, analogues, parodies, and plain misreadings" which, Baldick argues, "is not just a supplementary component of the myth" but "*is* the myth" (p. 5). Following an astute critical reading of the novel, Baldick shows how Victor Frankenstein's story was variously retold and reimagined as the Victorian Frankensteinian, figuring in representations of social insurgency, class struggle, industrial and capitalist fetishization, and imperialist politics. His analysis ranges from the cartoons of *Punch*, through the writings of Carlyle, Dickens, and Marx, to the mad scientists of Wells and others, the monstrosities of the artificial self in Stevenson and Wilde, and on to Conrad and D.H. Lawrence. One might argue with Baldick's definition of myth, or urge that many of his examples can be understood in a larger context than the Frankenstein story, but Baldick offers adept and convincing demonstrations of the complex and equivocal resonances of the story throughout Victorian culture. His subtle analyses illuminate the political and psychological ramifications both of the Frankenstein story and of the many works through which it reverberates.

Philip W. Martin's *Mad Women in Romantic Writing* takes up a fascinating topic, and offers intriguing background information about the conceptualization of madness in the nineteenth century, and splendid insights into writings on madness from Wordsworth's to Freud's. But the book is strangely incapacitated by theoretical scruples—Martin would like to speak as a feminist, but feels that as a man he cannot; he would like to write a book but feels that he must resist the impulse to create an "artificial synthesis" by making connections between texts, so he writes instead a series of disconnected chapters; he would like to talk about what his authors mean, but is determined to avoid any intentional fallacy, so he talks about "texts" as though they were self-generated. He is at his least inhibited, and at his best, in a long chapter about Wordsworth, where he draws on historical and textual scholarship to make an interesting, if somewhat overstated, case for the importance of mad women in Wordsworth's writing (he ignores mad men and idiot boys). Since the death of the author, the critical text can only elucidate, apparently, what the criticized "text is at pains to illustrate" (p. 117), so Martin's text is replete with remarks about the "text's intention" (p. 115). But somewhat surprisingly, he claims a control of his own text, with claims like "I have shown" (p. 116)—so he must be willing also to accept responsibility for the extraordinary number of typos and other errors, some of which, after all, may imply the text's autonomous desire to assert its loyalties ("She tears our Heathcliff's hair" [p. 110]), or to make puns, such as the one about the otherness of the "woman deserted at the alter" (p. 114).

Among general studies of the nineteenth-century novel are two Marxist works which both insist on the pun that literature's sentences sentence us. In *Consuming Fiction* Terry Lovell combines Marxism and feminism to provide a lucid and suggestive—if also sketchy and tentative—analysis of some of the ways in which fiction as a commodity in a capitalist market place is, or is not, raised to the status of "literature" that claims to transcend the realm of vulgar commerce. Her Marxist approach emphasizes the extent to which the conditions of production and distribution of fiction affected its class status and cultural role, and helps to explain why and how a certain kind of fiction ("formal realism") was ultimately established as "literature" while other kinds (gothic, sentimentalist) remained mere commodities. It also helps to explain why Marxism and feminism, despite some overlapping concerns, have tended to "talk past each other" (p. 161), since she argues that feminists have not fully realized the extent to which the role of women as writers, readers, and teachers has been to transmit an essentially bourgeois ideology—that the view of literature as a "civilizing" influence is a variant of the view of women themselves as civilizing agents, and that in both cases the granting of a high moral status actually disempowers both women and literature by removing them from the rough hurly-burly of life. Presumably many readers will be only half sympathetic to Lovell's arguments: many feminists will be offended by the view that even gains in the fairness with which women are treated in the academy may only move the nurturing angel from the house to the classroom, and many Marxists will see the gender issue as merely irrelevant. But her arguments, though sketchy, should at least help the two camps see their common ground. Few readers will be even half sympathetic to David E. Musselwhite's arguments in *Partings Welded Together: Politics and Desire in the Nineteenth-Century English Novel,* if only because he actively courts "anathematization" as "the price that one has to pay . . . within a discipline that is numbingly conformist" (p. 1). His essays on *Mansfield Park, Frankenstein,* the intellectual background of *Wuthering Heights, Vanity Fair,* and the "commodification" of Dickens draw on Marxism and various French theorists for their deliberately diverse approaches, but all argue in their different ways that the nineteenth-century novel was "a most important agency for [the] process of internalization, or subjectivization, of the 'idea of the state' " (p. 8). Along these lines he offers a powerful reading of *Mansfield Park* as a novel that aspires to be a saleable commodity in the largest possible market—a middle class market it helps to produce by appropriating "the popular appeal of egalitarian jacobinism" (p. 30) for the nascent bourgeois domestic ideology. The essay is characteristic in its combination of ingenious readings with an unnecessary imputation of hypocritical, merely greedy motives to Austen. But seeking anathematization, Musselwhite seeks to anathematize, and so finds out Austen's "guilty secret" of "meanness and betrayal" where the more likely explanation is that Austen was subject to the same ideological pressures as the readership she resembled even as she helped it into being. Similar excesses crop up in the analysis of *Frankenstein,* as Frankenstein's guilty secret is glossed as masturbation, and in the informative and thoughtful essay on some sources for *Wuthering Heights* in Brontë's Belgian education ("Yorkshire 'pudding' Emily was not; *Wuthering Heights* was very much a sprout of Brussels" [p. 105]), where far too much is made of a supposedly traumatic event in Brontë's childhood. By far the longest section of the book is a fascinating analysis of the transformation of "Boz" to Dickens. Musselwhite argues that Boz, the *flaneur* and myriad-eyed observer of London life was a far better writer than Dickens, the novelist who carefully crafted himself as a commodity—as "the great popular novelist" (p. 116). Not surprisingly, the incarnation of a capitalist, individualist ideology, as Musselwhite sees it, becomes incapable of writing a world that does not reflect himself—the novelist, having internalized the ideology, now mistakes ideology for inwardness. Musselwhite's point is that with this mechanism in place, the increasingly psychological bent of the novel is in the interests of the state: " 'the state' is quite happy for us to be 'inward'—'you don't hate Mrs Thatcher, you hate your mother' —what it can't stand is that we take to the streets" (p. 15).

In *The Novel and the Police,* D.A. Miller argues, somewhat

along the same lines as Musselwhite, that the nineteenth-century novel embodies, represents, and reinforces the internalization of a disciplinary ideology within the self—thus "moving the question of policing out of the streets, as it were, into the closet—I mean, into the private and domestic sphere on which the very identity of the liberal subject depends" (p. ix). Following Foucault, Miller maintains that the fundamental policing function in society is performed not by a legally constituted police force, but by the dispersed and ubiquitous disciplinary force of ideological discourse. Consequently, he is concerned with such officers of the law as Collins's Sergeant Cuff or Dickens's Inspector Bucket only as "drastic simplification[s] of power" (p. 69) that are more complexly and completely embodied in the social codes, their internalization, and their representation in novels. Miller's study focuses on works of Dickens as the first novelist to feature "a massive thematization of social discipline" (p. ix) and on Trollope and Collins as representative, respectively, of the novelistic extremes of "realism" and "sensation." Miller's readings are consistently brilliant, as they work through the ramifications of Dickens's simplifying displacement of ubiquitous social supervision by Inspector Bucket's all-seeing supervision, of the dependence of Trollope's ethos of liberal tolerance upon its precise supervision of what demands tolerance, of Collins's sensationalism as an actual physiological inscription of the mores of a patriarchal society. But the readings are also characterized by what Eve Kosofsky Sedgwick, on the jacket-liner, calls "farouche excess," and the essay on *The Woman in White*, especially, goes beyond the pale of its otherwise convincing thesis in local details that are often more clever than convincing—as the critical supervision detects what the narrative supervision could not see. Most of the "excesses" register impositions of contemporary "truths" about sexuality upon a Victorian text as though they were truths indeed. But Miller recognizes what he calls the pseudo-anachronism of imposing, for example, our "no less sensational staging of male homosexuality" (p. 189) upon Collins's sensationalism, and does so with a deliberate polemical purpose that makes the issues more immediate—in a sensational sort of way—for modern readers. Despite his excesses, Miller is never as outrageous as Musselwhite, if only because (as Musselwhite would probably argue) he writes as a liberal whose self-consciousness represents the extent to which he writes from within the policed terrain of an internalized liberal ideology. Nevertheless, writing as a liberal as I police the year's critical terrain, I find Miller's assumption that he and the authors he discusses are not immune to ideological constraint more compelling than Musselwhite's more radical trumpetings.

In *Romantic Vision and the Novel* Jay Clayton explores ways in which versions of romantic transcendence disrupt the novel, a form generally associated with terrestrial concerns. He first establishes two models of romantic transcendence, a Wordsworthian one in which visionary experience displaces and halts narrative sequence, and a Shelleyan one, in which apocalyptic experience itself is deconstructed. His analyses of *Clarissa, Mansfield Park, Wuthering Heights, Little Dorrit, Adam Bede,* and *Women in Love* show how the lyric, asocial, atemporal form of Romantic vision is at odds with the narrative, socially mimetic, time-bound structures generally associated with the novel. Examining the points at which the visionary and mimetic modes intersect in these novels, Clayton offers exciting new readings—particularly of *Mansfield Park, Little Dorrit,* and *Adam Bede*—and also offers some provocative suggestions about the novel as a genre. Clayton is, I think, more successful when working with the Wordsworthian model than with the more radically disruptive Shelleyan one, which leads him to somewhat predictable deconstuctive readings. Nevertheless, Clayton's approach results in a stimulating study of both specific works and of narrative theory.

A salutary result of the New Historicism has been to historicize psychological approaches to Victorian studies. John Kucich's *Repression in Victorian Fiction: Charlotte Brontë, George Eliot, and Charles Dickens* explicitly rejects the Freudian sense of repression with its essentialist assumptions about the self, and describes instead an understanding of repression as "the ideological instrument that actually produced a certain historical subject" (p. 3). Kucich argues that both the psychoanalytic model and the whole tendency of modern thought to exalt self-realization and self-expression as goals have led to a fundamental misunderstanding—and condescension towards—Victorian ideas of repression. He argues that for the Victorians repression, or self-renunciation, did not cripple or maim some essential self, but rather enlarged the sense of self by encouraging a greater introspective interiority: "Victorian repression produced a self that was actually more responsive libidinally, more self-sufficient, and—oddly enough—more antisocial than we have yet understood" (p. 3). Though the re-appropriation of the term from psychoanalysis is, as Kucich admits, "somewhat confusing" (p. 2), and though the term is used with considerable and sometimes confusing latitude, the understanding of repression that emerges significantly revises received ideas about character in the Victorian novel, and about Victorian understanding of the self. At times, however, as Kucich examines character after character from the novels, the specifically historical focus is lost and we seem once again to be examining characters as essential selves rather than constructs, but at the end of his discussion of each author he forcefully returns to his radical argument that, quite contrary to modern assumption, the Victorian cultivation of repression functioned to increase libidinal energy, and to increase self-sufficiency. But as Kucich points out, this construction of inwardness is not wholly positive, since it results, in the case of all three authors, in a privatization of self, a rejection of interpersonal or social models of the self.

In *The Politics of Story in Victorian Social Fiction,* Rosemarie Bodenheimer analyses a number of major and minor social problem novels to show that their greatest historical interest may lie not in their continuity with non-fictional discourse about social problems, but with the plot structures that have often been seen as "deflections from the delineation of social crisis or as evasion of its implications" (p. 5). Bodenheimer persuasively demonstrates that such plots, often confusedly pitting optimistic authorial fantasies of individual self-realization against despairing visions of the existing social order, lead to fissures and discontinuities in narrative coherence, and that such gaps show, more clearly than the authors could be aware, the cultural impasses to which conflicting Victorian ideologies were likely to lead. Bodenheimer's readings of novels by such authors as Frances Trollope, Elizabeth Stone, and Geraldine Jewsbury do not attempt to raise these novels to canonical status, but set forth their often preposterous failings as reflective of the ideological bewilderment of sensitive, reasonably intelligent writers in a confusing, rapidly changing age. Without either condescending to the novels or wishing away their structural and logical flaws, she demonstrates how the seemingly evasive plot lines of such better known novels as *Ruth, Oliver Twist, Hard Times, Sybil,* and *Felix Holt* reveal their authors' attitudes toward social issues more fully than do the more apparently straightforward sermons and polemics embedded in the texts.

In *Tradition Counter Tradition: Love and the Form of Fiction,* Joseph Allen Boone defines the "traditional" novel as that which formally and thematically reinforces the dominant, patriarchal ideological status of love and marriage in society. The "counter-traditional" novel is one that enters into a disruptive dialogue with the dominant ideology, subverting it either by rewriting the traditional love and courtship story, as in *Wuthering Heights* and *Daniel Deronda,* or by isolating men from women to examine "hidden sexual politics" as in the American quest romance, or by describing independent female communities, as in *Cranford* and *Herland.* Boone's vast scope takes in the entire history of the English and American novel, and even includes the ancients and the Renaissance, so his book is inevitably rife with generalizations and occasionally with reviews of familiar material—as in his description of the courtly love tradition. One might argue that no very detailed or nuanced account of these materials is possible in one book—neither tradition nor counter-tradition can be fully articulated in a study that barely mentions, for example, Sterne, Burney, Radcliffe, Scott, Dickens, Thackeray, Conrad, Ford, Faulkner, and Fitzgerald (to name only "canonized" authors). Inevitably the traditions are defined largely in the process of selection (or the selections are determined by the definitions of traditions) but, as he argues, the panoramic view avoids the parochialism of more restricted studies, and enables him to show how interlocked the western ideology of love is with the standard love and marriage plots of most novels, and how effectively some novelists have originated new formal structures to challenge the ideology. Finally, despite the unavoidable gaps resulting from the selection process, Boone makes a convincing case, and offers a forceful feminist analysis of major themes and forms in the history of the novel.

Not all of the year's studies in the novel are as compelling as those discussed above. In *Hidden Rivalries in Victorian Fiction: Dickens, Realism, and Revaluation* Jerome Meckier offers the plausible suggestion that Victorian novelists competed with one another in an effort to produce, in effect, the most real realism. Unfortunately Meckier's argument is marred by an irritating habit of referring to himself as "the modern revaluator," and by a tendency to assign the narrowest of imaginable motives to his rival novelists. He asserts, for example, that George Eliot invented "Bulstrode to revise [Dickens's] Jasper" (p. 201), that Dickens invented the Podsnaps to outdo Collins's attack on propriety in *The Woman in White* (p. 122). In general, Meckier's quite reasonable assumption that Victorian novelists responded to the challenges posed in one another's works too often leads him to reductive simplifications and occasional absurdities: "Trollope and George Eliot entered the fray in defense of the Victorian era because of Mrs. Gaskell's failure to repair the oppositions in *Hard Times* as decisively as she had hoped" (pp. 47-48). Lars Hartveit's *Workings of the Picaresque in the British Novel* includes chapters on *Rob Roy, Vanity Fair,* and *Great Expectations,* but his delineation of picaresque elements in those novels does not significantly alter conventional readings of those novels. In *The*

Novel and Authenticity David Holbrook stands up for good old-fashioned morals and the novelist's duty to promote them. He argues—or asserts—that "philosophical anthropology" demonstrates the falsity of postmodernist attacks on such concepts as being and self, that everyone has a "true self," that the "primary need of this true self is to find meaning in existence," and that it is the purpose of culture, and of the novel, to help us find such meaning. Not surprisingly, he finds that since Austen's *Mansfield Park* novelists have been falling down on the job—though even as late as Henry James they were still morally creditable.

Jane Austen continues to attract a vast amount of criticism of extremely uneven quality. In fact a valuable guide through an uneven seventy years of Austen criticism is *Jane Austen: The Critical Heritage, Volume 2: 1870-1940*, edited by Brian Southam. Southam's long and informative introductory essay surveys the various modes of criticism from the gushy "twaddle" of much Janeite commentary to the acerbic but sometimes uninformed attacks on the image of "gentle Jane" brought in by the rigors of New Criticism. As Southam demonstrates, however, the critical heritage is marked not only by general shifts in approach but also by a tendency of critics to simplify and falsify the critical heritage in order to make room for new critiques. The history of Austen criticism offers wonderful examples of the failures of critics to learn from one another, but it also offers a fascinating locus for the study of what Arac calls the "genealogies of criticism," for as Southam shows, the individual critical essays are intriguingly connected with historical changes in the institutional structures available for the study of literature. Southam's excerpts are well chosen, but he might have provided more of them, and at greater length—his introduction, valuable though it is, could certainly have been shortened (the 159-page introduction precedes only 152 pages of excerpts). Much current Austen criticism remains disappointing. In *Jane Austen and the State* Mary Evans argues that Austen was not a conservative, but only succeeds in showing, what few have doubted, that Austen was not a "simple-minded conservative" (p. 39). In *Mr. Collins Considered: Approaches to Jane Austen,* Ivor Morris writes as a devoted Janeite. His discussion of Austen's characters is engagingly chatty, if not very scholarly or innovative.

More scholarly and better focused studies are Claudia L. Johnson's *Jane Austen: Women, Politics, and the Novel* and Laura G. Mooneyham's *Romance, Language and Education in Jane Austen's Novels.* Johnson examines the literary and political milieu in which Austen wrote to show how extraordinarily politicized writing by and about women had become in the wake of the French Revolution and to demonstrate how Austen's writings exploit and undermine the Burkean idiom of conservative women novelists. Johnson argues that although Austen's socially incisive novels subvert rigid conservatism, they do not endorse outright radical positions—rather, Austen's depictions of the hypocrisy, exploitiveness, and oppressiveness of patriarchal society "defended and enlarged a progressive middle ground that had been eaten away by the polarizing polemics born of the 1790s" (p. 166). Johnson expertly situates the political implications of Austen's novels, and provides an excellent perspective on her politically charged, but non-doctrinaire understanding of social institutions and of the political implications of literary forms. Arguably, Johnson at times pushes Austen a little too far toward the radical camp by reading her caustic characterizations as necessarily attacks on social institutions rather than on the foibles of individuals and, arguably also, she is perhaps too ready at times to assume that her own modern perspective on the sexism of even the "benevolent patriarchs" was shared by Austen—even though, as she realizes, Austen "perforce wore" the ideological manacles of her time. Nevertheless, she offers some of the best readings of the novels in recent years, and situates Austen's writings in their political context with more precision than previous studies have done. Mooneyham's readings of the six novels go over a great deal of familiar ground about the moral education of the heroines, but offer some new insights by examining Austen's thematic emphasis on propriety in language. The emphasis Mooneyham puts on the primacy of correct use of language, however, may be a bit misleading—she does not, I think, succeed in showing that "Moral and intellectual achievement flows from linguistic achievement" (p. xi) rather than vice-versa, though she does convincingly make the point that correct use of language and correct moral behavior are inseparably interrelated. On the subject of virtue, Mooneyham is, if anything, more difficult to please than Austen—for her (as for Johnson) even Henry Tilney, even Edmund Bertram, are not merely fallible mortals, but "morally irresponsible," and their efforts to educate the heroines are "muddied by unacknowledged selfishness" (p. 107). Mooneyham, in other words, gives us a very stern Austen—certainly no gentle Jane—but perhaps at the expense of ignoring Austen's wit, or at least her humor.

Both the strengths and the potential weaknesses of the New Historicism are evident in Daniel Cottom's provocatively subversive *Social Figures: George Eliot, Social History, and Literary Representation*. Cottom's central theoretical argument, oft reiterated, is the Foucauldian one that all discourse is political, that discourse "constitutes [the] forms of authority" (p. xix), that "power lies in the production of meaning" (p. 120). Eliot's writings provide fascinating material for his analysis because her realism, still often understood as an apolitical, utterly "natural," historically accurate mirror of society is actually, as Cottom sees it, the formulation of a liberal intellectual discourse—a social reality not discovered but invented. Cottom's complex analyses reveal the ways in which Eliot exploited and explored a rhetoric that transfigured social actualities into the terms of a seamless discourse that equated liberal rationalism with universal truth, thus excluding even the possibility of other legitimate discourses. In the process Cottom explores the political implications of such seemingly neutral terms as rationalism ("the power to make nature appear as purely formal laws, whether of thought, economy, culture, or society, so that through these laws class interest can appear as universal truth" [p. 27]), education, character, "ordinary human life," and "moral sympathy" ("the discourse of a class presented as the discovery of psychology" [p. 190]). But a potential weakness of this kind of approach is that in resisting a collusive sympathy with the author, the critic may assume a smug superiority on the basis of a new and improved ideological perspective. Despite his assertion that he is not "making dogmatic judgments" (p. 206), Cottom often seems as patronizing to Eliot as he accuses her of being to the lower classes—as when he graciously admits that "she and her readers are not necessarily hypocrites" (p. 191). Very late in the book Cottom acknowledges that Eliot's writing was "a complex exploration of ideology rather than a conventional reproduction of ideology" (p. 199), but in general his determination to unmask Eliot's bourgeois ideology makes her appear almost deliberately pernicious. Surely there is something too narrow in a study that, according to Terry Eagleton's foreword, "ineluctably" raises the question: "Why, after this, read Eliot at all?" (p. xvi). One reason, perhaps, is that Eliot's "production of ideology," presented in other terms, is a profound attempt to make sense of the world. To Cottom's credit, he does make us see the nature and limitation of that effort in new ways. Jeanie Thomas's *Reading "Middlemarch": Reclaiming the Middle Distance* is the kind of book Cottom deplores—Thomas is unabashedly and unreservedly in sympathy with Eliot and with her interpretation of experience. Thomas uncritically reproduces Eliot's liberal ideology, and accepts her narrator's perception of life for "knowledge of life" (p. 29), but her sympathetic reading nevertheless provides an intelligent, if relatively unambitious, commentary on Eliot's art, particularly on her sense of the difficulties of adjusting desires and possibilities in a complex world.

In *From Copyright to Copperfield: The Identity of Dickens,* Alexander Welsh's purposes are to change the emphases from which biographical criticism of the novels has traditionally proceeded, to offer new perspectives on autobiographical elements in the works, and of course to provide fresh readings of the novels under consideration: *Martin Chuzzlewit, Dombey and Son,* and *David Copperfield.* Welsh persuasively argues that the Freudian procedure of looking back to the influences of traumas in early life on a writer's work may lead to neglect of biographical events more contemporary with the writing, and that in Dickens's case critical emphasis on the author's childhood experiences in Warren's Blacking Warehouse has contributed to neglect of his later perplexities as an advocate of international copyright laws during his American tour of 1842. Dickens, Welsh shows, was at a kind of hiatus in his career when he went to America, was troubled to a surprising extent by American attacks claiming that his advocacy of copyright was self-serving, that his guise as a seeker of justice was hypocritical. It was only after these attacks on his motives that Dickens, becoming introspective, wrote his autobiographical fragment, revealed his traumatic experiences as a child, and began a series of novels explicitly concerned with hypocrisy, pride, and the nature of individual identity. Looking at the novels from this perspective, Welsh advances fascinating analyses of the complexly devious ways in which Dickens constructs a sense of self by displacing and diffracting personal concerns in his characters, forms, and even literary borrowings.

Though relatively few studies of Victorian poetry were produced this year, it was a splendid year for Tennyson scholarship. A major boon to Tennysonians (and especially to reviewers who get free copies) is Christopher Ricks's long awaited second edition of *Tennyson's Poetry* (now in three volumes). The expanded edition takes advantage of the newly available Trinity College manuscripts, and "assimilates the Tennyson scholarship of the last fifteen years or so" to add "about a dozen poems, about a thousand lines of verse, and countless variants" (p. xii). It does not attempt to be definitive, to include all textual variants, but it does include those Ricks deems most important, and will certainly be the standard edition of Tennyson's poetry until—as Ricks anticipates—it is eventually superceded by an inclusive edition "in twenty volumes or so" (p. xiv). As his editors are well aware, Tennyson was not one of the nineteenth century's great letter writers, but volume 2 of *The Letters of Alfred Lord Tennyson,* superbly edited and annotated by Cecil Y. Lang and Edgar F.

Shannon Jr., provides surprisingly fascinating reading. Tennyson's own letters are not brilliant, are not introspective, are not often informative about the genesis or even the backgrounds of the poetry, but they do reflect clearly and engagingly the unaffected, sensitive, affectionate nature of the man as he copes with the pressures of his growing fame with varying degrees of petulance, modesty, and pride. Further, the letters, combined with letters and journal entries of others in Tennyson's circle and with the informative and often witty annotations, provide a remarkably coherent narrative of Tennyson's life from 1850-1870, and a still more remarkably broad panorama of Victorian life. Flitting and sometimes lingering on these pages are figures from across the class spectrum—from Victoria and Albert to Gladstone, from dentists to domestics.

Yet another major contribution to Tennyson studies is Herbert F. Tucker's massive and masterful *Tennyson and the Doom of Romanticism*. Tucker combines careful and subtle exegesis with a deep historical awareness to offer new insights into Tennyson's major poems, into the ways in which he self-consciously shaped his career, into the interplay of Romantic and Victorian modes in his verse, and into the ways in which ideological forces impinged upon Tennyson's writing, and upon its reception from his time to our own. The first section examines Tennyson's early efforts to achieve a kind of poetic authority by wedding the carefully crafted music of his poetry to his intuited sense of the "roar or pulse of an inevitable, unutterable power" from a source he calls "the deep" (p. 20). Tennyson's early and enduring "stylistic authority" is owing to his mastery of what Tucker calls his "measure of doom," a "rhythm of fatality . . . as imperturbable as Milton's God but even more distant in its nameless, faceless indifference" (p. 35). Submission to this sense of nameless power, however, involves the "dissolution of the self," so that Tennyson "owes his utter authority of manner" to a dissolution of his individual personality. Though Tucker recognizes this loss of self as a source of Tennyson's melancholy as well as of his authority, he may not do justice to the extent to which Tennyson clung to the idea of immortal personality. Nevertheless, his emphasis leads to brilliant analyses of the juvenilia, the 1830 and 1832 *Poems,* and the classical dramatic monologues, "Tiresias," "Ulysses," and "Tithonus,"—monologues which he sees as, in part, Tennyson's rewriting of Romanticism in his versions of the greater Romantic ode. Unlike Browning's, Tucker argues, Tennyson's dramatic monologues, far from exploring the intricacies of personality, aspire to pure lyric as they approach "the life beyond personality that had always been the poet's deepest faith and supremely generative fiction" (p. 266). But counter to this asocial lyric impulse in Tennyson is the desire to speak directly to and for Victorian ideological concerns, an impulse that Tucker examines in superb readings of the "distinctly bourgeois" (p. 273) English idylls, "The Gardener's Daughter," "Dora," and (interestingly in this category) "Morte D'Arthur." Finally, Tucker concludes with relatively brief, incisive analyses of Tennyson's explorations of his mixed impulses in the mixed genres of "The Princess," "In Memoriam," and "Maud."

Despite the seemingly narrow focus implied in its title, Daniel A. Harris's *Tennyson and Personification: The Rhetoric of "Tithonus"* ranges widely through Tennyson's works and more widely still through nineteenth-century thought about personification. Harris's exploration of "Tithonus" as a "core document through which to understand the Victorian mind in a very broad context" (p. 86) may lead him to occasional excess in teasing out the implications of the poem, but it also leads him to a fascinatingly complex reading of Tennyson's exploration of the trope of personification, and to intriguing insights into Victorian thought about such topics as imaginative sympathy, animism, incarnationism, and metaphor. The stylistic and thematic representation of the dissolving borders of the self in a kind of elegiac desire is characteristic not only of "Tithonus," but also, James Richardson argues, of Tennysonian and other Victorian poetry generally. In *Vanishing Lives: Style and Self in Tennyson, D.G. Rossetti, Swinburne, and Yeats,* Richardson explores what he sees as the characteristic Victorian interest in "dimness," in crepuscular states of mind in which self seems to flow outward, dissolving into impersonality and oblivion. Such terms, Richardson worries, might seem merely impressionistic, and Richardson's own uncommonly beautiful, highly figurative prose might at first seem a throwback to an earlier age of colorful, impressionistic criticism, as when he notes Tennyson's ability to render vagueness with precision, to use "smoke to find the shape of wind" (p. 90). But in fact Richardson is remarkably precise in describing what other critics usually gesture at in vague terms. He not only has a fine ear for subtle nuances of rhythm and tone, but he has the rare gift of making careful, often highly technical, prosodic analysis not only interesting, but absorbing, and he is able to show the careful craftsmanship with which his poets achieve their most characteristic effects. The results, as he traces large concerns through the minutest details of prosody, are stunning readings of particular passages, remarkably precise descriptions of vague poetic effects, and a compelling account of how hard poets work to achieve the seeming effortlessness of "self-expression." Consequently, his graceful, lucid study enlightens the dimness and outlines the dissolutions characteristic in various ways of Tennyson, Rossetti, Swinburne, and the young Yeats, and examines the techniques that the later Yeats used to check the elegiac flow of verse and poetic self.

In *Elizabeth Barrett Browning, Woman & Artist* Helen Cooper ably describes the difficulties of a woman poet in an almost parodically patriarchal situation. Cooper examines the difficulties of Barrett Browning's personal life, the condescension of the reviews to a "poetess," and especially the poor fit between the male poetic tradition and female poetic aspirations, and argues that Barrett Browning gradually found her own female voice, overcoming both the "anxiety of influence" and the "anxiety of authorship" (p. 190). In her chronologically ordered study of the poems, Cooper provides excellent thematic readings, particularly of *Casa Guidi Windows* and *Aurora Leigh*, and clearly demonstrates the poet's consistent concern with the role of women, and particularly with her own role as woman-poet. But in her account of Barrett Browning as a feminist thinker, she has little to say about the poetic techniques that characterize her efforts to find a "voice." She points out, for example, Barrett Browning's courageous desire to speak out boldly and in plain words, but does not discuss the paradox that the power of Barrett Browning's poetry, its outspokeness, often results from an extraordinary extravagance of style. Still, though Cooper asserts the presence of a uniquely female voice more than she demonstrates how it is poetically constituted, she nevertheless offers a fine introduction to and analysis of Barrett Browning's difficulties, ambitions, and achievements.

Mary Ellis Gibson's *History and the Prism of Art: Browning's Poetic Experiments* examines Robert Browning's views of history in the contexts of nineteenth-century historiography and Romantic theories of poetry that tend to disparage the historicizing imagination. Gibson argues that Browning's "contextualist" view of history is of major significance to our understanding of his experiments in poetic form. It leads him, for example, to prefer spatial form to straightforward narrative, to engage in forms of irony dependent on distanced historic perspectives, to use colloquial-sounding diction and meters. None of this is startlingly new, and it does not lead to a major "reassessment of Browning's poems" (p. 2), but Gibson does very successfully delineate "the intimate connections between [Browning's] contextualist conceptualization of history and his poetic forms" (p. 266), and along the way she offers fine insights into what she calls Browning's "poetry of obstacles" (p. 218)—his poetic struggle with the mire of historical actualities.

Everyone who writes about Christina Rossetti complains that she is unjustly neglected, but this year at least she seems to be getting her due, with two monographs and a collection of essays devoted to her. In *Christina Rossetti: The Poetry of Endurance*, Dolores Rosenblum makes the feminist argument that Rossetti, writing without a female tradition that could give her voice, and within a male tradition that reifies the female as a silent, passive icon, masqueraded in the role assigned, in a subtle parody that announces "both alienation and the means by which she overcomes alienation" (p. 6). The argument seems especially plausible for Rossetti, who was indeed reified as an icon in pre-Raphaelite paintings, and was explicitly excluded from the "Brotherhood" of art; but despite some suggestive readings and insights, Rosenblum is not entirely convincing about how Rossetti "overcomes alienation"—except, of course, in her thoroughly orthodox Christianity. Part of the problem, I think, is that Rosenblum tends to impose modern feminist and psychoanalytic readings on a poetic idiom that doesn't very convincingly support them. I doubt, for example, that "psychobiographical interpretation is unavoidable," or that much is gained but distortion by reading her poetry as an expression of "her poetic and Oedipal rivalry with her brother and her Oedipal rivalry with her mother" (p. 146). Still, Rosenblum's feminist perspective forcefully delineates the difficulties a female poet faced in the nineteenth century, and often leads to intriguing—if debatable—analyses of her personal and poetic responses to a patriarchal order. Antony Harrison's approach in *Christina Rossetti in Context* diverges sharply from Rosenblum's. He sets himself against "neo-Freudian interpretations" (p. 11) and, far from seeing Rossetti as cut off from any viable tradition, he argues that her work is best understood in terms of Pre-Raphaelitism, Tractarianism, Augustinian Christianity, the general tradition of courtly love, and Dantean neo-Platonism. On the whole, Harrison's approach is, I think, the more fruitful of the two, particularly in its insistence that Rossetti be treated first and foremost as a conscientious, self-consciously literary artist—and not as confessional versifier. Moreover, the contexts that Harrison discusses help to elucidate the complex, seemingly disparate strains of thought that contribute both to the tensions and to the ultimate unity of Rossetti's work—particularly of the magnificent sonnet sequence "Monna Innominata." Harrison's insistence on Rossetti's literariness, however, leads him to relative neglect of the non-literary historical context (though he occasionally glances at the socio-historical context), and so to slight the problems of gender explored by Rosenblum. Fittingly, Rosenblum and Harrison are both represented among the fifteen contributors to David A. Kent's *The Achievement of Christina Rossetti,* a collection of consistent excellence which, in its diversity of critical perspectives, reflects the diversity and scope of Rossetti's works.

If the Pre-Raphaelite poets have been relatively neglected this year, it is not the fault of Antony Harrison, who also wrote the year's only study of Swinburne, *Swinburne's Medievalism: A Study in Victorian Love Poetry*. Harrison counters what he sees as an undue critical neglect of Swinburne's medievalism by ably describing the poet's lifelong interest in medieval literature and history, by arguing for the importance of the courtly love tradition as an influence on Swinburne's love poetry, and by defending his high estimate of the medievalist poems with readings of some of the most significant among them, including "Laus Veneris," *Tristram of Lyonesse,* and *The Tale of Balen.* Convincing as Harrison is about the value of these poems, I would argue against his contention that the dozen or so works he discusses "represent systematically and coherently [Swinburne's] moral, literary, philosophical, and religious values" (p. 18). Surely no such overview is possible without extended consideration of Swinburne's Hellenism, Romanticism, Republicanism, late Imperialism, and a number of other -isms besides Medievalism.

William E. Buckler's premises in *Walter Pater: The Critic as Artist of Ideas* are that Pater's "criticism depends, not on abstract theory, but on informed imaginative intuition" (p. 25), and that his carefully crafted prose demands and rewards the kind of close attention usually reserved for the study of poetry. The first of these premises leads Buckler to what he sees as a Paterian avoidance of theory as he attempts to see and describe Pater's works with "complete loyalty to the object as it really is and to his impression of the object" (p. 25). But the theoretical assumption that one can work without theoretical assumptions combined with the uncritical acceptance of Pater's desperately valiant attempt to reconcile empiricism (loyalty to the object as it really is) and phenomenology (his impression of the object) seems somewhat naive. The second premise, that Pater's prose demands careful attention, certainly seems reasonable enough, but Buckler's paragraph-by-paragraph descriptions of various works are rather less rewarding than the works they describe. Interestingly enough, the kind of New Critical approach taken by Buckler is called into question by another book on Pater, written in 1960 when New Criticism was still dominant, but only translated into English in 1987. According to Wolfgang Iser, his *Walter Pater: The Aesthetic*

Movement (translated by David Henry Wilson) was originally conceived as part of the movement to free art from extrinsic concerns, and "to show through Pater's work what was entailed in the concept of autonomous art" (p. ix). Looking back, Iser now sees that his "approach sometimes seems rather intrinsic" (p. viii), but he also rightly sees that his examination of Pater's limited success in legitimizing the aesthetic ideal by attempts at historicization or renewal of myth gives his thirty-year-old study a distinctly modern tone. In the end, Iser's close readings, far more than Buckler's, end up not celebrating but problematizing the ideal of an autonomous art and therefore of a purely intrinsic criticism. In effect, Iser's book gives us a more modern Pater. A third study of Pater describes him as a reluctant English Nietzsche, powerfully drawn to the dark Greek gods of disorder, but usually unwilling to abandon the comforting Victorian image of classical Greek calm and serene order. But Robert and Janice A. Keefe at times obscure their own best insights by overstating their thesis in the almost melodramatic prose that sometimes characterizes *Walter Pater and the Gods of Disorder*. This is particularly a problem in their description of *The Renaissance,* which they see as structured around a submerged ritualistic pagan fertility cycle. Most of the paganism is supplied in the authors' paraphrases, not in Pater's prose. The authors also, I think, overstate the originality of Pater's recognition of the Dionysiac side of Greek myth, but they are very good at showing how and speculating on why he shied away from Dionysiac frenzy to embrace a morally and politically repressive idea of Apollonian order in his late works.

Literary criticism of late has been preoccupied with unmasking pernicious covert ideologies in literary works, but has tended to overlook the quite overtly pernicious Victorian ideology comprising racism, militarism, and imperialism. This year, however, such issues are addressed directly in Patrick Brantlinger's *Rule of Darkness: British Literature and Imperialism, 1830-1914,* and in Cecil D. Eby's *The Road to Armageddon: The Martial Spirit in English Popular Literature 1870-1914.* Brantlinger points out how widely and deeply virulent racism infects British thought not only late in the century, when imperialism was a conscious issue, but also earlier, when ideas of British racial superiority and right to rule were simply taken for granted. Not surprisingly, the most blatantly and mindlessly imperialist writing has not survived in the literary canon, though as Brantlinger shows, even in the high literary mode of domestic realism the empire serves as constant background, or as the periphery that defines the insular center—only occasionally pushing itself to prominence in the cynical racism of Thackeray, for example, or in the astonishingly vicious racism of Carlyle and Dickens. The vastness of his subject forces Brantlinger to devote substantial sections of his book to surveying various kinds of imperialist fiction, and perhaps to simplify the split between early and late Victorian attitudes, but the breadth of his study shows the ubiquity, the seeming inescapability, of imperialist ideology. *Rule of Darkness* makes one wonder at the ideological power of the selective processes of canon formation that give us the still prevalent, comfortable view of Victorian literature's universally humane, compassionate tendencies. The problematic relation of literature—or of writing, at any rate—to social attitudes is a prominent concern in Cecil D. Eby's examination of the militaristic ethos preceding the First World War. Eby surveys the literature of scare-mongering invasion fantasies, the militarism of Baden-Powell's Boy Scouts, the ludicrous public school ethos of "playing the game" on cricket pitch and battlefield, and he skillfully explicates works of Wells, Kipling, Barrie, Brooke, and infinitely dimmer lights in the context of these cultural manifestations. Since his focus is on the martial and the popular, it is perhaps not surprising that Eby finds scarcely a glimmer of intelligence in the half-century he examines, but the result is a slightly disturbing tone of sometimes indignant and sometimes bemused contempt for the whole age, and not merely for the abundance of contemptible ideas he examines. Still, the absurd and atrocious ideology he explores is fundamentally important to our understanding of the period, and he sets it forth skillfully, thoroughly, and vivaciously. The study provides a melancholy but salutary demonstration of the power of bad art to reinforce popular prejudice and promote hatred.

The year's work quite clearly reflects the eclipse of poststructuralist criticism by New Historicism, though post-structuralism has certainly left its mark—nearly all of the year's best books are very much influenced by it. And the guru is still French—though Foucault rather than Derrida seems to be the ultimate authority. Doubtless the New Historicism will soon go the way of all critical trends, or at least its jargon will soon grow stale. Indeed, it is already growing repetitious as one critic after another advances the same "revolutionary" claims about the displacement of history by the false consciousness of literature. But a New Historicism that is a little more careful to avoid totalizing claims about nebulous ideologies still has much to offer in opening the canon, examining the social functions of art and, above all, looking more closely at the socio-historical contexts that have too often been simultaneously described as all-important and generalized out of existence as symptoms of "ideology."

BOOKS RECEIVED

Abbey, Cherie D., and Mullane, Janet, eds. *Nineteenth-Century Literature Criticism.* Vol. 15. Detroit: Gale Research, 1987. Pp. 579. $92.00. ISBN 0-8103-5815-8.

Abbey, Cherie D., and Mullane, Janet, eds. *Nineteenth-Century Literature Criticism.* Vol. 16. Detroit: Gale Research, 1987. Pp. 597. $92.00. ISBN 0-8103-5816-6.

Allen, Michael. *Charles Dickens' Childhood.* New York: St. Martin's Press, 1988. Pp. x + 158. $29.95. ISBN 0-312-01275-6.

Altick, Richard D. *The Scholar Adventurers.* Columbus: Ohio State Univ. Press, 1987. Pp. xi + 338. $9.95. ISBN 0-8142-0435-X.

Anderson, Nancy Fix. *Woman against Woman in Victorian England: A Life of Eliza Lynn Linton.* Bloomington: Indiana Univ. Press, 1988. Pp. x + 260. $29.50. ISBN 0-243-36600-3.

ap Roberts, Ruth. *The Ancient Dialect: Thomas Carlyle and Comparative Religion.* Berkeley and London: Univ. of California Press, 1988. Pp. 126. $22.50. ISBN 0-520-06116-0.

Arac, Jonathan. *Critical Genealogies: Historical Situations for Postmodern Literary Studies.* New York: Columbia Univ. Press, 1987. Pp. 350. $32.50. ISBN 0-231-06254-0.

Arnold, Matthew. *Matthew Arnold.* Ed. Miriam Allott and Robert H. Super. Oxford and New York: Oxford Univ. Press, 1986. Pp. xxxi + 616. $35.00. ISBN 0-19-254187-0.

Attridge, Derek. *Peculiar Language: Literature as Difference from the Renaissance to James Joyce.* Ithaca: Cornell Univ. Press, 1988. Pp. xiii + 262. $9.95. ISBN 0-8014-9407-9.

Bachinger, Katrina. *The Multi-Man Genre and Poe's Byrons.* Salzburg: Universität Salzburg, 1987. Pp. vi + 140.

Baldick, Chris. *In Frankenstein's Shadow: Myth, Monstrosity, and Nineteenth-Century Writing.* Oxford: Clarendon Press, 1988. Pp. 207. $58.00. ISBN 0-19-811726-4.

Barry, Kevin. *Language, Music and the Sign: A Study in Aesthetics, Poetics and Poetic Practice from Collins to Coleridge.* Cambridge and New York: Cambridge Univ. Press, 1988. Pp. xii + 255. $39.50. ISBN 0-521-34175-2.

Beerbohm, Max. *Rossetti and His Circle.* Ed. N. John Hall. New Haven and London: Yale Univ. Press, 1987. Pp. 50 + 30 plates. $19.95. ISBN 0-300-03986-7.

Bennett, Sheila. *Imagination and Awareness: Literature as Society's Analyst.* New York: Vantage Press, 1988. Pp. x + 244. $15.95.

Bentman, Raymond. *Robert Burns.* Boston: Twayne, 1987. Pp. 155. $19.95. ISBN 0-8057-6952-8.

Berg, Maggie. *Jane Eyre, Portrait of a Life.* Boston: Twayne, 1987. Pp. xiv + 134. $17.95. ISBN 0-8057-7955-8.

Berggren, Ruth, ed. *The Definitive Four-Act Version of "The Importance of Being Earnest, a Trivial Comedy for Serious People," by Oscar Wilde.* New York: Vanguard Press, 1987. Pp. 192. $18.95. ISBN 0-8149-0930-2.

Blank, G. Kim. *Wordsworth's Influence on Shelley: A Study of Poetic Authority*. New York: St. Martin's Press, 1988. Pp. xii + 243. $45.00. ISBN 0-312-01179-2.

Bloom, Harold, ed. *Charles Dickens*. New York: Chelsea House, 1987. Pp. viii + 367. $29.50. ISBN 0-87754-690-8.

Bloom, Harold, ed. *Poets of Sensibility and the Sublime*. New York: Chelsea House, 1986. Pp. viii + 324. $29.50. ISBN 0-87754-679-7.

Bloom, Harold, ed. *John Ruskin*. New York: Chelsea House, 1986. Pp. viii + 196. $29.50. ISBN 0-87754-692-4.

Bodenheimer, Rosemarie. *The Politics of Story in Victorian Social Fiction*. Ithaca and New York: Cornell Univ. Press, 1988. Pp. 247. $24.95. ISBN 0-8014-2099-7.

Bolton, H. Philip. *Dickens Dramatized*. Boston: G.K. Hall, 1987. Pp. xviii + 501. $60.00. ISBN 0-8161-8924-2.

Boone, Joseph Allen. *Tradition Counter Tradition: Love and the Form of Fiction*. Chicago and London: Univ. of Chicago Press, 1987. Pp. xiii + 391. $27.50. ISBN 0-226-06464-6.

Bradley, John Lewis, and Ousby, Ian, eds. *The Correspondence of John Ruskin and Charles Eliot Norton*. Cambridge and New York: Cambridge Univ. Press, 1987. Pp. xiii + 537. $59.50. ISBN 0-521-32091-7.

Brantlinger, Patrick. *Rule of Darkness: British Literature and Imperialism, 1830-1914*. Ithaca and London: Cornell Univ. Press, 1988. Pp. xi + 309. $29.95. ISBN 0-8014-2090-3.

Bristow, Joseph, ed. *The Victorian Poet: Poetics and Persona*. London and New York: Croom Helm, 1988. Pp. xii + 208. $13.50. ISBN 0-70993977-9.

Bromwich, David, ed. *Romantic Critical Essays*. Cambridge and New York: Cambridge Univ. Press, 1988. Pp. viii + 269. $34.50. ISBN 0-521-24411-0.

Brontë, Charlotte. *The Professor*. Ed. Margaret Smith and Herbert Rosengarten. Oxford: Clarendon Press, and New York: Oxford Univ. Press, 1987. Pp. xl + 349. $79.00. ISBN 0-19-812694-8.

Buckler, William E. *Walter Pater: The Critic as Artist of Ideas*. New York and London: New York Univ. Press, 1987. Pp. xiii + 359. $45.00. ISBN 0-8147-1092-1.

Burrows, J. F. *Computation into Criticism: A Study of Jane Austen's Novels and an Experiment in Method*. Oxford: Clarendon Press, 1987. Pp. xii + 255. $48.00. ISBN 0-19-812856-8.

Carlyle, Thomas. *Sartor Resartus*. Oxford and New York: Oxford Univ. Press, 1987. Pp xlii + 273. $6.95. ISBN 0-19-281757-4.

Carroll, Lewis. *Sylvie and Bruno*. New York: Dover, 1988. Pp. xlv + 400. $7.95. ISBN 0-486-25588-3.

Clare, Johanne. *John Clare and the Bounds of Circumstance*. Kingston: McGill-Queen's Univ. Press, 1987. Pp. xiii + 217. $25.00. ISBN 0-7735-0606-3.

Clare, John. *Selected Poetry and Prose*. Ed. Merryn and Raymond Williams. Methuen English Texts. London and New York: Methuen, 1986. Pp. viii + 252. $7.95. ISBN 0-416-41120-7.

Clayton, Jay. *Romantic Vision and the Novel.* Cambridge and New York: Cambridge Univ. Press, 1987. Pp. x + 249. $34.50. ISBN 0-521-32776-8.

Cohen, Michael. *Engaging English Art: Entering the Work in Two Centuries of English Painting and Poetry.* Tuscaloosa and London: Univ. of Alabama Press, 1987. Pp. xii + 228. $28.95. ISBN 0-8173-0306-5.

Cohen, Morton N., and Gandolfo, Anita, eds. *Lewis Carroll and the House of Macmillan.* Cambridge and New York: Cambridge Univ. Press, 1987. Pp. ix + 384. ISBN 0-521-25602-X.

Cohn, Jan. *Romance and the Erotics of Property: Mass-Market Fiction for Women.* Durham and London: Duke Univ. Press, 1988. Pp. 181. $27.95. ISBN 0-8223-0799-5.

Coleridge, Samuel Taylor. *The Collected Works of Samuel Taylor Coleridge. Lectures 1808-1819: On Literature,* gen. ed. Kathleen Coburn. 2 vols. Princeton: Princeton Univ. Press, 1987. Vol. 1, pp. lxxxvi + 608. Vol. 2, pp. xi + 677. $75.00 the set. ISBN 0-691-09872-7.

Coleridge, Samuel Taylor. *Selected Letters.* Ed. H. J. Jackson. Oxford: Clarendon Press, 1987. pp. xxix + 306. $37.00. ISBN 0-19-818540-5.

Colls, Robert, and Dodd, Philip, eds. *Englishness: Politics and Culture 1880-1920.* London and New York: Croom Helm, 1987. Pp. 378. $16.95. ISBN 0-7099-4562-0.

Comstock, Cathy. *Disruption and Delight in the Nineteenth-Century Novel.* Ann Arbor: UMI Research Press, 1987. Pp. 95. $39.95. ISBN 0-8357-1812-3.

Conrad, Peter. *The History of English Literature: One Indivisible, Unending Book.* Philadelphia: Univ. of Pennsylvania Press, 1987. Pp. x + 740. $39.95. ISBN 0-8122-8067-9.

Coombs, James H., et al., eds. *A Pre-Raphaelite Friendship: the Correspondence of William Holman Hunt and John Lucas Tupper.* Ann Arbor: UMI Research Press, 1987. Pp. xxiv + 333. ISBN 0-8357-1745-3.

Cooper, Andrew M. *Doubt and Identity in Romantic Poetry.* New Haven and London: Yale Univ. Press, 1988. Pp. xi + 233. $24.50. ISBN 0-300-04004-0.

Cooper, Helen. *Elizabeth Barrett Browning, Woman & Artist.* Chapel Hill and London: Univ. of North Carolina Press, 1988. Pp. xii + 219. $25.00. ISBN 0-8078-1788-0.

Cosslett, Tess. *Woman to Woman: Female Friendship in Victorian Fiction.* Atlantic Highlands: Humanities Press, 1988. Pp. 211. $45.00. ISBN 0-391-03591-6.

Cottom, Daniel. *Social Figures: George Eliot, Social History, and Literary Representation.* Theory and History of Literature, Vol. 44. Minneapolis: Univ. of Minnesota Press, 1987. Pp. xxxiv + 241. $35.00 cloth, ISBN 0-8166-1547-0. $14.95 paper, ISBN 0-8166-1548-9.

Cox, Jeffrey N. *In the Shadows of Romance: Romantic Tragic Drama in Germany, England, and France.* Athens: Ohio Univ. Press, 1987. Pp. xiv + 335. $36.95. ISBN 0-8214-0858-5.

Curry, George. *Charles Dickens and Annie Fields.* San Marino: Huntington Library, 1988. Pp. vii + 71. $6.00. ISSN 0018-7895.

Cutsinger, James S. *The Form of Transcribed Vision: Coleridge and the Knowledge of God.* Macon: Mercer Univ. Press, 1988. Pp. xix + 136. $24.95. ISBN 0-86554-280-5.

Darwin, Charles. *The Correspondance of Charles Darwin.* Ed. Frederick Burkhardt and Sydney Smith. Vol. 3. 1844-1846. Cambridge and New York: Cambridge Univ. Press, 1988. Pp. xxix + 523. $37.50. ISBN 0-521-25589-9.

Darwin, Charles. *The Works of Charles Darwin.* Ed. Paul H. Barrett and R B. Freeman, vols. 1-10. New York: Columbia Univ. Press, 1987. Vol. 1. *Diary of the Voyage of the H.M.S. Beagle,* ed. Nora Barlow. Pp. 411. $75.00. ISBN 0-8147-1796-9. Vol. 2. *Journal of Researches,* pt. 1. Pp. 240. $75.00. ISBN 0-8147-1787-X. Vol. 3. *Journal of Researches,* pt. 2. Pp. 241-497. $75.00. ISBN 0-8147-1788-8. Vol. 4. *Zoology of the Voyage of the H.M.S. Beagle,* pts. 1 and 2. Pp. 145 + 140. $95.00. ISBN 0-8147-1789-6. Vol. 5. *The Zoology of the Voyage of the H.M.S. Beagle,* pt. 3. Pp. 244. $95.00. ISBN 0-8147-1790-X. Vol. 6. *The Zoology of the Voyage of the H.M.S. Beagle,* pts. 4 and 5. Pp. 253 + 83. $95.00. ISBN 0-8147-1791-8. Vol. 7. *The Geology of the Voyage of the H.M.S. Beagle,* pt. 1. Pp. 241. $75.00. ISBN 0-8147-1792-6. Vol. 8. *The Geology of the Voyage of the H.M.S. Beagle,* pt. 2. Pp. 142. $75.00. ISBN 0-8147-1793-4. Vol. 9. *The Geology of the Voyage of the H.M.S. Beagle,* pt. 3. Pp. 330. $75.00. ISBN 0-8147-1794-2. Vol. 10. *The Foundations of the Origins of Species.* Pp. 199. $75.00. ISBN 0-8147-1795-0.

David, Deirdre. *Intellectual Women and Victorian Patriarchy: Harriet Martineau, Elizabeth Barrett Browning, George Eliot.* Ithaca: Cornell Univ. Press, 1987. Pp. xvi + 273. $24.95. ISBN 0-8014-1965-4.

Dawson, Carl. *Prophets of Past Time: Seven British Autobiographers, 1880-1914.* Baltimore and London: Johns Hopkins Univ. Press, 1988. Pp. xx + 257. $29.50. ISBN 0-8018-3587-9.

De Paolo, Charles. *Coleridge's Philosophy of Social Reform.* New York and Bern: Peter Lang, 1988. Pp. xi + 273. $42.90. ISBN 0-8204-0531-0.

Dennis, Barbara, and Skilton, David, eds. *Reform and Intellectual Debate in Victorian England.* London and New York: Croom Helm, 1987. Pp. 223. ISBN 0-7099-5428-X.

Drabble, Margaret, ed. *The Concise Oxford Guide to English Literature.* Oxford and New York: Oxford Univ. Press, 1987. Pp. vi + 632. $24.95. ISBN 0-19-866140-1.

Dramin, Edward. *Light in a Dark Place: Romanticism in the Victorian Social-Political Novel: A Critical Anthology.* Lanham and London: Univ. Press of America, 1987. Pp. xviii + 335. $16.75. ISBN 0-8191-6403-8.

Eby, Cecil Degrotte. *The Road to Armageddon: The Martial Spirit in English Popular Literature, 1870-1914.* Durham and London: Duke Univ. Press, 1987. Pp. 280. $27.50. ISBN 0-8223-0775-8.

Eliot, George. *Daniel Deronda.* Oxford and New York: Oxford Univ. Press, 1988. Pp. xxii + 727. ISBN 0-19-281787-6.

Empson, William. *Argufying: Essays on Literature and Culture.* Ed. John Haffenden. Iowa City: Univ. of Iowa Press, 1987. Pp. ix + 657. $19.95. ISBN 0-87745-199-0.

Engelberg, Karsten Klejs. *The Making of the Shelley Myth: An Annotated Bibliography of Criticism of Percy Bysshe Shelley 1822-1860.* Meckler, Westport, CT: Mansell, 1988. Pp. xxiv + 468. $59.50. ISBN 0-7201-1968-5.

Evans, Mary. *Jane Austen and the State.* London and New York: Tavistock Publications, 1987. Pp. xi + 97. $6.95. ISBN 0-422-61370-3.

Fizer, John. *Alexander A. Potebnja's Psycholinguistic Theory of Literature: A Metacritical Inquiry.* Cambridge, MA: Harvard Univ. Press, 1988. Pp. viii + 164. $16.00. ISBN 0-916458-16-4.

Fletcher, Ian. *W. B. Yeats and His Contemporaries.* New York: St. Martin's Press, 1987. Pp. x + 350. ISBN 0-312-85306-8.

Flint, Kate ed. *The Victorian Novelist: Social Problems and Social Change.* London and New York: Croom Helm, 1988. Pp. 276. $13.95. ISBN 0-7099-1093-1.

Foltinek, Herbert. *Charles Dickens und der Zwang des Systems.* Wien: Verlag der Osterreichischen Akademie der Wissenschaften, 1987. Pp. 35. DM 14. ISBN 3-7001-1225-4.

Fowler, Alastair. *A History of English Literature.* Cambridge, MA: Harvard Univ. Press, 1987. Pp. ix + 395. $30.00. ISBN 0-674-39665-0.

Galt, John. *The Member: An Autobiography.* Ed. Ian A. Gordon. Edinburgh: Scottish Academic Press, The Association for Scottish Literary Studies, 1985. Pp. xiii + 128. ISBN 0-7073-0464-4.

Garber, Frederick. *Self, Text, and Romantic Irony: The Example of Byron.* Princeton: Princeton Univ. Press, 1988. Pp. xv + 322. $37.00. ISBN 0-691-06730-9.

Gaskell, Elizabeth. *Wives and Daughters.* Oxford and New York: Oxford Univ. Press, 1987. Pp. xxxvii + 740. ISBN 0-19-281702-7.

Gerould, Winifred Gregory, and Gerould, James Thayer. *A Guide to Trollope.* Princeton: Princeton Univ. Press, 1988. Pp. xxv + 256. $12.95. ISBN 0-691-01441-8.

Gibson, Mary Ellis. *History and the Prism of Art: Browning's Poetic Experiments.* Columbus: Ohio State Univ. Press, 1987. Pp. x + 341. $25.00. ISBN 0-8142-0418-X.

Girouard, Mark. *A Country House Companion.* New Haven and London: Yale Univ. Press, 1987. Pp. 192. $24.95. ISBN 0-300-04083-0.

Green, Michael, ed. *Broadening the Context.* London: John Murray, and Atlantic Highlands: Humanities Press, 1987. Pp. 128. $45.00. ISBN 0-391-03551-7.

Groves, David, ed. *James Hogg: Selected Poems and Songs.* Edinburgh: Scottish Academic Press, 1986. pp. xxxiii + 232. $15.25. ISBN 0-7073-0471-7.

von Hallberg, Robert, ed. *Politics and Poetic Value.* Chicago and London: Univ. of Chicago Press, 1988. Pp. 341. $30.00. ISBN 0-226-86496-0.

Halperin, John. *Gissing: A Life in Books.* Oxford and New York: Oxford Univ. Press, 1987. Pp. xiii + 426. $12.95. ISBN 0-19-282016-8.

Hardy, Thomas. *The Collected Letters of Thomas Hardy.* Ed. Richard Little Purdy and Michael Millgate. Vol. 6, 1920-1925. Oxford: Clarendon Press, 1987. Pp. x + 379. $52.00. ISBN 0-19-812623-9.

Hardy, Thomas. *Tess of the D'urbervilles.* Oxford and New York: Oxford Univ. Press, 1988. Pp. xxxiv + 410. $2.95. ISBN 0-19-281826-0.

Harpham, Geoffrey Galt. *The Ascetic Imperative in Culture and Criticism.* Chicago and London: Univ. of Chicago Press, 1988. Pp. xvii + 325. $29.95. ISBN 0-226-31691-2.

Harris, Daniel A. *Tennyson and Personification: The Rhetoric of "Tithonus."* Ann Arbor: UMI Research Press, 1987. Pp. xvi + 142. ISBN 0-8357-1736-4.

Harrison, Antony H. *Christina Rossetti in Context.* Chapel Hill and London: Univ. of North Carolina Press, 1988. Pp. xv + 231. $29.95. ISBN 0-8078-1755-4.

Harrison, Antony H. *Swinburne's Medievalism: A Study in Victorian Love Poetry.* Baton Rouge and London: Louisiana State Univ. Press, 1988. Pp. xi + 205. $27.50. ISBN 0-8071-1327-1.

Hartman, Geoffrey H. *The Unremarkable Wordsworth.* Minneapolis: Univ. of Minnesota Press, 1987. Pp. xxix + 249. $29.50. ISBN 0-8166-1175-0.

Hartman, Geoffrey H. *Wordsworth's Poetry 1787-1814.* Cambridge, MA, and London: Harvard Univ. Press, 1987. Pp. xxv + 418. $12.50. ISBN 0-674-95821-7.

Hartveit, Lars. *Workings of the Picaresque in the British Novel.* Oslo: Solum Forlag A. S., Atlantic Highlands, NJ: Humanities Press, 1987. Pp. 171. $39.95. ISBN 0-391-03477-4 (U.S.); 82-560-0417-7 (Norway).

Hodgson, Amanda. *The Romances of William Morris.* Cambridge and New York: Cambridge Univ. Press, 1987. Pp. xii + 219. ISBN 0-521-32075-5.

Hoge, James 0., and West, James L., III, eds. *Review.* Vol. 9. Charlottesville: Univ. Press of Virginia, 1987. Pp. xi + 356. $30.00. ISBN 0-8139-1160-5.

Holbrook, David. *The Novel and Authenticity.* Totowa: Barnes and Noble, 1987. Pp. xx + 247. $27.50. ISBN 0-389-20683-0.

Horn, Pamela. *Life and Labour in Rural England, 1760-1850.* Atlantic Highlands: Humanities Press, 1987. Pp. x + 184. $9.95. ISBN 0-333-37585-8.

Hornback, Bert G. *Middlemarch: A Novel of Reform.* Boston: Twayne, 1988. Pp. xii + 165. $17.95. ISBN 0-8057-7981-7.

Houghton, Walter, ed. *The Wellesley Index to Victorian Periodicals 1825-1900,* vol. 4. Toronto and Buffalo: Routledge & Kegan Paul, 1987. Pp. xx + 826. $175.00. ISBN 0-8020-5721-7.

Hubin, Allan J. *1981-1985 Supplement to Crime Fiction 1749-1980.* New York and London: Garland, 1988. Pp. xxi + 260. $32.00. ISBN 0-8240-7596-X.

Humm, Peter, Stigant, Paul, and Widdowson, Peter, eds. *Popular Fictions: Essays in Literature and History.* London and New York: Methuen, 1986. Pp. xiv + 265. $24.50 cloth, ISBN 0-416-90040-2. $10.95 paper, ISBN 0-416-90050-X.

Huntington Library Quarterly, ed. Guilland Sutherland. 51, 1 (Winter 1988). San Marino: Huntington Library. Pp. 71. $22.50 annually. ISSN 0018-7895.

Iser, Wolfgang. *Walter Pater: The Aesthetic Movement.* Cambridge and New York: Cambridge Univ. Press, 1987. Pp. xi + 212. ISBN 0-521-30962-X.

Jack, R.D.S. *Scottish Literature's Debt to Italy*. Edinburgh: Edinburgh Univ. Press, 1986, and NY: Columbia Univ. Press, 1987. Pp. vii + 86. $10.00. ISBN 0-85224-526-2.

Jakobson, Roman. *Language in Literature*. Ed. Krystyna Pomorska and Stephan Rudy. Cambridge, MA, and London: Belknap Press of Harvard Univ. Press, 1987. Pp. 548. $25.00. ISBN 0-674-51027-5.

Johnson, Claudia L. *Jane Austen: Women, Politics, and the Novel*. Chicago and London: Univ. of Chicago Press, 1988. Pp. xxv + 186. $27.50. ISBN 0-226-40138-3.

Johnston, Kenneth R., and Ruoff, Gene W. *The Age of William Wordsworth: Critical Essays on the Romantic Tradition*. New Brunswick and London: Rutgers Univ. Press, 1987. Pp. xviii + 390. $35.00. ISBN 0-8135-1273-5.

Katz, Wendy. *Rider Haggard and the Fiction of Empire: A Critical Study of British Imperial Fiction*. Cambridge and New York: Cambridge Univ. Press, 1987. Pp. ix + 171. ISBN 0-521-33425-X.

Kearney, Anthony. *The Louse on the Locks of Literature: John Churton Collins*. Edinburgh: Scottish Academic Press, 1986. Pp. xii + 125. $18.75. ISBN 0-7073-0480-6.

Keefe, Robert, and Keefe, Janice A. *Walter Pater and the Gods of Disorder*. Athens: Ohio Univ. Press, 1988. Pp. x + 184. $24.95. ISBN 0-8214-0892-5.

Keith, W. J. *Regions of the Imagination: The Development of British Rural Fiction*. Toronto, Buffalo, and London: Univ. of Toronto Press, 1988. Pp. ix + 199. $30.00. ISBN 0-8020-2654-0.

Kelley, Philip, and Hudson, Ronald, eds. *The Brownings' Correspondence*, vol. 5. January 1841-May 1842, Letters 784-966. Winfield, KS: Wedgestone Press, 1988. Pp. xii + 428. $55.00. ISBN 0-911459-09-X.

Kelley, Theresa M. *Wordsworth's Revisionary Aesthetics*. Cambridge and New York: Cambridge Univ. Press, 1988. Pp. xiv + 249. $39.50. ISBN 0-521-34398-4.

Kent, David A., ed. *The Achievement of Christina Rossetti*. Ithaca and London: Cornell Univ. Press, 1988. Pp. xi + 367. $37.50. ISBN 0-8014-1937-9.

Klaus, H. Gustav, ed. *The Rise of Socialist Fiction 1880-1914*. Sussex: Harvester Press and New York: St. Martin's Press, 1987. Pp. viii + 277. $35.00. ISBN 0-312-00949-6.

Kucich, John. *Repression in Victorian Fiction: Charlotte Brontë, George Eliot, and Charles Dickens*. Berkeley and London: Univ. of California Press, 1987. Pp. viii + 294. $32.00. ISBN 0-520-05980-8.

Kuznets, Lois R. *Kenneth Grahame*. Boston: Twayne Publishers, 1987. Pp. 156. $17.95. ISBN 0-8057-6943-9.

Langbaum, Robert. *The Word from Below: Essays on Modern Literature and Culture*. Madison: Univ. of Wisconsin Press, 1987. Pp. xv + 240. $12.95. ISBN 0-299-11184-9.

Latane, David E., Jr. *Browning's "Sordello" and the Aesthetics of Difficulty*. Victoria: Univ. of Victoria Press, 1987. Pp. 147. ISBN 0-920604-1.

Levine, George, ed. *One Culture: Essays in Science and Literature*. Madison: Univ. of Wisconsin Press, 1988. Pp. 359. $12.95. ISBN 0-299-11304-3.

Lister, Raymond. *Samuel Palmer, His Life and Art*. Cambridge and New York: Cambridge Univ. Press, 1988. Pp. xx + 272. $49.50. ISBN 0-521-32850-0.

Lovell, Terry. *Consuming Fiction*. London and New York: Verso, 1988. ISBN 0-86091-885-8.

Macey, Samuel L. *Patriarchs of Time: Dualism in Saturn-Cronos, the Watchmaker God, and Father Christmas*. Athens and London: Univ. of Georgia Press, 1987. pp. xiii + 216. $25.00. ISBN 0-8203-0934-6.

Magnuson, Paul. *Coleridge and Wordsworth: A Lyrical Dialogue*. Princeton: Princeton Univ. Press, 1988. Pp. xiv + 330. $35.00. ISBN 0-691-06732-5.

Markert, Lawrence W. *Arthur Symons, Critic of the Seven Arts*. Ann Arbor: UMI Research Press, 1988. Pp. xi + 176. $44.95. ISBN 0-8357-1845-X.

Marsh, Jan. *Jane and May Morris: A Biographical Story 1839-1938*. London and New York: Pandora, 1987. Pp. xvi + 328. $10.95. ISBN 0-86358-026-2.

Marshall, David. *The Surprising Effects of Sympathy: Marivaux, Diderot, Rousseau, and Mary Shelley*. Chicago and London: Univ. of Chicago Press, 1988. Pp. 286. $27.50. ISBN 0-226-50710-6.

Martin, Philip W. *Mad Women in Romantic Writing*. Sussex: Harvester Press and New York: St. Martin's Press. 1988. Pp. x + 198. $35.00. ISBN 0-312-01246-2.

McFarland, Thomas. *Romantic Cruxes: The English Essayists and the Spirit of the Age*. Oxford: Clarendon Press, and New York: Oxford Univ. Press, 1988. pp. xiii + 128. $32.50. ISBN 0-19-812895-9.

McGann, Jerome J. *Social Values and Poetic Acts: The Historical Judgment of Literary Work*. Cambridge, MA, and London: Harvard Univ. Press, 1988. Pp. xii + 279. ISBN 0-674-81495-9.

Meckier, Jerome. *Hidden Rivalries in Victorian Fiction: Dickens, Realism, and Revaluation*. Lexington: Univ. Press of Kentucky, 1987. Pp. x + 310. $29.00. ISBN 0-8131-1622-8.

Meisel, Perry. *The Myth of the Modern: A Study in British Literature and Criticism after 1850*. New Haven and London: Yale Univ. Press, 1987. Pp. x + 293. $24.00. ISBN 0-300-03946-8.

Mellor, Anne K., ed. *Romanticism and Feminism*. Bloomington: Indiana Univ. Press, 1988. Pp. 238. $12.95. ISBN 0-253-20462-3.

Melville, Joy. *Ellen and Edy: A Biography of Ellen Terry and Her Daughter, Edith Craig, 1847-1947*. London and New York: Pandora, 1988. pp, xv + 293. $10.95. ISBN 0-86358-078-5.

Miller, D. A. *The Novel and the Police*. Berkeley and London: Univ. of California Press, 1988. Pp. xv + 222. $22.50. ISBN 0-520-06281-7.

Miller, Dan, Bracher, Mark, and Ault, Donald, eds. *Critical Paths: Blake and the Argument of Method*. Durham and London: Duke Univ. Press, 1987. Pp. 382. $17.95. ISBN 0-8223-0792-8.

Millgate, Jane. *Scott's Last Edition: A Study in Publishing History*. Edinburgh: Edinburgh Univ. Press, 1987. Pp. x + 154. $17.50. ISBN 0-85224-541-6.

Mooneyham, Laura G. *Romance, Language and Education in Jane Austen's Novels.* New York: St. Martin's Press, 1988. Pp. xii + 199. $35.00. ISBN 0-312-01191-1.

Morris, Ivor. *Mr Collins Considered: Approaches to Jane Austen.* London and New York: Routledge & Kegan Paul, 1987. Pp. x + 173. $39.00. ISBN 0-7102-1005-1.

Morris, William. *The Collected Letters of William Morris,* vol. 2. Ed. Norman Kelvin. Princeton: Princeton Univ. Press, 1988. Pp. liii + 365 (1881-1884) and pp. 366-921 (1885-1888). Part A $45.00. ISBN 0-691-06723-6. Part B $49.50. ISBN 0-691-06723-6.

Morris, William. *The Story of the Glittering Plain.* New York: Dover Publications, 1987. Pp. 192. $7.95. ISBN 0-486-25467-4.

Mulvihill, James. *Thomas Love Peacock.* Boston: Twayne, 1987. Pp. 140. $24.95. ISBN 0-8057-6957-9.

Musselwhite, David E. *Partings Welded Together: Politics and Desire in the Nineteenth-Century English Novel.* New York and London: Methuen, 1988. Pp. ix + 278. $14.95. ISBN 0-416-06172-9.

Page, Norman. *A Dickens Chronology.* Boston: G. K. Hall, 1988. Pp. xiii + 156. $35.00. ISBN 0-8161-8949-8.

Page, Norman. *Speech in the English Novel,* 2nd. edn. Atlantic-Highlands: Humanities Press, 1987. Pp. 173. $35.00. ISBN 0-391-03562-2.

Page, Norman, ed. *Thomas Hardy Annual* 5. Atlantic Highlands: Humanities Press, 1987. Pp. xii + 217. $55.00. ISBN 0-333-38666-3. ISSN 0264-9454.

Pagliaro, Harold. *Selfhood and Redemption in Blake's "Songs."* University Park and London: Pennsylvania Univ. Press, 1987. Pp. xiv + 161. $20.00. ISBN 0-271-00603-X.

Parrish, Stephen Maxfield. *Coleridge's "Dejection": The Earliest Manuscripts and the Earliest Printings.* Ithaca and London: Cornell Univ. Press, 1988. Pp. xi + 142. $29.95. ISBN 0-8014-1255-2.

Peacock, Thomas Love. *Headlong Hall and Gryll Grange.* Oxford and New York: Oxford Univ. Press, 1987. Pp. xl + 425. ISBN 0-19-281693-4.

Peavler, Terry, J. *Individuations: The Novel as Dissent.* Lanham and London: Univ. Press of America, 1988. Pp. xiv + 155. $12.25. ISBN 0-8191-6442-9.

Pine, Richard. *The Dandy and the Herald: Manners, Mind, and Morals from Brummel to Durrell.* New York: St. Martin's Press, 1988. Pp. 254. $29.95. ISBN 0-312-00521-0.

Pinion, F. B. *A Wordsworth Chronology.* Boston: G. K. Hall, 1988. Pp. xx + 255. $35.00. ISBN 0-8161-8950-1.

Piper, H. W. *The Singing of Mount Abora: Coleridge's Use of Biblical Imagery and Natural Symbolism in Poetry and Philosophy.* Rutherford: Fairleigh Dickinson Univ. Press, and London and Toronto: Associated Univ. Presses, 1987. Pp. 124. $20.00. ISBN 0-8386-3295-5.

Rayan, Krishna. *Text and Sub-text: Suggestion in Literature.* Baltimore: Edward Arnold, 1987. Pp. xi + 236. $49.95. ISBN 0-7131-6514-6.

Raymond, Meredith B., and Mary Rose Sullivan, eds. *Women of Letters: Selected Letters of Elizabeth Barrett Browning and Mary Russell Mitford*. Boston: Twayne, 1987. Pp. xvii + 293. $29.95. ISBN 0-8057-9023-3.

Reiman, Donald H. *Intervals of Inspiration: The Skeptical Tradition and the Psychology of Romanticism*. Greenwood, FL: Penkevill, 1988. Pp. xxiii + 499. ISBN 0-913283-22-3.

Reiman, Donald H. *Romantic Texts and Contexts*. Columbia: Univ. of Missouri Press, 1987. Pp. xi + 395. $32.00. ISBN 0-8262-0649-2.

Richardson, Alan. *A Mental Theater: Poetic Drama and Consciousness in the Romantic Age*. University Park and London: Pennsylvania State Univ. Press, 1988. Pp. x + 224. $22.50. ISBN 0-271-00612-9.

Richardson, James. *Vanishing Lives: Style and Self in Tennyson, D.G. Rossetti, Swinburne, and Yeats*. Charlottesville: Univ. Press of Virginia, 1988. Pp. x + 240. $32.50. ISBN 0-8139-1165-6.

Ricks, Christopher, ed. *The New Oxford Book of Victorian Verse*. Oxford and New York: Oxford Univ. Press, 1987. Pp. xxxiv + 654. $30.00. ISBN 0-19-214154-6.

Ritvo, Harriet. *The Animal Estate: The English and Other Creatures in the Victorian Age*. Cambridge, MA, and London: Harvard Univ. Press, 1987. Pp. viii + 357. ISBN 0-674-03706-5.

Robb, David S. *George MacDonald*. Edinburgh: Scottish Academic Press, 1987. Pp. 136. $14.95. ISBN 0-7073-0523-3.

Roe, Nicholas. *Wordsworth and Coleridge: The Radical Years*. Oxford: Clarendon Press, and New York: Oxford Univ. Press, 1988. Pp. xvi + 306. $55.00. ISBN 0-19-812868-1.

Rogers, Pat, ed. *The Oxford Illustrated History of English Literature*. Oxford and New York: Oxford Univ. Press, 1987. Pp. xiv + 528. $30.00. ISBN 0-19-813816-9.

Rosenblum, Dolores. *Christina Rossetti: The Poetry of Endurance*. Carbondale: Southern Illinois Univ. Press, 1988. Pp. xvii + 247. $23.95. ISBN 0-8093-1269-7.

Ryals, Clyde de L., and Fielding, Kenneth, eds. *The Collected Letters of Thomas and Jane Welsh Carlyle,* vol. 13. Durham: Duke Univ. Press, 1987. Pp. xxvi + 333. $37.50. ISBN 0-8223-0702-2.

Ryals, Clyde de L., and Fielding, Kenneth, eds. *The Collected Letter of Thomas and Jane Welsh Carlyle,* vol. 14. Durham: Duke Univ. Press, 1987. Pp. 248. $37.50. ISBN 0-8223-0703-0.

Ryals, Clyde de L., and Fielding, Kenneth, eds. *The Collected Letters of Thomas and Jane Welsh Carlyle,* vol. 15. Durham: Duke Univ. Press, 1987. Pp. 293. $37.50. ISBN 0-8223-0704-9.

Rylance, Rick, ed. *Debating Texts: Readings in Twentieth-Century Literary Theory and Method*. Toronto and Buffalo: Univ. of Toronto Press, 1987. Pp. xi + 290. $14.95. ISBN 0-8020-6682-8.

Salusinszky, Imre. *Criticism in Society*. London and New York: Methuen, 1987. Pp. x 244. $18.95. ISBN 0-416-92270-8.

Schofield, Mary Anne, and Macheski, Cecelia, eds. *Fetter'd or Free? British Women Novelists, 1670-1815.* Athens and London: Ohio Univ. Press, 1986. Pp. xvii + 441. $38.50. ISBN 0-8214-0799-6.

Schreiner, Olive. *Olive Schreiner Letters,* vol. 1: 1871-1899. Ed. Richard Rive. Oxford and New York: Oxford Univ. Press, 1988. Pp. xiii + 409. $59.00. ISBN 0-19-812220-9.

Scott, Mary Jane W. *James Thomson, Anglo-Scot.* Athens and London: Univ. of Georgia Press, 1988. Pp. xiv + 373. ISBN 0-8203-0973-7.

Sharpe, William, and Wallock, Leonard, eds. *Visions of the Modern City: Essays in History, Art, and Literature.* Baltimore and London: Johns Hopkins Univ. Press, 1987. Pp. ix + 268. $10.95. ISBN 0-8018-3540-2.

Shatto, Susan. *The Companion to "Bleak House."* London and Boston: Unwin Hyman, 1988. Pp. 339. $49.95. ISBN 0-04-800047-7.

Shelley, Mary. *The Journals of Mary Shelley, 1814-1844.* Ed. Paula R. Feldman and Diane Scott-Kilvert. Oxford: Clarendon Press, 1987. Vol. 1. 1814-1822. Pp. xlii + 427. $96.00. ISBN 0-19-812571-2. Vol. 2. 1822-1844. Pp. x + 429-735. $84.00. ISBN 0-19-812674-3.

Shelley, Mary Wollstonecraft. *The Letters of Mary Wollstonecraft Shelley,* vol. 3. Ed. Betty T. Bennett. Baltimore and London: Johns Hopkins Univ. Press, 1988. Pp. li + 473. $37.50. ISBN 0-8018-2646-2.

Simpson, David. *Wordsworth's Historical Imagination: The Poetry of Displacement.* New York and London: Methuen, 1987. Pp. x + 239. $33.00. ISBN 0-416-03872-7.

Siskin, Clifford. *The Historicity of Romantic Discourse.* New York and Oxford: Oxford Univ. Press, 1988. Pp. viii + 225. $24.95. ISBN 0-19-504470-3.

Solokoff, Janice. *The Margin that Remains: A Study of Aging in Literature.* New York and Bern: Peter Lang, 1987. Pp. viii + 135. ISBN 0-8204-0287-7.

Southam, Brian, ed, *Jane Austen: The Critical Heritage,* vol. 2. The Critical Heritage Series. London and New York: Routledge & Kegan Paul, 1987. Pp. xii + 308. $45.00. ISBN 0-7102-0189-3.

Stanford, Derek. *Introduction to the Nineties.* Salzburg: Universität Salzburg, 1987. Pp. 124.

Stansky, Peter. *Redesigning the World: William Morris, the 1880s, and the Arts and Crafts.* Princeton: Princeton Univ. Press, 1987. Pp. xvi + 293. $12.95. ISBN 0-691-01411-6.

Stein, Richard L. *Victoria's Year: English Literature and Culture, 1837-1838.* New York and Oxford: Oxford Univ. Press, 1987. Pp. xiii + 314. $32.50. ISBN 0-19-504922-5.

Steiner, Wendy. *Pictures of Romance: Form Against Content in Painting and Literature.* Chicago and London: Univ. of Chicago Press, 1988. Pp. xi + 218. $27.95. ISBN 0-226-77229-2.

Stone, J. S. *George Meredith's Politics as Seen in His Life, Friendships, and Works.* Port Credit, Ont.: P. D. Meany, 1986. $45.00. ISBN 0-88835-020-1.

Tabachnick, Stephen E., ed. *Explorations in Doughty's Arabia Deserta.* Athens and London: Univ. of Georgia Press, 1987. Pp. vi + 275. $35.00. ISBN 0-8203-0899-4.

Taylor, Beverly, and Bain, Robert, eds. *The Cast of Consciousness: Concepts of the Mind in British and American Romanticism.* New York, Westport, and London: Greenwood Press, 1988. Pp. xv + 249. $35.95. ISBN 0-313-25891-0.

Taylor, Ina. *Victorian Sisters: The Remarkable Macdonald Women and the Great Men They Inspired.* Bethesda: Adler and Adler, 1987. Pp. xix + 218. $17.95. ISBN 0-917561-34-1.

Taylor, Joshua C. *Nineteenth Century Theories of Art.* Berkeley and London: Univ. of California Press, 1987. Pp. xii + 563. $38.50. ISBN 0-520-04887-3.

Tennyson, Alfred Lord. *The Letters of Alfred Lord Tennyson,* vol. 2, 1851-1870. Ed. Cecil Y. Lang and Edgar F. Shannon, Jr. Cambridge, MA: Belknap Press of Harvard Univ. Press, 1987. Pp. xii + 585. $35.00. ISBN 0-674-52583-3.

Tennyson, Alfred Lord. *The Poems of Tennyson in Three Volumes,* ed. Christopher Ricks. 2nd. edn. Berkeley, New York, and London: Univ. of California Press, 1987. Pp. vol. 1: xxxi + 662; vol. 2: ix + 746; vol. 3: ix + 674. $225.00. ISBN 0-520-06012-1.

Tennyson, G. B., and Wortham, Thomas, eds. *Nineteenth Century Literature.* Berkeley and London; Univ. of California Press, 1988. Vol. 42, no. 4. Pp. 415-538. $17.50 annual, $6.00 single copy. ISSN 0891-9456.

Terry, R. C., ed. *Trollope: Interviews and Recollections.* New York: St. Martin's Press, 1987. Pp. 257. $29.95. ISBN 0-312-00368-4.

Thesing, William B., ed. *Victorian Prose Writers Before 1867. Dictionary of Literary Biography,* vol. 55. Detroit: Gale Research, 1987. Pp. xiv + 379. $90.00. ISBN 0-8103-1733-8.

Thesing, William B., ed. *Victorian Prose Writers After 1867.* Dictionary of Literary Biography, vol. 57. Detroit: Gale Research, 1987. Pp. xiii + 571. $90.00. ISBN 0-8103-1735-4.

Thomas, Jeanie. *Reading Middlemarch: Reclaiming the Middle Distance.* Ann Arbor: UMI Research Press, 1987. Pp. xi + 111. ISBN 0-8357-1797-6.

Thornburg, Mary K. Patterson. *The Monster in the Mirror: Gender and the Sentimental/Gothic Myth in "Frankenstein."* Studies in Speculative Fiction 14. Ann Arbor: UMI Research Press, 1987. Pp. ix + 154. ISBN 0-8357-1798-4.

Thorpe, James. *The Sense of Style: Reading English Prose.* Hamden, CT: Archon Books, 1987. Pp. 185. $25.00. ISBN 0-208-02181-7.

Trollope, Anthony. *Collected Short Stories.* Ed. John Hampden. New York: Dover, 1988. Pp. 403. $7.95. ISBN 0-486-25484-4.

Trollope, Anthony. *The Macdermots of Ballycloran.* New York: Dover, 1988. Pp. 364. $8.95. ISBN 0-486-25572-7.

Tucker, Herbert F. *Tennyson and the Doom of Romanticism.* Cambridge, MA, and London: Harvard Univ. Press, 1988. Pp. 481. $37.50. ISBN 0-674-87430-7.

Van Boheemen-Saaf, Christine. *Between Sacred and Profane: Narrative Design and the Logic of Myth from Chaucer to Coover.* Amsterdam: Rodopi, and Atlantic Highlands: Humanities Press, 1987. Pp. 188. $39.95. ISBN 90-6203-589-2.

Veeder, William and Hirsch, Gordon, eds. *Dr. Jekyll and Mr. Hyde After One Hundred Years.* Chicago and London: Univ. of Chicago Press, 1988. Pp. xx + 312. $16.95. ISBN 0-226-85229-6.

Vendler, Helen. *The Music of What Happens: Poems, Poets, Critics.* Cambridge, MA, and London: Harvard Univ. Press, 1988. Pp. ix + 473. $29.50. ISBN 0-674-59152-6.

Victorian Poetry 24, 2(Summer 1987). Ed. John Stasny. Morgantown: West Virginia Univ., 1987. Pp. 101-257. $14.00 individuals, $20.00 institutions. ISSN 0042-5206.

Walvin, James. *Victorian Values.* Athens: Univ. of Georgia Press, 1988. Pp. 171. $9.95. ISBN 0-8203-1013-1.

Welsh, Alexander. *From Copyright to Copperfield: The Identity of Dickens.* Cambridge, MA, and London: Harvard Univ. Press, 1987. Pp. 200. $25.00. ISBN 0-674-32342-4.

Welsh, Alexander. *George Eliot and Blackmail.* Cambridge, MA, and London: Harvard Univ. Press, 1985. Pp. xii + 388. ISBN 0-674-34872-9.

White, R. S. *Keats as a Reader of Shakespeare.* Norman OK, and London: Univ. of Oklahoma Press, 1987. Pp. 250. $24.95. ISBN 0-8061-2053-3.

Williams, A. Susan. *The Rich Man and the Diseased Poor in Early Victorian Literature.* Atlantic Highlands: Humanities Press, 1987. Pp. xi + 152. $25.00. ISBN 0-391-03498-7.

Winnifrith, Tom. *A New Life of Charlotte Brontë.* New York: St. Martin's Press, 1988. Pp. 136. $29.95. ISBN 0-312-01578-X.

Wordsworth, Jonathan, Jaye, Michael C., and Woof, Robert. *William Wordsworth and the Age of English Romanticism.* New Brunswick and London: Rutgers Univ. Press, 1987. Pp. x + 261. $65.00. ISBN 0-8135-12735.

Wordsworth, William. *Selected Prose.* Ed. John O. Hayden. New York: Penguin, 1988. Pp. 514. $7.95. ISBN 0-14-043292-X.